MyBcommLab®

MyBcommLab is an online assessment and preparation solution that helps you actively study and prepare material for class. Chapter-by-chapter activities, including study plans, focus on what you need to learn and to review in order to succeed.

Visit **www.pearsoninternationaleditions.com/ mybcommlab** to learn more.

ALWAYS LEARNING

PEARSON

Tenth Edition

Excellence in Business Communication

Tenth Edition

Excellence in Business Communication

John V. Thill
Chairman and Chief Executive Officer
Global Communication Strategies

Courtland L. Bovée
Professor of Business Communication
C. Allen Paul Distinguished Chair
Grossmont College

International Edition contributions by

Rimi B. Chatterjee
Assistant Professor, Department of English
Jadavpur University, Kolkata

Karthik Subramanian

PEARSON

Boston   Columbus   Indianapolis   New York   San Francisco   Upper Saddle River
Amsterdam   Cape Town   Dubai   London   Madrid   Milan   Munich   Paris   Montreal
Toronto   Delhi   Mexico City   São Paulo   Sydney   Hong Kong   Seoul   Singapore   Taipei   Tokyo

Editorial Director: Sally Yagan
Director of Development: Stephen Deitmer
Acquisitions Editor: James Heine
Director of Editorial Services: Ashley Santora
Editorial Project Manager: Karin Williams
Editorial Assistant: Ashlee Bradbury
Director of Marketing: Maggie Moylan
Senior Marketing Manager: Nikki Jones
Marketing Assistant: Kim Lovato
Senior Managing Editor: Judy Leale
Senior Production Project Manager: Karalyn Holland
Publisher, International Edition: Angshuman Chakraborty
Acquisitions Editor, International Edition: Somnath Basu
Publishing Assistant, International Edition: Shokhi Shah

Print and Media Editor, International Edition: Ashwitha Jayakumar
Project Editor, International Edition: Jayashree Arunachalam
Senior Operations Specialist: Arnold Vila
Senior Media Project Manager: Allison Longley
Creative Director: Blair Brown
Senior Art Director/Cover Designer: Kenny Beck
Interior Designer: Laura C. Ierardi
Cover Art: Ljupco Smokovski/Shutterstock, EDHAR/Shutterstock
Media Project Manager, Production: Lisa Rinaldi
Full-Service Project Management: S4Carlisle Publishing Services
Cover Printer: Lehigh-Phoenix Color/Hagerstown

Pearson Education Limited
Edinburgh Gate
Harlow
Essex CM20 2JE
England

and Associated Companies throughout the world

Visit us on the World Wide Web at:
www.pearsoninternationaleditions.com

© Pearson Education Limited 2013

ISBN 13: 978-0-273-76889-0
ISBN 10: 0-273-76889-1

British Library Cataloguing-in-Publication Data
A catalogue record for this book is available from the British Library

10 9 8 7 6 5 4 3 2 1
14 13 12

Typeset in 10.5/12 Minion Pro by S4Carlisle Publishing Services
Printed and bound by Courier Kendallville

The publisher's policy is to use paper manufactured from sustainable forests.

Contents in Brief

Contents

14   Contents

PART 5
Writing Employment Messages and Interviewing for Jobs   527

CHAPTER 15
Building Careers and Writing Résumés   528
ON THE JOB: COMMUNICATING AT ATK   528

ON THE JOB: SOLVING COMMUNICATION DILEMMAS AT ATK   551

CHAPTER 16
Applying and Interviewing for Employment   560
ON THE JOB: COMMUNICATING AT ZAPPOS   560

ON THE JOB: SOLVING COMMUNICATION DILEMMAS AT ZAPPOS   585

Real-Time Updates—Learn More

Real-Time Updates "Learn More" is a unique feature that you will see strategically located throughout the text, connecting you with dozens of carefully selected online media items. These elements—categorized by the icons shown below representing interactive websites, online videos, PowerPoint presentations, podcasts, PDF files, and articles—complement the text's coverage by providing contemporary examples and valuable insights from successful professionals. See page 22 for an illustration of how Real-Time Updates works.

REAL-TIME UPDATES
Learn More by Reading This Article

REAL-TIME UPDATES
Learn More by Reading This PDF

REAL-TIME UPDATES
Learn More by Listening to This Podcast

REAL-TIME UPDATES
Learn More by Watching
This PowerPoint Presentation

REAL-TIME UPDATES
Learn More by Watching This Video

REAL-TIME UPDATES
Learn More by Exploring
This Interactive Website

Preface

Major Changes and Improvements in This Edition

Bovée and Thill texts have long set the benchmark in this field for rigorous, high-value revisions that make sure instructors and students have the most comprehensive, realistic, and contemporary materials available. The following table identifies the major changes and improvements in the tenth edition of *Excellence in Business Communication*.

Significant content additions and upgrades	In addition to numerous updates and streamlining rewrites throughout, the following sections are all new or substantially revised with new material: • *Understanding Why Communication Matters* (in Chapter 1) • *The Social Communication Model* (in Chapter 1) • *Committing to Ethical and Legal Communication* (in Chapter 1; new coverage of transparency) • *Distinguishing Ethical Dilemmas from Ethical Lapses* (in Chapter 1; revised and streamlined) • *Business Communication 2.0: Who's Responsible Here?* (in Chapter 1) • *Communicating Effectively in Teams* (in Chapter 2; new coverage of collaboration) • *Communicating Across Cultures: Whose Skin Is This, Anyway?* (in Chapter 2) • *Social Networks and Virtual Communities* (in Chapter 2; updated) • *Business Etiquette Online* (in Chapter 2; updated) • *Developing Cultural Competency* (in Chapter 3) • *Communicating Across Cultures: Us Versus Them: Generational Conflict in the Workplace* (in Chapter 3) • *Speaking and Listening Carefully* (in Chapter 3; updated with accommodation strategies) • *Business Communication 2.0: The Web 2.0 Way to Learn a New Language* (in Chapter 3) • *Analyzing the Situation* (in Chapter 4; revised) • *Practicing Ethical Communication: How Much Information Is Enough?* (in Chapter 4) • *Building Reader Interest with Storytelling Techniques* (in Chapter 4) • *Emphasizing the Positive* (in Chapter 5; revised coverage of euphemisms) • *Communicating Across Cultures: Protecting Patients with Reader-Friendly Prescription Labels* (in Chapter 6) • *Business Communication 2.0: Walking Around with the Entire Internet in Your Hands* (in Chapter 7) • *Compositional Modes for Electronic Media* (in Chapter 7) • *Creating Content for Social Media* (in Chapter 7; updated)

- *Social Networking and Community Participation Websites* (in Chapter 7)

  Social Networks

    Business Communication Uses of Social Networks

    Strategies for Business Communication on Social Networks

  User-Generated Content Sites

  Community Q&A Sites

  Community Participation Websites

- *Microblogging* (in Chapter 7)

- New two-page highlight feature: *Business Communicators Innovating with Social Media* (in Chapter 7)

- *Continuing with a Clear Statement of the Bad News* (in Chapter 9; revised coverage of using conditionals)

- *Closing on a Respectful Note* (in Chapter 9)

- *Making Negative Announcements on Routine Business Matters* (in Chapter 9)

- *Rejecting Suggestions and Proposals* (in Chapter 9)

- *Refusing Social Networking Recommendation Requests* (in Chapter 9)

- *Rejecting Job Applications* (in Chapter 9)

- *Giving Negative Performance Reviews* (in Chapter 9; substantially revised)

- *Business Communication 2.0: We're Under Attack! Responding to Rumors and Criticism in a Social Media Environment* (in Chapter 9; substantially revised)

- *Writing Promotional Messages for Social Media* (in Chapter 10; revised)

- *Online Monitoring Tools* (in Chapter 11)

- *Sharpening Your Career Skills: Creating an Effective Business Plan* (in Chapter 11; revised)

- *Data Visualization* (in Chapter 12; updated)

- *Maps and Geographic Information Systems* (in Chapter 12; updated)

- *Drawings, Diagrams, Infographics, and Photographs* (in Chapter 12; added coverage of infographics)

- *Presentation Close* (in Chapter 14; revised)

- *Embracing the Backchannel* (in Chapter 14)

- *Choosing Structured or Free-Form Slides* (in Chapter 14; expanded discussion)

- *Designing Effective Slides* (in Chapter 14)

- *Designing Slides Around a Key Visual* (in Chapter 14)

- *Creating Charts and Tables for Slides* (in Chapter 14)

- *Business Communication 2.0: Presentations Get Social* (in Chapter 14)

- *Creating Effective Handouts* (in Chapter 14; updated)

- *Finding the Ideal Opportunity in Today's Job Market* (in Chapter 15)

    Writing the Story of You

    Learning to Think Like an Employer

    Translating Your General Potential into a Specific Solution for Each Employer

    Taking the Initiative to Find Opportunities

    Building Your Network

    Avoiding Mistakes

- *Composing Your Résumé* (in Chapter 15; revised with the latest advice on keywords)
- *Producing Your Résumé* (in Chapter 15; with new coverage and cautions about infographic résumés)
- *Printing a Scannable Résumé* (in Chapter 15; updated to reflect the decline of this format)
- *Creating an Online Résumé* (in Chapter 15)
- *Following Up After Submitting a Résumé* (in Chapter 16)
- *Learning About the Organization and Your Interviewers* (in Chapter 16)

The social media revolution	This edition includes up-to-date coverage of the social communication model that is redefining business communication and reshaping the relationships between companies and their stakeholders. Social media concepts and techniques are integrated throughout the book, from career planning to presentations. Here are some examples: - Social media questions, activities, and cases appear throughout the book, involving Twitter, Facebook, LinkedIn, and other media that have taken the business world by storm in the past couple of years. - Three dozen examples of business applications of social media demonstrate how a variety of companies use these tools. - The social communication model is now covered in Chapter 1. - A new two-page, magazine-style feature in Chapter 7 highlights the innovative uses of social media by a variety of companies. - Social networking sites are now covered as a brief-message medium in Chapter 7. - The Twitter-enabled *backchannel*, which is revolutionizing electronic presentations, is covered in Chapter 14. - Social media tools are covered extensively in the career-planning Prologue and the two employment communication chapters (15 and 16).
Compositional modes for electronic media	For all the benefits they offer, social media and other innovations place new demands on business communicators. This edition introduces you to nine important modes of writing for electronic media.
Personal branding	As the workforce continues to evolve and with the employment situation likely to remain unstable for some time to come, it is more vital than ever for you to take control of your career. An important first step is to clarify and communicate your *personal brand*, a topic that is now addressed in the Prologue and carried through to the employment-message chapters.
Storytelling techniques	Some of the most effective business messages, from advertising to proposals to personal branding, rely on storytelling techniques. This edition offers hands-on advice and multiple activities to help you develop "business-class" narrative techniques.
Full implementation of objective-driven learning	Every aspect of this new edition is organized by learning objectives, from the chapter content to the student activities in the textbook and online at www.pearsoninternationaleditions.com/mybcommlab. This structure makes planning and course management easier for instructors and makes reading, studying, and practicing easier for students.
Deeper integration with MyBcommLab	This essential online resource now offers even more ways to test your understanding of the concepts presented in every chapter, practice vital skills, and create customized study plans.

Multimedia resources	Extend their learning experience with unique *Real-Time Updates* "Learn More" media elements that connect you with dozens of handpicked videos, podcasts, and other items that complement chapter content.
New On the Job communication vignettes and simulations	Chapter 1: Toyota's Auto-Biography user-generated content program Chapter 6: Noted web designer Jefferson Rabb's user-focused design principles Chapter 9: Chargify's communication errors regarding a price increase Chapter 11: MyCityWay's winning business plan Chapter 13: Garage Technology Ventures's advice for writing executive summaries Chapter 14: Comedy super-agent Peter Principato's techniques for effective presentations Chapter 15: ATK's cutting-edge workforce analytics Chapter 16: Zappos's free-spirited approach to recruiting free-spirited employees
New review and analysis questions and skills-development projects	Dozens of new questions and activities are offered in Learning Objectives Checkup, Apply Your Knowledge, and Practice Your Skills categories.
New communication cases	Communication cases give you the opportunity to solve real-world communication challenges using the media skills you'll be expected to have in tomorrow's workplace; 40 percent of the 125 cases are new in this edition.
New figures and more annotated model documents	The tenth edition offers an unmatched portfolio of business communication exhibits. Here are the highlights: • Nearly 70 new figures provide examples of the latest trends in business communication. • Nearly 80 annotated model documents, ranging from printed letters and reports to websites, blogs, and social networking sites, show you in detail how successful business messages work. • 70 exhibits feature communication examples from real companies, including Bigelow Tea, Burton Snowboards, Google, IBM, Microsoft Bing, Patagonia, Red Bull, Segway, Southwest Airlines, and Zappos. • More than 100 illustrated examples of communication technologies help students grasp the wide range of tools and media formats they will encounter on the job.
Critique the Professionals	This new activity invites you to analyze an example of professional communication using the principles learned in each chapter.
Quick Learning Guide	This convenient review tool at the end of every chapter lists the learning objectives with page references for review and defines essential terminology from the chapter.

Extend the Value of Your Textbook with Free Multimedia Content

Excellence in Business Communication's unique Real-Time Updates system automatically provides weekly content updates, including interactive games and tools, podcasts, PowerPoint presentations, online videos, PDF files, and articles. You can subscribe to updates chapter by chapter, so you get only the material that applies to the chapter you are studying. You can access Real-Time Updates through MyBcommLab or by visiting http://real-timeupdates.com/ebc10.

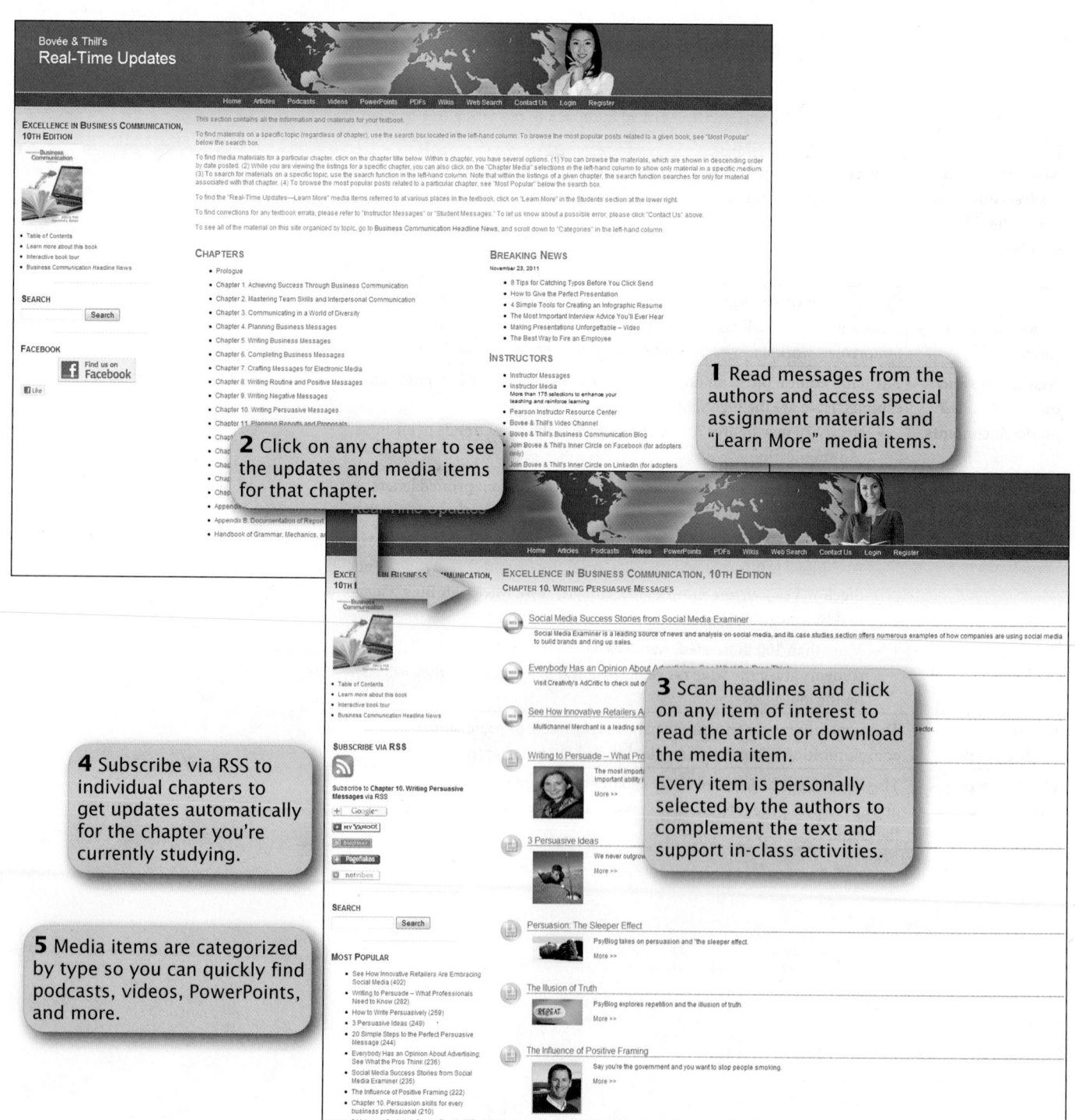

What Is the Single Most Important Step You Can Take to Enhance Your Career Prospects?

No matter what profession you want to pursue, the ability to communicate will be an essential skill—and a skill that employers expect you to have when you enter the workforce. This course introduces you to the fundamental principles of business communication and gives you the opportunity to develop your communication skills. You'll discover how business communication differs from personal and social communication, and you'll see how today's companies are using blogs, social networks, podcasts, virtual worlds, wikis, and other technologies. You'll learn a simple three-step writing process that works for all types of writing and speaking projects, both in college and on the job. Along the way, you'll gain valuable insights into ethics, etiquette, listening, teamwork, and nonverbal communication. Plus, you'll learn effective strategies for the many types of communication challenges you'll face on the job, from routine messages about transactions to complex reports and websites.

Colleges and universities vary in the prerequisites established for the business communication course, but we advise taking at least one course in English composition before enrolling in this class. Some coursework in business studies will also give you a better perspective on communication challenges in the workplace. However, we have taken special care not to assume any in-depth business experience, so you can use *Excellence in Business Communication* successfully even if you have limited on-the-job experience or business coursework.

HOW THIS COURSE WILL HELP YOU

Few courses can offer the three-for-the-price-of-one value you get from a business communication class. Check out these benefits:

- **In your other classes.** The communication skills you learn in this class can help you in every other course you take in college. From simple homework assignments to complicated team projects to class presentations, you'll be able to communicate more effectively with less time and effort.
- **During your job search.** You can reduce the stress of searching for a job and stand out from the competition. As you'll see in Chapters 15 and 16, every activity in the job search process relies on communication. The better you can communicate, the more successful you'll be at landing interesting and rewarding work.
- **On the job.** After you get that great job, the time and energy you have invested in this course will continue to yield benefits year after year. As you tackle each project and every new challenge, influential company leaders—the people who decide how quickly you'll get promoted and how much you'll earn—will be paying close attention to how well you communicate. They will observe your interactions with colleagues, customers, and business partners. They'll take note of how well you can collect data, find the essential ideas buried under mountains of information, and convey those points to other people. They'll observe your ability to adapt to different audiences and circumstances. They'll be watching when you encounter tough situations that require careful attention to ethics and etiquette. The good news: Every insight you gain and every skill you develop in this course will help you shine in your career.

HOW TO SUCCEED IN THIS COURSE

Although this course explores a wide range of message types and appears to cover quite a lot of territory, the underlying structure of the course is actually rather simple. You'll learn a few basic concepts, identify some key skills to use and procedures to follow—and then practice, practice, practice. Whether you're writing a blog posting in response to one of the real-company cases or drafting your own résumé, you'll be practicing the same skills again and again. With feedback and reinforcement from your instructor and your classmates, your confidence will grow and the work will become easier and more enjoyable.

The following sections offer advice on approaching each assignment, using your textbook, and taking advantage of some other helpful resources.

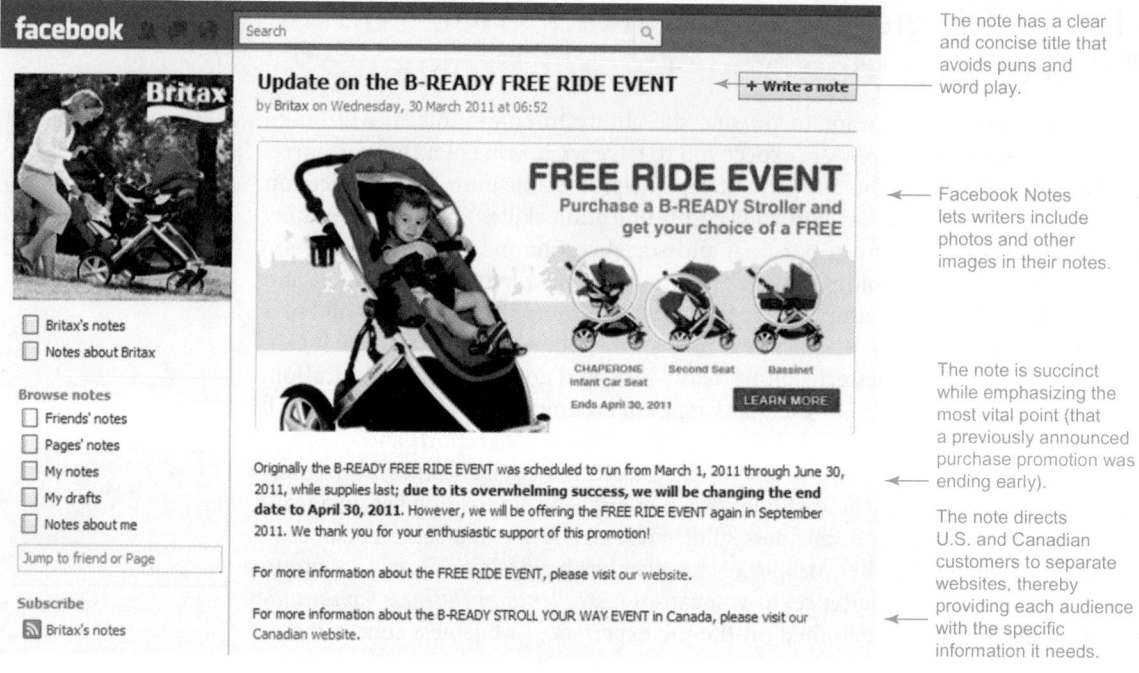

The note has a clear and concise title that avoids puns and word play.

Facebook Notes lets writers include photos and other images in their notes.

The note is succinct while emphasizing the most vital point (that a previously announced purchase promotion was ending early).

The note directs U.S. and Canadian customers to separate websites, thereby providing each audience with the specific information it needs.

Excellence in Business Communication uses contemporary examples of business communication while emphasizing the fundamentals of audience-focused writing.

Approaching Each Assignment

In the spirit of practice and improvement, you will have a number of writing (and possibly speaking) assignments throughout this course. These suggestions will help you produce better results with less effort:

- **First, don't panic!** If the thought of writing a report or giving a speech sends a chill up your spine, you're not alone. Everybody feels that way when first learning business communication skills, and even experienced professionals can feel nervous about major projects. Keeping three points in mind will help. First, every project can be broken down into a series of small, manageable tasks. Don't let a big project overwhelm you; it's nothing more than a bunch of smaller tasks. Second, remind yourself that you have the skills you need to accomplish each task. As you move through the course, the assignments are carefully designed to match the skills you've developed up to that point. Third, if you feel panic creeping up on you, take a break and regain your perspective.

- **Focus on one task at a time.** A common mistake writers make is trying to organize and express their ideas while simultaneously worrying about audience reactions, grammar, spelling, formatting, page design, and a dozen other factors. Fight the temptation to do everything at once; otherwise, your frustration will soar and your productivity will plummet. In particular, don't worry about grammar, spelling, and word choices during your first draft. Concentrate on the organization of your ideas first, then the way you express those ideas, and then the presentation and production of your messages. Following the three-step writing process is an ideal way to focus on one task at a time in a logical sequence.

- **Give yourself plenty of time.** As with every other school project, putting things off to the last minute creates unnecessary stress. Writing and speaking projects in particular are much easier if you tackle them in small stages with breaks in between, rather than trying to get everything done in one frantic blast. Moreover, there will be instances when you simply get stuck on a project, and the best thing to do is walk away and give your mind a break. If you allow room for breaks in your schedule, you'll minimize the frustration and spend less time overall on your homework, too.

- **Step back and assess each project before you start.** The writing and speaking projects you'll have in this course cover a wide range of communication scenarios, and it's essential that you adapt your approach to each new challenge. Resist the urge to dive in and start writing without a plan. Ponder the assignment for a while, consider the various approaches you might take, and think carefully about your objectives before you start writing. Nothing is more frustrating than getting stuck halfway through because you're not sure what you're trying to say or you've wandered off track. Spend a little time planning, and you'll spend a lot less time writing.

- **Use the three-step writing process.** Those essential planning tasks are the first step in the three-step writing process, which you'll learn about in Chapter 4 and use throughout the course. This process has been developed and refined by professional writers with decades of experience and thousands of projects ranging from short blog posts to 500-page textbooks. It works, so take advantage of it.
- **Learn from the examples and model documents.** This textbook offers dozens of realistic examples of business messages, many with notes along the sides that explain strong and weak points (see the example on this page). Study these and any other examples that your instructor provides. Learn what works and what doesn't, then apply these lessons to your own writing.

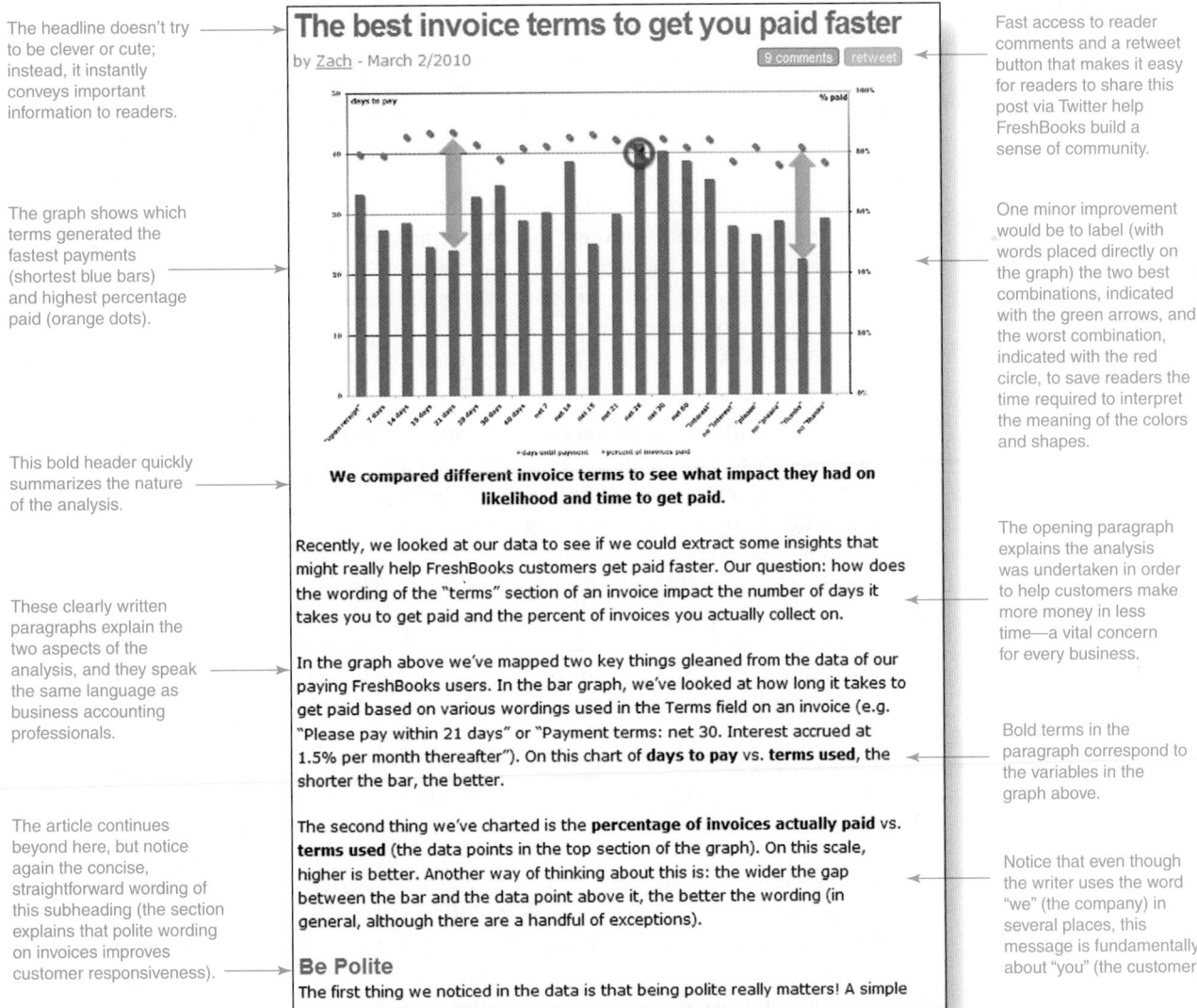

The headline doesn't try to be clever or cute; instead, it instantly conveys important information to readers.

The graph shows which terms generated the fastest payments (shortest blue bars) and highest percentage paid (orange dots).

This bold header quickly summarizes the nature of the analysis.

These clearly written paragraphs explain the two aspects of the analysis, and they speak the same language as business accounting professionals.

The article continues beyond here, but notice again the concise, straightforward wording of this subheading (the section explains that polite wording on invoices improves customer responsiveness).

Fast access to reader comments and a retweet button that makes it easy for readers to share this post via Twitter help FreshBooks build a sense of community.

One minor improvement would be to label (with words placed directly on the graph) the two best combinations, indicated with the green arrows, and the worst combination, indicated with the red circle, to save readers the time required to interpret the meaning of the colors and shapes.

The opening paragraph explains the analysis was undertaken in order to help customers make more money in less time—a vital concern for every business.

Bold terms in the paragraph correspond to the variables in the graph above.

Notice that even though the writer uses the word "we" (the company) in several places, this message is fundamentally about "you" (the customer).

Here is one of nearly 90 annotated model documents that point out what works (and sometimes, what doesn't work) in a variety of professional messages and documents.
Source: Used with permission of FreshBooks.

- **Learn from experience.** Finally, learn from the feedback you get from your instructor and from other students. Don't take the criticism personally; your instructor and your classmates are commenting about the work, not about you. View every bit of feedback as an opportunity to improve.

Using This Textbook Package

This book and its accompanying online resources introduce you to the key concepts in business communication while helping you develop essential skills. As you read each chapter, start by studying the learning objectives. They will help you identify the most important concepts in the chapter and give you a feel for what you'll be learning. Following the learning objectives, the "On the Job" communication vignette features a successful professional role model who uses the same skills you will be learning in the chapter.

As you work your way through the chapter, compare the advice with the various examples, both the brief in-text examples and the standalone model documents. Also, keep an eye out for the Real-Time Updates elements in each chapter. We have selected these videos, podcasts, presentations, and other online media to provide informative and entertaining enhancements to the text material.

At the end of each chapter, you'll revisit the "On the Job" story from the beginning of the chapter and imagine yourself in the role of a business professional solving four realistic communication dilemmas. Next, the "Learning Objectives Checkup" gives you the chance to quickly verify your grasp of important concepts. Each chapter includes a variety of questions and activities that help you gauge how well you've learned the material and are able to apply it to realistic business scenarios. Several chapters have activities with downloadable media such as podcasts; if your instructor assigns these, follow the instructions in the text to locate the correct files.

Several chapters have activities with downloadable media such as presentations and podcasts or the use of the Bovée-Thill wiki simulator. If your instructor assigns these activities, follow the instructions in the text to locate the correct files. And if you'd like some help getting started with Facebook, Twitter, or LinkedIn, we have created screencasts with helpful advice on these topics.

In addition to the 16 chapters of the text itself, here are some special features that will help you succeed in the course and on the job:

- **Prologue: Building a Career with Your Communication Skills.** This section (immediately following this Preface) helps you understand today's dynamic workplace, the steps you can take to adapt to the job market, and the importance of creating an employment portfolio and building your personal brand.
- **Handbook.** The Handbook of Grammar, Mechanics, and Usage (see page H-1) serves as a convenient reference of essential business English.
- **MyBcommLab.** If your course includes MyBcommLab, you can take advantage of this unique resource to test your understanding of the concepts presented in every chapter.
- **Real-Time Updates.** You can use this unique newsfeed service to make sure you're always kept up to date on important topics. Plus, at strategic points in every chapter, you will be directed to the Real-Time Updates website to get the latest information about specific subjects. To sign up, visit http://real-timeupdates.com/ebc10. You can also access Real-Time Updates through MyBcommLab.
- **Business Communication Web Search.** With our unique web search approach, you can quickly access more than 325 search engines. The tool uses a simple and intuitive interface engineered to help you find precisely what you want, whether it's PowerPoint files, Adobe Acrobat PDF files, Microsoft Word documents, Excel files, videos, or podcasts. Check it out at http://businesscommunicationblog .com/websearch.
- Instructor resources for the International Edition are available at http://www .pearsoninternationaleditions.com/thill.

About the Authors

Courtland L. Bovée and John V. Thill have been leading textbook authors for more than two decades, introducing millions of students to the fields of business and business communication. Their award-winning texts are distinguished by proven pedagogical features, extensive selections of contemporary case studies, hundreds of real-life examples, engaging writing, thorough research, and the unique integration of print and electronic resources. Each new edition reflects the authors' commitment to continuous refinement and improvement, particularly in terms of modeling the latest practices in business and the use of technology.

Professor Bovée has 22 years of teaching experience at Grossmont College in San Diego, where he has received teaching honors and was accorded that institution's C. Allen Paul Distinguished Chair. Mr. Thill is a prominent communications consultant who has worked with organizations ranging from Fortune 500 multinationals to entrepreneurial start-ups. He formerly held positions with Pacific Bell and Texaco.

Courtland Bovée and John Thill were recently awarded proclamations from the Governor of Massachusetts for their lifelong contributions to education and for their commitment to the summer youth baseball program that is sponsored by the Boston Red Sox.

Acknowledgments

The tenth edition of *Excellence in Business Communication* reflects the professional experience of a large team of contributors and advisors. We express our thanks to the many individuals whose valuable suggestions and constructive comments influenced the success of this book.

Donna R. Everett, *Morehead State University*
Randall J. Gerber, *Macomb Community College*
Alice Griswold, *Clarke University*
Karen Kendrick, *Nashville State Community College*
Christine Laursen, *Red Rocks Community College*
Gregory H. Morin, *University of Nebraska–Omaha*
Pamela G. Needham, *Northeast Mississippi Community College*
Jean Anna Sellers, *Fort Hays State University*
Cheryl L. Sypniewski, *Macomb Community College*
Scott T. Warman, *Skyline College*
Lucinda Willis, *Indiana University of Pennsylvania*

REVIEWERS OF PREVIOUS EDITIONS

We express our thanks to the many individuals whose valuable suggestions and constructive comments influenced the success of this book. The authors are deeply grateful to

Janet Adams, *Minnesota State University–Mankato*
Gus Amaya, *Florida International University*
Anita S. Bednar, *Central State University*
Donna Cox, *Monroe Community College*
Sauny Dills, *California Polytechnic State University–San Luis Obispo*
Ruthann Dirks, *Emporia State University*
Cynthia Drexel, *Western State College*
Mary DuBoise, *DeVry University–Dallas*
J. Thomas Dukes, *University of Akron*
Karen Eickhoff, *University of Tennessee*

Lindsay S. English, *Ursuline College*
Mike Flores, *Wichita State University*
Charlene A. Gierkey, *Northwestern Michigan College*
Sue Granger, *Jacksonville State University*
Bradley S. Hayden, *Western Michigan University*
Joyce Hicks, *Valparaiso University*
Michael Hignite, *Southwest Missouri State*
Mark Hilton, *Lyndon State College*
Cynthia Hofacker, *University of Wisconsin–Eau Claire*
Louise C. Holcomb, *Gainesville College*
Larry Honl, *University of Wisconsin–Eau Claire*
Kenneth Hunsaker, *Utah State University*
Sandie Idziak, *University of Texas*
Robert O. Joy, *Central Michigan University*
Paula R. Kaiser, *University of North Carolina–Greensboro*
Paul Killorin, *Portland Community College*
Linda M. LaDuc, *University of Massachusetts–Amherst*
Jennifer Loney, *Portland State University*
Al Lucero, *East Tennessee State University*
Rachel Mather, *Adelphi University*
Linda McAdams, *Westark Community College*
Melinda McCannon, *Gordon College*
Bronna McNeely, *Midwestern State University*
William McPherson, *Indiana University of Pennsylvania*
Russ Meade, *Tidewater Community College*
Betty Mealor, *Abraham Baldwin College*
Mary Miller, *Ashland University*
Joe Newman, *Faulkner University*
Barbara Oates, *Texas A&M University*
Richard Profozich, *Prince George's Community College*
Brian Railsback, *Western Carolina University*
John Rehfuss, *California State University–Sacramento*
Joan C. Roderick, *Southwest Texas State University*
Salvatore Safina, *University of Wisconsin*
Jean Anna Sellers, *Fort Hays State University*
Andrea Smith-Hunter, *Siena College*
Carol Smith White, *Georgia State University*
Karen Sneary, *Northwestern Oklahoma State University*
Jeanne Stannard, *Johnson County Community College*
Terisa Tennison, *Florida International University*
Michael Thompson, *Brigham Young University*
Betsy Vardaman, *Baylor University*
Robert von der Osten, *Ferris State University*
Billy Walters, *Troy State University*
George Walters, *Emporia State University*
John L. Waltman, *Eastern Michigan University*
F. Stanford Wayne, *Southwest Missouri State*
Robert Wheatley, *Troy State University*
Rosemary B. Wilson, *Washtenaw Community College*
Karl V. Winton, *Marshall University*
Beverly C. Wise, *SUNY–Morrisville*
Aline Wolff, *New York University*
Bonnie Yarbrough, *University of North Carolina–Greensboro*

We also appreciate the notable talents and distinguished contributions of

Anne Bliss, *University of Colorado–Boulder*
Carolyn A. Embree, *University of Akron*

Susan S. Rehwaldt, *Southern Illinois University*
Carla L. Sloan, *Liberty University*
Deborah Valentine, *Emory University*
Doris A. Van Horn Christopher, *California State University–Los Angeles*

REVIEWERS OF DOCUMENT MAKEOVERS

We sincerely thank the following reviewers for their assistance with the Document Makeover feature:

Lisa Barley, *Eastern Michigan University*
Marcia Bordman, *Gallaudet University*
Jean Bush-Bacelis, *Eastern Michigan University*
Bobbye Davis, *Southern Louisiana University*
Cynthia Drexel, *Western State College*
Kenneth Gibbs, *Worcester State College*
Ellen Leathers, *Bradley University*
Diana McKowen, *Indiana University*
Bobbie Nicholson, *Mars Hill College*
Andrew Smith, *Holyoke Community College*
Jay Stubblefield, *North Carolina Wesleyan College*
Dawn Wallace, *South Eastern Louisiana University*

REVIEWERS OF MODEL DOCUMENTS

In previous editions, model documents and their accompanying annotations received invaluable input from

Dacia Charlesworth, *Indiana University–Purdue University Fort Wayne*
Avon Crismore, *Indiana University*
Nancy Goehring, *Monterey Peninsula College*
James Hatfield, *Florida Community College at Jacksonville*
Estelle Kochis, *Suffolk County Community College*
Sherry Robertson, *Arizona State University*
Diane Todd Bucci, *Robert Morris University*

PERSONAL ACKNOWLEDGMENTS

We wish to extend a heartfelt thanks to our many friends, acquaintances, and business associates who provided materials or agreed to be interviewed so that we could bring the real world into the classroom.

A very special acknowledgment goes to George Dovel, whose superb writing skills, distinguished background, and wealth of business experience assured this project of clarity and completeness. Also, recognition and thanks to Jackie Estrada for her outstanding skills and excellent attention to details. Her creation of the "Peak Performance Grammar and Mechanics" material is especially noteworthy. Jill Gardner's professionalism and keen eye for quality were invaluable.

We also feel it is important to acknowledge and thank the Association for Business Communication, an organization whose meetings and publications provide a valuable forum for the exchange of ideas and for professional growth.

Additionally, we would like to thank the supplement authors who prepared material for this new edition. They include Gina Genova, University of California–Santa Barbara; Jay Stubblefield, North Carolina Wesleyan College; Randall J. Gerber, Macomb Community College; Danielle Scane, Orange Coast College; and Maureen Steddin.

The publishers would like to thank Dr. Bhavna Bhalla of IMT Ghaziabad, for reviewing the content of the International Edition.

Dedication

This book is dedicated to you and the many thousands of other students who have used this book in years past. We appreciate the opportunity to play a role in your education, and we wish you success and satisfaction in your studies and in your career.

John V. Thill
Courtland L. Bovée

Prologue

Building a Career with Your Communication Skills

Using This Course to Help Launch Your Career

This course will help you develop vital communication skills that you'll use throughout your career—and those skills can help you launch an interesting and rewarding career, too. This brief prologue sets the stage by helping you understand today's dynamic workplace, the steps you can take to adapt to the job market, and the importance of creating an employment portfolio and building your personal brand. Take a few minutes to read it while you think about the career you hope to create for yourself.

Understanding Today's Dynamic Workplace

There is no disguising the fact that you are entering a tough job market, but there are several reasons for at least some hope over the longer term. First, the U.S. economy will recover from the Great Recession, although it's going to take a while before the majority of employers feel confident enough to ramp up hiring significantly. Second, the large demographic bulge of Baby Boomers is moving into retirement, which should set off a chain reaction of openings from the tops of companies on downward. Third, political and business leaders here and abroad are keenly aware of the problem of unemployment among young adults, both as it affects people looking for work and in the loss of vitality to the economy. For example, programs aimed at helping graduates start companies right out of college, rather than entering the conventional job market, are springing up under government and philanthropic efforts.[1]

As the recovery plays out, you can count on a few other forces that are likely to affect your entry into the job market and your career options in years to come:[2]

- **Unpredictability.** Your career probably won't be as stable as careers were in your parents' generation. In today's business world, your career will likely be affected by globalization, mergers and acquisitions, a short-term mentality driven by the demands of stockholders, ethical upheavals, and the relentless quest for lower costs. On the plus side, new opportunities, new companies, and even entire industries can appear almost overnight. So while your career might not be as predictable as careers used to be, it could well be more of an adventure.
- **Flexibility.** As companies try to become more agile in a globalized economy, many employees—sometimes of their choice and sometimes not—are going solo and setting up shop as independent contractors. Innovations in electronic communication and social media will continue to spur the growth of *virtual organizations* and *virtual teams*, in which independent contractors and companies of various sizes join forces for long- or short-term projects, often without formal employment arrangements.
- **Economic globalization.** Commerce across borders has been going on for thousands of years, but the volume of international business has roughly tripled in the past 30 years. One significant result is *economic globalization*, the increasing integration

and interdependence of national economies around the world. Just as companies now compete across borders, as an employee or independent contractor you also compete globally. This situation can be disruptive and traumatic in some instances, but it also creates opportunities.

- **Growth of small business.** Small businesses employ about half of the private-sector workforce in this country and create somewhere between two-thirds and three-quarters of new jobs, so chances are good that you'll work for a small firm at some point.

What do all these forces mean to you? First, take charge of your career—and stay in charge of it. Understand your options, have a plan, and don't count on others to watch out for your future. Second, as you will learn throughout this course, understanding your audience is key to successful communication, so it is essential for you to understand how employers view the job market.

HOW EMPLOYERS VIEW TODAY'S JOB MARKET

From an employer's perspective, the employment process is always a question of balance. Maintaining a stable workforce can improve practically every aspect of business performance, yet many employers want the flexibility to shrink and expand payrolls as business conditions change. Employers obviously want to attract the best talent, but the best talent is more expensive and more vulnerable to offers from competitors, so there are always financial trade-offs to consider.

Employers also struggle with the ups and downs of the economy. When unemployment is low, the balance of power shifts to employees, and employers have to compete in order to attract and keep top talent. When unemployment is high, the power shifts back to employers, who can afford to be more selective and less accommodating. In other words, pay attention to the economy; at times you can be more aggressive in your demands, but at other times you need to be more accommodating.

Many employers now fill some labor needs by hiring temporary workers or engaging contractors on a project-by-project basis. Many U.S. employers are now also more willing to move jobs to cheaper labor markets outside the country and to recruit globally to fill positions in the United States. Both trends have stirred controversy, especially in the technology sector, as U.S. firms recruit top engineers and scientists from other countries while shifting mid- and low-range jobs to India, China, Russia, the Philippines, and other countries with lower wage structures.[3]

In summary, companies view employment as a complex business decision with lots of variables to consider. To make the most of your potential, regardless of the career path you pursue, you need to view employment in the same way.

WHAT EMPLOYERS LOOK FOR IN JOB APPLICANTS

Given the complex forces in the contemporary workplace and the unrelenting pressure of global competition, what are employers looking for in the candidates they hire? The short answer: a lot. Like all "buyers," companies want to get as much as they can for the money they spend. The closer you can present yourself as the ideal candidate, the better your chances of getting a crack at the most exciting opportunities.

Specific expectations vary by profession and position, of course, but virtually all employers look for the following general skills and attributes:[4]

- **Communication skills.** The reason this item is listed first isn't that you're reading a business communication textbook. Communication is listed first because it is far and away the most commonly mentioned skill set when employers are asked about what they look for in employees. Improving your communication skills will help in every aspect of your professional life.
- **Interpersonal and team skills.** You will have many individual responsibilities on the job, but chances are you won't work alone very often. Learn to work with others—and help them succeed as you succeed.

- **Intercultural and international awareness and sensitivity.** Successful employers tend to be responsive to diverse workforces, markets, and communities, and they look for employees with the same outlook.
- **Data collection, analysis, and decision-making skills.** Employers want people who know how to identify information needs, find the necessary data, convert the data into useful knowledge, and make sound decisions.
- **Computer and electronic media skills.** Today's workers need to know how to use common office software and to communicate using a wide range of electronic media.
- **Time and resource management.** If you've had to juggle multiple priorities during college, consider that great training for the business world. Your ability to plan projects and manage the time and resources available to you will make a big difference on the job.
- **Flexibility and adaptability.** Stuff happens, as they say. Employees who can roll with the punches and adapt to changing business priorities and circumstances will go further (and be happier) than employees who resist change.
- **Professionalism.** Professionalism is the quality of performing at the highest possible level and conducting oneself with confidence, purpose, and pride. True professionals strive to excel, continue to hone their skills and build their knowledge, are dependable and accountable, demonstrate a sense of business etiquette, make ethical decisions, show loyalty and commitment, don't give up when things get tough, and maintain a positive outlook.

Adapting to Today's Job Market

Adapting to the workplace is a lifelong process of seeking the best fit between what you want to do and what employers (or clients, if you work independently) are willing to pay you to do. It's important to know what you want to do, what you have to offer, and how to make yourself more attractive to employers.

WHAT DO YOU WANT TO DO?

Economic necessities and the vagaries of the marketplace will influence much of what happens in your career, of course; nevertheless, it's wise to start your employment search by examining your values and interests. Identify what you want to do first, then see whether you can find a position that satisfies you at a personal level while also meeting your financial needs. Consider these questions:

- **What would you like to do every day?** Research occupations that interest you. Find out what people really do every day. Ask friends, relatives, alumni from your school, and contacts in your social networks. Read interviews with people in various professions to get a sense of what their careers are like.
- **How would you like to work?** Consider how much independence you want on the job, how much variety you like, and whether you prefer to work with products, machines, people, ideas, figures, or some combination thereof.
- **How do your financial goals fit with your other priorities?** For instance, many high-paying jobs involve a lot of stress, sacrifices of time with family and friends, and frequent travel or relocation. If location, lifestyle, intriguing work, or other factors are more important to you, you may well have to sacrifice some level of pay to achieve them.
- **Have you established some general career goals?** For example, do you want to pursue a career specialty such as finance or manufacturing, or do you want to gain experience in multiple areas with an eye toward upper management?
- **What sort of corporate culture are you most comfortable with?** Would you be happy in a formal hierarchy with clear reporting relationships? Or do you prefer less structure? Teamwork or individualism? Do you like a competitive environment?

You might need some time in the workforce to figure out what you really want to do or to work your way into the job you really want, but it's never too early to start thinking

TABLE 1	Career Self-Assessment

What work-related activities and situations do you prefer? Evaluate your preferences in each of the following areas and use the results to help guide your job search.

Activity or Situation	Strongly Agree	Agree	Disagree	No Preference
1. I want to work independently.				
2. I want variety in my work.				
3. I want to work with people.				
4. I want to work with technology.				
5. I want physical work.				
6. I want mental work.				
7. I want to work for a large organization.				
8. I want to work for a nonprofit organization.				
9. I want to work for a small business.				
10. I want to work for a service business.				
11. I want to start or buy a business someday.				
12. I want regular, predictable work hours.				
13. I want to work in a city location.				
14. I want to work in a small town or suburb.				
15. I want to work in another country.				
16. I want to work outdoors.				
17. I want to work in a structured environment.				
18. I want to avoid risk as much as possible.				
19. I want to enjoy my work, even if that means making less money.				
20. I want to become a high-level corporate manager.				

about where you want to be. Filling out the assessment in Table 1 might help you get a clearer picture of the nature of work you would like to pursue in your career.

WHAT DO YOU HAVE TO OFFER?

Knowing what you want to do is one thing. Knowing what a company is willing to pay you to do is another thing entirely. You may already have a good idea of what you can offer employers. If not, some brainstorming can help you identify your skills, interests, and characteristics. Start by jotting down 10 achievements you're proud of, and think carefully about what specific skills these achievements demanded of you. For example, leadership skills, speaking ability, and artistic talent may have helped you coordinate a successful class project. As you analyze your achievements, you may well begin to recognize a pattern of skills. Which of them might be valuable to potential employers?

Next, look at your educational preparation, work experience, and extracurricular activities. What do your knowledge and experience qualify you to do? What have you learned from volunteer work or class projects that could benefit you on the job? Have you held any offices, won any awards or scholarships, mastered a second language? What skills have you developed in nonbusiness situations that could transfer to a business position?

Take stock of your personal characteristics. Are you aggressive, a born leader? Or would you rather follow? Are you outgoing, articulate, great with people? Or do you prefer working alone? Make a list of what you believe are your four or five most important qualities. Ask a relative or friend to rate your traits as well.

If you're having difficulty figuring out your interests, characteristics, or capabilities, consult your college career center. Many campuses administer a variety of tests that can help you identify interests, aptitudes, and personality traits. These tests won't reveal your "perfect" job, but they'll help you focus on the types of work best suited to your personality.

HOW CAN YOU MAKE YOURSELF MORE VALUABLE?

While you're figuring out what you want from a job and what you can offer an employer, you can take positive steps toward building your career. First, look for volunteer projects, temporary jobs, freelance work, or internships that will help expand your experience base and skill set.[5] You can look for freelance projects on Craigslist (www .craigslist.org) and numerous other websites; some of these jobs have only nominal pay, but they do provide an opportunity for you to display your skills. Also consider applying your talents to *crowdsourcing* projects, in which companies and nonprofit organizations invite the public to contribute solutions to various challenges.

These opportunities help you gain valuable experience and relevant contacts, provide you with important references and work samples for your *employment portfolio*, and help you establish your *personal brand* (see the following sections).

Second, learn more about the industry or industries in which you want to work and stay on top of new developments. Join networks of professional colleagues and friends who can help you keep up with trends and events. Many professional societies have student chapters or offer students discounted memberships. Take courses and pursue other educational or life experiences that would be difficult while working full time.

For more ideas and advice on planning your career, check out the resources listed in Table 2.

BUILDING AN EMPLOYMENT PORTFOLIO

Employers want proof that you have the skills to succeed on the job, but even if you don't have much relevant work experience, you can use your college classes to assemble that proof. Simply create and maintain an *employment portfolio*, which is a collection of projects that demonstrate your skills and knowledge. You can create a *print portfolio* and an *e-portfolio*; both can help with your career effort. A print portfolio gives you something tangible to bring to interviews, and it lets you collect project results that might not be easy to show online, such as a handsomely bound report.

An e-portfolio is a multimedia presentation of your skills and experiences.[6] Think of it as a website that contains your résumé, work samples, letters of recommendation, relevant videos or podcasts you have recorded, any blog posts or articles you have written, and other information about you and your skills. If you have set up a *lifestream* (a real-time aggregation of your content creation, online interests, and social media interactions) that is

TABLE 2	Career Planning Resources
Resource	**URL**
Career Rocketeer	www.careerrocketeer.com
The Creative Career	http://thecreativecareer.com
Brazen Careerist	www.brazencareerist.com
Daily Career Connection	http://dailycareerconnection.com
The Career Key	http://careerkey.blogspot.com
Rise Smart	www.risesmart.com/risesmart/blog
Women's Leadership Blog	http://blog.futurewomenleaders.net/blog
The Career Doctor	www.careerdoctor.org/career-doctor-blog

professionally focused, consider adding that to your e-portfolio. Be creative. For example, a student who was pursuing a degree in meteorology added a video clip of himself delivering a weather forecast.[7] The portfolio can be burned on a CD or DVD for physical distribution or, more commonly, it can be posted online—whether it's a personal website, your college's site (if student pages are available), a specialized portfolio hosting site such as Behance (www.behance.com), or a résumé hosting site such as VisualCV (www.visualcv.com) that offers multimedia résumés. To see a selection of student e-portfolios from colleges around the United States, go to http://real-timeupdates.com/ebc10, click on "Student Assignments," and then click on "Prologue" to locate the link to student e-portfolios.

Throughout this course, pay close attention to the assignments marked "Portfolio Builder" (they start in Chapter 7). These items will make particularly good samples of not only your communication skills but also your ability to understand and solve business-related challenges. By combining these projects with samples from your other courses, you can create a compelling portfolio when you're ready to start interviewing. Your portfolio is also a great resource for writing your résumé because it reminds you of all the great work you've done over the years. Moreover, you can continue to refine and expand your portfolio throughout your career; many professionals use e-portfolios to advertise their services. For example, Evan Eckard, a specialist in web design, marketing, and branding, promotes his capabilities by showing a range of successful projects in his online portfolio, which you can view at www.evaneckard.com.

As you assemble your portfolio, collect anything that shows your ability to perform, whether it's in school, on the job, or in other venues. However, you *must* check with employers before including any items that you created while you were an employee and check with clients before including any *work products* (anything you wrote, designed, programmed, and so on) they purchased from you. Many business documents contain confidential information that companies don't want distributed to outside audiences.

For each item you add to your portfolio, write a brief description that helps other people understand the meaning and significance of the project. Include such items as these:

- **Background.** Why did you undertake this project? Was it a school project, a work assignment, or something you did on your own initiative?
- **Project objectives.** Explain the project's goals, if relevant.
- **Collaborators.** If you worked with others, be sure to mention that and discuss team dynamics if appropriate. For instance, if you led the team or worked with others long distance as a virtual team, point that out.
- **Constraints.** Sometimes the most impressive thing about a project is the time or budget constraints under which it was created. If such constraints apply to a project, consider mentioning them in a way that doesn't sound like an excuse for poor quality. If you had only one week to create a website, for example, you might say that "One of the intriguing challenges of this project was the deadline; I had only one week to design, compose, test, and publish this material."
- **Outcomes.** If the project's goals were measurable, what was the result? For example, if you wrote a letter soliciting donations for a charitable cause, how much money did you raise?
- **Learning experience.** If appropriate, describe what you learned during the course of the project.

Keep in mind that the portfolio itself is a communication project too, so be sure to apply everything you'll learn in this course about effective communication and good design. Assume that every potential employer will find your e-portfolio site (even if you don't tell them about it), so don't include anything that could come back to haunt you. Also, if you have anything embarrassing on Facebook, MySpace, or any other social networking site, remove it immediately.

To get started, first check with the career center at your college; many schools now offer e-portfolio systems for their students. (Some schools now require e-portfolios, so you may already be building one.) You can also find plenty of advice online; search for "e-portfolio," "student portfolio," or "professional portfolio."

BUILDING YOUR PERSONAL BRAND

Products and companies have brands that represent collections of certain attributes, such as the safety emphasis of Volvo cars, the performance emphasis of BMW, or the luxury emphasis of Cadillac. Similarly, when people who know you think about you, they have a particular set of qualities in mind based on your professionalism, your priorities, and the various skills and attributes you have developed over the years. Perhaps without even being conscious of it, you have created a **personal brand** for yourself (see Figure 1).

As you plan the next stage of your career, start managing your personal brand deliberately. Branding specialist Mohammed Al-Taee defines personal branding succinctly as "a way of clarifying and communicating what makes you different and special."[8]

You can learn more about personal branding from the sources listed in Table 3, and you will have multiple opportunities to plan and refine your personal brand during this

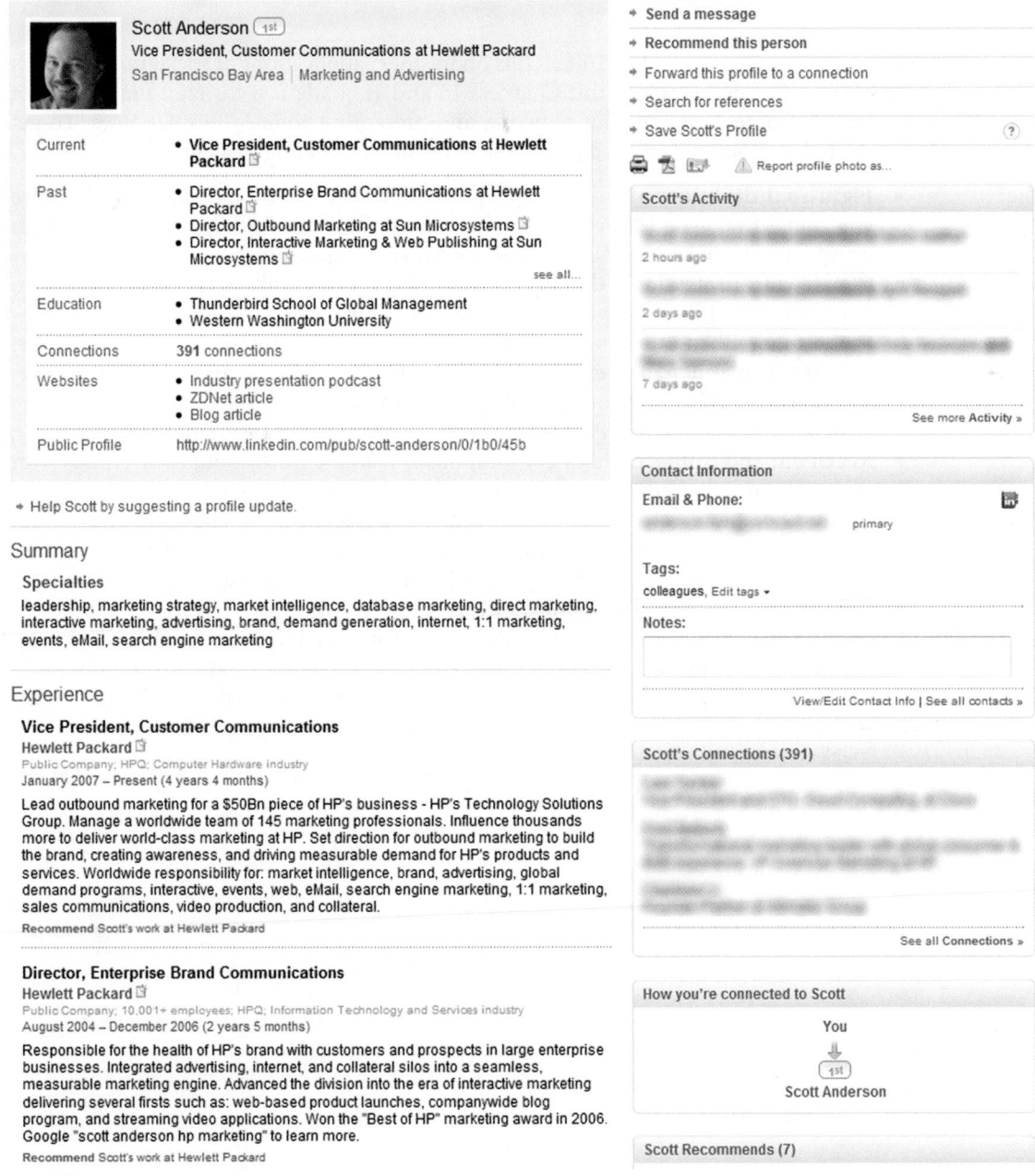

Figure 1   Personal Branding on LinkedIn
Scott Anderson, a marketing executive in the computer industry, makes good use of LinkedIn to present himself as an experienced professional capable of handling considerable levels of responsibility.

TABLE 3	Personal Branding Resources
Resource	**URL**
Personal Branding Blog	www.personalbrandingblog.com
Mohammed Al-Taee	http://altaeeblog.com
Brand Yourself	http://blog.brand-yourself.com
Krishna De	www.krishnade.com/blog
Cube Rules	http://cuberules.com
Jibber Jobber	www.jibberjobber.com/blog
The Engaging Brand	http://theengagingbrand.typepad.com
Brand-Yourself	http://blog.brand-yourself.com

course. For example, Chapter 7 offers tips on business applications of social media, which are key to personal branding, and Chapters 15 and 16 guide you through the process of creating a résumé, building your network, and presenting yourself in interviews. To get you started, here are the basics of a successful personal branding strategy:[9]

- **Figure out the "story of you."** Simply put, where have you been in life, and where are you going? Every good story has dramatic tension that pulls readers in and makes them wonder what will happen next. Where is your story going next?

- **Clarify your professional theme.** Volvos, BMWs, and Cadillacs can all get you from Point A to Point B in safety, comfort, and style—but each brand emphasizes some attributes more than others to create a specific image in the minds of potential buyers. Similarly, you want to be seen as something more than just an accountant, a supervisor, a salesperson. What will your theme be? Brilliant strategist? Hard-nosed, get-it-done tactician? Technical guru? Problem solver? Creative genius? Inspirational leader?

- **Reach out and connect.** Major corporations spread the word about their brands with multimillion-dollar advertising campaigns. You can promote your brand for free or close to it. The secret is networking, which you'll learn more about in Chapter 15. You build your brand by connecting with like-minded people, sharing information, demonstrating skills and knowledge, and helping others succeed.

- **Deliver on your brand's promise—every time, all the time.** When you promote a brand, you make a promise—a promise that whoever buys that brand will get the benefits you are promoting. All of this planning and communication is of no value if you fail to deliver on the promises that your branding efforts make. Conversely, when you deliver quality results time after time, your talents and your professionalism will speak for you.

We wish you great success in this course and in your career!

REFERENCES

1. Peter Coy, "The Youth Unemployment Bomb," *Bloomberg Businessweek*, 2 February 2011, www.businessweek.com.

2. Jeanne C. Meister and Karie Willyerd, "Leading Virtual Teams to Real Results," *Harvard Business Review* blogs, 30 June 2010, http://blogs.hbr.org; *The Small Business Economy, 2009*, U.S. Small Business Administration website, accessed 16 August 2010, www.sba.gov; Malik Singleton, "Same Markets, New Marketplaces," *Black Enterprise*, September 2004, 34; Edmund L. Andrews, "Where Do the Jobs Come From?" *New York Times*, 21 September 2004, E1, E11; Maureen Jenkins, "Yours for the Taking," *Boeing Frontiers Online*, June 2004, www.boeing.com; "Firm Predicts Top 10 Workforce/Workplace Trends for 2004," *Enterprise*, 8–14 December 2003, 1–2; Ricky W. Griffin and Michael W. Pustay, *International Business*, 6th ed. (Upper Saddle River, N.J.: Pearson Prentice Hall, 2010), 21.

3. Vivian Yeo, "India Still Top Choice for Offshoring," *BusinessWeek*, 27 June 2008, www.businessweek.com; Jim Puzzanghera, "Coalition of High-Tech Firms to Urge Officials to Help Keep U.S. Competitive," *San Jose Mercury News*, 8 January 2004, www.ebscohost.com.

4. Courtland L. Bovée and John V. Thill, *Business in Action*, 5th ed. (Upper Saddle River, N.J.: Pearson Prentice Hall, 2010), 18–21; Randall S. Hansen and Katharine Hansen, "What Do Employers Really Want? Top Skills and Values Employers Seek from Job-Seekers," QuintCareers.com, accessed 17 August 2010, www.quintcareers.com.

5. Nancy M. Somerick, "Managing a Communication Internship Program," *Bulletin of the Association for Business Communication* 56, no. 3 (1993): 10–20.

6. Jeffrey R. Young, "'E-Portfolios' Could Give Students a New Sense of Their Accomplishments," *The Chronicle of Higher Education*, 8 March 2002, A31.

7. Brian Carcione, e-portfolio, accessed 20 December 2006, http://eportfolio.psu.edu.

8. Mohammed Al-Taee, "Personal Branding," Al-Taee blog, accessed 17 August 2010 http://altaeeblog.com.

9. Pete Kistler, "Seth Godin's 7-Point Guide to Bootstrap Your Personal Brand," Personal Branding blog, 28 July 2010, www.personalbrandingblog; Kyle Lacy, "10 Ways to Building Your Personal Brand Story," Personal Branding blog, 5 August 2010, www.personalbrandingblog; Al-Taee, "Personal Branding"; Scot Herrick, "30 Career Management Tips—Marketing AND Delivery Support Our Personal Brand," Cube Rules blog, 8 September 2007, http://cuberules.com; Alina Tugend, "Putting Yourself Out There on a Shelf to Buy," *New York Times*, 27 March 2009, www.nytimes.com.

PART 1

Understanding the Foundations of Business Communication

No other skill can help your career in as many ways as communication. Discover what business communication is all about, why communication skills are essential to your career, and how to adapt your communication experiences in life and college to the business world. Improve your skills in such vital areas as team interaction, etiquette, listening, and nonverbal communication. Explore the advantages and the challenges of a diverse workforce, and develop the skills that every communicator needs to succeed in today's global business environment.

Asia Images Group-Royalty Free, Getty Images, Inc.

LEARNING OBJECTIVES   After studying this chapter, you will be able to

1 Explain the importance of effective communication to your career and to the companies where you will work

2 Describe the communication skills employers will expect you to have and the nature of communicating in an organization by using an audience-centered approach

3 Describe the communication process model and the ways that social media are changing the nature of business communication

4 List four general guidelines for using communication technology effectively

5 Define *ethics*, explain the difference between an ethical dilemma and an ethical lapse, and list six guidelines for making ethical communication choices

MyBcommLab **Where you see MyBcommLab in this chapter, go to** www.pearsoninternationaleditions.com/mybcommlab **for additional activities on the topic being discussed.**

ON THE JOB: COMMUNICATING AT TOYOTA

Toyota's user-generated content campaign, Auto-Biography, invited owners to submit stories, photos, and videos that describe their favorite moments and memories with their Toyota vehicles.
Source: Used with permission of Toyota.

Inviting Customers to Help Rejuvenate a Brand's Reputation

Imagine that you're in the market for a new car and need to learn about the various models, options, dealers, and other factors involved in this important purchase. Fortunately, a friend has just gone through this process and can provide valuable information from a consumer's perspective.

Now imagine that you have a hundred or a thousand or ten thousand friends who have recently purchased cars. Imagine how much information you could get from all these people—and all you need to do is jump on Facebook, Epinions, or another social media website.

Consumers have been sharing information online for as long as computers have been connected, but the rapid growth of social media has merged these isolated conversations into a global phenomenon that has permanently changed the nature of business communication. The Japanese automaker Toyota is one of the millions of companies around the world using social media to supplement or even replace traditional forms of customer communication.

Toyota was looking for some positive communication in 2010, after concerns about sticking gas pedals led to the recall of millions of vehicles and prompted the company to halt sales of eight models while it investigated the problem. The situation was potentially serious, to be sure, but Toyota executive Bob Zeinstra said that loyal Toyota owners responded with an "outpouring of support and care."

To capitalize on this goodwill, built up through years of delivering safe, dependable vehicles, Toyota invited owners to tell their stories through a Facebook campaign it called "Auto-Biography." The program featured a customized Facebook application that encouraged owners to "showcase your most memorable moments [with your Toyota] and get inspired by the stories of other loyal Toyota owners."

Thousands of Toyota owners contributed, sharing everything from the pet names they gave their cars to how they use their cars for work or play to the way their families passed down a Toyota from one generation to the next. Many listed the number of miles they had on their cars, some up to 300,000 or more, making strong statements to support the Toyota message of reliability. Many owners also personalized their stories with photos or videos of themselves and their cars. Toyota highlighted a small number of the stories through professionally produced animated or live videos, which it then featured prominently on the Auto-Biography page and used in print and television advertising.

By inviting satisfied customers to the tell their own stories through *user-generated content* (which you'll read more about in Chapter 7), the campaign helped Toyota repair its reputation among potential car buyers and respond to negative stories in the news media. Moreover, Zeinstra says the Facebook initiative also reminded current Toyota owners "why they love their cars so much."[1]

www.facebook.com/toyota

Understanding Why Communication Matters

Whether it's as simple as a smile or as ambitious as a Facebook campaign such as Toyota's (profiled in the chapter-opener), **communication** is the process of transferring information and meaning between *senders* and *receivers*, using one or more written, oral, visual, or electronic media. The essence of communication is sharing—providing data, information, insights, and inspiration in an exchange that benefits both you and the people with whom you are communicating.[2]

You will invest a lot of time and energy in this course to develop your communication skills, so it's fair to ask whether the effort will be worthwhile. This section outlines the many ways in which good communication skills are critical for your career and for any company you join.

1 **LEARNING OBJECTIVE**

Explain the importance of effective communication to your career and to the companies where you will work.

Communication is the process of transferring information and meaning between senders and receivers.

COMMUNICATION IS IMPORTANT TO YOUR CAREER

Improving your communication skills may be the single most important step you can take in your career. You can have the greatest ideas in the world, but they're no good to your company or your career if you can't express them clearly and persuasively. Some jobs, such as sales and customer support, are primarily about communicating. In fields such as engineering or finance, you often need to share complex ideas with executives, customers, and colleagues, and your ability to connect with people outside your field can be as important as your technical expertise. If you have the entrepreneurial urge, you will need to communicate with a wide range of audiences, from investors, bankers, and government regulators to employees, customers, and business partners.

Ambition and great ideas aren't enough; you need to be able to communicate with people in order to succeed in business.

As you take on leadership and management roles, communication becomes even more important. The higher you rise in an organization, the less time you will spend using the technical skills of your particular profession and the more time you will spend communicating. Top executives spend most of their time communicating, and businesspeople who can't communicate well don't stand much chance of reaching the top.

Many employers express frustration at the poor communication skills of many employees—particularly recent college graduates who haven't yet learned how to adapt their communication styles to a professional business environment. If you learn to write well, speak well, listen well, and recognize the appropriate way to communicate in any situation, you'll gain a major advantage that will serve you throughout your career.[3]

Strong communication skills give you an advantage in the job market.

This course teaches you how to send and receive information more effectively and helps you improve your communication skills through practice in an environment that provides honest, constructive criticism. You will discover how to collaborate in teams, listen effectively, master nonverbal communication, and participate in productive meetings. You'll learn about communicating across cultural boundaries. You'll learn a three-step process

MyBcommLab

● Access this chapter's simulation entitled Successful Business Communication, located at www.pearsoninternational editions.com/mybcommlab.

that helps you write effective business messages, and you'll get specific tips for crafting a variety of business messages using a wide range of media, from social networks to blogs to online presentations. Develop these skills, and you'll start your business career with a clear competitive advantage.

COMMUNICATION IS IMPORTANT TO YOUR COMPANY

Effective communication yields numerous business benefits.

Aside from the personal benefits, communication should be important to you because it is important to your company. Effective communication helps businesses in numerous ways. It provides:[4]

- Closer ties with important communities in the marketplace
- Opportunities to influence conversations, perceptions, and trends
- Increased productivity and faster problem solving
- Better financial results and higher return for investors
- Earlier warning of potential problems, from rising business costs to critical safety issues
- Stronger decision making based on timely, reliable information
- Clearer and more persuasive marketing messages
- Greater employee engagement with their work, leading to higher employee satisfaction and lower employee turnover

WHAT MAKES BUSINESS COMMUNICATION EFFECTIVE?

Effective communication strengthens the connections between a company and all of its **stakeholders**, those groups affected in some way by the company's actions: customers, employees, shareholders, suppliers, neighbors, the community, the nation, and the world as a whole.[5] Conversely, when communication is ineffective, the results can range from time wasting to tragic.

Effective messages are *practical, factual, concise, clear,* and *persuasive.*

To make your communication efforts as effective as possible, focus on making them practical, factual, concise, clear, and persuasive:

- **Provide practical information.** Give recipients useful information, whether it's to help them perform a desired action or understand a new company policy.
- **Give facts rather than vague impressions.** Use concrete language, specific detail, and information that is clear, convincing, accurate, and ethical. Even when an opinion is called for, present compelling evidence to support your conclusion.
- **Present information in a concise, efficient manner.** Concise messages show respect for people's time, and they increase the chances of a positive response.
- **Clarify expectations and responsibilities.** Craft messages to generate a specific response from a specific audience. When appropriate, clearly state what you expect from audience members or what you can do for them.
- **Offer compelling, persuasive arguments and recommendations.** Show your readers precisely how they will benefit from responding to your message the way you want them to.

Keep these five important characteristics in mind as you review Figures 1.1 and 1.2. At first glance, both emails appear to be well constructed, but Figure 1.2 is far more effective, as the comments in blue explain.

2 **LEARNING OBJECTIVE**

Describe the communication skills employers will expect you to have and the nature of communicating in an organization by using an audience-centered approach.

Communicating in Today's Global Business Environment

You've been communicating your entire life, of course, but if you don't have a lot of work experience yet, meeting the expectations of a professional environment might require some adjustment. This section offers a brief look at the unique challenges of business

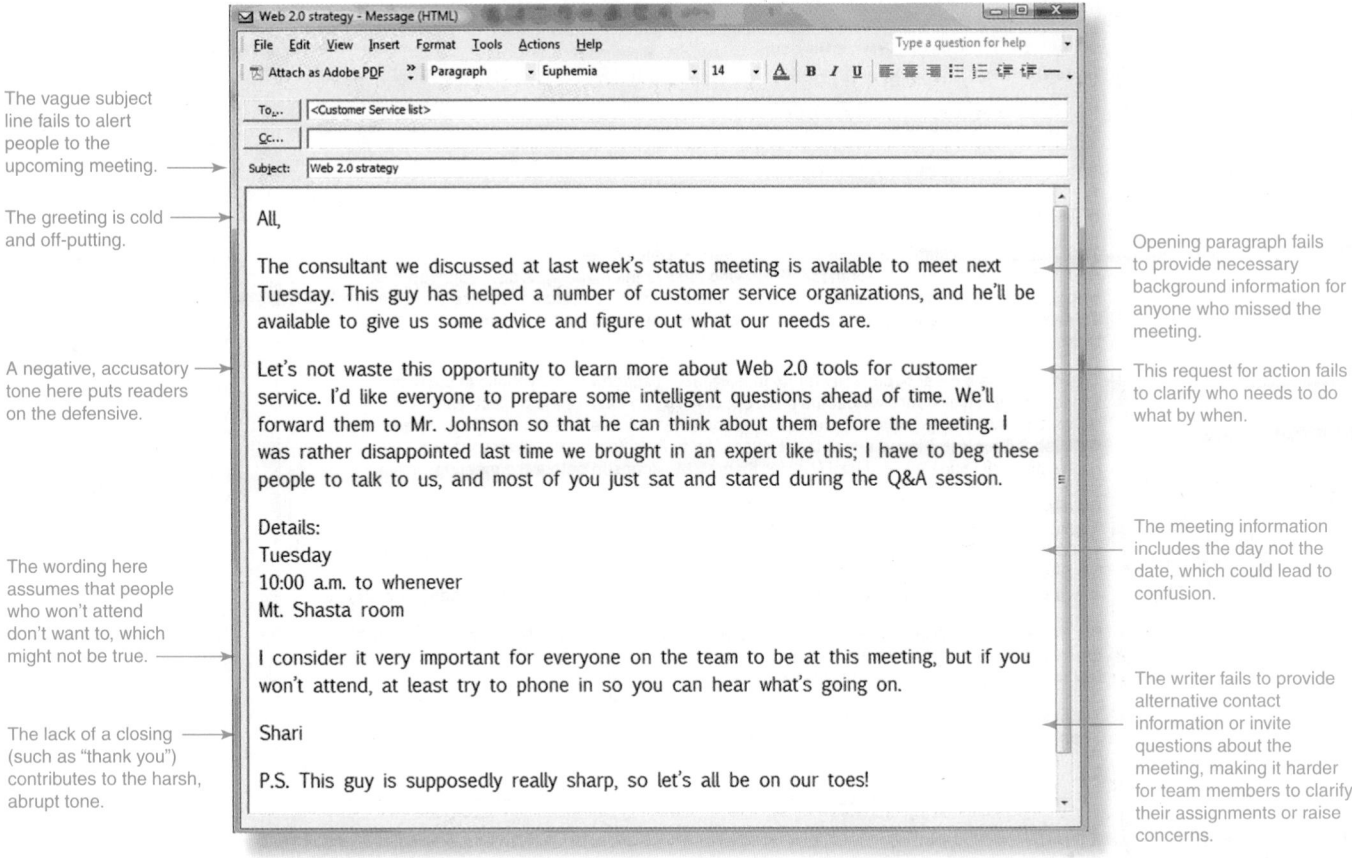

The vague subject line fails to alert people to the upcoming meeting.

The greeting is cold and off-putting.

A negative, accusatory tone here puts readers on the defensive.

The wording here assumes that people who won't attend don't want to, which might not be true.

The lack of a closing (such as "thank you") contributes to the harsh, abrupt tone.

Opening paragraph fails to provide necessary background information for anyone who missed the meeting.

This request for action fails to clarify who needs to do what by when.

The meeting information includes the day not the date, which could lead to confusion.

The writer fails to provide alternative contact information or invite questions about the meeting, making it harder for team members to clarify their assignments or raise concerns.

Figure 1.1   Ineffective Business Communication
At first glance, this email message looks like a reasonable attempt at communicating with the members of a project team. However, review the blue annotations to see just how many problems the message really has.

MyBcommLab

Apply Figure 1.1's key concepts by revising a new document. Go to Chapter 1 in www .pearsoninternationaleditions.com/mybcommlab and select Document Makeovers.

communication, the skills that employers will expect you to have, the nature of communication in an organizational environment, and the importance of adopting an audience-centered approach.

UNDERSTANDING THE UNIQUE CHALLENGES OF BUSINESS COMMUNICATION

Business communication is often more complicated and demanding than the social communication you typically engage in with family, friends, and school associates. This section highlights five issues that illustrate why business communication requires a high level of skill and attention.

You will need to adjust your communication habits to the more formal demands of business and the unique environment of your company.

The Globalization of Business and the Increase in Workforce Diversity

Today's businesses increasingly reach across international borders to market their products, partner with other businesses, and employ workers and executives—an effort known as **globalization**. Many U.S. companies rely on exports for a significant portion of their sales, sometimes up to 50 percent or more, and managers and employees in these firms need to communicate with many other cultures. Moreover, thousands of companies from all around the world vie for a share of the massive U.S. market, so chances are you'll do business with or even work for a company based in another country at some point in your career.

Businesses are paying more attention to **workforce diversity**—all the differences among people who work together, including differences in age, gender, sexual orientation, education, cultural background, religion, ability, and life experience. As Chapter 3

Smart employers recognize the benefits of a more diverse workforce—and the additional challenges of ensuring smooth communication between people from diverse backgrounds.

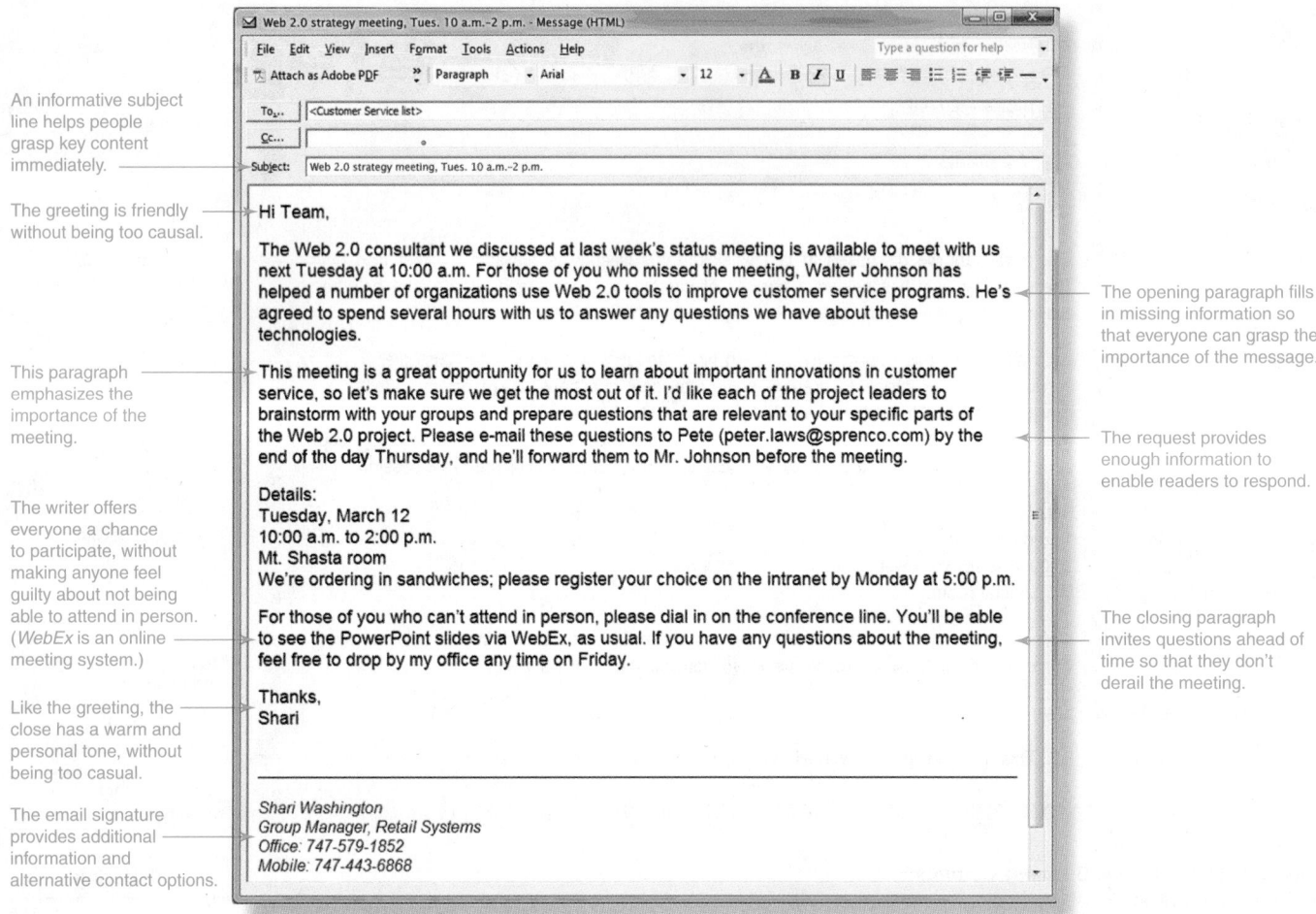

An informative subject line helps people grasp key content immediately.

The greeting is friendly without being too causal.

This paragraph emphasizes the importance of the meeting.

The writer offers everyone a chance to participate, without making anyone feel guilty about not being able to attend in person. (*WebEx* is an online meeting system.)

Like the greeting, the close has a warm and personal tone, without being too casual.

The email signature provides additional information and alternative contact options.

The opening paragraph fills in missing information so that everyone can grasp the importance of the message.

The request provides enough information to enable readers to respond.

The closing paragraph invites questions ahead of time so that they don't derail the meeting.

Figure 1.2   Effective Business Communication
This improved version of the email message from Figure 1.1 does a much better job of communicating the essential information these team members need in order to effectively prepare for the meeting.

discusses, successful companies realize that a diverse workforce can yield a significant competitive advantage, but it also requires a more conscientious approach to communication.

The Increasing Value of Business Information

Information has become one of the most important resources in business today.

As global competition for talent, customers, and resources continues to grow, the importance of information continues to escalate as well. Companies in virtually every industry rely heavily on *knowledge workers*, employees at all levels of an organization who specialize in acquiring, processing, and communicating information. Three examples help to illustrate the value of information in today's economy:

- **Competitive insights.** The more a company knows about its competitors and their plans, the better able it will be to adjust its own business plans.
- **Customer needs.** Information about customer needs is analyzed and summarized in order to develop goods and services that better satisfy customer demands.
- **Regulations and guidelines.** Today's businesses must understand and follow a wide range of government regulations and guidelines covering such areas as employment, environment, taxes, and accounting.

No matter what the specific type of information, the better you are able to understand it, use it, and communicate it to others, the more competitive you and your company will be.

The Pervasiveness of Technology

Business communication today is heavily dependent on a growing array of technologies.

Technology influences virtually every aspect of business communication today. To benefit from these tools, however, you need to have at least a basic level of skills. If your level of technical expertise doesn't keep up with that of your colleagues and coworkers, the imbalance can put you at a disadvantage and complicate the communication process. Throughout this course, you'll gain insights into using numerous tools and systems more effectively.

The Evolution of Organizational Structures and Leadership Styles

Every firm has a particular structure that defines the relationships among units in the company, and these relationships influence the nature and quality of communication throughout the organization. *Tall structures* have many layers of management between the lowest and highest positions, and they can suffer communication breakdowns and delays as messages are passed up and down through multiple layers.[6]

> Organizations with tall structures may unintentionally restrict the flow of information; flatter structures can make it easier to communicate effectively.

To overcome such problems, many businesses have adopted *flat structures* that reduce the number of layers and promote more open and direct communication. However, with fewer formal lines of control and communication in these organizations, individual employees are expected to assume more responsibility for communication.

Specific types of organization structures present unique communication challenges. In a *matrix structure*, for example, employees report to two managers at the same time, such as a project manager and a department manager. The need to coordinate workloads, schedules, and other matters increases the communication burden on everyone involved. In a *network structure*, sometimes known as a *virtual organization*, a company supplements the talents of its employees with services from one or more external partners, such as a design lab, a manufacturing firm, or a sales and distribution company.

> Newer types of organization structures such as matrices and networks present new communication challenges.

Regardless of the particular structure a company uses, your communication efforts will also be influenced by the organization's **corporate culture**: the mixture of values, traditions, and habits that gives a company its atmosphere and personality. Many successful companies encourage employee contributions by fostering *open climates* that promote candor and honesty, helping employees feel free enough to admit their mistakes, disagree with the boss, and share negative or unwelcome information.

> Open corporate cultures benefit from free-flowing information and employee input.

A Heavy Reliance on Teamwork

Both traditional and innovative company structures can rely heavily on teamwork, and you will probably find yourself on dozens of teams throughout your career. Teams are commonly used in business today, but they're not always successful—and a key reason that teams fail to meet their objectives is poor communication. Chapter 2 offers insights into the complex dynamics of team communication and identifies skills you need in order to be an effective communicator in group settings.

> Working in a team makes you even more responsible for communicating effectively.

UNDERSTANDING WHAT EMPLOYERS EXPECT FROM YOU

Today's employers expect you to be competent at a wide range of communication tasks. Fortunately, the skills that employers expect from you are the same skills that will help you advance in your career:[7]

- Organizing ideas and information logically and completely
- Expressing ideas and information coherently and persuasively
- Actively listening to others
- Communicating effectively with people from diverse backgrounds and experiences
- Using communication technologies effectively and efficiently
- Following accepted standards of grammar, spelling, and other aspects of high-quality writing and speaking

Successful companies know that diverse workforces can create powerful competitive advantages, but they require closer attention to communication in order to eliminate barriers between groups with different communication styles.
Source: © Corbis Super RF/Alamy.

Employers expect you to possess a wide range of communication skills.

- Communicating in a civilized manner that reflects contemporary expectations of business etiquette, even when dealing with indifferent or hostile audiences
- Communicating ethically, even when choices aren't crystal clear
- Managing your time wisely and using resources efficiently

You'll have the opportunity to practice these skills throughout this course—but don't stop there. Successful professionals continue to hone communication skills throughout their careers.

COMMUNICATING IN AN ORGANIZATIONAL CONTEXT

The formal communication network mirrors the company's organizational structure.

In addition to having the proper skills, you need to learn how to apply those skills in the business environment, which can be quite different from the social and scholastic environments you are accustomed to. Every organization has a *formal communication network*, in which ideas and information flow along the lines of command (the hierarchical levels) in the company's organization structure (see Figure 1.3). Throughout the formal network, information flows in three directions. *Downward communication* flows from executives to employees, conveying executive decisions and providing information that helps employees do their jobs. *Upward communication* flows from employees to executives, providing insight into problems, trends, opportunities, grievances, and performance—thus allowing executives to solve problems and make intelligent decisions. *Horizontal communication* flows between departments to help employees share information, coordinate tasks, and solve complex problems.[8]

Social media play an increasingly important role in the informal communication network.

Every organization also has an *informal communication network*, often referred to as the *grapevine* or the *rumor mill*, that encompasses all communication that occurs outside the formal network. Some of this informal communication takes place naturally as a result of employee interaction both on the job and in social settings, and some of it takes place when the formal network doesn't provide information that employees want. In fact, the inherent limitations of formal communication networks helped spur the growth of social media in the business environment.

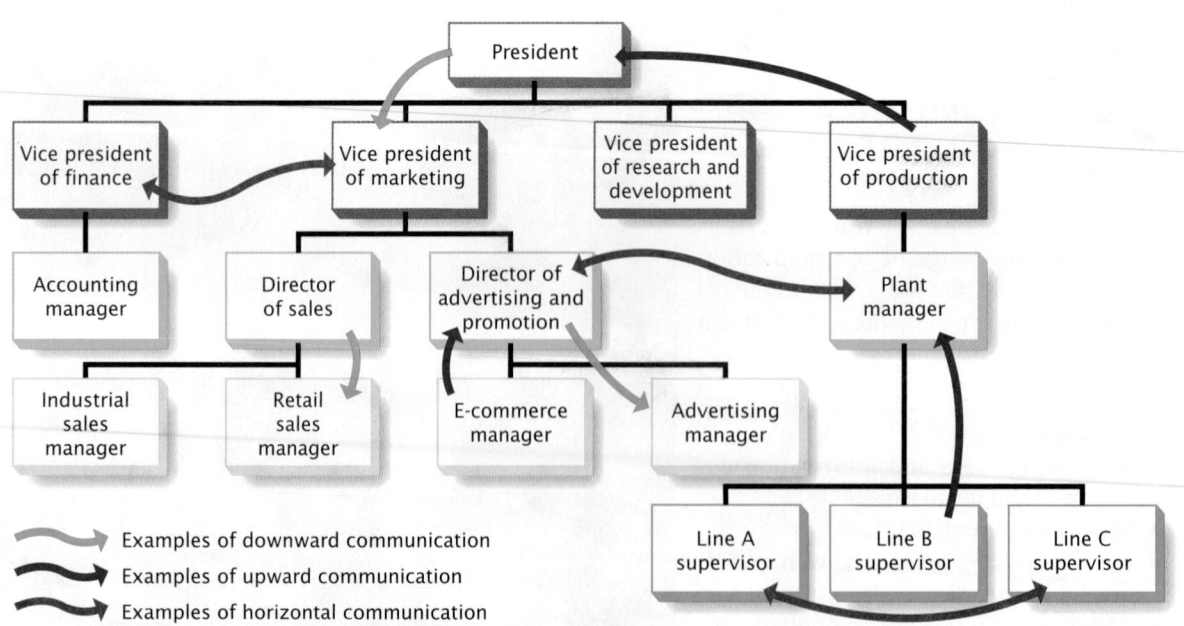

Figure 1.3 Formal Communication Network
The formal communication network is defined by the relationships between the various job positions in the organization. Messages can flow *upward* (from a lower-level employee to a higher-level employee), *downward* (from a higher-level employee to a lower-level employee), and *horizontally* (across the organization, between employees at the same or similar levels).

ADOPTING AN AUDIENCE-CENTERED APPROACH

An **audience-centered approach** involves understanding and respecting the members of your audience and making every effort to get your message across in a way that is meaningful to them (see Figure 1.4). This approach is also known as adopting the **"you" attitude**, in contrast to messages that are about "me." Learn as much as possible about the biases, education, age, status, style, and personal and professional concerns of your receivers. If you're addressing people you don't know and you're unable to find out more about them, try to project yourself into their position by using common sense and imagination. This ability to relate to the needs of others is a key part of *emotional intelligence*, which is widely considered to be a vital characteristic of successful managers and leaders.[9] The more you know about the people you're communicating with, the easier it will be to concentrate on their needs—which, in turn, will make it easier for them to hear your message, understand it, and respond positively.

An audience-centered approach involves understanding, respecting, and meeting the needs of your audience members.

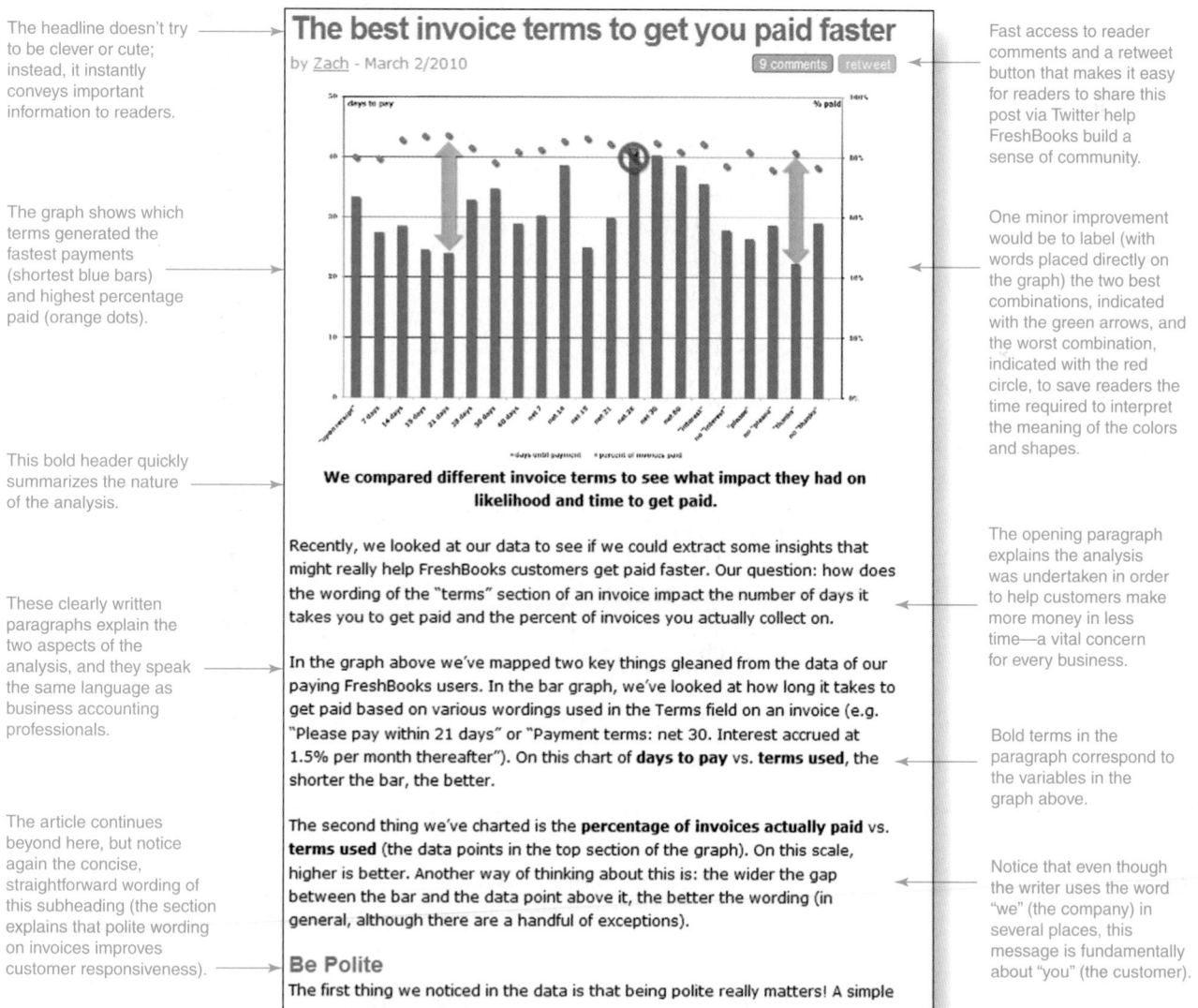

The headline doesn't try to be clever or cute; instead, it instantly conveys important information to readers.

The graph shows which terms generated the fastest payments (shortest blue bars) and highest percentage paid (orange dots).

This bold header quickly summarizes the nature of the analysis.

These clearly written paragraphs explain the two aspects of the analysis, and they speak the same language as business accounting professionals.

The article continues beyond here, but notice again the concise, straightforward wording of this subheading (the section explains that polite wording on invoices improves customer responsiveness).

Fast access to reader comments and a retweet button that makes it easy for readers to share this post via Twitter help FreshBooks build a sense of community.

One minor improvement would be to label (with words placed directly on the graph) the two best combinations, indicated with the green arrows, and the worst combination, indicated with the red circle, to save readers the time required to interpret the meaning of the colors and shapes.

The opening paragraph explains the analysis was undertaken in order to help customers make more money in less time—a vital concern for every business.

Bold terms in the paragraph correspond to the variables in the graph above.

Notice that even though the writer uses the word "we" (the company) in several places, this message is fundamentally about "you" (the customer).

Figure 1.4   Audience-Centered Communication

This blog post from the developers of the FreshBooks online business accounting system demonstrates audience focus in multiple ways, starting with the effort behind the message. Every company worries about how quickly customers will pay their bills, so FreshBooks analyzed the customer data it had on hand to see which payment terms and invoice messages generated the quickest responses. This alone is remarkable customer service; the audience-focused presentation of the information makes it that much better.

Source: Used with permission of FreshBooks.

Etiquette, the expected norms of behavior in any particular situation, can have a profound influence on your company's success and your career.

A vital element of audience-centered communication is **etiquette**, the expected norms of behavior in any particular situation. In today's hectic, competitive world, etiquette might seem a quaint and outdated notion. However, the way you conduct yourself and interact with others can have a profound influence on your company's success and your career. When executives hire and promote you, they expect your behavior to protect the company's reputation. The more you understand such expectations, the better chance you have of avoiding career-damaging mistakes. The principles of etiquette discussed in Chapter 2 will help you communicate with an audience-centered approach in a variety of business settings.

Exploring the Communication Process

3 **LEARNING OBJECTIVE**

Describe the communication process model and the ways that social media are changing the nature of business communication.

As you no doubt know from your personal interactions over the years, even well-intentioned communication efforts can fail. Messages can get lost or simply ignored. The receiver of a message can interpret it in ways the sender never imagined. In fact, two people receiving the same information can reach different conclusions about what it means.

Fortunately, by understanding communication as a process with distinct steps, you can improve the odds that your messages will reach their intended audiences and produce their intended effects. This section explores the communication process in two stages: first by following a message from one sender to one receiver in the basic communication model, and second by expanding on that basic scenario to include multiple messages and participants in the social communication model.

THE BASIC COMMUNICATION MODEL

Viewing communication as a process helps you identify steps you can take to improve your success as a communicator.

By viewing communication as a process (see Figure 1.5), you can identify and improve the skills you need in order to be more successful. Many variations on this process model exist, but these eight steps provide a practical overview:

1. **The sender has an idea.** Whether a communication effort will ultimately be effective starts right here. For example, if you have a clear idea about a procedure change that will save your company time and money, the communication process is off to a strong start. On the other hand, if all you want to do is complain about how the company is wasting time and money but don't have any solutions, you probably won't communicate anything of value to your audience.

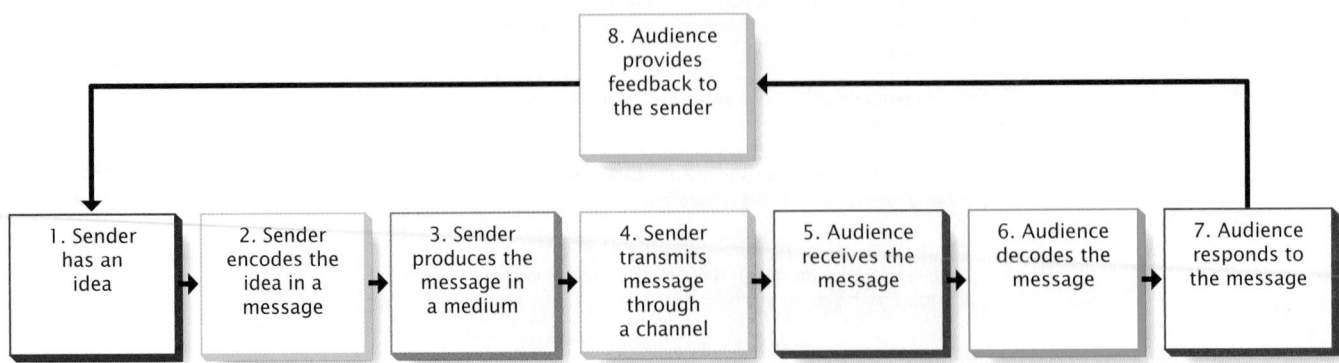

Figure 1.5   A Model of the Communication Process
These eight steps illustrate how an idea travels from a sender to a receiver. After you explore the process in more detail in the following pages, refer to Figure 1.7 on page 55 for advice on improving your skills at each step. This diagram offers a simplified view of a process that is both complex and subtle, but it provides a good foundation on which to build your understanding of communication.

2. **The sender encodes the idea as a message.** When someone puts an idea into a **message**—which you can think of as the "container" for an idea—he or she is **encoding** it, or expressing it in words or images. Much of the focus of this course is on developing the skills needed to successfully encode your ideas into effective messages.

3. **The sender produces the message in a transmittable medium.** With the appropriate message to express an idea, the sender now needs a **communication medium** to present that message to the intended audience. As you'll read in Chapter 4, media for transmitting messages can be divided into *oral, written, visual,* and *electronic* forms.

> The medium is the *form* a message takes and the channel is the system used to *deliver* the message.

4. **The sender transmits the message through a channel.** Just as technology continues to increase the number of media options at your disposal, it continues to provide new **communication channels** you can use to transmit your messages. The distinction between medium and channel can get a bit murky, but think of the medium as the *form* a message takes and the channel as the system used to *deliver* the message. The channel can be a face-to-face conversation, the Internet, another company—any method or system capable of delivering messages.

5. **The audience receives the message.** If the channel functions properly, the message reaches its intended audience. However, mere arrival at the destination is no guarantee that the message will be noticed or understood correctly. As "How Audiences Receive Messages" (page 52) explains, many messages are either ignored or misinterpreted as noise.

6. **The audience decodes the message.** After a message is received, the receiver needs to extract the idea from the message, a step known as **decoding**. "How Audiences Decode Messages" (page 53) takes a closer look at this complex and subtle step in the process.

7. **The audience responds to the message.** By crafting messages in ways that show the benefits of responding, senders can increase the chances that recipients will respond in positive ways. However, as "How Audiences Respond to Messages" (page 54) points out, whether a receiver responds as the sender hopes depends on the receiver (a) *remembering* the message long enough to act on it, (b) being *able* to act on it, and (c) being *motivated* to respond.

8. **The audience provides feedback to sender.** In addition to responding (or not responding) to the message, audience members may give **feedback** that helps the sender evaluate the effectiveness of the communication effort. Feedback can be verbal (using written or spoken words), nonverbal (using gestures, facial expressions, or other signals), or both. Just like the original message, however, this feedback from the receiver also needs to be decoded carefully. A smile, for example, can have many meanings.

The following sections take a closer look at two important aspects of the process: environmental barriers that can block or distort messages along the way, and the steps audiences take to receive, decode, and respond to messages.

Barriers in the Communication Environment

Within any communication environment, messages can be disrupted by a variety of **communication barriers**. These include noise and distractions, competing messages, filters, and channel breakdowns:

> A number of barriers can block or distort messages before they reach the intended audience.

- **Noise and distractions.** External distractions range from uncomfortable meeting rooms to crowded computer screens with instant messages and reminders popping up all over the place. Internal distractions are thoughts and emotions that prevent audiences from focusing on incoming messages. The common habit of *multitasking,* attempting more than one task at a time, is practically guaranteed to create communication distractions. Moreover, research suggests that "chronic multitasking" can reduce productivity and increase errors.[10]

- **Competing messages.** Having your audience's undivided attention is a rare luxury. In most cases, you must compete with other messages that are trying to reach your

audience at the same time, which is why it is so essential to craft messages that your audience will care about.

- **Filters.** Messages can be blocked or distorted by *filters*, any human or technological interventions between the sender and the receiver. Filtering can be both intentional (such as automatically filing incoming messages based on sender or content) or unintentional (such as an overly aggressive spam filter that deletes legitimate emails). As you read earlier, the structure and culture of an organization can also inhibit the flow of vital messages. And, in some cases, the people or companies you rely on to deliver your message can distort it or filter it to meet their own needs.

- **Channel breakdowns.** Sometimes the channel simply breaks down and fails to deliver your message at all. A colleague you were counting on to deliver a message to your boss might have forgotten to do so, or a computer server might have crashed and prevented your blog from updating.

Minimizing barriers and distractions in the communication environment is everyone's responsibility.

Everyone in an organization can help minimize barriers and distractions. In any situation, a small dose of common sense and courtesy goes a long way. Turn off that mobile phone before you step into a meeting. Don't talk across the tops of other people's cubicles. Be sensitive to personal differences, too. For instance, some people enjoy working with music on, but music is a huge distraction for others, so use headphones.[11]

Finally, take steps to insulate yourself from distractions. Don't let messages interrupt you every minute of the day. Instead, try to set aside time to attend to messages all at once so that you can focus the rest of the time.

Inside the Mind of Your Audience

After a message works its way through the communication channel and reaches the intended audience, it encounters a whole new set of challenges. Understanding how audiences receive, decode, and respond to messages will help you create more effective messages.

To actually receive a message, audience members need to sense it, select it, then perceive it as a message.

How Audiences Receive Messages   For an audience member to receive a message, three events need to occur: The receiver has to *sense* the presence of a message, *select* it from all the other messages clamoring for attention, and *perceive* it as an actual message (as opposed to random, pointless noise).[12] You can appreciate the magnitude of this challenge by driving down any busy street in a commercial section of town. You'll encounter literally hundreds of messages—billboards, posters, store window displays, car stereos, pedestrians waving or talking on mobile phones, car horns, street signs, traffic lights, and so on. However, you sense, select, and perceive only a small fraction of these messages.

Today's business audiences are much like drivers on busy streets. They are inundated with so many messages and so much noise that they can miss or ignore many of the messages intended for them. Through this course, you will learn a variety of techniques to craft messages that get noticed. In general, follow these five principles to increase your chances of success:

- **Consider audience expectations.** Deliver messages using the media and channels that the audience expects. If colleagues expect meeting notices to be delivered by email, don't suddenly switch gears and start delivering the notices via blog postings without telling anyone. Of course, sometimes going *against*

Message overload is a constant challenge in contemporary life; your messages must compete with many others clamoring for the audience's attention.
Source: © Extrastock/SuperStock.

expectations can stimulate audience attention, which is why advertisers sometimes do wacky and creative things to get your attention. However, for most business communication efforts, following the expectations of your audience is the most efficient way to get your message across.

- **Ensure ease of use.** Your audience will have a tough time receiving your messages if you make them hard to find, hard to access, or hard to read. Poorly designed websites with confusing navigation are common culprits in this respect.
- **Emphasize familiarity.** Use words, images, and designs that are familiar to your audience. For example, most visitors to company websites expect to see information about the company on a page called "About" or "About Us."
- **Practice empathy.** Make sure your messages speak to the audience by clearly addressing *their* wants and needs—not yours. People are inclined to notice messages that relate to their individual concerns.[13]
- **Design for compatibility.** For the many messages delivered electronically these days, be sure to verify technological compatibility with your audience. For instance, if your website requires visitors to have a particular video capability in their browsers, you won't reach those audience members who don't have that software installed.

To improve the odds that your messages will be successfully perceived by your audience, pay close attention to expectations, ease of use, familiarity, empathy, and technical compatibility.

How Audiences Decode Messages   A received message doesn't "mean" anything until the recipient decodes it and assigns meaning to it, and there is no guarantee that the receiver will assign the same meaning that the sender intended. Even well-crafted, well-intentioned communication efforts can fail at this stage, because assigning meaning through decoding is a highly personal process that is influenced by culture, individual experience, learning and thinking styles, hopes, fears, and even temporary moods. Moreover, audiences tend to extract the meaning they expect to get from a message, even if it's the opposite of what the sender intended.[14] In fact, rather than "extract" your meaning, it's more accurate to say that your audience members re-create their own meaning—or meanings—from the message.

Decoding is a complex process; receivers often extract different meanings from messages than the meanings senders intended.

Cultural and personal beliefs and biases influence the meaning that audiences get from messages. For instance, the human brain organizes incoming sensations into a mental "map" that represents the person's individual **perception** of reality. If an incoming detail doesn't fit into that perception, a message recipient may simply distort the information to make it fit rather than rearrange his or her mental map—a phenomenon known as **selective perception**.[15] For example, an executive who has staked her reputation on a particular business strategy might distort or ignore evidence that suggests the strategy is failing.

Selective perception occurs when people ignore or distort incoming information to fit their preconceived notions of reality.

Differences in language and usage also influence received meaning. If you ask an employee to send you a report on sales figures "as soon as possible," does that mean within 10 seconds, 10 minutes, or 10 days? By clarifying expectations and resolving potential ambiguities in your messages, you can minimize such uncertainties. In general, the more experiences you share with another person, the more likely you are to share perception and thus share meaning (see Figure 1.6).

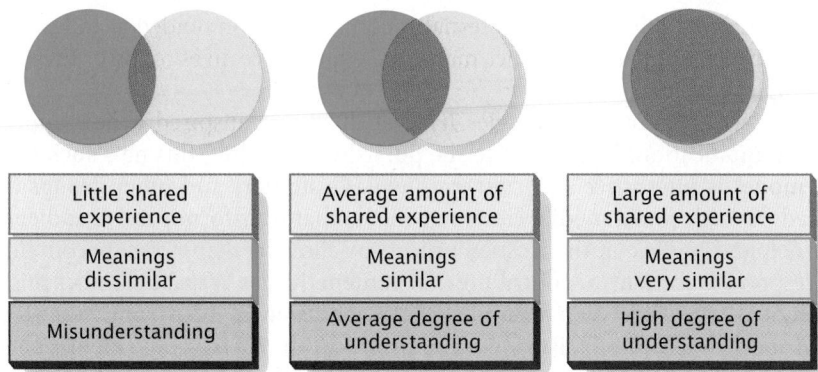

Little shared experience	Average amount of shared experience	Large amount of shared experience
Meanings dissimilar	Meanings similar	Meanings very similar
Misunderstanding	Average degree of understanding	High degree of understanding

Figure 1.6   How Shared Experience Affects Understanding
The more that two people or two groups of people share experiences—personal, professional, and cultural—the more likely it is that receivers will extract the intended meanings that senders encode into the messages.

Individual thinking styles are another important factor in message decoding. For example, someone who places a high value on objective analysis and clear logic might interpret a message differently than someone who values emotion or intuition (reaching conclusions without using rational processes).

How Audiences Respond to Messages   Your message has been delivered, received, and correctly decoded. Now what? Will audience members respond in the way you'd like them to? Only if three events occur.

First, the recipient has to *remember* the message long enough to act on it. Simplifying greatly, memory works in several stages: *Sensory memory* momentarily captures incoming data from the senses; then, whatever the recipient pays attention to is transferred to *short-term memory*. Information in short-term memory will quickly disappear if it isn't transferred to *long-term memory*, which can be done either actively (such as when a person memorizes a list of items) or passively (such as when a new piece of information connects with something else the recipient already has stored in long-term memory). Finally, the information needs to be *retrieved* when the recipient wants to act on it.[16] In general, people find it easier to remember and retrieve information that is important to them personally or professionally. Consequently, by communicating in ways that are sensitive to your audience's wants and needs, you greatly increase the chance that your messages will be remembered and retrieved.

Second, the recipient has to be *able* to respond as you wish. Obviously, if recipients simply cannot do what you want them to do, they will not respond according to your plan. By understanding your audience (you'll learn more about audience analysis in Chapter 4), you can work to minimize these unsuccessful outcomes.

Third, the recipient has to be *motivated* to respond. You'll encounter many situations in which your audience has the option of responding but isn't required to. For instance, a record company may or may not offer your band a contract, or your boss may or may not respond to your request for a raise. Throughout this course, you'll learn techniques for crafting messages that can help motivate readers to respond.

Now that you have some additional insights into what makes communication succeed, take another look at the communication process model. Figure 1.7 identifies the key challenges in the process and summarizes the steps you can take along the way to become a more effective communicator.

THE SOCIAL COMMUNICATION MODEL

The basic model presented in Figure 1.5 shows how a single idea moves from one sender to one receiver. In a larger sense, it also helps represent the traditional nature of much business communication, which was primarily defined by a *publishing* or *broadcasting* mindset. Externally, companies issued carefully scripted messages to a mass audience that often had few options for responding to those messages or initiating messages of their own. Customers and other interested parties had few ways to connect with one another to ask questions, share information, or offer support. Internally, communication tended to follow the same "we talk, you listen" model, with upper managers issuing directives to lower-level supervisors and employees.

However, a variety of technologies have enabled and inspired a new approach to business communication. In contrast to the publishing mindset, this new **social communication model** is *interactive* and *conversational*. Customers and other groups are now empowered through **social media**, electronic media that transform passive audiences into active participants in the communication process by allowing them to share content, revise content, respond to content, or contribute new content. Just as *Web 2.0* signifies this second generation of World Wide Web technologies (social networks, blogs, and other tools that you'll read about in Chapter 7), **Business Communication 2.0** is a convenient label for this new approach to business communication.

On the surface, this approach might look like it's just added some new media tools. However, as Figure 1.8 on page 56 shows, the changes are much deeper and more profound. In a typical 1.0 approach, messages are scripted by designated communicators, approved

Margin notes

Audiences will likely respond to a message if they remember it, if they're able to respond, and if they're properly motivated to respond.

By explaining how audiences will benefit by responding to your messages, you'll increase their motivation to respond.

The social communication model is interactive, conversational, and usually open to all who wish to participate.

The conversational and interactive *social communication model* is revolutionizing business communication.

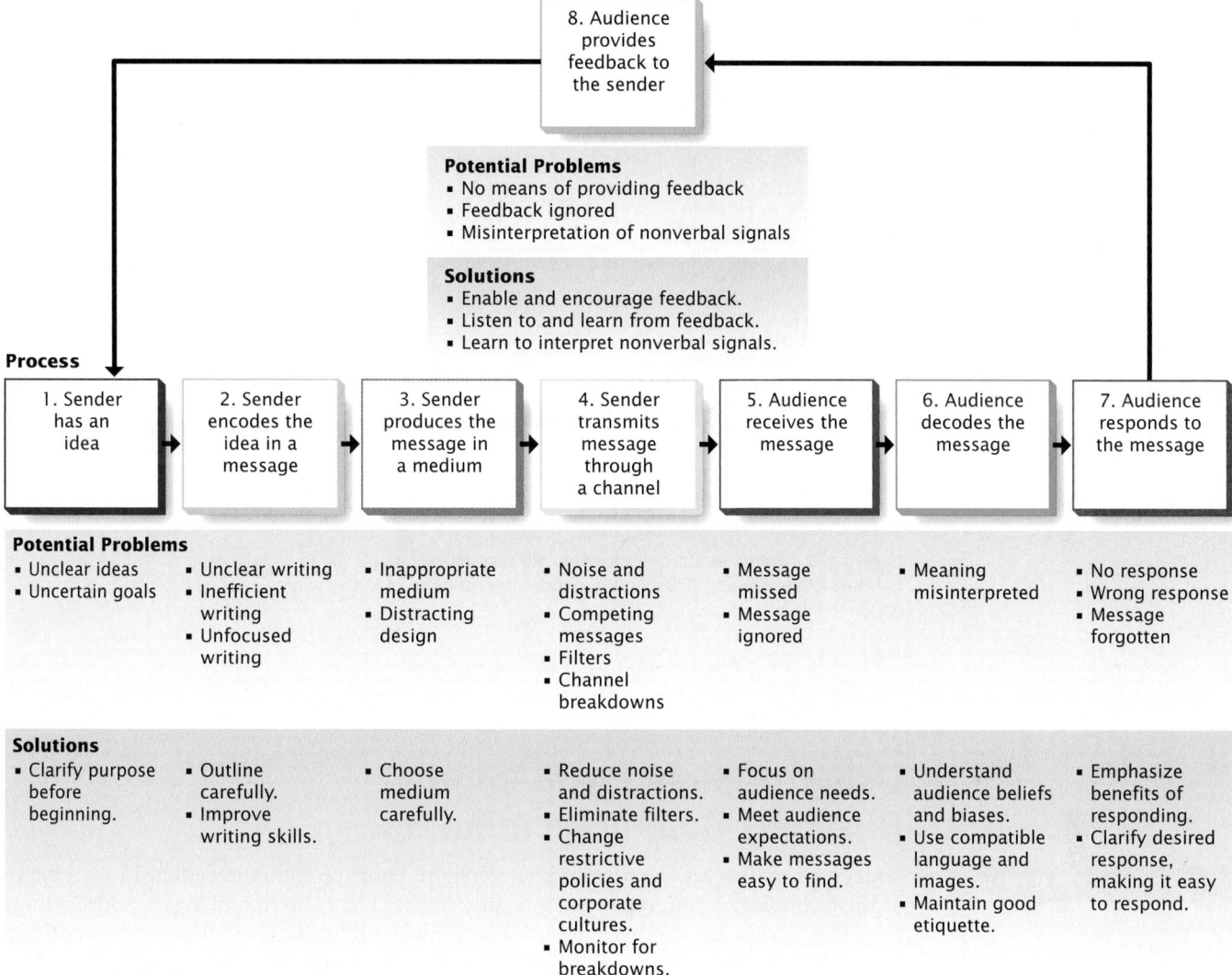

Figure 1.7 Becoming an Effective Business Communicator
The communication process presents many opportunities for messages to get lost, distorted, or misinterpreted as they travel from sender to receiver. Fortunately, you can take action at every step in the process to increase your chances of success.

by someone in authority, distributed through selected channels, and delivered without modification to a passive audience that is not invited or even expected to respond. In the 2.0 approach, the rules change dramatically. Customers and other stakeholders participate in, influence, and often take control of conversations in the marketplace. They rely on each other for information about products, offer technical support, and even participate in group buying using social tools.[17]

For both internal and external communication, Web 2.0 tools can increase the speed of communication, lower communication costs, improve access to pockets of expertise, and boost employee satisfaction.[18] Of course, no company, no matter how enthusiastically it embraces the 2.0 mindset, is going to be run as a social club in which everyone has a say and a vote. Instead, a hybrid approach is emerging in which some communications follow the traditional approach and others follow the 2.0 approach.[19]

If you're an active user of Web 2.0 technologies, you'll fit right in with this new communication environment—and possibly even have a head start on more experienced professionals who are still adapting to the new tools and techniques. For the latest information on communicating in a Web 2.0 environment, visit http://real-timeupdates.com/EBC10 and select Chapter 1.

The "Business Communication 2.0" approach can increase the speed of communication, lower costs, improve access to expertise, and boost employee satisfaction.

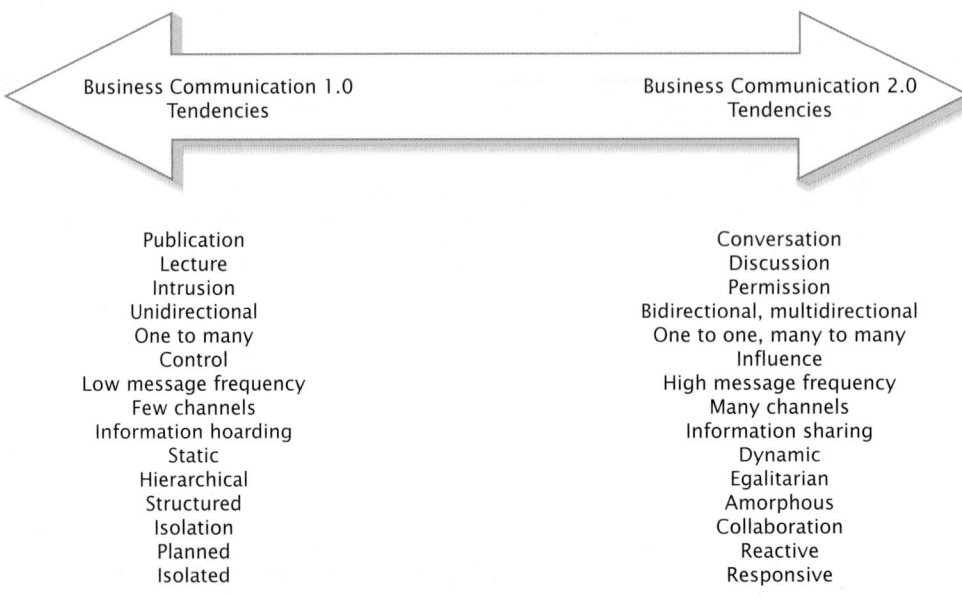

Business Communication 1.0 Tendencies	Business Communication 2.0 Tendencies
Publication	Conversation
Lecture	Discussion
Intrusion	Permission
Unidirectional	Bidirectional, multidirectional
One to many	One to one, many to many
Control	Influence
Low message frequency	High message frequency
Few channels	Many channels
Information hoarding	Information sharing
Static	Dynamic
Hierarchical	Egalitarian
Structured	Amorphous
Isolation	Collaboration
Planned	Reactive
Isolated	Responsive

Figure 1.8   Business Communication: 1.0 versus 2.0
Business Communication 2.0 differs from conventional communication strategies and practices in a number of significant ways.

Using Technology to Improve Business Communication

4   LEARNING OBJECTIVE

List four general guidelines for using communication technology effectively.

Today's businesses rely heavily on technology to enhance communication. In fact, many of the technologies you might use in your personal life, from microblogs to video games to virtual worlds, are also used in business. You will find technology discussed extensively throughout this book, with specific advice on using both common and emerging tools. The four-page photo essay "Powerful Tools for Communicating Efficiently" (see pages 58–61) provides an overview of the technologies that connect people in offices, factories, and other business settings.

Anyone who has used a computer, a smartphone, or other advanced gadget knows that the benefits of technology are not automatic. Poorly designed or inappropriately used technology can hinder communication more than help. To communicate effectively, learn to keep technology in perspective, guard against information overload and information addiction, use technological tools productively, and disengage from the computer frequently to communicate in person.

REAL-TIME UPDATES
Learn More by Reading This PDF

Steps you can take to help reduce information overload

Everyone needs to play a part in reducing the burden of too much data and information in the work environment; this document has plenty of helpful tips. Go to http://real-timeupdates.com/ebc10 and click on Learn More. If you are using MyBcommLab, you can access Real-Time Updates within each chapter or under Student Study Tools.

KEEPING TECHNOLOGY IN PERSPECTIVE

Perhaps the single most important point to remember about technology is that it is simply a tool, a means by which you can accomplish certain tasks. Technology is an aid to interpersonal communication, not a replacement for it. Technology can't think for you or communicate for you, and if you lack some essential skills, technology can't fill in the gaps.

While this advice might sound obvious, it is easy to get caught up in the "gee whiz" factor, particularly with new technologies. No matter how exotic or entertaining it may be, technology has business value only if it helps deliver the right information to the right people at the right time.

GUARDING AGAINST INFORMATION OVERLOAD

The overuse or misuse of communication technology can lead to **information overload**, in which people receive more information than they can effectively process. Information overload makes it difficult to discriminate between useful and useless information, lowers productivity, and amplifies employee stress both on the job and at home—even to the point of causing health and relationship problems.[20]

As a recipient, you often have some level of control over the number and types of messages you choose to receive. Use the filtering features of your communication systems to isolate high-priority messages that deserve your attention. Also, be wary of subscribing to too many blog feeds, Twitter follows, Facebook updates, and other sources of recurring messages. Focus on the information you truly need to do your job.

As a sender, you can help reduce information overload by making sure you don't send unnecessary messages. In addition, when you send messages that aren't crucial, let people know so they can prioritize. Even though most communication systems let you mark messages as urgent, use this feature only when it is truly needed. Overusing it leads to annoyance and anxiety, not action.

REAL-TIME UPDATES
Learn More by Reading This Article

Will your social media habits kill your career?

Follow these tips to make sure your social media habits don't keep you from getting a job or derail your career after it has begun. Go to http://real-timeupdates.com/ebc10 and click on Learn More. If you are using MyBcommLab, you can access Real-Time Updates within each chapter or under Student Study Tools.

Information overload results when people receive more information than they can effectively process.

USING TECHNOLOGICAL TOOLS PRODUCTIVELY

Facebook, Twitter, YouTube, IM, and other technologies are key parts of what has been called the "information technology paradox," in which information tools can waste as much time as they save. Concerns over inappropriate use of social networking sites, for example, have led many companies to ban employees from accessing them during work hours.[21]

Inappropriate web use not only distracts employees from work responsibilities but can leave employers open to lawsuits for sexual harassment if inappropriate images are displayed in or transmitted around the company.[22] Social media have created another set of managerial challenges, given the risk that employee blogs or social networking pages can expose confidential information or damage a firm's reputation in the marketplace. With all these technologies, the best solution lies in developing clear policies that are enforced evenly for all employees.[23]

In addition to using your tools appropriately, knowing how to use them efficiently can make a big difference in your productivity. You don't have to become an expert in most cases, but you need to be familiar with the basic features and functions of the tools you are expected to use on the job. As a manager, you also need to ensure that your employees have sufficient training to productively use the tools you expect them to use.

Communicating in today's business environment requires at least a basic level of technical competence.

RECONNECTING WITH PEOPLE

Let's say you IM a colleague asking how she did with her sales presentation to an important client, and her answer comes back simply as "Fine." What does *fine* mean? Is an order expected soon? Or did she lose the sale and doesn't want to talk about it? If you visit with her in person, or at least talk over the phone, she might provide additional information, or you might be able to offer advice or support during a difficult time.

Even enthusiastic users know that technology has limits. Jill Smart, an executive with the consulting firm Accenture, often takes advantage of the company's advanced *telepresence* videoconferencing systems (discussed in Chapter 2) but still travels frequently to meet with clients—particularly clients in other countries and cultures. She says, "You get things from being there, over breakfast and dinner, building relationships face to face."[24]

Remember to step out from behind your computer occasionally and connect in person.
Source: © Radius Images/Alamy.

Powerful Tools for Communicating Effectively

The tools of business communication evolve with every new generation of digital technology. Selecting the right tool for each situation can enhance your business communication in many ways. In today's flexible office settings, communication technology helps people keep in touch and stay productive. When coworkers in different cities or countries need to collaborate, they can meet and share ideas without costly travel. Companies use communication technology to keep track of parts, orders, and shipments—and to keep customers well-informed. Those same customers can also communicate with companies in many ways at any time of the day or night. For a closer look at the latest business uses of social media tools in particular, see pages 228-235 in Chapter 7.

Electronic Presentations

Source: Photodisc/Getty Images.

Electronic presentations, both on-site and online, are a mainstay of business communication.

Wireless Networks

Source: Belkin International, Inc.

Many business professionals today have only part-time offices or no offices at all, relying on wireless networks to stay connected with colleagues and customers.

REDEFINING THE OFFICE

Technology makes it easier for business professionals to stay connected with customers and colleagues, wherever their work takes them. Electronic presentations, shared workspaces, and virtual meeting spaces can bring professionals together at the same time or give them access to vital resources on their own schedules. Wireless networks and mobile-phone data services let workers "cut the wire" from the home office and move around as they need to.

Virtual Meeting Spaces

Source: Cranaial Tap, Inc.

A number of companies (such as Cranial Tap, whose virtual headquarters is shown here) now hold meetings, host conferences, and demonstrate products and services in virtual worlds such as Second Life.

Shared Workspaces

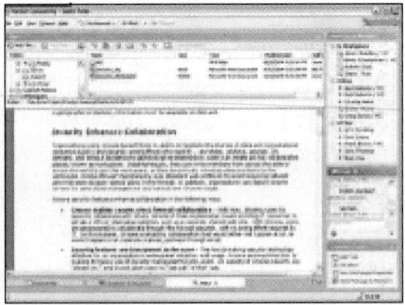

Source: EMC Documentum.

Online workspaces such as Documentum eRoom and Share Point Workspace make it easy for far-flung team members to access shared files anywhere at any time. The workspace can control which team members can read, edit, and save specific files.

Unified Communications

Many workers can now access their voice and electronic communication (including email and instant messaging) through a single portal. *Follow-me phone service* automatically forwards incoming calls. *Text-to-speech* features using voice synthesis can convert email and IM to voice messages.

Source: © 2002 Ethan Hill.

Wikis

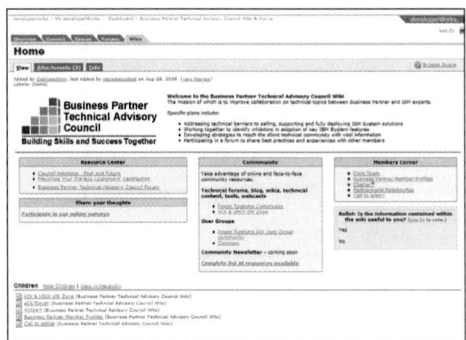

Source: Reprint Courtesy of International Business Machines Corporation, © 2011 International Business Machines Corporation.

Wikis promote collaboration by simplifying the process of creating and editing online content. Anyone with access (some wikis are private; some are public) can add and modify pages as new information becomes available.

Social Networking

Source: © 2010 Biznik, Inc.--Biznik is an online community of independent business people interested in helping each other succeed. Blending the best of social media with in-person events Biznik encourages collaboration, inspiration, education and ultimately... professional relationships that produce more business. (http://biznik.com).

Businesses use a variety of social networks as specialized networks to engage customers, find new employees, attract investors, and share ideas and challenges with peers.

COLLABORATING

Working in teams is essential in almost every business. Teamwork can become complicated, however, when team members work in different parts of the company, in different time zones, or even for different companies. Technology helps bridge the distance by making it possible to brainstorm, attend virtual meetings, share files, meet new business partners, and collaborate with experts outside the company from widely separated locations.

Crowdsourcing and Collaboration Platforms

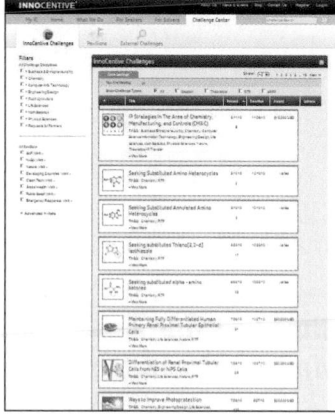

Source: Used with permission of Innocentive.

Crowdsourcing, inviting input from groups of people inside or outside the organization, can give companies access to a much wider range of ideas, solutions to problems, and insights into market trends.

Web-Based Meetings

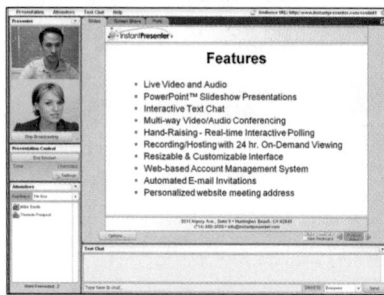

Source: InstantPresenter.

Web-based meetings allow team members from all over the world to collaborate online. Various systems support instant messaging, video, real-time editing tools, and more.

Videoconferencing and Telepresence

Source: © 2002 Ethan Hill.

Videoconferencing provides many of the benefits of in-person meetings at a fraction of the cost. Advanced systems feature *telepresence,* in which the video images are life-sized and extremely realistic.

RSS Newsfeeds and Aggregators

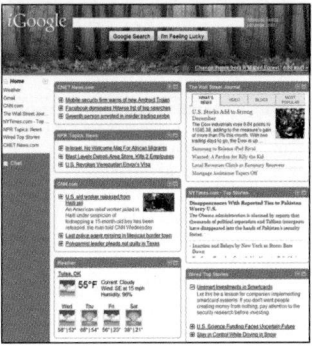

Aggregators, sometimes called *newsreaders*, automatically collect information about new blogposts, podcasts, and other content via Really Simple Syndication (RSS) newsfeeds, giving audiences more control over the content they receive.

Social Tagging and Bookmarking

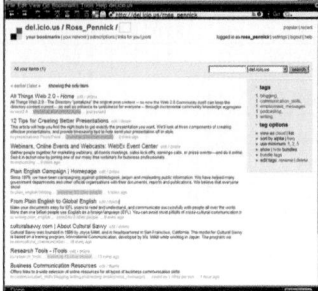

Source: del.icio.us/Ross_Pennick.

Audiences become part of the communication channel when they find and recommend online content through tagging and bookmarking sites such as Delicious and Digg.

SHARING INFORMATION

Companies use a variety of communication technologies to create products and services, deliver them to customers, and support users with vital information. The ability to easily access and share the latest information improves the flow and timing of supplies, lowers operating costs, improves customer satisfaction, and boosts financial performance. Easy information access also helps companies respond to customer needs by providing them accurate information and timely product deliveries.

Interactive Data Visualization

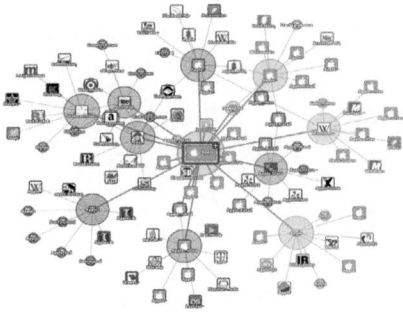

Source: Used with permission of TouchGraph.

A stunning array of new tools helps business professionals analyze, display, and share vast quantities of data and nonnumeric information.

Community Q&A

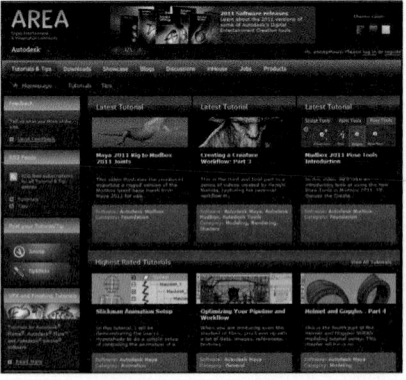

Source: Autodesk, Inc.

Many companies now rely heavily on communities of customers to help each other with product questions and other routine matters.

Supply Chain Management Software

Manufacturers, distributors, and retailers now automatically share information that used to require labor-intensive manual reporting. Improved information flow increases report accuracy and helps each company in the supply chain manage inventory.

Source: © Peter Christopher/Masterfile.

Online Customer Support

Source: CustomerReach.

For online shoppers who need instant help, many retail websites make it easy to connect with a live sales rep via phone or instant messaging. Alternatively, software tools known as *virtual agents* or *bots* can answer simple questions and respond to requests for electronic documents.

Podcast

Source: Marcio Jose Sanchez/AP Wide World Photos.

With the portability and convenience of downloadable audio and video recordings, podcasts have quickly become a popular means of delivering everything from college lectures to marketing messages. Podcasts are also used for internal communication, replacing conference calls, newsletters, and other media.

Microblogs

Microblogging services (of which Twitter is by far the best known) are a great way to share ideas, solicit feedback, monitor market trends, and announce special deals and events.

INTERACTING WITH CUSTOMERS

Maintaining an open dialogue is essential to finding, engaging, and supporting customers. Today's communication technologies, particularly the ever-evolving field of social media, make it easier for customers to interact with a company whenever, wherever, and however they wish. Companies that take the lead in fostering a conversation with their markets have a big advantage over companies that don't.

Source: Courtesy of Patagonia, Inc.

User-Generated Content

Source: Used with permission Segway, Inc.

User-generated content sites let businesses host photos, videos, software programs, technical solutions, and other valuable content for their customer communities.

Blogs

Source: Christine Winter, Xerox.

Blogs let companies connect with customers and other audiences in a fast and informal way. Commenting features let readers participate in the conversation, too.

Committing to Ethical and Legal Communication

Ethics are the accepted principles of conduct that govern behavior within a society. Ethical behavior is a companywide concern, but because communication efforts are the public face of a company, they are subjected to particularly rigorous scrutiny from regulators, legislators, investors, consumer groups, environmental groups, labor organizations, and anyone else affected by business activities. **Ethical communication** includes all relevant information, is true in every sense, and is not deceptive in any way. In contrast, unethical communication can distort the truth or manipulate audiences in a variety of ways. Examples of unethical communication include:[25]

Any time you try to mislead your audience, the result is unethical communication.

- **Plagiarism.** Plagiarism is presenting someone else's words or other creative products as your own. Note that plagiarism can be illegal if it violates a **copyright**, which is a form of legal protection for the expression of creative ideas.[26]
- **Omitting essential information.** Information is essential if your audience needs it to make an intelligent, objective decision.
- **Selective misquoting.** Distorting or hiding the true intent of someone else's words is unethical.
- **Misrepresenting numbers.** Statistics and other data can be unethically manipulated by increasing or decreasing numbers, exaggerating, altering statistics, or omitting numeric data.
- **Distorting visuals.** Images can be manipulated in unethical ways, such as making a product seem bigger than it really is or changing the scale of graphs and charts to exaggerate or conceal differences.
- **Failing to respect privacy or information security needs.** Failing to respect the privacy of others or failing to adequately protect information entrusted to your care can also be considered unethical (and is sometimes illegal).

Transparency gives audience members access to all the information they need in order to process messages accurately.

The widespread adoption of social media has increased the attention given to the issue of **transparency**, which in this context refers to a sense of openness, of giving all participants in a conversation access to the information they need to accurately process the messages they are receiving. A key aspect of transparency is knowing who is behind the messages one receives. Consider the promotional event that Netflix staged in Toronto to announce the launch of its streaming video service in Canada. The outdoor news conference seemed to attract dozens of curious people who were excited about the availability of Netflix. However, many of these people who "spontaneously" showed up were actually paid actors with instructions to "look really excited, particularly if asked by media to do any interviews about the prospect of Netflix in Canada." The company apologized when the stunt was exposed.[27]

The controversial practice of stealth marketing involves marketing to people without their knowledge.

A major issue in business communication transparency is *stealth marketing*, which involves attempting to promote products and services to customers who don't know they're being marketed to. A common stealth marketing technique is rewarding someone to promote products to his or her friends without telling them it's a form of advertising. Critics—including the U.S. Federal Trade Commission (FTC) and the Word of Mouth Marketing Association—assert that such techniques are deceptive because they don't give their targets the opportunity to raise their instinctive defenses against the persuasive powers of marketing messages.[28]

Aside from ethical concerns, trying to fool the public is simply bad for business. As LaSalle University communication professor Michael Smith puts it, "The public backlash can be long, deep, and damaging to a company's reputation."[29]

DISTINGUISHING ETHICAL DILEMMAS FROM ETHICAL LAPSES

An ethical dilemma is having to choose between alternatives that may all be ethical and valid.

Some ethical questions are easy to recognize and resolve, but others are not. Deciding what is ethical can be a considerable challenge in complex business situations. An **ethical dilemma** involves choosing among alternatives that aren't clear cut. Perhaps two conflicting alternatives are both ethical and valid, or perhaps the alternatives lie somewhere in the gray area between clearly right and clearly wrong. Every company has responsibilities to multiple groups of people inside and outside the firm, and those various groups often have competing interests. For instance, employees generally want higher wages and more benefits, but investors who have risked their money in the company want management to keep costs low so that profits are strong enough to drive up the stock price. Both sides have a valid ethical position.

In contrast, an **ethical lapse** is a clearly unethical choice. For example, homebuyers in an Orlando, Florida, housing development were sold houses without being told that the area was once a U.S. Army firing range and that live bombs and ammunition were still buried in multiple locations around the neighborhood.[30] By depriving buyers of vital information, the seller engaged in unethical communication.

> An ethical lapse is making a choice that you know to be unethical.

With both internal and external communication efforts, the pressure to produce results or justify decisions can make unethical communication a tempting choice. (Compare the messages in Figures 1.9 and 1.10.)

ENSURING ETHICAL COMMUNICATION

Ensuring ethical business communication requires three elements: ethical individuals, ethical company leadership, and the appropriate policies and structures to support employees' efforts to make ethical choices.[31] Moreover, these three elements need to work in harmony. If employees see company executives making unethical decisions and flouting company guidelines, they might conclude that the guidelines are meaningless and emulate their bosses' unethical behavior.

Employers have a responsibility to establish clear guidelines for ethical behavior, including ethical business communication. Many companies establish an explicit ethics policy by using a written **code of ethics** to help employees determine what is acceptable. For example, Gap Inc. (the owner of the Gap, Banana Republic, and Old Navy retail chains), publishes a detailed Code of Business Conduct for its employees, addressing such areas as conflicts of interest, product integrity, health and safety, protection of company assets and information, and political activities by employees.[32] A code is often part of a larger program of employee training and communication channels that allow employees to ask questions and report instances of questionable ethics. To ensure ongoing compliance with their code of ethics, many companies also conduct *ethics audits* to monitor ethical progress and to point out any weaknesses that need to be addressed.

> Responsible employers establish clear ethical guidelines for their employees to follow.

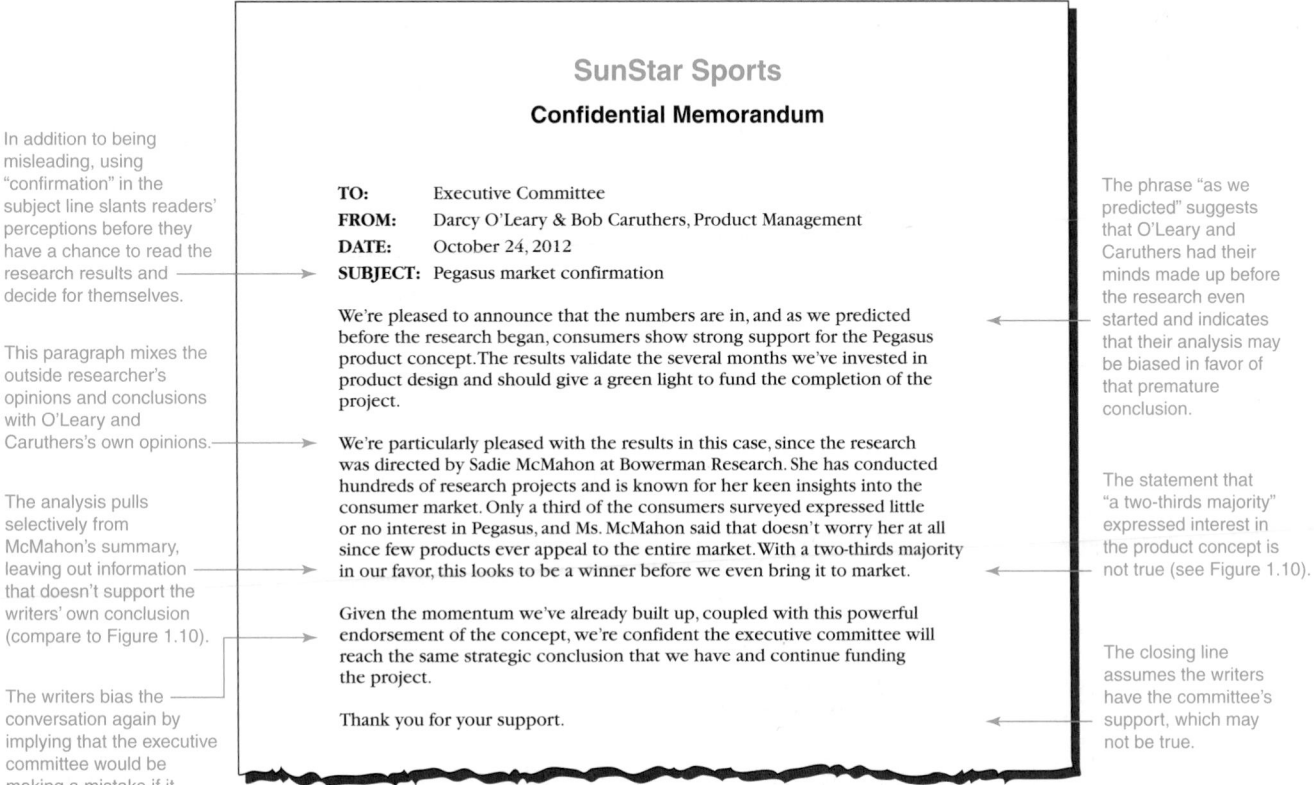

Figure 1.9   Unethical Communication
The writers of this memo clearly want the company to continue funding their pet project, even though the marketing research doesn't support such a decision. By comparing this memo with the version shown in Figure 1.10, you can see how the writers twisted the truth and omitted evidence in order to put a positive "spin" on the research.

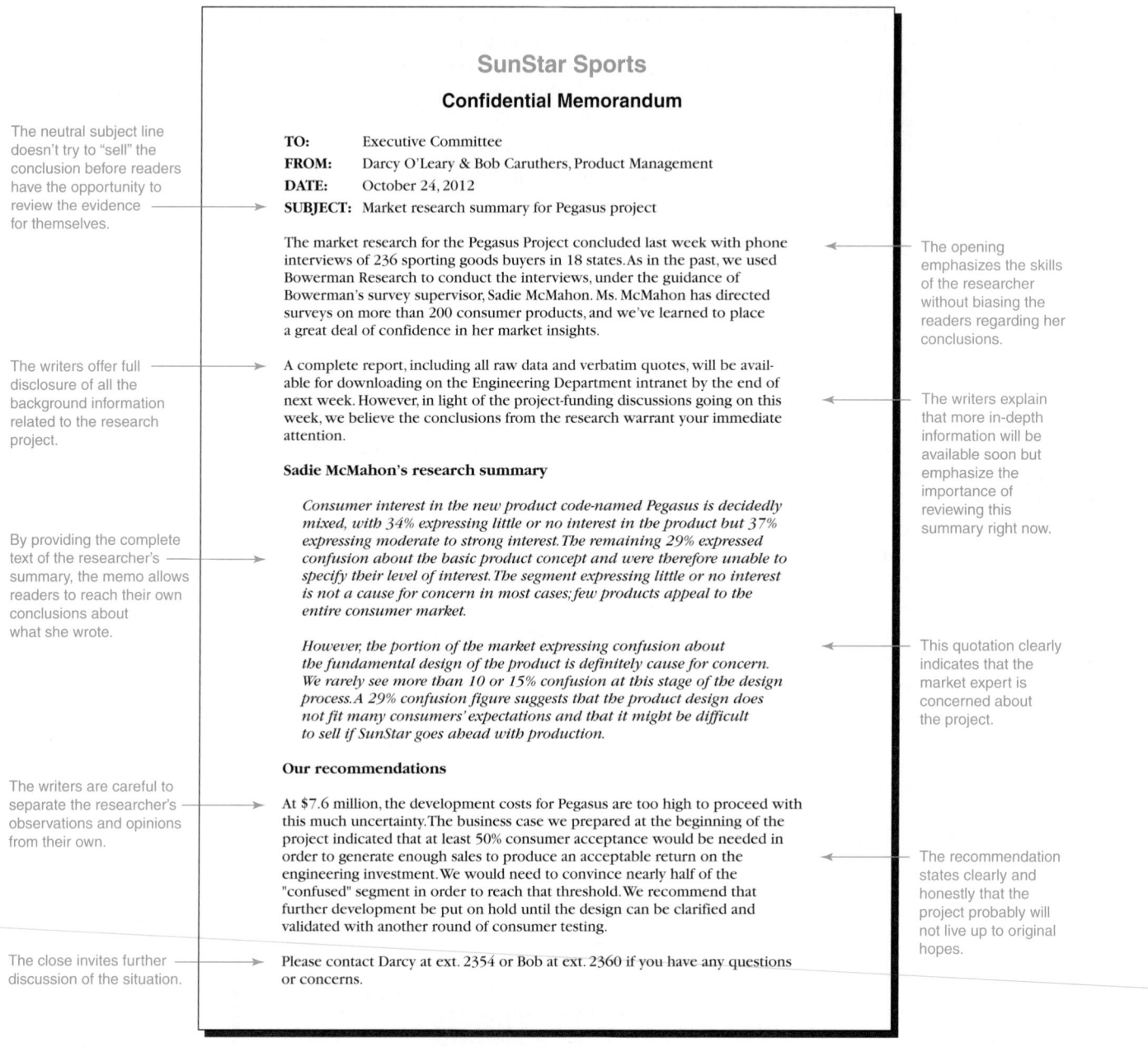

The neutral subject line doesn't try to "sell" the conclusion before readers have the opportunity to review the evidence for themselves.

The writers offer full disclosure of all the background information related to the research project.

By providing the complete text of the researcher's summary, the memo allows readers to reach their own conclusions about what she wrote.

The writers are careful to separate the researcher's observations and opinions from their own.

The close invites further discussion of the situation.

SunStar Sports
Confidential Memorandum

TO: Executive Committee
FROM: Darcy O'Leary & Bob Caruthers, Product Management
DATE: October 24, 2012
SUBJECT: Market research summary for Pegasus project

The market research for the Pegasus Project concluded last week with phone interviews of 236 sporting goods buyers in 18 states. As in the past, we used Bowerman Research to conduct the interviews, under the guidance of Bowerman's survey supervisor, Sadie McMahon. Ms. McMahon has directed surveys on more than 200 consumer products, and we've learned to place a great deal of confidence in her market insights.

A complete report, including all raw data and verbatim quotes, will be available for downloading on the Engineering Department intranet by the end of next week. However, in light of the project-funding discussions going on this week, we believe the conclusions from the research warrant your immediate attention.

Sadie McMahon's research summary

Consumer interest in the new product code-named Pegasus is decidedly mixed, with 34% expressing little or no interest in the product but 37% expressing moderate to strong interest. The remaining 29% expressed confusion about the basic product concept and were therefore unable to specify their level of interest. The segment expressing little or no interest is not a cause for concern in most cases; few products appeal to the entire consumer market.

However, the portion of the market expressing confusion about the fundamental design of the product is definitely cause for concern. We rarely see more than 10 or 15% confusion at this stage of the design process. A 29% confusion figure suggests that the product design does not fit many consumers' expectations and that it might be difficult to sell if SunStar goes ahead with production.

Our recommendations

At $7.6 million, the development costs for Pegasus are too high to proceed with this much uncertainty. The business case we prepared at the beginning of the project indicated that at least 50% consumer acceptance would be needed in order to generate enough sales to produce an acceptable return on the engineering investment. We would need to convince nearly half of the "confused" segment in order to reach that threshold. We recommend that further development be put on hold until the design can be clarified and validated with another round of consumer testing.

Please contact Darcy at ext. 2354 or Bob at ext. 2360 if you have any questions or concerns.

The opening emphasizes the skills of the researcher without biasing the readers regarding her conclusions.

The writers explain that more in-depth information will be available soon but emphasize the importance of reviewing this summary right now.

This quotation clearly indicates that the market expert is concerned about the project.

The recommendation states clearly and honestly that the project probably will not live up to original hopes.

Figure 1.10   Ethical Communication
This version of the memo presents the evidence in a more honest and ethical manner.

If you can't decide whether a choice is ethical, picture yourself explaining your decision to someone whose opinion you value.

However, whether or not formal guidelines are in place, every employee has a responsibility to communicate in an ethical manner. In the absence of clear guidelines, ask yourself the following questions about your business communications:[33]

- Have you defined the situation fairly and accurately?
- What is your intention in communicating this message?
- What impact will this message have on the people who receive it, or who might be affected by it?
- Will the message achieve the greatest possible good while doing the least possible harm?
- Will the assumptions you've made change over time? That is, will a decision that seems ethical now seem unethical in the future?
- Are you comfortable with your decision? Would you be embarrassed if it were printed in tomorrow's newspaper or spread across the Internet? Think about a person whom you admire and ask yourself what he or she would think of your decision.

BUSINESS COMMUNICATION 2.0

Who's Responsible Here?

When companies engage in *comparative advertising*, making explicit comparisons between their products and those of competitors, complaints of false statements and defamation are fairly common. In that sense, a lawsuit that Subway recently filed against Quiznos is not in itself unusual. Subway claimed that Quiznos made unfair and untrue comparisons about the size and meat content of one of its sandwiches and failed to disclose the fact that the larger Quiznos sandwich cost nearly twice as much as the Subway sandwich.

What made this case unusual—and gave it potentially far-reaching impact for business communication—is the Web 2.0 angle of *user-generated content* (UGC). As part of its efforts to promote this particular sandwich, Quiznos sponsored a contest in which members of the public were invited to create their own commercials. The contest encouraged people to highlight the "meat, no meat" theme, suggesting that the Quiznos sandwich had copious amounts of beef, while the Subway sandwich had far less. More than 100 people submitted videos, which were posted to a Quiznos website and to iFilm, a now-defunct video clip website owned by the media giant Viacom.

Subway's lawsuit claimed that some of the videos contained false and disparaging content for which Quiznos and iFilm should be held liable. Subway asserted that Quiznos specifically encouraged contestants to promote one product at the expense of the other, so it should not be immune from responsibility. Quiznos's lawyers responded by pointing out that the company did not create these videos and was therefore not liable. "We're just facilitating consumers who go out and create their own expression in the form of a commercial."

Quiznos first tried to have the UGC part of the lawsuit dismissed by claiming the same immunity that YouTube and similar services have regarding the content that members of the public post on their websites. However, a judge refused, saying the law protecting YouTube (the Communications Decency Act, or CDA) didn't necessarily protect Quiznos in this case. Quinzos subsequently asked for a summary judgment to avoid going to trial. When that request was also denied, the two companies settled out of court.

That private settlement closed the dispute between the two sandwich chains, but it left the matter of legal responsibility for UGC campaigns wide open. The central question is how much involvement a company sponsoring a UGC contest has in the content of the submissions. The court indicated that by sponsoring the contest and presenting the contest guidelines in a particular way, Quiznos played *some* role in the creation of the videos. However, because the case didn't go to trial, the question of whether that role was significant enough to strip the company of legal immunity under the CDA is still unresolved. Until clear legal guidelines are established, companies running UGC programs, such as Toyota's Auto-Biography campaign, will need to tread carefully to avoid legal problems.

CAREER APPLICATIONS

1. Legal issues aside, in your opinion, is Quiznos ethically responsible for any false or misleading information that may be found in the user-generated videos? Why or why not?
2. Most consumers lack the skills and equipment needed to produce professional-quality video commercials. Why would companies such as Quiznos invite them to create commercials?

Sources: Adapted from Joseph Lewczak, "Quiznos/Subway Settlement Poses Legal Threat to Future UGC Promos," *Promo*, 23 March 2010, www.promomagazine.com; United States District Court, District of Connecticut, "Memorandum of Decision Denying Defendants' Motion for Summary Judgment, *Doctor's Associates, Inc., v. Qip Holder LLC and Ifilm Corp.*," 19 February 2010; Louise Story, "Can a Sandwich Be Slandered?" *New York Times*, 29 January 2008, www.nytimes.com; David Ardia, "Slandering Sandwiches and User Submitted Content," Citizen Media Law Project website, 29 January 2008, www.citmedialaw.org; "Doctor's Associates Inc. vs. QIP Holders LLC: Complaint for Injunctive Relief and Damages," 27 October 2006, www.citmedialaw.org; "MTV to Run User Generated Ads," *Marketing*, 15 November 2006, 3.

ENSURING LEGAL COMMUNICATION

In addition to ethical guidelines, business communication is also bound by a wide variety of laws and regulations, including the following areas:

Business communication is governed by a wide variety of laws designed to ensure accurate, complete messages.

- **Promotional communication.** Marketing specialists need to be aware of the many laws that govern truth and accuracy in advertising. Chapter 10 explores this area in more detail.
- **Contracts.** A *contract* is a legally binding promise between two parties, in which one party makes a specified offer and the other party accepts. Contracts are fundamental to virtually every aspect of business, from product sales to property rental to credit cards and loans to professional service agreements.[34]
- **Employment communication.** A variety of local, state, and federal laws govern communication between employers and both potential and current employees.

For example, job descriptions must be written in a way that doesn't intentionally or unintentionally discriminate against women, minorities, or people with disabilities.[35]

- **Intellectual property. Intellectual property** includes patents, copyrighted materials, trade secrets, and even Internet domain names.[36] Bloggers in particular need to be careful about IP protection, given the carefree way that some post the work of others without offering proper credit. For guidelines on this hot topic, get the free *Legal Guide for Bloggers* at www.eff.org/bloggers/legal.

- **Financial reporting.** Finance and accounting professionals who work for publicly traded companies (those that sell stock to the public) must adhere to stringent reporting laws. For instance, a number of corporations have recently been targets of both government investigations and shareholder lawsuits for offering misleading descriptions of financial results and revenue forecasts.

- **Defamation.** Negative comments about another party raise the possibility of **defamation**, the intentional communication of false statements that damage character or reputation.[37] (Written defamation is called *libel*; spoken defamation is called *slander*.) Someone suing for defamation must prove (1) that the statement is false, (2) that the language is injurious to the person's reputation, and (3) that the statement has been published.

- **Transparency requirements.** Governments around the world are taking steps to help ensure that consumers and other parties know who is behind the information they receive, particularly from online sources. The European Union, for instance, outlaws a number of online marketing tactics, including "flogs," short for "fake blogs," in which an employee or a paid agent posing as an independent consumer posts positive stories about a company's products.[38] In the United States, the FTC recently adopted a requirement that product-review bloggers disclose any relationship—such as receiving payments or free goods—they have with the companies whose products they discuss in their blogs.[39]

If you have any doubts about the legality of a message you intend to distribute, ask for advice from your company's legal department. A small dose of caution can prevent huge legal headaches and protect your company's reputation in the marketplace.

For the latest information on ethical and legal issues in business communication, visit http://real-timeupdates.com/ebc10 and click on Chapter 1.

Applying What You've Learned

At the beginning of this chapter, you met Toyota's Bob Zeinstra in "On the Job: Communicating at Toyota." Zeinstra is just one of the many working business professionals you'll meet throughout this book—people who successfully handle the same communication challenges you'll face on the job. Each chapter opens with one of these slice-of-life vignettes. As you read through each chapter and become familiar with the concepts presented, imagine how they might apply to the person and company highlighted in the vignette.

At the end of each chapter, you'll take part in an innovative simulation called "On the Job: Solving Communication Dilemmas." You'll play the role of a person working in the highlighted organization, and you'll face situations you'd encounter on the job. You will be presented with several communication scenarios, each with several possible courses of action. It's up to you to recommend one course of action from each scenario as homework, as teamwork, as material for in-class discussion, or in a host of other ways. These scenarios let you explore various communication ideas and apply the concepts and techniques from the chapter.

Now you're ready for the first simulation. As you tackle each problem, think about the material you covered in this chapter and consider your own experience as a communicator. You'll probably be surprised to discover how much you already know about business communication.

Source: Used with permission of Toyota.

You've recently joined the staff of Bob Zeinstra, the executive in charge of product management, advertising, and communication strategy at Toyota Motor Sales, USA. In your role as a social media specialist, you look for opportunities to help Toyota build positive relationships with all its stakeholders. Use what you've learned in this chapter to address the following challenges.

1. You have been receiving complaints that the finance company that handles hire purchase for your cars has been overly aggressive in pursuing cases of default on installments. There have been two notorious cases where the customer has threatened to sue both you and the finance company. Although your lawyers reassure you that they have no case, you are concerned about the impact on relationships with existing and future hire purchasers. You and your boss brainstorm a number of possible solutions. Which of these will you finally choose and why?
   a. Drop the finance company and issue a public statement dissociating your name from theirs immediately. If they want to give themselves a bad image, that's their problem.
   b. Do nothing: the finance company was just doing its job and people have to put up with it. Defaulting is a crime and defaulters ought to take the consequences without complaining.
   c. Issue a statement of regret to the press while pointing out that it's not your fault. In private, tell the finance company it should immediately issue a public apology.
   d. Confront the finance company and get them to hammer out a compromise position on the issue, then meet with the aggrieved customers and their lawyers, and negotiate with them to defuse the situation.

2. One of your youngest sales employees seems overawed by the rest of his team, especially a legendary sales manager whom he reports to directly. She has complained that the employee is frequently tongue-tied at meetings, and even when he comes up with a good idea, he gives up too easily when challenged face to face, though he writes well. When he meets people one on one he is able to interact with them, but people in groups completely destroy his confidence. She thinks he won't make a successful sales executive and wants him transferred to another department, but you would like to give him another chance. Which strategy do you think will work best to build up his confidence?
   a. Take him out to dinner and dish the dirt on his co-workers. He'll lose his awe of them pretty quickly.
   b. Choose him to make a big solo presentation at the next sales meeting. Nothing like jumping in the deep end when learning to swim.

   c. Give him exclusive charge of the company blog for a week, with a mandate to write at least three new product profiles. That will give him the chance to discover his potential for himself, without the interference of others.
   d. Pass on his manager's reservations to him and give him three weeks to improve his behavior. Sales is a tough department and slacking can't be tolerated: he has to shape up or ship out.

3. The employees at your branch greatly covet the chance to be sent to the company headquarters for special training, which is seen as a reward for good service. However, due to cutbacks at headquarters, this is no longer being done, although no official notification has been issued to say that the policy has definitely been discontinued. You know for a fact that the company has sold off some of the guesthouses near HQ in which it used to house visiting employees, and the old scheme will never be revived. But your subordinates are getting restive, and one day they confront you and insist that you forward some of their names for training at HQ. What would you do?
   a. Tell them that those days are gone and they should get used to it, showing them the circulars relating to the guesthouse if they ask for proof.
   b. Tell them you will give them all a cash bonus instead, linked to performance, and start looking at local budgets you can squeeze for the money.
   c. Promise to forward the names and then do nothing. They'll soon forget about it.
   d. Produce, print, and distribute a pamphlet listing (with photographs) the employees who have performed the best, with personal congratulations from the CEO printed next to their names. Also make a site on the office intranet with the same content and email links to the whole staff. This will give the best workers a sense of connection with HQ without actually having to ship them there.

4. A rumor of a safety recall has got customers besieging your customer relationship sites, nearly causing them to crash. The rumor is partly true: a small number of cars containing a certain customization to the sun roof are at fault and are being recalled, as your boss has made clear in a statement to the press. However, the rumor has it that all new Toyotas with sunroofs are faulty and can short-circuit disastrously in wet weather. The only way you can deal with the flood is to have your customer care personnel do double shifts, manning the phones and the chat sites, help sites, bulletin boards, and blogs. How will you motivate your people to step up?
   a. Rotate your employees between handling customers over the phones and tweeting, posting, and blogging on the Internet. Have everyone do one shift of each till the crisis is over.
   b. Promise them cash bonuses when the crisis is over. A week or so should give you the time to rustle up the extra budget.
   c. Point out that this is a temporary situation and they should be grateful it's not like this every day.
   d. Subcontract the crisis handling to another firm. It's clearly outside your capacity.

LEARNING OBJECTIVES CHECKUP

Assess your understanding of the principles in this chapter by reading each learning objective and studying the accompanying exercises. For fill-in-the-blank items, write the missing text in the blank provided; for multiple-choice items, circle the letter of the correct answer. You can check your responses against the answer key on page AK-1.

Objective 1.1: Explain the importance of effective communication to your career and to the companies where you will work.

1. Which of the following is the most accurate description of the role that communication will play in your career?
   a. Ideas matter more than anything, so as long as you are creative and have strong business sense, you can hire people to take care of communication tasks.
   b. No matter what other skills, connections, and attributes you have, your prospects will be limited if you don't have good communication skills.
   c. In today's tough business world, performance is the most important differentiator; everything else is a distant second.
   d. As a "soft skill," communication is important in some careers, such as sales and human resources, but not in technical, financial, or administrative careers.

2. Effective business messages are
   a. Entertaining, blunt, direct, opinionated, and persuasive
   b. Practical, objective, concise, clear, and persuasive
   c. Personal, clear, short, catchy, and challenging

3. Why is it important for a business message to clearly state expectations regarding who is responsible for doing what in response to the message?
   a. To make sure other employees don't avoid their responsibilities
   b. To make sure that the person who sent the message isn't criticized if important tasks don't get completed
   c. To eliminate confusion by letting each affected person know what his or her specific responsibilities are

4. Which of the following is not a skill that employers will expect you to have?
   a. Communicating effectively with people from diverse backgrounds and experiences
   b. Using communication technologies effectively and efficiently
   c. Managing your time wisely and using resources efficiently
   d. Commanding employees to follow orders

Objective 1.2: Describe the communication skills employers will expect you to have and the nature of communicating in an organization by using an audience-centered approach.

5. An audience-centered approach to communication
   a. Starts with the assumption that the audience is always right
   b. Improves the effectiveness of communication by focusing on the information needs of the audience
   c. Is generally a waste of time because it doesn't accommodate the needs of the sender
   d. Always simplifies the tasks involved in planning and creating messages

6. Sensitivity to business etiquette
   a. Reduces the chance of interpersonal blunders that might negatively affect communication
   b. Is considered by most companies to be a waste of time in today's fast-paced markets
   c. Is now legally required in all 50 states
   d. Always increases the cost of business communication

Objective 1.3: Describe the communication process model and the ways that social media are changing the nature of business communication.

7. Communication style using the Business Communication 2.0 concept is best described as
   a. Conversational
   b. Multilingual
   c. Technical
   d. Playful

8. Which of the following pairs of attributes best describes the social communication model?
   a. Interactive and conversational
   b. Technical and instantaneous
   c. Electronic and print
   d. Relaxed and unrestricted

9. In order for audience members to successfully receive messages, they must first _____ the presence of the message, then _____ it from other sensory input, and then _____ it as a message.

10. In order for the receiver of a message to respond in the manner desired by the sender, the receiver needs to
   a. Remember the message
   b. Be able to respond to the message
   c. Have the motivation to respond to the message
   d. Do all of the above

Objective 1.4: List four general guidelines for using communication technology effectively.

11. Communication technology has value only if it helps deliver the right _____ to the right _____ at the right time.

12. The information technology paradox means that
   a. Communication tools can sometimes waste more time than they save
   b. Computers lose as much information as they save
   c. People are no longer needed to create messages
   d. Technology isn't as expensive as it used to be

13. Reconnecting frequently with colleagues and customers in person
   a. Is widely considered an inappropriate use of time, given all the electronic options now available
   b. Is frowned on by successful managers
   c. Is critical because it helps ensure that technology doesn't hinder human interaction

Objective 1.5: Define *ethics*, explain the difference between an ethical dilemma and an ethical lapse, and list six guidelines for making ethical communication choices.

14. Ethical communication
   a. Is the same thing as legal communication
   b. Costs more because there are so many rules to consider
   c. Is important only for companies that sell to consumers rather than to other businesses
   d. Includes all relevant information, is true in every sense, and is not deceptive in any way

15. An ethical _____ exists when a person is faced with two conflicting but ethical choices or alternatives that are neither entirely right nor entirely wrong; an ethical _____ occurs when a person makes an unethical choice.

MyBcommLab

Log on to www.pearsoninternationaleditions.com/mybcommlab to access study and assessment aids associated with this chapter. If you are not using MyBcommLab, you can access the Real-Time Updates at http://real-timeupdates.com/ebc10.

CHAPTER OUTLINE

Understanding Why Communication Matters

Communication Is Important to Your Career
Communication Is Important to Your Company
What Makes Business Communication Effective?

Communicating in Today's Global Business Environment

Understanding the Unique Challenges of Business Communication
Understanding What Employers Expect from You
Communicating in an Organizational Context
Adopting an Audience-Centered Approach

Exploring the Communication Process

The Basic Communication Model
The Social Communication Model

Using Technology to Improve Business Communication

Keeping Technology in Perspective
Guarding Against Information Overload
Using Technological Tools Productively
Reconnecting with People

Committing to Ethical and Legal Communication

Distinguishing Ethical Dilemmas from Ethical Lapses
Ensuring Ethical Communication
Ensuring Legal Communication

Applying What You've Learned

LEARNING OBJECTIVES

1. Explain the importance of effective communication to your career and to the companies where you will work. [page 43]

2. Describe the communication skills employers will expect you to have and the nature of communicating in an organization using an audience-centered approach. [page 44]

3. Describe the communication process model and the ways that social media are changing the nature of business communication. [page 50]

4. List four general guidelines for using communication technology effectively. [page 56]

5. Define *ethics*, explain the difference between an ethical dilemma and an ethical lapse, and list six guidelines for making ethical communication choices. [page 62]

KEY TERMS

audience-centered approach Understanding and respecting the members of your audience and making every effort to get your message across in a way that is meaningful to them

Business Communication 2.0 A new approach to business communication based on social communication

code of ethics A written set of ethical guidelines that companies expect their employees to follow

communication The process of transferring information and meaning using one or more written, oral, visual, or electronic media

communication barriers Forces or events that can disrupt communication, including noise and distractions, competing messages, filters, and channel breakdowns

communication channels Systems used to deliver messages

communication medium The form in which a message is presented; the four categories of media are oral, written, visual, and electronic

copyright A form of legal protection for the expression of creative ideas

corporate culture The mixture of values, traditions, and habits that give a company its atmosphere and personality

decoding Extracting the idea from a message

defamation The intentional communication of false statements that damage character or reputation

encoding Putting an idea into a message (words, images, or a combination of both)

ethical communication Communication that includes all relevant information, is true in every sense, and is not deceptive

ethical dilemma Situation that involves making a choice when the alternatives aren't completely wrong or completely right

ethical lapse A clearly unethical choice

ethics The accepted principles of conduct that govern behavior within a society

etiquette The expected norms of behavior in any particular situation

feedback Information from receivers regarding the quality and effectiveness of a message

information overload Condition in which people receive more information than they can effectively process

intellectual property Assets including patents, copyrighted materials, trade secrets, and even Internet domain names

message The "container" for an idea to be transmitted from a sender to a receiver

perception A person's awareness or view of reality; also, the process of detecting incoming messages

selective perception The inclination to distort or ignore incoming information rather than change one's beliefs

social communication model An interactive, conversational approach to communication in which formerly passive audience members are empowered to participate fully

social media Electronic media such as social networks and blogs that transform passive audiences into active participants in the communication process by allowing them to share content, revise content, respond to content, or contribute new content

stakeholders Groups affected by a company's actions: customers, employees, shareholders, suppliers, neighbors, the community, and the world at large

transparency Giving all participants in a conversation access to the information they need to accurately process the messages they are receiving

workforce diversity All the differences among the people who work together, including differences in age, gender, sexual orientation, education, cultural background, religion, ability, and life experience

"you" attitude Communicating with an audience-centered approach; creating messages that are about "you," the receiver, rather than "me," the sender

APPLY YOUR KNOWLEDGE

To review chapter content related to each question, refer to the indicated Learning Objective.

1. If you are an acknowledged expert in your field, do you really need to care about communication skills? Why or why not? [LO-1]

2. How does the presence of a reader comments feature on a corporate blog reflect audience-centered communication? [LO-2]

3. How are social networks, wikis, and other Web 2.0 technologies changing the practice of business communication? [LO-3]

4. Is it possible for companies to be too dependent on communication technology? Explain briefly. [LO-4]

5. Because of your excellent communication skills, your boss always asks you to write his reports for him. When you overhear the CEO complimenting him on his logical organization and clear writing style, your boss responds as if he'd written all those reports himself. What kind of ethical choice does your boss's response represent? What can you do in this situation? Briefly explain your solution and your reasoning. [LO-5]

PRACTICE YOUR SKILLS

Active links for all websites in this chapter can be found on MyBcommLab; see your User Guide for instructions on accessing the content for this chapter. Each activity is labeled according to the primary skill or skills you will need to use. To review relevant chapter content, you can refer to the indicated Learning Objective. In some instances, supporting information will be found in another chapter, as indicated.

Message for Analysis: Analyzing Communication Effectiveness [LO-1]

Read the following blog posting and then (1) analyze whether the message is effective or ineffective (be sure to explain why) and (2) revise the message so that it follows this chapter's guidelines.

It is totally out of order the way you people are wasting office supplies. This company spends thousands of dollars every month on consumables. Only yesterday, I found five hundred discarded copies of invitation letters to someone's farewell dinner in the waste bin next to the photocopier. Why not just send a group email? Or at least check that your document is error-free and you are printing an appropriate number. This senseless waste of paper is ridiculous when the company is trying to reduce its carbon footprint.

You all attended the workshop on waste that we had last January; I remember that some of you even came up with good ideas to reduce wastage in the office cafeteria. Why then do you throw away documents with the bulldog clips still attached? Is it my job to go through your waste bins and salvage stuff you're too lazy or careless to keep out of the trash? Here's a photograph of the waste bin in the copying room, and here's a selection of things you people have seen fit to throw away. Note the Parker Rollerball that just needs a new refill. If you're not careful, I will have to institute some sort of penalty for wastage to make you sit up and take notice.

Exercises

1. **Writing: Compositional Modes: Summaries [LO-1], Chapter 4** Write a paragraph introducing yourself to your instructor and your class. Address such areas as your background, interests, achievements, and goals. Submit your paragraph using email, blog, or social network, as indicated by your instructor.

2. **Media Skills: Microblogging [LO-1], Chapter 6** Write four effective messages of no more than 140 characters each (short enough to work as Twitter tweets, in other words) to put on posters in the subway on the consequences of bad communication skills in business. The four messages should describe four quite different consequences.

3. **Fundamentals: Analyzing Communication Effectiveness [LO-1]** Identify a video clip (on YouTube or another online source) that you believe represents an example of effective communication. It can be in any context, business or otherwise, but make sure it is something appropriate to discuss in class. Post a link to the video on your class blog, along with a brief written summary of why you think this example shows effective communication in action.

4. **Planning: Assessing Audience Needs [LO-2], Chapter 3** A friend of yours comes to you with a problem. She's trying to write her résumé for a job at a renowned HR firm. She dropped out of college when she was twenty but went back four years later and finished her degree in sociology. During the gap, she worked for a year at a wildlife reserve in Thailand and then for three years at an orphanage where she taught the children in the village primary school. She was also involved with an NGO there, where she helped rehabilitate trafficked women to their villages. She has now completed her college education with average grades and has also done a one-year diploma course in conflict management. She wants to work in HR but has no corporate experience and is very tense about her employability. Draft a sample email for her to send out to prospective employers outlining her experience and skills, and either submit a hard copy to your instructor or post it on the class blog.

5. **Communication Etiquette: Communicating with Sensitivity and Tact [LO-2]** You have only one coffee lounge in your company offices, and all the staff use it. Unfortunately it's also the only way to reach the conference room. You have noticed that guests often witness loud conversations and very casual behavior by the staff when they have to pass through this lounge to reach the conference rooms. You have repeatedly warned the staff that they should watch their manners in the lounge, but there is a core group of five or six people who regard it as 'their' place and won't listen. Write an email to the whole staff outlining the problem and gently warning them to be careful. Be careful to anticipate any possible counter-arguments the troublesome group might throw at you.

6. **Collaboration: Team Project; Planning: Assessing Audience Needs [LO-2], Chapter 2, Chapter 4** Your boss has asked your work group to research and report on the effect on employee satisfaction of a new performance-linked bonus scheme. Your boss, along with some of the other senior

managers, believes that it has actually decreased employee satisfaction, but the CEO loves the scheme. Of course, you'll want to know who (besides your boss) will be reading your report. Working with two team members, list four or five other things you'll want to know about the situation and about your audience before starting your research. Briefly explain why each of the items on your list is important.

7. **Planning: Constructing a Persuasive Argument [LO-3], Chapter 10** You are the customer service manager for a company that sells a software package used by not-for-profit organizations to plan and manage fundraising campaigns. The powerful software is complicated enough to require a fairly extensive user's manual, and the company has always provided a printed manual to customers. Customers frequently email your department with questions about using the software and suggestions for using the software to maximize fundraising efforts. You know that many customers could benefit from the answers to those questions and the suggestions from fellow customers, but with a printed manual issued once every couple years, you don't have any way to collect and distribute this information in a timely fashion.

You've been researching wikis and believe this would be a great way to let customers participate in an ongoing conversation about using the software. In fact, you'd like to convert the printed manual to a wiki on which any registered customer could add or edit pages. Rather than spend thousands of dollars printing a manual that is difficult to expand or update, the wiki would be a "living" document that continually evolves as people ask and answer questions and offer suggestions. The rest of the management team is extremely nervous, however. "We—not the customer—are the experts," one says. Another asks, "How can we ensure the quality of the information if any customer can change it?" They don't deny that customers have valuable information to add; they just don't want customers to have control of an important company document. Making up any information you need, write a brief email to your colleagues, explaining the benefits of letting customers contribute to a wiki-based user manual. (You can refer to pages 419–420 to learn more about wikis.)

8. **Planning: Constructing a Persuasive Argument [LO-3], Chapter 10** Blogging has become a popular way for employees to communicate with customers and other parties outside the company. In some cases, employee blogs have been quite beneficial for both companies and their customers by providing helpful information and "putting a human face" on other formal and imposing corporations. However, in some other cases, employees have been fired for posting information that their employers said was inappropriate. One particular area of concern is criticism of the company or individual managers. Should employees be allowed to criticize their employers in a public forum such as a blog? In a brief email message, argue for or against company policies that prohibit critical information in employee blogs.

9. **Fundamentals: Analyzing Communication Effectiveness [LO-3]** Use the eight phases of the communication process to analyze a miscommunication you've recently had with a co-worker, supervisor, classmate, teacher, friend, or family member. What idea were you trying to share? How did you encode and transmit it? Did the receiver get the message? Did the receiver correctly decode the message? How do you know? Based on your analysis, identify and explain the barriers that prevented your successful communication in this instance.

10. **Technology: Using Communication Tools [LO-4]** Find a free online communication service that you have no experience using as a content creator or contributor. Services to consider include blogging (such as Blogger), microblogging (such as Twitter), community Q&A sites (such as Yahoo! Answers), and user-generated content sites (such as Flickr). Perform a basic task such as opening an account or setting up a blog. Was the task easy to perform? Were the instructions clear? Could you find help online if you needed it? Is there anything about the experience that could be improved? Summarize your conclusions in a brief email message to your instructor.

11. **Communication Ethics: Distinguishing Ethical Dilemmas and Ethical Lapses [LO-5]** There is one person in your company who loves to play practical jokes on people. Recently you suspect he switched his colleague's pen drive for one that looked identical to it but contained a PowerPoint presentation of stills from popular cartoon shows. As a result of that embarrassment, the company lost a small but very stable client account. How will you confront him and get him to confess, and what penalty will you impose on him if he does confess?

12. **Communication Ethics: Distinguishing Ethical Dilemmas and Ethical Lapses [LO-5]** In less than a page, explain why you think each of the following is or is not ethical.
   a. Entering an earlier time next to your name in the signup book when you are late for work.
   b. Downloading a cracked version of an expensive software package from a torrent site.
   c. Telling a colleague she can have time off to look after her sick four-year-old and then telling your boss she took the day off even though you told her not to.
   d. Reading your boss's correspondence upside down when you sit across from her at her desk.

13. **Communication Ethics: Providing Ethical Leadership [LO-5]** Cisco, a leading manufacturer of equipment for the Internet and corporate networks, has developed a code of ethics that it expects employees to abide by. Visit the company's website, at www.cisco.com, and find its code of conduct. In a brief paragraph, describe three specific examples of things you could do that would violate these provisions; then list at least three opportunities that Cisco provides its employees to report ethics violations or to ask questions regarding ethical dilemmas.

EXPAND YOUR SKILLS

Critique the Professionals

Locate an example of professional communication from a reputable online source. It can reflect any aspect of business communication, from an advertisement or a press release to a company blog or website. Evaluate this communication effort in light of any aspect of this chapter that is relevant to the sample and interesting to you. For example, is the piece effective? Audience-centered? Ethical? Using whatever medium your instructor requests, write a brief analysis of the piece (no more than one page), citing specific elements from the piece and support from the chapter.

Sharpening Your Career Skills Online

Bovée and Thill's Business Communication Web Search, at http://businesscommunicationblog.com/websearch, is a unique research tool designed specifically for business communication research. Use the Web Search function to find an online video, a podcast, or a PowerPoint presentation that explains at least one essential business communication skill. Write a brief email message to your instructor or a post for your class blog, describing the item that you found and summarizing the career skills information you learned from it.

IMPROVE YOUR GRAMMAR, MECHANICS, AND USAGE

The following exercises help you improve your knowledge of and power over English grammar, mechanics, and usage. Turn to the Handbook of Grammar, Mechanics, and Usage at the end of this book and review all of Section 1.1 (Nouns). Then look at the following 10 items. Underline the preferred choice within each set of parentheses. (Answers to these exercises appear on page AK-3.)

1. I remember seeing your report on my (*superiors, superior's*) desk.
2. Some of the new employees are like (*fish, fishes*) out of water in this new project.
3. The worldwide recession of the mid- (*2000's, 2000s*) has affected us badly.
4. The (*Jameses, James'*) have requested that all (*faxs, faxes*) and mails be forwarded to them.
5. Seven (*companys, companies*) will be attending our talk about incorporation.
6. Make sure that all your team members have understood their (*dutys, duties*) completely.
7. Please ensure that all the (*member's, members'*) donations are collected by Friday.
8. John and his (*brothers-in-law, brother-in-laws*) have launched two online (*venture's, ventures*).
9. You need to add more (*analyses, analysis*) to your reports.
10. Director (*Leses, Les's*) memo details exactly what constitutes a (*months, month's*) work.

For additional exercises focusing on nouns, visit MyBcommLab. Click on Chapter 1, click on Additional Exercises to Improve Your Grammar, Mechanics, and Usage, and then click on 1. Possessive nouns or 2. Antecedents.

REFERENCES

1. Toyota Facebook page, accessed 22 December 2010, www.facebook.com/toyota; Lisa Lacy, "Toyota Pushes 'Auto-Biography' Facebook Campaign," ClickZ, 2 August 2010, www.clickz.com; Alan Ohnsman and Makiko Kitamura "Is Toyota's Reputation Finished?" *Bloomberg Businessweek*, 28 January 2010, www.businessweek.com.

2. Richard L. Daft, *Management*, 6th ed. (Cincinnati: Thomson South-Western, 2003), 580.

3. Julie Connelly, "Youthful Attitudes, Sobering Realities," *New York Times*, 28 October 2003, E1, E6; Nigel Andrews and Laura D'Andrea Tyson, "The Upwardly Global MBA," *Strategy + Business* 36:60–69; Jim McKay, "Communication Skills Found Lacking," *Pittsburgh Post-Gazette*, 28 February 2005, www.delawareonline.com.

4. Brian Solis, *Engage!* (Hoboken: John Wiley & Sons, 2010), 11–12; "Majority of Global Companies Face an Engagement Gap," Internal Comms Hub website, 23 October 2007, www.internalcommshub.com; Gary L. Neilson, Karla L. Martin, and Elizabeth Powers, "The Secrets to Successful Strategy Execution," *Harvard Business Review*, June 2008, 61–70; Nicholas Carr, "Lessons in Corporate Blogging," *Business-Week*, 18 July 2006, 9; Susan Meisinger, "To Keep Employees, Talk—and Listen—to Them!" *HR Magazine*, August 2006, 10.

5. Daft, *Management*, 147.

6. Don Hellriegel, Susan E. Jackson, and John W. Slocum, Jr., *Management: A Competency-Based Approach* (Cincinnati: Thomson South-Western, 2002), 447.

7. "CEOs to Communicators: 'Stick to Common Sense'," Internal Comms Hub website, 23 October 2007, www.internalcommshub.com; "A Writing Competency Model for Business," BizCom 101.com, 14 December 2007, www.business-writing-courses.com; Sue Dewhurst and Liam FitzPatrick, "What Should Be the Competency of Your IC Team?" white paper, 2007, http://competentcommunicators.com.

8. Philip C. Kolin, *Successful Writing at Work*, 6th ed. (Boston: Houghton Mifflin, 2001), 17–23.

9. Laura L. Myers and Mary L. Tucker, "Increasing Awareness of Emotional Intelligence in a Business Curriculum," *Business Communication Quarterly*, March 2005, 44–51.

10. Pete Cashmore, "10 Web Trends to Watch in 2010," CNN Tech, 3 December 2009, www.cnn.com.

11. Stephanie Armour, "Music Hath Charms for Some Workers—Others It Really Annoys," *USA Today*, 24 March 2006, B1–B2.

12. Paul Martin Lester, *Visual Communication: Images with Messages* (Belmont, Calif.: Thomson South-Western, 2006), 6–8.

13. Michael R. Solomon, *Consumer Behavior: Buying, Having, and Being*, 6th ed. (Upper Saddle River, N.J.: Pearson Prentice Hall, 2004), 65.

14. Anne Field, "What You Say, What They Hear," *Harvard Management Communication Letter*, Winter 2005, 3–5.

15. Chuck Williams, *Management*, 2nd ed. (Cincinnati: Thomson South-Western, 2002), 690.

16. Charles G. Morris and Albert A. Maisto, *Psychology: An Introduction*, 12th ed. (Upper Saddle River, N.J.: Pearson Prentice Hall, 2005), 226–239; Saundra K. Ciccarelli and Glenn E. Meyer, *Psychology* (Upper Saddle River, N.J.: Prentice Hall, 2006), 210–229; Mark H. Ashcraft, *Cognition*, 4th ed. (Upper Saddle River, N.J.: Prentice Hall, 2006), 44–54.

17. Niall Harbison, "Seven Important Social Media Trends for the Next Year," TNW Social Media, 12 September 2010, http://thenextweb.com.

18. Jacques Bughin and Michael Chu, "The Rise of the Networked Enterprise: Web 2.0 Finds Its Payday," *McKinsey Quarterly*, December 2010, www.mckinseyquarterly.com.

19. IBM Corporation, "Capitalizing on Complexity: Insights from the Global Chief Executive Study," May 2010, www.ibm.com.

20. Tara Craig, "How to Avoid Information Overload," *Personnel Today*, 10 June 2008, 31; Jeff Davidson, "Fighting Information Overload," *Canadian Manager*, Spring 2005, 16+.

21. "The Top Ten Ways Workers Waste Time Online," 24/7 Wall St., 30 September 2010, http://247wallst.com.

22. Eric J. Sinrod, "Perspective: It's My Internet—I Can Do What I Want," News.com, 29 March 2006, www.news.com.

23. Eric J. Sinrod, "Time to Crack Down on Tech at Work?" News.com, 14 June 2006, www.news.com.

24. Steve Lohr, "As Travel Costs Rise, More Meetings Go Virtual," *New York Times*, 22 July 2008, www.nytimes.com.

25. Kolin, *Successful Writing at Work*, 24–30.

26. Nancy K. Kubasek, Bartley A. Brennan, and M. Neil Browne, *The Legal Environment of Business*, 3rd ed. (Upper Saddle River, N.J.: Prentice Hall, 2003), 172.

27. Michael Oliveira, "Netflix Apologizes for Using Actors to Meet Press at Canadian Launch," *Globe and Mail*, 22 September 2010, www.theglobeandmail.com.

28. Word of Mouth Marketing Association, "WOM 101", http://womma.org; Nate Anderson, "FTC Says Stealth Marketing Unethical," *Ars Technica*, 13 December 2006, http://arstechnica.com; "Undercover Marketing Uncovered," CBSnews.com, 25 July 2004, www.cbsnews.com; Stephanie Dunnewind, "Teen Recruits Create Word-of-Mouth 'Buzz' to Hook Peers on Products," *Seattle Times*, 20 November 2004, www.seattletimes.com.

29. Linda Pophal, "Tweet Ethics: Trust and Transparency in a Web 2.0 World." *CW Bulletin*, September 2009, www.iabc.com

30. Rich Phillips and John Zarrella, "Live Bombs Haunt Orlando Neighborhood," CNN.com, 1 July 2008, www.cnn.com.

31. Daft, *Management*, 155.

32. Gap Inc., "Code of Business Conduct," updated 7 December 2009, www.gapinc.com.

33. Based in part on Robert Kreitner, *Management*, 9th ed. (Boston: Houghton Mifflin, 2004), 163.

34. Henry R. Cheeseman, *Contemporary Business and E-Commerce Law*, 4th ed. (Upper Saddle River, N.J.: Prentice Hall, 2003), 201.

35. John Jude Moran, *Employment Law: New Challenges in the Business Environment*, 2nd ed. (Upper Saddle River, N.J.: Prentice Hall, 2002), 186–187; Kubasek et al., *The Legal Environment of Business*, 562.

36. Cheeseman, *Contemporary Business and E-Commerce Law*, 325.

37. Kubasek et al., *The Legal Environment of Business*, 306.

38. Robert Plummer, "Will Fake Business Blogs Crash and Burn?" BBC News, 22 May 2008, http://news.bbc.co.uk.

39. Tim Arango, "Soon, Bloggers Must Give Full Disclosure," *New York Times*, 5 October 2009, www.nytimes.com.

Mastering Team Skills and Interpersonal Communication

LEARNING OBJECTIVES After studying this chapter, you will be able to

1 List the advantages and disadvantages of working in teams, describe the characteristics of effective teams, and highlight four key issues of group dynamics

2 Offer guidelines for collaborative communication, identify major collaboration technologies, and explain how to give constructive feedback

3 List the key steps needed to ensure productive team meetings

4 Identify the major technologies used to enhance or replace in-person meetings

5 Identify three major modes of listening, describe the listening process, and explain the problem of selective listening

6 Explain the importance of nonverbal communication, and identify six major categories of nonverbal expression

7 Explain the importance of business etiquette, and identify three key areas in which good etiquette is essential

MyBcommLab Where you see MyBcommLab in this chapter, go to www.pearsoninternationaleditions.com/mybcommlab for additional activities on the topic being discussed.

ON THE JOB: COMMUNICATING AT ROSEN LAW FIRM

The Wiki Way to Cut Costs and Build Team Spirit

When communication tools function at their best, they can go beyond mere facilitation to transformation. Such was the case at Rosen Law Firm, based in Raleigh, North Carolina. Lee Rosen, the firm's owner and chief executive, wanted to replace an expensive, complicated, and inflexible computer system that employees relied on for everything from contact lists to appointment calendars to document storage. The solution he chose was a wiki, the same technology that enables nearly 100,000 people around the world to contribute to Wikipedia.

The wiki certainly helped cut costs, and it did much more. Besides handling much of the firm's document storage and formal communication, the wiki introduced an informal social element that is helping employees bond as a community. Many have added personal pages with information about themselves, helping employees get to know their colleagues on a more intimate level.

In implementing the wiki, Rosen faced a common challenge with new communication tools: getting people to give up familiar ways of doing things and embrace change. Knowing that the value of a company wiki depends on the level of employee contribution—and that having some of the staff switch while others stuck to old ways would seriously disrupt communication—he encouraged use of the new wiki with a friendly competition. For each page an employee created during

Lee Rosen's Law Firm uses a wiki to manage thousands of documents while boosting teamwork and collaboration.
Source: Rosen Law Firm.

the three-month competition, he or she was given one possible combination to the company safe, which contained a $1,000 cash prize. From time to time, Rosen also forced use of the wiki by publishing important information only in that venue.

As often happens when companies face significant changes, the move to the wiki did cause some turmoil. Two camps of employees argued over the best way to organize information and got caught up in an "edit war," repeatedly undoing each other's decisions. They eventually reached a compromise that resolved the disagreement and had lasting benefits for teamwork and interpersonal communication across the firm. According to Rosen, "It forced everybody to learn about each other's job."[1]

www.rosen.com

Communicating Effectively in Teams

The teamwork interactions among the employees at Rosen Law Firm (profiled in the chapter opener) represent one of the most essential elements of interpersonal communication. **Collaboration**—working together to meet complex challenges—has become a core job responsibility for roughly half the U.S. workforce.[2] No matter what career path you pursue, it's a virtual guarantee that you will be expected to collaborate in at least some of your work activities. Your communication skills will pay off handsomely in these interactions, because the productivity and quality of collaborative efforts depend heavily on the communication skills of the professionals involved.

A **team** is a unit of two or more people who share a mission and the responsibility for working to achieve a common goal.[3] **Problem-solving teams** and **task forces** assemble to resolve specific issues and then disband when their goals have been accomplished. Such teams are often *cross-functional*, pulling together people from a variety of departments who have different areas of expertise and responsibility. The diversity of opinions and experiences can lead to better decisions, but competing interests can lead to tensions that highlight the need for effective communication. **Committees** are formal teams that usually have a long life span and can become a permanent part of the organizational structure. Committees typically deal with regularly recurring tasks, such as an executive committee that meets monthly to plan strategies and review results.

ADVANTAGES AND DISADVANTAGES OF TEAMS

When teams are successful, they can improve productivity, creativity, employee involvement, and even job security.[4] Teams are often at the core of **participative management**, the effort to involve employees in the company's decision making. A successful team can provide a number of advantages:[5]

- **Increased information and knowledge.** By pooling the experience of several individuals, a team has access to more information in the decision-making process.
- **Increased diversity of views.** Team members can bring a variety of perspectives to the decision-making process—as long as these diverse viewpoints are guided by a shared goal.[6]
- **Increased acceptance of a solution.** Those who participate in making a decision are more likely to support it and encourage others to accept it.
- **Higher performance levels.** Working in teams can unleash new levels of creativity and energy in workers who share a sense of purpose and mutual accountability. Effective teams can be better than top-performing individuals at solving complex problems.[7]

Although teamwork has many advantages, it also has a number of potential disadvantages. At the worst, working in teams can be a frustrating waste of time. Teams need to be aware of and work to counter the following potential disadvantages:

- **Groupthink.** Like other social structures, business teams can generate tremendous pressures to conform with accepted norms of behavior. **Groupthink** occurs when peer pressures cause individual team members to withhold contrary or unpopular opinions. The result can be decisions that are worse than the choices the team members might have made individually.

---

1   LEARNING OBJECTIVE

List the advantages and disadvantages of working in teams, describe the characteristics of effective teams, and highlight four key issues of group dynamics.

Collaboration, working together to solve complex problems, is an essential skill for knowledge workers in every profession.

Team members have a shared mission and are collectively responsible for their work.

Effective teams can pool knowledge, take advantage of diverse viewpoints, and increase acceptance of solutions the team proposes.

MyBcommLab

- Access this chapter's simulation entitled Interpersonal Communication and Teamwork, located at www .pearsoninternationaleditions .com/mybcommlab.

Teams need to avoid the negative impact of groupthink, hidden agendas, and excessive costs.

- **Hidden agendas.** Some team members may have a **hidden agenda**—private, counterproductive motives, such as a desire to take control of the group, to undermine someone else on the team, or to pursue a business goal that runs counter to the team's mission.
- **Cost.** Aligning schedules, arranging meetings, and coordinating individual parts of a project can eat up a lot of time and money.

CHARACTERISTICS OF EFFECTIVE TEAMS

Effective teams have a clear sense of purpose, open and honest communication, consensus-based decision making, creativity, and effective conflict resolution.

The most effective teams have a clear objective and shared sense of purpose, have a strong sense of trust, communicate openly and honestly, reach decisions by consensus, think creatively, and know how to resolve conflict.[8] Teams that have these attributes can focus their time and energy on their work, without being disrupted by destructive conflict (see page 78).

In contrast, teams that lack one or more of these attributes can get bogged down in conflict or waste time and resources pursuing unclear goals. Two of the most common reasons cited for unsuccessful teamwork are a lack of trust and poor communication. A lack of trust can result from team members being suspicious of one another's motives or ability to contribute.[9] Communication breakdowns are most likely to occur when teams operate across cultures, countries, or time zones.[10]

GROUP DYNAMICS

Group dynamics are the interactions and interpersonal processes that take place in a team.

The interactions and processes that take place among the members of a team are called **group dynamics**. Productive teams tend to develop clear **norms**, informal standards of conduct that members share and that guide member behavior. Group dynamics are influenced by several factors: the roles that team members assume, the current phase of team development, the team's success in resolving conflict, and the team's success in overcoming resistance.

Assuming Team Roles

Each member of a group plays a role that affects the outcome of the group's activities.

Members of a team can play various roles, which fall into three categories (see Table 2.1). Members who assume **self-oriented roles** are motivated mainly to fulfill personal needs, so they tend to be less productive than other members. "Dream teams" composed of multiple superstars often don't perform as well as one might expect because high-performing individuals can have trouble putting the team's needs ahead of their own.[11] In addition, highly skilled and experienced people with difficult personalities might not contribute for the simple reason that other team members may avoid interacting with them.[12] Far more likely to contribute to team goals are members who assume **team-maintenance roles** to

TABLE 2.1	Team Roles—Functional and Dysfunctional	
Dysfunctional: Self-Oriented Roles	**Functional: Team-Maintenance Roles**	**Functional: Task-Facilitating Roles**
Controlling: Dominating others by exhibiting superiority or authority	**Encouraging:** Drawing out other members by showing verbal and nonverbal support, praise, or agreement	**Initiating:** Getting the team started on a line of inquiry
Withdrawing: Retiring from the team either by becoming silent or by refusing to deal with a particular aspect of the team's work	**Harmonizing:** Reconciling differences among team members through mediation or by using humor to relieve tension	**Information giving or seeking:** Offering (or seeking) information relevant to questions facing the team
Attention seeking: Calling attention to oneself and demanding recognition from others	**Compromising:** Offering to yield on a point in the interest of reaching a mutually acceptable decision	**Coordinating:** Showing relationships among ideas, clarifying issues, summarizing what the team has done
Diverting: Focusing the team's discussion on topics of interest to the individual rather than on those relevant to the task		**Procedure setting:** Suggesting decision-making procedures that will move the team toward a goal

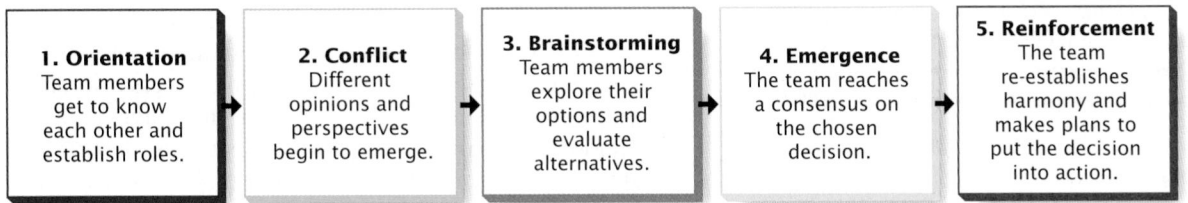

Figure 2.1   Phases of Group Development
Groups generally progress through several stages on their way to becoming productive and reaching their objectives.
Sources: Adapted from B. Aubrey Fisher, *Small Group Decision Making: Communication and the Group Process*, 2nd ed. (New York: McGraw-Hill, 1980), 145–149; Robbins and De Cenzo, *Fundamentals of Management*, 334–335; Richard L. Daft, *Management*, 6th ed. (Cincinnati: Thomson South-Western, 2003), 602–603.

help everyone work well together and those who assume **task-facilitating roles** to help the team reach its goals.[13]

Allowing for Team Evolution

Teams typically evolve through a number of phases on their way to becoming productive (see Figure 2.1). A variety of models have been proposed to describe the evolution toward becoming a productive team. Here is how one commonly used model identifies the phases a problem-solving team goes through as it evolves:[14]

1. **Orientation.** Team members socialize, establish their roles, and begin to define their task or purpose. Team-building exercises and activities can help teams break down barriers and develop a sense of shared purpose.[15] For geographically dispersed virtual teams, creating a "team operating agreement" that sets expectations for online meetings, communication processes, and decision making can help overcome the disadvantages of distance.[16]
2. **Conflict.** Team members begin to discuss their positions and become more assertive in establishing their roles. Disagreements and uncertainties are natural in this phase.
3. **Brainstorming.** Team members air all the options and fully discuss the pros and cons. At the end of this phase, members begin to settle on a single solution to the problem. Note that while group brainstorming remains a highly popular activity in today's companies, it may not always be the most productive way to generate new ideas. Some research indicates that having people brainstorm individually and then bring their ideas to a group meeting is more successful.[17]
4. **Emergence.** Consensus is reached when the team finds a solution that all members are willing to support (even if they have reservations).
5. **Reinforcement.** The team clarifies and summarizes the agreed-upon solution. Members receive their assignments for carrying out the group's decision, and they make arrangements for following up on those assignments.

You may also hear the process defined as *forming, storming, norming, performing,* and *adjourning,* the phases identified by researcher Bruce Tuckman when he proposed one of the earliest models of group development.[18] Regardless of the model you consider, these stages are a general framework for team development. Some teams may move forward and backward through several stages before they become productive, and other teams may be productive right away, even while some or all members are in a state of conflict.[19]

Resolving Conflict

Conflict in team activities can arise for a number of reasons: competition for resources, disagreement over goals or responsibilities, poor communication, power struggles, or fundamental differences in values, attitudes, and personalities.[20] Although the term *conflict* sounds negative, conflict isn't necessarily bad. Conflict can be *constructive* if

Teams typically evolve through a variety of phases, such as orientation, conflict, brainstorming, emergence, and reinforcement.

Conflict in teams can be either constructive or destructive.

REAL-TIME UPDATES
Learn More by Watching This Video

Use negotiation skills to resolve conflicts

Learn how to resolve conflicts through the win–win strategies of empathetic negotiation. Go to http://real-timeupdates.com/ebc10 and click on Learn More. If you are using MyBcommLab, you can access Real-Time Updates within each chapter or under Student Study Tools.

it forces important issues into the open, increases the involvement of team members, and generates creative ideas for solving a problem. Teamwork isn't necessarily about happiness and harmony; even teams that have some interpersonal friction can excel with effective leadership and team players committed to strong results. As teamwork experts Andy Boynton and Bill Fischer put it, "Virtuoso teams are not about getting polite results."[21]

In contrast, conflict is *destructive* if it diverts energy from more important issues, destroys the morale of teams or individual team members, or polarizes or divides the

> Destructive conflict can lead to win–lose or lose–lose outcomes.

team.[22] Destructive conflict can lead to *win–lose* or *lose–lose* outcomes, in which one or both sides lose, to the detriment of the entire team. If you approach conflict with the idea that both sides can satisfy their goals to at least some extent (a *win–win* strategy), you can minimize losses for everyone. For a win-win strategy to work, everybody must believe that (1) it's possible to find a solution that both parties can accept, (2) cooperation is better for the organization than competition, (3) the other party can be trusted, and (4) greater power or status doesn't entitle one party to impose a solution.

The following seven measures can help team members successfully resolve conflict:

- **Proactive behavior.** Deal with minor conflict before it becomes major conflict.
- **Communication.** Get those directly involved in a conflict to participate in resolving it.
- **Openness.** Get feelings out in the open before dealing with the main issues.
- **Research.** Seek factual reasons for a problem before seeking solutions.
- **Flexibility.** Don't let anyone lock into a position before considering other solutions.
- **Fair play.** Insist on fair outcomes and don't let anyone avoid a fair solution by hiding behind the rules.
- **Alliance.** Get opponents to fight together against an "outside force" instead of against each other.

Overcoming Resistance

One particular type of conflict that can affect team progress is resistance to change. Sometimes this resistance is clearly irrational, such as when people resist any kind of change, whether it makes sense or not. Sometimes, however, resistance is perfectly logical. A change may require someone to relinquish authority or give up comfortable ways of doing things. If someone is resisting change, you can be persuasive with calm, reasonable communication:

> When you encounter resistance or hostility, try to maintain your composure and address the other person's emotional needs.

- **Express understanding.** You might say, "I understand that this change might be difficult, and if I were in your position, I might be reluctant myself." Help the other person relax and talk about his or her anxiety so that you have a chance to offer reassurance.[23]
- **Bring resistance out into the open.** When people are noncommittal and silent, they may be tuning you out without even knowing why. Continuing with your argument is futile. Deal directly with the resistance, without accusing. You might say, "You seem to have reservations about this idea. Have I made some faulty assumptions?" Such questions force people to face and define their resistance.[24]
- **Evaluate others' objections fairly.** Use active listening to focus on what the other person is expressing, both the words and the feelings. Get the person to open up so that you can understand the basis for the resistance. Others' objections may raise legitimate points that you'll need to discuss, or they may reveal problems that you'll need to minimize.[25]

Hold your arguments until the other person is ready for them. Getting your point across depends as much on the other person's frame of mind as it does on your arguments. You can't assume that a strong argument will speak for itself. By becoming more audience centered, you will learn to address the other person's emotional needs first.

Collaborating on Communication Efforts

You should expect to collaborate on a wide variety of research, writing, design, and presentation projects in your career. When teams collaborate, the collective energy and expertise of the various members can lead to results that transcend what each individual could do otherwise.[26] However, collaborating on team messages requires special effort; the following section offers a number of helpful guidelines.

2   **LEARNING OBJECTIVE**

Offer guidelines for collaborative communication, identify major collaboration technologies, and explain how to give constructive feedback.

GUIDELINES FOR COLLABORATIVE WRITING

In any collaborative effort, team members coming from different backgrounds may have different work habits or priorities: A technical expert may focus on accuracy and scientific standards, an editor may be more concerned about organization and coherence, and a manager may focus on schedules, cost, and corporate goals. In addition, team members differ in writing styles, work habits, and personality traits.

To collaborate effectively, everyone involved must be flexible and open to other opinions, focusing on team objectives rather than on individual priorities.[27] Successful writers know that most ideas can be expressed in many ways, so they avoid the "my way is best" attitude. The following guidelines will help you collaborate more successfully:[28]

- **Select collaborators carefully.** Whenever possible, choose a combination of people who together have the experience, information, and talent needed for each project.
- **Agree on project goals before you start.** Starting without a clear idea of what the team hopes to accomplish inevitably leads to frustration and wasted time.
- **Give your team time to bond before diving in.** If people haven't had the opportunity to work together before, make sure they can get to know each other before being asked to collaborate.
- **Clarify individual responsibilities.** Because members will be depending on each other, make sure individual responsibilities are clear.
- **Establish clear processes.** Make sure everyone knows how the work will be managed from start to finish.
- **Avoid composing as a group.** The actual composition is the only part of developing team messages that usually does not benefit from group participation. Brainstorming the wording of short pieces of text, particularly headlines, slogans, and other high-visibility elements, can be an effective way to stimulate creative word choices. However, for longer projects, you will usually find it more efficient to plan, research, and outline together but assign the task of writing to one person or divide larger projects among multiple writers. If you divide the writing, try to have one person do a final revision pass to ensure a consistent style.
- **Make sure tools and techniques are ready and compatible across the team.** Even minor details such as different versions of software can delay projects.
- **Check to see how things are going along the way.** Don't assume that everything is working just because you don't hear anything negative.

Successful collaboration on writing projects requires a number of steps, from selecting the right partners and agreeing on project goals to establishing clear processes and avoiding writing as a group.

TECHNOLOGIES FOR COLLABORATIVE WRITING

A variety of collaboration tools exist to help teams write together. Among the simpler tools are group review and editing features in word processing software and the Adobe Acrobat electronic document system (PDF files) and web-based document systems such as Google Docs. More complex solutions include **content management systems** that organize and control the content for many websites (particularly larger corporate sites). As the chapter opening story about Rosen Law Firm discusses, a **wiki** (from the Hawaiian word for *quick*) is a website that allows anyone with access to add new material and edit existing material (see Figure 2.2 on the next page). Chapter 14 offers guidelines for effective wiki collaboration.

The key benefits of wikis include simple operation—writers don't need to know any of the techniques normally required to create web content—and the freedom to post new or revised material without prior approval. This approach is quite different from a content management

A wide variety of collaboration tools now exist to help professionals work on reports, presentations, and other communication efforts.

Wiki benefits include simple operation and the ability to post new or revised material instantly without a formal review process.

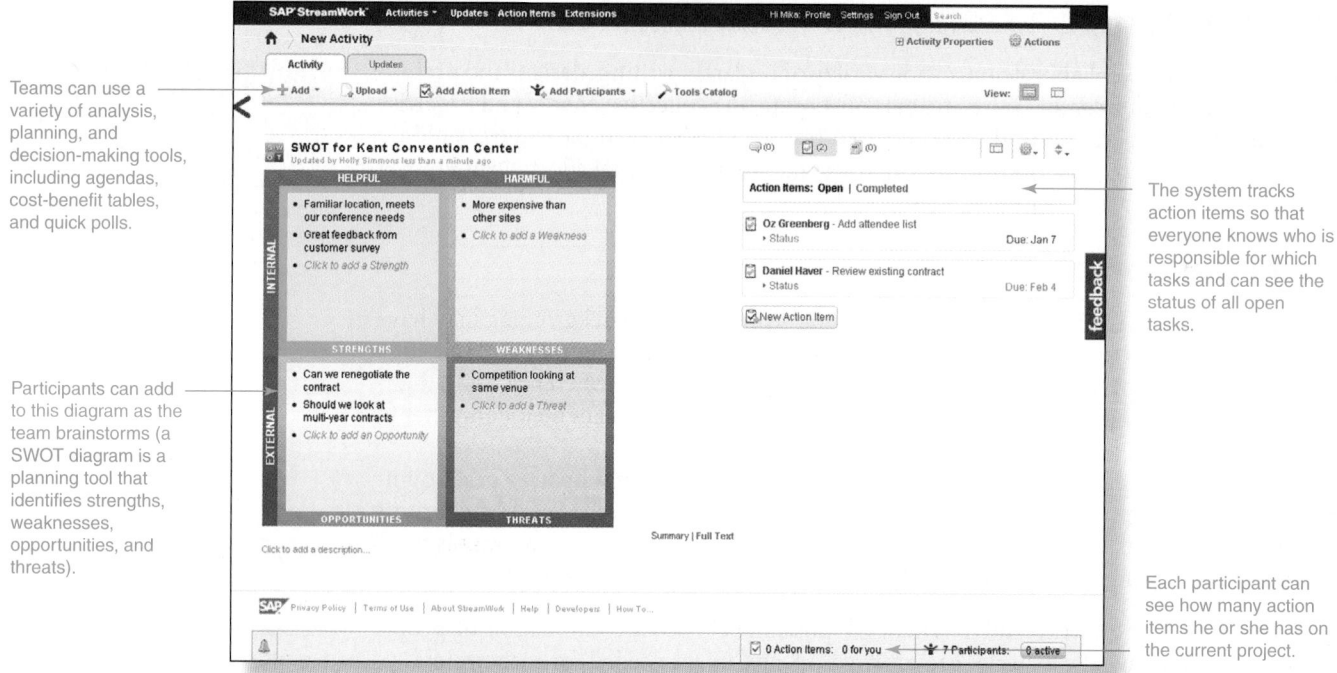

Teams can use a variety of analysis, planning, and decision-making tools, including agendas, cost-benefit tables, and quick polls.

Participants can add to this diagram as the team brainstorms (a SWOT diagram is a planning tool that identifies strengths, weaknesses, opportunities, and threats).

The system tracks action items so that everyone knows who is responsible for which tasks and can see the status of all open tasks.

Each participant can see how many action items he or she has on the current project.

Figure 2.2 Collaboration Technologies
Collaboration technologies such as SAP's StreamWork system help team members work together in real time, with documents, decisions, messages, and other vital project elements accessible to everyone.
Source: © Copyright 2011. SAP AG. All rights reserved.

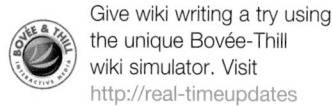

Give wiki writing a try using the unique Bovée-Thill wiki simulator. Visit http://real-timeupdates .com/ebc10, click on Student Assignments, and then click on any of the wiki exercises.

system, in which both the organization of the website and the *work flow* (the rules for creating, editing, reviewing, and approving content) are tightly controlled.[29] A content management system is a great tool for maintaining consistent presentation on a company's primary public website, whereas a wiki allows a team to collaborate with speed and flexibility.

Enterprise wiki systems extend the wiki concept with additional features for business use that ensure information quality and confidentiality and also provide the speed and flexibility of a wiki. For instance, *access control* lets a team leader identify who is allowed to read and modify a wiki. *Change monitoring* alerts team members when significant changes or additions are made. And *rollback* allows a team to "travel back in time" to see all previous versions of pages.[30]

Groupware is a general term for computer-based systems that let people communicate, share files, review previous message threads, work on documents simultaneously, and connect using social networking tools. These systems help companies capture and share knowledge from multiple experts, bringing greater insights to bear on tough challenges.[31] **Shared workspaces** are online "virtual offices" that give everyone on a team access to the same set of resources and information: databases, calendars, project plans, pertinent messaging and exchanges, reference materials, and team-created documents (see Figure 2.3). You may see some of these workspaces referred to as *intranets* (restricted-access websites that are open to employees only) or *extranets* (restricted sites that are available to employees and to outside parties by invitation only).

In the coming years, keep an eye out for emerging technologies that can help teams collaborate in new ways. For example, *cloud computing*, a somewhat vague term for "on-demand" software capabilities delivered over the Internet, promises to expand the ways in which geographically dispersed teams can collaborate quickly and inexpensively.[32]

SOCIAL NETWORKS AND VIRTUAL COMMUNITIES

Social networking technologies are becoming vital communication links in many companies.

Chapter 1 explains how social media and the Web 2.0 approach are revolutionizing business communication. Within that context, **social networking technologies** are redefining teamwork and team communication by helping erase the constraints of geographic and organization boundaries. In addition to enabling and enhancing teamwork, social networks have

Each project and program gets its own workspace, which can be shared with designated users inside or outside the company.

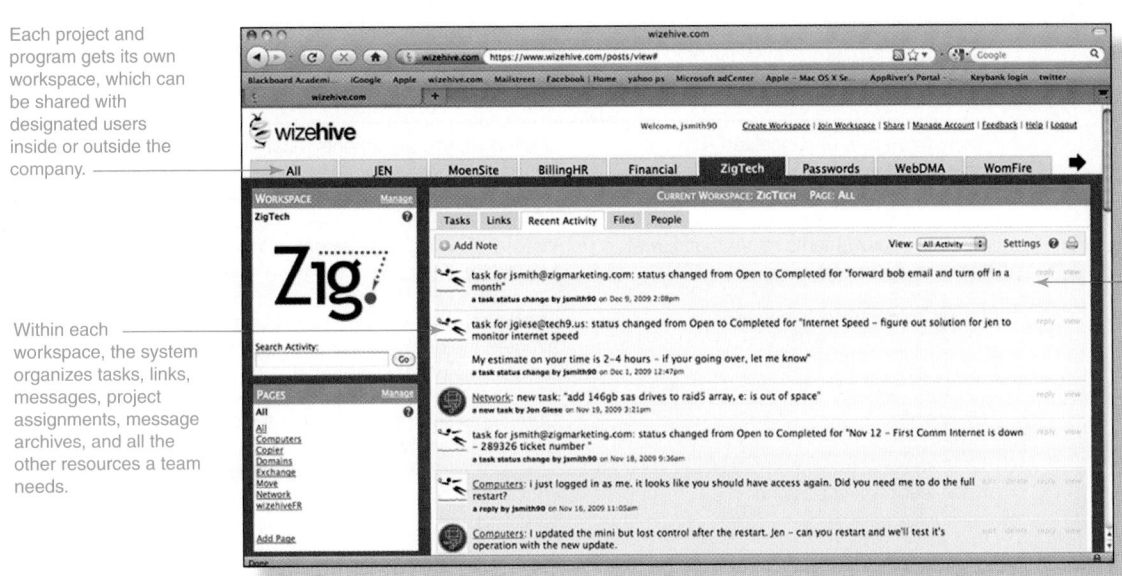

The system tracks all recent activity on a project, creating a searchable record of messages, task assignments, and other important details.

Within each workspace, the system organizes tasks, links, messages, project assignments, message archives, and all the other resources a team needs.

Figure 2.3   Shared Workspaces
Zig Marketing uses the WizeHive platform to create shared online workspaces for its employees, business partners, and clients.
Source: Used with permission of WizeHive-Zig Marketing.

numerous other business applications and benefits; see Table 7.1 on page 229 for more information.

The two fundamental elements of any social networking technology are *profiles* (the information stored about each member of the network) and *connections* (mechanisms for finding and communicating with other members).[33] If you're familiar with Facebook, you have a basic idea of how social networks function. Thousands of companies now use Facebook, but you may also encounter networks created specifically for business use, the most significant being LinkedIn (www.linkedin.com). Others include Ryze (www.ryze.com), Spoke (www.spoke.com), and Xing (www.xing.com).

Some companies use social networking technologies to form *virtual communities* or *communities of practice* that link employees with similar professional interests throughout the company and sometimes with customers and suppliers as well. The huge advantage that social networking brings to these team efforts is in identifying the best people to collaborate on each problem or project, no matter where they are around the world or what their official roles are in the organization. Such communities are similar to teams in many respects, but one major difference is in the responsibility for accumulating organizational knowledge over the long term. For example, the pharmaceutical company Pfizer has a number of permanent product safety communities that provide specialized advice on drug safety issues to researchers all across the company.[34]

A *community of practice* links professionals with similar job interests; a key benefit is accumulating long-term organizational knowledge.

Social networking can also help a company maintain a sense of community even as it grows beyond the size that normally permits a lot of daily interaction. At the online retailer Zappos, fostering a supportive work environment is the company's top priority. To encourage the sense of community among its expanding workforce, Zappos uses social networking tools to track employee connections and encourage workers to reach out and build relationships.[35]

REAL-TIME UPDATES
Learn More by Reading This PDF

Social networks for professionals

See several intriguing new examples of social networks designed exclusively for members of certain professions or industries. Go to http://real-timeupdates.com/ebc10 and click on Learn More. If you are using MyBcommLab, you can access Real-Time Updates within each chapter or under Student Study Tools.

GIVING—AND RESPONDING TO—CONSTRUCTIVE FEEDBACK

Aside from processes and tools, collaborative communication often involves giving and receiving feedback about writing efforts. **Constructive feedback**, sometimes called *constructive criticism*, focuses on the process and outcomes of communication, not on

When you give writing feedback, make it constructive by focusing on how the material can be improved.

TABLE 2.2	Giving Constructive Feedback
How to Be Constructive	**Explanation**
Think through your suggested changes carefully.	Many business documents must illustrate complex relationships between ideas and other information, so isolated and superficial edits can do more harm than good.
Discuss improvements rather than flaws.	Instead of saying "this is confusing," for instance, explain how the writing can be improved to make it clearer.
Focus on controllable behavior.	The writer may not have control over every variable that affected the quality of the message, so focus on those aspects the writer can control.
Be specific.	Comments such as "I don't get this" or "Make this clearer" don't give the writer much direction.
Keep feedback impersonal.	Focus comments on the message, not on the person who created it.
Verify understanding.	If in doubt, ask for confirmation from the recipient to make sure that the person understood your feedback.
Time your feedback carefully.	Respond in a timely fashion so that the writer will have sufficient time to implement the changes you suggest.
Highlight any limitations your feedback may have.	If you didn't have time to give the document a thorough edit, or if you're not an expert in some aspect of the content, let the writer know so that he or she can handle your comments appropriately.

the people involved (see Table 2.2). In contrast, **destructive feedback** delivers criticism with no guidance to stimulate improvement.[36] For example, "This proposal is a confusing mess, and you failed to convince me of anything" is destructive feedback. Your goal is to be more constructive: "Your proposal could be more effective with a clearer description of the manufacturing process and a well-organized explanation of why the positives outweigh the negatives." When giving feedback, avoid personal attacks and give the person clear guidelines for improvement. Also, think carefully about which media to use when you give feedback. For example, you might find it helpful to convey details in writing (such as when using revision marks and commenting features in word processing software) but discuss "big pictures" issues or sensitive matters in person or on the phone. Written feedback by itself can be jarring to the recipient, so a phone call to accompany your notes can help you maintain a positive working relationship. (You'll learn more about the strengths and weaknesses of various media in Chapter 4.)

When you receive constructive feedback on your writing, keep your emotions in check and view it as an opportunity to improve.

When you receive constructive feedback, resist the understandable urge to defend your work or deny the validity of the feedback. Remaining open to criticism isn't easy when you've poured your heart and soul into a project, but good feedback provides a valuable opportunity to learn and to improve the quality of your work.

Making Your Meetings More Productive

3   LEARNING OBJECTIVE

List the key steps needed to ensure productive team meetings.

Much of your workplace communication will occur during in-person or online meetings, so to a large degree, your ability to contribute to the company—and to be recognized for your contributions—will depend on your meeting skills. Well-run meetings can help companies solve problems, develop ideas, and identify opportunities. Meetings can also be a great way to promote team building through the experience of social interaction.[37] As useful as meetings can be, though, they can be a waste of time if they aren't planned and managed well. You can help ensure productive meetings by preparing carefully, conducting meetings efficiently, and using meeting technologies wisely.

Much of the communication you'll participate in will take place in meetings.

PREPARING FOR MEETINGS

The first step in preparing for a meeting is to make sure the meeting is really necessary. Meetings can consume hundreds or thousands of dollars of productive time while taking people away from other work, so don't hold a meeting if some other form of communication (such as a blog post) can serve the purpose as effectively.[38] If a meeting is truly necessary, proceed with these four planning tasks:

- **Clarify your purpose.** Most meetings are one of two types: *Informational meetings* involve sharing information and perhaps coordinating action. *Decision-making meetings* involve analysis, problem solving, and in many cases, persuasive communication. Whatever your purpose, make sure it is clear and specific—and clearly communicated to all participants.
- **Select participants for the meeting.** The rule here is simple: Invite everyone who really needs to be involved, and don't invite anyone who doesn't. For decision-making meetings, for example, invite only those people who are in a direct position to help the meeting reach its objective.
- **Choose the venue and the time.** Online meetings (see page 85 on the next page) are often the best way and sometimes the only way to connect people in multiple locations or to reach large audiences. For onsite meetings, review the facility and the seating arrangements. Are rows of chairs suitable, or do you need a conference table or some other arrangement? Pay attention to room temperature, lighting, ventilation, acoustics, and refreshments; these details can make or break a meeting. If you have control over the timing, morning meetings are often more productive because people are generally more alert and not yet engaged with the work of the day.
- **Set the agenda.** People who will be presenting information need to know what is expected of them, nonpresenters need to know what will be presented so they can prepare questions, and everyone needs to know how long the meeting will last. In addition, the agenda is an important tool for guiding the progress of the meeting (see Figure 2.4 on the next page).

To ensure a successful meeting, decide on your purpose ahead of time, select the right participants, choose the venue and time, and set a clear agenda.

CONDUCTING AND CONTRIBUTING TO EFFICIENT MEETINGS

Everyone in a meeting shares the responsibility for making the meeting productive. If you're the designated leader of a meeting, however, you have an extra degree of responsibility and accountability. The following guidelines will help leaders and participants contribute to more effective meetings:

Everyone shares the responsibility for successful meetings.

- **Keep the discussion on track.** A good meeting leader draws out the best ideas the group has to offer and resolves differences of opinion while maintaining progress toward achieving the meeting's purpose and staying on schedule.
- **Follow agreed-upon rules.** The larger the meeting, the more formal you need to be to maintain order. Formal meetings use **parliamentary procedure**, a time-tested method for planning and running effective meetings. The best-known guide to this procedure is *Robert's Rules of Order* (www.robertsrules.com).
- **Encourage participation.** On occasion, some participants will be too quiet and others too talkative. The quiet participants may be shy, they may be expressing disagreement or resistance, or they may be working on unrelated tasks. Draw them out by asking for their input on issues that pertain to them.
- **Participate actively.** If you're a meeting participant, look for opportunities to contribute to both the subject of the meeting and the smooth interaction of the group. Speak up

MyBcommLab

Apply Figure 2.4's key concepts by revising a new document. Go to Chapter 2 in www.pearsoninternationaleditions .com/mybcommlab and select Document Makeovers.

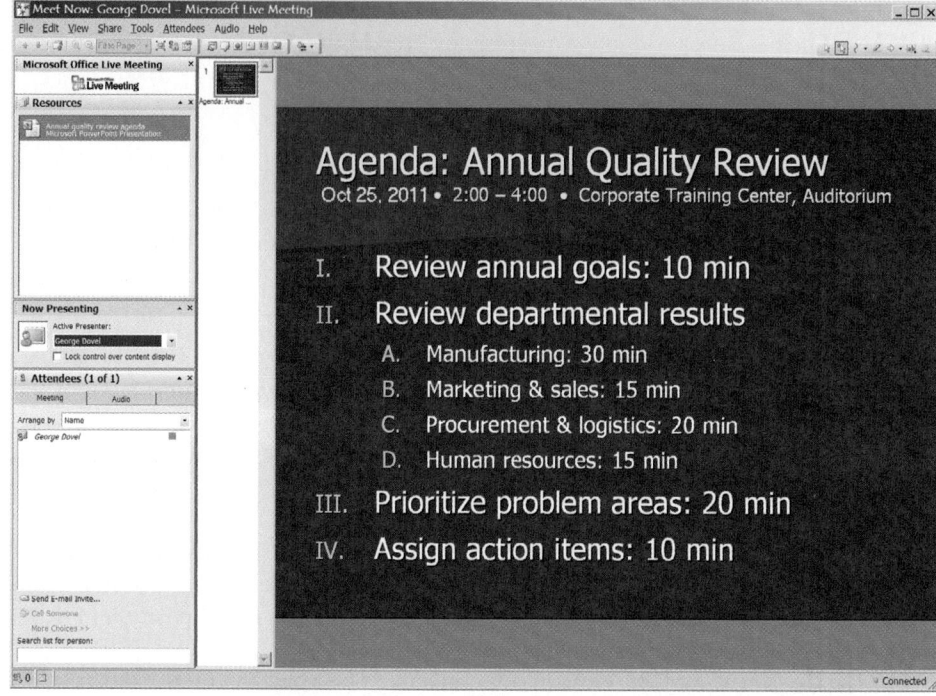

Figure 2.4   Typical Meeting Agenda
Agenda formats vary widely, depending on the complexity of the meeting and the presentation technologies that will be used. For an online meeting, for instance, a good approach is to first send a detailed planning agenda in advance of the meeting so that presenters know what they need to prepare, then create a simpler display agenda such as this to guide the progress of the meeting.

if you have something useful to say but don't monopolize the discussion or talk simply to bring attention to yourself.
- **Close effectively.** At the conclusion of the meeting, verify that the objectives have been met or arrange for follow-up work, if needed. Either summarize the general conclusion of the discussion or the actions to be taken. Make sure all participants have a chance to clear up any misunderstandings.

To review the tasks that contribute to productive meetings, refer to "Checklist: Improving Meeting Productivity."

For formal meetings, it's good practice to appoint one person to record the **minutes**, a summary of the important information presented and the decisions made during a meeting. In smaller or informal meetings, attendees often make their own notes on their copies of the agenda. In either case, a clear record of the decisions made and the people responsible for follow-up action is essential. If your company doesn't have a specific format for minutes, follow the generic format shown in Figure 2.5.

✓ **Checklist**   **Improving Meeting Productivity**

A. Prepare carefully.
- Make sure the meeting is necessary.
- Decide on your purpose.
- Select participants carefully.
- Choose the venue and the time.
- Establish and distribute a clear agenda.

B. Lead effectively and participate fully.
- Keep the meeting on track.
- Follow agreed-upon rules.
- Encourage participation.
- Participate actively.
- Close effectively.

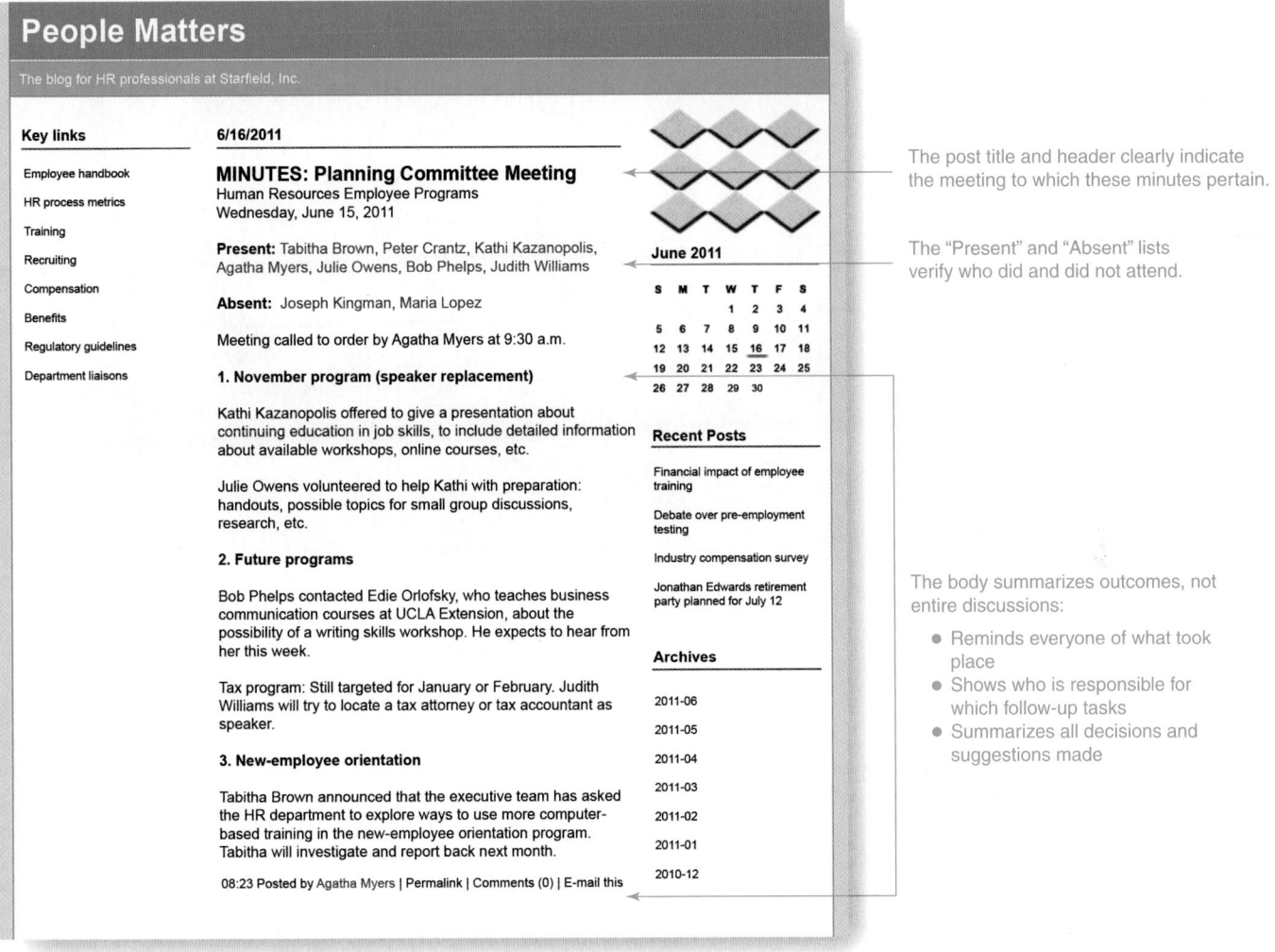

People Matters

The blog for HR professionals at Starfield, Inc.

Key links

Employee handbook

HR process metrics

Training

Recruiting

Compensation

Benefits

Regulatory guidelines

Department liaisons

6/16/2011

MINUTES: Planning Committee Meeting
Human Resources Employee Programs
Wednesday, June 15, 2011

Present: Tabitha Brown, Peter Crantz, Kathi Kazanopolis, Agatha Myers, Julie Owens, Bob Phelps, Judith Williams

Absent: Joseph Kingman, Maria Lopez

Meeting called to order by Agatha Myers at 9:30 a.m.

1. November program (speaker replacement)

Kathi Kazanopolis offered to give a presentation about continuing education in job skills, to include detailed information about available workshops, online courses, etc.

Julie Owens volunteered to help Kathi with preparation: handouts, possible topics for small group discussions, research, etc.

2. Future programs

Bob Phelps contacted Edie Orlofsky, who teaches business communication courses at UCLA Extension, about the possibility of a writing skills workshop. He expects to hear from her this week.

Tax program: Still targeted for January or February. Judith Williams will try to locate a tax attorney or tax accountant as speaker.

3. New-employee orientation

Tabitha Brown announced that the executive team has asked the HR department to explore ways to use more computer-based training in the new-employee orientation program. Tabitha will investigate and report back next month.

08:23 Posted by Agatha Myers | Permalink | Comments (0) | E-mail this

June 2011

S	M	T	W	T	F	S
			1	2	3	4
5	6	7	8	9	10	11
12	13	14	15	16	17	18
19	20	21	22	23	24	25
26	27	28	29	30		

Recent Posts

Financial impact of employee training

Debate over pre-employment testing

Industry compensation survey

Jonathan Edwards retirement party planned for July 12

Archives

2011-06
2011-05
2011-04
2011-03
2011-02
2011-01
2010-12

The post title and header clearly indicate the meeting to which these minutes pertain.

The "Present" and "Absent" lists verify who did and did not attend.

The body summarizes outcomes, not entire discussions:

- Reminds everyone of what took place
- Shows who is responsible for which follow-up tasks
- Summarizes all decisions and suggestions made

Figure 2.5   Typical Minutes of a Meeting
Intranet and blog postings are a common way to distribute meeting minutes. The specific format of the minutes is less important than making sure you record all the key information, particularly regarding responsibilities that were assigned during the meeting. Key elements include a list of those present and a list of those who were invited but didn't attend, followed by the times the meeting started and ended, all major decisions reached at the meeting, all assignments of tasks to meeting participants, and all subjects that were deferred to a later meeting. In addition, the minutes objectively summarize important discussions, noting the names of those who contributed major points. Outlines, subheadings, and lists help organize the minutes; additional documentation (such as tables or charts submitted by meeting participants) is noted in the minutes and attached. Many companies now post meeting minutes on internal websites for easy reference.

MyBcommLab

Apply Figure 2.5's key concepts by revising a new document. Go to Chapter 2 in www.pearsoninternationaleditions.com/mybcommlab and select Document Makeovers.

Using Meeting Technologies

A growing array of technologies enables professionals to enhance or even replace traditional meetings. Replacing in-person meetings with long-distance, virtual interaction can dramatically reduce costs and resource usage, reduce wear and tear on employees, and give teams access to a wider pool of expertise. For example, by meeting customers and business partners online instead of in person, during a recent 18-month period Cisco Systems cut its travel-related costs by $100 million, reduced its carbon footprint by millions of tons, and improved employee productivity and satisfaction.[39]

Meeting-replacement technologies have helped spur the emergence of **virtual teams**, whose members work in different locations and interact electronically through **virtual meetings**. Instant messaging (IM) and teleconferencing are the simplest forms of virtual

4   LEARNING OBJECTIVE

Identify the major technologies used to enhance or replace in-person meetings.

Virtual meeting technologies connect people spread around the country or around the world.

Figure 2.6 Telepresence
How many people are in this conference room in Chicago? Only the two people in the foreground are in the room; the other six are in Atlanta and London. Virtual meeting technologies such as this telepresence system connect people spread across the country or around the world.
Source: Peter Wynn Thompson/The New York Times, Redux Pictures.

meetings. Videoconferencing lets participants see and hear each other, demonstrate products, and transmit other visual information. *Telepresence* technologies (see Figure 2.6) enable realistic conferences in which participants thousands of miles apart almost seem to be in the same room.[40] The ability to convey nonverbal subtleties such as facial expressions and hand gestures makes these systems particularly good for negotiations, collaborative problem solving, and other complex discussions.[41]

The most sophisticated web-based meeting systems combine the best of real-time communication, shared workspaces, and videoconferencing with other tools, such as *virtual whiteboards*, that let teams collaborate in real time. Such systems are used for everything from spontaneous discussions among small groups to carefully planned, formal events such as customer training seminars or press conferences.[42]

Technology continues to create intriguing opportunities for online interaction. For instance, one of the newest virtual tools is online brainstorming, in which a company can conduct "idea campaigns" to generate new ideas from people across the organization. These sessions range from small team meetings to huge events such as IBM's giant Innovation-Jam, in which 100,000 IBM employees, family members, and customers from 160 countries were invited to brainstorm online for three days.[43]

Companies are also beginning to experiment with virtual meetings and other communication activities in virtual worlds that range from realistic-looking environments that represent offices and conference rooms (see Figure 2.7) to the otherworldly environment of Second Life (www.secondlife.com). In Second Life, professionals can create online *avatars* to represent themselves in meetings, training sessions, sales presentations, and even casual conversations with customers they happen to bump into (see pages 58 and 568 for examples of business communication in Second Life).

Conducting successful telephone or online meetings requires extra planning and more diligence during the meeting.

Conducting successful meetings over the phone or online requires extra planning before the meeting and more diligence during the meeting. Because virtual meetings offer less visual contact and nonverbal communication than in-person meetings, leaders need to make sure everyone stays engaged and has the opportunity to contribute. Paying attention during online meetings takes greater effort as well. Participants need to stay committed to the meeting and resist the temptation to work on unrelated tasks.[44]

For the latest information on meeting technologies, visit http://real-timeupdates .com/ebc10 and click on Chapter 2.

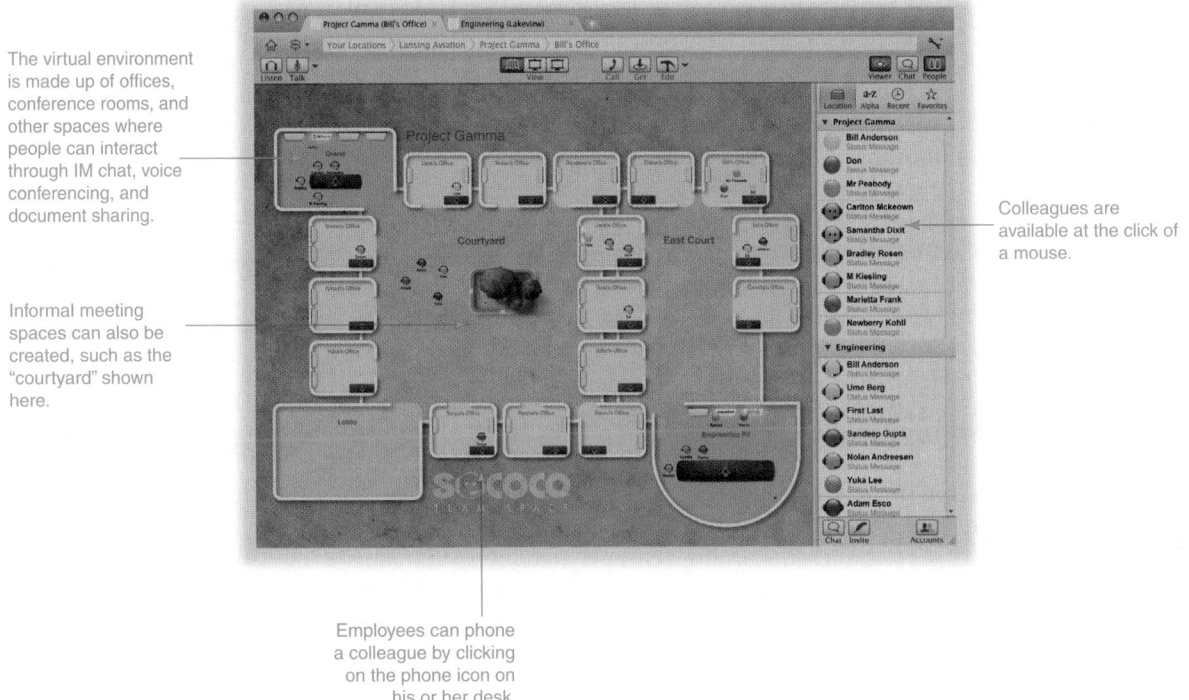

The virtual environment is made up of offices, conference rooms, and other spaces where people can interact through IM chat, voice conferencing, and document sharing.

Informal meeting spaces can also be created, such as the "courtyard" shown here.

Colleagues are available at the click of a mouse.

Employees can phone a colleague by clicking on the phone icon on his or her desk.

Figure 2.7   Virtual Meetings
Virtual meeting technologies offer a variety of ways to interact online. The Team Space system from Sococo mimics the layout of an office building, allowing users to click into offices, conference rooms, and other spaces to initiate virtual meetings and presentations, participate in phone and IM conferences, and share documents.
Source: Used with permission of Sococo.

Improving Your Listening Skills

Your long-term career prospects are closely tied to your ability and willingness to listen. Effective listening strengthens organizational relationships, alerts an organization to opportunities for innovation, and allows an organization to manage diversity both in the workforce and in the customers it serves.[45] Companies whose employees and managers listen effectively stay in touch, up to date, and out of trouble. Some 80 percent of top executives say that listening is the most important skill needed to get things done in the workplace.[46] Plus, today's younger employees place a high premium on being heard, so listening is becoming even more vital for managers.[47] In fact, many of the leading business schools in the United States have begun retooling their curricula in recent years to put more emphasis on "soft skills" such as listening.[48]

5   **LEARNING OBJECTIVE**

Identify three major modes of listening, describe the listening process, and explain the problem of selective listening.

Listening is one of the most important skills in the workplace.

RECOGNIZING VARIOUS TYPES OF LISTENING

Effective listeners adapt their listening approaches to different situations. The primary goal of **content listening** is to understand and retain the information in the speaker's message. Because you're not evaluating the information at this point, it doesn't matter whether you agree or disagree, approve or disapprove—only that you understand. Try to overlook the speaker's style and any limitations in the presentation; just focus on the information.[49]

The goal of **critical listening** is to understand and evaluate the meaning of the speaker's message on several levels: the logic of the argument, the strength of the evidence, the validity of the conclusions, the implications of the message, the speaker's intentions and motives, and the omission of any important or relevant points. If you're skeptical, ask questions to explore the speaker's point of view and credibility. Be on the lookout for bias that could color the way the information is presented and be careful to separate opinions from facts.[50]

The goal of **empathic listening** is to understand the speaker's feelings, needs, and wants so that you can appreciate his or her point of view, regardless of whether you share

To be a good listener, adapt the way you listen to suit the situation.

Listening actively means making the effort to turn off your internal filters and biases to truly hear and understand what the other person is saying.

that perspective. By listening with empathy, you help the individual vent the emotions that prevent a calm, clear-headed approach to the subject. Avoid the temptation to jump in with advice unless the person specifically asks for it. Also, don't judge the speaker's feelings and don't try to tell people they shouldn't feel this or that emotion. Instead, let the speaker know that you appreciate his or her feelings and understand the situation. After you establish that connection, you can help the speaker move on to search for a solution.[51]

No matter what mode they are using at any given time, effective listeners try to engage in **active listening**, making a conscious effort to turn off their own filters and biases to truly hear and understand what the other party is saying. They ask questions to verify key points and encourage the speaker through positive body language.[52]

UNDERSTANDING THE LISTENING PROCESS

Listening is a far more complex process than most people think—and most of us aren't very good at it. People typically listen at no better than a 25 percent efficiency rate, remember only about half of what's said during a 10-minute conversation, and forget half of that within 48 hours.[53] Furthermore, when questioned about material they've just heard, they are likely to get the facts mixed up.[54]

Why is such a seemingly simple activity so difficult? The reason is that listening is not a simple process, by any means. Listening follows the same sequence as the general communication process model described in Chapter 1 (page 50), with the added challenge that it happens in real time. To listen effectively, you need to successfully complete five separate steps:[55]

Listening involves five steps: receiving, decoding, remembering, evaluating, and responding.

1. **Receiving.** Start by physically hearing the message and recognizing it as incoming information.
2. **Decoding.** Assign meaning to sounds, according to your own values, beliefs, ideas, expectations, roles, needs, and personal history.
3. **Remembering.** Store the information for future processing.
4. **Evaluating.** Evaluate the quality of the information.
5. **Responding.** React based on the situation and the nature of the information.

If any one of these steps breaks down, the listening process becomes less effective or even fails entirely. As both a sender and a receiver, you can reduce the failure rate by recognizing and overcoming a variety of physical and mental barriers to effective listening.

OVERCOMING BARRIERS TO EFFECTIVE LISTENING

Good listeners actively try to overcome the barriers to successful listening.

Good listeners look for ways to overcome potential barriers throughout the listening process (see Table 2.3). Some factors you may not be able to control, such as conference room acoustics or poor phone reception. However, you can control other factors, such as not interrupting speakers and not creating distractions that make it difficult for others to pay attention. And don't think that you're not interrupting just because you're not talking. Such actions as texting or checking your watch can interrupt a speaker and lead to communication breakdowns.

Selective listening is one of the most common barriers to effective listening. If your mind wanders, you may stay tuned out until you hear a word or phrase that gets your attention again. But by that time, you're unable to recall what the speaker *actually* said; instead, you remember what you think the speaker *probably* said.[56]

REAL-TIME UPDATES
Learn More by Watching This PowerPoint Presentation

Simple tips to improve your listening skills

These concepts will help make you a better listener on the job and in every other aspect of life. Go to http://real-timeupdates.com/ebc10 and click on Learn More. If you are using MyBcommLab, you can access Real-Time Updates within each chapter or under Student Study Tools.

Your mind can process information much faster than most speakers talk, so you need to focus to listen effectively.

One reason listeners' minds tend to wander is that people think faster than they speak. Most people speak at about 120 to 150 words per minute, but listeners can process audio information at up to 500 words per minute or more.[57] Consequently, your brain has a lot of free time whenever you're listening, and if left unsupervised, it will find a thousand other things to think about. Make the effort to focus on the speaker and use the extra time to analyze and paraphrase what you hear or to take relevant notes.

TABLE 2.3	What Makes an Effective Listener?
Effective Listeners	**Ineffective Listeners**
• Listen actively	• Listen passively
• Take careful and complete notes, when applicable	• Take no notes or ineffective notes
• Make frequent eye contact with the speaker (depends on culture to some extent)	• Make little or no eye contact—or inappropriate eye contact
• Stay focused on the speaker and the content	• Allow their minds to wander, are easily distracted, work on unrelated tasks
• Mentally paraphrase key points to maintain attention level and ensure comprehension	• Fail to paraphrase
• Adjust listening style to the situation	• Listen with the same style, regardless of the situation
• Give the speaker nonverbal cues (such as nodding to show agreement or raising eyebrows to show surprise or skepticism)	• Fail to give the speaker nonverbal feedback
• Save questions or points of disagreement until an appropriate time	• Interrupt whenever they disagree or don't understand
• Overlook stylistic differences and focus on the speaker's message	• Are distracted by or unduly influenced by stylistic differences; are judgmental
• Make distinctions between main points and supporting details	• Unable to distinguish main points from details
• Look for opportunities to learn	• Assume they already know everything that's important to know

Sources: Adapted from Madelyn Burley-Allen, *Listening: The Forgotten Skill* (New York: Wiley, 1995), 70–71, 119–120; Judi Brownell, *Listening: Attitudes, Principles, and Skills* (Boston: Allyn and Bacon, 2002); 3, 9, 83, 89, 125; Larry Barker and Kittie Watson, *Listen Up* (New York: St. Martin's, 2000), 8, 9, 64.

Overcoming interpretation barriers can be difficult because you may not even be aware of them. As Chapter 1 notes, selective perception leads listeners to mold messages to fit their own conceptual frameworks. Listeners sometimes make up their minds before fully hearing the speaker's message, or they engage in *defensive listening*—protecting their egos by tuning out anything that doesn't confirm their beliefs or their view of themselves.

Even when your intentions are good, you can still misinterpret incoming messages if you and the speaker don't share enough language or experience. When listening to a speaker whose native language or life experience is different from yours, try to paraphrase that person's ideas. Give the speaker a chance to confirm what you think you heard or to correct any misinterpretation.

If the information you hear will be important to use later, write it down or otherwise record it. Don't rely on your memory. If you do need to memorize, you can hold information in short-term memory by repeating it silently or organizing a long list of items into several shorter lists. To store information in long-term memory, four techniques can help: (1) Associate new information with something closely related (such as the restaurant in which you met a new client), (2) categorize the new information into logical groups (such as alphabetizing a list of names), (3) visualize words and ideas as pictures, and (4) create mnemonics such as acronyms or rhymes.

For a reminder of the steps you can take to overcome listening barriers, see "Checklist: Overcoming Barriers to Effective Listening."

When information is crucial, don't count on your memory—record the information mechanically or electronically.

REAL-TIME UPDATES
Learn More by Watching This Video

Are you a good listener?

Most of us believe we are good listeners, but the constant communication breakdowns in business and personal settings is evidence that we could all improve. Go to http://real-timeupdates .com/ebc10 and click on Learn More. If you are using MyBcommLab, you can access Real-Time Updates within each chapter or under Student Study Tools.

✓ Checklist Overcoming Barriers to Effective Listening

- Lower barriers to physical reception whenever you can (such as avoiding interrupting speakers by asking questions or by exhibiting disruptive nonverbal behaviors).
- Avoid selective listening by focusing on the speaker and carefully analyzing what you hear.
- Keep an open mind by avoiding any prejudgment and by not listening defensively.

- Don't count on your memory; write down or record important information.
- Improve your short-term memory by repeating information or breaking it into shorter lists.
- Improve your long-term memory by using association, categorization, visualization, and mnemonics.

Improving Your Nonverbal Communication Skills

6 **LEARNING OBJECTIVE**

Explain the importance of nonverbal communication, and identify six major categories of nonverbal expression.

Nonverbal communication can supplement or even replace verbal messages (those that use words).

Nonverbal signals include facial expression, gesture and posture, vocal characteristics, personal appearance, touch, and time and space.

Nonverbal communication is the interpersonal process of sending and receiving information, both intentionally and unintentionally, without using written or spoken language. Nonverbal signals play a vital role in communication because they can strengthen a verbal message (when the nonverbal signals match the spoken words), weaken a verbal message (when nonverbal signals don't match the words), or replace words entirely. For example, you might tell a client that a project is coming along nicely, but your forced smile and nervous glances will send an entirely different message.

RECOGNIZING NONVERBAL COMMUNICATION

Paying special attention to nonverbal signals in the workplace will enhance your ability to communicate successfully. The range and variety of nonverbal signals are almost endless, but you can grasp the basics by studying six general categories:

- **Facial expression.** Your face is the primary vehicle for expressing your emotions; it reveals both the type and the intensity of your feelings.[58] Your eyes are especially effective for indicating attention and interest, influencing others, regulating interaction, and establishing dominance.[59]
- **Gesture and posture.** The way you position and move your body expresses both specific and general messages, some voluntary and some involuntary. Many gestures—a wave of the hand, for example—have specific and intentional meanings. Other types of body movement are unintentional and express more general messages. Slouching, leaning forward, fidgeting, and walking briskly are all unconscious signals that can reveal whether you feel confident or nervous, friendly or hostile, assertive or passive, powerful or powerless.
- **Vocal characteristics.** Voice carries both intentional and unintentional messages. A speaker can intentionally control pitch, pace, and stress to convey a specific message. For instance, compare "*What* are you doing?" and "What are *you* doing?" Unintentional vocal characteristics can convey happiness, surprise, fear, and other emotions (for example, fear often increases the pitch and the pace of your speaking voice).
- **Personal appearance.** People respond to others on the basis of their physical appearance, sometimes fairly and other times unfairly. Although an individual's body type and facial features impose limitations, you can control grooming, clothing, accessories, piercings, tattoos, and hairstyle. If your goal is to make a good impression, adopt the style of the people you want to impress.
- **Touch.** Touch is an important way to convey warmth, comfort, and reassurance—as well as control. Touch is so powerful, in fact, that it is governed by cultural customs that establish who can touch whom and how in various circumstances. In the United States and Great Britain, for instance, people usually touch less frequently than people in France or Costa Rica do. Even within each culture's norms, however, individual attitudes toward touch vary widely. A manager might be comfortable using hugs to

---

SHARPENING YOUR CAREER SKILLS

Sending the Right Signals

The nonverbal signals you send can enhance—or undermine—your verbal message, so make sure to use nonverbal cues to your advantage. In U.S. business culture, the following signals are key to building and maintaining professional credibility:

- **Eye behavior.** Maintain direct, but not continuous, eye contact. Don't look down before responding to a question, and be careful not to shift your eyes around. Don't look away from the other person for extended periods, and try not to blink excessively.
- **Gestures.** When using gestures to emphasize points or convey the intensity of your feelings, keep them spontaneous, unrehearsed, and relaxed. Keep your hands and elbows away from your body, and avoid hand-to-face gestures, throat clearing, fidgeting, and tugging at clothing. Don't lick your lips, wring your hands, tap your fingers, or smile out of context.
- **Posture.** Assume an open and relaxed posture. Walk confidently, with grace and ease. Stand straight, with both feet on the floor, and sit straight in your chair without

slouching. Hold your head level, and keep your chin up. Shift your posture while communicating, leaning forward and smiling as you begin to answer a question. Avoid keeping your body rigid or otherwise conveying a sense of tension.
- **Voice.** Strive for a conversational style, while speaking at a moderately fast rate. Use appropriate variation in pitch, rate, and volume. Avoid speaking in a monotone. Avoid sounding flat, tense, or nasal. Do your best to avoid ahs or ums, repeating words, interrupting or pausing mid-sentence, omitting parts of words, and stuttering.

CAREER APPLICATIONS

1. What message might you get if your boss smiles but looks away when you ask if you'll be getting a raise this year? Explain your interpretation of these nonverbal signals.
2. Would you be reluctant to hire a job candidate who stares intently at you through an entire job interview? Why or why not?

---

express support or congratulations, but his or her subordinates could interpret those hugs as a show of dominance or sexual interest.[60] Touch is a complex subject. The best advice: When in doubt, don't touch.

- **Time and space.** Like touch, time and space can be used to assert authority, imply intimacy, and send other nonverbal messages. For instance, some people try to demonstrate their own importance or disregard for others by making other people wait; others show respect by being on time. Similarly, taking care not to invade private space, such as standing too close when talking, is a way to show respect for others. Keep in mind that expectations regarding both time and space vary by culture.

USING NONVERBAL COMMUNICATION EFFECTIVELY

Paying attention to nonverbal cues will make you both a better speaker and a better listener. When you're talking, be more conscious of the nonverbal cues you could be sending. Are they effective without being manipulative? Consider a situation in which an employee has come to you to talk about a raise. This situation is stressful for the employee, so don't say you're interested in what she has to tell you and then spend your time glancing at your computer or checking your watch. Conversely, if you already know you won't be able to give her the raise, be honest in your expression of emotions. Don't overcompensate for your own stress by smiling too broadly or shaking her hand too vigorously. Both nonverbal signals would raise her hopes without justification. In either case, match your nonverbal cues to the tone of the situation.

Work to make sure your nonverbal signals match the tone and content of your spoken communication.

Also consider the nonverbal signals you send when you're not talking—the clothes you wear, the way you sit, the way you walk. Are you talking like a serious business professional but dressing like you belong in a dance club or a frat house? (Appropriate clothing for work situations is discussed in the next section, on business etiquette.)

What signals does your personal appearance send?

When you listen, be sure to pay attention to the speaker's nonverbal cues. Do they amplify the spoken words or contradict them? Is the speaker intentionally using nonverbal signals to send you a message that he or she can't put into words? Be observant but don't

Checklist   **Improving Nonverbal Communication Skills**

- Understand the roles that nonverbal signals play in communication, complementing verbal language by strengthening, weakening, or replacing words.
- Note that facial expressions (especially eye contact) reveal the type and intensity of a speaker's feelings.
- Watch for cues from gestures and posture.
- Listen for vocal characteristics that can signal the emotions underlying the speaker's words.

- Recognize that listeners are influenced by physical appearance.
- Be careful with physical contact; touch can convey positive attributes but can also be interpreted as dominance or sexual interest.
- Pay attention to the use of time and space.

assume that you can "read someone like a book." Nonverbal signals are powerful, but they aren't infallible, particularly if you don't know a person's normal behavioral patterns.[61] For example, contrary to popular belief, avoiding eye contact and covering one's face while talking are not reliable clues that someone is lying. Even when telling the truth, most people don't make uninterrupted eye contact with the listeners, and various gestures such as touching one's face might be normal behavior for particular people.[62] Moreover, these and other behaviors may be influenced by culture (in some cultures, sustained eye contact can be interpreted as a sign of disrespect) or might just be ways of coping with stressful situations.[63]

If something doesn't feel right, ask the speaker an honest and respectful question; doing so may clear everything up, or it may uncover issues you need to explore further. See "Checklist: Improving Nonverbal Communication Skills" for a summary of key ideas regarding nonverbal skills.

Developing Your Business Etiquette

Etiquette is an essential element of every aspect of business communication.

You may have noticed a common thread running through the topics of successful teamwork, productive meetings, effective listening, and nonverbal communication: All these activities depend on mutual respect and consideration among all participants. As Chapter 1 notes, etiquette is now considered an essential business skill. Nobody wants to work with someone who is rude to colleagues or an embarrassment to the company. Moreover, shabby treatment of others in the workplace can be a huge drain on morale and productivity.[64] Poor etiquette can drive away customers, investors, and other critical audiences—and it can limit your career potential.

This section addresses some key etiquette points to remember when you're in the workplace, out in public, and online. Long lists of etiquette rules can be difficult to remember, but you can get by in most every situation by being aware of your effect on others, treating everyone with respect, and keeping in mind that the impressions you leave behind can have a lasting effect on you and your company—so make sure to leave positive impressions wherever you go.

BUSINESS ETIQUETTE IN THE WORKPLACE

Personal appearance can have a considerable impact on your success in business.

Workplace etiquette includes a variety of behaviors, habits, and aspects of nonverbal communication. Although it isn't always thought of as an element of etiquette, your personal appearance in the workplace sends a strong signal to managers, colleagues, and customers. Pay attention to the style of dress where you work and adjust your style to match. Expectations for specific jobs, companies, and industries can vary widely. The financial industries tend to be more formal than high technology, for instance, and sales and executive positions usually involve more formal expectations than positions in engineering or manufacturing. Observe others, and don't be afraid to ask for advice. If you're not sure, dress modestly and simply—earn a reputation for what you can do, not for what you can wear. Table 2.4 offers some general guidelines on assembling a business wardrobe that's cost-effective and flexible.

TABLE 2.4	Assembling a Business Wardrobe		
1 **Smooth and Finished** **(Start with This)**	**2** **Elegant and Refined** **(To Column 1, Add This)**	**3** **Crisp and Starchy** **(To Column 2, Add This)**	**4** **Up-to-the-Minute Trendy** **(To Column 3, Add This)**
1. Choose well-tailored clothing that fits well; it doesn't have to be expensive, but it does have to fit and be appropriate for business. 2. Keep buttons, zippers, and hemlines in good repair. 3. Select shoes that are comfortable enough for long days but neither too casual nor too dressy for the office; keep shoes clean and in good condition. 4. Make sure the fabrics you wear are clean, are carefully pressed, and do not wrinkle easily. 5. Choose colors that flatter your height, weight, skin tone, and style; sales advisors in good clothing stores can help you choose.	1. Choose form-fitting (but not skin-tight) clothing—not swinging or flowing fabrics, frills, or fussy trimmings. 2. Choose muted tones and soft colors or classics, such as a dark blue suit or a basic black dress. 3. If possible, select a few classic pieces of jewelry (such as a string of pearls or diamond cuff links) for formal occasions. 4. Wear jackets that complement an outfit and lend an air of formality to your appearance. Avoid jackets with more than two tones; one color should dominate.	1. Wear blouses or shirts that are or appear starched. 2. Choose closed top-button shirts or button-down shirt collars, higher-neckline blouses, or long sleeves with French cuffs and cuff links. 3. Wear creased trousers or a longer skirt hemline.	1. Supplement your foundation with pieces that reflect the latest styles. 2. Add a few pieces in bold colors but wear them sparingly to avoid a garish appearance. 3. Embellish your look with the latest jewelry and hairstyles but keep the overall effect looking professional.

COMMUNICATING ACROSS CULTURES

Whose Skin Is This, Anyway?

Generational differences abound in the workplace, but few are quite as visible as *body art*: tattoos, piercings (other than ear lobes), and hair dyes in unconventional colors. According to survey data from the Pew Research Center, people younger than 40 are much more inclined than those over 40 to display some form of body art. For example, people 26 to 40 years old are four times more likely to have tattoos than people who are 41 to 64 years old.

With such profound differences, it's no surprise that body art has become a contentious issue in many workplaces, between employees wanting to express themselves and employers wanting to maintain particular standards of professional appearance. As employment law attorney Danielle S. Urban notes, the issue gets even more complicated when religious symbolism is involved.

Who is likely to win this battle? Will the body art aficionados who continue to join the workforce and who are now rising up the managerial ranks force a change in what is considered acceptable appearance in the workplace? Or will they be forced to cover up in order to meet traditional standards?

So far, most companies appear to be relying on the judgment of their employees and managers, rather than enforcing strict guidelines. Many seem to accept that tastes and norms are changing and that body art has become a widespread form of self-expression rather than a mode of rebellion. Job seekers are still advised to be discreet, however, particularly with facial piercings and large, visible tattoos. The nonverbal signals you think you are sending might not be the signals a hiring manager receives.

CAREER APPLICATIONS

1. Should companies have stricter standards of appearance for "customer-facing" employees than for employees who do not interact with customers? Why or why not?
2. Should companies allow their employees the same freedom of expression and appearance latitude as their customers exhibit? For example, if a firm's clientele tends to be heavily tattooed, should employees be allowed the same freedom? Why or why not?

Sources: Rita Pyrillis, "Body of Work," *Workforce Management*, November 2010, www.workforce.com; Danielle S. Urban, "What to Do About 'Body Art' at Work," *Workforce Management*, March 2010, www.workforce.com; "36% – Tattooed Gen Nexters," Pew Research Center [accessed 29 December 2010] http://pewresearch.org.

Grooming is as important as attire. Pay close attention to cleanliness and avoid using products with powerful scents, such as perfumed soaps, colognes, shampoos, and after-shave lotions (many people are bothered by these products, and some are allergic to them). Shampoo your hair frequently, keep your hands and nails neatly manicured, use mouthwash and deodorant, and make regular trips to a barber or hair stylist.[65]

If you work in an office setting, you'll spend as much time with your officemates as you do with family and friends. Personal demeanor is therefore a vital element of workplace harmony. No one expects (or wants) you to be artificially upbeat and bubbly every second of the day, but a single negative personality can make an entire office miserable. Rude behavior is more than an etiquette issue, too; it can have serious financial costs through lower productivity and lost business opportunities.[66] Every person in the company has a responsibility to contribute to a positive, energetic work environment.

Given the telephone's central role in business communication, phone skills are essential in most professions. Because phone calls lack the visual richness of face-to-face conversations, you have to rely on your attitude and tone of voice to convey confidence and professionalism. Table 2.5 summarizes helpful tips for placing and receiving phone calls in a confident, professional manner.

TABLE 2.5   Quick Tips for Improving Your Phone Skills

General Tips	Placing Calls	Receiving Calls	Using Voice Mail
• Use frequent verbal responses that show you're listening ("Oh yes," "I see," "That's right").	• Be ready before you call so that you don't waste the other person's time.	• Answer promptly and with a smile so that you sound friendly and positive.	• When recording your own outgoing message, make it brief and professional.
• Increase your volume just slightly to convey your confidence.	• Minimize the noise level in your environment as much as possible to avoid distracting the other party.	• Identify yourself and your company (some companies have specific instructions for what to say when you answer).	• If you can, record temporary greetings on days when you are unavailable all day so that callers will know you're gone for the day.
• Don't speak in a monotone; vary your pitch and inflections so people know you're interested.	• Identify yourself and your organization, briefly describe why you're calling, and verify that you've called at a good time.	• Establish the needs of your caller by asking, "How may I help you?" If you know the caller's name, use it.	• Check your voice-mail messages regularly and return all necessary calls within 24 hours.
• Slow down when conversing with people whose native language isn't the same as yours.	• Don't take up too much time. Speak quickly and clearly, and get right to the point of the call.	• If you can, answer questions promptly and efficiently; if you can't help, tell them what you can do for them.	• Leave simple, clear messages with your name, number (don't assume the recipient has caller ID), purpose for calling, and times when you can be reached.
• Stay focused on the call throughout; others can easily tell when you're not paying attention.	• Close in a friendly, positive manner and double-check all vital information such as meeting times and dates.	• If you must forward a call or put someone on hold, explain what you are doing first.	• State your name and telephone number slowly so that the other person can easily write them down; repeat both if the other person doesn't know you.
		• If you forward a call to someone else, try to speak with that person first to verify that he or she is available and to introduce the caller.	• Be careful what you say; most voice-mail systems allow users to forward messages to anyone else in the system.
		• If you take a message for someone else, be complete and accurate, including the caller's name, number, and organization.	• Replay your message before leaving the system to make sure it is clear and complete.

Sources: Alf Nucifora, "Voice Mail Demands Good Etiquette from Both Sides," *Puget Sound Business Journal,* 5–11 September 2003, 24; Ruth Davidhizar and Ruth Shearer, "The Effective Voice Mail Message," *Hospital Material Management Quarterly,* 45–49; "How to Get the Most Out of Voice Mail," *The CPA Journal,* February 2000, 11; Jo Ind, "Hanging on the Telephone," *Birmingham Post,* 28 July 1999, PS10; Larry Barker and Kittie Watson, *Listen Up* (New York: St. Martin's Press, 2000), 64–65; Lin Walker, *Telephone Techniques* (New York: Amacom, 1998), 46–47; Dorothy Neal, *Telephone Techniques,* 2nd ed. (New York: Glencoe McGraw-Hill, 1998), 31; Jeannie Davis, *Beyond "Hello"* (Aurora, Colo.: Now Hear This, Inc., 2000), 2–3; "Ten Steps to Caller-Friendly Voice Mail," *Managing Office Technology,* January 1995, 25; Rhonda Finniss, "Voice Mail: Tips for a Positive Impression," *Administrative Assistant's Update,* August 2001, 5.

Mobile phones are a contentious point of etiquette in today's workplace. They can boost productivity if used mindfully, but they can be a productivity- and morale-draining disruption when used carelessly. Be aware that attitudes about mobile phones vary widely, and don't be surprised if you encounter policies restricting their use in offices or meeting rooms. Nearly half of U.S. companies already have such policies.[67]

Inappropriate use of mobile phones and other devices is a sign of disrespect.
Source: © GlowImages/Alamy.

Like every other aspect of communication, your phone habits say a lot about how much respect you have for the people around you. Selecting obnoxious ring tones, talking loudly in open offices or public places, using your phone right next to someone else, making excessive or unnecessary personal calls during work hours, invading someone's privacy by using your camera phone without permission, taking or making calls in restrooms and other inappropriate places, texting while someone is talking to you, allowing incoming calls to interrupt meetings or discussions—all are disrespectful choices that will reflect negatively on you.[68]

BUSINESS ETIQUETTE IN SOCIAL SETTINGS

From business lunches to industry conferences, you may represent your company when you're out in public. Make sure your appearance and actions are appropriate to the situation. Get to know the customs of the culture when you meet new people. For example, in North America, a firm handshake is expected when two people meet, whereas a respectful bow of the head is more appropriate in Japan. If you are expected to shake hands, be aware that the passive "dead fish" handshake creates an extremely negative impression. If you are physically able, always stand when shaking someone's hand.

When introducing yourself, include a brief description of your role in the company. When introducing two other people, speak their first and last names clearly and then try to offer some information (perhaps a shared professional interest) to help the two people ease into a conversation.[69] Generally speaking, the lower-ranking person is introduced to the senior-ranking person, without regard to gender.[70]

You represent your company when you're out in public, so etiquette continues to be important.

Business is often conducted over meals, and knowing the basics of dining etiquette will make you more effective in these situations.[71] Start by choosing foods that are easy to eat. Avoid alcoholic beverages in most instances, but if drinking one is appropriate, save it for the end of the meal. Leave business documents under your chair until entrée plates have been removed; the business aspect of the meal doesn't usually begin until then.

Just as in the office, when you use your mobile phone around other people in public, you send the message that people around you aren't as important as your call and that you don't respect your caller's privacy.[72] If it's not a matter of life and death, or at least an urgent request from your boss or a customer, wait until you're back in the office.

Finally, always remember that business meals are a forum for business, period. Don't get on your soapbox about politics, religion, or any other topic that's likely to stir up emotions. Don't complain about work, don't ask deeply personal questions, avoid profanity, and be careful with humor—a joke that entertains some people could easily offend others.

REAL-TIME UPDATES
Learn More by Watching This PowerPoint Presentation

Don't let etiquette blunders derail your career

Get great advice on developing professional telephone skills, making a positive impression while dining, and dressing for success in any career environment (including great tips on buying business suits). Go to http://real-timeupdates.com/ebc10 and click on Learn More. If you are using MyBcommLab, you can access Real-Time Updates within each chapter or under Student Study Tools.

BUSINESS ETIQUETTE ONLINE

Electronic media seem to be a breeding ground for poor etiquette. Learn the basics of professional online behavior to avoid mistakes that could hurt your company or your career. Here are some guidelines to follow whenever you are representing your company while using electronic media:[73]

When you represent your company online, you must adhere to a high standard of etiquette and respect for others.

- **Avoid personal attacks.** The anonymous and instantaneous nature of online communication can cause even level-headed people to strike out in blog postings, social networks, and other media.
- **Stay focused on the original topic.** If you want to change the subject of an email exchange, a forum discussion, or a blog comment thread, start a new message.
- **Don't present opinions as facts, and support facts with evidence.** This guideline applies to all communication, of course, but online venues in particular seem to tempt people into presenting their beliefs and opinions as unassailable truths.
- **Follow basic expectations of spelling, punctuation, and capitalization.** Sending careless, acronym-filled messages that look like you're texting your high school buddies makes you look like an amateur.
- **Use virus protection and keep it up to date.** Sending or posting a file that contains a computer virus is rude.
- **Ask if this is a good time for an IM chat.** Don't assume that just because a person is showing as "available" on your IM system that he or she wants to chat with you right this instant.
- **Watch your language and keep your emotions under control.** A moment of indiscretion could haunt you forever.
- **Avoid multitasking while using IM and other tools.** You might think you're saving time by doing a dozen things at once, but you're probably making the other person wait while you bounce back and forth between IM and your other tasks.
- **Never assume privacy.** Assume that anything you type will be stored forever, could be forwarded to other people, and might be read by your boss or the company's security staff.
- **Don't use "reply all" in emails unless everyone can benefit from your reply.** If one or more recipients of an email message don't need the information in your reply, remove their addresses before you send.
- **Don't waste others' time with sloppy, confusing, or incomplete messages.** Doing so is disrespectful.

Respect personal and professional boundaries when using Facebook and other social networking tools.

- **Respect boundaries of time and virtual space.** For instance, don't start using an employee's personal Facebook page for business messages unless you've discussed it beforehand, and don't assume people are available to discuss work matters around the clock, even if you do find them online in the middle of the night.

You recently joined Rosen Law Firm and love the spirit of camaraderie and mutual support that most employees exhibit. Of course, even in the best work environments, conflicts and misunderstandings can arise. Study these scenarios and decide how to respond.

Source: Rosen Law Firm.

1. You are in charge of the company's wiki, and your boss has asked you to increase the rate of employee contribution to it. You announce a competition whereby the employee who contributes the most number of new pages gets a cash prize. However, after a couple of weeks, you find out that one of the employees, a new recruit who is very enthusiastic, has contributed an incredibly high number of pages. On inspection, you find that some of these have similar content, but with different titles, or are lists organized in different ways, or are possible Internet downloads. However, the other pages are worthwhile and well done. How should you handle it?
   a. Disqualify her for the prize on the ground of inflated page counts containing unsuitable matter, and send her a memo to that effect.
   b. Silently delete those of her pages that you think are irrelevant.
   c. Ask her to merge similar pages and delete superfluous ones before the deadline for the prize arrives.
   d. Take her aside and explain to her the basic principles of copyright, intellectual property, the wiki's purpose and methods, and then rationalize her pages, resolving to monitor her contributions in the future.

2. You discover that you have been assigned to a team which includes a senior employee whom you have worked under before. At that time, this senior employee denied you little favors such as leaving early if you had work to do, and generally behaved very negatively toward you. You are now equals on the new team, and you are aware that you have to get off on the right foot with this person. What do you do?
   a. Greet the person cordially and get down to business as if nothing ever happened.
   b. Greet him as an old friend and offer to take him out to lunch after the meeting.
   c. Tell him how far you've risen in the company since he was your boss.
   d. Stonewall everything he says because offense is the best defense.

3. You have been assigned to a team notorious for 'ownership issues' regarding information: although they are all very high-functioning, team members have got into the habit of keeping information to themselves and working on their own. The previous manager believed in 'competition' and encouraged team members to try and snatch assignments

from each other. There is a high level of legacy hostility and mistrust. You believe that the team would be even more efficient if members would cooperate, but this involves a change in philosophy as well as in routines and procedures. Which strategy will work best for you?
   a. Call a meeting and present a set of slides where you proactively sell the idea of cooperation to them, highlighting all the benefits they will reap from it.
   b. Penalize anyone who demonstrably fails to cooperate or withholds needed information, telling them that they are slowing the company down.
   c. Throw a lavish party for the whole team at company expense as a 'reward' for their good performance where you announce that everyone must work together from now on.
   d. Call an informal meeting and encourage members to talk about trust issues, following up if necessary with meetings with individuals. Outline new workflows and information-handling procedures.

4. You are sitting in on your boss's fifteen-minute interview with a client to observe the client's body language. During the interview, the client speaks with confidence and clarity. After the initial handshake and greetings, the client clasps his hands and rests them on his desk where they remain throughout the interview. While describing his company's case, the client does not correct himself even once. When your boss asks for additional documents, there is a tiny delay before the client smiles and says of course. At the end of the interview he gets up with an expansive gesture and shakes hands effusively with you and your boss. Afterwards, your boss asks for your reactions. How would you interpret the client's behavior?
   a. The client seemed confident and in control. He had all his facts at his fingertips. The fact that he did not fidget suggests he was relaxed, and his pause on the request of documents simply meant he was calculating how long it would take to get them together.
   b. The client's unnatural stillness suggests he was concentrating too hard on speaking. His lack of fumbling when describing his case suggests his speech was rehearsed. His sudden change in body language at the end of the interview suggests relief. However, it isn't certain that he was doing anything wrong. This client needs further investigation.
   c. The client was confident of his facts, but nervous about your boss's possible reaction to them. He must clearly have made this case before in internal meetings, hence the smoothness of his narration of the facts. His stillness was due to concentration and mindfulness. His relief at the end of the interview was because he was desperately hoping you would help him.
   d. The client was clearly lying throughout the interview, and his relief at the end was because he thought he had successfully fooled you and your boss. You should drop this client at once.

LEARNING OBJECTIVES CHECKUP

Assess your understanding of the principles in this chapter by reading each learning objective and studying the accompanying exercises. For fill-in-the-blank items, write the missing text in the blank provided; for multiple-choice items, circle the letter of the correct answer. You can check your responses against the answer key on page AK-1.

Objective 2.1: List the advantages and disadvantages of working in teams, describe the characteristics of effective teams, and highlight four key issues of group dynamics.

1. Teams can achieve a higher level of performance than individuals alone because
   a. They combine the intelligence and energy of multiple individuals
   b. Motivation and creativity flourish in team settings
   c. They involve more input and a greater diversity of views, which tends to result in better decisions
   d. They do all of the above

2. Which of the following is a potential disadvantage of working in teams?
   a. Teams always stamp out creativity by forcing people to conform to existing ideas and practices.
   b. Teams increase a company's clerical workload because of the additional government paperwork required for administering workplace insurance.
   c. Team members are never held accountable for their individual performance.
   d. Social pressure within the group can lead to group-think, in which people go along with a bad idea or poor decision even though they may not really believe in it.

3. Conflict in team settings can be _____ if it forces important issues into the open, increases the involvement of team members, and generates creative ideas for solving a problem.

Objective 2.2: Offer guidelines for collaborative communication, identify major collaboration technologies, and explain how to give constructive feedback.

4. Which of the following is the best way for a team of people to write a report?
   a. Each member should plan, research, and write his or her individual version and then the group can select the strongest report.
   b. The team should divide and conquer, with one person doing the planning, one doing the research, one doing the writing, and so on.

c. To ensure a true group effort, every task from planning through final production should be done as a team, preferably with everyone in the same room at the same time.
   d. Research and plan as a group but assign the actual writing to one person, or at least assign separate sections to individual writers and have one person edit them all to achieve a consistent style.

5. Which of the following steps should be completed before anyone from the team does any planning, researching, or writing?
   a. The team should agree on the project's goals.
   b. The team should agree on the report's title.
   c. To avoid compatibility problems, the team should agree on which word processor or other software will be used.
   d. The team should always step away from the work environment and enjoy some social time in order to bond effectively before starting work.

6. Which of the following is not a benefit of using social media for business communication?
   a. Social media are "out in the open," so messages are easier for managers to monitor and control.
   b. Social media help erase geographic and organization boundaries.
   c. Social media give customers an easy way to voice their opinions and concerns.
   d. Social media can help "faceless" companies adopt a more human, conversational tone.

Objective 2.3: List the key steps needed to ensure productive team meetings.

7. What are the three key steps to making sure meetings are productive?
   a. Planning, planning, and more planning
   b. Preparing carefully, conducting meetings efficiently, and using meeting technologies wisely
   c. Preparing carefully, conducting meetings using true democratic participation, and using meeting technologies wisely
   d. Preparing carefully, using meeting technologies wisely, and distributing in-depth minutes to everyone in the company

8. *Robert's Rules of Order* is a guide to _____ procedure.

Objective 2.4: Identify the major technologies used to enhance or replace in-person meetings.

9. _____ teams are teams whose members work in different locations and interact electronically.

10. _____ technologies enable realistic conferences in which participants thousands of miles apart almost seem to be in the same room.

Objective 2.5: Identify three major modes of listening, describe the listening process, and explain the problem of selective listening.

11. After receiving messages, listeners _____ what they've heard by assigning meaning to the sounds.

12. If you're giving an important presentation and notice that many of the audience members look away when you try to make momentary eye contact, which of the following is most likely going on?
   a. These audience members don't want to challenge your authority by making direct eye contact.
   b. You work with a lot of shy people.
   c. The information you're presenting is making your audience uncomfortable in some way.
   d. The audience is taking time to carefully think about the information you're presenting.

13. If you don't agree with something the speaker says in a large, formal meeting, the best response is to
   a. Signal your disagreement by folding your arms across your chest and staring defiantly back at the speaker
   b. Use your mobile phone to begin sending text messages to other people in the room, explaining why the speaker is wrong
   c. Immediately challenge the speaker so that the misinformation is caught and corrected
   d. Quietly make a note of your objections and wait until a question-and-answer period to raise your hand

Objective 2.6: Explain the importance of nonverbal communication, and identify six major categories of nonverbal expression.

14. Nonverbal signals can be more influential than spoken language because
   a. Body language is difficult to control and therefore difficult to fake, so listeners often put more trust in nonverbal cues than in the words a speaker uses
   b. Nonverbal signals communicate faster than spoken language, and most people are impatient
   c. Body language saves listeners from the trouble of paying attention to what a speaker is saying

15. Which of the following is true about nonverbal signals?
   a. They can strengthen a spoken message.
   b. They can weaken a spoken message.
   c. They can replace spoken messages.
   d. All of the above are true.

Objective 2.7: Explain the importance of business etiquette, and identify three key areas in which good etiquette is essential.

16. Which of the following is the best characterization of etiquette in today's business environment?
   a. Business etiquette is impossible to generalize because every company has its own culture; you have to make it up as you go along.
   b. With ferocious international competition and constant financial pressure, etiquette is an old-fashioned luxury that businesses simply can't afford today.
   c. Ethical businesspeople don't need to worry directly about etiquette because ethical behavior automatically leads to good etiquette.
   d. Etiquette plays an important part in the process of forming and maintaining successful business relationships.

17. If you forgot to shut off your mobile phone before stepping into a business meeting and you receive a call during the meeting, the most appropriate thing to do is to
   a. Lower your voice to protect the privacy of your phone conversation
   b. Answer the phone and then quickly hang it up to minimize the disruption to the meeting
   c. Excuse yourself from the meeting and find a quiet place to talk
   d. Continue to participate in the meeting while taking the call; this shows everyone that you're an effective multitasker

18. Your company has established a designated "quiet time" from 1:00 to 3:00 every afternoon, during which office phones, IM, and email are disabled so that people can concentrate on planning, researching, writing, and other intensive tasks without being interrupted. However, a number of people continue to flout the guidelines by leaving their mobile phones on, saying their families and friends need to able to reach them. With all the various ringtones going off at random, the office is just as noisy as it was before. What is the best response?
   a. Agree to reactivate the office phone system if everyone will shut off their mobile phones, but have all incoming calls routed through a receptionist who will take messages for all routine calls and deliver a note if an employee truly is needed in an emergency.
   b. Give up on quiet time; with so many electronic gadgets in the workplace today, you'll never achieve peace and quiet.
   c. Get tough on the offenders by confiscating mobile phones whenever they ring during quiet time.
   d. Without telling anyone, simply install one of the available mobile phone jamming products that block incoming and outgoing mobile phone calls.

19. Constantly testing the limits of your company's dress and grooming standards sends a strong signal that you
   a. Don't understand or don't respect your company's culture
   b. Are a strong advocate for workers' rights
   c. Are a creative and independent thinker who is likely to generate lots of successful business ideas
   d. Represent the leading edge of a new generation of enlightened workers who will redefine the workplace according to contemporary standards

MyBcommLab

CHAPTER OUTLINE

Communicating Effectively in Teams
Advantages and Disadvantages of Teams
Characteristics of Effective Teams
Group Dynamics

Collaborating on Communication Efforts
Guidelines for Collaborative Writing
Technologies for Collaborative Writing
Social Networks and Virtual Communities
Giving—and Responding to—Constructive Feedback

Making Your Meetings More Productive
Preparing for Meetings
Conducting and Contributing to Efficient Meetings

Using Meeting Technologies

Improving Your Listening Skills
Recognizing Various Types of Listening
Understanding the Listening Process
Overcoming Barriers to Effective Listening

Improving Your Nonverbal Communication Skills
Recognizing Nonverbal Communication
Using Nonverbal Communication Effectively

Developing Your Business Etiquette
Business Etiquette in the Workplace
Business Etiquette in Social Settings
Business Etiquette Online

LEARNING OBJECTIVES

1. List the advantages and disadvantages of working in teams, describe the characteristics of effective teams, and highlight four key issues of group dynamics. [page 75]

2. Offer guidelines for collaborative communication, identify major collaboration technologies, and explain how to give constructive feedback. [page 79]

3. List the key steps needed to ensure productive team meetings. [page 82]

4. Identify the major technologies used to enhance or replace in-person meetings. [page 85]

5. Identify three major modes of listening, describe the listening process, and explain the problem of selective listening. [page 87]

6. Explain the importance of nonverbal communication, and identify six major categories of nonverbal expression. [page 90]

7. Explain the importance of business etiquette, and identify three key areas in which good etiquette is essential. [page 92]

KEY TERMS

active listening Making a conscious effort to turn off filters and biases to truly hear and understand what someone is saying

collaboration Working together to meet complex challenges

committees Formal teams with long life spans that can become a permanent part of the organizational structure

constructive feedback Focuses on the process and outcomes of communication, not on the people involved

content listening Listening to understand and retain the speaker's message

content management systems Computer systems that organize website content

critical listening Listening to understand and evaluate the meaning of the speaker's message

destructive feedback Delivers criticism with no guidance to stimulate improvement

empathic listening Listening to understand the speaker's feelings, needs, and wants

group dynamics The interactions and processes that take place among the members of a team

groupthink Situation in which peer pressure causes individual team members to withhold contrary or unpopular opinions

hidden agenda Private, counterproductive motives, such as a desire to take control

minutes Written summary of the important information presented and the decisions made during a meeting

nonverbal communication Sending and receiving information, both intentionally and unintentionally, without using written or spoken language

norms Shared, informal standards of conduct that guide team behavior

parliamentary procedure A time-tested method for planning and running effective meetings; the best-known guide to this procedure is *Robert's Rules of Order*

participative management The effort to involve employees in the company's decision making

problem-solving teams Teams that assemble to resolve specific issues and then disband when their goals have been accomplished

selective listening Listening to only part of a message; ignoring the parts one doesn't agree with or find interesting

self-oriented roles Unproductive team roles in which people are motivated mainly to fulfill personal needs

shared workspaces Online "virtual offices" that give everyone on a team access to the same set of resources and information

social networking technologies Online technologies that help erase the constraints of geographic and organization boundaries

task forces Another form of problem-solving teams, often with members from more than one organization

task-facilitating roles Productive team roles directed toward helping the team reach its goals

team A unit of two or more people who share a mission and the responsibility for working to achieve a common goal

team-maintenance roles Productive team roles directed toward helping everyone work well together

virtual meetings Meetings that take place online rather than in person

virtual teams Teams whose members work in different locations and interact electronically

wiki Special type of website that allows anyone with access to add new material and edit existing material

APPLY YOUR KNOWLEDGE

To review chapter content related to each question, refer to the indicated Learning Objective.

1. You head up the interdepartmental design review team for a manufacturer of high-performance motorcycles, and things are not going well at the moment. The design engineers and marketing strategists keep arguing about which should be a higher priority, performance or aesthetics, and the accountants say both groups are driving the cost of the new model through the roof by adding too many new features. Everyone has valid points to make, but the team is bogging down in conflict. Explain how you could go about resolving the stalemate. [LO-1]

2. You and another manager in your company disagree about whether employees should be encouraged to create online profiles on LinkedIn and other business-oriented social networking websites. You say these connections can be valuable to employees by helping them meet their peers throughout the industry and valuable to the company by identifying potential sales leads and business partners. The other manager says that encouraging employees to become better known in the industry will only make it easier for competitors to lure them away with enticing job offers. Write a brief email message that outlines your argument. (Make up any information you need about the company and its industry.) [LO-2]

3. How can nonverbal communication help you run a meeting? How can it help you call a meeting to order, emphasize important topics, show approval, express reservations, regulate the flow of conversation, and invite a colleague to continue with a comment? [LO-3], [LO-6]

4. Considering what you've learned about nonverbal communication, what are some of the ways in which communication might break down during an online meeting in which the participants can see video images of only the person presenting at any given time—and then only his or her head? [LO-6]

5. Why do you think people are more likely to engage in rude behaviors during online communication than during in-person communication? [LO-7]

PRACTICE YOUR SKILLS

Active links for all websites in this chapter can be found on MyBcommLab; see your User Guide for instructions on accessing the content for this chapter. Each activity is labeled according to the primary skill or skills you will need to use. To review relevant chapter content, you can refer to the indicated Learning Objective. In some instances, supporting information will be found in another chapter, as indicated.

Message for Analysis: Planning Meetings [LO-3]

A project leader has made notes about covering the following items at the quarterly budget meeting. Prepare a formal agenda by putting these items into a logical order and rewriting, where necessary, to give phrases a more consistent sound.

- Budget Committee Meeting to be held on December 12, 2012, at 9:30 a.m., and we have allotted one hour for the meeting.
- I will call the meeting to order.
- Real estate director's report: A closer look at cost overruns on Greentree site. (10 minutes)
- The group will review and approve the minutes from last quarter's meeting. (5 minutes)
- I will ask the finance director to report on actual versus projected quarterly revenues and expenses. (15 minutes)
- I will distribute copies of the overall divisional budget and announce the date of the next budget meeting.
- Discussion: How can we do a better job of anticipating and preventing cost overruns? (20 minutes)
- Meeting will take place in Conference Room 3, with WebEx active for remote employees.
- What additional budget issues must be considered during this quarter?

Exercises

1. **Collaboration: Working in Teams [LO-1], [LO-2]** In teams assigned by your instructor, prepare a 10-minute presentation on the potential disadvantages of using social media for business communication. When the presentation is ready, discuss how effective the team was using the criteria of (1) having a clear objective and a shared sense of purpose, (2) communicating openly and honestly, (3) reaching decisions by consensus, (4) thinking creatively, and (5) knowing how to resolve conflict. Be prepared to discuss your findings with the rest of the class.

2. **Collaboration: Working in Teams [LO-1]** In teams of four or five classmates, role play a scenario in which the team is to decide which department at your college will receive a $1 million gift from an anonymous donor. The catch: Each member of the team will advocate for a different department (decide among yourselves who represents which departments), which means that all but one member will "lose" in the final decision. Working as a team, decide which department will receive the donation and discuss the results to help everyone on the team support the decision. Be prepared to present your choice and your justification for it to the rest of the class.

3. **Negotiation and Conflict Resolution: Resolving Conflicts; Communication Ethics: Providing Ethical Leadership [LO-1], Chapter 1** During team meetings, one member constantly calls for votes or decisions before all the members have voiced their views. As the leader, you asked this member privately about his behavior. He replied that he was trying to move the team toward its goals, but you are concerned that he is really trying to take control. How can you deal with this situation without removing the member from the group?

4. **Collaboration: Collaborating on Writing Projects; Media Skills: Blogging [LO-2]** In this project, you will conduct research on your own and then merge your results with those of the rest of your team. Search Twitter for messages on the subject of workplace safety. (You can use Twitter's

advanced search page at http://search.twitter.com/advanced or use the "site: twitter.com" qualifier on a regular search engine.) Compile at least five general safety tips that apply to any office setting, and then meet with your team to select the five best tips from all those the team has collected. Collaborate on a blog post that lists the team's top five tips.

 Learn how to use Twitter search. Access Real-Time Updates at www.pearsoninternationaleditions.com/mybcommlab or visit http://real-timeupdates.com/ebc10, click on Student Assignments and then click on Twitter Screencast.

5. **Communication Etiquette: Etiquette in the Workplace, Participating in Meetings [LO-3], [LO-7]** In group meetings, some of your colleagues have a habit of interrupting and arguing with the speaker, taking credit for ideas that aren't theirs, and shooting down ideas they don't agree with. You're the newest person in the group and not sure if this is accepted behavior in this company, but it concerns you both personally and professionally. Should you go with the flow and adopt their behavior or stick with your own communication style, even though you might get lost in the noise? In a two-paragraph email message or post for your class blog, explain the pros and cons of both approaches.

6. **Collaboration: Participating in Meetings [LO-3]** With a classmate, attend a local community or campus meeting where you can observe a group discussion, vote, or take other group action. During the meeting, take notes individually and, afterward, work together to answer the following questions.

   a. What is your evaluation of this meeting? In your answer, consider (1) the leader's ability to articulate the meeting's goals clearly, (2) the leader's ability to engage members in a meaningful discussion, (3) the group's dynamics, and (4) the group's listening skills.

   b. How did group members make decisions? Did they vote? Did they reach decisions by consensus? Did those with dissenting opinions get an opportunity to voice their objections?

   c. How well did the individual participants listen? How could you tell?

   d. Did any participants change their expressed views or their votes during the meeting? Why might that have happened?

   e. Did you observe any of the communication barriers discussed in Chapter 1? Identify them.

   f. Compare the notes you took during the meeting with those of your classmate. What differences do you notice? How do you account for these differences?

7. **Collaboration: Leading Meetings [LO-3], Chapter 3** Every month, each employee in your department is expected to give a brief oral presentation on the status of his or her project. However, your department has recently hired an employee who has a severe speech impediment that prevents people from understanding most of what he has to say. As department manager, how will you resolve this dilemma? Please explain.

8. **Collaboration: Using Collaboration Technologies [LO-4]** In a team assigned by your instructor, use Zoho (www.zoho.com; free for personal use), Google Docs (http://docs.google.com), or a comparable system to collaborate on a set of directions that out-of-town visitors could use to reach a specific point on your campus, such as a stadium or dorm. The team should choose the location and the mode(s) of transportation involved. Be creative—brainstorm the best ways to guide first-time visitors to the selected location using all the media at your disposal.

9. **Interpersonal Communication: Listening Actively [LO-5]** For the next several days, take notes on your listening performance during at least a half-dozen situations in class, during social activities, and at work, if applicable. Referring to the traits of effective listeners in Table 2.3, rate yourself using *always, frequently, occasionally,* or *never* on these positive listening habits. In a report no longer than one page, summarize your analysis and identify specific areas in which you can improve your listening skills.

10. **Interpersonal Communication: Listening to Empathize [LO-5]** Think back over conversations you have had with friends, family members, coworkers, or classmates in the past week. Select a conversation in which the other person wanted to talk about something that was troubling him or her—a bad situation at work, a scary exam on the horizon, difficulties with a professor, a health problem, financial concerns, or the like. As you replay this conversation in your mind, think about how well you did in terms of empathic listening (see page 87). For example, did you find yourself being critical when the person really just needed someone to listen? Did you let the person know, by your words or actions, that you cared about his or her dilemma, even if you were not able to help in any other way? Analyze your listening performance in a brief email message to your instructor. **Note:** Do not disclose any private information in your message; you can change the names of the people involved or the circumstances as needed to maintain privacy.

11. **Nonverbal Communication: Analyzing Nonverbal Signals [LO-6]** Select a business letter and envelope that you have received at work or home. Analyze their appearance. What nonverbal messages do they send? Are these messages consistent with the content of the letter? If not, what could the sender have done to make the nonverbal communication consistent with the verbal communication? Summarize your findings in a post on your class blog or in an email message to your instructor.

12. **Nonverbal Communication: Analyzing Nonverbal Signals [LO-6]** Describe what the following body movements suggest when someone exhibits them during a conversation. How do such movements influence your interpretation of spoken words? Summarize your findings in a post on your class blog or in an email message to your instructor.

   a. Shifting one's body continuously while seated

   b. Twirling and playing with one's hair

   c. Sitting in a sprawled position

   d. Rolling one's eyes

   e. Extending a weak handshake

13. **Communication Etiquette: Telephone Skills [LO-7]** Late on a Friday afternoon, you learn that the facilities department is going to move you—and your computer, your desk, and all your files—to another office first thing Monday morning. However, you have an important client meeting scheduled in your office for Monday afternoon, and you need to finalize some contract details on Monday morning. You simply can't lose access to your office at this point, and you're more than a little annoyed that your boss didn't ask you before approving the move. He has already left for the day, but you know he usually checks his voice mail over the weekend, so you decide to leave a message, asking him to cancel the move or at least call you at home as soon as possible. Using the voice-mail guidelines listed in Table 2.5, plan your message (use an imaginary phone number as your contact number and make up any other details you need for the call). As directed by your instructor, submit either a written script of the message or a podcast recording of the actual message.

14. **Communication Etiquette: Etiquette in the Workplace [LO-7]** As the local manager of an international accounting firm, you place high priority on professional etiquette. Not only does it communicate respect to your clients, it also instills confidence in your firm by showing that you and your staff are aware of and able to meet the expectations of almost any audience. Earlier today, you took four recently hired college graduates to lunch with an important client. You've done this for years, and it's usually an upbeat experience for everyone, but today's lunch was a disaster. One of the new employees made not one, not two, but three calls on his mobile phone during lunch. Another interrupted the client several times and even got into a mild argument. The third employee kept making sarcastic jokes about politics, making everyone at the table uncomfortable. And the fourth showed up dressed like she was expecting to bale hay or work in coal mine, not have a business lunch in a posh restaurant. You've already called the client to apologize, but now you need to coach these employees on proper business etiquette. Draft a brief memo to these employees, explaining why etiquette is so important to the company's success—and to their individual careers.

EXPAND YOUR SKILLS

Critique the Professionals

Celebrities can learn from successful businesses when it comes to managing their careers, but businesses can learn from successful celebrities, too—particularly when it comes to building communities online using social media. For instance, social media guru Dan Schawbel cites Vin Diesel, Ashton Kutcher, Lady Gaga, Lenny Kravitz, and Michael Phelps as celebrities who have used Facebook to build their personal brands.[74] Locate three celebrities (musicians, actors, authors, or athletes) who have sizable fan bases on Facebook and analyze how they use the social network. Using whatever medium your instructor requests, write a brief analysis (no more than one page) of the lessons, positive or negative, that a business could learn from these celebrities. Be sure to cite specific elements from the

Facebook pages you've chosen, and if you think any of the celebrities have made mistakes in their use of Facebook, describe those as well.

Sharpening Your Career Skills Online

Bovée and Thill's Business Communication Web Search, at http://businesscommunicationblog.com/websearch, is a unique research tool designed specifically for business communication research. Use the Web Search function to find an online video, a podcast, or a PowerPoint presentation that offers advice on improving your active listening skills in business situations. Write a brief email message to your instructor, describing the item that you found and summarizing the career skills information you learned from it.

IMPROVE YOUR GRAMMAR, MECHANICS, AND USAGE

The following exercises help you improve your knowledge of and power over English grammar, mechanics, and usage. Turn to the Handbook of Grammar, Mechanics, and Usage at the end of this book and review all of Section 1.2 (Pronouns). Then look at the following 10 items. Underline the preferred choice within each set of parentheses. (Answers to these exercises appear on page AK-3.)

1. The office is busy preparing (*their, its*) annual report.
2. Some members of John's team did not turn in (*their, its*) reports on time.
3. The Education Board has chosen (*their, its*) president.
4. Spade and Archer have informed (*their, his*) juniors about the new rules.
5. Every team leader has to increase (*his, their, his or her*) productivity next year.
6. Please find out if everyone has supplied (*his, their, his or her*) PAN number.
7. Every employee knows that they will get (*his, their, a*) raise this year; Lawrence told (*them, they, all*) about it last week.
8. Nicholas and Nora are both applying for the position of Project Manager. (*Who, Whom*) do you think is better suited for the role?
9. Infosys has just announced (*who, whom*) it will hire as the new COO.
10. Either of the products would make (*their, its*) mark by next month.

For additional exercises focusing on pronouns, visit MyBcommLab. Click on Chapter 2, click on Additional Exercises to Improve Your Grammar, Mechanics, and Usage, and then click on 3. Case of pronouns 4. Possessive pronouns.

REFERENCES

1. Evelyn Nussenbaum, "Boosting Teamwork with Wikis," *Fortune Small Business*, 12 February 2008, http://money.cnn.com; Doug Cornelius, "Wikis at the Rosen Law Firm," KM Space blog, 28 February 2008, http://kmspace.blogspot.com; Rosen Law Firm website, accessed 28 December 2010, www.rosen.com.

2. James Manyika, Kara Sprague, and Lareina Yee, "Using Technology to Improve Workforce Collaboration," What Matters (McKinsey & Company), 27 October 2009, http://whatmatters.mckinseydigital.com.

3. Courtland L. Bovée and John V. Thill, *Business in Action*, 5th ed. (Upper Saddle River, N.J.: Pearson Prentice Hall, 2011), 172.

4. "Five Case Studies on Successful Teams," *HR Focus*, April 2002, 18+.

5. Stephen R. Robbins, *Essentials of Organizational Behavior*, 6th ed. (Upper Saddle River, N.J.: Prentice Hall, 2000), 98.

6. Max Landsberg and Madeline Pfau, "Developing Diversity: Lessons from Top Teams," *Strategy + Business*, Winter 2005, 10–12.

7. "Groups Best at Complex Problems," *Industrial Engineer*, June 2006, 14.

8. Nicola A. Nelson, "Leading Teams," *Defense AT&L*, July–August 2006, 26–29; Larry Cole and Michael Cole, "Why Is the Teamwork Buzz Word Not Working?" *Communication World*, February–March 1999, 29; Patricia Buhler, "Managing in the 90s: Creating Flexibility in Today's Workplace," *Supervision*, January 1997, 241; Allison W. Amason, Allen C. Hochwarter, Wayne A. Thompson, and Kenneth R. Harrison, "Conflict: An Important Dimension in Successful Management Teams," *Organizational Dynamics*, Autumn 1995, 201.

9. Geoffrey Colvin, "Why Dream Teams Fail," *Fortune*, 12 June 2006, 87–92.

10. Vijay Govindarajan and Anil K. Gupta, "Building an Effective Global Business Team," *MIT Sloan Management Review*, Summer 2001, 631.

11. Colvin, "Why Dream Teams Fail," 87–92.

12. Tiziana Casciaro and Miguel Sousa Lobo, "Competent Jerks, Lovable Fools, and the Formation of Social Networks," *Harvard Business Review*, June 2005, 92–99.

13. Stephen P. Robbins and David A. DeCenzo, *Fundamentals of Management*, 4th ed. (Upper Saddle River, N.J.: Prentice Hall, 2004), 266–267; Jerald Greenberg and Robert A. Baron, *Behavior in Organizations*, 8th ed. (Upper Saddle River, N.J.: Prentice Hall, 2003), 279–280.

14. B. Aubrey Fisher, *Small Group Decision Making: Communication and the Group Process*, 2nd ed. (New York: McGraw-Hill, 1980), 145–149; Robbins and DeCenzo, *Fundamentals of Management*, 334–335; Richard L. Daft, *Management*, 6th ed. (Cincinnati: Thomson South-Western, 2003), 602–603.

15. Michael Laff, "Effective Team Building: More Than Just Fun at Work," *Training + Development*, August 2006, 24–35.

16. Claire Sookman, "Building Your Virtual Team," *Network World*, 21 June 2004, 91.

17. Jared Sandberg, "Brainstorming Works Best if People Scramble for Ideas on Their Own," *Wall Street Journal*, 13 June 2006, B1.

18. Mark K. Smith, "Bruce W. Tuckman—Forming, Storming, Norming, and Performing in Groups," Infed.org [accessed 5 July 2005] www.infed.org.

19. Robbins and DeCenzo, *Fundamentals of Management*, 258–259.

20. Daft, *Management*, 609–612.

21. Andy Boynton and Bill Fischer, *Virtuoso Teams: Lessons from Teams That Changed Their Worlds* (Harrow, UK: FT Prentice Hall, 2005), 10.

22. Thomas K. Capozzoli, "Conflict Resolution—A Key Ingredient in Successful Teams," *Supervision*, November 1999, 14–16.

23. Jesse S. Nirenberg, *Getting Through to People* (Paramus, N.J.: Prentice Hall, 1973), 134–142.

24. Nirenberg, *Getting Through to People*, 134–142.

25. Nirenberg, *Getting Through to People*, 134–142.

26. Jon Hanke, "Presenting as a Team," *Presentations*, January 1998, 74–82.

27. William P. Galle, Jr., Beverly H. Nelson, Donna W. Luse, and Maurice F. Villere, *Business Communication: A Technology-Based Approach* (Chicago: Irwin, 1996), 260.

28. Mary Beth Debs, "Recent Research on Collaborative Writing in Industry," *Technical Communication*, November 1991, 476–484.

29. Mark Choate, "What Makes an Enterprise Wiki?" CMS Watch website, 28 April 2006, www.cmswatch.com.

30. Choate, "What Makes an Enterprise Wiki?"

31. Rob Koplowitz, "Building a Collaboration Strategy," *KM World*, November/December 2009, 14–15.

32. Eric Knorr and Galen Gruman, "What Cloud Computing Really Means," *InfoWorld*, accessed 11 June 2010, www.infoworld.com; Lamont Wood, "Cloud Computing Poised to Transform Communication," LiveScience, 8 December 2009, www.livescience.com.

33. Christopher Carfi and Leif Chastaine, "Social Networking for Businesses & Organizations," white paper, Cerado website, accessed 13 August 2008, www.cerado.com.

34. Richard McDermott and Douglas Archibald, "Harnessing Your Staff's Informal Networks," *Harvard Business Review*, March 2010, 82–89.

35. Tony Hsieh, "Why I Sold Zappos," *Inc.*, 1 June 2010, www.inc.com.

36. Chuck Williams, *Management*, 2nd ed. (Cincinnati: Thomson South-Western, 2002), 706–707.

37. Ron Ashkenas, "Why We Secretly Love Meetings," *Harvard Business Review* blogs, 5 October 2010, http://blogs.hbr.org.

38. Douglas Kimberly, "Ten Pitfalls of Pitiful Meetings," Payroll Manager's Report, January 2010, 1, 11; "Making the Most of Meetings," *Journal of Accountancy*, March 2009, 22.

39. Manyika, Sprague, and Yee, "Using Technology to Improve Workforce Collaboration."

40. Roger O. Crockett, "The 21st Century Meeting," *Businessweek*, 26 February 2007, 72–79.

41. Steve Lohr, "As Travel Costs Rise, More Meetings Go Virtual," *New York Times*, 22 July 2008, www.nytimes.com.

42. "Unlock the Full Power of the Web Conferencing," CEOworld.biz, 20 November 2007, www.ceoworld.biz.

43. IBM Jam Events website, accessed 10 June 2010, www.collaborationjam.com; "Big Blue Brainstorm," BusinessWeek, 7 August 2006, www.businessweek.com.

44. "17 Tips for More Productive Conference Calls," AccuConference, accessed 30 January 2008, www.accuconference.com.

45. Augusta M. Simon, "Effective Listening: Barriers to Listening in a Diverse Business Environment," *Bulletin of the Association for Business Communication* 54, no. 3 (September 1991): 73–74.

46. Judi Brownell, *Listening*, 2nd ed. (Boston: Allyn & Bacon, 2002), 9, 10.

47. Carmine Gallo, "Why Leadership Means Listening," *BusinessWeek*, 31 January 2007, www.businessweek.com.

48. Anne Fisher, "The Trouble with MBAs," *Fortune International*, 30 April 2007, 33–34.

49. Dennis M. Kratz and Abby Robinson Kratz, *Effective Listening Skills* (New York: McGraw-Hill, 1995), 45–53; J. Michael Sproule, *Communication Today* (Glenview, Ill.: Scott Foresman, 1981), 69.

50. Brownell, *Listening*, 230–231.

51. Kratz and Kratz, *Effective Listening Skills*, 78–79; Sproule, *Communication Today*.

52. Bill Brooks, "The Power of Active Listening," *American Salesman*, June 2003, 12; "Active Listening," Study Guides and Strategies website, accessed 5 February 2005, www.studygs.net.

53. Bob Lamons, "Good Listeners Are Better Communicators," *Marketing News*, 11 September 1995, 13+; Phillip Morgan and H. Kent Baker, "Building a Professional Image: Improving Listening Behavior," *Supervisory Management*, November 1985, 35–36.

54. Clarke, "Do You Hear What I Hear?"; Dot Yandle, "Listening to Understand," *Pryor Report Management Newsletter Supplement* 15, no. 8 (August 1998): 13.

55. Brownell, *Listening*, 14; Kratz and Kratz, *Effective Listening Skills*, 8–9; Sherwyn P. Morreale and Courtland L. Bovée, *Excellence in Public Speaking* (Orlando, Fla.: Harcourt Brace, 1998), 72–76; Lyman K. Steil, Larry L. Barker, and Kittie W. Watson, *Effective Listening: Key to Your Success* (Reading, Mass.: Addison Wesley, 1983), 21–22.

56. Patrick J. Collins, *Say It with Power and Confidence* (Upper Saddle River, N.J.: Prentice Hall, 1997), 40–45.

57. Morreale and Bovée, *Excellence in Public Speaking*, 296.

58. Dale G. Leathers, *Successful Nonverbal Communication: Principles and Applications* (New York: Macmillan, 1986), 19.

59. Gerald H. Graham, Jeanne Unrue, and Paul Jennings, "The Impact of Nonverbal Communication in Organizations: A Survey of Perceptions," *Journal of Business Communication* 28, no. 1 (Winter 1991): 45–62.

60. Virginia P. Richmond and James C. McCroskey, *Nonverbal Behavior in Interpersonal Relations* (Boston: Allyn & Bacon, 2000), 153–157.

61. Mary Ellen Slayter, "Pamela Meyer on the Science Behind 'Liespotting,'" SmartBlog on Workforce, 14 September 2010, http://smartblogs.com.

62. Slayter, "Pamela Meyer on the Science Behind 'Liespotting.'"

63. Joe Navarro, "Body Language Myths," *Psychology Today*, 25 October 2009, www.psychologytoday.com; Richmond and McCroskey, *Nonverbal Behavior in Interpersonal Relations*, 2–3.

64. John Hollon, "No Tolerance for Jerks," *Workforce Management*, 12 February 2007, 34.

65. Marilyn Pincus, *Everyday Business Etiquette* (Hauppauge, N.Y.: Barron's Educational Series, 1996), 136.

66. Susan G. Hauser, "The Degeneration of Decorum," *Workforce Management*, January 2011, 16–18, 20–21.

67. "Use Proper Cell Phone Etiquette At Work," Kelly Services Website, accessed 11 June 2010, www.kellyservices.us.

68. J. J. McCorvey, "How to Create a Cell Phone Policy," *Inc.*, 10 February 2010, www.inc.com; "Use Proper Cell Phone Etiquette at Work."

69. Casperson, *Power Etiquette*, 10–14; Ellyn Spragins, "Introducing Politeness," *Fortune Small Business*, November 2001, 30.

70. Tanya Mohn, "The Social Graces as a Business Tool," *New York Times*, 10 November 2002, sec. 3, 12.

71. Casperson, *Power Etiquette*, 44–46.

72. Casperson, *Power Etiquette*, 109–110.

73. "Are You Practicing Proper Social Networking Etiquette?" *Forbes*, 9 October 2009, www.forbes.com; Pete Babb, "The Ten Commandments of Blog and Wiki Etiquette," *InfoWorld*, 28 May 2007, www.infoworld.com; Judith Kallos, "Instant Messaging Etiquette," NetM@nners blog, www.netmanners.com; Michael S. Hyatt, "Email Etiquette 101," From Where I Sit blog, 1 July 2007, www.michaelhyatt.com.

74. Dan Schawbel, "5 Lessons Celebrities Can Teach Us About Facebook Pages," Mashable, 15 May 2009, http://mashable.com.

Communicating in a World of Diversity

LEARNING OBJECTIVES After studying this chapter, you will be able to

1 Discuss the opportunities and challenges of intercultural communication

2 Define *culture*, explain how culture is learned, and define *ethnocentrism* and *stereotyping*

3 Explain the importance of recognizing cultural variations, and list eight categories of cultural differences

4 List four general guidelines for adapting to any business culture

5 Identify seven steps you can take to improve your intercultural communication skills

MyBcommLab Where you see MyBcommLab in this chapter, go to www.pearsoninternationaleditions.com/mybcommlab for additional activities on the topic being discussed.

ON THE JOB: COMMUNICATING AT IBM

Ron Glover oversees IBM's efforts to build competitive advantages by capitalizing on the benefits of a diverse workforce.
Source: Courtesy of International Business Machines Corporation. Unauthorized use not permitted.

Building Competitive Advantage by Embracing Diversity

The *I* in IBM stands for *International*, but it could just as easily stand for *Intercultural*, as a testament to the computer giant's long-standing commitment to embracing diversity. Ron Glover, IBM's vice president of global workforce diversity, knows from years of experience that communicating successfully across cultures is no simple task, however—particularly in a company that employs more than 350,000 people and sells to customers in roughly 175 countries around the world.

Language presents a formidable barrier to communication when you consider that IBM's employees speak more than 165 languages. But language is just one of many elements that play a role in communication between cultures. Differences in age, ethnic background, gender, sexual orientation, physical ability, and economic status can all affect the communication process. Glover emphasizes that "to operate successfully, we must be especially mindful of how we respect and value differences among people in countries and regions." He recognizes that these differences represent both a challenge and an opportunity, and a key part of his job is helping IBM executives and employees work together in a way that transforms their cultural differences into a critical business strength. Diversity, he explains, is "an essential aspect of IBM's broader business strategy." To emphasize this fact, managers cannot receive a top performance ranking unless they can demonstrate that they are practicing IBM's diversity values.

Throughout its long history of employing and working with people from a variety of cultures, IBM has learned some powerful lessons. Perhaps the most significant is its conclusion that successfully managing a diverse workforce and competing in a diverse marketplace starts with embracing those differences, not trying to ignore them or pretending they don't affect interpersonal communication. Take Ron Glover's advice when he says that even if your company never does business outside the United States, "you will need to effectively engage differences to remain viable in the economy of the future."[1]

www.ibm.com

Understanding the Opportunities and Challenges of Communication in a Diverse World

IBM's experience (profiled in the chapter opener) illustrates the opportunities and challenges for business professionals who know how to communicate with diverse audiences. Although the concept is often framed in terms of ethnic background, a broader and more useful definition of **diversity** includes "all the characteristics and experiences that define each of us as individuals."[2] As one example, the pharmaceutical company Merck identifies 19 separate dimensions of diversity in its discussions of workforce diversity, including race, age, military experience, parental status, marital status, and thinking style.[3] As you'll learn in this chapter, these characteristics and experiences can have a profound effect on the way businesspeople communicate.

Intercultural communication is the process of sending and receiving messages between people whose cultural backgrounds could lead them to interpret verbal and nonverbal signs differently. Every attempt to send and receive messages is influenced by culture, so to communicate successfully, you need a basic grasp of the cultural differences you may encounter and how you should handle them. Your efforts to recognize and bridge cultural differences will open up business opportunities throughout the world and maximize the contributions of all the employees in a diverse workforce.

THE OPPORTUNITIES IN A GLOBAL MARKETPLACE

Chances are good that you'll be working across international borders sometime in your career. Thanks to communication and transportation technologies, natural boundaries and national borders are no longer the impassable barriers they once were. Local markets are opening to worldwide competition as businesses of all sizes look for new growth opportunities outside their own countries. Thousands of U.S. businesses depend on exports for significant portions of their revenues. Every year, these companies export hundreds of billions of dollars worth of materials and merchandise, along with billions more in personal and professional services. If you work in one of these companies, you may well be called on to visit or at least communicate with a wide variety of people who speak languages other than English and who live in cultures quite different from what you're used to (see Figure 3.1 on the next page). Of the top 10 export markets for U.S. products, only two, Canada and Great Britain, have English as an official language—and Canada also has French as an official language.[4]

THE ADVANTAGES OF A DIVERSE WORKFORCE

Even if you never visit another country or transact business on a global scale, you will interact with colleagues from a variety of cultures, with a wide range of characteristics and life experiences. Over the past few decades, many innovative companies have changed the way they approach diversity, from seeing it as a legal requirement (providing equal opportunities for all) to seeing it as a strategic opportunity to connect with customers and take advantage of the broadest possible pool of talent.[5] Smart business leaders recognize the competitive advantages of a diverse workforce that offers a broader spectrum of viewpoints and ideas, helps companies understand and identify with diverse markets, and enables companies to benefit from a wider range of employee talents (see Figure 3.2 on page 109). "It just makes good business sense," says Gord Nixon, CEO of Royal Bank of Canada.[6] According to IBM's Ron Glover, more-diverse teams tend to be more innovative over the long

1   LEARNING OBJECTIVE

Discuss the opportunities and challenges of intercultural communication.

Diversity includes all the characteristics that define people as individuals.

You will communicate with people from other cultures throughout your career.

MyBcommLab

- Access this chapter's simulation titled Communicating in a World of Diversity, located at www.pearsoninternationaleditions.com/mybcommlab

The diversity of today's workforce brings distinct advantages to businesses:
- A broader range of views and ideas
- A better understanding of diverse, fragmented markets
- A broader pool of talent from which to recruit

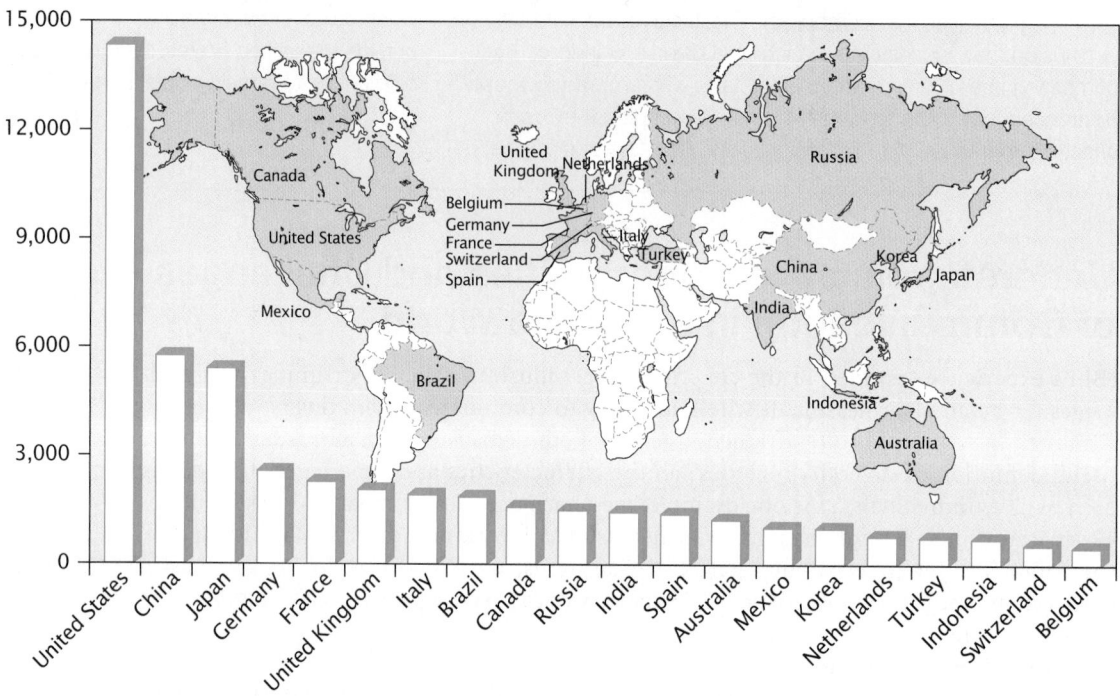

Figure 3.1   World's Biggest Economies
This snapshot of the world's 20 largest economies gives you an idea of the global nature of business today. Figures shown are estimates of 2010 gross domestic product (GDP) in billions of U.S. dollars. *Source:* Economic data from International Monetary Fund website, accessed 4 January 2011, www.imf.org.

term than more-homogeneous teams (those on which team members tend to have similar backgrounds).[7]

Diversity is simply a fact of life for all companies. The United States has been a nation of immigrants from the beginning, and that trend continues today. The western and northern Europeans who made up the bulk of immigrants during the nation's early years now share space with people from across Asia, Africa, Eastern Europe, and other parts of the world. Even the term *minority*, as it applies to nonwhite residents, makes less and less sense every year: In two states (California and New Mexico), several dozen large cities, and about 10 percent of the counties across the United States, Caucasian Americans make up less than half the population.[8] This pattern of immigration isn't unique to the United States. For example, workers from Africa, Asia, and the Middle East are moving to Europe in search of new opportunities, while workers from India, the Philippines, and Southeast Asia contribute to the employment base of the Middle East.[9]

However, you and your colleagues don't need to be recent immigrants to constitute a diverse workforce. Differences in everything from age and gender to religion and ethnic heritage to geography and military experience enrich the workplace. Both immigration and workforce diversity create advantages—and challenges—for business communicators throughout the world.

A company's cultural diversity affects how its business messages are conceived, composed, delivered, received, and interpreted.

Culture influences everything about communication, including
- Language
- Nonverbal signals
- Word meaning
- Time and space issues
- Rules of human relationships

THE CHALLENGES OF INTERCULTURAL COMMUNICATION

Today's increasingly diverse workforce encompasses a wide range of skills, traditions, backgrounds, experiences, outlooks, and attitudes toward work—all of which can affect communication in the workplace. Supervisors face the challenge of connecting with these diverse employees, motivating them, and fostering cooperation and harmony among them. Teams face the challenge of working together closely, and companies are challenged to coexist peacefully with business partners and with the community as a whole.

The interaction of culture and communication is so pervasive that separating the two is virtually impossible. The way you communicate is deeply influenced by the culture in which

Merck's top-line message about diversity acknowledges the strategic advantages available to companies that embrace diversity in their hiring and management practices.

Specific supporting points back up the high-level message about the company's commitment to embracing diversity in all facets of its business.

In addition to developing and supporting a diverse workforce, Merck also works closely with a diverse base of suppliers to its various business units.

This diagram lists the 19 dimensions of diversity that Merck takes into account in its management philosophy.

Significant awards and recognitions let potential employees and business partners know that Merck is serious about inclusivity.

Figure 3.2 Diversity at Merck
Like IBM (see page 106), the pharmaceutical company Merck approaches employee and supplier diversity as an opportunity and a strategy imperative.
Source: Courtesy of Merck, Global Communications, Reputation and Branding.

you were raised. The meaning of words, the significance of gestures, the importance of time and space, the rules of human relationships—these and many other aspects of communication are defined by culture. To a large degree, your culture influences the way you think, which naturally affects the way you communicate as both a sender and a receiver.[10] Intercultural communication is much more complicated than simply matching language between sender and receiver—it goes beyond mere words to beliefs, values, and emotions.

Elements of human diversity can affect communication at every stage of the communication process (see page 50), from the ideas a person deems important enough to share to the habits and expectations of giving feedback. In particular, your instinct is to encode your message using the assumptions of *your* culture. However, members of your audience decode your message according to the assumptions of *their* culture. The greater the difference between cultures, the greater the chance for misunderstanding.[11]

Throughout this chapter, you'll see examples of how communication styles and habits vary from one culture to another. These examples are intended to illustrate the

Communication among people of diverse cultural backgrounds and life experiences is not always easy, but doing it successfully can create tremendous strategic advantages.
Source: Blend Images/SuperStock.

major themes of intercultural communication, not to give an exhaustive list of styles and habits of any particular culture. With an understanding of these major themes, you'll be prepared to explore the specifics of any culture.

Developing Cultural Competency

Cultural competency requires a combination of attitude, knowledge, and skills.

Cultural competency is an appreciation for cultural differences that affect communication and the ability to adjust one's communication style to ensure that efforts to send and receive messages across cultural boundaries are successful. It requires a combination of attitude, knowledge, and skills.[12]

The good news is that you're already an expert in culture, at least in the culture in which you grew up. You understand how your society works, how people are expected to communicate, what common gestures and facial expressions mean, and so on. The bad news is that because you're such an expert in your own culture, your communication is largely automatic; that is, you rarely stop to think about the communication rules you're following. An important step toward successful intercultural communication is becoming more aware of these rules and of the way they influence your communication.

UNDERSTANDING THE CONCEPT OF CULTURE

Culture is a shared system of symbols, beliefs, attitudes, values, expectations, and behavior norms.

Culture is a shared system of symbols, beliefs, attitudes, values, expectations, and norms for behavior. Your cultural background influences the way you prioritize what is important in life, helps define your attitude toward what is appropriate in a situation, and establishes rules of behavior.[13]

You belong to several cultures, each of which affects the way you communicate.

Actually, you belong to several cultures. In addition to the culture you share with all the people who live in your own country, you belong to other cultural groups, including an ethnic group, possibly a religious group, and perhaps a profession that has its own special language and customs. With its large population and long history of immigration, the United States is home to a vast array of cultures. As one indication of this diversity, the inhabitants of this country now speak more than 170 languages.[14] In contrast, Japan is much more homogeneous, having only a few distinct cultural groups.[15]

Members of a given culture tend to have similar assumptions about how people should think, behave, and communicate, and they all tend to act on those assumptions in much the same way. Cultures can differ widely and vary in their rate of change, degree of complexity, and tolerance toward outsiders. These differences affect the level of trust and openness that can be achieved when communicating with people of other cultures.

You learn culture both directly (by being instructed) and indirectly (by observing others).

People learn culture directly and indirectly from other members of their group. As you grow up in a culture, you are taught by the group's members who you are and how best to function in that culture. Sometimes you are explicitly told which behaviors are acceptable; at other times you learn by observing which values work best in a particular group. In these ways, culture is passed on from person to person and from generation to generation.[16]

Cultures tend to offer both views of life that are both coherent (internally logical) and complete (able to answer all of life's big questions).

In addition to being automatic, culture tends to be *coherent*; that is, a culture appears to be fairly logical and consistent when viewed from the inside. Certain norms within a culture may not make sense to someone outside the culture, but they probably make sense to those inside. Such coherence generally helps a culture function more smoothly internally, but it can create disharmony between cultures that don't view the world in the same way.

Finally, cultures tend to be *complete*; that is, they provide most of their members with most of the answers to life's big questions. This idea of completeness dulls or even suppresses curiosity about life in other cultures. Not surprisingly, such completeness can complicate communication with other cultures.[17]

OVERCOMING ETHNOCENTRISM AND STEREOTYPING

Ethnocentrism is the tendency to judge all other groups according to the standards, behaviors, and customs of one's own group.

Ethnocentrism is the tendency to judge other groups according to the standards, behaviors, and customs of one's own group. Given the automatic influence of one's own culture, when people compare their culture to others, they often conclude that their own group is superior.[18] An even more extreme reaction is **xenophobia**, a fear of strangers and foreigners. Clearly, businesspeople who take these views are not likely to communicate successfully across cultures.

Distorted views of other cultures or groups also result from **stereotyping**, assigning a wide range of generalized attributes to an individual on the basis of membership in a particular culture or social group. For instance, assuming that an older colleague will be out of touch with the youth market and thinking that a younger colleague can't be an inspiring leader are examples of stereotyping age groups.

Those who want to show respect for other people and to communicate effectively in business need to adopt a more positive viewpoint, in the form of **cultural pluralism**—the practice of accepting multiple cultures on their own terms. When crossing cultural boundaries, you'll be even more effective if you move beyond simple acceptance and adapt your communication style to that of the new cultures you encounter—even integrating aspects of those cultures into your own.[19] A few simple habits can help:

- **Avoid assumptions.** Don't assume that others will act the same way you do, use language and symbols the same way you do, or even operate from the same values and beliefs. For instance, in a comparison of the 10 most important values in three cultures, people from the United States had *no* values in common with people from Japanese or Arab cultures.[20]
- **Avoid judgments.** When people act differently, don't conclude that they are in error or that their way is invalid or inferior.
- **Acknowledge distinctions.** Don't ignore the differences between another person's culture and your own.

Unfortunately, overcoming ethnocentrism and stereotyping is not a simple task, even for people who are highly motivated to do so. Moreover, research suggests that people often have beliefs and biases that they're not even aware of—and that may even conflict with the beliefs they *think* they have. (To see if you have some of these *implicit beliefs*, visit the Project Implicit website, at **https://implicit.harvard.edu/implicit**, and take some of the simple online tests.)[21]

Recognizing Variations in a Diverse World

You can begin to learn how people in other cultures want to be treated by recognizing and accommodating eight main types of cultural differences: contextual, legal and ethical, social, nonverbal, age, gender, religious, and ability.

CONTEXTUAL DIFFERENCES

Every attempt at communication occurs within a **cultural context**, the pattern of physical cues, environmental stimuli, and implicit understanding that convey meaning between two members of the same culture. However, cultures around the world vary widely in the role that context plays in communication.

In a **high-context culture**, people rely less on verbal communication and more on the context of nonverbal actions and environmental setting to convey meaning. For instance, a Chinese speaker expects the receiver to discover the essence of a message and uses indirectness and metaphor to provide a web of meaning.[22] The indirect style can be a source of confusion during discussions with people from low-context cultures, who are more accustomed to receiving direct answers. Also, in high-context cultures, the rules of everyday life are rarely explicit; instead, as individuals grow up, they learn how to recognize situational cues (such as gestures and tone of voice) and how to respond as expected.[23] The primary role of communication in high-context cultures is building relationships, not exchanging information.[24]

In a **low-context culture** such as the United States, people rely more on verbal communication and less on circumstances and cues to convey meaning. In such cultures, rules and expectations are usually spelled out through explicit statements such as "Please wait until I'm finished" or "You're welcome to browse."[25] The primary task of communication in low-context cultures is exchanging information.[26]

Stereotyping is assigning generalized attributes to an individual on the basis of membership in a particular group.

Cultural pluralism is the acceptance of multiple cultures on their own terms.

You can avoid ethnocentrism and stereotyping by avoiding assumptions and judgments and by accepting differences.

3 **LEARNING OBJECTIVE**
Explain the importance of recognizing cultural variations and list eight categories of cultural differences.

Cultural context is the pattern of physical cues, environmental stimuli, and implicit understanding that conveys meaning between members of the same culture.

High-context cultures rely heavily on nonverbal actions and environmental setting to convey meaning; low-context cultures rely more on explicit verbal communication.

Negotiations between businesspeople in low-context and high-context cultures can be hampered by the different communication styles of the two cultures.
Source: © Blend Images/Alamy.

Contextual differences are apparent in the way businesspeople approach situations such as decision making, problem solving, negotiating, interaction among levels in the organizational hierarchy, and socializing outside the workplace.[27] For instance, in low-context cultures, businesspeople tend to focus on the results of the decisions they face, a reflection of the cultural emphasis on logic and progress (for example, "Will this be good for our company? For my career?"). In comparison, higher-context cultures emphasize the means or the method by which a decision will be made. Building or protecting relationships can be as important as the facts and information used in making the decisions.[28] Consequently, negotiators working on business deals in such cultures may spend most of their time together building relationships rather than hammering out contractual details.

The distinctions between high and low context are generalizations, of course, but they are important to keep in mind as guidelines. Communication tactics that work well in a high-context culture may backfire in a low-context culture and vice versa.

LEGAL AND ETHICAL DIFFERENCES

Cultural context influences legal and ethical behavior, which in turn can affect communication. For example, the meaning of business contracts can vary from culture to culture. While a manager from a U.S. company would tend to view a signed contract as the end of the negotiating process, with all the details hammered out, his or her counterpart in many Asian cultures might view the signed contract as an agreement to do business—and only then begin to negotiate the details of the deal.[29]

As you conduct business around the world, you'll find that legal systems and ethical standards differ from culture to culture. Making ethical choices across cultures can seem complicated, but you can keep your messages ethical by applying four basic principles:[30]

- **Actively seek mutual ground.** To allow the clearest possible exchange of information, both parties must be flexible and avoid insisting that an interaction take place strictly in terms of one culture or another.
- **Send and receive messages without judgment.** To allow information to flow freely, both parties must recognize that values vary from culture to culture, and they must trust each other.
- **Send messages that are honest.** To ensure that information is true, both parties must see things as they are—not as they would like them to be. Both parties must be fully aware of their personal and cultural biases.
- **Show respect for cultural differences.** To protect the basic human rights of both parties, each must understand and acknowledge the other's needs and preserve each other's dignity by communicating without deception.

Honesty and respect are cornerstones of ethical communication, regardless of culture.

SOCIAL DIFFERENCES

Formal rules of etiquette are explicit and well defined, but informal rules are learned through observation and imitation.

The nature of social behavior varies among cultures, sometimes dramatically. Some behavioral rules are formal and specifically articulated (table manners are a good example), and others are informal and learned over time (such as the comfortable distance to stand from a colleague during a discussion). The combination of formal and informal rules influences the overall behavior of most people in a society most of the time. In addition to the factors already discussed, social norms can vary from culture to culture in the following areas:

- **Attitudes toward work and success.** In the United States, for instance, a widespread view is that material comfort earned by individual effort is a sign of superiority and that people who work hard are better than those who don't.
- **Roles and status.** Culture influences the roles that people play, including who communicates with whom, what they communicate, and in what way. For example, people in the United States show respect by addressing top managers as "Mr. Roberts" or "Ms. Gutierrez." However, people in China are addressed according to their official titles, such as "President" or "Manager."[31]
- **Use of manners.** What is polite in one culture may be considered rude in another. For instance, asking a colleague "How was your weekend?" is a common way of making small talk in the United States, but the question sounds intrusive to people in cultures in which business and private lives are seen as separate spheres.
- **Concepts of time.** People in low-context cultures see time as a way to plan the business day efficiently, often focusing on only one task during each scheduled period and viewing time as a limited resource. However, executives from high-context cultures often see time as more flexible. Meeting a deadline is less important than building a business relationship.[32]
- **Future orientation.** Successful companies tend to have a strong *future orientation*, planning for and investing in the future, but national cultures around the world vary widely in this viewpoint. Some societies encourage a long-term outlook that emphasizes planning and investing—making sacrifices in the short term for the promise of better outcomes in the future. Others are oriented more toward the present, even to the point of viewing the future as hopelessly remote and not worth planning for.[33]
- **Openness and inclusiveness.** At both the national level and within smaller groups, cultures vary on how open they are to accepting people from other cultures and people who don't necessarily fit the prevailing norms within the culture. An unwillingness to accommodate others can range from outright exclusion to subtle pressures to conform to majority expectations.

> Respect and rank are reflected differently from culture to culture in the way people are addressed and in their working environment.

> The rules of polite behavior vary from country to country.

> Attitudes toward time, such as strict adherence to meeting schedules, can vary throughout the world.

> Cultures around the world exhibit varying degrees of openness toward both outsiders and people whose personal identities don't align with prevailing social norms.

NONVERBAL DIFFERENCES

As discussed in Chapter 2, nonverbal communication can be a reliable guide to determining the meaning of a message—but this situation holds true only if the sender and receiver assign the same meaning to nonverbal signals. For instance, the simplest hand gestures have different meanings in different cultures. A gesture that communicates good luck in Brazil is the equivalent of giving someone "the finger" in Colombia.[34] Don't assume that the gestures you grew up with will translate to another culture; doing so could lead to embarrassing mistakes.

When you have the opportunity to interact with people in another culture, the best advice is to study the culture in advance and then observe the way people behave in the following areas:

- **Greetings.** Do people shake hands, bow, or kiss lightly (on one side of the face or both)? Do people shake hands only when first introduced or every time they say hello or good-bye?
- **Personal space.** When people are conversing, do they stand closer together or farther away than you are accustomed to?
- **Touching.** Do people touch each other on the arm to emphasize a point or slap each other on the back to show congratulations? Or do they refrain from touching altogether?
- **Facial expressions.** Do people shake their heads to indicate "no" and nod them to indicate "yes"? This is what people are accustomed to in the United States, but it is not universal.

> The meaning of nonverbal signals can vary widely from culture to culture, so you can't rely on assumptions.

REAL-TIME UPDATES
Learn More by Watching This Video

Putting culture in context

Enjoy a pictorial tour of cultures around the world as you learn more about communication across the spectrum of cultural context. Go to http://real-timeupdates.com/ebc10 and click on Learn More. If you are using MyBcommLab, you can access Real-Time Updates within each chapter or under Student Study Tools.

- **Eye contact.** Do people make frequent eye contact or avoid it? Frequent eye contact is often taken as a sign of honesty and openness in the United States, but in other cultures it can be a sign of aggressiveness or disrespect.
- **Posture.** Do people slouch and relax in the office and in public, or do they sit up and stand up straight?
- **Formality.** In general, does the culture seem more or less formal than yours?

Following the lead of people who grew up in the culture is not only a great way to learn but a good way to show respect as well.

AGE DIFFERENCES

In U.S. culture, youth is often associated with strength, energy, possibilities, and freedom, and age is sometimes associated with declining powers and the inability to keep pace. However, older workers can offer broader experience, the benefits of important business relationships nurtured over many years, and high degrees of "practical intelligence"—the ability to solve complex, poorly defined problems.[35]

In contrast, in cultures that value age and seniority, longevity earns respect and increasing power and freedom. For instance, in many Asian societies, the oldest employees hold the most powerful jobs, the most impressive titles, and the greatest degrees of freedom and decision-making authority. If a younger employee disagrees with one of these senior executives, the discussion is never conducted in public. The notion of "saving face," of avoiding public embarrassment, is too strong. Instead, if a senior person seems to be in error about something, other employees will find a quiet, private way to communicate whatever information they feel is necessary.[36]

In addition to cultural values associated with various life stages, the multiple generations within a culture present another dimension of diversity. Today's workplaces can have three or even four generations working side by side. Each of these generations has been shaped by dramatically different world events, social trends, and technological advances, so it is not surprising that they often have different values, expectations, and communication habits. For instance, Generation Y workers (see "Us Versus Them: Generational Conflict in the Workplace") have a strong preference for communicating via short electronic messages, but Baby Boomers and Generation Xers sometimes find these brief messages abrupt and impersonal.[37]

GENDER DIFFERENCES

The perception of men and women in business varies from culture to culture, and these differences can affect communication efforts. In some cultures, men hold most or all positions of authority, and women are expected to play a more subservient role. Female executives who visit these cultures may not be taken seriously until they successfully handle challenges to their knowledge, capabilities, and patience.[38]

As more women take on positions of greater responsibility, enlightened company leaders are making a point to examine past assumptions and practices.[39] For instance, company cultures that have been dominated by men for years may have adopted communication habits that some women have difficulty relating to—such as the frequent use of certain sports metaphors or the acceptance of coarse language.

Whatever the culture, evidence suggests that men and women tend to have slightly different communication styles. Broadly speaking, men tend to emphasize content in their communication efforts, whereas women place a higher premium on relationship maintenance.[40] This difference can create friction when two parties in a conversation have different needs and expectations from the interchange. Again, these are broad generalizations that do not apply to every person in every situation, but keeping them in mind can help men and women overcome communication hurdles in the workplace.

RELIGIOUS DIFFERENCES

Religion is a dominant force in many cultures and the source of many differences between cultures.[41] The effort to accommodate employees' life interests on a broader scale has led a number of companies to address the issue of religion in the workplace. As one of the most

Communication styles and expectations can vary widely among age groups, putting extra demands on teams that include workers of varying ages.
Source: Steve Cole/Getty Images—Photodisc-Royalty Free

A culture's views on youth and aging affect how people communicate with one another.

Broadly speaking, men tend to emphasize content in their messages, while women tend to emphasize relationship maintenance.

COMMUNICATING ACROSS CULTURES

Us Versus Them: Generational Conflict in the Workplace

The way people view the world as adults is profoundly shaped by the social and technological trends they experienced while growing up, so it's no surprise that each generation entering the workforce has a different perspective than the generations already at work. Throw in the human tendencies to resist change and to assume that whatever way one is doing something must be the best way to do it, and you have a recipe for conflict. Moreover, generations in a workplace sometimes find themselves competing for jobs, resources, influence, and control. The result can be tension, mistrust, and communication breakdowns.

Lumping people into generations is an imprecise science at best, but it helps to know the labels commonly applied to various age groups and to have some idea of their broad characteristics. These labels are not official, and there is no general agreement on when some generations start and end, but you will see and hear references to the following groups (approximate years of birth shown in parentheses):

- **The Radio Generation** (1925 to 1945). People in this group are beyond what was once considered the traditional retirement age of 65, but many want or need to continue working.
- **Baby Boomers** (1946 to 1964). This large segment of the workforce, which now occupies many mid- and upper-level managerial positions, got its name from the population boom in the years following World War II. The older members of this generation have reached retirement age, but many will continue to work beyond age 65—meaning that younger workers waiting for some of these management spots to open up might have to wait a while longer.
- **Generation X** (1965 to 1980). This relatively smaller "MTV generation" is responsible for many of the innovations that have shaped communication habits today but sometimes feels caught between the large mass of Baby Boomers ahead of them and the younger Generation Y employees entering the workforce. When Generation X does finally get the chance to take over starting in 2015 or 2020, it will be managing in a vastly different business landscape, one in which virtual organizations and networks of independent contractors replace much of the hierarchy inherited from the Baby Boomers.

- **Generation Y** (1981 to 1995). Also known as *millennials*, this youngest generation currently in the workforce is noted for its entrepreneurial instincts and technological savvy. This generation's comfort level with social networks and other Web 2.0 tools is helping to change business communication practices—but is also a source of concern for managers worried about information leaks and employee productivity.
- **Generation Z** (after 1996). If you're a member of Generation Y, those footsteps you hear behind you are coming from Generation Z, also known as *Generation I* (for Internet) or the *Net Generation*. The first full generation to be born after the World Wide Web was invented will be entering the workforce soon.

These brief summaries can hardly do justice to entire generations of workers, but they give you some idea of the different generational perspectives and the potential for communication problems. As with all cultural conflicts, successful communication starts with recognizing and understanding these differences.

CAREER APPLICATIONS

1. How would you resolve a conflict between a Baby Boomer manager who worries about the privacy and productivity aspects of social networking and a Generation Y employee who wants to use these tools on the job?
2. Consider the range of labels from the Radio Generation to the Net Generation. What does this tell you about the possible influence of technology on business communication habits?

Sources: Adapted from Anne Fisher, "When Gen X Runs the Show," *Time*, 14 May 2009, www.time.com; Deloitte, "Generation Y: Powerhouse of the Global Economy," research report, 2009, www.deloitte.com; "Generation Y," Nightly Business Report website, 30 June 2010, www.pbs.org; Sherry Posnick-Goodwin, "Meet Generation Z," *California Educator*, February 2010, www.cta.org; Ernie Stark, "Lost in a Time Warp," *People & Strategy*, Vol. 32 No. 4, 2009, 58–64; Nancy Sutton Bell and Marvin Narz, "Meeting the Challenges of Age Diversity in the Workplace," *The CPA Journal*, February 2007, www.nysscpa.org; Steff Gelston, "Gen Y, Gen X and the Baby Boomers: Workplace Generation Wars," *CIO*, 30 January 2008, www.cio.com; Heather Havenstein, "Generation Y in the Workplace: Digital Natives' Tech Needs Are Changing Companies Forever," *CIO*, 17 September 2008, www.cio.com.

personal and influential aspects of life, religion brings potential for controversy in a work setting. On the one hand, some employees feel they should be able to express their beliefs in the workplace and not be forced to "check their faith at the door" when they come to work. On the other hand, companies want to avoid situations in which openly expressed religious differences cause friction between employees or distract employees from their responsibilities.

To help address such concerns, a growing number of firms, including Ford, Intel, Texas Instruments, and American Airlines, allow employees to form faith-based employee support groups as part of their diversity strategies.[42] In contrast, Procter & Gamble, a company admired for its diversity policies, is among the firms that don't allow organized religious activities at their facilities.[43]

U.S. law requires employers to accommodate employees' religious beliefs to a reasonable degree.

Religion in the workplace is a complex and contentious issue—and it's getting more so every year, at least as measured by a significant rise in the number of religious discrimination lawsuits.[44] Beyond accommodating individual beliefs to a reasonable degree, as required by U.S. law, companies occasionally need to resolve situations that pit one group of employees against another or against the company's policies.[45] As more companies work to establish inclusive workplaces, and as more employees seek to integrate religious convictions into their daily work, you can expect this issue to be increasingly discussed at many companies in the coming years.

ABILITY DIFFERENCES

Colleagues and customers with disabilities that affect communication represent an important aspect of the diversity picture. People whose hearing, vision, cognitive ability, or physical ability to operate electronic devices is impaired can be at a significant disadvantage in today's workplace. As with other elements of diversity, success starts with respect for individuals and sensitivity to differences.

Assistive technologies help employers create more inclusive workplaces and benefit from the contribution of people with physical or cognitive impairments.

Employers can also invest in a variety of *assistive technologies* that help people with disabilities perform activities that might otherwise be difficult or impossible. These technologies include devices and systems that help workers communicate orally and visually, interact with computers and other equipment, and enjoy greater mobility in the workplace. For example, designers can emphasize *web accessibility*, taking steps to make websites more accessible to people whose vision is limited. Assistive technologies create a vital link for thousands of employees with disabilities, giving them opportunities to pursue a greater range of career paths and giving employers access to a broader base of talent. With the United States possibly heading for a serious shortage of workers in a few years, the economy will need all the workers who can make a contribution, and assistive technologies will be an important part of the solution.[46]

Adapting to Other Business Cultures

4 **LEARNING OBJECTIVE**

List four general guidelines for adapting to any business culture.

Whether you're trying to work productively with members of another generation in your own office or with a business partner on the other side of the world, adapting your approach is essential to successful communication. This section offers general advice on adapting to any business culture and specific advice for professionals from other cultures on adapting to U.S. business culture.

GUIDELINES FOR ADAPTING TO ANY BUSINESS CULTURE

You'll find a variety of specific tips in "Improving Intercultural Communication Skills," starting on the next page, but here are four general guidelines that can help all business communicators improve their cultural competency:

An important step in understanding and adapting to other cultures is to recognize the influences that your own culture has on your communication habits.

- **Become aware of your own biases.** Successful intercultural communication requires more than just an understanding of the other party's culture; you need to understand your own culture and the way it shapes your communication habits.[47] For instance, knowing that you value independence and individual accomplishment will help you communicate more successfully in a culture that values consensus and group harmony.
- **Ignore the "Golden Rule."** You probably heard this growing up: "Treat people the way you want to be treated." The problem with the Golden Rule is that other people don't always want to be treated the same way you want to be treated, particularly across cultural boundaries. The best approach: Treat people the way *they* want to be treated.
- **Exercise tolerance, flexibility, and respect.** As IBM's Ron Glover puts it, "To the greatest extent possible, we try to manage our people and our practices in ways that are respectful of the core principles of any given country or organization or culture."[48]
- **Practice patience and maintain a sense of humor.** Even the most committed and attuned business professionals can make mistakes in intercultural communication, so

it is vital for all parties to be patient with one another. As business becomes ever more global, even people in the most tradition-bound cultures are learning to deal with outsiders more patiently and overlook occasional cultural blunders.[49] A sense of humor is a helpful asset as well, allowing people to move past awkward and embarrassing moments. When you make a mistake, simply apologize and, if appropriate, ask the other person to explain the accepted way; then move on.

GUIDELINES FOR ADAPTING TO U.S. BUSINESS CULTURE

If you are a recent immigrant to the United States or grew up in a culture outside the U.S. mainstream, you can apply all the concepts and skills in this chapter to help adapt to U.S. business culture. Here are some key points to remember as you become accustomed to business communication in this country:[50]

- **Individualism.** In contrast to cultures that value group harmony and group success, U.S. culture generally expects individuals to succeed by their own efforts, and it rewards individual success. Even though teamwork is emphasized in many companies, competition between individuals is expected and even encouraged in many cases.

- **Equality.** Although the country's historical record on equality has not always been positive and some inequalities still exist, equality is considered a core American value. This principle applies to race, gender, social background, and age.

- **Privacy and personal space.** Although this appears to be changing somewhat with the popularity of social networking and other personal media, people in the United States are accustomed to a fair amount of privacy. That also applies to their "personal space" at work. For example, they expect you to knock before entering a closed office and to avoid asking questions about personal beliefs or activities until they get to know you well.

- **Time and schedules.** U.S. businesses value punctuality and the efficient use of time. For instance, meetings are expected to start and end at designated times.

- **Religion.** The United States does not have an official state religion. Many religions are practiced throughout the country, and people are expected to respect each other's beliefs.

- **Communication style.** Communication tends to be direct and focused more on content and transactions than on relationships or group harmony.

As with all observations about culture, these are generalizations, of course. Any nation of more than 300 million people will exhibit a wide variety of behaviors. However, following these guidelines will help you succeed in most business communication situations.

The values espoused by American culture include individualism, equality, and privacy.

REAL-TIME UPDATES
Learn More by Watching This Video

Overcoming culture shock

This entertaining five-part video series shares the experience of an Israeli journalist undergoing culture shock when coming to graduate school in New York City, and it offers help and encouragement to anyone living in a new culture for the first time. Go to http://real-timeupdates.com/ebc10 and click on Learn More. If you are using MyBcommLab, you can access Real-Time Updates within each chapter or under Student Study Tools.

Improving Intercultural Communication Skills

Communicating successfully between cultures requires a variety of skills (see Figure 3.3 on the next page). You can improve your intercultural skills throughout your career by studying other cultures and languages, respecting preferences for communication styles, learning to write and speak clearly, listening carefully, knowing when to use interpreters and translators, and helping others adapt to your culture.

 5   LEARNING OBJECTIVE

Identify seven steps you can take to improve your intercultural communication skills.

STUDYING OTHER CULTURES

Effectively adapting your communication efforts to another culture requires not only knowledge about the culture but also the ability and motivation to change your personal habits as needed.[51] Fortunately, you don't need to learn about the whole world all at once. Many companies appoint specialists for specific countries or regions, giving employees a chance to focus on just one culture at a time. Some firms also provide resources to help employees

Successful intercultural communication can require the modification of personal communication habits.

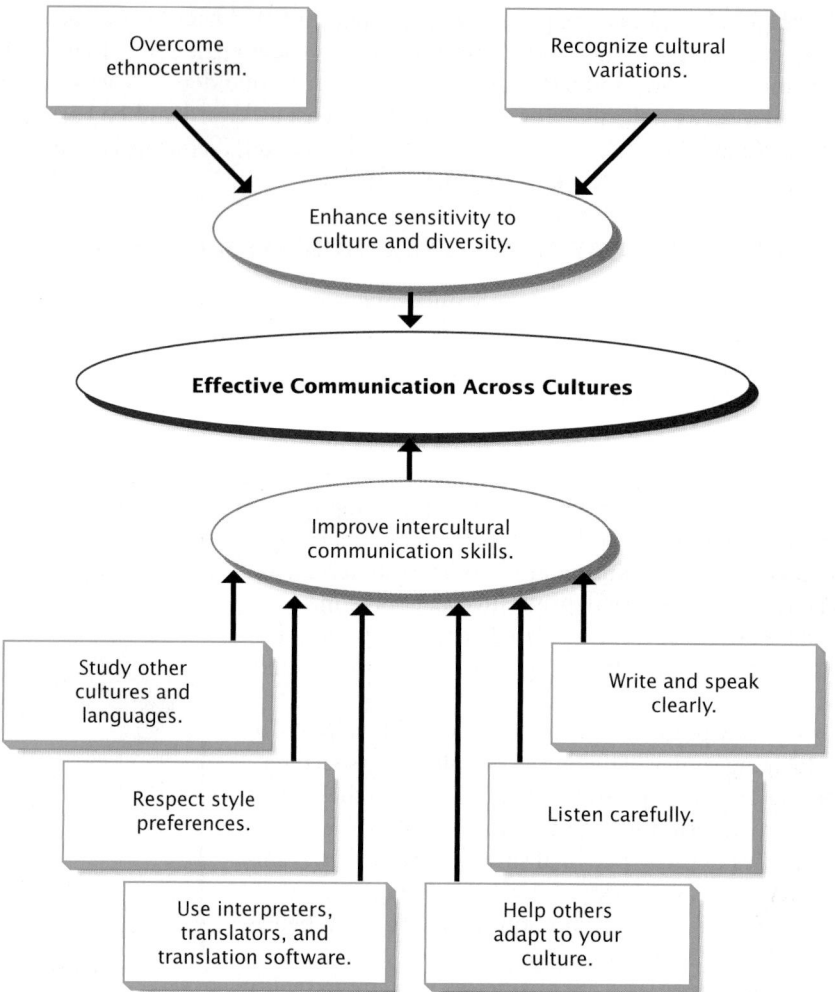

FIGURE 3.3   Components of Successful Intercultural Communication
Communicating in a diverse business environment is not always an easy task, but you can continue to improve your sensitivity and build your skills as you progress in your career.

prepare for interaction with other cultures. On IBM's Global Workforce Diversity intranet site, for instance, employees can click on the GoingGlobal link to learn about customs in specific cultures.[52]

Even a small amount of research and practice will help you get through many business situations. In addition, most people respond positively to honest effort and good intentions, and many business associates will help you along if you show an interest in learning more about their cultures. Don't be afraid to ask questions, either. People will respect your concern and curiosity. You will gradually accumulate considerable knowledge, which will help you feel comfortable and be effective in a wide range of business situations.

Numerous websites (such as www.kwintessential.co.uk) and books offer advice on traveling to and working in specific countries. Also try to sample newspapers, magazines, and even the music and movies of another country. For instance, a movie can demonstrate nonverbal customs even if you don't grasp the language. (However, be careful not to rely solely on entertainment products. If people in other countries based their opinions of U.S. culture only on the silly teen flicks and violent action movies that the United States exports around the globe, what sort of impression do you imagine they'd get?) For some of the key issues to research before doing business in another country, refer to Table 3.1.

Making an effort to learn about another person's culture is a sign of respect.

REAL-TIME UPDATES
Learn More by Watching This PowerPoint Presentation

Essential guidelines for adapting to other business cultures

Learn great etiquette tips for doing business in France, Germany, Japan, Mexico, and Russia. Go to http://real-timeupdates.com/ebc10 and click on Learn More. If you are using MyBcommLab, you can access Real-Time Updates within each chapter or under Student Study Tools.

TABLE 3.1	**Doing Business in Other Cultures**
Action	**Details to Consider**
Understand social customs	• How do people react to strangers? Are they friendly? Hostile? Reserved? • How do people greet each other? Should you bow? Nod? Shake hands? • How do you express appreciation for an invitation to lunch, dinner, or someone's home? Should you bring a gift? Send flowers? Write a thank-you note? • Are any phrases, facial expressions, or hand gestures considered rude? • How do you attract the attention of a waiter? Do you tip the waiter? • When is it rude to refuse an invitation? How do you refuse politely? • What topics may or may not be discussed in a social setting? In a business setting? • How do social customs dictate interaction between men and women? Between younger people and older people?
Learn about clothing and food preferences	• What occasions require special attire? • What colors are associated with mourning? Love? Joy? • Are some types of clothing considered taboo for one gender or the other? • How many times a day do people eat? • How are hands or utensils used when eating? • Where is the seat of honor at a table?
Assess political patterns	• How stable is the political situation? • Does the political situation affect businesses in and out of the country? • Is it appropriate to talk politics in social or business situations?
Understand religious and social beliefs	• To which religious groups do people belong? • Which places, objects, actions, and events are sacred? • Do religious beliefs affect communication between men and women or between any other groups? • Is there a tolerance for minority religions? • How do religious holidays affect business and government activities? • Does religion require or prohibit eating specific foods? At specific times?
Learn about economic and business institutions	• Is the society homogeneous or heterogeneous? • What languages are spoken? • What are the primary resources and principal products? • Are businesses generally large? Family controlled? Government controlled? • What are the generally accepted working hours? • How do people view scheduled appointments? • Are people expected to socialize before conducting business?
Appraise the nature of ethics, values, and laws	• Is money or a gift expected in exchange for arranging business transactions? • Do people value competitiveness or cooperation? • What are the attitudes toward work? Toward money? • Is politeness more important than factual honesty?

STUDYING OTHER LANGUAGES

Consider what it must be like to work at IBM, where the global workforce speaks more than 165 languages. Without the ability to communicate in more than one language, how could this diverse group of people ever conduct business? As commerce continues to become more globalized and many countries become more linguistically diverse, the demand for multilingual communicators continues to grow as well. The ability to communicate in more than one language can make you a more competitive job candidate and open up a wider variety of career opportunities (see "The Web 2.0 Way to Learn a New Language").

Even if your colleagues or customers in another country speak your language, it's worth the time and energy to learn common phrases in theirs. Learning the basics not only helps you get through everyday business and social situations but also demonstrates your commitment to the business relationship. After all, the other person probably spent years learning your language.

Finally, don't assume that people from two countries who speak the same language speak it the same way. The French spoken in Quebec and other parts of Canada is often noticeably different from the French spoken in France. Similarly, it's often said that the United States and the United Kingdom are two countries divided by a common language. For instance, *period* (punctuation), *elevator*, and *gasoline* in the United States are *full stop*, *lift*, and *petrol* in the United Kingdom.

English is the most prevalent language in international business, but don't assume that everyone understands it or speaks it the same way.

BUSINESS COMMUNICATION 2.0
The Web 2.0 Way to Learn a New Language

Taking classes with a skilled teacher and getting real-life practice while living in another country are proven ways to learn a new language, but what if neither of these options is available to you? Thanks to the growth of social networking technology and other Web 2.0 communication tools, independent language learners now have a multitude of online learning options.

Palabea (www.palabea.net) is a great example of the possibilities of the Web 2.0 approach to learning. By adapting social networking concepts for the unique demands of language learning, this service offers numerous helpful features:

- **Online chat with other language learners.** No matter what language you're trying to learn, someone somewhere in the world speaks it—and is trying to learn your language. Palabea lets you connect and help each other with text, audio, or video chat.
- **Connections to native speakers in your local area.** Palabea can connect you with nearby native speakers of the language you're trying to learn.

- **User-generated content.** Palabea offers a growing collection of podcasts, video lectures, documents, and other learning tools, all contributed by members.
- **Virtual classrooms.** Just as online meeting systems let business colleagues collaborate in real time on reports and other documents, Palabea's virtual classrooms let members meet online to review and correct translations and other projects.

Palabea is just one of many online resources that can help language learners. For example, the Free Language website (http://freelanguage.org) offers links to free resources for several dozen languages.

CAREER APPLICATIONS

1. How could a multinational company such as IBM benefit from the capabilities offered by Palabea and similar websites?
2. As a manager, would you be comfortable having employees use a free service such as Palabea before sending them on important overseas assignments? Why or why not?

Sources: Adapted from Palabea, accessed 30 October 2011, www.palabea.net; Free Language, accessed 30 October 2011, http://freelanguage.org.

RESPECTING PREFERENCES FOR COMMUNICATION STYLE

Communication style—including the level of directness, the degree of formality, media preferences, and other factors—varies widely from culture to culture. Knowing what your communication partners expect can help you adapt to their particular style. Once again, watching and learning are the best ways to improve your skills. However, you can infer some generalities by learning more about the culture. For instance, U.S. workers typically prefer an open and direct communication style; they find other styles frustrating or suspect. Directness is also valued in Sweden as a sign of efficiency; but, unlike with discussions in the United States, heated debates and confrontations are unusual. Italian, German, and French executives don't put colleagues at ease with praise before they criticize—doing so seems manipulative to them. However, professionals from high-context cultures, such as Japan or China, tend to be less direct.[53] Finally, in general, business correspondence in other countries is often more formal than the style used by U.S. businesspeople (see Figure 3.4).

WRITING CLEARLY

Writing clearly is always important, of course, but it is essential when you are writing to people whose first language is not English. Follow these recommendations to make sure your message can be understood:[54]

Clarity and simplicity are essential when writing to or speaking with people who don't share your native language.

- **Choose words carefully.** Use precise words that don't have the potential to confuse with multiple meanings. For instance, the word *right* has several dozen different meanings and usages, so look for a synonym that conveys the specific meaning you intend, such as *correct, appropriate, desirable, moral, authentic,* or *privilege.*[55]
- **Be brief.** Use simple sentences and short paragraphs, breaking information into smaller chunks that are easier for readers to process.
- **Use plenty of transitions.** Help readers follow your train of thought by using transitional words and phrases (see page 181). For example, tie related points together with expressions such as *in addition* and *first, second,* and *third.*

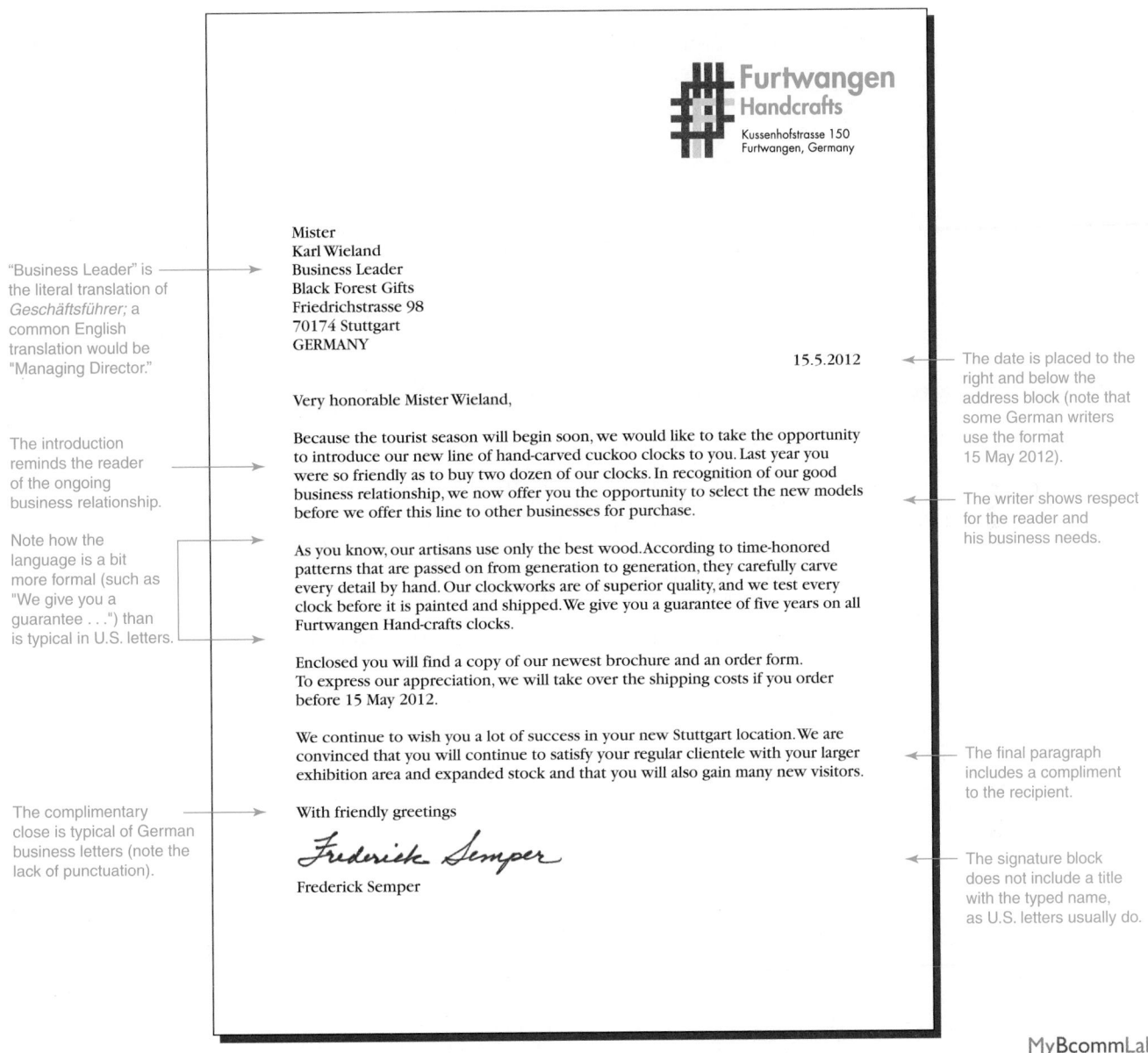

FIGURE 3.4   Effective German Business Letter (Translated)
In Germany, business letters usually open with a reference to the business relationship and close with a compliment to the recipient. In this letter written by a supplier to a nearby retailer, you can see that the tone is more formal than would typically be used in the United States.

Apply Figure 3.4's key concepts by revising a new document. Go to Chapter 3 in www .pearsoninternationaleditions.com/mybcommlab and select Document Makeovers.

- **Address international correspondence properly.** Refer to Tables A.1 through A.5 in Appendix A for an explanation of different address elements and salutations commonly used in various countries.
- **Cite numbers and dates carefully.** In the United States, 12-05-11 means December 5, 2011, but in many other countries, it means May 12, 2011. Dates in Japan and China are usually expressed with the year first, followed by the month and then the day; therefore, to write December 5, 2011, in Japan, write it as 2011-12-05. Similarly, in the United States and Great Britain 1.000 means one with three decimal places, but it means one thousand in many European countries.
- **Avoid slang, idiomatic phrases, and business jargon.** Everyday speech and writing are full of slang and **idiomatic phrases**—phrases that mean more than the sum of their literal parts. Examples from U.S. English include "Off the top of my head" and "More bang for the buck." Your audience may have no idea what you're talking about when you use such phrases.

The title and address are not formatted in French style.

Using the reader's first name is much too informal for most French business correspondence.

The use of slang and idioms throughout the message (such as *hammered, bottlenecks, shut-eye, crunch, struck out,* and *jam*) creates the potential for confusion.

The writer fails to provide a total of the extra expenses.

Bottom of the letter fails to alert the reader that other documents are enclosed.

This U.S. date format is not the format typically used by French writers.

This unnecessarily dramatic and long description of weather problems wastes the reader's time.

Important information on costs is buried in a long-winded paragraph.

The closing paragraph focuses on the writer's needs, not the reader's.

La Cristallerie

Troy Halford,   U.S. Sales Representative
163 Pico Boulevard
Los Angeles, CA 90032
Voice: (213) 975-8924
Fax: (213) 860-3489
halford@home.com

April 7, 2012

Mr. Pierre Coll
Director of Accounting
La Cristallerie
22 Marne Blvd.
Beaune, France 21200

Dear Pierre:

I know you've had gorgeous spring weather, with sunny skies and balmy days. But here in the States, it's been a spring of another color. We've been hammered with storms, flooding, and even late snow. Travel over here has been a night-mare, which is why you'll find my expenses a bit elevated this month.

I realize that you've asked all the reps to reduce rather than increase our expenses, but there were extenuating circumstances this last month. All the bad weather we've been having has caused major bottlenecks, with flights canceled and people forced to sleep in the terminals wherever they could find a spot.

After being stuck in the Chicago airport for 18 hours straight, I was desperate for a hotshower and some shut-eye, so I decided to wait out the crunch in a hotel. I know that hotels near airports are expensive, but I struck out trying to book a cheaper room intown. The bottom line is I had to spend extra funds for a hotel at $877; meals, which came to some $175; $72 just in transportation from the terminal to the hotel, and extra phone calls totaling $38.

I appreciate your understanding these unique circumstances. I was really in a jam.

Sincerely,

Troy Halford

Troy Halford
U.S. Sales Rep

FIGURE 3.5   Ineffective Intercultural Letter
This letter from a U.S. sales representative to a manager in France exhibits several intercultural mistakes, including the informal tone and use of U.S. slang. Compare this with the improved version in Figure 3.6.

Humor does not "travel well" because it usually relies on intimate knowledge of a particular culture.

- **Avoid humor and references to popular culture.** Jokes and references to popular entertainment usually rely on culture-specific information that might be completely unknown to your audience.

Although some of these differences may seem trivial, meeting the expectations of an international audience illustrates both knowledge of and respect for the other cultures (see Figures 3.5 and 3.6).

SPEAKING AND LISTENING CAREFULLY

Languages vary considerably in the significance of tone, pitch, speed, and volume, which can create challenges for people trying to interpret the explicit meaning of words themselves as well as the overall nuance of a message. The English word *progress* can be a noun or a verb, depending on which syllable you accent. In Chinese, the meaning of the word *mà* changes depending on the speaker's tone; it can mean *mother, pileup, horse,* or *scold.* And routine Arabic speech can sound excited or angry to an English-speaking U.S. listener.[56]

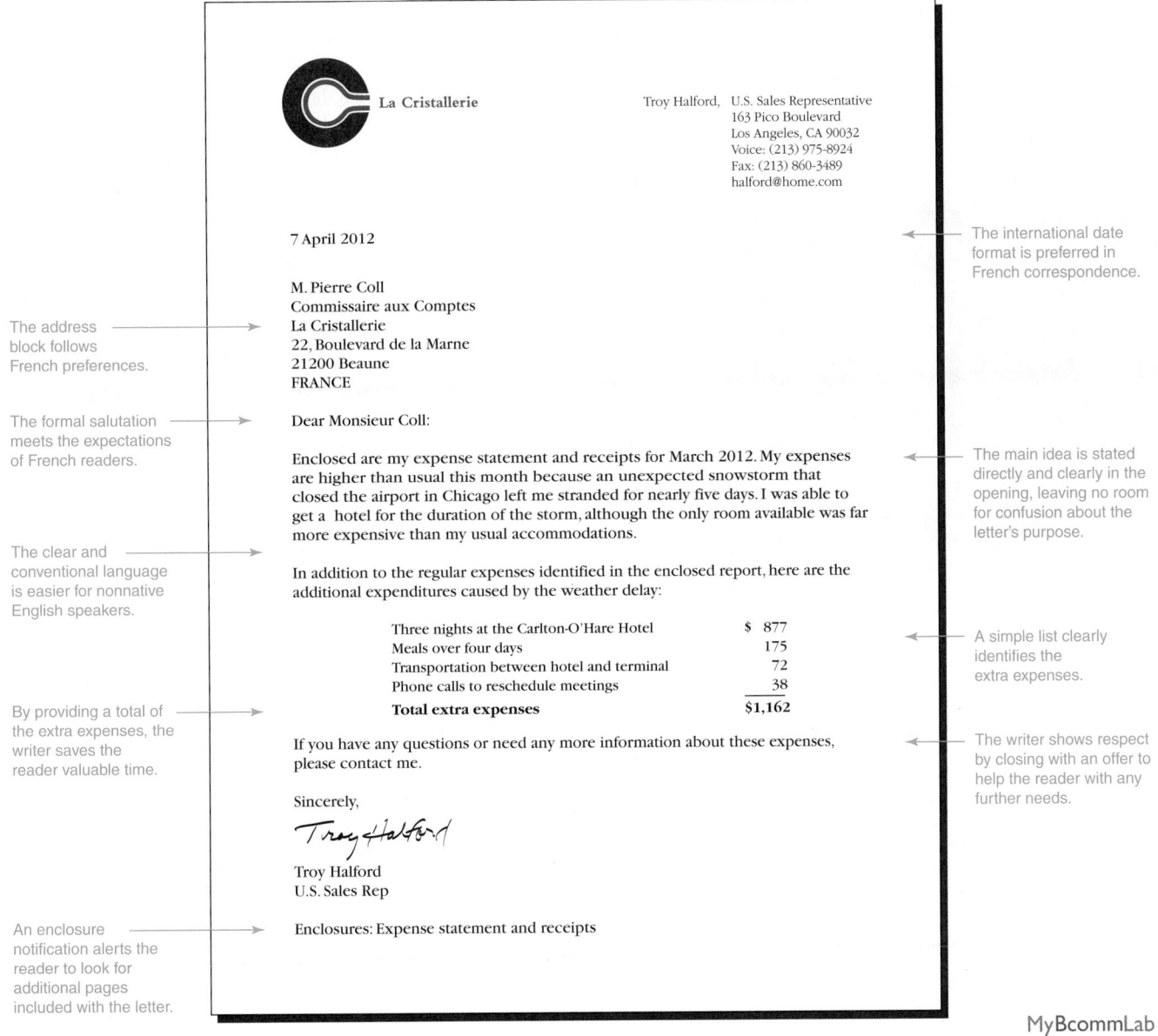

FIGURE 3.6   Effective Intercultural Letter
This version of the letter in Figure 3.5 follows French standards for correspondence and is also easier to read and to scan.

Apply Figure 3.6's key concepts by revising a new document. Go to Chapter 3 in www .pearsoninternationaleditions.com/mybcommlab and select Document Makeovers.

When talking with people whose native language is different from yours, remember that the processing of even everyday conversations can be difficult. For instance, speakers from the United States are notorious for stringing together multiple words into a single, mystifying pseudoword, such as turning "Did you eat yet?" into "Jeetyet?" The French language uses a concept known as *liaison*, in which one word is sometimes intentionally joined with the next. Without a lot of listening practice, new French speakers have a hard time telling when one word ends and the next one begins.

To be more effective in intercultural conversations, remember these tips: (1) Speak slowly and clearly; (2) don't rephrase until it's obviously necessary (immediately rephrasing something you've just said doubles the translation workload for the listener); (3) look for and ask for feedback to make sure your message is getting through; (4) don't talk down to the other person by overenunciating words or oversimplifying sentences; and (5) at the end of the conversation, double-check to make sure you and the listener agree on what has been said and decided.

As a listener, you'll need some practice to get a sense of vocal patterns. The key is simply to accept what you hear first, without jumping to conclusions about meaning or

Speaking clearly and getting plenty of feedback are two of the keys to successful intercultural conversations.

To listen more effectively in intercultural situations, accept what you hear without judgment and let people finish what they have to say.

香港中文大學
The Chinese University of Hong Kong

Microsoft

Experienced international speakers, such as Microsoft Chairman Bill Gates, are careful to incorporate culture and language variations into their communication efforts. *Source:* © AsiaPix/Alamy.

For important business communication, use a professional interpreter (for oral communication) or translator (for written communication).

Help others adapt to your culture; it will create a more productive workplace and teach you about their cultures as well.

motivation. Let other people finish what they have to say. If you interrupt, you may miss something important. You'll also show a lack of respect. If you do not understand a comment, ask the person to repeat it. Any momentary awkwardness you might feel in asking for extra help is less important than the risk of unsuccessful communication.

USING INTERPRETERS, TRANSLATORS, AND TRANSLATION SOFTWARE

You may encounter business situations that require using an *interpreter* (for spoken communication) or a *translator* (for written communication). Interpreters and translators can be expensive, but skilled professionals provide invaluable assistance for communicating in other cultural contexts.[57] Some companies use *back-translation* to ensure accuracy. Once a translator encodes a message into another language, a different translator retranslates the same message into the original language. This back-translation is then compared with the original message to discover any errors or discrepancies.

A variety of software products and websites offer translation capabilities, from individual words and phrases to documents and entire webpages. Although none of these tools can translate as well as human experts, they can often give you the overall gist of a message.[58]

HELPING OTHERS ADAPT TO YOUR CULTURE

Everyone can contribute to successful intercultural communication. Whether a younger person is unaccustomed to the formalities of a large corporation or a colleague from another country is working on a team with you, look for opportunities to help people fit in and adapt their communication style. For example, if a nonnative English speaker is making mistakes that could hurt his or her credibility, you can offer advice on the appropriate words and phrases to use. Most language learners truly appreciate this sort of assistance, as long as it is offered in a respectful manner. Moreover, chances are that while you're helping, you'll learn something about the other person's culture and language, too.

You can also take steps to simplify the communication process. For instance, oral communication in a second language is usually more difficult than written forms of communication, so instead of asking a foreign colleague to provide information in a conference call, you could ask for a written response instead of or in addition to the live conversation.

For a brief summary of ideas to improve intercultural communication in the workplace, see "Checklist: Improving Intercultural Communication Skills." For additional information on communicating in a world of diversity, visit http://real-timeupdates.com/ebc10 and click on Chapter 3.

✓ **Checklist**   **Improving Intercultural Communication Skills**

- Understand your own culture so that you can recognize its influences on your communication habits.
- Study other cultures so that you can appreciate cultural variations.
- Study the languages of people with whom you communicate, even if you can learn only a few basic words and phrases.
- Help nonnative speakers learn your language.
- Respect cultural preferences for communication style.
- Write clearly, using brief messages, simple language, generous transitions, and appropriate international conventions.

- Avoid slang, humor, and references to popular culture.
- Speak clearly and slowly, giving listeners time to translate your words.
- Ask for feedback to verify that communication was successful.
- Listen carefully and ask speakers to repeat anything you don't understand.
- Use interpreters and translators for important messages.

ON THE JOB: SOLVING COMMUNICATION DILEMMAS AT **IBM**

Source: Courtesy of International Business Machines Corporation. Unauthorized use not permitted.

Ron Glover is responsible for overall diversity planning and strategy at IBM, but every manager throughout the company is expected to foster a climate of inclusion and support for employees of every cultural background. As a team leader in one of IBM's software development labs, you're learning to exercise sound business judgment and use good listening skills to help resolve situations that arise within your diverse group of employees. How would you address each of these challenges?

1. You have a new hardware designer who has developed an idea for the architecture of processors that dispenses with the need for separate RAM chips. Unfortunately, your designer is not at all fluent in English and the notes which accompany the design are unintelligible. You can see from the diagrams that he is onto something very good, but the rest is a mystery. How will you get his notes into shape for presentation to the board?
   a. Give your designer a deadline and a dictionary, and tell him to write the simplest sentences he can think of.
   b. Find someone who speaks his language and get them to help him write the notes.
   c. Send him to take a crash course in written English and hope that he learns enough to get through the presentation.
   d. Rely on the visuals to make your point.

2. You're the assistant human resources manager, and your boss tells you about a group of employees who all come from the same town and belong to the same religious sect. They are in different departments but recently in a team building exercise, they met at a company guest house and became friends. Now, they sit together in the cafeteria and talk loudly in their native language which no one else understands. The HR manager is concerned about the effect on the other employees and wants you to deal with it. What do you think is the best option for solving the problem?
   a. Call the clique into your office and give them all a tough speech about workplace etiquette.
   b. Do nothing. The employees are excited to have discovered so many people from 'home' in the company, but after a while the novelty will wear off and they will get back to normal.
   c. Watch them closely and catch them in the act a few times. Give them disapproving looks. They will realize they aren't invisible.
   d. Speak to them individually and in confidence about workplace culture and make them see what's wrong in their behavior.

3. One of your employees prominently displays icons of faith on her desk and has put up religious posters not only in her office but in the adjacent coffee-making area as well. She has been known to pray in public also. Other than that she is an inoffensive person who is very good at looking after the troubled members of the company and making them feel better. Now, a new recruit has taken the desk next to her and calls you up to complain about the 'religious nutcase' with whom she shares the room. What should you do?
   a. Tell your senior employee to take down the posters and clear her desk, at least till the new person feels more comfortable.
   b. Tell your new recruit she should be more tolerant and that she's overreacting.
   c. Promise to move the new recruit to another room (although this will take a few days to organize).
   d. Take them both out to lunch and try to thaw the ice between them.

4. You've been assigned to a new liaison department that deals with overseas partners, and the team members come from a variety of cultures. Your boss's writing style was much appreciated in his previous department. However, recently his memos have been generating a lot of confusion with your team members. He calls you in and shows you a memo he's about to circulate. This reads as follows: "Good day, my fellow travelers, let's take a moment to look down the road to how we fared this time last year. This department had just kicked off and everything was in a shambles. A year of hard graft has passed and everything is now ship shape. We should all pat ourselves on the back for having climbed this Everest of a challenge, and, to spread the good cheer, I'm giving you all a sweetener for the holidays: a bonus! That should beat the Monday morning blues.'" He gives you the task of making this more readable to the new team. You come up with four possible drafts. Which do you think does the job best?
   a. "To all team members. To commemorate our first year of successful operation, everyone is going to get a bonus this month. Good work, everyone."
   b. "Fellow team members, I take this opportunity to congratulate you on a wonderful performance. Today is the anniversary of the setting up of this department, and the team has made great progress since we commenced operations. In celebration of that fact, everyone is to receive a gratuity with their compensation package this month. This reflects the tremendous value this department has added to the workings of the company."
   c. "Team, you have done us all proud. Who would have thought that such a diverse bunch of people could come together and work so well? We may have had our disagreements, but who does not? We all deserve a share in the bounty we've worked so hard to create, so everyone is getting a bonus this month. Well done."
   d. "Everything comes to he who waits. So they say, and we've waited a year for the fruits of our labor. Good news; they're here! Because of our great performance, we are all getting a bonus."

LEARNING OBJECTIVES CHECKUP

Assess your understanding of the principles in this chapter by reading each learning objective and studying the accompanying exercises. For fill-in-the-blank items, write the missing text in the blank provided; for multiple-choice items, circle the letter of the correct answer. You can check your responses against the answer key on page AK-1.

Objective 3.1: Discuss the opportunities and challenges of intercultural communication.

1. Which of the following factors is a significant reason U.S. business professionals often need to understand the cultures of other countries?
   a. Companies have to show that they have been trained in dealing with other cultures before they can be granted export licenses.
   b. Greater cultural exposure is an inevitable consequence of many companies shifting their back-office overseas.
   c. Immigrants from these countries may form part of the local workforce.
   d. The value of overseas markets is enormous and many companies already do a lot of business in them.

2. Which of the following is a benefit of a multicultural workforce?
   a. The company gets to benefit from its employees' different work styles, approaches, and ideas.
   b. Companies get the right personnel to tap new and emerging markets overseas.
   c. Conflict may arise if only two cultures are represented: the more cultures there are, the less chance there is of polarization.
   d. A and B but not C.

3. A culturally rich workforce, composed of employees representing a wide range of ethnicities, religions, ages, physical abilities, languages, and other factors
   a. Makes it harder to reach consensus.
   b. Makes heavy demands on additional resources, like childcare and medical plans.
   c. Requires tact and patience but pays off in greater productivity and more intelligent solutions.
   d. Is suitable only for export-oriented companies.

Objective 3.2: Define *culture,* explain how culture is learned, and define *ethnocentrism* and *stereotyping.*

4. Which of these definitions is closest to the idea of culture?
   a. A complete system of being which includes religious beliefs, language, social rules and roles, life patterns, philosophies, and self images.
   b. A particular way of dressing, behaving, and thinking
   c. A social construct with no real basis in human psychology
   d. A category of artistic creativity including music, dance, literature, painting, sculpture, drama, and poetry

5. Which of the following is *not* an example of a cultural group?
   a. Players of a particular online multiplayer game.
   b. Muslims.
   c. Kindergarten children.
   d. Biker gangs.

6. Culture is learned from
   a. Family members
   b. Explicit teaching by others in the culture
   c. Observations of the behavior of others in the culture
   d. All of the above

7. _____ is the tendency to judge all other groups according to the standards, behaviors, and customs of one's own group.

8. _____ is the mistake of assigning a wide range of generalized attributes to individuals on the basis of their membership in a particular culture or social group, without considering an individual's unique characteristics.

9. Which of the following is one of several techniques you can use to make sure you don't fall into the traps of ethnocentrism and stereotyping?
   a. Try not to speak a foreign language unless you are expert enough to write opinion pieces for the newspapers in it.
   b. See your own culture as one of many possible ones, and accept that it may not be the best system on every count.
   c. Make sure that "diverse" people don't rise beyond a certain point in your organization.
   d. Strictly penalize anyone who expresses a prejudice on company time.

Objective 3.3: Explain the importance of recognizing cultural variations, and list eight categories of cultural differences.

10. In business, recognizing cultural differences is important because
    a. Doing so helps reduce the chances for misunderstanding
    b. Someone from another culture may try to take advantage of your ignorance
    c. If you don't, you'll be accused of being politically incorrect
    d. Doing so helps you become more ethnocentric

11. An example of low-context cultural communication would be
    a. Someone using metaphors to convey meaning
    b. Someone insisting that the details of an agreement can be worked out later
    c. Someone vigorously arguing his point of view in a problem-solving situation
    d. Someone encouraging socializing before entering into official negotiations

12. Which of the following is generally true about high-context cultures?
    a. Employees work shorter hours in such cultures because context allows them to communicate less often.
    b. People rely less on verbal communication and more on the context of nonverbal actions and environmental setting to convey meaning.
    c. People rely more on verbal communication and less on the context of nonverbal actions and environmental setting to convey meaning.
    d. The rules of everyday life are explicitly taught to all people within the culture.

13. Differing attitudes toward greeting gestures, personal space, touching, facial expression, eye contact, posture, and formality are common examples of _____ differences between cultures.

Objective 3.4: List four general guidelines for adapting to any business culture.

14. Why is understanding your own culture an important step in learning to relate well with other cultures?
   a. Understanding your own culture is important because it helps you recognize biases you have that shape your communication habits.
   b. Understanding your own culture is important because it helps you identify the ways that other cultures are inferior (or at least might be inferior) to your own.
   c. Understanding your own culture is important because it helps you identify the ways that other cultures are superior (or at least might be superior) to your own.
   d. Understanding your own culture is not important when you are trying to reach out to other cultures.

Objective 3.5: Identify seven steps you can take to improve your intercultural communication skills.

15. When communicating orally to those who speak English as a second language, you should make a habit to always
   a. Immediately rephrase every important point you make in order to give your listeners two options to choose from
   b. Speak louder if listeners don't seem to understand you
   c. Ignore the other person's body language
   d. Rephrase your key points if you observe body language that suggests a lack of understanding

16. Understanding the nuances of a culture can take years to learn, so the best approach when preparing to communicate with people in a culture that you don't know well is to
   a. Learn as much as you can from websites, travel guides, and other resources and not be afraid to ask for help while you are communicating in that new culture
   b. Learn as much as you can from websites, travel guides, and other resources but never ask for help because doing so will only show everyone how ignorant you are
   c. Learn as much as you can from television shows and movies that feature the other culture; the combination of spoken words, visuals, and music is the best way to learn a culture
   d. Not worry about cultural variations; you'll never have time to understand them all, so your energy is better spent on other business issues

17. When writing for audiences who don't speak the same native language as you speak, you can improve communication by
   a. Spelling out numbers rather than writing them as figures
   b. Using simple sentences and careful word choices
   c. Using long paragraphs to reduce the number of visual breaks on the page
   d. Doing all of the above

18. When you are writing for multilanguage audiences, humor
   a. Should be used often because it makes your audience feel welcome on a personal level
   b. Should rarely, if ever, be used because humor is one of the most difficult elements of communication to encode or decode in a second language
   c. Should never be used because movies and other entertainment products rarely cross over national boundaries
   d. Should be used at least once per letter to show that you appreciate your audience as human beings

MyBcommLab

Log on to www.pearsoninternationaleditions .com/mybcommlab to access study and assessment aids associated with this chapter. If you are not using MyBcommLab, you can access the Real-Time Updates at http:// real-timeupdates.com/ebc10.

CHAPTER OUTLINE

Understanding the Opportunities and Challenges of Communication in a Diverse World
The Opportunities in a Global Marketplace
The Advantages of a Diverse Workforce
The Challenges of Intercultural Communication

Developing Cultural Competency
Understanding the Concept of Culture
Overcoming Ethnocentrism and Stereotyping

Recognizing Variations in a Diverse World
Contextual Differences
Legal and Ethical Differences
Social Differences
Nonverbal Differences
Age Differences
Gender Differences
Religious Differences
Ability Differences

Adapting to Other Business Cultures
Guidelines for Adapting to Any Business Culture
Guidelines for Adapting to U.S. Business Culture

Improving Intercultural Communication Skills
Studying Other Cultures
Studying Other Languages
Respecting Preferences for Communication Style
Writing Clearly
Speaking and Listening Carefully
Using Interpreters, Translators, and Translation Software
Helping Others Adapt to Your Culture

LEARNING OBJECTIVES

1 Discuss the opportunities and challenges of intercultural communication. [page 107]

2 Define *culture*, explain how culture is learned, and define *ethnocentrism* and *stereotyping*. [page 110]

3 Explain the importance of recognizing cultural variations, and list eight categories of cultural differences. [page 111]

4 List four general guidelines for adapting to any business culture. [page 116]

5 Identify seven steps you can take to improve your intercultural communication skills. [page 117]

KEY TERMS

cultural competency An appreciation for cultural differences that affect communication and the ability to adjust one's communication style to ensure that efforts to send and receive messages across cultural boundaries are successful

cultural context The pattern of physical cues, environmental stimuli, and implicit understanding that convey meaning between two members of the same culture

cultural pluralism The practice of accepting multiple cultures on their own terms

culture A shared system of symbols, beliefs, attitudes, values, expectations, and norms for behavior

diversity All the characteristics and experiences that define each of us as individuals

ethnocentrism The tendency to judge other groups according to the standards, behaviors, and customs of one's own group

high-context culture Culture in which people rely less on verbal communication

and more on the context of nonverbal actions and environmental setting to convey meaning

idiomatic phrases Phrases that mean more than the sum of their literal parts; such phrases can be difficult for nonnative speakers to understand

intercultural communication The process of sending and receiving messages between people whose cultural backgrounds could lead them to interpret verbal and nonverbal signs differently

low-context culture Culture in which people rely more on verbal communication and less on circumstances and cues to convey meaning

stereotyping Assigning a wide range of generalized attributes to an individual on the basis of membership in a particular culture or social group

xenophobia Fear of strangers and foreigners

 **Checklist**

Improving Intercultural Communication Skills

- Understand your own culture so that you can recognize its influences on your communication habits.
- Study other cultures so that you can appreciate cultural variations.
- Study the languages of people with whom you communicate, even if you can learn only a few basic words and phrases.
- Help nonnative speakers learn your language.
- Respect cultural preferences for communication style.

- Write clearly, using brief messages, simple language, generous transitions, and appropriate international conventions.
- Avoid slang, humor, and references to popular culture.
- Speak clearly and slowly, giving listeners time to translate your words.
- Ask for feedback to verify that communication was successful.
- Listen carefully and ask speakers to repeat anything you don't understand.
- Use interpreters and translators for important messages.

APPLY YOUR KNOWLEDGE

To review chapter content related to each question, refer to the indicated Learning Objective.

1. Is the United States a homogeneous culture? Explain. [LO-1]
2. Make a list of the top five priorities in your life (for example, fame, wealth, family, spirituality, peace of mind, individuality, artistic expression). Compare your list with the priorities that appear to be valued in the culture in which you are currently living. (You can be as broad or as narrow as you like in defining *culture* for this exercise, such as overall U.S. culture or culture in your college or university.) Do your personal priorities align with the culture's priorities? If not, how might this disparity affect your communication with other members of the culture? [LO-2]
3. How would you define cultural pluralism? Is there cultural pluralism in the room where you are sitting? In your family? In your hometown? [LO-3]
4. Discuss the cultural assumptions you see at work in the production of the following: a women's magazine, a fancy-dress party, a five star hotel. [LO-4]
5. Imagine that you are a foreigner from a particular country or culture. Watch your favorite movie or TV show (choose one that is rooted in your own culture). What kind of impression would a foreigner get of your culture from the show or movie? [LO-5]

PRACTICE YOUR SKILLS

Active links for all websites in this chapter can be found on MyBcommLab; see your User Guide for instructions on accessing the content for this chapter. Each activity is labeled according to the primary skill or skills you will need to use. To review relevant chapter content, you can refer to the indicated Learning Objective. In some instances, supporting information will be found in another chapter, as indicated.

Message for Analysis: Adapting to Cultural Differences [LO-5]

Your boss is very excited to soon be welcoming some Irish employees recently transferred to your department from the company's Belfast branch. He is a committed Hibernophile—that is, a lover of Ireland—but you are rather apprehensive that the Ireland he loves exists only in his imagination. Before he meets the new employees, he wants to send them an email message, and he shows it to you for your comments. What would you suggest your boss change in the message—and why? Would you consider this message to be culturally sensitive? Why or why not? (Hint: Do some research on Northern Ireland and its idiom and history.)

> "I'm pleased to be welcoming you all to green and fair America where your ancestors migrated so many centuries ago. I myself am part-Irish from County Cork, and we still go to the church that Father O'Rourke set up a hundred years ago. If you ever need a pint of stout or a good crack session, my door is always open."

Exercises

1. **Intercultural Communication: Recognizing Cultural Variations [LO-1], [LO-3], [LO-4]** Review the definitions of the

generations on page 115. Based on your year of birth, in which generation do you belong? Do you feel a part of this generation? Why or why not? If you were born outside the United States, do the generational boundaries seem accurate to you? Now consider the biases that you might have regarding other generations. For example, if you are a member of Generation Y, what do you think about the Baby Boomers and their willingness to embrace new ideas? Identify several of your generational biases that could create friction in the workplace. Summarize your responses to these questions in a post on your class blog or an email message to your instructor.

2. **Intercultural Communication: Adapting to Cultural Variations [LO-2]** You are a new manager at K & J Brick, a masonry products company that is now run by the two sons of the man who founded it 50 years ago. For years, the co-owners have invited the management team to a wilderness lodge for a combination of outdoor sports and annual business planning meetings. You don't want to miss the event, but you know that the outdoor activities weren't designed for someone like you, whose physical impairments prevent participation in the sporting events. Draft a short email message to the rest of the management team, suggesting changes to the annual event that will allow all managers to participate.

3. **Intercultural Communication: Recognizing Cultural Variations [LO-2]** Differences in gender, age, and physical abilities contribute to the diversity of today's workforce. Working with a classmate, role-play a conversation in which

   a. a woman is being interviewed for a job by a male personnel manager.

   b. an older person is being interviewed for a job by a younger personnel manager.

   c. an employee who is a native speaker of English is being interviewed for a job by a hiring manager who is a recent immigrant with relatively poor English skills.

   How did differences between the applicant and the interviewer shape the communication? What can you do to improve communication in such situations?

4. **Intercultural Communication: Recognizing Cultural Variations [LO-3]** You represent a German breakfast cereal company that's negotiating to buy nuts and dried fruits from a Lebanese family-run group of plantations. In your first meeting, you explain that your company has very high standards of quality control and you will expect to station your own experts at the packing and handling facility. This results in silence while the brothers who run the company look silently at each other. You try to assure them that you will not interfere with their operations. The brothers promise to meet you in a day, but the next day, repeated phone calls to them only produce evasions. What cultural differences may be interfering with effective communication in this situation? (Germany is considered a low-context culture; Lebanon is high-context.) In a brief email message to your instructor or a post on your class blog, share your analysis.

5. **Intercultural Communication: Writing for Multiple-Language Audiences [LO-5]** Reading English-language content written by non-native speakers of English can be a good

reminder of the challenges of communicating in another language. The writing can be confusing or even amusing at first glance, but the key to remember here is that your writing might sound just as confusing or amusing to someone else if your roles were reversed.

Find an English-language newspaper based in a non-English speaking country and look at its website. Does it sound as though it was written by someone adept at English? Are there differences in language between news and features? Are there any instances of a use of "mixed" language or native slang? Select a section of text, at least several sentences long, and rewrite it to sound more "American." Submit the original text and your rewritten version to your instructor.

6. **Intercultural Communication: Writing for Multiple-Language Audiences; Collaboration: Team Projects [LO-5], Chapter 2** With a team assigned by your instructor, review the Facebook pages of five companies, looking for words and phrases that might be confusing to a nonnative speaker of English. If you (or someone on the team) is a nonnative speaker, explain to the team why those word choices could be confusing. Choose three sentences, headlines, company slogans, or other pieces of text that contain potentially confusing words and rewrite them to minimize the chances of misinterpretation. As much as possible, try to retain the tone of the original—although you may find that this is impossible in some instances. Use Google Docs to compile the original selections and your revised versions, then email the documents to your instructor.

7. **Intercultural Communication: Speaking with Multiple-Language Audiences; Collaboration: Team Projects [LO-5], Chapter 2** Working with two other students, prepare a list of 10 examples of slang (in your own language) that might be misinterpreted or misunderstood during a business conversation with someone from another culture. Next to each example, suggest other words you might use to convey the same message. Do the alternatives mean *exactly* the same as the original slang or idiom? Submit your list of original words and suggested replacements, with an explanation of why each replacement is better than the original.

8. **Intercultural Communication: Studying Cultures [LO-5]** Choose a specific country, such as India, Portugal, Bolivia, Thailand, or Nigeria, with which you are not familiar. Research the culture and write a brief summary for your class blog of what a U.S. manager would need to know about concepts of personal space and rules of social behavior in order to conduct business successfully in that country.

9. **Intercultural Communication: Writing for Multiple-Language Audiences [LO-5]** Explore the powers and limitations of free online translation services such as Yahoo! Babel Fish (http://babelfish.yahoo.com) or Google Translate (http://translate.google.com). Enter a sentence from this chapter, such as "Local markets are opening to worldwide competition as businesses of all sizes look for new growth opportunities outside their own countries." First, translate the sentence from English to Spanish and click to complete the translation. Next, copy the Spanish version and paste it into the translation entry box and back-translate it from Spanish to English. Now repeat this test for

German, French, Italian, or another language. Did the sentence survive the round trip? Does it still sound like normal business writing when translated back into English?

(1) What are the implications for the use of automated translation services for international correspondence? (2) Would you feel comfortable using an online tool such as this to translate an important business message? (3) How might you use this website to sharpen your intercultural communication skills? Summarize your findings in a brief report.

10. **Intercultural Communication: Speaking with Multiple-Language Audiences; Media Skills: Podcasting [LO-5], Chapter 7** Your company was one of the first to use podcasting as a business communication tool. Executives frequently record messages (such as monthly sales summaries) and post them on the company's intranet site; employees from the 14 offices in Europe, Asia, and North America then download the files to their music players or other devices and listen to the messages while riding the train to work, eating lunch at their desks, and so on. Your boss asks you to draft an amusing opening statement for a podcast that will announce new facilities for crèches and carpooling for employees. She reviews your script and hands it back with a gentle explanation that it needs to be revised to be intelligible (and inoffensive) for all audiences. Improve the following statement in as many ways as you can:

> Howdy, ladies. Company rugrats can climb out of the playpen now; we're starting a 'take-your-kid-to-work' plan for all those single moms with baby on board bumper stickers. Each office will have a crèche with an onsite nurse and activities for the little tykes. Downside: bawling Junior is no longer an excuse to take the day off! If your kid won't sleep, forget dawn patrol: bring him here, we'll read him a round of sales figures and he'll be off to dreamland in no time while you wheel and deal with the big boys.

EXPAND YOUR SKILLS

Critique the Professionals

Find an online business document—such as a company webpage, blog post, Facebook Info tab, or LinkedIn profile—that you believe commits an intercultural communication blunder by failing to consider the needs of at least some of its target readers. For example, a website might use slang or idiomatic language that could confuse some readers, or it might use language that offends some readers. In a post on your class blog, share the text you found and explain why you think it does not succeed as effective intercultural communication. Be sure to include a link back to the original material.

Sharpening Your Career Skills Online

Bovée and Thill's Business Communication Web Search, at http://businesscommunicationblog.com/websearch, is a unique research tool designed specifically for business communication research. Use the Web Search function to find a website, video, podcast, or PowerPoint presentation that offers advice on communicating with business contacts in another country or culture. Write a brief email message to your instructor, describing the item that you found and summarizing the career skills information you learned from it.

IMPROVE YOUR GRAMMAR, MECHANICS, AND USAGE

The following exercises help you improve your knowledge of and power over English grammar, mechanics, and usage. Turn to the Handbook of Grammar, Mechanics, and Usage at the end of this book and review all of Section 1.3 (Verbs). Then look at the following 10 items. Circle the letter of the preferred choice in the following groups of sentences. (Answers to these exercises appear on page AK-3.)

1. Which sentence contains a verb in the present perfect form?
   a. Sheela should know his name, because she has attended every meeting.
   b. Sheela should know his name, because she attends every meeting.

2. Which sentence contains a verb in the simple past form?
   a. He stays in New York before he shifted to Atlanta.
   b. He stayed in New York before he shifted to Atlanta.

3. Which sentence contains a verb in the simple future form?
   a. Next month, John is going to come here to teach us about emerging trends in technology.
   b. Next month, John is coming here to teach us about emerging trends in technology.

4. Which sentence is in the active voice?
   a. Jonathan Wright will conduct the exam.
   b. The exam will be conducted by Jonathan Wright.

5. Which sentence is in the passive voice?
   a. I did not receive your note.
   b. Your note was not received by me.

6. Which sentence contains the correct verb form?
   a. Everyone gets their visiting cards printed by Annie.
   b. Everyone get their visiting cards printed by Annie.

7. Which sentence contains the correct verb form?
   a. Neither the director nor the team leader is here.
   b. Neither the director nor the team leader are here.

8. Which sentence contains the correct verb form?
   a. F&B Accounts are listed in the directory.
   b. F&B Accounts is listed in the directory.

9. Which sentence contains the correct verb form?
   a. When printing the banner, 4 feet is sufficient.
   b. When printing the banner, 4 feet are sufficient.

10. Which sentence contains the correct verb form?
    a. About 75 percent of the students wants to attend the conference.
    b. About 75 percent of the students want to attend the conference.

REFERENCES

1. IBM website, accessed 4 January 2011, www.ibm.com; "No. 10 IBM Corp.: Why It's on the DiversityInc Top 50," DiversityInc.com, 13 March 2009, http://diversityinc.com; "IBM Innovation Embraces All Races, Cultures and Genders," Diversity Careers website, accessed 16 August 2008, www .diversitycareers.com; Regina Tosca and Rima Matsumoto, "Diversity and Inclusion: A Driving Force for Growth and Innovation at IBM," 2 February 2007, Hispanic Association on Corporate Responsibility website, www.hacr.org; "Executive Corner: Letter from IBM's Vice President, Global Workforce Diversity," IBM website, www.ibm .com; "IBM—Diversity as a Strategic Imperative," TWI website, accessed 6 July 2005, www.diversityatwork.com; Cliff Edwards, "The Rewards of Tolerance," *BusinessWeek*, 15 December 2003, www.businessweek.com; David A. Thomas, "IBM Finds Profit in Diversity," *HBS Working Knowledge*, 27 September 2004, http://hbswk.hbs.edu; "IBM Diversity Executive to Speak at the University of Virginia," *University of Virginia News*, 7 November 2003, www.virginia.edu.

2. Michael R. Carrell, Everett E. Mann, and Tracey Honeycutt Sigler, "Defining Workforce Diversity Programs and Practices in Organizations: A Longitudinal Study," *Labor Law Journal*, Spring 2006, 5–12.

3. "Dimensions of Diversity—Workforce," Merck website, accessed 4 January 2011, www.merck.com.

4. "Top Ten Countries with Which the U.S. Trades," U.S. Census Bureau website, accessed 29 December 2010, www .census.gov.

5. Nancy R. Lockwood, "Workplace Diversity: Leveraging the Power of Difference for Competitive Advantage," *HR Magazine*, June 2005, Special Section 1–10.

6. Alan Kline, "The Business Case for Diversity," *USbanker*, May 2010, 10–11.

7. Podcast Interview with Ron Glover, IBM Website, accessed 17 August 2008, www.ibm.com.

8. "More Than 300 Counties Now 'Majority–Minority,'" press release, U.S. Census Bureau website, 9 August 2007, www .census.gov; Robert Kreitner, *Management*, 9th ed. (Boston: Houghton Mifflin, 2004), 84.

9. Linda Beamer and Iris Varner, *Intercultural Communication in the Workplace*, 2nd ed. (New York: McGraw-Hill Irwin, 2001), xiii.

10. Tracy Novinger, *Intercultural Communication, A Practical Guide* (Austin, Tex.: University of Texas Press, 2001), 15.

11. Larry A. Samovar and Richard E. Porter, "Basic Principles of Intercultural Communication," in *Intercultural Communication: A Reader*, 6th ed., edited by Larry A. Samovar and Richard E. Porter (Belmont, Calif.: Wadsworth, 1991), 12.

12. Arthur Chin, "Understanding Cultural Competency," *New Zealand Business*, December 2010/January 2011, 34–35; Sanjeeta R. Gupta, "Achieve Cultural Competency,"

Training, February 2009, 16–17; Diane Shannon, "Cultural Competency in Health Care Organizations: Why and How," *Physician Executive*, September–October 2010, 15–22.

13. Beamer and Varner, *Intercultural Communication in the Workplace*, 3.

14. "Languages of United States," Ethnologue website, accessed 29 December 2010, www.ethnologue.com.

15. Philip R. Harris and Robert T. Moran, *Managing Cultural Differences*, 3rd ed. (Houston: Gulf, 1991), 394–397, 429–430.

16. Lillian H. Chaney and Jeanette S. Martin, *Intercultural Business Communication*, 2nd ed. (Upper Saddle River, N.J.: Prentice Hall, 2000), 6.

17. Beamer and Varner, *Intercultural Communication in the Workplace*, 4.

18. Chaney and Martin, *Intercultural Business Communication*, 2nd ed., 9.

19. Richard L. Daft, *Management*, 6th ed. (Cincinnati: Thomson South-Western, 2003), 455.

20. Lillian H. Chaney and Jeanette S. Martin, *Intercultural Business Communication*, 4th ed. (Upper Saddle River, N.J.: Pearson Prentice Hall, 2007), 53.

21. Project Implicit website, accessed 29 December 2010, http://implicit.harvard.edu/implicit.

22. Linda Beamer, "Teaching English Business Writing to Chinese-Speaking Business Students," *Bulletin of the Association for Business Communication* 57, no. 1 (1994): 12–18.

23. Edward T. Hall, "Context and Meaning," in *Intercultural Communication*, 6th ed., edited by Larry A. Samovar and Richard E. Porter (Belmont, Calif.: Wadsworth, 1991), 46–55.

24. Daft, *Management*, 459.

25. Charley H. Dodd, *Dynamics of Intercultural Communication*, 3rd ed. (Dubuque, Ia.: Brown, 1991), 69–70.

26. Daft, *Management*, 459.

27. Hannah Seligson, "For American Workers in China, a Culture Clash," *New York Times*, 23 December 2009, accessed 1 January 2011, www.nytimes.com.

28. Beamer and Varner, *Intercultural Communication in the Workplace*, 230–233.

29. Ed Marcum, "More U.S. Businesses Abandon Outsourcing Overseas," *Seattle Times*, 28 August 2010, www.seattletimes.com.

30. Guo-Ming Chen and William J. Starosta, *Foundations of Intercultural Communication* (Boston: Allyn & Bacon, 1998), 288–289.

31. Robert O. Joy, "Cultural and Procedural Differences That Influence Business Strategies and Operations in the People's Republic of China," *SAM Advanced Management Journal*, Summer 1989, 29–33.

32. Chaney and Martin, *Intercultural Business Communication*, 2nd ed., 122–123.

33. Mansour Javidan, "Forward-Thinking Cultures," *Harvard Business Review*, July–August 2007, 20.

34. Novinger, *Intercultural Communication: A Practical Guide*, 54.

35. Peter Coy, "Old. Smart. Productive." *BusinessWeek*, 27 June 2005, www.businessweek.com; Beamer and Varner, *Intercultural Communication in the Workplace*, 107–108.

36. Beamer and Varner, *Intercultural Communication in the Workplace*, 107–108.

37. Steff Gelston, "Gen Y, Gen X and the Baby Boomers: Workplace Generation Wars," *CIO*, 30 January 2008, www.cio.com.

38. Tonya Vinas, "A Place at the Table," *IndustryWeek*, 1 July 2003, 22.

39. Daft, *Management*, 445.

40. John Gray, *Mars and Venus in the Workplace* (New York: HarperCollins, 2002), 10, 25–27, 61–63.

41. Chaney and Martin, *Intercultural Business Communication*, 4th ed., 62.

42. Fara Warner, "Professionals Tap a Higher Power in the Workplace," *Workforce Management*, April 2011, 20–22, 24–25.

43. "The DiversityInc Top 50 Companies for Diversity," DiversityInc, accessed 10 May 2011, www.diversityinc.com; Todd Henneman, "A New Approach to Faith at Work," *Workforce Management*, October 2004, 76–77.

44. Warner, "Professionals Tap a Higher Power in the Workplace"; Mark D. Downey, "Keeping the Faith," *HR Magazine*, January 2008, 85–88.

45. Vadim Liberman, "What Happens When an Employee's Freedom of Religion Crosses Paths with a Company's Interests?" *Conference Board Review*, September/October 2007, 42–48.

46. IBM Accessibility Center, accessed 24 August 2006, www-03.ibm.com/able; AssistiveTech.net, accessed 24 August 2006, www.assistivetech.net; Business Leadership Network website, accessed 24 August 2006, www.usbln.org; National Institute on Disability and Rehabilitation Research website, accessed 24 August 2006, www.ed.gov/about/offices/list/osers/nidrr; Rehabilitation Engineering & Assistive Technology Society of North America website, accessed 24 August 2006, www.resna.org.

47. Daphne A. Jameson, "Reconceptualizing Cultural Identity and its Role in Intercultural Business Communication," *Journal of Business Communication*, July 2007, 199–235.

48. Leslie Knudson, "Diversity on a Global Scale," *HR Management*, accessed 17 August 2008, www.hrmreport.com.

49. Craig S. Smith, "Beware of Green Hats in China and Other Cross-Cultural Faux Pas," *New York Times*, 30 April 2002, C11.

50. Sana Reynolds and Deborah Valentine, *Guide for Internationals: Culture, Communication, and ESL* (Upper Saddle River, N.J.: Pearson Prentice Hall, 2006), 3–11, 14–19, 25.

51. P. Christopher Earley and Elaine Mosakowsi, "Cultural Intelligence," *Harvard Business Review*, October 2004, 139–146.

52. Wendy A. Conklin, "An Inside Look at Two Diversity Intranet Sites: IBM and Merck," *The Diversity Factor*, Summer 2005.

53. Bob Nelson, "Motivating Workers Worldwide," *Global Workforce*, November 1998, 25–27.

54. Mona Casady and Lynn Wasson, "Written Communication Skills of International Business Persons," *Bulletin of the Association for Business Communication* 57, no. 4 (1994): 36–40.

55. Lynn Gaertner-Johnston, "Found in Translation," Business Writing blog, 25 November 2005, accessed 18 August 2008, www.businesswritingblog.com.

56. Myron W. Lustig and Jolene Koester, *Intercultural Competence*, 4th ed. (Boston: Allyn & Bacon, 2003), 196.

57. Wilfong and Seger, *Taking Your Business Global*, 232.

58. Sheridan Prasso, ed., "It's All Greek to These Sites," *BusinessWeek*, 22 July 2002, 18.

PART 2 | Applying the Three-Step Writing Process

CHAPTER 4	**Planning Business Messages**
CHAPTER 5	**Writing Business Messages**
CHAPTER 6	**Completing Business Messages**

Every professional can learn to write more effectively while spending less time and energy creating successful messages. Discover a proven writing process that works for everything from blog posts to formal reports to your résumé. With a bit of practice, you'll be using the process to write more effectively without even thinking about it.

ZanyZeus/Shutterstock

LEARNING OBJECTIVES After studying this chapter, you will be able to

1 Describe the three-step writing process

2 Explain why it's important to analyze a communication situation in order to define your purpose and profile your audience before writing a message

3 Discuss information-gathering options for simple messages, and identify three attributes of quality information

4 List the factors to consider when choosing the most appropriate medium for a message

5 Explain why good organization is important to both you and your audience, and list the tasks involved in organizing a message

MyBcommLab Where you see MyBcommLab in this chapter, go to www.pearsoninternationaleditions.com/mybcommlab for additional activities on the topic being discussed.

ON THE JOB: COMMUNICATING AT **H&R BLOCK**

The tax services giant H&R Block uses social media extensively to build relationships with clients and customers. The company's YouTube channel, for example, offers videos with tax tips and gives H&R Block employees the opportunity to answer questions from viewers.
Source: Provided courtesy of H&R Block Inc.

Adding Some Excitement to a Most Unexciting Task

Many U.S. taxpayers don't think about their taxes until they absolutely have to, and then they want to think about taxes as little as possible. In this context of extreme apathy, H&R Block certainly has a challenge on its hands when it wants to communicate with taxpayers about tax preparation products and services.

H&R Block is the leading tax preparation firm in the United States, with a range of options for virtually every class of taxpayer. Those who want to avoid the laborious chore of doing their own taxes can hand the job over to a tax professional in one of the company's 13,000 offices nationwide. In contrast, those taxpayers who are willing to do most or all of the work themselves can choose from a variety of digital alternatives, including both computer software and web-based solutions.

Although tax preparation is one of the least exciting consumer experiences, H&R Block has developed a reputation for creative communication efforts that make use of the latest innovations in social media. For example, in a recent product launch that noted media expert Shel Israel characterized as "among the most extensive business-to-consumer social media campaigns in history," the company used a variety of techniques to connect with potential customers: videos on YouTube (including a contest for user-created videos), profiles on MySpace and Facebook, Twitter microblogging, and "H&R Block Island" in the virtual world Second Life.

The innovations aren't simply about technology, however. In the spirit of Business Communication 2.0 (see Chapter 1), the company emphasizes a conversational, two-way approach in which the company listens as carefully as it speaks. For example, staffers follow a large number of Twitter users who have asked tax questions in the past, with the goal of maintaining an open channel of communication.

Particularly coming from a company that has a stodgy, old-school image in the minds of many people, this cutting-edge communication has surprised more than a few social media observers. Perhaps even more amazing is that H&R Block has actually generated some public interest in the field of tax preparation.[1]

www.hrblock.com

Understanding the Three-Step Writing Process

The emphasis that H&R Block (profiled in the chapter opener) puts on connecting with customers is a lesson that applies to business messages for all stakeholders. Fortunately, by following the process introduced in this chapter, you can learn to create successful messages that meet audience needs and highlight your skills as a perceptive business professional.

The three-step writing process (see Figure 4.1) helps ensure that your messages are both *effective* (meeting your audience's needs and getting your points across) and *efficient* (making the best use of your time and your audience's time):

- **Step 1: Planning business messages.** To plan any message, first *analyze the situation* by defining your purpose and developing a profile of your audience. When you're sure what you need to accomplish with your message, *gather information* that will meet your audience's needs. Next, *select the right medium* (oral, written, visual, or electronic) to deliver your message. Then *organize the information* by defining your main idea, limiting your scope, selecting the direct or indirect approach, and outlining your content. Planning messages is the focus of this chapter.

1 LEARNING OBJECTIVE

Describe the three-step writing process.

The three-step writing process consists of planning, writing, and completing your message.

1 Plan → 2 Write → 3 Complete

Analyze the Situation
Define your purpose and develop an audience profile.

Gather Information
Determine audience needs and obtain the information necessary to satisfy those needs.

Select the Right Medium
Select the best medium for delivering your message.

Organize the Information
Define your main idea, limit your scope, select a direct or an indirect approach, and outline your content.

Adapt to Your Audience
Be sensitive to audience needs by using a "you" attitude, politeness, positive emphasis, and unbiased language. Build a strong relationship with your audience by establishing your credibility and projecting your company's preferred image. Control your style with a conversational tone, plain English, and appropriate voice.

Compose the Message
Choose strong words that will help you create effective sentences and coherent paragraphs.

Revise the Message
Evaluate content and review readability, edit and rewrite for conciseness and clarity.

Produce the Message
Use effective design elements and suitable layout for a clean, professional appearance.

Proofread the Message
Review for errors in layout, spelling, and mechanics.

Distribute the Message
Deliver your message using the chosen medium; make sure all documents and all relevant files are distributed successfully.

Figure 4.1   The Three-Step Writing Process
This three-step process will help you create more effective messages in any medium. As you get more practice with the process, it will become easier and more automatic.
Sources: Adapted from Kevin J. Harty and John Keenan, *Writing for Business and Industry: Process and Product* (New York: Macmillan Publishing Company, 1987), 3–4; Richard Hatch, *Business Writing* (Chicago: Science Research Associates, 1983), 88–89; Richard Hatch, *Business Communication Theory and Technique* (Chicago: Science Research Associates, 1983), 74–75; Center for Humanities, *Writing as a Process: A Step-by-Step Guide* (Mount Kisco, N.Y.: Center for Humanities, 1987); Michael L. Keene, *Effective Professional Writing* (New York: D. C. Heath, 1987), 28–34.

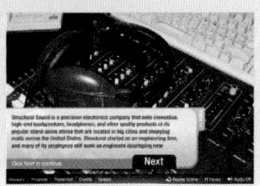

- **Step 2: Writing business messages.** After you've planned your message, *adapt to your audience* with sensitivity, relationship skills, and an appropriate writing style. Then you're ready to *compose your message* by choosing italic words, creating effective sentences, and developing coherent paragraphs. Writing business messages is discussed in Chapter 5.
- **Step 3: Completing business messages.** After writing your first draft, *revise your message* by evaluating the content, reviewing readability, and editing and rewriting until your message comes across concisely and clearly, with correct grammar, proper punctuation, and effective format. Next, *produce your message.* Put it into the form that your audience will receive and review all design and layout decisions for an attractive, professional appearance. *Proofread* the final product to ensure high quality and then *distribute your message.* Completing business messages is discussed in Chapter 6.

Throughout this book, you'll learn how to apply these steps to a wide variety of business messages: short messages such as social network and blog posts (Chapters 7 through 10), longer messages such as reports and wikis (Chapters 11 through 13), oral presentations (Chapter 14), and the employment messages you can use to build a great career (Chapters 15 and 16).

OPTIMIZING YOUR WRITING TIME

The more you use the three-step writing process, the more intuitive and automatic it will become. You'll also get better at allotting your time for each task during a writing project. Start by figuring out the total amount of time you have to spend. Then, as a general rule, set aside roughly 50 percent of that time for planning, 25 percent for writing, and 25 percent for completing.

As a starting point, allot half your available time for planning, one-quarter for writing, and one-quarter for completing your messages—but adjust these percentages for each project.

Allotting half your time for planning might seem excessive, but as the next section explains, careful planning usually saves time overall by focusing your writing and reducing the need to rework. Of course, the ideal time split varies from project to project. Simpler and shorter messages require less planning than long reports, websites, and other complex projects. Also, the time required to produce and distribute messages can vary depending on the media, the size of the audience, and other factors. However, start with the 50-25-25 split as a guideline and use your best judgment for each project.

PLANNING EFFECTIVELY

Trying to save time by skimping on planning usually costs you more time in the long run.

As soon as the need to create a message appears, inexperienced communicators are often tempted to dive directly into writing. However, skipping or shortchanging the planning stage often creates extra work and stress later in the process. First, thoughtful planning is necessary to make sure you provide the right information in the right format to the right people. Taking the time to understand your audience members and their needs helps you find and assemble the facts they're looking for and deliver that information in a concise and compelling way. Second, with careful planning, the writing stage is faster, easier, and a lot less stressful. Third, planning can save you from embarrassing blunders that could hurt your company or your career.

Analyzing the Situation

2   LEARNING OBJECTIVE

Explain why it's important to analyze a communication situation in order to define your purpose and profile your audience before writing a message.

Every communication effort takes place in a particular situation, meaning you have a specific message to send to a specific audience under a specific set of circumstances. For example, describing your professional qualifications in an email message to an executive in your own company differs significantly from describing your qualifications in your LinkedIn profile. The email message is likely to be focused on one specific goal, such as explaining why you would be a good choice to head up a major project, and you have the luxury of focusing on the needs of a single, personally identifiable reader. In contrast, your social networking profile could have multiple goals, such as connecting with your peers in other companies and presenting your qualifications to potential employers, and it might be viewed by hundreds or thousands of readers, each with his or her own needs.

The underlying information for these two messages could be roughly the same, but the level of detail to include, the tone of the writing, the specific word choices—these and other choices you need to make will differ from one situation to another. Making the right choices starts with defining your purpose clearly and understanding your audience's needs.

DEFINING YOUR PURPOSE

All business messages have a **general purpose**: to inform, to persuade, or to collaborate with the audience. This purpose helps define the overall approach you'll need to take, from gathering information to organizing your message. Within the scope of its general purpose, each message also has a **specific purpose**, which identifies what you hope to accomplish with your message and what your audience should do or think after receiving your message. For instance, is your goal simply to update your audience about some upcoming event, or do you want people to take immediate action? State your specific purpose as precisely as possible, even to the point of identifying which audience members should respond, how they should respond, and when.

After you have defined your specific purpose, take a moment for a reality check. Decide whether that purpose merits the time and effort required for you to prepare and send the message—and for your audience to spend the time required to read it, view it, or listen to it. Test your purpose by asking these four questions:

- **Will anything change as a result of your message?** Don't contribute to information overload by sending messages that won't change anything. For instance, if you don't like your company's latest advertising campaign but you're not in a position to influence it, sending a critical message to your colleagues won't change anything and won't benefit anyone.
- **Is your purpose realistic?** Recognizing whether a goal is realistic is an important part of having good business sense. For example, if you request a raise while the company is struggling, you might send the message that you're not tuned into the situation around you.
- **Is the time right?** People who are busy or distracted when they receive your message are less likely to pay attention to it. Many professions and departments have recurring cycles in their workloads, for instance, and messages sent during peak times may be ignored.
- **Is your purpose acceptable to your organization?** Your company's business objectives and policies, and even laws that apply to your particular industry, may dictate whether a particular purpose is acceptable.

When you are satisfied that you have a clear and meaningful purpose and that this is a smart time to proceed, your next step is to understand the members of your audience and their needs.

DEVELOPING AN AUDIENCE PROFILE

The more you know about your audience members, their needs, and their expectations, the more effectively you'll be able to communicate with them. Follow these steps to conduct a thorough audience analysis (see Figure 4.2 on the next page for an example):

- **Identify your primary audience.** For some messages, certain audience members may be more important than others. Don't ignore the needs of less influential members, but make sure you address the concerns of the key decision makers.
- **Determine audience size and geographic distribution.** A message aimed at 10,000 people spread around the globe will probably require a different approach than one aimed at a dozen people down the hall.
- **Determine audience composition.** Look for similarities and differences in culture, language, age, education, organizational rank and status, attitudes, experience,

Your general purpose may be to inform, to persuade, or to collaborate.

Your specific purpose is what you hope to accomplish with your message and what your audience should do or think after receiving your message.

Wait to send a message, or do not send it at all, if
- Nothing will change as a result of sending it
- The purpose is not realistic
- The timing is not right
- The purpose is not acceptable to your organization

REAL-TIME UPDATES
Learn More by Reading This PDF

Dig deep into audience needs with this planning tool

This in-depth audience analysis tool can help you analyze audience needs for even the most complex communication scenarios. Go to http://real-timeupdates.com/ebc10 and click on Learn More. If you are using MyBcommLab, you can access Real-Time Updates within each chapter or under Student Study Tools.

Audience analysis notes

Project: A report recommending that we close down the on-site exercise facility and subsidize private memberships at local health clubs.

- **Primary audience:** Nicole Perazzo, vice president of operations, and her supervisory team.

- **Size and geographic distribution:** Nine managers total; Nicole and five of her staff are here on site; three other supervisors are based in Hong Kong.

- **Composition:** All have experience in operations management, but several are new to the company.

- **Level of understanding:** All will no doubt understand the financial considerations, but the newer managers may not understand the importance of the on-site exercise facility to many of our employees.

- **Expectations and preferences.** They're expecting a firm recommendation, backed up with well-thought-out financial rationale and suggestions for communicating the bad news to employees. For a decision of this magnitude, a formal report is appropriate; email distribution is expected.

- **Probable reaction.** From one-on-one discussions, I know that several of the managers receiving this report are active users of the on-site facility and won't welcome the suggestion that we should shut it down. However, some nonexercisers generally think it's a luxury the company can't afford. Audience reactions will range from highly positive to highly negative; the report should focus on overcoming the highly negative reactions since they're the ones I need to convince.

Figure 4.2 Example of Using Audience Analysis to Plan a Message
For simple, routine messages, you usually don't need to analyze your audience in depth. However, for complex messages or messages for indifferent or hostile audiences, take the time to study their information needs and potential reactions to your message.

motivations, and any other factors that could affect the successful reception and decoding of your message.

- **Gauge audience members' level of understanding.** If audience members share your general background, they'll probably understand your material without difficulty. If not, your message will need an element of education to help people understand your message.

> If audience members have different levels of understanding of the topic, aim your message at the most influential decision makers.

- **Understand audience expectations and preferences.** For example, will members of your audience expect complete details or just a summary of the main points? In general, for internal communication, the higher up the organization your message goes, the fewer details people want to see.

- **Forecast probable audience reaction.** As you'll read later in the chapter, potential audience reaction affects message organization. If you expect a favorable response, you can state conclusions and recommendations up front and offer minimal supporting evidence. If you expect skepticism, you can introduce conclusions gradually and with more proof.

> To win over a skeptical audience, use a gradual approach and plenty of evidence.

Gathering Information

3 **LEARNING OBJECTIVE**

Discuss information-gathering options for simple messages, and identify three attributes of quality information.

When you have a clear picture of your audience, your next step is to assemble the information that you will include in your message. For simple messages, you may already have all the information at hand, but for more complex messages, you may need to do considerable research and analysis before you're ready to begin writing. Chapter 11 explores formal techniques for finding, evaluating, and processing information. Meanwhile, you can often use a variety of informal techniques to gather insights and guide your research efforts:

- **Consider the audience's perspective.** Put yourself in the audience's position; what are these people thinking, feeling, or planning? What information do they need to move in the direction you would like them to move?
- **Read reports and other company documents.** Annual reports, financial statements, news releases, blogs by industry experts, marketing reports, and customer surveys are just a few of the many potential sources. Find out whether your company has a *knowledge-management system*, a centralized database that collects the experiences and insights of employees throughout the organization.
- **Ask supervisors, colleagues, customers, or people in your online networks.** Fellow workers and customers may have information you need, or they may know what your audience will be interested in. And one of the huge advantages of social media is the ability to quickly locate experts and sources of vital information.
- **Ask your audience for input.** If you're unsure what audience members need from your message, ask them. Admitting you don't know but want to meet their needs will impress an audience more than guessing and getting it wrong.

UNCOVERING AUDIENCE NEEDS

In many situations, your audience's information needs will be obvious, or readers will be able to tell you what they need. In other situations, though, people may be unable to articulate exactly what is needed. If someone makes a vague or broad request, ask questions to narrow the focus. If your boss says, "Find out everything you can about Interscope Records," narrow the investigation by asking which aspect of the company and its business is most important. Asking a question or two often forces the person to think through the request and define more precisely what is required.

If you're given a vague request, ask questions to clarify it before you plan a response.

In addition, try to think of relevant information needs that your audience may not have expressed. Suppose you've been asked to compare two health insurance plans for your firm's employees, but your research has uncovered a third alternative that might be even better. You could then expand your report to include a brief explanation of why the third plan should be considered and compare it to the two original plans. Use judgment, however; in some situations you need to provide only what the audience expects and nothing more.

If appropriate, include additional information that might be helpful, even though the requester didn't specifically ask for it.

FINDING YOUR FOCUS

You may encounter situations in which the assignment or objective is so vague that you have no idea how to get started in determining what the audience needs to know. In such cases, you can use some *discovery techniques* to help generate ideas and uncover possible avenues to research. One popular technique is **free writing**, in which you write whatever comes to mind, without stopping to make any corrections, for a set period of time. The big advantage of free writing is that you silence your "inner critic" and just express ideas as they come to you. You might end up with a rambling mess by any conventional measure, but that's not important. Within that tangle of expressions, you might also find some useful ideas and angles that hadn't occurred to you yet—perhaps the crucial idea that will jumpstart the entire project.

If you're stuck for ideas, try free writing or sketching ideas instead of writing them.

The best discovery option in some cases might not be writing at all, but rather *sketching*. If you're unable to come up with any words, grab a sketchpad and starting drawing. While you're thinking visually, your brain might release some great ideas that were trapped behind words.

The techniques listed under "Defining Your Main Idea" on page 148 can also be helpful if you don't know where to start.

PROVIDING REQUIRED INFORMATION

After you've defined your audience's information needs, be ready to satisfy those needs completely (see "Practicing Ethical Communication: How Much Information Is Enough?").

REAL-TIME UPDATES
Learn More by Reading This Article

Need some fresh creative inspiration?

If you're stuck on a project and your brain could use a little spark, try these unusual creative techniques to break through tough problems. Go to http://real-timeupdates.com/ebc10 and click on Learn More. If you are using MyBcommLab, you can access Real-Time Updates within each chapter or under Student Study Tools.

Test the completeness of your document by making sure it answers all six journalistic questions: *who, what, when, where, why,* and *how.*

One good way to test the thoroughness of your message is to use the **journalistic approach**: Check to see whether your message answers *who, what, when, where, why,* and *how.* Using this method, you can quickly tell whether a message fails to deliver. For example, consider this message requesting information from employees:

> We are exploring ways to reduce our office space leasing costs and would like your input on a proposed plan in which employees who telecommute on alternate days could share offices. Please let me know what you think of this proposal.

The message fails to tell employees everything they need to know in order to provide meaningful responses. The *what* could be improved by identifying the specific information points the writer needs from employees (such as whether individual telecommuting patterns are predictable enough to allow scheduling of shared offices). The writer also doesn't specify *when* the responses are needed or *how* the employees should respond. By failing to address such points, the request is likely to generate a variety of responses, some possibly helpful but some probably not.

Be Sure the Information Is Accurate

Be certain that the information you provide is accurate and that the commitments you make can be kept.

The *quality* of the information you provide is every bit as important as the *quantity.* Inaccurate information in business messages can cause a host of problems, from embarrassment and lost productivity to serious safety and legal issues. You may commit the organization to promises it isn't able to keep—and the error could harm your reputation as a reliable businessperson. Thanks to the Internet, inaccurate information may persist for years after you distribute it.

You can minimize mistakes by double-checking every piece of information you collect. If you are consulting sources outside the organization, ask yourself whether the information is current and reliable. You must be particularly careful when using sources you find online; the simplicity of online publishing and the frequent lack of editorial oversight call for extra care in using online information. Be sure to review any mathematical or financial

---

PRACTICING ETHICAL COMMUNICATION
How Much Information Is Enough?

Imagine that your company creates a variety of home furniture products, with extensive use of fine woods. To preserve the look and feel of the wood, your craftspeople use an oil-based finish that you purchase from a local building products wholesaler. The workers apply the finish with rags, which are thrown away after each project. After a news report about spontaneous combustion of waste rags in other furniture shops, you grow concerned enough to contact the wholesaler and ask for verification of the product's safety. The wholesaler knows that you've been considering a nonflammable, water-based alternative from another source but tries to reassure you with the following email message:

> Seal the rags in an approved container and dispose of it according to local regulations. As you probably already know, county regulations require all commercial users of solvent-based materials to dispose of leftover finishes at the county's hazardous waste facility.

You're still not satisfied. You visit the website of the oil's manufacturer and find the following cautionary statement about the product you're currently using:

Improper disposal of oil-soaked rags and other materials can lead to serious fire hazards. As certain oil-based finishes cure, the chemical reactions that take place can generate enough heat to cause spontaneous combustion of vapors and oil-soaked material. To temporarily store oil-soaked rags and other waste safely, immerse them fully in water in a metal container and close the container with an airtight seal. Dispose of the container in accordance with local regulations.

CAREER APPLICATIONS

1. Was the wholesaler guilty of an ethical lapse in this case? If yes, explain what you think the lapse is and why you believe it is unethical. If no, explain why you think the statement qualifies as ethical.
2. Would the manufacturer's warning be as effective without the second sentence, which explains spontaneous combustion? Why or why not?

Source: Adapted in part from product warning message at the Minwax website, accessed 1 November 2003, www.minwax.com. The account depicted in this box is fictional; the Minwax website was referenced only for the product warning message included within the overall story.

calculations. Check all dates and schedules and examine your own assumptions and conclusions to be certain they are valid.

Be Sure the Information Is Ethical

By working hard to ensure the accuracy of the information you gather, you'll also avoid many ethical problems in your messages. If you do make an honest mistake, such as delivering information you initially thought to be true but later found to be false, contact the recipients of the message immediately and correct the error. No one can reasonably fault you in such circumstances, and people will respect your honesty.

A clear sense of ethics should guide your decisions when determining how much detail to include in your message.

Messages can also be unethical if important information is omitted. Of course, as a business professional, you may have legal or other sound business reasons for not including every detail about every matter. Just how much detail should you include? Make sure you include enough detail to avoid misleading your audience. If you're unsure how much information your audience needs, offer as much as you believe best fits your definition of complete and then offer to provide more upon request.

Be Sure the Information Is Pertinent

When gathering information for your message, remember that some points will be more important to your audience than others. Audience members will appreciate your efforts to prioritize the information they need and filter out the information they don't. Moreover, by focusing on the information that concerns your audience the most, you increase your chances of accomplishing your own communication goals.

Audiences respond best to information that has been filtered and prioritized to meet their needs.

If you don't know your audience or if you're communicating with a large group of people who have diverse interests, use common sense to identify points of interest. Audience factors such as age, job, location, income, and education can give you a clue. If you're trying to sell memberships in a health club, you might adjust your message for athletes, busy professionals, families, and people in different locations or in different income brackets. The comprehensive facilities and professional trainers would appeal to athletes, whereas the low monthly rates would appeal to college students on tight budgets.

Rely on common sense if you don't know enough about your audience to know exactly what will interest them.

Some messages necessarily reach audiences with a diverse mix of educational levels, subject awareness, and other variables. In these cases, your only choice is to try to accommodate the likely range of audience members.

Selecting the Right Medium

A **medium** is the form through which you choose to communicate a message. You may choose to talk with someone face to face, post to a blog, send an email message, or create a webcast. The range of media possibilities is wide and growing wider all the time. In fact, with so many options now available, selecting the best medium for a given message is itself an important communication skill (see Figure 4.3 on the next page).

4 LEARNING OBJECTIVE

List the factors to consider when choosing the most appropriate medium for a message.

Although media categories have become increasingly blurred in recent years, for the sake of discussion, you can think of media as being *oral, written, visual,* or *electronic* (which often combines several media types).

ORAL MEDIA

Oral media include face-to-face conversations, interviews, speeches, and in-person presentations and meetings. By giving communicators the ability to see, hear, and react to each other, oral media are useful for encouraging people to ask questions, make comments, and work together to reach a consensus or decision. For example, experts recommend that managers engage in frequent "walk-arounds," chatting with employees to get input, answer their questions, and interpret important business events and trends.[2]

Oral communication is best when you need to encourage interaction, express emotions, or monitor emotional responses.

Of course, if you don't want a lot of questions or interaction, using oral media can be an unwise choice. However, consider your audience carefully before deciding to limit interaction by choosing a different medium. As a manager, you will encounter unpleasant situations (declining an employee's request for a raise, for example) for which sending an

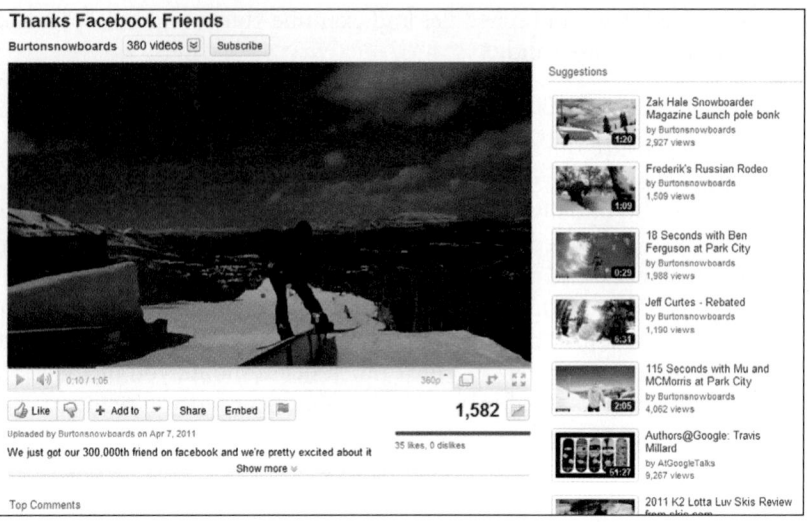

Figure 4.3   Media Choices
Online video has become one of the most important media for business communication. On its branded YouTube channel, Burton Snowboards offers numerous short videos that portray the excitement of snowboarding.
Source: Courtesy, Burton Snowboards.

email message or otherwise avoiding personal contact will seem appealing to you. In many such cases, though, you owe the other party the opportunity to ask questions or express concerns. Moreover, facing the tough situations in person will earn you a reputation as an honest, caring manager.

WRITTEN MEDIA

Nonelectronic written messages have been replaced in many instances by electronic media, although printed messages still have a place in business today.

Written messages take many forms, from traditional memos to glossy reports that rival magazines in production quality. **Memos** are brief printed documents traditionally used for the routine, day-to-day exchange of information within an organization. In many organizations, social networking, IM, email, blogs, and other electronic media have largely replaced paper memos.

Letters are brief written messages generally sent to recipients outside the organization. In addition to conveying a particular message, they perform an important public relations function in fostering good working relationships with customers, suppliers, and others. Many organizations save time and money on routine communication with *form letters*, in which a standard message is personalized as needed for each recipient.

Reports and proposals are usually longer than memos and letters, although both can be created in memo or letter format. These documents come in a variety of lengths, ranging from a few pages to several hundred, and are usually fairly formal in tone. Chapters 11 through 13 discuss reports and proposals in detail.

VISUAL MEDIA

In some situations, a message that is predominantly visual, with text used to support the illustration, can be more effective than a message that relies primarily on text.

Although you probably won't work with many messages that are purely visual (with no text), the importance of visual elements in business communication continues to grow. Traditional business messages rely primarily on text, with occasional support from graphical elements such as charts, graphs, or diagrams to help illustrate points discussed in the text. However, many business communicators are discovering the power of messages in which the visual element is dominant and supported by small amounts of text. For the purposes of this discussion, you can think of *visual media* as any format in which one or more visual elements play a central role in conveying the message content (see Figure 4.4).

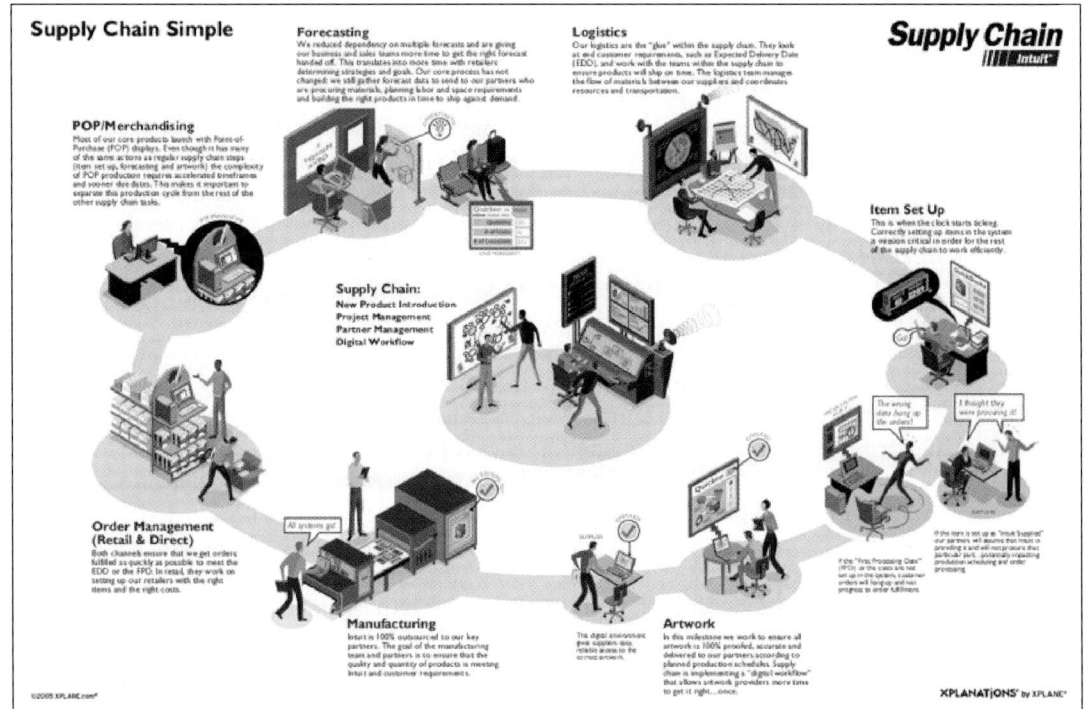

Figure 4.4   Visual Media
In traditional business messages, visual elements usually support the text. However, in some instances, the message can be presented more effectively by reversing that relationship—basing the message on a dominant visual and using text to support that image.
Source: Used with permission of Supply Chain Simple.

Messages that combine powerful visuals with supporting text, sometimes known as *infographics*, can be effective for a number of reasons. Today's audiences are pressed for time and bombarded with messages, so anything that communicates quickly is welcome. Visuals are also effective at describing complex ideas and processes because they can reduce the work required for an audience to identify the parts and relationships that make up the whole. Also, in a multilingual business world, diagrams, symbols, and other images can lower communication barriers by requiring less language processing. Finally, visual depictions can be easier to remember than purely textual descriptions or explanations. Chapter 12 offers more information on visual design.

ELECTRONIC MEDIA

The range of electronic media is broad and continues to grow even broader, from phone calls and podcasts to blogs and wikis to email and text messaging. When you want to make a powerful impression, using electronic media can increase the excitement and visual appeal with interactivity, animation, audio, and video.

The growth of electronic communication options is both a blessing and a curse for business communicators. On the one hand, you have more tools than ever before to choose from, with more ways to deliver rational and emotional content. On the other hand, the sheer range of choices can complicate your job, because you often need to choose among multiple media and you need to know how to use each medium successfully.

From the audience's perspective, a common frustration with electronic media is lack of integration, with people being forced to use to an ever-growing arsenal of separate but overlapping media options to stay informed.[3] As the options multiply, the struggle to monitor multiple sources of information can consume considerable time and energy. To minimize frustration and maximize productivity, company managers should establish clear expectations for the use of electronic media and carefully integrate—or officially choose *not* to use—each new media innovation.

In general, use electronic media to deliver messages quickly, to reach widely dispersed audiences, and to take advantage of rich multimedia formats.

Today's audiences can get frustrated with the sheer number of electronic media in the workplace.

You'll learn more about using electronic media throughout this book (in Chapter 7, in particular), but for now, here is a quick overview of the major electronic media being used in business:

- **Electronic versions of oral media.** These media include telephone calls, teleconferencing, voice-mail messages, audio recordings such as compact discs and podcasts, *voice synthesis* (creating audio signals from computer data), *voice recognition* (converting audio signals to computer data), and even animated online characters (see Figure 4.5). *Internet telephony* services such as Skype that use VoIP (which stands for *voice over IP*, the Internet protocol) continue to grow in popularity. Although audio-only telephone calls can't convey all the nonverbal signals of an in-person conversation, they can convey quite a few, including tone of voice, pace, laughter, pauses, and so on. Of course, video phone calls can replace much of the nonverbal content missing from audio calls; 40 percent of Skype's call volume is video calls.[4]

- **Electronic versions of written media.** These options range from email and IM to blogs, websites, social networks, and wikis. These media are in a state of constant change, in terms of both what is available and who tends to use which media. For example, email has been a primary business medium for the past decade or two, but it is being replaced in many cases by IM, blogs, text messaging, and communication via social networks.[5] Chapter 7 takes a closer look at email, IM, blogs, and social networks; Chapter 14 discusses wikis in more detail.

- **Electronic versions of visual media.** These choices can include electronic presentations (using Microsoft PowerPoint, Google Docs, Apple Keynote, and other software), computer animation (using software such as Adobe Flash to create many of the animated sequences you see on websites, for example), and video (YouTube quickly became a major business communication channel). **Multimedia** refers to the use of two or more media to craft a single message, typically some combination of audio, video, text, and visual graphics. Multimedia advances continue to create intriguing communication possibilities, such as *augmented reality*, in which computer-generated text, graphics, and sounds are superimposed onto a user's physical reality, either on a device display or directly onto the physical world itself.

For more on the latest innovations in electronic media, visit http://real-timeupdates .com/ebc10 and click on Chapter 4.

FACTORS TO CONSIDER WHEN CHOOSING MEDIA

In some situations, you have little or no choice of which medium to use. For instance, your department might use IM for all short internal messages and a wiki for longer status reports, and you'll be expected to use those media as well. In other situations, you'll have

Figure 4.5   Electronic Oral Media
Many websites now feature talking animated figures, sometimes called *avatars*, offering website visitors a more engaging experience.
Source: Used with permission of World Voyager Vacations.

TABLE 4.1	Media Advantages and Disadvantages	
Media Type	**Advantages**	**Disadvantages**
Oral	• Provide opportunity for immediate feedback • Promote interaction • Involve rich nonverbal cues (both physical gestures and vocal inflection) • Allow you to express the emotions behind the message	• Restrict participation to those physically present • Unless recorded, provide no permanent, verifiable record of the communication • In most cases, reduce communicator's control over the message • Other than for messages that are prewritten and rehearsed, offer no opportunity to revise or edit spoken words
Written	• Allow you to plan and control your message • Reach geographically dispersed audiences • Offer a permanent, verifiable record • Minimize the distortion that can result with oral and some forms of electronic messages • Can be used to avoid immediate interactions • Can help you control the emotional aspects of an interchange by eliminating interpersonal communication	• Offer limited opportunities for timely feedback • Lack the rich nonverbal cues provided by oral media • Can require more time and more resources to create and distribute, relative to oral media • Elaborate documents can require special skills in preparation and production
Visual	• Can convey complex ideas and relationships quickly • Often less intimidating than long blocks of text, particularly for nonnative readers • Can reduce the burden on the audience to figure out how the pieces of a message or concept fit together	• Can require artistic skills to design • Require some technical skills to create • Can require more time to create than an equivalent amount of text • Are more difficult to transmit and store than simple textual messages
Electronic	• Deliver messages quickly • Reach geographically dispersed audiences • Can offer the persuasive power of multimedia formats • Enable audience interaction through social media features • Can increase accessibility and openness within an organization and between an organization and its external stakeholders	• Are easy to overuse (sending too many messages to too many recipients) • Present privacy risks and concerns (exposing confidential data; employer monitoring; accidental forwarding) • Present security risks (viruses and spyware; network breaches) • Create productivity concerns (frequent interruptions, lack of integration among multiple electronic media in use at the same time, and time wasted on nonbusiness uses)

the opportunity to choose the medium (or media) for a particular message. Table 4.1 lists the general advantages and disadvantages of each medium. In addition, be sure to consider how your message is affected by these important factors:

- **Media richness.** *Richness* is a medium's ability to (1) convey a message through more than one informational cue (visual, verbal, vocal), (2) facilitate feedback, and (3) establish personal focus. The richest medium is face-to-face communication; it's personal, provides immediate feedback (verbal and nonverbal), and conveys the emotion behind a message.[6] Multimedia presentations and multimedia webpages are also quite rich, with the ability to present images, animation, text, music, sound effects, and other elements (see Figure 4.6 on the next page). Many electronic media are also *interactive*, in that they enable audiences to participate in the communication process. At the other extreme are the leanest media—those that communicate in the simplest ways, provide no opportunity for audience feedback, and aren't personalized. In general, use richer media to send nonroutine or complex messages, to humanize your presence throughout the organization, to communicate caring to employees, and to gain employee commitment to company goals. Use leaner media to send routine messages or to transfer information that doesn't require significant explanation.[7]

  > Media range from *rich* (many cues, simple feedback, personalization) to *lean* (few information cues, few feedback mechanisms, no personalization).

- **Message formality.** Your media choice is a nonverbal signal that affects the style and tone of your message. For example, a printed memo or letter is likely to be perceived as a more formal gesture than an email message.

- **Media limitations.** Every medium has limitations. For instance, IM is ideal for communicating simple, straightforward messages, but it is less effective for sending complex messages.

- **Urgency.** Some media establish a connection with the audience faster than others, so choose wisely if your message is urgent. However, be sure to respect audience members' time and workloads. If a message isn't urgent and doesn't require immediate feedback, choose a medium such as email that allows people to respond at their convenience.

  > Some media deliver messages faster than others, but instantaneous delivery shouldn't be used to create a false sense of urgency.

Leaner:
fewer cues,
no interactivity,
no personal focus

| Standard reports
Static webpages
Mass media
Posters & signs | Custom reports
Letters & memos
Email & IM
Wikis
Blogs
Podcasts | Telephone calls
Teleconferencing
Video | Face-to-face
conversations
Multimedia
presentations
Multimedia
webpages
Virtual reality |

Richer:
multiple cues,
interactive,
personalized

Figure 4.6 Media Richness
Business media vary widely in terms of *richness*, which is the number of informational cues available, their ability to incorporate feedback, and the degree to which they can be personalized.

- **Cost.** Cost is both a real financial factor and a perceived nonverbal signal. For example, depending on the context, extravagant (and expensive) video or multimedia presentations can send a nonverbal signal of sophistication and professionalism—or careless disregard for company budgets.
- **Audience preferences.** Be sure to consider which medium or media your audience expects or prefers.[8] For instance, businesspeople in the United States, Canada, and Germany emphasize written messages, whereas in Japan professionals tend to emphasize oral messages—perhaps because Japan's high-context culture carries so much of the message in nonverbal cues and "between-the-lines" interpretation.[9]

When choosing the appropriate medium, don't forget to consider your audience's preferences and expectations.

Organizing Your Information

5 **LEARNING OBJECTIVE**

Explain why good organization is important to both you and your audience, and list the tasks involved in organizing a message.

Organization can make the difference between success and failure. Compare the two versions of the message in Figure 4.7. The ineffective version exhibits several common organization mistakes: taking too long to get to the point, including irrelevant material, getting ideas mixed up, and leaving out necessary information.

RECOGNIZING THE IMPORTANCE OF GOOD ORGANIZATION

Good organization helps audience members understand your message, accept your message, and save time.

Good organization helps your readers or listeners in three key ways. First, it helps them understand your message. In a well-organized message, you make the main point clear at the outset, present additional points to support that main idea, and satisfy all the information needs of the audience. But if your message is poorly organized, your meaning can be obscured, and your audiences may form inaccurate conclusions about what you've written or said.

Second, good organization helps receivers accept your message. If your writing appears confused and disorganized, people will likely conclude that the *thinking* behind the writing is also confused and disorganized. Moreover, effective messages often require a bit more than simple, clear logic. A diplomatic approach helps receivers accept your message, even if it's not exactly what they want to hear. In contrast, a poorly organized message on an emotionally charged topic can alienate the audience before you have the chance to get your point across.

Third, good organization saves your audience time. Well-organized messages are efficient. They contain only relevant ideas, and they are brief. Moreover, each piece of information is located in a logical place in the overall flow; each section builds on the one before to create a coherent whole, without forcing people to look for missing pieces.

Good organization saves you time and energy in the writing and completing phases.

In addition to saving time and energy for your readers, good organization saves *you* time and consumes less of your creative energy. Writing moves more quickly because you don't waste time putting ideas in the wrong places or composing material that you don't need. You spend far less time rewriting, trying to extract sensible meaning from disorganized rambling. Last but far from least, organizational skills are good for your career because they help you develop a reputation as a clear thinker who cares about your readers.

Figure 4.7   Improving the Organization of a Message
The improved version of this email message is clear and efficient, presenting only the necessary information in a logical sequence.

MyBcommLab

Apply Figure 4.7's key concepts by revising a new document. Go to Chapter 4 in www .pearsoninternationaleditions.com/mybcommlab and select Document Makeovers.

DEFINING YOUR MAIN IDEA

The topic is the overall subject; the main idea is a specific statement about the topic.

The **topic** of your message is the overall subject, and your **main idea** is a specific statement about that topic (see Table 4.2). For example, if you believe that the current system of using paper forms for filing employee insurance claims is expensive and slow, you might craft a message in which the topic is employee insurance claims and the main idea is that a new web-based claim-filing system would reduce costs for the company and reduce reimbursement delays for employees.

In longer documents and presentations, you often need to unify a mass of material with a main idea that encompasses all the individual points you want to make. Finding a common thread through all these points can be a challenge. Sometimes you won't even be sure what your main idea is until you sort through the information. For tough assignments like these, consider a variety of techniques to generate creative ideas:

- **Brainstorming.** Working alone or with others, generate as many ideas and questions as you can, without stopping to criticize or organize. After you capture all these pieces, look for patterns and connections to help identify the main idea and the groups of supporting ideas. For example, if your main idea concerns whether to open a new restaurant in Denver, you'll probably find a group of ideas related to financial return, another related to competition, and so on. Identifying such groups helps you see the major issues that will lead you to a conclusion you can feel confident about.

- **Journalistic approach.** The journalistic approach (see page 140) asks *who, what, when, where, why,* and *how* questions to distill major ideas from unorganized information.
- **Question-and-answer chain.** Start with a key question, from the audience's perspective, and work back toward your message. In most cases, you'll find that each answer generates new questions until you identify the information that needs to be in your message.
- **Storyteller's tour.** Some writers find it best to talk through a communication challenge before they try to write. Record yourself as you describe what you intend to write. Then listen to the playback, identify ways to tighten and clarify the message, and repeat the process until you distill the main idea down to a single concise message.
- **Mind mapping.** You can generate and organize ideas using a graphic method called *mind mapping.* Start with a main idea and then branch out to connect every other related idea that comes to mind (see Figure 4.8). You can find a number of free mind mapping tools online, including http://bubbl.us.

LIMITING YOUR SCOPE

The scope of your message is the range of information you present to support your main idea.

The **scope** of your message is the range of information you present, the overall length, and the level of detail—all of which need to correspond to your main idea. The length of some business messages has a preset limit, whether from a boss's instructions, the technology you're using, or a time frame such as individual speaker slots during a seminar. Even if you

TABLE 4.2	Defining Topic and Main Idea		
General Purpose	**Example of Specific Purpose**	**Example of Topic**	**Example of Main Idea**
To inform	Teach customer service representatives how to edit and expand the technical support wiki	Technical support wiki	Careful, thorough edits and additions to the wiki help the entire department provide better customer support.
To persuade	Convince top managers to increase spending on research and development	Funding for research and development	Competitors spend more than we do on research and development, enabling them to create more innovative products.
To collaborate	Solicit ideas for a companywide incentive system that ties wages to profits	Incentive pay	Tying wages to profits motivates employees and reduces compensation costs in tough years.

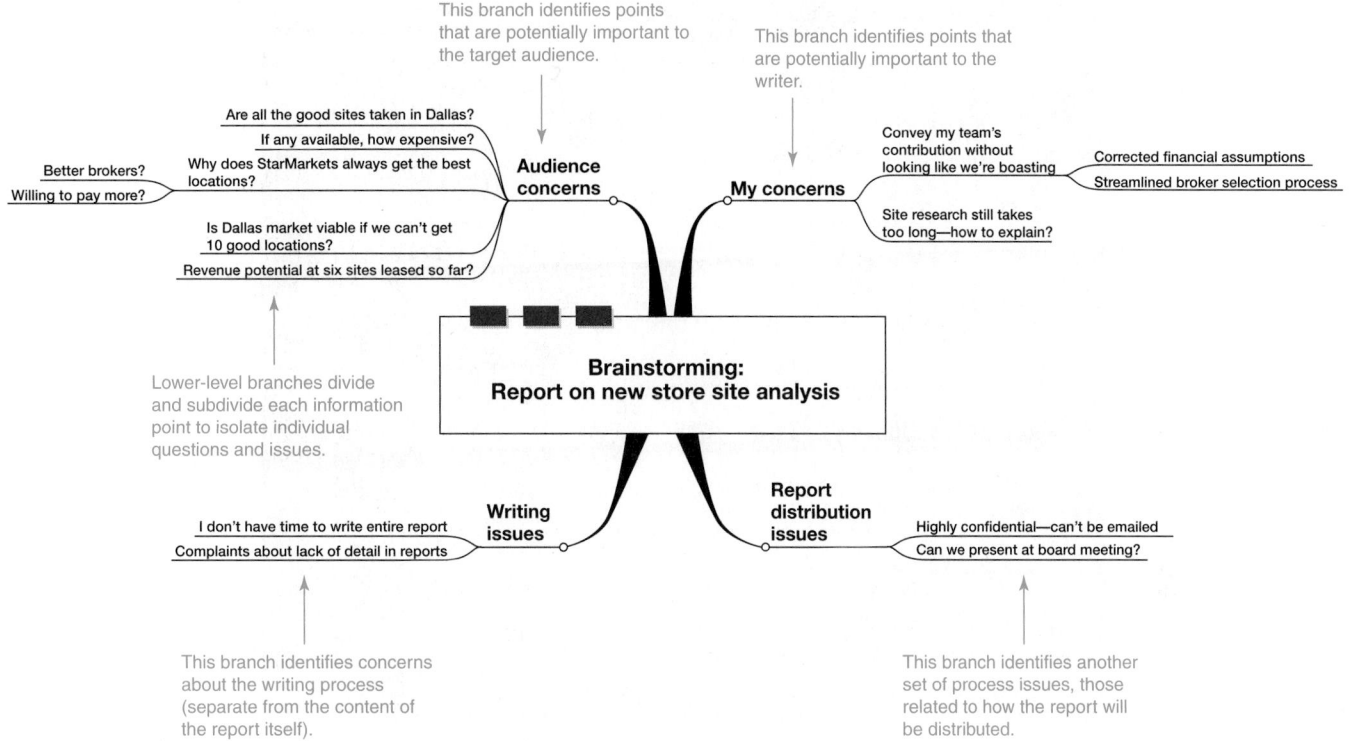

Figure 4.8   Using the Mind-Mapping Technique to Plan a Writing Project
Mind mapping is a helpful technique for identifying and organizing the many ideas and pieces of information that a complex writing task usually entails. Software (MindJet's MindManager in this case) makes it easy to create graphical output—such as this diagram, which shows the writer's own concerns about a report, her insights into the audience's concerns, and several issues related to writing and distributing the report.

don't have a preset length, it's vital to limit yourself to the scope needed to convey your main idea—and no more (see Figure 4.9 on the next page).

Whatever the length of your message, keep the number of major supporting points to half a dozen or so—and if you can get your idea across with fewer points, all the better. Listing 20 or 30 supporting points might feel as though you're being thorough, but your audience is likely to view such detail as rambling and mind numbing. Instead, group your supporting points under major headings, such as finance, customers, competitors, employees, or whatever is appropriate for your subject. Look for ways to distill your supporting points so that you have a smaller number with greater impact.

The number of words, pages, or minutes you need to communicate and support your main idea depends on your topic, your audience members' familiarity with the material, their receptivity to your conclusions, and your credibility. You'll need fewer words to present routine information to a knowledgeable audience that already knows and respects you. You'll need more words or time to build a consensus about a complex and controversial subject, especially if the members of your audience are skeptical or hostile strangers.

> Having fewer, stronger points is a better approach than using many, weaker points.

CHOOSING BETWEEN DIRECT AND INDIRECT APPROACHES

After you've defined your main idea and supporting points, you're ready to decide on the sequence you will use to present your information. You have two basic options:

- **The direct approach.** When you know your audience will be receptive to your message, use the **direct approach**: Start with the main idea (such as a recommendation, a conclusion, or a request) and follow that with your supporting evidence.

> Use the direct approach if the audience's reaction is likely to be positive and the indirect approach if it is likely to be negative.

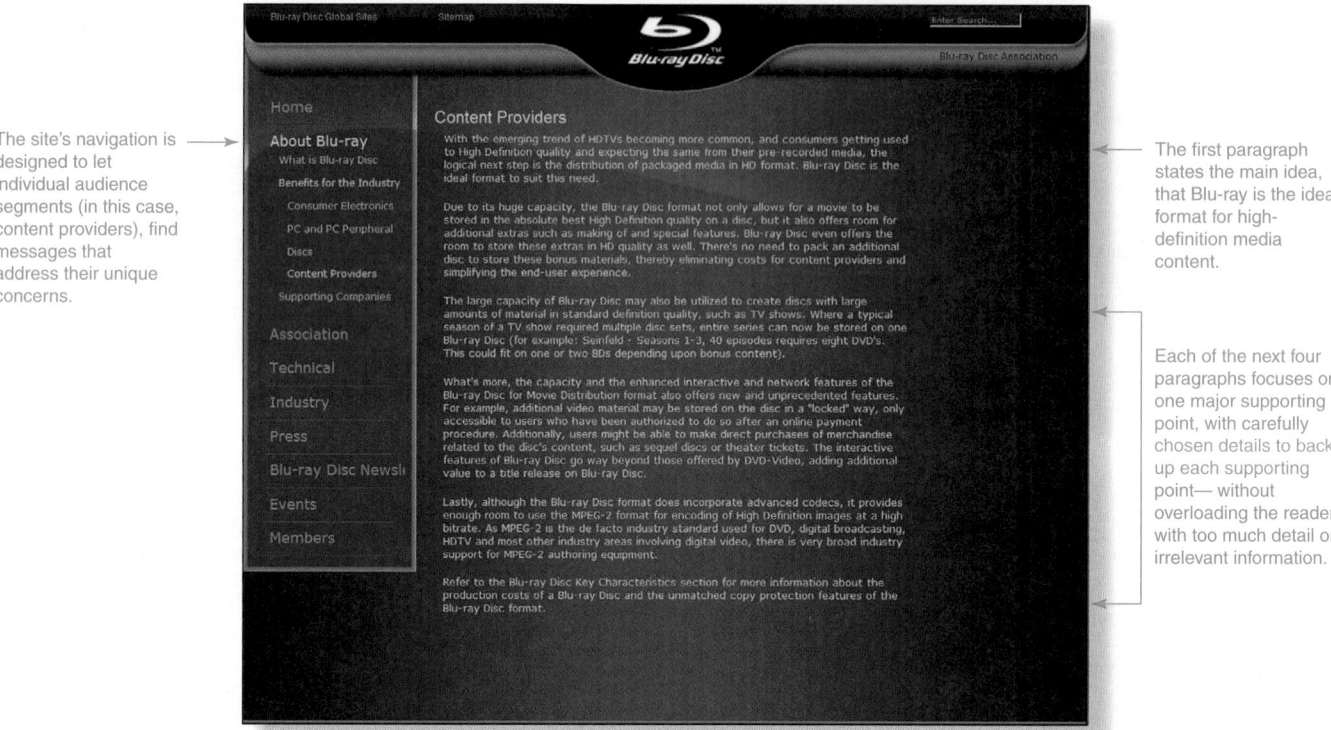

Figure 4.9   Limiting the Scope of a Message
The Blu-ray Disc Association is the industry consortium that oversees the technical standards and other matters related to Blu-ray discs used for movies, music, and data storage. In this section of its website, the association describes the benefits of the Blu-ray format, with a separate message for each of four stakeholder groups. This particular screen describes the benefits for one of those groups (*content providers*, such as movie studios). Notice how the scope of the message is limited to supporting a single main idea—the business benefits of Blu-ray for this specific audience.
Source: Used with permission of Limiting the Scope of a Message from Blue-ray Disc Association.

- **The indirect approach.** When your audience will be skeptical about or even resistant to your message, use the **indirect approach**: Start with the evidence first and build your case before presenting the main idea.

To choose between these two alternatives, analyze your audience's likely reaction to your purpose and message (see Figure 4.10). Bear in mind, however, that Figure 4.10 presents only general guidelines; always consider the unique circumstances of each message and audience situation. The following sections offer more insight on choosing the best approach for routine and positive messages, negative messages, and persuasive messages.

The type of message also influences the choice of the direct or indirect approach. In the coming chapters, you'll get specific advice on choosing the best approach for a variety of communication challenges.

OUTLINING YOUR CONTENT

After you have chosen the best approach, it's time to figure out the most logical and effective way to present your major points and supporting details. Get into the habit of creating outlines when you're preparing business messages. You'll save time, get better results, and do a better job of navigating through complicated business situations. Even if you're just jotting down three or four key points, making an outline will help you organize your thoughts for faster writing. When you're preparing a longer, more complex message, an outline is indispensable because it helps you visualize the relationships among the various parts.

REAL-TIME UPDATES
Learn More by Watching This
PowerPoint Presentation

Get helpful tips on creating an outline for any project

Learn these proven steps for creating robust, practical outlines. Go to http://real-timeupdates.com/ebc10 and click on Learn More. If you are using MyBcommLab, you can access Real-Time Updates within each chapter or under Student Study Tools.

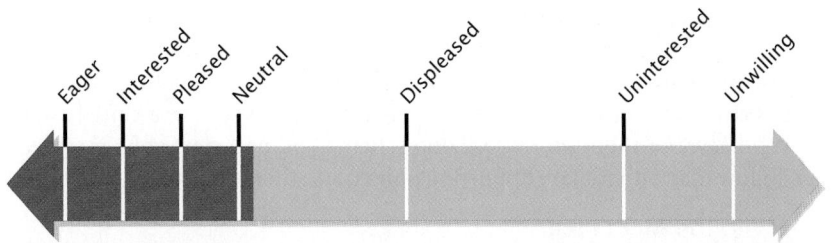

	Direct Approach	**Indirect Approach**	
Audience Reaction	Eager/interested/ pleased/neutral	Displeased	Uninterested/unwilling
Message Opening	Start with the main idea, the request, or the good news.	Start with a neutral statement that acts as a transition to the reasons for the bad news.	Start with a statement or question that captures attention.
Message Body	Provide necessary details.	Give reasons to build up to the negative answer or announcement. State or imply the bad news, and make a positive suggestion.	Arouse the audience's interest in the subject. Build the audience's desire to comply.
Message Close	Close with a cordial comment, a reference to the good news, or a statement about the specific action desired.	Close cordially.	Request action.

Figure 4.10   Choosing Between the Direct and Indirect Approaches
Think about the way your audience is likely to respond before choosing your approach.

You're no doubt familiar with the basic outline formats that identify each point with a number or letter and that indent certain points to show which ones are of equal status. A good outline divides a topic into at least two parts, restricts each subdivision to one category, and ensures that each subdivision is separate and distinct (see Figure 4.11).

Another way to visualize the outline of your message is to create an organization chart similar to the charts used to show a company's management structure (see Figure 1.3 on page 48 for an example). Put the main idea, like the top executive in a company, in the highest-level box to establish the big picture. The lower-level ideas, like lower-level employees, provide the details. All the ideas should be logically organized into divisions of thought, just

You may want to experiment with other organizational schemes in addition to traditional outlines.

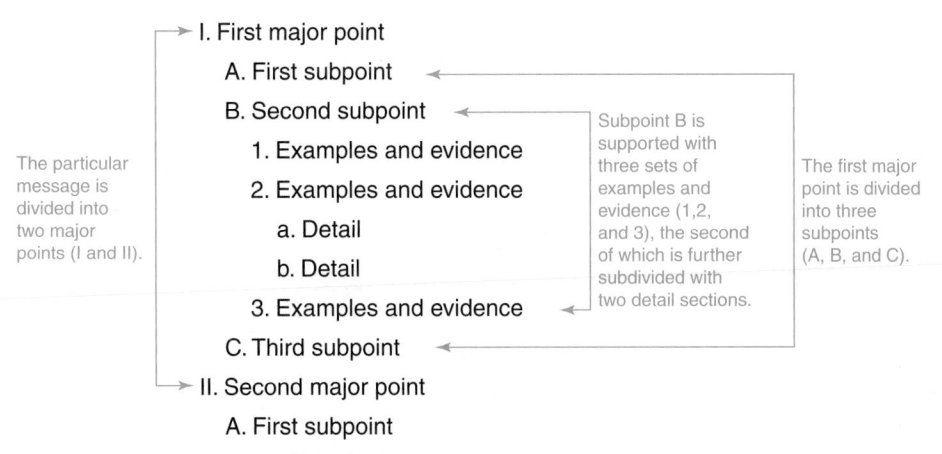

Figure 4.11   Organizing Your Thoughts with a Clear Outline
No matter what outlining format you use, think through your major supporting points and the examples and evidence that can support each point.

MyBcommLab

Apply Figure 4.11's key concepts by revising a new document. Go to Chapter 4 in www .pearsoninternationaleditions.com/mybcommlab and select Document Makeovers.

as a company is organized into divisions and departments.[10] Using a visual chart instead of a traditional outline has many benefits. Charts can help you see the various levels of ideas and how the parts fit together, develop new ideas, and restructure your information flow. The mind-mapping technique used to generate ideas works in a similar way.

Whichever outlining or organizing scheme you use, start your message with the main idea, follow that with major supporting points, and then illustrate these points with evidence.

Start with the Main Idea

The main idea is a specific statement about your topic.

The main idea helps you establish the goals and general strategy of the message, and it summarizes two vital considerations: (1) *what* you want your audience members to do or think and (2) *why* they should do so. Everything in your message should either support the main idea or explain its implications. As discussed earlier, the direct approach states the main idea quickly and directly, whereas the indirect approach delays the main idea until after the evidence is presented.

State the Major Points

Major supporting points clarify and explain your main idea.

You need to support your main idea with major points that clarify and explain the main idea in concrete terms. If your purpose is to inform and the material is factual, your major points may be based on something physical or financial—something you can visualize or measure, such as activities to be performed, functional units, spatial or chronological relationships, or parts of a whole. When you're describing a process, the major points are almost inevitably steps in the process. When you're describing an object, the major points often correspond to the parts of the object. When you're giving a historical account, major points represent events in the chronological chain of events. If your purpose is to persuade or to collaborate, select major points that develop a line of reasoning or a logical argument that proves your central message and motivates your audience to act.

Provide Examples and Evidence

Back up your supporting points with carefully selected examples and evidence.

After you've defined the main idea and identified major supporting points, think about examples and evidence that can confirm, illuminate, or expand on your supporting points. Choose examples and evidence carefully so that these elements support your overall message without distracting or overwhelming your audience. One good example, particularly if it is conveyed through a compelling story (see the next section), is usually more powerful than several weaker examples. Similarly, a few italic points of evidence are usually more persuasive than a large collection of minor details. Keep in mind that you can back up your major supporting points in a variety of ways, depending on the subject material and the available examples and evidence (see Table 4.3).

If your schedule permits, put your outline aside for a day or two before you begin composing your first draft. Then review it with a fresh eye, looking for opportunities to improve the flow of ideas.

BUILDING READER INTEREST WITH STORYTELLING TECHNIQUES

Storytelling might seem like an odd subject for a business course, but narrative techniques can be an effective way to organize messages in a surprising number of business communication situations, from recruiting and training employees to enticing investors and customers. Storytelling is such a vital means of communicating that, in the words of management consultant Steve Tobak, "It's hard to imagine your career going anywhere if you can't tell a story."[11] Fortunately, you've been telling stories all your life, so narrative techniques already come naturally to you; now it's just a matter of adapting those techniques to business situations.

You've already been on the receiving end of thousands of business stories—storytelling is one of the most common structures used in television commercials and other advertisements (see Figure 4.12 on page 154). People love to share stories about themselves and others, too, which makes social media ideal for storytelling.[12] User-generated content, such as Toyota's Auto-Biography campaign highlighted in Chapter 1, is usually all about storytelling.

Career-related stories, such as how someone sought and found the opportunity to work on projects he or she is passionate about, can entice skilled employees to consider joining a firm. Entrepreneurs use stories to help investors see how their new ideas have the potential

TABLE 4.3	Six Types of Detail	
Type of Detail	**Example**	**Comment**
Facts and figures	Sales are strong this month. We have two new contracts worth $5 million and a good chance of winning another worth $2.5 million.	Enhances credibility more than any other type. Can become boring if used excessively. Most common type used in business.
Example or illustration	We've spent four months trying to hire recent accounting graduates, but so far, only one person has joined our firm. One candidate told me that she would love to work for us, but she can get $10,000 more a year elsewhere.	Adds life to a message, but one example does not prove a point. Idea must be supported by other evidence as well.
Description	Upscale hamburger restaurants target burger lovers who want more than the convenience and low prices of a McDonald's burger. These places feature wine and beer, half-pound burgers, and generous side dishes (nachos, potato skins). Atmosphere is key.	Helps audience visualize the subject by creating a sensory impression. Does not prove a point but clarifies it and makes it memorable. Begins with an overview of the function; defines its purpose, lists major parts, and explains how it operates.
Narration (storytelling)	When Rita Longworth took over as CEO, she faced a tough choice: shut down the tablet PC division entirely or outsource manufacturing as a way to lower costs while keeping the division alive. As her first step, she convened a meeting with all the managers in the division to get their input on the two options. (Story continues from there.)	Stimulates audience interest throughout dramatic tension. In many instances, must be supplemented with statistical data in order to prove a point convincingly.
Reference to authority	I discussed this idea with Jackie Loman in the Chicago plant, and she was very supportive. As you know, Jackie has been in charge of that plant for the past six years. She is confident that we can speed up the number 2 line by 150 units an hour if we add another worker.	Bolsters a case while adding variety and credibility. Works only if authority is recognized and respected by audience.
Visual aids	Graphs, charts, tables, infographics, data visualization	Helps audience grasp the key points about sets of data or visualize connections betweeen ideas.

to affect people's lives (and therefore generate lots of sales). Stories can be cautionary tales as well, dramatizing the consequences of career blunders, ethical mistakes, and strategic missteps.

A key reason storytelling can be so effective is that stories help readers and listeners imagine themselves living through the experience of the person in the story. Chip Heath of Stanford University and his brother, Dan Heath of Duke University, have spent years exploring the question of why some ideas "stick" and others disappear. One of their conclusions is that ideas conveyed through storytelling tend to thrive because stories "put knowledge into a framework that is more lifelike, more true to our day-to-day existence."[13]

In addition, stories can demonstrate cause-and-effect relationships in a compelling fashion.[14] Imagine attending a new employee orientation and listening to the trainer read off a list of ethics rules and guidelines. Now imagine the trainer telling the story of someone who sounded a lot like you in the very near future, fresh out of college and full of energy and ambition. Desperate to hit demanding sales targets, the person in the story began entering transactions before customers had actually agreed to purchase, hoping the sales would eventually come through and no one would be the wiser. However, the scheme was exposed during a routine audit, and the rising star was booted out of the company with an ethical stain that would haunt him for years. You may not remember all the rules and guidelines, but chances are you will remember what happened to that person who sounded a lot like you. This ability to share organizational values is one of the major benefits of using storytelling in business communication, particularly across diverse workforces.[15]

A classic story has three basic parts. The beginning of the story presents someone whom the audience can identify with in some way, and this person has a dream to pursue or a problem to solve. (Think of how movies and novels often start by introducing a likable character who immediately gets into trouble, for example.) The middle of the story shows this character taking action and making decisions as he or she pursues the goal or tries to solve the problem. The storyteller's objective here is to build the audience's interest by increasing the tension: Will the "hero" overcome the obstacles in his or her path and eventually succeed or fail? The end of the story answers that question and usually offers a lesson to be learned about the outcome as well.

Storytelling is an effective way to organize many business messages because it helps readers personalize the message and understand causes and consequences.

Organize stories in three parts: a beginning that introduces a sympathetic person with a dream or a challenge, a middle that shows the complications to be overcome, and an ending that resolves the situation and shows the moral or message of the story.

Figure 4.12 Storytelling at Patagonia
Patagonia's Tin Shed website serves two storytelling functions. The tin shed (Patagonia's first building) plays a key role in the story of the company's founding and early years, and the online image of the shed offers gateways to a growing collection of stories on such topics as how various Patagonia products came into being, how outdoor enthusiasts use the company's products, and how Patagonia is engaged with various causes related to the outdoors.
Source: Courtesy of Patagonia, Inc.

By the way, even though these are "stories," they must not be made-up tales. Telling stories that didn't happen to people who don't exist while presenting them as real-life events is a serious breach of ethics that damages a company's credibility.[16]

Consider adding an element of storytelling whenever your main idea involves the opportunity to inspire, to persuade, to teach, or to warn readers or listeners about the potential outcomes of a particular course of action.

For fresh ideas and media materials on planning messages, visit http://real-timeupdates .com/ebc10 and click on Chapter 4. For a quick refresher on message-planning tasks, see "Checklist: Planning Business Messages."

✓ Checklist   Planning Business Messages

A. Analyze the situation.
- Determine whether the purpose of your message is to inform, persuade, or collaborate.
- Identify what you want your audience to think or do after receiving the message.
- Make sure your purpose is worthwhile and realistic.
- Make sure the time is right for your message.
- Make sure your purpose is acceptable to your organization.
- Identify the primary audience.
- Determine the size and composition of your audience.
- Estimate your audience's level of understanding and probable reaction to your message.

B. Gather information.
- Decide whether to use formal or informal techniques for gathering information.

- Find out what your audience needs to know.
- Provide all required information and make sure it's accurate, ethical, and pertinent.

C. Select the best medium for your message.
- Understand the advantages and disadvantages of oral, written, visual, and electronic media.
- Consider media richness, formality, media limitations, urgency, cost, and audience preference.

D. Organize your information.
- Define your main idea.
- Limit your scope.
- Choose the direct or indirect approach.
- Outline content by starting with the main idea, adding major points, and illustrating with evidence.
- Look for opportunities to use storytelling to build audience interest.

ON THE JOB: SOLVING COMMUNICATION DILEMMAS AT **H&R BLOCK**

Source: Provided courtesy of H&R Block Inc.

Robert Turtledove, H&R Block's chief marketing officer, was impressed enough with your communication skills and social media experience to add you to the team that markets H&R Block's digital tax preparation solutions. Using the insights you gained in this chapter, address these internal and external communication challenges.

1. You are asked to be part of a high-level brainstorming group at H&R Block. The group's task is to clearly define the motivations of customers who buy and use tax preparation packages so that the company can take audience expectations into account when designing marketing messages. In the course of brainstorming, the group comes up with a number of possible motivations to explain why people might want to use their tax preparation products. You know it is important to decide which of these is the most pivotal in a typical customer's decision-making process, as your communication must speak directly to this need in order to persuade customers to take a purchase or trial package. The most persuasive business message will be the one that most accurately anticipates the customer's needs and concerns. You have four choices on which to base your message: decide which is likely to be the closest match to your customers' state of mind.
   a. Taxes are scary and complicated, so people need a friendly guide to help them through the process of filing taxes. If they could afford it, individuals and small businesses would hire a real live person to provide this

service, but that is expensive. The experience that people want to have with the tax package is 'as good as' talking to a human being, because of the copious context-sensitive help that the package offers at every step.
   b. Accuracy in tax preparation is the most important requirement if one is to avoid penalties. The tax preparation software eliminates human error by providing automatic checks that compare data that is input in different forms to see whether it is consistent across the board. People are apprehensive of mistakes in their filing, so accuracy is what they most want to hear about.
   c. The H&R Block websites, blogs, and Facebook page offer access to a community of users. People can thus interact with other people who use the software. On these forums they can compare notes, report problems, and get help. This feeling of community is the most important aspect of their experience with the package.
   d. Using the package means that the confidentiality of the customer's data is protected. Since they are not disclosing their financial details to a person, the chances of sensitive information leaking out are minimal. This is the feature that is mostly likely to persuade people to buy the product.

2. You want to reach out to first-time tax filers and get them to use your product. You particularly want to target women. In order to do this, you need to know what a cross-section of women's experiences of tax filing has been, and you particularly want accounts of what it was like for them to file their first return. You have a week to do the necessary research. Which of these options do you think will provide you with the richest data?
   a. Reading books by social anthropologists who study women in the economy.

b. Looking at reports by market research companies and statistics aggregators on women's financial behavior, tax burdens, and buying of financial products.

c. Searching the Internet for posts or comments by women relating to filing taxes.

d. Posting messages on the company blogs and pages asking women to come forward with their stories.

3. A group of activists who believe that income tax should be abolished join your bulletin board, posing as legitimate users, and then post a slew of messages telling customers not to pay income tax, not to buy your product for a variety of fictitious reasons, and showing hostility toward anyone who has said good things about you on the site. You log in on Monday and find that this smear campaign has run for the whole weekend. You are facing scores of angry customers who have been bewildered, offended, and annoyed by the behavior of the activists. Your tech team gets busy blocking the offenders and deleting their posts (there are over 200 of them) but you still have to control the damage to your reputation. You decide to send out a circular email to all the users of the BBS. What should you begin your message with?

a. A reasoned explanation of what went wrong.

b. A promise that it will never happen again.

c. An apology to the users who were abused.

d. A detailed rebuttal of all the lies and misinformation spread by the group.

4. You have been doing some research, and you've found that the biggest cause of errors in tax filing is overlooked data. This is inevitable if people sit down at the end of a year and attempt to remember, or recover from documents, all of their transactions during that year. You realize that to reduce this quantum of error to zero, your package actually needs to be active all the year round. If people were to enter their income as and when it accrues: a bonus, a payoff from a project, a legacy, a gift, a windfall, with a very short description of the source and nature of the payment, they would only have to give a single command at the end of the financial year and their income statement would be auto-generated. However, you are aware that plugging this functionality into the present package requires a lot of technical input, and thus new investment. Nevertheless, you believe you are onto something and that the innovation might work. You therefore call a meeting where you and your team intend to present your proposal. What should be your approach to designing the presentation?

a. This is an important change and it makes most sense to come right out with it. The less time you waste on the preliminaries, the more you will be able to devote to the details of your idea, and most importantly, to discussing the cost to benefit ratio. Nothing persuades people like figures.

b. You're talking to an audience that is very comfortable with, and has invested a lot in, the current product. They'll sit down in the conference room completely convinced that they have done all they can to meet the needs of their customers. You must first destabilize this comfort zone by making them put themselves in the place of a customer who forgets an important transaction or mislays the papers six months down the line. Once they see that there is indeed a source of discomfort right in front of them, you will be able to bring them your idea.

c. Providing tax solutions is a competitive market with a lot of services to choose from. In this scenario, you are very concerned that someone will anticipate your idea and steal a march on your company, forcing you to play catch-up. Your first task is to paint this picture for them.

d. It's best to start with what they know: critique the existing package, doing a detailed SWOT analysis. Just when things seem most dismal, you can whip out your magic solution and show them a better way.

LEARNING OBJECTIVES CHECKUP

Assess your understanding of the principles in this chapter by reading each learning objective and studying the accompanying exercises. For fill-in-the-blank items, write the missing text in the blank provided; for multiple-choice items, circle the letter of the correct answer. You can check your responses against the answer key on page AK-1.

Objective 4.1: Describe the three-step writing process.

1. The three major steps in the three-step writing process are
   a. Writing, editing, and producing
   b. Planning, writing, and completing
   c. Writing, editing, and distributing
   d. Organizing, defining your purpose, and writing

2. The first step of the three-step writing process is
   a. Writing the first draft
   b. Organizing your information
   c. Planning your message
   d. Preparing an outline

3. Which of the following tasks should you do when you're planning a writing project?
   a. Define your purpose
   b. Revise carefully to make sure you haven't made any embarrassing mistakes
   c. Choose words and sentences carefully to make sure the audience understands your main idea
   d. Do all of the above

Objective 4.2: Explain why it's important to analyze a communication situation in order to define your purpose and profile your audience before writing a message.

4. The _____ _____ of a message indicates whether you intend to use the message to inform, to persuade, or to collaborate.

5. If you were to write a letter to a manufacturer complaining about a defective product and asking for a refund, your general purpose would be
   a. To inform
   b. To persuade
   c. To collaborate
   d. To entertain

6. No matter what the message is or the audience you want to reach, you should always
   a. Determine the information your audience needs in order to grasp your main idea
   b. Learn the names of everyone in the target audience
   c. Estimate the percentage of audience members who are likely to agree with your message
   d. Determine a complete demographic profile of your audience

7. If audience members will vary in terms of the amount of information they already know about your topic, your best approach is to
   a. Provide as much extra information as possible to make sure everyone gets every detail
   b. Provide just the basic information; if your audience needs to know more, they can find out for themselves
   c. Gear your coverage to your primary audience and provide the information most relevant to them
   d. Include lots of graphics

Objective 4.3: Discuss information-gathering options for simple messages, and identify three attributes of quality information.

8. To make sure you have provided all the necessary information, use the journalistic approach, which is to
   a. Interview your audience about its needs
   b. Check the accuracy of your information
   c. Verify whether your message answers the questions of *who, what, when, where, why,* and *how*
   d. Make sure your information is ethical

9. To determine whether the information you've gathered is good enough, verify that it is
   a. Accurate
   b. Ethical
   c. Pertinent to the audience's needs
   d. All of the above

10. If you realize you have given your audience incorrect information, the most ethical action would be to
    a. Say nothing and hope no one notices
    b. Wait until someone points out the error and then acknowledge the mistake
    c. Post a correction on your website
    d. Contact the audience immediately and correct the error

Objective 4.4: List the factors to consider when choosing the most appropriate medium for a message.

11. A medium's ability to convey a message using more than one informational cue, to facilitate feedback, and to establish personal focus is a measure of its _____.

12. Which of the following choices would be best for communicating a complex policy change to employees in a company with offices all over the world?
    a. A teleconference followed by an email message
    b. Instant messaging (IM)
    c. A traditional typed memo sent via regular postal mail
    d. A posting on an internal website with an email message alerting employees to the change and directing them to the website for more information

13. Media richness is a measure of
    a. A medium's ability to use more than one informational cue, facilitate feedback, and establish personal focus
    b. A medium's ability to use more than one informational cue, limit destructive feedback, and establish personal focus
    c. How expensive the delivery options are likely to be, particularly for large or geographically dispersed audiences
    d. How much total employee cost is involved in creating messages using a particular medium

Objective 4.5: Explain why good organization is important to both you and your audience, and list the tasks involved in organizing a message.

14. Which of the following is an important benefit of taking time to organize your business messages?
    a. You can delay the actual writing.
    b. You save time and conserve creative energy because the writing process is quicker.
    c. Organizing your thoughts and information saves you the trouble of asking colleagues for input.
    d. In many cases, you can simply send a detailed outline and save the trouble of writing the document.

15. The purpose of limiting your scope when planning a writing project is to
    a. Make your job easier
    b. Reduce the number of things you need to think about
    c. Make sure your memos are never longer than one page
    d. Make sure that your message stays focused on the main idea and any necessary supporting details

16. Starting with the main idea and then offering supporting evidence is known as the _____ approach.

17. Starting with evidence first and building toward your main idea is known as the _____ approach.

18. When your audience is likely to have a skeptical or even hostile reaction to your main idea, you should generally use
    a. The indirect approach
    b. The direct approach
    c. The open-ended approach
    d. The closed approach

19. Which of the following is one of the reasons that storytelling can be effective in business communication?
    a. Stories help readers and listeners imagine themselves living through the experience of the person in the story.
    b. Stories are entertaining, so they offer some diversion from the daily grind of work.
    c. Readers and listeners are overloaded with data, so avoiding facts and figures is a proven way to get their attention.
    d. Stories are inherently funny, and people are more receptive to new ideas when they are in a good mood.

Quick Learning Guide

MyBcommLab

Log on to www.pearsoninternationaleditions .com/mybcommlab to access study and assessment aids associated with this chapter. If you are not using MyBcommLab, you can access the Real-Time Updates http:// real-timeupdates.com/ebc10.

LEARNING OBJECTIVES

1 Describe the three-step writing process. [page 135]

2 Explain why it's important to analyze a communication situation in order to define your purpose and profile your audience before writing a message. [page 136]

3 Discuss information-gathering options for simple messages, and identify three attributes of quality information. [page 138]

4 List the factors to consider when choosing the most appropriate medium for a message. [page 141]

5 Explain why good organization is important to both you and your audience, and list the tasks involved in organizing a message. [page 146]

KEY TERMS

direct approach Message organization that starts with the main idea (such as a recommendation, a conclusion, or a request) and follows that with your supporting evidence

free writing An exploratory technique in which you write whatever comes to mind, without stopping to make any corrections, for a set period of time

general purpose The broad intent of a message—to inform, to persuade, or to collaborate with the audience

indirect approach Message organization that starts with the evidence and builds your case before presenting the main idea

journalistic approach Verifying the completeness of a message by making sure it answers the *who, what, when, where, why,* and *how* questions

letters Brief written messages generally sent to recipients outside the organization

main idea A specific statement about the topic

medium The form through which you choose to communicate a message

memos Brief printed documents traditionally used for the routine, day-to-day exchange of information within an organization; most have been replaced by electronic media

multimedia Refers to the use of two or more media to deliver a message, typically some combination of audio, video, text, and visual graphics

scope The range of information presented in a message, its overall length, and the level of detail provided

specific purpose Identifies what you hope to accomplish with your message and what your audience should do or think after receiving your message

topic The overall subject of a message

✔ Checklist

Planning Business Messages

A. Analyze the situation.
- Determine whether the purpose of your message is to inform, persuade, or collaborate.
- Identify what you want your audience to think or do after receiving the message.
- Make sure your purpose is worthwhile and realistic.
- Make sure the time is right for your message.
- Make sure your purpose is acceptable to your organization.
- Identify the primary audience.
- Determine the size and composition of your audience.
- Estimate your audience's level of understanding and probable reaction to your message.

B. Gather information.
- Decide whether to use formal or informal techniques for gathering information.
- Find out what your audience needs to know.
- Provide all required information and make sure it's accurate, ethical, and pertinent.

C. Select the best medium for your message.
- Understand the advantages and disadvantages of oral, written, visual, and electronic media.
- Consider media richness, formality, media limitations, urgency, cost, and audience preference.

D. Organize your information.
- Define your main idea.
- Limit your scope.
- Choose the direct or indirect approach.
- Outline content by starting with the main idea, adding major points, and illustrating with evidence.
- Look for opportunities to use storytelling to build audience interest.

APPLY YOUR KNOWLEDGE

To review chapter content related to each question, refer to the indicated Learning Objective.

1. Once one has planned a message, should one change the plan at any point during the writing process, or should one stick with it no matter what? Make a case for doing any one of these things. [LO-1]

2. You discover to your horror that one of your juniors has plagiarized a well-known business writer in making notes that you used in writing a blog post. Moreover, before you made the discovery, you had already commended the junior for her enterprise and good writing skills and sent a link to the blog post to your whole department. You have taken the post down. Now write an email to the junior explaining what she did wrong, to your department apologizing for the post, and to your boss, explaining what happened and the action you have taken. [LO-3]

3. To highlight your success in corporate social responsibility projects running at your head office, your boss has given you a small budget for either a twenty minute film or a printed brochure with a print run of ten thousand copies to be distributed to branches all over the world. Which medium do you think is preferable to carry this message? Write an email to your creative team justifying the use of either of these media for the purpose. [LO-4]

4. Would you use the direct or indirect approach to speak to an employee if you had to terminate her contract of service because of downsizing? Justify your answer. [LO-5]

5. You are about to make a big presentation to a potential client, and your boss is concerned that the PowerPoint presentation you have created is way too short with only twelve slides. Is his concern justified? Give reasons for your answer. [LO-5]

PRACTICE YOUR SKILLS

Active links for all websites in this chapter can be found on MyBcommLab; see your User Guide for instructions on accessing the content for this chapter. Each activity is labeled according to the primary skill or skills you will need to use. To review relevant chapter content, you can refer to the indicated Learning Objective. In some instances, supporting information will be found in another chapter, as indicated.

Message for Analysis: Outlining Your Content [LO-5]

A writer is working on an information brochure for a car repair and reconditioning company, and is having trouble grouping the ideas logically into an outline. Using the following information, prepare the outline, paying attention to the appropriate hierarchy of ideas. If necessary, rewrite phrases to make them all consistent.

- Urban Customs Auto Shop
- Used car sales

- All jobs quoted for on their merits
- Door-to-door service
- Very reasonable rates
- Skilled workers who can make parts by hand if required
- Master upholsterer on call for interiors
- Located in San Francisco
- State of the art workshop and paint shop
- Award winning designers on the job
- Extensive reference library of vintage and classic car designs, including exploded assembly schemes
- Real time uplink in case owners want to watch the work from home
- Custom designed paint jobs and refitting

Exercises

1. **Planning: Identifying Your Purpose; Media Skills: Email [LO-2]** Make a list of communication tasks you'll need to accomplish in the next week or so (for example, a homework assignment, an email message to an instructor, a job application, or a speech to a class). For each, determine a general and a specific purpose.

2. **Planning: Identifying Your Purpose [LO-2]** For each of the following communication tasks, state a specific purpose (if you have trouble, try beginning with "I want to . . .").

   a. A letter to a friend from your childhood whom you haven't seen for ten years.

   b. A memo to your junior about a report that is a week overdue.

   c. A letter to a bank that has failed to sanction a loan you requested.

   d. A memo to employees about keeping the cafeteria clean.

   e. A phone call to a creditor who hasn't paid dues for over three months.

   f. An email congratulating your best-performing employee in that quarter.

3. **Planning: Assessing Audience Needs [LO-2]** For each communication task that follows, write brief answers to three questions: Who is the audience? What is the audience's general attitude toward my subject? What does the audience need to know?

   a. A cease-and-desist letter to a company that is using a similar logo to yours.

   b. An invitation to your new collaborative blog for team projects.

   c. A warning to switch off computers at the end of the working day.

   d. A letter inviting a local school to bring the children on a tour of your chocolate factory.

   e. A cover letter sent along with your résumé to a potential employer

   f. A notice to be posted on your service website while you make essential repairs to it.

4. **Planning: Assessing Audience Needs [LO-2]** Choose a fairly simple electronic device (such as a digital music player or digital camera) that you know how to operate well. Write two sets of instructions for operating the device: one set for a reader who has never used that type of device and one set for someone who is generally familiar with that type of machine but has never operated the specific model. Briefly explain how your two audiences affect your instructions.

5. **Planning: Identifying Your Purpose [LO-2]** List five messages you have received lately, such as direct-mail promotions, letters, email messages, phone solicitations, and lectures. For each, determine the general purpose and the specific purpose; then answer the following questions: (1) Was the message personalized or impersonal? (2) Was the medium appropriate for the message? (3) Was the message clearly readable and aesthetically pleasing?

6. **Planning: Analyzing the Situation; Media Skills: Electronic Presentations [LO-2]** Go to the Microsoft website, at www.microsoft.com, and locate the latest annual report. Read the annual report's letter to shareholders. Who is the audience for this message? What is the general purpose of the message? What do you think this audience wants to know from the chairman of Microsoft? Summarize your answers in a one-page report or five-slide presentation, as your instructor directs.

7. **Planning: Analyzing the Situation; Collaboration: Planning Meetings [LO-2], Chapter 2** How can the material discussed in this chapter also apply to meetings, as discussed in Chapter 2? Outline your ideas in a brief presentation or a post for your class blog.

8. **Planning: Creating an Audience Profile; Collaboration: Team Projects [LO-2], [LO-3], Chapter 2** With a team assigned by your instructor, compare the Facebook pages of three companies in the same industry. Analyze the content on all the available tabs. What can you surmise about the intended audience for each company? Which of the three does the best job of presenting the information its target audience is likely to need? Prepare a brief presentation, including slides that show samples of the Facebook content from each company.

9. **Planning: Analyzing the Situation, Selecting Media; Media Skills: Email [LO-2], [LO-4], Chapter 9** You are the head of public relations for a company that organizes music tours for rock bands. Recently a disgruntled fan posted a bitter blog post about his experience at a concert organized by you, accompanied by a video clip of bouncers roughing him and his friends up. However, the video clip does not show him and his friends taunting the security men just before the incident. You have security camera footage of that. The video goes viral, and you are contacted by a journalist for your side of the story. Write (1) an email and (2) the transcript of a phone call demonstrating how you would talk to the journalist through these media and what you would say to de-escalate the situation.

10. **Planning: Assessing Audience Needs; Media Skills: Blogging; Communication Ethics: Making Ethical Choices [LO-3], Chapter 1** There has been a leakage of hazardous waste at your plant. The leakage is easily contained, but your boss doesn't want the details to make it into the routine work report. No harm was done, he tells you. Should you leave the information out, or report it? On the basis of the discussion in Chapter 1, would you consider this situation to be an ethical dilemma or an ethical lapse? Explain your analysis in a brief email message to your instructor.

11. **Planning: Limiting Your Scope [LO-5]** Suppose you are preparing to recommend that top management introduce a bio-composting system in the company grounds to deal with kitchen waste from the canteen. The following information is in your files. Eliminate topics that aren't essential and then arrange the other topics so that your report will give top managers a clear understanding of the heating system and a balanced, concise justification for installing it.
    - Theory of recycling and its many benefits to the Earth
    - Scientific credentials of the developers of the process
    - Exploded diagram of bio-digester and worm pit
    - Details of how you discovered this system and the supplier's contact information
    - Stories about the successful use of the bio-digester in comparable facilities
    - Forecasts of benefits to flower gardens and lawns
    - Costs of installing and running the new equipment, including the collection system in the kitchen
    - Advantages and disadvantages of using the new process
    - Detailed 10-year cost projections
    - Estimates of the time needed to phase in the new system
    - A critique of the present wasteful, costly, and unsustainable system

12. **Planning: Choosing the Direct or Indirect Approach [LO-5]** Indicate whether the direct or indirect approach would be best in each of the following situations and briefly explain why. Would any of these messages be inappropriate for email? Explain.
    a. A message to the owner of a hair salon, complaining about a bad haircut
    b. A message from a recent college graduate, requesting a letter of recommendation from a former instructor
    c. A message turning down a job applicant
    d. A message announcing that because of rising costs, pickups from the airport will be provided only for employees arriving between midnight and 6 am.
    e. A message from an organizer of trade fairs to a troublesome participant who has still not paid dues for last year's fair, turning down the participant's application for this year's fair.

13. **Planning: Choosing the Direct or Indirect Approach [LO-5]** If you were trying to persuade people to take the following actions, how would you organize your argument?
    a. You want your boss to approve your plan for hiring two new people.
    b. You want to be hired for a job.
    c. You want to be granted a business loan.
    d. You want to collect a small amount of money from a regular customer whose account is slightly past due.
    e. You want to collect a large amount of money from a customer whose account is seriously past due.

14. **Planning: Using Storytelling Techniques; Communication Ethics: Providing Ethical Leadership: Media Skills: Podcasting [LO-5], Chapter 1** Research recent incidents of ethical lapses by a business professional or executive in any industry. Choose one example that has a clear story "arc" from beginning to end. Outline a cautionary tale that explains the context of the ethical lapse, the choice the person made, and the consequences of the ethical lapse. Script a podcast (aim for roughly 3 to 5 minutes) that tells the story. If your instructor directs, record your podcast and post to your class blog.

EXPAND YOUR SKILLS

Critique the Professionals

Locate an example of professional communication in any medium that you think would work equally well—or perhaps better—in another medium. Using the media selection guidelines in this chapter and your understanding of the communication process, write a brief analysis (no more than one page) of the company's media choice and explain why your choice would be at least as effective. Use whatever medium your instructor requests for your report and be sure to cite specific elements from the piece and support from the chapter.

Sharpening Your Career Skills Online

Bovée and Thill's Business Communication Web Search, at http://businesscommunicationblog.com/websearch, is a unique research tool designed specifically for business communication research. Use the Web Search function to find a website, video, podcast, or PowerPoint presentation that offers advice on planning a report, speech, or other business message. Write a brief email message to your instructor, describing the item that you found and summarizing the career skills information you learned from it.

IMPROVE YOUR GRAMMAR, MECHANICS, AND USAGE

The following exercises help you improve your knowledge of and power over English grammar, mechanics, and usage. Turn to the "Handbook of Grammar, Mechanics, and Usage" at the end of this book and review all of Section 1.4 (Adjectives). Then look at the following 10 items. Underline the preferred choice within each set of parentheses. (Answers to these exercises appear on page AK-3.)

1. Of the two proposals received, Jonathan's has the (*better, best*) presentation.

2. The (*most appropriate, appropriate*) choice is *c*.

3. Here is the (*effective, most effective*) of all the solutions I have heard so far.

4. The (*bigger, biggest*) problem with this profile is the amount of paperwork.

5. Tom's (*expensively designed, expensively-designed*) house indicates that he is not in the (*low-budget, low budget*) category.

6. You must learn to include better (*cross references, cross-references*) in your report.

7. Smith has a (*ten year old, ten-year-old*) daughter.

8. His (*high-handed devil may care; high-handed, devil-may-care*) attitude is adversely affecting his position in the company.

9. The Xerox machine stopped working because there was a (*small plastic; small, plastic*) piece stuck inside.

10. I received his (*usual warm friendly; usual, warm, friendly; usual warm, friendly*) Christmas letter.

For additional exercises focusing on adjectives, visit MyBcommLab. Click on Chapter 4, click on Additional Exercises to Improve Your Grammar, Mechanics, and Usage, and then click on 8. Adjectives.

REFERENCES

1. H&R Block website, accessed 9 January 2011, www.hrblock.com; Paula Drum, "I Got People (Online): How H&R Block Connects by Using Social Media," presentation at BlogWell conference, 22 January 2009, www.socialmedia.org; Shel Israel, "Twitterville Notebook: H&R Block's Paula Drum," Global Neighbourhoods blog, 22 December 2008, http://redcouch.typepad.com/weblog; "H&R Block's Paula Drum Talks Up Value of Online 'Presence,'" The Deal website, video interview, 6 June 2008, www.thedeal.com; Shel Israel, "SAP Global Survey: H&R Block's Paula Drum," Global Neighbourhoods blog, 4 April 2008, http://redcouch.typepad.com/weblog; "Tango in Plain English," video, accessed 27 August 2008, www.youtube.com; "H&R Block, Inc.," Hoovers, accessed 28 August 2008, www.hoovers.com; Linda Zimmer, "H&R Block Tangoes into Second Life," Business Communicators of Second Life blog, 17 March 2007, http://freshtakes.typepad.com/sl_communicators; "H&R Block Launches First Virtual Tax Experience in Second Life," press release, accessed 27 August 2008, www.hrblock.com.

2. Linda Duyle, "Get Out of Your Office," *HR Magazine*, July 2006, 99–101.

3. Frank Martin Hein, "Making the Best Use of Electronic Media," *Communication World*, November–December 2006, 20–23.

4. "About Skype," Skype Website, accessed 7 January 2011, http://about.skype.com.

5. Caroline McCarthy, "The Future of Web Apps Will See the Death of Email," Webware blog, 29 February 2008, http://news.cnet.com; Kris Maher, "The Jungle," *Wall Street Journal*, 5 October 2004, B10; Kevin Maney, "Surge in Text Messaging Makes Cell Operators :-)," *USA Today*, 28 July 2005, B1–B2.

6. Laurey Berk and Phillip G. Clampitt, "Finding the Right Path in the Communication Maze," *IABC Communication World*, October 1991, 28–32.

7. Samantha R. Murray and Joseph Peyrefitte, "Knowledge Type and Communication Media Choice in the Knowledge Transfer Process," *Journal of Managerial Issues*, Spring 2007, 111–133.

8. Raymond M. Olderman, *10 Minute Guide to Business Communication* (New York: Alpha Books, 1997), 19–20.

9. Mohan R. Limaye and David A. Victor, "Cross-Cultural Business Communication Research: State of the Art and

Hypotheses for the 1990s," *Journal of Business Communication*, Summer 1991, 277–299.

10. Holly Weeks, "The Best Memo You'll Ever Write," *Harvard Management Communication Letter*, Spring 2005, 3–5.

11. Steve Tobak, "How to Be a Great Storyteller and Win Over Any Audience," BNET, 12 January 2011, www.bnet.com.

12. Debra Askanase, "10 Trends in Sustainable Social Media," Community Organizer 2.0 Blog, 13 May 2010, www.communityorganizer20.com.

13. Chip Heath and Dan Heath, *Made to Stick: Why Some Ideas Survive and Others Die* (New York: Random House: 2008), 214.

14. Heath and Heath, *Made to Stick: Why Some Ideas Survive and Others Die*, 206, 214.

15. Randolph T. Barker and Kim Gower, "Strategic Application of Storytelling in Organizations," *Journal of Business Communication*, Vol 47, No 3, July 2010, 295–312.

16. Jennifer Aaker and Andy Smith, "7 Deadly Sins of Business Storytelling," American Express Open Forum, accessed 21 March 2011, www.openforum.com.

Writing Business Messages

LEARNING OBJECTIVES   After studying this chapter, you will be able to

1 Identify the four aspects of being sensitive to audience needs when writing business messages

2 Explain how establishing your credibility and projecting your company's image are vital aspects of building strong relationships with your audience

3 Explain how to achieve a tone that is conversational but businesslike, explain the value of using plain language, and define active and passive voice

4 Describe how to select words that are not only correct but also effective

5 Define the four types of sentences, and explain how sentence style affects emphasis within a message

6 Define the three key elements of a paragraph, and list five ways to develop unified, coherent paragraphs

7 Identify the most common software features that help you craft messages more efficiently

MyBcommLab   Where you see MyBcommLab in this chapter, go to www.pearsoninternationaleditions.com/mybcommlab for additional activities on the topic being discussed.

ON THE JOB: COMMUNICATING AT CREATIVE COMMONS

Creative Commons, chaired by Joi Ito, uses a variety of communication vehicles to convince copyright owners to explore new ways of sharing and protecting their creative works.
Source: Mizuka Ito/Creative Commons.

Redefining Two Centuries of Copyright Law for the Digital Age

Have you ever noticed that tiny © symbol on books, DVDs, music CDs, and other media products? It means that the person or organization that created the item is granted *copyright* protection, the exclusive legal right to produce, distribute, and sell that creation. Anyone who wants to resell, redistribute, or adapt such works usually needs to secure permission from the current copyright holder.

However, what if you *want* people to remix the song you just recorded or use your graphic designs in whatever artistic compositions they might want to create? Or if you want to give away some of your creative works to get your name out there, without giving up all your legal rights to them? Alternatively, suppose you need a few photos or a video clip for a website. In all of these cases, permission would normally have to be sought and granted for use of the material. Other than for limited personal and educational use, a conventional copyright requires every person to negotiate a contract for every application or adaptation of every piece of work he or she wants to use.

The search for some middle ground between "all rights reserved" and simply giving your work away led to the founding of Creative Commons. This nonprofit organization's goal is to provide a simple, free, and legal way for musicians, artists, writers, teachers, scientists, and others to collaborate

163

and benefit through the sharing of art and ideas. Instead of the everything-or-nothing approach of traditional copyright, Creative Commons offers a more flexible range of "some rights reserved" options.

Through a variety of media, Creative Commons continues to promote the benefits of simplifying the legal constraints on sharing and reusing intellectual property, whether for creative expression or scientific research. Millions of Creative Commons licenses have been initiated for musical works, images, short films, educational materials, novels, and more. This approach can't solve the entire dilemma of copyrights in the digital age, and not everyone agrees with the Creative Commons model, but it has created an easier way for creative people to communicate and collaborate.[1]

http://creativecommons.org

Adapting to Your Audience: Being Sensitive to Audience Needs

1 LEARNING OBJECTIVE

Identify the four aspects of being sensitive to audience needs when writing business messages.

Readers and listeners want to know how your messages will benefit them.

As they work to persuade their audiences to consider new forms of copyright protection, Joi Ito and his colleagues at Creative Commons (profiled in the chapter opener) realize it takes more than just a great idea to change the way people think. Expressing ideas clearly and persuasively starts with adapting to one's audience.

Whether consciously or not, audiences greet most incoming messages with a selfish question: "What's in this for me?" If your intended audience members think a message does not apply to them or doesn't meet their needs, they won't be inclined to pay attention to it. Follow the example set by the Creative Commons website, which addresses a diverse audience of artists, lawyers, and business professionals but fine-tunes specific messages for each group of people.

If your readers or listeners don't think you understand or care about their needs, they won't pay attention, plain and simple. You can improve your audience sensitivity by adopting the "you" attitude, maintaining good standards of etiquette, emphasizing the positive, and using bias-free language.

USING THE "YOU" ATTITUDE

The "you" attitude is best implemented by expressing your message in terms of the audience's interests and needs.

Chapter 1 introduced the notion of audience-centered communication and the "you" attitude—speaking and writing in terms of your audience's wishes, interests, hopes, and preferences. On the simplest level, you can adopt the "you" attitude by replacing terms such as *I, me, mine, we, us,* and *ours* with *you* and *yours*:

Instead of This	Write This
Tuesday is the only day that we can promise quick response to purchase order requests; we are swamped the rest of the week.	If you need a quick response, please submit your purchase order requests on Tuesday.
We offer MP3 players with 50, 75, or 100 gigabytes of storage capacity.	You can choose an MP3 player with 50, 75, or 100 gigabytes of storage.

MyBcommLab

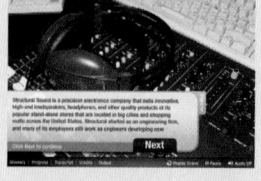

● Access this chapter's simulation entitled The Communication Process located at www .pearsoninternationaleditions.com/ mybcommlab.

Messages that emphasize "I" and "we" risk sounding selfish and uninterested in the audience. Such messages feel like they are all about the sender, not the receiver.

However, the "you" attitude is more than simply using particular pronouns; it's a matter of genuine interest and concern. You can use *you* 25 times in a single page and still ignore your audience's true concerns. If you're talking to a retailer, try to think like a retailer; if you're dealing with a production supervisor, put yourself in that position; if you're writing to a dissatisfied customer, imagine how you would feel at the other end of the transaction.

Be aware that on some occasions, it's better to avoid using *you*, particularly if doing so will sound overly authoritative or accusing:

Avoid using *you* and *yours* when doing so
- Makes you sound dictatorial
- Could make someone else feel unnecessarily guilty
- Is inappropriate for the culture
- Goes against your organization's style

Instead of This	Write This
You failed to deliver the customer's order on time.	The customer didn't receive the order on time. *or* Let's figure out a system that will ensure on-time deliveries.
You must correct all five copies by noon.	All five copies must be corrected by noon.

As you practice using the "you" attitude, be sure to consider the attitudes of other cultures and the policies of your organization. In some cultures, it is improper to single out one person's achievements, because the whole team is responsible for the outcome; in that case, using the pronoun *we* or *our* (when you and your audience are part of the same team) would be more appropriate. Similarly, some companies have a tradition of avoiding references to *you* and *I* in most messages and reports.

MAINTAINING STANDARDS OF ETIQUETTE

Good etiquette not only indicates respect for your audience but also helps foster a more successful environment for communication by minimizing negative emotional reaction:

Although you may be tempted now and then to be brutally frank, try to express the facts in a kind and thoughtful manner.

Instead of This	Write This
Once again, you've managed to bring down the entire website through your incompetent programming.	Let's review the last website update to explore ways to improve the process.
You've been sitting on our order for two weeks, and we need it now!	Our production schedules depend on timely delivery of parts and supplies, but we have not yet received the order you promised to deliver two weeks ago. Please respond today with a firm delivery commitment.

Of course, some situations require more diplomacy than others. If you know your audience well, a less formal approach may be more appropriate. However, when you are communicating with people who outrank you or with people outside your organization, an added measure of courtesy is usually needed.

Written communication and most forms of electronic media generally require more tact than oral communication (Figure 5.1 on the next page). When you're speaking, your words are softened by your tone of voice and facial expression. Plus, you can adjust your approach according to the feedback you get. If you inadvertently offend someone in writing or in a podcast, for example, you don't usually get the immediate feedback you would need in order to resolve the situation. In fact, you may never know that you offended your audience.

EMPHASIZING THE POSITIVE

You will encounter situations throughout your career in which you need to convey unwanted news. However, sensitive communicators understand the difference between delivering negative news and being negative. Never try to hide the negative news, but look for positive points that will foster a good relationship with your audience:[2]

You can communicate negative news without being negative.

Instead of This	Write This
It is impossible to repair your laptop today.	Your computer can be ready by Tuesday. Would you like a loaner until then?
We wasted $300,000 advertising in that magazine.	Our $300,000 advertising investment did not pay off. Let's analyze the experience and apply the insights to future campaigns.

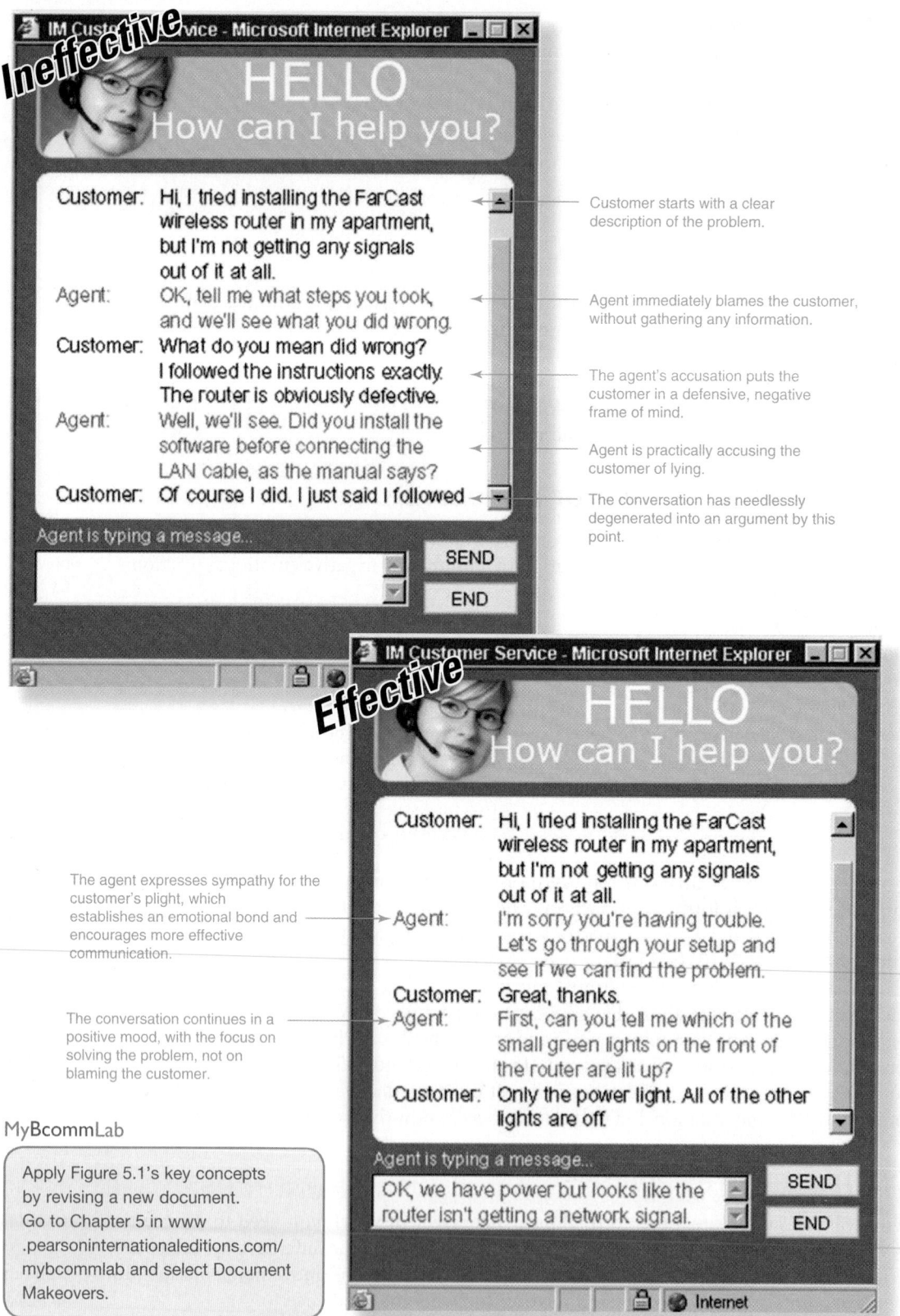

Ineffective

IM Customer Service - Microsoft Internet Explorer

HELLO
How can I help you?

Customer: Hi, I tried installing the FarCast
wireless router in my apartment,
but I'm not getting any signals
out of it at all.

Agent: OK, tell me what steps you took,
and we'll see what you did wrong.

Customer: What do you mean did wrong?
I followed the instructions exactly.
The router is obviously defective.

Agent: Well, we'll see. Did you install the
software before connecting the
LAN cable, as the manual says?

Customer: Of course I did. I just said I followed

Agent is typing a message...

SEND

END

Customer starts with a clear description of the problem.

Agent immediately blames the customer, without gathering any information.

The agent's accusation puts the customer in a defensive, negative frame of mind.

Agent is practically accusing the customer of lying.

The conversation has needlessly degenerated into an argument by this point.

Effective

IM Customer Service - Microsoft Internet Explorer

HELLO
How can I help you?

Customer: Hi, I tried installing the FarCast
wireless router in my apartment,
but I'm not getting any signals
out of it at all.

Agent: I'm sorry you're having trouble.
Let's go through your setup and
see if we can find the problem.

Customer: Great, thanks.

Agent: First, can you tell me which of the
small green lights on the front of
the router are lit up?

Customer: Only the power light. All of the other
lights are off.

Agent is typing a message...

OK, we have power but looks like the
router isn't getting a network signal.

SEND

END

The agent expresses sympathy for the customer's plight, which establishes an emotional bond and encourages more effective communication.

The conversation continues in a positive mood, with the focus on solving the problem, not on blaming the customer.

MyBcommLab

Apply Figure 5.1's key concepts by revising a new document. Go to Chapter 5 in www.pearsoninternationaleditions.com/mybcommlab and select Document Makeovers.

Figure 5.1   Fostering a Positive Relationship with an Audience
In the "ineffective" example, notice how the customer service agent's unfortunate word choices immediately derail this IM exchange. In the "effective" example, a more sensitive approach allows both people to focus on solving the problem.

If you find it necessary to criticize or correct, don't dwell on the other person's mistakes. Avoid referring to failures, problems, or shortcomings. Focus instead on what the audience members can do to improve the situation:

When you are offering criticism or advice, focus on what the person can do to improve.

Instead of This	Write This
People in this department consistently fail to keep their travel spending under budget.	By choosing travel options more carefully and avoiding last-minute trips whenever possible, this department will be able to meet its budgetary goals.
You failed to provide all the necessary information on the previous screen.	Please review the items marked in red on the previous screen so that we can process your order as quickly as possible.

If you're trying to persuade audience members to perform a particular action, point out how doing so will benefit them:

Show your audience members how they will benefit from responding to your message in the way you would like them to respond.

Instead of This	Write This
We will notify all three credit reporting agencies if you do not pay your overdue bill within 10 days.	Paying your overdue bill within 10 days will prevent a negative entry on your credit record.
I am tired of seeing so many errors in the customer service blog.	Proofreading your blog postings will help you avoid embarrassing mistakes that generate more customer service complaints.

Look for appropriate opportunities to use **euphemisms**, or milder synonyms, that convey your meaning without carrying negative connotations. For example, when referring to people beyond a certain age, use "senior citizens," rather than "old people." *Senior* conveys respect in a way that *old* doesn't.

However, take care when using euphemisms; it's easy to push the idea too far and wind up sounding ridiculous—or worse yet, obscuring the truth. Speaking to your local community about the disposal of "manufacturing by-products" would be unethical if you're really talking about toxic waste. Even if it is unpleasant, people respond better to an honest message delivered with integrity than they do to a sugar-coated message that obscures the truth.

Euphemisms, equivalent words or phrases that express a thought in milder terms, can ease the blow of negative news, but they must be used carefully to avoid annoying or misleading the audience.

USING BIAS-FREE LANGUAGE

Bias-free language avoids words and phrases that unfairly and even unethically categorize or stigmatize people in ways related to gender, race, ethnicity, age, disability, or other personal characteristics. Contrary to what some may think, biased language is not simply about "labels." To a significant degree, language reflects the way people think and what they believe, and biased language may well perpetuate the underlying stereotypes and prejudices that it represents.[3] Moreover, because communication is all about perception, simply *being* fair and objective isn't enough. To establish a good relationship with your audience, you must also *appear* to be fair.[4] Good communicators make every effort to change biased language (see Table 5.1 on the next page). Bias can come in a variety of forms:

Biased language can perpetuate stereotypes and prejudices.

- **Gender bias.** Avoid sexist language by using the same labels for everyone, regardless of gender. Don't refer to a woman as *chairperson* and then to a man as *chairman*. Use *chair*, *chairperson*, or *chairman* consistently. (Note that it is not uncommon to use *chairman* when referring to a woman who heads a board of directors. Avon's Andrea Jung, Ogilvy & Mather's Shelly Lazarus, and Xerox's Ursula Burns, for example, all refer to themselves as *chairman*.[5]) Reword sentences to use *they* or to use no pronoun at all rather than refer to all individuals as *he*. Note that the preferred title for women in business is *Ms.* unless the individual asks to be addressed as *Miss* or *Mrs.* or has some other title, such as *Dr.*

REAL-TIME UPDATES
Learn More by Reading This PDF

Get detailed advice on using bias-free language

This in-depth guide offers practical tips for avoiding many types of cultural bias in your writing and speaking. Go to http://realtimeupdates.com/ebc10 and click on "Learn More." If you are using MyBcommLab, you can access Real-Time Updates within each chapter or under Student Study Tools.

TABLE 5.1	**Overcoming Bias in Language**	
Examples	**Unacceptable**	**Preferable**
Gender Bias		
Using words containing *man* (note that *chairman* is a common exception to this rule)	Man-made	Artificial, synthetic, manufactured, constructed, human-made
	Mankind	Humanity, human beings, human race, people
	Manpower	Workers, workforce
	Businessman	Executive, manager, businessperson, professional
	Salesman	Sales representative, salesperson
	Foreman	Supervisor
Using female-gender words	Actress, stewardess	Actor, flight attendant
Using special designations	Woman doctor, male nurse	Doctor, nurse
Using *he* to refer to "everyone"	The average worker . . . he	The average worker . . . he or she *OR* Average workers . . . they
Identifying roles with gender	The typical executive spends four hours of his day in meetings.	Most executives spend four hours a day in meetings.
	the consumer . . . she	consumers . . . they
	the nurse/teacher . . . she	nurses/teachers . . . they
Identifying women by marital status	Mrs. Norm Lindstrom	Maria Lindstrom *OR* Ms. Maria Lindstrom
	Norm Lindstrom and Ms. Drake	Norm Lindstrom and Maria Drake *OR* Mr. Lindstrom and Ms. Drake
Racial and Ethnic Bias		
Assigning stereotypes	Not surprisingly, Shing-Tung Yau excels in mathematics.	Shing-Tung Yau excels in mathematics.
Identifying people by race or ethnicity	Mario M. Cuomo, Italian-American politician and ex-governor of New York	Mario M. Cuomo, politician and ex-governor of New York
Age Bias		
Including age when irrelevant	Mary Kirazy, 58, has just joined our trust department.	Mary Kirazy has just joined our trust department.
Disability Bias		
Putting the disability before the person	Disabled workers face many barriers on the job.	Workers with physical disabilities face many barriers on the job.
	An epileptic, Tracy has no trouble doing her job.	Tracy's epilepsy has no effect on her job performance.

- **Racial and ethnic bias.** Avoid identifying people by race or ethnic origin unless such a label is relevant to the matter at hand—and it rarely is.
- **Age bias.** Mention the age of a person only when it is relevant. Moreover, be careful of the context in which you use words that refer to age; such words carry a variety of positive and negative connotations. For example, *young* can imply energy, youthfulness, inexperience, or even immaturity, depending on how it's used.
- **Disability bias.** Physical, mental, sensory, or emotional impairments should never be mentioned in business messages unless those conditions are directly relevant to the subject. If you must refer to someone's disability, put the person first and the disability second.[6] For example, by saying "employees with physical handicaps," not "handicapped employees," you focus on the whole person, not the disability. Finally, never use outdated terminology such as *crippled* or *retarded*.

Adapting to Your Audience: Building Strong Relationships

Successful communication relies on a positive relationship between sender and receiver. Establishing your credibility and projecting your company's image are two vital steps in building and fostering positive business relationships.

ESTABLISHING YOUR CREDIBILITY

Audience responses to your messages depend heavily on your **credibility**, a measure of your believability, based on how reliable you are and how much trust you evoke in others. With audiences who already know you, you've already established some degree of credibility, based on past communication efforts. However, with audiences that don't know you, you need to establish credibility before they'll accept—or perhaps even pay attention to—your messages (see Figure 5.2). To build, maintain, or repair your credibility, emphasize the following characteristics:

- **Honesty.** Demonstrating honesty and integrity will earn you the respect of your audiences, even if they don't always agree with or welcome your messages.
- **Objectivity.** Show that you can distance yourself from emotional situations and look at all sides of an issue.
- **Awareness of audience needs.** Let your audiences know that you understand what's important to them.
- **Credentials, knowledge, and expertise.** Audiences need to know that you have whatever it takes to back up your message, whether it's education, professional certification, special training, past successes, or simply the fact that you've done your research.

2 LEARNING OBJECTIVE

Explain how establishing your credibility and projecting your company's image are vital aspects of building strong relationships with your audience.

People are more likely to react positively to your message when they have confidence in you.

To enhance your credibility, emphasize such factors as honesty, objectivity, and awareness of audience needs.

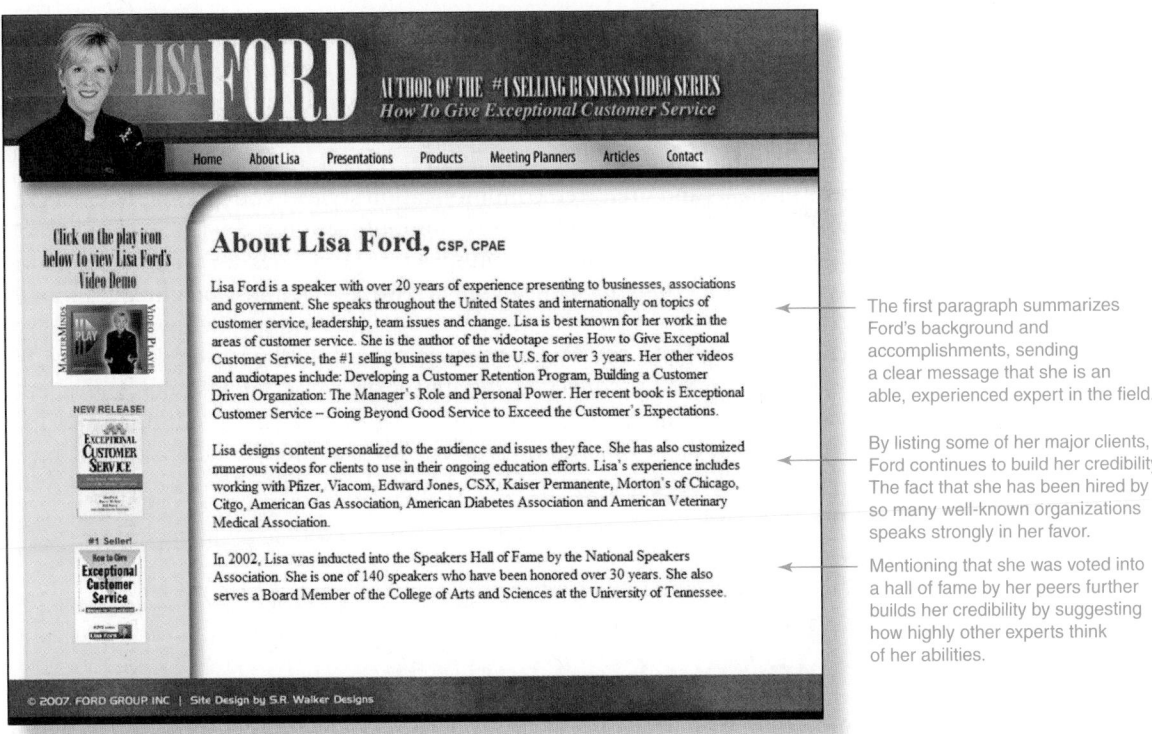

The first paragraph summarizes Ford's background and accomplishments, sending a clear message that she is an able, experienced expert in the field.

By listing some of her major clients, Ford continues to build her credibility. The fact that she has been hired by so many well-known organizations speaks strongly in her favor.

Mentioning that she was voted into a hall of fame by her peers further builds her credibility by suggesting how highly other experts think of her abilities.

Figure 5.2   Building Credibility
Lisa Ford is a highly regarded expert in the field of customer service, but she still takes care to communicate her qualifications as a presenter so that potential audience members who aren't familiar with her work can appreciate the expertise she has to offer.
Source: Used with permission of Lisa Ford.

REAL-TIME UPDATES
Learn More by Reading This Article

Building credibility online

Follow these steps to build your credibility as an online voice. Go to http://real-timeupdates.com/ebc10 and click on Learn More. If you are using MyBcommLab, you can access Real-Time Updates within each chapter or under Student Study Tools.

- **Endorsements.** An *endorsement* is a statement on your behalf by someone who is accepted by your audience as an expert.
- **Performance.** Demonstrating impressive communication skills is not enough; people need to know they can count on you to get the job done.
- **Sincerity.** When you offer praise, don't use *hyperbole*, such as "you are the most fantastic employee I could ever imagine." Instead, point out specific qualities that warrant praise.

In addition, audiences need to know that you believe in yourself and your message. Be careful with phrases containing words such as *hope* and *trust*, which can drain the audience's confidence in your message:

Instead of This	Write This
We hope this recommendation will be helpful.	We're pleased to make this recommendation.
We trust that you'll want to extend your service contract.	By extending your service contract, you can continue to enjoy top-notch performance from your equipment.

Finally, keep in mind that credibility can take a long time to establish—and it can be wiped out in an instant. An occasional mistake or letdown is usually forgiven, but major lapses in honesty or integrity can destroy your reputation.

PROJECTING YOUR COMPANY'S IMAGE

Your company's interests and reputation take precedence over your personal communication style.

When you communicate with anyone outside your organization, it is more than a conversation between two individuals. You represent your company and therefore play a vital role in helping the company build and maintain positive relationships with all its stakeholders. Most successful companies work hard to foster a specific public image, and your external communication efforts need to project that image. As part of this responsibility, the interests and preferred communication style of your company must take precedence over your own views and personal communication style.

Many organizations have specific communication guidelines that show everything from the correct use of the company name to preferred abbreviations and other grammatical details. Specifying a desired style of communication is more difficult, however. Observe more-experienced colleagues to see how they communicate, and never hesitate to ask for editorial help to make sure you're conveying the appropriate tone. For instance, with clients entrusting thousands or millions of dollars to it, an investment firm communicates in a style quite different from that of a clothing retailer. And a clothing retailer specializing in high-quality business attire communicates in a different style than a store catering to the latest trends in casual wear.

Adapting to Your Audience: Controlling Your Style and Tone

3   LEARNING OBJECTIVE

Explain how to achieve a tone that is conversational but businesslike, explain the value of using plain language, and define active and passive voice.

Your communication **style** involves the choices you make to express yourself: the words you select, the manner in which you use those words in sentences, and the way you build paragraphs from individual sentences. Your style creates a certain **tone**, or overall impression, in your messages. You can vary your style to sound forceful or objective, personal or formal, colorful or dry. The right choice depends on the nature of your message and your relationship with the reader.

USING A CONVERSATIONAL TONE

The tone of your business messages can range from informal to conversational to formal. When you're communicating with your superiors or with customers, your tone may tend to be more formal and respectful.[7] However, that formal tone might sound distant and cold if used with close colleagues.

Compare the three versions of the message in Table 5.2. The first is too formal and stuffy for today's audiences, whereas the third is inappropriately casual for business. The second message demonstrates the **conversational tone** used in most business communication—plain language that sounds businesslike without being stuffy at one extreme or too laid back and informal at the other extreme. You can achieve a tone that is conversational but still businesslike by following these guidelines:

- **Understand the difference between texting and writing.** The casual, acronym-laden language used in text messaging and instant messaging between friends is not considered professional business writing. Yes, texting style is an efficient way for friends to communicate—particularly taking into account the limitations of a phone keypad—but if you want to be taken seriously in business, you simply cannot write like this on the job.

- **Avoid stale and pompous language.** Most companies now shy away from such dated phrases as "attached please find" and "please be advised that." Similarly, avoid using obscure words, stale or clichéd expressions, and overly complicated sentences to impress others (see Table 5.3 on the next page).

- **Avoid preaching and bragging.** No one wants to listen to know-it-alls who like to preach or brag. However, if you need to remind your audience of something that should be obvious, try to work in the information casually, perhaps in the middle

> Most business messages aim for a conversational style that is warm but businesslike.

TABLE 5.2	Finding the Right Tone

Tone	Example
Stuffy: too formal for today's audiences	Dear Ms. Navarro:
	Enclosed please find the information that was requested during our telephone communication of May 14. As was mentioned at that time, Midville Hospital has significantly more doctors of exceptional quality than any other health facility in the state.
	As you were also informed, our organization has quite an impressive network of doctors and other health-care professionals with offices located throughout the state. In the event that you should need a specialist, our professionals will be able to make an appropriate recommendation.
	In the event that you have questions or would like additional information, you may certainly contact me during regular business hours.
	Most sincerely yours,
	Samuel G. Berenz
Conversational: just right for most business communication	Dear Ms. Navarro:
	Here's the information you requested during our phone conversation on Friday. As I mentioned, Midville Hospital has the highest-rated doctors and more of them than any other hospital in the state.
	In addition, we have a vast network of doctors and other health professionals with offices throughout the state. If you need a specialist, they can refer you to the right one.
	If you would like more information, please call any time between 9:00 and 5:00, Monday through Friday.
	Sincerely,
	Samuel G. Berenz
Unprofessional: too casual for business communication	Here's the 411 you requested. IMHO, we have more and better doctors than any other hospital in the state.
	FYI, we also have a large group of doctors and other health professionals w/offices close to U at work/home. If U need a specialist, they'll refer U to the right one.
	Any? just ring or msg.
	L8R,
	S

TABLE 5.3	Weeding Out Obsolete Phrases
Obsolete Phrase	**Up-to-Date Replacement**
we are in receipt of	we received
kindly advise	please let me/us know
attached please find	enclosed is or I/we have enclosed
it has come to my attention	I have just learned or [someone] has just informed me
the undersigned	I/we
in due course	(specify a time or date)
permit me to say that	(omit; just say whatever you need to say)
pursuant to	(omit; just say whatever you need to say)
in closing, I'd like to say	(omit; just say whatever you need to say)
we wish to inform you that	(omit; just say whatever you need to say)
please be advised that	(omit; just say whatever you need to say)

of a paragraph, where it will sound like a secondary comment rather than a major revelation.

- **Be careful with intimacy.** Business messages should generally avoid intimacy, such as sharing personal details or adopting a casual, unprofessional tone. However, when you have a close relationship with audience members, such as among the members of a close-knit team, a more intimate tone is sometimes appropriate and even expected.
- **Be careful with humor.** Humor can easily backfire and divert attention from your message. If you don't know your audience well or you're not skilled at using humor in a business setting, don't use it at all. Avoid humor in formal messages and when you're communicating across cultural boundaries.

USING PLAIN LANGUAGE

What do you think this sentence is trying to say?

> We continually exist to synergistically supply value-added deliverables such that we may continue to proactively maintain enterprise-wide data to stay competitive in tomorrow's world.[8]

If you don't have any idea what it means, you're not alone. However, this is a real sentence from a real company, written in an attempt to explain what the company does and why. This sort of incomprehensible, buzzword-filled writing is driving a widespread call to use *plain language* (or *plain English* specifically when English is involved).

Audiences can understand and act on plain language without reading it over and over.

Plain language presents information in a simple, unadorned style that allows your audience to easily grasp your meaning—language that recipients "can read, understand and act upon the first time they read it."[9] You can see how this definition supports using the "you" attitude and shows respect for your audience. In addition, plain language can make companies more productive and more profitable simply because people spend less time trying to figure out messages that are confusing or aren't written to meet their needs.[10] Finally, plain language helps nonnative speakers read your messages (see "Communicating Across Cultures: Can You Connect with a Global Audience on the Web?").

On the Creative Commons website, for instance, licensing terms are available in three versions: a complete "legal code" document that spells out contractual details in specific legal terms that meet the needs of legal professionals, a "human readable" version that explains the licensing

COMMUNICATING ACROSS CULTURES

Can You Connect with a Global Audience on the Web?

Reaching an international audience on the web involves more than simply offering translations of the English language. Successful global sites address the needs of international customers in five ways:

1. **Consider the reader's perspective.** Many communication elements that you take for granted may be interpreted differently by audiences in different countries. Should you use the metric system, different notations for times or dates, or even different names for countries? For example, German citizens don't refer to their country by the English word *Germany*; it's *Deutschland* to them. Review the entire online experience and look for ways to improve communication, including such helpful tools as interactive currency converters and translation dictionaries.

2. **Take cultural differences into account.** For instance, because humor is rooted in cultural norms, U.S. humor may not be so funny to readers from other countries. Avoid idioms and references that aren't universally recognized, such as "putting all your eggs in one basket" or "jumping out of the frying pan into the fire."

3. **Keep the message clear.** Choose simple, unambiguous words; construct short, clear, sentences; and write in the active voice whenever possible. Define abbreviations, acronyms, and words an international audience may not be familiar with.

4. **Complement language with visuals.** Use drawings, photos, videos, and other visual elements to support written messages.

5. **Consult local experts.** Seek the advice of local experts about phrases and references that may be expected. Even terms as simple as *homepage* differ from country to country. Spanish readers refer to the "first page," or *pagina inicial*, whereas the French term is "welcome page," or *page d'accueil*.

CAREER APPLICATIONS

1. Visit the U.S. website of HP at **www.hp.com** and find the links to country-specific HP websites by clicking on the world map next to the "United States" label. Choose any three countries and compare those sites to the U.S. site. How does HP localize its web presence for the countries you've chosen? Which textual or visual elements are consistent across all four countries? Write a two-paragraph summary of your analysis.

2. Repeat this comparison using the same three companies on IBM's website (**www.ibm.com**). After analyzing IBM's localization efforts, compare its approach with HP's. Which company does a more effective job of localization? Why?

Sources: Adapted from Laura Morelli, "Writing for a Global Audience on the Web," *Marketing News*, 17 August 1998, 16; Yuri and Anna Radzievsky, "Successful Global Web Sites Look Through Eyes of the Audience," *Advertising Age's Business Marketing*, January 1998, 17; Sari Kalin, "The Importance of Being Multiculturally Correct," *Computerworld*, 6 October 1997, G16–G17; B. G. Yovovich, "Making Sense of All the Web's Numbers," *Editor & Publisher*, November 1998, 30–31; David Wilford, "Are We All Speaking the Same Language?" *The Times*, (London), 20 April 2000, 4.

terms in nontechnical language that anyone can understand, and a "machine readable" version fine-tuned for search engines and other systems (see Figure 5.3 on the next page).[11]

SELECTING THE ACTIVE OR PASSIVE VOICE

Your choice of the active or passive voice affects the tone of your message. In a sentence written in the **active voice**, the subject performs the action and the object receives the action: "Jodi sent the email message." In a sentence written in the **passive voice**, the subject receives the action: "The email message was sent by Jodi." As you can see, the passive voice combines the helping verb *to be* with a form of the verb that is usually similar to the past tense.

Using the active voice helps make your writing more direct, livelier, and easier to read (see Table 5.4 on the next page). In contrast, the passive voice is often cumbersome, can be unnecessarily vague, and can make sentences overly long. In most cases, the active voice is your best choice.[12] Nevertheless, using the passive voice can help you demonstrate the "you" attitude in some situations:

- When you want to be diplomatic about pointing out a problem or an error of some kind (the passive version seems less like an accusation)
- When you want to point out what's being done without taking or attributing either the credit or the blame (the passive version shifts the spotlight away from the person or persons involved)
- When you want to avoid personal pronouns in order to create an objective tone (the passive version may be used in a formal report, for example)

Use passive sentences to soften bad news, to put yourself in the background, or to create an impersonal tone.

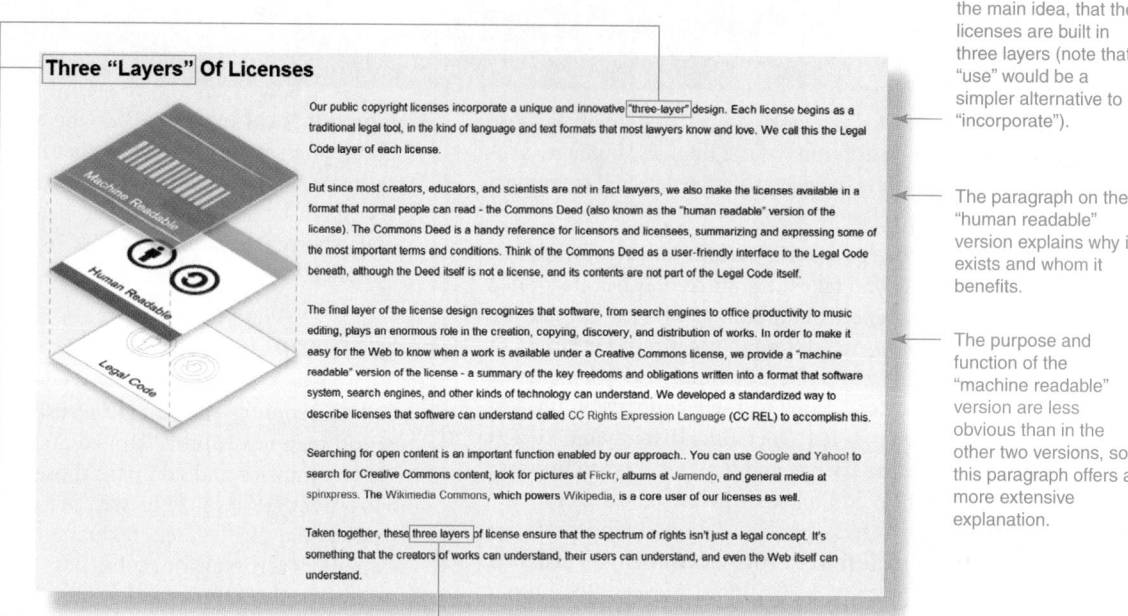

The notion of three layers is carried through the text and reinforced with the diagram.

The introductory sentence expresses the main idea, that the licenses are built in three layers (note that "use" would be a simpler alternative to "incorporate").

The paragraph on the "human readable" version explains why it exists and whom it benefits.

The purpose and function of the "machine readable" version are less obvious than in the other two versions, so this paragraph offers a more extensive explanation.

Figure 5.3 Plain Language at Creative Commons
Creative Commons uses this diagram and text to explain the differences among its three versions of content licenses.
Source: Courtesy of Creative Commons.

TABLE 5.4	Choosing Active or Passive Voice

In general, avoid passive voice in order to make your writing lively and direct.

Dull and Indirect in Passive Voice	Lively and Direct in Active Voice
The new procedure was developed by the operations team.	The operations team developed the new procedure.
Legal problems are created by this contract.	This contract creates legal problems.
Reception preparations have been undertaken by our PR people for the new CEO's arrival.	Our PR people have begun planning a reception for the new CEO.

However, passive voice is helpful when you need to be diplomatic or want to focus attention on problems or solutions rather than on people.

Accusatory or Self-Congratulatory in Active Voice	More Diplomatic in Passive Voice
You lost the shipment.	The shipment was lost.
I recruited seven engineers last month.	Seven engineers were recruited last month.
We are investigating the high rate of failures on the final assembly line.	The high rate of failures on the final assembly line is being investigated.

The second half of Table 5.4 illustrates several other situations in which the passive voice helps you focus your message on your audience.

Composing Your Message: Choosing Powerful Words

After you have decided how to adapt to your audience, you're ready to begin composing your message. As you write your first draft, let your creativity flow. Don't try to write and edit at the same time or worry about getting everything perfect. Make up words if you can't think of the right word, draw pictures, talk out loud—do whatever it takes to get the ideas out of your head and captured on screen or paper. If you've scheduled carefully, you should have time to revise and refine the material later, before showing it to anyone. In fact, many writers find it helpful to establish a personal rule of *never* showing a first draft to anyone. By working in this "safe zone," away from the critical eyes of others, your mind will stay free to think clearly and creatively.

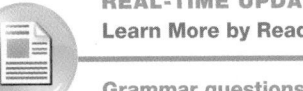

You may find it helpful to hone your craft by viewing your writing at three levels: strong words, effective sentences, and coherent paragraphs. Starting at the word level, successful writers pay close attention to the correct use of words.[13] If you make errors of grammar or usage, you lose credibility with your audience—even if your message is otherwise correct. Poor grammar suggests to readers that you're uninformed, and they may choose not to trust an uninformed source. Moreover, poor grammar can imply that you don't respect your audience enough to get things right.

> Hone your craft by viewing your writing at three levels: strong words, effective sentences, and coherent paragraphs.

The "rules" of grammar and usage can be a source of worry for writers because some of these rules are complex and some evolve over time. Even professional editors and grammarians occasionally have questions about correct usage, and they sometimes disagree about the answers. For example, the word *data* is the plural form of *datum*, yet some experts now prefer to treat *data* as a singular noun when it's used in nonscientific material to refer to a collection of facts or figures.

With practice, you'll become more skilled in making correct choices. If you have doubts about what is correct, you have many ways to find the answer. Check the "Handbook of Grammar, Mechanics, and Usage" at the end of this book, or consult the many special reference books and resources available in libraries, in bookstores, and on the Internet.

> If you're not sure of correct grammar or usage, look it up; you'll avoid embarrassing mistakes and learn at the same time.

In addition to using words correctly, successful writers and speakers take care to find the most effective words and phrases to convey their meaning. Selecting and using words effectively is often more challenging than using words correctly because it's a matter of judgment and experience. Careful writers continue to work at their craft to find words that communicate with power (see Figure 5.4 on the next page).

> Effectiveness is the second consideration when choosing words.

UNDERSTANDING DENOTATION AND CONNOTATION

A word may have both a denotative and a connotative meaning. The **denotative meaning** is the literal, or dictionary, meaning. The **connotative meaning** includes all the associations and feelings evoked by the word.

> Many words have both a *denotative* (explicit, specific) meaning and a *connotative* (implicit, associative) meaning.

The denotative meaning of *desk* is "a piece of furniture with a flat work surface and various drawers for storage." The connotative meaning of *desk* may include thoughts associated with work or study, but the word *desk* has fairly neutral connotations—neither strong nor emotional. However, some words have much stronger connotations than others and should be used with care. For example, the connotations of the word *fail* are negative and can carry strong emotional meaning. If you say that the sales department *failed* to meet its annual quota, the connotative meaning suggests that the group is inferior, incompetent, or below some standard of performance. However, the reason for not achieving 100 percent might be an inferior product, incorrect pricing, or some other factor outside the control of the sales department. In contrast, by saying that the sales department achieved 85 percent of its quota, you clearly communicate that the results were less than expected—without triggering all the negative emotions associated with *failure*.

BALANCING ABSTRACT AND CONCRETE WORDS

Words vary dramatically in their degree of abstraction or concreteness. An **abstract word** expresses a concept, quality, or characteristic. Abstractions are usually broad, encompassing a category of ideas, and they are often intellectual, academic, or philosophical. *Love, honor, progress, tradition,* and *beauty* are abstractions, as are such important business

> The more abstract a word is, the more it is removed from the tangible, objective world that can be perceived with the senses.

Two Sides of the Story

Growing interest in the global acceptance of a single set of robust accounting standards comes from all participants in the capital markets. Many multinational companies and national regulators and users support it because they believe that the use of common standards in the preparation of public company financial statements will make it easier to compare the financial results of reporting entities from different countries. They believe it will help investors understand opportunities better. Large public companies with subsidiaries in multiple jurisdictions would be able to use one accounting language company-wide and present their financial statements in the same language as their competitors.

Another benefit some believe is that in a truly global economy, financial professionals including CPAs will be more mobile, and companies will more easily be able to respond to the human capital needs of their subsidiaries around the world.

Nevertheless, many people also believe that U.S. GAAP is the gold standard, and something will be lost with full acceptance of IFRS. However, recent SEC actions and global trends have increased awareness of the need to address possible adoption. According to a survey conducted in the first half of 2008 by Deloitte & Touche among chief financial officers and other financial professionals, U.S. companies have an interest in adopting IFRS and this interest is steadily growing. Thirty percent would consider adopting IFRS now, another 28 percent are unsure or do not have sufficient knowledge to decide, while 42 percent said they would not. Still, an AICPA survey conducted in Fall 2008 among its CPA members shows a significant and positive shift in the number of firms and companies that are starting to prepare for eventual adoption of IFRS. A 55 percent majority of CPAs at firms and companies nationwide said they are preparing in a variety of ways for IFRS adoption, an increase of 14 percentage points over the 41 percent who were preparing for change, according to an April 2008 AICPA survey.

Another concern is that worldwide many countries that claim to be converging to international standards may never get 100 percent compliance. Most reserve the right to carve out selectively or modify standards they do not consider in their national interest, an action that could lead to incompatibility—the very issue that IFRS seek to address.

GAAP and IFRS, Still Differences

Great strides have been made by the FASB and the IASB to converge the content of IFRS and U.S. GAAP. The goal is that by the time the SEC allows or mandates the use of IFRS for U.S. publicly traded companies, most or all of the key differences will have been resolved.

Because of these ongoing convergence projects, the extent of the specific differences between IFRS and U.S. GAAP is shrinking. Yet significant differences do remain. For example:

- IFRS does not permit Last In First Out (LIFO) as an inventory costing method.
- IFRS uses a single-step method for impairment write-downs rather than the two-step method used in U.S. GAAP, making write-downs more likely.
- IFRS has a different probability threshold and measurement objective for contingencies.
- IFRS does not permit curing debt covenant violations after year-end.
- IFRS guidance regarding revenue recognition is less extensive than GAAP and contains relatively little industry-specific instructions.

5

Annotations (left margin):

In many cases, *global* is an absolute term and doesn't benefit from a modifier such as *truly*. However, economic globalization is occurring in stages, so *truly* here suggests the point at which globalization is nearly complete.

Claim is a powerful word here because it suggests a strong element of doubt.

The diplomatic use of passive voice keeps the focus on the issue at hand, rather than on the organizations that are involved.

Annotations (right margin):

Robust goes beyond simply *strong* to suggest *resilient* and *comprehensive* as well.

Gold standard (a term borrowed from economics) refers to something against which all similar entities are compared, an unsurpassed model of excellence.

In the context of a survey *significant* means more than just *important*; it indicates a statistical observation that is large enough to be more than mere chance. *Positive* indicates the direction of the change and suggests *affirmation* and *progress*.

Carve out is much stronger than *remove* because it could suggest surgical precision if done well or perhaps violent destruction if not done with finesse. In this context, *carve out* is meant to express a concern about countries weakening the international financial standards by modifying them to meet their own needs.

Figure 5.4   Choosing Powerful Words

Notice how careful word choices help this excerpt from a report published by the American Institute of Certified Public Accountants make a number of important points. The tone is formal, which is appropriate for a report with global, public readership. (GAAP refers to accounting standards currently used in the United States; IFRS refers to international standards.)

Source: Copyright 2011, American Institute of Certified Public Accountants. All rights reserved. Used with Permission.

---

concepts as *productivity, profits, quality,* and *motivation.* In contrast, a **concrete word** stands for something you can touch, see, or visualize. Most concrete terms are anchored in the tangible, material world. *Chair, table, horse, rose, kick, kiss, red, green,* and *two* are concrete words; they are direct, clear, and exact. Incidentally, technology continues to generate new words and new meanings that describe things that don't have a physical presence but are nonetheless concrete: *software, database,* and *website* are all concrete terms as well.

As you can imagine, abstractions tend to cause more trouble for writers and readers than concrete words. Abstractions tend to be "fuzzy" and can be interpreted differently, depending on the audience and the circumstances. The best way to minimize such problems is to blend abstract terms with concrete ones, the general with the specific.

State the concept, then pin it down with details expressed in more concrete terms. Save the abstractions for ideas that cannot be expressed any other way. In addition, abstract words such as *small, numerous, sizable, near, soon, good,* and *fine* are imprecise, so try to replace them with terms that are more accurate. Instead of referring to a *sizable loss,* give an exact number.

FINDING WORDS THAT COMMUNICATE WELL

By practicing your writing, learning from experienced writers and editors, and reading extensively, you'll find it easier to choose words that communicate exactly what you want to say. When you compose your business messages, think carefully to find the most powerful words for each situation and to avoid obscure words, clichés, and buzzwords that are turning into clichés (see Table 5.5 on the next page):

- **Choose strong, precise words.** Choose words that express your thoughts clearly, specifically, and dynamically. If you find yourself using a lot of adjectives and adverbs, you're probably trying to compensate for weak nouns and verbs. Saying that *sales plummeted* is stronger and more efficient than saying *sales dropped dramatically* or *sales experienced a dramatic drop.*
- **Choose familiar words.** You'll communicate best with words that are familiar to both you and your readers. Moreover, trying to use an unfamiliar word for the first time in an important document can lead to embarrassing mistakes.
- **Avoid clichés and use buzzwords carefully.** Although familiar words are generally the best choice, avoid *clichés*—terms and phrases so common that they have lost some of their power to communicate. *Buzzwords,* newly coined terms often associated with technology, business, or cultural changes, are more difficult to handle than clichés. In some situations, the careful use of a buzzword can signal that you're an insider, someone in the know.[14] However, buzzwords quickly become clichés, and using them too late in their "life cycle" can mark you as an outsider desperately trying to look like an insider.
- **Use jargon carefully.** *Jargon,* the specialized language of a particular profession or industry, has a bad reputation, but it's not always bad. Using jargon is usually an efficient way to communicate within the specific groups that understand these terms. After all, that's how jargon develops in the first place, as people with similar interests develop ways to communicate complex ideas quickly.

Try to use words that are powerful and familiar.

Avoid clichés, be extremely careful with trendy buzzwords, and use jargon only when your audience is completely familiar with it.

If you need help finding the right words, try some of the visual dictionaries and thesauruses available online. For example, Visuwords (www.visuwords.com) shows words that are similar to or different from a given word and helps you see subtle differences to find the perfect word.[15]

Composing Your Message: Creating Effective Sentences

Arranging your carefully chosen words in effective sentences is the next step in creating powerful messages. Start by selecting the best type of sentence to communicate each point you want to make.

5   LEARNING OBJECTIVE

Define the four types of sentences, and explain how sentence style affects emphasis within a message.

CHOOSING FROM THE FOUR TYPES OF SENTENCES

Sentences come in four basic varieties: simple, compound, complex, and compound–complex. A **simple sentence** has one main *clause* (a single subject and a single predicate), although it may be expanded by nouns and pronouns that serve as objects of the action and by modifying phrases. Here's an example with the subject noun underlined once and the predicate verb underlined twice:

A simple sentence has one main clause.

Profits increased in the past year.

TABLE 5.5	Finding Stronger Word Choices: Selected Examples

Potentially Weak Words and Phrases	Stronger Alternatives (effective usage depends on the situation)
Increase (as a verb)	Accelerate, amplify, augment, enlarge, escalate, expand, extend, magnify, multiply, soar, swell
Decrease (as a verb)	Curb, cut back, depreciate, dwindle, shrink, slacken
Large, small	(use a specific number, such as $100 million)
Good	Admirable, beneficial, desirable, flawless, pleasant, sound, superior, worthy
Bad	Abysmal, corrupt, deficient, flawed, inadequate, inferior, poor, substandard, worthless
We are committed to providing . . .	We provide . . .
It is in our best interest to . . .	We should . . .

Unfamiliar Words	Familiar Words
Ascertain	Find out, learn
Consummate	Close, bring about
Peruse	Read, study
Circumvent	Avoid
Unequivocal	Certain

Clichés and Buzzwords	Plain Language
An uphill battle	A challenge
Writing on the wall	Prediction
Call the shots	Lead
Take by storm	Attack
Costs an arm and a leg	Expensive
A new ballgame	Fresh start
Fall through the cracks	Be overlooked
Think outside the box	Be creative
Run it up the flagpole	Find out what people think about it
Eat our own dog food	Use our own products
Mission-critical	Vital
Disintermediate	Get rid of
Green light (as a verb)	Approve
Architect (as a verb)	Design
Space (as in, "we compete in the XYZ space")	Market or industry
Blocking and tackling	Basic skills
Trying to boil the ocean	Working frantically but without focus
Human capital	People, employees, workforce
Low-hanging fruit	Tasks that are easy to complete or sales that are easy to close
Pushback	Resistance

A **compound sentence** has two main clauses that express two or more independent but related thoughts of equal importance, usually joined by *and*, *but*, or *or*. In effect, a compound sentence is a merger of two or more simple sentences (independent clauses) that are related. For example:

> Wage rates have declined by 5 percent, and employee turnover has been high.

A compound sentence has two main clauses.

The independent clauses in a compound sentence are always separated by a comma or by a semicolon (in which case the conjunction—*and*, *but*, *or*—is dropped).

A **complex sentence** expresses one main thought (the independent clause) and one or more subordinate, related thoughts (dependent clauses that cannot stand alone as valid sentences). Independent and dependent clauses are usually separated by a comma. In this example, "Although you may question Gerald's conclusions" is a subordinate thought expressed in a dependent clause:

A complex sentence has one main clause and one subordinate clause.

> Although you may question Gerald's conclusions, you must admit that his research is thorough.

A **compound–complex sentence** has two main clauses, at least one of which contains a subordinate clause:

A compound–complex sentence has two main clauses and at least one dependent clause.

> Profits increased 35 percent in the past year, so although the company faces long-term challenges, I agree that its short-term prospects look quite positive.

To make your writing as effective as possible, strive for variety and balance using all four sentence types. If you use too many simple sentences, you won't be able to properly express the relationships among your ideas, and your writing will sound choppy and abrupt. At the other extreme, a long series of compound, complex, or compound-complex sentences can be tiring to read.

Writing is usually more interesting and effective if it balances all four sentence types.

USING SENTENCE STYLE TO EMPHASIZE KEY THOUGHTS

In every message of any length, some ideas are more important than others. You can emphasize these key ideas through your sentence style. One obvious technique is to give important points the most space. When you want to call attention to a thought, use extra words to describe it. Consider this sentence:

You can emphasize ideas in a sentence by
- Devoting more words to them
- Putting them at the beginning or at the end of the sentence
- Making them the subject of the sentence

> The chairperson called for a vote of the shareholders.

To emphasize the importance of the chairperson, you might describe her more fully:

> Having considerable experience in corporate takeover battles, the chairperson called for a vote of the shareholders.

You can increase the emphasis even more by adding a separate, short sentence to augment the first:

> The chairperson called for a vote of the shareholders. She has considerable experience in corporate takeover battles.

You can also call attention to a thought by making it the subject of the sentence. In the following example, the emphasis is on the person:

> I can write letters much more quickly by using a computer.

However, by changing the subject, the computer takes center stage:

> The computer enables me to write letters much more quickly.

Another way to emphasize an idea is to place it either at the beginning or at the end of a sentence:

> **Less emphatic:** We are cutting the price to stimulate demand.
> **More emphatic:** To stimulate demand, we are cutting the price.

In complex sentences, the placement of the dependent clause hinges on the relationship between the ideas expressed. If you want to emphasize the subordinate idea, put the dependent clause at the end of the sentence (the most emphatic position) or at the beginning (the second most emphatic position). If you want to downplay the idea, put the dependent clause within the sentence:

> **Most emphatic:** The electronic parts are manufactured in Mexico, <u>which has lower wage rates than the United States.</u>
> **Emphatic:** <u>Because wage rates are lower in Mexico than in the United States,</u> the electronic parts are manufactured there.
> **Least emphatic:** Mexico, <u>which has lower wage rates than the United States,</u> was selected as the production site for the electronic parts.

You can adjust the emphasis given to a subordinate idea by placing the dependent clause at the beginning, middle, or end of the sentence.

Techniques such as these give you a great deal of control over the way your audience interprets what you have to say.

Composing Your Message: Crafting Unified, Coherent Paragraphs

6   LEARNING OBJECTIVE

Define the three key elements of a paragraph, and list five ways to develop unified, coherent paragraphs.

Paragraphs organize sentences related to the same general topic. Readers expect every paragraph to be *unified*—focusing on a single topic—and *coherent*—presenting ideas in a logically connected way. By carefully arranging the elements of each paragraph, you help your readers grasp the main idea of your document and understand how the specific pieces of support material back up that idea.

CREATING THE ELEMENTS OF A PARAGRAPH

Paragraphs vary widely in length and form, but a typical paragraph contains three basic elements: a topic sentence, support sentences that develop the topic, and transitional words and phrases.

Topic Sentence

Most paragraphs consist of
• A topic sentence that reveals the subject of the paragraph
• Related sentences that support and expand the topic
• Transitions that help readers move between sentences and between paragraphs

An effective paragraph deals with a single topic, and the sentence that introduces that topic is called the **topic sentence**. In informal and creative writing, the topic sentence may be implied rather than stated. In business writing, the topic sentence is generally explicit and is often the first sentence in the paragraph. The topic sentence gives readers a summary of the general idea that will be covered in the rest of the paragraph. The following examples show how a topic sentence can introduce the subject and suggest the way the subject will be developed:

> The medical products division has been troubled for many years by public relations problems. [In the rest of the paragraph, readers will learn the details of the problems.]
>
> To get a refund, please supply us with the following information. [The details of the necessary information will be described in the rest of the paragraph.]

In addition to helping your readers, topic sentences help you as a writer because they remind you of the purpose of each paragraph and thereby encourage you to stay focused.

Support Sentences

In most paragraphs, the topic sentence needs to be explained, justified, or extended with one or more support sentences. These related sentences must all have a bearing on the general subject and must provide enough specific details to make the topic clear:

> The medical products division has been troubled for many years by public relations problems. Since 2002 the local newspaper has published 15 articles that portray the division in a negative light. We have been accused of everything from mistreating laboratory animals to polluting the local groundwater. Our facility has been described as a health hazard. Our scientists are referred to as "Frankensteins," and our profits are considered "obscene."

The support sentences are all more specific than the topic sentence. Each one provides another piece of evidence to demonstrate the general truth of the main thought. Also, each sentence is clearly related to the general idea being developed, which gives the paragraph unity. A paragraph is well developed if it contains enough information to make the topic sentence understood and convincing, and if it doesn't contain any extraneous, unrelated sentences.

Transitions

Transitions connect ideas by showing how one thought is related to another. They also help alert the reader to what lies ahead so that shifts and changes don't cause confusion. In addition to helping readers understand the connections you're trying to make, transitions give your writing a smooth, even flow.

Depending on the specific need within a document, transitional elements can range in length from a single word to an entire paragraph or more. You can establish transitions in a variety of ways:

- **Use connecting words.** Use conjunctions such as *and, but, or, nevertheless, however, in addition*, and so on.
- **Echo a word or phrase from a previous paragraph or sentence.** "A system should be established for monitoring inventory levels. *This system* will provide . . ."
- **Use a pronoun that refers to a noun used previously.** "Ms. Arthur is the leading candidate for the president's position. *She* has excellent qualifications."
- **Use words that are frequently paired.** "The machine has a *minimum* output of . . . Its *maximum* output is . . ."

> Transitional elements include
> - Connecting words (conjunctions)
> - Repeated words or phrases
> - Pronouns
> - Words that are frequently paired

Some transitions serve as mood changers, alerting the reader to a change in mood from the previous material. Some announce a total contrast with what's gone on before, some announce a causal relationship, and some signal a change in time. Here is a list of transitions frequently used to move readers smoothly between clauses, sentences, and paragraphs:

Additional detail: moreover, furthermore, in addition, besides, first, second, third, finally

Cause-and-effect relationship: therefore, because, accordingly, thus, consequently, hence, as a result, so

Comparison: similarly, here again, likewise, in comparison, still

Contrast: yet, conversely, whereas, nevertheless, on the other hand, however, but, nonetheless

Condition: although, if

Illustration: for example, in particular, in this case, for instance

Time sequence: formerly, after, when, meanwhile, sometimes

Intensification: indeed, in fact, in any event

Summary: in brief, in short, to sum up

Repetition: that is, in other words, as mentioned earlier

The three sentences in this paragraph start with the broad topic (social media for charities and nonprofits) and narrow down the main idea, which is that TwitCause is a good tool for this purpose. (Note that the third sentence is really a fragment, but Hayes is selectively breaking the rules here to emphasize the suitability of TwitCause.)

Echoing *TwitCause* at the beginning of this paragraph tells readers that this paragraph will continue on the same subject.

The transition *Additionally* signals that the topic in the previous paragraph will be expanded upon in this new paragraph.

In my opinion lets readers know she is transitioning from reporting to offering her personal thoughts on the subject at hand.

Following suit functions as a transition from the previous paragraph by linking Pepsi back to the description of Home Depot.

The second and third sentences in this paragraph provide an example of the observation made in the topic sentence at the beginning of the paragraph.

MyBcommLab

Apply Figure 5.5's key concepts by revising a new document. Go to Chapter 5 in www .pearsoninternationaleditions .com/mybcommlab and select Document Makeovers.

Figure 5.5   Crafting Unified, Coherent Paragraphs
Olivia Hayes, a copywriter with the social media marketing agency Ignite, demonstrates several aspects of effective writing in this blog post about the Twitter-based social contribution network TwitCause.
Source: Used with permission of Ignite Social Media.

Consider using a transition whenever it could help the reader understand your ideas and follow you from point to point. You can use transitions inside paragraphs to tie related points together and between paragraphs to ease the shift from one distinct thought to another. In longer reports, a transition that links major sections or chapters may be a complete paragraph that serves as a mini-introduction to the next section or as a summary of the ideas presented in the section just ending.

Figure 5.5 offers several examples of transitions and other features of effective paragraphs.

CHOOSING THE BEST WAY TO DEVELOP EACH PARAGRAPH

You have a variety of options for developing paragraphs, each of which can convey a specific type of idea. Five of the most common approaches are illustration, comparison or contrast, cause and effect, classification, and problem and solution (see Table 5.6).

Using Technology to Compose and Shape Your Messages

7 LEARNING OBJECTIVE

Identify the most common software features that help you craft messages more efficiently.

Be sure to take advantage of the tools in your word processor or online publishing system to write more efficiently and effectively. The features, functions, and names vary from system to system and version to version, but you'll encounter some combination of the following capabilities:

- **Style sheets, style sets, templates, and themes.** *Style sheets, style sets, templates,* and *themes* are various ways of ensuring consistency throughout a document and from document to document. These tools also make it easy to redesign an entire document

TABLE 5.6	Five Techniques for Developing Paragraphs	
Technique	**Description**	**Example**
Illustration	Giving examples that demonstrate the general idea	Some of our most popular products are available through local distributors. For example, Everett & Lemmings carries our frozen soups and entrees. The J. B. Green Company carries our complete line of seasonings, as well as the frozen soups. Wilmont Foods, also a major distributor, now carries our new line of frozen desserts.
Comparison or contrast	Using similarities or differences to develop the topic	When the company was small, the recruiting function could be handled informally. The need for new employees was limited, and each manager could comfortably screen and hire her or his own staff. However, our successful bid on the Owens contract means that we will be doubling our labor force over the next six months. To hire that many people without disrupting our ongoing activities, we will create a separate recruiting group within the human resources department.
Cause and effect	Focusing on the reasons for something	The heavy-duty fabric of your Wanderer tent probably broke down for one of two reasons: (1) a sharp object punctured the fabric, and without reinforcement, the hole was enlarged by the stress of pitching the tent daily for a week or (2) the fibers gradually rotted because the tent was folded and stored while still wet.
Classification	Showing how a general idea is broken into specific categories	Successful candidates for our supervisor trainee program generally come from one of several groups. The largest group by far consists of recent graduates of accredited business management programs. The next largest group comes from within our own company, as we try to promote promising staff workers to positions of greater responsibility. Finally, we occasionally accept candidates with outstanding supervisory experience in related industries.
Problem and solution	Presenting a problem and then discussing the solution	Selling handmade toys online is a challenge because consumers are accustomed to buying heavily advertised toys from major chain stores or well-known websites such as Amazon.com. However, if we develop an appealing website, we can compete on the basis of product novelty and quality. In addition, we can provide unusual crafts at a competitive price: a rocking horse of birch, with a hand-knit tail and mane; a music box with the child's name painted on the top; and a real teepee, made by Native American artisans.

or screen simply by redefining the various styles or selecting a different design theme. Style sheets or sets are collections of formatting choices for words, paragraphs, and other elements. Rather than manually formatting every element, you simply select one of the available styles. Templates usually set overall document parameters such as page size and provide a specific set of styles to use. Templates can be particularly handy if you create a variety of document types, such as letters, calendars, agendas, and so on. Themes tend to address the overall look and feel of the page or screen, including color palettes and background images.

Take full advantage of your software's formatting capabilities to help produce effective, professional messages in less time.

- **Boilerplate and document components.** *Boilerplate* refers to a standard block of saved text that is reused in multiple documents. Moving beyond simple text blocks, some systems can store fully formatted document components such as cover pages and sidebars.
- **Autocorrection or autocompletion.** Some programs can automate text entry and correction using a feature called autocompletion, autocorrection, or something similar. In Microsoft Word, for example, the AutoCorrect feature lets you build a library of actions that automatically fill in longer entries based on the first few characters you type (such as entering a full description of the company after you type the word "boilerplate") or correct common typing errors (such as typing *teh* instead of *the*). Use these features carefully, though. First, they can make changes you might not want in every instance. Second, you may grow to rely on them to clean up your typing, but they won't be there to help when you're using other systems.
- **File merge and mail merge.** Most word processing software makes it easy to combine files, which is an especially handy feature when several members of a team write

different sections of a report. Mail merge lets you personalize form letters by automatically inserting names and addresses from a database.

- **Endnotes, footnotes, indexes, and tables of contents.** Your computer can help you track footnotes and endnotes, renumbering them every time you add or delete references. For a report's indexes and table of contents, you can simply flag the items you want to include, and the software assembles the lists for you.

For new articles and advice on writing business messages, visit http://real-timeupdates .com/ebc10 and click on Chapter 5. For a reminder of the tasks involved in writing messages, see "Checklist: Writing Business Messages."

✓ Checklist | Writing Business Messages

A. Adapt to your audience.
- Use the "you" attitude.
- Maintain good etiquette through polite communication.
- Emphasize the positive whenever possible.
- Use bias-free language.
- Establish credibility in the eyes of your audience.
- Project your company's preferred image.
- Use a conversational but still professional and respectful tone.
- Use plain language for clarity.

B. Compose your message.
- Choose strong words that communicate efficiently.
- Pay attention to the connotative meaning of your words.
- Balance abstract and concrete terms to convey your meaning accurately.
- Avoid clichés and trendy buzzwords.
- Use jargon only when your audience understands it and prefers it.
- Vary your sentence structure for impact and interest.
- Develop coherent, unified paragraphs.
- Use transitions generously to help your audience follow your message.

ON THE JOB: SOLVING COMMUNICATION DILEMMAS AT **CREATIVE COMMONS**

Source: Mizuka Ito/Creative Commons.

To achieve their mission of popularizing a new approach to copyrighting songs, artwork, literature, and other creative works, the staff at Creative Commons need to convince people that the traditional approach to copyright protection doesn't meet all the needs of today's digital society. This is no small challenge: Not only do they need to convince people to reconsider more than 200 years of legal precedent and habit, they also need to communicate with an extremely diverse audience—everyone from lawyers and business managers to artists, writers, musicians, and scientists. After graduating with a business degree, you've joined Creative Commons as a communication intern for a year before entering law school. Apply your knowledge of effective writing to the following scenarios.[16]

1. You have been asked to help develop a brochure for distribution by email to a mailing list of independent filmmakers, writers, and artists. The purpose of the brochure is to familiarize your target audience with Creative Commons and its licenses. The people you are writing for mostly work commercially; in some cases they may create content pro bono and distribute it as a public service. You are keen to persuade them that Creative Commons can provide them

with a framework to control permissions and make sure that their content has the appropriate legal protection as it leaves their hands. You need to come up with an opening statement for the brochure. Which of these do you think will do the job?
a. In today's world of easily disseminated content, copyright has to be more than an on-off switch.
b. If you have ever distributed your creations for the public good and then worried about the possibility that your generosity might be abused, Creative Commons has just the solution for you.
c. Copyright has to become subtler to operate in today's multimedia environments. Pirates abound and you can bet they have little compunction in stealing your work.
d. Creative Commons licenses come in six flavors, created by combining four parameters. (1) attribution (giving credit to the creator), (2) the freedom to make derivatives based on original creations, (3) restrictions on whether someone can make commercial products or use a derivative commercially, and (4) requirements to share a derivative with exactly the same licensing terms.

2. As a representative of Creative Commons, you are invited to take part in a panel discussion at a prestigious university where you share a platform with a prominent writer. However, the writer starts showing hostility toward you, alleging that Creative Commons is anti-creator and is just a "Band-Aid of self-righteousness applied to the rampant theft of intellectual property that characterizes the modern age." You suspect that her attack is not specifically targeted at you but rather at those who treat the rights of writers without respect. You want to convince her you are on her side. Which of these statements is likely to be most successful in doing this?

a. I completely agree with everything you say. People don't respect writers enough these days.

b. You must be talking about someone else. We would never do such a thing.

c. The purpose of Creative Commons is not to condone theft, but to allow writers to apply the level of protection they feel is appropriate to their work.

d. I don't think your statement is based on facts. Have you any data to support it?

3. Your legal department calls you one morning to say that a well-known comic book creator is visiting the office and he has some queries. You meet the comic book creator and he asks you to explain this sentence: "The above rights may be exercised in all media and formats whether now known or hereafter devised. The above rights include the right to make such modifications as are technically necessary to exercise the rights in other media and formats, but otherwise you have no rights to make adaptations." You paraphrase the sentence as follows:

a. This license grants the rights to reproduce the material in any media, whether now existing or yet to be invented, and grants limited permission to modify the content as necessary for such reproduction.

b. You are hereby granted the right to use this material in any media, modifying it as you choose.

c. This contract grants you rights which include the right to use this material in any media that either exists now or might be devised in the future. Moreover, you are also granted the right to modify the material as any current or future media might technically demand.

d. You may reproduce this material in any present or future media. You may modify it only where you need to in order to reproduce it in your chosen medium.

4. The director of an experimental dance company comes to you with a problem. He and his partner created a dance using various items of cyber trash as props, and they had posted a video of a performance of it on their website under a Creative Commons license. They then discovered that a prominent maker of electronic goods has used the dance in creating an advertisement for itself. The dance company is rather heavily burdened with debt. They consulted a legal advisor, a personal friend who had no experience of Creative Commons licenses, who told them they had basically given their property away for free and that they didn't have a case. You consult your legal department, who tell you that the dance company does have a case but under U.S. law they might have to fight a rather long and expensive battle to win it. You now have to email the director with your professional opinion on what they should do next. Which of these is a good opening line?

a. I have some good news for you: you do have a case. However, you might have to brace for a long fight to win it.

b. My lawyers say you could win, but from what you told me, you can barely pay legal fees, so I guess it wouldn't be a good idea.

c. You most certainly haven't thrown the copyright away: my lawyers confirm that your friend doesn't know what he's talking about.

d. After putting so much work into your creation, it must be heartbreaking to see someone ripping you off like that. People are so lax about these things.

LEARNING OBJECTIVES CHECKUP

Assess your understanding of the principles in this chapter by reading each learning objective and studying the accompanying exercises. For fill-in-the-blank items, write the missing text in the blank provided; for multiple-choice items, circle the letter of the correct answer. You can check your responses against the answer key on page AK-1.

Objective 5.1: Identify the four aspects of being sensitive to audience needs when writing business messages.

1. Why should you take the time to adapt your messages to your audience?

   a. People are more inclined to read and respond to messages that they believe apply to them and their concerns.

   b. Adapting messages to audiences is corporate policy in nearly all large companies.

   c. Adapting your message saves time during planning and writing.

   d. You can manipulate audience responses more easily by adapting your messages.

2. How is your audience likely to respond to a message that doesn't seem to be about their concerns or that is written in language they don't understand?

   a. They will ignore the message.

   b. If they read the message, they will be less inclined to respond in a positive way.

   c. They will assume that the writer doesn't respect them enough to adapt the message.

   d. All of the above could occur.

Objective 5.2: Explain how establishing your credibility and projecting your company's image are vital aspects of building strong relationships with your audience.

3. Credibility is a measure of

   a. Your power within the organization

   b. The length of time the audience has known you

   c. Your confidence

   d. The audience's perception of your believability

4. If you have developed a reputation for missing deadlines on projects you manage, which of the following statements would do the best job of helping to rebuild your credibility? [You have previously committed to a project completion date of April 1.]
   a. No April foolin' this time; we'll be finished by April 1.
   b. After analyzing past projects, I now realize that a failure to clarify project objectives up front created significant delays down the line. In order to meet the April 1 deadline, I will make sure to clarify the objective as soon as the team assembles.
   c. I plan to work extra hard this time to make sure we will be finished by April 1.
   d. I hope that we will be finished by April 1.

Objective 5.3: Explain how to achieve a tone that is conversational but businesslike, explain the value of using plain language, and define active and passive voice.

5. A good way to achieve a businesslike tone in your messages is to
   a. Use formal business terminology, such as "In re your letter of the 18th"
   b. Brag about your company
   c. Use a conversational style that is not intimate or chatty
   d. Use plenty of humor
6. Plain English is
   a. Never recommended when speaking with people for whom English is a second language
   b. A movement toward using "English only" in American businesses
   c. A way of writing and arranging content to make it more readily understandable
   d. An attempt to keep writing at a fourth- or fifth-grade level
7. If you want to avoid attributing blame or otherwise calling attention to a specific person, the _____ voice is a more diplomatic approach.
8. The _____ voice usually makes sentences shorter, more direct, and livelier.

Objective 5.4: Describe how to select words that are not only correct but also effective.

9. Which of the following defines the connotative meaning of the word *flag*?
   a. A flag is a piece of material with a symbol of some kind sewn on it.
   b. A flag is a symbol of everything that a nation stands for.
   c. A flag is fabric on a pole used to mark a geographic spot.
   d. A flag is an object used to draw attention.
10. Which of the following is a concrete word?
    a. Little
    b. Mouse
    c. Species
    d. Kingdom
11. If you're not sure about the meaning of a word you'd like to use, which of the following is the most appropriate way to handle the situation?
    a. Your readers probably have instant access to online dictionaries these days, so go ahead and use the word.
    b. Use the word but include a humorous comment in parentheses saying that you're not really sure what this big, important word means.

c. Either verify the meaning of the word or rewrite the sentence so that you don't need to use it.
   d. Find a synonym in a thesaurus and use that word instead.
12. Using jargon is
    a. Often a good idea when discussing complex subjects with people who are intimately familiar with the subject and common jargon relating to it
    b. Never a good idea
    c. A good way to build credibility, no matter what the purpose of the message
    d. A sign of being an "insider"

Objective 5.5: Define the four types of sentences, and explain how sentence style affects emphasis within a message.

13. Where is the most emphatic place to put a dependent clause?
    a. At the end of the sentence
    b. At the beginning of the sentence
    c. In the middle of the sentence
    d. Anywhere in the sentence
14. Devoting a lot of words to a particular idea shows your audience that
    a. The idea is complicated
    b. The idea is the topic sentence
    c. The idea is important
    d. The idea is new and therefore requires more explanation

Objective 5.6: Define the three key elements of a paragraph, and list five ways to develop unified, coherent paragraphs.

15. When developing a paragraph, keep in mind
    a. That you should stick to one method of development within a single paragraph
    b. That once you use one method of development, you should use that same method for all the paragraphs in a section
    c. That your choice of technique should take into account your subject, your intended audience, and your purpose
    d. All of the above
16. To develop a paragraph by illustration, give your audience enough _____ to help them grasp the main idea.
17. Paragraphs organized by comparison and contrast point out the _____ or _____ between two or more items.
18. To explain the reasons something happened, which of these paragraph designs should you use?
    a. Cause–effect
    b. Opposition and argument
    c. Classification
    d. Prioritization

Objective 5.7: Identify the most common software features that help you craft messages more efficiently.

19. Which of the following is one of the risks of relying too heavily on autocorrection or autocompletion?
    a. Using these features slows down your writing.
    b. You might grow to depend on them to correct errors when using one system, but they might not be available when you use other systems.
    c. Using them makes you look unprofessional.
    d. If your computer crashes, you will lose all your saved correction settings.
20. _____ refers to a standard block of saved text that is reused in multiple documents.

MyBcommLab

Log on to www.pearsoninternationaleditions .com/mybcommlab to access study and assessment aids associated with this chapter. If you are not using MyBcommLab, you can access the Real-Time Updates at http:// real-timeupdates.com/ebc10.

LEARNING OBJECTIVES

1. Identify the four aspects of being sensitive to audience needs when writing business messages. [page 164]

2. Explain how establishing your credibility and projecting your company's image are vital aspects of building strong relationships with your audience. [page 169]

3. Explain how to achieve a tone that is conversational but businesslike, explain the value of using plain language, and define active and passive voice. [page 170]

4. Describe how to select words that are not only correct but also effective. [page 174]

5. Define the four types of sentences, and explain how sentence style affects emphasis within a message. [page 177]

6. Define the three key elements of a paragraph, and list five ways to develop unified, coherent paragraphs. [page 180]

7. Identify the most common software features that help you craft messages more efficiently. [page 182]

KEY TERMS

abstract word Word that expresses a concept, quality, or characteristic; abstractions are usually broad

active voice Sentence structure in which the subject performs the action and the object receives the action

bias-free language Language that avoids words and phrases that categorize or stigmatize people in ways related to gender, race, ethnicity, age, or disability

complex sentence Sentence that expresses one main thought (the independent clause) and one or more subordinate, related thoughts (dependent clauses that cannot stand alone as valid sentences)

compound–complex sentence Sentence with two main clauses, at least one of which contains a subordinate clause

compound sentence Sentence with two main clauses that express two or more independent but related thoughts of equal importance, usually joined by *and*, *but*, or *or*

concrete word Word that represents something you can touch, see, or visualize; most concrete terms are related to the tangible, material world

connotative meaning All the associations and feelings evoked by a word

conversational tone The tone used in most business communication; it uses plain language that sounds businesslike without being stuffy at one extreme or too laid-back and informal at the other extreme

credibility A measure of your believability, based on how reliable you are and how much trust you evoke in others

denotative meaning The literal, or dictionary, meaning of a word

euphemisms Words or phrases that express a thought in milder terms

passive voice Sentence structure in which the subject receives the action

simple sentence Sentence with one main *clause* (a single subject and a single predicate)

style The choices you make to express yourself: the words you select, the manner in which you use those words in sentences, and the way you build paragraphs from individual sentences

tone The overall impression in your messages, created by the style you use

topic sentence Sentence that introduces the topic of a paragraph

transitions Words or phrases that tie together ideas by showing how one thought is related to another

APPLY YOUR KNOWLEDGE

To review chapter content related to each question, refer to the indicated Learning Objective.

1. Many older people find it hard to read the labels on their medication. Nevertheless, pharmaceutical companies persist in using the smallest font possible on these vials and bottles, as if they are certain that only the caregivers need to read the labels, and the caregivers are always younger than fifty. This can result in potentially life-threatening situations. What do you think is the nature of the error made by the pharmaceutical companies, and where is their "communication circuit" defective? [LO-1]

2. Since you are a member of a company, should you ever use the pronoun "I" in your speech on official occasions when you are representing the company? Why or why not? [LO-2]

3. Can there be a useful role for jargon or tech-speak? Give instances. [LO-3]

4. Take this sentence: "It is very difficult to determine where the error may be occurring." What kind of audience, if any, is it suitable for? Try rephrasing it to make two different versions of the same sentence, and speculate on which audience the new versions might be best for. [LO-4]

5. What is the function of a transition in a paragraph? Give an example, and discuss how it is related to logical structure. [LO-6]

PRACTICE YOUR SKILLS

Message for Analysis: Creating a Businesslike Tone [LO-1], [LO-3]

Read the following email draft and then (1) analyze the strengths and weaknesses of each sentence and (2) revise the document so that it follows this chapter's guidelines. The message was written by the marketing manager of an online retailer of dog accessories in the hope of becoming a retail outlet for Bestfriends collars, leashes, muzzles, and grooming products. Bestfriends is a new company that uses hypoallergenic pet-friendly materials in all its products and has pioneered several new designs of head restraints, puppy beds, folding dog cages, and insect repellants.

> Our e-tailing site, www.doggonegood.com, specializes in only the very best products for owners of canines. We constantly scour the world looking for products that are good enough and well-built enough and classy enough—good enough, that is, to take their place alongside the hundreds of other carefully selected products that adorn the pages of our award-winning website. We aim for the fences every time we select a product to join this portfolio; we don't want to waste our time with onesey-twosey products that might sell a half dozen units per annum—no, we want every product to be a top-drawer success, selling at least one hundred units per specific model per year in order to justify our expense and hassle factor in adding it to the above mentioned portfolio. We thusly concluded that your Bestfriends lines meet our needs and would therefore like to add them to our inventory.

Exercises

Active links for all websites in this chapter can be found on MyBcommLab; see your User Guide for instructions on accessing the content for this chapter. Each activity is labeled according to the primary skill or skills you will need to use. To review relevant chapter content, you can refer to the indicated Learning Objective. In some instances, supporting information will be found in another chapter, as indicated.

1. **Writing: Communicating with Sensitivity and Tact [LO-1]** Substitute a better phrase for each of the following:
   a. You must inform us
   b. We do not consider it our obligation to
   c. You were deficient in attention
   d. Your point is not well made
   e. You seem to be dissatisfied
   f. I did not find your argument convincing
   g. We have no concern with the issue you raise
   h. I suspect that you have misunderstood me
   i. Your letter rambles excessively
   j. I am at pains to make clear to you

2. **Writing: Demonstrating the "You" Attitude [LO-1]** Rewrite these sentences to reflect your audience's viewpoint:
   a. Do not reply to this email: we do not monitor this inbox. Instead, use the form on our website.
   b. We cannot process your order without a valid address.
   c. We have too many doormats and rugs in store, so this week we are offering a 20 percent discount on selected lines.
   d. I am applying for the position of receptionist in your office. I feel I have a pleasing personality and good people skills and am well-suited to be the public face of your company to visitors.
   e. As requested, we are sending the brochure and a selection of samples from our catalogue.
   f. I don't understand how, after a month of working here, you still don't know how to use the photocopier.
   g. Your memo to the group was so elegantly put. You are such a good role model for me and my team and we are fortunate to have you steering this division.
   h. I know you are impatient for your money, but I have to counsel patience as the shift to our new offices is not yet complete and the accounts department will need another week to get settled in. You can bring up your complaint with them after that.
   i. With children in the house, you know how difficult it is to get anything done on time. The report may be overdue, but I am doing my best and, given how exhausted I am, it's a miracle I'm over halfway through.
   j. I saw your comments on the Biznews site article. Weren't you supposed to be researching possible retail partners instead of shooting your mouth off on it?

3. **Writing: Emphasizing the Positive [LO-1]** Revise these sentences to be positive rather than negative:
   a. To avoid closure of your account, please make sure that all dues are cleared within sixty days.
   b. Returns will not be accepted without the original packaging.

c. Your order is not in stock, so you will have to wait at least one month before we can ship to you.

d. Allowing the curtains to dry in the sun may seriously damage the dye and design of the fabric.

e. Had you read the manual correctly, you would have seen that the engine cleaner must not be used in conjunction with high-performance gasoline.

4. **Writing: Using Unbiased Language [LO-1]** Rewrite each of the following to eliminate bias:

a. Ji Xu learned to drive in Beijing, but nevertheless, he is an expert driver.

b. Even though Sheryl is completely deaf, she can follow a conversation provided she can see the face of her companion.

c. Receptionists can be given extra training sessions to help them cope with the new guest information database.

d. Dr. (Mrs.) Anne Rogers is a mother of three and an excellent orthopedist.

e. Roland Harcourt (56) is still the first man into the office every morning and the last man out.

5. **Writing: Establishing Your Credibility; Microblogging Skills [LO-2], Chapter 7** Search LinkedIn for the profile of an expert in any industry or profession. Now imagine that you are going to introduce this person as a speaker at a convention. You will make an in-person introduction at the time of the speech, but you decide to introduce him or her the day before on Twitter. Write four tweets: one that introduces the expert and three that cover three key supporting points that will enhance the speaker's credibility in the minds of potential listeners. Make up any information you need to complete this assignment, then email the text of your proposed tweets to your instructor.

6. **Writing: Using Plain Language; Communication Ethics: Making Ethical Choices [LO-3], Chapter 1** Your company has been a major employer in the local community for years, but shifts in the global marketplace have forced some changes in the company's long-term direction. In fact, the company plans to reduce local staffing by as much as 50 percent over the next 5 to 10 years, starting with a small layoff next month. The size and timing of future layoffs have not been decided, although there is little doubt that more layoffs will happen at some point. In the first draft of a letter aimed at community leaders, you write that "this first layoff is part of a continuing series of staff reductions anticipated over the next several years." However, your boss is concerned about the vagueness and negative tone of the language and asks you to rewrite that sentence to read "this layoff is part of the company's ongoing efforts to continually align its resources with global market conditions." Do you think this suggested wording is ethical, given the company's economic influence in the community? Explain your answer in an email message to your instructor.

7. **Writing: Using Plain Language; Media Skills: Blogging [LO-3]** Download *A Plain English Handbook* from the website of the Securities and Exchange Commission (SEC) at www.sec.gov/pdf/handbook.pdf. In one or two sentences, summarize what the SEC means by the phrase *plain English*. Now scan the SEC's introduction to mutual funds at www.sec.gov/investor/pubs/inwsmf.htm. Does this information follow the SEC's plain English guidelines? Cite several examples that support your assessment. Post your analysis on your class blog.

8. **Writing: Creating Effective Sentences; Media Skills: Social Networking [LO-4], Chapter 7** If you are interested in business, chances are you've had an idea or two for starting a company. If you haven't yet, go ahead and dream up an idea now. Make it something you are passionate about, something you could really throw yourself into. Now write a four-sentence summary that could appear on the Info tab on a Facebook profile. Make sure the first sentence is a solid topic sentence, and make sure the next three sentences offer relevant evidence and examples. Feel free to make up any details you need. Email your summary to your instructor or post it on your class blog.

 Learn the basics of creating a company profile on Facebook. Visit http://real-timeupdates.com/ebc10, click on Learn More and then click on Facebook Screencast.

9. **Writing: Choosing Powerful Words [LO-4]** Write a concrete phrase for each of these vague phrases:

a. Sometime next autumn

b. A considerable sum as seed capital

c. Quite a few attended

d. Better profits

e. Streamlined the work area

f. Flatten the company hierarchy

10. **Writing: Choosing Powerful Words [LO-4]** List terms that are stronger than the following:

a. Receded

b. A few kinks in the graph

c. Interesting

d. A measurable rise

e. Takes it forward

11. **Writing: Choosing Powerful Words [LO-4]** As you rewrite these sentences, replace the clichés and buzzwords with plain language (if you don't recognize any of these terms, you can find definitions online):

a. Being a know-it-all, Jason did well at technical tasks but had terrible people skills.

b. I had a few butterflies about giving Janice the new position, but she took to it like a duck to water.

c. My only takeaway from your lowdown was that you just made it under the wire, but that is unacceptable where the rubber meets the road.

d. Your jargon-heavy presentation was clear as mud. I need that kind of thing like I need a hole in the head.

e. The ROI by EOY that will accrue from the MOU as calculated by the SME is to be notified ASAP.

12. **Writing: Choosing Powerful Words [LO-4]** Suggest short, simple words to replace each of the following:

    a. Commence

    b. Prevaricate

    c. Disaggregate

    d. Notify

    e. Objective

    f. Determine

    g. Importune

    h. Procure

    i. Conclude

    j. Disengage

    k. Modification

    l. Encapsulate

13. **Writing: Choosing Powerful Words [LO-4]** Read this passage and change the phrases underlined to ones that have the same meaning but are less stilted and more contemporary.

    As per your missive of the 12th, I have looked into the matter and come to the conclusion that, in default of a more congenial option, we will have to solicit the assistance of an outside agency. This is deeply regrettable, but, at the present instance, unavoidable.

14. **Writing: Choosing Powerful Words [LO-4],** How do connotative meanings affect the overall reception of a message? Give three examples where apparently correctly used words sabotage the message by calling to mind unwanted connotations.

15. **Writing: Creating Effective Sentences [LO-5]** Rewrite each sentence so that is it active rather than passive:

    a. Many interesting speeches were delivered by former alumni.

    b. Your application will not be cleared until it has been vetted by the records department.

    c. The workshop was conducted by several highly skilled trainers.

    d. An impression was given by the franchisee that the customers were not at all willing to try out the samples.

    e. My concentration was being torn to shreds by her constant phone calls.

    f. Our doughnuts are made with the finest ingredients.

16. **Writing: Crafting Unified, Coherent Paragraphs; Media Skills: Email [LO-6], Chapter 7** Sam is an intern at a teaching hospital. He has been having trouble filing reports on time, and Lucy, the Resident Medical Officer, has asked for an explanation. Exhausted from a twelve-hour shift, Sam types this message, but asks you to have a look at it before he sends it. Advise him on how to improve this message so that Lucy will understand his point of view and perhaps be more sympathetic to his situation.

    I know I have been tardy in doing the requisite paperwork, but you must understand that I have a slight dyslexia problem that gets worse when I am under stress. I suffered from this in school and years of therapy have helped me get over it. My worst fear is that it will take over my life again. It is very bizarre; I can read single sentences but blocks of text appear to dance on the page: I can't tell if I'm reading a line or the line above or below it. You objected to my double-spacing the reports: well, now you know my dirty little secret. I'm not doing it to waste paper: just to make sure I can read what I've written. My apologies if it annoys you. I have been working very hard since I got here. Even my seniors recognize that I am good at reassuring nervous patients and in taking histories. That's just the trouble: people pour out their life stories to me, and then I can't boil down what they've said into a neat little report. It just seems so unfair to summarize a lifetime of suffering with "Chronic myalgia of unknown etiology". I can do it all right; it just takes longer than it ought to. I'm really grateful to you for giving me the chance to work here with you. I promise to do better in the future.

17. **Writing: Crafting Unified, Coherent Paragraphs [LO-6]** In the following paragraph, identify the topic sentence and the related sentences (those that support the idea of the topic sentence):

    You can take control of your time and space with Here&Now. Once you've input your home location on the system, Here&Now will provide you with a set of place-cards where you can input the details of the places you visit most frequently: work, the gym, your favorite café. Each of these will then generate a minischedule within the large framework of your overall schedule. If you link up these place-cards with local businesses with our mobile apps, they will automatically update with specials, game-times, or friends' tweets from that location. You'll never forget an appointment or miss that game again.

    Now add a topic sentence to this paragraph:

    Our analysis of the customer experience should start before families even walk through the front gate here at Funland. It should start when they reserve tickets online or over the phone, and continue up to our ticket windows. Nothing dampens a day out for the kids more than long lines: hence crowd management and smooth ticketing is essential. Once they're inside, we need to get people to move on quickly and leave the reception area clear for new arrivals. A number of avenues branching off from the reception space, down which different attractions can be clearly seen, will accomplish this. We have to be careful there is not too much initial choice, or people will be becalmed by decision problems.

18. **Writing: Crafting Unified, Coherent Paragraphs; Collaboration: Evaluating the Work of Others [LO-6], Chapter 6** Working with four other students, divide the following five topics among yourselves and each write one paragraph on your selected topic. Be sure each student uses a different technique when writing his or her paragraph: One student should use the illustration technique, one the comparison or contrast technique, one a discussion of cause and effect, one the classification technique, and one a discussion of problem and solution. Then exchange paragraphs within the team and pick out the main idea and general purpose of the paragraph one of your teammates wrote. Was everyone able to correctly identify the main idea and purpose? If not, suggest how the paragraph could be rewritten for clarity.

    a. Types of mobile phones available for sale

    b. Reading paper books versus reading online

    c. Deciding what one's goal is in life

    d. Living in cities compared with living in the countryside

    e. How to make a cake (or lasagna or coffee)

19. **Writing: Using Transitions [LO-6]** Add transitional elements to the following sentences to improve the flow of ideas. (*Note:* You may need to eliminate or add some words to smooth out your sentences.)

    a. Simon Carlyle pioneered microcredit in some of Scotland's most remote villages. Simon Carlyle grew up in Aberdeenshire. His family came from the same social group among whom he now works. This social group lived a hard life with few modern comforts, but they were also enterprising and hard working. Carlyle went to Edinburgh where he completed his BA in social anthropology. He returned and tried his hand at running an animal feed store. After two years he turned a meager profit. An old school friend, now a sheep farmer, borrowed fifty pounds from him to repair a shed. Carlyle saw that his friend could fix the shed permanently for two hundred pounds. He asked why his friend did not apply for a bank loan. His friend told him that the local banks regarded the sheep farmers as risky prospects. Carlyle contacted a college friend who was an actuary and did a careful risk assessment of his friend's business. He then loaned his friend the two hundred pounds. This was the beginning of Carlyle Credit.

    b. Ten years ago, Simple Gemstones nearly went under. The company was still churning out outdated designs and unimaginative products. The granddaughter of the founder, Megan Riley, came up with a plan to save her family's business. She left her job at a respected law firm and invested her meager savings in some new plant and hires. She scouted for young designers willing to think differently about jewelry. They came up with beautiful designs for crafted mobile phones, MP3 players, mobile ear pieces, and other products. Their designs were not only beautiful, but also ergonomic and functional. They won several industry awards for these designs. Their vision made the term "cyber bling" a marketable concept.

    c. Everyone knows what goes into a Granny's Cookie: pure love. Advertisements make this statement. The reality is somewhat different. Peanut residue in a "nut-free" cookie led to a damaging lawsuit. The problem is that this ninety-seven year old company hasn't evolved to keep pace with today's market. Granny's Goodness hasn't aged well. The company has patents on a number of baking processes and recipes that are rumored to be game-changers in the baked-goods industry. However, there is no money to increase plant capacity or upgrade old equipment. Venture capitalists have been slow to respond to appeals for new investment.

20. **Writing: Using Technology to Compose Messages; Designing for Readability [LO-7], Chapter 6** Team up with another student and choose some form of document or presentation software that allows you to create templates or another form of "master design." (Microsoft Word, Microsoft PowerPoint, Google Docs, or their equivalents are good choices for this assignment.) Your task is to design a report template for a company that you either know about firsthand or whose general communication style you are able to analyze from its website and other materials. You can start your template from scratch or adapt an existing template, but if you adapt another template, make sure the final design is largely your own. Chapter 6 offers information on document design.

EXPAND YOUR SKILLS

Critique the Professionals

Locate an example of professional communication from a reputable online source. Choose a paragraph that has at least three sentences. Evaluate the effectiveness of this paragraph at three levels, starting with the paragraph structure. Is the paragraph unified and cohesive? Does it have a clear topic sentence and sufficient support to clarify and expand on that topic? Second, evaluate each sentence. Are the sentences easy to read and easy to understand? Did the writer vary the types and lengths of sentences to produce a smooth flow and rhythm? Is the most important idea presented prominently in each sentence? Third, evaluate at least six word choices. Did the writer use these words correctly and effectively? Using whatever medium your instructor requests, write a brief analysis of the piece (no more than one page), citing specific elements from the piece and support from the chapter.

Sharpening Your Career Skills Online

Bovée and Thill's Business Communication Web Search, at http://businesscommunicationblog.com/websearch, is a unique research tool designed specifically for business communication research. Use the Web Search function to find a website, video, PDF document, or PowerPoint presentation that offers advice on writing effective sentences. Write a brief email message to your instructor, describing the item that you found and summarizing the career skills information you learned from it.

IMPROVE YOUR GRAMMAR, MECHANICS, AND USAGE

The following exercises help you improve your knowledge of and power over English grammar, mechanics, and usage. Turn to the "Handbook of Grammar, Mechanics, and Usage" at the end of this book and review all of Section 1.5 (Adverbs). Then look at the following 10 items. Underline the preferred choice within each set of parentheses. (Answers to these exercises appear on page AK-3.)

1. Today's meeting went (*good, well*).

2. You can (*sure, surely*) figure out how to solve this problem.

3. I didn't come to the office because I was feeling (*sick, sickly*).

4. Employees have a better chance of being promoted if they perform (*good, well*) in their jobs.

5. The new logo looks (*good, well*).

6. Which of the two algorithms is (*more better, better*) for this problem?

7. Of the two proposals, this one is the (*best, better*) written.

8. None of the employees had (*any, no*) suggestions.

9. We haven't (*never, ever*) changed our policy.

10. They (*can, can't*) hardly proceed without (*any, no*) more directions.

For additional exercises focusing on adverbs, visit MyBcommLab. Click on Chapter 5; click on Additional Exercises to Improve Your Grammar, Mechanics, and Usage; and then click on 9. Adverbs.

REFERENCES

1. Creative Commons website, accessed 26 May 2011, www.creativecommons.org; "An Interview with Joi Ito, CEO of Creative Commons," audio interview, accessed 6 September 2008, www.businessweek.com; Kenji Hall, "Online Sharing with Creative Commons," *BusinessWeek*, 15 August 2008, www.businessweek.com; Ariana Eunjung Cha, "Creative Commons Is Rewriting Rules of Copyright," *Washington Post*, 15 March 2005, www.washingtonpost.com; Steven Levy, "Lawrence Lessig's Supreme Showdown," Wired, October 2002, www.wired.com; "Happy Birthday: We'll Sue," Snopes.com, accessed 3 August 2005, www.snopes.com.

2. Annette N. Shelby and N. Lamar Reinsch, Jr., "Positive Emphasis and You-Attitude: An Empirical Study," *Journal of Business Communication* 32, no. 4 (1995): 303–322.

3. Sherryl Kleinman, "Why Sexist Language Matters," *Qualitative Sociology* 25, no. 2 (Summer 2002): 299–304.

4. Judy E. Pickens, "Terms of Equality: A Guide to Bias-Free Language," *Personnel Journal*, August 1985, 24.

5. Biography of Ursula M. Burns, Xerox website, accessed 25 June 2010, www.xerox.com; biography of Shelly Lazarus, Ogilvy & Mather website, accessed 25 June 2010, www.ogilvy.com; biography of Andrea Jung, Avon website, accessed 25 June 2010, www.avoncompany.com.

6. Lisa Taylor, "Communicating About People with Disabilities: Does the Language We Use Make a Difference?" *Bulletin of the Association for Business Communication* 53, no. 3 (September 1990): 65–67.

7. Susan Benjamin, *Words at Work* (Reading, Mass.: Addison-Wesley, 1997), 136–137.

8. Stuart Crainer and Des Dearlove, "Making Yourself Understood," *Across the Board*, May/June 2004, 23–27.

9. Plain English Campaign website, accessed 28 June 2010, www.plainenglish.co.uk.

10. Plain Language website, accessed 16 January 2011, www.plainlanguage.gov.

11. Creative Commons website, accessed 16 January 2011, www.creativecommons.org.

12. Susan Jaderstrom and Joanne Miller, "Active Writing," *Office Pro*, November/December 2003, 29.

13. Portions of this section are adapted from Courtland L. Bovée, *Techniques of Writing Business Letters, Memos, and Reports* (Sherman Oaks, Calif.: Banner Books International, 1978), 13–90.

14. Catherine Quinn, "Lose the Office Jargon; It May Sunset Your Career," *The Age* (Australia), 1 September 2007, www.theage.com.au.

15. Visuwords, accessed 16 January 2011, www.visuwords.com.

16. See Note 1.

17. Food Allergy Initiative website, accessed 5 September 2008, www.foodallergyinitiative.org; Diana Keough, "Snacks That Can Kill; Schools Take Steps to Protect Kids Who Have Severe Allergies to Nuts," *Plain Dealer*, 15 July 2003, E1; "Dawdling over Food Labels," *New York Times*, 2 June 2003, A16; Sheila McNulty, "A Matter of Life and Death," *Financial Times*, 10 September 2003, 14.

18. Apple iTunes website, accessed 23 September 2006, www.apple.com/itunes.

LEARNING OBJECTIVES   After studying this chapter, you will be able to

1. Discuss the value of careful revision, and describe the tasks involved in evaluating your first drafts and the work of other writers

2. List four techniques you can use to improve the readability of your messages

3. Describe eight steps you can take to improve the clarity of your writing, and give four tips on making your writing more concise

4. List four principles of effective design, and explain the role of major design elements in document readability

5. Explain the importance of proofreading, and give eight tips for successful proofreading

6. Discuss the most important issues to consider when distributing your messages

MyBcommLab   Where you see MyBcommLab in this chapter, go to www.pearsoninternationaleditions.com/mybcommlab for additional activities on the topic being discussed.

ON THE JOB: COMMUNICATING AT JEFFERSON RABB WEB DESIGN

Authors such as Monica Ali still rely on personal contact with readers to promote books, but websites—particularly interactive, multimedia websites—have become an increasingly important element in book promotion.
Source: © Kathy deWitt/Alamy.

Using Leading-Edge Electronic Media to Reach Today's Book Audience

As a composer, game designer, photographer, programmer, and website developer, Jefferson Rabb epitomizes the "multi" in multimedia. For all the technical and creative skills he brings, however, Rabb's work never loses sight of audiences and their desire to be informed and entertained when they visit a website.

Rabb's career history includes stints at MTV.com and Sephora.com, but most of his current work as an independent designer involves projects in the publishing industry. The best-selling authors he has helped bring to the web include Dan Brown, Gary Shteyngart, Jhumpa Lahiri, Laura Hillenbrand, and Anita Shreve.

For every project, Rabb starts his design work with an in-depth analysis of the audience. The questions he asks about site visitors include their familiarity with the author's work, the range of their reading interests, and their general demographics. He also wants to know whether a site needs to serve book reviewers, bookstore buyers, and other industry professionals, in addition to readers.

With some insight into who the target visitors are, Rabb puts himself in their place and imagines the knowledge and experiences they hope to gain during their visits. These needs can vary from biographical information about the author to multimedia exhibits (such as video interviews and photographs

193

depicting locations mentioned in a book) to complex games that extend a novel's storylines. Rabb makes a point to find compelling visual connections between a book and a website, too, such as basing the design of the site for Shteyngart's *Super Sad True Love Story* on the portable communication device featured in the story. Completing the multimedia experience, he often composes music to create a specific mood that reflects the themes of a book.[1]

Your business communication efforts may not always be as elaborate as Rabb's, but you can always apply his strategy of combining methodical analysis with creative design and implementation. This chapter addresses the third step in the three-step writing process, completing your messages—which includes the important tasks of revising, producing, proofreading, and distributing your messages.

www.jeffersonrabb.com

Revising Your Message: Evaluating the First Draft

1 **LEARNING OBJECTIVE**

Discuss the value of careful revision, and describe the tasks involved in evaluating your first drafts and the work of other writers.

The time required for revision can vary from just a moment or two for a simple message to many hours or even days for a complex report or multimedia document.

In any medium, readers tend to equate the quality of your writing with the quality of your thinking.

For longer documents, try to put aside your draft for a day or two before you begin the revision process.

Successful communicators like Jefferson Rabb (profiled in the chapter opener) recognize that the first draft is rarely as tight, clear, and compelling as it needs to be. Careful revision can mean the difference between a rambling, unfocused message and a lively, direct message that gets results. The third step of the three-step writing process involves four key tasks: revising your message to achieve optimum quality and then producing, proofreading, and distributing it.

The revision task can vary somewhat, depending on the medium and the nature of your message. For informal messages to internal audiences, particularly when using instant messaging, text messaging, email, or blogging, the revision process is often as simple as quickly looking over your message to correct any mistakes before sending or posting it. However, don't fall into the common trap of thinking that you don't need to worry about grammar, spelling, clarity, and other fundamentals of good writing when you use these media. These elements can be *especially* important in electronic media, particularly if these messages are the only contact your audience has with you. Audiences are likely to equate the quality of your writing with the quality of your thinking. Poor-quality messages create an impression of poor-quality thinking and can cause confusion, frustration, and costly delays.

With more-complex messages, try to put your draft aside for a day or two before you begin the revision process so that you can approach the material with a fresh eye. Then start with the "big picture," making sure that the document accomplishes your overall goals before moving to finer points, such as readability, clarity, and conciseness. Compare the letters in Figures 6.1 and 6.2 (on page 196) for an example of how careful revision improves a customer letter.

MyBcommLab

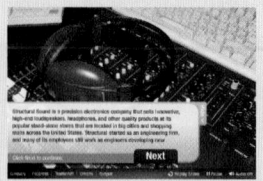

● Access this chapter's simulation entitled The Communication Process, located at www.pearsoninternationaleditions.com/mybcommlab.

EVALUATING YOUR CONTENT, ORGANIZATION, STYLE, AND TONE

When you begin the revision process, focus your attention on content, organization, style, and tone. To evaluate the content of your message, answer these questions:

- Is the information accurate?
- Is the information relevant to the audience?
- Is there enough information to satisfy the readers' needs?
- Is there a good balance between general information (giving readers enough background information to appreciate the message) and specific information (giving readers the details they need to understand the message)?

When you are satisfied with the content of your message, you can review its organization. Answer another set of questions:

- Are all the points covered in the most logical order?
- Do the most important ideas receive the most space, and are they placed in the most prominent positions?
- Would the message be more convincing if it were arranged in another sequence?
- Are any points repeated unnecessarily?
- Are details grouped together logically, or are some still scattered throughout the document?

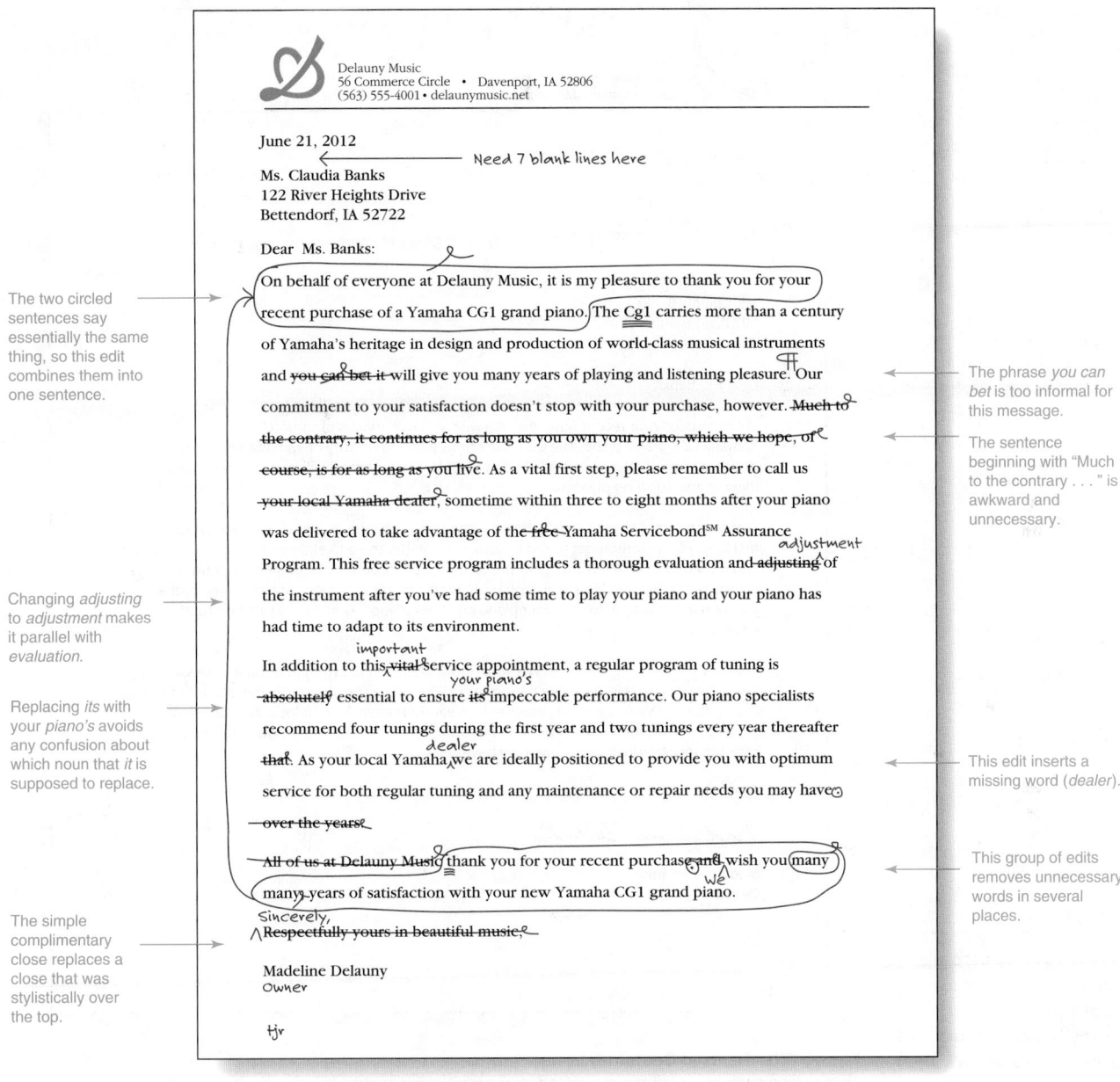

Figure 6.1   Improving a Customer Letter Through Careful Revision
Careful revision makes this draft shorter, clearer, and more focused. These *proofreading symbols* (see Appendix C) are still widely used when printed documents are edited and revised. However, in many instances you'll use the electronic markup features in your word processor or other software, as shown on page 204.

Delauny Music
56 Commerce Circle • Davenport, IA 52806
(563) 555-4001 • delaunymusic.net

June 21, 2012

Ms. Claudia Banks
122 River Heights Drive
Bettendorf, IA 52722

Dear Ms. Banks:

Thank you for your recent purchase. We wish you many years of satisfaction with your new Yamaha CG1 grand piano. The CG1 carries more than a century of Yamaha's heritage in design and production of world-class musical instruments and will give you many years of playing and listening pleasure.

Our commitment to your satisfaction doesn't stop with your purchase, however. As a vital first step, please remember to call us sometime within three to eight months after your piano was delivered to take advantage of the Yamaha Servicebond℠ Assurance Program. This free service program includes a thorough evaluation and adjustment of the instrument after you've had some time to play your piano and your piano has had time to adapt to its environment.

In addition to this important service appointment, a regular program of tuning is essential to ensure your piano's impeccable performance. Our piano specialists recommend four tunings during the first year and two tunings every year thereafter. As your local Yamaha dealer, we are ideally positioned to provide you with optimum service for both regular tuning and any maintenance or repair needs you may have.

Sincerely,

Madeline Delauny

Madeline Delauny
Owner

tjr

Figure 6.2 Revised Customer Letter
This revised letter provides the requested information more clearly, in a more organized fashion, with a friendlier style, and with precise mechanics.

The beginning and end of a message usually have the greatest impact on your readers, so make sure they are clear, concise, and compelling.

Next, consider whether you have achieved the right tone for your audience. Is your writing formal enough to meet the audience's expectations without being too formal or academic? Is it too casual for a serious subject?

Spend a few extra moments on the beginning and end of your message; these sections usually have the greatest impact on the audience. Be sure that the opening is relevant, interesting, and geared to the reader's probable reaction. In longer messages, ensure that the first few paragraphs establish the subject, purpose, and organization of the material. Review the conclusion to be sure that it summarizes the main idea and leaves the audience with a positive impression.

EVALUATING, EDITING, AND REVISING THE WORK OF OTHERS

At many points in your career, you will be asked to evaluate, edit, or revise the work of others. Whether you're suggesting improvements or actually making the improvements yourself (as you might on a wiki site, for example), you can make a contribution by using all the skills you have learned in Chapters 4 through 6.

Before you dive into someone else's work, recognize the dual responsibility that doing so entails. First, unless you've been specifically asked to rewrite something in your own style or to change the emphasis of the message, remember that your job is to help the other writer succeed at his or her task, not to impose your writing style or pursue your own agenda. In other words, make sure your input focuses on making the piece more effective, not on making it more like something you would've written. Second, make sure you understand the writer's intent before you begin suggesting or making changes. If you try to edit or revise without knowing what the writer hoped to accomplish, you run the risk of making the piece less effective, not more. With those thoughts in mind, answer the following questions as you evaluate someone else's writing:

> Before you evaluate and revise someone else's writing, make sure you understand the writer's intent with the message.

- What is the purpose of this document or message?
- Who is the target audience?
- What information does the audience need?
- Does the document provide this information in a well-organized way?
- Does the writing demonstrate the "you" attitude toward the audience?
- Is the tone of the writing appropriate for the audience?
- Can the readability be improved?
- Is the writing clear? If not, how can it be improved?
- Is the writing as concise as it could be?
- Does the design support the intended message?

You can read more about using these skills in the context of wiki writing in Chapter 14.

Revising to Improve Readability

After checking the content, organization, style, and tone of your message, make a second pass to improve *readability*. Most professionals are inundated with more reading material than they can ever hope to consume, and they'll appreciate your efforts to make your documents easier to read. You'll benefit from this effort, too: If you earn a reputation for creating well-crafted documents that respect the audience's time, people will pay more attention to your work.

> **2   LEARNING OBJECTIVE**
>
> List four techniques you can use to improve the readability of your messages.

You may be familiar with one of the many readability indexes, such as the Flesch-Kincaid Grade Level, that have been developed over the years in an attempt to measure readability. These indexes offer a useful reference point, but they are limited by what they are able to measure: word length, number of syllables, sentence length, and paragraph length. They can't measure any of the other factors that affect readability, such as document design, the "you" attitude, clear sentence structure, smooth transitions, and proper word usage. As a general rule, don't assume that a piece of text is readable if it scores well on a readability index—or that it is difficult to read if it doesn't score well.

> Readability formulas can't measure everything that affects readability, so don't rely on them as a test of true readability.

Beyond using shorter words and simpler sentences, you can improve the readability of a message by making the document interesting and easy to skim. Most business audiences—particularly influential senior managers—tend to skim documents, looking for key ideas, conclusions, and recommendations. If they determine that a document contains valuable information or requires a response, they will read it more carefully when time permits. Four techniques will make your message easier to read and easier to skim: varying sentence length, using shorter paragraphs, using lists and bullets instead of narrative, and adding effective headings and subheadings.

> Use effective headings, bullet lists, and other features to help your readers skim through documents quickly to find the major ideas, conclusions, and recommendations.

VARYING YOUR SENTENCE LENGTH

Varying sentence length is a good way to maintain reader interest and control the emphasis given to major and minor points. Look for ways to combine a mixture of sentences that are short (up to 15 words or so), medium (15–25 words), and long (more than 25 words). Each sentence length has advantages. Short sentences can be processed quickly and are easier for nonnative speakers and translators to interpret. Medium-length sentences are useful for showing the relationships among ideas. Long sentences are often the best way to convey complex ideas, to list a number of related points, or to summarize or preview information.

> To keep readers' interest, use a variety of long, medium, and short sentences.

Of course, each sentence length also has disadvantages. Too many short sentences in a row can make your writing choppy and disconnected. Medium sentences lack the punch of short sentences and the informative power of longer sentences. Long sentences are usually harder to understand than short sentences because they are packed with information; they are also harder to skim because readers can absorb only a few words per glance.

KEEPING YOUR PARAGRAPHS SHORT

Long paragraphs are visually intimidating and can be difficult to read.

Large blocks of text can be visually daunting, particularly on screen, so the optimum paragraph length is short to medium in most cases. Unless you break up your thoughts somehow, you'll end up with lengthy paragraphs that are guaranteed to intimidate even the most dedicated reader. Short paragraphs, generally 100 words or fewer (this paragraph has 84 words), are easier to read than long ones, and they make your writing look inviting. You can also emphasize ideas by isolating them in short, forceful paragraphs.

However, don't go overboard with short paragraphs. In particular, be careful to use one-sentence paragraphs only occasionally and only for emphasis. Also, if you need to divide a subject into several pieces in order to keep paragraphs short, be sure to help your readers keep the ideas connected by guiding them with plenty of transitional elements.

USING LISTS TO CLARIFY AND EMPHASIZE

Lists are effective tools for highlighting and simplifying material.

An effective alternative to using conventional sentences is to set off important ideas in a list—a series of words, names, or other items. Lists can show the sequence of your ideas, heighten their impact visually, and increase the likelihood that a reader will find key points. In addition, lists help simplify complex subjects, highlight main points, break up a page or screen visually, ease the skimming process for busy readers, and give readers a breather. Compare these two treatments of the same information:

Narrative	List
Owning your own business has many potential advantages. One is the opportunity to pursue your own personal passion. Another advantage is the satisfaction of working for yourself. As a sole proprietor, you also have the advantage of privacy because you do not have to reveal your financial information or plans to anyone.	Owning your own business has three advantages: • Opportunity to pursue personal passion • Satisfaction of working for yourself • Financial privacy

You can separate list items with numbers, letters, or bullets (a general term for any kind of graphical element that precedes each item). Bullets are generally preferred over numbers, unless the list is in some logical sequence or ranking or you need to refer to specific list items elsewhere in the document.

Regardless of the format you choose, the items in a list should be parallel; that is, they should all use the same grammatical pattern. For example, if one list item begins with a verb, every item should begin with a verb. You can create parallelism by repeating the pattern in words, phrases, clauses, or entire sentences (see Table 6.1).

ADDING HEADINGS AND SUBHEADINGS

Use headings and subheadings to show the organization of your material, draw the reader's attention to key points, and show connections between ideas.

A **heading** is a brief title that tells readers about the content of the section that follows. **Subheadings** are subordinate to headings, indicating subsections within a major section. Complex documents may have several levels of subheadings. Headings and subheadings help in three important ways: They show readers at a glance how the material is organized, they call attention to important points, and they highlight connections and transitions between ideas.

Informative headings are generally more helpful than descriptive ones.

Headings and subheadings fall into two categories. **Descriptive headings**, such as "Cost Considerations," identify a topic but do little more. **Informative headings**, such as "Redesigning Material Flow to Cut Production Costs," guide readers to think in a certain

TABLE 6.1	Achieving Parallelism
Method	**Example**
Parallel words	The letter was approved by Clausen, Whittaker, Merlin, and Carlucci.
Parallel phrases	We are gaining market share in supermarkets, in department stores, and in specialty stores.
Parallel clauses	I'd like to discuss the issue after Vicki gives her presentation but before Marvin shows his slides.
Parallel sentences	In 2011 we exported 30 percent of our production. In 2012 we exported 50 percent.

way about the topic. Well-written informative headings are self-contained, which means readers can read just the headings and subheadings and understand them without reading the rest of the document. Whatever types of headings you choose, keep them brief and use parallel construction throughout the document.

Editing for Clarity and Conciseness

After you have reviewed and revised your message for readability, your next step is to make sure your message is as clear and as concise as possible.

3   LEARNING OBJECTIVE

Describe eight steps you can take to improve the clarity of your writing, and give four tips on making your writing more concise.

EDITING FOR CLARITY

Make sure every sentence conveys the message you intend and that readers can extract that meaning without needing to read it more than once. To ensure clarity, look closely at your paragraph organization, sentence structure, and word choices. Can readers make sense of the related sentences in a paragraph. Is the meaning of each sentence easy to grasp? Is each word clear and unambiguous (meaning it doesn't have any risk of being interpreted in more than one way)?

Clarity is essential to getting your message across accurately and efficiently.

See Table 6.2 on the next page for examples of the following tips:

- **Break up overly long sentences.** If you find yourself stuck in a long sentence, you're probably trying to make the sentence do more than it can reasonably do, such as expressing two dissimilar thoughts or peppering the reader with too many pieces of supporting evidence at once. (Did you notice how difficult this long sentence was to read?)
- **Rewrite hedging sentences.** *Hedging* means pulling back from making a confident, definitive statement about a topic. Granted, sometimes you have to write *may* or *seems* to avoid stating a judgment as a fact. However, when you hedge too often or without good reason, you come across as being unsure of what you're saying.

Hedging, or qualifying your statements, is sometimes necessary, but doing it too often undermines your credibility.

- **Impose parallelism.** When you have two or more similar ideas to express, make them parallel by using the same grammatical construction. Parallelism shows that the ideas are related, of similar importance, and on the same level of generality.
- **Correct dangling modifiers.** Sometimes a modifier is not just an adjective or an adverb but an entire phrase modifying a noun or a verb. Be careful not to leave this type of modifier *dangling*, with no connection to the subject of the sentence.
- **Reword long noun sequences.** When multiple nouns are strung together as modifiers, the resulting sentence can be hard to read. See if a single well-chosen word will do the job. If the nouns are all necessary, consider moving one or more to a modifying phrase, as shown in Table 6.2.

Camouflaged verbs are verbs that have been changed into nouns; they often increase the length of a sentence without adding any value.

- **Replace camouflaged verbs.** Watch for words that end in *-ion, -tion, -ing, -ment, -ant, -ent, -ence, -ance,* and *-ency.* These endings often change verbs into nouns and adjectives, requiring you to add a verb in order to get your point across.
- **Clarify sentence structure.** Keep the subject and predicate of a sentence as close together as possible. Similarly, adjectives, adverbs, and prepositional phrases usually

Keep the subject and predicate as close together as possible, and keep modifiers close to the words they modify.

TABLE 6.2	Revising for Clarity	
Issues to Review	**Ineffective**	**Effective**
Overly Long Sentences		
Taking compound sentences too far	The magazine will be published January 1, and I'd better meet the deadline if I want my article included because we want the article to appear before the trade show.	The magazine will be published January 1. I'd better meet the deadline because we want the article to appear before the trade show.
Hedging Sentences		
Overqualifying sentences	I believe that Mr. Johnson's employment record seems to show that he may be capable of handling the position.	Mr. Johnson's employment record shows that he is capable of handling the position.
Unparallel Sentences		
Using dissimilar construction for similar ideas	Mr. Simms had been drenched with rain, bombarded with telephone calls, and his boss shouted at him.	Mr. Sims had been drenched with rain, bombarded with telephone calls, and shouted at by his boss.
	To waste time and missing deadlines are bad habits.	Wasting time and missing deadlines are bad habits.
Dangling Modifiers		
Placing modifiers close to the wrong nouns and verbs	Walking to the office, a red sports car passed her. [suggests that the car was walking to the office]	A red sports car passed her while she was walking to the office.
	Reduced by 25 percent, Europe had its lowest semiconductor output in a decade. [suggests that Europe shrank by 25 percent]	Europe reduced semiconductor output by 25 percent, its lowest output in a decade.
Long Noun Sequences		
Stringing too many nouns together	The window sash installation company will give us an estimate on Friday.	The company that installs window sashes will give us an estimate on Friday.
Camouflaged Verbs		
Changing verbs and nouns into adjectives	The manager undertook implementation of the rules.	The manager implemented the rules.
	Verification of the shipments occurs weekly.	We verify shipment weekly.
Changing verbs into nouns	reach a conclusion about	conclude
	give consideration to	consider
Sentence Structure		
Separating subject and predicate	A 10 percent decline in market share, which resulted from quality problems and an aggressive sales campaign by Armitage, the market leader in the Northeast, was the major problem in 2010.	The major problem in 2010 was a 10 percent loss of market share, which resulted from quality problems and an aggressive sales campaign by Armitage, the market leader in the Northeast.
Separating adjectives, adverbs, or prepositional phrases from the words they modify	Our antique desk lends an air of strength and substance with thick legs and large drawers.	With its thick legs and large drawers, our antique desk lends an air of strength and substance.
Awkward References	The Law Office and the Accounting Office distribute computer supplies for legal secretaries and beginning accountants, respectively.	The Law Office distributes computer supplies for legal secretaries; the Accounting Office distributes those for beginning accountants.

make the most sense when they're placed as close as possible to the words they modify.

- **Clarify awkward references.** If you want readers to refer to a specific point in a document, avoid vague references such as *the above-mentioned, as mentioned above, the aforementioned, the former, the latter,* and *respectively.* Use a specific pointer such as "as described in the second paragraph on page 22."

COMMUNICATING ACROSS CULTURES
Protecting Patients with Reader-Friendly Prescription Labels

Few messages in life are as important as the instructions for prescription medications. Yet, according to the American Academy of Pediatrics, nearly half of all parents fail to correctly follow the information contained on the labels of medications prescribed for their children. Errors also abound among elderly patients, who often need to take multiple medications every day. Blaming the parents and patients for these errors may be tempting, but evidence suggests that the labels themselves are responsible for many mistakes.

Experts cite such communication problems as confusing terminology, information overload, and poor prioritization—emphasizing nonessential information such as the name of the pharmacy at the expense of truly critical information, such as the correct dosage, drug interaction warnings, or even the name of the medication itself. The situation can get even worse in households where two or more people have prescriptions, creating the possibility of patients accidentally taking the wrong medication. Moreover, the information now included with many medications is split among the label on the bottle, the box the bottle comes in, and a government-mandated printed insert. Those inserts are meant to clarify important information for the patient, but many patients toss them aside rather than read what can be several pages of dense, tiny type and unfamiliar terminology.

Fortunately, some improvements are taking place. After her grandmother accidentally took some of her grandfather's pills, graphic designer Deborah Adler decided that a major change was needed. Overhauling the round pill bottle that has been in use and unchanged for 60 years, Adler and industrial designer Klaus Rosburg crafted a new design that features a large, flat labeling surface that wraps over the top of the bottle. The label makes vital information—particularly the name of the drug, the patient's name, and dosage instructions—easy to find and easy to read. Color-coded bands can be attached as well to help various members of a household identify the right bottles. Adler's design, named ClearRx, is now in use at Target pharmacies nationwide.

CAREER APPLICATIONS
1. Why is information prioritization so important with medicine labels?
2. Aside from medications, what other situations have you encountered in your life in which confusing labels, signs, instructions, or other messages created health or safety hazards? Choose one of these situations and write a brief description of the poor communication and your advice on how it could have been improved.

Sources: "ClearRx," Target website, accessed 21 January 2011, www.target.com; "Medications—The Importance of Reading the Label," American Academy of Pediatrics, accessed 9 September 2008, www.medem.com; Sarah Bernard, "The Perfect Prescription," *New York Magazine*, 18 April 2005, www.newyorkmetro.com.

EDITING FOR CONCISENESS

Efforts to improve clarity often reduce overall word count, so at this point you've probably eliminated most of the excess verbiage in your document. The next step is to examine the text with the specific goal of reducing the number of words you use. Readers appreciate conciseness and are more likely to read your documents if you have a reputation for efficient writing. See Table 6.3 on the next page for examples of the following tips:

> Improving clarity often makes messages shorter, but you can make them shorter still by using some specific revision techniques.

- **Delete unnecessary words and phrases.** If you can remove a word or phrase without changing the meaning of a sentence, leave it out.
- **Shorten long words and phrases.** Short words and phrases are generally more vivid and easier to read than long ones. Also, by using infinitives (the "to" form of a verb) in place of some phrases, you can often shorten sentences while making them clearer.
- **Eliminate redundancies.** In some word combinations, the words say the same thing. For instance, "visible to the eye" is redundant because *visible* is enough without further clarification; "to the eye" adds nothing.
- **Recast "It is/There are" starters.** If you start a sentence with an indefinite pronoun such as *it* or *there*, odds are the sentence could be shorter and more active. For instance, "We believe . . ." is a stronger opening than "It is believed that . . ." because it is shorter and because it identifies who is doing the believing.

> Early drafts often have words and phrases that don't add anything and can easily be cut out.

As you rewrite, concentrate on how each word contributes to an effective sentence and on how each sentence helps build a coherent paragraph. For a reminder of the tasks involved in revision, see "Checklist: Revising Business Messages."

TABLE 6.3	Revising for Conciseness	
Issues to Review	**Ineffective**	**Effective**
Unnecessary Words and Phrases		
Using wordy phrases	for the sum of	for
	in the event that	if
	prior to the start of	before
	in the near future	soon
	at this point in time	now
	due to the fact that	because
	in view of the fact that	because
	until such time as	when
	with reference to	about
Using too many relative pronouns	Cars that are sold after January will not have a six-month warranty.	Cars sold after January will not have a six-month warranty.
	Employees who are driving to work should park in the underground garage.	Employees driving to work should park in the underground garage.
		OR
		Employees should park in the underground garage.
Using too few relative pronouns	The project manager told the engineers last week the specifications were changed.	The project manager told the engineers last week that the specifications were changed.
		OR
		The project manager told the engineers that last week the specifications were changed.
Long Words and Phrases		
Using overly long words	During the preceding year, the company accelerated productive operations.	Last year the company sped up operations.
	The action was predicated on the assumption that the company was operating at a financial deficit.	The action was based on the belief that the company was losing money.
Using wordy phrases rather than infinitives	If you want success as a writer, you must work hard.	To succeed as a writer, you must work hard.
	He went to the library for the purpose of studying.	He went to the library to study.
	The employer increased salaries so that she could improve morale.	The employer increased salaries to improve morale.
Redundancies		
Repeating meanings	absolutely complete	complete
	basic fundamentals	fundamentals
	follows after	follows
	free and clear	free
	refer back	refer
	repeat again	repeat
	collect together	collect
	future plans	plans
	return back	return
	important essentials	essentials
	end result	result
	actual truth	truth
	final outcome	outcome
	uniquely unusual	unique
	surrounded on all sides	surrounded
Using double modifiers	modern, up-to-date equipment	modern equipment
It Is/There Are Starters		
Starting sentences with *It* or *There*	It would be appreciated if you would sign the lease today.	Please sign the lease today.
	There are five employees in this division who were late to work today.	Five employees in this division were late to work today.

✓ Checklist   Revising Business Messages

A. Evaluate content, organization, style, and tone.
- Make sure the information is accurate, relevant, and sufficient.
- Check that all necessary points appear in logical order.
- Verify that you present enough support to make the main idea convincing and compelling.
- Be sure the beginning and ending of the message are effective.
- Make sure you've achieved the right tone for the audience and the situation.

B. Review for readability.
- Consider using a readability index but be sure to interpret the outcome carefully.
- Use a mix of short, medium, and long sentences.
- Keep paragraphs short.
- Use bulleted and numbered lists to emphasize key points.

- Make the document easy to skim with headings and subheadings.

C. Edit for clarity.
- Break up overly long sentences and rewrite hedging sentences.
- Impose parallelism to simplify reading.
- Correct dangling modifiers.
- Reword long noun sequences and replace camouflaged verbs.
- Clarify sentence structure and awkward references.

D. Edit for conciseness.
- Delete unnecessary words and phrases.
- Shorten long words and phrases.
- Eliminate redundancies.
- Rewrite sentences that start with "It is" or "There are."

USING TECHNOLOGY TO REVISE YOUR MESSAGE

When it's time to revise and polish your message, software features can help you add, delete, and move text, using functions such as *cut and paste* (taking a block of text out of one section of a document and pasting it in somewhere else) and *search and replace* (finding words or phrases and changing them if you need to). Be careful using the "Replace all" option; it can result in unintended errors. For example, finding *power* and replacing all occurrences with *strength* will also change the word *powerful* to *strengthful*, which isn't a word.

To assist with revision, software features such as *revision marks* or *change tracking* (see Figure 6.3 on page 204) and *commenting* (see Figure 6.4 on page 205) show proposed editing changes electronically and provide a history of a document's revisions. Using revision marks and commenting features is a great way to keep track of editing changes made by multiple reviewers, too.

In addition to the many revision tools, four software functions can help bring out the best in your documents. First, a *spell checker* compares your document with an electronic dictionary, highlights unrecognized words, and suggests correct spellings. Spell checkers are wonderful for finding typos, but they are no substitute for good spelling skills and careful work. For example, if you use *their* when you mean to use *there*, your spell checker won't notice because *their* is spelled correctly (although a grammar checker might; see below).

Second, a computer *thesaurus* (either within your software or on a website such as http://thesaurus.com) offers alternatives to a particular word. The best uses of a thesaurus are to find fresh, interesting words when you've been using the same word too many times and to find words that most accurately convey your intended meaning. Don't use a thesaurus simply to find impressive-sounding words, however, and don't assume that all the alternatives suggested are correct for each situation.

Third, a *grammar checker* tries to do for your grammar what a spell checker does for your spelling. Because the program doesn't have a clue about what you're trying to say, it can't tell whether you've said it clearly or completely. However, grammar checkers can highlight items you should consider changing, such as passive voice, long sentences, and words that tend to be misused (such as *their* versus *there*).

Fourth, a style checker can monitor your word and sentence choices and suggest alternatives that might produce more effective writing. Style-checking options can range from basic issues, such as the spelling out of numbers and use of contractions, to more subjective matters, such as sentence structure and the use of technical terminology.

By all means, use any software tools that you find helpful when revising your documents. Just remember that it's unwise to rely on them to do all your revision work and that you're responsible for the final product.

Revision marks and commenting features are great ways to track the revision process when multiple reviewers are involved.

Spell checkers, grammar checkers, and computerized thesauruses can all help with the revision process, but they can't take the place of good writing and editing skills.

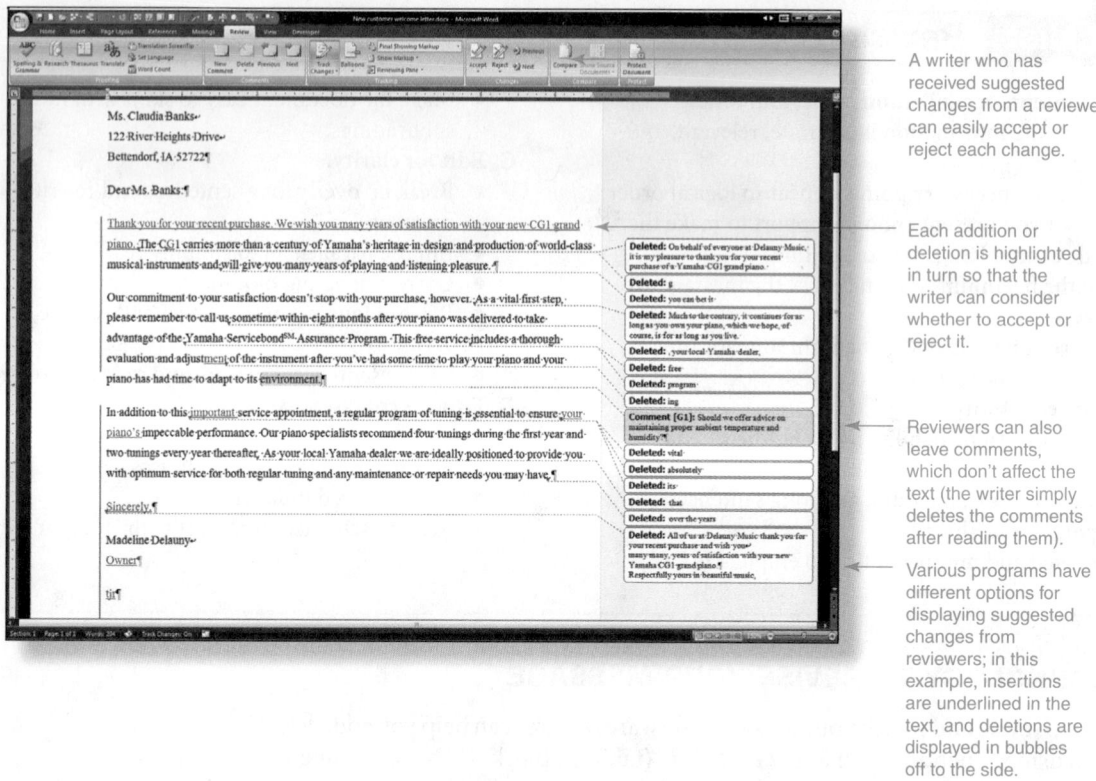

A writer who has received suggested changes from a reviewer can easily accept or reject each change.

Each addition or deletion is highlighted in turn so that the writer can consider whether to accept or reject it.

Reviewers can also leave comments, which don't affect the text (the writer simply deletes the comments after reading them).

Various programs have different options for displaying suggested changes from reviewers; in this example, insertions are underlined in the text, and deletions are displayed in bubbles off to the side.

Figure 6.3 Revision Marks in Microsoft Word
Microsoft Word, the most commonly used word processor in business offices, offers handy tools for reviewing draft documents. In this example, text to be added is shown in red, and text to be deleted is shown in balloons in the right margin. The writer can then choose to accept or reject each suggested change.

Producing Your Message

4   LEARNING OBJECTIVE

List four principles of effective design, and explain the role of major design elements in document readability.

Now it's time to put your hard work on display. The *production quality* of your message—the total effect of page or screen design, graphical elements, typography, and so on—plays an important role in the effectiveness of your message. A polished, inviting design not only makes your material easier to read but also conveys a sense of professionalism and importance.[2]

DESIGNING FOR READABILITY

Production quality affects readability and audience perceptions of you and your message.

Design affects readability in two important ways. First, if used carefully, design elements can improve the effectiveness of your message. If used poorly, design elements can act as barriers, blocking your communication. Second, the visual design sends a nonverbal message to your readers, influencing their perceptions of the communication before they read a single word.

Document design sends strong nonverbal signals—make sure the signals you send are positive and appropriate.

Effective design helps you establish the tone of your document and helps guide your readers through your message (see Figure 6.5). To achieve an effective design, pay careful attention to the following design elements:

Aim for consistent design within each message and from message to message.

- **Consistency.** Throughout each message, be consistent in your use of margins, typeface, type size, and space. Also be consistent when using recurring design elements, such as vertical lines, columns, and borders. In many cases, you'll want to be consistent from message to message as well; that way, audiences who receive multiple messages from you recognize your documents and know what to expect.
- **Balance.** Balance is an important but subjective issue. One document may have a formal, rigid design in which the various elements are placed in a grid pattern, whereas

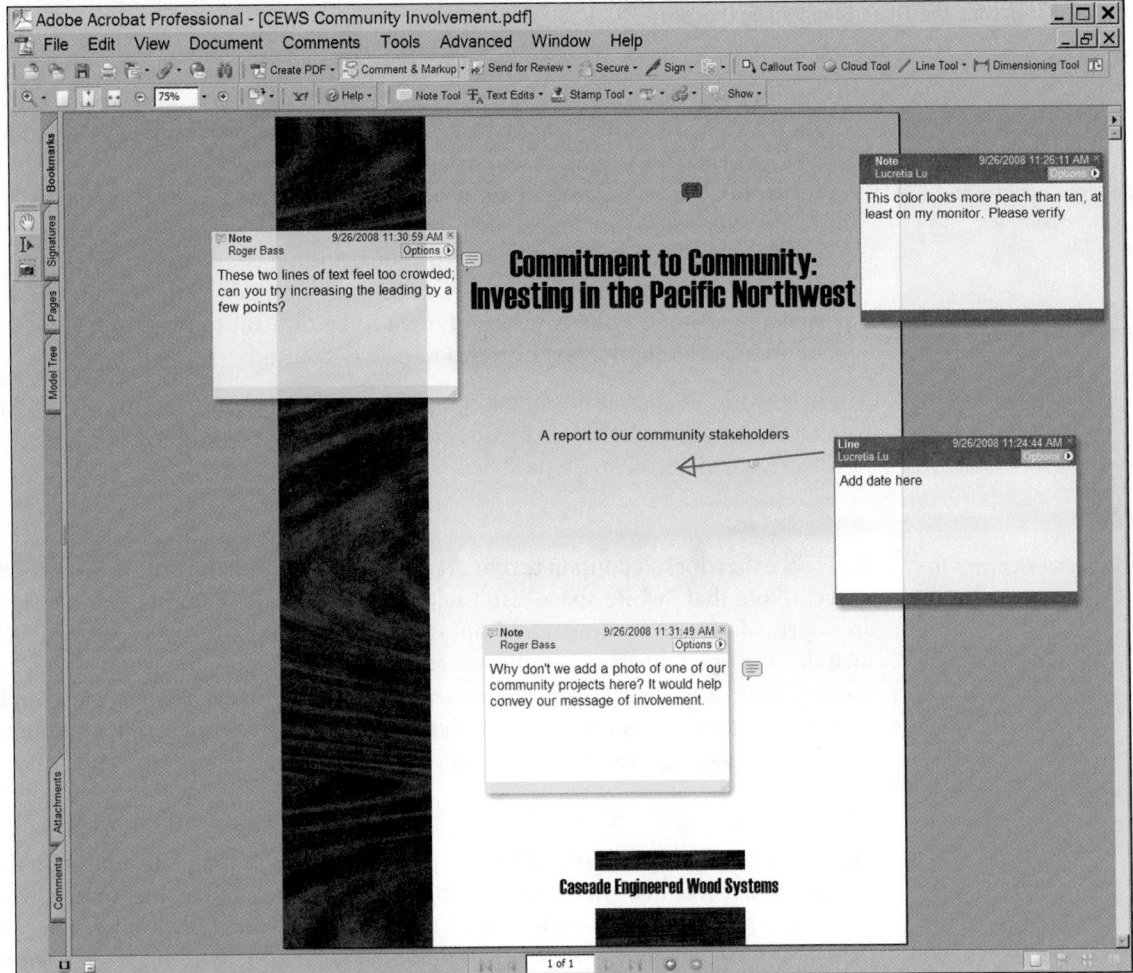

Figure 6.4 Comments Attached to a PDF File
Adobe Acrobat lets reviewers attach comments to any document in PDF format, even if it was originally created using software that the reviewers don't have.

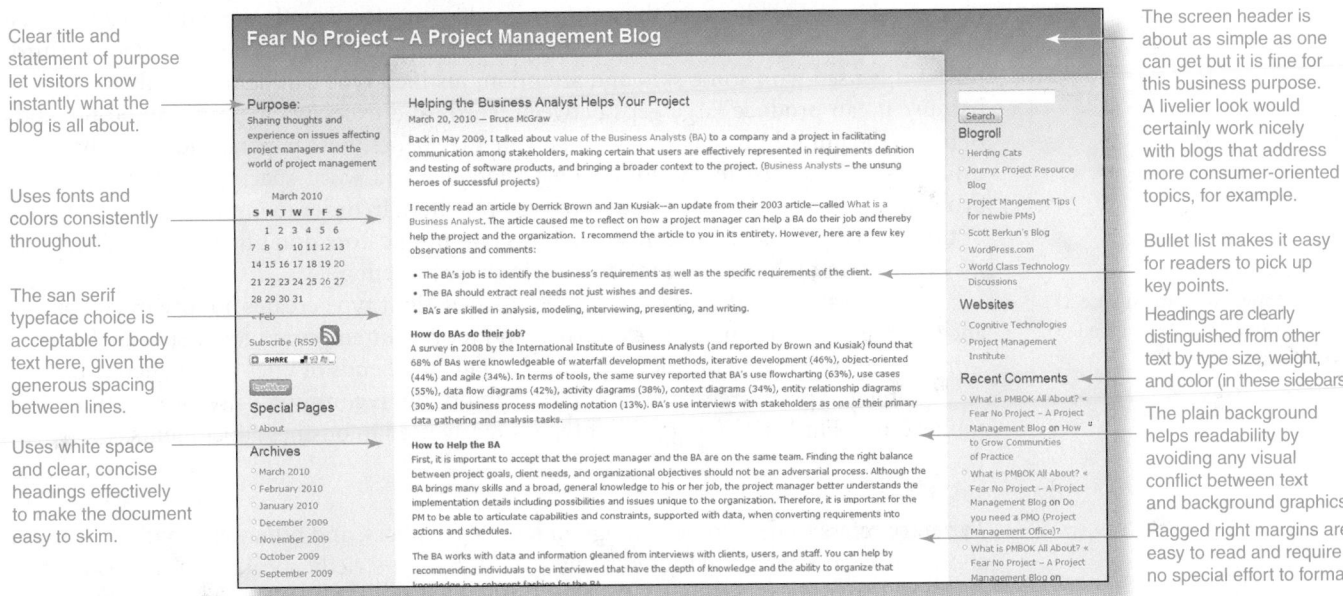

Figure 6.5 Designing for Readability
This blog uses a clean, restrained design that is more than adequate for its purpose, which is sharing ideas on project management strategies and techniques.

Apply Figure 6.5's key concepts by revising a new document. Go to Chapter 6 in www.pearsoninternationaleditions.com/ mybcommlab and select Document Makeovers.

MyBcommLab

another may have a less formal design in which elements flow more freely across the page—and both could be in balance. Like the tone of your language, visual balance can be too formal, just right, or too informal for a given message.

- **Restraint.** Strive for simplicity in design. Don't clutter your message with too many design elements, too much highlighting, too many colors, or too many decorative touches. Let "simpler" and "fewer" be your guiding concepts.
- **Detail.** Pay attention to details that affect your design and thus your message. For instance, extremely wide columns of text can be difficult to read; in many cases a better solution is to split the text into two narrower columns.

Even without special training in graphic design, you can make your printed and electronic messages more effective by understanding the use of white space, margins and line justification, typefaces, and type styles.

White Space

Any space that doesn't contain text or artwork, both in print and online, is considered **white space**. (Note that "white space" isn't necessarily white; it is simply blank.) These unused areas provide visual contrast and important resting points for your readers. White space includes the open area surrounding headings, margins, paragraph indents, space around images, vertical space between columns, and horizontal space between paragraphs or lines of text. To increase the chance that readers will read your messages, be generous with white space; it makes pages and screens feel less intimidating and easier to read.[3]

Margins and Justification

Margins define the space around text and between text columns. In addition to their width, the look and feel of margins is influenced by the way you arrange lines of text, which can be set (1) *justified* (which means they are *flush*, or aligned vertically, on both the left and the right), (2) flush left with a *ragged-right* margin, (3) flush right with a *ragged-left* margin, or (4) centered. This paragraph is justified, whereas the paragraphs in Figure 6.2 on page 196 are flush left with a ragged-right margin.

Magazines, newspapers, and books often use justified type because it can accommodate more text in a given space. However, justified type needs to be used with care. First, it creates a denser look because the uniform line lengths decrease the amount of white space along the right margin. Second, it produces a more formal and less personalized look. Third, unless it is used with some skill and attention, justified type can be more difficult to read because it can produce large gaps between words and excessive hyphenation at the ends of lines. The publishing specialists who create magazines, newspapers, and books have the time and skill needed to carefully adjust character and word spacing to eliminate these problems. (In some cases, sentences are even rewritten in order to improve the appearance of the printed page.) Because most business communicators don't have that time or skill, it's best to avoid justified type in most business documents.

In contrast to justified type, flush-left, ragged-right type creates a more open appearance on the page, producing a less formal and more contemporary look. Spacing between words is consistent, and only long words that fall at the ends of lines are hyphenated.

Centered type is rarely used for text paragraphs but is commonly used for headings and subheadings. Flush-right, ragged-left type is rarely used in business documents.

Typefaces

Typeface refers to the physical design of letters, numbers, and other text characters. (*Font* and *typeface* are often used interchangeably, although strictly speaking, a font is a set of characters in a given typeface.) Typeface influences the tone of your message, making it look authoritative or friendly, businesslike or casual, classic or modern, and so on (see Table 6.4). Be sure to choose fonts that are appropriate for your message; many of the fonts on your computer are not appropriate for business use.

Serif typefaces have small crosslines (called serifs) at the ends of each letter stroke. Serif typefaces such as Times New Roman are commonly used for regular paragraph text (as in this book), but they can look busy and cluttered when set in large sizes for headings.

Simple designs are usually more effective than more complex designs.

White space separates elements in a document and helps guide the reader's eye.

Most business documents use a flush-left margin and a ragged-right margin.

The classic style of document design uses a sans serif typeface for headings and a serif typeface for regular paragraph text; however, many contemporary documents now use all sans serif.

TABLE 6.4	Typeface Purposes and Personalities	
Serif Typefaces (Best for Text)	**Sans Serif Typefaces (Best for Headlines; Some Work Well for Text)**	**Speciality Typefaces (For Decorative Purposes Only)**
Bookman Old Style	**Arial**	ANNA
Century Schoolbook	**Eras Bold**	Bauhaus
Courier	Franklin Gothic Book	*Edwardian*
Garamond	Frutiger	*Lucida Handwriting*
Rockwell	Gill Sans	Old English
Times New Roman	Verdana	**STENCIL**

Sans serif typefaces have no serifs (*sans* is French for "without"). The visual simplicity of sans serif typefaces such as Helvetica and Arial makes them ideal for the larger sizes used in headlines. Sans serif faces can be difficult to read in long blocks of text, however, unless they are formatted with generous amounts of *leading* (pronounced *ledding*), or spacing between lines.

The classic style of document design uses a sans serif typeface for headings and a serif typeface for regular paragraph text. However, many contemporary documents and websites now use a sans serif face for both. Whichever combination you use, make sure that the result is reader-friendly and that it conveys the right personality for the situation.

For most documents, generally avoid using more than two typefaces, although if you want to make captions or another special text element stand out, you can use a third font for that.[4] Using too many typefaces clutters a document and can produce an amateurish look.

Type Styles

Type style refers to any modification that lends contrast or emphasis to type, including boldface, italic, underlining, color, and other highlighting and decorative styles. Using boldface type for subheads breaks up long expanses of text. You can also boldface individual words or phrases to draw more attention to them. For example, the key terms in each chapter in this book are set in bold. Italic type also creates emphasis, although not as pronounced as boldface. Italic type has specific uses as well, such as highlighting quotations and indicating foreign words, irony, humor, book and movie titles, and unconventional usage.

As a general rule, avoid using any style in a way that slows your audience's progress through the message. For instance, underlining or using all-uppercase letters can interfere with a reader's ability to recognize the shapes of words, and shadowed or outlined type can seriously hinder legibility. Also, avoid overusing any type style. For example, putting too many words in boldface dilutes the impact of the special treatment by creating too many focal points in the paragraph.

Avoid using any type style in ways that might interfere with reading.

Type size is an important consideration as well. For most printed business messages, use a size of 10 to 12 points for regular text and 12 to 18 points for headings and subheadings (1 point is approximately 1/72 inch). Resist the temptation to reduce type size too much in order to squeeze in extra text or to enlarge it to fill up space. Type that is too small is hard to read, whereas extra-large type consumes more space and can look unprofessional. Be particularly careful with small type online. Small type that looks fine on a medium-resolution screen can be hard to read on both low-resolution screens (because these displays can make letters look jagged or fuzzy) and high-resolution screens (because these monitors reduce the apparent size of the type even further).

DESIGNING MULTIMEDIA DOCUMENTS

A **multimedia document** contains a combination of text, graphics, photographs, audio, animation, video, and interactivity (such as hyperlinks that access webpages or software programs). As rich media, multimedia documents can convey large amounts of information quickly, engage people in multiple ways, express emotions, and allow recipients to personalize the communication process to their own needs. However, these documents are more difficult to create than documents that contain only text and static images. To design and create multimedia documents, you need to consider the following factors:

Multimedia documents can be powerful communication vehicles, but they require more time, tools, and skills to create.

- **Creative and technical skills.** Depending on what you need to accomplish, creating and integrating multimedia elements can require some creative and technical skills. Fortunately, many basic tasks, such as adding photographs or video clips to a webpage, have gotten much easier in recent years. And even if you don't have the advantage of formal training in design, by studying successful examples, you can start to get a feel for what works and what doesn't.
- **Tools.** The hardware and software tools needed to create and integrate media elements are now widely available and generally affordable. For example, with simpler and less expensive consumer versions of professional photo and video editing software, you can often perform all the tasks you need for business multimedia (see Figure 6.6).
- **Time and cost.** The time and cost of creating multimedia documents has dropped dramatically in recent years. However, you still need to consider these elements—and exercise good judgment when deciding whether to include multimedia and how much to include. Make sure the time and money you plan to spend will be paid back in communication effectiveness.
- **Content.** To include various media elements in a document, you obviously need to create them if you have the time, tools, and skills or acquire them if you don't. Millions of graphics, photos, video clips, and other elements are available online, but you need to make sure you can legally use each item. One good option is to search Creative Commons (http://creativecommons.org) for multimedia elements available for use at no charge but with various restrictions (such as giving the creator credit).

Make sure you have the legal right to use any media elements that you include in your documents.

Figure 6.6   Multimedia Tools
Software such as Adobe Photoshop Elements makes it easy for anyone with basic computer skills to create and modify content for multimedia documents. A simple *cropping* operation, which selects a portion of the overall image and deletes the rest, is shown here.
Source: Photo by Ryan Lackey. Adobe product screen shot(s) reprinted with permission from Adobe Systems Incorporated.

- **Message structure.** Multimedia documents often lack a rigid linear structure from beginning to end, which means you need to plan for readers to take multiple, individualized paths through the material. Chapter 13 discusses the challenge of *information architecture*, the structure and navigational flow of websites and other multimedia documents.
- **Compatibility.** Some multimedia elements require specific software to be installed on the recipient's viewing device. Another challenge is the variety of screen sizes and resolutions, from large, high-resolution computer monitors to tiny mobile phone displays. Make sure you understand the demands your message will place on the audience.

USING TECHNOLOGY TO PRODUCE YOUR MESSAGE

Production tools vary widely, depending on the software and systems you're using. Some IM and email systems offer limited formatting and production capabilities, whereas some word processors now offer capabilities that rival those of professional publishing software for many day-to-day business needs. *Desktop publishing* software such as Adobe InDesign goes beyond word processing, offering more advanced and precise layout capabilities that meet the technical demands of publication-quality printing. (Such programs are used mainly by design professionals.) For online content, web publishing and blogging systems make it easy to post great-looking content quickly without worrying too much about design or production.

No matter what system you're using, become familiar with the basic formatting capabilities. A few hours of exploration on your own or an introductory training course can help you dramatically improve the production quality of your documents. Depending on the types of messages you're creating, you'll benefit from being proficient with the following features:

> Learning to use the basic features of your communication tools will help you produce better messages in less time.

- **Templates, themes, and stylesheets.** As Chapter 5 notes, you can save a tremendous amount of time by using templates, themes, and stylesheets. Many companies provide these tools to their employees to ensure a consistent look and feel for all print and online documents.
- **Page setup.** Use page setup to control margins, orientation (*portrait* is vertical; *landscape* is horizontal), and the location of *headers* (text and graphics that repeat at the top of every page) and *footers* (similar to headers but at the bottom of the page).
- **Column formatting.** Most business documents use a single column of text per page, but multiple columns can be an attractive format for documents such as newsletters. Columns are also handy for formatting long lists.
- **Paragraph formatting.** Take advantage of paragraph formatting controls to enhance the look of your documents. For instance, you can offset quotations by increasing margin width around a single paragraph, subtly compress line spacing to fit a document on a single page, or use *hanging indents* to offset the first line of a paragraph.
- **Numbered and bulleted lists.** Let your software do the busywork of formatting numbered and bulleted lists. It can also automatically renumber lists when you add or remove items.
- **Tables.** Tables are great for displaying any information that lends itself to rows and columns, including calendars, numeric data, comparisons, and multicolumn lists. Use paragraph and font formatting thoughtfully within tables for the best look.
- **Pictures, text boxes, and objects.** Print and online publishing software lets you insert a wide variety of elements. *Text boxes* are small blocks of text that stand apart from the main text and can be placed anywhere on the page; they are great for captions, callouts, margin notes, and so on. *Objects* can be anything from a spreadsheet to a sound clip to an engineering drawing.

FORMATTING FORMAL LETTERS AND MEMOS

> Business letters typically have the following elements:
> - Preprinted letterhead
> - Date
> - Inside address
> - Salutation
> - Complimentary close
> - Signature block

Formal business letters usually follow certain design conventions, as the letter in Figure 6.2 (see page 196) illustrates. Most business letters are printed on *letterhead stationery*, which includes the company's name, address, and other contact information. The first element to appear after the letterhead is the date, followed by the inside address, which identifies the person receiving the letter. Next is the salutation, usually in the form of *Dear Mr.* or *Ms. Last Name*. The message comes next, followed by the complimentary close, usually *Sincerely* or *Cordially*. And last comes the signature block: space for the signature, followed by the sender's printed name and title. For in-depth information on letter formats, see Appendix A, "Format and Layout of Business Documents."

Memos are usually identified by a title such as Memo or Memorandum.

Like letters, business memos usually follow a preset design (see Figure 6.7). Memos have largely been replaced by electronic media in many companies, but if they are still in use at the firm you join, the company may have a standard format or template for you to use. Most memos begin with a title such as *Memo, Memorandum,* or *Interoffice Correspondence*. Following that are usually four headings: *Date, To, From,* and *Subject* (*Re:,* short for *Regarding,* is sometimes used instead of *Subject*). Memos usually don't use a salutation, complimentary close, or signature, although signing your initials next to your name on the *From* line is standard practice in most companies. Bear in mind that memos are often distributed without sealed envelopes, so they are less private than most other message formats.

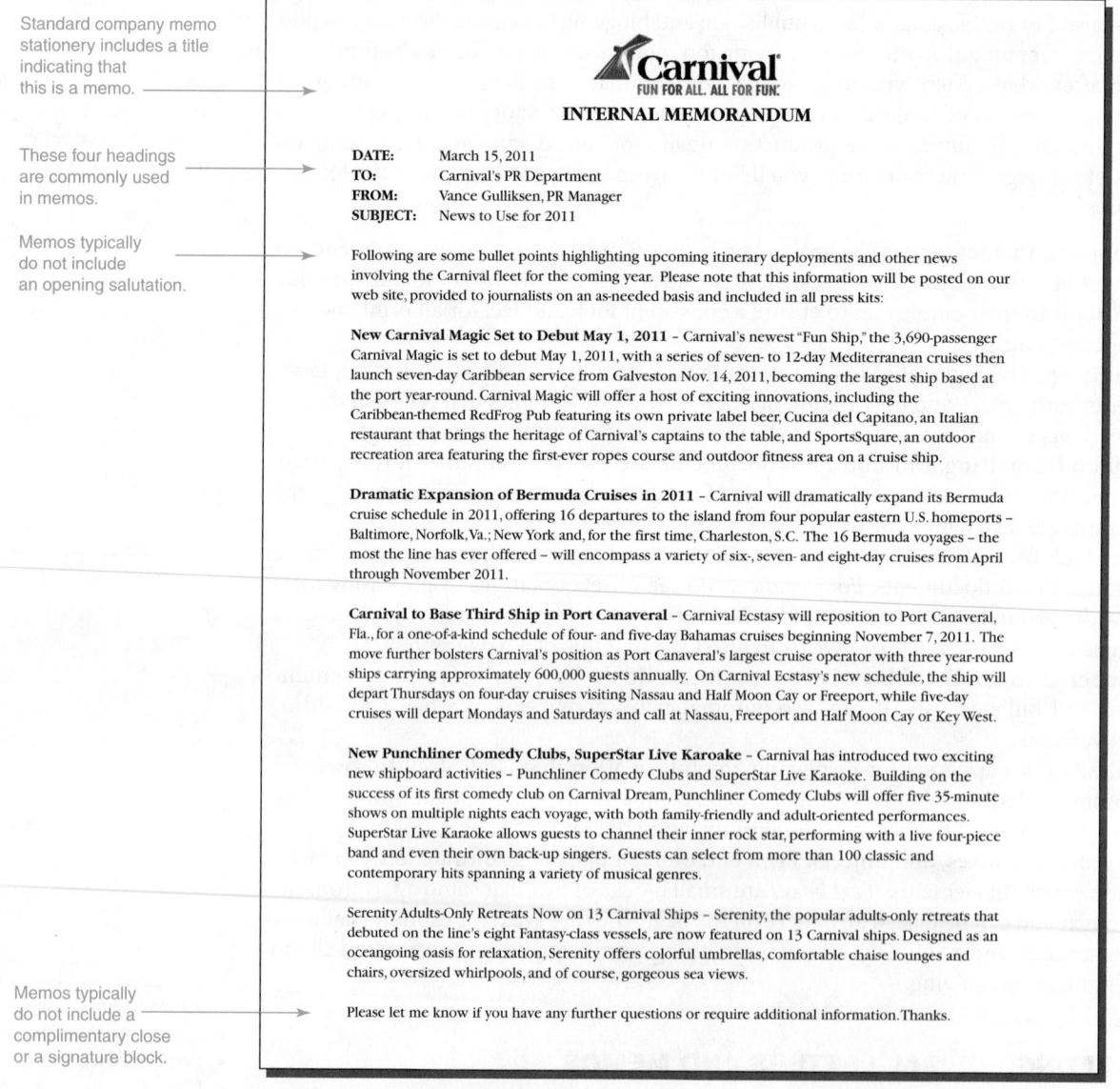

Standard company memo stationery includes a title indicating that this is a memo.

These four headings are commonly used in memos.

Memos typically do not include an opening salutation.

Memos typically do not include a complimentary close or a signature block.

Figure 6.7   A Typical Business Memo
This document shows the elements usually included in a formal business memo.
Source: Carnival Cruise Lines © 2011. All Rights Reserved.

Proofreading Your Message

Proofreading is the quality inspection stage for your documents, your last chance to make sure that your document is ready to carry your message—and your reputation—to the intended audience. Even a small mistake can doom your efforts, so take proofreading seriously.

Look for two types of problems: (1) undetected mistakes from the writing, design, and layout stages and (2) mistakes that crept in during production. For the first category, you can review format and layout guidelines in Appendix A on page A-1 and brush up on writing basics with the "Handbook of Grammar, Mechanics, and Usage" on page H-1. The second category can include anything from computer glitches such as missing fonts to broken web links to problems with the ink used in printing. Be particularly vigilant with complex documents and complex production processes that involve teams of people and multiple computers. Strange things can happen as files move from computer to computer, especially when lots of fonts and multimedia elements are involved.

Resist the temptation to treat proofreading as a casual scan up and down the page or screen. Instead, approach it as a methodical procedure in which you look for specific problems that may occur. Start by reviewing the advice in "Sharpening Your Career Skills: Proofread Like a Pro to Create Perfect Documents." You might also find it helpful to create a checklist of items to review; it can come in handy whether you need to review one of your own documents or you're asked to review someone else's work.

The amount of time you need to spend on proofing depends on the length and complexity of the document and the situation. A typo in an email message to your team may not be a big deal, but a typo in a financial report, a contract, or a medical file certainly could be serious. As with every other task in the writing process, practice helps—you become more familiar with what errors to look for and more skilled in identifying those errors. See "Checklist: Proofing Business Messages" for a handy list of items to review during proofing.

5 LEARNING OBJECTIVE

Explain the importance of proofreading, and give eight tips for successful proofreading.

A methodical approach to proofreading will help you find the problems that need to be fixed.

REAL-TIME UPDATES
Learn More by Watching This PowerPoint Presentation

Practical advice for thorough proofreading

Identify and correct common problems in business writing with this handy guide. Go to http://real-timeupdates.com/ebc10 and click on Learn More. If you are using MyBcommLab, you can access Real-Time Updates within each chapter or under Student Study Tools.

REAL-TIME UPDATES
Learn More by Reading This PDF

Proofread with advice from Stanford Business School

Prepare world-class business documents with help from this 32-page writing and editing style guide. Go to http://real-timeupdates.com/ebc10 and click on Learn More. If you are using MyBcommLab, you can access Real-Time Updates within each chapter or under Student Study Tools.

Distributing Your Message

With the production finished, you're ready to distribute your message. You often have several options for distribution; consider the following factors when making your choice:

6 LEARNING OBJECTIVE

Discuss the most important issues to consider when distributing your messages.

- **Cost.** Cost isn't a major concern for most messages, but for lengthy reports or multimedia productions, it may well be. Printing, binding, and delivering reports can be expensive, so weigh the cost versus the benefits before you decide. Be sure to consider the nonverbal message you send regarding cost as well. Overnight delivery of a printed report could look responsive in one situation but wasteful in another, for example.

- **Convenience.** How much work is involved for you and your audience? For instance, if you use a file-compression utility to shrink the size of email attachments, make sure your recipients have the means to expand the files on arrival. For extremely large files, consider recordable media such as DVDs or a file-hosting site such as MediaFire (www.mediafire.com).

Make sure your delivery method is convenient for your audience members.

- **Time.** How soon does the message need to reach the audience? Don't waste money on overnight delivery if the recipient won't read the report for a week. And speaking of time, don't mark any messages, printed or electronic, as "urgent" if they aren't truly urgent.

- **Security and privacy.** The convenience offered by electronic communication needs to be weighed against security and privacy concerns. For the most sensitive messages, your company will probably restrict both the people who can receive the messages and

SHARPENING YOUR CAREER SKILLS

Proofread Like a Pro to Create Perfect Documents

Before you click on "Send" or tote that stack of reports off to the shipping department, make sure your document represents the best possible work you can do. Your colleagues will usually overlook errors in everyday emails, but higher-profile mistakes in messages to outside audiences can damage your company and hinder your career.

Use these techniques from professional proofreaders to help ensure high-quality output:

- **Make multiple passes.** Go through the document several times, focusing on a different aspect each time. The first pass may be to look for omissions and errors in content; the second pass may be to check for typographical, grammatical, and spelling errors; and a final pass could be for layout, spacing, alignment, colors, page numbers, margins, and other design features.
- **Use perceptual tricks.** You've probably experienced the frustration of reading over something a dozen times and still missing an obvious error that was staring you right in the face. This happens because your brain has developed a wonderful skill of subconsciously supplying missing pieces and correcting mistakes when it "knows" what is supposed to be on the page. To keep your brain from tricking you, you need to trick it by changing the way you process the visual information. Try (1) reading each page backward, from the bottom to the top; (2) placing your finger under each word and reading it silently; (3) making a slit in a sheet of paper that reveals only one line of type at a time; (4) reading the document aloud and pronouncing each word carefully; and (5) temporarily reformatting the document so that it looks fresh to your eyes.
- **Double-check high-priority items.** Double-check the spelling of names and the accuracy of dates, addresses, and any number that could cause grief if incorrect (such as telling a potential employer that you'd be happy to work for $5,000 a year when you meant to say $50,000).
- **Give yourself some distance.** If possible, don't proofread immediately after finishing a document; let your brain wander off to new topics and then come back fresh later on.
- **Be vigilant.** Avoid reading large amounts of material in one sitting and try not to proofread when you're tired.
- **Stay focused.** Concentrate on what you're doing. Try to block out distractions and focus as completely as possible on your proofreading task.
- **Review complex electronic documents on paper.** Some people have trouble proofreading webpages, online reports, and other electronic documents on-screen. If you have trouble, try to print the materials so you can review them on paper.
- **Take your time.** Quick proofreading is not careful proofreading.

CAREER APPLICATIONS

1. Why is it so valuable to have other people proofread your documents?
2. Proofread and correct the following sentence:

   aplication of thse methods in stores in San Deigo nd Cinncinati have resultted in a 30 drop in roberies an a 50 precent decling in violnce there, acording ot thedevelpers if the securty sytem, Hanover brothrs, Inc.

✓ Checklist Proofing Business Messages

A. Look for writing errors.
- Typographical mistakes
- Misspelled words
- Grammatical errors
- Punctuation mistakes

B. Look for missing elements.
- Missing text sections
- Missing exhibits (drawings, tables, photographs, charts, graphs, online images, and so on)
- Missing source notes, copyright notices, or other reference items

C. Look for design, formatting, and programming mistakes.
- Incorrect or inconsistent font selections
- Problems with column sizing, spacing, and alignment
- Incorrect margins
- Incorrect special characters
- Clumsy line and page breaks
- Problems with page numbers
- Problems with page headers and footers
- Lack of adherence to company standards
- Inactive or incorrect links
- Missing files

---

the means you can use to distribute them. In addition, most computer users are wary of opening attachments these days, particularly word processor files.

For the latest news on revision, proofreading, and other topics related to this chapter, visit http://real-timeupdates.com/ebc10 and click on Chapter 6.

ON THE JOB: SOLVING COMMUNICATION DILEMMAS AT JEFFERSON RABB WEB DESIGN

Jefferson Rabb's web business is doing so well that he has hired you to help with a variety of writing and design tasks. Use what you've learned in this chapter about revising messages, designing for readability, and distributing messages to address the following challenges.[5]

Source: © Kathy deWitt/Alamy.

1. You received some draft copy for an author website that contains the following rather long sentence:

   Jhumpa Lahiri is the recipient of a Guggenheim Fellowship, and has won the Pulitzer Prize, the PEN/Hemingway Award and *The New Yorker* Debut of the Year for her debut collection of stories, *Interpreter of Maladies,* while her novel *The Namesake was a New York Times* Notable Book, a *Los Angeles Times* Book Prize finalist and was selected as one of the best books of the year *by USA Today* and *Entertainment Weekly,* among other publications.

   Which of these four alternatives does the best job of revising the material to improve its readability without losing any of the original information or introducing any new information?
   a. Jhumpa Lahiri is the recipient of a Guggenheim Fellowship. Her debut collection of stories, *Interpreter of Maladies,* was awarded the Pulitzer Prize, the PEN/Hemingway Award, and The New Yorker Debut of the Year. Her novel *The Namesake was a New York Times* Notable Book, a *Los Angeles Times* Book Prize finalist, and was selected as one of the best books of the year by *USA Today* and *Entertainment Weekly,* among other publications.
   b. Recipient of a Guggenheim Fellowship, Jhumpa Lahiri first shot to fame with a collection of short stories. Titled *Interpreter of Maladies,* it was awarded the Pulitzer Prize, the PEN/Hemingway Award, and *The New Yorker* Debut of the Year. With her novel *The Namesake* she entered the lists of the *New York Times* Notable Books, and was a *Los Angeles Times* Book Prize finalist. *The Namesake* was selected as one of the best books of the year by *USA Today* and *Entertainment Weekly,* among other publications.
   c. Jhumpa Lahiri was a Guggenheim Fellow. *Interpreter of Maladies,* her first book, won the Pulitzer Prize, the PEN/Hemingway Award, and *The New Yorker* Debut of the Year. Her novel *The Namesake* was a *New York Times* Notable Book, a *Los Angeles Times* Book Prize finalist, and was named one of the best books of the year by *USA Today* and *Entertainment Weekly,* among other publications.
   d. Guggenheim Fellow Jhumpa Lahiri shot to fame with *Interpreter of Maladies,* her first book, which won the Pulitzer Prize, the PEN/Hemingway Award, and *The New Yorker* Debut of the Year. *The Namesake,* her novel, was named a *New York Times* Notable Book, a *Los Angeles Times* Book

   Prize finalist, and one of the best books of the year by *USA Today* and *Entertainment Weekly,* among other publications.

2. David Shipley and Will Shwalbe's book *Think Before You Send* has a section detailing the schedule of their book tours, lectures, and readings. What title do you think this section should have?
   a. Readings
   b. Tours
   c. Lectures
   d. Appearances

3. The following sentence appears on the website for Tom Vanderbilt's *Traffic,* a study of the technical and social evolution of traffic and the never-ending attempts to making driving less dangerous and more efficient:

   Based on exhaustive research and interviews with driving experts and traffic officials around the globe, *Traffic* gets under the hood of the everyday activity of driving to uncover the surprisingly complex web of physical, psychological, and technical factors that explain how traffic works, why we drive the way we do, and what our driving says about us. [57 words]

   Which of the following does the best job of reducing the length and complexity of this sentence without significantly altering its meaning?
   a. *Traffic* explores the surprisingly complex web of physical, psychological, and technical factors that explain how traffic works, why we drive the way we do, and what our driving says about us. [31 words]
   b. *Traffic* relies on extensive global research to explore the surprisingly complex web of physical, psychological, and technical factors that explain how traffic works, why we drive the way we do, and what our driving says about us. [37 words]
   c. How traffic works, why we drive the way we do, and what our driving says about us—these are the questions addressed and answered in the exhaustively researched book *Traffic.* [30 words]
   d. *Traffic* gets under the hood of the everyday activity of driving to uncover the surprisingly complex web of physical, psychological, and technical factors that explain how traffic works, why we drive the way we do, and what our driving says about us. [42 words]

4. A number of authors reach out to their reader bases by offering to participate in book group discussions via Skype. If you wanted to get the word out that a new author was available to talk with book groups via Skype, which of the following distribution methods would you choose? (For this exercise, assume that you can choose only one of these.)
   a. Posters in book stores
   b. A message printed somewhere on the cover of the book
   c. A Twitter update from the author
   d. A wall posting on the author's Facebook page

LEARNING OBJECTIVES CHECKUP

Assess your understanding of the principles in this chapter by reading each learning objective and study the accompanying exercises. For fill-in-the-blank items, write the missing text in the blank provided; for multiple-choice items, circle the letter of the correct answer. You can check your responses against the answer key on page AK-1.

Objective 6.1: Discuss the value of careful revision, and describe the tasks involved in evaluating your first drafts and the work of other writers.

1. Which of these is the most important reason you should take care to revise messages before sending them?
   a. Revising shows your audience how hard you work.
   b. Revising lowers the word count.
   c. Revising makes it cheaper to email messages.
   d. Revising can usually make your messages more successful.

2. Which of the following is not one of the main tasks involved in completing a business message?
   a. Drafting the message
   b. Revising the message
   c. Producing the message
   d. Proofreading the message

Objective 6.2: List four techniques you can use to improve the readability of your messages.

3. Regarding sentence length, the best approach for business messages is to
   a. Keep all sentences as short as possible
   b. Make most of your sentences long since you will usually have complex information to impart
   c. Vary the length of your sentences
   d. Aim for an average sentence length of 35 words

4. Regarding paragraph length, the best approach for business messages is to
   a. Keep paragraphs short
   b. Make most of your paragraphs long since that is standard practice in business writing
   c. Make most of your paragraphs one sentence in length
   d. Aim for an average paragraph length of 200 words

5. Regarding the use of lists, the best approach for business messages is to
   a. Avoid using lists except where absolutely necessary
   b. Make sure listed items are in parallel form
   c. Use numbered lists rather than bulleted ones
   d. Do all of the above

6. Which of the following is not an informative heading?
   a. Why We Need a New Distributor
   b. Five Challenges Facing Today's Distributors
   c. Distributors Are a Better Choice for Us Than Wholesalers
   d. Distributor Choices

Objective 6.3: Describe eight steps you can take to improve the clarity of your writing, and give four tips on making your writing more concise.

7. Which of the following sentences contains hedging words?
   a. It appears that we may have a problem completing the project by May 20.
   b. There is a possibility that the project might be done by May 20.
   c. It seems that the project could possibly miss its completion date of May 20.
   d. All of the above contain hedging words.

8. Which of the following sentences lacks parallelism?
   a. Consumers can download stock research, electronically file their tax returns, create a portfolio, or choose from an array of recommended mutual funds.
   b. Consumers can download stock research, can electronically file their tax returns, create a portfolio, or they can choose from an array of recommended mutual funds.
   c. Consumers can download stock research, can electronically file their tax returns, can create a portfolio, or can choose from an array of recommended mutual funds.
   d. Consumers can download stock research, they can electronically file their tax returns, they can create a portfolio, or they can choose from an array of recommended mutual funds.

9. Which of the following sentences does not have a dangling modifier?
   a. Lacking brand recognition, some consumers are wary of using Internet-only banks.
   b. Because Internet-only banks lack brand recognition, some consumers are wary of using them.
   c. Because of a lack of brand recognition, some consumers are wary of using Internet-only banks.
   d. All have dangling modifiers.

10. When editing for conciseness, you should look for
    a. Unnecessary words and phrases
    b. Dangling modifiers
    c. Lack of parallelism
    d. Awkward references

11. Which of the following is not an example of a redundancy?
    a. Visible to the eye
    b. Free gift
    c. Very useful
    d. Repeat again

Objective 6.4: List four principles of effective design, and explain the role of major design elements in document readability.

12. A well-designed document
    a. Includes a wide variety of typefaces
    b. Balances the space devoted to text, artwork, and white space
    c. Fills as much of the available space as possible with text and art
    d. Does all of the above

13. Any blank areas in a document are referred to as _____ _____.

14. Type that is "justified" is
    a. Flush on the left and ragged on the right
    b. Flush on the right and ragged on the left
    c. Flush on both the left and the right
    d. Centered

15. A sans serif typeface would be best for
    a. The headings in a report
    b. The text of a report
    c. Both the headings and the text of a report
    d. Elements such as footnotes and endnotes

Objective 6.5: Explain the importance of proofreading, and give eight tips for successful proofreading.

16. The best time to proofread is
    a. As you are writing
    b. Immediately after you finish the first draft, while the information is still fresh in your mind
    c. A day or so after you finish the first draft
    d. After you distribute the document
17. When proofreading, you should look for errors in
    a. Spelling and punctuation
    b. Grammar and usage
    c. Typography and format
    d. All of the above

Objective 6.6: Discuss the most important issues to consider when distributing your messages.

18. As a general rule, the cost of distributing a business message should be balanced against
    a. The importance and urgency of the message
    b. The length of the message
    c. Your career goals as they relate to the message
    d. The number of recipients
19. Which of the following concerns is the most important to consider when distributing messages through electronic media such as email?
    a. The difficulty of reading on-screen
    b. Privacy and security
    c. Differences between flat-panel and CRT monitors
    d. The difficulty of keeping email addresses current

MyBcommLab

Log on to www.pearsoninternationaleditions
.com/mybcommlab to access study and
assessment aids associated with this chapter.
If you are not using MyBcommLab, you can
access the Real-Time Updates at http://
real-timeupdates.com/ebc10.

CHAPTER OUTLINE

**Revising Your Message:
Evaluating the First Draft**
 Evaluating Your Content, Organization, Style,
 and Tone
 Evaluating, Editing, and Revising the Work of
 Others

Revising to Improve Readability
 Varying Your Sentence Length
 Keeping Your Paragraphs Short
 Using Lists to Clarify and Emphasize
 Adding Headings and Subheadings

Editing for Clarity and Conciseness
 Editing for Clarity
 Editing for Conciseness
 Using Technology to Revise Your Message

Producing Your Message
 Designing for Readability
 Designing Multimedia Documents
 Using Technology to Produce Your Message
 Formatting Formal Letters and Memos

Proofreading Your Message

Distributing Your Message

 **Checklists**

Revising Business Messages

**A. Evaluate content, organization, style,
 and tone.**
 - Make sure the information is accurate,
  relevant, and sufficient.
 - Check that all necessary points appear
  in logical order.
 - Verify that you present enough
  support to make the main idea
  convincing and compelling.
 - Be sure the beginning and ending of
  the message are effective.
 - Make sure you've achieved the
  right tone for the audience and the
  situation.

B. Review for readability.
 - Consider using a readability index
  but be sure to interpret the outcome
  carefully.
 - Use a mix of short, medium, and long
  sentences.
 - Keep paragraphs short.

LEARNING OBJECTIVES

1. Discuss the value of careful revision, and identify the three key aspects to consider when evaluating your first drafts. [page 194]

2. List four techniques you can use to improve the readability of your messages. [page 197]

3. Describe eight steps you can take to improve the clarity of your writing, and give four tips on making your writing more concise. [page 199]

4. List four principles of effective design, and explain the role of major design elements in document readability. [page 204]

5. Explain the importance of proofreading, and give eight tips for successful proofreading. [page 211]

6. Discuss the most important issues to consider when distributing your messages. [page 211]

KEY TERMS

descriptive headings Headings that simply identify a topic

heading A brief title that tells readers about the content of the section that follows

informative headings Headings that guide readers to think in a certain way about the topic

multimedia document Electronic document that contains a combination of text, graphics, photographs, audio, animation, video, and interactivity

sans serif typefaces Typefaces whose letters lack serifs: This is sans serif type.

serif typefaces Typefaces with small crosslines (called serifs) at the ends of letter strokes: This is serif type.

subheadings Titles that are subordinate to headings, indicating subsections with a major section

type style Any modification that lends contrast or emphasis to type, including boldface, italic, underlining, color, and other highlighting and decorative styles

typeface The physical design of letters, numbers, and other text characters (*font* and *typeface* are often used interchangeably, although strictly speaking, a font is a set of characters in a given typeface)

white space Space (of any color) in a document or screen that doesn't contain any text or artwork

 - Use bulleted and numbered lists to emphasize key points.
 - Make the document easy to skim with headings and subheadings.

C. Edit for clarity.
 - Break up overly long sentences and rewrite hedging sentences.
 - Impose parallelism to simplify reading.
 - Correct dangling modifiers.
 - Reword long noun sequences and replace camouflaged verbs.
 - Clarify sentence structure and awkward references.

D. Edit for conciseness.
 - Delete unnecessary words and phrases.
 - Shorten long words and phrases.
 - Eliminate redundancies.
 - Rewrite sentences that start with "It is" or "There are."

Proofing Business Messages

A. Look for writing errors.
 - Typographical mistakes
 - Misspelled words

 - Grammatical errors
 - Punctuation mistakes

B. Look for missing elements.
 - Missing text sections
 - Missing exhibits (drawings, tables, photographs, charts, graphs, online images, and so on)
 - Missing source notes, copyright notices, or other reference items

C. Look for design, formatting, and programming mistakes.
 - Incorrect or inconsistent font selections
 - Problems with column sizing, spacing, and alignment
 - Incorrect margins
 - Incorrect special characters
 - Clumsy line and page breaks
 - Problems with page numbers
 - Problems with page headers and footers
 - Lack of adherence to company standards
 - Inactive or incorrect links
 - Missing files

APPLY YOUR KNOWLEDGE

To review chapter content related to each question, refer to the indicated Learning Objective.

1. What can go wrong if you try to revise your first draft immediately after you finish writing it? [LO-1]

2. Is a message with a bad beginning more likely to be misunderstood than a message with a bad ending? Why, or why not? [LO-1]

3. Is the ClearRx medicine labeling and packaging system (see page 201) designed to solve an ethical or an aesthetic problem? Give reasons for your opinion. [LO-3]

4. Why should you limit the number of typefaces and type styles in most business documents? [LO-4]

5. What are the factors involved in choosing the medium for your message? Can you rank them by importance on general principles? Justify your ranking. [LO-6]

PRACTICE YOUR SKILLS

Message for Analysis 6.A:
Revising to Improve Readability [LO-2]

Analyze the strengths and weaknesses of this message, then revise it so that it follows the guidelines in Chapters 4 through 6:

> We at Hope in the Clouds are committed to making sure that there is never any chance that our tours affect the fragile Himalayan environment adversely. We assist local people and non-governmental organizations and other concerned authorities along the designated routes of our treks to ensure that these areas benefit from, and are not harmed by, their interaction with us. We leave no trash behind, we compost and biodegrade our biological waists, we donate part of our expedition fees to local schools and healthcare centers, and we enjoy the hospitality of locale people, paying for the raw ingredients, the fuel and the labor required to cater for us. This has made our local trek partners happier and healthier, and also means that our members have a much more positive and welcoming experience when they trak with us.

Message for Analysis 6.B:
Designing for Readability [LO-4]

To access this message, visit http://real-timeupdates.com/ebc10, click on "Student Assignments," select Chapter 6, and then select page 217, Message 6.B. Download and open the Microsoft Word document. Using the various page, paragraph, and font formatting options available in your word processor, modify the formatting of the document so that its visual tone matches the tone of the message.

Message for Analysis 6.C:
Evaluating the Work of Another Writer [LO-1]

To access this message, visit http://real-timeupdates.com/ebc10, click on "Student Assignments" select Chapter 6, and then select page 217, Message 6.C. Download and open the Microsoft Word document. Using your knowledge of effective writing and the tips on page 197 for evaluating the work of other writers, evaluate this message. After you set Microsoft Word to track changes, make any necessary corrections. Insert comments, as needed, to explain your changes to the author.

Exercises

Active links for all websites in this chapter can be found on MyBcommLab; see your User Guide for instructions on accessing the content for this chapter. Each activity is labeled according to the primary skill or skills you will need to use. To review relevant chapter content, you can refer to the indicated Learning Objective. In some instances, supporting information will be found in another chapter, as indicated.

1. **Evaluating the Work of Other Writers [LO-1]** Find a blog post (at least three paragraphs long) on any business-related topic. Evaluate it using the 10 questions on page 197. Email your analysis to your instructor, along with a permalink (a permanent link to this specific post, rather than to the blog overall) to the blog post.

2. **Revising for Readability (Sentence and Paragraph Length) [LO-2]** Rewrite the following paragraph to vary the length of the sentences and to shorten the paragraph so it looks more inviting to readers:

   > Very few gamers today are aware, or care to be aware, that fantasy role-playing games began long before the Internet. The premier example of this genre of game is Dungeons and Dragons. Players of this game would dress up in the costume of their character (partly self-created and partly based on a complex template) and sit around a table. There would be a master of ceremonies, the Dungeon Master, and he or she would apply the rules of the game to the interactions of the players. Given certain parameters, and relying on the roll of dice for a random choice generator, the players would indulge in collaborative storytelling. To "win" meant to either earn powers for one's own character or team mates by completing quests or defeating enemies, or to maneuver other characters into positions of weakness. Not enough research has been done on this fascinating, though short-lived, sociological phenomenon.

3. **Revising for Readability (Using Lists) [LO-2]** Rewrite the following paragraph using a parallel bulleted list and one introductory sentence:

   > We offer a wide range of pathological tests. We have state-of-the-art medical scanning equipment, including CT scanning, magnetic resonance imaging, positron emission tomography, as well as traditional ultrasound and X-ray facilities. All our tests are administered by qualified radiologists and carried out to international standards of accuracy, quality, and safety.

4. **Revising for Readability (Sentence Length) [LO-2]** Break the following sentences into shorter ones by adding more periods and revise as needed for smooth flow:

   a. There is no need to look up every word you may have doubts about until the writing process is finished and you are ready to move on to the next step: the editorial process.

   b. A lot of people feel nervousness in airplanes, but in very few cases can this be traced to any actual underlying medical condition; it is far more likely to be caused by a kind of philosophical unease with the obvious absurdity of flying.

c. Reading your work aloud after you have written it is an excellent way to put some distance between you and the thing you have written, because, as your ears consume what your mouth produces, you can vicariously experience the reader's most likely reaction to your offering.

d. Rhetoric was the ancient science of influencing people with words, and experiments have shown that language rich in rhetoric or figures of speech is more memorable and persuasive than plain, undecorated prose, provided it is not overdone.

e. Machine translation has its limitations, as was seen when a machine was asking to translate "put the red block on the green block" and came up with "Place the communist political affiliation above the environmentalist special interest group."

5. **Editing for Conciseness (Unnecessary Words) [LO-3]** Cross out unnecessary words in the following phrases:

a. At this point in time

b. Outstanding excellence

c. A large sum of money

d. Continues uninterruptedly

e. Rising uptick

6. **Editing for Conciseness (Long Words) [LO-3]** Revise the following sentences, using shorter, simpler words:

a. The innovative and novel concept she proposes in her presentation has been expounded very competently.

b. I'm afraid I must recommend that the inordinate duration of the delay you have demonstrated in delivering the results of your research be taken into consideration when your remuneration is discussed.

c. There is no cause for concern surrounding the media reports of closure of our branch factories as we have shown with overwhelming veracity that these bulletins are unfounded on fact.

d. Our partners in other national territories have acquiesced to the mooted profit-sharing stipulations that we outlined in our draft contract.

e. The balance of probability tilts in the direction of grave irregularities in the reporting and recording of day to day financial transactions.

7. **Editing for Conciseness (Lengthy Phrases) [LO-3]** Use infinitives as substitutes for the overly long phrases in these sentences:

a. Editing is never optional for making sure the work is readable.

b. I am not convinced by your explanation of why you failed in cleaning the office up in time for the meeting.

c. Carrying a grudge for so many years is only destroying your own happiness.

8. **Editing for Conciseness (Lengthy Phrases) [LO-3]** Rephrase the following in fewer words:

a. In the foreseeable future

b. Assuming the possibility that

c. In order that

d. In a manner of speaking

e. As it were

f. Suffice it to say

g. In a majority of cases

h. Notwithstanding the fact that

i. With reference to

j. Without any reasonable doubt

9. **Editing for Conciseness (Lengthy Phrases) [LO-3]** Revise to condense these sentences to as few words as possible:

a. In all honesty, I have to tell you that I did not like your idea the first time round.

b. An approximate guess is that we can cover these costs in the next quarter.

c. We are strongly purposed toward finding a solution to this difficulty.

d. At the end of the day, one has to face the fact that, after all, business competencies have to be leveraged.

e. In these times of recession and market shrinkage, we have to be cautiously complacent that we have managed to retain our continuing 31 percent market share.

10. **Editing for Conciseness (Unnecessary Modifiers) [LO-3]** Remove all the unnecessary modifiers from these sentences:

a. Generous compensation packages were offered to the highly qualified and immensely sought after marketing mavens.

b. The watchdog body made numerous sweeping, generalized and across-the-board statements.

11. **Editing for Clarity (Hedging) [LO-3]** Rewrite these sentences so that they no longer contain any hedging:

a. The success of the project, given enough time and resources and the requisite commitment from senior management, is virtually assured.

b. I can definitely speculate that sometime in the near future our difficulties may move toward a possible solution.

c. The possibility of financial loss, while vanishingly small, cannot, under certain circumstances, be entirely ruled out.

d. It seems to me that you have been devoting rather more time than is normally expected on identifying employees who don't perform at par.

e. I believe you wish to submit this letter of resignation because you have some intention of leaving us.

12. **Editing for Clarity (Indefinite Starters) [LO-3]** Rewrite these sentences to eliminate the indefinite starters:

a. In quite a few instances I have seen that you overwork yourself unreasonably.

b. It would be very fortunate if that report could be found.

c. It is regrettable that in several cases the people who joined our offshore facility left after less than a year.

d. There is a rule that states that you cannot use office equipment for your personal projects.

e. Owing to several losses it would be a good gesture if this department forgoes its yearly bonus this year.

13. **Editing for Clarity (Parallelism) [LO-3]** Revise these sentences in order to present the ideas in parallel form:

a. This machine can clean sidewalks, sweep leaves, and can also polish any stone surface.

b. She is passionate about gardening and she is good at playing the piano too.

c. In order to be a successful accountant, you have to have a feel for figures, you must be interested in describing things with numbers, and your analytical skills must be top notch.

d. This book was well plotted, racy, and had a beautiful cover.

14. **Editing for Clarity (Awkward References) [LO-3]** Revise the following sentences to delete the awkward references:

a. The Chief Operating Officer and the network manager have each in their possession a key to the large and the small server room, respectively.

b. The keys to the large and the small server rooms are in executive hands, with the former belonging to the chief operating officer and the latter belonging to the network manager.

c. The keys to 34A and 35A have been given to the network manager, with the aforementioned keys being gold embossed.

d. I got a chocolate donut and a Danish for Sarah and Neill, respectively.

e. The hardback book is more expensive than the paperback; the former is priced at $27 and the latter is only $10.

15. **Editing for Clarity (Dangling Modifiers) [LO-3]** Rewrite these sentences to clarify the dangling modifiers:

a. Sat upon by goats and nibbled by puppies, I hung onto the corners of my sorry manuscript as it disappeared between the jaws of my brother's prize Jersey cow.

b. Locked up in the safe, Lionel found the keycodes to the server settings five days after he first began looking for them.

c. With a leaky bottom and misshapen sides, that woman is selling you bankruptcy disguised as a sailboat.

d. After scrubbing and tidying all afternoon, the room was back to Sally's idea of a cozy lounge.

e. Soaring five hundred metres into the sky, David was deeply impressed by the new headquarters.

16. **Editing for Clarity (Noun Sequences) [LO-3]** Rewrite the following sentences to eliminate the long strings of nouns:

a. Your report evaluation group feedback taking procedures leave much to be desired.

b. As per your post meeting debrief letter, we have decided not to go forward with the overflow containment building annexe plans.

c. The customer satisfaction assurance program requires that you make targeted scheduled post-service feedback calls to all tagged customers.

d. All of our pre-publication expert focused readers' reports must be in by the beginning of the last pre-production month.

e. Our yummylicious low-fat frozen desserts are on the summer sale special discount racks.

17. **Editing for Clarity (Sentence Structure) [LO-3]** Rearrange the following sentences to bring the subjects closer to their verbs:

a. Lucy, when she was absolutely sure that nothing could save her from the runaway train hurtling unstoppably down the track, ran for her life.

b. I think your coat, which looks like you bought it at a prewar garage sale with the money you saved from washing windows and delivering paper rounds, has accidentally fallen into the trash compactor.

c. Martin, who prides himself on being the best organizer among the lot of us in this department even though it's actually Jenny who keeps track of things for him, has left the presentation notes at home.

d. Ingrid opened the oven, and finding that the special cake she had made with the recipe handed down to her by her grandmother had dried to a brick, picked up the phone and ordered takeout.

18. **Editing for Clarity (Camouflaged Verbs) [LO-3]** Rewrite each sentence so that the verbs are no longer camouflaged:

a. Flotation after a water landing is achieved by means of the seat bottom cushion.

b. My boss will make an assessment of the liability before we contact you again.

c. I will carry out the investigation as discreetly as possible.

d. I will be obliged if you grant me permission to leave early today.

e. The editing procedure on the final report should be performed by the section head.

19. **Completing: Designing for Readability; Media Skills: Blogging [LO-4], Chapter 7** Compare the home pages of Bloomberg (www.bloomberg.com) and MarketWatch (www.marketwatch.com), two websites that cover financial markets. What are your first impressions of these two sites? How do their overall designs compare in terms of information delivery and overall user experience? Choose three pieces of information that a visitor to these sites would be likely to look for, such as a current stock price, news from international markets, and commentary from market experts. Which site makes it easier to find this information? Why? Present your analysis in a post for your class blog.

20. **Communication Ethics: Making Ethical Choices; Media Skills: Blogging [LO-3], Chapter 7** Say you are the public relations liaison officer for a medium-sized garment factory. You are adding a new section to your plant, and the construction will disrupt a major road in your town for nearly a year, according to estimates, and cause quite a bit of noise and air pollution. Given that your product does not sell in the local area and none of those affected by the upgrades are your customers, is it worth your while blogging and putting up notices with detailed information to help people adjust their routes and schedules and minimize the inconvenience the work will cause to them? Or would your time be better spent looking after "real" customers? Give reasons for your answer.

21. **Proofreading [LO-5]** Proofread the following email message and revise it to correct any problems you find:

   Pleas wellcome our new recruits when they finally join us tomorow morning after the orientatation session in the large meeting room. There will be an informla receptions in the foyer followed by a speech by our head of Human resources. Cooffee and snacks will be served.

EXPAND YOUR SKILLS

Critique the Professionals

Identify a company website that in your opinion violates one or more of the principles of good design discussed on pages 204–206. Using whatever medium your instructor requests, write a brief analysis of the site (no more than one page), citing specific elements from the piece and support from the chapter.

Sharpening Your Career Skills Online

Bovée and Thill's Business Communication Web Search, at http://businesscommunicationblog.com/websearch, is a unique research tool designed specifically for business communication research. Use the Web Search function to find a website, video, PDF document, or PowerPoint presentation that offers advice on effective proofreading. Write a brief email message to your instructor, describing the item that you found and summarizing the career skills information you learned from it.

IMPROVE YOUR GRAMMAR, MECHANICS, AND USAGE

The following exercises help you improve your knowledge of and power over English grammar, mechanics, and usage. Turn to the "Handbook of Grammar, Mechanics, and Usage" at the end of this book and review Section 1.6.1 (Prepositions). Then look at the following 10 items. Underline the preferred choice within each set of parentheses. (Answers to these exercises appear on page AK-3.)

1. Are the figures (*approaching to, approaching*) our target?

2. Are you coming (*to home, home*) with me?

3. You must remember to read and (*reply, reply to*) your client's email.

4. Dr. Smith (*said, told*) me he will be conducting the marketing class today.

5. You must divide the gifts (*in between, between*) all eight of you.

6. I am taking my daughter out (*to, for*) the theater today.

7. All these books are different (*from, to*) each other.

8. Henry's car's number-plate is the same (*as, to*) the one we saw outside James' house.

9. She has decided (*to not, not to*) talk to him anymore.

10. Margaret told Jacques to put the oranges (*onto, on*) the kitchen counter.

For additional exercises focusing on prepositions, visit MyBcommLab or go to www.pearsoninternationaleditions.com/thill, then locate your text and click on its Companion Website link. Click on Chapter 6; click on Additional Exercises to Improve Your Grammar, Mechanics, and Usage; and then click on 10. Prepositions.

REFERENCES

1. Jefferson Rabb website, accessed 22 January 2011, www.jeffersonrabb.com; Joshua Bodwell, "Artful Author Web Sites," *Poets & Writers*, January/February 2011, 79–84; *Super Sad True Love Story* website, accessed 22 January 2011, http://supersadtruelovestory.com; *Beat the Reaper* website, accessed 22 January 2011, www.beatthereaper.com.

2. Deborah Gunn, "Looking Good on Paper," *Office Pro*, March 2004, 10–11.

3. Jacci Howard Bear, "Desktop Publishing Rules of Page Layout," About.com, accessed 22 August 2005, www.about.com.

4. Jacci Howard Bear, "Desktop Publishing Rules for How Many Fonts to Use," About.com, accessed 22 August 2005, www.about.com.

5. The writing samples in this exercise were taken or adapted from the Alexander McCall Smith website, accessed 2 June 2011, www.alexandermccallsmith.com; Anita Shreve website, accessed 2 June 2011, www.anitashreve.com; *Traffic* website, accessed 2 June 2011, http://tomvanderbilt.com/traffic.

6. The writing sample in this exercise was adapted from material on the Marsh Risk Consulting website, accessed 2 October 2006, www.marshriskconsulting.com.

PART 3 | Crafting Brief Messages

Most of your communication on the job will be through brief messages, from Twitter updates and blog posts to formal letters that might run to several pages. Learning how to write these messages effectively is key to maintaining productive working relationships with colleagues and customers. Start by adapting what you already know about electronic media to the professional challenges of business communication. Then learn specific techniques for crafting routine, positive, negative, and persuasive messages—techniques that will help you in everything from getting a raise to calming an angry customer to promoting your next great idea.

Goodluz/Shutterstock

7 Crafting Messages for Electronic Media

LEARNING OBJECTIVES   After studying this chapter, you will be able to

1 Identify the electronic media available for short messages, list nine compositional modes used in electronic media, and discuss the challenges of communicating through social media

2 Describe the use of social networks, user-generated content sites, community Q&A sites, and community participation sites in business communication

3 Describe the evolving role of email in business communication, and explain how to adapt the three-step writing process to email messages

4 Describe the business benefits of instant messaging (IM), and identify guidelines for effective IM in the workplace

5 Describe the role of blogging and microblogging in business communication today, and explain how to adapt the three-step writing process to blogging

6 Explain how to adapt the three-step writing process to podcasting

MyBcommLab   Where you see MyBcommLab in this chapter, go to www.pearsoninternationaleditions.com/mybcommlab for additional activities on the topic being discussed.

ON THE JOB: COMMUNICATING AT SOUTHWEST AIRLINES

Southwest Airline's multimedia, multiauthor blog, Nuts About Southwest, features a variety of entertaining writers from around the company.
Source: Courtesy Southwest Airlines, Co.

Online Uproar Triggers Change in Company Policy

Southwest Airlines's blog is usually a love fest—or a "luv" fest, to use one of the company's favorite words. In fact, the blog's official name is Nuts About Southwest. A typical post might highlight the community service efforts of a group of employees or congratulate a team of Southwest mechanics for winning gold at the Aviation Maintenance Olympics. Devoted customers post enthusiastic comments on nearly every article, and many seem to have bonded in virtual friendship with the 30 Southwest employees who take turns writing the blog.

Bill Owen probably didn't expect a bubbly reception to a rather workaday post titled "Why can't I make reservations further in advance?" in which he calmly explained why the company usually didn't let customers make reservations as far into the future as other airlines do. But he probably wasn't expecting the response he *did* get, either. In his words, "Talk about sticking your head in a hornet's nest!" Instead of the usual dozen or so happy responses to a typical post, he received several hundred responses—many of which expressed disappointment, unhappiness, and downright anger. Customers described one scenario after another in which they had a real need to book travel further in advance than Southwest allowed, and many complained that the policy was forcing them to fly other airlines. Some Southwest employees chimed in, too, expressing their frustration with not being able to meet customer needs at times.

After bravely and patiently addressing specific customer responses over a period of several months, Owen responded with a new post titled "I blogged. You flamed. We changed." In this message, he explained that the company had listened and was changing its scheduling policies to better accommodate customer needs.

In fact, feedback from blog readers is so important that Southwest considers the blog a "customer service laboratory" that helps the company learn how to better serve its customers.[1]

www.blogsouthwest.com

Electronic Media for Business Communication

Bill Owen from Southwest Airlines (profiled in the chapter opener) might've used any number of media to convey the company's message about reservation policies. However, the choice of a blog post is significant because it represents a fundamental change in business communication and the relationships between companies and their stakeholders, a change enabled by the rapid growth of social media (see Figure 7.1 on the next page).

The considerable range of electronic media available for brief business messages continues to grow as communication technologies evolve:

- **Social networking and community participation websites.** Social networking sites such as Facebook and LinkedIn, user-generated content (UGC) sites such as Flickr and YouTube, community Q&A sites, and a variety of social bookmarking and tagging sites provide an enormous range of communication tools.
- **Email.** Conventional email has long been a vital medium for business communication, although it is replaced in many instances by other tools that provide better support for instant communication and real-time collaboration.
- **Instant messaging (IM).** IM usage now rivals email in many companies. IM offers even greater speed than email, as well as simple operation and fewer problems with unwanted messages or security and privacy problems.
- **Text messaging.** Phone-based text messaging has a number of applications in business communication, including order and status updates, marketing and sales messages, electronic coupons, and customer service.[2]
- **Blogging and microblogging.** The ability to update content quickly and easily makes blogs and microblogs (such as Twitter) a natural medium when communicators want to get messages out in a hurry.
- **Podcasting.** You may be familiar with podcasts as the online equivalent of recorded radio or video broadcasts (video podcasts are often called *vidcasts* or *vodcasts*). Businesses are now using podcasts to replace or supplement some conference calls, newsletters, training courses, and other communication activities.
- **Online video.** Now that YouTube and similar websites have made online video available to hundreds of millions of web users, video has been transformed from a fairly specialized tool to a mainstream business communication medium. More than half of the world's largest companies now have their own *branded channels* on YouTube, for example.[3]

The lines between these media often get blurry as systems expand their capabilities or people use them in new ways (see "Business Communication 2.0: Walking Around with the Entire Internet in Your Hands"). For example, Facebook Messages integrates IM, text messages, and email capabilities, in addition to being a social networking system.[4] Similarly, some people consider Twitter to be a social network, and it certainly offers some of that capability. However, because blog-like messaging is Twitter's core function, this chapter classifies it as a microblogging system.

Most of your business communication is likely to be via electronic means, but don't overlook the benefits of printed messages. (For more on formatting printed letters and

MyBcommLab

- Access this chapter's simulation entitled Crafting Messages for Electronic Media located at www.pearsoninternational editions.com/mybcommlab.

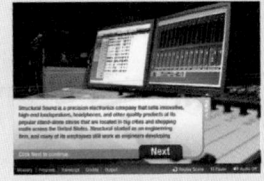

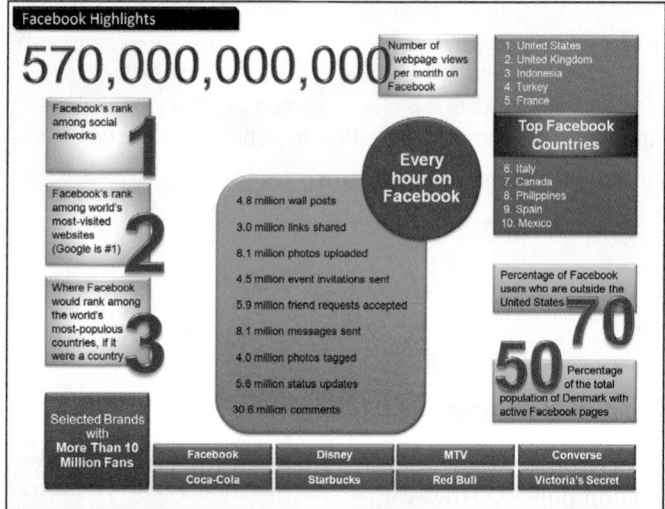

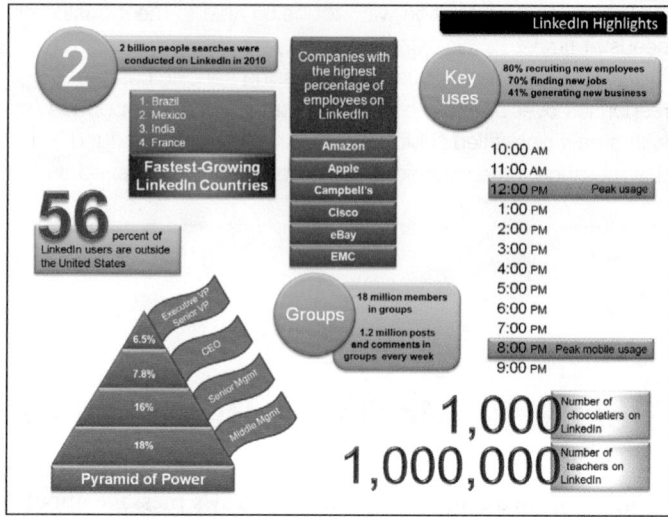

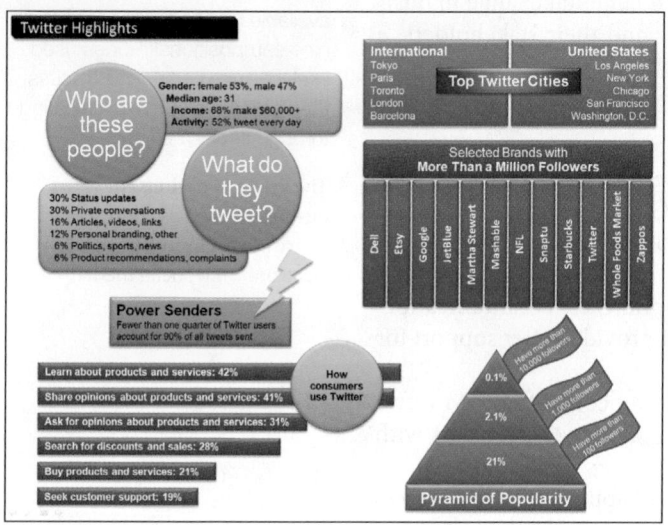

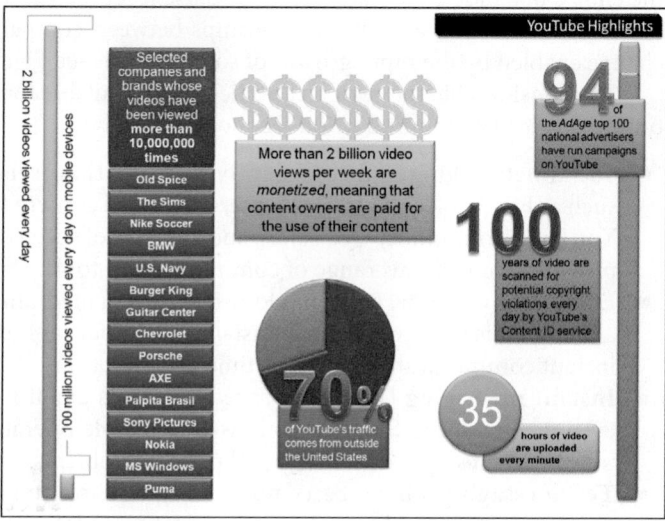

Figure 7.1 **The Rise and Reach of Social Media**
This infographic shows the rapid rise and wide reach of four major social media platforms: Facebook, Twitter, LinkedIn, and YouTube.

Sources: Adapted from "About Us," LinkedIn, accessed 2 May 2011, http://press.linkedin.com/about/; Ben Parr, "LinkedIn Surpasses 100 Million Users," Mashable, 22 March 2011, http://mashable.com; "Franky Branckaute, "Facebook Statistics: The Numbers Game Continues," The Blog Herald blog, 11 August 2010, www.blogherald.com; Stan Schroeder, "Facebook: Facts You Probably Didn't Know," Mashable, 13 May 2010, http://mashable.com; "The 1000 Most-Visited Sites on the Web," Doubleclick Ad Planner, February 2011, www.google.com/adplanner; Willis Wee, "The Facebook Story in an Infographic," Penn Olson blog 2 April 2010, www.penn-olson.com; "Statistics," YouTube, accessed 2 May 2011, www.youtube.com; "LinkedIn by the Numbers," HubSpot Blog, 29 June 2010, http://blog.hubspot.com; "Top Corporate Brands on Twitter," Fan Page List, http://fanpagelist.com; "Top Corporate Brands on Facebook," Fan Page List, accessed 2 May 2011, http://fanpagelist.com; "Twitter Statistics for 2010," Sysomos, December 2010, www.sysomos.com; Shiva Chettri, "The Meteoric Rise of Twitter," NetChunks, 10 July 2010, www.netchunks.com.

memos, see Chapter 6 and Appendix A.) Here are several situations in which you should consider using a printed message rather than electronic alternatives:

> Even with the widespread use of electronic media, printed memos and letters still play an important role in business communication.

- **When you want to make a formal impression.** For special messages, such as sending congratulations or condolences, the formality of printed documents usually makes them a much better choice than electronic messages.
- **When you are legally required to provide information in printed form.** Business contracts and government regulations sometimes require that information be provided on paper.
- **When you want to stand out from the flood of electronic messages.** If your audience's computers are overflowing with Twitter updates, email, and IM, sometimes a printed message can stand out enough to get noticed.

- **When you need a permanent, unchangeable, or secure record.** Letters and memos are reliable. Once printed, they can't be erased with a single keystroke or surreptitiously modified the way some electronic messages can be. Printed documents are also more difficult to copy and forward.

Again, most of your on-the-job communication is going to be through electronic media. This chapter focuses on electronic media for brief business messages, while the report writing chapters (Chapters 13 through 15) address writing for the web and wikis.

COMPOSITIONAL MODES FOR ELECTRONIC MEDIA

As you practice using electronic media in this course, it's best to focus on the principles of social media communication and the fundamentals of planning, writing, and completing messages, rather than on the specific details of any one medium or system.[5] Fortunately, the basic communication skills required usually transfer from one system to another. You can succeed with written communication in virtually all electronic media by using one of nine *compositional modes*:

Communicating successfully with electronic media requires a wide range of writing approaches.

- **Conversations.** IM is a great example of a written medium that mimics spoken conversation. With IM, the ability to think, compose, and type relatively quickly is important to maintaining the flow of an electronic conversation.
- **Comments and critiques.** One of the most powerful aspects of social media is the opportunity for interested parties to express opinions and provide feedback. Sharing helpful tips and insightful commentary is also a great way to build your personal brand. To be an effective commenter, focus on short chunks of information that a broad spectrum of other site visitors will find helpful.

BUSINESS COMMUNICATION 2.0

Walking Around with the Entire Internet in Your Hands

Although strictly speaking not a separate medium, the *mobile web*—the capability of connecting to the Internet with smartphones and other mobile devices—is expanding rapidly for business communication. As two indications of the growth of mobile access, YouTube serves up more than 100 million videos a day to mobile devices, and more than 40 percent of Facebook's half-billion-plus members interact with the social network using their mobile devices.

Beyond just the unwired web, though, a growing variety of location-based information services help personalize communication, down to a specific time and place. For example, the ability to scan coded labels such as barcodes or the similar *Quick Response (QR) codes* attached to printed materials, products, or stores and other buildings (or the ability to pick up radio signals from new *near-field communication* tags) gives smartphone users a way to get more information—from the companies themselves and from other consumers providing reviews on social websites.

The combination of mobile phone service, social networking, and GPS navigation has given rise to a new form of communication known as *location-based social networking* through services such as Foursquare and Loopt. Key features of these systems include *check-ins*, in which mobile consumers can indicate presence at specific locations, and "gamification,"

encouraging specific types of consumer behavior through the use of mobile games (such as Foursquare's competitions to become "mayor" of a location by checking in more than anyone else during a given time frame). Location-based networking promises to become an important business communication medium because mobile consumers are a significant economic force—through the purchases they make directly and through their ability to influence other consumers.

CAREER APPLICATIONS

1. When potential customers can show up on a business's doorstep with the Internet literally in their hands, what effect might this development have on the company's communication efforts?

2. How can businesses use Foursquare and other location-based services to build stronger relationships with customers and potential customers?

Sources: Adapted from Foursquare Support, accessed 10 July 2011, http://support.foursquare.com; Mark Sullivan, "The Buzzwords of South by Southwest," PCWorld, 15 March 2011, www.pcworld.com; Facebook Press Room, accessed 29 January 2011, www.facebook.com; Adam Ostrow, "A Look Back at the Last 5 Years in Social Media," Mashable, 20 July 2010, www.mashable.com; Peter Koeppel, "How Do I Love Thee, Smartphone?" Adotas, 25 January 2011, www.adotas.com; Jennifer Van Grove, "Why Google's Slapping Decals on Small Businesses," Mashable, 7 December 2009, http://mashable.com; Jennifer Van Grove, "5 Huge Trends in Social Media Right Now," Mashable, 20 August 2010, http://mashable.com.

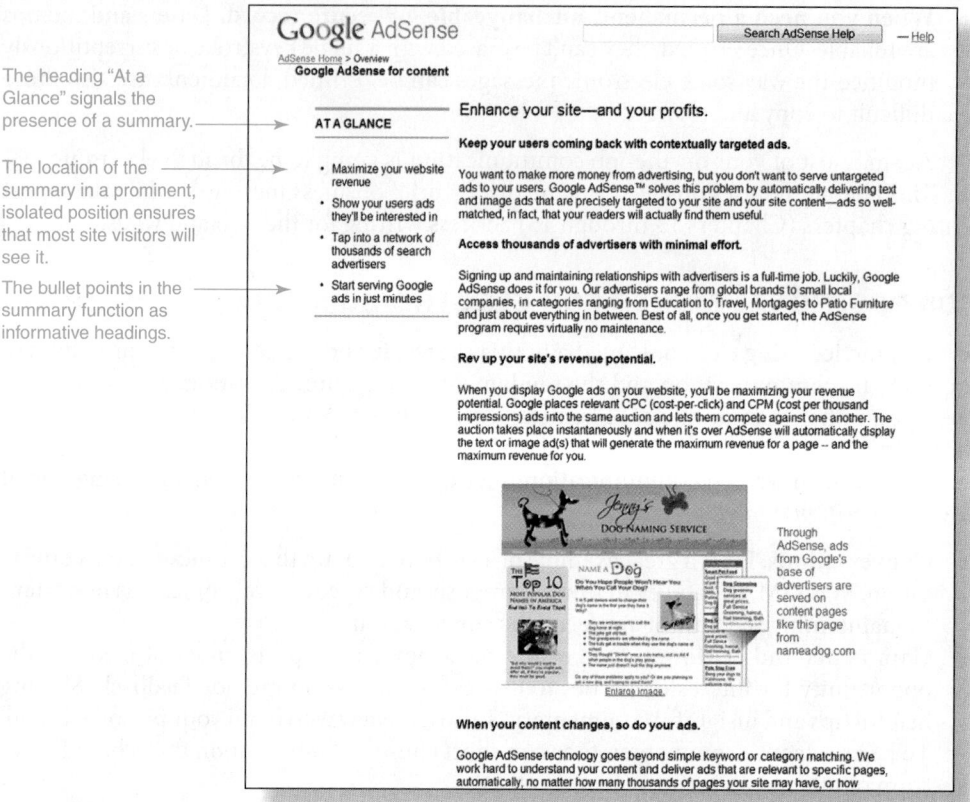

The heading "At a Glance" signals the presence of a summary.

The location of the summary in a prominent, isolated position ensures that most site visitors will see it.

The bullet points in the summary function as informative headings.

Figure 7.2   Writing Summaries for Electronic Media
This "At a Glance" sidebar serves as a helpful summary of Google's AdSense program, while also promoting the program's benefits.
Source: Courtesy of Google.

- **Orientations.** The ability to help people find their way through an unfamiliar system or new subject is a valuable writing skill and a talent that readers greatly appreciate. Unlike summaries (see next item), orientations don't give away the key points in the collection of information but rather tell readers where to find those points and how to navigate through the collection.
- **Summaries.** At the beginning of an article or webpage, a summary functions as a miniature version of the document, giving readers all the key points while skipping over details (see Figure 7.2). In some instances, this is all a reader needs. At the end of an article or webpage, a summary functions as a review, reminding readers of the key points they've just read.
- **Reference material.** One of the challenges of planning and writing reference material is that people typically don't read such material in a linear sense but rather search through to find particular data points, trends, or other specific elements. Making the information accessible via search engines is an important step. However, readers don't always know which search terms will yield the best results, so include an orientation and organize the material in logical ways with clear headings that promote skimming.
- **Narratives.** The storytelling techniques covered in Chapter 4 (see page 152) can be effective in a wide variety of situations. Narratives work best when they have an intriguing beginning that ignites readers' curiosity, a middle section that moves quickly through the challenges that an individual or company faced, and an inspiring or instructive ending that gives readers information they can apply in their own lives and jobs.
- **Teasers.** Teasers intentionally withhold key pieces of information as a way to pull readers or listeners into a story or other document. In electronic media, the space limitations and URL linking capabilities of Twitter and other microblogging systems make them a natural tool for the teaser approach. Be sure that the *payoff*, the information a teaser links to, is valuable and legitimate.

With Twitter and other super-short messaging systems, the ability to write a compelling *teaser* is an important skill.

- **Status updates and announcements.** If you use social media frequently, much of your writing will involve status updates and announcements. Be sure to post only those updates that readers will find useful, and include only the information they need.
- **Tutorials.** Given the community nature of social media, the purpose of many messages is to share how-to advice. Becoming known as a reliable expert is a great way to build customer loyalty for your company while enhancing your own personal value.

As you approach a new communication task using electronic media, ask yourself what kind of information audience members are likely to need and then choose the appropriate compositional mode. Of course, many of these modes are also used in written media, but over time you may find yourself using all of them in various electronic and social media contexts.

REAL-TIME UPDATES
Learn More by Reading This Article

Integrating social media in a global corporation

IBM's Social Computing Guidelines offer practical advice for any company that wants to incorporate social media. Go to http://real-timeupdates.com/ebc10 and click on Learn More. If you are using MyBcommLab, you can access Real-Time Updates within each chapter or under Student Study Tools.

CREATING CONTENT FOR SOCIAL MEDIA

No matter what media or compositional mode you are using for a particular message, writing for social media requires a different approach than traditional media. As Chapter 1 points out in the discussion of Business Communication 2.0, social media have changed the relationship between sender and receiver, so the nature of the messages needs to change as well. Whether you're writing a blog or posting a product demonstration video to YouTube, consider these tips for creating successful content for social media:[6]

- **Remember that it's a conversation, not a lecture or a sales pitch.** One of the great appeals of social media is the feeling of conversation, of people talking *with* one another instead of one person talking *at* everyone else. For all its technological sophistication, in an important sense social media provide a new spin on the age-old practice of *word-of-mouth* communication. As more and more people gain a voice in the marketplace, companies that try to maintain the old "we talk, you listen" mindset are likely to be ignored in the social media landscape.
- **Write informally but not carelessly.** Write as a human being, not as a cog in a faceless corporate machine. At the same time, don't get sloppy; no one wants to slog through misspelled words and half-baked sentences to find the message.
- **Create concise, specific, and informative headlines.** Avoid the temptation to engage in clever wordplay with headlines. This advice applies to all forms of business communication, of course, but it is essential for social media. Readers don't want to spend time and energy figuring out what your witty headlines mean. Search engines won't know what they mean, either, so fewer people will find your content.
- **Get involved and stay involved.** Social media understandably make some businesspeople nervous because they don't permit a high level of control over messages. However, don't hide from criticism. Take the opportunity to correct misinformation or explain how mistakes will be fixed.
- **If you need to promote something, do so indirectly.** Just as you wouldn't hit people with a company sales pitch during an informal social gathering, refrain from blatant promotional efforts in social media.
- **Be transparent and honest.** Honesty is always essential, of course, but a particular issue that has tripped up a few companies in recent years is hiding behind an online blogging persona—either a fictitious character whose writing is actually done by a corporate marketing specialist or a real person who fails to disclose an affiliation with a corporate sponsor.
- **Think before you post!** Because of careless messages, individuals and companies have been sued for Twitter

REAL-TIME UPDATES
Learn More by Listening to This Podcast

Exploring ethical expectations in social media

Listen in on this corporate training session regarding ethical issues in social media. Go to http://real-timeupdates.com/ebc10 and click on Learn More. If you are using MyBcommLab, you can access Real-Time Updates within each chapter or under Student Study Tools.

A momentary lapse of concentration while using social media can cause tremendous career or company damage.

updates, employees have been fired for Facebook wall postings, vital company secrets have been leaked, and business and personal relationships have been strained. Unless you are sending messages through a private channel, assume that every message will be read by people far beyond your original audience.

Social Networking and Community Participation Websites

2   LEARNING OBJECTIVE

Describe the use of social networks, user-generated content sites, community Q&A sites, and community participation sites in business communication.

Social networks, online services that enable individual and organizational members to form connections and share information, have become a major force in business communication in recent years. For example, Facebook is now the most-visited website on the Internet, and a number of companies, such as Adidas, Red Bull, and Starbucks, have millions of fans on their Facebook pages.[7] This section takes a look at the business communication uses of social networks and a range of related technologies, including *user-generated content (UGC) sites, community Q&A sites,* and *community participation sites.*

SOCIAL NETWORKS

The business world currently has a complicated relationship with the idea of social networks. Some companies embrace these media wholeheartedly and encourage employees to use them to reach out to customers. Other companies ban employees from using them at work, particularly networks such as Facebook that weren't originally designed for business use (unlike LinkedIn, for example). No matter what an individual company's take on the topic might be, few observers would deny that social networking is already a major force in business communication and promises to get even bigger as networks grow in size and offer more communication features. In addition to connecting hundreds of millions of consumers to each other and to the companies they buy from, social networks are likely to become the primary communication system for a significant portion of the workforce over the next few years.[8]

Business communicators make use of a wide range of social networks, in addition to the well-known Facebook.

Businesses now use several types of social networks, including public, general-purpose networks such as Facebook and Google+; public, business-oriented networks (LinkedIn is the largest of these—see page 37 in the Prologue for an example); and a variety of specialized networks. This last group includes networks that help small-business owners get support and advice, those that connect entrepreneurs with investors, and those such as Segway Social and Specialized (see page 230) created by individual companies to enhance the sense of community among their customer bases. Some companies have built private social networks for internal use only. For example, the defense contractor Lockheed Martin created its Unity network, complete with a variety of social media applications, to meet the expectations of younger employees accustomed to social media and to capture the expert knowledge of older employees nearing retirement.[9]

Business Communication Uses of Social Networks

With their ability to reach virtually unlimited numbers of people through a variety of electronic formats, social networks are a great fit for many business communication needs (see Table 7.1). In fact, a significant majority of consumers now want the businesses they patronize to use social networking for distributing information and interacting with customers—and companies that aren't active in social networking risk getting left behind.[10]

Social networks are vital tools for distributing information as well as gathering information about the business environment.

In addition to the collaboration uses discussed in Chapter 2, here are some of the key business applications of social networks:

- **Gathering market intelligence.** With hundreds of millions of people expressing themselves via social media, you can be sure that smart companies are listening. For example, *sentiment analysis* is an intriguing research technique in which companies track social networks and other media with automated language-analysis software that

TABLE 7.1	Business Uses of Social Networking Technology
Business Challenge	**Example of Social Networking in Action**
Supporting customers	Allowing customers to develop close relationships with product experts within the company
Integrating new employees	Helping new employees navigate their way through the organization, finding experts, mentors, and other important contacts
Easing the transition after reorganizations and mergers	Helping employees connect and bond after internal staff reorganizations or mergers with other organizations
Overcoming structural barriers in communication channels	Bypassing the formal communication system in order to deliver information where it is needed in a timely fashion
Assembling teams	Identifying the best people, both inside the company and in other companies, to collaborate on projects
Fostering the growth of communities	Helping people with similar—or complementary—interests and skills find each other in order to provide mutual assistance and development
Solving problems	Finding "pockets of knowledge" within the organization—the expertise and experience of individual employees
Preparing for major meetings and events	Giving participants a way to meet before an event takes place, helping to ensure that the meeting or event becomes more productive more quickly
Accelerating the evolution of teams	Accelerating the sometimes slow process of getting to know one another and identifying individual areas of expertise
Maintaining business relationships	Giving people an easy way to stay in contact after meetings and conferences
Sharing and distributing information	Making it easy for employees to share information with people who may need it and for people who need information to find employees who might have it
Finding potential customers, business partners, and employees	Identifying strong candidates by matching user profiles with current business needs and linking from existing member profiles

Sources: Adapted from Christopher Carfi and Leif Chastaine, "Social Networking for Businesses & Organizations," white paper, Cerado website, accessed 13 August 2008, www.cerado.com; Anusorn Kansap, "Social Networking," PowerPoint presentation, Silpakorn University, accessed 14 August 2008, http://real-timeupdates.com; "Social Network Websites: Best Practices from Leading Services," white paper, 28 November 2007, FaberNovel Consulting, www.fabernovel.com.

tries to take the pulse of public opinion and identify influential opinion makers. Social media can be "an incredibly rich vein of market intelligence," says Margaret Francis of San Francisco's Scout Labs (**www.scoutlabs.com**).[11]

- **Recruiting new employees and finding business partners.** Companies use social networks to find potential employees, short-term contractors, subject-matter experts, product and service suppliers, and business partners. On LinkedIn, for example, members can recommend each other based on current or past business relationships, which helps remove the uncertainty of initiating business relationships with complete strangers.

- **Sharing product information.** Businesses don't invest time and money in social networking simply to gain fans. The ultimate goal is profitable, sustainable relationships with customers, and attracting new customers is one of the primary reasons businesses use networks and other social media.[12] However, the traditional notions

Product promotion can be done on social networks, but it needs to be done in a low-key, indirect way.

Business Communicators Innovating with Social Media

Companies in virtually every industry have been adopting social media and experimenting with new ways to connect with customers and other stakeholders. From offering helpful tips on using products to helping customers meet each other, these companies show the enormous range of possibilities that new media bring to business communication.

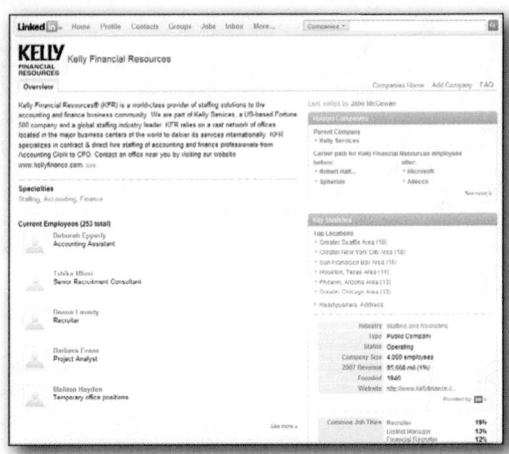

General-Purpose Social Networks: Business Focus

Most everyone is familiar with Facebook these days, and thousands of companies are active on the world's most popular social network. However, a number of social networks exist just for businesses and business professionals, including LinkedIn, the largest of the business networks. Kelly Financial Resources, part of the Kelly Services staffing company, maintains a profile on LinkedIn, as do several hundred of its employees.

Source: Used with permission of Kelly Services, Inc.

Specialized Social Networks: Business Focus

"Biznik is a social network designed for use by entrepreneurs and small business people to aid them in connecting and collaborating with their peers and contemporaries," explains Biznik's Andrew Lippert. A great example of these groups is The Marketing Crowd. "This Biznik group consists of professionals in the marketing profession who connect with one another and discuss issues relevant to their industry. The group is an online extension of their community, which facilitates their interaction and the development of real relationships supporting and benefiting the group members' professional careers and businesses."

Source: © 2010 Biznik, Inc - Biznik is an online community of independent business people interested in helping each other succeed. Blending the best of social media with in-person events Biznik encourages collaboration inspiration, education and ultimately . . . professional relationships that produce more business. (http://biznik.com).

Specialized Social Networks: Consumer Focus

A number of companies now host their own social networking sites, where product enthusiasts interact by sharing personal stories, offering advice, and commenting on products and company news—all brief-message functions that replace more traditional media options. For example, Specialized, a major bicycle manufacturer based in Morgan Hill, California, hosts the Specialized Riders Club (www.specializedriders.com), where customers can interact with each other and the professional riders the company sponsors. Similarly, the Segway Social network connects owners of these unique personal vehicles, including helping teams organize for Segway polo matches and other events.

Source: Used with permission of Segway, Inc.

User-Generated Content

Many companies now encourage *user-generated content* as a way to engage their stakeholders and provide additional value through shared expertise. The online shoe and apparel retailer Zappos, for example, invites customers to create and upload videos that communicate their experiences with Zappos and its products.

Value-Added Content via Blogging

One of the best ways to become a valued member of a network is to provide content that is useful to others in the network. The Quizzle personal finance blog offers a steady stream of articles and advice that help people manage their finances.

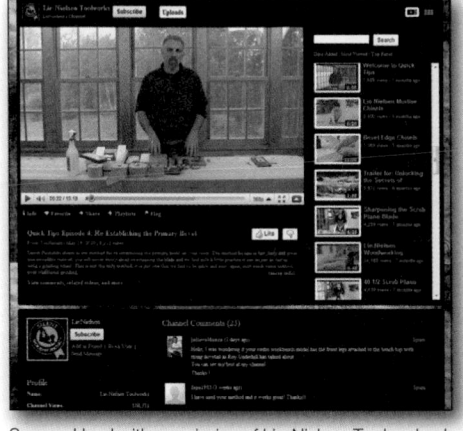

Value-Added Content via Online Video

Lie-Nielsen Toolworks of Warren, Maine, uses its YouTube channel to offer valuable information on choosing and using premium woodworking tools. By offering sought-after information for both current and potential customers free of charge, these videos help Lie-Nielsen foster relationships with the worldwide woodworking community and solidify its position as one of the leaders in this market. Animal Planet, Best Western, and Taco Bell are among the many other companies that make effective use of branded channels on YouTube.

Idea Generation Through Community Feedback

Starbucks has collected tens of thousands of ideas for new products and service enhancements through its community website, My Starbucks Idea. The company makes the clear request: "You know better than anyone else what you want from Starbucks. So tell us."

of marketing and selling need to be adapted to the social networking environment because customers and potential customers don't join a network merely to be passive recipients of advertising messages. They want to participate, to connect with fellow enthusiasts, to share knowledge about products, to communicate with company insiders, and to influence the decisions that affect the products they value. This notion of interactive participation is the driving force behind **conversation marketing**, in which companies *initiate* and *facilitate* conversations in a networked community of customers and other interested parties.

- **Fostering brand communities.** Social networking is playing an important role in the rapid spread of **brand communities**, groups of people united by their interest in and ownership or use of particular products (see Figure 7.3). These communities can be formal membership organizations, such as the Harley Owners Group, or informal networks of people with similar interests. They can be fairly independent from the company behind the brand or can have the active support and involvement of company management.[13] A strong majority of consumers now trust their peers more than any other source of product information—including conventional advertising techniques—so formal and informal brand communities are becoming an essential information source in consumer buying decisions.[14] Continuing innovations such as Google+'s Sparks feature, which helps people connect with others with common interests, will make social networks even more important in the development of brand communities.

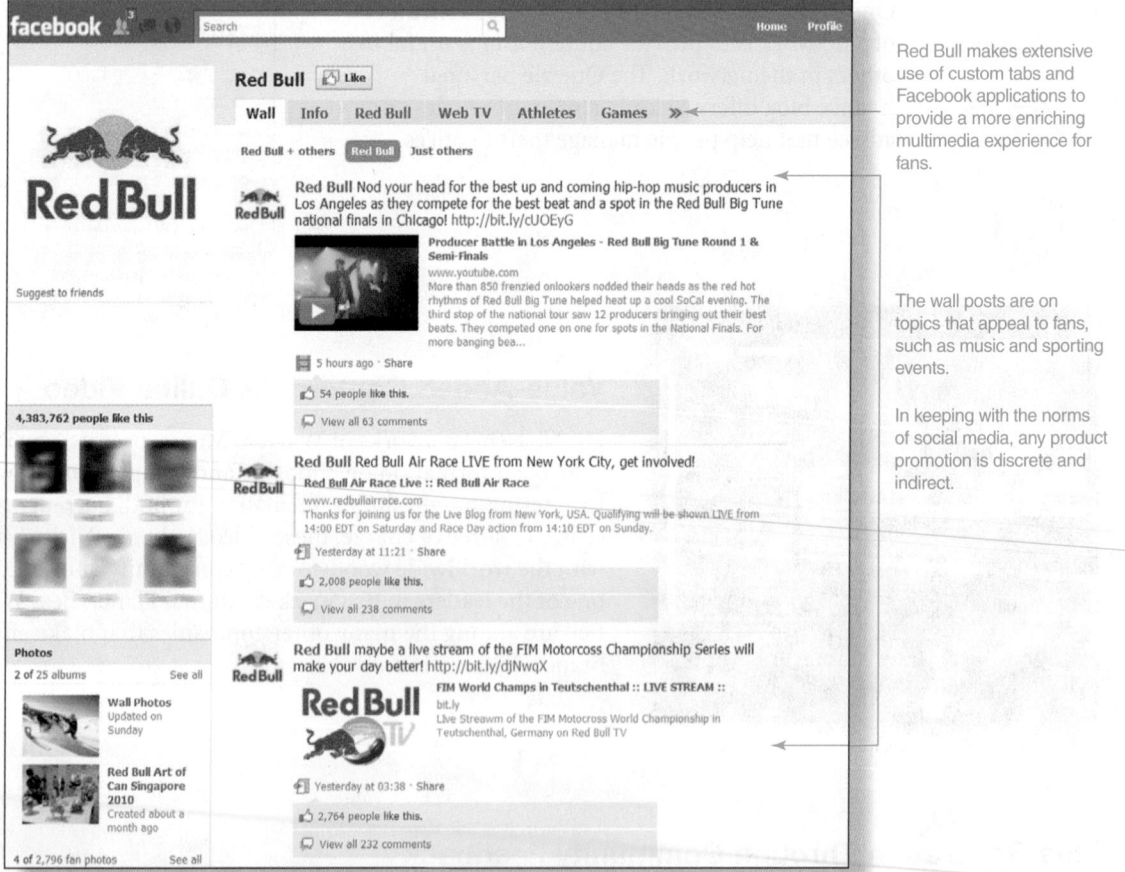

Red Bull makes extensive use of custom tabs and Facebook applications to provide a more enriching multimedia experience for fans.

The wall posts are on topics that appeal to fans, such as music and sporting events.

In keeping with the norms of social media, any product promotion is discrete and indirect.

Figure 7.3   Business Communication on Social Networks
The energy drink company Red Bull has one of the largest fan bases on Facebook, giving the company the opportunity to connect with millions of enthusiastic customers.
Source: Used with permission of Red Bull.

Strategies for Business Communication on Social Networks

Social networks offer lots of communication options, but with those opportunities comes a certain degree of complexity. Moreover, the norms and practices of business social networking continue to evolve. Follow these guidelines to make the most of social networks for both personal branding and company communication:[15]

- **Choose the best compositional mode for each message, purpose, and network.** As you visit various social networks, take some time to observe the variety of message types you see in different parts of each website. For example, the informal status update mode works well for Facebook Wall posts but would be less effective for company overviews and mission statements.

- **Join existing conversations, in addition to starting your own.** Search for online conversations that are already taking place. Answer questions, solve problems, and respond to rumors and misinformation.

- **Anchor your online presence in your hub.** Although it's important to join conversations and be visible where your stakeholders are active, it's equally important to anchor your presence at your own central *hub*—a web presence that you own and control. This can be a conventional website or a combination of a website, a blog, and a company-sponsored online community, for example.[16] Use the hub to connect the various "spokes" of your online presence (as an individual or a company) to better coordinate outgoing messages and to provide a clear inbound path for people who want to engage with you. As part of this, take advantage of the many automated links that are available on social media platforms. For example, you can link to your blog from your LinkedIn profile or automatically feed your blog entries into the Notes tab on your Facebook page.

- **Facilitate community building.** Make it easy for customers and other audiences to connect with the company and with each other. For example, you can use the group feature on Facebook, LinkedIn, and other social networks to create and foster special-interest groups within your networks. Groups are a great way to connect people who are interested in specific topics, such as owners of a particular product.

- **Restrict conventional promotional efforts to the right time and right place.** Persuasive communication efforts are still valid for specific communication tasks, such as regular advertising and the product information pages on a website, but efforts to inject blatant "salespeak" into social networking conversations will usually be rejected by the audience.

- **Maintain a consistent personality.** Each social network is a unique environment with particular norms of communication.[17] For instance, as a business-oriented network, LinkedIn has a more formal "vibe" than Facebook. However, while adapting to the expectations of each network, be sure to maintain a consistent personality.[18] The computer giant HP uses the same (fairly formal-sounding) company overview on LinkedIn and Facebook, while its Wall updates on Facebook are "chattier" and more in keeping with the tone expected by Facebook visitors.[19]

- **Manage conversational threads.** Conversations with customers and other important parties often carry over to multiple messages, involve multiple employees, and sometimes cross over multiple media as well (such as when a Twitter conversation is moved to direct messaging for privacy). With so many channels in place today, companies are beginning to use systems to track these *conversational threads* so that messages aren't dropped and all parties can communicate productively.

See "Writing Promotional Messages for Social Media" in Chapter 10 (page 349) for more tips.

Communicating via social networks is complicated and requires a thoughtful, well-integrated strategy.

REAL-TIME UPDATES
Learn More by Reading This Article

Get inspired to build a great Facebook Page

Facebook Pages are the service that companies use to build a presence on Facebook. See how these Facebook innovators use the social network to build online communities. Go to http://real-timeupdates.com/ebc10 and click on Learn More. If you are using MyBcommLab, you can access Real-Time Updates within each chapter or under Student Study Tools.

USER-GENERATED CONTENT SITES

YouTube is now a major channel for business communicators, hosting everything from product demonstration videos to television commercials.

User-generated content (UGC) sites, where users rather than website owners contribute most or all of the content, have also become serious business tools. In fact, a recent survey suggested that video company profiles on YouTube have more measurable impact than company profiles on Facebook, LinkedIn, and other prominent sites.[20]

Video (including *screencasts*, recordings of on-screen activity on a computer with audio narration) is a powerful medium for product demonstrations, interviews, industry news, training, facility tours, and other uses. Moreover, the business communication value of sites such as YouTube goes beyond the mere ability to deliver content. The social aspects of these sites, including the ability to vote for, comment on, and share material, encourage enthusiasts to spread the word about the companies and products they endorse.[21]

Creating compelling and useful content is the key to leveraging the reach of social networks.

As with other social media, the keys to effective user-generated content are making it valuable and making it easy. First, provide content that people want to see and to share with colleagues. A video clip that explains how to use a product more effectively will be more popular than a clip that talks about how amazing the company behind the product is. Also, keep videos short, generally no longer than 3 to 5 minutes if possible.[22]

Second, make material easy to find, consume, and share. For example, a *branded channel* on YouTube (see the Lie-Nielsen Toolworks screen on page 231) lets a company organize all its videos in one place, making it easy for visitors to browse the selection or subscribe to get automatic updates of future videos. Sharing features let fans share videos through email or their accounts on Twitter, Facebook, and other platforms.

COMMUNITY Q&A SITES

Community Q&A sites, where visitors answer questions posted by other visitors or by representatives of companies, are becoming increasingly an important venue for routine communication such as customer support questions. Examples include dedicated customer support communities such as those hosted on Get Satisfaction (http://getsatisfaction .com), public sites such as Yahoo! Answers (http://answers.yahoo.com) and Quora (www .quora.com), and member-only sites such as LinkedIn Answers (www.linkedin.com/ answers). Responding to questions on Q&A sites can be a great way to build your personal brand, to demonstrate your company's commitment to customer service, and to counter misinformation about your company and its products.

Community Q&A sites offer great opportunities for building your personal brand.

COMMUNITY PARTICIPATION WEBSITES

Community participation websites pool the input of multiple users in order to benefit the community as a whole.

Some of the more intriguing developments in business communication are taking place in a diverse group of **community participation websites**, designed to pool the inputs of multiple users in order to benefit the community as a whole (see Figure 7.4). These include *social bookmarking* or *content recommendation sites* such as Delicious (http://delicious .com), Digg (www.digg.com), and StumbleUpon (www.stumbleupon.com); *group buying sites* such as Groupon (www.groupon.com); *crowdsourcing sites* such as InnoCentive (www .innocentive.com) that invite people to submit or collaborate on research challenges and product designs; and *product and service review* websites that compile reviews from people who have purchased products or patronized particular businesses.

As one example of the way these sites are changing business communication, Yelp (www.yelp.com) has become a major influence on consumer behavior at a local level by aggregating millions of reviews of stores, restaurants, and other businesses in large cities across the United States.[23] With the voice of the crowd affecting consumer behavior, businesses need to (a) focus on performing at a high level so that customers reward them with positive reviews and (b) get involved on Yelp (the site encourages business owners to tell potential customers about themselves as well). These efforts could pay off much more handsomely than advertising and other conventional communication efforts.

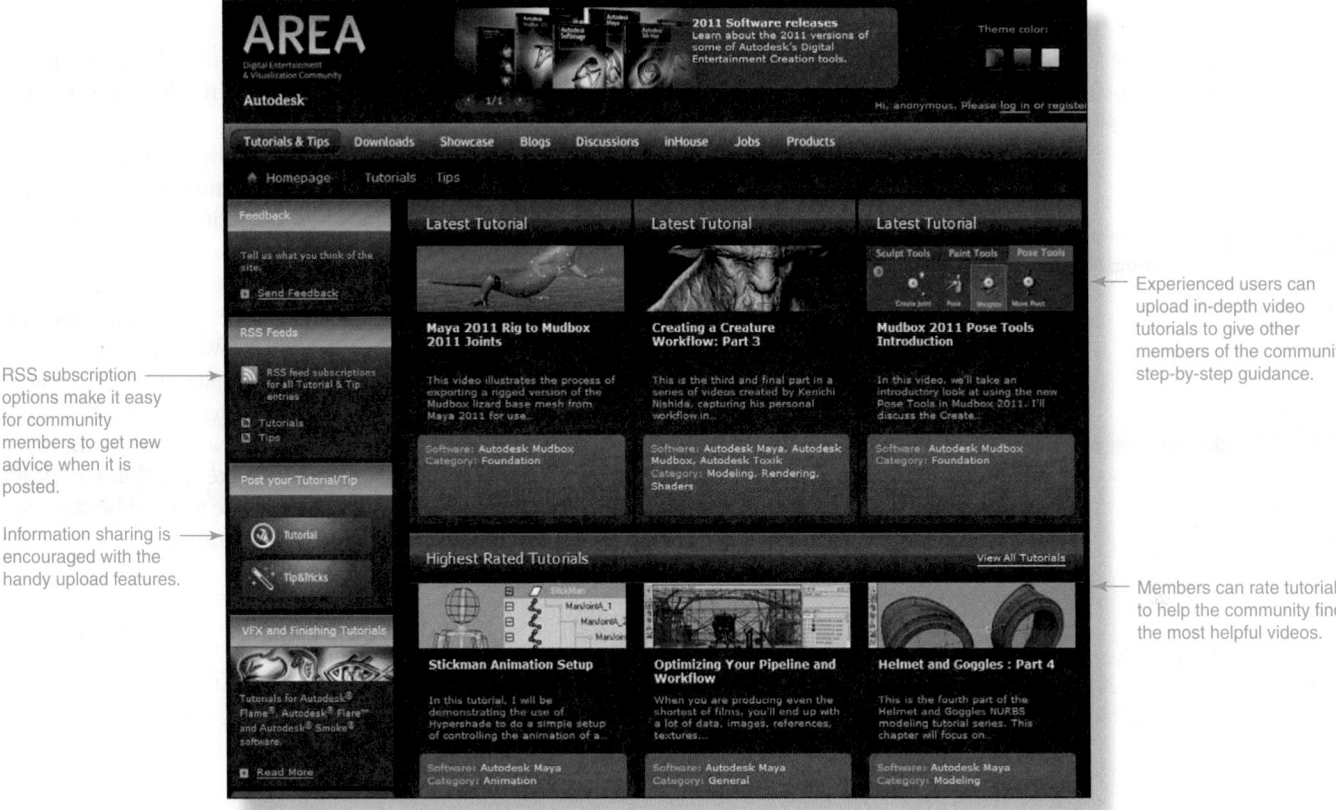

Figure 7.4   Community Participation Sites

The software company Autodesk hosts this community participation website for customers who work in the fields of digital entertainment and visualization. Users share quick tips, advice, and in-depth tutorials about using Autodesk software in video games, animations, product designs, and other creative projects.

Source: Used with permission of Autodesk Area.

Email

Email has been a primary business communication medium for many years, although newer tools such as instant messaging, blogs, microblogs, social networks, and shared workspaces are taking over specialized tasks for which they are better suited.[24] In fact, email can seem out of step in a world of instantaneous and open communication, where many users are accustomed to rapid-fire updates from Twitter, public forums on social networks, and never-ending streams of incoming information.[25]

However, email still has compelling advantages that will keep it in steady use in many companies, even as it evolves and becomes integrated with other electronic media. First, email is universal. Anybody with an email address can reach anybody else with an email address, no matter which systems the senders and receivers are on. You don't need to join a special group or be friended by anyone in order to correspond. Second, email is still the best medium for many private, short- to medium-length messages. Unlike with microblogs and IM, for instance, midsize messages are easy to compose and easy to read on email. Third, email's noninstantaneous nature is an advantage when used properly. Many business messages don't need the rapid update rates of IM or Twitter, and the implied urgency of those systems can be a productivity-sapping interruption. Email allows senders to compose substantial messages in private and on their own schedule, and it allows recipients to read those messages at their leisure.

3 LEARNING OBJECTIVE

Describe the evolving role of email in business communication, and explain how to adapt the three-step writing process to email messages.

Email can seem a bit "old school" in comparison to social networks and other technologies, but it is still one of the more important business communication media.

REAL-TIME UPDATES

Learn More by Watching This PowerPoint Presentation

Take a crash course in email etiquette

Learn career-enhancing tips on using email in professional settings. Go to http://real-timeupdates.com/ebc10 and click on Learn More. If you are using MyBcommLab, you can access Real-Time Updates within each chapter or under Student Study Tools.

PLANNING EMAIL MESSAGES

Do your part to stem the flood of email by making sure you don't send unnecessary messages or "cc" people who don't really need to see particular messages.

The biggest complaints about email are that there is just too much of it and that too many messages are of little or no value. You can help with this problem during the planning step by making sure every message has a useful, business-related purpose.

Email presents considerable legal hazards, and many companies have formal email policies.

Be aware that many companies now have formal email policies that specify how employees can use email, including restrictions against using company email service for personal messages and sending material that might be deemed objectionable. In addition, many employers now monitor email, either automatically with software programmed to look for sensitive content or manually via security staff actually reading selected email messages. Regardless of formal policies, though, every email user has a responsibility to avoid actions that could cause trouble, from downloading virus-infected software to sending inappropriate photographs. *Email hygiene* refers to all the efforts that companies are making to keep email clean and safe—from spam blocking and virus protection to content filtering.[26]

Respect the chain of command in your company when sending email messages.

Finally, be sure to respect the chain of command. In many companies, any employee can email anyone else, including the president and CEO. However, take care that you don't abuse this freedom. For instance, don't send a complaint straight to the top just because it's easy to do so. Your efforts will be more effective if you follow the organizational hierarchy and give each person a chance to address the situation in turn.

WRITING EMAIL MESSAGES

Business email messages are more formal than the email messages you send to family and friends.

Business email is a more formal medium than you are probably accustomed to with email for personal communication (see Figure 7.5). The expectations of writing quality for

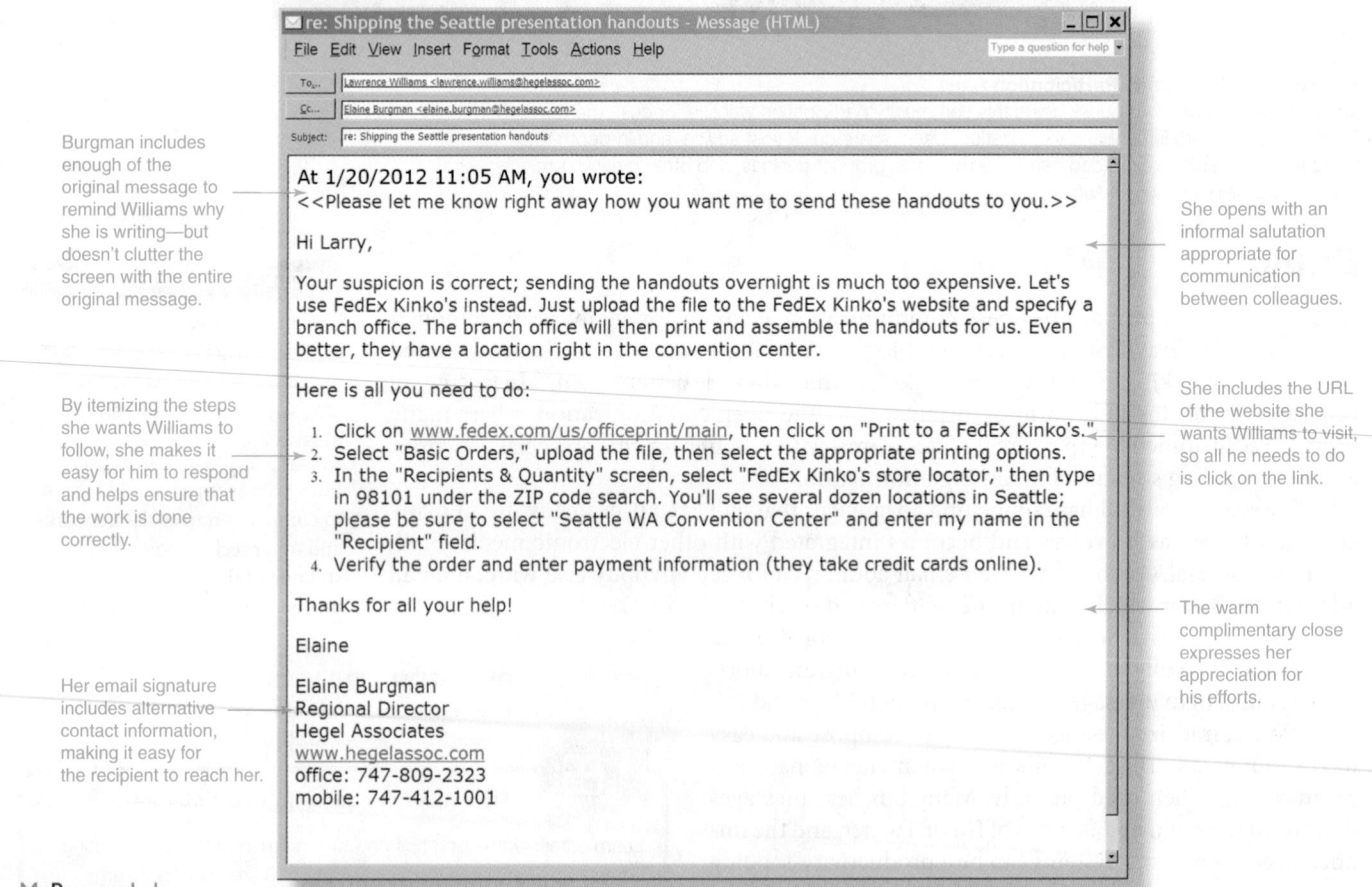

Burgman includes enough of the original message to remind Williams why she is writing—but doesn't clutter the screen with the entire original message.

By itemizing the steps she wants Williams to follow, she makes it easy for him to respond and helps ensure that the work is done correctly.

Her email signature includes alternative contact information, making it easy for the recipient to reach her.

She opens with an informal salutation appropriate for communication between colleagues.

She includes the URL of the website she wants Williams to visit, so all he needs to do is click on the link.

The warm complimentary close expresses her appreciation for his efforts.

MyBcommLab

Apply Figure 7.5's key concepts by revising a new document. Go to Chapter 7 in www.pearsoninternational editions.com/mybcommlab and select Document Makeovers.

Figure 7.5   Email for Business Communication

In this response to an email query from a colleague, Elaine Burgman takes advantage of her email system's features to create an efficient and effective message.

business email are higher than for personal email, and the consequences of bad writing or poor judgment can be much more serious. For example, email messages and other electronic documents have the same legal weight as printed documents, and they are often used as evidence in lawsuits and criminal investigations.[27]

The email subject line is one of the most important parts of an email message because it helps recipients decide which messages to read and when to read them. To capture your audience's attention, make your subject lines informative and compelling. Go beyond simply describing or classifying your message; use the opportunity to build interest with keywords, quotations, directions, or questions.[28]

A poorly written subject line could lead to a message being deleted or ignored.

For example, "July sales results" accurately describes the content of the message, but "July sales results: good news and bad news" is more intriguing. Readers will want to know why some news is good and some is bad.

In addition, many email programs display the first few words or lines of incoming messages, even before the recipient opens them. As noted by social media public relations expert Steve Rubel, you can "tweetify" the opening lines of your email messages to make them stand out. In other words, choose the first few words carefully to grab your reader's attention.[29]

COMPLETING EMAIL MESSAGES

Particularly for important messages, taking a few moments to revise and proofread might save you hours of headaches and damage control. The more important the message, the more carefully you need to proof. Also, favor simplicity when it comes to producing your email messages. A clean, easily readable font, in black on a white background, is sufficient for nearly all email messages. Take advantage of your email system's ability to include an **email signature**, a small file that automatically includes such items as your full name, title, company, and contact information at the end of your messages.

When you're ready to distribute your message, pause to verify what you're doing before you click "Send." Make sure you've included everyone necessary—and no one else. Don't click "Reply All" when you mean to click only "Reply." The difference could be embarrassing or even career threatening. Don't include people in the "cc" (courtesy copy) or "bcc" (blind courtesy copy) fields unless you know how these features work. (Everyone who receives the message can see who is on the cc line but not who is on the bcc line.) Also, don't set the message priority to "high" or "urgent" unless your message is truly urgent. And if you intend to include an attachment, be sure that it is indeed attached.

Think twice before hitting "Send." A simple mistake in your content or distribution can cause major headaches.

To review the tips and techniques for successful email, see Table 7.2 on the next page and "Checklist: Creating Effective Email Messages" or click on Chapter 7 at http://real-timeupdates.com/ebc10.

✓ Checklist | Creating Effective Email Messages

A. Planning email messages.
- Make sure every email message you send is necessary.
- Don't cc or bcc anyone who doesn't really need to see the message.
- Follow company email policy; understand the restrictions your company places on email usage.
- Practice good email hygiene by not opening suspicious messages, keeping virus protection up to date, and following other company guidelines.
- Follow the chain of command.

B. Writing email messages.
- Remember that business email is more formal than personal email.
- Recognize that email messages carry the same legal weight as other business documents.
- Pay attention to the quality of your writing and use correct grammar, spelling, and punctuation.

- Make your subject lines informative by clearly identifying the purpose of your message.
- Make your subject lines compelling by wording them in a way that intrigues your audiences.
- Use the first few words of the email body to catch the reader's attention.

C. Completing email messages.
- Revise and proofread carefully to avoid embarrassing mistakes.
- Keep the layout of your messages simple and clean.
- Use an email signature file to give recipients your contact information.
- Double-check your recipient list before sending.
- Don't mark messages as "urgent" unless they truly are urgent.

TABLE 7.2	Tips for Effective Email Messages
Tip	**Why It's Important**
When you request information or action, make it clear what you're asking for, why it's important, and how soon you need it; don't make your reader write back for details.	People will be tempted to ignore your messages if they're not clear about what you want or how soon you want it.
When responding to a request, either paraphrase the request or include enough of the original message to remind the reader what you're replying to.	Some businesspeople get hundreds of email messages a day and may need reminding what your specific response is about.
If possible, avoid sending long, complex messages via email.	Long messages are easier to read as attached reports or web content.
Adjust the level of formality to the message and the audience.	Overly formal messages to colleagues can be perceived as stuffy and distant; overly informal messages to customers or top executives can be perceived as disrespectful.
Activate a signature file, which automatically pastes your contact information into every message you create.	A signature saves you the trouble of retyping vital information and ensures that recipients know how to reach you through other means.
Don't let unread messages pile up in your in-basket.	You'll miss important information and create the impression that you're ignoring other people.
Never type in all caps.	ALL CAPS ARE INTERPRETED AS SCREAMING.
Don't overformat your messages with background colors, multicolored type, unusual fonts, and so on.	Such messages can be difficult and annoying to read on screen.
Remember that messages can be forwarded anywhere and saved forever.	Don't let a moment of anger or poor judgment haunt you for the rest of your career.
Use the "return receipt requested" feature only for the most critical messages.	This feature triggers a message back to you whenever someone receives or opens your message; many consider this an invasion of privacy.
Make sure your computer has up-to-date virus protection.	One of the worst breaches of "netiquette" is infecting other computers because you haven't bothered to protect your own system.
Pay attention to grammar, spelling, and capitalization.	Some people don't think email needs formal rules, but careless messages make you look unprofessional and can annoy readers.
Use acronyms sparingly.	Shorthand such as IMHO (in my humble opinion) and LOL (laughing out loud) can be useful in informal correspondence with colleagues, but avoid using them in more formal messages.

Instant Messaging and Text Messaging

Computer-based **instant messaging (IM)**, in which users' messages appear on each other's screens instantly, is used extensively for internal and external communication. IM is available in both stand-alone systems and as a function embedded in groupware, collaboration systems, social networks, and other platforms.

Phone-based **text messaging** (sometimes known as *short messaging service* or *SMS*) has many applications in business, including marketing (alerting customers about new sale prices, for example), customer service (such as airline flight status, order status, package tracking, and appointment reminders), security (for example, authenticating mobile banking transactions), crisis management (such as updating all employees working at a disaster scene), and process monitoring (alerting computer technicians to system failures, for example).[30] As it becomes more tightly integrated with other communication media, text messaging is likely to find even more widespread use in business communication. For example, texting is now integrated into systems such as Facebook Messages and GMail, and branded "StarStar numbers" can deliver web-based content such as videos, software apps, and electronic coupons to mobile phones.[31]

The advice offered in this section applies primarily to IM but is relevant to text messaging as well.

UNDERSTANDING THE BENEFITS AND RISKS OF IM

The benefits of IM include rapid response to urgent messages, lower cost than phone calls, ability to mimic conversation more closely than email, and availability on a wide range of devices and systems.[32] In addition, because it more closely resembles one-on-one conversation, IM doesn't get misused as a one-to-many broadcast method as often as email does.[33]

The potential drawbacks of IM include security problems (computer viruses, network infiltration, and the possibility that sensitive messages might be intercepted by outsiders), the need for *user authentication* (making sure that online correspondents are really who they appear to be), the challenge of logging messages for later review and archiving (a legal requirement in some industries), incompatibility between competing IM systems, and *spim* (unsolicited commercial messages, similar to email spam). Fortunately, with the growth of *enterprise instant messaging* (*EIM*), or IM systems designed for large-scale corporate use, many of these problems are being overcome.

IM offers many benefits:
- Rapid response
- Low cost
- Ability to mimic conversation
- Wide availability

ADAPTING THE THREE-STEP PROCESS FOR SUCCESSFUL IM

Although instant messages are often conceived, written, and sent within a matter of seconds, the principles of the three-step process still apply:

- **Planning instant messages.** View every IM exchange as a conversation; while you may not deliberately plan every individual statement you make or question you pose, take a moment to plan the overall exchange. If you're requesting something, think through exactly what you need and the most effective way to ask for it. If someone is asking you for something, consider his or her needs and your ability to meet them before you respond. And although you rarely need to organize instant messages in the sense of creating an outline, try to deliver information in a coherent, complete way that minimizes the number of individual messages required.

- **Writing instant messages.** As with email, the appropriate writing style for business IM is more formal than the style you may be accustomed to with personal IM or text messaging. You should generally avoid IM acronyms (such as *FWIW* for "for what it's worth" or *HTH* for "hope that helps") except when communicating with close colleagues. In the IM exchange in Figure 7.6 on the next page, notice how the participants communicate quickly and rather informally but still maintain good etiquette and a professional tone. This style is even more important if you or your staff use IM to communicate with customers and other outside audiences.

- **Completing instant messages.** One of the biggest attractions of IM is that the completing step is so easy. You don't have to produce the message in the usual sense, and distribution is as simple as hitting "Enter" or clicking a "Send" button. However, don't skip over the revising and proofreading tasks. Quickly scan each message before you send it, to make sure you don't have any missing or misspelled words and that your message is clear and complete.

Although you don't plan individual instant messages in the usual way, view important IM exchanges as conversations with specific goals in mind.

Regardless of the system you're using, you can make IM more efficient and effective by following these tips:[34]

Understand the guidelines for successful business IM before you begin to use it.

- Unless an IM conversation or meeting is scheduled, make yourself unavailable when you need to focus on other work.
- If you're not on a secure system, don't send confidential information.
- Be extremely careful about sending personal messages—they have a tendency to pop up on other people's computers at embarrassing moments.
- Don't use IM for important but impromptu meetings if you can't verify that everyone concerned will be available.
- Unless your system is set up for it, don't use IM for lengthy, complex messages; email is better for those.
- Try to avoid carrying on multiple IM conversations at once, to minimize the chance of sending messages to the wrong people or making one person wait while you tend to another conversation.
- Follow all security guidelines designed to keep your company's information and systems safe from attack.

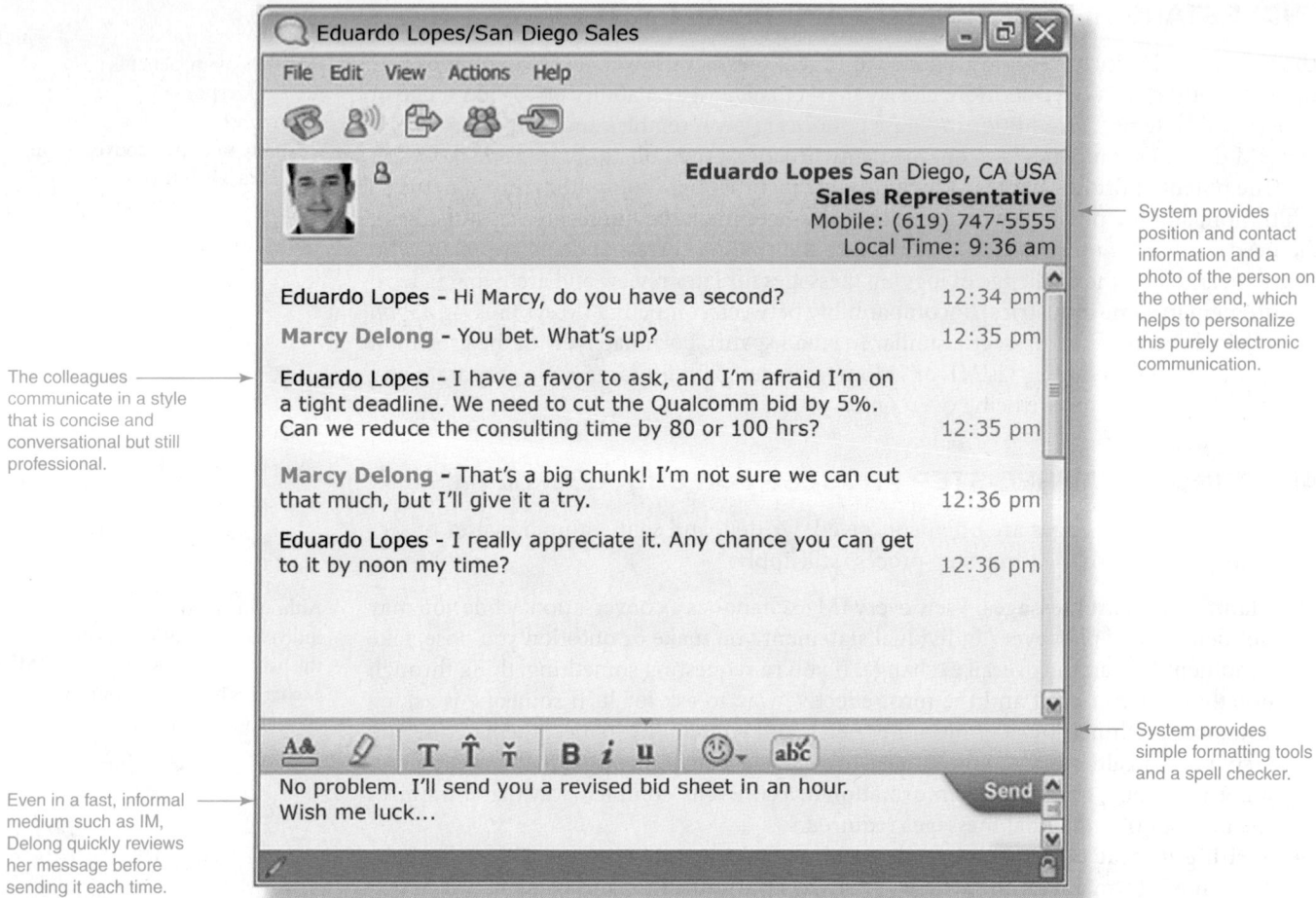

The colleagues communicate in a style that is concise and conversational but still professional.

System provides position and contact information and a photo of the person on the other end, which helps to personalize this purely electronic communication.

Even in a fast, informal medium such as IM, Delong quickly reviews her message before sending it each time.

System provides simple formatting tools and a spell checker.

MyBcommLab

Apply Figure 7.6's key concepts by revising a new document. Go to Chapter 7 in www.pearsoninternationaleditions.com/ mybcommlab and select Document Makeovers.

Figure 7.6 Instant Messaging for Business Communication
Instant messaging is widely used in business, but you should not use the same informal style of communication you probably use for IM with your friends and family.

✓ Checklist Using IM Productively

- Pay attention to security and privacy issues and be sure to follow all company guidelines.
- Treat IM as a professional communication medium, not an informal, personal tool; avoid using IM slang with all but close colleagues.
- Maintain good etiquette, even during simple exchanges.

- Protect your own productivity by making yourself unavailable when you need to focus.
- In most instances, don't use IM for confidential messages, complex messages, or personal messages.

To review the advice for effective IM in the workplace, see "Checklist: Using IM Productively" or click on Chapter 7 at http://real-timeupdates.com/ebc10.

Blogging and Microblogging

5 LEARNING OBJECTIVE

Describe the role of blogging and microblogging in business communication today, and explain how to adapt the three-step writing process to blogging.

A **blog** (short for *weblog*) is an easily updatable online journal that can combine the global reach and reference value of a conventional website with the conversational exchanges of email or IM. Blogging first began to catch on in business communication because blogs provided a much easier way for senders to update and distribute fresh content and for receivers to get new information automatically (through *feeds* or *newsfeeds*, of which *RSS* is the best known). Blogging also began to take on a more personal and informal tone than regular business websites, helping to "put a human face" on companies and increase the lines of communication between experts and executives on the inside and customers and other stakeholders on the outside. Another important role that blogging has acquired is making individuals and companies more easily findable through search engines.[35] With all these benefits, blogs are now a common tool in business communication, and many companies have multiple bloggers, writing either as a team on an individual blog (as with Southwest) or on their own blogs (as with Xerox, see page 61).

Blogs can combine the global reach and reference value of a conventional website with the conversational exchanges of email or IM.

Good business bloggers pay close attention to several important elements:

- **Communicating with personal style and an authentic voice.** Traditional business messages designed for large audiences tend to be carefully scripted and written in a "corporate voice" that is impersonal and objective. In contrast, successful business blogs such as Southwest Airlines's are written by individuals and exhibit their personal style. Audiences relate to this fresh approach and often build closer emotional bonds with the blogger's organization as a result.
- **Delivering new information quickly.** The ability to post new material as soon as you create it helps you to respond quickly when needed (such as during a crisis), and it lets your audiences know that an active conversation is taking place.
- **Choosing topics of peak interest to audiences.** Successful blogs cover topics that readers care about, and they emphasize useful information while downplaying product promotion.[36] These topics don't need to be earth shaking or cutting edge—they just need to be things that matter to target readers. For instance, a pair of researchers at Clorox blog for the company under the name "Dr. Laundry," dispensing helpful advice on removing stains and tackling other household chores.[37]
- **Encouraging audiences to join the conversation.** Not all blogs invite comments, although most do. These comments can be a valuable source of news, information, and insights. In addition, the relatively informal nature of blogging seems to make it easier for company representatives to let their guards down and converse with their audiences. Of course, not all comments are helpful or appropriate, which is why many bloggers *moderate* comments, previewing them before allowing them to be displayed.

Most business blogs invite readers to leave comments as a way to encourage participation among stakeholders.

Table 7.3 on the next page offers a number of specific suggestions for successful business blogging.

UNDERSTANDING THE BUSINESS APPLICATIONS OF BLOGGING

Blogs are a potential solution whenever you have a continuing stream of information to share with an online audience—and particularly when you want the audience to have the opportunity to respond. Here are some of the many ways businesses are using blogs:[38]

The business applications of blogs include a wide range of internal and external communication tasks.

- **Anchoring the social media presence.** As noted on page 233, the multiple threads of any social media program should be anchored in a central hub that the company or individual owns and controls. Blogs make an ideal social media hub.
- **Project management and team communication.** Using blogs is a good way to keep project teams up to date, particularly when team members are geographically dispersed. For instance, the trip reports that employees file after visiting customers or other external parties can be enhanced vividly with *mobile blogs*, or *moblogs*.
- **Internal company news.** Companies can use blogs to keep employees informed about general business matters, from facility news to benefit updates. By reducing the need for grapevines to spring up, blogs can enhance communication across all levels of a company.
- **Customer support.** Customer support blogs answer questions, offer tips and advice, and inform customers about new products.
- **Public relations and media relations.** Many company employees and executives now share company news with both the general public and journalists via their blogs.
- **Recruiting.** Using a blog is a great way to let potential employees know more about your company, the people who work there, and the nature of the company culture

TABLE 7.3	Tips for Effective Business Blogging
Tip	**Why It's Important**
Don't blog without a clear plan.	Without a clear plan, your blog is likely to wander from topic to topic and fail to build a sense of community with your audience.
Post frequently; the whole point of a blog is fresh material.	If you won't have a constant supply of new information or new links, create a traditional website instead.
Make it about your audience and the issues that are important to them.	Readers want to know how your blog will help them, entertain them, or give them a chance to communicate with others who have similar interests.
Write in an authentic voice; never create an artificial character who supposedly writes a blog.	*Flogs*, or fake blogs, violate the spirit of blogging, show disrespect for your audience, and will turn audiences against you as soon as they uncover the truth. Fake blogs used to promote products are now illegal in some countries.
Link generously—but carefully.	Providing interesting links to other blogs and websites is a fundamental aspect of blogging, but make sure the links will be of value to your readers and don't point to inappropriate material.
Keep it brief.	Most online readers don't have the patience to read lengthy reports. Rather than writing long, report-style posts, write brief posts that link to in-depth reports on your website.
Don't post anything you wouldn't want the entire world to see.	Future employers, government regulators, competitors, journalists, and community critics are just a few of the people who might eventually see what you've written.
Don't engage in blatant product promotion.	Readers who think they're being advertised to will stop reading.
Take time to write compelling, specific headlines for your postings.	Readers usually decide within a couple of seconds whether to read your postings; boring or vague headlines will turn them away instantly.
Pay attention to spelling, grammar, and mechanics.	No matter how smart or experienced you are, poor-quality writing undermines your credibility with intelligent audiences.
Respond to criticism openly and honestly.	Hiding sends the message that you don't have a valid response to the criticism. If your critics are wrong, patiently explain why you think they're wrong. If they are right, explain how you'll fix the situation.
Listen and learn.	If you don't take the time to analyze the comments people leave on your blog or the comments other bloggers make about you, you're missing out on one of the most valuable aspects of blogging.
Respect intellectual property.	Improperly using material you don't own is not only unethical but can be illegal as well.
Be scrupulously honest and careful with facts.	Honesty is an absolute requirement for every ethical business communicator, of course, but you need to be extra careful online because inaccuracies (both intentional and unintentional) are likely to be discovered quickly and shared widely.
If you review products on your blog, disclose any beneficial relationships you have with the companies that make those products.	Bloggers who receive free products or other compensation from companies whose products they write about are now required to disclose the nature of these relationships.

Sources: Adapted from Robert Scoble and Shel Israel, *Naked Conversations* (Hoboken, N.J.: John Wiley & Sons, 2006), 78–81, 190–194; Paul McFedries, *The Complete Idiot's Guide to Creating a Web Page & Blog*, 6th ed. (New York: Alpha, 2004), 206–208; 272–276; Shel Holtz and Ted Demopoulos, *Blogging for Business* (Chicago: Kaplan, 2006), 54–59, 113–114; Denise Wakeman, "Top 10 Blog Writing Tips," Blogarooni.com, accessed 1 February 2006, www.blogarooni.com; Dennis A. Mahoney, "How to Write a Better Weblog," 22 February 2002, A List Apart, www.alistapart.com.

(see Figure 7.7 on page 244). Conversely, companies can scan blogs and microblogs to find promising candidates.

- **Policy and issue discussions.** Executive blogs in particular provide a public forum for discussing legislation, regulations, and other broad issues of interest to an organization.
- **Crisis communication.** Using blogs is an efficient way to provide up-to-the-minute information during emergencies, correct misinformation, or respond to rumors.

| BUSINESS COMMUNICATION 2.0 | Help! I'm Drowning in Social Media! |

Anyone who has sampled today's social media offerings has probably experienced this situation: You find a few fascinating blogs, a few interesting people to follow on Twitter, a couple of podcast channels with helpful business tips, and then *wham*—within a few hours of signing up, your computer is overflowing with updates. Even if every new item is useful (which is unlikely), you receive so many that you can't stay ahead of the incoming flood. Between Twitter updates, newsfeeds, email, instant messaging, and social networks—not to mention a desk phone and a mobile phone—today's business professionals could easily spend their entire days just trying to keep up with incoming messages and never get any work done.

To keep social media from turning into a source of stress and information anxiety, consider these tips:

- **Understand what information you really need in order to excel in your current projects and along your intended career path.** Unfortunately, taking this advice is even trickier than it sounds because you can't always know what you need to know, so you can't always predict which sources will be helpful. However, don't gather information simply because it is interesting or entertaining; collect information that is useful or at least potentially useful.

- **Face the fact that you cannot possibly handle every update from every potentially interesting and helpful source.** You have to set priorities and make tough choices to protect yourself from information overload.
- **Add new information sources slowly.** Give yourself a chance to adjust to the flow and judge the usefulness of each new source.
- **Prune your sources vigorously and frequently.** Bloggers run out of things to say; your needs and interests change; higher-priority sources appear.
- **Remember that information is an enabler, a means to an end.** Collecting vast amounts of information won't get you a sweet promotion with a big raise. *Using* information creatively and intelligently will.

CAREER APPLICATIONS

1. How can you determine whether a social media source is worth paying attention to?
2. Should you allow any information source to interrupt your work flow during the day (even just to signal that a new message is available)? Why or why not?

- **Market research.** Blogs can be a clever mechanism for soliciting feedback from customers and experts in the marketplace. In addition to using its own blogs for research, every company needs to monitor blogs that are likely to discuss its operations, executives, and products. Negative product reviews, rumors, and other information can spread across the globe in a matter of hours, and managers need to know what the online community is saying—whether it's positive or negative. *Reputation analysts* such as Evolve24 (www.evolve24.com) have developed ways to automatically monitor blogs and other online sources to see what people are saying about their corporate clients and evaluate risks and opportunities in the global online conversation.[39]
- **Brainstorming.** Online brainstorming via blogs offers a way for people to toss around ideas and build on each others' contributions.
- **Word-of-mouth marketing.** Bloggers and microbloggers often make a point of providing links to other blogs and websites that interest them, giving marketers a great opportunity to have their messages spread by enthusiasts. (Word-of mouth marketing is often called *viral marketing* in reference to the transmission of messages in much the same way that biological viruses are transmitted from person to person. However, viral marketing is not really an accurate metaphor. As author Brian Solis puts it, "There is no such thing as viral marketing."[40] Real viruses spread from host to host on their own, whereas word-of-mouth marketing spreads *voluntarily* from person to person. The distinction is critical, because you need to give people a good reason—good content, in other words—to pass along your message.)
- **Influencing traditional media news coverage.** According to social media consultant Tamar Weinberg, "the more prolific bloggers who provide valuable and consistent content are often considered experts in their subject matter" and are often called upon when journalists need insights into various topics.[41]
- **Community building.** Blogging is a great way to connect people with similar interests, and popular bloggers often attract a community of readers who connect with one another through the commenting function.

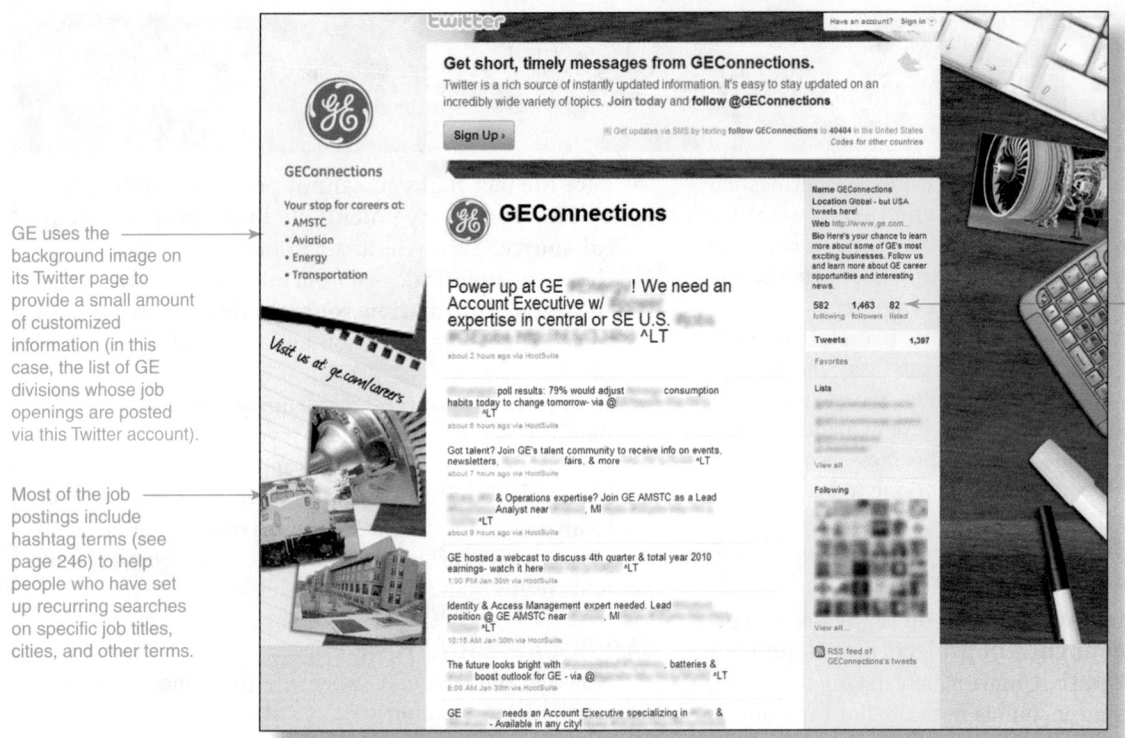

GE uses the background image on its Twitter page to provide a small amount of customized information (in this case, the list of GE divisions whose job openings are posted via this Twitter account).

Most of the job postings include hashtag terms (see page 246) to help people who have set up recurring searches on specific job titles, cities, and other terms.

Note that while this Twitter account doesn't have a huge number of followers, anyone can find the information by searching or monitoring for hashtag terms.

FIGURE 7.7   Recruiting on Twitter
GE is just one of many companies now recruiting on Twitter.
Source: Used with permission of GE Counsel-Trademarks.

The possibilities of blogs are almost unlimited, so be on the lookout for new ways to use them to foster positive relationships with colleagues, customers, and other important audiences.

ADAPTING THE THREE-STEP PROCESS FOR SUCCESSFUL BLOGGING

The three-step writing process is easy to adapt to blogging tasks. The planning step is particularly important if you're considering starting a blog, because you're planning an entire communication channel, not just a single message. Pay close attention to your audience, your purpose, and your scope:

Before you launch a blog, make sure you have a clear understanding of your target audience, the purpose of your blog, and the scope of subjects you plan to cover.

- **Audience.** Defining the target audience for a blog can be challenging. You want an audience large enough to justify the time you'll be investing but narrow enough that you can meet readers' needs and not try to be all things to all people.
- **Purpose.** A business blog needs to have a business-related purpose that is important to your company and to your chosen audience (see Figure 7.8). Moreover, the purpose has to "have legs"—that is, it needs to be something that can drive the blog's content for months or years. For instance, if you're a technical expert, you might create a blog to give the audience tips and techniques for using your company's products more effectively—a never-ending subject that's important to both you and your audience. This would be the general purpose of your blog; each posting would have a specific purpose within the context of that general purpose. Finally, whether you are writing on a company blog or your own personal blog, make sure you understand your employer's blogging guidelines.[42]
- **Scope.** Defining the scope of your blog can be a bit tricky. You want to cover a subject area that is broad enough to offer discussion possibilities for months or years but narrow enough to have an identifiable focus. For instance, GM's FastLane blog (http://fastlane.gmblogs.com/) is about GM automobiles only—not GM's stock price, labor negotiations, or other topics.

Reed posts articles that interest her readers and encourage them to engage with her.

This post describes a contest conducted on her Twitter account.

By posting comments from some of her Twitter followers, Reed helps to build the sense of community among her fans.

Giveaways and other techniques help her build an audience on various social media sites.

Offering discounts for readers of her blog adds financial value to the sense of being part of her community.

Category listings make it easy for readers to find posts of interest.

Figure 7.8   Elements of an Effective Business Blog
Amy Reed, owner of Pittsburgh's Chickdowntown clothing store, uses her blog and a variety of other social media tools to build a sense of community among her customers and to promote the store in a way that is compelling without being obtrusive.
Source: Used with permission of chickdowntown.com.

Use a comfortable, personal writing style. Blog audiences don't want to hear from your company; they want to hear from *you*. Bear in mind, though, that comfortable does not mean careless. Sloppy writing damages your credibility. Successful blog content also needs to be interesting, valuable to readers, and as brief as possible.[43] In addition, although audiences expect you to be knowledgeable in the subject area your blog covers, you don't need to know everything about a topic. If you don't have all the information yourself, provide links to other blogs and websites that supply relevant information. In fact, *media curation*, selecting content that will be useful and interesting to your target audience, in much the same way that museum curators decide which pieces of art to display, is one of the most valuable aspects of blogging.

As with email subject lines, compelling headlines for blog posts are an essential tool to draw in readers. A headline needs to grab the reader's attention in a split second by promising something useful, surprising, challenging, or otherwise different from what the reader already knows. Headlines should be as short as possible and suggest that the information in the post will be easy to read and use. "List" headlines that cut right to the heart of something readers care about, such as "10 Reasons You Didn't Get that Promotion" or "Seven Ways to Save Money with Your Smartphone," are particularly popular among bloggers.

Completing messages for your blog is usually quite easy. Evaluate the content and readability of your message, proofread to correct any errors, and post using your blogging system's tools. Be sure to include one or more *newsfeed options* (often called RSS newsfeeds) so that your audience can automatically receive headlines and summaries of new blog posts. Whatever blogging system you are using can provide guidance on setting up newsfeeds. Finally, make your material easier to find by **tagging** it with descriptive words. Visitors to your blog who want to read everything you've written about recruiting just click on that word to see all your posts on that subject. Tagging can also help audiences locate

Write blog postings in a comfortable—but not careless—style.

your posts on blog trackers such as Technorati (http://technorati.com) and on social bookmarking sites.

MICROBLOGGING

A **microblog** is a variation on blogging in which messages are restricted to specific character counts. Twitter (http://twitter.com) is the best known of these systems, but many others exist. Some companies have private microblogging systems for internal use only; these systems are sometimes referred to as *enterprise microblogging* or *internal micromessaging*.[44]

Many of the concepts of regular blogging apply to microblogging as well, although the severe length limitations call for a different approach to composition. The current limit on Twitter, for instance, is 140 characters, including spaces, and if you include a URL, the limit for the rest of the message is 120 characters.

Microblog messages often involve short summaries or teasers that provide links to more information. In fact, Twitter updates are frequently used to announce or promote new posts on regular blogs. In addition, microblogs tend to have a stronger social networking aspect that makes it easier for writers and readers to forward messages and for communities to form around individual writers.[45]

Like Facebook and YouTube, Twitter quickly became an important business communication medium.

Like regular blogging, microblogging quickly caught on with business users and is now a mainstream business medium. Microblogs are used for virtually all of the blog applications mentioned on pages 241–243. In addition, microblogs are frequently used for providing company updates, offering coupons and notice of sales, presenting tips on product usage, sharing relevant and interesting information from experts, serving as the backchannel in meetings and presentations (see page 515 for more on backchannels), and interacting with customers individually (see Figure 7.9).

As microblogging evolves, the technology is gaining features that continue to enhance its value as a business communication medium. On Twitter, for instance, users have adopted the *hashtag* (the # symbol followed by a unique term) to help readers track topics of interest. For example, to establish a backchannel for a conference, you can create a unique hashtag (such as #WBSDCC, the hashtag used by Warner Brothers during a recent San Diego Comic-Con[46]) to help people follow messages on a particular subject. *Retweeting*, the practice of forwarding messages from other Twitter users, is the microblogging equivalent of sharing other content from other bloggers via media curation.

Finally, keep in mind that Twitter is a publishing platform. Unless you set your account to private, anyone can see and search for your tweets—and every public tweet from every Twitter user is being archived by the Library of Congress.[47]

"Checklist: Blogging for Business" summarizes some of the key points to remember when creating and writing a business blog. You can also visit http://real-timeupdates.com/ebc10 and click on Chapter 7 for the latest advice on blogging.

REAL-TIME UPDATES
Learn More by Reading This Article

Tweets from the boss: CEOs on Twitter

See how a number of CEOs are putting microblogging to work for their companies. Go to http://real-timeupdates.com/ebc10 and click on Learn More. If you are using MyBcommLab, you can access Real-Time Updates within each chapter or under Student Study Tools.

✓ Checklist   Blogging for Business

- Consider creating a blog or microblog account whenever you have a continuing stream of information to share with an online audience.
- Identify an audience that is broad enough to justify the effort but narrow enough to have common interests.
- Identify a purpose that is comprehensive enough to provide ideas for a continuing stream of posts.
- Consider the scope of your blog carefully; make it broad enough to attract an audience but narrow enough to keep you focused.

- Communicate with a personal style and an authentic voice but don't write carelessly.
- Deliver new information quickly.
- Choose topics of peak interest to your audience.
- Encourage audiences to join the conversation.
- Consider using Twitter or other microblog updates to alert readers to new posts on your regular blog.

Retweeting items of interest to Patagonia's environmentally aware customer base provides value while building the sense of shared interests.

Like many companies, Patagonia also responds to customer queries and complaints posted on Twitter.

Figure 7.9   Customer Service on Twitter
The outdoor clothing and equipment supplier Patagonia uses Twitter both as a general communication tool and as a way to interact with individual customers to answer questions and solve problems.
Source: Courtesy of Patagonia, Inc.

Podcasting

Podcasting is the process of recording audio or video files and distributing them online. Although podcasting is not used as widely as blogging and some other electronic media, it does offer a number of interesting possibilities for business communication.

> **6   LEARNING OBJECTIVE**
>
> Explain how to adapt the three-step writing process to podcasting.

UNDERSTANDING THE BUSINESS APPLICATIONS OF PODCASTING

The most obvious use of podcasting is to replace existing audio and video messages, such as one-way teleconferences in which a speaker provides information without expecting to engage in conversation with the listeners. Training is another good use of podcasting; you may have already taken a college course via podcasts. Marketing departments can replace expensive printed brochures with video podcasts that demonstrate new products in action. Sales representatives who travel to meet with potential customers can listen to audio podcasts or view video podcasts to get the latest information on their companies' products. Human resources departments can offer video tours of their companies to entice new recruits. Podcasts are also an increasingly common feature on blogs, letting audiences listen to or watch recordings of their favorite bloggers. Some services can even transcribe blogs into podcasts and vice versa.[48]

> Podcasting can be used to deliver a wide range of audio and video messages.

ADAPTING THE THREE-STEP PROCESS FOR SUCCESSFUL PODCASTING

The three-step process adapts quite well to podcasting.

Although it might not seem obvious at first, the three-step writing process adapts quite nicely to podcasting. First, focus the planning step on analyzing the situation, gathering the information you'll need, and organizing your material. One vital planning step depends on whether you intend to create podcasts for limited use and distribution (such as a weekly audio update to your virtual team) or a **podcasting channel** with regular recordings on a consistent theme, designed for a wider public audience. As with planning a blog, if you intend to create a podcasting channel, be sure to think through the range of topics you want to address over time to verify that you have a sustainable purpose.[49]

Steering devices such as transitions, previews, and reviews are vital in podcasts.

As you organize the content for a podcast, pay close attention to previews, transitions, and reviews. These steering devices are especially vital in audio recordings because audio lacks the headings and other elements that audiences rely on in print media. Moreover, scanning back and forth to find specific parts of an audio or video message is much more difficult than with textual messages, so you need to do everything possible to make sure your audience successfully receives and interprets your message on the first try.

One of the attractions of podcasting is the conversational, person-to-person feel of the recordings, so unless you need to capture exact wording, speaking from an outline and notes rather than a prepared script is often the best choice. However, no one wants to listen to rambling podcasts that take several minutes to get to the topic or struggle to make a point, so don't try to make up your content on the fly. Effective podcasts, like effective stories, have a clear beginning, middle, and end.

Plan your podcast content carefully; editing is more difficult with podcasts than with textual messages.

The completing step is where podcasting differs most dramatically from written communication, for the obvious reason that you are recording and distributing audio or video files. Particularly for more formal podcasts, start by revising your script or thinking through your speaking notes before you begin to record. The closer you can get to recording your podcasts in one take, the more productive you'll be, because editing audio is more time-consuming than editing text.

Figure 7.10 illustrates the basic process of recording and distributing podcasts, but the process can vary depending on such factors as the production quality you need to achieve and whether you plan to record in a studio setting or on the go (using a mobile phone or digital recorder to capture your voice).

For basic podcasts, your computer and perhaps even your smartphone might have the hardware you already need, and you can download free recording software.

Most personal computers, smartphones, and other devices now have basic audio recording capability, including built-in microphones, and free editing software is available online (at http://audacity.sourceforge.net, for example). If you need higher production quality or greater flexibility, you'll need additional pieces of hardware and software, such as an audio processor (to filter out extraneous noise and otherwise improve the audio signal), a mixer (to combine multiple audio or video signals), a better microphone, more sophisticated recording and editing software, and perhaps some physical improvements in your recording location to improve the acoustics. You can find more information at Podcast Alley (www.podcastalley.com/forum) and Podcast Bunker (www.podcastbunker.com; click on "Podcasting Tips & Tools").

Podcasts can be distributed in several ways, including through media stores such as iTunes, by dedicated podcast hosting services, or on a blog with content that supports the podcast channel. If you distribute your podcast on a blog, you can provide additional information and use the commenting feature of the blog to encourage feedback from your audience.[50]

For a quick review of the key points of business podcasting, see "Checklist: Planning and Producing Business Podcasts." For news on the latest developments in podcasting, visit http://real-timeupdates.com/ebc10 and click on Chapter 7.

REAL-TIME UPDATES
Learn More by Watching This Video

Step-by-step advice for recording your first podcast

You'll be podcasting in no time with this helpful advice, which includes step-by-step instructions for using the free Audacity audio recording software. Go to http://real-timeupdates.com/ebc10 and click on Learn More. If you are using MyBcommLab, you can access Real-Time Updates within each chapter or under Student Study Tools.

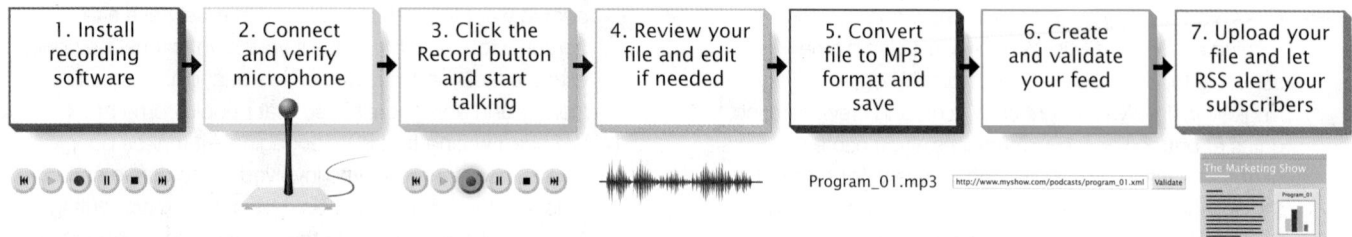

Figure 7.10   The Podcasting Process
Creating a podcast requires a few easy steps, and basic podcasts can be created using free or low-cost hardware and software.

✓ Checklist   Planning and Producing Business Podcasts

- Consider podcasting whenever you have the opportunity to replace existing audio or video messages.
- If you plan a podcast channel with a regular stream of new content, make sure you've identified a theme or purpose that is rich enough to sustain your effort.
- Pay close attention to previews, transitions, and reviews to help prevent your audience from getting lost.

- Decide whether you want to improvise or speak from a written script.
- If you improvise, do enough planning and organization to avoid floundering and rambling in search of a point.
- Remember that editing is much more difficult to do with audio or video than with textual media and plan your content and recording carefully.

ON THE JOB: SOLVING COMMUNICATION DILEMMAS AT **SOUTHWEST AIRLINES**

You recently joined the corporate communications group at Southwest Airlines, and one of your responsibilities is overseeing the Nuts About Southwest blog. Study the scenarios that follow and apply what you learned about blogging in this chapter to choose the best course of action.

Source: Courtesy Southwest Airlines, Co.

1. Pressure is building to stop the practice of moderating the blog by reviewing reader comments and selecting which ones will appear on the blog. You've received a number of adamant messages saying that Nuts About Southwest won't be a "real" blog until anyone is allowed to write any sort of comment without being "censored" by the company. However, you know that every blog is vulnerable to rude, inappropriate, and irrelevant comments, and you don't want Nuts About Southwest to turn into a free-for-all shouting match. Which of the following messages should you post on the blog to explain that the current policy of reviewing and filtering comments will continue?

   a. There are plenty of free-for-all blogs and websites on the Internet; if you want to rant and rave, I suggest you try one of those.
   b. Please bear in mind that this blog is a Southwest company commercial communication endeavor and,

as such, it must adhere to company standards for communication style. I therefore regret to inform you that we cannot allow a free-form, unmonitored exchange as part of this blog.

   c. Our blog; our rules. Seriously, though, this is a professional communication channel designed primarily to give Southwest employees the opportunity to share their thoughts with customers and vice versa. As such, we need to make sure that primary messaging effort doesn't get lost in the noise that can flare up in unregulated online forums.
   d. Every web surfer knows that online discussions can get a little out of hand at times, degenerating into shouting matches, name calling, and off-topic rants. In order to continue providing the congenial, information-driven blog that readers have come to expect, we believe it is necessary to exercise a minimal amount of control over the content.

2. Southwest's change in scheduling policy (allowing customers to reserve seats slightly further into the future) placated many customers but not everyone. Some still want to book travel up to a year or more in advance. You don't want to ignore these complaints, but the company has decided that scheduling that far out just isn't feasible. You therefore decide to post a few representative complaints and respond to them as best you can. In addition to letting customers know that the schedule window won't be extended that far, you'd like to curtail any further discussion on this topic. Which of the following would be the best way to respond to these complaints?

a. Folks, you don't really understand how complicated running an airline truly is. You can't just slap a time schedule together and have it magically happen. Every single flight involves a flight crew, a ground crew, catering, gates at both ends, fees, clearances—you name it. Zillions of details have to be coordinated for every flight we put on the schedule, and it's a major job. We manage to handle 3,000 flights a day, so trust us; we know what we're doing.

b. Thanks for your input. We realize air travel isn't as smooth or as simple as we'd all like, so it's helpful to hear from all of our valued customers. I'll make sure the rest of the scheduling team reads your comments, and if anything changes in the scheduling policy, I'll post the new information here immediately.

c. Thanks for taking the time to post your comments. You're certainly welcome to book your travel on other airlines if you need to nail down a reservation 6 to 12 months into the future. However, I should warn you that the further into the future you make a reservation, the greater the chances that the airline will change the schedule on you. Let's say it's January 10, and you want to book a flight from Denver to San Jose on December 20. Fine, you're all set. Then along comes October or November, and the airline realizes it needs that plane for the Denver to Chicago leg on December 20 instead. What happens then? You get a phone call or email saying "Sorry, we've had to book you on a different flight at a different time." What's the point of nailing down your plans 11 or 12 months in advance if they're just going to change on you?

d. Thanks for taking the time to post your comments. When we're considering the scheduling question, let's remember why all of us—employees included—are nuts about flying Southwest: low fares, predictable schedules, and on-time performance. In order to maintain those benefits, we've learned over the years that we need to make certain choices about how we run the airline. One of those choices is to operate a shorter reservation window than many other airlines. I realize this doesn't meet the needs of every passenger in every situation, but experience shows that it's the best way to make most passengers happy most of the time. In that light, I hope the decision not to extend scheduling beyond six months makes sense to everyone.

3. The multiauthor concept generally works well for Nuts About Southwest. It divides the writing workload, and it gives readers the opportunity to hear from a variety of voices across the company. One member of the team is retiring, so you need to recruit a new blogger to replace her. Your plan is to send an email message to everyone in the company, providing a brief reminder of the blog's purpose, describing the writing style you're looking for, and inviting interested writers to submit sample blog entries for evaluation. Which of the following paragraphs is the best way to describe the preferred writing style for the blog? (This message is for employees only; it won't be seen by the public.)

a. Here's your chance to get noticed: write for Nuts about Southwest. Your writing must be engaging and make people want to read and respond, it must have a few personal touches that make it your own, it must be honest with the facts and in facing criticism, and it must sound friendly and approachable so that people come back.

b. We need writing that is (a) engaging—it makes people want to read and become involved in the conversation. Plus, (b), the writing must be personal; you are writing as yourself and not just as the voice of the company. However, (c), we, of course (!), need writing that is consistent with Southwest's culture that combines honesty with friendliness.

c. You should be able to produce copy that meets the following criteria: Your writing must be engaging, personal, honest, and friendly. Writing that does not meet these criteria, no matter how well written, will not be accepted for online publication.

d. I'll be short and to the point: the writing we want for this blog must be engaging and honest and have a personal and friendly tone.

4. For the sample blog entries you solicited in your email message, you asked candidates to start their entries with a brief paragraph introducing themselves. Which of the following seems like the most compatible style for Nuts About Southwest?

a. Hi everyone! I'm Janice McNathan, and I couldn't be more excited to be joining the Nuts About Southwest blog cuz—hey, I'm nuts! I've worked at some goofball companies before, but nobody has as much fun as the loonies here at Southwest, so I know I'm going to have a great time writing for this blog!

b. Howdy folks, Charlie Parker here. No, not the famous jazz musician! I'm just a lowly fuel inventory auditor here in Dallas. Pretty much, I keep tabs on the fuel that goes into our planes and I make sure we get the best deals possible and all the paperwork stays in order. I can't promise any exciting stories of adventure like the pilots and other people write here, but I'll keep my eyes peeled around the airport here, and maybe something interesting will come up.

c. I'm Rick Munoz, and I've always wanted to be a professional writer. My career sort of took a detour, though, and I wound up as a programmer who works behind the scenes at the Southwest website. I really appreciate this opportunity to hone my craft, and who knows—maybe this will be the break I need to make it as a "real" writer. You'll be able to say "I knew that guy before he became famous!"

d. Excuse me while I wipe the grease off my hands; I don't want to mess up this shiny new keyboard! Hi, I'm Kristal Yan, an airframe and powerplant mechanic at Southwest's facility in Oakland, California. I've been an avid reader of Nuts About Southwest since it started, and I really look forward to participating in this wonderful worldwide conversation. I hope to provide some interesting observations from a mechanic's perspective, and I hope you'll feel free to ask any questions you may have about how we keep Southwest's planes running smoothly and safely.

LEARNING OBJECTIVES CHECKUP

Assess your understanding of the principles in this chapter by reading each learning objective and studying the accompanying exercises. For fill-in-the-blank items, write the missing text in the blank provided; for multiple-choice items, circle the letter of the correct answer. You can check your responses against the answer key on page AK-1.

Objective 7.1: Identify the electronic media available for short messages, list nine compositional modes used in electronic media, and discuss the challenges of communicating through social media.

1. To give final notice of legal action to a customer who has repeatedly defaulted on payments, which of these media would you choose and why?
   a. Facebook wall post
   b. Printed letter
   c. Email
   d. Instant message

2. Which of the following is not listed in the chapter as one of the compositional modes for electronic media?
   a. Conversations
   b. Redacting
   c. Comments and critiques
   d. Narratives

3. Which of these descriptions best captures the preferred style of writing for social media in business?
   a. Corporate and correct
   b. Off the cuff, flippant, by the way
   c. Conversational, willing to listen, ready to respond quickly
   d. Full of humor and amusing quirks

Objective 7.2: Describe the use of social networks, user-generated content sites, community Q&A sites, and community participation sites in business communication.

4. A _____ is a site where people post and share content they have generated themselves.

5. Why should a company have a *hub* to anchor its online presence?
   a. A hub is more aesthetically appealing than the chaos of social media sites as it can be designed and customized.
   b. A hub can be easily controlled as the company owns it and decides what should be shown on it.
   c. A hub can provide a clear inbound path for people seeking information about the company and can be linked with any number of new or existing conversations.
   d. Maintaining a hub is an essential part of the branding process.

6. A _____ _____ website is designed to pool the inputs of multiple users in order to benefit the community as a whole.

Objective 7.3: Describe the evolving role of email in business communication, and explain how to adapt the three-step writing process to email messages.

7. Email hygiene prevents
   a. Viruses from entering the company network.

b. Not-safe-for-work visuals from opening on office machines.
   c. Catching germs from infected keyboards.
   d. Spam messages from clogging your inbox.

8. A subject line should
   a. Give the same information as the message.
   b. Give less information than the message.
   c. Give the most important point of the message.
   d. Be a "teaser" to make people read more.

9. Which of the following is the most effective email subject line?
   a. Problem with stocking: multiple entries last week.
   b. Whose brilliant idea was this?
   c. Stock: FYI
   d. I cannot find the correct figures for the stock intakes last week because someone has entered them in three places.

10. You work in a customer service department, answering emails from customers. This morning you received an angry message from a customer who has a legitimate complaint about your company's warranty policies. After responding to the message as best you can, which of the following steps should you take?
    a. Forward the message to your immediate supervisor and suggest that the company might want to reconsider its warranty policies.
    b. Forward the message to the CEO and suggest that the company might want to reconsider its warranty policies.
    c. Forward the message to everyone in the department so they are aware of the problem with the warranty policy.
    d. Delete the customer's message; you can't fix the warranty policy.

Objective 7.4: Describe the business benefits of instant messaging (IM), and identify guidelines for effective IM in the workplace.

11. Which of the following reasons helps explain why IM usage is overtaking email in some companies?
    a. Emoticons convey a writer's feelings about a piece of information and therefore IM communication is richer than text.
    b. IM saves time and can be done while doing other things, thus allowing people to multitask.
    c. IM is faster than email and mimics human conversation better than email, so many people find it a more natural way to communicate.
    d. IM is similar to SMS and therefore familiar to most people, whereas email is more technical.

12. Which of these statements best describes how the three-step writing process applies to IM?
    a. Because there is no planning step and no completing step in IM, the three-step process does not apply.

b. The real beauty of IM in the business world is that people don't have to spend so much time composing; they just zap out whatever is on their minds and get back to work.

c. The three-step process for IM works exactly the same way as it does with letters, memos, and reports. Every message requires audience analysis, information gathering, and outlining.

d. IM exchanges should be planned the same way conversations are planned to minimize confusion and the number of messages required. And instant messages don't have to be great works of literature, but they do need to be efficient and effective, so some degree of care in writing and revising is important.

13. Which of the following types of messages are most appropriate for IM?
   a. Long, complex messages
   b. Brief conversational messages
   c. Confidential or highly personal messages
   d. All of the above

Objective 7.5: Describe the role of blogging and microblogging in business communication today, and explain how to adapt the three-step writing process to blogging.

14. Which of the following is a good strategy for using blogs to promote products and services?
   a. Find ways to promote your product indirectly. Help out with issues that don't get addressed through normal channels, add a personal take on company events like new product launches, connect with customers, and be willing to have conversations that aren't wholly focused on selling and promoting your wares.
   b. People are constantly distracted by videos, messages, and other content on the web. Make the most of your eyeballs; even someone who views your blog for a few seconds should get the message: buy this product.
   c. Blogging is just business communication by another name: get your superiors to approve all your posts and make sure nothing you post would sound out of place in the CEO's mouth.
   d. A blog is an online diary. Using it for marketing or selling is a perversion of what blogs are about.

15. Which of the following best describes the idea of an "authentic voice" in blogging?
   a. A voice that is hip, uses the latest SMS slang, is peppered with animated emoticons, and speaks to the predominantly young, trendy crowd on the web.
   b. A voice that always speaks perfect textbook English. The informality of the blogosphere is no excuse for sloppiness.
   c. A voice that is personal, informal, and individual but at the same time clear and easily understood.
   d. A voice that gives no clue as to the personality of the writer and offers no opinion, but is always accurate on facts and information, because ultimately that is what people want.

16. Which of the following best describes the optimum audience of a blog?
   a. Always the largest audience possible.
   b. Self-selected experts who can enhance the value of the blog with their helpful comments and observations.
   c. You can't control who your audience will be.
   d. People who are interested enough to take the blog seriously, but not so general as to dilute the focus.

17. Which of the following is *not* a good general purpose for a blog?
   a. Sharing news from the ramp, describing new fashion lines and trends and how designers we stock are faring.
   b. Commenting on new policies in health care and social welfare that affect local hospitals.
   c. Announcing the company's decision not to branch out into soft-toy manufacture.
   d. Following robot wars, a competition for student builders of household robots sponsored by your company.

18. Which of the following would be a good use of retweeting for an independent consulting engineer who uses Twitter to build relationships with potential clients?
   a. Avoiding retweeting under any circumstances, because it is tantamount to plagiarizing
   b. Retweeting every Tweet he or she receives so that clients know how well-rounded and well-read she is
   c. Retweeting fun and interesting messages on non-business topics as a way to build an emotional bond with potential clients
   d. Retweeting selectively, sharing only messages that meet two strict criteria: providing information that followers can use in their work and portraying the consultant as an expert who is up on the latest developments in her field

Objective 7.6: Explain how to adapt the three-step writing process to podcasting.

19. Which of these is the most important consequence of not using a script when recording a podcast?
   a. The podcast might be a bit more chaotic, but it will be more lively and spontaneous.
   b. The podcaster will have to edit the podcast after recording.
   c. The podcast might miss important points, resulting in more time spent recording but less usable material.
   d. The podcast will be more vulnerable to unplanned interference, like people talking in the background.

20. A/an _____ _____ is like a podcast except that it uses video.

21. Which of the following tools is used to collect new blog postings, podcasts, and other fresh content automatically?
   a. A newsreader or aggregator
   b. A feedburner
   c. A bot
   d. A spider

MyBcommLab

CHAPTER OUTLINE

Electronic Media for Business Communication
- Compositional Modes for Electronic Media
- Creating Content for Social Media

Social Networking and Community Participation Websites
- Social Networks
- User-Generated Content Sites
- Community Q&A Sites
- Community Participation Websites

Email
- Planning Email Messages
- Writing Email Messages
- Completing Email Messages

Instant Messaging and Text Messaging
- Understanding the Benefits and Risks of IM
- Adapting the Three-Step Process for Successful IM

Blogging and Microblogging
- Understanding the Business Applications of Blogging
- Adapting the Three-Step Process for Successful Blogging
- Microblogging

Podcasting
- Understanding the Business Applications of Podcasting
- Adapting the Three-Step Process for Successful Podcasting

 **Checklist**

Using IM Productively

- Pay attention to security and privacy issues and be sure to follow all company guidelines.
- Treat IM as a professional communication medium, not an informal, personal tool; avoid using IM slang with all but close colleagues.
- Maintain good etiquette, even during simple exchanges.
- Protect your own productivity by making yourself unavailable when you need to focus.
- In most instances, don't use IM for confidential messages, complex messages, or personal messages.

LEARNING OBJECTIVES

1. Identify the electronic media available for short messages, list nine compositional modes used in electronic media, and discuss the challenges of communicating through social media. [page 223]

2. Describe the use of social networks, user-generated content sites, community Q&A sites, and community participation sites in business communication. [page 228]

3. Describe the evolving role of email in business communication, and explain how to adapt the three-step writing process to email messages. [page 235]

4. Describe the business benefits of instant messaging (IM), and identify guidelines for effective IM in the workplace. [page 238]

5. Describe the role of blogging and microblogging in business communication today, and explain how to adapt the three-step writing process to blogging. [page 240]

6. Explain how to adapt the three-step writing process to podcasting. [page 247]

KEY TERMS

blog An easily updatable online journal; short for *weblog*

brand communities Groups of people united by their interest in and ownership or use of particular products

community participation websites Websites designed to pool the inputs of multiple users in order to benefit the community as a whole

community Q&A sites Websites on which visitors answer questions posted by other visitors or by representatives of companies

conversation marketing Communication in which companies initiate and facilitate conversations in a networked community of customers and other interested parties

email signature A small file that automatically includes such items as your full name, title, company, and contact information at the end of your messages

instant messaging (IM) Communication system in which users' messages appear on each other's screens instantly, without the need to be opened individually, as with email

microblog A variation on blogging in which messages are restricted to specific character counts; Twitter is the best-known example

podcasting The process of recording audio or video files and distributing them online

podcasting channel Series of regular recordings on a consistent theme

social networks Online services that enable individual and organizational members to form connections and share information

tagging Attaching descriptive terms to blog posts and other articles to facilitate searching

text messaging Phone-based messaging capability, also known as *short messaging service* (SMS)

user-generated content (UGC) sites Websites on which users rather than website owners contribute most or all of the content

✓ **Checklist**

Blogging for Business

- Consider creating a blog or microblog account whenever you have a continuing stream of information to share with an online audience.
- Identify an audience that is broad enough to justify the effort but narrow enough to have common interests.
- Identify a purpose that is comprehensive enough to provide ideas for a continuing stream of posts.
- Consider the scope of your blog carefully; make it broad enough to attract an audience but narrow enough to keep you focused.
- Communicate with a personal style and an authentic voice but don't write carelessly.
- Deliver new information quickly.
- Choose topics of peak interest to your audience.
- Encourage audiences to join the conversation.
- Consider using Twitter or other microblog updates to alert readers to new posts on your regular blog.

APPLY YOUR KNOWLEDGE

To review chapter content related to each question, refer to the indicated Learning Objective.

1. Given the strict limits on length, should all your microblogging messages function as teasers that link to more detailed information on a blog or website? Why or why not? [LO-1]
2. Would you use your Facebook or LinkedIn contacts as a focus group to market your new product? Why or why not? [LO-2]
3. Your team has got into the habit of sending instant messages not only for important work-related reasons, but as a pastime. You have seen screens with more than 14 different chat windows open at once. You are concerned that while IM is an important communication tool in the office, this might be too much of a good thing. Which of these is the best option to deal with the situation? [LO 4]
   a. Call a face-to-face meeting and take them to task about their IM manners. They should know not to waste time while at work.
   b. Ban IM from the office. The benefits aren't worth the time lost.
   c. Have your network manager log all IM chat and penalize those who break the rules. That way only the wrongdoers get penalized.
   d. Call a face-to-face meeting to draw up some IM guidelines.
4. Does good grammar and conventional syntax take away the personal, intimate feel of blogging? Why or why not? [LO-5]
5. In your work as a fashion designer, you know that both buyers and rival designers search the web for any scrap of information they can find about new lines. Of course, you want to drop hints to the buyers about the exciting new designs you're working on, but you're also concerned that rival houses might steal your ideas. You've been running a blog with your boss's permission on your work and your ideas, and particularly your technical innovations in cut, stitching, and fabric choice, but now your boss has seen a rival house's line which has suspicious resemblances to yours, and wants you to shut your blog down. Would this be a wise move? Why or why not? [LO-5]

PRACTICE YOUR SKILLS

Message 7.A: Media Skills:
IM, Creating a Businesslike Tone [LO-4]

Review this IM exchange and explain how the customer service agent could have handled the situation more effectively.

Agent: Thanks for contacting Bicycles R Us. What's up?
Customer: I bought a commuter bike from you but now I'm having trouble putting it together.
Agent: I hear that a lot! LOL
Customer: This was advertised as easy to knock down and reassemble. But the instructions are in Chinese!
Agent: That doesn't matter, the pictures are self-explanatory. Do you have a specific problem?
Customer: The front wheel won't go on.
Agent: Try to be a bit more graphic. Which part is giving trouble?
Customer: The front wheel has a tiny axle thingy. It should slot into the forks, but it doesn't.
Agent: Are you sure?

Message 7.B: Media Skills:
Blogging, Creating a Businesslike Tone [LO-5]

Revise this blog post based on what you've learned in this chapter.

[headline]

We're DOOMED!!!!!

[post]

I went down to Honda the other day and my eyes nearly fell out of my head. They're working on a fuel system that uses conventional petrol but consumes forty percent of the fuel used by the most efficient engine to date. You can fill it up at your local station, but it drinks less than half of what your family car guzzles and it costs the same to buy. From what I gathered from the Honda people, this prototype is ready for exhibition at the next expo and the car will go into production early next year. They're already taking bookings for it. Apparently the car is pretty low tech; it just uses microchips and catalysts to get the most out of the existing internal combustion engine.

I've been saying for years that rather than think about fancy fuel cells and dodgy fuels, we should apply good common sense to what we have. Now they're stealing a march on us and all the other manufacturers in the market. We could have beaten them if you'd only listened to me and not frittered away our budget on science-fiction airy fairy schemes. I hope you're happy now.

Message 7.C: Media Skills: Podcasting, Planning: Outlining Your Content [LO-6]

To access this message, visit **http://real-timeupdates.com/ebc10**, click on Student Assignments and select Chapter 7, page 254, Message 7.C to listen to this podcast. Identify at least three ways in which the podcast could be improved and draft a brief email message that you could send to the podcaster, giving your suggestions for improvement.

Exercises

Active links for all websites in this chapter can be found on MyBcommLab; see your User Guide for instructions on accessing the content for this chapter. Each activity is labeled according to the primary skill or skills you will need to use. To review relevant chapter content, you can refer to the indicated Learning Objective. In some instances, supporting information will be found in another chapter, as indicated.

1. **Collaboration: Working in Teams; Planning: Selecting Media [LO-1] Chapter 2** For each of these message needs, choose a medium that you think would work effectively and explain your choice. (More than one medium could work in some cases; just be able to support your particular choice.)
   a. A technical support service for the customers of a company selling dishwashers.
   b. A message of condolence to the family of an employee who died in an accident at work.

c. A message from the new manager of a small company that has just been bought by a larger one, introducing herself to the employees.

d. A series of observations on family law, intended mostly for lawyers working in the field.

e. A series of messages, questions, and answers between members of a lab group developing a new product.

2. **Media Skills: Social Networking [LO-2]** Pick a company in any industry that interests you. Imagine you are doing strategic planning for this firm, and identify one of your company's key competitors. (Hint: You can use the free listings on **www.hoovers.com** to find several top competitors for most medium and large companies in the United States; click on the Competition tab.) Now search through social media sources to find three strategically relevant pieces of information about this competitor, such as the hiring of a new executive, the launch of a major new product, or a significant problem of some kind. In a post on your class blog, identify the information you found and the sources you used. (If you can't find useful information, pick another firm or try another industry.)

3. **Media Skills: Writing Email Subject Lines [LO-3]** Using your imagination to make up whatever details you need, revise the following email subject lines to make them more informative:

a. New sales statistics

b. Marketing brochure—feedback please

c. Seminar schedule

4. **Media Skills: Email [LO-3]** The following email message contains numerous errors related to what you've learned about planning and writing business messages. Using the information it contains, write a more effective version.

TO: Felicia August <fb_august@evertrust.com>
SUBJECT: Puff policy

We know that the terrace on the first floor has become a smokers' paradise. Till now we have had a turn-a-blind-eye deal running with you guys, but that's going to change. The terrace is right next to the air-conditioning intake and the smell of stale cigarette smoke is trapped in all our ducts. It is worst in John Saville's office and he is an asthmatic. Furthermore, some people are getting more breaks than others because of this disgusting habit. As of tomorrow we are putting the terrace out of bounds for everything except coffee breaks for department heads and above. If any of you don't like it, you can go down to the car park and smoke there where you will have no chance of disturbing anyone or polluting the building.

I am very sorry to have to do this, this is not discriminatory to anyone, but you all have to admit that the company must be careful of the health and safety of its employees and the current situation is neither.

Thank you for your cooperation
Felicia August
Manager
Billing and Accounting

5. **Media Skills: IM, Creating a Businesslike Tone [LO-4]** Your firm, which makes car alarm systems, uses IM for internal communication as well as external communication with customers and suppliers. Several customers have recently forwarded copies of messages they've received from your staff, asking if you know how casually some employees are treating this important medium. You decide to revise parts of several messages to show your staff a more appropriate writing style. Rewrite these sentences, making up any information you need, to convey a more businesslike style and tone. (Look up the acronyms online if you need to.)

a. AFAIK, water damage will not affect DEFENDER per4mnc.

b. Dis is best model fr small cr BICBW

c. U can try out but IMHO u need XPERT premium mdl

d. Dont use w/o earthing BTW.

6. **Media Skills: Blogging, Creating a Businesslike Tone [LO-5]** The members of the project team of which you are the leader have enthusiastically embraced blogging as a communication medium. Unfortunately, as emotions heat up during the project, some of the blog posts are getting too casual, too personal, and even sloppy. Because your boss and other managers around the company also read this project blog, you don't want the team to look unprofessional in anyone's eyes. Revise the following blog post so that it communicates in a more businesslike manner while retaining the informal, conversational tone of a blog. (Be sure to correct any spelling and punctuation mistakes you find as well.)

So we're going to miss the second deadline for delivering the website design! Whoda thunk it? Our problem is that we cannot, just cannot let a job go unless its absolutely perfect, even if it takes us all year! That's what happened with the flash animation for the front page and the new logo design. We looked at over twenty options from the desin team, we even liked a coupla, they said they needed more polishing, then six weeks go by with no further submissions! Meanwhile we programmers are sitting on our hands. Me? I prefer to meet dead lines rather than face the shame of broken promises. What use is something which is perfect if the contract's gone to another company because we just couldn't move fast enough? This isn't the first time I've had to tear my hare over this. But what the hell, I'm only a junior programmer. I don't even have a fancy design degree.

7. **Media Skills: Microblogging [LO-5]** Busy knitters can go through a lot of yarn in a hurry, so most keep a sharp eye out for sales. You're on the marketing staff of Knitting-Warehouse, and you like to keep your loyal shoppers up to date with the latest deals. Visit the Knitting-Warehouse website at www .knitting-warehouse.com, select any on-sale product that catches your eye, and write a Twitter update that describes the product and the sale. Be sure to include a link back to the

website so your Twitter followers can learn more. (Unless you are working on a private Twitter account that is accessible only by your instructor and your classmates, don't actually send this Twitter update. Email it to your instructor instead.)

8. **Media Skills: Podcasting, Planning: Outlining Your Content [LO-6]** You began recording a weekly podcast to share information with your large and far-flung staff. After a month, you ask for feedback from several of your subordinates, and you're disappointed to learn that some people stopped listening to the podcast after the first couple weeks. Someone eventually admits that many staffers feel the recordings are too long and rambling, and the information they contain isn't valuable enough to justify the time it takes to listen. You aren't pleased, but you want to improve. An assistant transcribes the introduction to last week's podcast so you can review it. You immediately see two problems. Revise the introduction based on what you've learned in this chapter.

Well, I strolled over to the presentation on the new shows we're putting up this season. Bumped into Harrison Medlen, the guy who's headlining *The Season*, about all the exciting stuff that goes on at comic cons. Looks like an exciting set of episodes lined up for that. We've also got a new feature series on comics called *Framed!* and one on animation called *24 Per Second*. Shows which are shooting include GOD, about gamers. Sound design people still required for that. *Framed!* is doing some great reporting on indie comics publishers in the third world. I saw a mind-blowing pilot episode on the Philippines. While I was at the presentation, I caught a glimpse of our new studio head, the enigmatic Britta Mason. She said we'll soon be putting out a new schedule. Makeup people, you will need to change your shift timings soon. Britta is going to put out a notice on the intranet about this in a couple of days, so watch this space. She also told me she's a World of Warcraft fan and gave me the URL of her game blog www.chicattack.com. Check it out, it's uber cool. Also the advertising department is making some changes to the break schedule. For live shows, we're going to get a new blog to be run by the recruiting department for studio audiences to better attract people for our game show series. And I'm almost forgetting, we need a bunch of young people to get our Twitter accounts and Youtube channels humming. Apply to Britta if you're interested in that, with some writing samples.

EXPAND YOUR SKILLS

Critique the Professionals

Locate the YouTube channel page of any company you find interesting and assess its social networking presence using the criteria for effective communication discussed in this chapter and your own experience using social media. What does this company do well with its YouTube channel? How might it improve? Using whatever medium your instructor requests, write a brief analysis of the company's YouTube presence (no more than one page), citing specific elements from the piece and support from the chapter.

Sharpening Your Career Skills Online

Bovée and Thill's Business Communication Web Search, at http://businesscommunicationblog.com/websearch, is a unique research tool designed specifically for business communication research. Use the Web Search function to find a website, video, PDF document, podcast, or PowerPoint presentation that offers advice on using social media in business. Write a brief email message to your instructor, describing the item that you found and summarizing the career skills information you learned from it.

IMPROVE YOUR GRAMMAR, MECHANICS, AND USAGE

The following exercises help you improve your knowledge of and power over English grammar, mechanics, and usage. Turn to the "Handbook of Grammar, Mechanics, and Usage" at the end of this book and review Section 1.6.1 (Prepositions), Section 1.6.2 (Conjunctions), and Section 1.6.3 (Articles and Interjections). Then look at the following 10 items. Circle the letter of the preferred choice in the following groups of sentences. (Answers to these exercises appear on page AK-3.)

1. a. The report was not only late but it was also incomplete.
   b. The report was not only late but also incomplete.

2. a. Make sure you mark the copy up before mailing it.
   b. Make sure you mark up the copy before mailing it.

3. a. We didn't get the permission because our safety measures didn't conform with the guidelines.
   b. We didn't get the permission because our safety measures didn't conform to the guidelines.

4. a. Clarence must of remembered to copy the Director in the mail.
   b. Clarence must have remembered to copy the Director in the mail.

5. a. The features of the Nokia E-series are similar to those of the Blackberry Curve.
   b. The features of the Nokia E-series are similar with those of the Blackberry Curve.

6. a. What are you talking about?
   b. About what are you talking?

7. a. Have you sent an RFP?
   b. Have you sent a RFP?

8. a. The new employee has proved neither to be honest nor hardworking.
   b. The new employee has proved to be neither honest nor hardworking.

9. a. If you carry on this way, you will definitely lose your job!
   b. If you carry on this way, you will definitely lose your job.

10. a. She was involved in an horrific accident.
    b. She was involved in a horrific accident.

For additional exercises focusing on conjunctions, articles, and prepositions, visit MyBcommLab. Click on Chapter 7, click on Additional Exercises to Improve Your Grammar, Mechanics, and Usage, and click on 11. Conjunctions, articles, and interjections.

CASES

SOCIAL NETWORKING SKILLS

1. Media Skills: Social Networking; Media Skills: Microblogging [LO-2] [LO-5]   Foursquare (http://foursquare.com/) is one of the leading providers of location-based social networking services. Millions of people use Foursquare for social engagement and friendly competition, and many business owners are starting to recognize the marketing potential of having people who are on the move in local areas, broadcasting their locations and sharing information about stores, restaurants, clubs, and other merchants. (Review the highlight box "Walking Around with the Entire Internet in Your Hands" on page 225 for more on the mobile-local web.)

Your task: Review the information on Foursquare's Merchant Platform at http://foursquare.com/business/venues. Now write four brief messages, no more than 140 characters long (including spaces). The first should summarize the benefits to stores, restaurants, and other "brick and mortar" businesses of participating in Foursquare, and the next three messages should convey three compelling points that support that overall benefit statement. If your class is set up with private Twitter accounts, use your private account to send your messages. Otherwise, email your four messages to your instructor or post them on your class blog, as your instructor directs.

SOCIAL NETWORKING SKILLS

2. Media Skills: Social Networking; Online Etiquette [LO-2], Chapter 2   Employees who take pride in their work are a practically priceless resource for any business. However, pride can sometimes manifest itself in negative ways when employees come under criticism—and public criticism is a fact of life in social media. Imagine that your company has recently experienced a rash of product quality problems, and these problems have generated some unpleasant and occasionally unfair criticism on a variety of social media sites. Someone even set up a Facebook page specifically to give customers a place to vent their frustrations.

You and your public relations team jumped into action, responding to complaints with offers to provide replacement products and help customers who have been affected by the quality problems. Everything seemed to be going as well as could be expected, when you were checking a few industry blogs one evening and discovered that a couple of engineers in your company's product design lab have been responding to complaints on their own. They identified themselves as company employees and defended their product design, blaming the company's production department and even criticizing several customers for lacking the skills needed to use such a sophisticated product. Within a matter of minutes, you see their harsh comments being retweeted and reposted on multiple sites, only fueling the fire of negative feedback against your firm. Needless to say, you are horrified.

Your task: You manage to reach the engineers by private message and tell them to stop posting messages, but you realize you have a serious training issue on your hands. Write a post for the internal company blog that advises employees on how to respond appropriately when they are representing the company online. Use your imagination to make up any details you need.

SOCIAL NETWORKING SKILLS
PRESENTATION SKILLS

3. Media Skills: Social Networking; Media Skills: Presentations [LO-2], Chapters 16–17   Daniel Gordon, the fourth-generation jeweler who is CEO of Samuel Gordon Jewelers in Oklahoma City, has turbocharged the century-old company with social media. During some of the roughest economic times in memory, the company's revenues and foot traffic have grown steadily while its advertising costs have dropped by 90 percent. Gordon is an active social media user, using a variety of media tools to educate jewelry buyers, let customers know about new products, and guide customers through the process of selecting wedding rings and other significant jewelry purchases.

Your task: With a team of classmates, study the company's website (www.samuelgordons.com/) and its social media presence (you can find various social media links on the website). You can read more about the company's social media strategy by visiting http://real-timeupdates.com/ebc10, clicking on "Student Assignments" and selecting "Chapter 7 Case 3." Now identify a business near your college that could benefit from a similar social media strategy. Devise a social media strategy that could help this company expand its customer base and forge stronger links with the local community. Prepare a brief class presentation that describes the business and explains your proposed strategy. (Your instructor may ask you to undertake this as a service project, in which you meet with the company owner and present your proposed social media strategy.)

SOCIAL NETWORKING SKILLS

4. Media Skills: Social Networking [LO-2]   Social media can be a great way to, well, socialize during your college years, but employers are increasingly checking up on the online activities of potential hires to avoid bringing in employees who may reflect poorly on the company.

Your task: Team up with another student and review each other's public presence on Facebook, Twitter, Flickr, blogs, and any other website that an employer might check during the interview and recruiting process. Identify any photos, videos, messages, or other material that could raise a red flag when an employee is evaluating a job candidate. Write your teammate an email message that lists any risky material.

E-MAIL SKILLS

5. Media Skills: Email; Career Management: Personal Branding [LO-3], Prologue   You've been laboring all summer at an internship, learning how business is conducted. You've done work nobody else wanted to do, but that's okay. Even the smallest tasks can make a good impression on your future résumé.

This morning, your supervisor asks you to write a description of the job you've been doing. "Include everything, even the filing," she suggests, "and address it to me in an email message." She says a future boss might assign such a task prior to a performance review. "You can practice describing your work without exaggeration—or too much modesty," she says, smiling.

Your task: Using good techniques for short messages and relying on your real-life work experience, write an email that will impress your supervisor. Make up any details you need.

E-MAIL SKILLS   PORTFOLIO BUILDER

6. Media Skills: Email; Message Strategies: Marketing and Sales Messages [LO-3] Chapter 10   One-quarter of all motor vehicle accidents that involve children under age 12 are side-impact crashes—and these crashes result in higher rates of injuries and fatalities than those with front or rear impacts.[51]

Your task: You work in the consumer information department at Britax, a leading manufacturer of car seats. Your manager has asked you to prepare an email message that can be sent out whenever parents request information about side-impact crashes and the safety features of Britax seats. Start by researching side-impact crashes at www.britaxusa.com/learning-center/side-impact-protection-revealed. Write a three-paragraph message that explains the seriousness of side-impact crashes, describes how injuries and fatalities can be minimized in these crashes, and describes how Britax's car seats are designed to help protect children in side-impact crashes.

E-MAIL SKILLS

7. Media Skills: Email; Message Strategies: Negative Messages [LO-3] Chapter 9   Many companies operate on the principle that the customer is always right, even when the customer *isn't* right. They take any steps necessary to ensure happy customers, lots of repeat sales, and a positive reputation among potential buyers. Overall, this is a smart and successful approach to business. However, most companies eventually encounter a nightmare customer who drains so much time, energy, and profits that the only sensible option is to refuse the customer's business. For example, the nightmare customer might be someone who constantly berates you and your employees, repeatedly makes outlandish demands for refunds and discounts, or simply requires so much help that you not only lose money on this person but also no longer have enough time to help your other customers. "Firing" a customer is an unpleasant step that should be taken only in the most extreme cases and only after other remedies have been attempted (such as talking with the customer about the problem), but it is sometimes necessary for the well-being of your employees and your company.

Your task: If you are currently working or have held a job in the recent past, imagine that you've encountered just such a customer. If you don't have job experience to call on, imagine that you work in a retail location somewhere around campus or in your neighborhood. Identify the type of behavior this imaginary customer exhibits and the reasons the behavior can no longer be accepted. Write a brief email message to the customer to explain that you will no longer be able to accommodate him or her as a customer. Calmly explain why you have had to reach this difficult decision. Maintain a professional tone and keep your emotions in check.

E-MAIL SKILLS   TEAM SKILLS

8. Media Skills: Email; Collaboration: Team Projects [LO-3] Chapter 2   For the first time in history (aside from special situations such as major wars), more than half—51 percent—of all U.S.

adult women now live without a spouse. (In other words, they live alone, with roommates, or as part of an unmarried couple.) Twenty-five percent have never married, and 26 percent are divorced, widowed, or married but living apart from their spouses. In the 1950s and into the 1960s, only 40 percent of women lived without a spouse, but every decade since, the percentage has increased. In your work as a consumer trend specialist for Seymour Powell (www.seymourpowell.com), a product design firm based in London that specializes in the home, personal, leisure, and transportation sectors, it's your business to recognize and respond to demographic shifts such as this.

Your task: With a small team of classmates, brainstorm possible product opportunities that respond to this trend. In an email message to be sent to the management team at Seymour Powell, list your ideas for new or modified products that might sell well in a society in which more than half of all adult women live without a spouse. For each idea, provide a one-sentence explanation of why you think the product has potential.[52]

IM SKILLS

9. Media Skills: IM; Compositional Modes: Tutorials [LO-1] [LO-4]   High-definition television can be a joy to watch—but, oh, what a pain to buy. The field is littered with competing technologies and arcane terminology that is meaningless to most consumers. Moreover, it's nearly impossible to define one technical term without invoking two or three others, leaving consumers swimming in an alphanumeric soup of confusion. The manufacturers themselves can't even agree on which of the *18* different digital TV formats truly qualify as "high definition." As a sales support manager for Crutchfield, www.crutchfield.com, a leading online retailer of audio and video systems, you understand the frustration buyers feel; your staff is deluged daily by their questions.

Your task: To help your staff respond quickly to consumers who ask questions via Crutchfield's online IM chat service, you are developing a set of "canned" responses to common questions. When a consumer asks one of these questions, a sales advisor can simply click on the ready-made answer. Start by writing concise, consumer-friendly definitions of the following terms: *resolution*, *HDTV*, *1080p*, and *HDMI*. Explore the Learning Center on the Crutchfield website to learn more about these terms. Answers.com and CNET.com are two other handy sources.[53]

IM SKILLS

10. Media Skills: IM; Collaboration: Working in Teams [LO-4]   Instant messaging is frequently used in customer support situations where a customer needs help selecting, using, or troubleshooting a problem. In this activity, two two-person teams will use IM to simulate problem solving by helping classmates discuss important academic or life decisions. One team will be the "clients," who are struggling with the decisions, and the other will be the "advisors," who coach them toward solutions.

Your task: First choose a free IM/chat system such as Google Talk, Facebook chat, or any other system on which you can communicate privately in real time. Now choose two decision-making scenarios from your school or personal lives, such as deciding on a major, choosing whether to work during the upcoming summer or attend class, figuring out where to live next year, or any other decision that you're willing to have the group discuss and then later to discuss in front of the whole class. Choose decisions that are complicated enough to support an IM conversation lasting at least five minutes.

Decide which team will be the advisors and which will be the clients and move the teams to separate locations (make sure you have Internet access). In each team, one person will be the communicator first, and the other will be the observer, monitoring how well the IM conversation progresses and making note of any confusion, inefficiencies, or other issues.

When you're set up in your separate locations, begin the IM exchange with the communicator from the client team asking the advisor for help with a decision. The advisor should ask probing questions to find out what the client really wants to gain from the decision and help him or her work through the various alternatives. Discuss the decision scenario for at least five minutes. The observers should take notes but should not be involved in the IM exchange in any way.

After working through one of the decision scenarios, swap roles inside each team so that the observer becomes the communicator and vice versa. Now work through the second decision scenario.

Afterward, meet as a full team after the role playing and compare notes about how well each conversation went, how well the technology supported the communicators' needs, and what you might do differently in a business context to ensure smooth communication and customer satisfaction. Be prepared to discuss your observations and conclusions with the rest of the class.

BLOGGING SKILLS

11. Media Skills: Blogging; Compositional Modes: Tutorials [LO-5] Studying abroad for a semester or a year can be a rewarding experience in many ways—improving your language skills, experiencing another culture, making contacts in the international business arena, and building your self-confidence.

Your task: Write a post for your class blog that describes your college's study abroad program and summarizes the steps involved in applying for international study. If your school doesn't offer study-abroad opportunities, base your post on the program offered at another institution in your state.

BLOGGING SKILLS   PORTFOLIO BUILDER

12. Media Skills: Blogging [LO-5] U.S. automakers haven't had much good news to share lately. GM, in particular, has been going through a rough time, entering bankruptcy, shedding assets, and relying on bailouts from the U.S. and Canadian governments to stay in business. The news isn't entirely bleak, however. Chevrolet, one of the brands in the GM automotive stable, has recently introduced the Volt, a gas/electric hybrid that might finally give drivers a viable alternative to the wildly popular Toyota Prius.

Your task: Working with a team assigned by your instructor, write a post for GM's dealer-only blog that describes the new Volt and the benefits it offers car owners. Include at least one photo and one link to the Volt section of GM's website. You can learn more about the Volt at Chevy's website, www.chevrolet.com.

BLOGGING SKILLS

13. Media Skills: Blogging [LO-5] Comic-Con International is an annual convention that highlights a wide variety of pop culture and entertainment media, from comic books and collectibles to video games and movies. From its early start as a comic book convention that attracted several hundred fans and publishing industry insiders, Comic-Con has become a major international event with more than 125,000 attendees.

Your task: Several readers of your pop culture blog have been asking for your recommendation about visiting Comic-Con in San Diego next summer. Write a two- or three-paragraph posting for your blog that explains what Comic-Con is and what attendees can expect to experience at the convention. Be sure to address your posting to fans, not industry insiders. You can learn more at www.comic-con.org.[54]

BLOGGING SKILLS

14. Media Skills: Blogging [LO-5] You work for PreVisor, one of many companies that offer employee screening and testing services. PreVisors's offerings include a variety of online products and consulting services, all designed to help employers find and develop the best possible employees.

To help explain the value of its products and services, PreVisor publishes a variety of customer *case studies* on its website. Each case study describes the staffing challenges a particular company faces, the solution PreVisor was able to provide, and the results the company experienced after using PreVisor products or services.

Your task: Select one of the customer case studies on the PreVisor website (www.previsor.com/results/clients). Write a post that could appear on PreVisor's blog, summarizing the challenges, solutions, and results in no more than 100 words. Include a link to the complete case study on the PreVisor website.

BLOGGING SKILLS

15. Media Skills: Blogging [LO-5] The fact that 97 percent of American youth ages 12 to 17 play video games is not much of a surprise, but more than a few nongaming adults might be surprised to learn that game playing might not be quite the social and civic catastrophe it is sometimes made out to be. A recent study by the Pew Internet & American Life Project puts a least a few cracks in the stereotyped image of gamers being loners who live out violent fantasies while learning few if any skills that could make them positive members of society.[55]

Your task: Imagine that you're on the public relations staff at the Entertainment Software Association (ESA), an industry group that represents the interests of video game companies. You'd like to share the results of the Pew survey with parents to help ease their concerns. Visit http://real-timeupdates.com/ebc10, click on Student Assignments and then Chapter 7, page 259, Case 15. Download this PDF file, which is a summary of the Pew results. Find at least three positive aspects of video game playing and write a brief message that could be posted on an ESA public affairs blog.

MICROBLOGGING SKILLS

16. Media Skills: Microblogging [LO-5] Consumers looking for beauty, health, and lifestyle magazines have an almost endless array of choices, but even in this crowded field, Logan Olson found her own niche. Olson, who was born with congenital heart disease, suffered a heart attack at age 16 that left her in a coma and caused serious brain damage. The active and outgoing teen had to relearn everything from sitting up to feeding herself. As she recovered, she looked for help and advice in conquering such daily challenges as finding fashionable clothes that were easier to put on and makeup that was easier to apply. Mainstream beauty magazines didn't seem to offer any information for young women with disabilities, so she started her own magazine. Oprah Winfrey has *Oprah*, and Logan Olson has *Logan*. The magazine not only gives young women tips on buying and using a variety of products but lets women with disabilities know there are others like them, facing and meeting the same challenges.

Your task: Write a 120-character message suggesting a gift subscription to *Logan* magazine as a nice birthday gift for any young woman who might benefit from the magazine. Assume that your readers are not familiar with *Logan*. (Limiting your message to 120 characters allows room for a 20-character URL, which you don't need to include in your message.) You can learn more about *Logan* at www.loganmagazine.com or on Facebook (search for Logan Magazine).[56] If your class is set up with private Twitter accounts, use your private account to send your message. Otherwise, email it to your instructor.

17. Media Skills: Microblogging; Compositional Modes: Teasers [LO-1], [LO-5] Twitter updates are a great way to alert people to helpful articles, videos, and other online resources.

Your task: Find an online resource (it can be a website quiz, a YouTube video, a PowerPoint presentation, a newspaper article, or anything else appropriate) that offers some great tips to help college students prepare for job interviews. Write a teaser of no more than 120 characters that hints at the benefits other students can get from this resource. If your class is set up with private Twitter accounts, use your private account to send your message. Otherwise, email it to your instructor. Be sure to include the URL; if you're using a Twitter account, the system should shorten it to 20 characters to keep you within the 140-character limit.

MICROBLOGGING SKILLS

18. Media Skills: Microblogging; Compositional Modes: Updates and Announcements [LO-1], [LO-5] JetBlue is known for its innovations in customer service and customer communication, including its pioneering use of the Twitter microblogging system. Nearly two million JetBlue fans and customers follow the company on Twitter to get updates on flight status during weather disruptions, facility upgrades, and other news.[57]

Your task: Write a message of no more than 120 characters that announces the limited-time availability of flights and travel packages—flights plus hotel rooms, for example—at JetBlue's store on eBay. (Limiting your message to 120 characters allows room for a 20-character URL, which you don't need to include in your message.) The key selling point is that travelers may be able to purchase flights they want at steep discounts. If your class is set up with private Twitter accounts, use your private account to send your message. Otherwise, email it to your instructor.

PODCASTING SKILLS

19. Media Skills: Podcasting; Career Management: Personal Branding [LO-6], Prologue While writing the many letters and email messages that are part of the job search process, you find yourself wishing that you could just talk to some of these companies so your personality could shine through. Well, you've just gotten that opportunity. One of the companies that you've applied to has emailed you back, asking you to submit a two-minute podcast, introducing yourself and explaining why you would be a good person to hire.

Your task: Identify a company that you'd like to work for after graduation and select a job that would be a good match for your skills and interests. Write a script for a two-minute podcast (roughly 250 words). Introduce yourself and the position you're applying for, describe your background, and explain why you think you're a good candidate for the job. Make up any details you need. If your instructor asks you to do so, record the podcast and submit the file.

PODCASTING SKILLS   **PORTFOLIO BUILDER**

20. Media Skills: Podcasting; Message Strategies: Marketing and Sales Messages [LO-6] Chapter 10 With any purchase decision, from a restaurant meal to a college education, recommendations from satisfied customers are often the strongest promotional messages.

Your task: Write a script for a one- to two-minute podcast (roughly 150 to 250 words), explaining why your college or university is a good place to get an education. Your audience is high school juniors and seniors. You can choose to craft a general message, something that would be useful to all prospective students, or you can focus on a specific academic discipline, the athletic program, or some other important aspect of your college experience. Either way, make sure your introductory comments make it clear whether you are offering a general recommendation or a specific recommendation. If your instructor asks you to do so, record the podcast and submit the file electronically.

REFERENCES

1. Southwest Airlines, Nuts About Southwest blog, accessed 1 February 2011, www.blogsouthwest.com; Bill Owens, "Why Can't I Make Reservations Further in Advance?" Nuts About Southwest blog, 24 January 2007, www.blogsouthwest.com; Bill Owens, "I Blogged. You Flamed. We Changed." Nuts About Southwest blog, 18 April 2007, www.blogsouthwest .com; "Southwest Airlines Is Nuts About Blogging," Southwest Airlines press release, 27 April 2007, www.prnewswire.com.

2. "Ten Ways to Use Texting for Business," *Inc.*, accessed 21 July 2010, www.inc.com; Kate Maddox, "Warrillow Finds 39% of Small-Business Owners Use Text Messaging," BtoB, 1 August 2008, www.btobonline.com; Dave Carpenter, "Companies Discover Marketing Power of Text Messaging," *Seattle Times*, 25 September 2006, www.seattletimes.com.

3. "Burson-Marsteller Fortune Global 10 Social Media Study," The Burson-Marsteller Blog, 23 February 2010, www.burson-marsteller.com.

4. "The New Messages," Facebook.com, accessed 30 January 2011, www.facebook.com.

5. Richard Edelman, "Teaching Social Media: What Skills Do Communicators Need?" in *Engaging the New Influencers; Third Annual Social Media Academic Summit* (white paper), accessed 7 June 2010, www.newmediaacademicsummit.com.

6. Catherine Toole, "My 7 Deadly Sins of Writing for Social Media—Am I Right?" Econsultancy blog, 19 June 2007, www.econsultancy.com; Muhammad Saleem, "How to Write a Social Media Press Release," Copyblogger, accessed 16 September 2008, www.copyblogger.com; Melanie McBride, "5 Tips for (Better) Social Media Writing," Melanie McBride Online, 11 June 2008, http://melaniemcbride.net.

7. "Facebook Analytics: Full-on Facebook Tracking and Measurement," Webtrends, accessed 10 July 2010, www.webtrends.com; Facebook statistics page, Facebook.com, accessed 10 July 2010, www.facebook.com; Facebook pages of Adidas, Red Bull, and Starbucks, accessed 11 July 2010, www.facebook.com.

8. "Gartner Says Social-Networking Services to Replace Email as the Primary Vehicle for Interpersonal Communications for 20 Percent of Business Users by 2014," Gartner press release, 11 November 2010, www.gartner.com; Sarah Perez, "Social Networking More Popular Than Voice, SMS by 2015," ReadWriteWeb.com, 15 November 2010, www.readwriteweb.com.

9. Todd Henneman, "At Lockheed Martin, Social Networking Fills Key Workforce Needs While Improving Efficiency and Lowering Costs," *Workforce Management*, March 2010, www.workforce.com.

10. Sheryl Kingstone and Zeus Kerravala, "Social Media Means Serious Business," Yankee Group white paper, June 2010, www.siemens-enterprise.com; Sharon Gaudin, "Companies Not Using Social Nets at Risk, Report Says," *Computerworld*, 15 July 2010, www.computerworld.com.

11. Alex Wright, "Mining the Web for Feelings, Not Facts," *New York Times*, 23 August 2009, www.nytimes.com.

12. Erica Swallow, "How to Use Social Media for Lead Generation," Mashable, 24 June 2010, http://mashable.com.

13. Susan Fournier and Lara Lee, "Getting Brand Communities Right," *Harvard Business Review*, April 2009, 105–111.

14. Patrick Hanlon and Josh Hawkins, "Expand Your Brand Community Online," *Advertising Age*, 7 January 2008, 14–15.

15. Josh Bernoff, "Social Strategy for Exciting (and Not So Exciting) Brands," *Marketing News*, 15 May 2009, 18; Larry Weber, *Marketing to the Social Web* (Hoboken, N.J.: Wiley, 2007), 12–14; David Meerman Scott, *The New Rules of Marketing and PR* (Hoboken, N.J.: Wiley, 2007), 62; Paul Gillin, *The New Influencers* (Sanger, Calif.: Quill Driver Books, 2007), 34–35; Jeremy Wright, *Blog Marketing: The Revolutionary Way to Increase Sales, Build Your Brand, and Get Exceptional Results* (New York: McGraw-Hill, 2006), 263–365.

16. Matt Rhodes, "Build Your Own Community or Go Where People Are? Do Both," FreshNetworks blog, 12 May 2009, www.freshnetworks.com.

17. Brian Solis, *Engage!* (Hoboken, N.J.: Wiley, 2010), 13.

18. Zachary Sniderman, "5 Ways to Clean Up Your Social Media Identity," Mashable, 7 July 2010, http://mashable.com.

19. HP company profiles on LinkedIn and Facebook, accessed 21 July 2010, www.facebook.com/hp and www.linkedin.com/hp.

20. Ben Hanna, *2009 Business Social Media Benchmarking Study* (published by Business.com), 2 November 2009, 22.

21. Vanessa Pappas, "5 Ways to Build a Loyal Audience on You-Tube," Mashable, 15 June 2010, www.mashable.com.

22. Tamar Weinberg, *The New Community Rules: Marketing on the Social Web* (Sebastapol, Calif.: O'Reilly Media, 2009), 288.

23. "About Us," Yelp, accessed 30 January 2011, www.yelp.com; Lisa Barone, "Keynote Conversation with Yelp Chief Operating Officer Geoff Donaker," 5 October 2010, http://outspokenmedia.com.

24. Reid Goldborough, "More Trends for 2009: What to Expect with Personal Technology," *Public Relations Tactics*, February 2009, 9.

25. Jessica E. Vascellaro, "Why Email No Longer Rules. . ." *Wall Street Journal*, 12 October 2008, http://online.wsj.com.

26. Matt Cain, "Managing Email Hygiene," ZD Net Tech Update, 5 February 2004, www.techupdate.zdnet.com.

27. Hilary Potkewitz and Rachel Brown, "Spread of Email Has Altered Communication Habits at Work," *Los Angeles Business Journal*, 18 April 2005, www.findarticles.com; Nancy Flynn, *Instant Messaging Rules* (New York: AMACOM, 2004), 47–54.

28. Mary Munter, Priscilla S. Rogers, and Jone Rymer, "Business Email: Guidelines for Users," *Business Communication Quarterly*, March 2003, 26+; Renee B. Horowitz and Marian G. Barchilon, "Stylistic Guidelines for Email," *IEEE Transactions on Professional Communication* 37, no. 4 (December 1994): 207–212.

29. Steve Rubel, "Tip: Tweetify the Lead of Your Emails," The Steve Rubel Stream blog, 20 July 2010, www.steverubel.com.

30. Jack Aronson, "Use Text Messaging in Your Business," ClickZ, 12 June 2009, www.clickz.com; Paul Mah, "Using Text Messaging in Business," Mobile Enterprise blog, 4 February 2008, http://blogs.techrepublic.com.com/wireless; Paul Kedrosky, "Why We Don't Get the (Text) Message," *Business 2.0*, 2 October 2006, www.business2.com; Carpenter, "Companies Discover Marketing Power of Text Messaging."

31. "About StarStar Numbers," Zoove website, accessed 7 July 2011, www.zoove.com.

32. Mark Gibbs, "Racing to Instant Messaging," *NetworkWorld*, 17 February 2003, 74.

33. "E-Mail Is So Five Minutes Ago," *BusinessWeek*, 28 November 2005, www.businessweek.com.

34. Clint Boulton, "IDC: IM Use Is Booming in Business," InstantMessagingPlanet.com, 5 October 2005, accessed 22 January 2006, www.instantmessagingplanet.com; Jenny Goodbody, "Critical Success Factors for Global Virtual Teams," *Strategic Communication Management*, February/March 2005, 18–21; Ann Majchrzak, Arvind Malhotra,

Jeffrey Stamps, and Jessica Lipnack, "Can Absence Make a Team Grow Stronger?" *Harvard Business Review*, May 2004, 131–137; Christine Y. Chen, "The IM Invasion," *Fortune*, 26 May 2003, 135–138; Yudhijit Bhattacharjee, "A Swarm of Little Notes," *Time*, September 2002, A3–A8; Mark Bruno, "Taming the Wild Frontiers of Instant Messaging," *Bank Technology News*, December 2002, 30–31; Richard Grigonis, "Enterprise-Strength Instant Messaging," Convergence.com, accessed March 2003, www.convergence.com; Pallato, "Instant Messaging Unites Work Groups and Inspires Collaboration," 14+.

35. Valeria Maltoni, "Corporate Blogs: How's Your Elevator Pitch These Days?" Conversation Agent blog, 6 July 2010, www.conversationagent.com.

36. Amy Porterfield, "10 Top Business Blogs and Why They Are Successful," Social Media Examiner, 25 January 2011, www.socialmediaexaminer.com.

37. Dr. Laundry blog, www.drlaundryblog.com.

38. Debbie Weil, Why Your Blog Is the Hub of Social Media Marketing," Social Media Insights Blog, 12 January 2010, http://debbieweil.com; Ross Dawson, "A List of Business Applications for Blogging in the Enterprise," Trends in the Living Network blog, 7 July 2009, http://rossdawsonblog.com; Fredrik Wackå, "Six Types of Blogs—A Classification," CorporateBlogging.Info website, 10 August 2004, www.corporateblogging.info; Stephen Baker, "The Inside Story on Company Blogs," *BusinessWeek* 14 February 2006, www.businessweek.com; Jeremy Wright, *Blog Marketing* (New York: McGraw-Hill, 2006), 45–56; Paul Chaney, "Blogs: Beyond the Hype!" 26 May 2005, http://radiantmarketinggroup.com.

39. Evolve24 website, accessed 31 January 2011, www.evolve24.com.

40. Solis, *Engage!*, 86.

41. Weinberg, The New Community Rules: Marketing on the Social Web, 89.

42. Stephen Baker and Heather Green, "Blogs Will Change Your Business," *BusinessWeek*, 2 May 2005, 57–67.

43. Joel Falconer, "Six Rules for Writing Great Web Content," Blog News Watch, 9 November 2007, www.blognewswatch.com.

44. Dion Hinchcliffe, "Twitter on Your Intranet: 17 Microblogging Tools for Business," ZDNet, 1 June 2009, www.zdnet.com.

45. Hinchcliffe, "Twitter on Your Intranet: 17 Microblogging Tools for Business."

46. "Warner Brothers Television Group Social Media Contacts," The WB website, accessed 9 August 2010, www.thewb.com.

47. "Social Media Policies Reduce Discovery Risks: Are You Prepared?" Armstrong Teasdale, 3 November 2010, www.jdsupra.com; "The Library of Congress Is Archiving Your Tweets," NPR, 19 July 2010, www.npr.org; Simon Quance, "The Guide to Social Media Etiquette for Businesses," MyCustomer.com, 16 August 2010, www.mycustomer.com; Tony Schwartz, "Digital Incivility: The Unseemly Rise of Rudeness," Harvard Business Review blogs, 14 September 2010, http://blogs.hbr.org; Gillian Shaw, "Twitter Can Be a Legal Minefield: Watch What You Say," Vancouver Sun, 17 October 2009, www.vancouversun.com.

48. "Turn Your Feed into a Podcast," Lifehacker blog, 12 January 2006, www.lifehacker.com.

49. "Set Up Your Podcast for Success," FeedForAll website, accessed 4 October 2006, www.feedforall.com.

50. Shel Holtz, "Ten Guidelines for B2B Podcasts," Webpronews.com, 12 October 2005, www.webpronews.com.

51. Adapted from "Side Impact Protection Explained," Britax website, accessed 18 September 2008, www.britaxusa.com.

52. Adapted from Seymour Powell website, accessed 16 January 2007, www.seymourpowell.com; Sam Roberts, "51% of Women Now Living Without a Spouse," *New York Times*, 16 January 2007, www.nytimes.com.

53. Adapted from Crutchfield website, accessed 3 February 2011, www.crutchfield.com.

54. Adapted from Comic-Con website, accessed 19 July 2010, www.comic-con.org; Tom Spurgeon, "Welcome to Nerd Vegas: A Guide to Visiting and Enjoying Comic-Con International in San Diego, 2006!" The Comics Reporter.com, 11 July 2006, www.comicsreporter.com; Rebecca Winters Keegan, "Boys Who Like Toys," *Time*, 19 April 2007, www.time.com.

55. Adapted from "Major New Study Shatters Stereotypes About Teens and Video Games," MacArthur Foundation, 16 September 2008, www.macfound.org.

56. Adapted from *Logan* website, accessed 3 February 2011, www.loganmagazine.com.

57. JetBlue Twitter page, accessed 3 February 2011, http://twitter.com/JetBlue; "JetBlue Lands on eBay," JetBlue website, accessed 18 September 2008, http://jetblue.com/ebay.

LEARNING OBJECTIVES   After studying this chapter, you will be able to

1   Outline an effective strategy for writing routine business requests

2   Describe three common types of routine requests

3   Outline an effective strategy for writing routine replies and positive messages

4   Describe six common types of routine replies and positive messages

MyBcommLab   Where you see MyBcommLab in this chapter, go to www.pearsoninternationaleditions.com/mybcommlab for additional activities on the topic being discussed.

ON THE JOB: COMMUNICATING AT GET SATISFACTION

Get Satisfaction uses Web 2.0 tools such as community Q&A websites to address the widespread frustration with traditional approaches to customer support.
Source: © MGPhoto/Alamy

Using New Media Concepts to Solve an Age-Old Problem

For about as long as Internet communication has been possible, frustrated customers have been going online to complain about faulty products, confusing instructions, and poor service. When Web 2.0 tools hit the scene a few years ago, giving even nontechnical consumers a ready voice, the stream of "I need help!" messages turned into a full-time flood. On product review and shopping websites, enthusiast blogs, and various "complaint sites," consumers can vent their frustrations and ask for help when they feel they aren't getting satisfaction from the companies with which they do business.

These complaint sites can occasionally provide answers for visitors, but they suffer from four fundamental drawbacks. First, they are randomly scattered all over the Web, so many consumers are never quite sure where to look for help. Second, the right experts from the right companies are rarely involved, meaning that customers often have to rely on each other—which sometimes works but sometimes doesn't. Third, even companies that make a valiant effort to keep their customers satisfied know that everyone can benefit if customers can share ideas, learn from one another, and participate in ongoing conversations. Fourth, companies often find that multiple customers have the same routine questions, but communicating with all of them individually can be time-consuming and expensive.

The San Francisco–based company Get Satisfaction is working to address all these issues. CEO Thor Muller explains that the company is "creating a kind of social network designed for companies and customers to communicate with each other." Consumers can post questions or complaints and request email notification whenever a response is posted. If someone else has already posted the same complaint, all a visitor needs to do is ask to be notified when the issue is resolved, saving time for the people asking and answering questions. Consumers can also suggest ideas for new products and services or improvements to existing offerings.

On the other side of the relationship, employees from companies that sell products and services can register as official representatives to answer questions, solve problems, and solicit feedback. As both knowledgeable consumers and company representatives provide answers and solutions, the responses voted most useful rise to the top, ensuring that visitors always get the most helpful information available. Companies that use Get Satisfaction's services can deploy customer service capabilities on Facebook, Twitter, and their own company blogs to try to capture as many customer service conversations as possible.

As Muller explains, "When customers start to converge and talk, for many companies this is gold—real engagement with current or future customers." The idea certainly seems to be catching on, with nearly 50,000 companies now using Get Satisfaction to help their customers get satisfaction from the products and services they buy.[1]

http://getsatisfaction.com

Strategy for Routine Requests

Get Satisfaction's Thor Muller (profiled in the chapter opener) knows that much of the vital communication between a company and its customers is about routine matters, from product operation hints and technical support to refunds and ordering glitches. These messages fall into two groups: requests for information or action from another party, and a variety of routine and positive messages. Chapter 8 addresses these types of messages here; Chapter 9 covers messages in which you convey negative information, and Chapter 10 addresses persuasive messages.

Making requests is a routine part of business. In most cases, your audience will be prepared to comply, as long as you're not being unreasonable or asking people to do something they would expect you to do yourself. By applying a clear strategy and tailoring your approach to each situation, you'll be able to generate effective requests quickly.

For routine requests and positive messages
- State the request or main idea
- Give necessary details
- Close with a cordial request for specific action

Like all other business messages, a routine request has three parts: an opening, a body, and a close. Using the direct approach, open with your main idea, which is a clear statement of your request. Use the body to give details and justify your request. Finally, close by requesting specific action.

STATING YOUR REQUEST UP FRONT

Begin routine requests by placing your initial request first; up front is where it stands out and gets the most attention. Of course, getting right to the point should not be interpreted as license to be abrupt or tactless:

Take care that your direct approach doesn't come across as abrupt or tactless.

- **Pay attention to tone.** Even though you expect a favorable response, the tone of your initial request is important. Instead of demanding action ("Send me the latest personnel cost data"), soften your request with words such as *please* and *I would appreciate*.
- **Assume that your audience will comply.** An impatient demand for rapid service isn't necessary. You can generally assume that your readers will comply with your request when they clearly understand the reason for it.
- **Be specific.** State precisely what you want. For example, if you request the latest market data from your research department, be sure to say whether you want a 1-page summary or 100 pages of raw data.

EXPLAINING AND JUSTIFYING YOUR REQUEST

Use the body of your message to explain your request. Make the explanation a smooth and logical outgrowth of your opening remarks. If possible, point out how complying with the request could benefit the reader. For instance, if you would like some assistance interpreting complex quality-control data, you might point out how a better understanding of quality-control issues would improve customer satisfaction and ultimately lead to higher profits for the entire company.

Whether you're writing a formal letter or a simple instant message, you can use the body of your request to list a series of questions. These questions help organize your message and help your audience identify the information you need. Just keep in mind a few basics:

- **Ask the most important questions first.** If cost is your main concern, you might begin with a question such as "What is the cost for shipping the merchandise by air versus truck?" Then you might want to ask more specific but related questions about, say, discounts for paying early.
- **Ask only relevant questions.** To help expedite the response to your request, ask only questions that are central to your main request. Doing so will generate an answer sooner and make better use of the other person's time.
- **Deal with only one topic per question.** If you have an unusual or complex request, break it down into specific, individual questions so that the reader can address each one separately. Don't put the burden of untangling a complicated request on your reader. This consideration shows respect for your audience's time, and it probably will get you a more accurate answer in less time.

> If you have multiple requests or questions, start with the most important one.

REQUESTING SPECIFIC ACTION IN A COURTEOUS CLOSE

Close your message with three important elements: (1) a specific request, (2) information about how you can be reached (if it isn't obvious), and (3) an expression of appreciation or goodwill. When you ask readers to perform a specific action, ask for a response by a specific date or time, if appropriate (for example, "Please send the figures by May 5 so that I can return first-quarter results to you before the May 20 conference."). Plus, by including your phone number, email address, office hours, and other contact information, you help readers respond easily.

Conclude your message by sincerely expressing your goodwill and appreciation. However, don't thank the reader "in advance" for cooperating; many people find that presumptuous. And if the reader's reply warrants a word of thanks, send it after you've received the reply. To review, see "Checklist: Writing Routine Requests."

> Close request messages with
> - A request for some specific action
> - Information about how you can be reached
> - An expression of appreciation

Common Examples of Routine Requests

Many of the routine messages you'll be writing will likely fall into a few main categories: asking for information and action, asking for recommendations, and making claims and requesting adjustments.

2   LEARNING OBJECTIVE

Describe three common types of routine requests.

✓ Checklist | Writing Routine Requests

A. State your request up front.
- Write in a polite, undemanding, personal tone.
- Use the direct approach because your audience will probably respond favorably to your request.
- Be specific and precise in your request.

B. Explain and justify your request.
- Justify the request or explain its importance.

- Explain any potential benefits of responding.
- Ask the most important questions first.
- Break complex requests into individual questions that are limited to only one topic each.

C. Request specific action in a courteous close.
- Make it easy to comply by including appropriate contact information.
- Express your gratitude.
- Clearly state any important deadlines for the request.

ASKING FOR INFORMATION AND ACTION

When you need to know about something, elicit an opinion from someone, or request a simple action, you usually need only ask. In essence, simple requests say

- What you want to know or what you want the reader to do
- Why you're making the request
- Why it may be in your reader's interest to help you

Routine requests can be handled with simple, straightforward messages, but more complicated requests can require additional justification and explanation.

If your reader is able to do what you want, such a straightforward request will get the job done quickly. Use the direct approach by opening with a clear statement of your reason for writing. In the body, provide whatever explanation is needed to justify your request. Then close with a specific description of what you expect and include a deadline, if appropriate (see Figure 8.1). In some situations, readers might be unwilling to respond unless they understand how the request benefits them, so be sure to include this information in your explanation. You can assume some shared background when communicating about a routine matter to someone in the same company.

In contrast to requests sent internally, those sent to people outside the organization usually adopt a more formal tone, as in the following example:

Dear Bioverse:

The opening makes an overall request in polite question form (no question mark).

Please provide additional information on distribution opportunities for your Healthy Ponds product line, as mentioned on your website. Enviro Domestic is a 20-year-old firm with a well-established design, retail, and service presence in the Oklahoma City area, and we believe your bioremediation products would make a compelling addition to our offerings.

The writer identifies an affiliation and reason for writing.

The body specifies exactly what the writer wishes to know to assist the recipient in responding.

In particular, we would appreciate answers to the following questions:

1. Do you offer exclusive regional distribution contracts?
2. Do you offer factory training for sales and service specialists?
3. Do you plan to expand beyond water bioremediation solutions into other landscaping products?

The close makes a polite request and gives a specific answer deadline.

Please let us hear from you by February 15.

A more complex request might require not only greater detail but also information on how responding will benefit the reader.

ASKING FOR RECOMMENDATIONS

Always ask for permission before using someone as a reference.

The need to inquire about people arises often in business. For example, before extending credit or awarding contracts, jobs, promotions, or scholarships, companies often ask applicants to supply references: a list of people who can vouch for their ability, skills, integrity, character, and fitness for the job. Before you volunteer someone's name as a reference, ask permission to do so. Some people don't want you to use their names, perhaps because they don't know enough about you to feel comfortable writing a letter or because they or their employers have a policy of not providing recommendations.

Because requests for recommendations and references are routine, you can organize your inquiry using the direct approach. Open your message by clearly stating why the recommendation is needed (if it's not for a job, be sure to explain what it is for) and that you would like your reader to write the letter. If you haven't had contact with the person for

REAL-TIME UPDATES
Learn More by Reading This PDF

The right way to ask for recommendations on LinkedIn

Follow LinkedIn's etiquette guide for students and recent graduates to increase your response rate and to maintain positive networking connections. Go to http://real-timeupdates.com/ebct10 and click on Learn More. If you are using MyBcommLab, you can access Real-Time Updates within each chapter or under Student Study Tools.

1 Plan → 2 Write → 3 Complete

Analyze the Situation
Verify that the purpose is to request information from company managers.

Gather Information
Gather accurate, complete information about local competitive threats.

Select the Right Medium
Choose email for this internal message, which also allows the attachment of a Word document to collect the information.

Organize the Information
Clarify that the main idea is collecting information that will lead to a better competitive strategy, which will in turn help the various district managers.

Adapt to Your Audience
Show sensitivity to audience needs with a "you" attitude, politeness, positive emphasis, and bias-free language. The writer already has credibility, as manager of the department.

Compose the Message
Maintain a style that is conversational but still businesslike, using plain English and appropriate voice.

Revise the Message
Evaluate content and review readability; avoid unnecessary details.

Produce the Message
Simple email format is all the design this message needs.

Proofread the Message
Review for errors in layout, spelling, and mechanics.

Distribute the Message
Deliver the message via the company's email system.

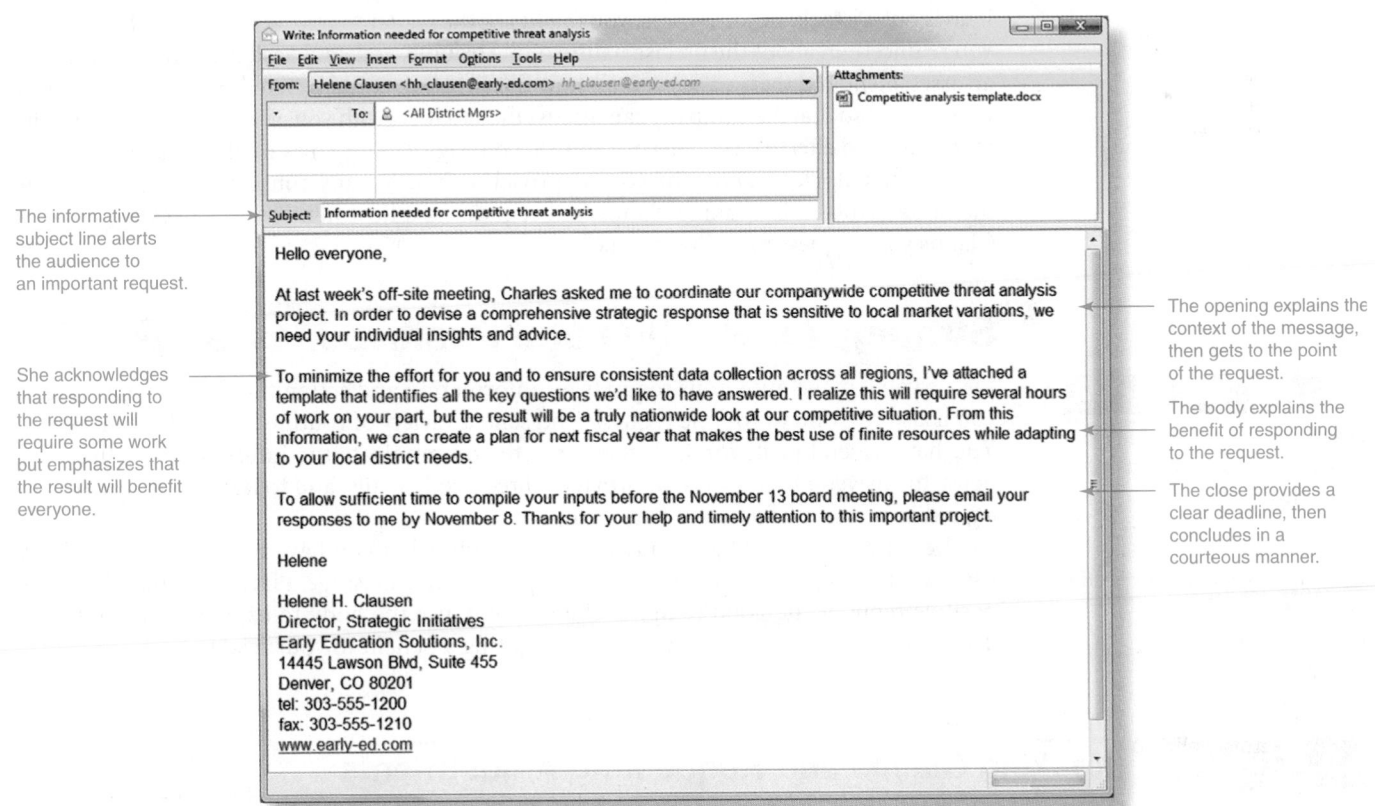

The informative subject line alerts the audience to an important request.

She acknowledges that responding to the request will require some work but emphasizes that the result will benefit everyone.

The opening explains the context of the message, then gets to the point of the request.

The body explains the benefit of responding to the request.

The close provides a clear deadline, then concludes in a courteous manner.

Figure 8.1 Effective Message Requesting Action
In this email request to district managers across the country, Helene Clausen asks them to fill out an attached information collection form. Although the request is not unusual and responding to it is part of the managers' responsibility, Clausen asks for their help in a courteous manner and points out the benefits of responding.

Refresh the memory of any potential references you haven't been in touch with for a while.

some time, use the opening to trigger the reader's memory of the relationship you had, the dates of association, and any special events that might bring a clear and favorable picture of you to mind. Consider including an updated résumé if you've had significant career advancement since your last contact.

Close your message with an expression of appreciation and the full name and address of the person to whom the letter should be sent. When asking for an immediate recommendation, you should also mention the deadline. Always be sure to enclose a stamped, preaddressed envelope as a convenience to the other party. Figure 8.2 provides an example of a request that follows these guidelines.

MAKING CLAIMS AND REQUESTING ADJUSTMENTS

If you're dissatisfied with a company's product or service, you can opt to make a **claim** (a formal complaint) or request an **adjustment** (a settlement of a claim). In either case, it's important to maintain a professional tone in all your communication, no matter how angry or frustrated you are. Keeping your cool will help you get the situation resolved sooner.

When making a claim
• Explain the problem and give details
• Provide backup information
• Request specific action

Be prepared to document any claims you make with a company. Send copies and keep the original documents.

In most cases, and especially in your first message, assume that a fair adjustment will be made, and use a direct request. Open with a straightforward statement of the problem. In the body, give a complete, specific explanation of the details; provide any information an adjuster would need to verify your complaint. In your close, politely request specific action or convey a sincere desire to find a solution. And, if appropriate, suggest that the business relationship will continue if the problem is solved satisfactorily. Be prepared to back up your claim with invoices, sales receipts, canceled checks, dated correspondence, and any other relevant documents. Send copies and keep the originals for your files.

If the remedy is obvious, tell your reader exactly what you expect from the company, such as exchanging incorrectly shipped merchandise for the right item or issuing a refund if the item is out of stock. In some cases, you might ask the reader to resolve a problem. However, if you're uncertain about the precise nature of the trouble, you could ask the company to make an assessment and then advise you on how the situation could be fixed. Supply your contact information so that the company can discuss the situation with you, if necessary. Compare the ineffective and effective versions in Figure 8.3 on page 270 for an example of making a claim.

A rational, clear, and courteous approach is best for any routine request. To review the tasks involved in making claims and requesting adjustments, see "Checklist: Making Claims and Requesting Adjustments."

Strategy for Routine and Positive Messages

3 **LEARNING OBJECTIVE**

Outline an effective strategy for writing routine replies and positive messages.

Just as you'll make numerous requests for information and action throughout your career, you'll also respond to routine requests and send a variety of routine and positive messages. You have several goals for such messages: to communicate the information or the good news, to answer all questions, to provide all required details, and to leave your reader with a good impression of you and your firm.

Use a direct approach for routine messages.

Because readers will generally be interested in what you have to say, you can usually use the direct approach with a routine reply or positive message. Place your main idea (the positive reply or the good news) in the opening, use the body to explain all the relevant details, and close cordially—perhaps highlighting a benefit to your reader.

✓ **Checklist** **Making Claims and Requesting Adjustments**

• Maintain a professional tone, even if you're extremely frustrated.
• Open with a straightforward statement of the problem.
• Provide specific details in the body.
• Present facts honestly and clearly.

• Politely summarize the desired action in the closing.
• Clearly state what you expect as a fair settlement or ask the reader to propose a fair adjustment.
• Explain the benefits of complying with the request, such as your continued patronage.

1 Plan → **2 Write** → **3 Complete**

Analyze the Situation
Verify that the purpose is to request a recommendation letter from a college professor.

Gather Information
Gather information on classes and dates to help the reader recall you and to clarify the position you seek.

Select the Right Medium
The letter format gives this message an appropriate level of formality, although many professors prefer to be contacted by an email.

Organize the Information
Messages like this are common and expected, so a direct approach is fine.

Adapt to Your Audience
Show sensitivity to audience needs with a "you" attitude, politeness, positive emphasis, and bias-free language.

Compose the Message
Style is respectful and businesslike, while still using plain English and appropriate voice.

Revise the Message
Evaluate content and review readability; avoid unnecessary details.

Produce the Message
Simple letter format is all the design this message needs.

Proofread the Message
Review for errors in layout, spelling, and mechanics.

Distribute the Message
Deliver the message via postal mail or email if you have the professor's email address.

1181 Ashport Drive
Tate Springs, TN 38101
March 14, 2012

Professor Lyndon Kenton
School of Business
University of Tennessee, Knoxville
Knoxville, TN 37916

Dear Professor Kenton:

I recently interviewed with Strategic Investments and have been called for a second interview for their Analyst Training Program (ATP). They have requested at least one recommendation from a professor, and I immediately thought of you. May I have a letter of recommendation from you?

As you may recall, I took BUS 485, Financial Analysis, from you in the fall of 2010. I enjoyed the class and finished the term with an "A." Professor Kenton, your comments on assertiveness and cold-calling impressed me beyond the scope of the actual course material. In fact, taking your course helped me decide on a future as a financial analyst.

My enclosed résumé includes all my relevant work experience and volunteer activities. I would also like to add that I've handled the financial planning for our family since my father passed away several years ago. Although I initially learned by trial and error, I have increasingly applied my business training in deciding what stocks or bonds to trade. This, I believe, has given me a practical edge over others who may be applying for the same job.

If possible, Ms. Blackmon in Human Resources needs to receive your letter by March 30. For your convenience, I've enclosed a preaddressed, stamped envelope.

I appreciate your time and effort in writing this letter of recommendation for me. It will be great to put my education to work, and I'll keep you informed of my progress. Thank you for your consideration in this matter.

Sincerely,

Joanne Tucker

Joanne Tucker

Enclosure

The opening states the purpose of the letter and makes the request, assuming the reader will want to comply with the request.

Tucker includes information near the opening to refresh her professor's memory.

The body refers to the enclosed résumé and mentions experience that could set the applicant apart from other candidates—information the professor could use in writing the recommendation.

She provides a deadline for response and includes information about the person who is expecting the recommendation.

The close mentions the preaddressed, stamped envelope to encourage a timely response.

Figure 8.2 Effective Letter Requesting a Recommendation
This writer uses the direct approach when asking for a recommendation from a former professor. Note how she takes care to refresh the professor's memory because she took the class a year and a half ago. She also indicates the date by which the letter is needed and points to the enclosure of a stamped, preaddressed envelope.

MyBcommLab

Apply Figure 8.3's key concepts by revising a new document. Go to Chapter 8 in www .pearsoninternationaleditions.com/mybcommlab and select Document Makeovers.

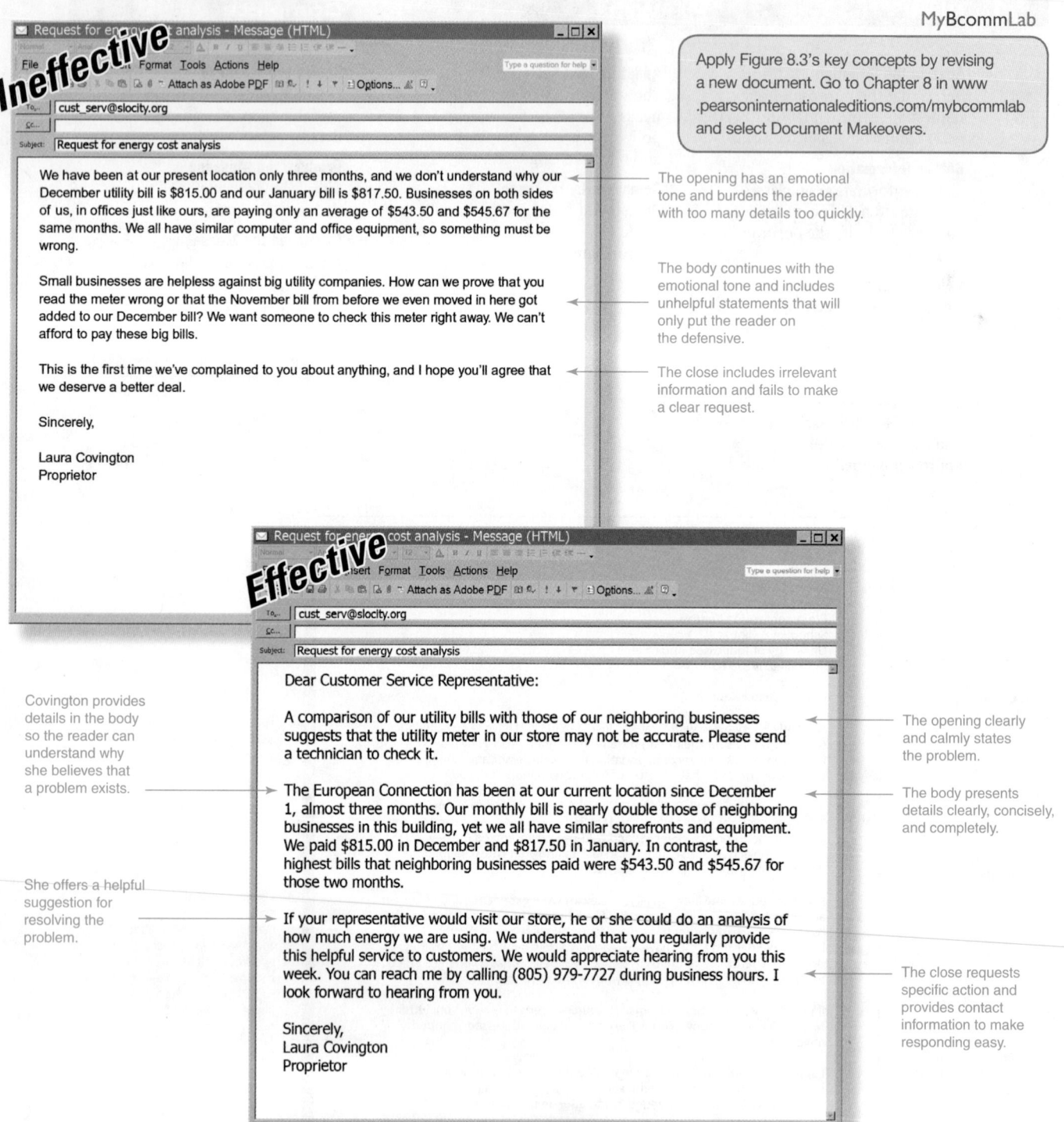

Ineffective

Request for energy cost analysis - Message (HTML)

To: cust_serv@slocity.org
Cc:
Subject: Request for energy cost analysis

We have been at our present location only three months, and we don't understand why our December utility bill is $815.00 and our January bill is $817.50. Businesses on both sides of us, in offices just like ours, are paying only an average of $543.50 and $545.67 for the same months. We all have similar computer and office equipment, so something must be wrong.

Small businesses are helpless against big utility companies. How can we prove that you read the meter wrong or that the November bill from before we even moved in here got added to our December bill? We want someone to check this meter right away. We can't afford to pay these big bills.

This is the first time we've complained to you about anything, and I hope you'll agree that we deserve a better deal.

Sincerely,

Laura Covington
Proprietor

The opening has an emotional tone and burdens the reader with too many details too quickly.

The body continues with the emotional tone and includes unhelpful statements that will only put the reader on the defensive.

The close includes irrelevant information and fails to make a clear request.

Effective

Request for energy cost analysis - Message (HTML)

To: cust_serv@slocity.org
Cc:
Subject: Request for energy cost analysis

Dear Customer Service Representative:

A comparison of our utility bills with those of our neighboring businesses suggests that the utility meter in our store may not be accurate. Please send a technician to check it.

The European Connection has been at our current location since December 1, almost three months. Our monthly bill is nearly double those of neighboring businesses in this building, yet we all have similar storefronts and equipment. We paid $815.00 in December and $817.50 in January. In contrast, the highest bills that neighboring businesses paid were $543.50 and $545.67 for those two months.

If your representative would visit our store, he or she could do an analysis of how much energy we are using. We understand that you regularly provide this helpful service to customers. We would appreciate hearing from you this week. You can reach me by calling (805) 979-7727 during business hours. I look forward to hearing from you.

Sincerely,
Laura Covington
Proprietor

Covington provides details in the body so the reader can understand why she believes that a problem exists.

She offers a helpful suggestion for resolving the problem.

The opening clearly and calmly states the problem.

The body presents details clearly, concisely, and completely.

The close requests specific action and provides contact information to make responding easy.

Figure 8.3   Ineffective and Effective Versions of a Claim
Note the difference in tone and information content in these two versions. The ineffective version is emotional and unprofessional, whereas the effective version communicates calmly and clearly.

STARTING WITH THE MAIN IDEA

By opening routine and positive messages with the main idea or good news, you're preparing your audience for the details that follow. Make your opening clear and concise. Although the following introductory statements make the same point, one is cluttered with unnecessary information that buries the purpose, whereas the other is brief and to the point:

With the direct approach, open with a clear and concise expression of the main idea or good news.

Instead of This	Write This
I am pleased to inform you that after careful consideration of a diverse and talented pool of applicants, each of whom did a thorough job of analyzing Trask Horton Pharmaceuticals's training needs, we have selected your bid.	Trask Horton Pharmaceuticals has accepted your bid to provide public speaking and presentation training to the sales staff.

The best way to write a clear opening is to have a clear idea of what you want to say. Ask yourself, "What is the single most important message I have for the audience?"

PROVIDING NECESSARY DETAILS AND EXPLANATION

Use the body to explain your point completely so that your audience won't be confused or doubtful about your meaning. As you provide the details, maintain the supportive tone established in the opening. This tone is easy to continue when your message is entirely positive, as in this example:

> Your educational background and internship have impressed us, and we believe you would be a valuable addition to Green Valley Properties. As discussed during your interview, your salary will be $4,300 per month, plus benefits. Please plan to meet with our benefits manager, Paula Sanchez, at 8 a.m. on Monday, March 21. She will assist you with all the paperwork necessary to tailor our benefit package to your family situation. She will also arrange various orientation activities to help you acclimate to our company.

However, if your routine message is mixed and must convey mildly disappointing information, put the negative portion of your message into as favorable a context as possible:

Try to embed any negative information in a positive context.

Instead of This	Write This
No, we no longer carry the Sportsgirl line of sweaters.	The new Olympic line has replaced the Sportsgirl sweaters that you asked about. Olympic features a wider range of colors and sizes and more contemporary styling.

In this example, the more complete description is less negative and emphasizes how the recipient can benefit from the change. Be careful, though: You can use negative information in this type of message *only* if you're reasonably sure the audience will respond positively. Otherwise, use the indirect approach (discussed in Chapter 9).

If you are communicating with a customer, you might also want to use the body of your message to assure the customer of the wisdom of his or her purchase selection (without being condescending or self-congratulatory). Using such favorable comments, often known as *resale*, is a good way to build customer relationships. These comments are commonly included in acknowledgments of orders and other routine announcements to customers, and they are most effective when they are relatively short and specific:

> The KitchenAid mixer you ordered is our best-selling model. It should meet your cooking needs for many years.

 **Checklist** | **Writing Routine Replies and Positive Messages**

A. Start with the main idea.
- Be clear and concise.
- Identify the single most important message before you start writing.

B. Provide necessary details and explanation.
- Explain your point completely to eliminate any confusion or lingering doubts.
- Maintain a supportive tone throughout.

- Embed negative statements in positive contexts or balance them with positive alternatives.
- Talk favorably about the choices the customer has made.

C. End with a courteous close.
- Let your readers know that you have their personal well-being in mind.
- If further action is required, tell readers how to proceed and encourage them to act promptly.

ENDING WITH A COURTEOUS CLOSE

Make sure audience members understand what to do next and how that action will benefit them.

Your message is more likely to succeed if your readers are left feeling that you have their best interests in mind. You can accomplish this task either by highlighting a benefit to the audience or by expressing appreciation or goodwill. If follow-up action is required, clearly state who will do what next. See "Checklist: Writing Routine Replies and Positive Messages" to review the primary tasks involved in this type of business message.

Common Examples of Routine and Positive Messages

4 LEARNING OBJECTIVE

Describe six common types of routine replies and positive messages.

Most routine and positive messages fall into six main categories: answers to requests for information and action, grants of claims and requests for adjustment, recommendations, routine information, good-news announcements, and goodwill messages.

ANSWERING REQUESTS FOR INFORMATION AND ACTION

Every professional answers requests for information and action from time to time. If the response to a request is a simple yes or some other straightforward information, the direct approach is appropriate. A prompt, gracious, and thorough response will positively influence how people think about you and the organization you represent.

When you're answering requests and a potential sale is involved, you have three main goals: (1) to respond to the inquiry and answer all questions, (2) to leave your reader with a good impression of you and your firm, and (3) to encourage the future sale. The following message meets all three objectives:

Here is the brochure "Entertainment Unlimited" that you requested. This booklet describes the vast array of entertainment options available to you with an Ocean Satellite Device (OSD).

On page 12 you'll find a list of the 338 channels that the OSD brings into your home. You'll have access to movies, sports, and music channels; 24-hour news channels; local channels; and all the major television networks. OSD gives you a clearer picture and more precise sound than those old-fashioned dishes that took up most of your yard—and OSD uses only a small dish that mounts easily on your roof.

More music, more cartoons, more experts, more news, and more sports are available to you with OSD than with any other cable or satellite connection in this region. It's all there, right at your fingertips.

Just call us at 1-800-786-4331, and an OSD representative will come to your home to answer your questions. You'll love the programming and the low monthly cost. Call us today!

GRANTING CLAIMS AND REQUESTS FOR ADJUSTMENT

Even the best-run companies make mistakes, from shipping the wrong order to billing a customer's credit card inaccurately. In other cases, a customer or a third party might be responsible for a mistake, such as misusing a product or damaging a product in shipment. Each of these events represents a turning point in your relationship with your customer. If you handle the situation well, your customer is likely to be even more loyal than before because you've proven that you're serious about customer satisfaction. However, if a customer believes that you mishandled a complaint, you'll make the situation even worse. Dissatisfied customers often take their business elsewhere without notice and tell numerous friends and colleagues about the negative experience. A transaction that might be worth only a few dollars by itself could cost you many times that amount in lost business. In other words, every mistake is an opportunity to improve a relationship.

Your response to a customer complaint depends on your company's policies for resolving such issues and your assessment of whether the company, the customer, or some third party is at fault.

Responding to a Claim When Your Company Is at Fault

Before you respond after your company has made a mistake, make sure you know your company's policies, which might dictate specific legal and financial steps to be taken. For serious problems that go beyond routine errors, your company should have a *crisis management plan* that outlines communication steps both inside and outside the organization (see Chapter 9).

Most routine responses should take your company's specific policies into account and do the following:

- Acknowledge receipt of the customer's claim or complaint.
- Sympathize with the customer's inconvenience or frustration.
- Take (or assign) personal responsibility for setting matters straight.
- Explain precisely how you have resolved, or plan to resolve, the situation.
- Take steps to repair the relationship.
- Follow up to verify that your response was correct.

In addition to taking these positive steps, maintain a professional demeanor. Don't blame anyone in your organization by name; don't make exaggerated, insincere apologies; don't imply that the customer is at fault; and don't promise more than you can deliver. See how this message acknowledges the problem, describes the action being taken, and works to rebuild the customer relationship:

> Maintain a sincere, professional tone when responding to a complaint.

Your email message concerning your recent Klondike order has been forwarded to our director of order fulfillment. Your complete satisfaction is our goal, and a customer service representative will contact you within 24 hours to assist with the issues raised in your letter.

In the meantime, please accept the enclosed $5 gift certificate as a token of our appreciation for your business. Whether you're skiing or driving a snowmobile, Klondike Gear offers you the best protection from wind, snow, and cold—and Klondike has been taking care of customers' outdoor needs for over 27 years.

Thank you for taking the time to write to us. Your input helps us better serve you and all our customers.

Responding to a Claim When the Customer Is at Fault

Communication about a claim is a delicate matter when the customer is clearly at fault. If you refuse the claim, you may lose your customer—as well as many of the customer's friends and colleagues, who will hear only one side of the dispute. You must weigh the cost of making the adjustment against the cost of losing future business from one or more customers. Some companies have strict guidelines for responding to such claims, whereas others give individual employees and managers some leeway in making case-by-case decisions.

If you choose to grant a claim, you can simply open with the good news, being sure to specify exactly what you're agreeing to do. The body of the message is tricky because you want to discourage such claims in the future by steering the customer in the right direction. For example, customers sometimes misuse products or fail to follow the terms of service agreements, such as forgetting to cancel hotel reservations at least 24 hours in advance and thereby incurring the cost of one night's stay. Even if you do grant a particular claim, you don't want to imply that you will grant similar claims in the future. The challenge is to diplomatically remind the customer of proper usage or procedures without being condescending ("Perhaps you failed to read the instructions carefully") or preachy ("You should know that wool shrinks in hot water"). Close in a courteous manner that expresses your appreciation for the customer's business (see Figure 8.4).

> To grant a claim when the customer is at fault, try to discourage future mistakes without insulting the customer.

Responding to a Claim When a Third Party Is at Fault

Sometimes neither your company nor your customer is at fault. For example, ordering a book from Amazon involves not only Amazon but also a delivery service such as UPS or the U.S. Postal Service, the publisher and possibly a distributor of the book, a credit card issuer, and a company that processes credit card transactions. Any one of these other partners might be at fault in the event of a problem, but the customer is likely to blame Amazon because that is the entity primarily responsible for the transaction.

> When a third party is at fault, your response depends on your company's agreements with that organization.

No general scheme applies to every case involving a third party, so evaluate the situation carefully and know your company's policies before responding. For instance, an online retailer and the companies that manufacture its merchandise might have an agreement which specifies that the manufacturers automatically handle all complaints about product quality. However, regardless of who eventually resolves the problem, if customers contact you, you need to respond with messages that explain how the problem will be solved. Pointing fingers is unproductive and unprofessional; resolving the situation is the only issue customers care about. See "Checklist: Granting Claims and Adjustment Requests" to review the tasks involved in these kinds of business messages.

PROVIDING RECOMMENDATIONS

When writing a letter of recommendation, your goal is to convince readers that the person being recommended has the characteristics necessary for the job, project assignment, scholarship, or other objective the person is seeking. A successful recommendation letter contains a number of relevant details (see Figure 8.5 on page 276):

- The candidate's full name
- The position or other objective the candidate is seeking

✔ Checklist | Granting Claims and Adjustment Requests

A. Responding when your company is at fault
- Be aware of your company's policies in such cases before you respond.
- For serious situations, refer to the company's crisis management plan.
- Start by acknowledging receipt of the claim or complaint.
- Take or assign personal responsibility for resolving the situation.
- Sympathize with the customer's frustration.
- Explain how you have resolved the situation (or plan to).
- Take steps to repair the customer relationship.
- Verify your response with the customer and keep the lines of communication open.

B. Responding when the customer is at fault
- Weigh the cost of complying with or refusing the request.
- If you choose to comply, open with the good news.
- Use the body of the message to respectfully educate the customer about steps needed to avoid a similar outcome in the future.
- Close with an appreciation for the customer's business.

C. Responding when a third party is at fault
- Evaluate the situation and review your company's policies before responding.
- Avoid placing blame; focus on the solution.
- Regardless of who is responsible for resolving the situation, let the customer know what will happen to resolve the problem.

1 Plan →

Analyze the Situation
The purpose is to grant the customer's claim, tactfully educate him, and encourage further business.

Gather Information
Gather information on product care, warranties, and resale information.

Select the Right Medium
An email message is appropriate in this case because the customer contacted the company via email.

Organize the Information
You're responding with a positive answer, so a direct approach is fine.

2 Write →

Adapt to Your Audience
Show sensitivity to audience needs with a "you" attitude, politeness, positive emphasis, and bias-free language.

Compose the Message
Style is respectful while still managing to educate the customer on product usage and maintenance.

3 Complete

Revise the Message
Evaluate content and review readability; avoid unnecessary details.

Produce the Message
Emphasize a clean, professional appearance.

Proofread the Message
Review for errors in layout, spelling, and mechanics.

Distribute the Message
Email the reply.

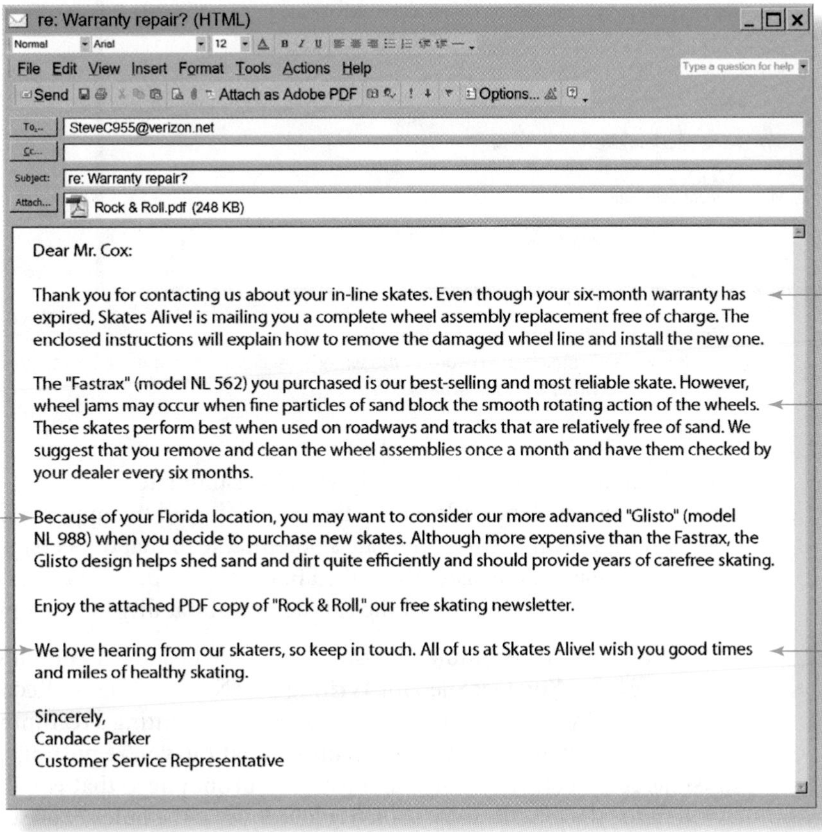

---

re: Warranty repair? (HTML)

File Edit View Insert Format Tools Actions Help

Send … Attach as Adobe PDF … Options…

To.. SteveC955@verizon.net
Cc..
Subject: re: Warranty repair?
Attach.. Rock & Roll.pdf (248 KB)

Dear Mr. Cox:

Thank you for contacting us about your in-line skates. Even though your six-month warranty has expired, Skates Alive! is mailing you a complete wheel assembly replacement free of charge. The enclosed instructions will explain how to remove the damaged wheel line and install the new one.

The "Fastrax" (model NL 562) you purchased is our best-selling and most reliable skate. However, wheel jams may occur when fine particles of sand block the smooth rotating action of the wheels. These skates perform best when used on roadways and tracks that are relatively free of sand. We suggest that you remove and clean the wheel assemblies once a month and have them checked by your dealer every six months.

Because of your Florida location, you may want to consider our more advanced "Glisto" (model NL 988) when you decide to purchase new skates. Although more expensive than the Fastrax, the Glisto design helps shed sand and dirt quite efficiently and should provide years of carefree skating.

Enjoy the attached PDF copy of "Rock & Roll," our free skating newsletter.

We love hearing from our skaters, so keep in touch. All of us at Skates Alive! wish you good times and miles of healthy skating.

Sincerely,
Candace Parker
Customer Service Representative

Annotations:

The opening acknowledges the customer's message, keeps the tone positive by avoiding words such as *mistake* or *failure*, and conveys the good news right away.

The body explains the problem without blaming the customer by avoiding the pronoun *you* and by suggesting ways to avoid future problems.

The writer subtly promotes a more appropriate product for the customer.

She closes on a positive note that conveys an attitude of excellent customer service.

The close gives the reader a glimpse into the corporate culture and encourages continued correspondence.

Figure 8.4   Responding to a Claim When the Buyer Is at Fault
In the interest of positive customer relationships, this company agreed to provide replacement parts for a customer's in-line skates, even though the product is outside its warranty period. (For the sake of clarity, the content of the customer's original email message is not reproduced here.)

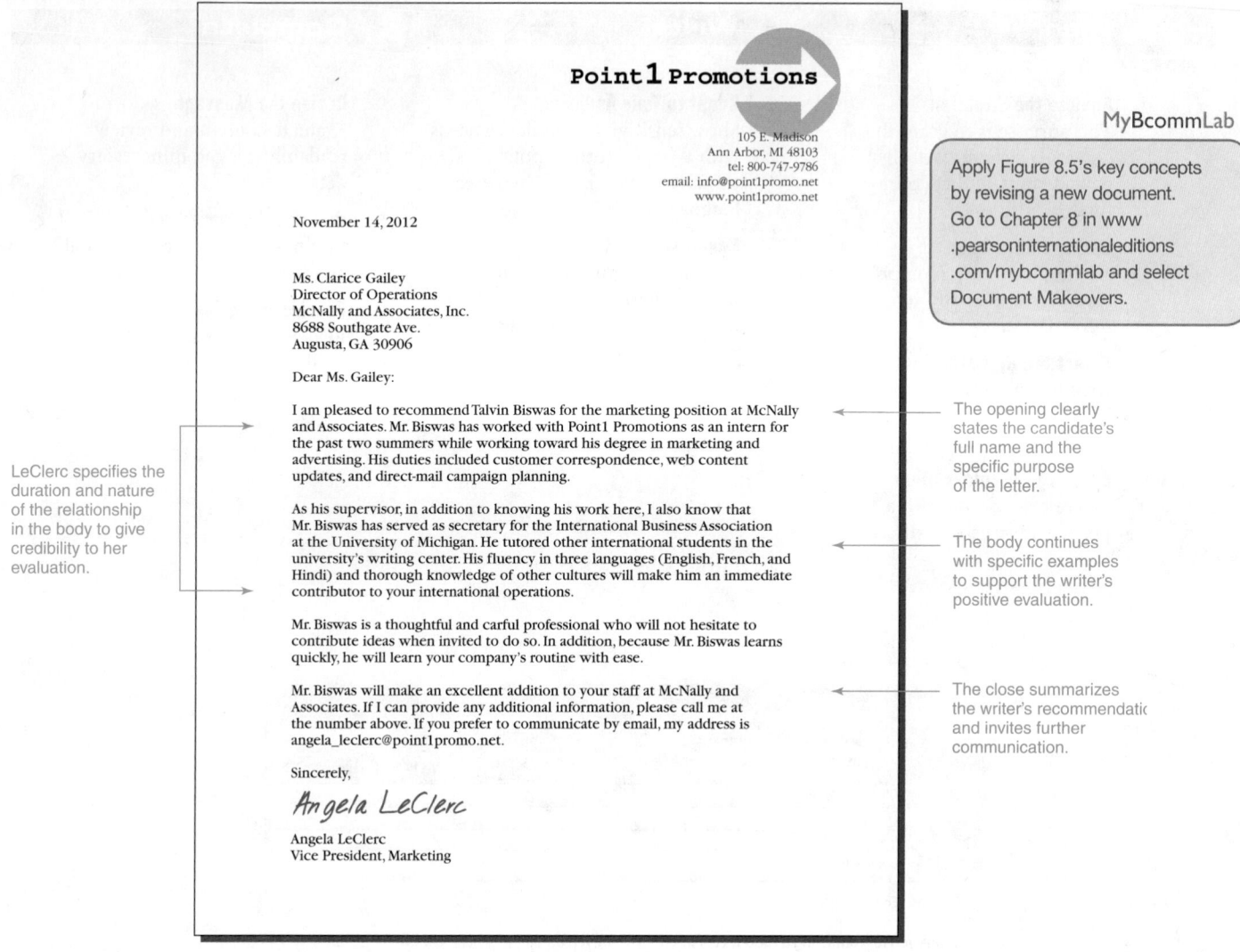

Figure 8.5 Effective Recommendation Letter
This letter clearly states the nature of the writer's relationship to the candidate and provides specific examples to support the writer's endorsements.

- The nature of your relationship with the candidate
- Facts and evidence relevant to the candidate and the opportunity
- A comparison of this candidate's potential with that of peers, if available (for example, "Ms. Jonasson consistently ranked in the top 10 percent of her class")
- Your overall evaluation of the candidate's suitability for the opportunity

Recommendation letters are vulnerable to legal complications, so consult with your company's legal department before writing one.

Be aware that recommendation letters have become a complex legal matter in recent years (see "Can You Get Sued for Writing—or Not Writing—a Recommendation Letter?"), so be sure to check your company's policies before writing a recommendation. Also, keep in mind that every time you write a recommendation, you're putting your own reputation on the line. If the person's shortcomings are so pronounced that you don't think he or she is a good fit for the job, the only choice is to not write the letter at all. Unless your relationship with the person warrants an explanation, simply suggest that someone else might be in a better position to provide a recommendation.

SHARING ROUTINE INFORMATION

When writing routine informational messages
- State the purpose at the beginning and briefly mention the nature of the information you are providing
- Provide the necessary details
- End with a courteous close

Many messages involve sharing routine information, such as project updates and order status notifications. Use the opening of these routine messages to state the purpose and briefly

COMMUNICATION MISCUES

Can You Get Sued for Writing— or Not Writing—a Recommendation Letter?

Recommendation letters are classified as routine messages, but with all the legal troubles they can cause employers these days, they've become anything but routine. Over the years, employees have won lawsuits that charged former employers with defamation related to job recommendations. In addition to defamation charges—which can be successfully defended if the "defamatory" statements are proven to be true—employers have been sued for retaliation by ex-employees who believed that negative letters were written expressly for purposes of revenge. And as if that weren't enough, employers have even sued each other over recommendation letters when the recipient of a letter believed the writer failed to disclose important negative information.

No wonder many companies now refuse to divulge anything more than job titles and dates of employment. But even that doesn't always solve the problem: Ex-employees have been known to sue for retaliation when their employers refused to write on their behalf. As you can imagine, this refusal to write recommendations creates worries for hiring companies. If they can't get any real background information on job candidates, they risk hiring employees who lack the necessary skills or who are disruptive or even dangerous in the workplace.

For companies that let managers write recommendations, what sort of information should or should not be included? Even though the majority of states now have laws protecting companies against recommendation-related lawsuits when the employer acts in good faith, individual cases vary so much that no specific guidelines can ever apply to all cases. However, answering the following questions before drafting a recommendation letter will help you avoid trouble:

- Does the party receiving this personal information have a legitimate right to it?

- Does all the information I've presented relate directly to the job or benefit being sought?
- Have I put the candidate's case as strongly and as honestly as I can?
- Have I avoided overstating the candidate's abilities or otherwise misleading the reader?
- Have I based all my statements on firsthand knowledge and provable facts?

No matter what the circumstances, experts also advise that you always consult your human resources or legal department for advice.

CAREER APPLICATIONS

1. A former employee was often late for work but was an excellent and fast worker who got along well with everyone. Do you think it's important to mention the tardiness to potential employers? If so, how would you handle it?
2. Step outside yourself for a moment and write a letter of recommendation about you from a former employer's perspective. Make sure your letter embodies honesty, integrity, and prudence.

Sources: Adapted from "How to Write Reference Letters," National Association of Colleges and Employers website, accessed 5 July 2010, www.naceweb.org; Diane Cadrain, "HR Professionals Stymied by Vanishing Job References," *HR Magazine*, November 2004, 31–40; "Five (or More) Ways You Can Be Sued for Writing (or Not Writing) Recommendation Letters," *Fair Employment Practice Guidelines*, July 2006, 1, 3–4; Rochelle Kaplan, "Writing a Recommendation Letter," National Association of Colleges and Employers website, accessed 12 October 2006, www.naceweb.org; Maura Dolan and Stuart Silverstein, "Court Broadens Liability for Job References," *Los Angeles Times*, 28 January 1997, A1, A11; David A. Price, "Good References Pave Road to Court," *USA Today*, 13 February 1997, 11A; Frances A. McMorris, "Ex-Bosses Face Less Peril Giving Honest Job References," *Wall Street Journal*, 8 July 1996, B1, B8.

mention the nature of the information you are providing. Provide the necessary details in the body and end your message with a courteous close (see Figure 8.6 on the next page).

Most routine communications are neutral. That is, they stimulate neither a positive nor a negative response from readers. For example, when you send departmental meeting announcements and reminder notices, you'll generally receive a neutral response from your readers (unless the purpose of the meeting is unwelcome). Simply present the factual information in the body of the message and don't worry too much about the reader's attitude toward the information.

Some routine informative messages may require additional care. For instance, policy statements or procedural changes may be good news for a company, perhaps by saving money. However, it may not be obvious to employees that such savings may make additional employee resources available or even lead to pay raises. In instances in which the reader may not initially view the information positively, use

REAL-TIME UPDATES
Learn More by Reading This Article

Get expert tips on writing (or requesting) a letter of recommendation

Find helpful advice on employment recommendations, academic recommendations, and character references. Go to http://realtimeupdates.com/ebct10 and click on Learn More. If you are using MyBcommLab, you can access Real-Time Updates within each chapter or under Student Study Tools.

The note has a clear and concise title that avoids puns and wordplay.

Facebook Notes lets writers include photos and other images in their notes.

The note is succinct while emphasizing the most vital point (that a previously announced purchase promotion was ending early).

The note directs U.S. and Canadian customers to separate websites, thereby providing each audience with the specific information it needs.

Figure 8.6 Routine Informational Message
Many companies use the Notes tab on their Facebook pages to share routine informational messages with their customers and other parties.
Source: www.facebook.com/Britax.

If a policy change or other announcement could have a profound negative effect on the audience, the indirect approach covered in Chapter 9 is usually preferred.

the body of the message to highlight the potential benefits from the reader's perspective. (For situations in which negative news will have a profound effect on the recipients, consider the indirect techniques discussed in Chapter 9.)

ANNOUNCING GOOD NEWS

To develop and maintain good relationships, smart companies recognize that it's good business to spread the word about positive developments. Such developments can include opening new facilities, hiring a new executive, introducing new products or services, or sponsoring community events. Because good news is always welcome, use the direct approach (see Figure 8.7).

A news release, also known as a press release, is a standardized way to share information with the news media.

Good-news announcements are often communicated in a **news release**, also known as a *press release*, a specialized document used to share relevant information with the news media. (News releases are also used to announce negative news, such as plant closings.) In most companies, news releases are usually prepared or at least supervised by specially trained writers in the public relations department. The content follows the customary pattern for a positive message: good news followed by details and a positive close. However, traditional news releases have a critical difference: You're not writing directly to the ultimate audience (such as the readers of a newspaper); you're trying to interest an editor or a reporter in a story, and that person will then write the material that is eventually read by the larger audience. To write a successful news release, keep the following points in mind:[2]

- Above all else, make sure your information is newsworthy and relevant to the specific publications or websites to which you are sending it.
- Focus on one subject; don't try to pack a single news release with multiple, unrelated news items.
- Put your most important idea first. Don't force editors to hunt for the news.
- Be brief: Break up long sentences and keep paragraphs short.

- Eliminate clutter, such as redundancy and extraneous facts.
- Be as specific as possible.
- Minimize self-congratulatory adjectives and adverbs; if the content of your message is newsworthy, the media professionals will be interested in the news on its own merits.
- Follow established industry conventions for style, punctuation, and format.

Until recently, news releases were crafted in a way to provide information to reporters, who would then write their own articles if the subject matter was interesting to their readers. Thanks to the Internet and social media, however, the nature of the news release is changing. Many companies now view it as a general-purpose tool for communicating directly with customers and other audiences, creating *direct-to-consumer news releases*. As media expert David Meerman Scott puts it, "Millions of people read press releases directly, unfiltered by the media. You need to be speaking directly to them."[3]

The newest twist on news releases is the *social media release*, which has several advantages over the traditional release. First, the social media release emphasizes bullet-point content over narrative paragraphs so that bloggers, editors, and others can assemble their own stories, rather than being forced to rewrite the material in a traditional release. Second, as an electronic-only document (a specialized webpage, essentially), the social media release offers the ability to include videos and other multimedia elements. Third, social bookmarking buttons make it easy for people to help publicize the content.[4]

> Many companies now release news directly to the public, rather than relying on the news media to share it.

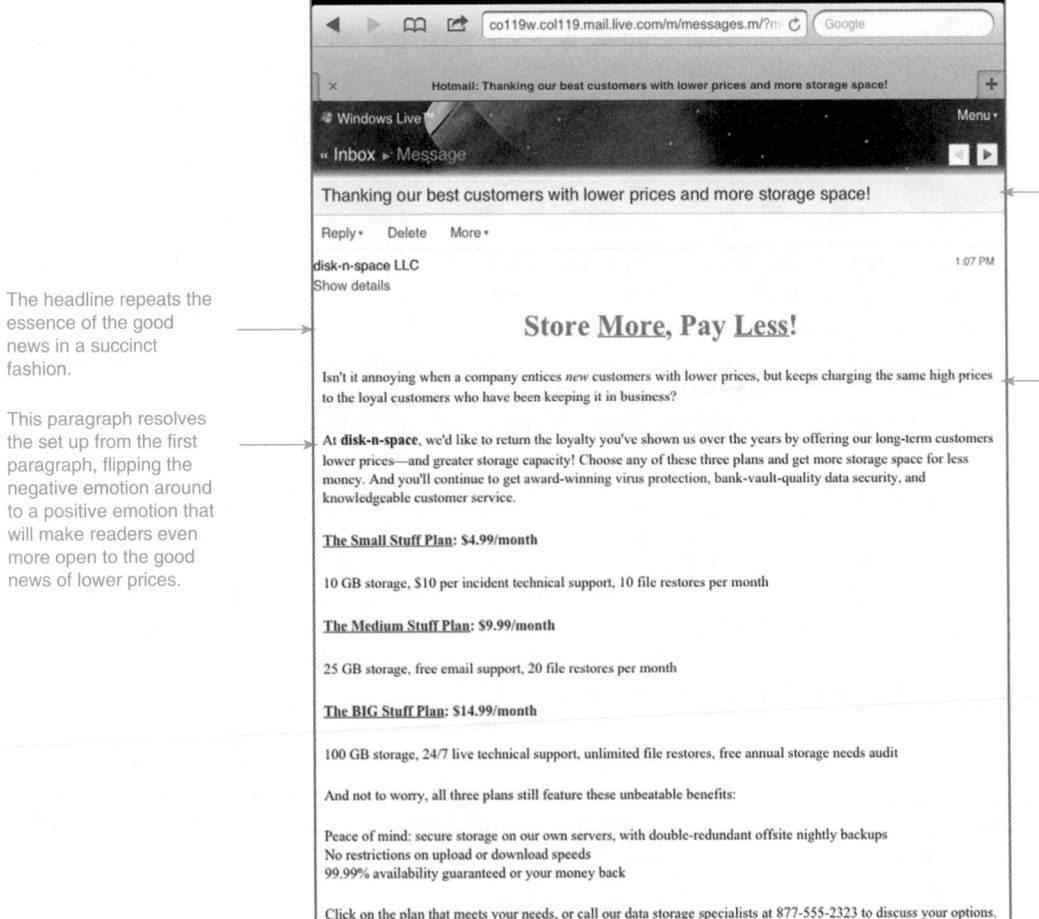

> The headline repeats the essence of the good news in a succinct fashion.

> This paragraph resolves the set up from the first paragraph, flipping the negative emotion around to a positive emotion that will make readers even more open to the good news of lower prices.

> The email subject line announces the good news.

> In this slightly modified version of the direct approach, this sentence builds on the idea of "thanking our best customers" by hitting an emotional hot button for many customers. This "set up" is then resolved in the next paragraph.

Figure 8.7   Announcing Positive News
This email message announcing lower prices for online backup service uses the direct approach, starting with sharing the positive news in the subject line.

FOSTERING GOODWILL

Goodwill is the positive feeling that encourages people to maintain a business relationship.

All business messages should be written with an eye toward fostering goodwill among business contacts, but some messages are written primarily and specifically to build goodwill. You can use these messages to enhance your relationships with customers, colleagues, and other business-people by sending friendly—even unexpected—notes with no direct business purpose.

Make sure your compliments are both sincere and honest.

Effective goodwill messages must be sincere and honest. Otherwise, you'll appear to be interested in personal gain rather than in benefiting customers, fellow workers, or your organization. To come across as sincere, avoid exaggerating and back up any compliments with specific points. In addition, readers often regard more restrained praise as being more sincere. Consider the following example:

Instead of This	Write This
Words cannot express my appreciation for the great job you did. Thanks. No one could have done it better. You're terrific! You've made the whole firm sit up and take notice, and we are ecstatic to have you working here.	Thanks again for taking charge of the meeting in my absence and doing such an excellent job. With just an hour's notice, you managed to pull the legal and public relations departments together so that we could present a united front in the negotiations. Your dedication and communication abilities have been noted and are truly appreciated.

Even though the second version is longer, it is a more effective message because it is specific and sincere.

Sending Congratulations

One prime opportunity for sending goodwill messages is to congratulate individuals or companies for significant business achievements (see Figure 8.8). Other reasons for sending congratulations include the highlights in people's personal lives, such as weddings, births, graduations, and success in nonbusiness competitions. Obviously, the nature of your relationship with a recipient determines the ranges of appropriate subjects for congratulations.

Taking note of significant events in someone's personal life helps foster the business relationship.

Sending Messages of Appreciation

An important managerial quality is the ability to recognize the contributions of employees, colleagues, suppliers, and other associates. Your praise does more than just make the person feel good; it encourages further excellence. Moreover, a message of appreciation may become an important part of someone's personnel file. So when you write a message of appreciation, try to specifically mention the person or people you want to praise. The brief message that follows expresses gratitude and reveals the happy result:

An effective message of appreciation documents a person's contributions.

Thank you and everyone on your team for the heroic efforts you took to bring our servers back up after last Friday's flood. We were able to restore business right on schedule first thing Monday morning. You went far beyond the level of contractual service in restoring our data center within 16 hours. I would especially like to highlight the contribution of networking specialist Julienne Marks, who worked for 12 straight hours to reconnect our Internet service. If I can serve as a reference in your future sales activities, please do not hesitate to ask.

The primary purpose of condolence messages is to let the audience know that you and the organization you represent care about the person's loss.

Hearing a sincere thank you can do wonders for morale.[5] Moreover, in today's electronic media environment, a handwritten thank-you note can be a particularly welcome acknowledgment.[6]

Offering Condolences

In times of serious trouble and deep sadness, well-written condolences and expressions of sympathy can mean a great deal to people who've experienced loss. This type of message is difficult to write, but don't let the difficulty of the task keep you from responding promptly.

REAL-TIME UPDATES
Learn More by Reading This Article

Simple rules for writing effective thank-you notes

These tips are easy to adapt to any business or social occasions in which you need to express appreciation. Go to http://real-timeupdates.com/ebct10 and click on Learn More. If you are using MyBcommLab, you can access Real-Time Updates within each chapter or under Student Study Tools.

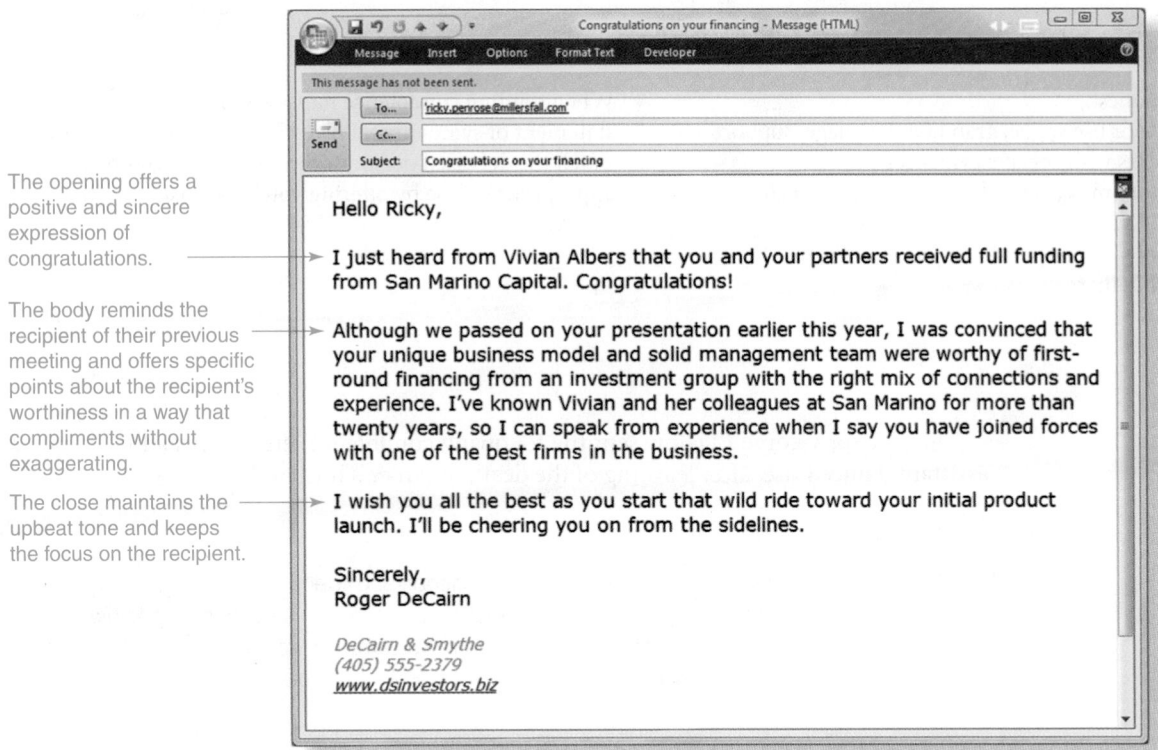

The opening offers a positive and sincere expression of congratulations.

The body reminds the recipient of their previous meeting and offers specific points about the recipient's worthiness in a way that compliments without exaggerating.

The close maintains the upbeat tone and keeps the focus on the recipient.

Figure 8.8 Goodwill Messages
Goodwill messages serve a variety of business functions. In this email message, investor Roger DeCairn congratulates an entrepreneur who had previously sought start-up capital from his firm but later secured funding from another firm. The message may ultimately benefit DeCairn and his company by building goodwill, but it doesn't serve an immediate business purpose.

Open a condolence message with a brief statement of sympathy, such as "I am deeply sorry to hear of your loss" in the event of a death, for example. In the body, mention the good qualities or the positive contributions made by the deceased. State what the person meant to you or your colleagues. In closing, you can offer your condolences and your best wishes. Here are a few general suggestions for writing condolence messages:[7]

- **Keep reminiscences brief.** Recount a memory, if appropriate, but don't dwell on the details of the loss.
- **Write in your own words.** Write as if you were speaking privately to the person. Don't quote "poetic" passages or use stilted or formal phrases.
- **Be tactful.** Mention your shock and dismay but remember that bereaved and distressed loved ones take little comfort in lines such as "Richard was too young to die" or "Starting all over again will be so difficult." Try to strike a balance between superficial expressions of sympathy and painful references to a happier past or the likelihood of a bleak future.
- **Take special care.** Be sure to spell names correctly and be accurate in your review of facts. Write and deliver your message promptly.
- **Write about special qualities of the deceased.** You may have to rely on reputation to do this, but let the grieving person know you valued his or her loved one.
- **Consider mentioning special attributes or resources of the bereaved person.** If you know that the bereaved person has attributes or resources that will be a comfort in the time of loss, such as personal resilience, religious faith, or a circle of close friends, mentioning these can make the reader feel more confident about handling the challenges he or she faces.

✔ Checklist Sending Goodwill Messages

- Be sincere and honest.
- Don't exaggerate or use vague, grandiose language; support positive statements with specific evidence.
- Use congratulatory messages to build goodwill with clients and colleagues.
- Send messages of appreciation to emphasize how much you value the work of others.

- When sending condolence messages, open with a brief statement of sympathy followed by an expression of how much the deceased person meant to you or your firm (as appropriate); close by offering your best wishes for the future.

Supervisor George Bigalow sent the following condolence letter to his administrative assistant, Janice Case, after learning of the death of Janice's husband:

> My sympathy to you and your children. All your friends at Carter Electric were so sorry to learn of John's death. Although I never had the opportunity to meet him, I do know how special he was to you. Your tales of your family's camping trips and his rafting expeditions were always memorable.

To review the tasks involved in writing goodwill messages, see "Checklist: Sending Goodwill Messages." For the latest information on writing routine and positive messages, visit http://real-timeupdates.com/ebct10.

ON THE JOB: SOLVING COMMUNICATION DILEMMAS AT **GET SATISFACTION**

Source: MGPhoto/Alamy

After reading the many helpful responses you, as a representative of your company, posted on the Get Satisfaction website, new CEO Wendy Lea invited you to join the Get Satisfaction team as a customer service specialist; your job is to communicate with the companies that use Get Satisfaction's online services. Take what you've learned in this chapter and put it to good use as you address the following challenges. (View some of the postings for various companies on http://getsatisfaction.com to get a feel for how the system works.)[8]

1. When people are frustrated with a problem and are trying to discuss it via a lean medium such as online postings, emotions can sometimes boil over. You've been monitoring a conversation between a representative for one of the companies that uses Get Satisfaction and one of its customers. Over the past couple of days, their online conversation has turned into an ugly argument, with accusations of incompetence and even dishonesty flying back and forth. Although the situation doesn't involve Get Satisfaction directly, you think it reflects poorly on your company because the dispute is taking place in full public view on your website—and it certainly isn't doing anybody any good to let this "flame war" keep raging. What is the best way to handle this situation?
   a. Email the company representative privately and offer to mediate the dispute.
   b. Post a public message offering to mediate the dispute.
   c. Post a public message reminding both sides to be civil.
   d. Ignore the dispute; it's between the company and its customer.

2. Web-based businesses occasionally suffer from "page loading" problems, when a particular webpage that a visitor requests will not display, even when the rest of a website seems to be working normally. Get Satisfaction recently had a spate of these problems. Which of these is the best way to respond to queries while the company is working to fix the situation?
   a. Yes, we've noticed this problem ourselves, but we hope to have everything stabilized soon.

b. We are soooooo sorry! We're working to resolve the situation as soon as possible.

c. Don't you just hate computers sometimes? We're working to resolve the situation as soon as possible.

d. We're having some problems with our host, which seems to be resulting in a lot of these errors. We're working on it now and hope to have everything stabilized soon.

3. Get Satisfaction recently released version 2.0 of its software. Which of the following is the best one-sentence summary of this major milestone?

a. Version 2.0 is a major update that unleashes the full value of the customer community to answer questions, solve problems, and collect ideas for developing the next generation of your products and services.

b. Version 2.0 rocks in every way imaginable.

c. Version 2.0 is our best work yet. It clearly shows how far we've come as a company and how much we've learned in the last two years.

d. Version 2.0 is a major update, incorporating multiple new features, expanded customizability, and a vastly improved and simplified user interface.

4. Get Satisfaction has just announced an *enterprise* version of its customer support software that companies can customize as part of their own information systems. The software is available in *beta release* form, a free prerelease version that software companies often release to encourage people to use as a way to see if anything needs to be changed or fixed before the official product is released. Get Satisfaction hasn't yet announced how much the software is going to cost when it is officially released, so not surprisingly, more than a few interested customers have written questions about the anticipated price. Small business owners in particular want to know if a less expensive version will be available to small companies. The company is working on a pricing structure that would charge by the volume of usage, meaning that small companies would probably pay less than large companies. Which of the following responses is the most effective response to this question?

a. The pricing structure will be announced when the product is ready for formal release.

b. We can't specify exact pricing yet, because we're still working on those details.

c. We can't specify exact pricing yet, because we're still working on those details. We will make sure that the pricing structure does in fact work both for small companies and large ones, and that if there is a tiered structure, that it scales according to a reliable set of figures/metrics that reflect those size differences.

d. We can't specify exact pricing yet, because we're still working on those details. However, we are trying to figure out a tiered pricing structure that would be fair to both large and small companies.

LEARNING OBJECTIVES CHECKUP

Assess your understanding of the principles in this chapter by reading each learning objective and studying the accompanying exercises. For fill-in-the-blank items, write the missing text in the blank provided; for multiple-choice items, circle the letter of the correct answer. You can check your responses against the answer key on page AK-2.

Objective 8.1: Outline an effective strategy for writing routine requests.

1. When it comes to routine messages, you can
   a. Skip the planning stage
   b. Keep the planning stage brief
   c. Begin by gathering all the information you'll need
   d. Begin by choosing the channel and medium

2. When writing routine messages, you
   a. Can assume that your readers will be interested or neutral
   b. Should open with an "attention getter"
   c. Should use the indirect approach with most audiences
   d. Need not allow much time for revision, production, or proofreading

3. When writing a routine request, the best approach is to begin
   a. With a personal introduction, such as "My name is Lee Marrs, and I am . . ."
   b. With a vague reference to what you are writing about, such as "I have something to ask you."
   c. With a strong demand for action
   d. By politely stating your request

4. What should you do when asking questions in a routine request?
   a. Begin with the least important question and work your way up to the most important question.
   b. Include all possible questions about the topic, even if the list gets long.
   c. Deal with only one topic per question.
   d. Do all of the above.

5. Which of the following should you do when closing a routine request?
   a. Be sure to thank the reader "in advance" for complying with the request.
   b. Ask the reader to respond by a specific and appropriate time.
   c. Ask any remaining questions you have.
   d. Do all of the above.

6. A courteous close contains
   a. A specific request
   b. Information about how you can be reached (if it isn't obvious)
   c. An expression of appreciation or goodwill
   d. All of the above

Objective 8.2: Describe three common types of routine requests.

7. Which of the following would be an inappropriate goal for a routine, simple request?
   a. Explaining what you want to know or what you want the reader to do
   b. Explaining why you're making the request
   c. Explaining how you can use your position in the company to force the reader to comply
   d. Explaining why it may be in your reader's interest to help you

8. Requests for recommendations and references are routine messages, so you can organize your inquiry using the _____ approach.

9. If you are requesting an adjustment from a company but you're not sure what the best solution would be, which of the following tactics would be best?
   a. Ask the company to assess the situation and offer advice on solving the problem
   b. Don't ask for a solution, because doing so could lead to a suboptimal outcome for you
   c. Subtly hint that legal action could light a fire under the company
   d. Demand that the company solve the problem immediately; after all, it's the right thing to do

Objective 8.3: Outline an effective strategy for writing routine replies and positive messages.

10. If you are making a routine reply to a customer, it's a good idea to
    a. Leave out any negative information
    b. Include resale information to assure the customer of the wisdom of his or her purchase
    c. Leave out sales promotion material, which would be tacky to include
    d. Do all of the above

11. A positive message should open with a clear and concise statement of the _____ _____.

12. If a message has both positive and negative elements, you should
    a. Always start with the bad news to get it out of the way first
    b. Write two separate messages; never mix good and bad news
    c. Put the bad news in a postscript (p.s.) at the bottom of the letter
    d. Try to put the negative news in a positive context

Objective 8.4: Describe six common types of routine replies and positive messages.

13. Which of the following is not among the recommended elements to include in your message if you are responding to a claim or complaint when your company is at fault?
    a. An acknowledgement that you received the customer's claim or complaint
    b. An expression of sympathy for the inconvenience or loss the customer has experienced
    c. An explanation of how you will resolve the situation
    d. Complete contact information for your corporate legal staff

14. If a customer who is clearly at fault requests an adjustment, you should
    a. Ignore the request; the customer is clearly wasting your time
    b. Carefully weigh the cost of complying with the request against the cost of denying it and then decide how to respond based on the overall impact on your company
    c. Always agree to such requests because unhappy customers spread bad publicity about a company
    d. Suggest in a firm but professional tone that the customer take his or her business elsewhere in the future

15. If a third party (such as a shipping company) is at fault when one of your customers makes a claim or requests an adjustment, the best response is to
    a. Follow the terms of whatever customer service agreement your company has with the third party
    b. Explain to the customer that your company is not at fault
    c. Always grant the request; after all, it's your customer, and the customer holds you responsible
    d. Forward the message to the third party as quickly as possible

16. The purpose of goodwill messages is to
    a. Generate sales
    b. Impress others
    c. Make yourself feel better
    d. Enhance relationships with customers, colleagues, and other businesspeople

17. The most effective goodwill messages
    a. Always try to find an "angle" that benefits the sender in addition to the receiver
    b. Avoid details and focus on the emotions of the situation
    c. Are sincere and honest
    d. Do all of the above

MyBcommLab

CHAPTER OUTLINE

Strategy for Routine Requests

Stating Your Request Up Front

Explaining and Justifying Your Request

Requesting Specific Action in a Courteous Close

Common Examples of Routine Requests

Asking for Information and Action

Asking for Recommendations

Making Claims and Requesting Adjustments

Strategy for Routine and Positive Messages

Starting with the Main Idea

Providing Necessary Details and Explanation

Ending with a Courteous Close

Common Examples of Routine and Positive Messages

Answering Requests for Information and Action

Granting Claims and Requests for Adjustment

Providing Recommendations

Sharing Routine Information

Announcing Good News

Fostering Goodwill

LEARNING OBJECTIVES

1. Outline an effective strategy for writing routine business requests. [page 264]
2. Describe three common types of routine requests. [page 265]
3. Outline an effective strategy for writing routine replies and positive messages. [page 268]
4. Describe six common types of routine replies and positive messages. [page 272]

KEY TERMS

claim A formal complaint made in response to dissatisfaction over a product or service

adjustment The settlement of a claim

news release Also known as a *press release*, a specialized document traditionally used to share relevant information with the local or national news media; today, many companies issue news releases directly to the public as well

✓ Checklist

Writing Routine Requests

A. **State your request up front.**
  - Write in a polite, undemanding, personal tone.
  - Use the direct approach because your audience will probably respond favorably to your request.
  - Be specific and precise in your request.

B. **Explain and justify your request.**
  - Justify the request or explain its importance.
  - Explain any potential benefits of responding.
  - Ask the most important questions first.
  - Break complex requests into individual questions that are limited to only one topic each.

C. **Request specific action in a courteous close.**
  - Make it easy to comply by including appropriate contact information.
  - Express your gratitude.
  - Clearly state any important deadlines for the request.

✓ Checklist

Writing Routine Replies and Informational Messages

A. **Start with the main idea.**
  - Be clear and concise.
  - Identify the single most important message before you start writing.

B. **Provide necessary details and explanation.**
  - Explain your point completely to eliminate any confusion or lingering doubts.
  - Maintain a supportive tone throughout.

  - Embed negative statements in positive contexts or balance them with positive alternatives.
  - Talk favorably about the choices the customer has made, if appropriate.

C. **End with a courteous close.**
  - Let your readers know that you have their personal well-being in mind.
  - If further action is required, tell readers how to proceed and encourage them to act promptly.

✓ Checklist

Sending Goodwill Messages

  - Be sincere and honest.
  - Don't exaggerate or use vague, grandiose language; support positive statements with specific evidence.
  - Use congratulatory messages to build goodwill with clients and colleagues.
  - Send messages of appreciation to emphasize how much you value the work of others.
  - When sending condolence messages, open with a brief statement of sympathy followed by an expression of how much the deceased person meant to you or your firm (as appropriate); close by offering your best wishes for the future.

APPLY YOUR KNOWLEDGE

To review chapter content related to each question, refer to the indicated Learning Objective.

1. Is deciding the nature of your claim an important part of the planning process for a claim request? What happens if this part of the process is not done well? [LO-1]

2. Should you always have documentation to back your claim? Under what circumstances, if any, would you make a claim without the proper documentation? [LO-2]

3. You are an out-of-work hair stylist, and you've just seen in your local newspaper that the proprietor of a local salon has won an important industry award. Your roommate suggests that you write the proprietor a congratulatory letter, mentioning in passing your qualifications and the fact that you are looking for work. Do you think this is a good idea? Why, or why not? [LO-4]

4. You're a busy head of Human Resources. You get a letter from Elizabeth Severn, claiming that she worked in your office seven years ago, after which she left to have a baby. She requests you to write a recommendation for her. You look up your records and see that she did indeed work for a year in your office, but you can't remember anything specific about her. Should you go ahead and write the letter anyway? [LO-4]

5. If you have inadvertently caused a business partner a financial loss, would you prefer to take responsibility and apologize immediately, or would you rather highlight the positive aspects of your relationship up to now, and promise that the mistake won't happen again? [LO-4]

PRACTICE YOUR SKILLS

Messages for Analysis

Read the following messages and then (1) analyze the strengths and weaknesses of each sentence and (2) revise each document so that it follows this chapter's guidelines.

Message 8.A: Message Strategies: Routine Requests [LO-2]

Why have the photographs from the ad shoots taken so long to reach my desk? I thought we agreed that from now on, photographs will come to us directly from the art department and not routed through editorial. Last time we met, we agreed that we waste too much time looking at each set of photographs twice. What is still taking so long? My designers have been twiddling their thumbs since 10 A.M. Next time you have a deadline crunch, don't blame us; blame your irrational office procedure which we asked you to streamline.

Message 8.B: Message Strategies: Requesting an Adjustment [LO-2]

I recently bought your high-end printer/scanner/copier from my local retail store (see enclosed bill). It clearly said on the box that it will work with "all known current versions"

of Windows, Mac OS, and Linux. I have Linux on my office system, but your printer did not work on it. I looked at some forums and they all said that for your printers, the only source for the Linux driver is you. Your website does not have the driver, and the store where I bought it refused to help. I am losing time and money on this as I have to pay the office next door to give me needed printouts. What can you do for me?

Message 8.C: Message Strategies: Responding to Claims and Requests for Adjustments [LO-4]

We got your letter explaining why you and your wife were late for the embarkation call for the cruise ship for which you had booked tickets. It seems you are correct that there is no provision in the cruise application form for "nationality of spouse," but, all of our retail partners are trained to elicit this information in a face-to-face meeting and take the necessary steps to get the required visas. You were detained at immigration at the port of origin because your wife, who is an Ethiopian citizen, did not have a valid visa for Indonesia.

While this could have been avoided if you had disclosed all the information to the travel agent, we accept that perhaps we could have done more to make the process smoother, so we're accepting your claim for a refund.

Even better, we're sending you a replacement ticket valid for travel any time within the next six months on any of our cruise ships anywhere in the world except the Caribbean. Don't forget your visas, though! Enjoy your holiday.

Message 8.D: Message Strategies: Providing Recommendations [LO-4]

Hi, I've just received your note asking about Ken Nobuyama which the CEO passed me at lunch today because the guy you wrote it to doesn't work here anymore. Let me introduce myself: I'm Walt Larmin, head of HR here, and I've been with the company for three years now. Your man Nobuyama left two months into my time here, so I pulled up his records to see what I could dig up for you.

Yeah, he was one of the old-timers; he joined at the founding of the company in 1995 and stayed till 2007; we all thought he was a keeper. It was a bit of a shock when he moved to Baltimore to be with his daughter. He was a whiz at looking at a project site. He was a good hand at a pencil too, and when they started the CAD/CAM thing they say he was the first one of us at the office who got it. Heck, he even taught me a few tricks once. Anyway, if he'd stuck around, I'm sure we would have become friends. You guys will be lucky to have him.

Exercises

Active links for all websites in this chapter can be found on MyBcommLab; see your User Guide for instructions on accessing the content for this chapter. Each activity is labeled according to the primary skill or skills you will need to use. To review relevant chapter content, you can refer to the indicated

Learning Objective. In some instances, supporting information will be found in another chapter, as indicated.

1. **Message Strategies: Routine Requests; Revising for Conciseness [LO-1] Chapter 6** Critique the following closing paragraphs. How would you rewrite each to be concise, courteous, and specific?

   a. Please complete all the formalities in time so I can open your trading account promptly. If your information is not complete, there may be delays and I may have to hold up your application. To benefit from our award-winning money management strategies, be on time and complete.

   b. The file closet you sold me is awesome. It totally replaces the old one and makes better use of the office space and looks cool too. I'm telling all my friends.

   c. To book an appointment with our home improvement team, call 1-800-BUILDHOME. We'll add up everything from floor to ceiling and make it all happen in a flash. Remember, once your job is assessed and quoted, the quote stays valid for three months only. Starting the job after that will require a requote.

2. **Message Strategies: Routine Responses; Media Skills: Email [LO-3], Chapter 7** Revise the following short email messages so that they are more direct and concise; develop a subject line for each revised message.

   a. I'm contacting you about your recent email request regarding your crashed laptop. You may have noticed that in the online support request form, there are a number of fields to enter the model number of your laptop, your operating system, software packages loaded, and so on. While you did tell us your system was freezing occasionally before the crash, you didn't tell us what software you have loaded, whether you had antivirus protection, or what you were doing at the time of the freeze. Your hardware profile is also incomplete. Please return to our support website and resubmit your request; then we'll be able to help you.

   b. Thank you for contacting us about the fabric you were desperately looking for. Betty in Purchase has tracked your bale to a supplier in Bangladesh and requested that they look for any more of the fabric, and this morning I got a favorable response from the supplier. He had to buy it back, however, and presents me with a bill for $1800. With my costs of $1450, that makes the total cost for you of $3250 plus freight. Sorry we can't reduce this; we went out of our way to help you in a crisis. On the bright side, you won't have to change the designs for the bridesmaids' dresses at your wedding.

   c. Sorry it took us so long to get back to you. Anyway, your résumé made the final cut, and we've now scheduled meetings with all the finalists. Will you be able to come into the office next Tuesday after lunch? Please tell us if this is convenient because we have to interview at least 20 people this week. As you can imagine, this is our busy season.

   d. As part of our drive to reduce waste in the workplace, henceforth, the little paper sachets of sugar, cream, etc., that used to be available in the cafeteria are being phased out. Instead, attractive pottery dispensers will be available on all tables for brown and white sugar, and cream will be given on request.

3. **Message Strategies: Routine and Positive Messages; Revising for Conciseness [LO-3], Chapter 6** Rewrite the following sentences so that they are direct and concise. If necessary, break your answer into two sentences.

   a. Please visit our store on November 9, which is going to be our big sale with attractive discounts on all end-of-line merchandise, and free gifts on selected purchases.

   b. You'll be delighted to hear that every donation you make to ChildNeed is tax deductible and helps a child who would otherwise not have a chance at education.

   c. The heads of departments will all be at the general operations meeting scheduled to be held a little after 11 A.M.

   d. Our guest today will be Fiona Ryderr, who last week posted the highest rate of conversion for first time expressions of interest into real sales; well done, Fiona!

4. **Message Strategies: Responding to Claims and Requests for Adjustments [LO-4]** Your company markets a line of "desk adjusters," which allow the typing/writing angles and heights of laptops to be adjusted for individual workers. A customer contacts you to say that your product is causing his laptop to overheat. Initially, you say that isn't possible; but he then sends you photographs and you realize his laptop is a nonstandard design and your product is indeed blocking the fan vents. Your company has a standard refund process to handle situations such as this, and the complaint is clearly both legitimate and unforeseeable. You think you can suggest a different model of your product that will work with the customer's machine, but by now the customer is so abusive that you don't feel obligated to help. Is this an appropriate response? Why, or why not?

 Learn how to set up a Twitter account and begin tweeting. Visit http://real-timeupdates.com/ebct10, click on Student Assignments and then click on Twitter Screencast.

5. **Message Strategies: Writing Positive Messages; Media Skills: Microblogging [LO-4], Chapter 7** Locate an online announcement for a new product that you find interesting or useful. Read enough about the product to be able to describe it to someone else in your own words and then write four Twitter tweets: one to introduce the product to your followers and three follow-on tweets that describe three particularly compelling features or benefits of the product.

6. **Message Strategies: Goodwill Messages [LO-4]** Visit the Workplace eCards section of the Blue Mountain site, at www.bluemountain.com, and analyze one of the electronic greeting cards bearing a goodwill message of appreciation for good performance. Under what circumstances would you send this electronic message? How could you personalize it for the recipient and the occasion? What would be an appropriate close for this message?

EXPAND YOUR SKILLS

Critique the Professionals

Locate an online example of a news release in which a company announces good news, such as a new product, a notable executive hire, an expansion, strong financial results, or an industry award. Analyze the release using the bullet list on pages 278–279 as a guide. In what ways did the writer excel? What aspects of the release could be improved? Using whatever medium your instructor requests, write a brief analysis of the piece (no more than one page), citing specific elements from the piece and support from the chapter.

Sharpening Your Career Skills Online

Bovée and Thill's Business Communication Web Search, at http://businesscommunicationblog.com/websearch, is a unique research tool designed specifically for business communication research. Use the Web Search function to find a website, video, PDF document, podcast, or PowerPoint presentation that offers advice on writing goodwill messages such as thank-you notes or congratulatory letters. Write a brief email message to your instructor, describing the item that you found and summarizing the career skills information you learned from it.

IMPROVE YOUR GRAMMAR, MECHANICS, AND USAGE

The following exercises help you improve your knowledge of and power over English grammar, mechanics, and usage. Turn to the "Handbook of Grammar, Mechanics, and Usage" at the end of this book and review all of Section 1.7 (Sentences). Then look at the following 10 items. Circle the letter of the preferred choice within each group of sentences. (Answers to these exercises appear on page AK-3.)

1. **a.** Constance Smith prepares every annual report. Because she is in charge of all operations.
   b. Constance Smith prepares every annual report. She is in charge of all operations.

2. **a.** The senior manager, along with his project leaders, is working overtime to finish the project by Friday.
   b. The senior manager, along with his project leaders, are working overtime to finish the project by Friday.

3. **a.** Reading the final chapter, the shortcomings of the new model were understood by the senior technician.
   b. Reading the final chapter, the senior technician understood the shortcomings of the new model.

4. **a.** First the project was carried out by our in-house team. Then we decided to outsource it.
   b. First the project was carried out by our in-house team then we decided to outsource it.

5. **a.** Simon was our top salesman, however he was able to convert only three accounts in one month.
   b. Simon was our top salesman; however, he was able to convert only three accounts in one month.

6. **a.** To identify the security leak, every single employee was grilled for hours.
   b. Every single employee was grilled for hours to identify the security leak.

7. **a.** Having finally been promoted to executive assistant, the director is accompanied by John everywhere.
   b. Having finally been promoted to executive assistant, John accompanies the director everywhere.

8. **a.** Roger was hiring for his new global team, he assured them tremendous performance-linked bonuses.
   b. Because Roger was hiring for his new global team, he assured them tremendous performance-linked bonuses.

9. **a.** He left the report in plain view on his desk. This was an unpardonable error, considering the extreme sensitivity of the data it contained.
   b. He left the report in plain view on his desk. An unpardonable error, considering the extreme sensitivity of the data it contained.

10. **a.** When it comes to improving security, Systech's new alarm system, with its multiple features, are the better choice.
    b. When it comes to improving security, Systech's new alarm system, with its multiple features, is the better choice.

For additional exercises focusing on sentences, visit MyBcommLab. Click on Chapter 8, click on Additional Exercises to Improve Your Grammar, Mechanics, and Usage, and click on 12. Longer sentences, 13. Sentence fragments, 15. Misplaced modifiers, or 24. Transitional words and phrases.

CASES

Routine Requests

BLOGGING SKILLS

1. Message Strategies: Requesting Information [LO-2] You are writing a book about the advantages and potential pitfalls of using viral advertising. You would like to include several dozen real-life examples from people in a variety of industries.

Fortunately, you publish a highly respected blog on the subject, with several thousand regular readers.

Your task: Write a post for your blog that asks readers to submit moderately detailed descriptions of their attempts, successful or otherwise, to use viral advertising. You are particularly interested in the "runaway" nature of these media: people don't always take away the message they were supposed to get. Ask your readers to email you stories of successes, failure, and their take on what went right or wrong. Explain that they will receive an autographed copy of the book as thanks, but they will need to sign a release form if their stories are used. In addition, emphasize that you would like to use real names—of people, companies, and products—but you can keep the anecdotes anonymous if readers require. To stay on schedule, you need to have these stories by May 20.

EMAIL SKILLS

2. Message Strategies: Requesting a Recommendation [LO-2]

Your company is starting a new department that you believe you would be the best choice to head. There are three other people in the running, but you believe you are closest to Karen Tan who is a powerful voice in the selection committee that will make the decision. Karen joined the company with you and was on your team for a number of important projects, but that was ten years ago, and although you're still friends, the demands of family and other responsibilities mean that you don't hang out as often as you used to. You suspect she will want to appear impartial, but on the basis of qualifications and experience, you believe you are the best choice.

Your task: Write an email message to Tan, telling her that you are definitely interested in leading the project and asking her to put in a good word for you with the committee. Mention four attributes that you believe would serve you well in the role: a dozen years of experience in the industry, an engineering degree that helps you understand the technologies involved in product design, a consistent record of excellent or exceptional ratings in annual employee evaluations, and the three years you spent working in the company's customer support group, which gave you a firsthand look at customer satisfaction and quality issues. Make up any additional details you need to write the message.

MICROBLOGGING SKILLS

3. Message Strategies: Routine Requests; Media Skills: Microblogging [LO-2], Chapter 7

A growing number of companies now monitor Twitter to pick up on messages from frustrated customers. Given the public visibility of such complaints, smart companies are eager to jump to the customer's aid.

Your task: Identify a real customer support situation in your own life in which you need information or some form of resolution from a company. This could be anything from a broken product that you're having trouble getting repaired to an erroneous charge on a credit card. If you can't identify a situation in your life, "borrow" a situation from a friend, a student in another class, or a family member that you can try to resolve on Twitter. This is going to be a "live" exercise that consumes a company's time and resources, so make sure you have a real problem to solve. Also, your messages will be available for all the world to see, so be sure to communicate in a calm, respectful manner, and do not disclose any confidential or personal information in your tweets. (If your problem requires sharing such information, the company should ask you to switch to direct messaging for privacy.)

First, search Twitter to see if the company has an account. If the company is on Twitter, its account should show up in the "People results for . . ." listing. Make sure you choose the most appropriate account; many companies have more than one

Twitter account. When you've located the right account, follow it from your Twitter account.

Next, send a Tweet that includes the company's account name and describes your problem clearly and as completely as possible within the character limit. Double-check the spelling of the account name, the company name, and any product name you use. Then be sure to monitor your Twitter account closely to watch for a message from the company, and send a follow-up response in a timely fashion. Work with the customer support person who contacts you to resolve the problem. Along the way, keep a copy of all the messages you send and receive.

As your instructor directs, write a summary or prepare a presentation of your experience and your analysis of the effectiveness of Twitter as a customer service tool.

EMAIL SKILLS

4. Message Strategies: Requesting a Recommendation [LO-2]

After five years of work in the human resources department at Dynacorp (a company that is developing novel human computer interfaces), you were laid off in a round of cost-cutting moves that rippled through the applied computing industry in recent years. The good news is that you found stable employment in the bakery business. The bad news is that in the three years since you left Dynacorp, you have truly missed working in the exciting field of HCI and having the opportunity to be a part of something as important as finding new ways to get computers to talk to people and vice versa. You know that careers in experimental applications of this sort are uncertain, but you have a few dollars in the bank now, and you're willing to ride that rollercoaster again.

Your task: Draft an email to Grant Selfridge, your old boss at Dynacorp, reminding him of the time you worked together and asking him to write a letter of recommendation for you.

IM SKILLS

5. Message Strategies: Requesting Information [LO-2]

Thank goodness your company, Diagonal Imports, chose the Sametime enterprise instant messaging software produced by IBM Lotus. Other products also allow you to carry on real-time exchanges with colleagues on the other side of the planet, but Sametime supports bidirectional machine translation, and you're going to need it.

The problem is that production on a popular line of nano-bonded unbreakable glassware produced at your Chinese manufacturing plant inexplicably came to a halt last month. As the product manager in the United States, you have many resources you could call on for help, such as a manufacturer in the Philippines who makes the same product on contract, though not quite as cheaply as your Chinese partners. But you can't do anything if you don't know the details. You've tried telephoning top managers in China, but they're evasive, telling you only what they think you want to hear.

Your friend Kuei-chen Tsao has returned from a business trip. You met her during your trip to China last year. She doesn't speak English, but she's the line engineer responsible for this particular product: a tableware set that has a unique internal crystal structure that makes it change color from different angles. You have orders from household goods stores all over the United States waiting to be filled. Kuei-chen should be able to explain the problem, determine whether you can help, and tell you how long before regular shipping resumes.

Your task: Write the first of what you hope will be a productive instant message exchange with Kuei-chen. Remember that your words will be machine translated.[9]

TEXT MESSAGING SKILLS

6. Message Strategies: Requesting Information [LO-2] The vast God Conclave is the premier promotional event in the gaming industry. More than 130,000 industry insiders from all over the world come to see the new gameware. You've just stumbled on the Punchbag: a new gel-filled device that fits to the hand and allows gamers to do complex actions like turning a doorknob or opening a letter. You also make game controllers, and you're worried that your customers will flock to this interface. You need to know how much buzz is circulating around the show: Have people seen it? What are they saying about it? Are they excited about it? Have game developers picked up on it in the design of their control interfaces?

Your task: Compose a text message to your colleagues at the show, alerting them to the new interface and asking them to listen for any buzz it might be generating among the attendees at the Convention Center and the several surrounding hotels where the show takes place. Here's the catch: Your text-messaging service limits messages to 160 characters, including spaces and punctuation, so your message can't be any longer than this.

EMAIL SKILLS

7. Message Strategies: Requesting an Adjustment [LO-2] You recently acquired a boisterous three-month-old German Shepherd–St Bernard cross from your local shelter. She's your first dog, so you wanted to get professional help with her training. There are no puppy schools near where you are, so you joined Puptalk, the mailing list of a reputed dog trainer for $10.99 a month, paid upfront for twelve months. Initially, the advice you were getting in weekly bulk postings seemed good, but, when you posted a specific query about how to leash-train your puppy, you got no answer. You also placed an order for a special leash available on the Puptalk website, for which you paid by credit card, but the leash never arrived. You are now fed up and figure you have got all the good advice you are going to get from this service. You still have seven months to run on your subscription. The Puptalk website says "Your money back if not fully satisfied," but gives no details.

Your task: Write an email to Trudy Laws, (trudylaws@puptalk .com) the customer support officer for Puptalk, asking for your subscription to be discontinued, and the balance of the money for the remaining seven months to be returned to you, as well as a refund for the undelivered leash.

EMAIL SKILLS

8. Message Strategies: Requesting Action [LO-2] You head the marketing division of a popular youth clothing store. You have 87 stores around the country. You have decided you need to penetrate deeper into the college market, and you've come up with a scheme to do this. You want to appoint young people—"Captains of Cool," who will go into college campuses in their lunch hours and hand out vouchers for your clothing. You would prefer to do this without a lot of new hires, and you figure you already have a young work-force on your shop floors. You want to appoint four Captains of Cool, two of each gender, from the stores nearest to college campuses, and pay them a percentage on the number of referrals they can generate. To do this, you need the managers of each store to identify those members of the shop floor staff most likely to have what it takes to rustle up business. Each manager can nominate up to three candidates, who will then go through a screening process.

Your task: Write an email to go out to the managers outlining your plan and explaining what they have to do. Since not all of them will know you personally, don't forget to introduce yourself. Make up any additional information you may need.

Routine Messages

EMAIL SKILLS

9. Message Strategies: Granting Claims [LO-4] You run a jewelry design firm. Carlton Hughes, a TV personality, orders a locket for his wife, Lara, but his not-so-legible handwriting on the form results in her name being misspelled as Laura in the engraving. Outraged, he sends you a heated email promising to "out" you on his TV show.

Your task: Respond to his email, promising alteration at no charge within 12 hours of his bringing the piece into your shop and apologizing for his, and his wife's, distress.

EMAIL SKILLS

10. Message Strategies: Granting Claims [LO-4] You are the customer service officer at Quicksilver Bicycles, makers of BMX-type sports bikes. You've been contacted by Leda Malmo, a 16-year-old who attempted to become the youngest female entrant in a BMX biking competition in Stockholm. She did okay, but damaged her bike beyond repair in the last round. She has written to you saying her parents can't afford to buy her a new bike, and would you please replace it with a new one. You think it might be worth your while allowing her claim, because she may turn out to be a good brand ambassador.

Your task: Write an email to her congratulating her on her efforts (make sure you are not condescending, however) and offering her a new bike. Also gently make it clear that this is not a regular thing, and you are making an exception for her.

BLOGGING SKILLS

11. Message Strategies: Providing Routine Information; Compositional Modes: Tutorials [LO-4] Austin, Texas, advertising agency GSD&M Idea City brainstorms new advertising ideas using a process it calls *dynamic collaboration*. A hand-picked team of insiders and outsiders is briefed on the project and given a key question or two to answer. The team members then sit down at computers and anonymously submit as many responses as they can within five minutes. The project moderators then pore over these responses, looking for any sparks that can ignite new ways of understanding and reaching out to consumers.

Your task: For these brainstorming sessions, GSD&M recruits an eclectic mix of participants from inside and outside the agency—figures as diverse as economists and professional video gamers. To make sure everyone understands the brainstorming guidelines, prepare a message to be posted on the project blog. In your own words, convey the following four points as clearly and succinctly as you can:

- **Be yourself.** We want input from as many perspectives as possible, which is why we recruit such a diverse array of participants. Don't try to get into what you believe is the mindset of an advertising specialist; we want you to approach the given challenge using whatever analytical and creative skills you normally employ in your daily work.

- **Create, don't edit.** Don't edit, refine, or self-censor] while you're typing during the initial five-minute session. We don't care if your ideas are formatted beautifully, phrased poetically, or even spelled correctly. Just crank' em out as quickly as you can.

- **It's about the ideas, not the participants.** Just so you know up front, all ideas are collected anonymously. We can't tell who submitted the brilliant ideas, the boring ideas, or the already-tried-that ideas. So while you won't get personal credit, you can also be crazy and fearless. Go for it!

- **The winning ideas will be subjected to the toughest of tests.** Just in case you're worried about submitting ideas that could be risky, expensive, or difficult to implement— don't fret. As we narrow down the possibilities, the few that remain will be judged, poked, prodded, and assessed from every angle. In other words, let us worry about containing the fire; you come up with the sparks.[10]

PODCASTING SKILLS   PORTFOLIO BUILDER

12. Message Strategies: Providing Routine Information; Media Skills: Podcasting [LO-4] As a training specialist in Winnebago Industry's human resources department, you're always on the lookout for new ways to help employees learn vital job skills. While watching a production worker page through a training manual while learning how to assemble a new recreational vehicle, you get what seems to be a great idea: Record the assembly instructions as audio files that workers can listen to while performing the necessary steps. With audio instructions, they wouldn't need to keep shifting their eyes between the product and the manual—and constantly losing their place. They could focus on the product and listen for each instruction. Plus, the new system wouldn't cost much at all; any computer can record the audio files, and you'd simply make them available on an intranet site for download into iPods or other digital music players.

Your task: You immediately run your new idea past your boss, who has heard about podcasting but doesn't think it has any place in business. He asks you to prove the viability of the idea by recording a demonstration. Choose a process that you engage in yourself—anything from replacing the strings on a guitar to sewing a quilt to changing the oil in a car—and write a brief (one page or less) description of the process that could be recorded as an audio file. Think carefully about the limitations of the audio format as a replacement for printed text (for instance, do you need to tell people to pause the audio while they perform a time-consuming task?). If directed by your instructor, record your instructions as a podcast.

BLOGGING SKILLS   PORTFOLIO BUILDER

13. Message Strategies: Providing Routine Information [LO-4] You are normally an easygoing manager who gives your employees a lot of leeway in using their own personal communication styles. However, the weekly staff meeting this morning pushed you over the edge. People were interrupting one another, asking questions that had already been answered, sending text messages during presentations, and exhibiting just about every other poor listening habit imaginable.

Your task: Review the advice in Chapter 2 on good listening skills and then write a post for the internal company blog. Emphasize the importance of effective listening and list at least five steps your employees can take to become better listeners.

Routine Replies

LETTER WRITING SKILLS   TEAM SKILLS

14. Message Strategies: Providing Recommendations [LO-4] You're a project manager at SpaceCookies, a company that uses NASA data and findings to make interactive space-themed information videos for school libraries. You have an intern program, whereby students from a design school nearby work with you over the summer. One of these, Lilly Das, a fledgling animator and story developer, has impressed you greatly. She has a strong sense of story and came up with some fantastic ideas to animate some rather dull facts and make them accessible to primary school kids. She was also popular in the office and quickly made friends with her team.

The only issue you might have had with her was her habit of calling her parents three or four times a day. You once had to tell her to get off the phone just before a meeting, and you had a word with her about it afterwards; the problem never came up again.

You'll be sorry to see Lilly leave when she returns to school in the fall, but you're pleased to respond when she asks you for a letter of recommendation. She's not sure where she'll apply for work after graduation, so she asks you to keep the letter fairly general.

Your task: Working with a team of your classmates, discuss what should and should not be in the letter. Prepare an outline based on your discussion and then draft the letter.

 Learn how to add Notes to your Facebook page. Visit http://real-timeupdates.com/ebct10, click on Student Assignments and then click on Facebook Screencast.

15. Message Strategies: Writing Routine Informative Messages; Composition Modes: Summarizing [LO-4] As energy costs trend ever upward and more people become attuned to the environmental and geopolitical complexities of petroleum-based energy, interest in solar, wind, and other alternative energy sources continues to grow. In locations with high *insolation*, a measure of cumulative sunlight, solar panels can be cost-effective solutions over the long term. However, the upfront costs are still daunting for most homeowners. To help lower the entry barrier, the Foster City, California–based firm SolarCity now lets homeowners lease solar panels for monthly payments that are less than their current electricity bills.[11]

Your task: Visit www.solarcity.com, click on "Residential," and then click "SolarLease" to read about the leasing program. Next, study SolarCity's presence on Facebook (www.facebook.com/solarcity) to get a feel for how the company presents itself in a social networking environment. Now assume that you have been assigned the task of writing a brief summary of the SolarLease program that will appear on the Notes tab of SolarCity's Facebook page. In your own language and in 200 words or less, write an introduction to the SolarLease program and email it to your instructor.

Positive Messages

BLOGGING **SKILLS**

16. Message Strategies: Good News Messages [LO-4] Amateur and professional golfers in search of lower scores want to find clubs that are optimized for their individual swings. This process of *club fitting* has gone decidedly high tech in recent years, with fitters using Doppler radar, motion-capture video, and other tools to evaluate golfers' swing and ball flight characteristics. Hot Stix Golf (www.hotstixgolf.com) is a leader in this industry, having fitted more than two hundred professionals and thousands of amateurs.[12]

Your task: Imagine that you are the communications director at the Indian Wells Golf Resort (www.indianwellsgolfresort.com) in Indian Wells, California. Your operation has just signed a deal with Hot Stix to open a fitting center on site. Write a three-paragraph message that could be posted on the resort blog. The first paragraph should announce the news that the Hot Stix center will open in six months, the second should summarize the benefits of club fitting, and the third should offer a brief overview of the services that will be available at the Indian Wells Hot Stix Center. Information on club fitting can be found on the Hot Stix website; make up any additional information you need to complete the post.

BLOGGING **SKILLS**   PORTFOLIO **BUILDER**

17. Message Strategies: Good-News Messages [LO-4] In both print and online communication, it's hard to escape the impact of Adobe Systems, the company behind Acrobat, Photoshop, Flash, InDesign, and other programs used to create and share textual and visual content. Even as its impact on the communication professions continues to increase, though, Adobe works to decrease its impact on the natural environment. The company invests in a variety of techniques and technologies to reduce its energy usage, and Adobe was the first company ever to receive the Platinum Certification from the U.S. Green Building Council.

Your task: Write a one- or two-paragraph post for an internal blog at Adobe, letting employees know how well the company is doing in its efforts to reduce energy usage and thanking employees for the energy-saving ideas they've submitted and the individual efforts they've made to reduce, reuse, and recycle. You can learn more about the company's efforts and accomplishments at www.adobe.com/corporateresponsibility/environmental.html.[13]

LETTER WRITING **SKILLS**

18. Message Strategies: Goodwill Messages [LO-4] You've been working for two years as administrative assistant to Ron Glover, vice president of global workforce diversity at IBM in Armonk, New York. Chana Panichpapiboon has been with Glover even longer than you have, and, sadly, her husband was killed (along with 19 others) in a bus accident yesterday. The bus skidded on icy pavement into a deep ravine, tipping over and crushing the occupants before rescue workers could get to them.

You met Surin last year at a company banquet. You can still picture his warm smile and the easy way he joked with you and others over chicken Florentine, even though you were complete strangers to him. He was only 32 years old, and he left Chana with two children, a 12-year-old boy, Arsa, and a 10-year-old girl, Veera. His death is a terrible tragedy.

Normally, you'd write a condolence letter immediately. But Chana is a native of Thailand, and so was Surin. You know you'd better do a little research first. Is Chana Buddhist or Catholic? Is there anything about the typical Western practice of expressing sympathy that might be inappropriate? Offensive?

After making some discreet inquiries among Chana's closest friends at work, you've learned that she is Theravada Buddhist, as are most people in Thailand. From a reference work in the company library about doing business around the world, you've gleaned only that, in the beliefs of many people in Thailand, "the person takes precedence over rule or law" and "people gain their social position as a result of karma, not personal achievement," which means Chana may believe in reincarnation. But the book also says that Theravada Buddhists are free to choose which precepts of their religion, if any, they will follow. So Chana's beliefs are still a mystery.

You do know that her husband was very important to her and much loved by all their family. That, at least, is universal. And you're toying with a phrase you once read, "The hand of time lightly lays, softly soothing sorrow's wound." Is it appropriate?

Your task: You've decided to handwrite the condolence note on a blank greeting card you've found that bears a peaceful, "Eastern-flavor" image. You know you're risking a cultural gaffe, but at least you won't commit the greater offense of not writing at all. Choose the most sincere wording you can, which should resonate through any differences in custom or tradition.[14]

LETTER WRITING **SKILLS**

19. Message Strategies: Condolence Messages [LO-4] As chief administrator for the underwriting department of Aetna Health Plans in Walnut Creek, California, you're facing a difficult task. One of your best underwriters, Hector Almeida, recently lost his wife in an automobile accident (he and his teenage daughter weren't with her at the time). Because you're the boss, everyone in the close-knit department is looking to you to communicate the group's sympathy and concern.

Someone suggested a simple greeting card that everyone could sign, but that seems so impersonal for someone you've worked with every day for nearly five years. So you decided to write a personal note on behalf of the whole department. Although you met Hector's wife, Rosalia, at a few company functions, you knew her mostly through Hector's frequent references to her. You didn't know her well, but you do know important things about her life, which you can celebrate in the letter.

Right now, he's devastated by the loss. But if anyone can overcome this tragedy, Hector can. He's always determined to get a job done, no matter what obstacles present themselves, and he does it with an upbeat attitude. That's why everyone in the office likes him so much.

You also plan to suggest that when he returns to work, he might like to move his schedule up an hour so that he'll have more time to spend with his daughter, Lisa, after school. It's your way of helping make things a little easier for them during this period of adjustment.

Your task: Write the letter to Hector Almeida, who lives at 47 West Ave., #10, Walnut Creek, CA 94596. (Feel free to make up any details you need.)[15]

SOCIAL NETWORKING SKILLS

20. Message Strategies: Goodwill Messages [LO-4]   As the largest employer in Loganville, your construction company provides jobs, purchasing activity, and tax payments that make up a vital part of the city's economy. In your role as CEO, however, you realize that the relationship between your company and the community is mutually beneficial, and the company could not survive without the efforts of its employees, the business opportunities offered by a growing marketplace, and the physical and legal infrastructure that the government provides.

The company's dependence on the community was demonstrated in a moving and immediate way last weekend, when a powerful storm pushed the Logan River past flood stage and threatened to inundate your company's office and warehouse facilities. More than two hundred volunteers worked alongside your employees through the night to fill and stack sandbags to protect your buildings, and the city council authorized the deployment of heavy equipment and additional staff to help in the emergency effort. As you watched the water rise nearly 10 feet high behind the makeshift dike, you realized that the community came together to save your company.

Your task: Write a Wall post for your company's Facebook page, thanking the citizens and government officials of Loganville for their help in protecting the company's facilities during the storm. Use your creativity to make up any details you need to write a 100- to 200-word message.

REFERENCES

1. Get Satisfaction website, accessed 4 February 2011, http://getsatisfaction.com; Dan Fost, "On the Internet, Everyone Can Hear You Complain," *New York Times*, 25 February 2008, www.nytimes.com.

2. Fraser P. Seitel, *The Practice of Public Relations*, 9th ed. (Upper Saddle River, N.J.: Prentice Hall, 2004), 402–411; *Techniques for Communicators* (Chicago: Lawrence Ragan Communication, 1995), 34, 36.

3. David Meerman Scott, *The New Rules of Marketing and PR*, (Hoboken, N.J., Wiley, 2007), 62.

4. Shel Holz, "Next-Generation Press Releases," CW Bulletin, September 2009, www.iabc.com; Steph Gray, "Baby Steps in Social Media News Releases," Helpful Technology blog, 15 May 2009, http://blog.helpfultechnology.com.

5. Pat Cataldo, "Op-Ed: Saying 'Thank You'; Can Open More Doors Than You Think," Penn State University Smeal College of Business website, accessed 19 February 2008, www.smeal.psu.edu.

6. Jackie Huba, "Five Must-Haves for Thank-You Notes," Church of the Customer Blog, 16 November 2007, www.churchofthecustomer.com.

7. Mary Mitchell, "The Circle of Life—Condolence Letters," LiveandLearn.com, accessed 18 July 2005, www.liveandlearn.com; Donna Larcen, "Authors Share the Words of Condolence," *Los Angeles Times*, 20 December 1991, E11.

8. See Note 1; some exercise questions adapted from content on the Get Satisfaction website.

9. Adapted from Lisa DiCarlo, "IBM Gets the Message—Instantly," Forbes.com, 7 July 2002, www.forbes.com; "IBM Introduces Breakthrough Messaging Technology for Customers and Business Partners," *M2 Presswire*, 19 February 2003, accessed 24 July 2003, www.proquest.com; "IBM and America Online Team for Instant Messaging Pilot," *M2 Presswire*, 4 February 2003, www.proquest.com.

10. Adapted from GSD&M Idea City website, accessed 7 July 2010, www.ideacity.com; Burt Helm, "Wal-Mart, Please Don't Leave Me," *BusinessWeek*, 9 October 2006, 84–89.

11. Adapted from SolarCity website, accessed 7 July 2010, www.solarcity.com.

12. Adapted from Hot Stix Golf website, accessed 8 February 2011, www.hotstixgolf.com.

13. Adapted from Adobe website, accessed 8 February 2011, www.adobe.com; Jeff Nachtigal, "It's Easy and Cheap Being Green," *Fortune*, 16 October 2006, 53; "Adobe Wins Platinum Certification Awarded by U.S. Green Building Council," press release, 3 July 2006, www.adobe.com.

14. Adapted from Keith H. Hammonds, "Difference Is Power," *Fast Company*, 36, 258, accessed 11 July 2000, www.fastcompany.com; Terri Morrison, Wayne A. Conaway, and George A. Borden, Ph.D., *Kiss, Bow, or Shake Hands* (Holbrook, Mass.: Adams Media Corporation, April 1995).

15. Adapted from Mitchell, "The Circle of Life—Condolence Letters"; Larcen, "Authors Share the Words of Condolence."

LEARNING OBJECTIVES   After studying this chapter, you will be able to

1   Apply the three-step writing process to negative messages

2   Explain how to use the direct approach effectively when conveying negative news

3   Explain how to use the indirect approach effectively when conveying negative news

4   Explain the importance of maintaining high standards of ethics and etiquette when delivering negative messages

5   Describe successful strategies for sending negative messages on routine business matters

6   List the important points to consider when conveying negative organizational news

7   Describe successful strategies for sending negative employment-related messages

MyBcommLab **Where you see MyBcommLab in this chapter, go to** www.pearsoninternationaleditions.com/ mybcommlab **for additional activities on the topic being discussed.**

ON THE JOB: COMMUNICATING AT **CHARGIFY**

Chargify, which offers online billing services to other companies, caused a ruckus among its own customer base when it raised prices without giving any advance notice.
Source: © D. Hurst/Alamy.

Communication Gaffe Makes an Unpleasant Situation Worse

If you've ever purchased anything online using a credit or debit card, you've used some form of an automated billing system. From a consumer's point of view, in which all you do is fill in a form and a charge eventually shows up on your monthly statement, billing looks fairly simple. However, a lot of tasks need to be done behind the scenes to make billing work, and they need to be done accurately, quickly, and securely. Many e-commerce companies therefore turn to specialists such as Boston-based Chargify to handle this vital business function.

Chargify charges its e-commerce clients flat monthly fees based on the number of customers *they* have. This tiered pricing plan keeps costs low for e-commerce startups that still have few revenue-generating customers. Up until late 2010, the lowest tier in Chargify's pricing plan had an extremely attractive price point—it was free.

The idea behind the free tier was to attract e-commerce companies still in their startup phase; as they grew, they would advance into the higher tiers and become paying clients. However, Chargify discovered that many companies in the free tier grew very slowly, if at all, and Chargify wound up supporting a lot of users that weren't bringing in any revenue.

To generate enough revenue to support the dependable, sustainable company that its clients needed, Chargify co-founder David Hauser realized he needed to raise prices, and that included charging lowest-tier clients for the first time. The company announced its new pricing structure in October 2010—and immediately came under attack from many of its clients for the price increases, for the lack of any advance notice, and for Chargify's refusal to "grandfather" existing customers under their original pricing plans. Some called the company "greedy" or "stupid," and a few went so far as to accuse it of bait-and-switch tactics. As bloggers and commentators across the Internet piled on, the technology news site TechCrunch summed up the situation with an article that began, "It's been a rough day for Chargify . . ."

After spending two long days responding to criticisms on Twitter, industry blogs, and other venues, Hauser wrote an unusually frank blog post titled "How to Break the Trust of Your Customers in Just One Day: Lessons Learned from a Major Mistake." He said the company made "a massive mistake"

in the way it handled the changes to its pricing model. By failing to alert customers well in advance of the change, he continued, Chargify "broke a trust that we had developed with our customers over a long period of time, and will take much to repair. We should have communicated our need and desire to remove free plans and provided more information about how this would happen, and over a period of time leading up to the change."

The kinds of services Chargify provides take money to deliver, and the price increases were necessary, but everyone involved agrees that the situation was not handled well. Hauser and his team will continue to learn new lessons as they expand Chargify, but you can bet they won't initiate any new price increases without giving their customers plenty of warning.[1]

http://chargify.com

Using the Three-Step Writing Process for Negative Messages

David Hauser and the rest of the executive team at Chargify (profiled in the chapter opener) are experienced and successful entrepreneurs, but even they discovered how tricky it can be to share unexpected and unwelcome news with audiences that have a lot riding on the information. Communicating negative information is a fact of life for all business professionals, whether it's saying no to a request, sharing unpleasant or unwelcome information, or issuing a public apology. With the techniques you'll learn in this chapter, however, you can communicate unwelcome news successfully while minimizing unnecessary stress for everyone involved.

Depending on the situation, you can have as many as five distinct goals when you need to convey negative information: (1) to convey the bad news, (2) to gain acceptance for the bad news, (3) to maintain as much goodwill as possible with your audience, (4) to maintain a good image for your organization, and (5) if appropriate, to reduce or eliminate the need for future correspondence on the matter. Five goals are clearly a lot to accomplish in one message, so careful planning and execution are critical with negative messages.

STEP 1: PLANNING A NEGATIVE MESSAGE

When planning negative messages, you can't avoid the fact that your audience does not want to hear what you have to say. To minimize the damage to business relationships and to encourage the acceptance of your message, analyze the situation carefully to better understand the context in which the recipient will process your message.

Be sure to consider your purpose thoroughly—whether it's straightforward (such as rejecting a job applicant) or more complicated (such as drafting a negative performance review, in which you not only give the employee feedback on past performance but also help the person develop a plan to improve future performance). With a clear purpose and your audience's needs in mind, identify and gather the information your audience requires in order to understand and accept your message. Negative messages can be intensely personal to the recipient, and in many cases, recipients have a right to expect a thorough explanation of your message.

Selecting the right medium is critical. For instance, bad news for employees should be delivered in person whenever possible, to guard their privacy, demonstrate respect, and give them an opportunity to ask questions. Doing so isn't always possible or feasible, though, so you will have times when you need to share important negative information through written or electronic media.

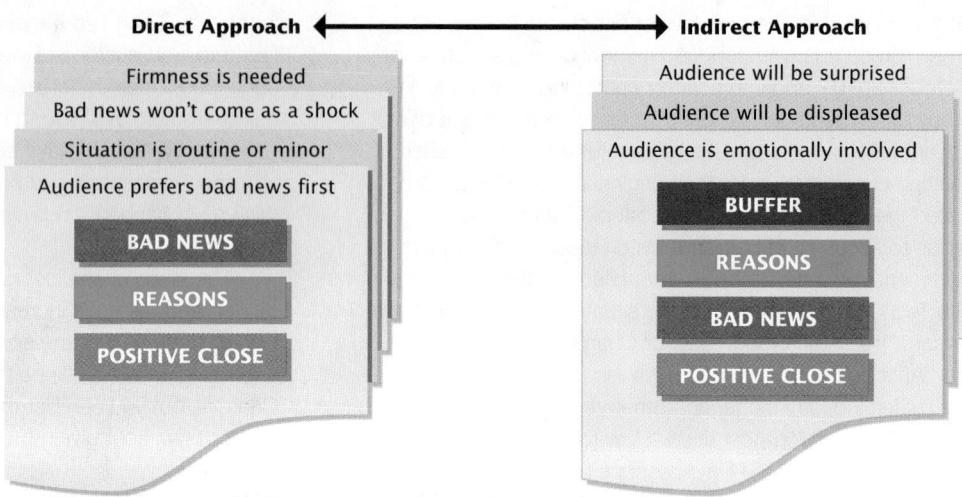

Figure 9.1 **Choosing the Indirect or Direct Approach for Negative Messages**
Analyze the situation carefully before choosing your approach to organizing negative messages.

Defining your main idea in a negative message is often more complicated than simply saying no. For instance, if you need to respond to a hardworking employee who requested a raise, your message might go beyond saying no to explaining how she can improve her performance by working smarter, not just harder.

Appropriate organization helps readers accept your negative news.

Finally, the organization of a negative message requires particular care. One of the most critical planning decisions is choosing whether to use the direct or indirect approach (see Figure 9.1). A negative message using the direct approach opens with the bad news, proceeds to the reasons for the situation or the decision, and ends with a positive statement aimed at maintaining a good relationship with the audience. In contrast, the indirect approach opens with the reasons behind the bad news before presenting the bad news itself.

You need to consider a variety of factors when choosing between direct and indirect approaches for negative messages.

To help decide which approach to take in any situation you encounter, ask yourself the following questions:

- **Will the bad news come as a shock?** The direct approach is fine for many business situations in which people understand the possibility of receiving bad news. However, if the bad news might come as a shock to readers, use the indirect approach to help them prepare for it.
- **Does the reader prefer short messages that get right to the point?** For example, if you know that your boss always wants messages that get right to the point, even when they deliver bad news, use the direct approach.
- **How important is this news to the reader?** For minor or routine scenarios, the direct approach is nearly always best. However, if the reader has an emotional investment in the situation or the consequences to the reader are considerable, the indirect approach is often better.
- **Do you need to maintain a close working relationship with the reader?** The indirect approach lets you soften the blow of bad news and preserve a positive business relationship.
- **Do you need to get the reader's attention?** If someone has ignored repeated messages, the direct approach can help you get his or her attention.
- **What is your organization's preferred style?** Some companies have a distinct communication style, ranging from blunt and direct to gentle and indirect.

STEP 2: WRITING A NEGATIVE MESSAGE

When you are adapting a negative message to your audience, pay close attention to effectiveness and diplomacy. After all, your audience does not want to hear bad news or something

TABLE 9.1	Choosing Positive Words	
Examples of Negative Phrasings		**Positive Alternatives**
Your request *doesn't make any sense*.		Please clarify your request.
The *damage won't be fixed* for a week.		The item will be repaired next week.
Although it wasn't *our fault*, there will be an *unavoidable delay* in your order.		We will process your order as soon as we receive an aluminum shipment from our supplier, which we expect to happen within 10 days.
You are clearly *dissatisfied*.		I recognize that the product did not live up to your expectations.
I was *shocked* to learn that you're *unhappy*.		Thank you for sharing your concerns about your shopping experience.
Unfortunately, we haven't received it.		The item hasn't arrived yet.
The enclosed statement is *wrong*.		Please verify the enclosed statement and provide a correct copy.

they will disagree with, so messages perceived as being unclear or unkind will amplify the audience's stress. "Continuing with a Clear Statement of the Bad News" on page 301 has advice on conveying unpleasant news with care and tact. Cultural expectations also play a role, from the organizational culture within a company to the regional variations around the world.

The disappointing nature of negative messages requires that you maintain your audience focus and be as sensitive as possible to audience needs. For example, internal audiences often have expectations regarding negative messages that differ from those of external audiences. In some cases, the two groups can interpret the news in different or even opposite ways. Employees will react negatively to news of an impending layoff, for instance, but company shareholders might welcome the news as evidence that management is trying to control costs. In addition, if a negative message such as news of a layoff is being sent to internal and external audiences, employees will expect not only more detail but also to be informed before the public is told.

> Compared to external audiences, internal audiences often expect more detail in negative messages.

Negative messages to outside audiences require attention to the diverse nature of the audience and the concern for confidentiality of internal information. A single message might have a half-dozen audiences, all with differing opinions and agendas. You may not be able to explain things to the level of detail that some of these people want if doing so would release proprietary information such as future product plans.

> You may need to adjust the content of negative messages for various external audiences.

If your credibility hasn't already been established with the audience, lay out your qualifications for making the decision in question. Recipients of negative messages who don't think you are credible are more likely to challenge your decision or reject your message. And, as always, projecting and protecting your company's image are prime concerns; if you're not careful, a negative answer could spin out of control into negative feelings about your company.

When you use language that conveys respect and avoids an accusing tone, you protect your audience's pride. This kind of communication etiquette is always important, but it demands special care with negative messages. Moreover, you can ease the sense of disappointment by using positive words rather than negative, counterproductive ones (see Table 9.1).

STEP 3: COMPLETING A NEGATIVE MESSAGE

The need for careful attention to detail continues as you complete your message. Revise your content to make sure everything is clear, complete, and concise—bearing in mind that even small flaws are magnified as readers react to your negative news. Produce clean, professional documents and proofread carefully to eliminate mistakes. Finally, be especially sure that your negative messages are delivered promptly and successfully. Delaying when you need to convey negative news can be a serious breach of etiquette.

Using the Direct Approach for Negative Messages

2 LEARNING OBJECTIVE

Explain how to use the direct approach effectively when conveying negative news.

Use the direct approach when your negative answer or information will have minimal personal impact.

A negative message using the direct approach opens with the bad news, proceeds to the reasons for the situation or the decision, and ends with a positive statement aimed at maintaining a good relationship with the audience. Depending on the circumstances, the message may also offer alternatives or a plan of action to fix the situation under discussion. Stating the bad news at the beginning can have two advantages: (1) It makes a shorter message possible, and (2) it allows the audience to reach the main idea of the message in less time.

OPENING WITH A CLEAR STATEMENT OF THE BAD NEWS

No matter what the news is, come right out and say it. However, even if the news is likely to be devastating, maintain a calm, professional tone that keeps the focus on the news and not on individual failures or other personal factors. Also, if necessary, remind the reader why you're writing.

PROVIDING REASONS AND ADDITIONAL INFORMATION

The amount of detail you should provide depends on your relationship with the audience.

In most cases, you follow the direct opening with an explanation of why the news is negative. The extent of your explanation depends on the nature of the news and your relationship with the reader. For example, if you want to preserve a long-standing relationship with an important customer, a detailed explanation could well be worth the extra effort such a message would require.

However, you will encounter some situations in which explaining negative news is neither appropriate nor helpful, such as when the reasons are confidential, excessively complicated, or irrelevant to the reader. To maintain a cordial working relationship with the reader, you might want to explain why you can't provide the information.

Should you apologize when delivering bad news? The answer isn't quite as simple as one might think, partly because the notion of *apology* is hard to pin down. To some people, it simply means an expression of sympathy that something negative has happened to another person. At the other extreme, it means admitting fault and taking responsibility for specific compensations or corrections to atone for the mistake.

Some experts have advised that a company should never apologize, even when it knows it has made a mistake, as the apology might be taken as a confession of guilt that could be used against the company in a lawsuit. However, several states have laws that specifically prevent expressions of sympathy from being used as evidence of legal liability. In fact, judges, juries, and plaintiffs tend to be more forgiving of companies that express sympathy for wronged parties; moreover, an apology can help repair a company's reputation. Recently, some prosecutors have begun pressing executives to publicly admit guilt and apologize as part of the settlement of criminal cases—unlike the common tactic of paying fines but refusing to admit any wrongdoing.[3]

After an explosion that killed one employee and worried local residents about the potential release of toxic chemicals, Bayer CropScience plant manager Nick Crosby said, "We are truly sorry for the serious issues caused by the incident at our facility . . . we understand the anxiety in the community resulting from the incident." He also apologized to people living near the Institute, West Virginia, plant for failing to clarify that there was no danger of toxic emissions. "We could have communicated, and we should have communicated, much better with the community that night."[2]
Source: Tom Hindman/Ap Wide World Photos.

Apologies can have legal ramifications, but refusing to apologize out of fear of admitting guilt can damage a company's relationships with its stakeholders.

The best general advice in the event of a serious mistake or accident is to immediately and sincerely express sympathy and offer help if appropriate, without admitting guilt; then seek the advice of your company's lawyers before elaborating. As one survey concluded, "The risks of making an apology are low, and the potential reward is high."[4]

If you do apologize, make it a real apology. Don't say "I'm sorry if anyone was offended" by what you did—this statement implies that you're not sorry at all and that it's the other party's fault for being offended.[5] For example, when Sony's PlayStation Network was breached and disabled by hackers, CEO Howard Stringer included the following statement in a post on the company's blog: "As a company we—and I—apologize for the inconvenience and concern caused by this attack."[6] Note that he did not say "*if* anyone was inconvenienced" or "*if* the attack caused any concern."

Note that you can also express sympathy with someone's plight without suggesting that you are to blame. For example, if a business customer damaged a product through misuse and suffered a financial loss as a result of not being able to use the product, you can say something along the lines of "I'm sorry to hear of your difficulties." This demonstrates sensitivity without accepting blame.

CLOSING ON A RESPECTFUL NOTE

After you've explained the negative news, close the message in a manner that respects the impact the negative news is likely to have on the recipient. If appropriate, consider offering your readers an alternative solution if you can and if doing so is a good use of your time. Look for opportunities to include positive statements, but avoid creating false hopes or writing in a way that seems to suggest that something negative didn't just happen to the recipient. Ending on a false positive can leave readers feeling "disrespected, disregarded, or deceived."[7]

In many situations, an important aspect of a respectful close is describing the actions being taken to avoid similar mistakes in the future. Offering such explanations can underline the sincerity of an apology because doing so signals that the person or organization is serious about not repeating the error. When the credit rating agency Standard & Poor's issued a statement expressing regret for its role in the 2007–2008 subprime mortgage meltdown that helped throw the economy into a deep recession, the company also described the changes it was making "to restore investor confidence in our ratings," as company president Deven Sharma explained.[8]

Using the Indirect Approach for Negative Messages

The indirect approach helps readers prepare for the bad news by presenting the reasons for it first. However, the indirect approach is *not* meant to obscure bad news, delay it, or limit your responsibility. Rather, the purpose of this approach is to ease the blow and help readers accept the situation. When done poorly, the indirect approach can be disrespectful and even unethical. But when done well, it is a good example of audience-oriented communication crafted with attention to ethics and etiquette. Showing consideration for the feelings of others is never dishonest.

OPENING WITH A BUFFER

Messages using the indirect approach open with a **buffer**: a neutral, noncontroversial statement that establishes common ground with the reader (refer to Figure 9.1). A good buffer can express your appreciation for being considered (if you're responding to a request), assure the reader of your attention to the request, or indicate your understanding of the reader's needs. A good buffer also needs to be relevant and sincere. In contrast, a poorly written buffer might trivialize the reader's concerns, divert attention from the problem with insincere flattery or irrelevant material, or mislead the reader into thinking your message actually contains good news.

3 **LEARNING OBJECTIVE**

Explain how to use the indirect approach effectively when conveying negative news.

Use the indirect approach when some preparation will help your audience accept your bad news.

A well-written buffer establishes common ground with the reader.

Consider these possible responses to a manager of the order-fulfillment department who requested some temporary staffing help from your department (a request you won't be able to fulfill):

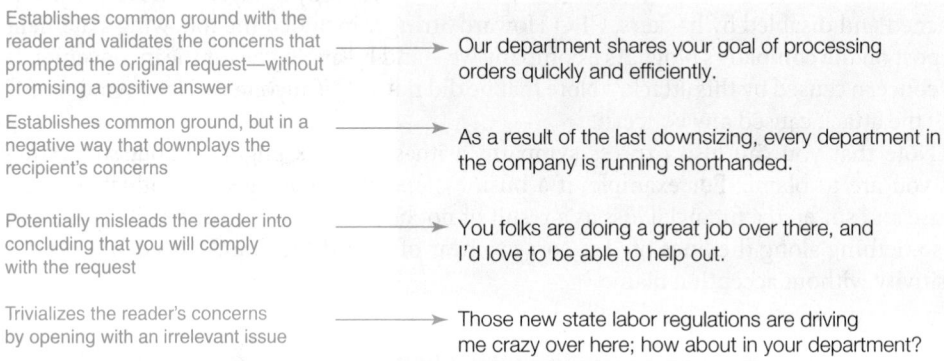

Establishes common ground with the reader and validates the concerns that prompted the original request—without promising a positive answer
→ Our department shares your goal of processing orders quickly and efficiently.

Establishes common ground, but in a negative way that downplays the recipient's concerns
→ As a result of the last downsizing, every department in the company is running shorthanded.

Potentially misleads the reader into concluding that you will comply with the request
→ You folks are doing a great job over there, and I'd love to be able to help out.

Trivializes the reader's concerns by opening with an irrelevant issue
→ Those new state labor regulations are driving me crazy over here; how about in your department?

Only the first of these buffers can be considered effective; the other three are likely to damage your relationship with the other manager—and lower his or her opinion of you. Table 9.2 shows several types of effective buffers you could use to tactfully open a negative message.

Poorly written buffers may mislead or insult the reader.

Given the damage that a poorly composed buffer can do, consider every buffer carefully before you send it. Is it respectful? Is it relevant? Does it avoid any chance of misleading the reader? Does it provide a smooth transition to the reasons that follow? If you can answer yes to every question, you can proceed confidently to the next section of your message. However, if a little voice inside your head tells you that your buffer sounds insincere or misleading, it probably is, in which case you'll need to rewrite it.

TABLE 9.2   Types of Buffers

Buffer Type	Strategy	Example
Agreement	Find a point on which you and the reader share similar views.	We both know how hard it is to make a profit in this industry.
Appreciation	Express sincere thanks for receiving something.	Your check for $127.17 arrived yesterday. Thank you.
Cooperation	Convey your willingness to help in any way you realistically can.	Employee Services is here to assist all associates with their health insurance, retirement planning, and continuing education needs.
Fairness	Assure the reader that you've closely examined and carefully considered the problem, or mention an appropriate action that has already been taken.	For the past week, we have had our bandwidth monitoring tools running around the clock to track your actual upload and download speeds.
Good news	Start with the part of your message that is favorable.	We have credited your account in the amount of $14.95 to cover the cost of return shipping.
Praise	Find an attribute or an achievement to compliment.	The Stratford Group clearly has an impressive record of accomplishment in helping clients resolve financial reporting problems.
Resale	Favorably discuss the product or company related to the subject of the letter.	With their heavy-duty, full-suspension hardware and fine veneers, the desks and file cabinets in our Montclair line have long been popular with value-conscious professionals.
Understanding	Demonstrate that you understand the reader's goals and needs.	So that you can more easily find the printer with the features you need, we are enclosing a brochure that describes all the Epson printers currently available.

PROVIDING REASONS AND ADDITIONAL INFORMATION

An effective buffer serves as a transition to the next part of your message, in which you build up the explanations and information that will culminate in your negative news. An ideal explanation section leads readers to your conclusion before you come right out and say it. In other words, before you actually say no, the reader has followed your line of reasoning and is ready for the answer. By giving your reasons effectively, you help maintain focus on the issues at hand and defuse the emotions that always accompany significantly bad news. In the blog post that announced Chargify's new pricing model (see page 304), for example, CEO Lance Walley explained how the company's costs had risen as it worked to improve the reliability and security of its services.[9]

Phrase your reasons to signal the negative news ahead.

As you lay out your reasons, guide your reader's response by starting with the most positive points first and moving forward to increasingly negative ones. Be concise, but provide enough detail for the audience to understand your reasons. You need to convince your audience that your decision is justified, fair, and logical. If appropriate, you can use the explanation section to suggest how the negative news might in fact benefit your reader in some way—but only if that is true and only if you can do so without offending your audience.

Avoid hiding behind company policy to cushion your bad news. If you say, "Company policy forbids our hiring anyone who does not have two years' supervisory experience," you imply that you won't consider anyone on his or her individual merits. Skilled and sympathetic communicators explain company policy (without referring to it as "policy") so that the audience can try to meet the requirements at a later time. Consider this response to an employee:

Don't hide behind "company policy" when you deliver bad news; present logical answers instead.

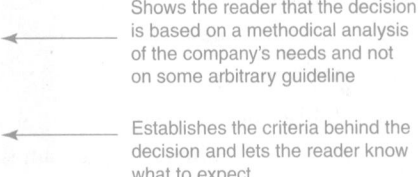

Because these management positions are quite challenging, the human relations department has researched the qualifications needed to succeed in them. The findings show that the two most important qualifications are a bachelor's degree in business administration and two years' supervisory experience.

⟵ Shows the reader that the decision is based on a methodical analysis of the company's needs and not on some arbitrary guideline

⟵ Establishes the criteria behind the decision and lets the reader know what to expect

This paragraph does a good job of stating reasons for the refusal:

- It provides enough detail to logically support the refusal.
- It implies that the applicant is better off avoiding a program in which he or she might fail.
- It shows that the company's policy is based on experience and careful analysis.
- It doesn't offer an apology for the decision because no one is at fault.
- It avoids negative personal expressions (such as "You do not meet our requirements").

Well-written reasons are
- *Detailed*
- *Tactful*
- *Individualized*
- *Unapologetic if no one is at fault*
- *Positive*

Even valid, well-thought-out reasons won't convince every reader in every situation. However, if you've done a good job of laying out your reasoning, you've done everything you can to prepare the reader for the main idea, which is the negative news itself.

CONTINUING WITH A CLEAR STATEMENT OF THE BAD NEWS

After you've thoughtfully and logically established your reasons and readers are prepared to receive the bad news, you can use three techniques to convey the negative information as clearly and as kindly as possible. First, deemphasize the bad news:

To handle bad news
- *Deemphasize the bad news visually and grammatically*
- *Use a conditional statement, if appropriate*
- *Tell what you did do, not what you didn't do*

- Minimize the space or time devoted to the bad news—without trivializing it or withholding any important information.
- Subordinate bad news in a complex or compound sentence ("My department is already shorthanded, so I'll need all my staff for at least the next two months"). This construction presents the bad news in the middle of the sentence, the point of least emphasis.
- Embed bad news in the middle of a paragraph or use parenthetical expressions ("Our profits, which are down, are only part of the picture").

However, keep in mind that it's possible to abuse deemphasis. For instance, if the primary point of your message is that profits are down, it would be inappropriate to marginalize that news by burying it in the middle of a sentence. State the negative news clearly and then make a smooth transition to any positive news that might balance the story.

Second, if appropriate, use a conditional (*if* or *when*) statement to imply that the audience could have received, or might someday receive, a favorable answer under different circumstances ("When you have more managerial experience, you are welcome to apply for any openings that we may have in the future"). Such a statement could motivate applicants to improve their qualifications. However, you must avoid any suggestion that you might reverse the decision you've just made or any phrasing that could give a rejected applicant false hope.

Third, emphasize what you can do or have done rather than what you cannot do. Say "We sell exclusively through retailers, and the one nearest you that carries our merchandise is . . ." rather than "We are unable to serve you, so please call your nearest dealer." Also, by implying the bad news, you may not need to actually state it ("The five positions have been filled with people whose qualifications match those uncovered in our research"). By focusing on the facts and implying the bad news, you make the impact less personal.

When implying bad news, however, be sure your audience will be able to grasp the entire message—including the bad news. Withholding negative information or overemphasizing positive information is unethical and unfair to your reader. If an implied message might lead to uncertainty, state your decision in direct terms. Just be sure to avoid overly blunt statements that are likely to cause pain and anger:

Instead of This	Write This
I *must refuse* your request.	I will be out of town on the day you need me.
We *must deny* your application.	The position has been filled.
I *am unable* to grant your request.	Contact us again when you have established . . .
We *cannot afford to* continue the program.	The program will conclude on May 1.
Much as I would like to attend . . .	Our budget meeting ends too late for me to attend.
We *must turn down* your extension request.	Please send in your payment by June 14.

Don't disguise bad news when you emphasize the positive.

CLOSING ON A RESPECTFUL NOTE

A positive close
- *Builds goodwill*
- *Offers a suggestion for action*
- *Provides a look toward the future*

As in the direct approach, the close in the indirect approach offers an opportunity to emphasize your respect for your audience, even though you've just delivered unpleasant news. Express best wishes without being falsely upbeat. If you can find a positive angle that's meaningful to your audience, by all means consider adding it to your conclusion. However, don't try to pretend that the negative news didn't happen or that it won't affect the reader. Suggest alternative solutions if such information is available. If you've asked readers to decide between alternatives or to take some action, make sure that they know what to do, when to do it, and how to do it. Whatever type of conclusion you use, follow these guidelines:

- **Avoid a negative or uncertain conclusion.** Don't belabor the bad news. Refrain from expressing any doubt that your reasons will be accepted. (Avoid statements such as "I trust our decision is satisfactory.")
- **Manage future correspondence.** Encourage additional communication *only* if you're willing to discuss the situation further. (If you're not, avoid statements such as "If you have further questions, please write.")
- **Be optimistic about the future, as appropriate.** Don't anticipate problems that haven't occurred yet. (Avoid statements such as "Should you have further problems, please let us know.")
- **Be sincere.** Steer clear of clichés that are insincere in view of the bad news. (If you can't help, don't say, "If we can be of any help, please contact us.")

Keep in mind that the close is the last thing audience members have to remember you by. Even though they're disappointed, leave them with the impression that they were treated with respect.

Maintaining High Standards of Ethics and Etiquette

All business messages demand attention to ethics and etiquette, of course, but these considerations take on special importance when you are delivering bad news—for several reasons. First, a variety of laws and regulations dictate the content and delivery of many business messages with potentially negative content, such as the release of financial information by a public company. Second, negative messages can have a significant negative impact on the lives of those receiving them. Even if the news is conveyed legally and conscientiously, good ethical practice demands that these situations be approached with care and sensitivity. Third, emotions often run high when negative messages are involved, for both the sender and the receiver. Senders need to manage their own emotions and consider the emotional state of their audiences.

For example, in a message announcing or discussing workforce cutbacks, you have the emotional needs of several stakeholder groups to consider. The employees who lost their jobs are likely to experience fear about their futures and possibly a sense of betrayal. The employees who kept their jobs are likely to feel anxiety about the long-term security of their jobs, the ability of company management to turn things around, and the level of care and respect the company has for its employees. These "survivors" may also feel guilty about keeping their jobs while some colleagues lost theirs. Outside the company, investors, suppliers, and segments of the community affected by the layoffs (such as retailers and homebuilders) will have varying degrees of financial interest in the outcome of the decision. Writing such messages requires careful attention to all these needs, while balancing respect for the departing employees with a positive outlook on the future.

The challenge of sending—and receiving—negative messages fosters a tendency to delay, downplay, or distort the bad news.[10] However, doing so may be unethical, if not illegal. In recent years, numerous companies have been sued by shareholders, consumers, employees, and government regulators for allegedly withholding or delaying negative information in such areas as company finances, environmental hazards, and product safety. In many of these cases, the problem was slow, incomplete, or inaccurate communication between the company and external stakeholders. In others, problems stemmed from a reluctance to send or receive negative news within the organization.

Effectively sharing bad news within an organization requires commitment from everyone involved. Employees must commit to sending negative messages when necessary and to doing so in a timely fashion, even when that is unpleasant or difficult. Conversely, managers must commit to maintaining open communication channels, truly listening when employees have negative information to share, and not punishing employees who deliver bad news.

Employees who observe unethical or illegal behavior within their companies and are unable to resolve the problems through normal channels may have no choice but to resort to **whistleblowing**, expressing their concerns internally through company ethics hot lines—or externally through social media or the news media if they perceive no other options. The decision to "blow the whistle" on one's own employer is rarely easy or without consequences; more than 80 percent of whistleblowers in one survey said they were punished in some way for coming forward with their concerns.[11] Although whistleblowing is sometimes characterized as "ratting on" colleagues or managers, it has an essential function. According to international business expert Alex MacBeath, "Whistleblowing can be an invaluable way to alert management to poor business practices within the workplace. Often whistleblowing can be the only way that information about issues such as rule breaking, criminal activity, cover-ups, and fraud can be brought to management's attention before serious damage is suffered."[12] Recognizing the value of this feedback, many companies have formal reporting mechanisms that give employees a way to voice ethical and legal concerns to management. Various government bodies have also instituted protections for

4   LEARNING OBJECTIVE

Explain the importance of maintaining high standards of ethics and etiquette when delivering negative messages.

Sharing bad news effectively requires commitment from everyone in the organization.

✔ Checklist | Creating Negative Messages

A. Choose the better approach.
- Consider using the direct approach when the audience is aware of the possibility of negative news, when the reader is not emotionally involved in the message, when you know that the reader would prefer the bad news first, when you know that firmness is necessary, and when you want to discourage a response.
- Consider using the indirect approach when the news is likely to come as a shock or surprise, when your audience has a high emotional investment in the outcome, and when you want to maintain a good relationship with the audience.

B. For the indirect approach, open with an effective buffer.
- Establish common ground with the audience.
- Validate the request, if you are responding to a request.
- Don't trivialize the reader's concerns.
- Don't mislead the reader into thinking the coming news might be positive.

C. Provide reasons and additional information.
- Explain why the news is negative.
- Adjust the amount of detail to fit the situation and the audience.

- Avoid explanations when the reasons are confidential, excessively complicated, or irrelevant to the reader.
- If appropriate, state how you plan to correct or respond to the negative news.
- Seek the advice of company lawyers if you're unsure what to say.

D. Clearly state the bad news.
- State the bad news as positively as possible, using tactful wording.
- To help protect readers' feelings, deemphasize the bad news by minimizing the space devoted to it, subordinating it, or embedding it.
- If your response might change in the future if circumstances change, explain the conditions to the reader.
- Emphasize what you can do or have done rather than what you can't or won't do.

E. Close on a respectful note.
- Express best wishes without being falsely positive.
- Suggest actions readers might take, if appropriate, and provide them with necessary information.
- Encourage further communication only if you're willing to discuss the situation further.

---

whistleblowers, partly in recognition of the role that workers play in food safety and other vital areas.[13]

Finally, recognize that some negative news scenarios will test your self-control and tempt you to respond with a personal attack. Customer service employees often undergo training specifically to help them keep their own emotions on an even keel when they are on the receiving end of anger or criticism from upset customers.[14] However, keep in mind that negative messages can have a lasting impact on the people who receive them and the people who send them. As a communicator, you have a responsibility to minimize the negative impact of your negative messages through careful planning and sensitive, objective writing. As much as possible, focus on the actions or conditions that led to the negative news, not on personal shortcomings or character issues. Develop a reputation as a professional who can handle the toughest situations with dignity.

For a reminder of successful strategies for creating negative messages, see "Checklist: Creating Negative Messages."

> Negative situations can put your sense of self-control and business etiquette to the test.

Sending Negative Messages on Routine Business Matters

5 LEARNING OBJECTIVE

Describe successful strategies for sending negative messages on routine business matters.

Professionals and companies receive a wide variety of requests and proposals and cannot respond positively to every single one. In addition, mistakes and unforeseen circumstances can lead to delays and other minor problems that occur in the course of business. Occasionally, companies must send negative messages to suppliers and other parties. Whatever the purpose, crafting routine negative responses and messages quickly and graciously is an important skill for every businessperson.

MAKING NEGATIVE ANNOUNCEMENTS ON ROUTINE BUSINESS MATTERS

Many negative messages are written in response to requests from an internal or external correspondent, but on occasion managers need to make unexpected announcements of a negative nature. For example, a company might decide to consolidate its materials purchasing with fewer suppliers and thereby need to tell several firms it will no longer be buying from them. Internally, management may need to announce the elimination of an employee benefit or other changes that employees will view negatively.

Although such announcements happen in the normal course of business, they are generally unexpected. Accordingly, except in the case of minor changes, the indirect approach is usually the better choice. Follow the steps outlined for indirect messages: open with a buffer that establishes some mutual ground between you and the reader, advance your reasoning, announce the change, and close with as much positive information and sentiment as appropriate under the circumstances.

> Negative announcements on routine business matters usually should be handled with the indirect approach because the news is unexpected.

REJECTING SUGGESTIONS AND PROPOSALS

Managers receive a variety of suggestions and proposals, both solicited and unsolicited, from internal and external sources. For an unsolicited proposal from an external source, you may not even need to respond if you don't already have a working relationship with the sender. However, if you need to reject a proposal that you solicited, you owe the sender an explanation, and because the news will be unexpected, the indirect approach is better. In general, the closer your working relationship, the more thoughtful and complete you need to be in your response. For example, if you are rejecting a proposal from an employee, explain your reasons fully and carefully so that the employee can understand why the proposal was not accepted and so that you don't damage an important working relationship.

REFUSING ROUTINE REQUESTS

When you are unable to meet a request, your primary communication challenge is to give a clear negative response without generating negative feelings or damaging either your personal reputation or the company's. As simple as such messages may appear to be, they can test your skills as a communicator because you often need to deliver negative information while maintaining a positive relationship with the other party.

The direct approach works best for most routine negative responses. It not only helps your audience get your answer quickly and move on to other possibilities but also helps you save time, because messages with the direct approach are often easier to write than those with the indirect approach.

REAL-TIME UPDATES
Learn More by Watching This Video

Take some of the sting out of delivering bad news

No one likes to deliver bad news, but these techniques can make it easier for you and the recipient. Go to http://real-timeupdates .com/ebc10 and click on Learn More. If you are using MyBcommLab, you can access Real-Time Updates within each chapter or under Student Study Tools.

The indirect approach is preferable when the stakes are high for you or for the receiver, when you or your company has an established relationship with the person making the request, or when you're forced to decline a request that you might have said yes to in the past (see Figure 9.2 on the next page).

Consider the following points as you develop your routine negative messages:

- Manage your time carefully; focus on the most important relationships and requests.
- If the matter is closed, don't imply that it's still open by using phrases such as "Let me think about it and get back to you" as a way to delay saying no.
- Offer alternative ideas if you can, particularly if the relationship is important.
- Don't imply that other assistance or information might be available if it isn't.

> If you aren't in a position to offer additional information or assistance, don't imply that you are.

HANDLING BAD NEWS ABOUT TRANSACTIONS

Bad news about transactions is always unwelcome and usually unexpected. When you send such messages, you have three goals: (1) modify the customer's expectations, (2) explain how you plan to resolve the situation, and (3) repair whatever damage might have been done to the business relationship.

1 Plan →	**2 Write** →	**3 Complete**
Analyze the Situation Verify that the purpose is to decline a request and offer alternatives; audience is likely to be surprised by the refusal. **Gather Information** Determine audience needs and obtain the necessary information. **Select the Right Medium** For formal messages, printed letters on company letterhead are best. **Organize the Information** The main idea is to refuse the request so limit your scope to that; select the indirect approach based on the audience and the situation.	**Adapt to Your Audience** Adjust the level of formality based on your degree of familiarity with the audience; maintain a positive relationship by using the "you" attitude, politeness, positive emphasis, and bias-free language. **Compose the Message** Use a conversational but professional style and keep the message brief, clear, and as helpful as possible.	**Revise the Message** Evaluate content and review readability to make sure the negative information won't be misinterpreted; make sure your tone stays positive without being artificial. **Produce the Message** Maintain a clean, professional appearance on company letterhead. **Proofread the Message** Review for errors in layout, spelling, and mechanics. **Distribute the Message** Deliver your message using the chosen medium.

The buffer eases the recipient into the message by demonstrating respect and recapping the request.

Kwan suggests an alternative, showing that she cares about the college and has given the matter some thought.

She provides a meaningful reason for the negative response, without apologizing (because the company is not at fault).

Her close emphasizes the importance of the relationship and the company's continuing commitment.

InfoTech

927 Dawson Valley Road, Tulsa, Oklahoma 74151
Voice: (918) 669-4428   Fax: (918) 669-4429
www.infotech.com

March 6, 2012

Dr. Sandra Wofford, President
Whittier Community College
333 Whittier Avenue
Tulsa, OK 74150

Dear Dr. Wofford:

Infotech has been happy to support Whittier Community College in many ways over the years, and we appreciate the opportunities you and your organization provide to so many deserving students. Thank you for considering our grounds for your graduation ceremony on June 3.

We would certainly like to accommodate Whittier as we have in years past, but our companywide sales meetings will be held this year during the weeks of May 29 and June 5. With more than 200 sales representatives and their families from around the world joining us, activities will be taking place throughout our facility.

My assistant, Robert Seagers, suggests you contact the Municipal Botanical Gardens as a possible graduation site. He recommends calling Jerry Kane, director of public relations.

We remain firm in our commitment to you, President Wofford, and to the fine students you represent. Through our internship program, academic research grants, and other initiatives, we will continue to be a strong corporate partner to Whittier College and will support your efforts as you move forward.

Sincerely,

May Yee Kwan

May Yee Kwan
Public Relations Director

lc

Figure 9.2 Effective Message Declining a Routine Request
May Yee Kwan's company has a long-standing relationship with the college Sandra Wofford represents and wants to maintain that positive relationship, but she can't meet this particular request. To communicate negative news, she therefore uses an indirect approach. If Kwan and Wofford shared a closer relationship (if they worked together in a volunteer organization, for instance), the direct approach might have been more appropriate.

The specific content and tone of each message can vary widely, depending on the nature of the transaction and your relationship with the customer. Telling an individual consumer that his new sweater will be arriving a week later than you promised is a much simpler task than telling GM that 30,000 transmission parts will be a week late, especially if you know the company will be forced to idle a multimillion-dollar production facility as a result.

If you haven't done anything specific to set the customer's expectations—such as promising delivery within 24 hours—the message simply needs to inform the customer of the situation, with little or no emphasis on apologies (see Figure 9.3).

If you did set the customer's expectations and now find that you can't meet them, your task is more complicated. In addition to resetting those expectations and explaining how you'll resolve the problem, you should include an apology as part of your message. The scope of the apology depends on the magnitude of the mistake. For the customer who ordered the sweater, a simple apology followed by a clear statement of when the sweater will arrive would probably be sufficient. For larger business-to-business transactions, the customer may want an explanation of what went wrong to determine whether you'll be able to perform as you promise in the future.

To help repair the damage to the relationship and encourage repeat business, many companies offer discounts on future purchases, free merchandise, or other considerations. Even modest efforts can go a long way to rebuilding a customer's confidence in your company. However, you don't always have a choice. Business-to-business purchasing contracts often include performance clauses that legally entitle the customer to discounts or other

Some negative messages regarding transactions carry significant financial and legal ramifications.

Your approach to bad news about business transactions depends on what you've done previously to set the customer's expectations.

If you've failed to meet expectations that you set for the customer, you should include an element of apology.

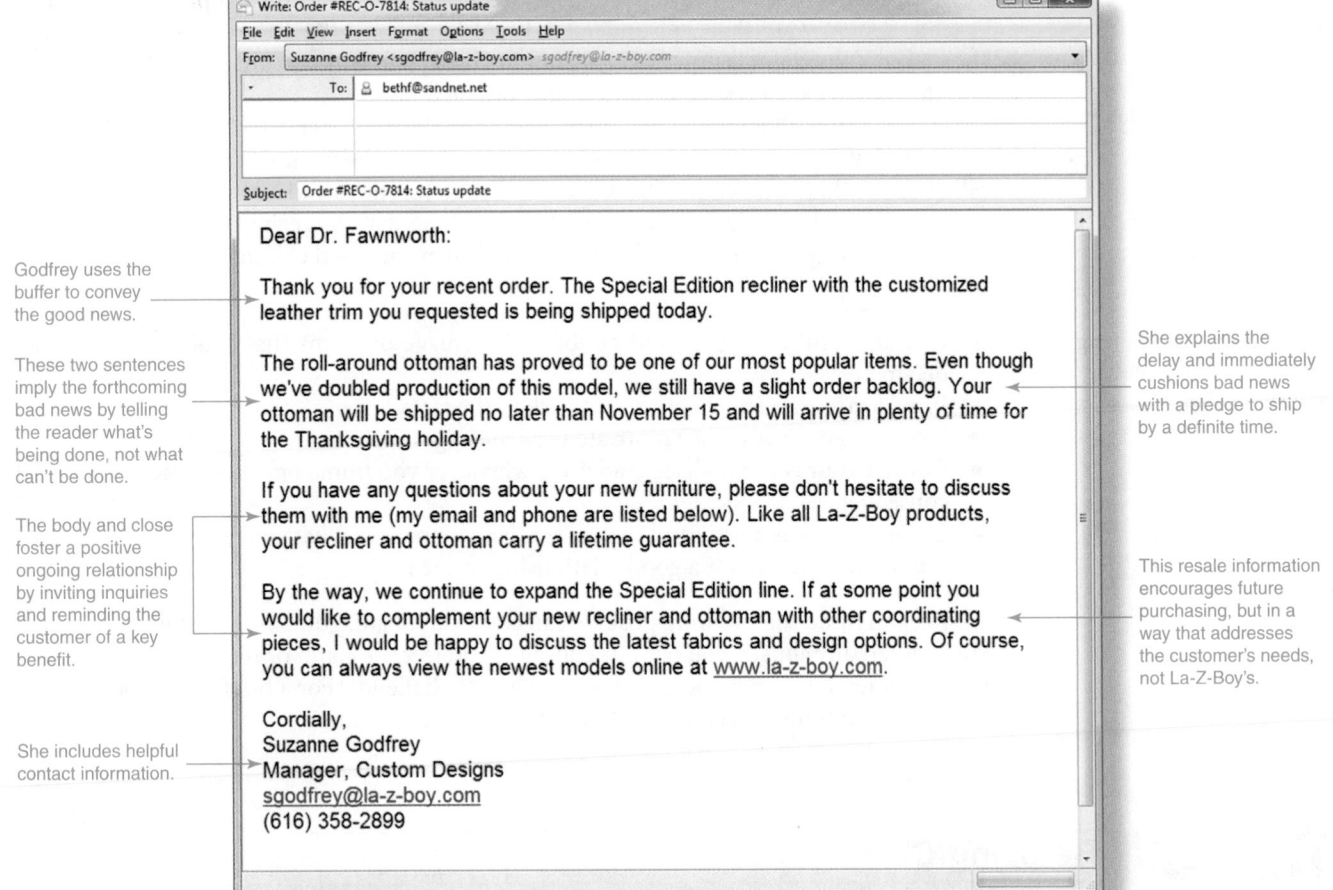

Figure 9.3 Effective Negative Message Regarding a Transaction
This message, which is a combination of good and bad news, uses the indirect approach—with the good news serving as a buffer for the bad news. In this case, the customer wasn't promised delivery by a certain date, so the writer simply informed the customer when to expect the rest of the order. The writer also took steps to repair the relationship and encourage future business with her firm.

MyBcommLab

Apply Figure 9.3's key concepts by revising a new document. Go to Chapter 9 in www.pearsoninternationaleditions.com/mybcommlab and select Document Makeovers.

✔ **Checklist** | **Handling Bad News About Transactions**

- Reset the customer's expectations regarding the transaction.
- Explain what happened and why, if appropriate.
- Explain how you will resolve the situation.

- Repair any damage done to the business relationship, perhaps offering future discounts, free merchandise, or other considerations.
- Offer a professional, businesslike expression of apology if your organization made a mistake.

restitution in the event of late delivery. To review the concepts covered in this section, see "Checklist: Handling Bad News About Transactions."

REFUSING CLAIMS AND REQUESTS FOR ADJUSTMENT

Use the indirect approach in most cases of refusing a claim.

Customers who make a claim or request an adjustment tend to be emotionally involved, so the indirect approach is usually the better choice. To avoid accepting responsibility for the unfortunate situation and avoid blaming or accusing the customer, pay special attention to the tone of your letter. A tactful and courteous message can build goodwill even while denying the claim (see Figure 9.4).

When refusing a claim
- *Demonstrate your understanding of the complaint*
- *Explain your refusal*
- *Suggest alternative action*

When refusing a claim, avoid language that might have a negative impact on the reader. Instead, demonstrate that you understand and have considered the complaint carefully. Then, even if the claim is unreasonable, rationally explain why you are refusing the request. End the message on a respectful and action-oriented note.

If you deal with enough customers over a long enough period, chances are you'll get a request that is particularly outrageous. You might even be positive that the person is not telling the truth. However, you need to control your emotions and approach the situation as calmly as possible to avoid saying or writing anything that the recipient might interpret as defamation (see page 66 in Chapter 1). To avoid being accused of defamation, follow these guidelines:

You can help avoid committing defamation by not responding emotionally or abusively.

- Refrain from using any kind of abusive language or terms that could be considered defamatory.
- Provide accurate information and stick to the facts.
- Never let anger or malice motivate your messages.
- Consult your company's legal advisers whenever you think a message might have legal consequences.
- Communicate honestly and make sure that you believe what you're saying is true.
- Emphasize a desire for a good relationship in the future.

Keep in mind that nothing positive can come out of antagonizing a customer, even one who has verbally abused you or your colleagues. Reject the claim or request for adjustment in a professional manner and move on to the next challenge. For a brief review of the tasks involved when refusing claims, see "Checklist: Refusing Claims."

✔ **Checklist** | **Refusing Claims**

- Use the indirect approach because the reader is expecting or hoping for a positive response.
- Indicate your full understanding of the nature of the complaint.
- Explain why you are refusing the request, without hiding behind company policy.
- Provide an accurate, factual account of the transaction.

- Emphasize ways things should have been handled rather than dwell on the reader's negligence.
- Avoid any appearance of defamation.
- Avoid expressing personal opinions.
- End with a positive, friendly, helpful close.
- Make any suggested action easy for readers to comply with.

1 Plan → **2 Write** → **3 Complete**

Analyze the Situation

Verify that the purpose is to refuse a warranty claim and offerre pairs; the audience's likely reaction will be disappointment and surprise.

Gather Information

Gather information on warranty policies and procedures, repair services, and resale information.

Select the Right Medium

Choose the best medium for delivering your message; for formal messages, printed letters on company letterhead are best.

Organize the Information

Your main idea is to refuse the claim and promote an alternative solution; select an indirect approach based on the audience and the situation.

Adapt to Your Audience

Adjust the level of formality based on degree of familiarity with the audience; maintain a positive relationship by using the "you" attitude, politeness, positive emphasis, and bias-free language.

Compose the Message

Use a conversational but professional style and keep the message brief, clear, and as helpful as possible.

Revise the Message

Evaluate content and review readability to make sure the negative information won't be misinterpreted; make sure your tone stays positive without being artificial.

Produce the Message

Emphasize a clean, professional appearance appropriate for a letter on company stationery.

Proofread the Message

Review for errors in layout, spelling, and mechanics.

Distribute the Message

Deliver your message using the chosen medium; make sure the reader receives any necessary support documents as well.

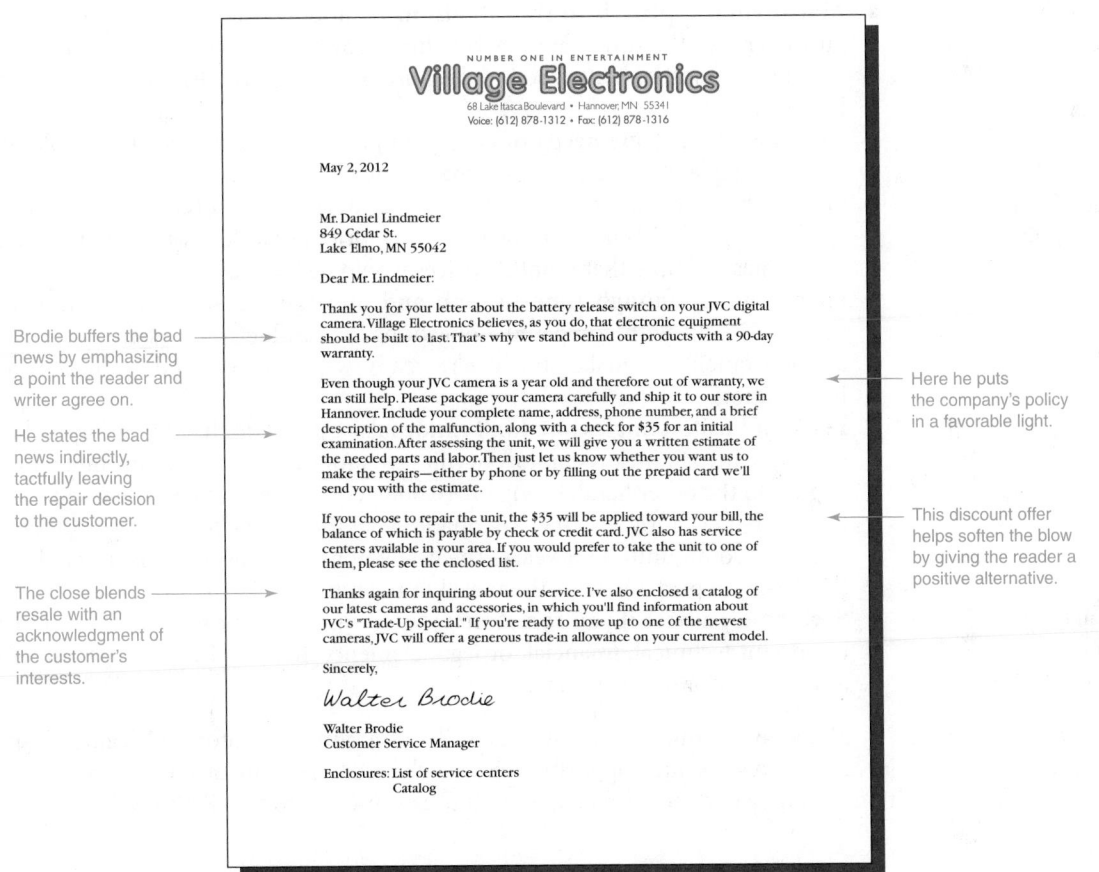

Figure 9.4 Effective Message Refusing a Claim

Daniel Lindmeier, who purchased a digital video camera from Village Electronics a year ago, wrote to say that the unit doesn't work properly and to inquire about the warranty. He incorrectly believed that the warranty covers one year, when it actually covers only three months. In this response, Walter Brodie uses an indirect approach to convey the bad news and to offer additional helpful information.

Sending Negative Organizational News

The messages described in the previous section deal with internal matters or individual interactions with external parties. From time to time, managers must also share negative information with the public at large, and sometimes respond to negative information as well. Most of these scenarios have unique challenges that must be addressed on a case-by-case basis, but the general advice offered here applies to all of them. One key difference among all these messages is whether you have time to plan the announcement. The following section addresses negative messages that you do have time to plan for, and the section after that, "Communicating in a Crisis," offers advice on communication during emergencies.

COMMUNICATING UNDER NORMAL CIRCUMSTANCES

Negative organizational messages to external audiences can require extensive planning.

Businesses must convey a range of negative messages regarding their ongoing operations. As you plan such messages, take extra care to consider all your audiences and their unique needs. Keep in mind that a significant negative event such as a plant closing can affect hundreds or thousands of people in many organizations. Employees need to find new jobs, get training in new skills, or perhaps get emergency financial help. School districts may have to adjust budgets and staffing levels if many of your employees plan to move in search of new jobs. Your customers need to find new suppliers. Your suppliers may need to find other customers of their own. Government agencies may need to react to everything from a decrease in tax revenues to an influx of people seeking unemployment benefits.

When making negative announcements, follow these guidelines:

- **Match your approach to the situation.** A modest price increase won't shock most customers, so the direct approach is fine. However, canceling a product that people count on is another matter, so building up to the news via the indirect approach might be better.
- **Consider the unique needs of each group.** As the plant closing example illustrates, various people have different information needs.

Give people as much time as possible to react to negative organizational news.

- **Give each audience enough time to react as needed.** One of the key mistakes Chargify made (see page 294) in announcing its new pricing model was failing to let customers know ahead of time that monthly prices would be increasing.
- **Give yourself enough time to plan and manage a response.** Chances are you're going to be hit with complaints, questions, or product returns after you make your announcement, so make sure you're ready with answers and additional follow-up information.
- **Look for positive angles but don't exude false optimism.** If eliminating a seldom-used employee benefit means employees will save money, by all means promote that positive angle. On the other hand, laying off 10,000 people does not give them "an opportunity to explore new horizons." It's a traumatic event that can affect employees, their families, and their communities for years. The best you may be able to do is to thank people for their past support and wish them well in the future.

Ask for legal help and other assistance if you're not sure how to handle a significant negative announcement.

- **Seek expert advice if you're not sure.** Many significant negative announcements have important technical, financial, or legal elements that require the expertise of lawyers, accountants, or other specialists.

Negative situations will test your skills as a communicator and leader. Inspirational leaders try to seize such opportunities as a chance to reshape or reinvigorate the organization, and they offer encouragement to those around them (see Figure 9.5).

COMMUNICATING IN A CRISIS

Some of the most critical instances of business communication occur during crises, which can include industrial accidents, crimes or scandals involving company employees, on-site

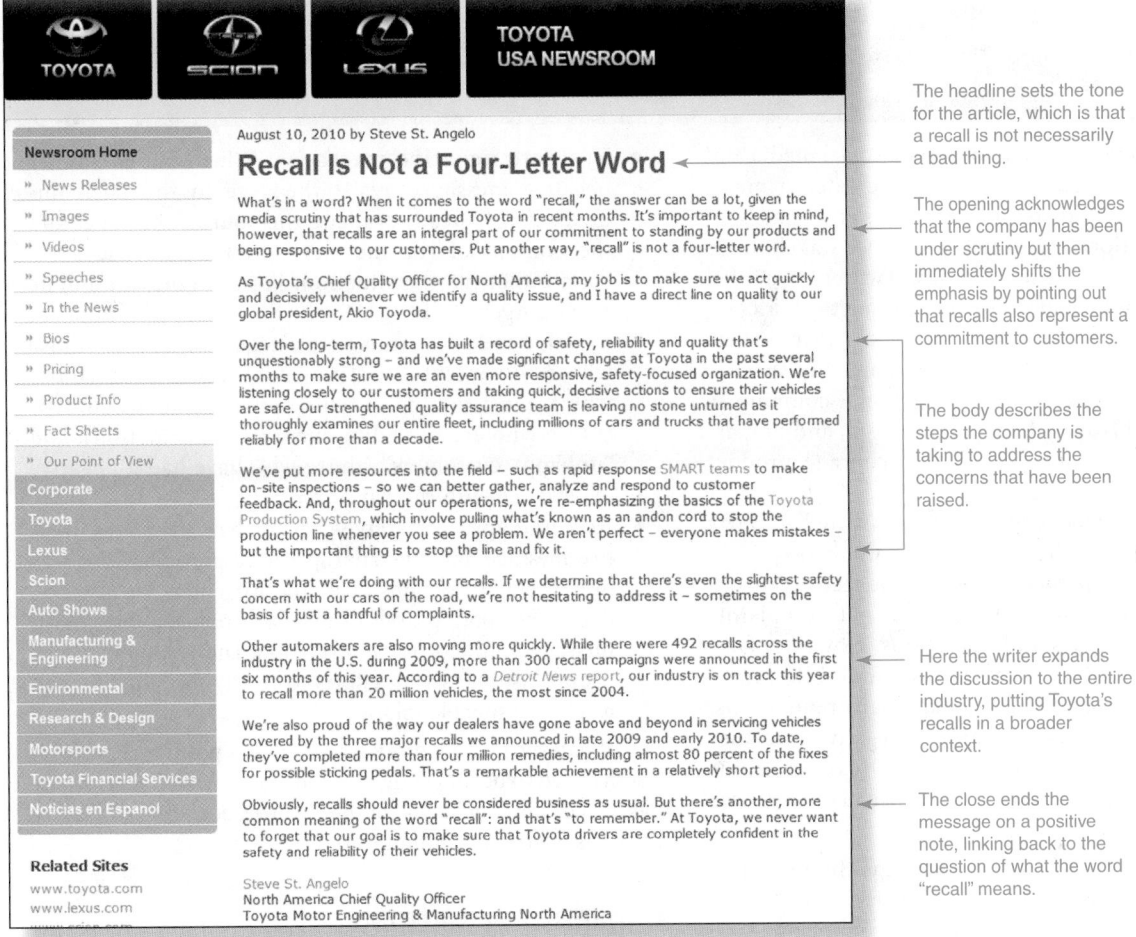

Figure 9.5   Using Negative Situations as Opportunities to Convey Positive Information
Situations that involve negative news are sometimes opportunities in disguise. After Toyota had issued several vehicle recalls and been subjected to quite a bit of media scrutiny regarding product quality, the company's chief quality officer took the opportunity to discuss the meaning of a product recall.
Source: Used with permission of Toyota.

hostage situations, terrorist attacks, information theft, product tampering incidents, and financial calamities. During a crisis, customers, employees, local communities, and others will demand information. In addition, rumors can spread unpredictably and uncontrollably (see "Business Communication 2.0: We're Under Attack! Responding to Rumors and Criticism in a Social Media Environment"). You can also expect the news media to descend quickly, asking questions of anyone they can find.

Although you can't predict these events, you can prepare for them. Analysis of corporate crises over the past several decades reveals that companies that respond quickly with the information people need tend to fare much better in the long run than those that go into hiding or release inconsistent or incorrect information.[15]

The key to successful communication efforts during a crisis is having a **crisis management plan**. In addition to defining operational procedures to deal with the crisis, this plan outlines communication tasks and responsibilities, which can include everything from media contacts to news release templates (see Table 9.3 on page 313). The plan should clearly specify which people are authorized to speak for the company, provide contact information for all key executives, and include a list of the news outlets and social media tools that will be used to disseminate information.

Anticipation and planning are key to successful communication in a crisis.

BUSINESS COMMUNICATION 2.0

We're Under Attack! Responding to Rumors and Criticism in a Social Media Environment

For all the benefits they bring to business, social media and other communication technologies have created a major new challenge: responding to online rumors and attacks on a company's reputation. Consumers and other stakeholders can now communicate through blogs, Twitter, YouTube, Facebook, advocacy sites such as www.walmartwatch.com, community participation websites such as www.epinions.com and www.planetfeedback.com, company-specific sites such as www.verizonpathetic.com, community Q&A sites such as http://getsatisfaction.com, and numerous e-commerce shopping sites that encourage product reviews.

Customers who feel they have been treated unfairly like these sites because they can use the public exposure as leverage. Many companies appreciate the feedback from these sites, too, and many actively seek out complaints to improve their products and operations. However, false rumors and unfair criticisms can spread around the world in a matter of minutes and endanger company reputations. Responding to rumors and countering negative information requires an ongoing effort and case-by-case decisions about which messages require a response. Follow these four steps:

- **Engage early, engage often.** Perhaps the most important step in responding to negative information has to be done *before* the negative information appears, and that is to engage with communities of stakeholders as a long-term strategy. Companies that have active, mutually beneficial relationships with customers and other interested parties are less likely to be attacked unfairly online and more likely to survive such attacks if they do occur. In contrast, companies that ignore constituents or jump into "spin doctoring" mode when a negative situation occurs don't have the same credibility as companies that have done the long, hard work of fostering relationships within their physical and online communities.

- **Monitor the conversation.** If people are interested in what your company does, chances are they are blogging, tweeting, podcasting, posting videos, writing on Facebook walls, and otherwise sharing their opinions. Use the available technologies to listen to what people are saying.

- **Evaluate negative messages.** When you encounter negative messages, resist the urge to fire back immediately. Instead, evaluate the source, the tone, and the content of the message and then choose a response that fits the situation. For example, the Public Affairs Agency of the U.S. Air Force groups senders of negative messages into four categories: "trolls" (those whose only intent is to stir up conflict), "ragers" (those who are just ranting or telling jokes), "the misguided" (those who are spreading incorrect information), and "unhappy customers" (those who have had a negative experience with the Air Force).

- **Respond appropriately.** After you have assessed a negative message, take the appropriate response based on an overall public relations plan. The Air Force, for instance, doesn't respond to trolls or ragers, responds to misguided messages with correct information, and responds to unhappy customers with efforts to rectify the situation and reach a reasonable solution.

Whatever you do, don't assume that a positive reputation doesn't need to be diligently guarded and defended. Everybody has a voice now, and some of those voices don't care to play by the rules of ethical communication.

CAREER APPLICATIONS

1. A legitimate complaint about your restaurant on Yelp also contains a statement that your company "doesn't care about its customers." How should you respond?

2. A few bloggers are circulating false information about your company, but the problem is not widespread—yet. Should you jump on the problem now and tell the world the rumor is false, even though most people haven't heard it yet? Explain your answer.

Sources: "When Fans Attack: How to Defend a Brand's Reputation Online," Crenshaw Communications blog, 20 May 2010, http://crenshawcomm.com; David Meerman Scott, "The US Air Force: Armed with Social Media," WebInkNow blog, 15 December 2008,www.webinknow.com; Matt Rhodes, "How to React If Somebody Writes About Your Brand Online," FreshNetworks blog, 9 January 2009, www.freshnetworks.com; Matt Rhodes, "Social Media as a Crisis Management Tool," Social Media Today blog, 21 December 2009, www.socialmediatoday.com; Jack Neff, "What to Do When Social Media Spreads Marketing Myth," *Advertising Age*, 7 September 2009, 4, 24.

TABLE 9.3	How to Communicate in a Crisis

WHEN A CRISIS HITS

Do	Don't
Prepare for trouble ahead of time by identifying potential problems, appointing and training a response team, and preparing and testing a crisis management plan.	Don't blame anyone for anything.
Get top management involved immediately.	Don't speculate in public.
Set up a news center for company representatives and the media that is equipped with phones, computers, and other electronic tools for preparing news releases and online updates. At the news center, take the following steps:	Don't refuse to answer questions.
• Issue frequent news updates, and have trained personnel available to respond to questions around the clock.	Don't release information that will violate anyone's right to privacy.
• Provide complete information packets to the news media as soon as possible.	Don't use the crisis to pitch products or services.
• Prevent conflicting statements and provide continuity by appointing a single person trained in advance to speak for the company.	Don't play favorites with media representatives.
• Tell receptionists and other employees to direct all phone calls to the designated spokesperson in the news center.	
• Provide updates when new information is available via blog postings, microblog updates, text messaging, Facebook, and other appropriate media.	
Tell the whole story—openly, completely, and honestly. If you are at fault, apologize.	
Demonstrate the company's concern by your statements and your actions.	

Sending Negative Employment Messages

Most managers must convey bad news about or to individual employees from time to time. Recipients have an emotional stake in your message, so taking the indirect approach is usually advised. In addition, use great care in choosing media for these messages. For instance, email and other written forms let you control the message and avoid personal confrontation, but one-on-one conversations are more sensitive and facilitate questions and answers.

7   LEARNING OBJECTIVE

Describe successful strategies for sending negative employment-related messages.

REFUSING REQUESTS FOR EMPLOYEE REFERENCES AND RECOMMENDATION LETTERS

When sending refusals to prospective employers who have requested information about past employees, your message can be brief and direct:

Our human resources department has authorized me to confirm that Yolanda Johnson worked for Tandy, Inc., for three years, from June 2007 to July 2009. Best of luck as you interview applicants.

← Implies that company policy prohibits the release of any more information but does provide what information is available

← Ends on a positive note

This message doesn't need to say, "We cannot comply with your request." It simply gives the reader all the information that is allowable.

Refusing an applicant's direct request for a recommendation letter is another matter. Any refusal to cooperate may seem to be a personal slight and a threat to the applicant's future. Diplomacy and preparation help readers accept your refusal.

The following message tactfully avoids hurting the reader's feelings because it makes positive comments about the reader's recent activities, implies the refusal, suggests an alternative, and uses a polite close:

Uses the indirect approach since the other party is probably expecting a positive response → Thank you for letting me know about your job opportunity with Coca-Cola. Your internship there and the MBA you've worked so hard to earn should place you in an excellent position to land the marketing job.

Announces that the writer cannot comply with the request, without explicitly blaming it on "policy" → Although we do not send out formal recommendations here at PepsiCo, I can certainly send Coca-Cola a confirmation of your employment dates. And if you haven't considered this already, be sure to ask several of your professors to write evaluations of your marketing skills. Best of luck to you in your career.

Ends on a positive note →

REFUSING SOCIAL NETWORKING RECOMMENDATION REQUESTS

One of the greatest values offered by business social networks is the opportunity for members to make introductions and recommendations. However, the situation with recommendations in a social networking environment is more complicated than with a traditional recommendation letter because the recommendations you make become part of your online profile. With a traditional letter, only a few hiring managers might read your recommendations, but on a network such as LinkedIn, other network members (or even the general public, in some instances) can see whom you've recommended and what you've written about these people. Much more so than with traditional letters, then, the recommendations you make in a social network become part of your brand.[16] Moreover, networks make it easy to find people and request recommendations, so chances are you will get more requests than you would have otherwise—and sometimes from people you don't know well.

Social networks have created new challenges in recommendation requests, but they also offer more flexibility in responding to these requests.

Fortunately, social networks give you a bit more flexibility when it comes to responding to these requests. One option is to simply ignore or delete the request. Some people make it personal policy to ignore requests from networkers they don't know. Of course, if you do know a person, ignoring a request could create an uncomfortable situation, so you will need to decide each case based on your relationship with the requester. Another option is to refrain from making recommendations at all, and just letting people know this policy when they ask. Whatever you decide, remember that it is your choice.[17]

If you choose to make recommendations and want to respond to a request, you can write as much or as little information about the person as you are comfortable sharing. Unlike an offline recommendation, you don't need to write a complete letter. You can write a briefer statement, even just a single sentence that focuses on one positive aspect.[18] This flexibility allows you to respond positively in those situations in which you have mixed feelings about a person's overall abilities.

REJECTING JOB APPLICATIONS

Poorly written rejection letters tarnish your company's reputation and can even invite legal troubles.

Application rejection messages are routine communications, but saying no is never easy, and recipients are emotionally invested in the decision. Moreover, companies must be aware of the possibility of employment discrimination lawsuits, which have been on the rise in recent years.[19] Of course, having fair and nondiscriminatory hiring practices is essential, but rejections must also be written in a way that doesn't inadvertently suggest any hint of discrimination. Expert opinions differ on the level of information to include in a rejection message, but the safest strategy is to avoid sharing any explanations for the company's decision and to avoid making or implying any promises of future consideration (see Figure 9.6):[20]

- **Personalize the email message or letter by using the recipient's name.** For example, mail merge makes it easy to insert each recipient's name into a form letter.
- **Open with a courteous expression of appreciation for having applied.** In a sense, this is like the buffer in an indirect message because it gives you an opportunity to begin the conversation without immediately and bluntly telling the reader that his or her application has been rejected.
- **Convey the negative news politely and concisely.** The passive voice is helpful in this situation because it shifts focus away from the people involved and thereby depersonalizes the response. For example, "Your application was not among those selected for an interview," is less blunt than the active phrase "We have rejected your application."

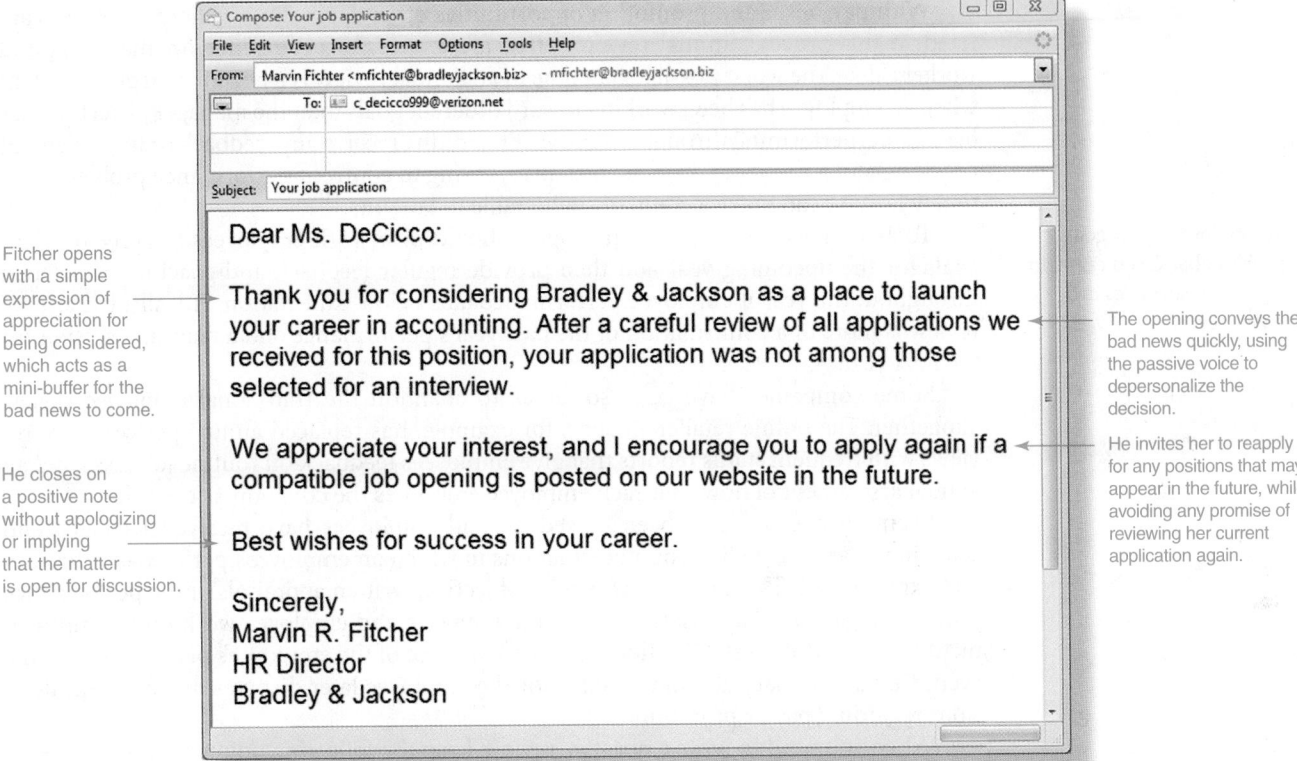

Fitcher opens with a simple expression of appreciation for being considered, which acts as a mini-buffer for the bad news to come.

The opening conveys the bad news quickly, using the passive voice to depersonalize the decision.

He closes on a positive note without apologizing or implying that the matter is open for discussion.

He invites her to reapply for any positions that may appear in the future, while avoiding any promise of reviewing her current application again.

MyBcommLab

Figure 9.6   Effective Message Rejecting a Job Applicant
This message rejecting a job applicant takes care to avoid making or implying any promises about future opportunities, beyond inviting the person to apply for positions that may appear in the future. Note that this would not be appropriate if the company did not believe the applicant was a good fit for the company in general.

Apply Figure 9.6's key concepts by revising a new document. Go to Chapter 9 in www.pearsoninternationaleditions.com/ mybcommlab and select Document Makeovers.

- **Avoid explaining why an applicant was rejected or why other applicants were chosen instead.** Although it was once more common to offer such explanations, and some experts still advocate this approach, the simplest strategy from a legal standpoint is to avoid offering reasons for the decision. Avoiding explanations lowers the possibility that an applicant will perceive discrimination in the hiring decision or be tempted to challenge the reasons given.
- **Don't state or imply that the application will be reviewed at a later date.** Saying that "we will keep your résumé on file for future consideration" can create false hopes for the recipient and leave the company vulnerable to legal complaints if a future hiring decision is made without actually reviewing this candidate's application again. If the candidate might be a good fit for another position in the company in the future, you can suggest he or she reapply if a new job opening is posted.
- **Close with positive wishes for the applicant's career success.** A brief statement such as "We wish you success in your career" is sufficient.

Naturally, you should adjust your tactics to the circumstances. A simple and direct message is fine when someone has only submitted a job application, but rejecting a candidate who has made it at least partway through the interview process requires greater care. Personal contact has already been established through the interview process, so a phone call may be more appropriate.

GIVING NEGATIVE PERFORMANCE REVIEWS

The main purpose of a **performance review** is to improve employee performance by (1) emphasizing and clarifying job requirements, (2) giving employees feedback on their efforts toward fulfilling those requirements, and (3) guiding continued efforts by developing a plan of action, which includes rewards and opportunities. Performance reviews help companies set organizational standards and communicate organizational values.[21] Documentation of performance problems can also protect a company from being sued for unlawful termination.[22]

An important goal of any performance evaluation is to give the employee a plan of action for improving his or her performance.

With pay raises and promotion opportunities often depending on how employees are rated in this process, annual reviews often are a stressful occurrence for managers and workers alike. The worst possible outcome in an annual review is a negative surprise, such as when an employee has been working toward different goals than the manager expects or has been underperforming throughout the year but didn't receive any feedback or improvement coaching along the way.[23] In some instances, failing to confront performance problems in a timely fashion can make a company vulnerable to lawsuits.[24]

By giving employees clear goals and regular feedback, you can help avoid unpleasant surprises in a performance review.

To avoid negative surprises, managers should meet with employees to agree on clear goals for the upcoming year and then provide regular feedback and coaching as needed throughout the year if employee performance falls below expectations. Ideally, the annual review is more of a confirmation of the past year's performance and a planning session for the next year.

Some companies have gone so far as to abandon the traditional employee review altogether. The online retailer Zappos, for example, has replaced annual performance reviews with frequent status reports that give employees feedback on routine job tasks and an annual assessment of how well each employee embodies the company's core values.[25]

Even when goals have been agreed on and employees have received feedback and coaching, managers will encounter situations in which an employee's performance has not met expectations. These situations require objective, written appraisals of the performance shortcomings. Such appraisals can help the manager and employee work on an improvement plan. They also establish documentary evidence of the employee's performance in the event that disciplinary action is needed, or the employee later disputes management decisions regarding pay or promotions.[26]

When you need to write a negative review, keep the following points in mind:[27]

Negative evaluations should provide careful documentation of performance concerns.

- **Document performance problems.** As you provide feedback throughout the year, keep a written record of performance issues. You will need this information in order to write an effective appraisal and to support any decisions that need to be made about pay, promotions, or termination.
- **Evaluate all employees consistently.** Consistency is not only fair but also helps protect the company from claims of discriminatory practices.
- **Write in a calm, objective voice.** The employee is not likely to welcome your negative assessment, but you can manage the emotions of the situation by maintaining professional reserve in your writing.
- **Focus on opportunities for improvement.** As you document performance problems, identify specific steps the employee can take to correct them. This information can serve as the foundation for an improvement plan for the coming year.
- **Keep job descriptions up to date.** Performance evaluations should be based on the criteria listed in an employee's job description. However, if a job evolves over time in response to changes in the business, the employees' current activities may no longer match an outdated job description.

TERMINATING EMPLOYMENT

If an employee's performance cannot be brought up to company standards or if other factors such as declining sales cause a reduction in the workforce, a company often has no choice but to terminate employment. As with other negative employment messages, termination is fraught with emotions and legal ramifications, so careful planning, complete documentation, and sensitive writing are essential.

Carefully word a termination message to avoid creating undue ill will and grounds for legal action.

Termination messages should always be written with input from the company's legal staff, but here are general writing guidelines to bear in mind:[28]

- Clearly present the reasons for this difficult action, whether it is the employee's performance or a business decision unrelated to specific employees.
- Make sure the reasons are presented in a way that cannot be construed as unfair or discriminatory.
- Follow company policy and any relevant legal guidelines (such as employment contracts) to the letter.

- Avoid personal attacks or insults of any kind.
- Ask another manager to review the letter before issuing it. An objective reviewer who isn't directly involved might spot troublesome wording or faulty reasoning.
- Deliver the termination letter in person if at all possible. Arrange a meeting that will ensure privacy and freedom from interruptions.

Any termination is clearly a negative outcome for both employer and employee, but careful attention to content and tone in the termination message can help the employee move on gracefully and minimize the misunderstandings and anger that can lead to expensive lawsuits. To review the tasks involved in this type of message, see "Checklist: Writing Negative Employment Messages." For the latest information on writing negative messages, visit http://real-timeupdates.com/ebc10 and click on Chapter 9.

✓ Checklist | Writing Negative Employment Messages

A. Refusing requests for employee references and recommendations
- Don't feel obligated to write a recommendation letter if you don't feel comfortable doing so.
- Take a diplomatic approach to minimize hurt feelings.
- Compliment the reader's accomplishments.
- Suggest alternatives, if available.
- Use the options available to you on social networks, such as ignoring a request from someone you don't know or writing a recommendation on a single positive attribute.

B. Rejecting job applicants
- If possible, respond to all applications, even if you use only a form message to acknowledge receipt.
- If you use the direct approach, take care to avoid being blunt or cold.
- If you use the indirect approach, don't mislead the reader in your buffer or delay the bad news for more than a sentence or two.
- Avoid explaining why the applicant was rejected.
- Suggest alternatives if possible.

C. Giving negative performance reviews
- Document performance problems throughout the year.
- Evaluate all employees consistently.
- Keep job descriptions up to date as employee responsibilities change.
- Maintain an objective and unbiased tone.
- Use nonjudgmental language.
- Focus on problem resolution.
- Make sure negative feedback is documented and shared with the employee.
- Don't avoid confrontations by withholding negative feedback.
- Ask the employee for a commitment to improve.

D. Terminating employment
- State your reasons accurately and make sure they are objectively verifiable.
- Avoid statements that might expose your company to a wrongful termination lawsuit.
- Consult company lawyers to clarify all terms of the separation.
- Deliver the letter in person if at all possible.
- End the relationship on terms as positive as possible.

ON THE JOB: SOLVING COMMUNICATION DILEMMAS AT **CHARGIFY**

Source: © D. Hurst/Alamy.

Thanks to your effective leadership skills, you didn't take long to move up to a management position in Chargify's human resources (HR) department. Use what you've learned about negative messages to address these communication dilemmas.

1. Another manager stopped by this morning with a request to borrow two of your best employees for a three-week emergency.

Under normal conditions, you wouldn't hesitate to help, but your team has its own scheduling challenges to deal with. Plus, this isn't the first time this manager has run into trouble, and you are confident that poor project management is the reason. Which of the following is the most diplomatic way to state your refusal while suggesting that your colleague's management skills need improvement?

a. With the commitments we've made on our own projects, we won't be able to bail you out this time.

b. I sympathize with the trouble you've gotten yourself into again, I really do, but the commitments we've made on our own projects prevent us from releasing any employees for temporary assignments.

c. The commitments we've made on our own projects prevent us from releasing any workers for temporary assignments. However, I would be happy to meet with you to discuss the techniques I've been using to manage project workloads.

d. Instead of shifting resources around as usual, why don't we meet to discuss some new strategies for staffing and project management?

2. The HR department acts as an internal service provider, helping various departments throughout the company with hiring, benefits, training, and other employment functions. An HR rep is assigned to each division, working with the managers and employees in that department, but reporting to HR managers. As in all other professional relationships, personal aspects can enter the relationship. Even competent professionals can start to rub each other the wrong way at a personal level, which can corrode the business relationship over time. Unfortunately, that has happened with one of your best staff members. Shirley Jackson is widely admired for her HR skills, but the general manager of the department where she is assigned has asked you to replace her with a new HR representative. Although you'd prefer to tell Jackson in person, schedule conflicts dictate that you send her an email. Which of these buffers would be the best way to open the message?

a. Your work for the customer support department continues to be first rate, but you never can tell how these things are going to work out, can you?

b. If it were up to me, Shirley, I would never deliver a message like this, but the customer support department has asked me to reevaluate the HR staffing assignments.

c. As I've expressed on many occasions, thank you once again for the top-quality work you've done for the customer support department over the years.

d. As you know, Shirley, I continually evaluate the HR staffing assignments to make sure the various departments are satisfied with the quality of our work and the overall nature of our relationship with them.

3. Although your project management skills are quite good, you do occasionally run into unforeseen circumstances that lead to less-than-ideal results. Halfway through the installation of a new applicant tracking system, you realized that you underestimated the complexity of linking this new technology to the company's information systems. You now have the unpleasant task of explaining to your boss that the project will be coming in at least 20 percent over budget and possibly as high as 30 percent over. Which of the following is the best way to begin an email message to your boss?

a. I messed up, big time. The applicant tracking project is going to come in over budget.

b. The applicant tracking project is going to come in at least 20 percent over budget and possibly as much as 30 percent over.

c. I recently discovered that linking the applicant tracking to our existing IT systems was more complicated than anyone realized when we established the budget for this project. As a result of the extra work required to customize the software, the project is going to run 20 to 30 percent over budget.

d. I recently discovered that linking the applicant tracking system to our existing IT systems was more complicated than anyone realized when we established the budget for this project. The fact that there is extra work is not really my fault, per se, since it would've been necessary in any case, but as a result of the extra work required to customize the software, the project is going to run 20 to 30 percent over budget.

4. You've found it easy to say "yes" to recommendation letter requests from former employees who were top performers, and you've learned to say "no" to people who didn't perform so well. The requests you struggle with are from employees in the middle, people who didn't really excel but didn't really cause any trouble, either. You've just received a request from an HR specialist who falls smack in the middle of the middle. Unfortunately, he's applying for a job at a firm that you know places high demands on its employees and generally hires the best of the best. He's a great person, and you'd love to help, but in your heart, you know that if by some chance he does get the job, he probably won't last. Plus, you don't want to get a reputation in the industry for recommending weak candidates. How do you set the stage for the negative news?

a. As your former manager, I'd like to think I can still look out for your best interests, and I'm sorry to say, but based on what I know about the position you're applying for, this might not be the best career move for you at this point.

b. In my view, the responsibility of writing a letter of recommendation goes beyond simply assessing a person's skills; it must consider whether the person is applying for the right job.

c. One of the most important factors I consider when deciding whether to endorse an applicant is whether he or she is pursuing an opportunity that offers a high probability of success.

d. Writing recommendation letters bears a heavy responsibility for the job applicant and the person writing the letter. After all, I have my own reputation to protect, too.

LEARNING OBJECTIVES CHECKUP

Assess your understanding of the principles in this chapter by reading each learning objective and studying the accompanying exercises. For fill-in-the-blank items, write the missing text in the blank provided; for multiple-choice items, circle the letter of the correct answer. You can check your responses against the answer key on page AK-2.

Objective 9.1: Apply the three-step writing process to negative messages.

1. Which of the following should be a goal of every negative message?
   a. To convey the bad news clearly
   b. To gain audience acceptance for the news
   c. To maintain as much goodwill as possible with the audience
   d. To maintain a good image for your organization
   e. To reduce or eliminate the need for future correspondence on the matter, if appropriate
   f. None of the above
   g. (a), (c), and (d)
   h. All of the above

2. Which of the following is an effective way to maintain the "you" attitude when crafting negative messages?
   a. Make sure the reader clearly understands that he or she is at fault; after all, recognizing a mistake is the first step toward improvement.
   b. Make it clear that you don't enjoy giving out bad news.
   c. Show respect for the reader by "soft peddling" the negative news, implying it without really coming out and saying it directly.
   d. Show respect for the reader by avoiding negative, accusatory language and emphasizing positives whenever possible.

Objective 9.2: Explain how to use the direct approach effectively when conveying negative news.

3. When using the direct approach with negative messages, you begin with
   a. A buffer
   b. An attention-getter
   c. The bad news
   d. Any of the above

4. An advantage of using the direct approach with negative messages is that it
   a. Saves readers time by helping them reach the main idea more quickly
   b. Eases readers into the message
   c. Is diplomatic
   d. Does all of the above

Objective 9.3: Explain how to use the indirect approach effectively when conveying negative news.

5. When using the indirect approach with negative messages, you begin with
   a. A buffer
   b. An attention-getter
   c. The bad news
   d. Any of the above

6. Which of the following is an advantage of using the indirect approach with negative messages?
   a. Most readers prefer the direct approach for such messages.
   b. It makes a shorter message possible.
   c. It eases the reader into the message.
   d. It does all of the above.

7. The purpose of using the indirect approach is to
   a. Help the writer avoid the unpleasant task of delivering bad news
   b. Help the reader avoid the unpleasant task of receiving bad news
   c. Soften the blow of the bad news for the reader
   d. Reduce the word count in your messages

8. A/an _____ is a neutral, noncontroversial opening statement that establishes common ground with your reader.

9. Which of the following is a good possibility to consider for use in writing a buffer?
   a. Look for subtle opportunities to promote your company and its products.
   b. Assure the reader that your company always follows all applicable laws and regulations.
   c. Indicate your understanding of the reader's situation.
   d. All of the above are useful approaches.

Objective 9.4: Explain the importance of maintaining high standards of ethics and etiquette when delivering negative messages.

10. Which of the following is an important reason to take particular care to maintain ethics and etiquette when crafting negative messages?
    a. In many cases, the communicator needs to adhere to a variety of laws and regulations when delivering negative messages.
    b. Good ethical practice demands care and sensitivity in the content and delivery of negative messages, as these messages can have a profoundly negative effect on the people who receive them.
    c. Communicators need to manage their own emotions when crafting and distributing negative messages while at the same time considering the emotional needs of their audiences.
    d. All of the above are important reasons to maintain ethics and etiquette in negative messages.

11. Which of the following is most characteristic of organizational cultures that emphasize open communication?
    a. Managers are willing to listen to bad news from employees, but they understand if employees don't want to deliver bad news.
    b. Managers expect employees to alert them to problems so that corrective action can be taken.
    c. Managers reward employees who deliver bad news with extra vacation time, extra pay, or both.
    d. None of the above are true.

Objective 9.5: Describe successful strategies for sending negative messages on routine business matters.

12. If you need to reject a solicited proposal from an employee, which of the following approaches is best?
    a. Use the indirect approach, but avoid explaining exactly why the proposal does not meet your needs; it's up to the employee to figure that out.
    b. Use the direct approach; rejected proposals are a fact of life of business.
    c. Use the indirect approach, and provide a thoughtful and complete explanation of why the proposal does not meet your needs.
    d. Don't respond at all; doing so will only create an uncomfortable situation for the employee.

13. Which of the following is not a normal goal when sending bad-news messages about transactions?
    a. Modifying the customer's expectations
    b. Explaining how you plan to resolve the situation
    c. Identifying who is responsible for the situation so that the customer understands you are serious about correcting the error
    d. Repair whatever damage might have been done to the business relationship

Objective 9.6: List the important points to consider when conveying negative organizational news.

14. Which of the following best characterizes the nature of crisis management planning?
    a. Good managers should be able to anticipate the specific crisis scenarios their companies might encounter and therefore should be able to plan for every crisis in a specific way.
    b. Faced with everything from terrorism to technological disasters, there's no way for managers to anticipate which crisis might hit any given business, so it's a waste of time to plan a response.
    c. Although you can't anticipate the nature and circumstance of every possible crisis, you can prepare by deciding how to handle such issues as communication with employees and the public.
    d. Only negatively focused managers worry about crisis planning; positive managers keep their organizations moving toward company goals.

15. Continuing advances in communication technology make it
    a. Easier to control rumors through Internet filters and other means
    b. More difficult to control rumors
    c. Easier to find the people who start rumors
    d. Illegal to spread false rumors about public corporations

Objective 9.7: Describe successful strategies for sending negative employment-related messages.

16. Why do many experts recommend using an indirect approach when rejecting job applicants?
    a. Applicants have a deep emotional investment in the decision.
    b. Laws in most states require an indirect approach.
    c. Indirect approaches are easier to write.
    d. Indirect approaches are shorter.

17. When explaining why an applicant wasn't chosen for a position, you should
    a. Be specific without being too personal, such as explaining that the position requires specific skills that the applicant doesn't yet possess
    b. Point out the person's shortcomings as that's the honest way and the only way the person knows what he or she needs to improve
    c. Be as vague as possible to avoid hurting the person's feelings
    d. Avoid explaining why an applicant wasn't chosen

MyBcommLab

CHAPTER OUTLINE

Using the Three-Step Writing Process for Negatives Messages

Step 1: Planning a Negative Message
Step 2: Writing a Negative Message
Step 3: Completing a Negative Message

Using the Direct Approach for Negative Messages

Opening with a Clear Statement of the Bad News
Providing Reasons and Additional Information
Closing on a Respectful Note

Using the Indirect Approach for Negative Messages

Opening with a Buffer
Providing Reasons and Additional Information
Continuing with a Clear Statement of the Bad News
Closing on a Respectful Note

Maintaining High Standards of Ethics and Etiquette

Sending Negative Messages on Routine Business Matters

Making Negative Announcements on Routine Business Matters
Rejecting Suggestions and Proposals
Refusing Routine Requests
Handling Bad News About Transactions
Refusing Claims and Requests for Adjustment

Sending Negative Organizational News

Communicating Under Normal Circumstances
Communicating in a Crisis

Sending Negative Employment Messages

Refusing Requests for Employee References and Recommendation Letters
Refusing Social Networking Recommendation Requests
Rejecting Job Applications
Giving Negative Performance Reviews
Terminating Employment

LEARNING OBJECTIVES

1. Apply the three-step writing process to negative messages. [page 295]
2. Explain how to use the direct approach effectively when conveying negative news. [page 298]
3. Explain how to use the indirect approach effectively when conveying negative news. [page 299]
4. Explain the importance of maintaining high standards of ethics and etiquette when delivering negative messages. [page 303]
5. Describe successful strategies for sending negative messages on routine business matters. [page 304]
6. List the important points to consider when conveying negative organizational news. [page 310]
7. Describe successful strategies for sending negative employment-related messages. [page 313]

KEY TERMS

buffer A neutral, noncontroversial statement that establishes common ground with the reader in an indirect negative message
crisis management plan Plan that defines operational procedures to deal with a crisis, including communication tasks and responsibilities

performance review Employee evaluation procedure giving feedback on performance and guidance for future efforts
whistleblowing Efforts by employees to report concerns about unethical or illegal behavior

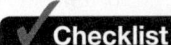 **Checklist**

Creating Negative Messages

A. Choose the better approach.
- Consider using the direct approach when the audience is aware of the possibility of negative news, when the reader is not emotionally involved in the message, when you know that the reader would prefer the bad news first, when you know that firmness is necessary, and when you want to discourage a response.
- Consider using the indirect approach when the news is likely to come as a shock or surprise, when your audience has a high emotional investment in the outcome, and when you want to maintain a good relationship with the audience.

B. For the indirect approach, open with an effective buffer.
- Establish common ground with the audience.
- Validate the request, if you are responding to a request.
- Don't trivialize the reader's concerns.
- Don't mislead the reader into thinking the coming news might be positive.

C. Provide reasons and additional information.
- Explain why the news is negative.
- Adjust the amount of detail to fit the situation and the audience.
- Avoid explanations when the reasons are confidential, excessively complicated, or irrelevant to the reader.
- If appropriate, state how you plan to correct or respond to the negative news.
- Seek the advice of company lawyers if you're unsure what to say.

D. Clearly state the bad news.
- State the bad news as positively as possible, using tactful wording.
- To help protect readers' feelings, deemphasize the bad news by minimizing the space devoted to it, subordinating it, or embedding it.
- If your response might change in the future if circumstances change, explain the conditions to the reader.
- Emphasize what you can or have done rather than what you can't or won't do.

E. Close on a respectful note.
- Express best wishes without being falsely positive.
- Suggest actions readers might take, if appropriate, and provide them with necessary information.
- Encourage further communication only if you're willing to discuss the situation further.

APPLY YOUR KNOWLEDGE

To review chapter content related to each question, refer to the indicated Learning Objective.

1. Would you choose the direct or indirect approach to announce that a popular employee benefit is being eliminated for cost reasons? Why? [LO-1]

2. Is intentionally deemphasizing bad news the same as distorting graphs and charts to deemphasize unfavorable data? Why or why not? [LO-3]

3. Why is whistleblowing a controversial activity? [LO-4]

4. If a company can't predict every specific calamity that might occur, does it still make sense to have a crisis plan? Why or why not? [LO-6]

5. How do social networks make the practices of requesting and granting or denying recommendations both easier and more difficult? [LO-7]

PRACTICE YOUR SKILLS

Messages for Analysis

Read the following messages and then (1) analyze the strengths and weaknesses of each sentence and (2) revise each message so that it follows this chapter's guidelines.

Message 9.A: Sending Negative Organizational News [LO-6]

From: A. Kosca, Travel & Meeting Services
To: [mailing list]
Subject: Travel

Dear Traveling Executives:

A notice will shortly reach you on the kind of expenses we want you to cut from your operating budgets. I don't need to repeat the reasons why we are all tightening our belts. Your target, as it is for the rest of the company, is to cut costs by at least half: the accounts department assures me that this is the only way we can hope to stretch our meager resources to cover this year's outlay.

Here is what you have to do: The biggest item of costs seems to be conference trips, which can be further broken down under the heads of air travel, hotel stays, and local transport and hospitality. First, ask yourself: is it necessary to travel at all? Would a video call or a teleconference work just as well? Next, I have gone over the bills and some things spring to my notice. The excessive use of hotel laundry services, mini-bar items, Wi-Fi and room service is evident everywhere. You are traveling on business on behalf of the company, not having an all-expenses-paid holiday. I notice also that in cities where you are staying within walking or busing distance of the meeting place, there are multiple vouchers for car hire. This makes no sense. If you really must take a car, henceforth, you'll have to pay for it yourself.

I'd like to see an immediate drop in these irrational expenditures. I'm afraid we're all going to have to sacrifice a little until things get better.

Sincerely,
A. Kosca
Travel & Meeting Services

Message 9.B: Refusing Requests for Claims and Adjustments [LO-5]

I am very sorry to hear that you have broken your Capo di Altamonte handcrafted porcelain figurine of John Lennon while unpacking it. We ship all our products packed in international standard packaging material, configured in a tried and tested system developed by our engineers. It is practically impossible for a correctly handled product to break or be damaged while it is in the original polyurethane molded cocoon (patent pending): believe me, we have conducted multiple tests in controlled conditions to establish this. It is still possible that the shipper did not follow best practice while handling your item, but you will, of course, understand that we cannot be responsible for that, and you had best take it up with the shipper directly.

We are executing your pending orders on a priority basis for the rest of the set: the Paul McCartney, Ringo Starr and George Harrison figurines. They should reach you by the end of next week. Congratulations on purchasing this beautiful and coveted tableau. We hope that we will get an opportunity to serve you again in the near future.

Message 9.C: Rejecting Job Applications [LO-7]

Hey Charlie, thanks for sending your CV over for the summer program. Sorry I forgot to tell you about it till there were only four days left till the deadline. Anyway, I put it with the others on my boss's desk and he said 'What? Jimmy, you can't be serious.' Turned out he had a headache and didn't want to go through them all. He just skimmed off the first 25 that had all the qualifications and dumped the rest back in the file. I tell you, I was pretty bummed. But don't worry buddy, I'm sure you'll find yourself something good somewhere else.

Exercises

Active links for all websites in this chapter can be found on MyBcommLab; see your User Guide for instructions on accessing the content for this chapter. Each activity is labeled according to the primary skill or skills you will need to use. To review relevant chapter content, you can refer to the indicated Learning Objective. In some instances, supporting information will be found in another chapter, as indicated.

1. **Planning: Choosing the Direct or Indirect Approach [LO-1]** Select which approach you would use (direct or indirect) for the following negative messages.

   a. An email message to your boss, informing her that a project for which you had pitched has gone to a rival firm.

   b. An instant message to a customer, explaining that the custom paint job he's asked for on his vintage car will take 12 days and he has a car show to attend in a week.

   c. A blog post to all employees, notifying them that the main lobby will be under repair for a week and they will have to use the stairs. The only working elevator will be reserved for those with physical impairments and those moving heavy loads.

   d. A form letter from a U.S. airline to a customer, explaining that the company cannot extend the expiration date of the customer's frequent flyer miles, even though the customer was living overseas for the past three years and unable to use the miles during that time.

e. A letter from an insurance company to a policyholder, denying a claim for reimbursement for the accidental destruction of the policyholder's garden, as the garden was not covered under the house insurance policy.

f. A letter from an electronics store, stating that the customer will not be reimbursed for a malfunctioning mobile phone that is still under warranty (because the terms of the warranty do not cover damages to phones sucked on by toddlers).

2. **Message Strategies: Refusing Routine Requests [LO-4]** As a customer service supervisor for a telephone company, you're in charge of responding to customers' requests for refunds. You've just received an email from a customer who unwittingly ran up a $100 bill for long-distance calls when he tried to call 911 about his stolen car and ended up dialing a number in New Delhi, India, belonging to a paid helpline for people filing lawsuits in the United States. He spoke with the helpline staff for several minutes (including being put on hold several times) before they were able to work out what he actually wanted. He has now discovered that he has been billed for the entire call. Draft an email message sympathizing with the customer's plight but preparing him for the bad news that, much as you'd like to, you really can't give him a refund in this case, as company policy prohibits it.

3. **Etiquette: Communicating with Sensitivity and Tact; Collaboration: Team Projects [LO-4]** Working alone, revise the following statements to deemphasize the bad news. Then team up with a classmate and read each other's revisions. Did you both use the same approach in every case? Which approach seems to be most effective for each of the revised statements?

a. The airline only refunds money in very rare cases. The "Conditions" section on the back of your ticket states that there are no refunds for missed flights. In your case, you missed your flight because of the encores to your stage performance. We do not think this is an adequately grave reason to refund your ticket money, especially as your ticket will remain valid for travel on any of our flights for a year.

b. I'm sorry to tell you, we can't supply the Indonesian wood paneling you requested. We called every supplier, including some outside our regular ones, and none of them were able to source the wood on such short notice. You can, however, get a Norwegian pine veneer which looks similar and (this is fortunate) costs maybe two-thirds of the original quote within the time you have stipulated. I found a supplier that stocks this. However, as it is a veneer, it may buckle and peel in the future.

c. We can't refund your money for the malfunctioning MP3 player. We aren't clear from your letter as to what went wrong with it, but the circumstances of its malfunction are clearly not covered by the warranty document. As you know, we are legally obliged only to provide replacements only for products which are damaged under the conditions described in the warranty.

4. **Communication Ethics [LO-4]** The kindergarten school where you work is planning to shift to new premises further out of town as part of a cost-cutting measure, resulting in a longer commute for parents bringing their kids to and from school. The head teacher calls you in to read the draft letter she is sending out to the parents. You find that the first two paragraphs of the letter are full of promises of cleaner air, bigger playgrounds, and better car parking. It is only in the last line of the letter that the readers get to learn of the move, which is happening in a week. What are the ethical implications of this letter? Would you redraft it? Why (or why not) and how?

5. **Sending Negative Organizational News [LO-6]** Public companies occasionally need to issue news releases to announce or explain downturns in sales, profits, demand, or other business factors. Search the web to locate a company that has issued a press release that recently reported lower earnings or other bad news and access the news release on that firm's website. Alternatively, find the type of press release you're seeking by reviewing press releases at www.prnewswire.com or www.businesswire.com. How does the headline relate to the main message of the release? Is the release organized according to the direct or the indirect approach? What does the company do to present the bad news in a favorable light— and does this effort seem sincere and ethical to you?

EXPAND YOUR SKILLS

Critique the Professionals

Locate an example online of a negative-news message from any company. Possible examples include announcements of product recalls, poor financial results, layoffs, and fines or other legal troubles. Analyze the approach the company took; was it the most effective strategy possible? Did the company apologize, if doing so would have been appropriate under the circumstances, and does the apology seem sincere? Does the tone of the message match the seriousness of the situation? Does the message end on a positive note, as appropriate? Using whatever medium your instructor requests, write a brief analysis of the message (no more than one page), citing specific elements from the piece and support from the chapter.

Sharpening Your Career Skills Online

Bovée and Thill's Business Communication Web Search, at http://businesscommunicationblog.com/websearch, is a unique research tool designed specifically for business communication research. Use the Web Search function to find a website, video, PDF document, podcast, or PowerPoint presentation that offers advice on writing messages that convey negative information. Write a brief email message to your instructor, describing the item that you found and summarizing the career skills information you learned from it.

IMPROVE YOUR GRAMMAR, MECHANICS, AND USAGE

The following exercises help you improve your knowledge of and power over English grammar, mechanics, and usage. Turn to the "Handbook of Grammar, Mechanics, and Usage" at the end of this book and review all of Section 2.6 (Commas). Then look at the following 10 items. Circle the letter of the preferred choice in the following groups of sentences. (Answers to these exercises appear on page AK-3.)

1. **a.** Please make out an order for three screwdrivers four sets of spanners and a box of screws.
   b. Please make out an order for three screwdrivers, four sets of spanners and a box of screws.
   c. Please make out an order for three screwdrivers, four sets of spanners, and a box of screws.

2. **a.** Your report, therefore, should have only one hundred pages.
   b. Your report therefore should have only one hundred pages.
   c. Your report, therefore should have only one hundred pages.

3. **a.** As a case in point, you could consider Enron.
   b. As a case in point you could consider Enron.

4. **a.** After June 17, 2000, your reports will not be accepted.
   b. After June 17, 2000 your reports will not be accepted.

5. **a.** Systech, Inc. officially declared bankruptcy on April 2nd 2011.
   b. Systech, Inc. officially declared bankruptcy on April 2nd, 2011.
   c. Systech, Inc., officially declared bankruptcy on April 2nd, 2011.

6. **a.** "Ask Jonathan" he said "before sending in the report."
   b. "Ask Jonathan," he said "before sending in the report."
   c. "Ask Jonathan," he said, "before sending in the report."

7. **a.** The company managed to stay relatively clean through the troubled scandal-hit mid-2000s.
   b. The company managed to stay relatively clean through the troubled, scandal-hit mid-2000s.
   c. The company managed to stay relatively clean through the troubled scandal-hit, mid-2000s.

8. **a.** Mail the envelope to this address: 124 Westbury Ave., Stanford CA 75628.
   b. Mail the envelope to this address: 124 Westbury Ave., Stanford, CA 75628
   c. Mail the envelope to this address: 124 Westbury Ave., Stanford, CA, 75628.

9. **a.** Roger has been transferred from Dayton, Ohio to Annapolis, Maryland.
   b. Roger has been transferred from Dayton Ohio, to Annapolis Maryland.
   c. Roger has been transferred from Dayton, Ohio, to Annapolis, Maryland.

10. **a.** Sheila Johnson his executive assistant is on leave tomorrow.
    b. Sheila Johnson, his executive assistant, is on leave tomorrow.
    c. Sheila Johnson, his executive assistant is on leave tomorrow.

For additional exercises focusing on commas, visit MyBcommLab. Click on Chapter 9, click on Additional Exercises to Improve Your Grammar, Mechanics, and Usage, and then click on 14. Fused sentences and comma splices.

CASES

Negative Messages on Routine Business Matters

IM SKILLS

1. Message Strategies: Refusing Claims and Requests for Adjustment: Media Skills: Instant Messaging [LO-5], Chapter 7   Your company has learned that selling instructional videos presents a difficult business dilemma. For its first five years of operation, the company had a generous return policy in which customers could return any DVD after ten days, even if it had been opened. However, as return rates began to climb, management began to suspect that some customers were abusing the policy by watching DVDs long enough to learn whatever they wanted to learn and then returning them and asking for refunds. The company disliked penalizing the majority of its customer base by changing the policy, but returns cost money, and the company's profits were taking a bigger and bigger hit every year. Starting last year, the company now accepts returns only if the product packaging has not been opened.

Your task: Team up with two other students. One of you will play the role of a customer who purchased the "Kickboxing Fundamentals" DVD two weeks ago. One of you will play the role of a service agent who assists customers with orders and returns.

Using Facebook's chat function or any other free IM service, role play an exchange in which the customer initiates the conversation and asks for a refund, saying that the program doesn't meet his or her needs. The reason offered is that the techniques shown in the video are quite basic, and he or she is already past that skill level.

Early in the exchange, the service agent needs to ask whether the DVD package has been unsealed. The customer replies that it has, after which the agent will respond that the company can accept only unopened DVDs for refund or exchange. The customer can continue to argue that there is no way to truly evaluate a DVD without watching the entire program, because every person might have a different understanding of what "fundamentals" means. However, the company's policy is firm.

Make up whatever details you need to complete the exchange, keeping in mind the following points:

- The video title and the product description on the website clearly indicate that this kickboxing program is intended for beginners.

- The website clearly states that DVDs can be returned only if they are unopened.
- In addition, the online shopping cart requires customers to check a box to indicate that they have read the return policy.
- The agent might suggest to the customer that he or she could offer it for sale on Craigslist, sell it to a store that buys used movies, or donate it to a library.

The third member of the team should sit beside either the customer or the agent and evaluate the IM exchange, without participating. If possible, capture the IM stream for offline analysis. The evaluator will then give both participants written feedback on the content and tone of their messages, offering suggestions for improvement. Be prepared to discuss the experience and the analysis with your class.

E-MAIL SKILLS

2. Message Strategies: Rejecting Suggestions and Proposals [LO-5] Kate Mitchell is a valued senior member of your team. She has been with you ever since you started in this company, working alongside you to make instructional videos for corporate trainers, and has always advised you well. She is usually worth listening to, but the email she sent you yesterday certainly wasn't up to her usual standard. In it, she proposed that the company dump the recording studio it has used for a decade and go instead to some new studio you've never heard of. The only reasons she offered were that the existing studio "was outdated" and that "their attitude is problematic." On the contrary, you know the studio has recently put in new equipment and opened a new sound stage. Mitchell didn't go into details about costs, facilities, or equipment at the new place, saying only that it was "run by a pair of award-winning film makers."

Your task: Draft an email message to Mitchell, rejecting her proposal. (Note that in a real-life setting, you would want to discuss this with Mitchell in person, rather than through email, but use email for the purposes of this exercise.)

E-MAIL SKILLS

3. Message Strategies: Making Routine Negative Announcements [LO-5] You've been proud of many things your gardening tool company has accomplished as it has grown from just you working in your basement shop to a nationally known company that employs over 200 people. However, nothing has made you prouder than the company's Helping Our Hometown Grow program, in which employees volunteer on company time to help residents in your city start their own vegetable gardens, using tools donated by the company. Nearly 50 employees have participated directly, helping some 500 families supplement their grocery budgets with home-grown produce. Virtually everyone in the company has contributed, though, because employees who didn't volunteer to help in the gardens pitched in to cover the work responsibilities of the volunteers.

Sadly, ten years after you launched the program, you have reached the inescapable conclusion that the company can no longer afford to keep the program going. With consumers around the country still struggling with the aftereffects of a deep recession, sales have been dropping for the past three years—even as lower cost competitors step up their presence in the market. To save the program, you would have to lay off several employees, but your employees come first.

Your task: Write an email to the entire company, announcing the cancellation of the program.

TELEPHONE SKILLS

4. Message Strategies: Making Routine Negative Announcements [LO-5] Loop-de-Loop Products of Toledo, Ohio, manufactures a line of novelty slides, climbing frames, and swings for school playgrounds. The company is particularly known for its Very-Go-Round pocket carousel. However, there is a design defect in this carousel: it is possible for a child's foot to get caught under it and be seriously injured. Loop-de-Loop has issued a recall for these products. However, the recall is not really a recall. Loop-de-Loop will not be replacing or modifying the carousels, nor will it accept returns. Instead, the company is urging institutions to lock or remove these rides. In the meantime, the line has been discontinued.

Your task: A flurry of phone calls from concerned teachers, parents, and education officials is overwhelming the support staff. As a writer in Loop-de-Loop's corporate communications office, you've been asked to draft a short script to be recorded on the company's phone system. When people call the main number, they'll hear "Press 1 for information regarding the recall of Whirligig, Planet Dizzy, and the Very-Go-Round carousels." After they press 1, they'll hear the message you're about to write, explaining that although the action is classified as a recall, Loop-de-Loop will not be accepting returned rides, nor will it replace any of the affected ones. The message should also assure customers that Loop-de-Loop has discontinued these lines. The phone system has limited memory, and you've been directed to keep the message to 75 words or less.

EMAIL SKILLS   PORTFOLIO BUILDER

5. Message Strategies: Rejecting Suggestions and Proposals; Communication Ethics: Making Ethical Choices [LO-5] A not-so-secret secret is getting more attention than you'd really like after an article in *BusinessWeek* gave the world an inside look at how much money you and other electronics retailers make from extended warranties (sometimes called service contracts). The article explained that typically half of the warranty price goes to the salesperson as a commission and that only 20 percent of the total amount customers pay for warranties eventually goes to product repair.

You also know why extended warranties are such a profitable business. Many electronics products follow a predictable pattern of failure: a high failure rate early in their lives, then a "midlife" period during which failures go way down, and concluding with an "old age" period when failure rates ramp back up again (engineers refer to the phenomenon as the *bathtub curve* because it looks like a bathtub from the side—high at both ends and low in the middle). The early failures are usually covered by manufacturers' warranties, and the extended warranties you sell are designed to cover that middle part of the life span. In other words, many extended warranties cover the period of time during which consumers are *least* likely to need them and offer no coverage when consumers need them *most*. (Consumers can actually benefit from extended warranties in a few product categories, including laptop computers and plasma televisions. Of course, the more sense the warranty makes for the consumer, the less financial sense it makes for your company.)[29]

Your task: Worried that consumers will stop buying so many extended warranties, your boss has directed you to put together a sales training program that will help cashiers sell the extended warranties even more aggressively. The more you ponder this challenge, though, the more you're convinced that your company should change its strategy so it doesn't rely on profits from these warranties so much. In addition to offering questionable value to the consumer, the warranties risk creating a consumer backlash that could lead to lower sales of all your products. You would prefer to voice your concerns to your boss in person, but both of you are traveling on hectic schedules for the next week. You'll have to write an email instead. Draft a brief message, explaining why you think the sales training specifically and the warranties in general are both bad ideas.

MICROBLOGGING SKILLS

6. Message Strategies: Making Routine Negative Announcements [LO-5] JetBlue was one of the first companies to incorporate the Twitter microblogging service into its customer communications, and thousands of fliers and fans now follow the airline's Twittering staff members. Messages include announcements about fare sales (such as limited-time auctions on eBay or special on-site sales at shopping malls), celebrations of company milestones (such as the opening of the carrier's new terminal at New York's JFK airport), schedule updates, and even personalized responses to people who Twitter with questions or complaints about the company.[30]

Your task: Write a Tweet alerting JetBlue customers to the fact that a volcano has erupted in the Mediterranean, spewing ash into the upper atmosphere, and is causing flight delays and reroutings. Try to minimize the chances of setting off a panic. Tell them that decisions about delays and cancellations will be made on a city-by-city basis and will be announced on Twitter and the company's website. The URL will take 20 characters, so you have 120 characters (including spaces) for your message.

EMAIL SKILLS

7. Message Strategies: Rejecting Suggestions and Proposals [LO-5] Lee Valley Tools (www.leevalley.com) sells high-quality woodworking tools across Canada through its retail stores and around the world through its website and catalogs. While weekend hobbyists can pick up a mass-produced hand plane (a tool for smoothing wood) for $20 or $30 at the local hardware

store, serious woodworkers pay five or ten times that much for one of Lee Valley's precision Veritas planes. For the price, they get top-quality materials, precision manufacturing, and innovative designs that help them do better work in less time.

Lee Valley sells both its own Veritas brand tools as well as 5,000 tools made by other manufacturers. One of those companies has just emailed you to ask if Lee Valley would like to carry a new line of midrange hand planes that would cost more than the mass-market, hardware-store models but less than Lee Valley's own Veritas models. Your job is to filter requests such as this, rejecting those that don't meet Lee Valley's criteria and forwarding those that do to the product selection committee for further analysis. After one quick read of this incoming email message, you realize there is no need to send this idea to the committee. While these planes are certainly of decent quality, they achieve their lower cost through lower-quality steel that won't hold an edge as long and through thinner irons (the element that holds the cutting edge) that will be more prone to vibrate during use and thus produce a rougher finish. These planes have a market, to be sure, but they're not a good fit for Lee Valley's top-of-the-line product portfolio. Moreover, the planes don't offer any innovations in terms of ease of use or any other product attribute.[31]

Your task: Reply to this email message, explaining that the planes appear to be decent tools, but they don't fit Lee Valley's strategy of offering only the best and most innovative tools. Support your decision with the three criteria described above. Choose the direct or indirect approach carefully, taking into consideration your company's relationship with this other company.

LETTER WRITING SKILLS   PORTFOLIO BUILDER

8. Message Strategies: Negative Announcements on Routine Matters [LO-5] You're a marketing manager for Stanton, one of the premier suppliers of DJ equipment (turntables, amplifiers, speakers, mixers, and related accessories). Your company's latest creation, the FinalScratch system, has been flying off retailers' shelves. Both professional and amateur DJs love the way that FinalScratch gives them the feel of working with vinyl records by letting them control digital music files from any analog turntable or CD player while giving them access to the endless possibilities of digital music technology. (For more information about the product, go to www.stantondj.com.) Sales are strong everywhere except in Music99 stores, a retail chain in the Mid-Atlantic region. You suspect the cause: The owners of this chain refused to let their salespeople attend the free product training you offered when FinalScratch was introduced, claiming their people were smart enough to train themselves.

To explore the situation, you head out from Stanton headquarters in Hollywood, Florida, on an undercover shopping mission. After visiting a few Music99 locations, you're appalled by what you see. The salespeople in these stores clearly don't understand the FinalScratch concept, so they either give potential customers bad information about it or steer them to products from your competitors. No wonder sales are so bad at this chain.

Your task: You're tempted to pull your products out of this chain immediately, but you know how difficult and expensive it is to recruit new retailers in this market. However, this situation can't go on; you're losing thousands of dollars of potential business every week. Write a letter to Jackson Fletcher, the CEO of Music99 (14014 Preston Pike, Dover, DE 19901), expressing your disappointment in what you observed and explaining that the Music99 sales staff will need to agree to attend product training or else your company's management team will consider terminating the business relationship. You've met Mr. Fletcher in person once and talked to him on the phone several times, and you know him well enough to know that he will not be pleased by this ultimatum. Music99 does a good job selling other Stanton products—and he'll probably be furious to learn that you were "spying" on his sales staff.[32]

PODCASTING SKILLS

9. Message Strategies: Negative Announcements on Routine Matters [LO-5] An employee concierge seemed like a great idea when you added it as an employee benefit last year. The concierge handles a wide variety of personal chores for employees, everything from dropping off dry cleaning to ordering event tickets to sending flowers. Employees love the service, and you know that the time they save can be devoted to work or family activities. Unfortunately, profits are way down, and concierge usage is up—up so far that you'll need to add a second concierge to keep up with the demand. As painful as it will be for everyone, you decide that the company needs to stop offering the service.

Your task: Script a brief podcast, announcing the decision and explaining why it was necessary. Make up any details you need. If your instructor asks you to do so, record your podcast and submit the file.

LETTER WRITING SKILLS

10. Message Strategies: Negative Announcements on Routine Matters [LO-5] Your company, PolicyPlan Insurance Services, is a 120-employee insurance claims processor based in Milwaukee. PolicyPlan has engaged Midwest Sparkleen for interior and exterior cleaning for the past five years. Midwest Sparkleen did exemplary work for the first four years, but after a change of ownership last year, the level of service has plummeted. Offices are no longer cleaned thoroughly, you've had to call the company at least six times to remind them to take care of spills and other messes that they're supposed to address routinely, and they've left toxic cleaning chemicals in a public hallway on several occasions. You have spoken with the owner about your concerns twice in the past three months, but his assurances that service would improve have not resulted in any noticeable improvements. When the evening cleaning crew forgot to lock the lobby door last Thursday—leaving your entire facility vulnerable to theft from midnight until 8 A.M. Friday morning—you decided it was time for a change.

Your task: Write a letter to Jason Allred, owner of Midwest Sparkleen, 4000 South Howell Avenue, Milwaukee, WI, 53207, telling him that PolicyPlan will not be renewing its annual cleaning contract with Midwest Sparkleen when the current contract expires at the end of this month. Cite the examples identified above, and keep the tone of your letter professional.

Negative Organizational News

SOCIAL NETWORKING SKILLS

11. Message Strategies: Negative Organizational Announcements [LO-6] Caught in a perfect storm of online retailing, downloadable e-books, low-cost mass merchandisers, a fragmented audience with multiple entertainment options, and the worst recession in memory, the giant Borders bookstore chain was forced to file for bankruptcy protection in 2011.

Your task: Download the Borders press release at http://real-timeupdates.com/ebc10 (click on Student Assignments, and then Chapter 9, Page 327, Case 11). Review the information, and then write a 100- to 150-word summary of the bankruptcy announcement that could be posted on the company's Facebook page.

BLOGGING SKILLS

12. Message Strategies: Negative Organizational Announcements [LO-6] XtremityPlus is known for its outlandish extreme-sports products, and the Looney Launch is no exception. Fulfilling the dream of every childhood daredevil, the Looney Launch is an aluminum and fiberglass contraption that quickly unfolds to create the ultimate bicycle jump. The product has been selling as fast as you can make it, even though it comes plastered with warning labels proclaiming that its use is inherently dangerous.

As XtremityPlus's CEO, you were nervous about introducing this product, and your fears were just confirmed: You've been notified of the first lawsuit by a parent whose child broke several bones after crash-landing off a Looney Launch.

Your task: Write a post for your internal blog, explaining that the Looney Launch is being removed from the market immediately. Tell your employees to expect some negative reactions from enthusiastic customers and retailers but explain that (a) the company can't afford the risk of additional lawsuits; and (b) even for XtremityPlus, the Looney Launch pushes the envelope a bit too far. The product is simply too dangerous to sell in good conscience.

EMAIL SKILLS

13. Message Strategies: Negative Organizational Announcements [LO-6] Now it's time to follow up the internal employee message about the Looney Launch (see Case 12) with a message to the retailers that carry the product.

Your task: Write an email message to retailers, explaining that the Looney Launch is being removed from the market and explaining why you've reached this decision. Apologize for the temporary disruption this will cause to their businesses but emphasize that it's the right decision from both legal and social perspectives. Thank them for their continuing efforts to sell XtremityPlus products and assure them that your company will continue to offer exciting and innovative products for extreme-sports enthusiasts.

BLOGGING SKILLS

14. Message Strategies: Negative Organizational Announcements [LO-6] As the U.S. economy continued to sag after receiving multiple blows from the housing and financial sectors, plant closures were a common tragedy across many industries.

Shaw Industries, the world's largest manufacturer of carpeting, was among those suppliers to the housing industry that suffered as fewer houses were built or remodeled.

Your task: Write a brief message for Shaw's corporate blog, covering the following points:

- With more than $5 billion in annual sales, Shaw Industries is the world's number one carpet manufacturer.
- Shaw's Milledgeville, Georgia, plant makes yarn used in the manufacture of carpeting.
- The continuing struggles in the new-housing market and the inability of many current homeowners to afford remodeling projects have lowered demand for carpet. With less demand for carpet, the Milledgeville plant can no longer operate at a profit.
- Shaw is forced to close the Milledgeville plant and lay off all 150 employees at the plant.
- The plant will close in three to four weeks from the current date.
- As openings become available in other Shaw facilities, the company hopes to be able to place some of the workers in those jobs.
- Georgia Labor Commissioner Michael Thurmond promised to help the affected employees. "The layoff at Shaw Industries in Milledgeville will create a difficult situation for the workers and their families, and I want them to know they're not alone in dealing with this problem. Our staff will work closely with the laid-off workers, company officials, and local elected officials in determining how to best assist the affected employees."
- Assistance to be provided by the State of Georgia includes career counseling, unemployment benefits, and job retraining.[33]

EMAIL SKILLS

15. Message Strategies: Negative Organizational Announcements [LO-6]   People who live for an adrenaline rush can find a way to go fast from Canada's Bombardier Recreational Products. Bombardier is one of the world's top makers of snowmobiles, personal watercraft, engines for motorboats, and all-terrain vehicles (ATVs)—all designed for fast fun.

Because it sends customers hurtling across snow, water, or land at high speeds, Bombardier takes safety quite seriously. However, problems do arise from time to time, requiring a rapid response with clear communication to the company's customer base. Bombardier recently became aware of a potentially hazardous situation with the "race-ready" version of its Can-Am DS 90 X ATVs. This model is equipped with a safety device called a tether engine shutoff switch, in which a cord is connected to a special switch that turns off the engine in the event of an emergency. On the affected units, pulling the cord might not shut off the motor, which is particularly dangerous if the rider falls off—the ATV will continue on its own until the engine speed returns to idle.

Your task: Write an email message that will be sent to registered owners of 2008 and 2009 DS 90 X ATVs that include the potentially faulty switch. Analyze the situation carefully as you choose the direct or indirect approach for your message. Explain that the tether engine shutoff switch may not deactivate the engine when it is pulled in an emergency situation. To prevent riders from

relying on a safety feature that might not work properly, Bombardier, in cooperation with transportation safety authorities in the United States and Canada, is voluntarily recalling these models to have the tether switch removed. Emphasize the serious nature of the situation by explaining that if the rider is ejected and the engine shutoff switch does not work properly, the ATV will run away on its own, potentially resulting in significant injuries or deaths. Owners should stop riding their vehicles immediately and make an appointment with an authorized dealer to have the switch removed. The service will be performed at no charge, and customers will receive a $50 credit voucher for future purchases of Bombardier accessories. Include the following contact information: www.can-am.brp.com and 1-888-638-5397.[34]

16. Message Strategies: Communicating in a Crisis [LO-6]
One of your company's worst nightmares has just come true. EQ Industrial Services (EQIS), based in Wayne, Michigan, operates a number of facilities around the country that dispose of, recycle, and transport hazardous chemical wastes. Last night, explosions and fires broke out at the company's Apex, North Carolina, facility, forcing the evacuation of 17,000 local residents.

Your task: It's now Friday, the day after the fire. Write a brief post for the company's blog, covering the following points:

- A fire broke out at the Apex facility at approximately 10 P.M. Thursday.
- No one was in the facility at the time.
- Because of the diverse nature of the materials stored at the plant, the cause of the fire is not yet known.
- Rumors that the facility stores extremely dangerous chlorine gas and that the fire was spreading to other nearby businesses are not true.
- Special industrial firefighters hired by EQIS have already brought the fire under control.
- Residents in the immediate area were evacuated as a precaution, and they should be able to return to their homes tomorrow, pending permission from local authorities.
- Several dozen residents were admitted to local hospitals with complaints of breathing problems, but most have been released already; about a dozen emergency responders were treated as well.
- At this point (Friday afternoon), tests conducted by the North Carolina State Department of Environment and Natural Resources "had not detected anything out of the ordinary in the air."

Conclude by thanking the local police and fire departments for their assistance and directing readers to EQIS's toll-free hot line for more information.[35]

BLOGGING SKILLS

17. Message Strategies: Responding to Rumors and Public Criticism [LO-6]   Spreading *FUD*—fear, uncertainty, and doubt—about other companies is one of the less-honorable ways of dealing with competition in the business world. For example, someone can start a "whisper campaign" in the marketplace, raising fears that a particular company is struggling financially.

Customers who don't want to risk future instability in their supply chains might then shift their purchasing away from the company, based on nothing more than the false rumor.

Your task: Find the website of any company that you find interesting and imagine that you are the CEO and that the company is the subject of an online rumor about impending bankruptcy. Explore the website to get a basic feel for what the company does. Making up any information you need, write a post for the company's blog, explaining that the rumors of bankruptcy are false and that the company is on solid financial ground and plans to keep serving the industry for many years to come. (Be sure to review "We're Under Attack! Responding to Rumors and Criticism in a Social Media Environment" on page 312 for tips.)

SOCIAL NETWORKING SKILLS

18. Message Strategies: Responding to Rumors and Public Criticism [LO-6] The consumer reviews on Yelp (www.yelp.com) can be a promotional boon to any local business—provided the reviews are positive, of course. Negative reviews, fair or not, can affect a company's reputation and drive away potential customers. Fortunately for business owners, sites like Yelp give them the means to respond to reviews, whether they want to apologize for poor service, offer some form of compensation, or correct misinformation in a review.

Your task: Search Yelp for a negative review (one or two stars) on any business in any city. Find a review that has some substance to it, not just a simple, angry rant. Now imagine that you are the owner of that business, and write a reply that could be posted via the "Add Owner Comment" feature. Use information you can find on Yelp about the company and fill in any details by using your imagination. Remember that your comment will be visible to everyone who visits Yelp. (Be sure to review "We're Under Attack! Responding to Rumors and Criticism in a Social Media Environment" on page 312 for tips.)

Negative Employment Messages

SOCIAL NETWORKING SKILLS   EMAIL SKILLS

19. Message Strategies: Refusing Requests for Recommendations [LO-7] You're delighted to get a message from an old friend and colleague, Heather Lang. You're delighted right up to the moment you read her request that you write a recommendation about her web design and programming skills for your LinkedIn profile. You would do just about anything for Lang—anything except recommend her web design skills. She is a master programmer whose technical wizardry saved more client projects than you can count, but when it comes to artistic design, Lang simply doesn't have "it." From gaudy color schemes to unreadable type treatment to confusing layouts, her design sense is as weak as her technical acumen is strong.

Your task: First, write a brief email to Lang, explaining that you would be most comfortable highlighting her technical skills because that is where you believe her true strengths lie. Second, write a two-sentence recommendation that you could include in your LinkedIn profile, recommending Lang's technical skills. Make up or research any details you need.

MEMO WRITING SKILLS   PORTFOLIO BUILDER

20. Message Strategies: Negative Performance Reviews [LO-7] Elaine Bridgewater, the former professional golfer you hired to oversee your golf equipment company's relationship with retailers, knows the business inside and out. As a former touring pro, she has unmatched credibility. She also has seemingly boundless energy, solid technical knowledge, and an engaging personal style. Unfortunately, she hasn't been quite as attentive as she needs to be when it comes to communicating with retailers. You've been getting complaints about voice-mail messages gone unanswered for days, confusing emails that require two or three rounds of clarification, and reports that are haphazardly thrown together. As valuable as Bridgewater's other skills are, she's going to cost the company sales if this goes on much longer. The retail channel is vital to your company's survival, and she's the employee most involved in this channel.

Your task: Draft a brief (one page maximum) informal performance appraisal and improvement plan for Bridgewater. Be sure to compliment her on the areas in which she excels but don't shy away from highlighting the areas in which she needs to improve, too: punctual response to customer messages; clear writing; and careful revision, production, and proofreading. Use what you've learned in this course so far to supply any additional advice about the importance of these skills.

REFERENCES

1. Chargify website, accessed 18 February 2011, http://chargify.com; David Hauser, "How to Break the Trust of Your Customers in Just One Day: Lessons Learned from a Major Mistake," David Hauser blog, 13 October 2010, http://davidhauser.com; Jason Kincaid, "Subscription Billing System Chargify Missteps as It Switches from Freemium to Premium," TechCrunch, 11 October 2010, http://techcrunch.com; Lance Walley, "Chargify News: New Pricing, Features & More," 11 October 2010, http://chargify.com; "Chargify New Pricing" comment thread, Hacker News, accessed 18 February 2011, http://news.ycombinator.com.

2. James Manyika, Kara Sprague, and Lareina Yee, "Using Technology to Improve Workforce Collaboration," What Matters (McKinsey & Company), 27 October 2009, http://whatmatters.mckinseydigital.com.

3. Ian McDonald, "Marsh Can Do $600 Million, but Apologize?" *Wall Street Journal*, 14 January 2005, C1, C3; Adrienne Carter and Amy Borrus, "What If Companies Fessed Up?" *Business-Week*, 24 January 2005, 59–60; Patrick J. Kiger, "The Art of the Apology," *Workforce Management*, October 2004, 57–62.

4. Ameeta Patel and Lamar Reinsch, "Companies Can Apologize: Corporate Apologies and Legal Liability," *Business Communication Quarterly*, March 2003, accessed 1 December 2003, www.elibrary.com.

5. John Guiniven, "Sorry! An Apology as a Strategic PR Tool," *Public Relations Tactics*, December 2007, 6.

6. Howard Stringer, "A Letter from Howard Stringer," PlayStation Blog, 5 May 2011, http://blog.us.playstation.com.

7. Quinn Warnick, "A Close Textual Analysis of Corporate Layoff Memos," *Business Communication Quarterly*, September 2010, 322–326.

8. Deven Sharma, "Standard & Poor's Commitment to Reform: Restoring Confidence in the Credit Markets," Standard & Poor's, accessed 13 July 2010, www.standardandpoors.com.

9. Walley, "Chargify News: New Pricing, Features & More."

10. "Advice from the Pros on the Best Way to Deliver Bad News," Report on *Customer Relationship Management,* 1 February 2003, www.elibrary.com.

11. Ben Levisohn, "Getting More Workers to Whistle," *Business-Week,* 28 January 2008, 18.

12. "Less Than Half of Privately Held Businesses Support Whistleblowing," Grant Thornton website, accessed 13 October 2008, www.internationalbusinessreport.com.

13. Steve Karnowski, "New Food Safety Law Protects Whistleblowers," *Bloomberg Businessweek,* 11 February 2011, www.businessweek.com.

14. Sue Shellenbarger, "How to Keep Your Cool in Angry Times," *Wall Street Journal,* 22 September 2010, http://online.wsj.com.

15. Courtland L. Bovée, John V. Thill, George P. Dovel, and Marian Burk Wood, *Advertising Excellence* (New York: Mc-Graw-Hill, 1995), 508–509; John Holusha, "Exxon's Public-Relations Problem," *New York Times,* 12 April 1989, D1.

16. Omowale Casselle, "Really, You Want ME to Write YOU a LinkedIn Recommendation," RecruitingBlogs, 22 April 2010, www.recruitingblogs.com.

17. "LinkedIn Profiles to Career Introductions: When You Can't Recommend Your Friend," Seattle Post-Intelligencer Personal Finance blog, 16 November 2010, http://blog.seattlepi.com.

18. Neal Schaffer, "How Should I Deal with a LinkedIn Recommendation Request I Don't Want to Give?" Social Web School, 20 January 2010, http://humancapitalleague.com.

19. Dawn Wolf, "Job Applicant Rejection Letter Dos and Donts—Writing an Appropriate 'Dear John' Letter to an Unsuccessful Applicant," 31 May 2009, Employment Blawg .com, www.employmentblawg.com.

20. Wolf, "Job Applicant Rejection Letter Dos and Donts—Writing an Appropriate 'Dear John' Letter to an Unsuccessful Applicant"; "Prohibited Employment Policies/Practices," U.S. Equal Employment Opportunity Commission, accessed 14 July 2010, www.eeoc.gov; Susan M. Heathfield, "Candidate Rejection Letter," about.com, accessed 14 July 2010, http://humanresources.about.com; "Rejection Letters Under Scrutiny: 7 Do's & Don'ts," *Business Management Daily,* 1 April 2009, www.businessmanagementdaily.com.

21. Judi Brownell, "The Performance Appraisal Interviews: A Multipurpose Communication Assignment," *Bulletin of the Association for Business Communication* 57, no. 2 (1994): 11–21.

22. Gary Dessler, *A Framework for Human Resource Management,* 3rd ed. (Upper Saddle River, N.J.: Pearson Prentice Hall, 2004), 198.

23. Kelly Spors, "Why Performance Reviews Don't Work—And What You Can Do About It," Independent Street blog, *Wall Street Journal,* 21 October 2008, http://blogs.wsj.com.

24. Carrie Brodzinski, "Avoiding Wrongful Termination Suits," *National Underwriter Property & Casualty—Risk & Benefits Management,* 13 October 2003, www.elibrary.com.

25. Rita Pyrillis, "Is Your Performance Review Underperforming?" *Workforce Management,* May 2011, 20–22, 24–25.

26. Susan Friedfel, "Protecting Yourself in the Performance Review Process," *Workforce Management,* April 2009, www.workforce.com.

27. Friedfel, "Protecting Yourself in the Performance Review Process."

28. E. Michelle Bohreer and Todd J. Zucker, "Five Mistakes Managers Make When Terminating Employees," *Texas Lawyer,* 2 May 2006, www.law.com; Deborah Muller, "The Right Things to Do to Avoid Wrongful Termination Claims," *Workforce Management,* October 2008, www.workforce.com; Maria Greco Danaher, "Termination: Telling an Employee," *Workforce Management,* accessed 14 July 2010, www.workforce.com.

29. Adapted from "Bathtub Curve," *Engineering Statistics Handbook,* National Institute of Standards and Technology website, accessed 16 April 2005, www.nist.gov; Robert Berner, "The Warranty Windfall," *BusinessWeek,* 20 December 2004, 84–86; Larry Armstrong, "When Service Contracts Make Sense," *BusinessWeek,* 20 December 2004, 86.

30. Adapted from Twitter/JetBlue website, accessed 29 October 2008, http://twitter.com/JetBlue.

31. Adapted from Lee Valley website, accessed 29 October 2008, www.leevalley.com.

32. Adapted from Stanton website, accessed 18 August 2005, www.stantondj.com.

33. Adapted from Rodney Manley, "Milledgeville Plant to Close; 150 to Lose Jobs," Macon.com, 28 January 2009, www.macon.com; Jamie Jones, "Shaw Plant Closing in Milledgeville," *The Daily Citizen* (Dalton, Georgia), 29 January 2009, www.northwestgeorgia.com.

34. Adapted from "Recall Safety Notice," Bombardier Recreational Products website, 10 September 2008, www.brp.com; Bombardier Recreational Products website, accessed 30 October 2008, www.brp.com.

35. Adapted from Environmental Quality Company press releases, accessed 27 October 2006, www.eqonline.com; "N.C. Residents to Return After Fire," Science Daily, 6 October 2006, www.sciencedaily.com; "Hazardous Waste Plant Fire in N.C. Forces 17,000 to Evacuate," FOXNews.com, 6 October 2006, www.foxnews.com.

Writing Persuasive Messages 10

LEARNING OBJECTIVES   After studying this chapter, you will be able to

1 Apply the three-step writing process to persuasive messages

2 Describe an effective strategy for developing persuasive business messages, and identify the three most common categories of persuasive business messages

3 Describe an effective strategy for developing marketing and sales messages

4 Explain how to modify your approach when writing promotional messages for social media

5 Identify steps you can take to avoid ethical lapses in marketing and sales messages

MyBcommLab Where you see MyBcommLab in this chapter, go to www.pearsoninternationaleditions.com/mybcommlab for additional activities on the topic being discussed.

ON THE JOB: COMMUNICATING AT **CAFEMOM**

CafeMom uses social media to replicate the in-person experience of parents sharing information, advice, and emotional support.
Source: © Vibe Images/Alamy.

Creating a Business by Connecting Mothers Everywhere

Few roles in life require more information and insight than parenting. From prenatal care to early childhood development to education to socialization issues, parents are in continuous learning mode as their children grow. Parents also need to learn about themselves as they grow in their roles, from balancing work and home life to nurturing their own relationships. At the same time, parenting can be one of the most isolating experiences for people, often making it difficult for them to acquire the information and support they need in order to succeed as parents.

Two lifelong friends, actor and activist Andrew Shue and entrepreneur Michael Sanchez, pondered this age-old challenge and saw the web as a solution. The pair co-founded CafeMom, an online community and information resource that helps mothers find answers, insights, and each other.

Information resources and social networks abound on the web, and like any other web start-up, CafeMom faced the challenge of standing apart from the crowd and growing its membership large enough to create a viable business. One of the keys to its success is crafting clear, audience-focused messages that make a compelling case for joining CafeMom. Using straightforward statements such as "CafeMom is an online community where thousands of moms come together every day to connect with each other" and "Whatever you're going through, chances are another mom has been there and can help," the company communicates the features of its various online services and the benefits of joining.

The persuasive communication effort certainly seems to have been successful: CafeMom is now the largest social networking community for mothers and continues to expand as more mothers join in search of helpful insights and friendly support from their peers.[1]

www.cafemom.com

Using the Three-Step Writing Process for Persuasive Messages

Persuasion is the attempt to change someone's attitudes, beliefs, or actions.

Professionals such as Michael Sanchez, CEO of CafeMom (profiled in the chapter opener), understand that successful businesses rely on persuasive messages in both internal and external communication. Whether you're trying to convince your boss to open a new office in Europe or to encourage potential customers to try your products, you need to call on your abilities of **persuasion**—the attempt to change an audience's attitudes, beliefs, or actions.[2] As with every other type of business message, the three-step writing process improves persuasive messages.

STEP 1: PLANNING A PERSUASIVE MESSAGE

Having a great idea or a great product is not enough; you need to be able to convince others of its merits.

In today's information-saturated business environment, having a great idea or a great product is no longer enough. Every day, untold numbers of good ideas go unnoticed (or get misunderstood) and good products go unsold simply because the messages meant to promote them aren't compelling enough to be heard above the competitive noise. Creating successful persuasive messages in these challenging situations demands careful attention to all four tasks in the planning step, starting with an insightful analysis of your purpose and your audience.

Analyzing the Situation

Effective persuasive messages are closely aligned with audience motivations, those forces that drive people to satisfy their needs.

Demographics include characteristics such as age, gender, occupation, income, and education.

Psychographics include characteristics such as personality, attitudes, and lifestyle.

In defining your purpose, make sure you're clear about what you really hope to achieve. Suppose you want to persuade company executives to support a particular research project. But what does "support" mean? Do you want them to pat you on the back and wish you well? Or do you want them to give you a staff of five researchers and a $1 million annual budget?

The best persuasive messages are closely connected to your audience's desires and interests (see Figure 10.1).[3] Consider these important questions: Who is my audience? What are my audience members' needs? What do I want them to do? How might they resist? Are there alternative positions I need to examine? What does the decision maker consider to be the most important issue? How might the organization's culture influence my strategy?

To understand and categorize audience needs, you can refer to specific information, such as **demographics** (the age, gender, occupation, income, education, and other quantifiable characteristics of the people you're trying to persuade) and **psychographics** (personality, attitudes, lifestyle, and other psychological characteristics). When analyzing your audiences, take into account their cultural expectations and practices so that you don't undermine your persuasive message by using an inappropriate appeal or by organizing your message in a way that seems unfamiliar or uncomfortable to your readers.

If you aim to change someone's attitudes, beliefs, or actions through a persuasive message, it is vital to understand his or her **motivation**—the combination of forces that drive people to satisfy their needs. Table 10.1 on page 334 lists some of the needs that psychologists have identified or suggested as being important in influencing human motivation. Obviously, the more closely a persuasive message aligns with a recipient's existing motivation, the more effective the message is likely to be. For example, if you try to persuade consumers to purchase a product on the basis of its fashion appeal, that message will connect with consumers who are motivated by a desire to be in style, but it probably won't connect with consumers driven by functional or financial concerns.

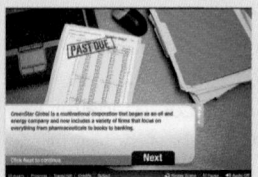

The main idea of "choose TD Ameritrade" is echoed from the webpage tab, through the introductory text, and down to the specific details.

The headline and introductory paragraph address universal concerns among investors.

These six supporting points—each of which reflects a key audience need—back up the top-level message of "A better way to invest."

An endorsement from a well-known source boosts the credibility of the company's promotional message.

Each of the six supporting points is presented at three levels of detail: (1) the short message of the button labels at the far left, (2) a short paragraph with a headline that echoes audience needs, and (3) additional pages (accessed via the link) with full details.

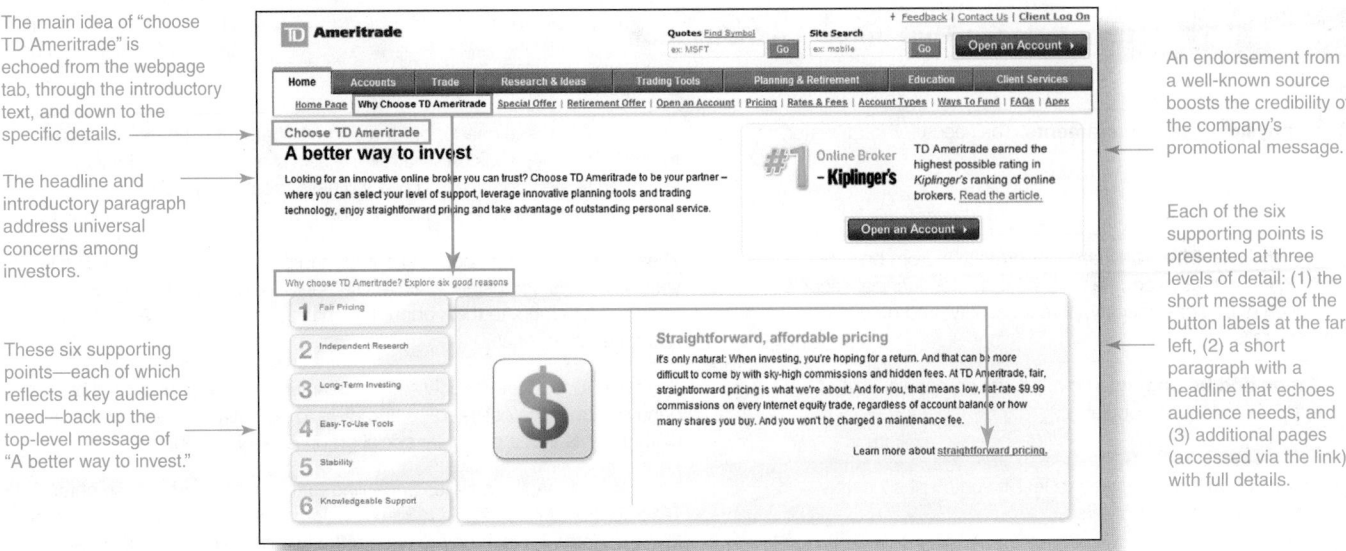

Figure 10.1 Appealing to Audience Needs

On this expertly written and designed webpage, TD Ameritrade echoes back the concerns that individual investors are likely to have when selecting a stockbroker. Notice how well the writing moves the reader from the high-level message to six individual supporting points—each of which is a major audience need—and then on to more detailed information. The clean, focused design is equally effective and works in close harmony with the text. The layout guides the reader's eye from the upper left corner, downward to the six key support points, and then across to the right for additional layers of detail.

Source: Image Courtesy TD Ameritrade IP Company, Inc.

Gathering Information

Once your situation analysis is complete, you need to gather the information necessary to create a compelling persuasive message. You'll learn more about the types of information to include in persuasive business messages and marketing and sales messages later in this chapter. Chapter 11 presents advice on how to find the information you need.

Selecting the Right Medium

Persuasive messages can be found in virtually every communication medium, from instant messages and podcasts to radio advertisements and skywriting. In fact, advertising agencies employ media specialists whose only jobs are to analyze the media options available and select the most cost-effective combination for each client and each advertising campaign (see Figure 10.2 on page 335).

In some situations, various members of your audience might prefer different media for the same message. Some consumers like to do all their car shopping in person, whereas others do most of their car-shopping research online. Some people don't mind promotional emails for products they're interested in; others resent every piece of commercial email they receive. If you can't be sure you can reach most or all of your audience through a single medium, you need to use two or more, such as following up an email campaign with printed letters.

Social media (see Chapter 7) provide some exciting options for persuasive messages, particularly marketing and sales messages. However, as "Writing Promotional Messages for Social Media" on page 349 explains, messages in these media require a unique approach.

Another important area of development is combining personal attention with technological reach and efficiency. For example, a customer support agent can carry on multiple instant messaging conversations at once, responding to one customer while other customers are typing messages. Even perceptions of human interaction created by animated

REAL-TIME UPDATES
Learn More by Watching This Video

Persuasion skills for every business professional

Persuasion is an essential business skill, no matter what career path you follow. This video offers great tips for understanding, practicing, and applying persuasive skills. Go to http://real-timeupdates.com/ebc10 and click on Learn More. If you are using MyBcommLab, you can access Real-Time Updates within each chapter or under Student Study Tools.

You may need to use multiple media to reach your entire audience.

TABLE 10.1 Human Needs That Influence Motivation	
Need	**Implications for Communication**
Basic physiological requirements: The needs for food, water, sleep, oxygen, etc.	Everyone has these needs, but the degree of attention an individual gives to them often depends on whether the needs are being met; for instance, an advertisement for sleeping pills will have greater appeal to someone suffering from insomnia than to someone who has no problem sleeping.
Safety and security: The needs for protection from bodily harm, to know that loved ones are safe, and for financial security, protection of personal identity, career security, and other assurances	These needs influence both consumer and business decisions in a wide variety of ways; for instance, advertisements for life insurance often encourage parents to think about the financial security of their children and other loved ones.
Affiliation and belonging: The needs for companionship, acceptance, love, and popularity	The need to feel loved, accepted, or popular drives a great deal of human behavior, from the desire to be attractive to potential mates to wearing the clothing style that a particular social group is likely to approve.
Power and control: The need to feel in control of situations or to exert authority over others	You can see many examples appealing to this need in advertisements: *Take control of your life, your finances, your future, your career*, and so on. Many people who lack power want to know how to get it, and people who have power often want others to know they have it.
Achievement: The need to feel a sense of accomplishment— or to be admired by others for accomplishments	This need can involve both *knowing* (when people experience a feeling of accomplishment) and *showing* (when people are able to show others that they've achieved success); advertising for luxury consumer products frequently appeals to this need.
Adventure and distraction: The need for excitement or relief from daily routine	People vary widely in their need for adventure; some crave excitement— even danger—while others value calmness and predictability. Some needs for adventure and distraction are met *virtually*, such as through horror movies, thriller novels, and violent video games.
Knowledge, exploration, and understanding: The need to keep learning	For some people, learning is usually a means to an end, a way to fulfill some other need; for others, acquiring new knowledge is the goal.
Aesthetic appreciation: The desire to experience beauty, order, and symmetry	Although this need may seem "noncommercial" at first glance, advertisers appeal to it frequently, from the pleasing shape of a package to the quality of the gemstones in a piece of jewelry.
Self-actualization: The need to "be all that one can be," to reach one's full potential as a human being	Psychologists Kurt Goldstein and Abraham Maslow popularized self-actualization as the desire to make the most of one's potential, and Maslow identified it as one of the higher-level needs in his classic hierarchy; even if people met most or all of their other needs, they would still feel the need to self-actualize. An often-quoted example of appealing to this need is the U.S. Army's one-time advertising slogan "Be all you can be."
Helping others: The need to believe that one is making a difference in the lives of other people	This need is the central motivation in fundraising messages and other appeals to charity.

Sources: Adapted from Saundra K. Ciccarelli and Glenn E. Meyer, *Psychology* (Upper Saddle River, N.J.: Prentice Hall, 2006), 336–346; Courtland L. Bovée and John V. Thill, *Business in Action,* 5th ed. (Upper Saddle River, N.J.: Prentice Hall, 2011), 213–217; Abraham H. Maslow, "A Theory of Human Motivation," *Psychological Review* 50 (1943): 370–396.

avatars such as IKEA's "Anna" (www.ikea.com) can create a more sociable experience for shoppers, which can make websites more effective as a persuasive medium.[4]

Organizing Your Information

The most effective main ideas for persuasive messages have one thing in common: They are about the receiver, not the sender. For instance, if you're trying to convince others to join you in a business venture, explain how it will help them, not how it will help you.

Limit your scope to include only the information needed to help your audience take the next step toward making a favorable decision.

Limiting your scope is vital. If you seem to be wrestling with more than one main idea, you haven't zeroed in on the heart of the matter. If you try to craft a persuasive message without focusing on the one central problem or opportunity your audience truly cares about, chances are you won't be able to persuade successfully.[5]

Because the nature of persuasion is to convince people to change their attitudes, beliefs, or actions, most persuasive messages use the indirect approach. That means you'll want

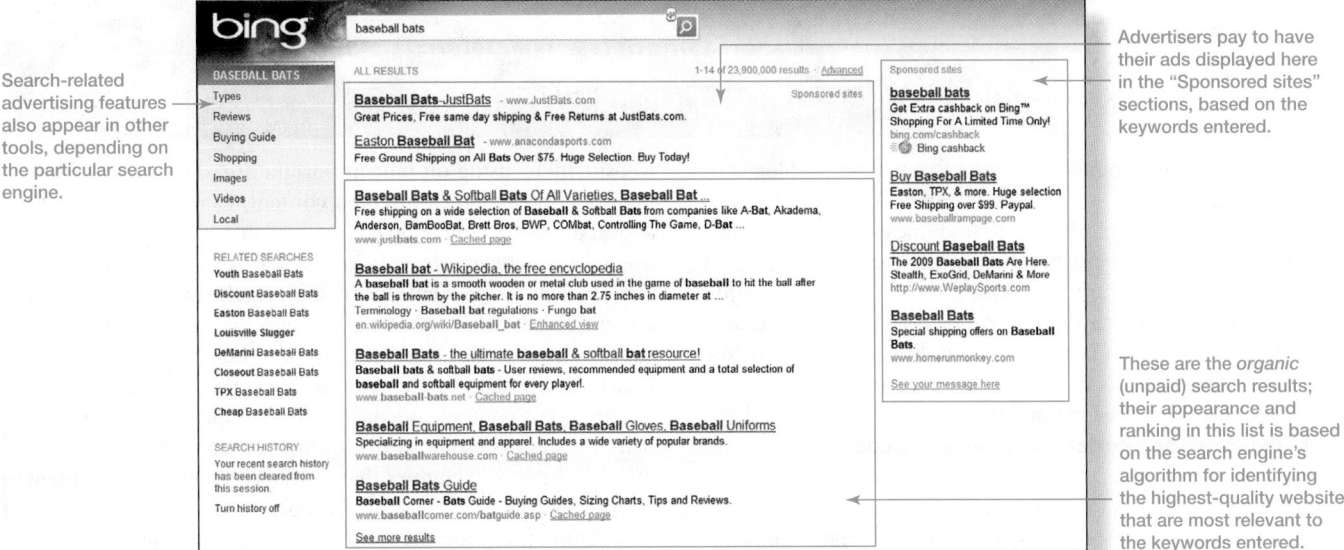

Figure 10.2 Media Choices: Search Engine Marketing

Search engines now play a central role in online promotion, both as search tools and as an advertising medium themselves. See "Please Find Us: Building an Audience Through Search Engine Optimization" on page 296 for more information.

Source: Courtesy of Microsoft.

to explain your reasons and build interest before asking for a decision or for action—or perhaps even before revealing your purpose. In contrast, when you have a close relationship with your audience and the message is welcome or at least neutral, the direct approach can be effective.

Use the direct approach if your audience is ready to hear your proposal.

For persuasive business messages, the choice between the direct and indirect approaches is also influenced by the extent of your authority, expertise, or power in an organization. For instance, if you are a highly regarded technical expert with years of experience, you might use the direct approach in a message to top executives. In contrast, if you aren't well known and therefore need to rely more on the strength of your message than the power of your reputation, the indirect approach will probably be more successful.

For persuasive business messages, the choice of approach is influenced by your position (or authority within the organization) relative to your audience's.

STEP 2: WRITING A PERSUASIVE MESSAGE

Encourage a positive response to your persuasive messages by (1) using positive and polite language, (2) understanding and respecting cultural differences, (3) being sensitive to organizational cultures, and (4) taking steps to establish your credibility.

Positive language usually happens naturally with persuasive messages because you're promoting an idea or a product you believe in. However, take care not to inadvertently insult your readers by implying that they've made poor choices in the past.

Be sure to understand cultural expectations as well. For example, a message that seems forthright and direct in a low-context culture might seem brash and intrusive in a high-context culture.

Make sure your persuasive messages consider the culture of your audience.

Just as social culture affects the success of a persuasive message, so too does the culture within various organizations. Some organizations handle disagreement and conflict in an indirect, behind-the-scenes way, whereas others accept and even encourage open discussion and sharing of differing viewpoints.

Finally, when you are trying to persuade a skeptical or hostile audience, credibility is essential. You must convince people that you know what you're talking about and that you're not trying to mislead them. Use these techniques:

- Use simple language to avoid suspicions of fantastic claims and emotional manipulation.
- Provide objective evidence for the claims and promises you make.
- Identify your sources, especially if your audience already respects those sources.

Audiences often respond unfavorably to over-the-top language, so keep your writing simple and straightforward.

Please Find Us: Building an Audience Through Search Engine Optimization

Have you ever wondered why certain websites and blogs appear at the top of the list when you use an online search engine? Or why a site you might expect to find doesn't show up at all? Such questions are at the heart of one of the most important activities in online communication: *search engine optimization* (SEO). (SEO applies to the *natural* or *organic* search results, not the sponsored, paid results you see above, beside, or below the main search results listing.)

SEO involves three major parties: web users, website owners, and search engine developers such as Google, Yahoo!, and Microsoft. Most web users rely heavily on search engines to find relevant websites for shopping, research, and other online tasks. Website owners rely heavily on search engines to steer potential customers and other valuable visitors their way. To bring these two parties together while building lots of web traffic and advertising opportunities for themselves, search engine developers constantly fine-tune their engines to produce relevant, helpful search results.

And that's where things get interesting. Using sophisticated—and secret—algorithms, search engines rank search results by relevance to the user's input terms, starting with the most relevant results at the top of the list. Web users typically choose sites that show up in the first few pages of search results, so site owners naturally want to be ranked as high as possible.

Given the secrecy and the high stakes, the online search business has become something of a cat-and-mouse game in which website owners try to figure out what they can do to improve their rankings, while search engine developers work to improve the quality of results—partly by blocking website owners' attempts to "game" the system. For instance, in the early days of online searches, some website owners would embed dozens of popular search terms in their websites, even if those terms had nothing to do with their site content. Search engine developers responded with ways to detect such tactics and penalize sites that use them by either lowering the sites' rankings in the search results or leaving them out entirely.

SEO has become a complex topic as search engines and the web itself have continued to evolve and as motivated website owners have looked for ways to boost their rankings. For instance, Google now evaluates more than 100 factors to determine search rankings. Without becoming an expert in SEO, however, you can work toward improving rankings for your website by focusing on four important areas. First, offer fresh, high-quality, audience-oriented content. Content that doesn't appeal to people won't appeal to search engines, either. Second, use relevant keywords judiciously, particularly in important areas such as the page title that displays at the top of the browser screen. Third, don't try to trick search engines with keyword stuffing, sneaky link redirects, or any other shady schemes. Fourth, encourage links to your site from other high-quality sites with relevant content. According to SEO experts who analyze search results, these links from other sites are crucial because they tell the search engines that other people find your content interesting and useful. Not surprisingly, given the importance of links from other sites, the content sharing encouraged by social media has had a huge impact on SEO in recent years.

You can learn more from Google's Webmaster Guidelines at www.google.com/support/webmasters and from Copyblogger at www.copyblogger.com/seo-copywriting.

CAREER APPLICATIONS

1. Locate a website for any company that sells products to consumers and write a new title for the site's homepage (the title that appears at the top of a web browser). Make the title short enough to read quickly while still summarizing what the company offers. Be sure to use one or more keywords that online shoppers would likely use when searching for the types of products the company sells.

2. Identify three high-quality websites that would be good ones to link to the site you chose in Question 1. For instance, if you chose a website that sells automotive parts and supplies, one of the three linking sites could be a popular blog that deals with automotive repair. Or if the site you chose sells golf equipment, you might find a sports website that covers the professional golf tours or one that provides information about golf courses around the world.

Sources: Adapted from "Webmaster Guidelines," Google, www.google.com; Brian Clark, "How to Create Compelling Content that Ranks Well in Search Engines," Copyblogger, May 2010, www.copyblogger.com; P.J. Fusco, "How Web 2.0 Affects SEO Strategy," ClickZ, 23 May 2007, www.clickz.com; "Law Firm Marketing Now Dependent on Search Engine Optimization," *Law Office Management & Administration Report*, June 2006, 1, 10–12; *Pandia Search Engine Marketing 101*, Pandia website, www.pandia.com; Mike Grehan, "Does Textbook SEO Really Work Anymore?" 17 April 2006, Clickz, www.clickz.com; Shari Thurow, "Web Positioning Metrics and SEO," Clickz.com, 24 October 2005, www.clickz.com.

- Establish common ground by emphasizing beliefs, attitudes, and background experiences you have in common with the audience.
- Be objective and present fair and logical arguments.
- Display your willingness to keep your audience's best interests at heart.
- Persuade with logic, evidence, and compelling narratives, rather than trying to coerce with high-pressure, "hard sell" tactics.
- Whenever possible, try to build your credibility before you present a major proposal or ask for a major decision. That way, audiences don't have to evaluate both you and your message at the same time.[6]

Audiences resist the high-pressure tactics of the "hard sell" and tend to distrust communicators who take this approach.

STEP 3: COMPLETING A PERSUASIVE MESSAGE

The pros know from experience that details can make or break a persuasive message, so they're careful not to skimp on this part of the writing process. For instance, advertisers may have a dozen or more people review a message before it's released to the public.

When you evaluate your content, try to judge your argument objectively and not overestimate your credibility. If possible, ask an experienced colleague who knows your audience well to review your draft. Make sure your design elements complement, rather than detract from, your persuasive argument. In addition, meticulous proofreading will help you identify any mechanical or spelling errors that would weaken your persuasive potential. Finally, make sure your distribution methods fit your audience's expectations and preferences.

With the three-step model in mind, you're ready to begin composing persuasive messages, starting with *persuasive business messages* (those that try to convince audiences to approve new projects, enter into business partnerships, and so on), followed by *marketing and sales messages* (those that try to convince audiences to consider and then purchase products and services).

Developing Persuasive Business Messages

Persuasive business messages comprise a broad and diverse category, with audiences that range from a single person in your own department to government agencies, investors, business partners, community leaders, and other external groups. Your success as a businessperson is closely tied to your ability to convince others to accept new ideas, change old habits, or act on your recommendations. As you move into positions of greater responsibility in your career, your persuasive messages could start to influence multimillion-dollar investments and the careers of hundreds or thousands of employees. Obviously, you need to match the increase in your persuasive skills with the care and thoroughness of your analysis and planning so that the ideas you convince others to adopt are sound.

2   LEARNING OBJECTIVE

Describe an effective strategy for developing persuasive business messages, and identify the three most common categories of persuasive business messages.

No matter where your career leads, your success will depend on your ability to craft effective persuasive messages.

STRATEGIES FOR PERSUASIVE BUSINESS MESSAGES

Even if you have the power to compel others to do what you want them to do, persuading them is more effective than forcing them. People who are forced into accepting a decision or plan are less motivated to support it and more likely to react negatively than if they're persuaded.[7] Within the context of the three-step process, effective persuasion involves four essential strategies: framing your arguments, balancing emotional and logical appeals, reinforcing your position, and anticipating objections. (Note that all these concepts in this section apply as well to marketing and sales messages, covered later in the chapter.)

Framing Your Arguments

As noted earlier, most persuasive messages use the indirect approach. Experts in persuasive communication have developed a number of indirect models for such messages. One of the best known is the **AIDA model**, which organizes messages into four phases:

- **Attention.** Your first objective is to engage your readers or listeners in a way that encourages them to want to hear about your main idea. Write a brief and compelling sentence, without making extravagant claims or irrelevant points. Look for some common ground on which to build your case (see Figure 10.3 on the next page). And while you want to be positive and confident, make sure you don't start out with a *hard sell*—a pushy, aggressive opening. Doing so often puts audiences on guard and on the defensive.
- **Interest.** Emphasize the relevance of your message to your audience. Continuing the theme you started with, paint a more detailed picture of the problem you propose to solve with the solution you're offering (whether it's a new idea, a new process, a new product, or whatever).

Using the AIDA model is an effective way to organize most persuasive messages:
- Attention
- Interest
- Desire
- Action

1 Plan →

Analyze the Situation
Verify that the purpose is to solve an ongoing problem, so the audience will be receptive.

Gather Information
Determine audience needs and obtain the necessary information on recycling problem areas.

Select the Right Medium
Verify that an email message is appropriate for this communication.

Organize the Information
Limit the scope to the main idea, which is to propose a recycling solution; use the indirect approach to lay out the extent of the problem.

2 Write →

Adapt to Your Audience
Adjust the level of formality based on the degree of familiarity with the audience; maintain a positive relationship by using the "you" attitude, politeness, positive emphasis, and bias-free language.

Compose the Message
Use a conversational but professional style and keep the message brief, clear, and as helpful as possible.

3 Complete

Revise the Message
Evaluate content and review readability to make sure the information is clear and complete without being overwhelming.

Produce the Message
Emphasize a clean, professional appearance.

Proofread the Message
Review for errors in layout, spelling, and mechanics.

Distribute the Message
Verify that the right file is attached and then deliver the message.

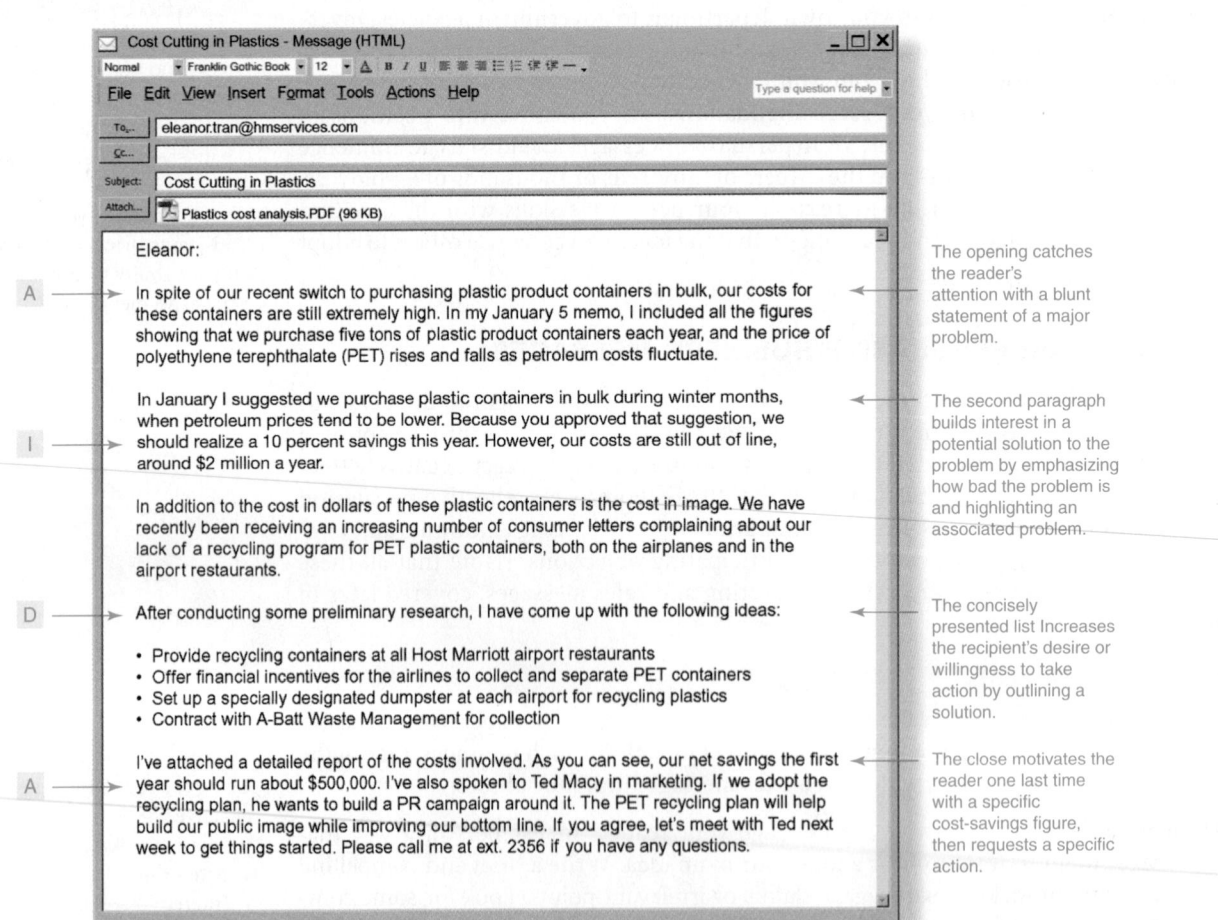

Figure 10.3 Persuasive Message Using the AIDA Model
Randy Thumwolt uses the AIDA model in a message about a program that would reduce Host Marriott's annual plastics costs and address consumer complaints about the company's recycling record. Note how Thumwolt "sells the problem" before attempting to sell the solution. Few people are interested in hearing about solutions to problems they don't know about or don't believe exist.

MyBcommLab

Apply Figure 10.3's key concepts by revising a new document. Go to Chapter 10 in www.pearsoninternationaleditions.com/ mybcommlab and select Document Makeovers.

- **Desire.** Help audience members embrace your idea by explaining how the change will benefit them, either personally or professionally. Reduce resistance by identifying and answering in advance any questions the audience might have. If your idea is complex, you might need to explain how you would implement it. Back up your claims in order to increase audience willingness to take the action you suggest in the next section.

- **Action.** Suggest the action you want readers to take and phrase it in a way that emphasizes the benefits to them or to the organization they represent. Make the action as easy as possible to take, including offering to assist, if appropriate. Be sure to provide all the information the audience needs to take the action, including deadlines and contact details.

The AIDA model is tailor-made for using the indirect approach, allowing you to save your main idea for the action phase. However, you can also use AIDA for the direct approach, in which case you use your main idea as an attention-getter, build interest with your argument, create desire with your evidence, and reemphasize your main idea in the action phase with the specific action you want your audience to take.

> The AIDA model and similar plans are ideal for the indirect approach.

When your AIDA message uses the indirect approach and is delivered by memo or email, keep in mind that your subject line usually catches your reader's eye first. Your challenge is to make it interesting and relevant enough to capture reader attention without revealing your main idea. If you put your request in the subject line, you might just get a quick no before you've had a chance to present your arguments:

Instead of This	Write This
Request for development budget to add automated IM response system	Reducing the cost of customer support inquiries

With either the direct or indirect approach, AIDA and similar models do have limitations. First, AIDA is a unidirectional method that essentially talks *at* audiences, not *with* them. Second, AIDA is built around a single event, such as asking an audience for a decision, rather than on building a mutually beneficial, long-term relationship.[8] AIDA is still a valuable tool for the right purposes, but as you'll read later in the chapter, a conversational approach is more compatible with today's social media.

> The AIDA approach has limitations:
> - It essentially talks *at* audiences, not *with* them
> - It focuses on one-time events, not long-term relationships

Balancing Emotional and Logical Appeals

Imagine you're sitting at a control panel with one knob labeled "logic" and another labeled "emotion." As you prepare your persuasive message, you carefully adjust each knob, tuning the message for maximum impact. Too little emotion, and your audience might not care enough to respond. Too much emotion, and your audience might think you are ignoring tough business questions or even being irrational.

Generally speaking, persuasive business messages rely more heavily on logical appeals than on emotional appeals because the main idea is usually to save money, increase quality, or improve some other practical, measurable aspect of business. To find the optimum balance, consider four factors: (1) the actions you hope to motivate, (2) your readers' expectations, (3) the degree of resistance you need to overcome, and (4) how far you feel empowered to go in order to sell your point of view.[9]

> Emotional appeals attempt to connect with the reader's feelings or sympathies.

Emotional Appeals As its name implies, an **emotional appeal** calls on audience feelings and sympathies rather than facts, figures, and rational arguments. For instance, you can make use of the emotions surrounding certain words. The word *freedom* evokes strong feelings, as do words such as *success, prestige, compassion, security,* and *comfort.* Such words can help put your audience members in a positive frame of mind and help them accept your message. However, emotional appeals in business messages aren't usually effective by themselves because the audience wants proof that you can solve a business problem. Even if your audience members reach a conclusion based primarily on emotions, they'll look to you to provide logical support as well.

Logical Appeals A **logical appeal** calls on reasoning and evidence. The basic approach with a logical appeal is to make a claim based on a rational argument, supported by solid evidence. When appealing to your audience's logic, you might use three types of reasoning:

Logical appeals are based on the reader's notions of reason; these appeals can use analogy, induction, or deduction.

- **Analogy.** With analogy, you reason from specific evidence to specific evidence, in effect "borrowing" from something familiar to explain something unfamiliar. For instance, to convince management to add chat room capability to the company's groupware system, you could explain that it is like a neighborhood community center, only online.
- **Induction.** With inductive reasoning, you work from specific evidence to a general conclusion. To convince your team to change to a new manufacturing process, for example, you could point out that every company that has adopted it has increased profits, so it must be a smart idea.
- **Deduction.** With deductive reasoning, you work from a generalization to a specific conclusion. To persuade your boss to hire additional customer support staff, you might point to industry surveys that show how crucial customer satisfaction is to corporate profits.

Every method of reasoning is vulnerable to misuse, both intentional and unintentional, so verify your rational arguments carefully. For example, in the case of the manufacturing process, are there any other factors that affect the integrity of your reasoning? What if that process works well only for small companies with few products, and your firm is a multinational behemoth with 10,000 products? To guard against faulty logic, follow these guidelines:[10]

Logical flaws include hasty generalizations, circular reasoning, attacks on opponents, oversimplifications, false assumptions of cause and effect, faulty analogies, and illogical support.

- **Avoid hasty generalizations.** Make sure you have plenty of evidence before drawing conclusions.
- **Avoid circular reasoning.** *Circular reasoning* is a logical fallacy in which you try to support your claim by restating it in different words. The statement "We know temporary workers cannot handle this task because temps are unqualified for it" doesn't prove anything because the claim and the supporting evidence are essentially identical. It doesn't prove *why* the temps are unqualified.
- **Avoid attacking an opponent.** If your persuasive appeal involves countering a competitive appeal made by someone else, make sure you attack the argument your opponent is making, not his or her character or qualifications.
- **Avoid oversimplifying a complex issue.** Make sure you present all the factors and don't reduce a wide range of choices to a simple "either/or" scenario if that isn't the case.
- **Avoid mistaken assumptions of cause and effect.** If you can't isolate the impact of a specific factor, you can't assume it's the cause of whatever effect you're discussing. The weather improves in spring, and people start playing baseball in spring. Does good weather cause baseball? No. There is a *correlation* between the two—meaning the data associated with them tend to rise and fall at the same time, but there is no *causation*— no proof that one causes the other. The complexity of many business situations makes cause and effect a particular challenge. You lowered prices, and sales went up. Were lower prices the cause of the increased sales? Perhaps, but the increase in sales might have been caused by a better advertising campaign, a competitor's delivery problems, or some other factor.
- **Avoid faulty analogies.** Be sure that the two objects or situations being compared are similar enough for the analogy to hold. For instance, explaining that an Internet firewall is like a prison wall is a poor analogy, because a firewall keeps things out, whereas a prison wall keeps things in.
- **Avoid illogical support.** Make sure the connection between your claim and your support is truly logical and not based on a leap of faith, a missing premise, or irrelevant evidence.

Reinforcing Your Position

After you've worked out the basic elements of your argument, step back and look for ways to bolster the strength of your position. Are all your claims supported by believable evidence? Would a quotation from a recognized expert help make your case?

Next, examine your language. Can you find more powerful words to convey your message? For example, if your company is in serious financial trouble, talking about *fighting for survival* is a more powerful emotional appeal than talking about *ensuring continued operations*. As with any other powerful tool, though, use vivid language and abstractions carefully and honestly.

Choose your words carefully and use abstractions to enhance emotional content.

In addition to examining individual word choices, consider using metaphors and other figures of speech. If you want to describe a quality-control system as being designed to detect every possible product flaw, you might call it a "spider web" to imply that it catches everything that comes its way. Similarly, anecdotes (brief stories) can help your audience grasp the meaning and importance of your arguments. Instead of just listing the number of times the old laptop computers in your department have failed, you could describe how you lost a sale when your computer broke down during a critical sales presentation.

Beyond specific words and phrases, look for other factors that can reinforce your position. When you're asking for something, your audience members will find it easier to grant your request if they stand to benefit from it as well.

Anticipating Objections

Even the most compelling ideas and proposals can be expected to encounter some initial resistance. The best way to deal with audience resistance is to anticipate as many objections as you can and address them in your message before your audience can even bring them up. For instance, if you know that your proposal to switch to lower-cost materials will raise concerns about product quality, address this issue head-on in your message. If you wait until people raise the concern after reading your message, they may gravitate toward another firm before you have a chance to address their concerns. By bringing up such potential problems right away, you also demonstrate a broad appreciation of the issue and imply confidence in your message.[11] This anticipation is particularly important in written messages, when you don't have the opportunity to detect and respond to objections on the spot.

Even powerful persuasive messages can encounter resistance from the audience.

To uncover potential audience objections, try to poke holes in your own theories and ideas before your audience does. Then find solutions to the problems you've uncovered. If possible, ask your audience members for their thoughts on the subject before you put together your argument; people are more likely to support solutions they help create.

Keep three things in mind when anticipating objections. First, you don't always have to explicitly discuss a potential objection. You could simply mention that the lower-cost materials have been tested and approved by the quality-control department. Second, if you expect a hostile audience, one biased against your plan from the beginning, present all sides of the story. As you cover each option, explain the pros and cons. You'll gain additional credibility if you present these options before presenting your recommendation or decision.[12] Third, successful persuasion is often a process of give-and-take, particularly in the case of persuasive business messages, where you don't always get everything you asked for in terms of budgets, investments, and other commitments. Be open to compromise.

Present all sides of an issue when you expect to encounter strong resistance.

To review the steps involved in developing persuasive messages, refer to "Checklist: Developing Persuasive Messages."

COMMON EXAMPLES OF PERSUASIVE BUSINESS MESSAGES

Throughout your career, you'll have numerous opportunities to write persuasive messages within your organization, such as reports suggesting more efficient operating procedures or memos requesting money for new equipment. Similarly, you may produce a variety of persuasive messages for people outside the organization, such as websites shaping public

✓ Checklist Developing Persuasive Messages

A. Get your reader's attention.
- Open with an audience benefit, a stimulating question, a problem, or an unexpected statement.
- Establish common ground by mentioning a point on which you and your audience agree.
- Show that you understand the audience's concerns.

B. Build your reader's interest.
- Expand and support your opening claim or promise.
- Emphasize the relevance of your message to your audience.

C. Increase your reader's desire.
- Make audience members want to change by explaining how the change will benefit them.
- Back up your claims with relevant evidence.

D. Motivate your reader to take action.
- Suggest the action you want readers to take.
- Stress the positive results of the action.
- Make the desired action clear and easy.

E. Balance emotional and logical appeals.
- Use emotional appeals to help the audience accept your message.
- Use logical appeals when presenting facts and evidence for complex ideas or recommendations.
- Avoid faulty logic.

F. Reinforce your position.
- Provide additional evidence of the benefits of your proposal and your own credibility in offering it.
- Use abstractions, metaphors, and other figures of speech to bring facts and figures to life.

G. Anticipate objections.
- Anticipate and answer potential objections.
- Present the pros and cons of all options if you anticipate a hostile reaction.

---

opinions or letters requesting adjustments that go beyond a supplier's contractual obligations. In addition, some of the routine requests you studied in Chapter 8 can become persuasive messages if you want a nonroutine result or believe that you haven't received fair treatment. Most of these messages can be divided into persuasive requests for action, persuasive presentations of ideas, and persuasive claims and requests for adjustment.

Persuasive Requests for Action

Most persuasive business messages involve a request for action.

The bulk of your persuasive business messages will involve requests for action. In some cases, your request will be anticipated or will require minimal effort on the recipient's part, so the direct approach is fine. In others, you'll need to introduce your intention indirectly. Open with an attention-getting device and show readers that you know something about their concerns, such as maintaining customer satisfaction. Use the interest and desire sections of your message to demonstrate that you have good reasons for making such a request and to cover what you know about the situation: the facts and figures, the benefits of helping, and any history or experience that will enhance your appeal. Your goals are (1) to gain credibility and (2) to make your readers believe that helping you will indeed help solve a significant problem. When you've demonstrated that your message is relevant to your readers, you can close with a request for some specific action or decision.

Persuasive Presentations of Ideas

Sometimes the objective of persuasive messages is simply to encourage people to consider a new idea.

You may encounter situations in which you simply want to change attitudes or beliefs about a particular topic, without asking the audience to decide or do anything—at least not yet. The goal of your first message might be nothing more than convincing your audience to reexamine long-held opinions or admit the possibility of new ways of thinking.

For instance, the World Wide Web Consortium (a global association that defines many of the guidelines and technologies behind the World Wide Web) has launched a campaign called the Web Accessibility Initiative. Although the consortium's ultimate goal is making websites more accessible to people who have disabilities or age-related limitations, a key interim goal is simply making website developers more aware of the need. As part of this effort, the consortium has developed a variety of presentations and documents that highlight the problems many web visitors face.[13]

Persuasive Claims and Requests for Adjustments

If a routine claim or request did not meet your needs, you may need to craft a more persuasive message to explain why you deserve a more satisfactory response.

Most claims and requests for adjustment are routine messages and use the direct approach discussed in Chapter 8. However, consumers and professionals sometimes encounter situations in which they believe they haven't received a fair deal by following normal procedures. These situations require a more persuasive message.

The key ingredients of a good persuasive claim are a complete and specific review of the facts and a confident and positive tone. Keep in mind that you have the right to be satisfied with every transaction. Begin persuasive claims by outlining the problem and continue by reviewing what has been done about it so far, if anything. The recipient might be juggling numerous claims and other demands on his or her attention, so be clear, calm, and complete when presenting your case. Be specific about how you would like to see the situation resolved.

Next, give your reader a good reason for granting your claim. Show how the individual or organization is responsible for the problem and appeal to your reader's sense of fair play, goodwill, or moral responsibility. Explain how you feel about the problem but don't get carried away, don't complain too much, and don't make threats. People generally respond most favorably to requests that are both calm and reasonable. Close on a positive note that reflects how a successful resolution of the situation will repair or maintain a mutually beneficial working relationship.

The ability to persuade others to accept and support your ideas is an essential career skill.
Source: © Image Source/SuperStock.

Developing Marketing and Sales Messages

Marketing and sales messages use the same basic techniques as other persuasive messages, with the added emphasis of encouraging someone to participate in a commercial transaction. Although the terms *marketing message* and *sales message* are often used interchangeably, they are slightly different: **Marketing messages** usher potential buyers through the purchasing process without asking them to make an immediate decision (see Figure 10.4 on the next page). **Sales messages** take over at that point, encouraging potential buyers to make a purchase decision then and there. Marketing messages focus on such tasks as introducing new brands to the public, providing competitive comparisons, encouraging customers to visit websites for more information, and reminding buyers that a particular product or service is available. In contrast, a sales message makes a specific request for people to place an order for a particular product or service. (The text of marketing and sales messages is usually referred to as "copy," by the way.)

Most marketing and sales messages, particularly in larger companies, are created and delivered by professionals with specific training in marketing, advertising, sales, or public relations. However, as a manager, you may be called on to review the work of these specialists or even to write such messages in smaller companies, and having a good understanding of how these messages work will help you be a more effective manager. The essential steps to address include assessing customer needs; analyzing your competition; determining key selling points and benefits; anticipating purchase objections; applying the AIDA model or a similar organizational plan; adapting your writing to social media, as needed; and maintaining high standards of ethics, legal compliance, and etiquette.

ASSESSING AUDIENCE NEEDS

Successful marketing and sales messages start with an understanding of audience needs. For some products and services, this assessment is a fairly simple matter. For instance, customers compare only a few basic attributes when purchasing paper, including its size,

3 LEARNING OBJECTIVE

Describe an effective strategy for developing marketing and sales messages.

Marketing and sales messages use many of the same techniques as persuasive business messages.

Understanding the purchase decision from the buyer's perspective is a vital step in framing an effective marketing or sales message.

The site offers handy links to earlier and later blog posts, making it easy for readers to browse.

Embedded links provide additional information about wedding dress designers, content that many readers will find helpful as well.

The page margin promotes a sale on wedding gowns but does so in a subtle way that doesn't hinder a reader's appreciation of the information offered in the article.

The list of recent posts helps readers find other marketing messages that may address their needs.

Also provided are links to product selections (organized by designer name).

Figure 10.4   Marketing Versus Sales Messages

This article on the Bridepower blog functions as a marketing message, rather than a sales message. It provides information that is potentially useful for many brides and indirectly promotes products offered elsewhere on the website, but it doesn't encourage shoppers to make a decision right away.
Source: Used with permission of Bridepower

MyBcommLab

Apply Figure 10.4's key concepts by revising a new document. Go to Chapter 10 in www.pearsoninternationaleditions.com/ mybcommlab and select Document Makeovers.

weight, brightness, color, and finish. In contrast, they might consider dozens of features when shopping for real estate, cars, professional services, and other complex purchases. In addition, customer needs often extend beyond the basic product or service. For example, clothes do far more than simply keep you warm. What you wear can also make a statement about who you are, which social groups you want to be associated with (or not), and how you view your relationships with the people around you.

Begin by assessing audience needs, interests, and emotional concerns—just as you would for any other business message. Try to form a mental image of the typical buyer for the product you want to sell. Ask yourself what your audience members might want to know about this product. How can your product help them? Are they driven by price, or is quality more important to them?

ANALYZING YOUR COMPETITION

Most marketing and sales messages have to compete for the audience's attention.

Marketing and sales messages nearly always compete with messages from other companies trying to reach the same audience. When Nike plans a marketing campaign to introduce a new shoe model to current customers, the company knows that its audience has also been exposed to messages from New Balance, Reebok, and numerous other shoe companies. In crowded markets, writers sometimes have to search for words and phrases that other companies aren't already using. They might also want to avoid themes, writing styles, or creative approaches that are too similar to those of competitors' messages.

TABLE 10.2	**Features Versus Benefits**
Product or Service Feature	**Customer Benefit**
Carrier's Hybrid Heat dual-fuel system combines our Infinity 19 fuel pump with our Infinity 96 furnace.[14]	Carrier's Hybrid Heat dual-fuel system provides the optimum balance of comfort and energy efficiency.
Our marketing communication audit accurately measures the impact of your advertising and public relations efforts.	Find out whether your message is reaching the target audience and whether you're spending your marketing budget in the best possible manner.
The spools in our fly-fishing reels are machined from solid blocks of aircraft-grade aluminum.	Go fishing with confidence: These lightweight reels will stand up to the toughest conditions.

DETERMINING KEY SELLING POINTS AND BENEFITS

With some insight into audience needs and existing messages from the competition, you're ready to decide which aspects of your product or service to highlight. For all but the simplest products and services, you want to prioritize the items you plan to discuss. You also want to distinguish between the features of the product or service and the benefits that those features offer the customers. As Table 10.2 shows, **selling points** are the most attractive features of a product or service, whereas **benefits** are the particular advantages that readers will realize from those features. Put another way, selling points focus on the product or service, whereas benefits focus on the user.

Selling points focus on the product; benefits focus on the user.

For example, CafeMom doesn't stress the online networking feature of its services; rather, it stresses the opportunity to connect with other moms who have similar concerns and interests—which is the benefit enabled by the networking feature. A common approach to communicating features and benefits is to show them in a list or a table, identifying each feature and describing the benefits it offers.

ANTICIPATING PURCHASE OBJECTIONS

As with persuasive business messages, marketing and sales messages often encounter objections; once again, the best way to handle them is to identify them up front and try to address as many as you can. Objections can include perceptions of high price, low quality, incompatibility, or unacceptable risk. Consumers might worry that a car won't be safe enough for a family, that a jacket will make them look unattractive, or that a hair salon will botch a haircut. Business buyers might worry about disrupting operations or failing to realize the financial returns on a purchase.

Anticipating objections is crucial to effective marketing and sales messages.

Price can be a particularly tricky issue in any message. Whether you highlight or downplay the price of your product, prepare your readers for it. Words such as *luxurious* and *economical* provide clues about how your price compares with that of competitors. Such words help your readers accept your price when you finally state it.

If price is a major selling point, give it a position of prominence, such as in the headline or as the last item in a paragraph. If price is not a major selling point, you can handle it in several ways: You can leave the price out altogether or deemphasize it by putting the figure in the middle of a paragraph that comes well after you've presented the benefits and selling points. Here's an example:

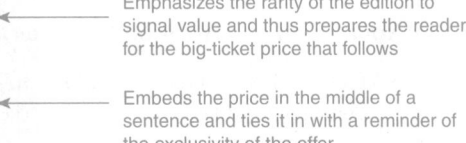

Only 100 prints of this exclusive, limited-edition lithograph will be created. On June 15, they will be made available to the general public, but you can reserve one now for only $350, the special advance reservation price. Simply rush the enclosed reservation card back today so that your order is in before the June 15 publication date.

Emphasizes the rarity of the edition to signal value and thus prepares the reader for the big-ticket price that follows

Embeds the price in the middle of a sentence and ties it in with a reminder of the exclusivity of the offer

Whenever price is likely to cause an objection, look for ways to increase the perceived value of the purchase and decrease the perceived cost. For example, to help blunt the impact of the price of a home gym, you might say that it costs less than a year's worth of health club dues—plus, customers save on transportation costs by exercising at home. Of course, any attempts to minimize perceptions of price or other potential negatives must be ethical.

APPLYING AIDA OR A SIMILAR MODEL

Most marketing and sales messages are prepared according to the AIDA model or some variation of it. (But compare this approach with how *conversation marketing* messages are prepared in "Writing Promotional Messages for Social Media" on page 349.) A typical AIDA-organized message begins with an attention-getting introduction, generates interest by describing some of the product's or service's unique features, increases desire by highlighting the benefits that are most appealing to the audience, and closes by suggesting the action the sender would like the audience members to take.

Getting Attention

You can use a wide range of techniques to attract your audience's attention:

You can use a variety of attention-getting devices in marketing and sales messages.

- **Your product's strongest feature or benefit.** "Game on. And on. And on" (promoting the game-playing aspects of Apple's iPod Touch).[15]
- **A piece of genuine news.** "HealthGrades Reveals America's Best Hospitals."[16]
- **A point of common ground with the audience.** "Tough on Dirt, Gentle on the Earth" (promoting the environmentally friendly aspects of Biokleen cleaning products).[17]
- **A personal appeal to the reader's emotions or values.** "Up to 35 mpg. Unlimited Fun" (promoting the fuel efficiency and sporty driving characteristics of the Ford Focus).[18]
- **The promise of insider information.** "France may seem familiar, but nearly everything—from paying taxes to having a baby—is done quite differently. Get the practical answers to nearly 300 questions about making a life in France."[19]
- **The promise of savings.** "Summer Clearance: Nearly 10,000 Books, Savings up to 90%."[20]
- **A sample or demonstration of the product.** "These videos can provide more detail on Mint's unique and award-winning approach to personal financial management."[21]
- **A solution to a problem.** "Fees to check a bag can add $50 to the cost of a round trip. So the FlightWise Carry-On Backpack is designed to fit in all carry-on storage spaces, even underseat, saving you money with every flight."[22]

Of course, words aren't the only attention-getting device at your disposal. Strong, evocative images are common attention-getters. With online messages, you have even more options, including audio, animation, and video. Even more so than in persuasive business messages, it's important to carefully balance emotion and logic in marketing and sales messages (see Figure 10.5).

Building Interest

To build interest, expand on and support the promises in your attention-getting opening.

Use the interest section of your message to build on the intrigue you created with your opening. This section should also offer support for any claims or promises you made in the opening. For instance, after opening with the headline, "Game on. And on. And on," the Apple iPod Touch web presentation continues with the following:[23]

> **Get Your Game on with Friends Across the Room or Across the Globe**
>
> Games for iPod Touch are made to take advantage of its built-in technologies such as the accelerometer, Multi-Touch, Wi-Fi, and Bluetooth wireless technology. The result is truly immersive gameplay—whether you're playing alone or with others in multiplayer mode. And with an App Store that offers thousands of games ready to download and play, the fun of iPod Touch never ends.

The red-orange color of the tea, enhanced with the glow of backlighting through the translucent liquid, speaks of warmth and comfort.

Without using any images of people, the solitary teacup (left), the multiple glasses of iced tea (center), and the brunch setting suggested by the tea and food (right) convey both the pleasures of a quiet time alone as well as the pleasures of sharing tea with friends and family.

Complementary colors suggest freshness and elegance, adding to the emotional appeal.

The text uses the storytelling technique to explain the creation of Bigelow's signature Constant Comment tea flavor and does so in a way that highlights the emotional appeal of drinking tea.

Figure 10.5   Emotional and Logical Appeals
Bigelow Tea uses an effective combination of visual and textual messages in this emotional appeal.
Source: Used with permission of R.C. Bigelow, Inc.

Notice how this paragraph highlights key game-related features of the iPod Touch and the key benefit ("truly immersive gameplay") that those features enable. The paragraph also addresses a potential objection that some readers might have, which is the number of games available for the device. At this point, anyone interested in portable gaming devices is probably intrigued enough to keep reading, and the website continues with deeper levels of information on each of the key features.

Increasing Desire

To build desire for a product, a service, or an idea, continue to expand on and explain how accepting it will benefit the recipient. Think carefully about the sequence of support points and use plenty of subheadings, hyperlinks, and other devices to help people quickly find the information they need. For example, after reading this much about the iPod touch, some users might want to know more about specific technical points such as the accelerometer, the speed and quality of the graphics, or software apps available. The iPod touch product page continues with detailed discussions of various product features and benefits, and it also offers numerous links to pages with other kinds of support information. The ability to provide flexible access to information is just one of the reasons the web is such a powerful medium for marketing and sales. As the TD Ameritrade webpage in Figure 10.1 shows, the ability to provide flexible access to information is just one of the reasons the web is such a powerful medium for marketing and sales.

> Add details and audience benefits to increase desire for the product or service.

Throughout the body of your message, remember to keep the focus on the audience, not on your company or your product. When you talk about product features, remember to stress the benefits and talk in terms that make sense to users. For instance, rather than going into a technical description of what an accelerometer is, the webpage offers several examples of what it does, such as how in racing games it turns the iPod into a virtual steering wheel.[23]

As you work to build reader interest, be careful not to get so enthusiastic that you lose credibility. If Apple said that the video viewing experience on the iPod touch was as

> Avoid being so enthusiastic that you lose credibility.

"satisfying as watching a full-size TV," most people would scoff at the notion of comparing a 3.5-inch display with a full-size television.

To increase desire, as well as boost your credibility, provide support for your claims. Creative writers find many ways to provide support, including testimonials from satisfied users, articles written by industry experts, competitive comparisons, product samples and free demonstrations, independent test results, and movies or computer animations that show a product in action. YouTube and other video hosting sites in particular have been a boon to marketers because they offer an easy, inexpensive way to demonstrate products. You can also highlight guarantees that demonstrate your faith in your product and your willingness to back it up.

Motivating Action

After you've generated sufficient interest and desire, you're ready to persuade readers to take the preferred action.

After you have raised interest and built up the reader's desire for your product or service, you're ready to ask your audience to take action. Whether you want people to pick up the phone to place an order or visit your website to download a free demo version of your software, try to persuade them to do it right away with an effective *call to action*. You might offer a discount to the first 1,000 people who order, put a deadline on the offer, or simply remind shoppers that the sooner they order, the sooner they'll be able to enjoy the product's benefits (see Figure 10.6). Even potential buyers who want the product can get distracted or forget to respond, so encouraging immediate action is important. Make the response action as simple and as risk-free as possible. If the process is confusing or time-consuming, you'll lose potential customers.

The primary visual encourages trainers to become ACE-certified and to enroll in continuing education courses.

The call to action helps trainers find courses that will expand their knowledge and skills.

The site offers to help trainers build their businesses.

Training courses offer to help trainers build their businesses.

The general public is encouraged to sign up for regular email updates.

Figure 10.6   The Call to Action in a Persuasive Message
Notice how many calls to action are built into the homepage of the American Council on Exercise's website. ACE is a not-for-profit organization committed to encouraging physical fitness through safe and effective exercise. In pursuit of that goal, it offers certification and training for people who want to become personal trainers, and it helps consumers find certified trainers.
Source: Courtesy of the American Council on Exercise® (ACE®) www.acefitness.org.

Writing Promotional Messages for Social Media

The AIDA model and similar approaches have been successful with marketing and sales messages for decades, but communicating with customers in the social media landscape requires a different approach. As earlier chapters emphasize, potential buyers in a social media environment are no longer willing to be passive recipients in a structured, one-way information delivery process or to rely solely on promotional messages from marketers. In addition, they tend to trust each other more than they trust advertisers and many shoppers rely on social media to learn about products before making purchase decisions.[24]

This notion of interactive participation is the driving force behind **conversation marketing**, in which companies initiate and facilitate conversations in a networked community of customers, journalists, bloggers, and other interested parties. The term **social commerce** encompasses any aspect of buying and selling products and services or supporting customers through the use of social media.

Given this shift from unidirectional talks to multidirectional conversations, marketing and sales professionals must adapt their approach to planning, writing, and completing persuasive messages. Follow these guidelines:[25]

- **Facilitate community building.** Make sure customers and other audiences can connect with your company and each other. Accomplishing this goal can be as simple as activating the commenting feature on a blog, or it may involve having a more elaborate social commerce system.
- **Listen at least as much as you talk.** Listening is just as essential for online conversations as it is for in-person conversations. Of course, trying to stay on top of a social media universe composed of millions of potential voices is no easy task. A variety of automated tools can help, from free alerts on search engines to sophisticated linguistic monitoring systems.
- **Initiate and respond to conversations within the community.** Through content on your website, blog postings, social network profiles and messages, newsletters, and other tools, make sure you provide the information customers need in order to evaluate your products and services. Use an objective, conversational style; people in social networks want useful information, not "advertising speak."
- **Provide information that people want.** Whether through industry-insider news, in-depth technical guides to using your products, video tutorials, or brief answers to questions posted on community Q&A sites, fill the information gaps about your company and its products. This strategy of *content marketing* helps you build trusted relationships with potential buyers by repeatedly demonstrating that you understand and care about meeting their needs.[26]
- **Identify and support your champions.** In marketing, *champions* are enthusiastic fans of your company and its products. Champions are so enthusiastic that they help spread your message (through their blogs, for instance), defend you against detractors, and help other customers use your products. As Michael Zeisser of Liberty Interactive put it, "We concluded that we could succeed only by being genuinely useful to the individuals who initiate or sustain virtual word-of-mouth conversations."[27]
- **Be authentic; be transparent; be real.** Trying to fool the public through fake blogs and other tactics is not only unethical (and possibly illegal) but almost guaranteed to eventually backfire in a world where people have unprecedented access to information. Similarly, trying to tack social media onto a consumer-hostile business is likely to fail as soon as stakeholders see through the superficial attempt to "be social." In contrast, social media audiences respond positively to companies that are open and conversational about themselves, their products, and subjects of shared interest.
- **Don't rely on the news media to distribute your message.** In traditional public relations efforts, marketers have to persuade the news media to distribute their messages to consumers and other audiences by producing news stories. These media

4   LEARNING OBJECTIVE

Explain how to modify your approach when writing promotional messages for social media.

Social commerce involves the use of social media in buying, selling, and customer support.

Promoting products and services through social media requires a more conversational approach.

are still important, but you can also speak directly to these audiences through blogs and other electronic tools.

- **Integrate conventional marketing and sales strategies at the right time and in the right places.** AIDA and similar approaches are still valid for specific communication tasks, such as conventional advertising and the product promotion pages on your website.

For the latest information on using social media for persuasive communication, visit http://real-timeupdates.com/ebc10 and click on Chapter 10.

Maintaining High Standards of Ethics, Legal Compliance, and Etiquette

5 LEARNING OBJECTIVE

Identify steps you can take to avoid ethical lapses in marketing and sales messages.

Marketing and sales messages are covered by a wide range of laws and regulations.

The word *persuasion* has negative connotations for some people, especially in a marketing or sales context. They associate persuasion with dishonest and unethical practices that lead unsuspecting audiences into accepting unworthy ideas or buying unneeded products.

However, effective businesspeople view persuasion as a positive force, aligning their own interests with what is best for their audiences. They influence audience members by providing information and aiding understanding, which allows audiences the freedom to choose.[28] To maintain the highest standards of business ethics, always demonstrate the "you" attitude by showing honest concern for your audience's needs and interests.

As marketing and selling grow increasingly complex, so do the legal ramifications of marketing and sales messages. In the United States, the Federal Trade Commission (www.ftc.gov) has the authority to impose penalties (ranging from cease-and-desist orders to multimillion-dollar fines) against advertisers who violate federal standards for truthful advertising. Other federal agencies have authority over advertising in specific industries, such as transportation and financial services. Individual states have additional laws that apply. The legal aspects of promotional communication can be quite complex, varying from state to state and from country to country, and most companies require marketing and salespeople to get clearance from company lawyers before sending messages.

Moreover, communicators must stay on top of changing regulations, such as the latest laws governing unsolicited bulk email ("spam"), disclosure requirements for bloggers who review products, privacy, and data security. Two of the latest ethical concerns that could produce new legislation are *behavioral targeting*, which tracks the online behavior of website visitors and serves up ads based on what they appear to be interested in, and *remarketing*, in which behaviorally targeted ads follow users even as they move on to other websites.[29]

For all marketing and sales efforts, pay close attention to the following legal considerations:[30]

- **Marketing and sales messages must be truthful and nondeceptive.** The FTC considers messages to be deceptive if they include statements that are likely to mislead reasonable customers and the statements are an important part of the purchasing decision. Failing to include important information is also considered deceptive. The FTC also looks at *implied claims*—claims you don't explicitly make but that can be inferred from what you do or don't say.
- **You must back up your claims with evidence.** According to the FTC, offering a money-back guarantee or providing letters from satisfied customers is not enough; you must still be able to support claims for your product with objective evidence such as a survey or scientific study (see Figure 10.7). If you claim that your food product lowers cholesterol, you must have scientific evidence to support that claim.

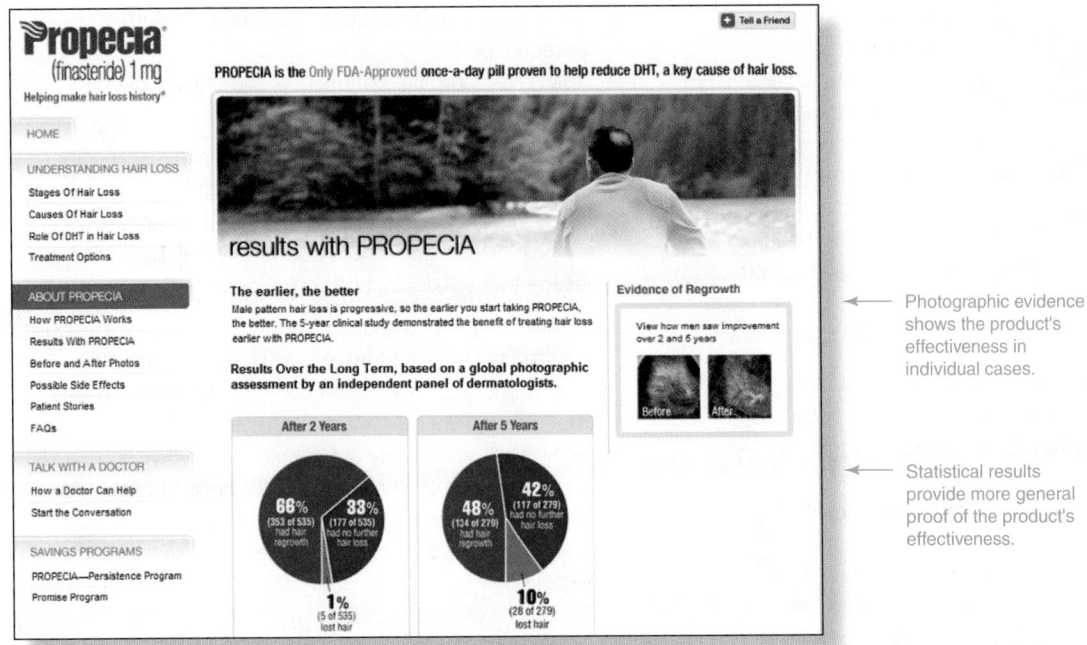

Figure 10.7   Backing Up Promotional Claims with Solid Evidence
Merck, the company that makes the hair-loss treatment Propecia, takes care to back up its product claims with solid evidence, out of respect for its audience and to ensure compliance with regulations regarding marketing and sales messages. The series of photos available through the "Evidence of Regrowth" link provides additional visual confirmation of the product's benefits.
Source: Reproduced with permission of Merck Sharp & Dohme Corp., subsidiary of Merck & Co., Inc. All rights reserved. PROPECIA® is a registered trademark of Merck Sharp & Dohme Corp.

- **"Bait and switch" advertising is illegal.** Trying to attract buyers by advertising a product that you don't intend to sell—and then trying to sell them another (and usually more expensive) product—is illegal.
- **Marketing messages and websites aimed at children are subject to special rules.** For example, online marketers must obtain consent from parents before collecting personal information about children under age 13.
- **Marketing and sales messages are considered binding contracts in many states.** If you imply or make an offer and then can't fulfill your end of the bargain, you can be sued for breach of contract.
- **In most cases, you can't use a person's name, photograph, or other identity without permission.** Doing so is considered an invasion of privacy. You can use images of people considered to be public figures as long as you don't unfairly imply that they endorse your message.

Meeting your ethical and legal obligations will go a long way toward maintaining good communication etiquette as well. However, you may still face etiquette decisions within ethical and legal boundaries. For instance, you can produce a marketing campaign that complies with all applicable laws and yet is offensive or insulting to your audience. Taking an audience-centered approach, involving respect for your readers and their values, should help you avoid any such etiquette missteps.

Technology also gives communicators new ways to demonstrate sensitivity to user needs. For, example automated RSS newsfeeds from blogs and updates sent from company pages on Facebook can alert customers to information in which they've expressed an interest. *Opt-in* email newsletters, sent only to those people who have specifically requested information, are another technology that shows the "you" attitude at work.

Maintaining high ethical standards is a key aspect of good communication etiquette.

Communication technologies such as RSS, opt-in email, and Facebook page updates can help you be sensitive to audience needs.

Source: © Vibe Images/Alamy.

You're the vice president of member services at CafeMom, reporting to CEO Michael Sanchez. In addition to developing new online services, a key part of your job responsibility is crafting messages that describe the new services and persuade members to try them. Use what you've learned in this chapter and in your own experiences as a consumer (and as a parent, if applicable) to address these challenges.

1. You asked one of your staffers to write a benefit statement to communicate the advantages of the Groups section of the CafeMom website, which lets members find and join any of the thousands of existing groups or create new groups focused on just about any topic imaginable. She emails the following sentence: "We've worked hard to define and create a powerful online group capability; you can search far and wide on the Web, but you won't find anything as great as what we've created." You then write back, explaining why it's important to make marketing messages about the *customer*, not about the *company*. Which of these versions best illustrates this vital aspect of the "you" attitude? (You can learn more about the Groups feature at the CafeMom website, **www.cafemom.com/groups**.)

   a. Group members at CafeMom support one another and share their knowledge, experience, and opinions on a wide variety of subjects, from pregnancy to schooling to religion.
   b. Get support, information, and thought-provoking opinions from CafeMom groups.
   c. Join a ClubMom group (or start your own) to get support, information, and thought-provoking opinions from other moms on a wide variety of subjects, from pregnancy to schooling to religion.
   d. Social networking has rapidly become a popular way for web surfers to get insights, information, and thought-provoking opinions, and the CafeMom groups will help you, too.

2. A common challenge in marketing communication is distilling a long list of features to a single compelling message that can serve as the product's "headline." Review the following list of features and benefits (extracted from various communications presented by CafeMom and its business partners):
   - The experiences of thousands of moms are now aggregated in a single place online.
   - Connect with moms like you; search for moms by personal and family challenges, interests, age of kids, or location.
   - Get and give support; find support and swap advice with other moms on a wide range of topics that matter most to you.
   - Post questions online and get input from mothers who've been there before.
   - Joining CafeMom is absolutely free.
   - Setting up your own personal profile is fast and easy.
   - Join groups who share your likes and concerns.
   - Write as much or as little as you want to share in your personal profile.
   - You have complete control over the privacy of your information.

   Which of these statements is the best single-sentence encapsulation of the wide range of benefits that CafeMom offers? Obviously, a single sentence can't communicate every point listed; think more about an initial, high-level message that will entice people to keep reading.

   a. Connecting and collecting; caring and sharing: The online community at CafeMom lets you network with other moms and find information you can use to help make motherhood successful and satisfying.
   b. The online community at CafeMom lets you connect with other moms and find valuable information to help make motherhood successful and satisfying.
   c. CafeMom offers moms everywhere a unique online experience.
   d. CafeMom offers the best moms everywhere an absolutely unique online experience, with unparalleled access to valuable knowledge and rewarding camaraderie.

3. Membership in CafeMom is free, so price isn't a potential purchase objection. However, CafeMom does collect a fair amount of information from its members, including information about members themselves, their families, and their product purchase and usage habits. Which of the following statements would you put on the website to encourage anyone who is concerned about privacy and data security to read CafeMom's privacy policy? You can read the policy by clicking on "Privacy Policy" at the bottom of the CafeMom homepage. (Assume that the statement will contain the necessary hyperlink to take visitors to the privacy policy page on the website.)

   a. See why you never have to worry about data security or personal privacy on CafeMom.
   b. Learn more about how we protect the information we collect in order to continue making CafeMom a great web destination.
   c. We implement SSL for credit card transactions and other sensitive transactions.
   d. Like most websites, we collect only the information necessary to provide the valuable services we offer on this website.

4. Which of the following is the most effective call to action to encourage interested moms to sign up for free CafeMom membership?

   a. Sign up for your free Join CafeMom membership today and get knowledge and camaraderie you can't get anywhere else.
   b. Visit **cafemom.com** today and learn about the many benefits of free membership.
   c. Every mom belongs in CafeMom; won't you please join today?
   d. CafeMom will change your life in ways you could never have imagined, and it's free!

LEARNING OBJECTIVES CHECKUP

Assess your understanding of the principles in this chapter by reading each learning objective and studying the accompanying exercises. For fill-in-the-blank items, write the missing text in the blank provided; for multiple-choice items, circle the letter of the correct answer. You can check your responses against the answer key on page AK-2.

Objective 10.1: Apply the three-step writing process to persuasive messages.

1. Which of the following is an accurate general statement about good ideas in the business world?
   a. Newer employees are not expected to contribute fresh ideas.
   b. Many good ideas pass unnoticed or are misunderstood because they are communicated poorly.
   c. Business leaders always jump on new ideas, even if they are poorly presented.
   d. Good ideas speak for themselves and don't need to be "communicated" in today's social media environment.

2. Why is the indirect approach often used in persuasive messages?
   a. It is more courteous and therefore gives the writer the opportunity to build up goodwill before slipping in the sales pitch.
   b. It takes less time.
   c. It is the traditional way to do persuasive messages and therefore expected.
   d. It lets the writer build audience interest and desire before asking for action or commitment.

3. Which of the following is not a good way to establish credibility with your audience?
   a. Support your argument with clear reasoning and objective evidence.
   b. Identify your sources.
   c. Establish common ground with your readers.
   d. Present only your side of the argument to avoid reminding the audience of alternatives.

Objective 10.2: Describe an effective strategy for developing persuasive business messages, and identify the three most common categories of persuasive business messages.

4. The first phase in the AIDA model is to
   a. Do your research
   b. Gain the audience's attention
   c. Analyze the audience
   d. Call for action

5. The body of a message that follows the AIDA model
   a. Captures the audience's attention
   b. Contains the buffer
   c. Generates interest and heightens desire
   d. Calls for action

6. Which of the following is a good way to build desire using the AIDA approach?
   a. Explain how the proposed change will help your audience.
   b. Reduce resistance by addressing objections the audience might have.
   c. Explain complex ideas or products in more detail.
   d. Do all of the above.

7. The final phase of the AIDA method
   a. Provides in-depth information to help generate interest
   b. Reduces resistance by increasing the audience's desire
   c. Calls for action
   d. Captures the audience's attention

8. An argument that is based on human feelings is known as a/an _____ appeal.

9. An argument that is based on facts and reason is known as a/an _____ appeal.

10. The best approach to using emotional appeals is usually to
    a. Use them by themselves
    b. Use them in conjunction with logical appeals
    c. Use them only when the audience is particularly hostile
    d. Avoid them in all business messages

Objective 10.3: Describe an effective strategy for developing marketing and sales messages.

11. Why is it important to anticipate objections when planning and writing persuasive messages?
    a. You are legally required to anticipate audience objections in all marketing messages.
    b. By anticipating potential objections, you have the opportunity to address them in a persuasive manner before the audience settles on a firm no answer.
    c. By anticipating potential objections, you have the opportunity to explain to audience members why they are viewing the situation incorrectly.
    d. By anticipating potential objections, you can explain to the audience all the negative consequences of accepting your message.

12. Prioritizing which features and benefits to write about is
    a. A waste of time because people don't read in sequential order
    b. Important because doing so lets you start with low-priority issues and work your way up to high-priority issues
    c. Important because it helps you focus your message on items and issues that the audience cares about the most
    d. Important because it helps ensure that you remember to talk about every single feature and benefit, no matter how inconsequential

13. How do marketing messages and sales messages differ?
    a. Sales messages use oral media exclusively.
    b. Sales messages are "hard sell," whereas marketing messages are "soft sell."
    c. Marketing messages move audiences toward a purchase decision without actually asking them to make a decision; sales messages ask them to make a decision then and there.
    d. The vast majority of marketing messages are still legal, but most traditional sales messages have been outlawed in both the United States and the European Union.

14. What is the relationship between features and benefits?
    a. They are different words for the same idea.
    b. Features are aspects of an idea or product; benefits are the advantages that readers will realize from those features.
    c. Features tell people how to use a product; benefits tell them how a product differs from the competition.
    d. Features are the primary advantages of a product; benefits are the secondary advantages.

Objective 10.4: Explain how to modify your approach when writing promotional messages for social media.

15. Which of the following is the best definition of social commerce?
    a. It encompasses any aspect of buying and selling products and services or supporting customers through the use of social media.
    b. It is another term for group buying or committee buying within corporations.
    c. It encompasses all of the communication traffic on a given social network.
    d. It refers to the communication aspects of marketing and selling, as distinct from the transactional and financial aspects.

16. Which of the following is not a good guideline for using social media in sales and marketing?
    a. Rely on the conventional news media to distribute your messages; frequent outages and too much "chatter" make social networks unreliable.
    b. Identify and support your *champions*, those people who are enthusiastic fans of your company and its products.
    c. Initiate and respond to conversations within the community.
    d. Integrate conventional marketing and sales strategies at the right time and in the right places.

Objective 10.5: Identify steps you can take to avoid ethical lapses in marketing and sales messages.

17. Which of the following steps should you take to make sure your persuasive messages are ethical?
    a. Align your interest with your audience's interests.
    b. Choose words that offer multiple interpretations.
    c. Limit the amount of information you provide to avoid overloading the audience and thereby confusing your readers.
    d. Do all of the above.

18. If it adheres to all applicable federal laws, a marketing or sales message
    a. Is certain to be both legal and ethical
    b. Could still violate some state laws
    c. Could still be unethical
    d. Both b and c

MyBcommLab

CHAPTER OUTLINE

Using the Three-Step Writing Process for Persuasive Messages

- Step 1: Planning a Persuasive Message
- Step 2: Writing a Persuasive Message
- Step 3: Completing a Persuasive Message

Developing Persuasive Business Messages

- Strategies for Persuasive Business Messages
- Common Examples of Persuasive Business Messages

Developing Marketing and Sales Messages

- Assessing Audience Needs
- Analyzing Your Competition
- Determining Key Selling Points and Benefits
- Anticipating Purchase Objections
- Applying AIDA or a Similar Model

Writing Promotional Messages for Social Media

Maintaining High Standards of Ethics, Legal Compliance, and Etiquette

LEARNING OBJECTIVES

1. Apply the three-step writing process to persuasive messages. [page 332]
2. Describe an effective strategy for developing persuasive business messages, and identify the three most common categories of persuasive business messages. [page 337]
3. Describe an effective strategy for developing marketing and sales messages. [page 343]
4. Explain how to modify your approach when writing promotional messages for social media. [page 349]
5. Identify steps you can take to avoid ethical lapses in marketing and sales messages. [page 350]

KEY TERMS

AIDA model Message sequence that involves attention, interest, desire, and action

benefits The particular advantages that readers will realize from a product's selling points

conversation marketing Approach in which companies initiate and facilitate conversations in a networked community of customers, journalists, bloggers, and other interested parties

demographics Quantifiable characteristics of a population, including age, gender, occupation, income, and education

emotional appeal Persuasive approach that calls on audience feelings and sympathies rather than facts, figures, and rational arguments

logical appeal Persuasive approach that calls on reasoning and evidence

marketing messages Promotional messages that usher potential buyers through the purchasing process without asking them to make an immediate decision

motivation The combination of forces that drive people to satisfy their needs

persuasion The attempt to change an audience's attitudes, beliefs, or actions

psychographics Psychological characteristics of an audience, including personality, attitudes, and lifestyle

sales messages In contrast to marketing messages, sales messages encourage potential buyers to make a purchase decision then and there

selling points The most attractive features of a product or service

social commerce Encompasses any aspect of buying and selling products and services or supporting customers through the use of social media

✓ Checklist

Developing Persuasive Messages

A. Get your reader's attention.
- Open with an audience benefit, a stimulating question, a problem, or an unexpected statement.
- Establish common ground by mentioning a point on which you and your audience agree.
- Show that you understand the audience's concerns.

B. Build your reader's interest.
- Expand and support your opening claim or promise.
- Emphasize the relevance of your message to your audience.

C. Increase your reader's desire.
- Make audience members want to change by explaining how the change will benefit them.
- Back up your claims with relevant evidence.

D. Motivate your reader to take action.
- Suggest the action you want readers to take.
- Stress the positive results of the action.
- Make the desired action clear and easy.

E. Balance emotional and logical appeals.
- Use emotional appeals to help the audience accept your message.
- Use logical appeals when presenting facts and evidence for complex ideas or recommendations.
- Avoid faulty logic.

F. Reinforce your position.
- Provide additional evidence of the benefits of your proposal and your own credibility in offering it.
- Use abstractions, metaphors, and other figures of speech to bring facts and figures to life.

G. Anticipate objections.
- Anticipate and answer potential objections.
- Present the pros and cons of all options if you anticipate a hostile reaction.

APPLY YOUR KNOWLEDGE

To review chapter content related to each question, refer to the indicated Learning Objective.

1. Why is it essential to consider your readers' motivations before writing a persuasive message? [LO-1]
2. Why is it important to present both sides of an argument when writing a persuasive message to a potentially hostile audience? [LO-2]
3. Are emotional appeals ethical? Why or why not? [LO-2]
4. What is likely to happen if a promotional message starts immediately with a call to action? Why? [LO-3]
5. Why do the AIDA model and similar approaches need to be modified when writing persuasive messages in social media? [LO-4]

PRACTICE YOUR SKILLS

Messages for Analysis

For Message 10.A and Message 10.B, read the following documents and then (1) analyze the strengths and weaknesses of each sentence and (2) revise each document so that it follows this chapter's guidelines.

Message 10.A: Message Strategies: Persuasive Claims and Requests for Adjustment [LO-2]

Dear TechStar Computing:

Last week, I bought a new stylus tablet from you after looking at your catalog. I chose that model because it was ultra-slim and promised a high resolution. However, when I got home, I found the resolution was half what it said on the box, and moreover, the stylus had a slippery grip. This was not evident from either your catalog or the publicity photos you showed me. I can't be sure, but the tablet also looks smaller than how it looked on your website. Please, I need this tablet for my next design project. What are you going to do to help me?

Message 10.B: Message Strategies: Sales Messages [LO-3]

Fed up of that old typewriter in the attic? Don't throw it away! We at Colorqwerty will convert it into an art machine for you. Our patented system involves fitting the metal keys of your typewriter with colored ink-filled pads, so instead of typing words, you can type art using at least 45 different colors! Give it a try. Drop into any of our showrooms and try out the colorqwerty for free. If you like it, it's yours to own for just $70 ($30 for the color refill kit).

Message 10.C: Media Skills: Podcasting [LO-2]

To access this message, visit http://real-timeupdates.com/ebc10, click on "Student Assignments," and select Chapter 10, page 356, Message 10.C. Download and listen to this podcast. Identify at least three ways in which the podcast could be more persuasive and draft a brief email message that you could send to the podcaster with your suggestions for improvement.

Exercises

Active links for all websites in this chapter can be found on MyBcommLab; see your User Guide for instructions on accessing the content for this chapter. Each activity is labeled according to the primary skill or skills you will need to use. To review relevant chapter content, you can refer to the indicated Learning Objective. In some instances, supporting information will be found in another chapter, as indicated.

1. **Choosing a Message Strategy: [LO-1], Chapters 8–9** Now that you've explored routine, positive, negative, and persuasive messages, review the following message scenarios and identify which of the four message strategies would be most appropriate for the situation. Offer a brief justification for each choice. (Depending on the particular circumstances, a scenario might lend itself to more than one type of message; just be sure to offer compelling reasons for your choices.)

   a. An unsolicited message to your department manager, explaining why you believe that the company's experiment with self-managed work teams has not been successful

   b. An unsolicited message to your department manager, explaining why you believe that the company's experiment with self-managed work teams has not been successful and suggesting that one of the more experienced employees (such as yourself) should be promoted to supervisor

   c. A message to a long-time industrial customer, explaining that a glitch in your accounting system resulted in the customer being overcharged on its last five orders, apologizing for the problem, and assuring the customer that you will refund the overcharged amount immediately

   d. A news release announcing that your company plans to invite back 50 employees who were laid off earlier in the year

2. **Message Strategies: Persuasive Business Messages; Collaboration: Team Projects [LO-2]** With another student, analyze the persuasive email message to Eleanor Tran at Host Marriott (Figure 10.3) by answering the following questions:

   a. What techniques are used to capture the reader's attention?

b. Does the writer use the direct or indirect organizational approach? Why?

c. Is the subject line effective? Why or why not?

d. Does the writer use an emotional or a logical appeal? Why?

e. What reader benefits are included?

f. How does the writer establish credibility?

g. What tools does the writer use to reinforce his position?

3. **Message Strategies: Persuasive Business Messages, Marketing and Sales Messages: Media Skills: Email [LO-2], [LO-3]** Compose effective subject lines for the following persuasive email messages:

a. A recommendation was sent by email to your branch manager to install wireless networking throughout the facility. The primary reason is that management has encouraged more teamwork, but teams often congregate in meeting rooms, the cafeteria, and other places that lack network access—without which they can't do much of the work they are expected to do.

b. A message to area residents, soliciting customers for your new business, "Meals à la Car," a carryout dining service that delivers from most of the local restaurants. All local restaurant menus are on the Internet. Mom and Dad can dine on egg rolls and chow mein while the kids munch on pepperoni pizza.

c. An email message to the company president, asking that employees be allowed to carry over their unused vacation days to the following year. Apparently, many employees canceled their fourth-quarter vacation plans to work on the installation of a new company computer system. Under their current contract, vacation days not used by December 31 can't be carried over to the following year.

4. **Communication Ethics: Making Ethical Choices [LO-2], [LO-5]** Your boss has asked you to post a message on the company's internal blog, urging everyone in your department to donate money to the company's favorite charity, an organization that operates a summer camp for children with physical challenges. You wind up writing a lengthy posting, packed with facts and heartwarming anecdotes about the camp and the children's experiences. When you must work that hard to persuade your audience to take an action such as donating money to a charity, aren't you being manipulative and unethical? Explain.

5. **Message Strategies: Marketing and Sales Messages (Customer Benefits)[LO-3]** Determine whether the following sentences focus on features or benefits; rewrite as necessary to focus all the sentences on benefits.

a. All-Cook skillets are coated with a durable, patented nonstick surface.

b. You can call anyone and talk as long as you like on Saturdays and Sundays with our new FamilyTalk wireless plan.

c. With 8-millisecond response time, the Samsung LN-S4095D 40-inch LCD TV delivers fast video action that is smooth and crisp.[31]

6. **Message Strategies: Marketing and Sales Messages [LO-3]** The daily mail often brings a selection of sales messages. Find a direct-mail package from your mailbox that includes a sales letter. Then answer the following questions to help analyze and learn from the approach used by the communication professionals who prepare these glossy sales messages. Your instructor might also ask you to share the package and your observations in a class discussion.

a. Who is the intended audience?

b. What are some of the demographic and psychographic characteristics of the intended audience?

c. What is the purpose of the direct-mail package? Has it been designed to solicit a phone-call response, make a mail-order sale, obtain a charitable contribution, or do something else?

d. What technique was used to encourage you to open the envelope?

e. Did the letter writer follow the AIDA model or something similar? If not, explain the letter's organization.

f. What emotional appeals and logical arguments does the letter use?

g. What selling points and consumer benefits does the letter offer?

h. Did the letter and the rest of the package provide convincing support for the claims made in the letter? If not, what is lacking?

EXPAND YOUR SKILLS

Critique the Professionals

Visit the Facebook pages of six companies in several industries. How do the companies make use of their Wall? Do any of the companies use Wall posts to promote their products? Compare the material on the Info tabs. Which company has the most compelling information here? How about the use of custom tabs; which company does the best job of using this Facebook feature? Using whatever medium your instructor requests, write a brief analysis of the message (no more than one page), citing specific elements from the piece and support from the chapter.

Sharpening Your Career Skills Online

Bovée and Thill's Business Communication Web Search, at http://businesscommunicationblog.com/websearch, is a unique research tool designed specifically for business communication research. Use the Web Search function to find a website, video, PDF document, podcast, or PowerPoint presentation that offers advice on writing persuasive messages (either persuasive business messages or marketing and sales messages). Write a brief email message to your instructor, describing the item that you found and summarizing the career skills information you learned from it.

IMPROVE YOUR GRAMMAR, MECHANICS, AND USAGE

The following exercises help you improve your knowledge of and power over English grammar, mechanics, and usage. Turn to the "Handbook of Grammar, Mechanics, and Usage" at the end of this book and review all of Sections 2.4 (Semicolons) and 2.5 (Colons). Then look at the following 10 items. Circle the letter of the preferred choice in the following groups of sentences. (Answers to these exercises appear on page AK-4.)

1. **a.** This memo is well-written; that one isn't.
   b. This memo is well-written: that one isn't.

2. **a.** Please understand one thing: You will have to send in your report by Wednesday.
   b. Please understand one thing; you will have to send in your report by Wednesday.
   c. Please understand one thing: You will have to send in your report; by Wednesday.

3. **a.** My car has a flat tire, however I am sure I can find a taxi.
   b. My car has a flat tire, however, I am sure I can find a taxi.
   c. My car has a flat tire; however, I am sure I can find a taxi.

4. **a.** Her goal was apparent from the start: to become the CEO.
   b. Her goal was apparent from the start; to become the CEO.

5. **a.** There are only two companies worth considering; George P. Johnson and Krayonz.
   b. There are only two companies worth considering: George P. Johnson and Krayonz.

6. **a.** Please remember to invite: Nancy Jones, COO, Robert Patz, CFO, and James Metzger, President.
   b. Please remember to invite Nancy Jones, COO; Robert Patz, CFO; and James Metzger, President.
   c. Please remember to invite Nancy Jones COO; Robert Patz CFO; and James Metzger President.

7. **a.** She sent three cases yesterday; therefore, you should receive them by tomorrow.
   b. She sent three cases yesterday, therefore; you should receive them by tomorrow.
   c. She sent three cases yesterday; therefore you should receive them by tomorrow.

8. **a.** The CEO was very angry: his secretary had mislaid the meeting notes.
   b. The CEO was very angry; because his secretary had mislaid the meeting notes.
   c. The CEO was very angry; his secretary had mislaid the meeting notes.

9. **a.** Jones is an excellent speechwriter however; he suffers from stage fright.
   b. Jones is an excellent speechwriter; however, he suffers from stage fright.
   c. Jones is an excellent speechwriter: however he suffers from stage fright.

10. **a.** There are three avenues; feedback forms; questionnaires; and focus groups.
    b. There are three avenues; feedback forms, questionnaires, and focus groups.
    c. There are three avenues: feedback forms, questionnaires, and focus groups.

For additional exercises focusing on semicolons and colons, visit MyBcommLab. Click on Chapter 10, click on Additional Exercises to Improve Your Grammar, Mechanics, and Usage, and click on 16. Punctuation A.

CASES

Persuasive Business Messages

Learn how to set up a Twitter account and begin tweeting. Visit http://real-timeupdates.com/ebc10, click on Student Assignments and then click on Twitter Screencast.

MICROBLOGGING SKILLS

1. Message Strategies: Persuasive Business Messages [LO-3] You've been trying for months to convince CEO Hannah Schmidt, your boss at Meltpot, a company that makes and sells specialty chocolates, to start using Twitter. Her main objection is that she doesn't think anything useful can be said in 140 characters. You get talking about this one day and she gives you a challenge: write five tweets with embedded URLs to drive traffic to your company site. If your network manager records a hundred

hits from people clicking the tweets, Schmidt will allow you to set up and run the company's Twitter account. The URLs will be 20 characters each. Your boss makes one more condition: you can't offer any rewards or prizes of the type: "Click here and get a free box of Praline Assortments," so, you'll have to be creative. Meltpot is particularly known for combining unusual fruits, spices, and even vegetables like carrots, beets, and peas in its chocolates.

Your task: Use the company's core asset of beautifully designed, creative, and healthy chocolates to intrigue people to come over and check it out. Brainstorm on what might set Meltpot apart from its competitors and highlight this in your tweets. Make up any additional information you might need.

BLOGGING SKILLS   TEAM SKILLS

2. Message Strategies: Persuasive Business Messages [LO-3] You have campaigned long and hard to get the people in your company, DeskEggs Stationery and Office Supplies, to use Twitter, IM, wikis, Youtube, and podcasting to interact with the public. You have now succeeded—and your boss is livid. He has looked through the online performance of the employees and identified four of the worst offenders. They are:

Bonnie: She tweets all the time, in SMSese without grammar or spelling. Sometimes it can take all day to figure out what she means.

Larry and Tod: Every blog post on the company's blog is a gladiatorial arena for them; they take turns posting comments and hijack the conversation, while the other commenters look on helplessly.

Matt: He's posted 17 videos about the production line on YouTube: all very useful, but none less than 12 minutes long. The first few minutes of each video usually show him setting up the shot, chatting with his buddies, eating his sandwiches, dropping things, and yelling at people.

Lorna: She's the Assistant Marketing Manager and she's known for her sharp tongue. Unfortunately her reputation has spread further than you'd like. In a couple of posts on the company blog she's been very frank and free with her opinion of your competitors, to the point where your boss got a phone call from one of them asking him to take the post down or face action.

Because this was your idea, your boss wants you to sort this out. However, he doesn't want you naming names.

Your task: Working with two other students, write four posts for the company's internal blog (which is not viewable outside the company), outlining your concerns about these communication practices. Use the examples mentioned above but change the names and details, and make up any additional details you need. Emphasize that, while social media communication is often less formal and more flexible than traditional business communication, it shouldn't be unprofessional. You are thinking of proposing a social media training program for everyone in the company, but for this message you just want to bring attention to the problem.

LETTER WRITING SKILLS

3. Message Strategies: Persuasive Business Messages [LO-3] The coffee shop across the street from your tiny apartment is your haven-away-from-home—great beverages, healthy snacks, an atmosphere that is convivial but not so lively that you can't focus on your homework, and free wireless. It lacks only one thing: some way to print out your homework and other files when you need hardcopy. Your college's libraries and computer labs provide printers, but you live three miles from campus, and it's a long walk or an inconvenient bus ride.

Your task: Write a letter to the owner of the coffee shop, encouraging her to set up a printing service to complement the free wireless access. Propose that the service run at break-even prices, just enough to pay for paper, ink cartridges, and the cost of the printer itself. The benefit to the shop would be enticing patrons to spend more time—and therefore more of their coffee and tea

money—in the shop. You might also mention that you had to take the bus to campus in order to print this letter, so you bought your afternoon latte somewhere else.

4. Message Strategies: Persuasive Business Messages [LO-2] Like your colleagues at the predominantly young and net-savvy company you have just joined, you are a regular user of Facebook, LinkedIn, Twitter, Google Plus, and other social networking tools, as well as email, IM, and your own personal blog. As you did at your previous company, you expect to use these tools in your work, but you are stunned by the news that your boss, who's in his fifties, has fired off an email message to the whole company stating that the use of all social networking tools barring email is to be banned from the company premises as of today. You ask around and discover from a colleague that your boss happened to be in the office of one of the department heads from where he could see the screens of several employees, and they were all busily surfing Facebook. He jumped to the conclusion that they were wasting time, and got usage statistics from the network manager that seemed to support his views.

Your task: You have to persuade your boss that he's got the wrong idea. Using not just facts about your own colleagues, but also research and statistics available on the Internet, and examples from Facebook, LinkedIn, and other sites, write an email explaining to him just how these tools can help your company communicate better. Particularly highlight the differences from and advantages over plain email. Make up any additional information you need.

IM SKILLS

5. Message Strategies: Requests for Action [LO-2] At IBM, you're one of the coordinators for the annual Employee Charitable Contributions Campaign. Since 1978, the company has helped employees contribute to more than 2,000 health and human service agencies. These groups may offer child care; treat substance abuse; provide health services; or fight illiteracy, homelessness, and hunger. Some offer disaster relief or care for the elderly. All deserve support. They're carefully screened by IBM, one of the largest corporate contributors of cash, equipment, and people to nonprofit organizations and educational institutions in the United States and around the world. As your literature states, the program "has engaged our employees more fully in the important mission of corporate citizenship."

During the winter holidays, you target agencies that cater to the needs of displaced families, women, and children. It's not difficult to raise enthusiasm. The prospect of helping children enjoy the holidays—children who otherwise might have nothing—usually awakens the spirit of your most distracted workers. But some of them wait until the last minute and then forget.

They have until December 16 to come forth with cash contributions. To make it in time for holiday deliveries, they can also bring in toys, food, and blankets through Tuesday, December 20. They shouldn't have any trouble finding the collection bins; they're everywhere, marked with bright red banners. But some will want to call you with questions or (you hope) to make credit card contributions: 800-658-3899, ext. 3342.

Your task: It's December 14. Write a 75- to 100-word instant message, encouraging last-minute holiday gifts.[32]

MEMO WRITING SKILLS

6. Message Strategies: Requests for Action [LO-2] This morning as you drove to your job as food services manager at the Pechanga Casino Entertainment Center in Temecula, California, you were concerned to hear on the radio that the local Red Cross chapter put out a call for blood because national supplies have fallen dangerously low. During highly publicized disasters, people are emotional and eager to help out by donating blood. But in calmer times, only 5 percent of eligible donors think of giving blood. You're one of those few.

Not many people realize that donated blood lasts only 72 hours. Consequently, the mainstay of emergency blood supplies must be replenished in an ongoing effort. No one is more skilled, dedicated, or efficient in handling blood than the American Red Cross, which is responsible for half the nation's supply of blood and blood products.

Donated blood helps victims of accidents and disease, as well as surgery patients. Just yesterday you were reading about a girl named Melissa, who was diagnosed with multiple congenital heart defects and underwent her first open-heart surgery at 1 week old. Now 5, she's used well over 50 units of donated blood, and she wouldn't be alive without them. In a thank-you letter, her mother lauded the many strangers who had "given a piece of themselves" to save her precious daughter—and countless others. You also learned that a donor's pint of blood can benefit up to four other people.

Today, you're going to do more than just roll up your own sleeve. You know the local Red Cross chapter takes its blood donation equipment to corporations, restaurants, beauty salons—any place willing to host public blood drives. What if you could convince the board of directors to support a blood drive at the casino? The slot machines and gaming tables are usually full, hundreds of employees are on hand, and people who've never visited before might come down to donate blood. The positive publicity will boost Pechanga's community image, too. With materials from the Red Cross, you're confident you can organize Pechanga's hosting effort and handle the promotion. (Last year, you headed the casino's successful Toys for Tots drive.)

To give blood, one must be healthy, be at least 17 years old (with no upper age limit), and weigh at least 110 pounds. Donors can give every 56 days. You'll be urging Pechanga donors to eat well, drink water, and be thoroughly rested before donating.[33]

Your task: Write a memo persuading the Pechanga board of directors to host a public Red Cross blood drive. You can learn more about what's involved in hosting a blood drive at www .redcrossblood.org (click on Hosting a Blood Drive). Ask the board to provide water, orange juice, and snacks for donors. You'll organize food service workers to handle the distribution, but you'll need the board's approval to let your team volunteer during work hours. Use a combination of logical and emotional appeals.

EMAIL SKILLS   PORTFOLIO BUILDER

7. Message Strategies: Requests for Action [LO-2] Your new company, Shoeprints, uses 3D imaging technology to create "footmaps" and a database of shoe designs to predict the right shape and style of shoe for your foot, along with a range of brand and model suggestions. You estimate that you can save a customer hundreds of dollars and much pain by helping them avoid unsuitable shoe choices. At present, you have a diehard set of local fans, but to expand beyond your Kansas City home market, you need a one-time infusion of cash to open branch offices in other cities around the Southeast, and to market your product more effectively. At the Entrepreneur's Lunch Forum you attended yesterday, you learned about several angels, as they are called in the investment community—private individuals who invest money in small companies in exchange for a share of ownership. One such angel, Susan Chen told the audience that she is looking for investment opportunities outside of dotcom applications, where angels often invest their money. She is looking for locally grounded entrepreneurs who can build a market, fill a need, who are passionate about the value they bring to the marketplace, who are committed to growing their businesses, and who have a solid plan for how they will spend an investor's money. Fortunately, you meet all of her criteria.

Your task: Draft an email message to Chen, introducing yourself and your business and asking for a meeting at which you can present your business plan in more detail. Mention that your "Happy Feet Club" has several thousand members and is growing by 10 to 20 members a day. Making up any information you need, draft a four-paragraph message following the AIDA model, ending with a request for a meeting within the next four weeks.

BLOGGING SKILLS   PORTFOLIO BUILDER

8. Message Strategies: Persuasive Presentation of Ideas [LO-2] You work for RiddleRabbit, makers of puzzles and board games. You are looking for ways to jazz up your company website, which was set up in the nineties and still has a nineties look and feel to it. It occurs to you that it might be interesting to have an animated avatar who will answer questions, present interesting facts and generally be the face of the company. Your bosses are willing to consider the idea, but they first want to try it out on the company blog before they put it on the website.

Your task: Write a blog post that will accompany a still picture of the new avatar, introducing it to the public and describing its functions. You can do this in third or first person, whichever you think is suitable.

EMAIL SKILLS

9. Message Strategies: Persuasive Claims and Requests for Adjustment [LO-2] While you were in transit from Chicago to Cancun, your worst nightmare came true: your suitcase, with an external hard drive in it, was misplaced by the airline. This contained the most up-to-date versions of some very large design files that you hadn't had time to sync with your laptop. You had backups on your personal cloud, but the datastream was so heavy you had to use a paid broadband connection in a local Internet cafe to download them. Five hours after the meeting, the airline returned your bag intact, but by then, you had had to spend almost $200 on account of its temporary absence, not to mention undergo much hassle. You call up the airline's local office to complain, and are asked to write an email to Danielle Martin, customer care officer.

Your task: Decide how much of an adjustment you think you deserve under the circumstances, and then send an email message to Martin to request it. Write a summary of events in chronological order, supplying exact dates for maximum effectiveness. Make up any information you need.

Marketing and Sales Messages: Conventional Media

LETTER WRITING SKILLS   PORTFOLIO BUILDER

10. Message Strategies: Marketing and Sales Messages [LO-4] Like all other states, Kentucky works hard to attract businesses that are considering expanding into the state or relocating entirely from another state. The Kentucky Cabinet for Economic Development is responsible for reaching out to these companies and overseeing the many incentive programs the state offers to new and established businesses.

Your task: As the communication director of the Kentucky Cabinet for Economic Development, you play the lead role in reaching out to companies that want to expand or relocate to Kentucky. Visit www.thinkkentucky.com and download the *Kentucky Facts* brochure (look under the "Why Kentucky" link). Identify the major benefits the state uses to promote Kentucky as a great place to locate a business. Summarize these reasons in a one-page form letter that will be sent to business executives throughout the country. Be sure to introduce yourself and your purpose in the letter, and close with a compelling call to action (have them reach you by telephone at 800-626-2930 or by email at econdev@ky.gov). As you plan your letter, try to imagine yourself as the CEO of a company and consider what a complex choice it would be to move to another state.[34]

LETTER WRITING SKILLS   PORTFOLIO BUILDER

11. Message Strategies: Marketing and Sales Messages [LO-3] Aikido is a martial art that involves locking the joints of an opponent and using their force against them. It can be used irrespective of one's strength or agility and requires only balance, inner calm, and a very good technique. It is always a defensive strategy and is particularly good for girls and women. See http://www.aikidofaq.com/ for more details.

Your task: Write a one-page letter to the parents of the members of a girls' club (for girls between 8 and 16 years of age) promoting aikido as a self-defense technique and proposing to start aikido training once a week at the club.

WEB WRITING SKILLS

12. Message Strategies: Marketing and Sales Messages [LO-3] Natalie Sisson bills herself as the "Suitcase Entrepreneur," and she's living proof that one can live an adventurous life and build a thriving business—she has been traveling the world since she left her native New Zealand in 2006. She offers business and social media coaching, and she recently compiled her social media advice in a PDF e-book, *The Entrepreneur's Social Media Workout*.

Your task: Sisson has been offering her social media e-book for free to anyone who subscribes to her email newsletter. However, as the assistant she recently hired, you convinced her the book was valuable enough on its own to warrant a small purchase price. She decided to give it a try and set the price at $10.00, with one catch: you need to write the website copy to promote the e-book.

First, visit http://real-timeupdates.com/ebc10, click on Student Assignments and then Chapter 10, Page 361, Case 12 to download the e-book. Then visit Sisson's website at http://womanzworld.com to learn more about her business experiences. Now write webpage copy (at least 200 words but no more than 400) to promote the e-book and encourage people to place an order.

EMAIL SKILLS

13. Message Strategies: Marketing and Sales Messages [LO-3] The oud (rhymes with "mood") is a popular musical instrument in many cultures from northern Africa to southwest Asia, enjoying the same status in these countries as the guitar enjoys in Europe and the Americas. The oud, which dates back to the seventh century, was also the ancestor of the European-style lute that had its heyday during the Renaissance.

Many guitar players are familiar with the lute, but probably fewer with the oud. As the marketing director for Your World Instruments (www.yourworldinstruments.com) you'd like to encourage guitar players to consider the oud. Some might want to just explore another musical heritage. Others might want to expand their sonic palettes, so to speak, giving their music a broader range of sounds.

Your task: Write a brief email message that encourages guitar players to try something new. Or something old, more precisely. The people to whom you will be writing have heard from the company before, many are past customers, and all have opted-in to the email list. The call to action is encouraging these musicians to click through to the website to watch videos of expert oud players and to learn more about these storied instruments.[35]

14. Message Strategies: Marketing and Sales Messages [LO-3] You never intended to become an inventor, but you saw a way to make something work more easily, so you set to work. You developed a model, found a way to mass-produce it, and set up a small manufacturing studio in your home. You know that other people are going to benefit from your invention. Now all you need to do is reach that market.

Your task: Team up with other students assigned by your instructor and imagine a useful product that you might have invented—perhaps something related to a hobby or sporting activity. List the features and benefits of your imaginary product, and describe how it helps customers. Then write the copy for a webpage that would introduce and promote this product, using what you've learned in this chapter and making up details as you need them. As your instructor indicates, submit the copy as a word processor file or as a webpage using basic HTML formatting.

15. Message Strategies: Marketing and Sales Messages [LO-3] Your new podcast channel, School2Biz, offers advice to business students making the transition from college to career. You provide information on everything from preparing résumés to interviewing to finding a place in the business world and building a successful career. As you expand your audience, you'd eventually like to turn School2Biz into a profitable operation (perhaps by selling advertising time during your podcasts). For now, you're simply offering free advice.

Your task: You've chosen Podcast Bunker (www.podcastbunker .com) the first website on which to promote School2Biz. This site lets podcasters promote their feeds with brief text listings, such as this description of Toolmonger Tool Talk: "Chuck and Sean from the web's first tool blog, Toolmonger.com, keep you up-to-date on the newest hand and power tools, and answer your home improvement, automotive, and tool-related questions."

As your instructor directs, either write a 50-word description of your new podcast that can be posted on Podcast Bunker or record a 30-second podcast describing the new service. Make up any information you need to describe School2Biz. Be sure to mention who you are and why the information you present is worth listening to.[36]

16. Message Strategies: Marketing and Sales Messages [LO-3] You are starting up a literary agency in a new market in which, hitherto, authors interacted directly with publishers. This

used to be fine when the market was small, but now there are many more publishers and a whole lot more authors out there with all kinds of books to offer. People in the market are unfamiliar with the concept of literary agents, however. Literary agents typically take a percentage of the author's royalties, usually 10 to 20 percent, when they place a book, and they may also offer editing services to the authors they represent. When an author signs on with them, they go round to the offices of publishers they know, and try to place the book with one of them; when the book is placed, the agent takes a commission from the author. Typically, the agent will try to place the book for a given period, a year to five years, after which, if the book fails to find a publisher, the rights revert to the author. Authors cannot give a book to be placed by more than one agent and are usually bound by contract to give the agent exclusive rights to represent the book for the duration of the contract.

Your task: Write a web-based ad of about 100 words introducing the new literary agency to this market. Imagine any necessary visuals or multimedia content.

Marketing and Sales Messages: Social Media

17. Message Strategies: Marketing and Sales Messages; Media Skills: Blogging [LO-4], Chapter 7 Your company manufactures plastic made from hemp. Because of the associations of the word "hemp," you get a lot of interest from fringe groups and ageing hippies, but you have yet to persuade serious businesses that your product is indeed a viable alternative to ordinary plastic. The hemp that you use is different from marijuana and the plastic it produces is as good as the normal kind; better, in fact, for it is less flammable. The plastic can do everything that normal plastic can, and is only slightly more expensive. This is offset by its completely sustainable manufacturing process.

Your task: Because many consumers aren't familiar with hemp plastic, they tend to dismiss the idea as a New Age fad. However, this plastic is fully biodegradable, slightly stronger than normal plastic, and fire retardant. Write a post for the company blog, explaining the good things about hemp plastic. Limit yourself to 400 words. You can learn more about industrial hemp at http://www.hempplastic.com/what-hemp.html.

18. Message Strategies: Marketing and Sales Messages; Media Skills: Social Networking [LO-4], Chapter 7 Curves is a fitness center franchise that caters to women who may not feel at home in traditional gyms. With its customer-focused and research-based approach, Curves has become a significant force in the fitness industry and one of the most successful franchise operations in history.[37]

Your task: Read the Overview and History sections at www .curves.com/about-curves. Imagine that you are adapting this material for the Info tab on the company's Facebook page. Write a "Company Overview" (95–100 words) and a "Mission" statement (45–50 words).

SOCIAL NETWORKING SKILLS
TEAMWORK SKILLS

19. Message Strategies: Marketing and Sales Messages; Media Skills: Social Networking [LO-4], Chapter 7 You chose your college or university based on certain expectations, and you've been enrolled long enough now to have some idea about whether those expectations have been met. In other words, you are something of an expert about the "consumer benefits" your school can offer prospective students.

Your task: In a team of four students, interview six other students who are not taking this business communication course. Try to get a broad demographic and psychographic sample, including students in a variety of majors and programs. Ask these students (1) why they chose this college or university and (2) whether the experience has met their expectations so far. To ensure the privacy of your respondents, do not record their names with their answers. Each member of the team should then answer these same two questions, so that you have responses from a total of ten students.

After compiling the responses (you might use Google Docs or a similar collaboration tool so that everyone on the team has easy access to the information), analyze them as a team to look for any recurring "benefit themes." Is it the quality of the education? Research opportunities? Location? The camaraderie of school sporting events? The chance to meet and study with fascinating students from a variety of backgrounds? Identify two or three strong benefits that your college or university can promise—and deliver—to prospective students.

Now nominate one member of the team to draft a short marketing message that could be posted on the Notes tab of your school's Facebook page. The message should include a catchy title that makes it clear the message is a student's perspective on why this is a great place to get a college education. When the draft is ready, the other members of the team should review it individually. Finally, meet as a team to complete the message.

MICROBLOGGING SKILLS

20. Message Strategies: Marketing and Sales Messages; Media Skills: Microblogging [LO-4], Chapter 7 Effective microblogging messages emphasize clarity and conciseness—and so do effective sales messages.

Your task: Find the website of any product that can be ordered online (any product you find interesting and that is appropriate to use for a class assignment). Adapt the information on the website, using your own words, and write four tweets to promote the product. The first should get your audience's attention (with

an intriguing benefit claim, for example), the second should build audience interest by providing some support for the claim you made in the first message, the third should increase readers' desire to have the product by layering on one or two more buyer benefits, and the fourth should motivate readers to take action to place an order. Your first three tweets can be up to 140 characters, but the fourth should be limited to 120 to accommodate a URL (you don't need to include the URL in your message, however).

If your class is set up with private Twitter accounts, use your private account to send your messages. Otherwise, email your four messages to your instructor or post them on your class blog, as your instructor directs.

REFERENCES

1. CafeMom website, accessed 19 February 2011, www .cafemom.com; "ClubMom Introduces the MomNetwork—The Web's First Social Network for Moms," press release, 8 May 2006, www.hcp.com; "Laura Fortner Named Senior Vice President, Business Development at ClubMom," press release, 20 September 2006, http://newyork.dbusinessnews.com.
2. Jay A. Conger, "The Necessary Art of Persuasion," *Harvard Business Review*, May–June 1998, 84–95; Jeanette W. Gilsdorf, "Write Me Your Best Case for . . . ," *Bulletin of the Association for Business Communication* 54, no. 1 (March 1991): 7–12.
3. Mary Cross, "Aristotle and Business Writing: Why We Need to Teach Persuasion," *Bulletin of the Association for Business Communication* 54, no. 1 (March 1991): 3–6.
4. IKEA website, accessed 19 February 2011, www.ikea.com; Liz C. Wang, Julie Baker, Judy A. Wagner, and Kirk Wakefield, "Can a Retail Web Site Be Social?" *Journal of Marketing* 71, no. 3 (July 2007), 143–157.
5. Stephen Bayley and Roger Mavity, "How to Pitch," *Management Today*, March 2007, 48–53.
6. Robert B. Cialdini, "Harnessing the Science of Persuasion," *BusinessWeek*, 4 December 2007, www.businessweek.com.
7. Wesley Clark, "The Potency of Persuasion," *Fortune*, 12 November 2007, 48; W. H. Weiss, "Using Persuasion Successfully," *Supervision*, October 2006, 13–16.
8. Tom Chandler, "The Copywriter's Best Friend," *The Copywriter Underground blog*, 20 December 2006, http://copywriterunderground.com.
9. Raymond M. Olderman, *10-Minute Guide to Business Communication* (New York: Macmillan Spectrum/Alpha Books, 1997), 57–61.
10. John D. Ramage and John C. Bean, *Writing Arguments: A Rhetoric with Readings*, 3rd ed. (Boston: Allyn & Bacon, 1995), 430–442.
11. Philip Vassallo, "Persuading Powerfully: Tips for Writing Persuasive Documents," *Et Cetera*, Spring 2002, 65–71.
12. Dianna Booher, *Communicate with Confidence* (New York: McGraw-Hill, 1994), 102.
13. "Social Factors in Developing a Web Accessibility Business Case for Your Organization," W3C website, accessed 17 July 2010, www.w3.org.

14. Adapted from "What Is the HYBRID HEAT Dual Fuel System by Carrier?" Carrier website, accessed 5 November 2008, www.residential.carrier.com.

15. iPod main product page, Apple website, accessed 17 July 2010, www.apple.com/ipod.

16. "HealthGrades Reveals America's Best Hospitals," 27 February 2008, www.ivanhoe.com.

17. Biokleen home page, accessed 17 July 2010, http://biokleen-home.com.

18. Ford Focus product page, Ford website, accessed 17 July 2010, www.fordvehicles.com.

19. *Living in France* product page, Insider Paris Guides website, accessed 4 March 2008, www.insiderparisguides.com.

20. Barnes & Noble website, accessed 17 July 2010, www.barnesandnoble.com.

21. Mint.com website, accessed 17 July 2010, www.mint.com.

22. FlightWise Carry-on Backpack product page, Lands End website, accessed 17 July 2010, www.landsend.com.

23. iPod Touch product page, Apple website, accessed 17 July 2010, www.apple.com/ipodtouch/what-is/gaming-device.html.

24. iPod Touch product page.

25. "More Than Virtual: Marketing the Total Brand 'Experience'" Knowledge@Wharton, 7 June 2011, http://knowledge.wharton.upenn.edu.

26. Larry Weber, *Marketing to the Social Web* (Hoboken, N.J.: Wiley, 2007), 12–14; David Meerman Scott, *The New Rules of Marketing and PR* (Hoboken, N.J.: Wiley, 2007), 62; Paul Gillin, *The New Influencers* (Sanger, Calif.: Quill Driver Books, 2007), 34–35; Jeremy Wright, *Blog Marketing: The Revolutionary Way to Increase Sales, Build Your Brand, and Get Exceptional Results* (New York: McGraw-Hill, 2006), 263–365.

27. "Content Marketing 101: How to Build Your Business with Content," Copyblogger, accessed 19 February 2011, www.copyblogger.com.

28. Michael Zeisser, "Unlocking the Elusive Potential of Social Networks," *McKinsey Quarterly*, June 2010, www.mckinseyquarterly.com.

29. Gilsdorf, "Write Me Your Best Case for. . . ."

30. Miguel Helft and Tanzina Vega, "Retargeting Ads Follow Surfers to Other Sites," *New York Times*, 29 August 2010, www.nytimes.com.

31. "How to Comply with the Children's Online Privacy Protection Rule," U.S. Federal Trade Commission website, accessed 17 July 2010, www.ftc.gov; "Frequently Asked Advertising Questions: A Guide for Small Business," U.S. Federal Trade Commission website, accessed 17 July 2010, www.ftc.gov.

32. Adapted from Samsung website, accessed 22 October 2006, www.samsung.com.

33. Adapted from IBM website, accessed 15 January 2004, www.ibm.com; "DAS Faces an Assured Future with IBM," IBM website, accessed 16 January 2004, www.ibm.com; "Sametime," IBM website, accessed 16 January 2004, www.ibm.com.

34. Adapted from Web Accessibility Initiative, World Wide Web Consortium website, accessed 7 November 2008, www.w3.org.

35. Kentucky Cabinet for Economic Development website, accessed 19 July 2010, www.thinkkentucky.com.

36. Adapted from Your World Instruments website, accessed 21 February 2011, www.yourworldinstruments.com; "Ud," *Encyclopedia Britannica*, accessed 21 February 2011, www.brittanica.com.

37. Adapted from Curves website, accessed 19 July 2010, www.curves.com.

PART 4 | Preparing Reports and Oral Presentations

Reports and presentations offer important opportunities to demonstrate your value to the organization. Depending on the project, you might analyze complex problems, educate audiences, address opportunities in the marketplace, win contracts, or even launch an entire company with the help of a compelling business plan. Adapt what you've learned so far to the particular challenges of long-format messages, including some special touches that can make formal reports stand out from the crowd. Learn how to plan effective presentations, overcome the anxieties that every speaker feels, and respond to questions from the audience. Discover some tips and techniques for succeeding with the Twitter-enabled *backchannel* and with online presentations. Finally, complement your talk with compelling visual materials and learn how to create presentation slides that engage and excite your audience.

wavebreakmedia ltd./
Shutterstock

11 Planning Reports and Proposals

LEARNING OBJECTIVES   After studying this chapter, you will be able to

1 Adapt the three-step writing process to reports and proposals

2 Describe an effective process for conducting business research, explain how to evaluate the credibility of an information source, and identify the five ways to use research results

3 Explain the role of secondary research, and describe the two major categories of online research tools

4 Explain the role of primary research, and identify the two most common forms of primary research for business communication purposes

5 Explain how to plan informational reports and website content

6 Identify the three most common ways to organize analytical reports

7 Explain how to plan proposals

MyBcommLab Where you see MyBcommLab in this chapter, go to www.pearsoninternationaleditions.com/mybcommlab for additional activities on the topic being discussed.

ON THE JOB: COMMUNICATING AT MYCITYWAY

MyCityWay's effective use of a business plan helped secure financing that allowed the company to expand far beyond its initial New York City market.
Source: Courtesy of Sonpreet Bhatia, Archana Patchirajan, and Puneet Mehta, mycityway.com.

Transforming a Great Idea into a Great Business

Any experienced entrepreneur will tell you there's a big difference between having a great idea for a business and actually building a successful business. Many things have to go right, from creating a compelling product or service to finding the right employees to getting enough money to launch, expand, and sustain operations.

For Archana Patchirajan, Sonpreet Bhatia, and Puneet Mehta, the adventure started with the NYC BigApps competition. This contest is sponsored by the city of New York as a way to encourage entrepreneurs to create better ways for people to use the NYC Data Mine, a huge trove of data created by all the government departments and agencies in the city.

The three partners jumped on the opportunity with NYC Way, a mobile application that helps people "navigate and explore" the city, whether they are residents looking for apartment deals or visitors looking for a great restaurant. One key aspect of the BigApps competition is that entrepreneurs must put their apps online for people to try out. By the time the contest ended, 100,000 people were using NYC Way.

Patchirajan, Bhatia, and Mehta clearly had a hit product on their hands. The next challenge was to turn it into a thriving business. As with most startups, that meant getting money to expand operations. The competition garnered the new firm, MyCityWay, priceless publicity and a small amount of *seed funding* that let the team set up offices and begin hiring.

Momentum continued to build as they enhanced the product and several hundred thousand more people began using it. After a successful launch in the New York City market, the next step was to conquer the world. That would require a significant infusion of capital, and to attract that, the three founders knew they needed a formal *business plan* to show potential investors why MyCityWay would be a smart place to invest their money.

With their Wall Street backgrounds, Patchirajan, Bhatia, and Mehta understood the fundamentals of business finance, which gave them a good foundation for their plan. They also got smart advice on what today's investors are looking for: short, compelling documents that strike a balance between providing enough information to be persuasive and providing so much information that potential investors balk at reading it. With so

many plans crossing their desks day after day, most venture capitalists and other investors don't have the time to slog through 50 or 60 pages of details to judge whether a company might be worth pursuing as an investment candidate. They want to be captivated in a matter of seconds and persuaded to learn more in a matter of minutes.

MyCityWay clearly found the right balance with its plan, as a second round of funding brought in $1 million in capital and then luxury carmaker BMW invested $5 million as part of its "BMW i" program, which promotes the development of innovative automotive materials and technologies. By early 2011, the company had apps for several dozen cities around the world and was launching a new city app about every week. Thanks to a great product and a compelling business plan, MyCityWay is now well on its way to becoming a global player in the world of mobile information.[1]

www.mycityway.com

Applying the Three-Step Writing Process to Reports and Proposals

Whether you're sharing your latest great idea with your boss or launching an entirely new company (see the profile of MyCityWay in the chapter opener), reports will play a vital role in your business career. Reports fall into three basic categories (see Figure 11.1 on the next page):

- **Informational reports** offer data, facts, feedback, and other types of information, without analysis or recommendations.
- **Analytical reports** offer both information and analysis, and they can also include recommendations.
- **Proposals** offer structured persuasion for internal or external audiences.

The nature of reports varies widely, from one-page trip reports that follow a standard format to detailed business plans and proposals that can run hundreds of pages. No matter what the circumstances, try to view every business report as an opportunity to demonstrate your understanding of your audience's challenges and your ability to contribute to your organization's success.

The three-step process you studied in Chapters 4 through 6 and applied to short messages in Chapters 7 through 10 is even more beneficial with reports and proposals because a methodical, efficient approach to planning, writing, and completing is even more valuable with these larger projects (see Figure 11.2 on page 369). This chapter addresses the planning step, focusing on two major areas that require special attention in long documents: gathering and organizing information. Chapter 12 covers the writing step and also includes advice on creating effective visuals for your reports and proposals. Chapter 13 describes the tasks involved in completing reports and proposals.

ANALYZING THE SITUATION

Reports can be complex, time-consuming projects, so be sure to analyze the situation carefully before you begin to write. Pay special attention to your **statement of purpose**, which explains *why* you are preparing the report and *what* you plan to deliver in the report (see Table 11.1 on page 369).

The most useful way to phrase a purpose statement is to begin with an infinitive phrase (*to* plus a verb), which helps pin down your general goal (*to inform, to identify, to analyze,*

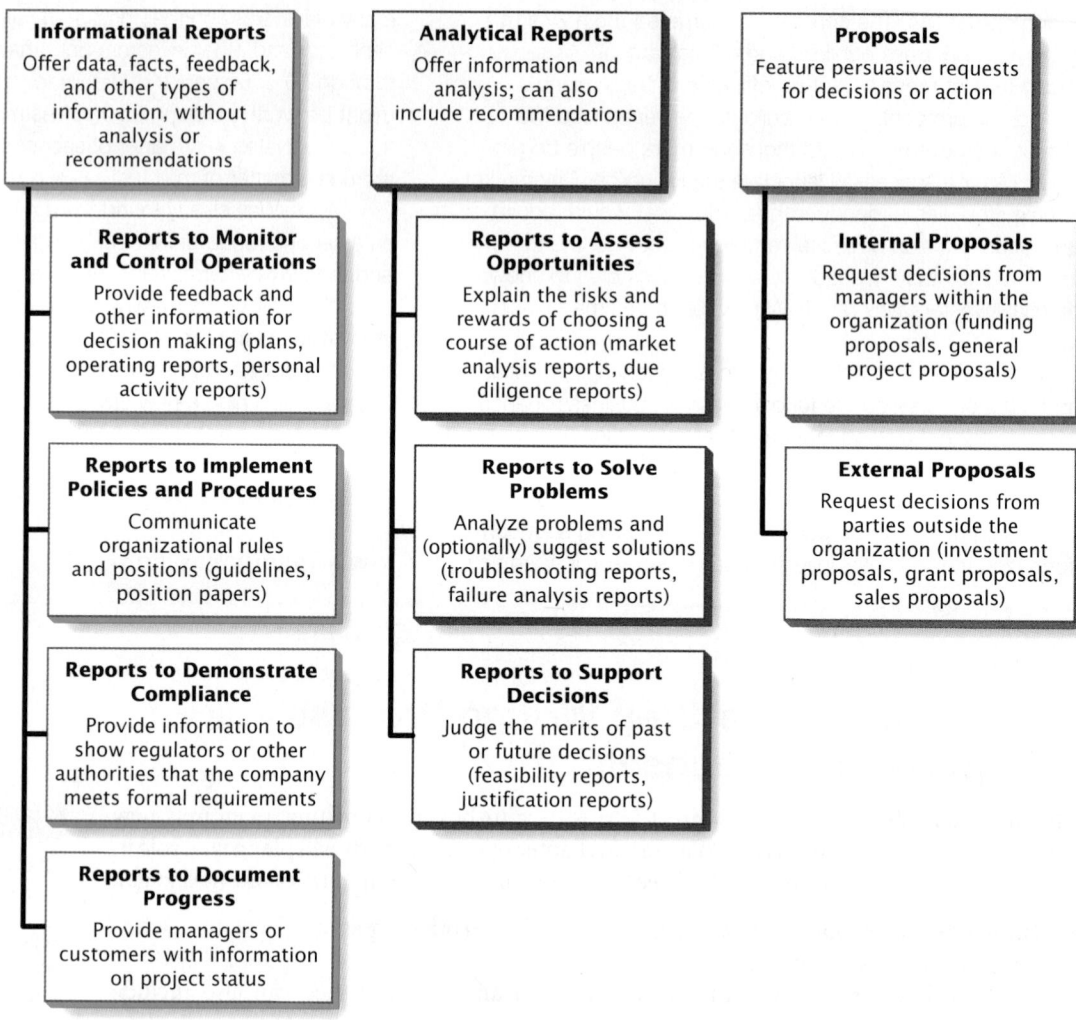

Figure 11.1   Common Types of Business Reports and Proposals
You will have the opportunity to read and write many types of reports in your career; here are some of the most common.

and so on). For instance, in an informational report, your statement of purpose can be as simple as one of these:

> To identify potential markets for our new smartphone apps
> To update the board of directors on the progress of our research into carbon-fiber composites
> To submit required information to the Securities and Exchange Commission

Your statement of purpose for an analytical report often needs to be more comprehensive. When Linda Moreno, the cost accounting manager for an electronics company, was asked to find ways of reducing employee travel and entertainment costs, she phrased her statement of purpose accordingly:

> . . . to analyze the T&E [travel and entertainment] budget, evaluate the impact of recent changes in airfares and hotel costs, and suggest ways to tighten management's control over T&E expenses.

Because Moreno was assigned an analytical report rather than an informational report, she had to go beyond merely collecting data; she had to draw conclusions and make recommendations. You'll see her complete report in Chapter 13.

1 Plan →	**2** Write →	**3** Complete
Analyze the Situation Clarify the problem or opportunity at hand, define your purpose, develop an audience profile, and develop a work plan. **Gather Information** Determine audience needs and obtain the information necessary to satisfy those needs; conduct a research project, if necessary. **Select the Right Medium** Choose the best medium for delivering your message; consider delivery through multiple media. **Organize the Information** Define your main idea, limit your scope, select the direct or indirect approach, and outline your content using an appropriate structure for an informational report, an analytical report, or a proposal.	**Adapt to Your Audience** Be sensitive to audience needs with a "you" attitude, politeness, positive emphasis, and bias-free language. Build a strong relationship with your audience by establishing your credibility and projecting your company's image. Control your style with a tone and voice appropriate to the situation. **Compose the Message** Choose strong words that will help you create effective sentences and coherent paragraphs throughout the introduction, body, and close of your report or proposal.	**Revise the Message** Evaluate content and review readability, then edit and rewrite for conciseness and clarity. **Produce the Message** Use effective design elements and suitable layout for a clean, professional appearance; seamlessly combine text and graphical elements. **Proofread the Message** Review for errors in layout, spelling, and mechanics. **Distribute the Message** Deliver your report using the chosen medium; make sure all documents and all relevant files are distributed successfully.

Figure 11.2   Three-Step Writing Process for Reports and Proposals
The three-step writing process is especially valuable with reports and proposals. By guiding your work at each step, the process helps you make the most of the time and energy you invest.

When writing a proposal, you must also be guided by a clear statement of purpose to help focus on crafting a persuasive message. Here are several examples:

The statement of purpose for a proposal should help guide you in developing a persuasive message.

> To secure funding in next year's budget for new conveyor systems in the warehouse
> To get management approval to reorganize the North American salesforce
> To secure $2 million from outside investors to start production of the new titanium mountain bike

In addition to considering your purpose carefully, you will also want to prepare a *work plan* for most reports and proposals in order to make the best use of your time. For simpler

A detailed work plan saves time and often produces more effective reports.

TABLE 11.1	Problem Statements Versus Purpose Statements
Problem Statement	**Statement of Purpose**
Our company's market share is steadily declining.	To explore new ways of promoting and selling our products and to recommend the approaches most likely to stabilize our market share
Our current computer network lacks sufficient bandwidth and cannot be upgraded to meet our future needs.	To analyze various networking options and to recommend the system that will best meet our company's current and future needs
We need $2 million to launch our new product.	To convince investors that our new business would be a sound investment so that we can obtain desired financing
Our current operations are too decentralized and expensive.	To justify the closing of the Newark plant and the transfer of East Coast operations to a single Midwest location in order to save the company money

The problem statement clearly and succinctly defines the problem the writers intend to address.

This section explains how the researchers will find the data and information they need.

The assignments and schedule section clearly lists responsibilities and due dates.

This paragraph identifies exactly what will be covered by the research and addressed in the final report.

The preliminary outline has enough detail to guide the research and set reader expectations.

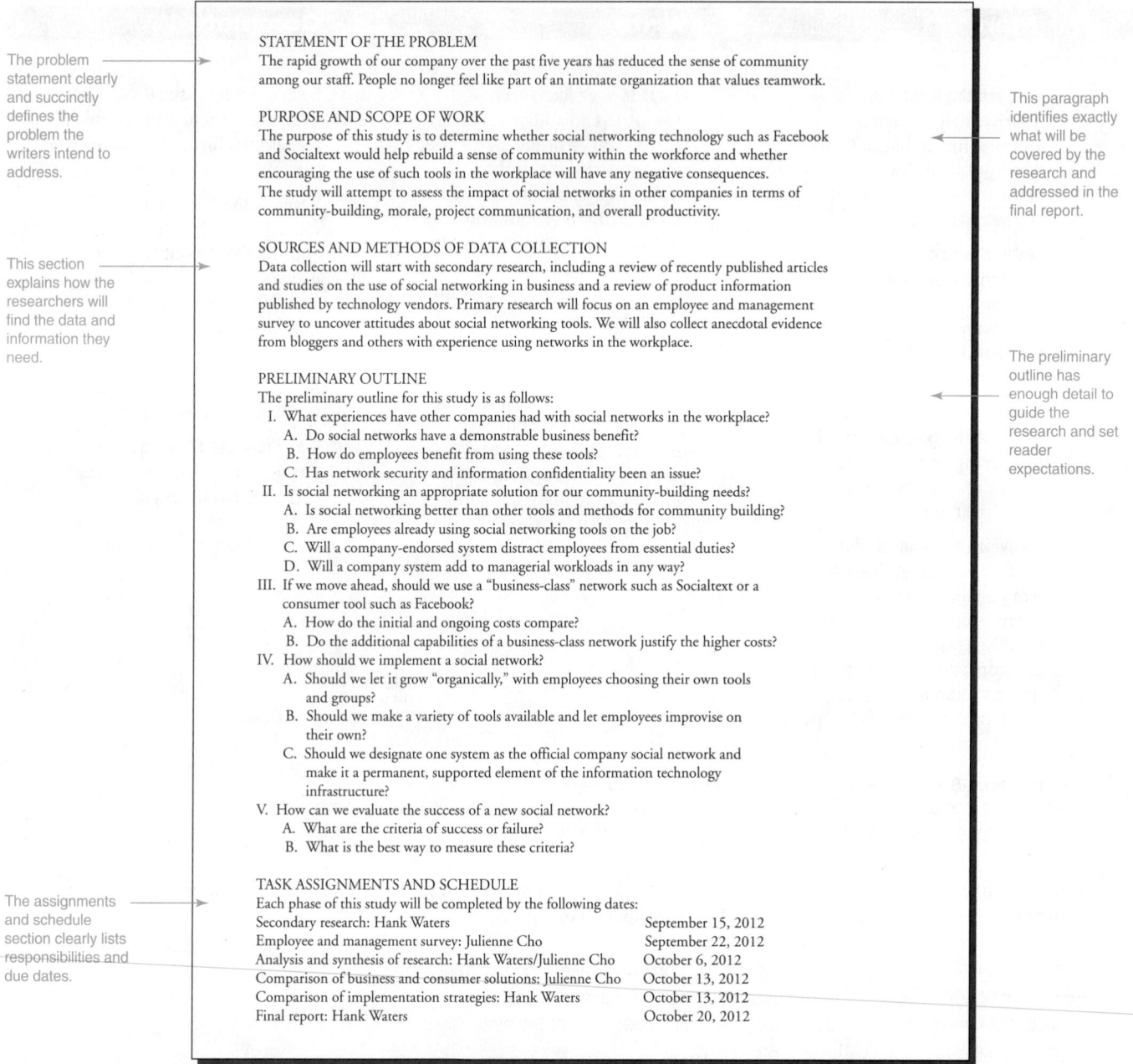

STATEMENT OF THE PROBLEM
The rapid growth of our company over the past five years has reduced the sense of community among our staff. People no longer feel like part of an intimate organization that values teamwork.

PURPOSE AND SCOPE OF WORK
The purpose of this study is to determine whether social networking technology such as Facebook and Socialtext would help rebuild a sense of community within the workforce and whether encouraging the use of such tools in the workplace will have any negative consequences.
The study will attempt to assess the impact of social networks in other companies in terms of community-building, morale, project communication, and overall productivity.

SOURCES AND METHODS OF DATA COLLECTION
Data collection will start with secondary research, including a review of recently published articles and studies on the use of social networking in business and a review of product information published by technology vendors. Primary research will focus on an employee and management survey to uncover attitudes about social networking tools. We will also collect anecdotal evidence from bloggers and others with experience using networks in the workplace.

PRELIMINARY OUTLINE
The preliminary outline for this study is as follows:
I. What experiences have other companies had with social networks in the workplace?
   A. Do social networks have a demonstrable business benefit?
   B. How do employees benefit from using these tools?
   C. Has network security and information confidentiality been an issue?
II. Is social networking an appropriate solution for our community-building needs?
   A. Is social networking better than other tools and methods for community building?
   B. Are employees already using social networking tools on the job?
   C. Will a company-endorsed system distract employees from essential duties?
   D. Will a company system add to managerial workloads in any way?
III. If we move ahead, should we use a "business-class" network such as Socialtext or a consumer tool such as Facebook?
   A. How do the initial and ongoing costs compare?
   B. Do the additional capabilities of a business-class network justify the higher costs?
IV. How should we implement a social network?
   A. Should we let it grow "organically," with employees choosing their own tools and groups?
   B. Should we make a variety of tools available and let employees improvise on their own?
   C. Should we designate one system as the official company social network and make it a permanent, supported element of the information technology infrastructure?
V. How can we evaluate the success of a new social network?
   A. What are the criteria of success or failure?
   B. What is the best way to measure these criteria?

TASK ASSIGNMENTS AND SCHEDULE
Each phase of this study will be completed by the following dates:

Secondary research: Hank Waters	September 15, 2012
Employee and management survey: Julienne Cho	September 22, 2012
Analysis and synthesis of research: Hank Waters/Julienne Cho	October 6, 2012
Comparison of business and consumer solutions: Julienne Cho	October 13, 2012
Comparison of implementation strategies: Hank Waters	October 13, 2012
Final report: Hank Waters	October 20, 2012

Figure 11.3 Work Plan for a Report
A formal work plan such as this is a vital tool for planning and managing complex writing projects. The preliminary outline here helps guide the research; as the writers move forward with the project and begin drafting the report, they may modify the outline to improve the flow or to incorporate new information uncovered during their research.

MyBcommLab

Apply Figure 11.3's key concepts by revising a new document. Go to Chapter 11 in www.pearsoninternationaleditions.com/mybcommlab and select Document Makeovers.

reports, the work plan can be an informal list of tasks and a simple schedule. However, if you're preparing a lengthy report, particularly when you're collaborating with others, you'll want to develop a more detailed work plan (see Figure 11.3).

GATHERING INFORMATION

Some reports require formal research projects in order to gather all the necessary information.

Obtaining the information needed for many reports and proposals requires careful planning, and you may even need to do a separate research project just to acquire the data and information you need (see "Supporting Your Messages with Reliable Information" on page 373). To stay on schedule and on budget, be sure to review both your statement of purpose and your audience's needs so that you collect all the information you need—and only the information you need. In some cases, you won't be able to collect every piece of information you'd like, so prioritize your needs up front and focus on the most important questions.

SELECTING THE RIGHT MEDIUM

Just as you would for other business messages, select the medium for your report based on the needs of your audience and the practical advantages and disadvantages of the choices available to you. In addition to the general media selection criteria discussed in Chapter 4, consider several points for reports and proposals. First, for many reports and proposals, audiences have specific media requirements, and you might not have a choice. For instance, executives in many corporations now expect to review reports via their in-house intranets, sometimes in conjunction with an *executive dashboard* (see Figure 11.4), a customized online presentation of key operating variables such as revenue, profits, quality, customer satisfaction, and project progress. Second, consider how your audience wants to provide feedback on your report or proposal, if applicable. Will your readers prefer to write comments on a printed document or to use the commenting and markup features in a word processing program or Adobe Acrobat? Third, will multiple people need to update the document over time? A wiki could be an ideal choice. Fourth, bear in mind that your choice of media also sends a nonverbal message. For instance, a routine sales report dressed up in fancy covers or multimedia could look like a waste of time and money.

The best medium for any given report might be anything from a professionally printed and bound document to an online executive dashboard that displays only report highlights.

ORGANIZING YOUR INFORMATION

The direct approach is used often for reports because it is efficient and easy to follow. When an audience is likely to be receptive or at least open minded, use the direct approach: Lead with a summary of your key findings, conclusions, recommendations, or proposal, whichever is relevant. This "up-front" arrangement is by far the most popular and convenient for business reports. It saves time and makes the rest of the report easier to follow. For those who have questions or want more information, later parts of the report provide complete findings and supporting details.

Use the direct approach for most reports; consider the indirect approach if you haven't established credibility with your readers, or if your main idea will be met with resistance.

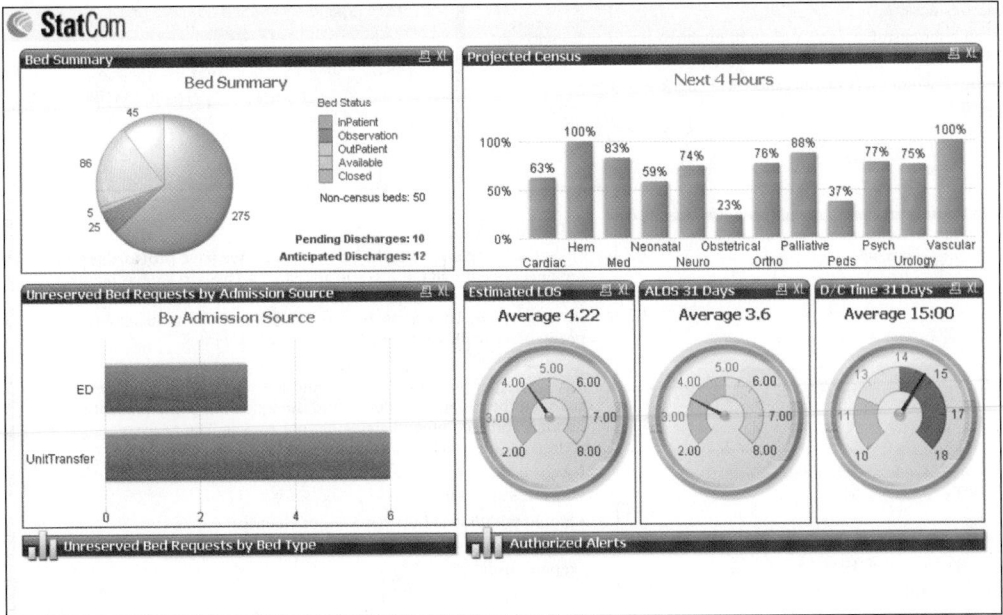

Figure 11.4   Executive Dashboards
To help managers avoid information overload, many companies now use executive dashboards to present carefully filtered highlights of key performance parameters. Dashboards are essentially super-summarized, live reports. The latest generation of software makes it easy to customize screens to show each manager the specific summaries he or she needs to see.
Source: Used with permission of StatCom.

However, if the audience is unsure about your credibility or is not ready to accept your main idea without first seeing some reasoning or evidence, the indirect approach is a better choice because it gives you a chance to prove your points and gradually overcome audience reservations. To enable the use of AIDA-style persuasion, unsolicited proposals in particular often use the indirect approach. Bear in mind, though, that the longer the document, the less effective the indirect approach is likely to be.

Both approaches have merit, so businesspeople often combine them, revealing their conclusions and recommendations in stages as they go along rather than putting them all first or last (see Figure 11.5).

When you outline your content, use informative ("talking") headings rather than simple descriptive ("topical") headings (see Table 11.2). When in question or summary form, informative headings force you to really think through the content rather than simply identify the general topic area. Using informative headings will not only help you plan more effectively but also facilitate collaborative writing. A heading such as "Industry Characteristics" could mean five different things to the five people on your writing team, so use a heading that conveys a single, unambiguous meaning, such as "Flour milling is a mature industry."

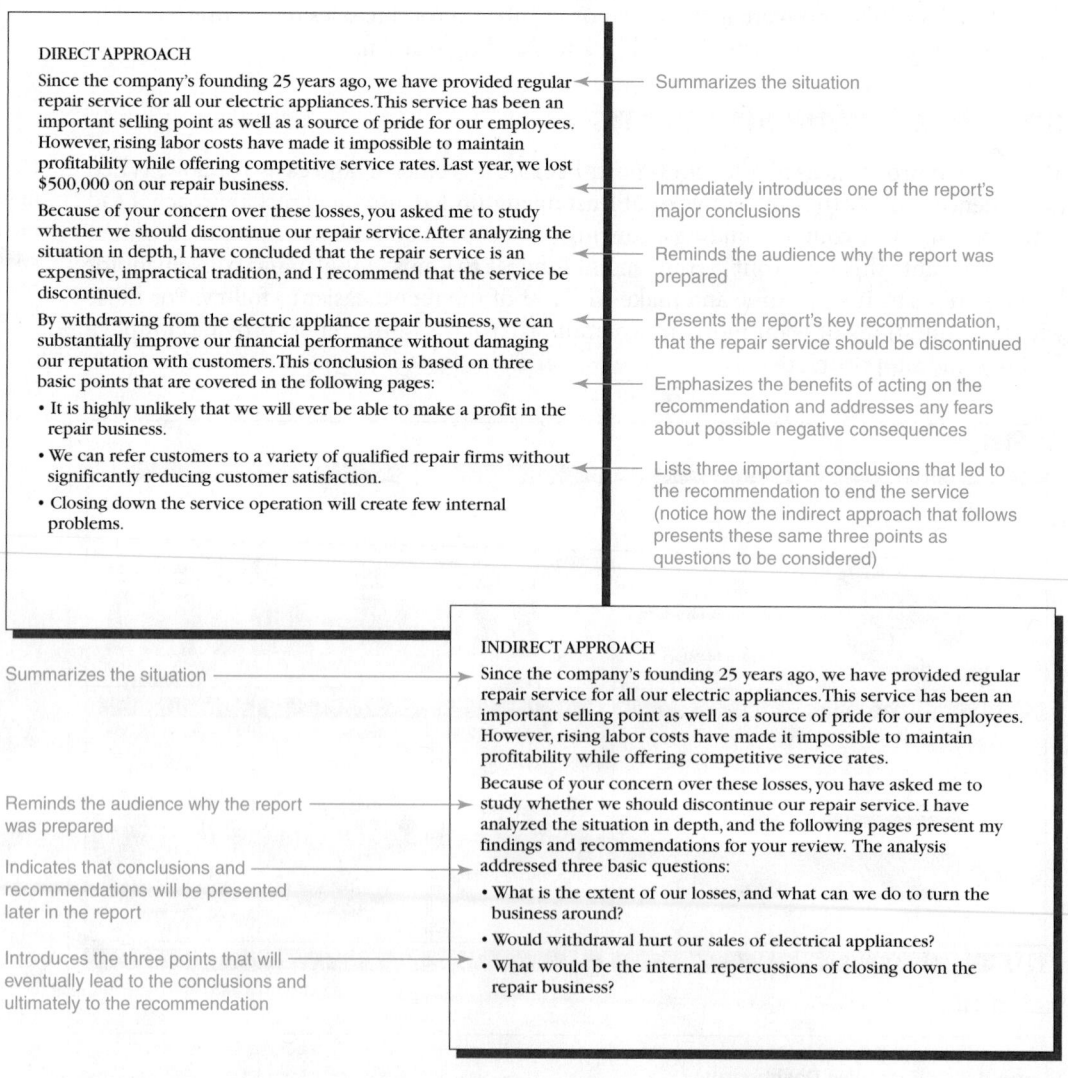

Figure 11.5   Direct Approach Versus Indirect Approach in an Introduction
In the direct version of this introduction, the writer quickly presents the report's recommendation, followed by the conclusions that led to that recommendation. In the indirect version, the same topics are introduced in the same order, but no conclusions are drawn about them; the conclusions and the ultimate recommendation appear later, in the body of the report.

TABLE 11.2	Types of Outline Headings		

DESCRIPTIVE (TOPICAL) OUTLINE	INFORMATIVE (TALKING) OUTLINE	
	Question Form	**Summary Form**

I. Industry Characteristics
 a. Annual sales
 b. Profitability
 c. Growth rate
  1. Sales
  2. Profit
	I. What is the nature of the industry?
	 a. What are the annual sales?
	 b. Is the industry profitable?
	 c. What is the pattern of growth?
	  1. Sales growth?
	  2. Profit growth?
		I. Flour milling is a mature industry.
		 a. Market is large.
		 b. Profit margins are narrow.
		 c. Growth is modest.
		  1. Sales growth averages less than 3 percent a year.
		  2. Profits are flat.

For a quick review of adapting the three-step process to long reports, refer to "Checklist: Adapting the Three-Step Writing Process to Informational and Analytical Reports." Sections later in this chapter provide specific advice on how to plan informational reports, analytical reports, and proposals.

Supporting Your Messages with Reliable Information

Audiences expect you to support your message with solid research. As you've probably discovered while doing school projects, effective research involves a lot more than simply typing a few terms into a search engine. Save time and get better results by using a clear process:

1. **Plan your research.** A solid plan yields better results in less time.
2. **Locate the data and information you need.** The research plan tells you *what* to look for; your next step is to figure out *where* the data and information are and *how* to access them.
3. **Process the data and information you've located.** The data and information you find probably won't be in a form you can use immediately and will require some processing, which might involve anything from statistical analysis to resolving the differences between two or more expert opinions.
4. **Apply your findings.** You can apply your research findings in three ways: summarizing information for someone else's benefit, drawing conclusions based on what you've learned, or developing recommendations.

2   LEARNING OBJECTIVE

Describe an effective process for conducting business research, explain how to evaluate the credibility of an information source, and identify the five ways to use research results.

Researching without a plan wastes time and usually produces unsatisfactory results.

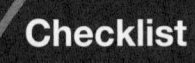 **Checklist   Adapting the Three-Step Writing Process to Informational and Analytical Reports**

A. Analyze the situation.
- Clearly define your purpose before you start writing.
- If you need to accomplish several goals in the report, identify all of them in advance.
- Prepare a work plan to guide your efforts.

B. Gather information.
- Determine whether you need to launch a separate research project to collect the necessary information.
- Reuse or adapt existing information whenever possible.

C. Select the right medium.
- Base your decision on audience expectations (or requirements, as the case may be).

- Consider the need for commenting, revising, distributing, and storing.
- Remember that the medium you choose also sends a message.

D. Organize your information.
- Use the direct approach if your audience is receptive.
- Use the indirect approach if your audience is skeptical.
- Use the indirect approach when you don't want to risk coming across as arrogant.
- Combine approaches if doing so will help build support for your primary message.

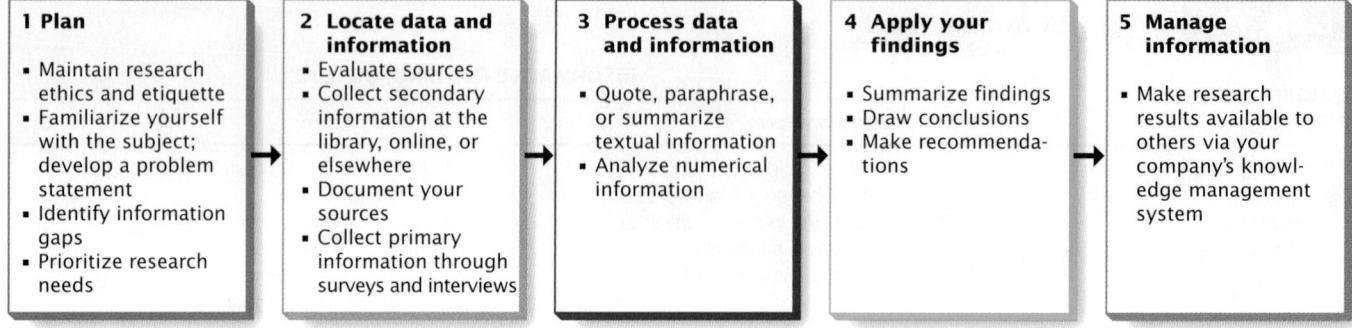

Figure 11.6 The Research Process
By following a methodical research process, you can save time and money while uncovering better information.

5. **Manage information efficiently.** Many companies today are trying to maximize the return on the time and money they invest in business research by collecting and sharing research results in a variety of computer-based systems, known generally as **knowledge management (KM)** systems. At the very least, be sure to share your results with any colleagues who may be able to benefit from them.

You can see the sequence of these steps in Figure 11.6; the following sections offer more details, starting with planning your research.

PLANNING YOUR RESEARCH

With so much information online these days, it's tempting just to punch some keywords into a search engine and then grab something from the first screen or two of results. However, this haphazard approach limits your effectiveness and can lead to expensive and embarrassing mistakes.

To maximize your chances of finding useful information and minimize the time you spend looking for it, start by familiarizing yourself with the subject so that you can frame insightful questions. As you explore the general subject area, try to identify basic terminology, significant trends, important conflicts, influential people, and potential sources of information. Next, develop a **problem statement** that will define the purpose of your research. This statement should explicitly define the decision you need to make or the conclusion you need to reach at the end of the process. For example, a retailer might want to know whether consumers are starting to turn away from bottled water because of concerns about cost and the environmental impact of plastic packaging and transportation. The problem statement could be "We need to determine whether we should reduce the number or variety of bottled water brands carried in our stores."

> The problem statement guides your research by focusing on the decision you need to make or the conclusion you need to reach.

Before you begin your research project, recognize that research carries some significant ethical responsibilities. To avoid ethical lapses, keep the following points in mind:

- Don't force a specific outcome by skewing your research.
- Respect the privacy of your research participants.
- Document sources and give appropriate credit.
- Respect *intellectual property rights*, the ownership of unique ideas that have commercial value in the marketplace.[2]
- Don't distort information from your sources.
- Don't misrepresent who you are or what you intend to do with the research results.

In addition to ethics, research etiquette deserves careful attention. For example, respect the time of anyone who agrees to be interviewed or to be a research participant, and maintain courtesy throughout the interview or research process.

LOCATING DATA AND INFORMATION

The range of sources available to business researchers today can be overwhelming. The good news is that if you have a question about an industry, a company, a market, a new technology, or a financial topic, somebody else has probably already researched the subject. Research done previously for another purpose is considered **secondary research** (covered on pages 378–383) when the results are reused in a new project. This secondary information can be anything from magazine articles to survey results. Don't let the name *secondary* fool you, though. You want to start with secondary research because it might save you considerable time and money. If you can't find existing research that meets your needs, you'll have to engage in **primary research** (covered on pages 383–386), which is new research done specifically for the current project.

Primary research involves collecting information for the first time, specifically for a new project; secondary research involves finding and reusing information that others have gathered in previous projects.

EVALUATING SOURCES

No matter where you're searching, it is your responsibility to separate quality information from unreliable junk, so you don't taint your results or damage your reputation. Web 2.0 tools have complicated this challenge by making many new sources of information available. On the positive side, independent sources communicating through blogs, Twitter and other microblogging sites, wikis, user-generated content sites, and podcasting channels can provide valuable and unique insights, often from experts whose voices might never be heard otherwise. On the negative side, these nontraditional information sources often lack the editorial boards and fact checkers commonly used in traditional publishing. You cannot assume that the information you find in blogs and other sources is accurate, objective, and current. Answer the following questions about each piece of material:

You have the responsibility to evaluate your sources carefully to avoid embarrassing and potentially damaging mistakes.

- **Does the source have a reputation for honesty and reliability?** Generally speaking, you can feel more comfortable using information from an established source that has a reputation for accuracy. For sources that are new or obscure, your safest bet is to corroborate anything you learn with information from several other sources.
- **Is the source potentially biased?** To interpret an organization's information, you need to know its point of view. For example, information about a particular company can be presented quite differently by a competitor, a union trying to organize the company's work force, an investment research firm, and an environmental advocacy group. Information from a source with a particular point of view isn't necessarily bad, of course, but knowing this context is always helpful and sometimes essential for interpreting the information correctly.
- **What is the purpose of the material?** For instance, was the material designed to inform others of new research, advance a political position, or promote a product? Was it designed to promote or sell a product? Be sure to distinguish among advertising, advocating, and informing. And don't lower your guard just because an organization has a reassuring name like the American Institute for the Advancement of All Things Good and Wonderful; many innocuously labeled groups advocate a particular line of political, social, or economic thinking.
- **Is the author credible?** Is the author a professional journalist? An industry insider? An informed amateur? Merely someone with an opinion?
- **Where did the source get *its* information?** Try to find out who collected the data, the methods they used, their qualifications, and their professional reputation.
- **Can you verify the material independently?** Verification can uncover biases or mistakes, which is particularly important when the information goes beyond simple facts to include projections, interpretations, and estimates. The more independent sources you can find that verify a piece of information, the more confidence you can have in it—as long as they're not all quoting the same source, naturally.
- **Is the material current?** Make sure you are using the most current information available by checking the publication date of a source. Look for a "posted on" or "updated

on" date with online material. If you can't find a date, don't assume the information is current without verifying it through some other channel.

- **Is the material complete?** Have you accessed the entire document or only a selection from it? If it's a selection, which parts were excluded? Do you need more detail?

You probably won't have time to conduct a thorough background check on all your sources, so focus your efforts on the most important or most suspicious pieces of information. And if you can't verify critical facts or figures, be sure to let your readers know that.

USING YOUR RESEARCH RESULTS

After you've collected all the necessary information, the next step is to transform it into the specific content you need. For simple projects, you may be able to drop your material directly into your report, presentation, or other application. However, when you have gathered a significant amount of information or raw data from surveys, you need to process the material before you can use it. This step can involve analyzing numeric data; quoting, paraphrasing, or summarizing textual material; drawing conclusions; and making recommendations.

Analyzing Data

Business research often yields numeric data, but these numbers alone might not provide the insights managers need in order to make good business decisions. Fortunately, even without advanced statistical techniques, you can use simple arithmetic to help extract meaning from sets of research data. Table 11.3 shows several answers you can gain about a collection of numbers, for instance. The **mean** (which is what people are usually referring to when they use the term *average*) is the sum of all the items in the group divided by the number of items in that group. The **median** is the "middle of the road," or the midpoint of a series, with an equal number of items above and below. The **mode** is the number that occurs more often than any other in the sample; it's the best answer to a question such as "What is the usual amount?" Each of the three measures can tell you different things about a set of data.

Mean, *median*, and *mode* provide specific insights into sets of numerical data.

It's also helpful to look for **trends**, any repeatable patterns taking place over time, including growth, decline, and cyclical trends that vary between growth and decline. Trend analysis is common in business. By looking at data over a period of time, you can detect patterns and relationships that help you answer important questions. In addition, researchers frequently explore the relationships between subsets of data, using a technique called *cross-tabulation*. For instance, if you're trying to figure out why total sales

Trends suggest directions or patterns in a series of data points.

TABLE 11.3	Three Types of Data Measures: Mean, Median, and Mode	
Wilson	$ 3,000	
Green	5,000	
Carrick	6,000	
Cho	7,000	Mean
Keeble	7,500	Median
Lopes	8,500	
O'Toole	8,500	Mode
Mannix	8,500	
Caruso	9,000	
Total	$63,000	

rose or fell, you might look separately at sales data by customer age, gender, location, and product type.

Whenever you process numeric data, make sure to double-check all your calculations and document the operation of any spreadsheets you plan to share with colleagues. Also, step back and look at your entire set of data before proceeding with any analysis. Do the numbers make sense based on what you know about the subject? Are there any individual data points that stand out as suspect? Business audiences like the clarity of numbers; it's your responsibility to deliver numbers they can count on.

Quoting, Paraphrasing, and Summarizing Information

You can use textual information from sources in three ways. *Quoting* a source means you reproduce it exactly as you found it, and you either set it off with quotation marks (for shorter passages) or extract it in an indented paragraph (for longer passages). Use direct quotations when the original language will enhance your argument or when rewording the passage would lessen its impact. However, try not to quote sources at great length. Too much quoting creates a choppy patchwork of varying styles and gives the impression that all you've done is piece together the work of other people.

> Quoting a source means reproducing the content exactly and indicating who created the information originally.

You can often maximize the impact of secondary material in your own writing by *paraphrasing* it, restating it in your own words and with your own sentence structures.[3] Paraphrasing helps you maintain a consistent tone while using vocabulary familiar to your audience. Of course, you still need to credit the originator of the information, but not with quotation marks or indented paragraphs.

> Paraphrasing is expressing someone else's ideas in your own words.

To paraphrase effectively, follow these tips:[4]

- Reread the original passage until you fully understand its meaning and are able to express it in your own words.
- Use language that matches the flow and tone of the rest of your report and that your audience is familiar with.
- Check your version with the original source to verify that you have not altered the meaning.
- Use quotation marks to identify any unique terms or phrases you have borrowed exactly from the source.
- Record the source so that you can give proper credit if you use this material in your report.

Summarizing is similar to paraphrasing but presents the gist of the material in fewer words than the original. An effective summary identifies the main ideas and major support points from your source material but leaves out most details, examples, and other information that is less critical to your audience. Summarizing is not always a simple task, and your audience will judge your ability to separate significant issues from less significant details. Identify the main idea and the key support points, and separate these from details, examples, and other supporting evidence (see Table 11.4 on the next page).

> Summarizing is similar to paraphrasing but distills the content into fewer words.

Of course, all three approaches require careful attention to ethics. When quoting directly, take care not to distort the original intent of the material by quoting selectively or out of context. And never resort to plagiarism.

Drawing Conclusions

A **conclusion** is a logical interpretation of the facts and other information in a report. A sound conclusion is not only logical but flows from the information included in a report, meaning that it should be based on the information included in the report and shouldn't rely on information that isn't in the report. Moreover, if you or the organization you represent have certain biases that influence your conclusion, ethics obligate you to inform the audience accordingly.

> A conclusion is a logical interpretation of the information at hand.

Reaching good conclusions based on the evidence at hand is one of the most important skills you can develop in your business career. In fact, the ability to see patterns and possibilities that others can't see is one of the hallmarks of innovative business leaders.

TABLE 11.4	Summarizing Effectively		
Original Material (116 Words)	**45-Word Summary**	**22-Word Summary**	
Our facilities costs spiraled out of control last year. The 23 percent jump **was far ahead of every other cost category in the company and many times higher than the 4 percent average rise for commercial real estate in the Portland metropolitan area.** The rise can be attributed to many factors, but **the major factors include repairs** (mostly electrical and structural problems at the downtown office), **energy** (most of our offices are heated by electricity, the price of which has been increasing much faster than for oil or gas), and last but not least, **the loss of two sublease tenants** whose rent payments made a substantial dent in our cost profile for the past five years.	Our facilities costs jumped 23 percent last year, far ahead of every other cost category in the company and many times higher than the 4 percent local average. The major factors contributing to the increase are repairs, energy, and the loss of two sublease tenants.	Our facilities costs jumped 23 percent last year, primarily because of rising repair and energy costs and the loss of sublease income.	

Main idea

Major support points

Details

Consequently, take your time with this part of the process. Play "devil's advocate," attacking your conclusion as an audience might to make sure it stands up to rigorous scrutiny.

Making Recommendations

A recommendation is a suggested course of action based on what you have concluded about a particular situation.

Whereas a conclusion interprets information, a **recommendation** suggests action—what to do in response to the information. The following example illustrates the difference between a conclusion and a recommendation:

Conclusion	Recommendation
On the basis of its track record and current price, I believe that this company is an attractive buy.	I recommend that we offer to buy the company at a 10 percent premium over the current market value of its stock.

To be credible, recommendations must be based on logical analysis and sound conclusions. They must also be practical and acceptable to the people who have to make your recommendations work. Finally, when making a recommendation, be certain that you have adequately described the steps needed to implement your recommendation.

Conducting Secondary Research

Explain the role of secondary research, and describe the two major categories of online research tools.

You'll want to start most projects by conducting secondary research first.

Even if you intend to eventually conduct primary research, start with a review of any available secondary research. Inside your company, you might be able to find a variety of reports and other documents that could help. Outside the company, business researchers can choose from a wide range of print and online resources, both in libraries and online. Table 11.5 provides a small sample of the many secondary resources available.

FINDING INFORMATION AT A LIBRARY

Libraries offer information and resources you can't find anywhere else—including experienced research librarians.

Public, corporate, and university libraries offer printed sources with information that is not available online and online sources that are available only by subscription. Libraries are also where you'll find one of your most important resources: librarians. Reference librarians are trained in research techniques and can often help you find obscure information you can't

TABLE 11.5   **Important Resources for Business Research**

COMPANY, INDUSTRY, AND PRODUCT RESOURCES (URLs are provided for online resources)

AnnualReports.com (www.annualreports.com). Free access to annual reports from thousands of public companies.

Brands and Their Companies/Companies and Their Brands. Contains data on more than 430,000 consumer products and 100,000 manufacturers, importers, marketers, and distributors. Also available as an online database; ask at your library.

CNN/Money (http://money.cnn.com). News, analysis, and financial resources covering companies, industries, and world markets.

D&B Directories. A variety of directories, including *America's Corporate Families* (ownership connections among companies), *Business Rankings* (25,000 leading companies), *Directory of Service Companies* (more than 50,000 companies in the service sector), and *Industrial Guide* (more than 120,000 manufacturing companies).

Hoover's Handbook of American Business. Profiles of 750 influential public and private corporations.

Hoover's Online (www.hoovers.com). Database of millions of companies worldwide, including in-depth coverage of thousands of leading companies around the world. Basic information available free; in-depth information requires a subscription.

Manufacturing and Distribution USA. Data on thousands of companies in the manufacturing, wholesaling, and retailing sectors.

NAICS Codes (www.census.gov/eos/www/naics). North American Industry Classification System.

Reference USA. Concise information on millions of U.S. companies; subscription database.

SEC filing (www.sec.gov/edgar.shtml). SEC filings, including 10Ks, 10Qs, annual reports, and prospectuses for U.S. public firms.

Standard & Poor's NetVantage. Comprehensive range of directories and databases focusing on publicly traded companies and their industries and markets.

ThomasNet (www.thomasnet.com). Information on thousands of U.S. manufacturers, indexed by company name and product.

RESEARCH DIRECTORIES AND INDEXES

Books in Print. Database indexes nearly 20 million books, audio books, and video titles from around the world. Available in print and professional online versions.

Directories in Print. Information on more than 15,000 business and industrial directories.

Encyclopedia of Associations. Index of thousands of associations, listed by broad subject category, specific subject, association, and location. Available as an online database as well.

Reader's Guide to Periodical Literature. Classic index of general-interest magazines, categorized by subject and author; also available in electronic format, including a version with the full text of thousands of articles.

TRADEMARKS AND PATENTS

Official Gazette of the United States Patent and Trademark Office (www.uspto.gov). Weekly publication (one for trademarks and one for patents) providing official record of newly assigned trademarks and patents, product descriptions, and product names.

United States Patent and Trademark Office (www.uspto.gov). Trademark and patent information records.

STATISTICS AND OTHER BUSINESS DATA

Bureau of Economic Analysis (www.bea.gov). Large collection of economic and government data.

Europa—The European Union Online (http://europa.eu/index_en.htm). A portal that provides up-to-date coverage of current affairs, legislation, policies, and EU statistics.

FedStats (www.fedstats.gov). Access to a full range of statistics and information from more than 70 U.S. government agencies.

Key Business Ratios (Dun & Bradstreet). Industry, financial, and performance ratios.

Information Please Almanac. Compilation of broad-range statistical data, with strong focus on labor force.

Annual Statement Studies. Industry, financial, and performance ratios published by the Risk Management Association.

Statistical Abstract of the United States (www.census.gov). Annual compendium of U.S. economic, social, political, and industrial statistics.

The World Almanac and Book of Facts. Facts on economic, social, educational, and political events for major countries.

U.S. Bureau of Labor Statistics (www.bls.gov). Extensive national and regional information on labor and business, including employment, industry growth, productivity, the Consumer Price Index (CPI), and the overall U.S. economy.

U.S. Census Bureau (www.census.gov). Demographic data and analysis on consumers and businesses based on census results.

COMMERCIAL DATABASES (Require subscriptions; check with your school library)

ABI/INFORM Trade & Industry. Access to more than 750 periodicals and newsletters that focus on specific trades or industries.

Business Source Premier (Ebsco). Access to a variety of databases on a wide range of disciplines from leading information providers.

ProQuest Dialog. Hundreds of databases that include areas such as business and finance, news and media, medicine, pharmaceuticals, references, social sciences, government and regulation, science and technology, and more.

ProQuest. Thousands of periodicals and newspapers with extensive archives.

HighBeam Research. Thousands of full-text newspaper, magazine, and newswire sources, plus maps and photographs.

Gale Business & Company Resource Center. A comprehensive research tool designed for undergraduate and graduate students, job searchers, and investors; offers a wide variety of information on companies and industries.

LexisNexis. Several thousand databases covering legal, corporate, government, and academic subjects.

find on your own. They can also direct you to the typical library's many sources of business information:

- **Newspapers and periodicals.** Libraries offer access to a wide variety of popular magazines, general business magazines, *trade journals* (which provide information about specific professions and industries), and *academic journals* (which provide research-oriented articles from researchers and educators).
- **Business books.** Although less timely than newspapers, periodicals, and online sources, business books provide comprehensive coverage, in-depth analysis, and broad perspective that often can't be found anywhere else.
- **Directories.** Thousands of directories are published in print and electronic formats in the United States, and many include membership information for all kinds of professions, industries, and special-interest groups.
- **Almanacs and statistical resources.** Almanacs are handy guides to factual and statistical information about countries, politics, the labor force, and so on. One of the most extensive is the *Statistical Abstract of the United States* (available at www .census.gov).
- **Government publications.** Information on laws, court decisions, tax questions, regulatory issues, and other governmental concerns can often be found in collections of government documents.
- **Electronic databases.** Databases offer vast collections of computer-searchable information, often in specific areas such as business, law, science, technology, and education. Some of these are available only by institutional subscription, so the library can be your only way to gain access to them. Some libraries offer remote online access to some or all databases; for others, you'll need to visit in person.

> Local, state, and federal government agencies publish a huge array of information that is helpful to business researchers.

FINDING INFORMATION ONLINE

> Internet research tools fall into two basic categories: search tools and monitoring tools.

The Internet can be a tremendous source of business information, provided that you know where to look and how to use the tools available. Roughly speaking, the tools fall into two categories: those you can use to actively *search* for existing information and those you can use to *monitor* selected sources for new information. (Some tools can perform both functions.)

Online Search Tools

> General-purpose search engines are tremendously powerful tools, but they do have several shortcomings that you need to consider.

The most familiar search tools are general-purpose **search engines**, such as Google and Bing, which scan millions of websites to identify individual webpages that contain a specific word or phrase and then attempt to rank the results from most useful to least useful. Website owners use *search engine optimization* techniques (see page 336) to help boost their rankings in the results, but the ranking algorithms are kept secret to prevent unfair manipulation of the results.

For all their ease and power, conventional search engines have three primary shortcomings: (1) no human editors are involved to evaluate the quality or ranking of the search results; (2) various engines use different search techniques, so they often find different material; and (3) search engines can't reach all the content on some websites (this part of the Internet is sometimes called the *hidden Internet* or the *deep Internet*).

> "Human-powered search engines" and web directories rely on human editors to evaluate and select content.

A variety of tools are available to overcome the three main weaknesses of general-purpose search engines, and you should consider one or more of them in your business research. First, "human-powered search engines" such as Mahalo (www.mahalo.com) offer manually compiled results for popular search queries that aim to provide more accurate and more meaningful information, although for a much narrower range of topics than a regular search engine.[5] Similarly, **web directories**, such as the Open Directory Project at www.dmoz.org use human editors to categorize and evaluate websites. A variety of other directories focus on specific media types, such as blogs or podcasts.

Second, *metacrawlers* or *metasearch engines* (such as Bovée and Thill's Web Search, at http://businesscommunicationblog.com/websearch) help overcome the differences among search engines by formatting your search request for multiple search engines,

TABLE 11.6	The Broad Spectrum of Online Search Tools

GENERAL-PURPOSE SEARCH ENGINES

AOL Search	http://search.aol.com	Bing	www.bing.com
AlltheWeb	www.alltheweb.com	Google	www.google.com
AltaVista	www.altavista.com	Yahoo! Search	http://search.yahoo.com
Ask.com	www.ask.com		

METACRAWLERS, CLUSTERING ENGINES, AND HYBRID SITES

Bovée & Thill Web Search	http://businesscommunicationblog.com/websearch/	Search.com	www.search.com
Dogpile	www.dogpile.com	SurfWax	www.surfwax.com
ixquick	www.ixquick.com	WebBrain	www.webbrain.com
Mamma	www.mamma.com	WebCrawler	www.webcrawler.com
MetaCrawler	www.metacrawler.com	ZapMeta	www.zapmeta.com

WEB DIRECTORIES AND ONLINE LIBRARIES

About	www.about.com	Internet Public Library	www.ipl.org
Answers.com	www.answers.com	Library of Congress	www.loc.gov/rr/business
CEOExpress	http://ceoexpress.com	Library Spot	www.libraryspot.com
Digital Librarian	www.digital-librarian.com/business.html	Open Directory Project	www.dmoz.com
Google Directory	www.google.com/dirhp	Questia (requires subscription)	www.questia.com
INFOMINE	http://infomine.ucr.edu	USA.gov (U.S. government portal)	www.usa.gov

NEWS SEARCH ENGINES AND SOCIAL TAGGING SITES

10 x 10	http://tenbyten.org	NewsNow	www.newsnow.co.uk
Delicious	http://delicious.com	Newseum	www.newseum.org
Digg	www.digg.com	WorldNews	www.wn.com
Google News	http://news.google.com	Yahoo! News	http://news.yahoo.com

BLOG, VIDEO, AND PODCAST SEARCH ENGINES AND DIRECTORIES

American Rhetoric (speeches)	www.americanrhetoric.com	Podcast Alley	www.podcastalley.com
Bing videos	www.bing.com/videos	Podcast Bunker	www.podcastbunker.com
blinkx	www.blinkx.com	Podcast Network	www.thepodcastnetwork.com
Bloglines	www.bloglines.com	podscope	www.podscope.com
BlogPulse	www.blogpulse.com	Technorati	www.technorati.com
Google Blog search	http://blogsearch.google.com	Yahoo! Video search	http://video.search.yahoo.com
Google Video search	http://video.google.com	YouTube	www.youtube.com

PERIODICAL AND BOOK SEARCH ENGINES

Google Scholar search	http://scholar.google.com	Google Book search	http://books.google.com

making it easy to find a broader range of results. With a few clicks, you can compare results from multiple search engines to make sure you are getting a broad view of the material. Table 11.6 lists some of the most popular search engines, metacrawlers, and directories.

Third, **online databases** help address the challenge of the hidden Internet by offering access to newspapers, magazines, journals, electronic copies of books, and other resources often not available with standard search engines. Some of these databases offer free access to

Online databases and specialty search engines can help you access parts of the hidden Internet.

The tools available for monitoring online sources for new information can help you track industry trends, consumer sentiment, and other information.

Search tools work in different ways, and you can get unpredictable results if you don't know how each one operates.

Before you begin searching, think about where the information you need might be located, how it might be structured, and what terms might be used to describe it.

the public, but others require a subscription (check with your library). Also, a variety of specialized search engines now exist to reach various parts of the hidden Internet.

Online Monitoring Tools

One of the most powerful aspects of online research is the ability to automatically monitor selected sources for new information. The possibilities include subscribing to newsfeeds from blogs and websites, following people on Twitter and other microblogs, setting up alerts on search engines and online databases, and using specialized monitors such as TweetBeep (http://tweetbeep.com) and TweetDeck (www.tweetdeck.com) to track tweets that mention specific companies or other terms.

Exercise some care when setting up monitoring tools, however, because it's easy to get overwhelmed by the flood of information. Remember that you can always go back and search your information sources if you need to gather additional information.

Search Tips

Search engines, web directories, and databases work in different ways, so make sure you understand how to optimize your search and interpret the results. With a *keyword search*, the engine or database attempts to find items that include all the words you enter. A *Boolean search* lets you define a query with greater precision, using such operators as AND (the search must include two terms linked by AND), OR (it can include either or both words), or NOT (the search ignores items with whatever word comes after NOT). *Natural language searches* let you ask questions in everyday English. *Forms-based searches* help you create powerful queries by simply filling out an online form.[6]

To make the best use of any search tool, keep the following points in mind:

- Think before you search. The results you get from a search engine can create the illusion that the Internet is a neatly organized warehouse of all the information in the universe, but the reality is far different. The Internet is an incomplete, unorganized hodgepodge of millions of independent websites with information that ranges in value from priceless to utter rubbish. After you have identified what you need to know, spend a few moments thinking about where that information might be found, how it might be structured, and what terms various websites might use to describe it.
- Read the instructions and pay attention to the details. A few minutes of learning can save hours of inefficient search time.
- Review the search and display options carefully so you don't misinterpret the results; some kinds of settings can make a huge difference in the results you see.
- Try variations of your terms, such as *adolescent* and *teenager* or *management* and *managerial*.
- User fewer search terms to find more results; use more search terms to find fewer results.
- Look beyond the first page of results. Don't assume that the highest-ranking results are the best sources for you. For example, materials that haven't been optimized for search engines won't rank as highly (meaning they won't show up in the first few pages of results), but they may be far better for your purposes.

Search technologies continue to evolve rapidly, so look for new ways to find the information you need. Some new tools search specific areas of information (such as Twitter) in better ways, whereas others approach search in new ways. For instance, Yolink (www.yolink.com) finds webpages like a regular search engine does but then also searches through documents and webpages that are linked to those first-level results.[7]

Other powerful search tools include *desktop search engines* that search all the files on your personal computer, *enterprise search engines* that search all the computers on a company's network, *research and content managers* such as the free Zotero browser extension (www.zotero.com), and *social tagging* or *bookmarking sites* such as Digg (http://digg.com) and Delicious (http://delicious.com).

For information on the latest online research tools and techniques, visit http://real-timeupdates.com/ebc10 and click on Chapter 11.

DOCUMENTING YOUR SOURCES

Documenting your sources serves three important functions: It properly and ethically credits the person who created the original material, it shows your audience that you have sufficient support for your message, and it helps readers explore your topic in more detail, if desired. Be sure to take advantage of the source documentation tools in your software, such as automatic endnote or footnote tracking.

Appendix B discusses the common methods of documenting sources. Whatever method you choose, documentation is necessary for books, articles, tables, charts, diagrams, song lyrics, scripted dialogue, letters, speeches—anything that you take from someone else, including ideas and information that you've presented through paraphrasing or summarizing. However, you do not have to cite a source for knowledge that's generally known among your readers, such as the fact that Facebook is a large social network or that computers are pervasive in business today.

> Proper documentation of the sources you use is both ethical and an important resource for your readers.

REAL-TIME UPDATES
Learn More by Reading This Article

Get clear answers to murky copyright questions

Find out what is covered by copyright, what isn't, and how to secure a copyright for your own work. Go to http://real-timeupdates.com/ebc10 and click on Learn More. If you are using MyBcommLab, you can access Real-Time Updates within each chapter or under Student Study Tools.

Conducting Primary Research

If secondary research can't provide the information and insights you need, you may need to gather the information yourself with primary research. The two most common primary research methods are surveys and interviews. Other primary techniques are observations (including tracking the behavior of website visitors) and experiments in special situations such as test marketing, but they're less commonly used for day-to-day business research.

> **4 LEARNING OBJECTIVE**
>
> Explain the role of primary research, and identify the two most common forms of primary research for business communication purposes.

CONDUCTING SURVEYS

A carefully prepared and conducted survey can provide invaluable insights, but only if it is *reliable* (would produce identical results if repeated under similar conditions) and *valid* (measures what it's supposed to measure). To conduct a survey that generates reliable and valid results, you need to choose research participants carefully and develop an effective set of questions. A good research handbook can guide you through the process of selecting a sufficient number of representative participants. For important surveys on strategically important topics with lots at stake, you're usually better off hiring a research specialist who knows how to avoid errors during planning, execution, and analysis.

> Surveys and interviews are the most common primary research techniques.
>
> Surveys need to be reliable, valid, and representative in order to be useful.

When selecting people to participate in a survey, the most critical task is getting a representative *sample* of the entire population in question. For instance, if you want to know how U.S. consumers feel about something, you can't just survey a few hundred people in a shopping mall. Different types of consumers shop at different times of the day and different days of the week, and many consumers do not shop at malls. The online surveys you see on many websites today potentially suffer from the same *sampling bias*: They capture only the opinions of people who visit the sites and want to participate, which might not be a representative sample of the population. A good handbook on survey research will help you select the right people for your survey, including selecting enough people to have a statistically valid survey.[8]

To develop an effective survey questionnaire, start with the information needs you identified at the beginning of the research process. Then break these points into specific questions, choosing an appropriate type of question for each point (see Figure 11.7). The following guidelines will help you produce results that are valid and reliable:[9]

Provide clear instructions to prevent mistaken answers.

- **Provide clear instructions.** Entry mistakes will distort your results.
- **Don't ask for information that people can't be expected to remember.** For instance, a question such as "How many times did you go grocery shopping last year?" will generate unreliable answers.
- **Keep the questionnaire short and easy to answer.** Don't expect people to give you more than 10 or 15 minutes of their time.

QUESTION TYPE	EXAMPLE
Open-ended	How would you describe the flavor of this ice cream?
Either-or	Do you think this ice cream is too rich? _____ Yes _____ No
Multiple choice	Which description best fits the taste of this ice cream? (Choose only one.) a. Delicious b. Too fruity c. Too sweet d. Too intense e. Bland f. Stale
Scale	Please mark an X on the scale to indicate how you perceive the texture of this ice cream. Too light Light Creamy Too creamy
Checklist	Which of the following ice cream brands do you recognize? (Check all that apply.) _____ Ben & Jerry's _____ Breyers _____ Carvel _____ Dreyer's _____ Häagen-Dazs
Ranking	Rank these flavors in order of your preference, from 1 (most preferred) to 5 (least preferred): _____ Vanilla _____ Cherry _____ Strawberry _____ Chocolate _____ Coconut
Short-answer	In the past 2 weeks, how many times did you buy ice cream in a grocery store? _____ In the past 2 weeks, how many times did you buy ice cream in an ice cream shop? _____

Figure 11.7   Types of Survey Questions
For each question you have in your survey, choose the type of question that will elicit the most useful answers.

MyBcommLab

Apply Figure 11.7's key concepts by revising a new document. Go to Chapter 11 in www .pearsoninternationaleditions.com/ mybcommlab and select Document Makeovers.

- **Whenever possible, formulate questions to provide answers that are easy to analyze.** Numbers and facts are easier to summarize than opinions, for instance.
- **Avoid leading questions that could bias your survey.** If you ask, "Do you prefer that we stay open in the evenings for customer convenience?" many people will say yes even if they don't shop in the evenings. Instead, ask, "What time of day do you normally do your shopping?"
- **Avoid ambiguous questions.** If you ask, "Do you shop online often?" some people might interpret *often* to mean "every day," whereas others might think it means "once a week" or "once a month."
- **Ask only one thing at a time.** A compound question such as "Do you read books and magazines?" doesn't allow for the respondent who reads one but not the other.
- **Make the survey adaptive.** With an online survey, you can program the software to branch automatically based on audience inputs. Not only does this sort of real-time adaptation deliver better answers, but it reduces frustration for survey respondents as well.[10]

You have probably noticed simple polls and surveys on many websites. Online surveys (see Figure 11.8) offer a number of advantages, including speed, cost, and the ability to adapt the question set along the way based on a respondent's answers. However, to deliver reliable and valid results, they must be designed and administered as carefully as offline surveys. For example, you can't assume that the results from a survey on your company's website reflect the attitudes, beliefs, or behaviors of the population as a whole, because the visitors to your website are almost guaranteed not to be an accurate cross-section of the entire population.

Online surveys are fast and convenient, but in order to produce meaningful data, they must be designed with the same care as offline surveys.

CONDUCTING INTERVIEWS

Getting in-depth information straight from an expert or an individual concerned about an issue can be a great method for collecting primary information. Interviews can dig deeper

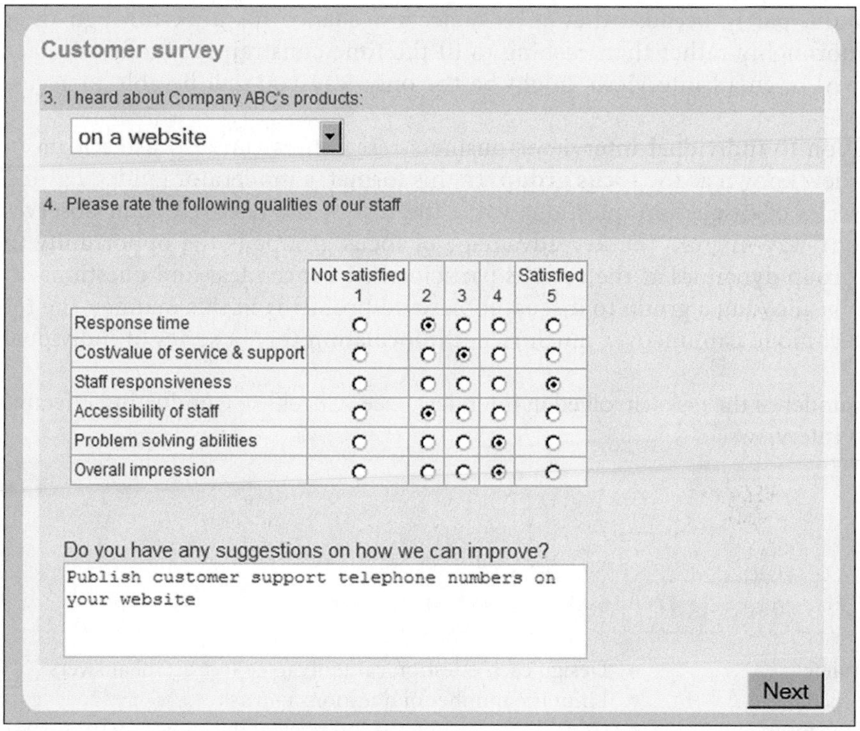

Figure 11.8 Online Survey Tools
Online survey systems such as this one, offered by Object Planet, make it easy to create, administer, and analyze surveys.

Interviews can take place online, over the phone, or in person, and they can involve individuals or groups.

than the "hands-off" approach of surveys, and skilled interviewers can also watch for non-verbal signals that provide additional insights. Interviews can take a variety of formats, from email exchanges to group discussions. For example, the British supermarket chain Tesco invites thousands of customers to visit its stores every year for meetings known as Customer Question Time, when it asks customers how the company can serve them better.[11]

Be aware that the answers you receive in an interview are influenced by the types of questions you ask, by the way you ask them, and by each subject's cultural and language background. Potentially significant factors include the person's race, gender, age, educational level, and social status.[12]

Open-ended questions, which can't be answered with a simple yes or no, can provide deeper insights, opinions, and information.

Ask **open-ended questions** (such as "Why do you believe that South America represents a better opportunity than Europe for this product line?") to solicit opinions, insights, and information. Ask **closed questions** to elicit a specific answer, such as yes or no. However, don't use too many closed questions in an interview, or the experience will feel more like a simple survey and won't take full advantage of the interactive interview setting.

Arrange the sequence of questions to help uncover layers of information.

Think carefully about the sequence of your questions and the subject's potential answers so you can arrange questions in an order that helps uncover layers of information. Also consider providing the other person with a list of questions at least a day or two before the interview, especially if you'd like to quote your subject in writing or if your questions might require your subject to conduct research or think extensively about the answers. If you want to record the interview, ask the person ahead of time and respect his or her wishes.

As soon as possible after the interview, take a few moments to write down your thoughts, go over your notes, and organize your material. Look for important themes, helpful facts or statistics, and direct quotes. If you made a tape recording, *transcribe* it (take down word for word what the person said) or take notes from the recording just as you would while listening to someone in person.

Face-to-face interviews give you the opportunity to gauge the reaction to your questions and observe the nonverbal signals that accompany the answers, but interviews don't necessarily have to take place in person. Email interviews are becoming more common, partly because they give subjects a chance to think through their responses thoroughly rather than rushing to fit the time constraints of a face-to-face interview.[13] Also, email interviews might be the only way you will be able to access some experts.

In addition to individual interviews, business researchers can also use a form of group interview known as the **focus group**. In this format, a moderator guides a group through a series of discussion questions while the rest of the research team observes through a one-way mirror. The key advantage of focus groups is the opportunity to learn from group dynamics as the various participants bounce ideas and questions off each other. By allowing a group to discuss topics and problems in this manner, the focus group technique can uncover much richer information than a series of individual interviews.[14]

As a reminder of the tasks involved in interviews, see "Checklist: Conducting Effective Information Interviews."

✓ Checklist Conducting Effective Information Interviews

- Learn about the person you are going to interview.
- Formulate your main idea to ensure effective focus.
- Choose the length, style, and organization of the interview.
- Select question types to elicit the specific information you want.

- Design each question carefully to collect useful answers.
- Limit the number of questions you ask.
- Consider recording the interview if the subject permits.
- Review your notes as soon as the interview ends.

Planning Informational Reports

Informational reports provide the material that employees, managers, and others need in order to make decisions, take action, and respond to dynamic conditions inside and outside the organization. Although these reports come in dozens of particular formats, they can be grouped into four general categories:

- **Reports to monitor and control operations.** Managers rely on a wide range of reports to see how well their companies are functioning. *Plans* establish expectations and guidelines to direct future action. Some of the most significant of these are *business plans* (see "Sharpening Your Career Skills: Creating an Effective Business Plan"). Many business plans are actually a combination of an informational report (describing conditions in the marketplace), an analytical report (analyzing threats and opportunities and recommending specific courses of action), and a proposal (persuading investors to put money into the firm in exchange for a share of ownership). *Operating reports* provide feedback on a wide variety of an organization's functions, including sales, inventories, expenses, shipments, and so on. *Personal activity reports* provide information regarding an individual's experiences during sales calls, industry conferences, market research trips, and so on.
- **Reports to implement policies and procedures.** *Policy reports* range from brief descriptions of business procedures to manuals that run dozens or hundreds of pages. *Position papers*, sometimes called *white papers* or *backgrounders*, outline an organization's official position on issues that affect the company's success.
- **Reports to demonstrate compliance.** Businesses are required to submit a variety of *compliance reports*, from tax returns to reports that describe the proper handling of hazardous materials.
- **Reports to document progress.** Supervisors, investors, and customers frequently expect to be informed of the status of projects and other activities via *progress reports*.

ORGANIZING INFORMATIONAL REPORTS

In most cases, the direct approach is the best choice for informational reports. However, if the information is both surprising and disappointing, such as a project that is behind schedule or over budget, you might consider using the indirect approach to build up to the bad news. Most informational reports use a **topical organization**, arranging material in one of the following ways (see Figure 11.9 on page 389):

- **Comparison.** Showing similarities and differences (or advantages and disadvantages) between two or more entities
- **Importance.** Building up from the least important item to the most important (or from most important to the least, if you don't think your audience will read the entire report)
- **Sequence.** Organizing the steps or stages in a process or procedure
- **Chronology.** Organizing a chain of events in order from oldest to newest or vice versa
- **Geography.** Organizing by region, city, state, country, or other geographic unit
- **Category.** Grouping by topical category, such as sales, profit, cost, or investment

Whichever pattern you choose, use it consistently so that readers can easily follow your discussion from start to finish. Bear in mind, however, that in many instances, you might be expected to follow a particular type of organization.

Of course, effective informational reports must also be audience centered, logical, focused, and easy to follow, with generous use of previews and summaries. Your audience expects you to sort out the details and separate major points from minor points.

5 LEARNING OBJECTIVE

Explain how to plan informational reports and website content.

Informational reports are used to monitor and control operations, to implement policies and procedures, to demonstrate compliance, and to document progress.

MyBcommLab

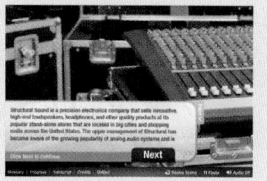

- Access this chapter's simulation entitled Business Reports located at www.pearsoninternationaleditions.com/mybcommlab.

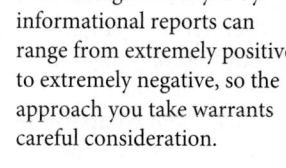

The messages conveyed by informational reports can range from extremely positive to extremely negative, so the approach you take warrants careful consideration.

REAL-TIME UPDATES
Learn More by Watching This Video

Is it necessary—or even smart—to spend months writing a business plan?

Some entrepreneurs don't agree that writing a comprehensive business plan is always a good idea. See what Kevin Ryan has to say in this interview. Go to http://real-timeupdates.com/ebc10 and click on Learn More. If you are using MyBcommLab, you can access Real-Time Updates within each chapter or under Student Study Tools.

SHARPENING YOUR CAREER SKILLS: Creating an Effective Business Plan

As the founders of MyCityWay (see page 366) can attest, the most important report you may ever get the chance to write is a business plan for a new or growing young company. A comprehensive business plan forces you to think about personnel, marketing, facilities, suppliers, distribution, and a host of other issues that are vital to your success. If you are starting out on a small scale and using your own money, your business plan may be relatively informal. But at a minimum, you should describe the basic concept of the business and outline its specific goals, objectives, and resource requirements. A formal plan, suitable for use with banks or investors, should cover these points:

- **Summary.** In one or two paragraphs, summarize your business concept, particularly the *business model*, which defines how the company will generate revenue and produce a profit. The summary must be compelling, catching the investor's attention and giving him or her reasons to keep reading. Describe your product or service and its market potential. Highlight some things about your company and its leaders that will distinguish your firm from the competition. Summarize your financial projections and indicate how much money you will need from investors or lenders and where it will be spent.
- **Mission and objectives.** Explain the purpose of your business and what you hope to accomplish.
- **Company and industry.** Give full background information on the origins and structure of your venture and the characteristics of its industry.
- **Products or services.** Give a complete but concise description of your products or services, focusing on their unique attributes.
- **Market and competition.** Provide data that will persuade investors that you understand your target market and can achieve your sales goals. Be sure to identify the strengths and weaknesses of your competitors.
- **Management.** Summarize the background and qualifications of the key management personnel in your company. Include résumés in an appendix.
- **Marketing strategy.** Provide projections of sales and market share and outline a strategy for identifying and contacting customers, setting prices, providing customer services, advertising, and so forth. Whenever possible, include evidence of customer acceptance, such as advance product orders.

- **Design and development plans.** If your product requires design or development, describe the nature and extent of what needs to be done, including costs and possible problems.
- **Operations plan.** Provide information on facilities, equipment, and personnel requirements.
- **Overall schedule.** Forecast important milestones in the company's growth and development, including when you need to be fully staffed and when your products will be ready for the market.
- **Critical risks and problems.** Identify all negative factors and discuss them honestly.
- **Financial projections and requirements.** Include a detailed budget of start-up and operating costs, as well as projections for income, expenses, and cash flow for the first three years of business. Identify the company's financing needs and potential sources, if appropriate.
- **Exit strategy.** Explain how investors will be able to cash out or sell their investment, such as through a public stock offering, sale of the company, or a buyback of the investors' interest.

A complete business plan obviously requires a considerable amount of work. However, by thinking your way through all these issues, you'll enjoy a smoother launch and a greater chance of success in your new adventure. (For an alternative view on the value of business plans and how much time you should spend writing one, watch the video in the Real-Time Updates "Learn More" on the preceding page. For more insider advice on writing business plans, see page 450 in Chapter 13.)

CAREER APPLICATIONS

1. Why is it important to identify critical risks and problems in a business plan?
2. Many experts suggest that you write a business plan yourself rather than hire a consultant to write it for you. Why is this a good idea?

Sources: Adapted from Heidi Brown, "How to Write a Winning Business Plan," *Forbes*, 18 June 2010, www.forbes.com; Michael Gerber, "The Business Plan That Always Works," *Her Business*, May/June 2004, 23–25; J. Tol Broome, Jr., "How to Write a Business Plan," *Nation's Business*, February 1993, 29–30; Albert Richards, "The Ernst & Young Business Plan Guide," *R & D Management*, April 1995, 253; David Lanchner, "How Chitchat Became a Valuable Business Plan," *Global Finance*, February 1995, 54–56; Marguerita Ashby-Berger, "My Business Plan—And What Really Happened," *Small Business Forum*, Winter 1994–1995, 24–35; Stanley R. Rich and David E. Gumpert, *Business Plans That Win $$$* (New York: Harper & Row, 1985).

ORGANIZING WEBSITE CONTENT

Many websites, particularly company websites, function as informational reports, offering sections with information about the company, its history, its products and services, its executive team, and so on. While most of what you've already learned about informational reports applies to website writing, the online experience requires some special considerations and practices.

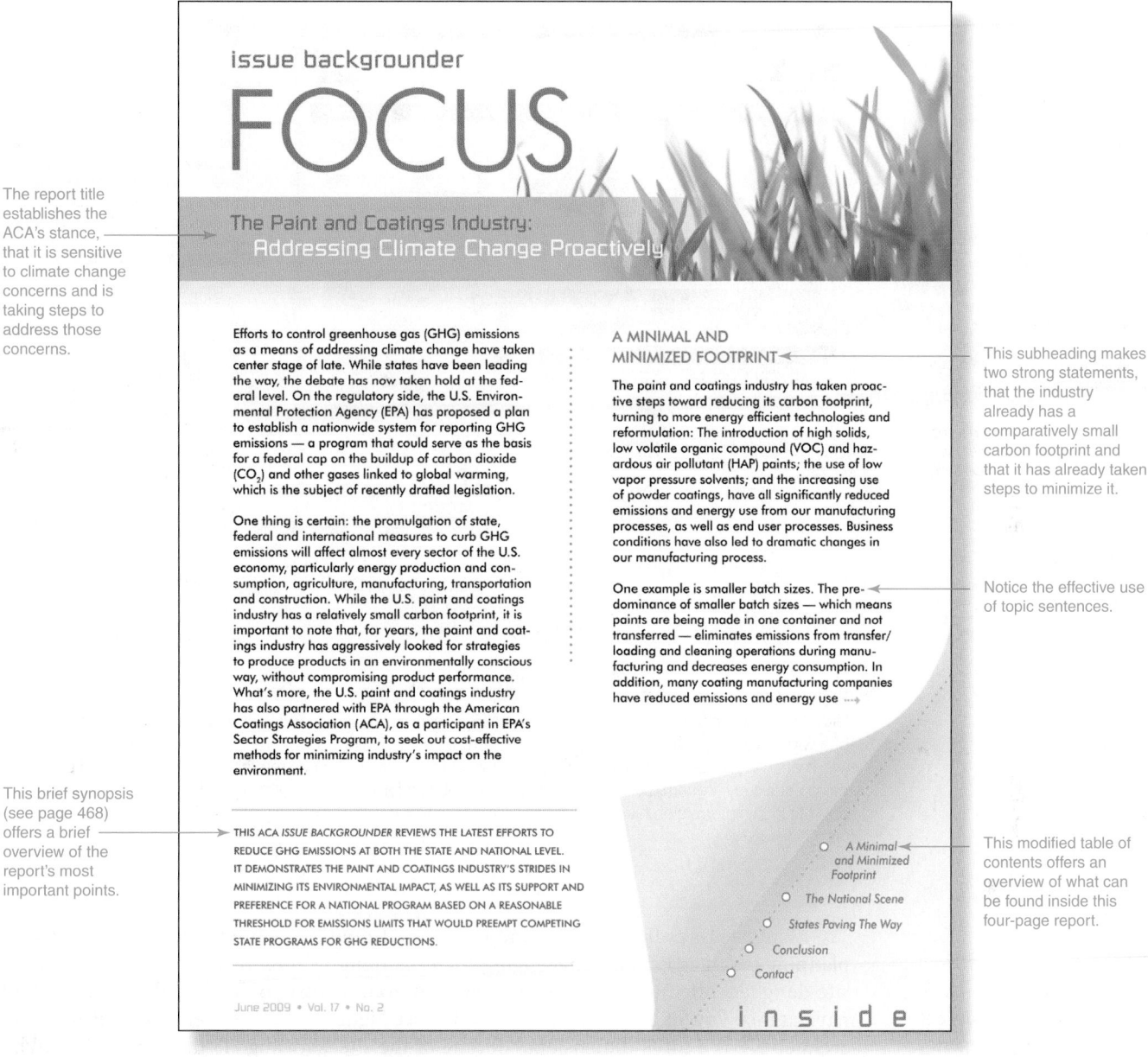

The report title establishes the ACA's stance, that it is sensitive to climate change concerns and is taking steps to address those concerns.

This brief synopsis (see page 468) offers a brief overview of the report's most important points.

This subheading makes two strong statements, that the industry already has a comparatively small carbon footprint and that it has already taken steps to minimize it.

Notice the effective use of topic sentences.

This modified table of contents offers an overview of what can be found inside this four-page report.

Figure 11.9 Effective Informational Report (Excerpt)
This background from the American Coatings Association (ACA), an organization that represents paint and coatings manufacturers, lays out the ACA's position on pending emissions legislation.
Source: Used with permission of the American Coatings Association, Inc.

As you begin to plan a website, start by recognizing the unique nature of online communication:

- **Web readers are demanding.** If site visitors can't find what they're looking for in a matter of minutes, they'll leave and look elsewhere.[15]
- **Reading online can be difficult.** Studies show that reading speeds are about 25 percent slower on a monitor than on paper.[16] Reading from computer screens can also be tiring on the eyes, even to the point of causing headaches, double vision, blurred vision, and other physical problems.[17]
- **The web is a nonlinear, multidimensional medium.** Readers of online material move around in any order they please; there often is no beginning, middle, or end. As a web writer, you need to anticipate the various paths your readers will want to follow and to make sure you provide the right hyperlinks in the right places to help readers explore successfully.

When planning online reports or other website content, remember that the online reading experience differs from offline reading in several important ways.

The six major sections of the information hierarchy are identified in the top navigation bar.

The page shown here is the top-level page of the first of these six major sections, "Starting & Managing a Business."

This graphic directs users to four general topics that are likely to be on the minds of site visitors: thinking about starting a business, starting a business, managing a business, and growing a business, represented visually by the seed, the sprout, the sapling, and tree.

The bulk of the section's content is accessed through these two content lists, each representing one half of "Starting & Managing a Business."

Notice how two-thirds of the screen (the left and middle columns in this three-column layout) are devoted to static information and one-third to dynamic information and special features.

Social media and community features are grouped in this corner, where they are accessible but not in the way.

Tabbed boxes such as this are a handy way to provide one-click access to a variety of lower-level pages. Rankings such as "most visited" and "top rated" let new visitors know what other people like them find valuable.

"SBA Direct" is another user-focused feature of the information architecture that lets visitors jump to the information that pertains specifically to their local areas.

Another tabbed box offers access to news stories, blog posts, and other updates.

Figure 11.10 Information Architecture
Like many corporate websites, the site of the U.S. Small Business Administration has to balance the needs of a wide variety of visitors looking for many different types of information. The challenges include grouping information in a meaningful hierarchy that minimizes the number of clicks required to access desired pages, mixing static and dynamic information, and finding places for the odd but important bits of information that don't fit in the information hierarchy.
Source: Courtesy of SBA.gov.

The *information architecture* of a website is the equivalent of the outline for a paper report, but it tends to be much more complicated than a simple linear outline.

Many websites have multiple audiences and multiple communication functions, so planning websites is more challenging than planning printed reports. Professional website designers often use the term **information architecture** to describe the structure and navigational flow of all the parts of a website (see Figure 11.10). In a sense, the information architecture is a three-dimensional outline of the site, showing (1) the vertical hierarchy of pages from the homepage down to the lower level, (2) the horizontal division of pages across the various sections of the site, and (3) the links that tie all these pages together, both internally (between various pages on the site) and externally (between your site and other websites).

To organize your site effectively, keep the following advice in mind:

- Plan your site structure and navigation before you write.[18]
- Let your readers be in control; give them clearly labeled pathways that let them explore on their own.
- Help online readers scan and absorb information by breaking it into self-contained, easily readable chunks that are linked together logically.

Planning Analytical Reports

The purpose of analytical reports is to analyze, to understand, to explain—to think through a problem or an opportunity and figure out how it affects the company and how the company should respond. In many cases, you'll also be expected to make a recommendation based on your analysis. As you saw in Figure 11.1, analytical reports fall into three basic categories:

- **Reports to assess opportunities.** Every business opportunity carries some degree of risk and also requires a variety of decisions and actions in order to capitalize on the opportunity. You can use analytical reports to assess risk and required decisions and actions. For instance, *market analysis reports* are used to judge the likelihood of success for new products or sales. *Due diligence reports* examine the financial aspects of a proposed decision, such as acquiring another company.
- **Reports to solve problems.** Managers often ask for *troubleshooting reports* when they need to understand why something isn't working properly and what needs to be done to fix it. A variation, the *failure analysis report*, studies events that happened in the past, with the hope of learning how to avoid similar failures in the future.
- **Reports to support decisions.** *Feasibility reports* are called for when managers need to explore the ramifications of a decision they're about to make, such as switching materials used in a manufacturing process. *Justification reports* explain a decision that has already been made.

Analytical reports are used to assess opportunities, to solve problems, and to support decisions.

Writing analytical reports presents a greater challenge than writing informational reports because you need to use your reasoning abilities and persuasive skills in addition to your writing skills. With analytical reports, you're doing more than simply delivering information: You're also thinking through a problem or an opportunity and presenting your conclusions in a compelling and persuasive manner. Finally, because analytical reports often convince other people to make significant financial and personnel decisions, your reports carry the added responsibility of the consequences of these decisions.

To help define the problem that your analytical report will address, answer these questions:

- What needs to be determined?
- Why is this issue important?
- Who is involved in the situation?
- Where is the trouble located?
- How did the situation originate?
- When did it start?

Not all of these questions apply in every situation, but asking them helps you define the problem being addressed and limits the scope of your discussion.

Also try **problem factoring**, dividing the problem into a series of logical, connected questions that try to identify cause and effect. When you speculate on the cause of a problem, you're forming a **hypothesis**, a potential explanation that needs to be tested. By subdividing a problem and forming hypotheses based on available evidence, you can tackle even the most complex situations.

Problem factoring is the process of breaking a problem down into smaller questions to help identify causes and effects.

As with all other business messages, the best organizational structure for each analytical report depends largely on your audience's likely reaction. The three basic structures involve focusing on conclusions, focusing on recommendations, and focusing on logic (see Table 11.7 on the next page).

FOCUSING ON CONCLUSIONS

When writing for audiences that are likely to accept your conclusions—either because they've asked you to perform an analysis or they trust your judgment—consider using a direct approach that focuses immediately on your conclusions. This structure communicates the main idea quickly, but it presents some risks. Even if audiences trust your judgment, they may have questions about your data or the methods you used. Moreover, starting with the conclusion may create the impression that you have oversimplified the situation. You're generally better off taking the direct approach in a report only when your credibility is high—when your readers trust you and are willing to accept your conclusions (see Figure 11.11 on the next page).

Focusing on conclusions is often the best approach when you're addressing a receptive audience.

TABLE 11.7	Common Ways to Structure Analytical Reports		
	Focus on Conclusions or Recommendations	**Focus on Logical Argument**	
Element		**Use 2 + 2 = 4 Model**	**Use Yardstick Model**
Reader mindset	Likely to accept	Hostile or skeptical	Hostile or skeptical
Approach	Direct	Indirect	Indirect
Writer credibility	High	Low	Low
Advantages	Readers quickly grasp conclusions or recommendations	Works well when you need to show readers how you built toward an answer by following clear, logical steps	Works well when you have a list of criteria (standards) that must be considered in a decision; alternatives are all measured against same criteria
Drawbacks	Structure can make topic seem too simple	Can make report longer	Readers must agree on criteria; can be lengthy because of the need to address each criteria for every alternative

FOCUSING ON RECOMMENDATIONS

When readers want to know what you think they should do, organize your report to focus on recommendations.

A slightly different approach is useful when your readers want to know what they ought to do in a given situation (as opposed to what they ought to conclude). Start with the following general outline and adapt it as needed:

1. Establish the need for action in the introduction by briefly describing the problem or opportunity.

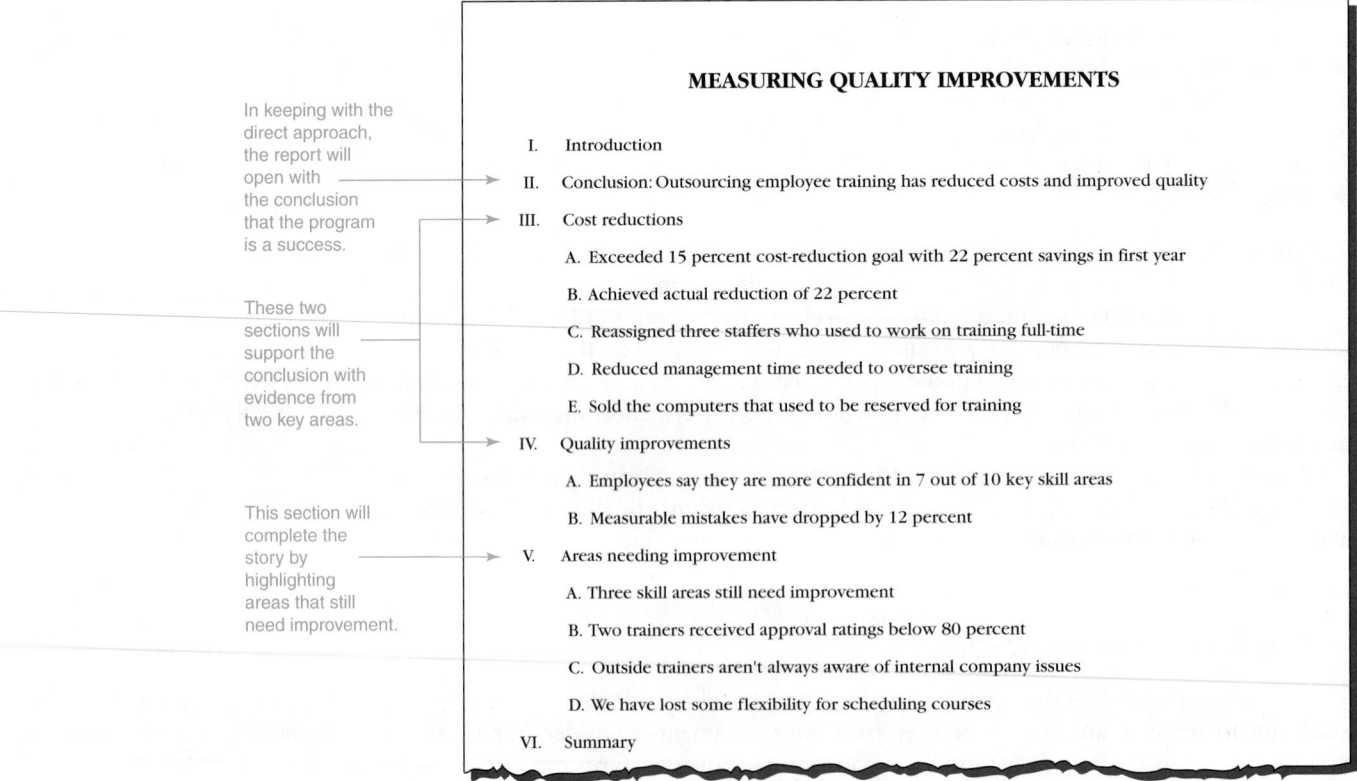

In keeping with the direct approach, the report will open with the conclusion that the program is a success.

These two sections will support the conclusion with evidence from two key areas.

This section will complete the story by highlighting areas that still need improvement.

MEASURING QUALITY IMPROVEMENTS

I.   Introduction

II. Conclusion: Outsourcing employee training has reduced costs and improved quality

III. Cost reductions

    A. Exceeded 15 percent cost-reduction goal with 22 percent savings in first year

    B. Achieved actual reduction of 22 percent

    C. Reassigned three staffers who used to work on training full-time

    D. Reduced management time needed to oversee training

    E. Sold the computers that used to be reserved for training

IV. Quality improvements

    A. Employees say they are more confident in 7 out of 10 key skill areas

    B. Measurable mistakes have dropped by 12 percent

V.   Areas needing improvement

    A. Three skill areas still need improvement

    B. Two trainers received approval ratings below 80 percent

    C. Outside trainers aren't always aware of internal company issues

    D. We have lost some flexibility for scheduling courses

VI. Summary

Figure 11.11 **Preliminary Outline of a Research Report Focusing on Conclusions**
Cynthia Zolonka works on the human resources staff of a bank in Houston, Texas. Her company decided to have an outside firm handle its employee training, and a year after the outsourcing arrangement was established, Zolonka was asked to evaluate the results. Her analysis shows that the outsourcing experiment was a success; she opens with that conclusion and supports it with clear evidence. Readers who accept the conclusion can stop reading, and those who desire more information can continue.

2. Introduce the benefit(s) that can be achieved if the recommendation is adopted, along with any potential risks.
3. List the steps (recommendations) required to achieve the benefit, using action verbs for emphasis.
4. Explain each step more fully, giving details on procedures, costs, and benefits; if necessary, also explain how risks can be minimized.
5. Summarize your recommendations.

FOCUSING ON LOGICAL ARGUMENTS

When readers are skeptical or hostile to the conclusion or recommendation you plan to make, use an indirect approach that logically builds toward your conclusion or recommendation. If you guide the audience along a rational path toward the answer, they are more likely to accept it when they encounter it. The two most common logical approaches are known as the *2 + 2 = 4 approach* and the *yardstick approach*.

Logical arguments can follow two basic approaches: 2 + 2 = 4 (adding everything up) and the yardstick method (comparing ideas against a predetermined set of standards).

The 2 + 2 = 4 Approach

The **2 + 2 = 4 approach** is so named because it convinces readers of your point of view by demonstrating that everything adds up. The main points in your outline are the main reasons behind your conclusions and recommendations. You support each reason with the evidence you collected during your analysis. With its natural feel and versatility, the 2 + 2 = 4 approach is generally the most persuasive and efficient way to develop an analytical report for skeptical readers, so try this structure first. You'll find that most of your arguments fall naturally into this pattern.

The troubleshooting report shown in Figure 11.12 on the next page is built on the main idea that the company should establish separate sales teams for major national accounts, rather than continuing to service them through the company's four regional divisions. The writer knew his plan would be controversial because it required a big change in the company's organization and in the way sales representatives are paid. His thinking had to be clear and easy to follow, so he used the 2 + 2 = 4 approach to focus on his reasons.

The Yardstick Approach

The **yardstick approach** is useful when you need to use a number of criteria to decide which option to select from two or more possibilities. With this approach, you begin by discussing the problem or opportunity, and then you list the criteria that will guide the decision. The body of the report then evaluates the alternatives against those criteria. Figure 11.13 on page 396 is an outline of a feasibility report that uses the yardstick approach, using five criteria to evaluate two alternative courses of action.

The yardstick approach has two potential drawbacks. First, your audience needs to agree with the criteria you're using in your analysis. If they don't, they won't agree with the results of the evaluation. If you have any doubt about their agreement, build consensus before you start your report, if possible, or take extra care to explain why the criteria you're using are the best ones in this particular case. Second, the yardstick approach can get a little boring when you have many options to consider or many criteria to compare them against. One way to minimize the repetition is to compare the options in tables and then highlight the most unusual or important aspects of each alternative in the text so that you get the best of both worlds. This approach allows you to compare all the alternatives against the same yardstick while calling attention to the most significant differences among them.

Planning Proposals

The specific formats for proposals are innumerable, but they can be grouped into two general categories. *Internal proposals* request decisions from managers within the organization, such as proposals to buy new equipment or launch new research projects. *External proposals* request decisions from parties outside the organization. Examples of external proposals

7 LEARNING OBJECTIVE

Explain how to plan proposals.

include *investment proposals*, which request funding from external investors; *grant proposals*, which request funds from government agencies and other sponsoring organizations; and *sales proposals*, which suggest individualized solutions for potential customers and request purchase decisions.

The best strategy for a proposal depends on whether it is unsolicited or solicited.

The most significant factor in planning a proposal is whether the recipient has asked you to submit a proposal. *Solicited proposals* are generally prepared at the request of external parties that require a product or a service, but they may also be requested by such internal sources as management or the board of directors. To solicit proposals from potential suppliers, an organization might prepare a formal invitation to bid, called a **request for proposals (RFP)**, which includes instructions that specify exactly the type of work to be performed or products to be delivered, along with budgets, deadlines, and other requirements. Companies then respond by preparing proposals that show how they would meet

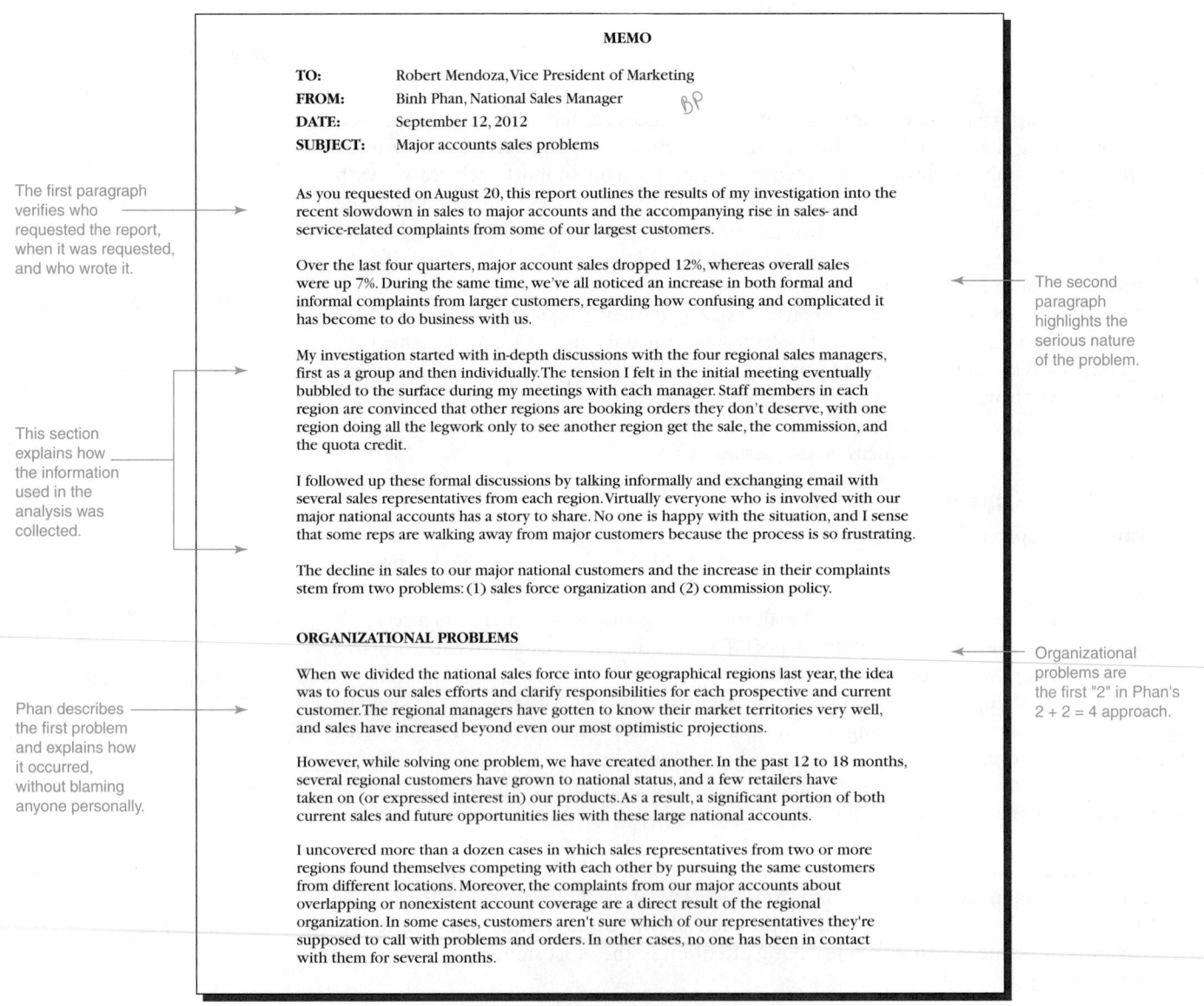

The first paragraph verifies who requested the report, when it was requested, and who wrote it.

This section explains how the information used in the analysis was collected.

Phan describes the first problem and explains how it occurred, without blaming anyone personally.

The second paragraph highlights the serious nature of the problem.

Organizational problems are the first "2" in Phan's 2 + 2 = 4 approach.

MEMO

TO: Robert Mendoza, Vice President of Marketing
FROM: Binh Phan, National Sales Manager
DATE: September 12, 2012
SUBJECT: Major accounts sales problems

As you requested on August 20, this report outlines the results of my investigation into the recent slowdown in sales to major accounts and the accompanying rise in sales- and service-related complaints from some of our largest customers.

Over the last four quarters, major account sales dropped 12%, whereas overall sales were up 7%. During the same time, we've all noticed an increase in both formal and informal complaints from larger customers, regarding how confusing and complicated it has become to do business with us.

My investigation started with in-depth discussions with the four regional sales managers, first as a group and then individually. The tension I felt in the initial meeting eventually bubbled to the surface during my meetings with each manager. Staff members in each region are convinced that other regions are booking orders they don't deserve, with one region doing all the legwork only to see another region get the sale, the commission, and the quota credit.

I followed up these formal discussions by talking informally and exchanging email with several sales representatives from each region. Virtually everyone who is involved with our major national accounts has a story to share. No one is happy with the situation, and I sense that some reps are walking away from major customers because the process is so frustrating.

The decline in sales to our major national customers and the increase in their complaints stem from two problems: (1) sales force organization and (2) commission policy.

ORGANIZATIONAL PROBLEMS

When we divided the national sales force into four geographical regions last year, the idea was to focus our sales efforts and clarify responsibilities for each prospective and current customer. The regional managers have gotten to know their market territories very well, and sales have increased beyond even our most optimistic projections.

However, while solving one problem, we have created another. In the past 12 to 18 months, several regional customers have grown to national status, and a few retailers have taken on (or expressed interest in) our products. As a result, a significant portion of both current sales and future opportunities lies with these large national accounts.

I uncovered more than a dozen cases in which sales representatives from two or more regions found themselves competing with each other by pursuing the same customers from different locations. Moreover, the complaints from our major accounts about overlapping or nonexistent account coverage are a direct result of the regional organization. In some cases, customers aren't sure which of our representatives they're supposed to call with problems and orders. In other cases, no one has been in contact with them for several months.

(continued)

Figure 11.12   Analytical Report Using the 2 + 2 = 4 Approach
To make his argument clear and compelling, Binh Phan used the 2 + 2 = 4 approach.

2

Phan brings the first problem to life by complementing the general description with a specific example.

For example, having retail outlets across the lower tier of the country, AmeriSport received pitches from reps out of our West, South, and East regions. Because our regional offices have a lot of negotiating freedom, the three were offering different prices. But all AmeriSport buying decisions were made at the Tampa headquarters, so all we did was confuse the customer. The irony of the current organization is that we're often giving our weakest selling and support efforts to the largest customers in the country.

COMMISSION PROBLEMS

Commission problems are the second "2" in Phan's 2 + 2 = 4 approach.

In discussing the second problem, he simplifies the reader's task by maintaining a parallel structure: a general description followed by a specific example.

The regional organization problems are compounded by the way we assign commissions and quota credit. Salespeople in one region can invest a lot of time in pursuing a sale, only to have the customer place the order in another region. So some sales rep in the second region ends up with the commission on a sale that was partly or even entirely earned by someone in the first region. Therefore, sales reps sometimes don't pursue leads in their regions, thinking that a rep in another region will get the commission.

For example, Athletic Express, with outlets in 35 states spread across all four regions, finally got so frustrated with us that the company president called our headquarters. Athletic Express has been trying to place a large order for tennis and golf accessories, but none of our local reps seem interested in paying attention. I spoke with the rep responsible for Nashville, where the company is headquartered, and asked her why she wasn't working the account more actively. Her explanation was that last time she got involved with Athletic Express, the order was actually placed from their L.A. regional office, and she didn't get any commission after more than two weeks of selling time.

RECOMMENDATIONS

Phan concludes the 2 + 2 = 4 approach: organizational problems + commission problems = the need for a new sales structure.

He explains how his recommendation (a new organizational structure) will solve both problems.

He acknowledges that the recommended solution does create a temporary compensation problem but expresses confidence that a solution to that can be worked out.

Our sales organization should reflect the nature of our customer base. To accomplish that goal, we need a group of reps who are free to pursue accounts across regional borders— and who are compensated fairly for their work. The most sensible answer is to establish a national account group. Any customers whose operations place them in more than one region would automatically be assigned to the national group.

In addition to solving the problem of competing sales efforts, the new structure will also largely eliminate the commission-splitting problem because regional reps will no longer invest time in prospects assigned to the national accounts team. However, we will need to find a fair way to compensate regional reps who are losing long-term customers to the national team. Some of these reps have invested years in developing customer relationships that will continue to yield sales well into the future, and everyone I talked to agrees that reps in these cases should receive some sort of compensation. Such a "transition commission" would also motivate the regional reps to help ensure a smooth transition from one sales group to the other. The exact nature of this compensation would need to be worked out with the various sales managers.

3

SUMMARY

The summary concisely restates both the problem and the recommended solution.

The regional sales organization is effective at the regional and local levels but not at the national level. We should establish a national accounts group to handle sales that cross regional boundaries. Then we'll have one set of reps who are focused on the local and regional levels and another set who are pursuing national accounts.

To compensate regional reps who lose accounts to the national team, we will need to devise some sort of payment to reward them for the years of work invested in such accounts. This can be discussed with the sales managers once the new structure is in place.

Figure 11.12 Analytical Report Using the 2 + 2 = 4 Approach *(continued)*

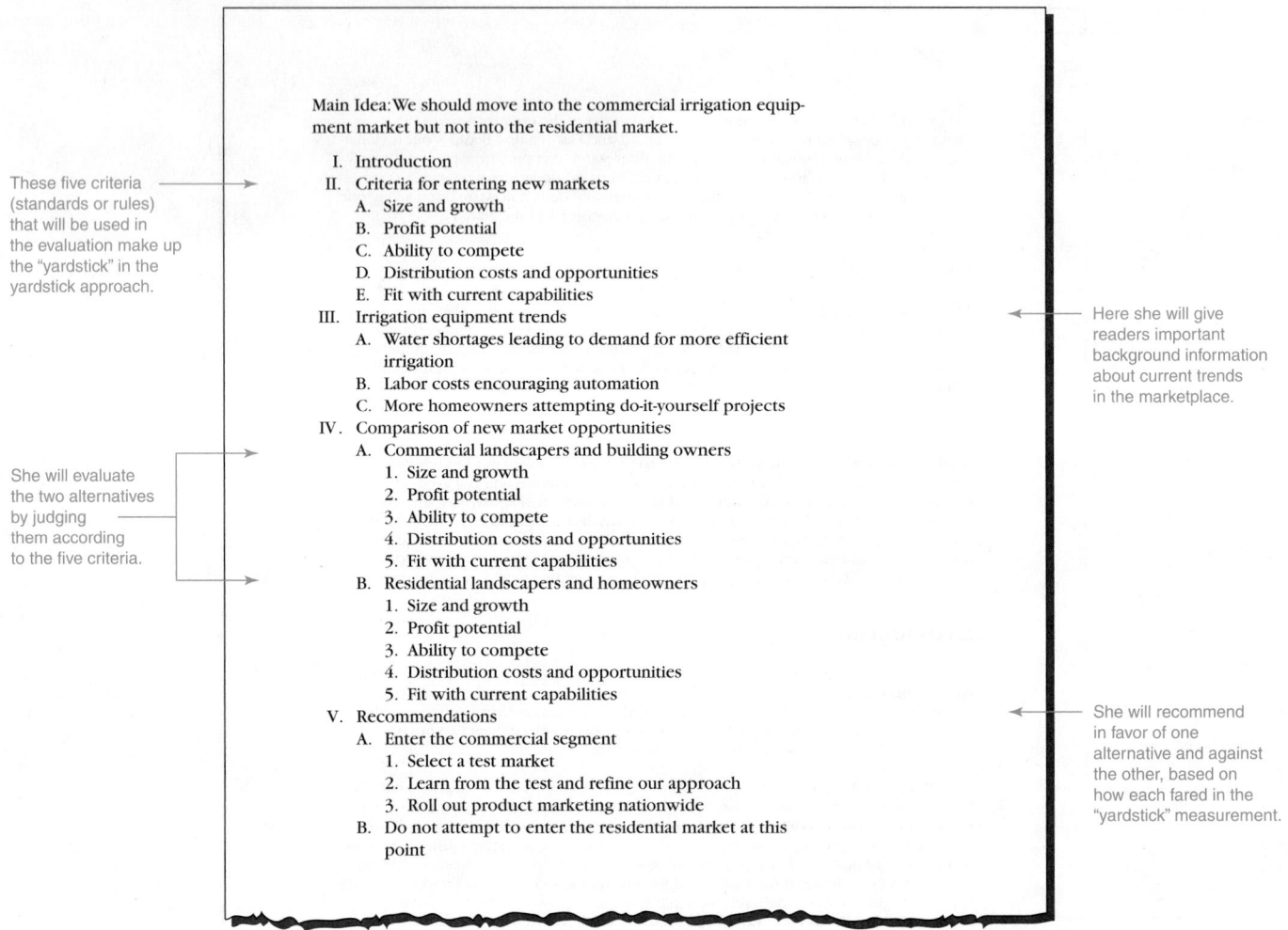

Main Idea: We should move into the commercial irrigation equipment market but not into the residential market.

I. Introduction
II. Criteria for entering new markets
    A. Size and growth
    B. Profit potential
    C. Ability to compete
    D. Distribution costs and opportunities
    E. Fit with current capabilities
III. Irrigation equipment trends
    A. Water shortages leading to demand for more efficient irrigation
    B. Labor costs encouraging automation
    C. More homeowners attempting do-it-yourself projects
IV. Comparison of new market opportunities
    A. Commercial landscapers and building owners
       1. Size and growth
       2. Profit potential
       3. Ability to compete
       4. Distribution costs and opportunities
       5. Fit with current capabilities
    B. Residential landscapers and homeowners
       1. Size and growth
       2. Profit potential
       3. Ability to compete
       4. Distribution costs and opportunities
       5. Fit with current capabilities
V. Recommendations
    A. Enter the commercial segment
       1. Select a test market
       2. Learn from the test and refine our approach
       3. Roll out product marketing nationwide
    B. Do not attempt to enter the residential market at this point

These five criteria (standards or rules) that will be used in the evaluation make up the "yardstick" in the yardstick approach.

She will evaluate the two alternatives by judging them according to the five criteria.

Here she will give readers important background information about current trends in the marketplace.

She will recommend in favor of one alternative and against the other, based on how each fared in the "yardstick" measurement.

Figure 11.13 Outline of an Analytical Report Using the Yardstick Approach
This report was provided by J. C. Hartley, a market analyst for a large Sacramento company that makes irrigation equipment for farms and ranches. "We've been so successful in the agricultural market that we're starting to run out of customers to sell to," says Hartley. "To keep the company growing, we needed to find another market. Two obvious choices to consider were commercial buildings and residences, but we needed to evaluate them carefully before making a decision."

the requirements spelled out in the RFP. In most cases, organizations that issue RFPs also provide strict guidelines on what the proposals should include, and you need to follow these guidelines carefully in order to be considered.

Unsolicited proposals offer more flexibility but a completely different sort of challenge than solicited proposals because recipients aren't expecting to receive them. In fact, your audience may not be aware of the problem or opportunity you are addressing, so before you can propose a solution, you might first need to convince your readers that a problem or an opportunity exists. Consequently, using an indirect approach is often a wise choice for unsolicited proposals.

Regardless of its format and structure, a good proposal explains what a project or course of action will involve, how much it will cost, and how the recipient and his or her organization will benefit. You can see all these elements in Figure 11.14.

A subject line with a compelling promise catches the reader's attention.

"The Solution" explains the proposed solution in enough detail to make it convincing, without burdening the reader with excessive detail.

"The Problem" describes the current situation and explains why it should be fixed.

Listing a number of compelling benefits as subheadings builds reader interest in the proposed solution.

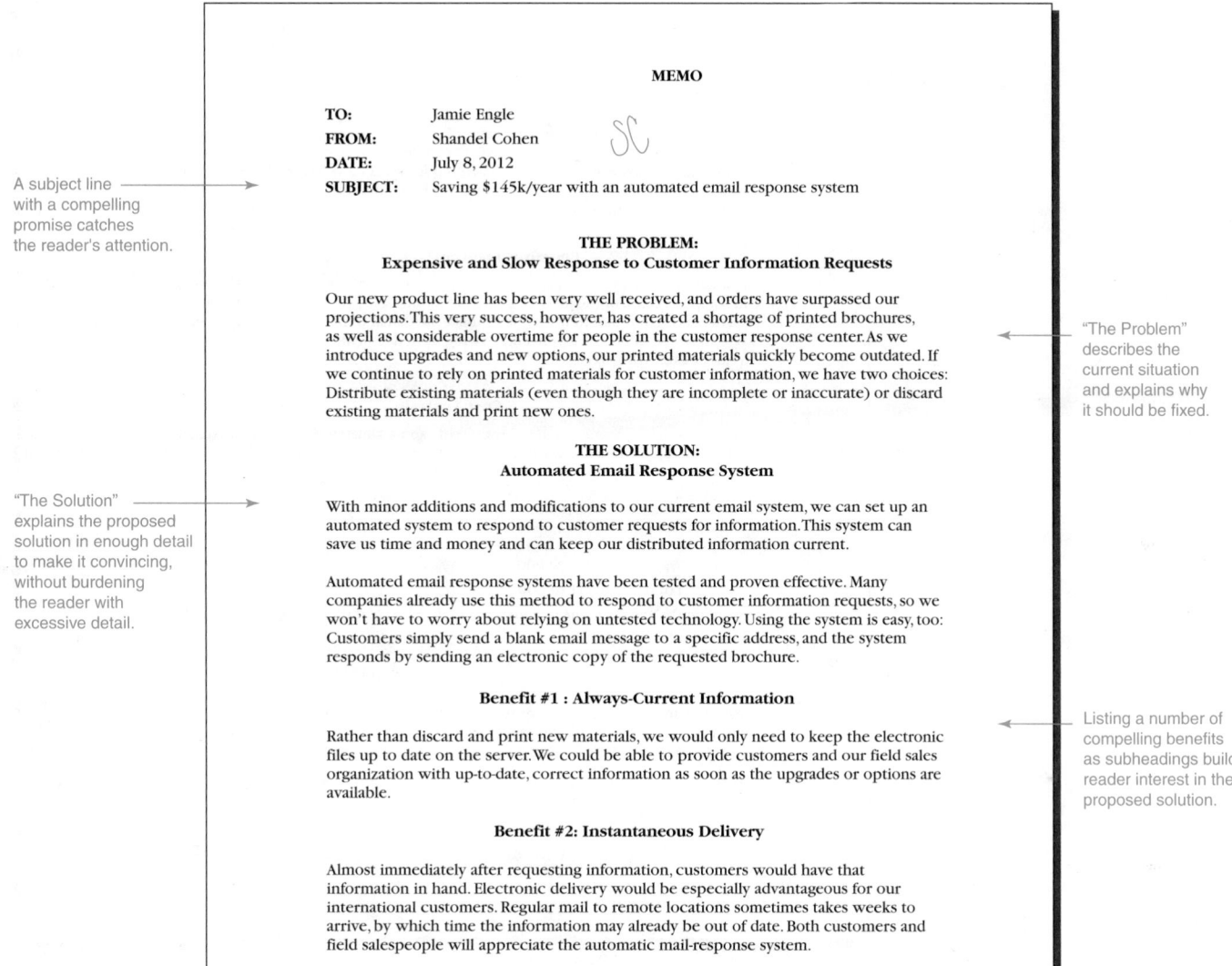

MEMO

TO: Jamie Engle
FROM: Shandel Cohen
DATE: July 8, 2012
SUBJECT: Saving $145k/year with an automated email response system

THE PROBLEM:
Expensive and Slow Response to Customer Information Requests

Our new product line has been very well received, and orders have surpassed our projections. This very success, however, has created a shortage of printed brochures, as well as considerable overtime for people in the customer response center. As we introduce upgrades and new options, our printed materials quickly become outdated. If we continue to rely on printed materials for customer information, we have two choices: Distribute existing materials (even though they are incomplete or inaccurate) or discard existing materials and print new ones.

THE SOLUTION:
Automated Email Response System

With minor additions and modifications to our current email system, we can set up an automated system to respond to customer requests for information. This system can save us time and money and can keep our distributed information current.

Automated email response systems have been tested and proven effective. Many companies already use this method to respond to customer information requests, so we won't have to worry about relying on untested technology. Using the system is easy, too: Customers simply send a blank email message to a specific address, and the system responds by sending an electronic copy of the requested brochure.

Benefit #1 : Always-Current Information

Rather than discard and print new materials, we would only need to keep the electronic files up to date on the server. We could be able to provide customers and our field sales organization with up-to-date, correct information as soon as the upgrades or options are available.

Benefit #2: Instantaneous Delivery

Almost immediately after requesting information, customers would have that information in hand. Electronic delivery would be especially advantageous for our international customers. Regular mail to remote locations sometimes takes weeks to arrive, by which time the information may already be out of date. Both customers and field salespeople will appreciate the automatic mail-response system.

Benefit #3: Minimized Waste

With our current method of printing every marketing piece in large quantities, we discard thousands of pages of obsolete catalogs, data sheets, and other materials every year. By maintaining and distributing the information electronically, we would eliminate this waste. We would also free up a considerable amount of expensive floor space and shelving that is required for storing printed materials.

(continued)

Figure 11.14   Internal Proposal
Shandel Cohen's internal proposal seeks management's approval to install an automatic mail-response system. She lays out the problem concisely, describes her proposed solution, itemizes the four benefits it would provide, and provides a clear analysis of the financial impact.

2

She acknowledges one potential shortcoming with the new approach but provides a convincing solution to that as well.

Of course, some of our customers may still prefer to receive printed materials, or they may not have access to electronic mail. For these customers, we could simply print copies of the files when we receive such requests. The new Xerox DocuColor printer just installed in the Central Services building would be ideal for printing high-quality materials in small quantities.

Benefit #4: Lower Overtime Costs

In addition to saving both paper and space, we would also realize considerable savings in wages. Because of the increased interest in our new products, we must continue to work overtime or hire new people to meet the demand. An automatic mail response system would eliminate this need, allowing us to deal with fluctuating interest without a fluctuating workforce.

Cost Analysis

The necessary equipment and software costs approximately $15,000. System maintenance and upgrades are estimated at $5,000 per year. However, those costs are offset many times over by the predicted annual savings:

A detailed breakdown of cost savings provides credible support for the $145k/year claim made in the subject line.

Printing	$100,000
Storage	25,000
Postage	5,000
Wages	20,000
Total	**$150,000**

Based on these figures, the system would save $130,000 the first year and $145,000 every year after that.

CONCLUSION

Her conclusion summarizes the benefits and invites further discussion.

An automated email response system would yield considerable benefits in both customer satisfaction and operating costs. If you approve, we can have it installed and running in 6 weeks. Please give me a call if you have any questions.

Figure 11.14   Internal Proposal (continued)

ON THE JOB: SOLVING COMMUNICATION DILEMMAS AT MYCITYWAY

Source: Courtesy of Sonpreet Bhatia, Archana Patchirajan, and Puneet Mehta, mycityway.com.

You recently joined MyCityWay as a market development manager, working on a variety of research, planning, and customer communication projects. Using what you've learned in this chapter about effective research methods and report planning, choose appropriate solutions to these report-writing challenges.

1. MyCityWay faces a problem that bedevils most smartphone app developers: an extremely crowded marketplace. The iTunes app store alone, for example, has more than 4,000 apps in its travel category. You are planning a research project to help identify tactics that

MyCityWay could use to stand out from the crowd. Which of the following problem statements would do the best job of guiding this research?
   a. We need to figure out how we can stand out from the crowd.
   b. We need to identify how leading software apps gained the brand recognition they have and whether we could adapt those tactics to our brand.
   c. We need to know if we should pursue more brand partnerships like the arrangement with BMW.
   d. We need to know if changing our brand name would improve our brand recognition.

2. Your readers appreciate how easy your reports are to read, with their generous use of previews, reviews, and transitions. For a section in the body of a report that describes the range of advertising possibilities in electronic media, which of these is the best review?

a. As this section has shown, today's new media landscape if full of intriguing, but challenging, choices, from advertising on blogs to advertising in video games.

b. As this section has shown, today's new media landscape is full of intriguing, but challenging, choices, including product placement in traditional movies and television programs, product placement in and sponsorship of online movies, webcasts, advertising on blogs and in podcasts, advertising in video games, advertising on social networks, stealth marketing and buzz marketing, and music and fashion sponsorships.

c. As this section has shown, today's new media landscape is full of intriguing, but challenging, choices:

- Product placement in traditional movies and television programs
- Product placement in and sponsorship of online movies
- Webcasts
- Advertising on blogs and in podcasts
- Advertising in video games
- Advertising on social networks
- Stealth marketing and buzz marketing
- Music and fashion sponsorships

d. As this section has shown, today's advertisers have a staggering array of new choices when it comes to connecting with target customers.

3. With several years of experience, you now find routine business reports to be fairly easy. It's usually just a matter of quickly assessing the situation at hand, gathering the information you'll need, and getting to work with organizing and writing. This morning, however, you were given an assignment that is anything but routine. The three founders have asked you to spend the next month on an analytical report that will answer a single question: What's next? They're not asking for a detailed business plan, but rather your advice on the overall direction the company should take over the next five years, after the company has created mobile apps for all the major cities around the world. Should it go after smaller cities next? Should it expand into other lines of businesses? Settle into a "maintain and protect" mode, in which it just keeps its existing products up to date, without attempting to grow? Faced with such an open-ended question, which of the following research and report writing strategies should you use?

a. Gather all the secondary research you can find on the market for mobile apps of any kind. Study these reports in depth to look for promising opportunities, and then describe the top 10 opportunities in a well-written report.

b. Design and conduct a consumer survey that is integrated with the MyCityWay app—this way you'll get data directly from the people who use the company's products. Split the survey into two audiences. Ask one group closed-ended questions, in which you identify a number of new product possibilities and ask customers to indicate which ones they would be most likely to buy. Ask the other group open-ended questions about which products the company should develop and which market opportunities it should go after. Compile the results in an analytical report focused on recommendations.

c. Conduct in-depth individual interviews with MyCityWay's founders, its major investors, and the company's top marketing and technology experts. Ask each person to give candid and complete assessments of the company's strengths and weaknesses as well as the opportunities and threats they see in the marketplace. Spend some time analyzing these in-depth answers and identify a strategic direction that has a good balance of risks and rewards and that is achievable, given the company's capabilities. Explain your analysis and recommendations in a concise report.

d. Research the history of one hundred of the world's most successful corporations to find out how they grew, and then distill those insights into a "wisdom handbook" that contains the best ideas adopted by the best companies in history.

4. MyCityWay's director of product planning believes that a great opportunity exists to convert the company's consumer-oriented mobile apps to commercial use. For example, real estate agents could use the information to scout out various neighborhoods and help buyers find the locations they'll really like. You've been assigned to write an analytical report on competition in this market segment, with the directive to study the major competitors and assess each one's strengths and weaknesses in preparation for MyCityWay's entry into the market. The report will be distributed to all executives in the company. In the course of your research, however, you conclude that the entire strategy is a mistake, that the competition in the commercial apps market is already too well-entrenched and too strong for MyCityWay to make any sort of meaningful progress. You believe the company will waste millions of dollars on the venture and that it should stay focused on the consumer segment. How should you handle this unexpected conclusion?

a. The decision to enter the commercial market has already been made, and it's not your job to question it. Don't mention this conclusion at all in your report.

b. Discuss your concerns with the director of product planning before you write your first draft and don't add this conclusion to your report unless he instructs you do to so.

c. Your conclusion is more important than following your instructions to the letter. Moreover, your discovery is too important to keep from the executive team. Organize your report with the direct approach, opening immediately with conclusion and then offering supporting evidence and reasons.

d. Add your conclusion to the report but organize the report indirectly. Insert your surprising conclusion at the very end of the report, after you've discussed the competitive situation in detail.

LEARNING OBJECTIVES CHECKUP

Assess your understanding of the principles in this chapter by reading each learning objective and studying the accompanying exercises. For fill-in-the-blank items, write the missing text in the blank provided; for multiple-choice items, circle the letter of the correct answer. You can check your responses against the answer key on page AK-2.

Objective 11.1: Adapt the three-step writing process to reports and proposals.

1. Why is it particularly important in long reports to clearly identify your purpose before you begin writing?
   a. A clear statement of purpose helps you avoid extensive revisions.
   b. A clear statement of purpose gives you the opportunity to decline projects that don't match your skill set or professional interests.
   c. A clear statement of purpose helps you avoid time-consuming research.
   d. All of the above are important factors.

2. _____ reports focus on the delivery of facts, figures, and other types of information, without making recommendations or proposing new ideas or solutions.

3. _____ reports assess a situation or problem and recommend a course of action in response.

4. _____ present persuasive messages that encourage readers to take a specific course of action.

Objective 11.2: Describe an effective process for conducting business research, explain how to evaluate the credibility of an information source, and identify the five ways to use research results.

5. Which of the following is the appropriate first step in any research project?
   a. Evaluate secondary research to see if you can reuse anything from earlier research projects.
   b. Conduct a preliminary phone survey to measure the extent of the issue you're about to research.
   c. Conduct a thorough statistical analysis of any existing data.
   d. Develop a research plan by familiarizing yourself with the subject, identifying information gaps, and prioritizing research needs.

6. Consider this series of values: 14, 37, 44, 44, 44, 74, 76, 88, 93, 100, and 112.
   a. The mean is 66.
   b. The median is 74.
   c. The mode is 44.
   d. All of the above are correct.

7. Research being conducted for the first time is called _____ research.

8. Research that was conducted for other projects but is being considered for a new project is called _____ research.

9. Why is it important to understand the purpose for which source material was created?
   a. Knowing the purpose helps alert you to any potential biases.
   b. You are required to indicate this purpose in your bibliography.
   c. The purpose tells you whether the material is copyrighted.
   d. The purpose tells you whether you need to pay usage rights.

10. If you uncover critically important information (the sort that could make or break your company) that is from a credible source and appears to be unbiased, well documented, current, and complete but is the only source of this information you can find, how should you handle this situation in your subsequent reporting?
    a. Use it as you would use any other information.
    b. Use it but clearly indicate the source in your report.
    c. Use it but clearly indicate in your report that this is the only source of the information and you weren't able to verify it through a second, independent source.
    d. Don't use it.

11. What is the difference between quoting and paraphrasing?
    a. Quoting is for printed sources; paraphrasing is for electronic sources.
    b. Quoting is legal (as long as appropriate credit is given); paraphrasing is not.
    c. Paraphrasing is just a shorter version of quoting.
    d. Quoting is reproducing someone else's writing exactly as you found it; paraphrasing is expressing someone else's ideas in your own words.

Objective 11.3: Explain the role of secondary research, and describe the two major categories of online research tools.

12. Secondary research is
    a. Generally used before primary research
    b. Generally used after primary research
    c. Generally used at the same time as primary research
    d. Another name for unpaid research

13. Why is it important to fully understand the instructions for using an individual search engine, web directory, database, or other computer-based research tool?
    a. You can be fined if you use these tools improperly.
    b. Most search tools don't return any results if you don't know how to use them.
    c. Using the tool without understanding how it works can produce unpredictable and misleading results.
    d. Today's search tools are so easy to use that you don't need to worry about learning the details.

Objective 11.4: Explain the role of primary research, and identify the two most common forms of primary research for business communication purposes.

14. What does it mean for a survey to be valid?
    a. It works every time.
    b. It returns the data and information the researchers expect it to return.
    c. Meets all ethical and legal criteria in a given industry.
    d. It measures what it was intended to measure.

15. "Why do some consumers refuse to switch to smartphones?" is an example of
    a. An open-ended question
    b. A value statement
    c. A closed question
    d. An in-depth question

Objective 11.5: Explain how to plan informational reports and website content.

16. Which of the following is not a common way to organize informational reports?
    a. Comparison
    b. Section size
    c. Sequence
    d. Chronology

17. The structure and navigational flow of all the parts of a website are commonly referred to as _____ _____.

Objective 11.6: Identify the three most common ways to organize analytical reports.

18. If you have a long history of success in business and are highly regarded by your audience, which two organizing models will probably be sufficient for most reports to this audience?
    a. Focusing on conclusions or focusing on recommendations
    b. Focusing on conclusions and focusing on troubleshooting
    c. Focusing on logic or focusing on analysis
    d. Focusing on reason and focusing on logic

Objective 11.7: Explain how to plan proposals.

19. What is the most significant factor to consider when planning a business proposal?
    a. Whether the recipient prefers printed or electronic media
    b. Whether the proposal is solicited or unsolicited
    c. The number of writers who will be involved
    d. Whether the audience will be receptive to new ideas

20. RFP stands for
    a. Request for proposals
    b. Reason for proposing
    c. Release form project
    d. Research for proposal

Quick Learning Guide

MyBcommLab

Log on to www.pearsoninternationaleditions
.com/mybcommlab to access study and
assessment aids associated with this chapter.
If you are not using MyBcommLab, you can
access the Real-Time Updates http://real-
timeupdates.com/ebc10.

LEARNING OBJECTIVES

1. Adapt the three-step writing process to reports and proposals. [page 367]

2. Describe an effective process for conducting business research, explain how to evaluate the credibility of an information source, and identify the five ways to use research results. [page 373]

3. Explain the role of secondary research and describe the two major categories of online research tools. [page 378]

4. Explain the role of primary research and identify the two most common forms of primary research for business communication purposes. [page 383]

5. Explain how to plan informational reports and website content. [page 387]

6. Identify the three most common ways to organize analytical reports. [page 390]

7. Explain how to plan proposals. [page 393]

KEY TERMS

2 + 2 = 4 approach Logical argumentation approach that convinces readers of your point of view by demonstrating how everything "adds up"

analytical reports Reports that offer both information and analysis; they can also include recommendations

closed questions Questions with a fixed range of possible answers

conclusion A logical interpretation of the facts and other information in a report

focus group A form of group interview in which a moderator leads participants through a series of questions while a research team hidden behind a one-way mirror listens to their responses and observes their nonverbal behavior.

hypothesis A potential explanation that needs to be tested and verified

information architecture The structure and navigational flow of all the parts of a website

informational reports Reports that offer data, facts, feedback, and other types of information, without analysis or recommendations

knowledge management (KM) Set of technologies, policies, and procedures that let colleagues capture and share information throughout an organization

mean Equal to the sum of all the items in the group divided by the number of items in that group; what people refer to when they use the term *average*

median The midpoint of a series, with an equal number of items above and below

mode The number that occurs more often than any other in a sample

online databases Online compilations of newspapers, magazines, journals, and other information sources

open-ended questions Questions without simple, predetermined answers; used to solicit opinions, insights, and information

primary research New research done specifically for the current project

problem factoring Dividing a problem into a series of smaller questions that try to identify cause and effect

problem statement Defines the problem for which a research project will be designed to collect data and information

proposals Reports that combine information delivery and persuasive communication

recommendation A suggested course of action

request for proposals (RFP) A formal invitation to bid on a contract

search engines Online search tools that identify individual webpages that contain specific words or phrases you've asked for

secondary research Research done previously for another purpose is considered

statement of purpose Planning statement that defines why you are preparing the report

topical organization Arranging material according to comparisons, importance, sequence, chronology, spatial orientation, geography, or category

trends Repeatable patterns taking place over time

web directories Online lists of websites selected by human editors

yardstick approach Logical argumentation approach that uses a number of criteria to evaluate one or more possible solutions

APPLY YOUR KNOWLEDGE

To review chapter content related to each question, refer to the indicated Learning Objective.

1. Why must you be careful when using information from the Internet in a business report? [LO-2]

2. Companies occasionally make mistakes that expose confidential information, such as when employees lose laptop computers containing sensitive data files or webmasters forget to protect confidential webpages from search engine indexes. If you conducted an online search that turned up competitive information on webpages that were clearly intended to be private, what would you do? Explain your answer. [LO-3]

3. Can you use the same approach for planning website content as you use for planning printed reports? Why or why not? [LO-5]

4. If you were writing a recommendation report for an audience that doesn't know you, would you use the direct approach, focusing on the recommendation, or the indirect approach, focusing on logic? Why? [LO-6]

5. Why are unsolicited proposals more challenging to write than solicited proposals? [LO-7]

PRACTICE YOUR SKILLS

Message for Analysis: Evaluating a Report
[LO-1], [LO-5]

The Securities and Exchange Commission (SEC) requires every public company to file a comprehensive annual report (form 10-K) electronically. Many companies post links to these reports on their websites, along with links to other company reports. Visit the website of Dell, at www.dell.com, and find the company's most recent annual reports: 10-K and Year in Review. Compare the style and format of the two reports. For which audience(s) is the Year in Review targeted? Who besides the SEC might be interested in the Annual Report 10-K? Which report do you find easier to read? More interesting? More detailed?

Exercises

Active links for all websites in this chapter can be found on MyBcommLab; see your User Guide for instructions on accessing the content for this chapter. Each activity is labeled according to the primary skill or skills you will need to use. To review relevant chapter content, you can refer to the indicated Learning Objective. In some instances, supporting information will be found in another chapter, as indicated.

1. **Planning: Analyzing the Situation [LO-1]** South by Southwest (SXSW) is a family of conferences and festivals in Austin, Texas, that showcase some of the world's most creative talents in music, interactive media, and film. In addition to being a major entertainment venue for a week every March, SXSW is also an increasingly important *trade show*, an opportunity for companies to present products and services to potential customers and business partners. You work for a company that makes music training equipment, such as an electronic keyboard with an integrated computer screen that guides learners through every step of learning to play the keyboard. Your manager has asked you to look into whether the company should rent an exhibition booth at SXSW next year. Prepare a work plan for an analytical report that will assess the promotional opportunities at SXSW and make a recommendation on exhibiting. Include the statement of purpose, a problem statement for any research you will conduct, a description of what will result from your investigation, the sources and methods of data collection, and a preliminary outline. Visit the SXSW website, at http://sxsw.com, for more information.[19]

2. **Planning: Analyzing the Situation [LO-1]** Sales at The Style Shop, a clothing store for men, have declined for the third month in a row. Your boss is not sure if this decline is due to a weak economy or if it's due to another unknown reason. She has asked you to investigate the situation and to submit a report to her highlighting some possible reasons for the decline. Develop a statement of purpose for your report.

3. **Research: Documenting Sources [LO-2]** Select five business articles from a combination of print and online sources. Develop a resource list, using Appendix B as a guideline.

4. **Research: Evaluating Sources; Collaboration: Team Projects [LO-2], Chapter 2** Break into small groups and find four websites that provide business information such as company or industry news, trends, analysis, facts, or performance data. Using the criteria discussed under "Evaluating Your Sources," evaluate the credibility of the information presented on these websites.

5. **Research: Using Research Results [LO-3]** Select an article from a reputable business magazine, blog, or website. Read the article and highlight its key points. Summarize the article in fewer than 100 words, paraphrasing the key points.

6. **Research: Conducting Secondary Research [LO-3]** Using online, database, or printed sources, find the following information. Be sure to properly cite your source, using the formats discussed in Appendix B.

   a. Contact information for the American Management Association

   b. Median weekly earnings of men and women by occupation

   c. Current market share for Perrier water

   d. Performance ratios for office supply retailers

   e. Annual stock performance for Hewlett-Packard

   f. Number of franchise outlets in the United States

   g. Composition of the U.S. workforce by profession

7. **Research: Conducting Secondary Research [LO-3]** Select any public company and find the following information.

   a. Names of the company's current officers

   b. List of the company's products or services (if the company has a large number of products, list the product lines instead)

   c. Current issues in the company's industry

   d. Outlook for the company's industry as a whole

8. **Research: Using Research Results [LO-3]** Your boss has asked you to analyze and report on your division's sales for the first nine months of this year. Using the following data from company invoices, calculate the mean for each quarter and all averages for the year to date. Then identify and discuss the quarterly sales trends.

January	$24,600	August	30,500
April	21,200	March	23,000
July	29,900	June	26,800
February	25,900	September	26,600
May	24,600		

9. **Research: Conducting Primary Research (Surveys) [LO-4]** You work for a movie studio that is producing a young director's first motion picture—the story of a group of unknown musicians finding work and making a reputation in a competitive industry. Unfortunately, some of your friends say that the 182-minute movie is simply too long. Others say they couldn't imagine any sequences to cut out. Your boss wants to test the movie on a regular audience and ask viewers to complete a questionnaire that will help the director decide whether edits are needed and, if so, where. Design a questionnaire that you can use to solicit valid answers for a report to the director about how to handle the audience's reaction to the movie.

10. **Research: Conducting Primary Research (Interviews) [LO-4]** You're conducting an information interview with a manager in another division of your company. Partway through the interview, the manager shows clear signs of impatience. How should you respond? What might you do differently to prevent this from happening in the future? Explain your answers.

11. **Message Strategies: Informational Reports [LO-5]** Imagine you're the manager of campus recruiting for Nortel, a Canadian telecommunications firm. Each of your four recruiters interviews up to 11 college seniors every day. What kind of personal activity report can you design to track the results of these interviews? List the areas you would want each recruiter to report on and explain how each would help you manage the recruiting process (and the recruiters) more effectively.

12. **Message Strategies: Informational Reports [LO-5]** Assume that your college president has received many student complaints about campus parking problems. You are appointed to chair a student committee organized to investigate the problems and recommend solutions. The president gives you a file labeled "Parking: Complaints from Students," and you jot down the essence of the complaints as you inspect the contents. Your notes look like this:

- Inadequate student spaces at critical hours
- Poor night lighting near the computer center
- Inadequate attempts to keep resident neighbors from occupying spaces
- Dim marking lines
- Motorcycles taking up full spaces
- Discourteous security officers
- Spaces (usually empty) reserved for college officials
- Relatively high parking fees
- Full fees charged to night students even though they use the lots only during low demand periods
- Vandalism to cars and a sense of personal danger
- Inadequate total space
- Harassment of students parking on the street in front of neighboring house

Now prepare an outline for an informational report to be submitted to committee members. Use a topical organization for your report that categorizes this information.

13. **Message Strategies: Informational Reports [LO-5]** From your college library, company websites, or an online service such as www.annualreportservice.com, find the annual reports recently released by two corporations in the same industry. Analyze each report and be prepared to discuss the following questions in class.

   a. What organizational differences, if any, do you see in the way each corporation discusses its annual performance? Are the data presented clearly so that shareholders can draw conclusions about how well the company performed?

   b. What goals, challenges, and plans do top managers emphasize in their discussion of results?

   c. How do the format and organization of each report enhance or detract from the information being presented?

14. **Message Strategies: Analytical Reports [LO-6]** Three years ago, your company (a carpet manufacturer) modernized its Georgia plant in anticipation of increasing demand for carpets. Because of the depressed housing market, the increase in demand for new carpets has been slow to materialize. As a result, the company has excess capacity at its Georgia and California plants. On the basis of your research, you have recommended that the company close the California plant. The company president has asked you to prepare a justification report to support your recommendation. Here are the facts you gathered by interviewing the respective plant managers:

Operational Statistics

- *Georgia plant:* This plant has newer equipment, productivity is higher, it employs 100 nonunion production workers, and it ships $12 million in carpets a year. The hourly base wage is $16.
- *California plant:* California plant employs 80 union production workers and ships $8 million in carpets a year. The hourly base wage is $20.

Financial Implications

- *Savings by closing California plant:* (1) Increase productivity by 17 percent; (2) reduce labor costs by 20 percent (total labor savings would be $1 million per year; see assumptions); (3) annual local tax savings of $120,000 (Georgia has a more favorable tax climate).

- *Sale of Pomona, California, land:* Purchased in 1952 for $200,000. Current market value $2.5 million. Net profit (after capital gains tax) over $1 million.
- *Sale of plant and equipment:* Fully depreciated. Any proceeds are a windfall.
- *Costs of closing California plant:* One-time deductible charge of $250,000 (relocation costs of $100,000 and severance payments totaling $150,000).

Assumptions

- Transfer 5 workers from California to Georgia.
- Hire 45 new workers in Georgia.
- Lay off 75 workers in California.
- Georgia plant would require a total of 150 workers to produce the combined volume of both plants.

  a. Which approach (focus on conclusions, recommendations, or logical arguments) will you use to structure your report to the president? Why?

  b. Suppose this report were to be circulated to plant managers and supervisors instead. What changes, if any, might you make in your approach?

  c. List some conclusions that you might draw from the above information to use in your report.

  d. Using the structure you selected for your report to the president, draft a final report outline with first- and second-level informative headings.

15. **Message Strategies: Proposals; Collaboration: Team Projects [LO-7], Chapter 2** Break into small groups and identify an operational problem occurring at your campus that involves either registration, university housing, food services, parking, or library services. Then develop a workable solution to that problem. Finally, develop a list of pertinent facts that your team will need to gather to convince the reader that the problem exists and that your solution will work.

16. **Message Strategies: Proposals [LO-7]** Read the step-by-step hints and examples for writing a funding proposal at www.learnerassociates.net/proposal. Review the entire sample proposal online. What details did the writer decide to include in the appendixes? Why was this material placed in the appendixes and not the main body of the report? According to the writer's tips, when is the best time to prepare a project overview?

EXPAND YOUR SKILLS

Critique the Professionals

Company websites function as multidimensional informational reports, with numerous sections and potentially endless ways for visitors to navigate through all the various pages. Locate the website of a public corporation with a fairly complex website. Imagine that you are approaching the site as (a) a potential employee, (b) a potential investor (purchaser of stock), (c) a member of one of the local communities in which this company operators, and (d) a potential customer of the company's products and services. Analyze how easy or difficult it is to find the information that each of these four visitors would typically be looking for. Using whatever medium your instructor requests, write a brief analysis of the information architecture of the website, describing what works well and what doesn't work well.

Sharpening Your Career Skills Online

Bovée and Thill's Business Communication Web Search, at http://businesscommunicationblog.com/websearch, is a unique research tool designed specifically for business communication research. Use the Web Search function to find a website, video, PDF document, podcast, or PowerPoint presentation that offers advice on conducting research for business reports. Write a brief email message to your instructor, describing the item that you found and summarizing the career skills information you learned from it.

IMPROVE YOUR GRAMMAR, MECHANICS, AND USAGE

The following exercises help you improve your knowledge of and power over English grammar, mechanics, and usage. Turn to the "Handbook of Grammar, Mechanics, and Usage" at the end of this book and review all of Sections 2.1 (Periods), 2.2 (Question Marks), and 2.3 (Exclamation Points). Then look at the following 10 items. Circle the letter of the preferred choice in the following groups of sentences. (Answers to these exercises appear on page AK-4.)

1. a. Eugene ordered a report to be prepared on Animaster, Inc.?
   b. Eugene ordered a report to be prepared on Animaster, Inc.

2. a. This award means that they are the best-run new enterprise, don't you agree?
   b. This award means that they are the best-run new enterprise, don't you agree.

3. a. He has done his MBA, so I hired him for our HR department.
   b. He has done his M.B.A, so I hired him for our HR department.

4. a. He can be reached at 5624 S. Edward St., Pittsburgh, PA 15205.
   b. He can be reached at 5624 S. Edward St., Pittsburgh, PA. 15205.

5. a. Deb exclaimed, "Does he know what he has done! Things like this will get him fired."
   b. Deb exclaimed, "Does he know what he has done? Things like this will get him fired!"

6. a. Our hotel rates depend on the stability of the US economy.
   b. Our hotel rates depend on the stability of the U.S. economy.

7. a. Do market surveys work as effectively as we think they do? Yes and no!
   b. Do market surveys work as effectively as we think they do? Yes and no.

8. a. Can you give her your address so that she can send it to you by mail?
   b. Can you give her your address so that she can send it to you by mail.

9. **a.** Have you found a replacement for Phil, or should we put an ad in the paper.
   b. Have you found a replacement for Phil, or should we put an ad in the paper?

10. **a.** What I say is, "Should you quit if this happens?" No!
    b. What I say is, "Should you quit if this happens"? No!

For additional exercises focusing on periods, question marks, and exclamation points, visit MyBcommLab. Click on Chapter 11, click on Additional Exercises to Improve Your Grammar, Mechanics, and Usage, and click on 17. Punctuation B.

REFERENCES

1. Adapted from MyCityWay website, accessed 5 March 2011, http://mycityway.com; BMW i website, accessed 5 March 2011, www.bmw-i.com; Adam Bluestein and Amy Barrett, "How Business-Plan Competitions Reward Innovation," Inc., 1 July 2010, www.inc.com; Nick Saint, "Mayor Bloomberg Announces First Investment by NYC-Sponsored Venture Fund: MyCityWay," SAI Business Insider, 25 May 2010, www.businessinsider.com; Heidi Brown, "How to Write a Winning Business Plan," Forbes, 18 June 2010, www.forbes.com; NYC DataMine website, accessed 5 March 2011, www.nyc.gov.

2. Legal-Definitions.com, accessed 17 December 2003, www.legal-definitions.com.

3. Lynn Quitman Troyka, *Simon & Schuster Handbook for Writers,* 6th ed. (Upper Saddle River, N.J.: Simon & Schuster, 2002), 481.

4. "How to Paraphrase Effectively: 6 Steps to Follow," Research-Paper.com, accessed 26 October 1998, www.researchpaper.com/writing_center/30.html.

5. "Mahalo," CrunchBase, accessed 25 July 2010, www.crunchbase.com.

6. AllTheWeb.com advanced search page, accessed 27 August 2005, www.alltheweb.com; Google advanced search page, accessed 27 August 2005, www.google.com; Yahoo! advanced search page, accessed 27 August 2005, www.yahoo.com.

7. Christina Warren, "Yolink Helps Web Researchers Search Behind Links," Mashable, 24 July 2010, http://mashable.com.

8. A. B. Blankenship and George Edward Breen, *State of the Art Marketing Research* (Chicago: NTC Business Books, 1993), 136.

9. Naresh K. Malhotra, *Basic Marketing Research* (Upper Saddle River, N.J.: Prentice-Hall, 2002), 314–317; "How to Design and Conduct A Study," *Credit Union Magazine,* October 1983, 36–46.

10. Product features page, SurveyMonkey.com, accessed 29 October 2006, www.surveymonkey.com.

11. Tesco website, accessed 25 July 2010, www.tesco.com.

12. Sherwyn P. Morreale and Courtland L. Bovée, *Excellence in Public Speaking* (Fort Worth, Tex.: Harcourt Brace College Publishers, 1998), 177.

13. Morreale and Bovée, *Excellence in Public Speaking,* 182.

14. A. B. Blankenship and George Edward Breen, *State of the Art Marketing Research* (Lincolnwood, Ill.: NTC Business Books, 1992), 225.

15. Jakob Nielsen, "How Users Read on the Web," accessed 11 November 2004, www.useit.com/alertbox/9710a.html.

16. Reid Goldsborough, "Words for the Wise," *Link-Up,* September–October 1999, 25–26.

17. Julie Rohovit, "Computer Eye Strain: The Dilbert Syndrome," Virtual Hospital website, accessed 9 November 2004, www.vh.org.

18. Holtz, "Writing for the Wired World," 28–29.

19. Adapted from SXSW website, accessed 27 July 2010, http://sxsw.com; Catherine Holahan and Spencer E. Ante, "SXSW: Where Tech Mingles with Music," *BusinessWeek,* 7 March 2008, www.businessweek.com.

Writing Reports and Proposals

12

LEARNING OBJECTIVES   After studying this chapter, you will be able to

1 Explain how to adapt to your audiences when writing reports and proposals, and describe the choices involved in drafting report and proposal content

2 Identify five characteristics of effective writing in online reports, and explain how to adapt your writing approach for wikis

3 Discuss six principles of graphic design, and identify the most common types of visuals used to present data, information, concepts, and ideas

4 Explain how to integrate visuals with text effectively and how to verify the quality of your visuals

MyBcommLab Where you see MyBcommLab in this chapter, go to www.pearsoninternationaleditions.com/mybcommlab for additional activities on the topic being discussed.

ON THE JOB: COMMUNICATING AT **TELLABS**

The annual reports written by Tellabs's George Stenitzer go beyond regulatory compliance to helping investors understand the business and its financial performance.
Source: Courtesy Tellabs. Photo by Robert Seale.

Redefining the Annual Report with Audience-Focused Writing

Few reports get as much scrutiny as corporate annual reports, and the feedback from many readers is not particularly positive.

These compliance reports are required of every company listed on U.S. stock exchanges, and investors pore over them, looking for clues about a company's financial health and prospects. However, investor surveys suggest that many readers don't believe they are getting the information they need in order to make intelligent decisions about investing in a company's stock. Some companies have even been sued in recent years over their annual reports, with investors accusing them of withholding or obscuring vital information.

In this environment of uncertainty and outright mistrust, writers who communicate clearly and openly tend to stand out from the crowd. One such writer is George Stenitzer, vice president of corporate communication for Tellabs, a major producer of equipment for Internet service providers based in Naperville, Illinois. According to one widely respected consultant who assesses the quality of annual reports, Stenitzer's work practically demands to be read, thanks to its brevity, forthright style, full disclosure of important financial information, numerous features that enhance readability, and attractive design.

While annual report writers must comply with a complex array of legal requirements, Stenitzer's view is that accuracy and compliance—while vital—are not enough. He recognizes that many companies still lean in the direction of minimal disclosure, saying just enough to satisfy government regulations, but Stenitzer's goal is to help investors truly understand the nature of Tellabs's business and its financial performance. As he puts it, "The test for investor communications is shifting from technical accuracy and legal compliance to clear communication and investor understanding."

The proof of his approach seems to bear out in investor surveys. In an environment in which many investors are extremely skeptical of, or even confused by, what they read in annual reports, one of Tellabs's recent annual reports was rated "good" or "very good" by an overwhelming 83 percent of readers.[1]

www.tellabs.com

Composing Reports and Proposals

George Stenitzer (profiled in the chapter opener) can tell you how important the writing stage is in the development of successful reports and proposals. This chapter builds on the writing techniques and ideas you learned in Chapter 5, focusing on issues that are particularly important when preparing longer message formats, including website and wiki content. In addition, you'll get an introduction to creating effective visuals, which are a vital aspect of many reports and proposals.

As with shorter messages, take a few moments before you start writing to make sure you're ready to adapt your approach to your audience.

ADAPTING TO YOUR AUDIENCE

Successful report writers adapt to their intended audiences by being sensitive to audience needs, building strong relationships with the audience, and controlling style and tone.

Long or complex reports demand a lot from readers, making the "you" attitude especially important.

Chapter 5 introduced four aspects of audience sensitivity, and all four apply to reports and proposals: adopting the "you" attitude, maintaining a strong sense of etiquette, emphasizing the positive, and using bias-free language. Reports and proposals that are highly technical, complex, or lengthy can put heavy demands on your readers, so the "you" attitude is especially important with these long messages.

Many companies have specific guidelines for reports, particularly those intended for external audiences.

Be sure to plan how you will adapt your style and your language to reflect the image of your organization. Many companies have specific guidelines for communicating with public audiences, so make sure you're aware of these preferences before you start writing.

If you know your readers reasonably well and your report is likely to meet with their approval, you can adopt a fairly informal tone (as long as that is appropriate in your organization, of course). A more formal tone is appropriate for longer reports, especially those that deal with controversial or complex information. You also need a more formal tone when your report will be sent to other parts of the organization or to outsiders, such as customers, suppliers, or members of the community (see Figure 12.1).

Reports destined for audiences outside the United States often require a more formal tone to match the expectations of audiences in many other countries.

Communicating with people in other cultures often calls for more formality, for two reasons. First, the business environment outside the United States tends to be more formal in general, and that formality must be reflected in your communication. Second, the things you do to make a document informal (such as using humor and idiomatic language) often translate poorly from one culture to another, so you risk offending or confusing your readers.

DRAFTING REPORT CONTENT

Your credibility and career advancement are on the line with every business report you write, so make sure your content is

- **Accurate.** Be sure to double-check your facts and references and to check for typos. If an audience ever gets an inkling that your information is shaky, they'll start to view all your work with skepticism.
- **Complete.** Tell your readers what they need to know—no more, no less—and present the information in a way that is geared to their needs. In a recent Tellabs annual report, for example, George Stenitzer and his team provided a concise and easily understandable overview of the company's complex and technical product line. The subject matter is presented in a way that any investor interested in the company's stock can comprehend.[2]

- **Balanced.** Present all sides of the issue fairly and equitably and include all the essential information, even if some of the information doesn't support your line of reasoning. Omitting relevant information or facts can bias your report.
- **Clear and logical.** Save your readers time by making sure your writing is uncluttered, and proceeds logically from point to point.
- **Documented properly.** If you use primary and secondary sources for your report or proposal, be sure to properly document and give credit to your sources.

Long and somewhat rigorous sentences help give the report its formal tone. For a more consumer-oriented publication, this writing could certainly be simplified.

Eating and physical activity patterns that are focused on consuming fewer calories, making informed food choices, and being physically active can help people attain and maintain a healthy weight, reduce their risk of chronic disease, and promote overall health. The *Dietary Guidelines for Americans, 2010* exemplifies these strategies through recommendations that accommodate the food preferences, cultural traditions, and customs of the many and diverse groups who live in the United States.

By law (Public Law 101-445, Title III, 7 U.S.C. 5301 et seq.), *Dietary Guidelines for Americans* is reviewed, updated if necessary, and published every 5 years. The U.S. Department of Agriculture (USDA) and the U.S. Department of Health and Human Services (HHS) jointly create each edition. *Dietary Guidelines for Americans, 2010* is based on the *Report of the Dietary Guidelines Advisory Committee on the Dietary Guidelines for Americans, 2010* and consideration of Federal agency and public comments.

Dietary Guidelines recommendations traditionally have been intended for healthy Americans ages 2 years and older. However, *Dietary Guidelines for Americans, 2010* is being released at a time of rising concern about the health of the American population. Poor diet and physical inactivity are the most important factors contributing to an epidemic of overweight and obesity affecting men, women, and children in all segments of our society. Even in the absence of overweight, poor diet and physical inactivity are associated with major causes of morbidity and mortality in the United States. Therefore, the *Dietary Guidelines for Americans, 2010* is intended for Americans ages 2 years and older, including those at increased risk of chronic disease.

Dietary Guidelines for Americans, 2010 also recognizes that in recent years nearly 15 percent of American households have been unable to acquire adequate food to meet their needs.[1] This dietary guidance can help them maximize the nutritional content of

A less-formal report might've said something along the lines of "Poor diet and physical inactivity are killing U.S. citizens" instead of the more formal (and more precise) "are associated with major causes of morbidity and mortality."

This paragraph mentions the troubling statistic that 15 percent of U.S. households can't afford to meet basic nutritional requirements, but because the report is presenting dietary recommendations and not public policy statements about economics or other issues, the tone is objective and dispassionate.

1. Nord M, Coleman-Jensen A, Andrews M, Carlson S. Household food security in the United States, 2009. Washington (DC): U.S. Department of Agriculture, Economic Research Service. 2010 Nov. Economic Research Report No. ERR-108. Available from http://www.ers.usda.gov/publications/err108.

viii   DIETARY GUIDELINES FOR AMERICANS, 2010

(continued)

Figure 12.1   Choosing the Appropriate Tone for a Report
This report excerpt (part of the executive summary of the *Dietary Guidelines for Americans* published by the U.S. Department of Agriculture and the U.S. Department of Health and Human Services), uses a number of techniques to create a formal tone. This is a formal policy document whose intended readers are educators, government regulators, and others charged with using the information to help inform consumers. If the document had been written with consumers in mind, you can imagine how the tone might have been lighter and less formal.
Source: Courtesy of Dietary Guidelines for Americans published by the U.S. Department of Agriculture and the U.S. Department of Health and Human Services.

their meals. Many other Americans consume less than optimal intake of certain nutrients even though they have adequate resources for a healthy diet. This dietary guidance and nutrition information can help them choose a healthy, nutritionally adequate diet.

The intent of the Dietary Guidelines is to summarize and synthesize knowledge about individual nutrients and food components into an interrelated set of recommendations for healthy eating that can be adopted by the public. Taken together, the Dietary Guidelines recommendations encompass two over-arching concepts:

- **Maintain calorie balance over time to achieve and sustain a healthy weight.** People who are most successful at achieving and maintaining a healthy weight do so through continued attention to consuming only enough calories from foods and beverages to meet their needs and by being physically active. To curb the obesity epidemic and improve their health, many Americans must decrease the calories they consume and increase the calories they expend through physical activity.

- **Focus on consuming nutrient-dense foods and beverages.** Americans currently consume too much sodium and too many calories from solid fats, added sugars, and refined grains.[2] These replace nutrient-dense foods and beverages and make it difficult for people to achieve recommended nutrient intake while controlling calorie and sodium intake. A healthy eating pattern limits intake of sodium, solid fats, added sugars, and refined grains and emphasizes nutrient-dense foods and beverages—vegetables, fruits, whole grains, fat-free or low-fat milk and milk products,[3] seafood, lean meats and poultry, eggs, beans and peas, and nuts and seeds.

A basic premise of the Dietary Guidelines is that nutrient needs should be met primarily through consuming foods. In certain cases, fortified foods and dietary supplements may be useful in providing one or more nutrients that otherwise might be consumed in less than recommended amounts. Two eating patterns that embody the Dietary Guidelines are the USDA Food Patterns and their vegetarian adaptations and the DASH (Dietary Approaches to Stop Hypertension) Eating Plan.

A healthy eating pattern needs not only to promote health and help to decrease the risk of chronic diseases, but it also should prevent foodborne illness. Four basic food safety principles (Clean, Separate, Cook, and Chill) work together to reduce the risk of foodborne illnesses. In addition, some foods (such as milks, cheeses, and juices that have not been pasteurized, and undercooked animal foods) pose high risk for foodborne illness and should be avoided.

The information in the *Dietary Guidelines for Americans* is used in developing educational materials and aiding policymakers in designing and carrying out nutrition-related programs, including Federal food, nutrition education, and information programs. In addition, the *Dietary Guidelines for Americans* has the potential to offer authoritative statements as provided for in the Food and Drug Administration Modernization Act (FDAMA).

The following are the *Dietary Guidelines for Americans, 2010* Key Recommendations, listed by the chapter in which they are discussed in detail. These Key Recommendations are the most important in terms of their implications for improving public health.[4] To get the full benefit, individuals should carry out the Dietary Guidelines recommendations in their entirety as part of an overall healthy eating pattern.

This is an example of a sentence that is precise and uses language appropriate for the purpose of this report. In contrast, a document aimed primarily at consumers might've said "We've converted the latest nutritional insights into recommendations for healthy eating."

In a less-formal report, the authors might've written "One of our basic premises is that nutrient needs should be met primarily through consuming foods" or even "You should meet your nutrient needs by eating food, not by taking supplements." However, to maintain a formal tone, they avoid both first and second person usage.

2. Added sugars: Caloric sweeteners that are added to foods during processing, preparation, or consumed separately. Solid fats: Fats with a high content of saturated and/or *trans* fatty acids, which are usually solid at room temperature. Refined grains: Grains and grain products missing the bran, germ, and/or endosperm; any grain product that is not a whole grain.
3. Milk and milk products also can be referred to as dairy products.
4. Information on the type and strength of evidence supporting the Dietary Guidelines recommendations can be found at http://www.nutritionevidencelibrary.gov.

DIETARY GUIDELINES FOR AMERICANS, 2010   ix

Figure 12.1 Choosing the Appropriate Tone for a Report *(continued)*

Keeping these points in mind will help you draft the most effective introduction, body, and close for your report.

Report Introduction

As with other written business communications, the text of reports and proposals has three main sections: an introduction, a body, and a close. The *introduction* (or *opening*) is the first section in the text of any report or proposal. An effective introduction accomplishes at least four things:

Your introduction needs to put the report in context for the reader, introduce the subject, preview main ideas, and establish the tone of the document.

- Puts the report or proposal in a broader context by tying it to a problem or an assignment
- Introduces the subject or purpose of the report or proposal and indicates why the subject is important
- Previews the main ideas and the order in which they'll be covered
- Establishes the tone of the document and the writer's relationship with the audience

The specific elements you should include in an introduction depend on the nature and length of the report, the circumstances under which you're writing the report, and your relationship with the audience. An introduction could contain any or all of the following:

- **Authorization.** When, how, and by whom the report was authorized; who wrote it; and when it was submitted. This material is especially important when you don't accompany the report with a *letter of transmittal* (see Chapter 13).
- **Problem/opportunity/purpose.** The reason the report was written and what is to be accomplished as a result of your having written it.
- **Scope.** What is and what isn't covered in the report. The scope also helps with the critical job of setting the audience's expectations.
- **Background.** Any relevant historical conditions or factors that can help readers grasp the report's message.
- **Sources and methods.** The primary and secondary sources of information used. As appropriate, this section can also explain how the information was collected.
- **Definitions.** Definitions of important terms used in the report. Define any terms that might be unfamiliar to the audience or any terms you use in an unfamiliar way.
- **Limitations.** Factors beyond your control that affect the quality of the report, such as budgets, schedule constraints, or limited access to information or people. However, don't apologize or try to explain away personal shortcomings, such as your own poor planning.
- **Report organization.** The organization of the report. This "road map" helps readers understand what's coming in the report and why.

> Carefully select the elements to include in your introduction; strive for a balance between necessary, expected information and brevity.

In a brief report, these topics may be discussed in only a paragraph or two. In a longer formal report, the discussion of these topics may span several pages and constitute a significant section within the report.

Report Body

The report's *body* presents, analyzes, and interprets the information gathered during your investigation and supports the recommendations or conclusions discussed in your document (see Figure 12.2 on the next page). As with the introduction, the body of your report can require some tough decisions about which elements to include and how much detail to offer. Here again, your decisions depend on many variables, including the needs of your audience. Provide only enough detail in the body to support your conclusions and recommendations.

The topics commonly covered in a report body include

> The body of your report presents, analyzes, and interprets the information you gathered during your investigation.

- Explanations of a problem or opportunity
- Facts, statistical evidence, and trends
- Results of studies or investigations
- Discussion and analyses of potential courses of action
- Advantages, disadvantages, costs, and benefits of a particular course of action
- Procedures or steps in a process
- Methods and approaches
- Criteria for evaluating alternatives and options
- Conclusions and recommendations
- Supporting reasons for conclusions or recommendations

> The report body should contain only enough information to convey your message in a convincing fashion; don't overload readers with interesting but unnecessary material.

For analytical reports that use the direct approach, you generally state your conclusions or recommendations in the introduction and use the body to provide your evidence and support. If you're using the indirect approach, you're likely to use the body to discuss your logic and reserve your conclusions or recommendations until the very end.

Report Close

A report's *close* has three important functions:

- Emphasizes the main points of the message
- Summarizes the benefits to the reader if the document suggests a change or some other course of action
- Brings all the action items together in one place and gives the details about who should do what, when, where, and how

The close might be the only part of your report some readers have time for, so make sure it conveys the full weight of your message.

The nature of your close depends on the type of report (informational or analytical) and the approach (direct or indirect).

Research shows that the final section of a report or proposal leaves a lasting impression. The close gives you one last chance to make sure your report says what you intended.[3]

The content and length of your report close depend on your choice of direct or indirect order, among other variables. If you're using the direct approach, you can end with a summary of key points, listed in the order in which they appear in the report body. If you're using the indirect approach, you can use the close to present your conclusions or recommendations if you didn't end the body with them. Just remember that a conclusion or recommendation isn't the place to introduce new facts; your readers should have all the information they need by the time they reach this point in your report.

If your report is intended to prompt others to action, use the ending to spell out exactly what should happen next and who is responsible for each task. If you'll be taking all the

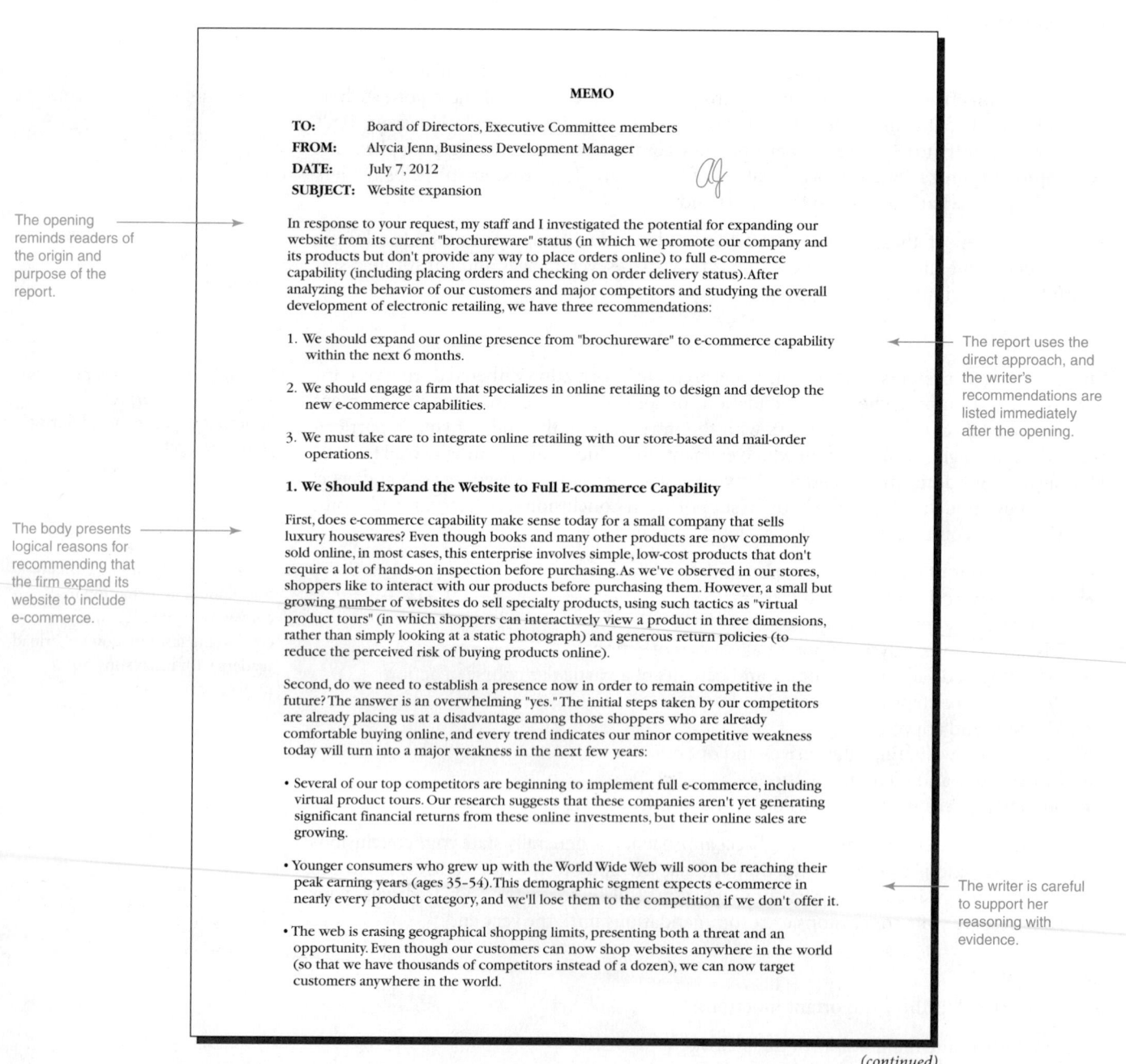

The opening reminds readers of the origin and purpose of the report.

The body presents logical reasons for recommending that the firm expand its website to include e-commerce.

The report uses the direct approach, and the writer's recommendations are listed immediately after the opening.

The writer is careful to support her reasoning with evidence.

(continued)

Figure 12.2   Effective Problem-Solving Report Focusing on Recommendations

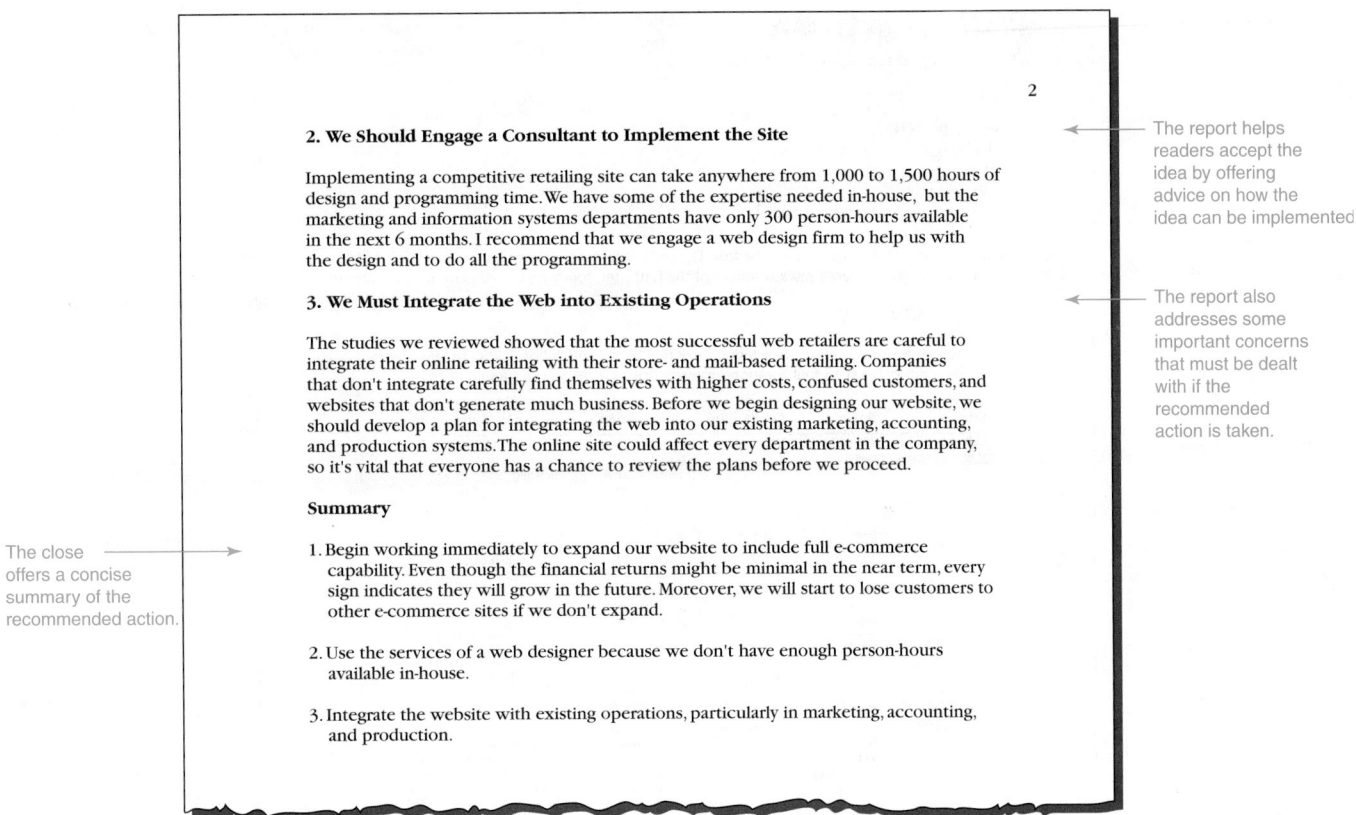

2. We Should Engage a Consultant to Implement the Site

Implementing a competitive retailing site can take anywhere from 1,000 to 1,500 hours of design and programming time. We have some of the expertise needed in-house, but the marketing and information systems departments have only 300 person-hours available in the next 6 months. I recommend that we engage a web design firm to help us with the design and to do all the programming.

3. We Must Integrate the Web into Existing Operations

The studies we reviewed showed that the most successful web retailers are careful to integrate their online retailing with their store- and mail-based retailing. Companies that don't integrate carefully find themselves with higher costs, confused customers, and websites that don't generate much business. Before we begin designing our website, we should develop a plan for integrating the web into our existing marketing, accounting, and production systems. The online site could affect every department in the company, so it's vital that everyone has a chance to review the plans before we proceed.

Summary

1. Begin working immediately to expand our website to include full e-commerce capability. Even though the financial returns might be minimal in the near term, every sign indicates they will grow in the future. Moreover, we will start to lose customers to other e-commerce sites if we don't expand.

2. Use the services of a web designer because we don't have enough person-hours available in-house.

3. Integrate the website with existing operations, particularly in marketing, accounting, and production.

The report helps readers accept the idea by offering advice on how the idea can be implemented

The report also addresses some important concerns that must be dealt with if the recommended action is taken.

The close offers a concise summary of the recommended action.

Figure 12.2   Effective Problem-Solving Report Focusing on Recommendations (continued)

actions yourself, make sure your readers understand this fact so that they know what to expect from you (see Figure 12.3 on the next page).

In a short report, the close may be only a paragraph or two. However, the close of a long report may have separate sections for conclusions, recommendations, and actions. Using separate sections helps your reader locate this material and focus on each element. Such an arrangement also gives you a final opportunity to emphasize this important content. If you have multiple conclusions, recommendations, or actions, you may want to number and list them as well for easier reference.

For long reports, you may need to divide your close into separate sections for conclusions, recommendations, and actions.

DRAFTING PROPOSAL CONTENT

With proposals, the content for each section is governed by many variables—the most important of which is the source of your proposal. If your proposal is unsolicited, you have some latitude in the scope and organization of content. However, if you are responding to a request for proposals (RFP), you need to follow the instructions in the RFP in every detail. Most RFPs spell out precisely what a proposal must cover and in what order so that all bids will be similar in form and therefore easier to compare.

The general purpose of any proposal is to persuade readers to do something, such as purchase goods or services, fund a project, or implement a program. Thus, your writing approach for a proposal is similar to that used for persuasive messages (see Chapter 10). As with other persuasive messages, the AIDA model of gaining attention, building interest, creating desire, and motivating action is an effective structure. Here are key strategies to strengthen your argument:[4]

Approach proposals the same way you approach persuasive messages.

- Demonstrate your knowledge in terms that are meaningful to the audience.
- Provide concrete information and examples.

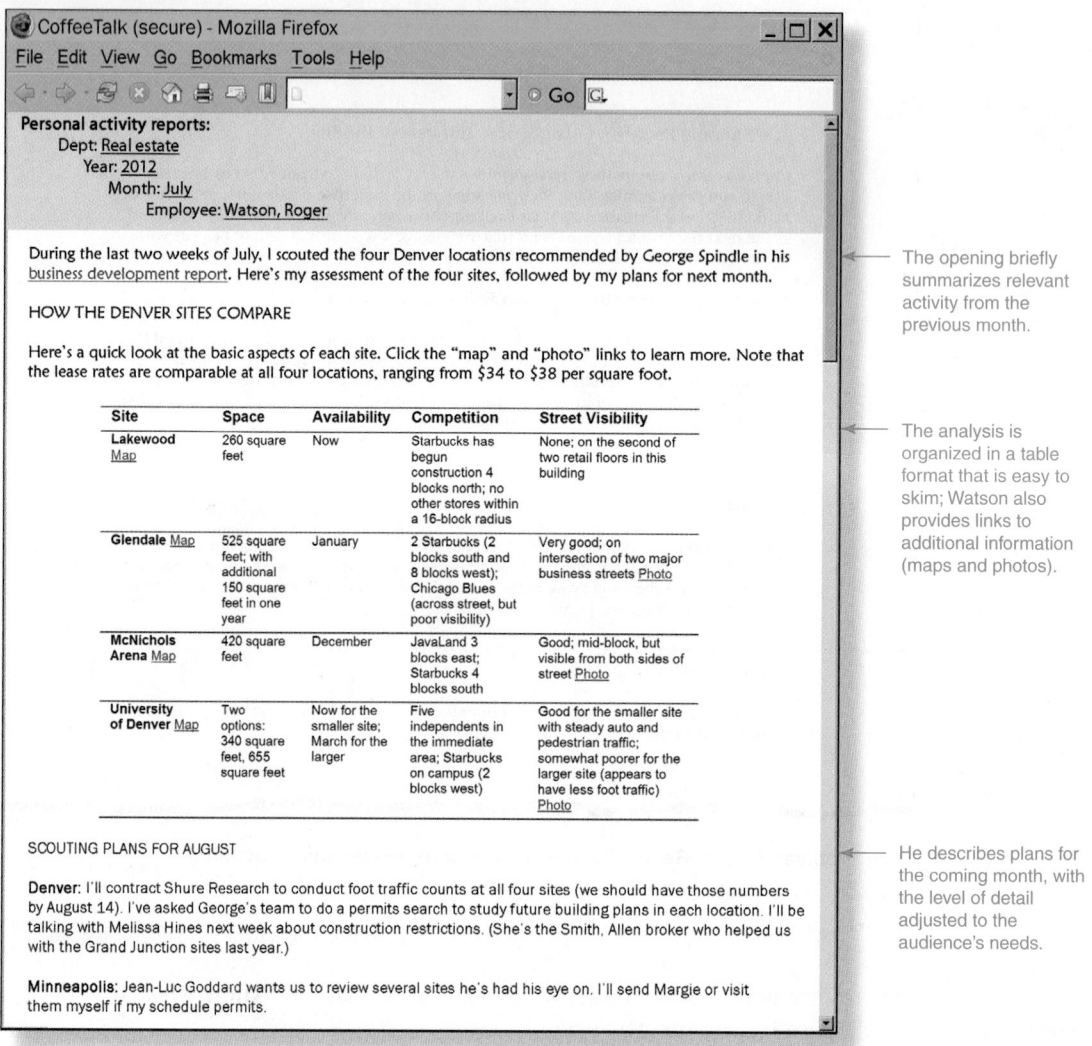

Figure 12.3 Clarifying Action Items in a Report Close
Roger Watson's personal activity report for July is a good example of efficiently conveying key information points, including a concise plan of action in the close. Note the use of hyperlinks to maps, photos, and a related report, all of which are stored on the same secure intranet site.

- Research the competition so you know what other proposals your audience is likely to read.
- Prove that your proposal is appropriate and feasible for your audience.
- Relate your product, service, or personnel to the reader's exact needs.
- Package your proposal attractively.

In addition, make sure your proposal is letter perfect, inviting, and readable. Readers will prejudge the quality of your products, services, and capabilities by the quality of the proposal you submit.

Proposal Introduction

The introduction of a proposal presents and summarizes the problem or opportunity you want to address, along with your proposed solution. If your proposal is solicited, follow the RFP's instructions about indicating which RFP you're responding to. If your proposal is unsolicited, your introduction should mention any factors that led you to submit your proposal, such as previous conversations you've had with readers. The following topics are commonly covered in a proposal introduction:

In an unsolicited proposal, your introduction needs to convince readers that a problem or an opportunity exists.

- **Background or statement of the problem or opportunity.** Briefly review the reader's situation and establish the need for action. Remember that readers may not perceive a problem or an opportunity the same way you do. In unsolicited proposals, you need to convince them that a problem or an opportunity exists before you can convince them to accept your solution.

- **Solution.** Briefly describe the change you propose and highlight your key selling points and their benefits, showing how your proposal will help readers meet their business objectives.
- **Scope.** States the boundaries of the proposal—what you will and will not do. Sometimes called "Delimitations."
- **Organization.** Orients the reader to the remainder of the proposal and calls attention to the major divisions of information.

In short proposals, your discussion of these topics will be brief—perhaps only a sentence or two for each. For long, formal proposals, each topic may warrant separate subheadings and several paragraphs of discussion.

Proposal Body

The proposal's body gives complete details on the proposed solution and specifies what the anticipated results will be. Because a proposal is by definition a persuasive message, your audience expects you to promote your offering in a confident but professional manner.

In addition to providing facts and evidence to support your conclusions, an effective body covers this information:

- **Proposed solution.** Describe what you have to offer: your concept, product, or service. Stress the benefits of your product, service, or investment opportunity that are relevant to your readers' needs and point out any advantages that you have over your competitors.
- **Work plan.** Explain the steps you'll take, the methods or resources you'll use, and the person(s) responsible. For solicited proposals, make sure your dates match those specified in the RFP. Keep in mind that if your proposal is accepted, the work plan is contractually binding, so don't promise more than you can deliver.
- **Statement of qualifications.** Describe your organization's experience, personnel, and facilities—all in relation to reader needs. You can supplement your qualifications by including a list of client references, but get permission ahead of time to use those references.
- **Costs.** Cover pricing, reimbursable expenses, discounts, and other financial concerns.

In an informal proposal, discussion of some or all of these elements may be grouped together and presented in a letter format, such as in the proposal in Figure 12.4 on the next page. In a formal proposal, the discussion of these elements can be quite long and thorough. The format may resemble long reports with multiple parts, as Chapter 13 discusses.

Proposal Close

The final section of a proposal generally summarizes your key points, emphasizes the benefits readers will get from your solution, and asks for a decision from the reader. The close is your last opportunity to persuade readers to accept your proposal. In both formal and informal proposals, make this section relatively brief, assertive (but not brash or abrupt), and confident.

HELPING REPORT READERS FIND THEIR WAY

Today's time-pressed readers want to browse reports and quickly find information of interest. To help them find what they're looking for and stay on track as they navigate through your documents, learn to make good use of headings and links, smooth transitions, and previews and reviews:

- **Headings and links.** Readers should be able to follow the structure of your document and pick up the key points of your message from the headings and subheadings.

Readers understand that a proposal is a persuasive message, so they're willing to accommodate a degree of promotional emphasis—as long as it is focused on their needs.

The work plan indicates exactly how you will accomplish the solution presented in the proposal.

The close is your last chance to convince the reader of the merits of your proposal, so make especially sure it's clear, compelling, and audience oriented.

Help your audiences navigate through your reports by providing clear directions to key pieces of content.

(See Chapter 6 for a review of what makes an effective heading.) Follow a simple, consistent arrangement that clearly distinguishes levels.

- **Transitions.** Chapter 5 defines transitions as words or phrases that tie ideas together and show how one thought is related to another. In a long report, an entire paragraph might be used to highlight transitions from one section to the next.
- **Previews and reviews.** *Preview sections* introduce important or complex topics by helping readers get ready for new information. *Review sections* come after a body of material and summarize key points to help readers absorb the information just read.

> Previews help readers prepare for upcoming information, and reviews help them verify and clarify what they've just read.

To review the tasks discussed in this section, see "Checklist: Composing Business Reports and Proposals" on page 418.

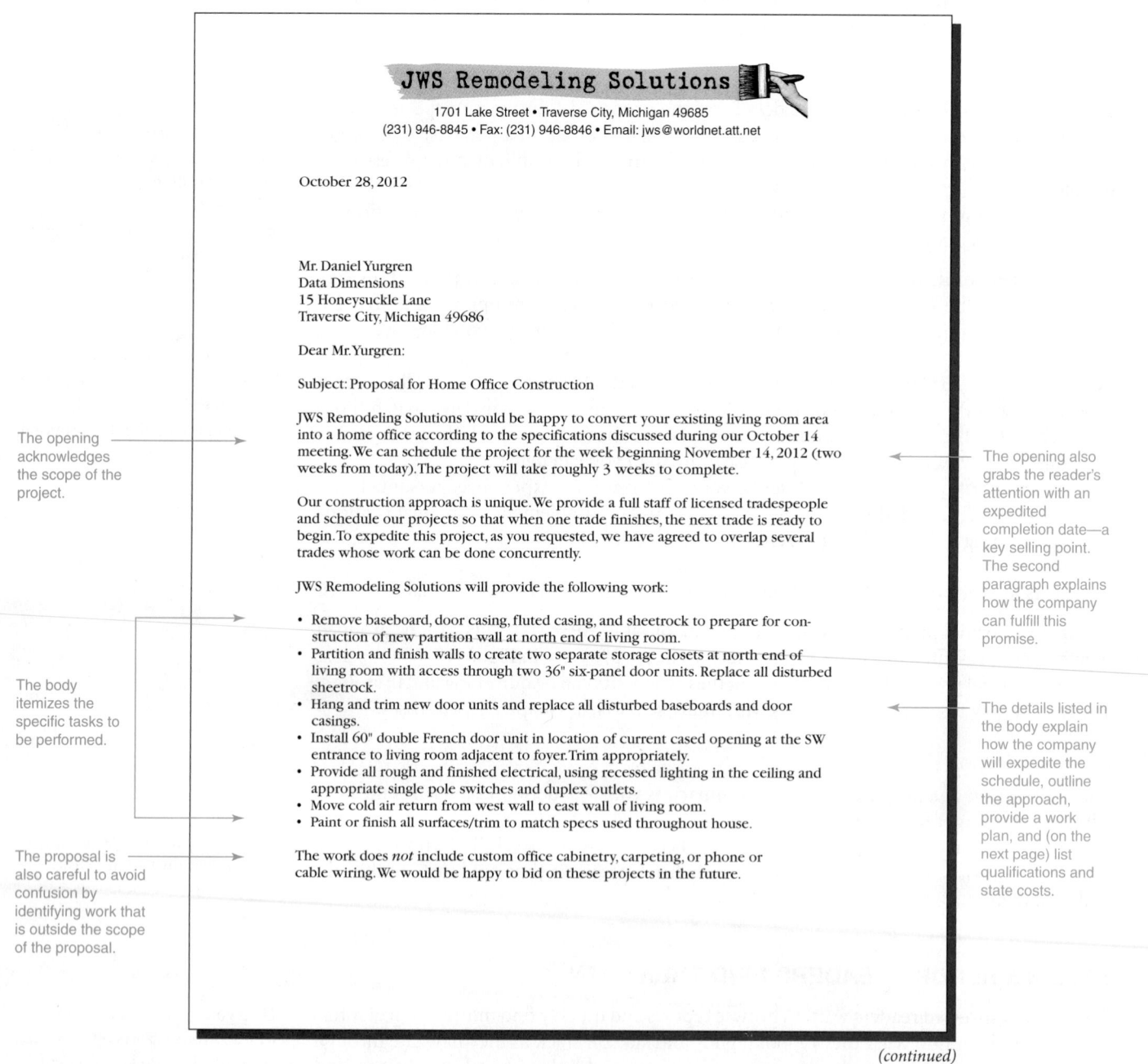

JWS Remodeling Solutions
1701 Lake Street • Traverse City, Michigan 49685
(231) 946-8845 • Fax: (231) 946-8846 • Email: jws@worldnet.att.net

October 28, 2012

Mr. Daniel Yurgren
Data Dimensions
15 Honeysuckle Lane
Traverse City, Michigan 49686

Dear Mr. Yurgren:

Subject: Proposal for Home Office Construction

JWS Remodeling Solutions would be happy to convert your existing living room area into a home office according to the specifications discussed during our October 14 meeting. We can schedule the project for the week beginning November 14, 2012 (two weeks from today). The project will take roughly 3 weeks to complete.

Our construction approach is unique. We provide a full staff of licensed tradespeople and schedule our projects so that when one trade finishes, the next trade is ready to begin. To expedite this project, as you requested, we have agreed to overlap several trades whose work can be done concurrently.

JWS Remodeling Solutions will provide the following work:

- Remove baseboard, door casing, fluted casing, and sheetrock to prepare for construction of new partition wall at north end of living room.
- Partition and finish walls to create two separate storage closets at north end of living room with access through two 36" six-panel door units. Replace all disturbed sheetrock.
- Hang and trim new door units and replace all disturbed baseboards and door casings.
- Install 60" double French door unit in location of current cased opening at the SW entrance to living room adjacent to foyer. Trim appropriately.
- Provide all rough and finished electrical, using recessed lighting in the ceiling and appropriate single pole switches and duplex outlets.
- Move cold air return from west wall to east wall of living room.
- Paint or finish all surfaces/trim to match specs used throughout house.

The work does *not* include custom office cabinetry, carpeting, or phone or cable wiring. We would be happy to bid on these projects in the future.

The opening acknowledges the scope of the project.

The body itemizes the specific tasks to be performed.

The proposal is also careful to avoid confusion by identifying work that is outside the scope of the proposal.

The opening also grabs the reader's attention with an expedited completion date—a key selling point. The second paragraph explains how the company can fulfill this promise.

The details listed in the body explain how the company will expedite the schedule, outline the approach, provide a work plan, and (on the next page) list qualifications and state costs.

(continued)

Figure 12.4   Effective Solicited Proposal in Letter Format
This informal solicited proposal in letter format provides the information the customer needs to make a purchase. Note that by signing the proposal and returning it, the customer will enter into a legal contract to pay for the services described.

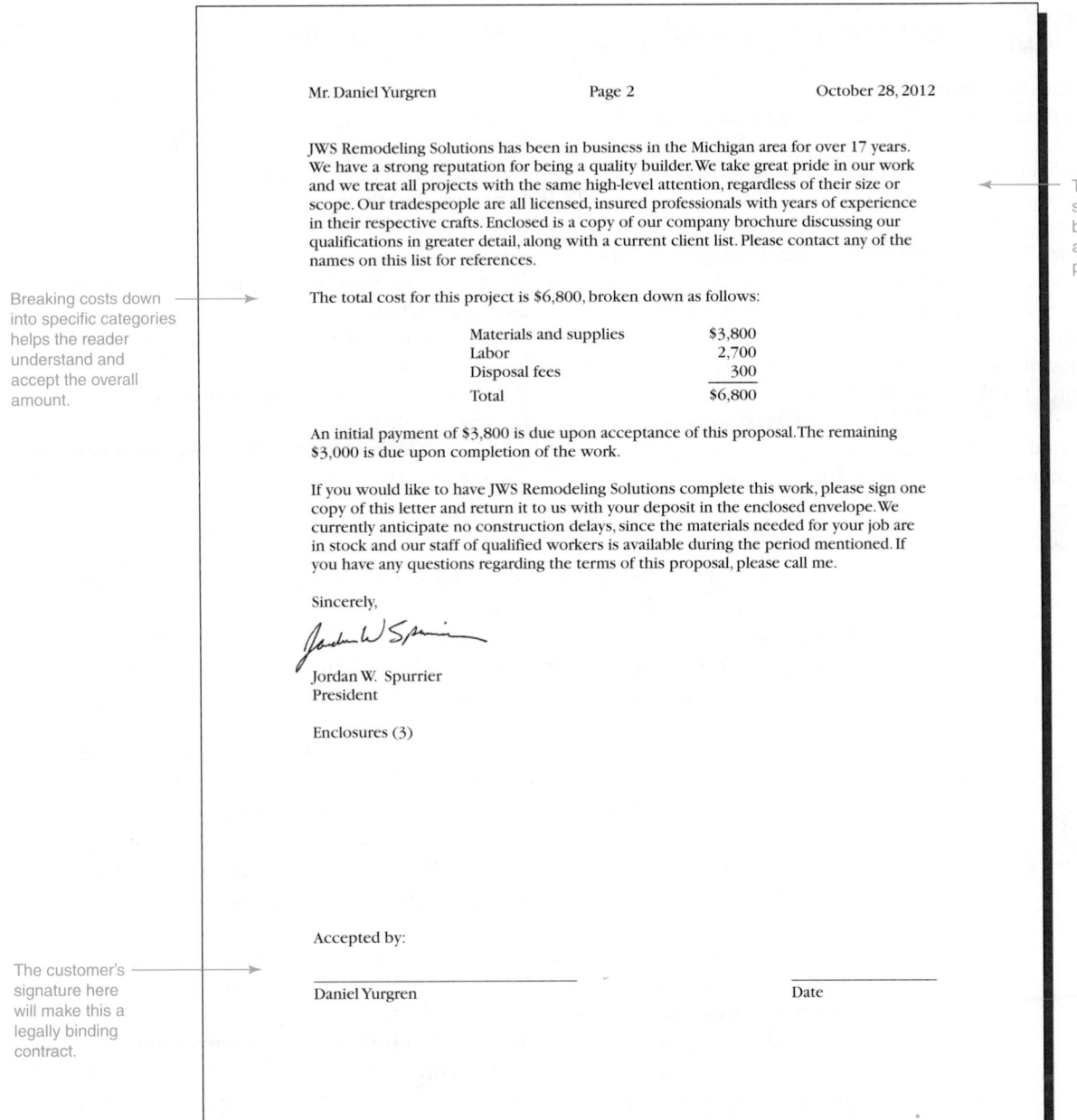

Mr. Daniel Yurgren   Page 2   October 28, 2012

JWS Remodeling Solutions has been in business in the Michigan area for over 17 years. We have a strong reputation for being a quality builder. We take great pride in our work and we treat all projects with the same high-level attention, regardless of their size or scope. Our tradespeople are all licensed, insured professionals with years of experience in their respective crafts. Enclosed is a copy of our company brochure discussing our qualifications in greater detail, along with a current client list. Please contact any of the names on this list for references.

The qualifications section helps reduce buyer uncertainty and prompt a positive response.

The total cost for this project is $6,800, broken down as follows:

Materials and supplies	$3,800
Labor	2,700
Disposal fees	300
Total	$6,800

Breaking costs down into specific categories helps the reader understand and accept the overall amount.

An initial payment of $3,800 is due upon acceptance of this proposal. The remaining $3,000 is due upon completion of the work.

If you would like to have JWS Remodeling Solutions complete this work, please sign one copy of this letter and return it to us with your deposit in the enclosed envelope. We currently anticipate no construction delays, since the materials needed for your job are in stock and our staff of qualified workers is available during the period mentioned. If you have any questions regarding the terms of this proposal, please call me.

Sincerely,

Jordan W. Spurrier

Jordan W. Spurrier
President

Enclosures (3)

Accepted by:

_____   _____
Daniel Yurgren   Date

The customer's signature here will make this a legally binding contract.

Figure 12.4   Effective Solicited Proposal in Letter Format *(continued)*

MyBcommLab

Apply Figure 12.4's key concepts by revising a new document. Go to Chapter 12 in www.pearsoninternationaleditions.com/mybcommlab and select Document Makeovers.

USING TECHNOLOGY TO CRAFT REPORTS AND PROPOSALS

Writing lengthy reports and proposals can be a huge task, so be sure to take advantage of technological tools to help throughout the process. In addition to the tools described under "Using Technology to Compose and Shape Your Messages" on pages 182–184, be sure to explore the advantages of these capabilities:

Look for ways to use technology to reduce the mechanical work involved in writing long reports.

- **Linked and embedded documents.** In many reports and proposals, you'll include graphics, spreadsheets, databases, and other elements produced in other software programs. Make sure you know how your software handles the files. For instance, in Microsoft Office, *linking* to a file maintains a "live" connection to it, so changes in the original file will show up in the document you're working on. However, *embedding* a

✓ Checklist | Composing Business Reports and Proposals

A. Review and fine-tune your outline.
- Match your parallel headings to the tone of your report or proposal.
- Understand how the introduction, body, and close work together to convey your message.

B. Draft report content.
- Use the introduction to establish the purpose, scope, and organization of your report or proposal.
- Use the body to present and interpret the information you gathered.
- Use the close to summarize major points, discuss conclusions, or make recommendations.

C. Draft proposal content.
- Use the introduction to discuss the background or problem, your solution, the scope, and organization.

- Use the body to persuasively explain the benefits of your proposed approach.
- Use the close to emphasize reader benefits and summarize the merits of your approach.

D. Help readers find their way.
- Provide headings to improve readability and clarify the framework of your ideas.
- Use hyperlinks online to allow readers to jump from section to section.
- Create transitions that tie together ideas and show how one thought relates to another.
- Preview important topics to help readers get ready for new information.
- Review key information to help readers absorb details and keep the big picture in mind.

---

file "breaks the link," so to speak, so changes in the original will not automatically appear in the new document.

- **Electronic forms.** For recurring reports such as sales reports and compliance reports, consider creating a document that uses *form tools* such as text boxes (in which users can type new text) and check boxes (which can be used to select from a set of predetermined choices).

- **Electronic documents.** Portable document format (PDF) files have become a universal replacement for printed reports and proposals. Using Adobe Acrobat or similar products, you can quickly convert reports and proposals to PDF files that are easy to share electronically. Note that PDFs have long been considered safer than word processor files, but recent discoveries indicate that PDFs could also be used to transmit computer viruses.[5] For information on protecting yourself when using Adobe Reader for PDFs, visit **www.adobe.com/security**.

- **Multimedia documents.** Video clips, animation, presentation software slides, screencasts (recordings of on-screen activity), and other media elements can enhance the communication and persuasion powers of the written word.

- **Proposal-writing software.** Proposal-writing software can automatically personalize proposals, ensure proper structure (making sure you don't forget any sections, for instance), organize storage of all your boilerplate text, integrate contact information from sales databases, and scan RFPs to identify questions and requirements and fill in potential answers from a centralized knowledge base.[6]

Writing for Websites and Wikis

In addition to standalone reports and proposals, you may be asked to write in-depth content for websites or to collaborate on a wiki. The basic principles of report writing apply to both formats, but each has some unique considerations as well.

DRAFTING WEBSITE CONTENT

Major sections on websites, particularly those that are fairly static (unlike, say, a blog) function in much the same way as reports. The skills you've developed for report writing adapt easily to this environment, as long as you keep a few points in mind:

- Take special care to build trust with your intended audiences because careful readers can be skeptical of online content. Make sure your content is accurate, current, complete, and authoritative.

- As much as possible, adapt your content for a global audience. Translating content is expensive, so some companies compromise by *localizing* the homepage while keeping the deeper, more detailed content in its original language.
- In an environment that presents many reading challenges, compelling, reader-oriented content is key to success.[7] Wherever you can, use the *inverted pyramid* style, in which you cover the most important information briefly at first and then gradually reveal successive layers of detail—letting readers choose to see those additional layers if they want to.
- Present your information in a concise, skimmable format. Effective websites use a variety of means to help readers skim pages quickly, including lists, careful use of color and boldface, informative headings, and helpful summaries that give readers a choice of learning more if they want to.
- Write effective links that serve for both site navigation and content skimming. Above all else, clearly identify where a link will take readers. Don't rely on cute wordplay that obscures the content, and don't force readers to click through and try to figure out where they're going.

COLLABORATING ON WIKIS

As Chapter 2 points out, using wikis is a great way for teams and other groups to collaborate on writing projects, from brief articles to long reports and reference works (see Figure 12.5). The benefits of wikis are compelling, but they do require a unique approach to writing. To be a valuable wiki contributor, keep these points in mind:[8]

- Let go of traditional expectations of authorship, including individual recognition and control.
- Encourage all team members to improve each other's work.
- Use page templates and other formatting options to make sure your content matches the rest of the wiki.
- Use the separate editing and discussion capabilities appropriately.
- Take advantage of the *sandbox*, if available; this is a "safe," nonpublished section of the wiki where team members can practice editing and writing.

Wikis usually have guidelines to help new contributors integrate their work into the group's ongoing effort. Be sure to read and understand these guidelines, and don't be afraid to ask for help.

Being an effective wiki collaborator requires a different writing mindset.

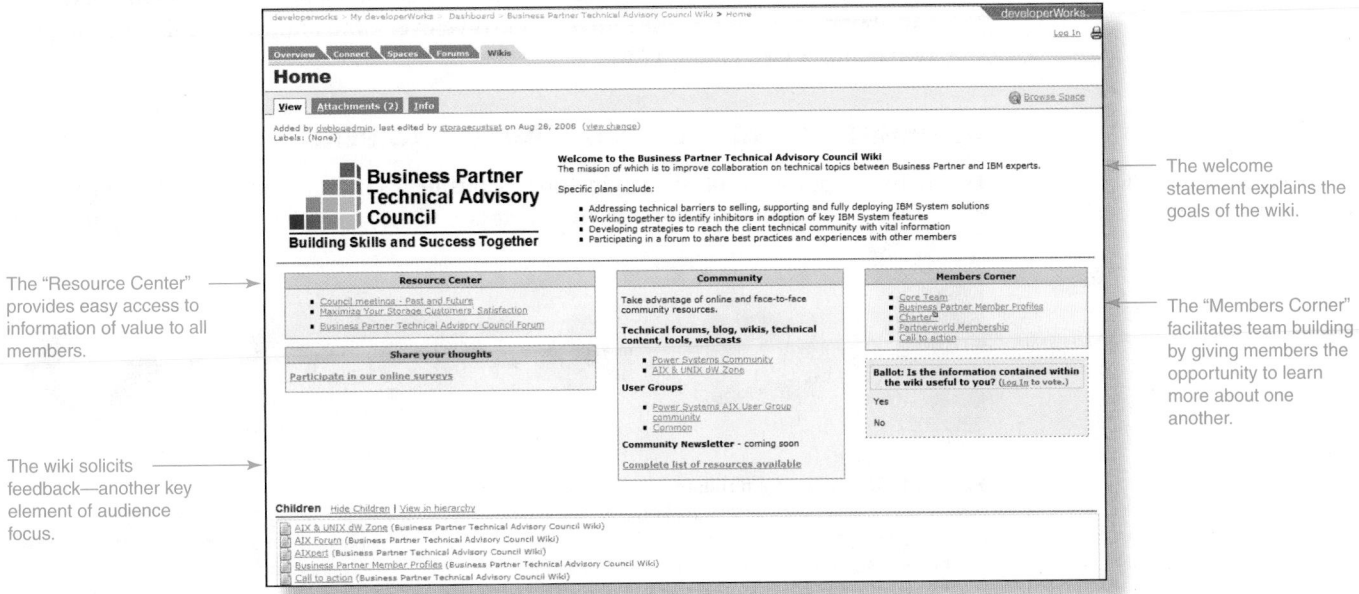

The "Resource Center" provides easy access to information of value to all members.

The wiki solicits feedback—another key element of audience focus.

The welcome statement explains the goals of the wiki.

The "Members Corner" facilitates team building by giving members the opportunity to learn more about one another.

Figure 12.5 IBM Business Partner Wiki
IBM created this wiki to facilitate collaboration with its external business partners.
Source: Reprint Courtesy of International Business Machines Corporation, © 2011 International Business Machines Corporation. First published by IBM developerWorks at http://www.ibm.com/developerWorks.

If you are creating a new wiki, think through your long-term purpose carefully, just as you would with a new blog or podcast channel. Doing so will help you craft appropriate guidelines, editorial oversight, and security policies. For instance, the PlayStation development team at Sony uses a wiki to keep top managers up to date on new products, and because this information is highly confidential, access to the wiki is tightly controlled.[9]

If you are adding a page or an article to an existing wiki, figure out how this new material fits in with the existing organization. Also, learn the wiki's preferred style for handling incomplete articles. For example, on the wiki that contains the user documentation for the popular WordPress blogging software, contributors are discouraged from adding new pages until the content is "fairly complete and accurate."[10]

If you are revising or updating an existing wiki article, use the list of questions on page 197 in Chapter 6 to evaluate the content before you make changes. If you don't agree with published content and plan to revise it, you can use the wiki's discussion facility to share your concerns with other contributors. The wiki environment should encourage discussions and even robust disagreements, as long as everyone remains civil and respectful.

Make sure you understand how a new wiki page will fit in with the existing content.

Illustrating Your Reports with Effective Visuals

3   LEARNING OBJECTIVE

Discuss six principles of graphic design, and identify the most common types of visuals used to present data, information, concepts, and ideas.

Well-designed visual elements can enhance the communication power of textual messages and, in some instances, even replace textual messages. Visuals can often convey some message points (such as spatial relationships, correlations, procedures, and emotions) more effectively and more efficiently than words. Generally speaking, in a given amount of time, well-designed images can convey much more information than text.[11] Visuals attract and hold people's attention, helping your audience understand and remember your message. Busy readers often jump to visuals to try to get the gist of a message, and attractive visuals can draw readers more deeply into your reports and presentations. Using pictures is also an effective way to communicate with the diverse audiences that are common in today's business environment.

Like words, visuals often carry connotative or symbolic meanings.

As you read in Chapter 5, many words and phrases carry connotative meanings, which are all the mental images, emotions, and other impressions that the word or phrase evokes in audience members. A significant part of the power—and risk—of visual elements derives from their connotative meanings as well. Even something as simple as a watermark symbol embedded in letterhead stationery can boost reader confidence in the message printed on the paper.[12] Many colors, shapes, and other design elements have **visual symbolism**, and their symbolic, connotative meanings can evolve over time and mean different things in different cultures (see Figure 12.6).

UNDERSTANDING VISUAL DESIGN PRINCIPLES

Visual literacy is the ability to create and interpret visual messages.

Given the importance of visuals in today's business environment, **visual literacy**—the ability (as a sender) to create effective images and (as a receiver) to correctly interpret

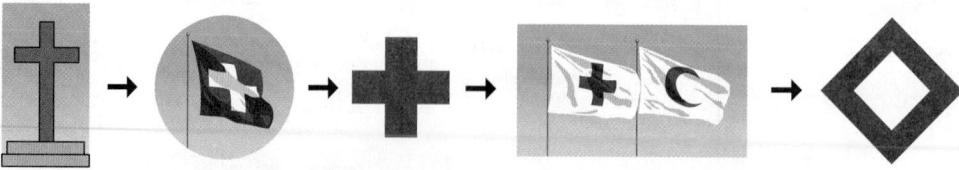

Figure 12.6   Visual Symbolism
A red cross (with equal-length arms) on a white background is the well-known symbol of the Red Cross relief organization. It is also used to indicate the medical branches of many nations' military services. The red cross symbol is based on the flag of Switzerland (where the first Red Cross organization was formed), which over the course of hundreds of years developed from battle flags that originally used the Christian cross symbol. Although the Red Cross emblem is not based directly on the Christian symbol, the organization uses a red crescent in countries where Islam is the dominant religion and is known as the Red Crescent. To avoid association with religious symbols, the International Federation of Red Cross and Red Crescent Societies (the global umbrella organization for all national Red Cross and Red Crescent organizations) recently adopted the Red Crystal as its new symbol.

visual messages—has become a key business skill.[13] Just as creating effective sentences, paragraphs, and documents requires working knowledge of the principles of good writing, creating effective visuals requires some knowledge of the principles of good design. Even if you have no formal training in design, being aware of the following six principles will help you be a more effective visual communicator:

- **Consistency.** Think of continuity as *visual parallelism*, in the same way that textual parallelism helps audiences understand and compare a series of ideas.[14] You can achieve visual parallelism in a variety of ways, through the consistent use of color, shape, size, texture, position, scale, or typeface.

- **Contrast.** Use visual choices such as size and color to emphasize contrasting quantities or ideas. To emphasize similarities, on the other hand, make the visual differences more subtle.

- **Balance.** Images that appear to be out of balance can be as unsettling as a building that looks like it's about to tip over. Balance can be either *formal*, in which the elements in the images are arranged symmetrically around a central point or axis, or *informal*, in which elements are not distributed evenly but visually stronger and weaker elements are arranged in a way that achieves an overall effect of balance. Generally speaking, formal balance is calming and serious, whereas informal balance tends to feel dynamic and engaging (which is why most advertising uses this approach, for example).

- **Emphasis.** Audiences usually assume that the dominant element in a design is the most important, so make sure that the visually dominant element really does represent the most important information. You can do this through color, position, size, or placement, for instance.

- **Convention.** Visual communication is guided by a variety of generally accepted rules or conventions, just as written communication is guided by an array of spelling, grammar, punctuation, and usage conventions. These conventions dictate virtually every aspect of design.[15] Moreover, many conventions are so ingrained that people don't even realize they are following these rules. For example, if English is your native language, you assume that ideas progress across the page from left to right because that's the direction in which English text is written. However, if you are a native Arabic or Hebrew speaker, you might automatically assume that flow on a page or screen is from right to left because that is the direction in which those languages are written. Similarly, Japanese audiences are used to reading publications from back to front, right to left. Flouting conventions often causes breakdowns in communication, but in some cases, it can be done to great effect.[16] For instance, flipping an organization chart upside down to put the customers at the top, with frontline employees directly beneath them and on down to the chief executive at the bottom, can be an effective way to emphasize that customers come first and that the managers are responsible for supporting employees in their efforts to satisfy customers.

- **Simplicity.** As Figure 12.7 on the next page indicates, simpler is usually better when it comes to visuals for business communication. When you're designing graphics for your documents, remember that you're conveying information, not decorating an apartment or creating artwork. Limit the number of colors and design elements you use and take care to avoid *chartjunk*, a term coined by visual communication specialist Edward R. Tufte for decorative elements that clutter documents and potentially confuse readers without adding any relevant information.[17] Be aware that computers make it far too easy to add chartjunk, from clip art illustrations to three-dimensional charts that display only two dimensions of data.

MyBcommLab

- Access this chapter's simulation entitled Business Presentations located at www.pearsoninternationaleditions.com/mybcommlab.

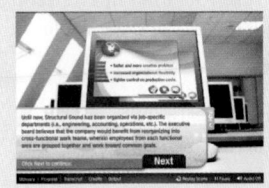

UNDERSTANDING THE ETHICS OF VISUAL COMMUNICATION

Power always comes with responsibility—and the potential power of visuals places an ethical burden on every business communicator. Ethical problems, both intentional and unintentional, can range from photos that play on racial or gender stereotypes to images that imply cause-and-effect relationships that may not exist to graphs that distort data.

Visuals are powerful, and you have the responsibility to use them ethically.

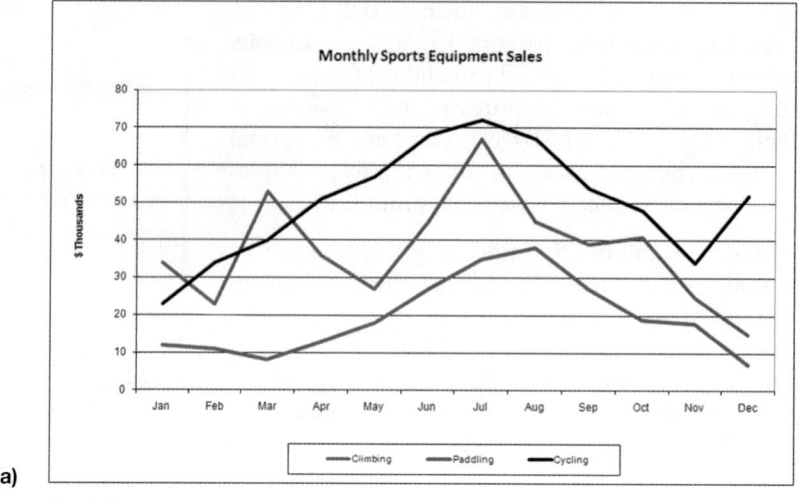

(a)

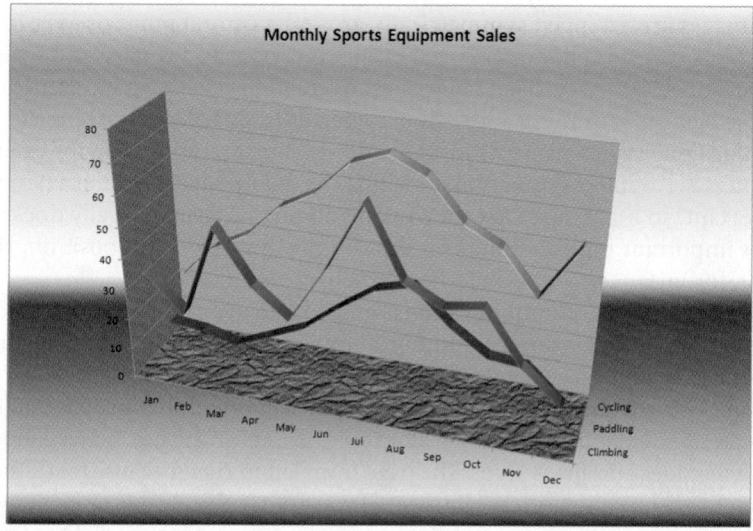

(b)

Figure 12.7 **The Power of Simplicity**
These two graphs contain the same information, but Figure 12.7a is much easier to interpret. None of the additional elements in Figure 12.7b add any information value—and they make the graph harder to interpret. Adding a false third dimension to two-dimensional information such as these sales figures is a common mistake.

You can take many steps to emphasize or deemphasize specific elements in your visuals, but make sure you don't inadvertently commit an ethical lapse while doing so.

Visuals can't always speak for themselves; make sure your audience has enough context to interpret your visuals correctly.

Altering the scale of items in a visual is just one of many ways to emphasize or deemphasize certain aspects of information. For example, to increase the perceived size of a product, an advertiser might show a close-up of it being held by someone with smaller-than-average hands. Conversely, a large hand would make the product seem smaller.

You can work to avoid ethical lapses in your visuals by following these guidelines:[18]

- Consider all possible interpretations—and misinterpretations.
- Provide enough background information to help audiences interpret the visual information correctly.
- Don't hide or minimize visual information that runs counter to your argument—and don't exaggerate visual information that supports your argument.
- Don't oversimplify complex situations by hiding complications that are important to the audience's understanding of the situation.
- Don't imply cause-and-effect relationships without providing proof that they exist.
- Avoid emotional manipulation or other forms of coercion.
- Be careful with the way you *aggregate*, or group, data. For example, aggregating daily sales data by weeks or months can obscure daily fluctuations that could be meaningful to your audience.

IDENTIFYING POINTS TO ILLUSTRATE

To help identify which parts of your message can benefit from visuals, step back and consider the flow of the entire message from the audience's point of view. Which parts might seem complex, open to misinterpretation, or even just a little bit dull? Are there any connections between ideas or data sets that might not be obvious if they are addressed only in text? Does the material have a lot of numeric data or other discrete factual content that would be difficult to read if presented in paragraph form? Is there a chance the main idea won't "jump off the page" if it's covered only in text? Will readers greet the message with skepticism and therefore look for plenty of supporting evidence?

If you answer yes to any of these questions, you probably need one or more visuals. When you're deciding which points to present visually, think of the five Cs:

- **Clear.** If you're having difficultly conveying an idea in words, take a minute to brainstorm some visual possibilities for clarifying the topic.
- **Complete.** Visuals, particularly tables, can complement your text to provide readers all the information they need.
- **Concise.** If a particular section of your message seems to require extensive description or explanation, see whether there's a way to convey that information visually in order to reduce your word count.
- **Connected.** A key purpose of many business messages is to show connections of some sort—similarities or differences, correlations, cause-and-effect relationships, and so on.
- **Compelling.** Will one or more illustrations make your message more persuasive, more interesting, or more likely to get read?

As you identify which points in your document would benefit from visuals, make sure that each visual you decide on has a clear purpose (see Table 12.1).

REAL-TIME UPDATES
Learn More by Exploring This Interactive Website

Quickly peruse dozens of data and information display techniques

This "periodic table of visualization methods" shows dozens of ways to display data, information, concepts, strategies, and more. Go to http://real-timeupdates.com/ebc10 and click on Learn More. If you are using MyBcommLab, you can access Real-Time Updates within each chapter or under Student Study Tools.

SELECTING THE RIGHT TYPE OF VISUAL

After you've identified which points would benefit most from visual presentation, your next decision is choosing what type of visual to use for each message point (see Figure 12.8 on the next page). For certain types of information, the decision is usually obvious. To present a large set of numeric values or detailed textual information, a table is the obvious choice in most cases. However, if you're presenting data broken down geographically, a color-coded map might be more effective. Also, certain visuals are commonly used for certain applications, such as line charts for showing trends over time. (Note that *chart* and *graph* are used interchangeably for most of the display formats discussed here.)

You have many types of visuals to choose from, and each is best suited to particular communication tasks.

TABLE 12.1	When to Use Visuals
Purpose	**Applications**
To clarify	Support text descriptions of quantitative or numeric information, trends, spatial relationships, and physical constructions.
To simplify	Break complicated descriptions into components that can be depicted with conceptual models, flowcharts, organization charts, or diagrams.
To emphasize	Call attention to particularly important points by illustrating them with line, bar, and pie and other types of charts.
To summarize	Review major points in the narrative by providing a chart or table that summarizes key items.
To reinforce	Present information in both visual and written forms to increase readers' retention.
To attract	Engage readers visually and emotionally; provide visual relief from long blocks of text.
To impress	Build credibility by putting ideas into visual form to convey the impression of authenticity and precision.
To unify	Depict the relationship among points, such as visually connecting the steps in a process by presenting them in a flowchart.

Communication Challenge	Effective Visual Choice

Presenting Data

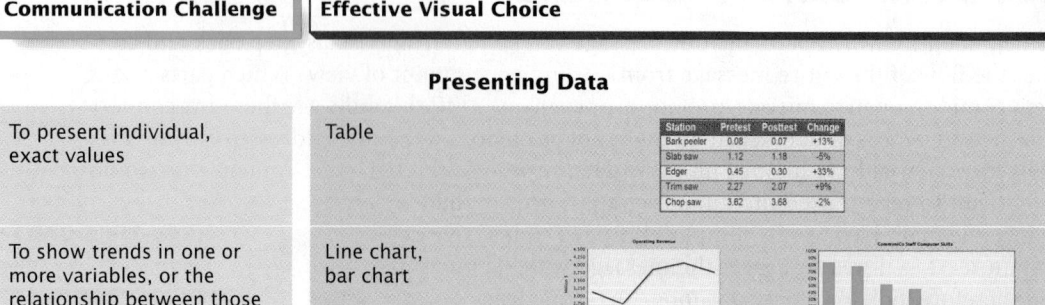

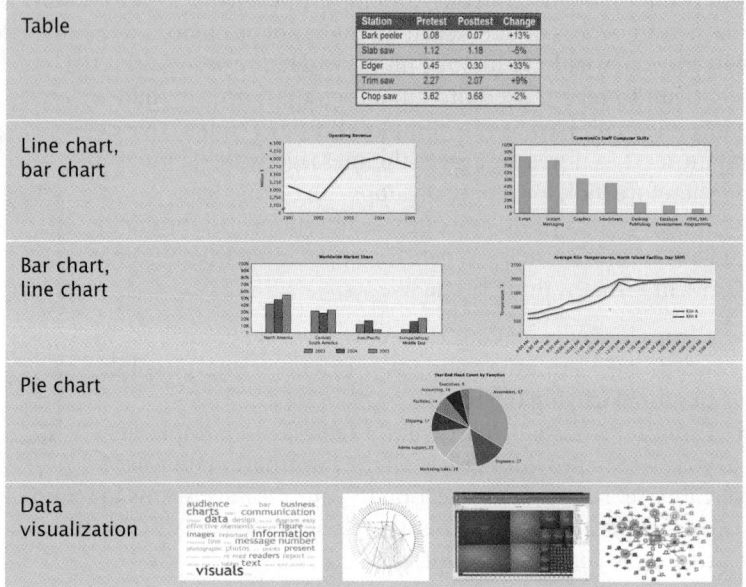

To present individual, exact values	Table
To show trends in one or more variables, or the relationship between those variables, over time	Line chart, bar chart
To compare two or more sets of data	Bar chart, line chart
To show frequency or distribution of parts in a whole	Pie chart
To show massive data sets, complex quantities, or dynamic data	Data visualization

Presenting Information, Concepts, and Ideas

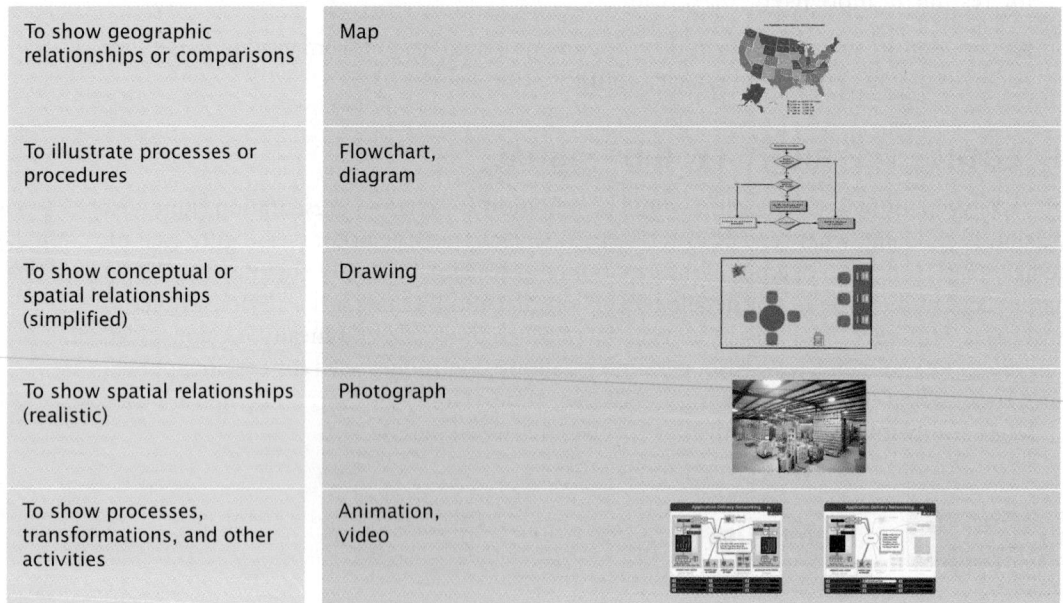

To show geographic relationships or comparisons	Map
To illustrate processes or procedures	Flowchart, diagram
To show conceptual or spatial relationships (simplified)	Drawing
To show spatial relationships (realistic)	Photograph
To show processes, transformations, and other activities	Animation, video

Figure 12.8   Selecting the Best Visual
For each point you want to illustrate, make sure to choose the most effective type of visual.

Visuals for Presenting Data

Business professionals have a tremendous number of choices for presenting data, from general-purpose line, bar, and pie charts to specialized charts for product portfolios, financial analysis, and other professional functions. The visuals most commonly used to present data include tables, line and surface charts, bar charts, and pie charts.

Printed tables can display extensive amounts of data, but tables for websites and presentations need to be simpler.

Tables   When you need to present detailed, specific information, choose a **table**, a systematic arrangement of data in columns and rows. Most tables contain the standard parts

	Multicolumn Heading			Single-Column Heading
	Column Subheading	Column Subheading	Column Subheading	
Row Heading	xxx	xxx	xxx	xxx
Row Heading	xxx	xxx	xxx	xxx
Row Subheading	xxx	xxx	xxx	xxx
Row Subheading	xxx	xxx	xxx	xxx
Row Heading	xxx	xxx	xxx	xxx
Row Heading	xxx	xxx	xxx	xxx
TOTALS	xxx	xxx	xxx	xxx

Figure 12.9 Parts of a Table
Here are the standard parts of a table. No matter which design you choose, make sure the layout is clear and that individual rows and columns are easy to follow.

MyBcommLab

Apply Figure 12.9's key concepts by revising a new document. Go to Chapter 12 in www.pearsoninternationaleditions.com/mybcommlab and select Document Makeovers.

illustrated in Figure 12.9. For printed documents, you can adjust font size and column/row spacing to fit a considerable amount of information on the page and still maintain readability. For online documents, you often need to reduce the number of columns and rows to make sure your tables are easily readable online. Tables for oral presentations usually need to be the simplest of all because you can't expect audiences to read detailed information from the screen.

Although complex information may require formal tables that are set apart from the text, you can present some data more simply within the text. Such text tables are usually introduced with a sentence that leads directly into the tabular information. Here's an example:[19]

Here is how five leading full-service restaurant chains compare in terms of number of locations and annual revenue:

	OSI Restaurant Partners	DineEquity	Carlson	Brinker	Darden
Major Chain(s)	Outback Steakhouse, Carrabba's	Applebee's, IHOP	Friday's, Pick Up Stix	Chili's, Maggiano's	Red Lobster, Olive Garden
Locations	1,470	3,300	990	1,550	1,800
Revenue ($ Million)	$3,600	$1,414	N/A	$2,859	$7,113

Sources: Hoover's Online, accessed 25 February 2011, www.hoovers.com; "America's Largest Private Companies," *Forbes,* accessed 25 February 2011, www.forbes.com; company financial reports accessed on Google Finance, accessed 25 February 2011, www.google.com/finance.

When you prepare tables, follow these guidelines to make your tables easy to read:

- Use common, understandable units and clearly identify the units you're using.
- Express all items in a column in the same unit and round off for simplicity.
- Label column headings clearly and use a subhead, if necessary.
- Separate columns or rows with lines or extra space to make the table easy to follow; in complex tables, consider highlighting every other row or column in a pale contrasting color.
- Provide totals or averages of columns or rows when relevant.
- Document the source of the data, using the same format as for a text footnote (see Appendix B).

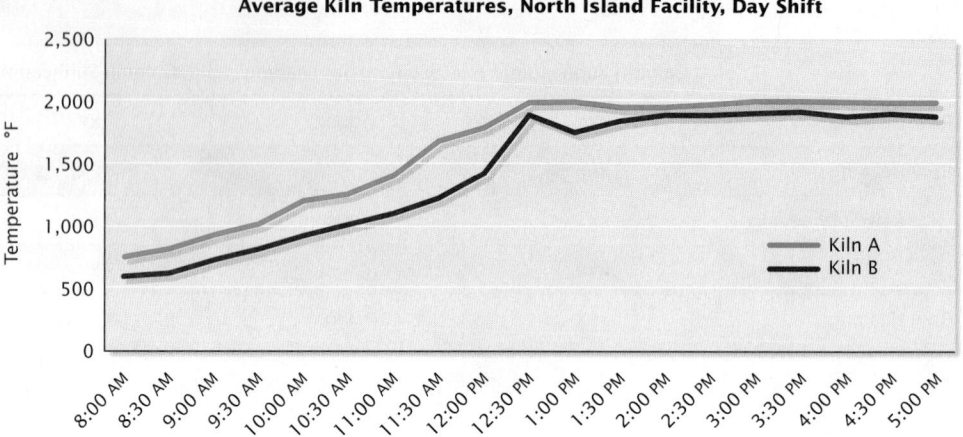

Figure 12.10 Line Chart
This two-line line chart compares the temperatures measured inside two cement kilns from 8:00 A.M. to 5:00 P.M.

Tables can contain numerals, words, symbols, or other facts and figures. Word tables are particularly useful for presenting survey findings or for comparing various items against a specific standard.

Line charts are commonly used to show trends over time or the relationship between two variables.

Line Charts and Surface Charts A **line chart**, or *line graph*, illustrates trends over time or plots the relationship of two variables. In line charts that show trends, the vertical, or *y*, axis shows the amount, and the horizontal, or *x*, axis shows the time or other quantity against which the amount is being measured. Moreover, you can plot just a single line or overlay multiple lines to compare different entities (see Figure 12.10).

A **surface chart**, also called an **area chart**, is a form of line chart that shows a cumulative effect; all the lines add up to the top line, which represents the total (see Figure 12.11). This form of chart helps you illustrate changes in the composition of something over time. When preparing a surface chart, put the most important segment against the baseline and restrict the number of strata to four or five.

Bar Charts and Pie Charts A **bar chart**, or *bar graph*, portrays numbers with the height or length of its rectangular bars, making one or more series of numbers easy to read or understand. Bar charts are particularly valuable when you want to show or compare quantities over time. As the charts in Figure 12.12 suggest, bar charts can appear in various forms.

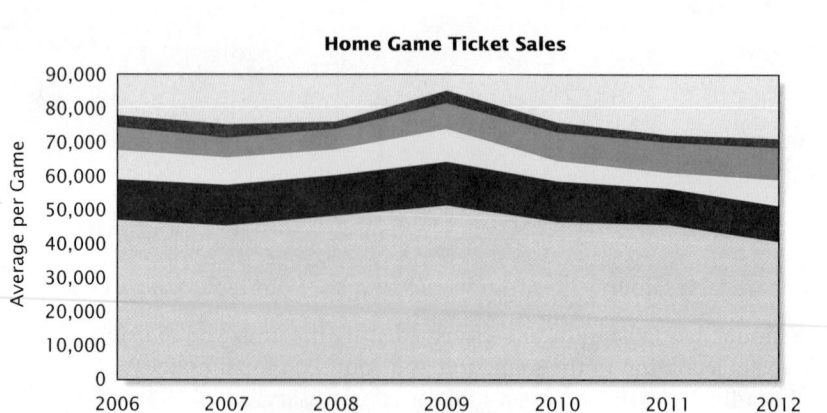

Figure 12.11 Surface Chart
Surface, or area, charts can show a combination of trends over time and the individual contributions of the components of a whole.

Specialized bar charts such as *timelines* and *Gantt charts* are used often in project management, for example.

A **pie chart** is a commonly used tool for showing how the parts of a whole are distributed. Although pie charts are popular and can quickly highlight the dominant parts of a whole, they are often not as effective as bar charts or tables. For example, comparing percentages accurately is often difficult with a pie chart but can be fairly easy with a bar chart (see Figure 12.13 on page 429). Making pie charts easier to read with accuracy can require labeling each slice with data values, in which case a table might serve the purpose more effectively.[20]

Data Visualization Conventional charts and graphs are limited in several ways: Most types can show only a limited number of data points before becoming too cluttered to interpret; they often can't show complex relationships among data points; and they can represent only numeric data. As computer technologies continue to generate massive amounts of data that can be combined and connected in endless ways, a diverse class of display capabilities known as **data visualization** works to overcome all these drawbacks.

Unlike charts and graphs, data visualization is less about clarifying individual data points and more about extracting broad meaning from giant masses of data or putting the data in context.[21] For instance, the Facebook "friend wheel" in Figure 12.14b on page 430 offers a visual sense of this particular Facebook user's network by showing which of his friends are friends of each other and thereby indicating "clustering"

Pie charts are effective if you want to show dramatic differences in proportions; to convey specific details, however, a bar chart or table is often more effective.

Data visualization tools let you display vast data sets, dynamic data, and textual information graphically.

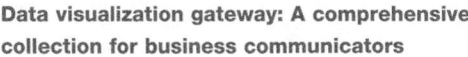

REAL-TIME UPDATES
Learn More by Exploring This Interactive Website

Data visualization gateway: A comprehensive collection for business communicators

This unique web resource offers links to a vast array of data visualization techniques and examples. Go to http://real-timeupdates.com/ebc10 and click on Learn More. If you are using MyBcommLab, you can access Real-Time Updates within each chapter or under Student Study Tools.

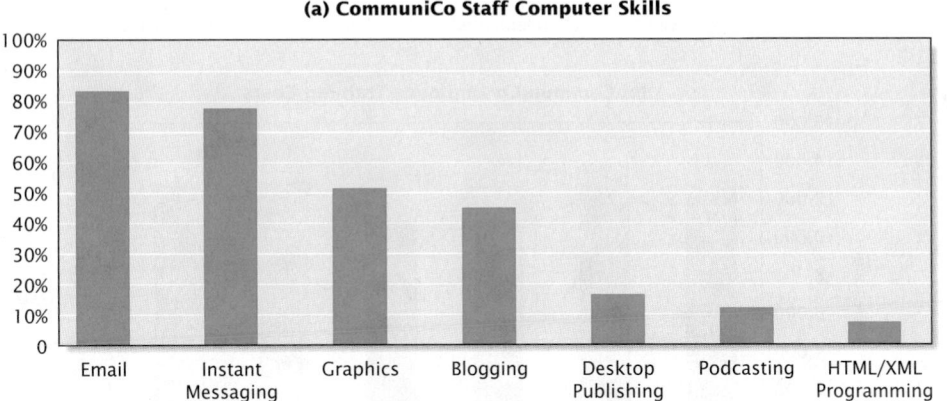

(a) CommuniCo Staff Computer Skills

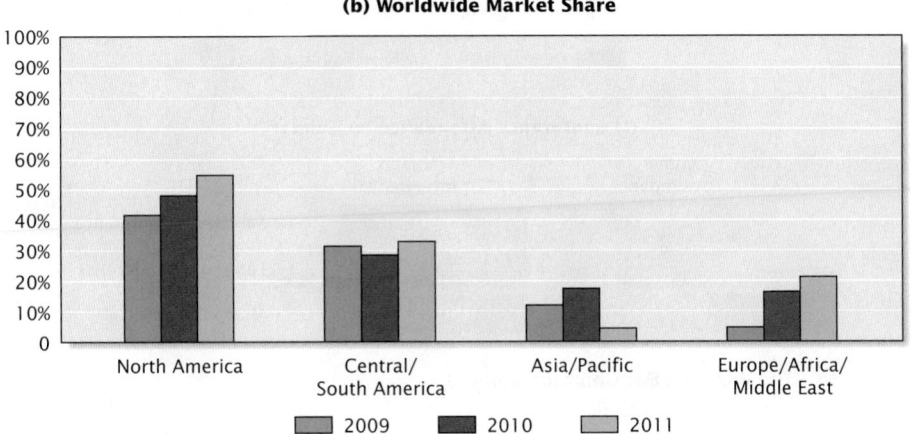

(b) Worldwide Market Share

(continued)

Figure 12.12 The Versatile Bar Chart
Here are six of the dozens of variations possible with bar charts: singular (12.12a), grouped (12.12b), deviation (12.12c), segmented (12.12d), combination (12.12e), and paired (12.12f).

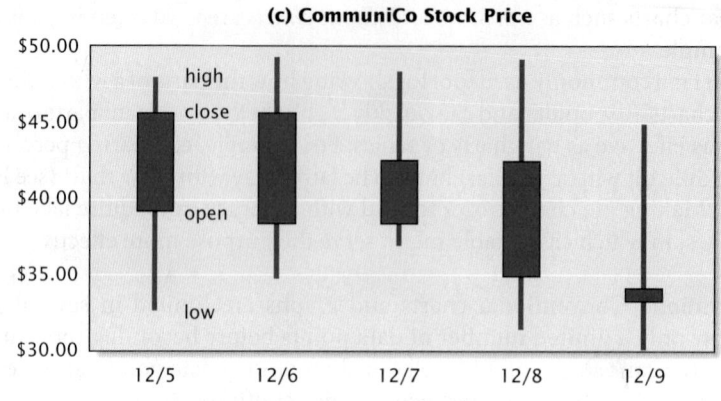

(c) CommuniCo Stock Price

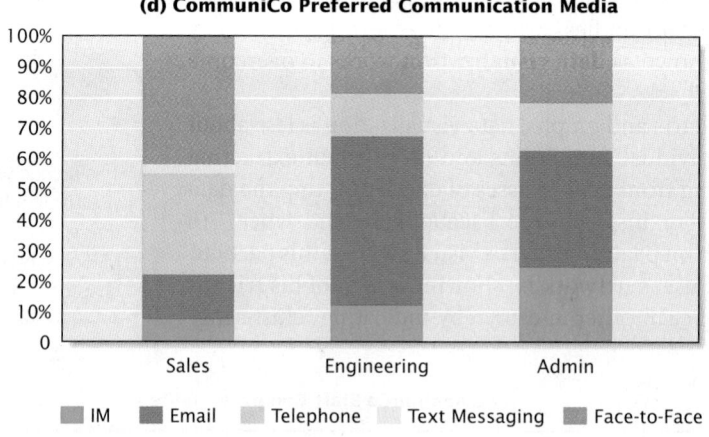

(d) CommuniCo Preferred Communication Media

■ IM ■ Email □ Telephone □ Text Messaging ■ Face-to-Face

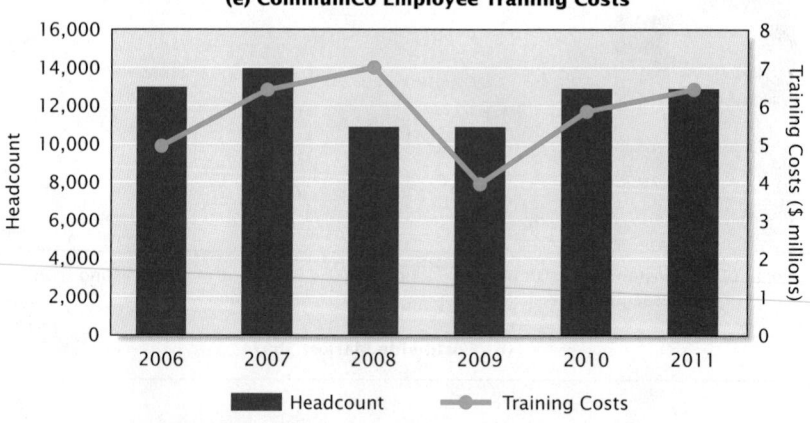

(e) CommuniCo Employee Training Costs

■ Headcount ━●━ Training Costs

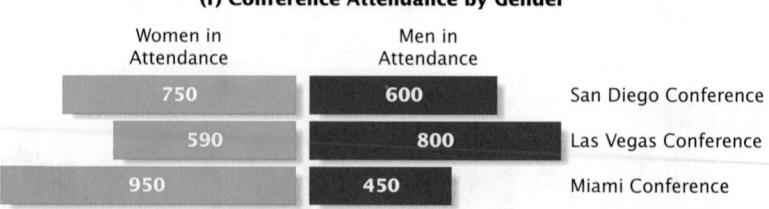

(f) Conference Attendance by Gender

Figure 12.12 **The Versatile Bar Chart** *(continued)*

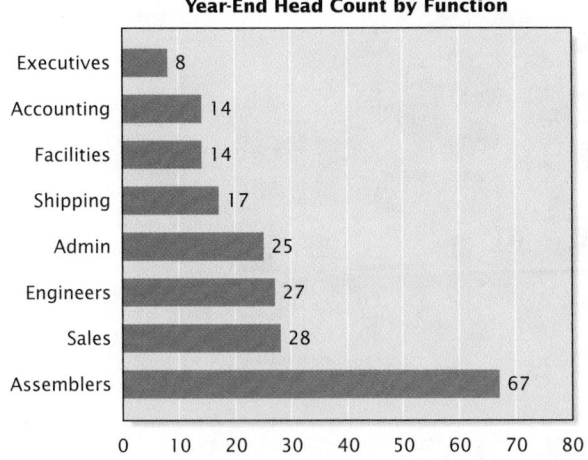

Figure 12.13 Pie Charts Versus Bar Charts
Pie charts are used frequently, but they aren't necessarily the best choice for many data presentations. This pie chart does make it easy to see that assemblers are the largest employee category, but other comparisons of slice sizes (such as Sales, Engineers, and Admin) are not as easy to make and require a numerical rather than a visual comparison. In contrast, the bar chart gives a quick visual comparison of every data point.

within the network (work friends, social friends, and so on). The diagram doesn't attempt to show quantities, but rather the overall nature of the network.

In addition to displaying large data sets and linkages within data sets, other kinds of visualization tools combine data with textual information to communicate complex or dynamic data much faster than conventional presentations can. For example, a *tag cloud* shows the relative frequency of terms, or tags (user-applied content labels), in an article, a blog, a website, survey data, or another collection of text.[22] Figure 12.14 on the next page shows a few of the many data visualization tools now available.

Data visualization is less about showing specific data points and more about extracting broad meaning from giant masses of data or putting data in context.

Visuals for Presenting Information, Concepts, and Ideas

In addition to facts and figures, you may need to present other types of information, from spatial relationships (such as the floor plan for a new office building) to abstract ideas (such as progress or competition). The most common types of visuals for these applications include flowcharts, organization charts, maps, drawings, diagrams, infographics, photographs, animation, and video.

Flowcharts and Organization Charts A **flowchart** (see Figure 12.15 on page 431) illustrates a sequence of events from start to finish; it is an indispensable tool for illustrating processes, procedures, and sequential relationships. For general business purposes, you don't need to be too concerned about the specific shapes in a flowchart, but use them consistently. However, you should be aware of the formal flowchart "language," in which each shape has a specific meaning (diamonds are decision points, rectangles are process steps, and so on). If you're communicating with computer programmers and others who are accustomed to formal flowcharting, make sure you use the correct symbols to avoid confusion.

As the name implies, an **organization chart** illustrates the positions, units, or functions of an organization and the way they interrelate. An organization's normal communication channels are almost impossible to describe without the benefit of a chart like the one in Figure 1.3 on page 48. These charts aren't limited to organization structures, of course; as you saw in Chapter 4, they can also be used to outline messages.

Maps and Geographic Information Systems Maps can show location, distance, points of interest (such as competitive retail outlets), and geographic distribution of data, such as sales by region or population by state. In addition to presenting facts and figures, maps are useful for showing market territories, distribution routes, and facilities locations.

When combined with databases and aerial or satellite photography in *geographic information systems (GIS)*, maps become extremely powerful visual reporting tools (see Figure 12.16 on page 431). As one example, retailing specialists can explore the demographic

Use maps to represent statistics by geographic area and to show spatial relationships.

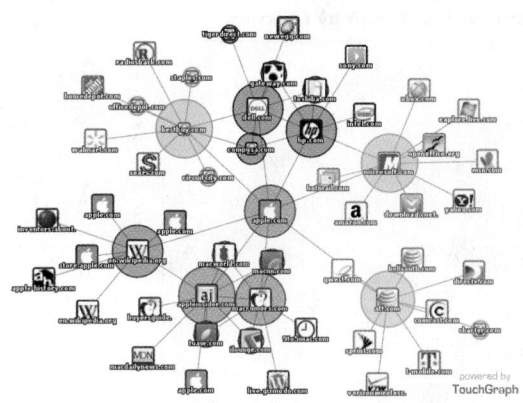

(a) Website Linkage Map. This interactive network diagram shows the most active links to and from Apple's homepage (**www.apple.com**). *Website linkage map by TouchGraph.com*

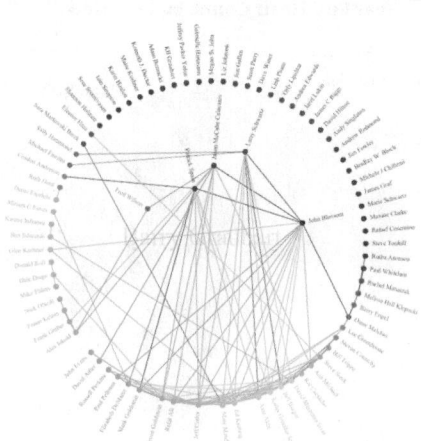

(b) Facebook Friend Wheel. This network diagram shows how the connections of Barry Graubart (an executive with an e-commerce company) are connected with one another.

(c) Tag Cloud. This "word chart" shows the relative frequency of the 50 most-used words in this chapter (other than common words such as *and, or,* and *the*).

(d) Interactive Data Display. This interactive display conveys two company performance variables at once (sales and profits) for a large data set by using the size and color of the individual blocks.

Figure 12.14   Data Visualization
The range of data visualization displays is virtually endless; here are a few of the many different ways to display complex sets of data.
Sources: (a) Used with permission by TouchGraph.com. (b) Visualize Your Facebook Social Network with a Friend Wheel. Courtesy of Facebook. (d) Used with permission from Microsoft®. Microsoft Dynamics NAV 2009 can be accessed at: www.microsoft.com/presspass/gallery.

and psychographic makeup of neighborhoods within various driving distances from a particular store location. Using such information, managers can plan everything from new building sites to delivery routes to marketing campaigns.

Drawings, Diagrams, Infographics, and Photographs   The opportunities to use drawings, diagrams, and photographs are virtually endless. Drawings can show everything from building sites to product concepts. Simple diagrams can show the network of suppliers in an industry, the flow of funds through a company, or the process for completing the payroll each week. More complex diagrams can convey technical topics such as the operation of a machine or repair procedures. Drawings or diagrams that contain enough visual and textual information to function as independent, standalone documents are sometimes called **infographics**. Figure 4.4 on page 143 and Figure 7.1 on page 224 are good examples. (Note that infographics are not the same as the often dysfunctional "slideuments" discussed in the presentations chapter on page 505.)

Word processors and presentation software now offer fairly advanced drawing capabilities, but for more precise and professional illustrations, you may need a specialized

Infographics are diagrams that contain enough textual information to function as standalone documents.

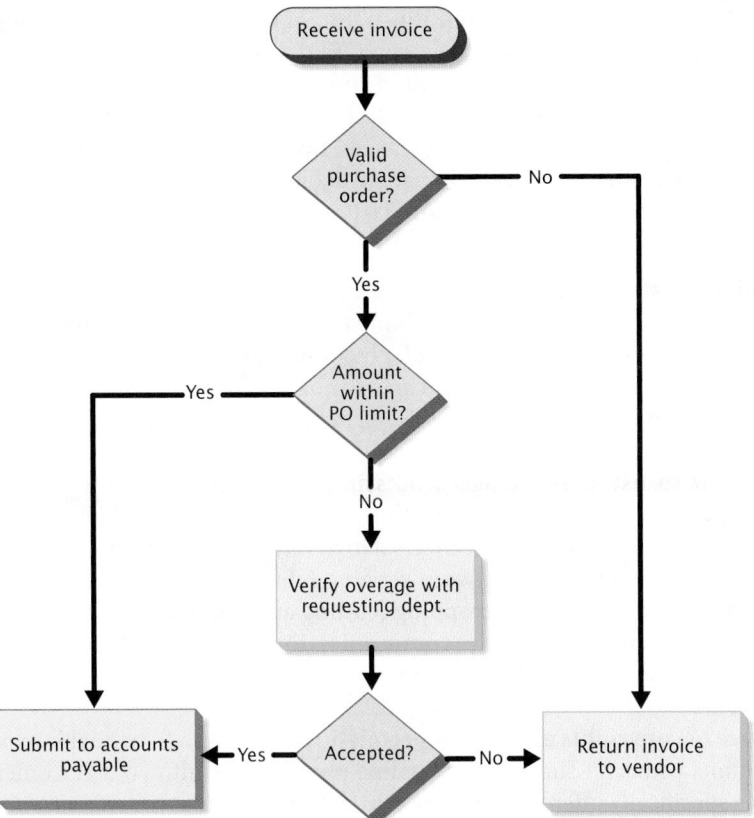

Figure 12.15 Flowchart
Flowcharts show sequences of events and are most valuable when the process or procedure has a number
of decision points and variable paths.

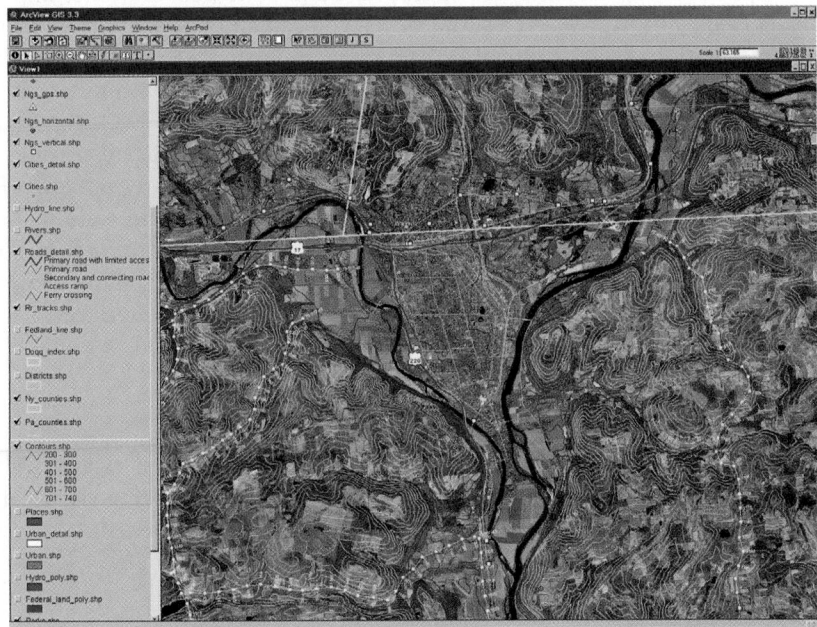

Figure 12.16 Geographic Information Systems
Businesses use geographic information systems (GIS) in a variety of ways. By overlaying maps and aerial or
satellite imagery with descriptive data, companies can use these displays for such purposes as planning sales
campaigns, optimizing transportation routing, and selecting retail or production sites.
Source: Image courtesy of Satellite Imaging Corporation.

package such as Microsoft Visio, Adobe Illustrator, or Google SketchUp. Moving a level beyond those programs, *computer-aided design* (CAD) systems such as Autodesk's AutoCAD can produce extremely detailed architectural and engineering drawings.

Photographs offer both functional and decorative value, and nothing can top a photograph when you need to show exact appearances. Because audiences expect photographs to show literal visual truths, you must take care to avoid misleading results when using image processing tools such as Adobe Photoshop. To use photographs successfully, consider these guidelines:

> *Use photographs for visual appeal and for showing exact appearances.*

- **Consider whether a diagram would be more effective than a photograph.** Photographs are often unmatched in their ability to communicate spatial relationships, sizes, shapes, and other physical parameters, but sometimes they communicate too much information. A simplified diagram can be more effective for some purposes because it allows you to emphasize the specific elements of the scene that are relevant to the problem at hand.
- **Learn how to use basic image-processing functions.** For most business reports, websites, and presentations, you won't need to worry about more advanced image-processing functions and special effects. However, you need to know such basic operations such as the difference between resizing (changing the size of an image without removing any parts of it) and cropping (cutting away parts of the image).
- **Make sure the photographs have communication value.** Except for covers, title slides, and other special uses, it's usually best to avoid including photographs simply for decorative value.
- **Be aware of copyrights and model permissions.** Just as with textual information you find online, you can't simply insert online photographs into your documents. Unless they are specifically offered for free, you have to assume that someone owns the photos and is entitled to payment or at least a photo credit. When you find a photo you'd like to use, see whether the owner has posted licensing terms. In addition, professional photographers are careful to have any person who poses in photos sign a model release form, which gives the photographer permission to use the person's image.

> *Make sure you have the right to use photographs you find online.*

Animation and Video   Computer animation and video are among the most specialized forms of business visuals; when they are appropriate and done well, they offer unparalleled visual impact (see Figure 12.17). At a simple level, you can animate shapes and text within electronic presentations (see Chapter 14). At a more sophisticated level, software such as Adobe Flash enables the creation of multimedia files that include computer animation, digital video, and other elements.

The combination of low-cost digital video cameras and video-sharing websites such as YouTube has spurred a revolution in business video applications in recent years. Product demonstrations, company overviews, promotional presentations, and training seminars are among the most popular applications of business video. *Branded channels* on YouTube, such as the Lie-Nielsen example presented on page 231 in Chapter 7, allow companies to present their videos as an integrated collection in a customized user interface.

> *Branded channels on YouTube have become an important business communication outlet.*

Producing and Integrating Visuals

4   **LEARNING OBJECTIVE**

Explain how to integrate visuals with text effectively and how to verify the quality of your visuals.

After you have chosen the best visuals to illustrate key points in your report, website, or presentation, it's time to get creative. This section offers advice on creating visuals, integrating them with your text, and verifying the quality of your visual elements.

CREATING VISUALS

> *Computer software offers a variety of tools but doesn't automatically give you the design sensibility that is needed for effective visuals.*

Computers make it easy to create visuals, but they also make it easy to create ineffective, distracting, and even downright ugly visuals. However, by following the basic design principles discussed on pages 420–421, you can create all the basic visuals you need—visuals that are attractive and effective. If possible, have a professional designer set up a *template* for the various types of visuals you and your colleagues need to create. In addition to helping

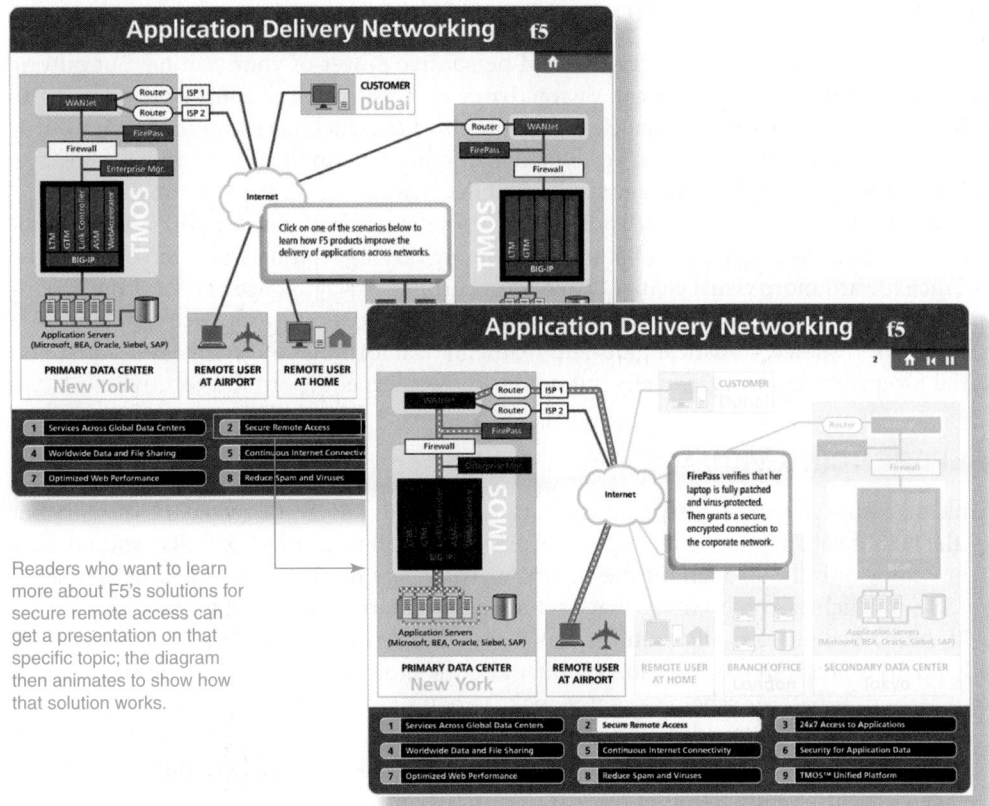

Readers who want to learn more about F5's solutions for secure remote access can get a presentation on that specific topic; the diagram then animates to show how that solution works.

Figure 12.17 Interactive, Animated Diagram
Clearly drawn diagrams help audiences grasp complex ideas quickly. Extending this capability with interactivity and animation, as F5 Networks did with this networking visual, can make a diagram even more audience-focused by letting website visitors choose the information most relevant to their individual needs. You can interact with the diagram yourself at **www.f5.com/flash/product-demo/**.
Source: Reproduced by permission of F5 Networks, Inc. © 2011 F5 Networks, Inc. All Rights Reserved.

ensure an effective design, using templates saves you the time of making numerous design decisions every time you create a chart or graphic.

Remember that the style and quality of your visuals communicate a subtle message about your relationship with the audience. A simple sketch might be fine for a working meeting but inappropriate for a formal presentation or report. On the other hand, elaborate, full-color visuals may be viewed as extravagant for an informal report but may be entirely appropriate for a message to top management or influential outsiders.

INTEGRATING VISUALS WITH TEXT

For maximum effectiveness and minimum disruption for the reader, visual elements need to be carefully integrated with the text of your message. In some instances, visual elements are somewhat independent from the text, as in the *sidebars* that occasionally accompany magazine articles. Such images are related to the content of the main story, but they aren't referred to by a specific title or figure number. For reports and most other business documents, however, visuals are tightly integrated with the text so that readers can move back and forth between text and visuals with as little disruption as possible. Successful integration involves four decisions: maintaining a balance between visuals and text, referring to visuals in the text, placing the visuals in a document, and writing titles and other descriptions.

REAL-TIME UPDATES
Learn More by Reading This PDF

Jumpstart your visual creativity

The notion that visual creativity is a skill that only artists have—or should care about—is simply not true. Every professional can develop visual thinking and design skills that will improve problem solving and communication. Go to http://real-timeupdates.com/ebc10 and click on Learn More. If you are using MyBcommLab, you can access Real-Time Updates within each chapter or under Student Study Tools.

BALANCING ILLUSTRATIONS AND WORDS

Maintain a balance between text and visuals and pace your visuals in a way that emphasizes your key points.

Strong visuals enhance the descriptive and persuasive power of your writing, but putting too many visuals into a report can distract your readers. If you're constantly referring to tables, drawings, and other visual elements, the effort to switch back and forth from words to visuals can make it difficult for readers to maintain focus on the thread of your message. The space occupied by visuals can also disrupt the flow of text on the page or screen.

As always, take into account your readers' specific needs. If you're addressing an audience with multiple language backgrounds or widely varying reading skills, you can shift the balance toward more visual elements to help get around any language barriers. The professional experience, education, and training of your audience should influence your approach as well. For instance, statistical plots and mathematical formulas are everyday reading material for quality-control engineers but not for most salespeople or top executives.

REFERENCING VISUALS

To tie visuals to the text, introduce them in the text and place them near the points they illustrate.

Unless a visual element clearly stands on its own, visuals should be referred to by number in the text of your report. Some report writers refer to all visuals as "exhibits" and number them consecutively throughout the report; many others number tables and figures separately (in which case everything that isn't a table is regarded as a figure). In a long report with numbered sections, illustrations may have a double number (separated by a period or a hyphen) representing the section number and the individual illustration number within that section. Whatever scheme you use, make sure it's clear and consistent.

Help your readers understand the significance of visuals by referring to them before readers encounter them in the document or onscreen. The following examples show how you can make this connection in the text:

Figure 1 summarizes the financial history of the motorcycle division over the past five years, with sales broken into four categories.

Total sales were steady over this period, but the mix of sales by category changed dramatically (see Figure 12.2).

The underlying reason for the remarkable growth in our sales of youth golf apparel is suggested by Table 4, which shows the growing interest in junior golf around the world.

When describing the data shown in your visuals, be sure to emphasize the main point you are trying to make. Don't make the mistake of simply repeating the data to be shown.

Placing Visuals

Try to position your visuals so that your audience doesn't have to flip back and forth (in printed documents) or scroll (onscreen) between the visuals and the text. Ideally, it's best to place each visual within, beside, or immediately after the paragraph it illustrates so that readers can consult the explanation and the visual at the same time. If possible, try to avoid bunching several visuals in one section of the document. (Bunching is unavoidable in some cases, such as when multiple visuals accompany a single section of text—as in this chapter, for instance.)

Writing Titles, Captions, and Legends

Use titles, captions, and legends to help audiences interpret visuals quickly and successfully.

Titles, captions, and legends provide more opportunities to connect your visual and textual messages. A **title** is similar to a subheading, providing a short description that identifies the content and purpose of the visual, along with whatever label and number you're using to refer to the visual. A **caption** usually offers additional discussion of the visual's content and can be several sentences long, if appropriate. Captions can also alert readers that additional discussion is available in the accompanying text. Titles usually appear above visuals, and captions appear below, but effective designs can place these two elements in other positions. Sometimes titles and captions are combined in a single block of text as well. As with all other design decisions, be consistent throughout your report or website. A **legend** helps readers decode the visual by explaining what various colors, symbols, or other design choices mean.

Readers should be able to grasp the point of a visual without digging into the surrounding text. For instance, a title that says simply "Refineries" doesn't say much at all. A **descriptive title** that identifies the topic of the illustration, such as "Relationship Between Petroleum Demand and Refinery Capacity in the United States" provides a better idea of what the chart is all about. An **informative title** tells even more by calling attention to the conclusion that ought to be drawn from the data, such as "Refinery Capacity Declines as Petroleum Demand Continues to Grow."

REAL-TIME UPDATES
Learn More by Reading This Article

Understand why some visuals work and some don't

Learn from the insightful analysis of more than a dozen commonly used displays for data and information, along with redesigned visuals that address the identified problems. Go to http://real-timeupdates.com/ebc10 and click on Learn More. If you are using MyBcommLab, you can access Real-Time Updates within each chapter or under Student Study Tools.

VERIFYING THE QUALITY OF YOUR VISUALS

Visuals have a particularly strong impact on your readers and on their perceptions of you and your work, so verifying their quality is vital. Ask yourself three questions about every visual element:

- **Is the visual accurate?** Be sure to check visuals for mistakes such as typographical errors, inconsistent color treatment, confusing or undocumented symbols, and misaligned elements. Does each visual deliver your message accurately? For data presentations, particularly if you're producing charts with a spreadsheet, verify any formulas used to generate the numbers and make sure you've selected the right numbers for each chart.
- **Is the visual properly documented?** As with the textual elements in your reports and presentations, visuals based on other people's research, information, and ideas require full citation. (Note that in many books, source notes for visuals are collected in one place at the end of the book.)
- **Is the visual honest?** As a final precaution, step back and make sure your visuals communicate truthful messages (see "Practicing Ethical Communication: Distorting the Data").

Review each visual to make sure it doesn't intentionally or unintentionally distort the meaning of the underlying information.

For the latest information on report writing and visuals, visit **http://real-timeupdates .com/ebc10** and select Chapter 12. For a review of the important points to remember when creating visuals, see "Checklist: Creating Effective Visuals."

✓ Checklist   Creating Effective Visuals

- Emphasize visual consistency to connect parts of a whole and minimize audience confusion.
- Avoid arbitrary changes of color, texture, typeface, position, or scale.
- Highlight contrasting points through color, position, and other design choices.
- Decide whether you want to achieve formal or informal balance.
- Emphasize dominant elements and deemphasize less important pieces in a design.
- Understand and follow (at least most of the time) the visual conventions your audience expects.
- Strive for simplicity and clarity; don't clutter your visuals with meaningless decoration.
- Follow the guidelines for avoiding ethical lapses.
- Carefully consider your message, the nature of your information, and your audience to choose which points to illustrate.

- Select the proper types of graphics for the information at hand and for the objective of the message.
- Be sure the visual contributes to overall understanding of the subject.
- Understand how to use your software tools to maximize effectiveness and efficiency.
- Integrate visuals and text by maintaining a balance between illustrations and words, clearly referring to visuals within the text, and placing visuals carefully.
- Use titles, captions, and legends to help readers understand the meaning and importance of your visuals.
- Verify the quality of your visuals by checking for accuracy, proper documentation, and honesty.

Distorting the Data

Take a quick look at these three line charts, all of which display the level of impurities found in a particular source of drinking water. Chart A suggests that the source has a consistently high level of impurities throughout the year, Chart B indicates that the level of impurities jumps up and down throughout the year, and Chart C shows an impurity level that is fairly consistent throughout the year—and fairly low.

Here's the catch: All three charts are displaying *exactly the same data*.

Look again at Chart A. The vertical scale is set from 0 to 120, sufficient to cover the range of variations in the data.

However, what if you wanted to persuade an audience that the variations from month to month were quite severe? In Chart B, the scale is "zoomed in" on 60 to 110, making the variations look much more dramatic. The result could be a stronger emotional impact on the reader, creating the impression that these impurities are out of control.

On the other hand, what if you wanted to create the impression that things were humming along just fine, with low levels of impurities and no wild swings from month to month? You would follow the example in Chart C, where the scale is expanded from 0 to 200, which appears to minimize the

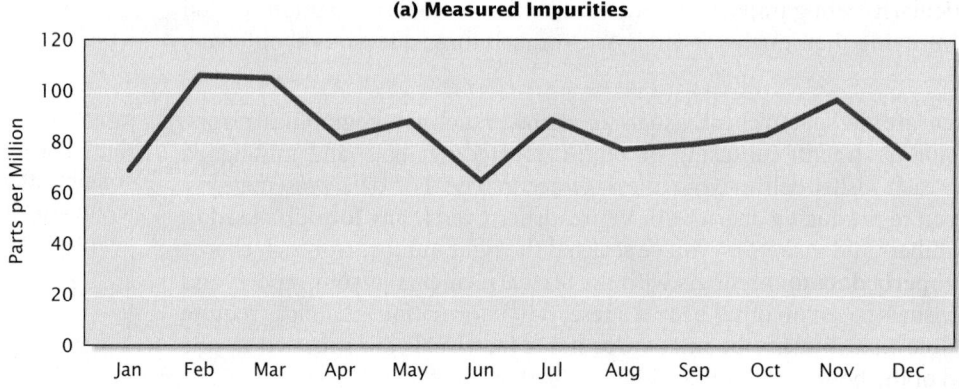

(a) Measured Impurities

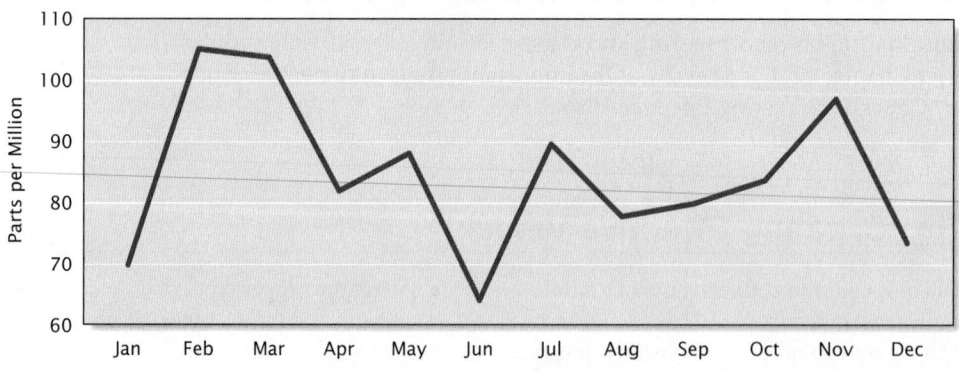

(b) Measured Impurities

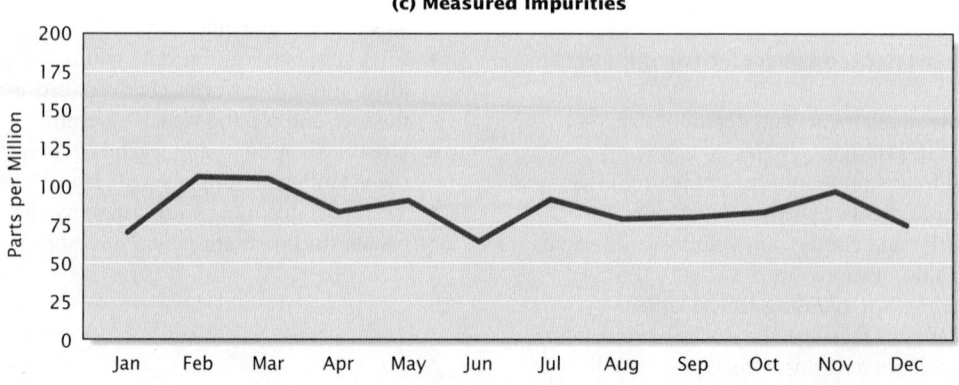

(c) Measured Impurities

variations in the data. This graph is visually "calmer," potentially creating the impression that there's really nothing to worry about.

If all three graphs show the same data, is any one of them more honest than the others? The answer to this question depends on your intent and your audience's information needs. For instance, if dramatic swings in the measurement from month to month suggest a problem with the quality of your product or the safety of a process that affects the public,

then visually minimizing the swings might well be considered dishonest.

CAREER APPLICATIONS

1. What sort of quick visual impression would such a chart give if the vertical scale is set to 0 to 500? Why?
2. If the acceptable range of impurities in this case is from 60 to 120 parts per million, which of these three charts is the fairest way to present the data? Why?

ON THE JOB: SOLVING COMMUNICATION DILEMMAS AT **TELLABS**

Source: Courtesy Tellabs. Photo by Robert Seale.

You wanted to start your career in corporate communications with an opportunity to learn from one of the best, so you're excited to be on George Stenitzer's team at Tellabs. Using the skills you've been practicing in this course, respond to these challenges.

1. The "CEO's letter" in a corporate annual report serves as an introduction to the rest of the report. In a recent report, CEO Krish Prabhu opened his letter with the following:

> More. I can't think of a better word to describe what's happening in communications today. All across the world, people want to see more. Do more. Interact more. Learn more. And everywhere we look, the world's communications providers are rushing to respond.
>
> This transition to tomorrow's networks represents a unique growth opportunity for Tellabs. That's because making more possible is what this company is all about. We do it by supplying the solutions that providers need to make their networks smarter, faster and better-suited to the kinds of high-bandwidth applications that will define the future of communications.
>
> In fact, that future is already with us. As I write this, YouTube, the immensely popular videosharing Web site, is already one of the top 15 Web sites in the world, even though it has yet to celebrate its second birthday. YouTube originates an average of 100 million video streams each day. And thanks to a partnership with Verizon, those videos are now accessible even when we're away from our computers.
>
> The YouTube success story is merely one illustration of the remarkable changes that are taking place in the way we communicate and entertain ourselves.

After reviewing a draft, Stenitzer suggested that a heading would help intrigue and prepare readers for the information in this section. Which of the following headings does the best job of introducing this section of Prabhu's letter? (The purpose of discussing these changes in online

communication and networking is to convince investors that the market opportunities for Tellabs's products will continue to grow.)
   a. There's No Stopping Us Now!
   b. Exciting Opportunities in the Exciting New World of High-Bandwidth Communication
   c. Growth Opportunities in a Growing Market
   d. Growth Opportunities: Market Drivers

2. Like many other companies associated with the Internet, Tellabs's business declined when the dot-com boom of the late 1990s began to fizzle out by early 2001. The following excerpt from one of the company's recent annual report describes the effect this had on the company's operations. (The *carriers* and *service providers* referred to are the companies that buy Tellabs's products; *material charges* are expenses that are significant enough to affect the company's stock price.) As you review these two paragraphs (don't worry about all the technical and financial details), you can see that the first discusses the period from 2001 to 2003, when the company's financial results suffered. The second discusses the upturn that began in 2003 and continued through 2005.

> The markets for our products have undergone dynamic change over the last few years. Beginning in 2001, carrier overcapacity, a softening economy and other factors caused our customers to reduce their capital spending significantly. The impact on Tellabs was a dramatic decline in revenue for each of the years 2001 through 2003. In addition, we had manufacturing overcapacity, excess inventories and a cost structure that could not be supported by our smaller revenue base. We responded by closing manufacturing facilities, reducing global head count, consolidating office space, exiting certain product lines and instituting cost controls across the organization. We also reviewed our product portfolio and cut back or stopped development efforts on some products. In addition, at the end of 2003, we moved to outsource the majority of our remaining manufacturing operations to third-party electronics manufacturing services providers to take advantage of their greater purchasing power and other efficiencies. These actions caused us to record material

charges in 2001 through 2005 for excess and obsolete inventory and excess purchase commitments, severance costs, facilities shutdown costs, including accelerated depreciation on certain manufacturing and office buildings and equipment due to shortened useful lives, and various contractual obligations. We also recorded charges for other impaired and surplus assets.

Market stability began in 2003 and continued in 2004 and 2005 as service providers invested in their networks at levels at or above 2003. This stability enabled us to post year-over-year revenue growth in 2004 for the first time since fiscal year 2000. Growing demand for wireless services, including third-generation (3G) services, drove capital investments by both wireless and wireline service providers and helped drive sales of our transport and managed access products.

Which of the following transition sentences would be the best choice to add at the beginning of the second paragraph, signaling to readers that the story is about to change from the negative news of 2001 to 2003 to the more positive results that began in 2003?

a. Were we glad to see the dark days of 2001 to 2003 behind us!

b. Fortunately, those bad times didn't last forever.

c. These aggressive measures helped the company survive the extended downturn and prepared us to grow again when the market recovered.

d. Transitioning forward, the situation began to improve beginning in 2003.

3. You've just helped a team from the marketing and engineering departments draft a report on the prospects for the electronic communication market over the next five years. Thanks to the team's diligent research, you're confident that the information is as about as current as it could possibly be. However, so many things associated with the Internet can change so quickly that you can't guarantee the information will be accurate several months from now, much less several years from now. Which of the following statements would be the best way to express this limitation of the report?

a. It must be pointed out that the information in this report may become obsolete as market conditions change. This is a function of the dynamic nature of the market and is not an issue with the quality of our research.

b. The information contained herein was current as of the time of publication. We cannot guarantee its accuracy in the future.

c. The dynamic nature of the electronic communication industry means that information is likely to change over time. Please accept our apologies for this limitation.

d. The dynamic nature of the electronic communication industry means that information is likely to change over time. Please check with us for the latest news and insights before making any major strategic or financial decisions based on the content of this report.

4. To help readers quickly assess the relative contributions of Tellabs's various product lines to the company's overall revenues, year by year over a 10-year period, which type of visual would be most effective?

a. Ten pie charts, one per year, showing the breakdown of sales by product line

b. A table, with the years in columns and the product lines in rows

c. An area chart

d. A bar chart

LEARNING OBJECTIVES CHECKUP

Assess your understanding of the principles in this chapter by reading each learning objective and studying the accompanying exercises. For fill-in-the-blank items, write the missing text in the blank provided; for multiple-choice items, circle the letter of the correct answer. You can check your responses against the answer key on page AK-2.

Objective 12.1: Explain how to adapt to your audiences when writing reports and proposals, and describe the choices involved in drafting report and proposal content.

1. Why is the "you" attitude particularly important with long or complex reports and proposals?

   a. The "you" attitude takes less time to write, so you'll save considerable time with long documents.

   b. Professionals are accustomed to reading long reports, so they don't require a lot of "hand holding."

   c. People simply don't read reports that don't demonstrate good business etiquette.

   d. The length and complexity of these reports put a heavy demand on readers, making it particularly important to be sensitive to their needs.

2. Which of these sentences has the most formal tone?

   a. We discuss herein the possibility of synergistic development strategies between our firm and U.S. Medical.

   b. This report explores the potential for a strategic partnership with U.S. Medical.

   c. My report is the result of a formal investigation into the possibility of a strategic partnership with U.S. Medical.

   d. In this report, I address the potential for a strategic partnership with U.S. Medical.

3. Which of these does not belong in the body of an informational or analytical report?

   a. An explanation of weaknesses in the report

   b. Facts, statistical evidence, and trends

   c. Conclusions and recommendations

   d. Criteria for evaluating alternatives and options

4. Where would you list action items in a report?

   a. In the opening

   b. In the body

   c. In the close

   d. Action items are never listed in reports.

5. How are audiences likely to react if they spot several errors in your reports?
   a. They'll become skeptical about the quality of all your work.
   b. They'll forgive you and move on without thinking any more about it; everybody makes mistakes.
   c. They'll stop reading your reports.
   d. They'll respect the fact that you don't waste time proofreading.

6. Which of the following is not a recommended strategy for strengthening your proposal argument?
   a. Provide concrete examples of the value of your proposal.
   b. Demonstrate your knowledge.
   c. Identify the amount of time you've invested in the proposal.
   d. Adopt a "you" attitude.

7. If packaging and presentation are only superficial, why are they so important in proposal writing?
   a. Readers tend to prejudge the quality of your products and services based on the quality of your proposal.
   b. They show that you're more than just a "numbers" person—that you can think creatively.
   c. They show the audience that you're willing to invest time and money in getting your proposal accepted.
   d. Attractive documents almost always have high-quality information in them.

8. Which of the following elements is usually *not* part of a proposal's introduction?
   a. Background or statement of the problem
   b. Detailed cost analysis
   c. Organization of the proposal
   d. Scope of the proposal

9. The primary purpose of the body of a proposal is to
   a. List your firm's qualifications for the project in question
   b. Explain why the recipient needs to address a particular problem or opportunity
   c. Communicate your passion for solving the problem or addressing the opportunity
   d. Give complete details on the proposed solution and its anticipated benefits

10. If a proposal is being sent in response to an RFP, how should the body of the proposal address the issue of costs?
    a. It should avoid any mention of costs.
    b. It should provide a total cost figure without wasting the reader's time with a lot of details.
    c. It should follow whatever your company's policy is regarding cost estimates.
    d. It should follow the instructions in the RFP exactly.

Objective 12.2: Identify five characteristics of effective writing in online reports, and explain how to adapt your writing approach for wikis.

11. _____ goes a step beyond translating, making sure web content reflects not only the native language of your readers but also their cultural norms, weights, measures, currency, and other specific elements.

12. Which of the following is the most effectively worded link to a webpage that describes a company's products and services?
    a. <u>Click here</u> to learn more about what we do.
    b. Learn more about <u>our products and services</u>.
    c. <u>Next page</u>
    d. You have problems? We have <u>solutions</u>.

13. Which of the following best summarizes some key advice for wiki collaboration?
    a. Because so many writers can be involved in a wiki, managerial control of content and process is essential.
    b. Personal responsibility is paramount with wikis, so all contributors must safeguard their contributions against unwelcome editing.
    c. Conventional web security measures such as access control should never be used on wikis because they inhibit free collaboration.
    d. Wikis writers need to let go of traditional expectations of authorship, including individual recognition and control.

Objective 12.3: Discuss six principles of graphic design, and identify the most common types of visuals used to present data, information, concepts, and ideas.

14. Why is consistency important in visual design?
    a. It shows the audience that you're not wasting precious time doing artistic designs.
    b. It reduces confusion by eliminating arbitrary changes that force people to relearn your design scheme every time they encounter another visual.
    c. It saves on ink and toner when reports are printed.
    d. It shows the audience that you're serious and businesslike.

15. Which of the following steps could you take to call attention to the most important elements in a visual?
    a. Use a dominant color for the important elements.
    b. Call attention to the important elements in the caption or in the text of your report.
    c. Make the important elements larger.
    d. Do all of the above.

16. Which of the following is a good candidate for illustrating in a report?
    a. Comparison of customer satisfaction ratings of 12 stores across a 12-month period
    b. Percentage of employees who have attended 10 different training courses
    c. Ranking of webpages on a website, from most visited to least visited
    d. All of the above

17. Which of the following is *not* a good reason to use a visual in a report?
    a. To communicate more effectively with multilingual audiences
    b. To help unify the separate parts of a process, an organization, or another entity, such as by using a flowchart to depict the various steps in a process
    c. To simplify access to specific data points, such as by listing them in a quick-reference table
    d. To demonstrate your creative side

18. _____ _____ overcomes several shortcomings of conventional charts and graphs—the inability to show only a limited number of data points before becoming too cluttered to interpret, a limited ability to show complex relationships among data points, and the ability to represent only numeric data.

19. Which of these is a good reason to use a diagram instead of a photograph?
    a. Diagrams are more colorful and aren't limited to colors found in real life.
    b. Diagrams are more realistic than photographs.
    c. Diagrams allow you to control the amount of detail shown to focus reader attention on particular parts of the image.
    d. All of the above are true.

Objective 12.4: Explain how to integrate visuals with text effectively and how to verify the quality of your visuals.

20. Which of the following steps should you take to verify the accuracy of the visuals in your reports?
    a. Make sure that data presentations such as line charts and bar charts accurately portray the data that you intended to show.
    b. Make sure flowcharts and other computer-generated artwork are correct and clear.
    c. Make sure that you've inserted the correct visuals at each place in your report.
    d. Do all of the above.

21. Assume that you have a line chart with a vertical axis scaled from 0 to 100 and data points that vary within a range of roughly 10 to 90. How would you influence audience perceptions if you increased the vertical scale so that it stretched from 0 to 200 instead of 0 to 100?
    a. The scaling change would have no affect on audience perceptions.
    b. The scaling change would maximize the perceived variations in the data.
    c. The scaling change would minimize the perceived variations in the data.
    d. You have no way of predicting in advance how the scaling change would affect perceptions.

MyBcommLab

Log on to www.pearsoninternationaleditions.com/mybcommlab to access study and assessment aids associated with this chapter. If you are not using MyBcommLab, you can access the Real-Time Updates http://real-timeupdates.com/ebc10.

LEARNING OBJECTIVES

1. Explain how to adapt to your audiences when writing reports and proposals, and describe the choices involved in drafting report and proposal content. [page 408]
2. Identify five characteristics of effective writing in online reports, and explain how to adapt your writing approach for wikis. [page 418]
3. Discuss six principles of graphic design, and identify the most common types of visuals used to present data, information, concepts, and ideas. [page 420]
4. Explain how to integrate visuals with text effectively and how to verify the quality of your visuals. [page 432]

KEY TERMS

area chart Another name for a surface chart

bar chart Chart that portrays quantities by the height or length of its rectangular bars

caption Brief commentary or explanation that accompanies a visual

data visualization A diverse class of displays that can show enormous sets of data in a single visual or show text and other complex information visually

descriptive title Title that simply identifies the topic of an illustration

flowchart Process diagram that illustrates a sequence of events from start to finish

infographics Diagrams that contain enough visual and textual information to function as independent documents

informative title Title that highlights the conclusion to be drawn from the data

legend A "key" that helps readers decode a visual by explaining what various colors, symbols, or other design choices mean

line chart Chart that illustrates trends over time or plots the relationship of two or more variables

organization chart Diagram that illustrates the positions, units, or functions of an organization and their relationships

pie chart Circular chart that shows how the parts of a whole are distributed

surface chart Form of line chart with a cumulative effect; all the lines add up to the top line, which represents the total

table A systematic arrangement of numerical or textual in columns and rows

title Identifies the content and purpose of a visual

visual literacy The ability (as a sender) to create effective images and (as a receiver) to correctly interpret visual messages

visual symbolism The connotative (as opposed to the denotative, or literal) meaning of visuals

 **Checklist**

Composing Business Reports and Proposals

A. Review and fine-tune your outline.
- Match your parallel headings to the tone of your report or proposal.
- Understand how the introduction, body, and close work together to convey your message.

B. Draft report content.
- Use the introduction to establish the purpose, scope, and organization of your report or proposal.
- Use the body to present and interpret the information you gathered.
- Use the close to summarize major points, discuss conclusions, or make recommendations.

C. Draft proposal content.
- Use the introduction to discuss the background or problem, your solution, the scope, and organization.
- Use the body to persuasively explain the benefits of your proposed approach.
- Use the close to emphasize reader benefits and summarize the merits of your approach.

D. Help readers find their way.
- Provide headings to improve readability and clarify the framework of your ideas.
- Use hyperlinks online to allow readers to jump from section to section.
- Create transitions that tie together ideas and show how one thought relates to another.
- Preview important topics to help readers get ready for new information.
- Review key information to help readers absorb details and keep the big picture in mind.

APPLY YOUR KNOWLEDGE

To review chapter content related to each question, refer to the indicated Learning Objective.

1. Why is it important to write clear, descriptive headings and link titles with online content, as opposed to clever, word-play headings? [LO-2]

2. Should the most experienced member of a department have final approval of the content for the department's wiki? Why or why not? [LO-3]

3. For providing illustration in a report or proposal, when is a diagram a better choice than a photograph? [LO-4]

4. If you wanted to compare average monthly absenteeism for five divisions in your company over the course of a year, which type of visual would you use? Explain your choice. [LO-4]

5. If a company receives a solicited formal proposal outlining the solution to a particular problem, is it ethical for the company to adopt the proposal's recommendations without hiring the firm that submitted the proposal? Why or why not? [LO-5]

PRACTICE YOUR SKILLS

Messages for Analysis

 Learn the basics of creating a company profile on Facebook. Visit http://realtimeupdaates.com/ebc10, click on Learn More and then click on Facebook Screencast.

Memco Construction
187 W. Euclid Avenue, Glenview, IL 60025
www.memco.com
April 19, 2012

Dear Mr. Estes:

PROJECT: IDOT Letting Item #83 Contract No. 79371 DuPage County

Memco Construction proposes to furnish all labor, material, equipment, and supervision to provide Engineered Fill—Class II and IV—for the following unit prices.

Engineered Fill—Class II and IV

Description	Unit	Quantity	Unit Price	Total
Mobilization*	Lump Sum	1	$4,500.00	$4,500.00
Engineered Fill Class II	Cubic Yards	1,267	$33.50	$41,811.00
Engineered Fill Class IV	Cubic Yards	1,394	$38.00	$52,972.00

* Mobilization includes one move-in. Additional move-ins to be billed at $1,100.00 each.

The following items clarify and qualify the scope of our subcontracting work:
1. All forms, earthwork, clearing, etc., to be provided and maintained by others at no cost to Memco Construction.
2. General Contractor shall provide location for staging, stockpiling material, equipment, and storage at the job site.
3. Memco Construction shall be paid strictly based upon the amount of material actually used on the job.
4. All prep work, including geotechnical fabrics, geomembrane liners, etc., to be done by others at no cost to Memco Construction.
5. Water is to be available at project site at no charge to Memco Construction.
6. Dewatering to be done by others at no cost to Memco Construction.
7. Traffic control setup, devices, maintenance, and flagmen are to be provided by others at no cost to Memco Construction.
8. Memco Construction LLC may withdraw this bid if we do not receive a written confirmation that we are the apparent low sub-bidder within 10 days of your receipt of this proposal.
9. Our F.E.I.N. is 36-4478095.
10. Bond is not included in above prices. Bond is available for an additional 1 percent.

If you have any questions, please contact me at the phone number listed below.

Sincerely

Kris Beiersdorf

Kris Beiersdorf
Memco Construction
187 W. Euclid Avenue, Glenview, IL 60025
Office: (847) 352-9742, ext. 30
Fax: (847) 352-6595
Email: Kbeiersdorf@memco.com

Figure 12.18 **Solicited Proposal** *(for Message 12.C on page 443)*

Message 12.A: Revising Web Content with a "You" Attitude [LO-3]

To access this wiki exercise, visit http://real-timeupdates.com/ ebc10, click on Student Assignments, and select Chapter 12, page 443, Message 12.A. Follow the instructions for evaluating the existing content and revising it to make it more reader oriented.

Message 12.B: Improving the Effectiveness of a Wiki Article [LO-3]

To access this wiki exercise, go to http://real-timeupdates.com/ ebc10, click on Student Assignments, and select Chapter 12, page 443, Message 12.B. Follow the instructions for evaluating the existing content and revising it to make it clear and concise.

Message 12.C: Improving a Solicited Proposal [LO-1]

Read Figure 12.18 (on the preceding page), a solicited proposal, and then (1) analyze the strengths and weaknesses of this document and (2) revise the document so that it follows this chapter's guidelines.

Exercises

Active links for all websites in this chapter can be found on MyBcommLab; see your User Guide for instructions on accessing the content for this chapter. Each activity is labeled according to the primary skill or skills you will need to use. To review relevant chapter content, you can refer to the indicated Learning Objective. In some instances, supporting information will be found in another chapter, as indicated.

1. **Adapting to Your Audience [LO-1]** Review the reports shown in Figures 12.1 through 12.4. Give specific examples of how each of these reports establishes a good relationship with the audience. Consider such things as using the "you" attitude, emphasizing the positive, establishing credibility, being polite, using bias-free language, and projecting a good company or organizational image.

2. **Drafting Report Content [LO-1]** You are writing an analytical report on the U.S. sales of your newest product. Of the following topics, identify those that should be covered in the report's introduction, body, and close. Briefly explain your decisions.

   a. Regional breakdowns of sales across the country

   b. Date the product was released in the marketplace

   c. Sales figures from competitors selling similar products worldwide

   d. Predictions of how the struggling U.S. economy will affect sales over the next six months

   e. Method used for obtaining the above predictions

   f. The impact of similar products being sold in the United States by Japanese competitors

   g. Your recommendation as to whether the company should sell this product internationally

   h. Actions that must be completed by year end if the company decides to sell this product internationally

3. **Drafting Report Content [LO-1]** Your boss, Len Chow (vice president of corporate planning), has asked you to research opportunities in the cosmetics industry and to prepare a report that presents your findings and your recommendation for where you think the company should focus its marketing efforts. Here's a copy of your note cards (data were created for this exercise):

Topic: Demand
Industrywide sales have grown consistently for several decades, fueled by both a growing population and increased per capita consumption
Topic: Competition
700 companies currently in cosmetics industry
Topic: Niches
Focusing on special niches avoids head-on competition with industry leaders
Topic: Competition
Industry dominated by market leaders: Revlon, Procter & Gamble, Avon, Gillette
Topic: Demand
Industry no longer recession-proof: Past year, sales sluggish; consumer spending is down; most affected were mid- to high-priced brands; consumers traded down to less expensive lines
Topic: Competition
Smaller companies (Neutrogena, Mary Kay, Softsoap, and Noxell) survive by: specializing in niches, differentiating product line, focusing on market segment
Topic: Demand
Consumption of cosmetics relatively flat for past five years
Topic: Competition
Prices are constant while promotion budgets are increasing
Topic: Niches
Men: 50 percent of adult population; account for one-fifth of cosmetic sales; market leaders have attempted this market but failed
Topic: Demand
Cosmetic industry is near maturity, but some segments may vary. Total market currently produces annual retail sales of $14.5 billion: Cosmetics/lotions/fragrances—$5.635 billion; Personal hygiene products—$4.375 billion; Hair-care products—$3.435 billion; Shaving products—$1.055 billion
Topic: Niches
Ethnic groups: Some firms specialize in products for African Americans; few firms oriented toward Hispanic, Asian, or Native Americans, which tend to be concentrated geographically
Topic: Demand
Average annual expenditure per person for cosmetics is $88
Topic: Competition
Competition is intensifying and dominant companies are putting pressure on smaller ones
Topic: Demand
First quarter of current year, demand is beginning to revive; trend expected to continue well into next year
Topic: Niches
Senior citizens: large growing segment of population; account for 6% of cosmetic sales; specialized needs for hair and skin not being met; interested in appearance
Topic: Demand
Demographic trends: (1) Gradual maturing of baby-boomer generation will fuel growth by consuming greater quantities of shaving cream, hair-coloring agents, and skin creams; (2) population is increasing in the South and Southwest, where some brands have strong distribution

List the main idea of your message (your recommendation), the major points (your conclusions), and supporting evidence. Then construct a final report outline with first- and second-level informative headings focusing on your conclusions. Because Chow requested this report, you can feel free to use the direct approach. Finish by writing a draft of your memo report to Chow.

4. **Drafting Report Content [LO-1]** Find an article in a business newspaper or journal (in print or online) that recommends a solution to a problem. Identify the problem, the recommended solution(s), and the supporting evidence provided by the author to justify his or her recommendation(s). Did the author cite any formal or informal studies as evidence? What facts or statistics did the author include? Did the author cite any criteria for evaluating possible options? If so, what were they?

5. **Drafting Online Content [LO-2]** Compare the "About Us" pages on the websites of three companies in the same industry. Which page is the most reader-friendly? Which is the worst? What specific elements make each of these pages effective or ineffective?

6. **Drafting Report Content; Communication Ethics: Making Ethical Choices [LO-1], Chapter 1** Your boss has asked you to prepare a feasibility report to determine whether the company should advertise its custom-crafted cabinetry in the weekly neighborhood newspaper. Based on your primary research, you think they should. As you draft the introduction to your report, however, you discover that the survey administered to the neighborhood newspaper subscribers was flawed. Several of the questions were poorly written and misleading. You used the survey results, among other findings, to justify your recommendation. The report is due in three days. What actions might you want to take, if any, before you complete your report?

7. **Applying Visual Design Principles [LO-3]** Review one of the client stories in the portfolio section of the Xplane website (www.xplane.com/portfolio). Briefly describe how a visual was used to address a business problem and why a visual approach worked better in this instance than a conventional text approach would've worked.

8. **Applying Visual Design Principles [LO-3]** From online sources, find three visual presentations of data, information, or concepts. Which of the three presents its data or information most clearly? What design choices promote this level of clarity? What improvements would you make to the other visuals to make them clearer?

9. **Communication Ethics [LO-3]** Using a spreadsheet, create a bar chart or line chart, using data you find online or in a business publication. Alter the horizontal and vertical scales in several ways to produce different displays of the original data. How do the alterations distort the information? How might a reader detect whether a chart's scale has been altered?

10. **Visual Communication: Choosing the Best Visual [LO-3]** You're preparing the annual report for FretCo Guitar Corporation. For each of the following types of information,

select an appropriate chart or visual to illustrate the text. Explain your choices.

a. Data on annual sales for the past 20 years

b. Comparison of FretCo sales, product by product (electric guitars, bass guitars, amplifiers, acoustic guitars), for this year and last year

c. Explanation of how a FretCo acoustic guitar is manufactured

d. Explanation of how the FretCo Guitar Corporation markets its guitars

e. Data on sales of FretCo products in each of 12 countries

f. Comparison of FretCo sales figures with sales figures for three competing guitar makers over the past 10 years

11. **Presenting Data (Line Charts) [LO-3]** Here are last year's sales figures for the appliance and electronics megastore where you work. Construct a line chart based on these figures to help explain to the store's general manager seasonal variations in each department.

Store Sales in 2010 (In $ Thousands)

Month	Home Electronics	Computers	Appliances
January	$68	$39	$36
February	72	34	34
March	75	41	30
April	54	41	28
May	56	42	44
June	49	33	48
July	54	31	43
August	66	58	39
September	62	58	36
October	66	44	33
November	83	48	29
December	91	62	24

12. **Visual Communication: Creating Visuals (Maps) [LO-4]** You work for C & S Holdings, a company that operates coin-activated, self-service car washes. Research shows that the farther customers live from a car wash, the less likely they are to visit. You know that 50 percent of customers at each of your car washes live within a 4-mile radius of the location, 65 percent live within 6 miles, 80 percent live within 8 miles, and 90 percent live within 10 miles. C & S's owner wants to open two new car washes in your city and has asked you to prepare a report recommending locations. Using a map of your city (print or online), choose two possible locations for car washes and create a visual depicting the customer base surrounding each location. (Make up whatever population data you need.)

13. **Presenting Data (Data Visualization) [LO-3]** Explore several of the data visualization tools available through the Bovée & Thill Data Visualization and Infographics Gateway. (Go to http://real-timeupdates.com/ebct10, click on "Learn More" and the selection "Chapter 12. Data Visualization and Infographics Gateway." If you are using MyBcommLab, you can access Real-Time Updates within each chapter or under Student Study Tools.) Select one that has the potential to help business managers make decisions. Write a post for your class blog, explaining how this tool could assist with decision making. Be sure to include a link to the site where you found it.

14. **Presenting Information, Concepts, and Ideas (Photographs) [LO-3]** As directed by your instructor, team up with other students, making sure that at least one of you has a digital camera or phone capable of downloading images to your word-processing software. Find a busy location on campus or in the surrounding neighborhood, someplace with lots of signs, storefronts, pedestrians, and traffic. Scout out two different photo opportunities, one that maximizes the visual impression of crowding and clutter, and one that minimizes this impression. For the first, assume that you are someone who advocates reducing the crowding and clutter, so you want to show how bad it is. For the second, assume that you are a real estate agent or someone else who is motivated to show people that even though the location offers lots of shopping, entertainment, and other attractions, it's actually a rather calm and quiet neighborhood. Insert the two images in a word-processing document and write a caption for each that emphasizes the two opposite messages just described. Finally, write a brief paragraph, discussing the ethical implications of what you've just done. Have you distorted reality or just presented it in ways that work to your advantage? Have you prevented audiences from gaining the information they would need to make informed decisions?

EXPAND YOUR SKILLS

Critique the Professionals

Download the latest issue of the *International Trade Update* from http://trade.gov (look under "Publications"). What techniques does the report use to help readers find their way through the document or direct readers to other sources of information? What techniques are used to highlight key points in the document? Are these techniques effective? Using whatever medium your instructor requests, write a brief summary of your analysis.

Sharpening Your Career Skills Online

Bovée and Thill's Business Communication Web Search, at http://businesscommunicationblog.com/websearch, is a unique research tool designed specifically for business communication research. Use the Web Search function to find a website, video, PDF document, podcast, or PowerPoint presentation that offers advice on writing business reports or on creating effective visuals for documents and presentations. Write a brief email message to your instructor, describing the item that you found and summarizing the career skills information you learned from it.

IMPROVE YOUR GRAMMAR, MECHANICS, AND USAGE

The following exercises help you improve your knowledge of and power over English grammar, mechanics, and usage. Turn to the "Handbook of Grammar, Mechanics, and Usage" at the end of this book and review all of Sections 2.7 (Dashes) and 2.8 (Hyphens). Then look at the following 10 items. Circle the letter of the preferred choice in the following groups of sentences. (Answers to these exercises appear on page AK-4.)

1. a. Three features—size, processor speed, and durability are the main considerations.
    b. Three features—size, processor speed, and durability—are the main considerations.

2. a. The brightly lit room is the result of the top-notch lighting system.
    b. The brightly-lit room is the result of the top-notch lighting system.
    c. The brightly lit room is the result of the top notch lighting system.

3. a. I've heard your report—no—I haven't read it yet has many mistakes.
    b. I've heard your report, no—I haven't read it yet—has many mistakes.
    c. I've heard your report—no, I haven't read it yet—has many mistakes.

4. a. She bought a low-grade TV set for her house.
    b. She bought a low grade TV set for her house.

5. a. Jonathan, Shirley, Bill—these are our three top performers.
    b. Jonathan, Shirley, Bill—these are our three—top performers.

6. a. I heard that there were three maybe four—vacancies.
    b. I heard that there were three—maybe four—vacancies.

7. a. Do you know many writer directors?
    b. Do you know many writer—directors?
    c. Do you know many writer-directors?

8. a. Johanna's ever-obedient secretary—without any questions—gave me her papers.
    b. Johanna's ever obedient secretary—without any questions—gave me her papers.

9. a. The ducts and vents are badly maintained—in this apartment block—unlike those in the neighboring building.
    b. The ducts and vents are badly-maintained in this apartment block—unlike those in the neighboring building.
    c. The ducts and vents are badly maintained in this apartment block—unlike those in the neighboring building.

10. a. His never-say-die approach inspires everyone on his team, as does his desire to be bias-free in his work.
    b. His never say die approach inspires everyone on his team, as does his desire to be bias-free in his work.
    c. His never-say-die approach inspires everyone on his team, as does his desire to be bias free in his work.

For additional exercises focusing on dashes and hyphens, visit MyBcommLab. Click on Chapter 12, click on Additional Exercises to Improve Your Grammar, Mechanics, and Usage, and click on 18. Punctuation C.

CASES

Informational Reports

1. Message Strategies: Informational Reports [LO-1] As you may already know, the procedural requirements involved in getting a degree or certificate can be nearly as challenging as any course you could take.

Your task: Prepare an interim progress report detailing the steps you've taken toward completing your graduation or certification requirements. After examining the requirements listed in your college catalog, indicate a realistic schedule for completing those that remain. In addition to course requirements, include steps such as completing the residency requirement, filing necessary papers, and paying necessary fees. Use memo format for your report, and address it to anyone who is helping or encouraging you through school.

2. Message Strategies: Informational Reports [LO-1] Success in any endeavor doesn't happen all at once. For example, success in college is built one quarter or semester at a time, and the way to succeed in the long term is to make sure you succeed in the short term. After all, even a single quarter or semester of college involves a significant investment of time, money, and energy.

Your task: Imagine you work for a company that has agreed to send you to college full time, paying all your educational expenses. You are given complete freedom in choosing your courses, as long as you graduate by an agreed-upon date. All your employer asks in return is that you develop your business skills and insights as much as possible so that you can make a significant contribution to the company when you return to full-time work after graduation. To make sure that you are using your time—and your company's money—wisely, the company requires a brief personal activity report at the end of every quarter or semester (whichever your school uses). Write a brief informational report that you can email to your instructor, summarizing how you spent your quarter or semester. Itemize the classes you took, how much time you spent studying and working on class projects, whether you got involved in campus activities and organizations that help you develop leadership or communication skills, and what you learned that you can apply in a business career. (For the purposes of this assignment, your time estimates don't have to be precise.)

WIKI SKILLS   **TEAM SKILLS**

3. Message Strategies: Informational Reports; Media Skills: Wiki Writing [LO-1], [LO-2] The use of social networks by employees during work hours remains a controversial topic, with some companies encouraging networking, some at least allowing it, and others prohibiting it.

Your task: Using the free wiki service offered by Zoho (www.zoho.com/wiki/) or a comparable system, collaborate on a report that summarizes the potential advantages and disadvantages of allowing social network usage in the workplace.

WEB WRITING   **SKILLS TEAM SKILLS**

4. Message Strategies: Online Content; Collaboration: Team Projects [LO-2], Chapter 2. If you're like many other college students, your first year was more than you expected: more difficult, more fun, more frustrating, more expensive, more exhausting, more rewarding—more of everything, positive and negative. Oh, the things you know now that you didn't know then!

Your task: With several other students, identify five or six things you wish you would've realized or understood better before you started your first year of college. These can relate to your school life (such as "I didn't realize how much work I would have for my classes" or "I should've asked for help as soon as I got stuck") and your personal and social life ("I wish I would've been more open to meeting people"). Use these items as the foundation of a brief informational report that you could post on a blog that is read by high school students and their families. Your goal with this report is to help the next generation of students make a successful and rewarding transition to college.

WEB WRITING SKILLS

5. Message Strategies: Online Content [LO-2] As you probably experienced, trying to keep all the different schools straight in one's mind while researching and applying for colleges can be rather difficult. Applicants and their families would no doubt appreciate a handy summary of your college or university's key points as they relate to the selection and application process.

Your task: Adapt content from your college or university's website to create a one-page "Quick Facts" sheet about your school. Choose the information that you think prospective students and their families would find most useful. (Note that adapting existing content would be acceptable in a real-life scenario like this, because you would be re-using content on behalf of the content owner. Doing so would definitely *not* be acceptable if you were using the content for yourself or for someone other than the original owner.)

Analytical Reports

6. Message Strategies: Analytical Reports [LO-1] Mistakes can be wonderful learning opportunities if we're honest with ourselves and receptive to learning from the mistake.

Your task: Identify a mistake you've made—something significant enough to have cost you a lot of money, wasted a lot of time, harmed your health, damaged a relationship, created serious problems at work, prevented you from pursuing what could've been a rewarding opportunity, or otherwise had serious consequences. Now figure out why you made that mistake. Did you let emotions get in the way of clear thinking? Did you make a serious financial blunder because you didn't take the time to understand the consequences of a decision? Were you too cautious? Not cautious enough? Perhaps several factors led to a poor decision.

Write a brief analytical report to your instructor that describes the situation and outlines your analysis of why the failure occurred and how you can avoid making a similar mistake in the future. If you can't think of a significant mistake or failure that you're comfortable sharing with your instructor, write about a mistake that a friend or family member made (without revealing the person's identify or potentially causing him or her any embarrassment).

EMAIL SKILLS

7. Message Strategies: Analytical Reports (2 + 2 = 4 Approach) [LO-1] Think of a course you would love to see added to the core curriculum at your school. Conversely, if you would like to see a course offered as an elective rather than being required, write your email report accordingly.

Your task: Write a short email proposal using the 2 + 2 = 4 approach (refresh your memory in Chapter 11, if necessary). Prepare your proposal to be submitted to the academic dean by email. Be sure to include all the reasons that support your idea.

8. Message Strategies: Analytical Reports (Yardstick Approach) [LO-1] Assume that you will have time for only one course next term.

Your task: List the pros and cons of each of four or five courses that interest you and use the yardstick approach to settle on the course that is best for you to take at this time. Write your report in memo format and address it to your academic adviser.

LETTER WRITING SKILLS

9. Message Strategies: Analytical Reports [LO-1] Visit any restaurant, including your school cafeteria.

Your task: After your visit, write a short letter to the owner or manager, explaining (1) what you did and what you observed, (2) any violations of policy that you observed, and (3) your recommendations for improvement. The first part of your report (what you did and what you observed) will be the longest. Include a description of the premises, inside and out. Tell how long it took for each step in ordering and receiving your meal. Describe the service and food thoroughly. You are interested in both the good and bad aspects of the establishment's décor, service, and food. For the second section (violations of policy), use some common sense. If all the servers but one have their hair covered, you may assume that policy requires hair to be covered; a dirty window or restroom obviously violates policy. The last section (recommendations for improvement) involves professional judgment. What management actions would improve the restaurant?

Proposals

10. Message Strategies: Proposals [LO-1] One of the banes of apartment living is those residents who don't care about the condition of their shared surroundings. They might leave trash all over the place, dent walls when they move furniture, spill food and beverages in common areas, destroy window screens, and otherwise degrade living conditions for everyone. Landlords obviously aren't thrilled about this behavior, either, because it raises the costs of cleaning and maintaining the facility.

Your task: Assume that you live in a fairly large apartment building some distance from campus. Write an email proposal that you could send to your landlord, suggesting that fostering a sense of stronger community among residents in your building might help reduce incidents of vandalism and neglect. Propose that the little-used storage area in the basement of the building be converted to a community room, complete with a simple kitchen and a large-screen television. By attending Super Bowl parties and other events there, residents could get to know one another and perhaps forge bonds that would raise the level of shared concern for their living environment. You can't offer any proof of this in advance, of course, but share your belief that a modest investment in this room could pay off long term in lower repair and maintenance costs. Moreover, it would be an attractive feature to entice new residents.

11. Message Strategies: Proposals [LO-1] Select a product you are familiar with and imagine that you are the manufacturer trying to get a local retail outlet to carry it. Use the Internet and other resources to gather information about the product.

Your task: Write an unsolicited sales proposal in letter format to the owner (or manager) of the store, proposing that the item be stocked. Use the information you gathered to describe some of the product's features and benefits to the store. Then make up some reasonable figures, highlighting what the item costs, what it can be sold for, and what services your company provides (return of unsold items, free replacement of unsatisfactory items, necessary repairs, and so on).

PORTFOLIO BUILDER

12. Message Strategies: Proposals [LO-1] As a sales manager for Air-Trak, one of your responsibilities is writing sales proposals for potential buyers of your company's Air-Trak tracking system. The system uses global positioning system (GPS) technology to track the location of vehicles and other assets. For example, the dispatcher for a trucking company can simply click a map display on a computer screen to find out where all the company's trucks are at that instant. Air-Trak lists the following as benefits of the system:

- Making sure vehicles follow prescribed routes with minimal loitering time
- "Geofencing," in which dispatchers are alerted if vehicles leave
- Route optimization, in which fleet managers can analyze routes and destinations to find the most time- and fuel-efficient path for each vehicle
- Comparisons between scheduled and actual travel
- Enhanced security to protect both drivers and cargos

Your task: Write a brief proposal to Doneta Zachs, fleet manager for Midwest Express, 338 S.W. 6th, Des Moines, Iowa, 50321. Introduce your company, explain the benefits of the Air-Trak system, and propose a trial deployment in which you would equip five Midwest Express trucks. For the purposes of this assignment, you don't need to worry about the technical details of the system; focus on promoting the benefits and asking for a decision regarding the test project. (You can learn more about Air-Trak at www.air-trak.com.)[23]

REFERENCES

1. Adapted from George Stenitzer profile on LinkedIn, accessed 4 March 2011, www.linkedin.com/in/stenitzer; Tellabs website, accessed 4 March 2011, www.tellabs.com; Sid Cato, "World's Best 2005 Reports," Sid Cato's Office Annual Report Website, accessed 11 November 2006, www.sidcato.com; George Stenitzer, "New Challenges for Annual Reports," Presentation to National Investor Relations Institute, November 2005, www.niri-chicago.org.

2. Tellabs Solutions and Applications," Tellabs 2005 Annual Report, www.tellabs.com.

3. A. S. C. Ehrenberg, "Report Writing—Six Simple Rules for Better Business Documents," *Admap,* June 1992, 39–42.

4. Philip C. Kolin, *Successful Writing at Work,* 6th ed. (Boston: Houghton Mifflin, 2001), 552–555.

5. Martin James, "PDF Virus Spreads Without Exploiting any Flaw," IT Pro, 8 April 2010, www.itpro.co.uk.

6. Sant Corporation website, accessed 29 July 2010, www.santcorp.com.

7. "Web Writing: How to Avoid Pitfalls," *Investor Relations Business,* 1 November 1999, 15.

8. "Codex: Guidelines," WordPress website, accessed 16 February 2008, http://wordpress.org; Michael Shanks, "Wiki Guidelines," Traumwerk website, accessed 18 August 2006, http://metamedia.stanford.edu/projects/traumwerk/home; Joe Moxley, MC Morgan, Matt Barton, and Donna Hanak, "For Teachers New to Wikis," Writing Wiki, accessed 18 August 2006, http://writingwiki.org; "Wiki Guidelines," Psi, accessed 18 August 2006, http://psi-im.org.

9. Rachael King, "No Rest for the Wiki," *BusinessWeek,* 12 March 2007, www.businessweek.com.

10. "Codex: Guidelines," WordPress website, accessed 14 February 2008, http://wordpress.org.

11. Alexis Gerard and Bob Goldstein, *Going Visual* (Hoboken, N.J.: Wiley, 2005), 18.

12. Charles Kostelnick and Michael Hassett, *Shaping Information: The Rhetoric of Visual Conventions* (Carbondale, Ill.: Southern Illinois University Press, 2003), 177.

13. Gerard and Goldstein, *Going Visual,* 103–106.

14. Edward R. Tufte, *Visual Explanations: Images and Quantities, Evidence and Narrative* (Cheshire, Conn.: Graphics Press, 1997), 82.

15. Kostelnick and Hassett, *Shaping Information: The Rhetoric of Visual Conventions,* 17.

16. Kostelnick and Hassett, *Shaping Information: The Rhetoric of Visual Conventions,* 216.

17. Edward R. Tufte, *The Visual Display of Quantitative Information* (Cheshire, Conn.: Graphic Press, 1983), 113.

18. Based in part on Tufte, *Visual Explanations: Images and Quantities, Evidence and Narrative,* 29–37, 53; Paul Martin Lester, *Visual Communication: Images with Messages,* 4th ed. (Belmont, Calif.: Thomson Wadsworth, 2006), 95–105, 194–196.

19. Hoover's Online, accessed 3 December 2008, www.hoovers.com.

20. Stephen Few, "Save the Pies for Dessert," *Visual Business Intelligence Newsletter,* August 2007, www.perceptualedge.com.

21. Maria Popova, "Data Visualization: Stories for the Information Age," *BusinessWeek,* 12 August 2009, www.businessweek.com.

22. "Data Visualization: Modern Approaches," Smashing Magazine Website, 2 August 2007, www.smashingmagazine.com; "7 Thinks You Should Know About Data Visualization," Educause Learning Initiative, accessed 15 March 2008, www.educause.edu; Tagcrowd Website, accessed 15 March 2008, www.tagcrowd.com.

23. Adapted from Air-Trak website, accessed 26 July 2010, www.air-trak.com.

LEARNING OBJECTIVES   After studying this chapter, you will be able to

1 Describe the process of revising formal reports and proposals

2 Identify the major components of formal reports

3 Identify the major components of formal proposals

4 Describe an effective plan for proofreading reports and proposals

5 Describe the decision process for distributing reports and proposals

MyBcommLab **Where you see MyBcommLab in this chapter, go to** www.pearsoninternationaleditions.com/mybcommlab **for additional activities on the topic being discussed.**

ON THE JOB: COMMUNICATING AT GARAGE TECHNOLOGY VENTURES

Scanning Business Plans to Find the Next Big Thing

The "garage" is a well-known metaphor in entrepreneurial circles that dates back at least to the founding of the giant technology company Hewlett-Packard, which was literally started in a garage in the late 1930s by Bill Hewlett and Dave Packard. More than just the physical space of a workshop, the garage suggests a mindset, with inspired visionaries working on shoestring budgets in humble surroundings but pouring their hearts and minds into business ideas that can change the world—or at least make a lot of money.

Noted entrepreneur, author, speaker, and investor Guy Kawasaki and his colleagues carry on this tradition with a venture capital firm called, appropriately enough, Garage Technology Ventures. Garage is based in the heart of Silicon Valley: Palo Alto, California (which also happens to be the current and ancestral home of Hewlett-Packard).

Venture capitalists (VCs) invest in young companies, primarily in high-technology fields, and help them through the early growth stages with an eye toward recouping their investments when the company gets big enough to go public or is sold to another company. The personal finance website Motley Fool and the online music service Pandora are among the many firms in which Garage has invested in recent years.

In the Silicon Valley VC culture, the process of presenting a new company to potential investors usually involves a short presentation, "the pitch," that is supported by the executive summary from a business plan. The entire plan might become part of the conversation later, but in the early stages the executive summary has to carry the load by itself.

Guy Kawasaki, one of the founders of the venture capital firm Garage Technology Ventures, advises entrepreneurs to craft concise, compelling summaries of their businesses before pitching their ideas to investors.
Source: Courtesy of Guy Kawasaki.

449

After listening to thousands of pitches and reading thousands of business plans, the Garage team has a clear idea of what it takes for entrepreneurs to get the attention—and money—of a VC. Garage advises entrepreneurs to keep their executive summaries under 20 pages and to include nine particular elements, starting with "the grab," a compelling one- or two-sentence statement that gets an investor's attention. Following that are the customer problems the entrepreneurs aim to solve, the solution they propose, and the business opportunity that this offering represents. The next three items describe the new company's competitive advantages, its business model (how it will generate revenue), and the key personnel involved in the new venture—including why these are the right people to drive this new company forward. The final two elements are directly about money: "the promise," which is how much investors can expect to earn from their stake in the company, followed by "the ask," how much money the new company wants.

This is a lot of information to pack into a relatively short document, but doing so is essential. If investors don't understand the business model or don't think the start-up team has honed in on a real market opportunity, they won't keep listening. Fortunately, entrepreneurs can tap into the expertise of those who have gone before them and use this advice to craft powerful business plans that get noticed. The Garage team is waiting with enthusiastic encouragement, too. As the company puts it, "We are on your side. So please help us get to know you better by telling your story clearly and concisely."[1]

www.garage.com

Revising Reports and Proposals

1 **LEARNING OBJECTIVE**

Describe the process of revising formal reports and proposals.

Experienced business communicators such as Guy Kawasaki (profiled in the chapter opener) recognize that the process of writing a report or proposal doesn't end with a first draft. This chapter addresses all four tasks involved in completing longer messages: revising, producing, proofreading, and distributing. Although the tasks covered in this chapter are similar in concept to those you studied for short messages in Chapter 6, the completion stage for reports and proposals can require a lot more work. And as you've probably already experienced while doing school reports, computers, printers, network connections, and other resources have an uncanny knack for going haywire when you're frantic to finish and have no time to spare. When you're completing an important report on the job, try to leave yourself double or even triple the amount of time you think you'll need so that last-minute glitches don't compromise the quality of all your hard work.

Formal reports have a higher degree of polish and production quality, and they often contain elements not found in informal reports.

Most of the discussion in this chapter applies to *formal* reports and proposals, documents that require an extra measure of polish and professionalism and often include packaging elements not used in informal reports and other documents. Few reports and proposals require every component described in this chapter, but be sure to carefully select the elements you want to include in each of your documents.

Revising for clarity and conciseness is especially important for online reports because reading online can be difficult.

The revision process is essentially the same for reports as for any other business message, although it may take considerably more time, depending on the length of your document. Evaluate your organization, style, and tone, making sure that you've said what you want to say and that you've said it in the most logical order and in a way that responds to your audience's needs. Then work to improve the report's readability by varying sentence length, keeping paragraphs short, using lists and bullets, adding headings and subheadings, and making generous use of transitions. Keep revising the content until it is clear, concise, and compelling.

Tight, efficient writing that is easy to skim is always a plus, but it's especially important for impatient online audiences.[2] Review online report content carefully; strip out all information that doesn't directly meet audience needs, and condense everything else as much as possible. Audiences will gladly return to sites that deliver quality information quickly—and they'll avoid sites that don't.

Producing Formal Reports

2 **LEARNING OBJECTIVE**

Identify the major components of formal reports.

When you are satisfied with the quality of your text, you're ready to produce your report by incorporating the design elements discussed in Chapter 6. At this point, you should also start to add charts, graphs, and other visuals, as well as any missing text elements, such as previews and reviews.

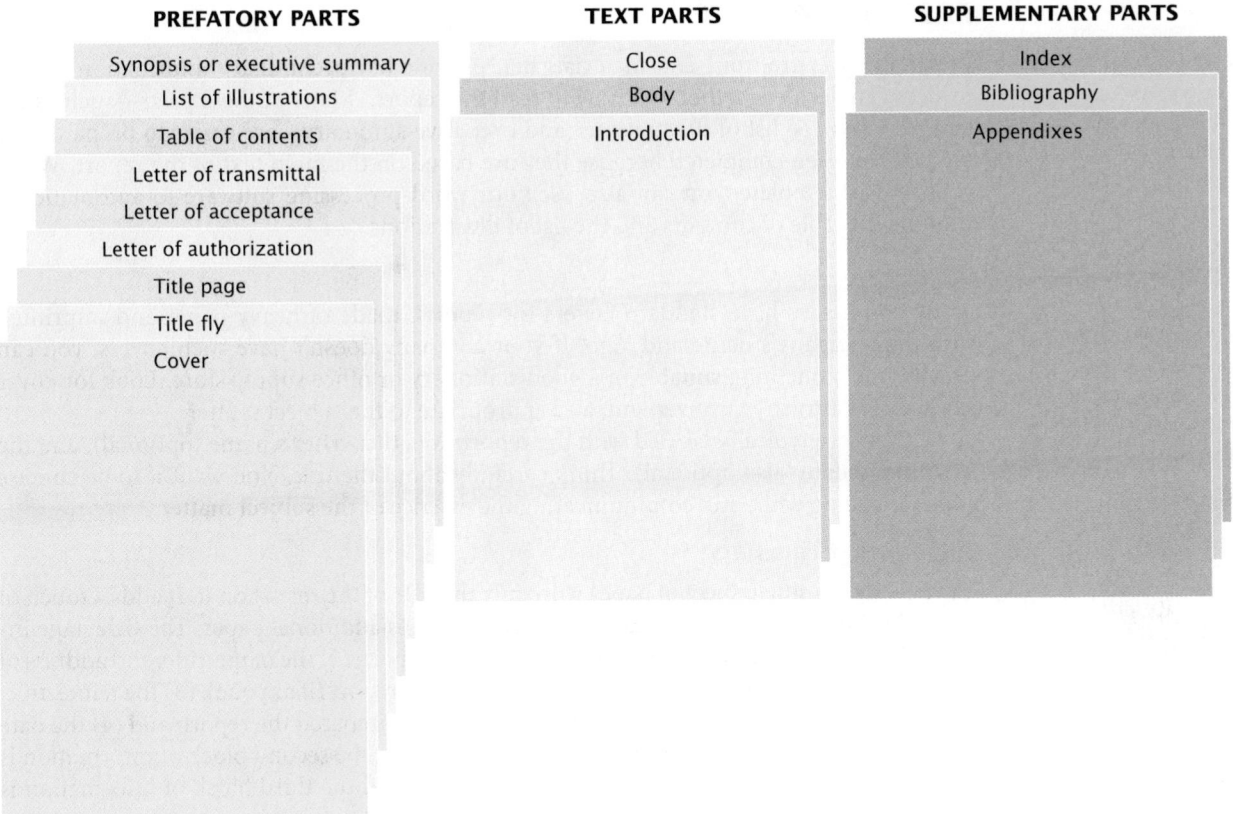

Figure 13.1   Parts of a Formal Report
Depending on the level of formality you need to achieve, you can select from these elements to complete a formal report.

In some organizations, you'll be able to rely on the help of specialists in design and production, particularly when you are working on important, high-visibility reports. You may also have clerical help available to assist with the mechanical assembly and distribution. However, for most reports in many of today's leanly staffed companies, you should count on doing most or all of the production work yourself.

In today's leanly staffed companies, you should be prepared to produce formal reports with little or no assistance from design specialists or other professionals.

The parts you include in a report depend on the type of report you are writing, its length, your audience's expectations and requirements, and your organization's preferences. The components listed in Figure 13.1 fall into three categories: prefatory parts, text of the report, and supplementary parts. For an illustration of how the various parts fit together, see Linda Moreno's Electrovision report in "Report Writer's Notebook: Analyzing a Formal Report."

A component of a formal report may start on a new page, but not always. Inserting page breaks consumes more paper and adds to the bulk of your report. On the other hand, starting a section on a new page helps readers navigate the report and recognize transitions between major sections or features.

If you want a section to stand out, start it on a new page.

When you want a particular section to stand apart, start it on a new page (in the same way that each chapter in this book starts on a new page). Most prefatory parts, such as the table of contents, should also be placed on their own pages. However, the various parts in the report text are often run together. If your introduction is only a paragraph long, don't bother with a page break before moving into the body of your report. If the introduction runs longer than a page, however, a page break can signal the reader that a major shift is occurring in the flow of the report.

REAL-TIME UPDATES
Learn More by Reading This Article

Get practical advice on developing research reports

The Online Writing Lab offers advice on developing all the sections of a typical research report. Go to http://real-timeupdates.com/ebc10 and click on Learn More. If you are using MyBcommLab, you can access Real-Time Updates within each chapter or under Student Study Tools.

PREFATORY PARTS

Formal reports can contain a variety of prefatory parts, from a cover page to a synopsis or executive summary.

Prefatory parts are front-end materials that provide key preliminary information so that readers can decide whether and how to read the report.[3] Many of these parts—such as the table of contents, list of illustrations, and executive summary—are easier to prepare after the text has been completed because they are based on the main text of the report. When your text is complete, you can also use your word-processing software to automatically compile the table of contents and the list of illustrations.

Cover

Many companies have standard covers for reports, made of heavy paper and imprinted with the company's name and logo. If your company doesn't have such covers, you can usually find something suitable in a good stationery or office supply store. Look for cover stock that is attractive, convenient, and appropriate to the subject matter.

Covers are typically labeled with the report title, the writer's name (optional), and the submission date (also optional). Think carefully about the title. You want it to be concise and compelling while still communicating the essence of the subject matter.

Title Fly and Title Page

The **title fly** is a single sheet of paper with only the title of the report on it. It adds a touch of formality, but it isn't really necessary, and it consumes additional paper. The **title page** includes four blocks of information: (1) the title of the report; (2) the name, title, and address of the person, group, or organization that authorized the report (if anyone); (3) the name, title, and address of the person, group, or organization that prepared the report; and (4) the date on which the report was submitted. On some title pages, the second block of information is preceded by the words *Prepared for* or *Submitted to*, and the third block of information is preceded by *Prepared by* or *Submitted by*. In some cases, the title page serves as the cover of the report, especially if the report is relatively short and is intended solely for internal use.

Letter of Authorization and Letter of Acceptance

A letter of authorization is a document that instructs you to produce a report; a letter of acceptance is your written agreement to produce the report.

If you received written authorization to prepare a report, you might want to include that **letter of authorization** (or *memo of authorization*) in your report. If you wrote a **letter of acceptance** (or *memo of acceptance*) in response to that communication, accepting the assignment and clarifying any conditions or limitations, you might also include that letter here, in the report's prefatory parts. In general, letters of authorization and acceptance are included in only the most formal reports. However, consider including one or both if a significant amount of time has passed since you started the project or if you do not have a close working relationship with the audience. These pieces help make sure everyone is clear about the report's intent and the approach you took to create it.

Letter of Transmittal

A letter or memo of transmittal introduces your report to your audience.

The **letter of transmittal** (or *memo of transmittal*), a specialized form of a cover letter that is usually positioned right before the table of contents, introduces your report to the audience. This piece says what you would say if you were handing the report directly to the person who authorized it, so the style is often less formal than the rest of the report.

If your readers are likely to be skeptical of or even hostile to something in your report, the letter of transmittal is a good place to acknowledge their concerns and explain how the report addresses the issues they care about. Also, if you need to convey sensitive information to selected audience members, you can opt to include the letter in just those copies.

Depending on the nature of your report, your letter of transmittal can follow either the direct approach for routine or positive messages described in Chapter 8 or the indirect approach for negative messages described in Chapter 9. Open by introducing the report and summarizing its purpose, with a statement such as "Here is the report you asked me to prepare on. . . ." The rest of the introduction includes information about the scope of the report, the methods used to complete the study, limitations, and any special messages you need to convey. If the report does not have a synopsis, the letter of transmittal may summarize the major findings, conclusions, and recommendations.

If you don't include a synopsis, you can summarize the report's content in your letter of transmittal.

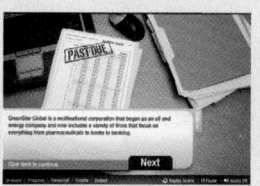

MyBcommLab

- Access this chapter's simulation entitled Completing Reports and Proposals located at www.pearsoninternationaleditions.com/mybcommlab.

(continued on page 468)

Analyzing a Formal Report

The report presented in the following pages was prepared by Linda Moreno, manager of the cost accounting department at Electrovision, a high-tech company based in Los Gatos, California. Electrovision's main product is optical character recognition equipment, which is used by the U.S. Postal Service for sorting mail. Moreno's job is to help analyze the company's costs. She has this to say about the background of the report:

> For the past three or four years, Electrovision has been on a roll. Our A-12 optical character reader was a real breakthrough, and the post office grabbed up as many as we could make. Our sales and profits kept climbing, and morale was fantastic. Everybody seemed to think that the good times would last forever. Unfortunately, everybody was wrong. When the Postal Service announced that it was postponing all new equipment purchases because of cuts in its budget, we woke up to the fact that we are essentially a one-product company with one customer. At that point, management started scrambling around looking for ways to cut costs until we could diversify our business a bit.
>
> The vice president of operations, Dennis McWilliams, asked me to help identify cost-cutting opportunities in travel and entertainment. On the basis of his personal observations, he felt that Electrovision was overly generous in its travel

policies and that we might be able to save a significant amount by controlling these costs more carefully. My investigation confirmed his suspicion.

> I was reasonably confident that my report would be well received. I've worked with Dennis for several years and know what he likes: plenty of facts, clearly stated conclusions, and specific recommendations for what should be done next. I also knew that my report would be passed on to other Electrovision executives, so I wanted to create a good impression. I wanted the report to be accurate and thorough, visually appealing, readable, and appropriate in tone.

When writing the analytical report that follows, Moreno based the organization on conclusions and recommendations presented in direct order. The first two sections of the report correspond to Moreno's two main conclusions: that Electrovision's travel and entertainment costs are too high and that cuts are essential. The third section presents recommendations for achieving better control over travel and entertainment expenses. As you review the report, analyze both the mechanical aspects and the way Moreno presents her ideas. Be prepared to discuss the way the various components convey and reinforce the main message.

MyBcommLab

Apply Report Writer's Notebook's key concepts
by revising a new document. Go to Chapter 13 in
www.pearsoninternationaleditions.com/mybcommlab
and select Document Makeovers.

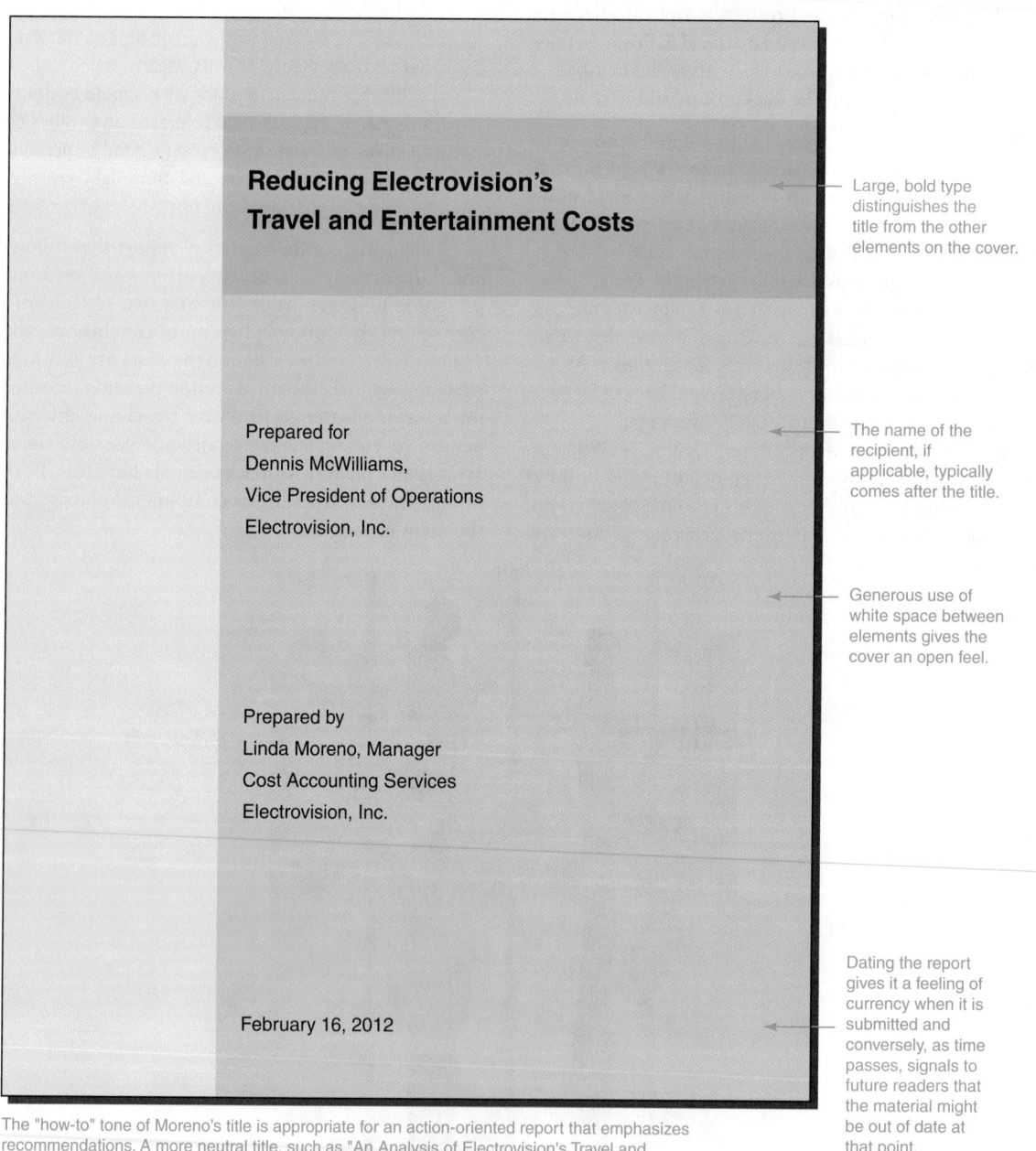

**Reducing Electrovision's
Travel and Entertainment Costs**

Large, bold type distinguishes the title from the other elements on the cover.

Prepared for
Dennis McWilliams,
Vice President of Operations
Electrovision, Inc.

The name of the recipient, if applicable, typically comes after the title.

Generous use of white space between elements gives the cover an open feel.

Prepared by
Linda Moreno, Manager
Cost Accounting Services
Electrovision, Inc.

February 16, 2012

Dating the report gives it a feeling of currency when it is submitted and conversely, as time passes, signals to future readers that the material might be out of date at that point.

The "how-to" tone of Moreno's title is appropriate for an action-oriented report that emphasizes recommendations. A more neutral title, such as "An Analysis of Electrovision's Travel and Entertainment Costs," would be more suitable for an informational report.

The memo format is appropriate for this internal report; the letter format would be used for transmitting an external report.

MEMORANDUM

TO: Dennis McWilliams, Vice President of Operations
FROM: Linda Moreno, Manager of Cost Accounting Services *LM*
DATE: February 16, 2012
SUBJECT: Reducing Electrovision's Travel and Entertainment Costs

Here is the report you requested January 28 on Electrovision's travel and entertainment costs.

Your suspicions were right. We are spending far too much on business travel. Our unwritten policy has been "anything goes," leaving us with no real control over T&E expenses. Although this hands-off approach may have been understandable when Electrovision's profits were high, we can no longer afford the luxury of going first class.

Moreno expects a positive response, so she presents her main conclusion right away.

The tone is conversational yet still businesslike and respectful.

The solutions to the problem seem rather clear. We need to have someone with centralized responsibility for travel and entertainment costs, a clear statement of policy, an effective control system, and a business-oriented travel service that can optimize our travel arrangements. We should also investigate alternatives to travel, such as videoconferencing. Perhaps more important, we need to change our attitude. Instead of viewing travel funds as a bottomless supply of money, all traveling employees need to act as if they were paying the bills themselves.

Getting people to economize is not going to be easy. In the course of researching this issue, I've found that our employees are deeply attached to their generous travel privileges. I think some would almost prefer a cut in pay to a loss in travel status. We'll need a lot of top management involvement to sell people on the need for moderation. One thing is clear: People will be very bitter if we create a two-class system in which top executives get special privileges while the rest of the employees make the sacrifices.

Acknowledging help given by others is good etiquette and a way to foster positive working relationships.

I'm grateful to Mary Lehman and Connie McIllvain for their considerable help in rounding up and sorting through five years' worth of expense reports.

Thanks for giving me the opportunity to work on this assignment. It's been a real education. If you have any questions about the report, please give me a call.

She closes graciously, with thanks and an offer to discuss the results.

In this report, Moreno decided to write a brief memo of transmittal and include a separate executive summary. Short reports (fewer than 10 pages) often combine the synopsis or executive summary with the memo or letter of transmittal.

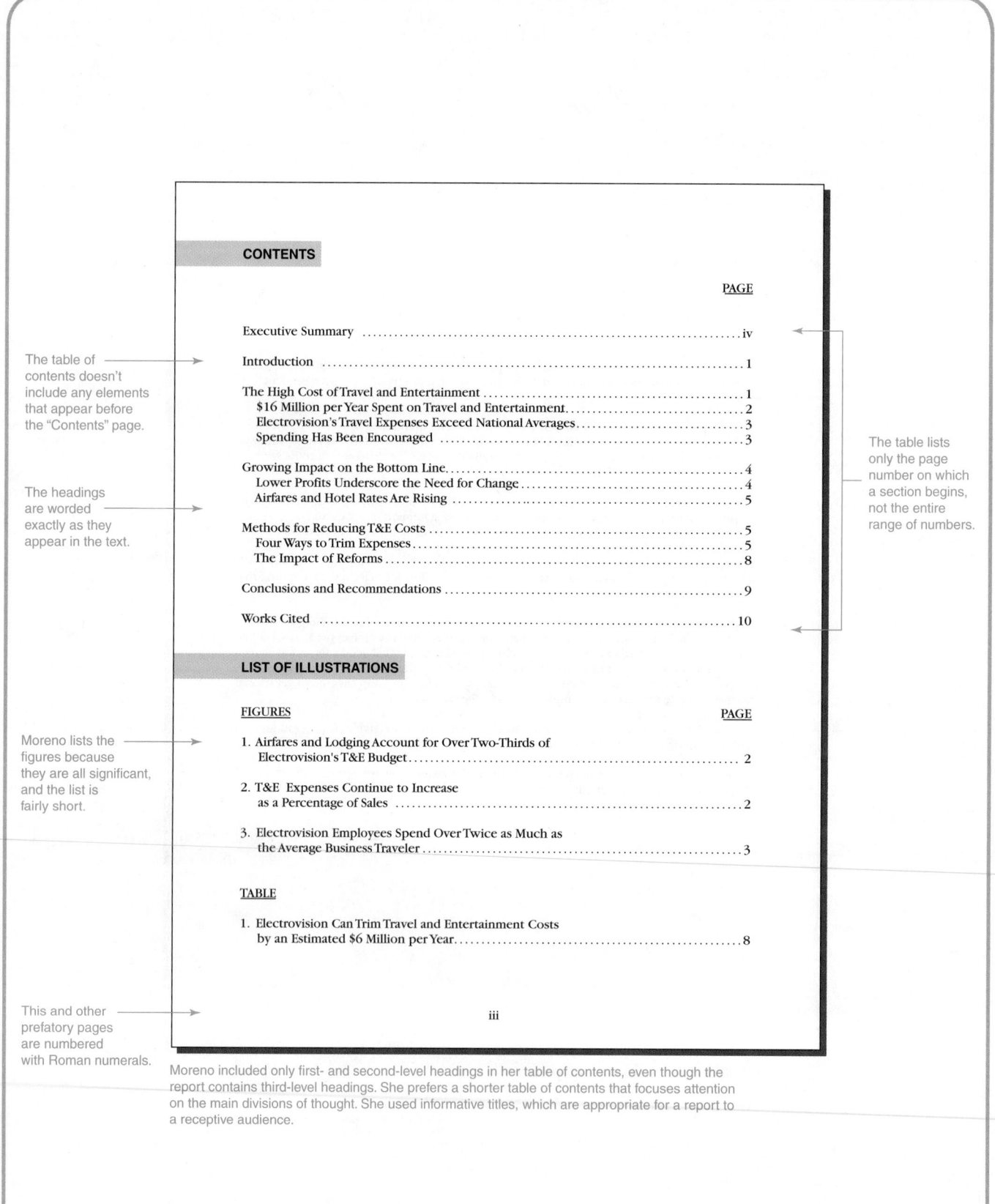

The table of contents doesn't include any elements that appear before the "Contents" page.

The headings are worded exactly as they appear in the text.

Moreno lists the figures because they are all significant, and the list is fairly short.

This and other prefatory pages are numbered with Roman numerals.

The table lists only the page number on which a section begins, not the entire range of numbers.

CONTENTS

LIST OF ILLUSTRATIONS

iii

Moreno included only first- and second-level headings in her table of contents, even though the report contains third-level headings. She prefers a shorter table of contents that focuses attention on the main divisions of thought. She used informative titles, which are appropriate for a report to a receptive audience.

The executive summary begins by stating the purpose of the report.

EXECUTIVE SUMMARY

This report analyzes Electrovision's travel and entertainment (T&E) costs and presents recommendations for reducing those costs.

Moreno presents the points in the executive summary in the same order as they appear in the report, using subheadings that summarize the content of the main sections of the report.

Travel and Entertainment Costs Are Too High

Travel and entertainment is a large and growing expense category for Electrovision. The company spends over $16 million per year on business travel, and these costs have been increasing by 12 percent annually. Company employees make roughly 3,390 trips each year at an average cost per trip of $4,720. Airfares are the biggest expense, followed by hotels, meals, and rental cars.

The nature of Electrovision's business does require extensive travel, but the company's costs are excessive: Our employees spend more than twice the national average on travel and entertainment. Although the location of the company's facilities may partly explain this discrepancy, the main reason for our high costs is a management style that gives employees little incentive to economize.

Cuts Are Essential

Electrovision management now recognizes the need to gain more control over this element of costs. The company is currently entering a period of declining profits, prompting management to look for every opportunity to reduce spending. At the same time, rising airfares and hotel rates are making T&E expenses more significant.

Her audience is receptive, so the tone in the executive summary is forceful; a more neutral approach would be better for hostile or skeptical readers.

Electrovision Can Save $6 Million per Year

Fortunately, Electrovision has a number of excellent opportunities for reducing T&E costs. Savings of up to $6 million per year should be achievable, judging by the experience of other companies. A sensible travel-management program can save companies as much as 35 percent a year (Gilligan 39–40), and we should be able to save even more, since we purchase many more business-class tickets than the average. Four steps will help us cut costs:

1. Hire a director of travel and entertainment to assume overall responsibility for T&E spending, policies, and technologies, including the hiring and management of a national travel agency.
2. Educate employees on the need for cost containment, both in avoiding unnecessary travel and reducing costs when travel is necessary.
3. Negotiate preferential rates with travel providers.
4. Implement technological alternatives to travel, such as virtual meetings.

As necessary as these changes are, they will likely hurt morale, at least in the short term. Management will need to make a determined effort to explain the rationale for reduced spending. By exercising moderation in their own travel arrangements, Electrovision executives can set a good example and help other employees accept the changes. On the plus side, using travel alternatives such as web conferencing will reduce the travel burden on many employees and help them balance their business and personal lives.

The executive summary uses the same font and paragraph treatment as the text of the report.

The page numbering in the executive summary continues with Roman numerals.

iv

Moreno decided to include an executive summary because her report is aimed at a mixed audience, some of whom are interested in the details of her report and others who just want the "big picture." The executive summary is aimed at the second group, giving them enough information to make a decision without burdening them with the task of reading the entire report.

Her writing style matches the serious nature of the content without sounding distant or stiff. Moreno chose the formal approach because several members of her audience are considerably higher up in the organization, and she did not want to sound too familiar. In addition, her company prefers the impersonal style for formal reports.

A color bar highlights the report title and the first-level headings; a variety of other design treatments are possible as well.

REDUCING ELECTROVISION'S TRAVEL AND ENTERTAINMENT COSTS

INTRODUCTION

Electrovision has always encouraged a significant amount of business travel. To compensate employees for the stress and inconvenience of frequent trips, management has authorized generous travel and entertainment (T&E) allowances. This philosophy has been good for morale, but last year Electrovision spent $16 million on travel and entertainment—$7 million more than it spent on research and development.

The introduction opens by establishing the need for action.

This year's T&E costs will affect profits even more, due to increases in airline fares and hotel rates. Also, the company anticipates that profits will be relatively weak for a variety of other reasons. Therefore, Dennis McWilliams, Vice President of Operations, has asked the accounting department to explore ways to reduce the T&E budget.

The purpose of this report is to analyze T&E expenses, evaluate the effect of recent hotel and airfare increases, and suggest ways to tighten control over T&E costs. The report outlines several steps that could reduce Electrovision's expenses, but the precise financial impact of these measures is difficult to project. The estimates presented here provide a "best guess" view of what Electrovision can expect to save.

In preparing this report, the accounting department analyzed internal expense reports for the past five years to determine how much Electrovision spends on travel and entertainment. These figures were then compared with average statistics compiled by Dow Jones (publisher of the *Wall Street Journal*) and presented as the Dow Jones Travel Index. We also analyzed trends and suggestions published in a variety of business journal articles to see how other companies are coping with the high cost of business travel.

Moreno mentions her sources and methods to increase credibility and to give readers a complete picture of the study's background.

THE HIGH COST OF TRAVEL AND ENTERTAINMENT

Although many companies view travel and entertainment as an incidental cost of doing business, the dollars add up. At Electrovision the bill for airfares, hotels, rental cars, meals, and entertainment totaled $16 million last year. Our T&E budget has increased by 12 percent per year for the past five years. Compared to the average U.S. business traveler, Electrovision's expenditures are high, largely because of management's generous policy on travel benefits.

A *running footer* that contains the report title and the page number appears on every page.

In her brief introduction, Moreno counts on topic sentences and transitions to indicate that she is discussing the purpose, scope, and limitations of the study.

$16 Million per Year Spent on Travel and Entertainment

Electrovision's annual budget for travel and entertainment is only 8 percent of sales. Because this is a relatively small expense category compared with such things as salaries and commissions, it is tempting to dismiss T&E costs as insignificant. However, T&E is Electrovision's third-largest controllable expense, directly behind salaries and information systems.

Last year Electrovision personnel made about 3,390 trips at an average cost per trip of $4,720. The typical trip involved a round-trip flight of 3,000 miles, meals, and hotel accommodations for two or three days, and a rental car. Roughly 80 percent of trips were made by 20 percent of the staff—top management and sales personnel traveled most, averaging 18 trips per year.

Figure 1 illustrates how the T&E budget is spent. The largest categories are airfares and lodging, which together account for $7 out of $10 that employees spend on travel and entertainment. This spending breakdown has been relatively steady for the past five years and is consistent with the distribution of expenses experienced by other companies.

The visual is placed as close as possible to the point it illustrates.

Figure 1
Airfares and Lodging Account for Over
Two-Thirds of Electrovision's T&E Budget

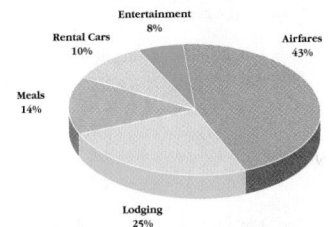

Although the composition of the T&E budget has been consistent, its size has not. As mentioned earlier, these expenditures have increased by about 12 percent per year for the past five years, roughly twice the rate of the company's sales growth (see Figure 2). This rate of growth makes T&E Electrovision's fastest-growing expense item.

Each visual has a title that clearly indicates what it's about; titles are consistently placed to the left of each visual.

Figure 2
T&E Expenses Continue to Increase as a
Percentage of Sales

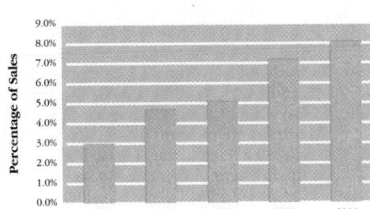

Moreno opens the first main section of the body with a topic sentence that introduces an important fact about the subject of the section. Then she orients the reader to the three major points developed in the section.

Electrovision's Travel Expenses Exceed National Averages

Much of our travel budget is justified. Two major factors contribute to Electrovision's high T&E budget:

- With our headquarters on the West Coast and our major customer on the East Coast, we naturally spend a lot of money on cross-country flights.

- A great deal of travel takes place between our headquarters here on the West Coast and the manufacturing operations in Detroit, Boston, and Dallas. Corporate managers and division personnel make frequent trips to coordinate these disparate operations.

However, even though a good portion of Electrovision's travel budget is justifiable, the company spends considerably more on T&E than the average business traveler (see Figure 3).

Figure 3
Electrovision Employees Spend Over Twice as Much as the Average Business Traveler

Source: *Wall Street Journal* and company records

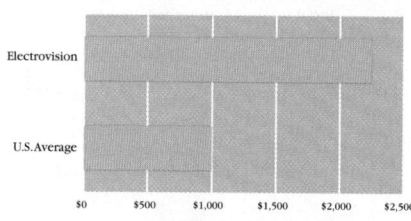

Dollars Spent per Day

The Dow Jones Travel Index calculates the average cost per day of business travel in the United States, based on average airfare, hotel rates, and rental car rates. The average fluctuates weekly as travel companies change their rates, but it has been running at about $1,000 per day for the last year or so. In contrast, Electrovision's average daily expense over the past year has been $2,250—a hefty 125 percent higher than average. This figure is based on the average trip cost of $4,720 listed earlier and an average trip length of 2.1 days.

Spending Has Been Encouraged

Although a variety of factors may contribute to this differential, Electrovision's relatively high T&E costs are at least partially attributable to the company's philosophy and management style. Since many employees do not enjoy business travel, management has tried to make the trips more pleasant by authorizing business-class airfare, luxury hotel accommodations, and full-size rental cars. The sales staff is encouraged to entertain clients at top restaurants and to invite them to cultural and sporting events.

The visuals are numbered consecutively and referred to by their numbers in the text.

Moreno introduces visuals before they appear and indicates what readers should notice about the data.

The chart in Figure 3 is simple but effective; Moreno includes just enough data to make her point. Notice how she is as careful about the appearance of her report as she is about the quality of its content.

A bulleted list makes it easy for readers to identify and distinguish related points.

The cost of these privileges is easy to overlook, given the weakness of Electrovision's system for keeping track of T&E expenses:

- The monthly financial records do not contain a separate category for travel and entertainment; the information is buried under Cost of Goods Sold and under Selling, General, and Administrative Expenses.

- Each department head is given authority to approve any expense report, regardless of how large it may be.

- Receipts are not required for expenditures of less than $100.

- Individuals are allowed to make their own travel arrangements.

- No one is charged with the responsibility for controlling the company's total spending on travel and entertainment.

GROWING IMPACT ON THE BOTTOM LINE

During the past three years, the company's healthy profits have resulted in relatively little pressure to push for tighter controls over all aspects of the business. However, as we all know, the situation is changing. We're projecting flat to declining profits for the next two years, a situation that has prompted all of us to search for ways to cut costs. At the same time, rising airfares and hotel rates have increased the impact of T&E expenses on the company's financial results.

Lower Profits Underscore the Need for Change

The next two years promise to be difficult for Electrovision. After several years of steady increases in spending, the Postal Service is tightening procurement policies for automated mail-handling equipment. Funding for the A-12 optical character reader has been canceled. As a consequence, the marketing department expects sales to drop by 15 percent. Although Electrovision is negotiating several other promising R&D contracts, the marketing department does not foresee any major procurements for the next two to three years.

At the same time, Electrovision is facing cost increases on several fronts. As we have known for several months, the new production facility now under construction in Salt Lake City, Utah, is behind schedule and over budget. Labor contracts in Boston and Dallas will expire within the next six months, and plant managers there anticipate that significant salary and benefits concessions may be necessary to avoid strikes.

Moreover, marketing and advertising costs are expected to increase as we attempt to strengthen these activities to better cope with competitive pressures. Given the expected decline in revenues and increase in costs, the Executive Committee's prediction that profits will fall by 12 percent in the coming fiscal year does not seem overly pessimistic.

Informative headings focus reader attention on the main points. Such headings are appropriate when a report uses the direct order and is intended for a receptive audience. However, descriptive headings are more effective when a report uses the indirect order and readers are less receptive.

Moreno designed her report to include plenty of white space so even those pages that lack visuals are still attractive and easy to read.

Airfares and Hotel Rates Are Rising

Business travelers have grown accustomed to frequent fare wars and discounting in the travel industry in recent years. Excess capacity and aggressive price competition, particularly in the airline business, made travel a relative bargain.

However, that situation has changed as weaker competitors have been forced out and the remaining players have grown stronger and smarter. Airlines and hotels are better at managing inventory and keeping occupancy rates high, which translates into higher costs for Electrovision. Last year saw some of the steepest rate hikes in years. Business airfares (tickets most likely to be purchased by business travelers) jumped more than 40 percent in many markets. The trend is expected to continue, with rates increasing another 5 to 10 percent overall (Phillips 331; "Travel Costs Under Pressure" 30; Dahl B6).

Given the fact that air and hotel costs account for almost 70 percent of our T&E budget, the trend toward higher prices in these two categories will have serious consequences, unless management takes action to control these costs.

METHODS FOR REDUCING T&E COSTS

By implementing a number of reforms, management can expect to reduce Electrovision's T&E budget by as much as 40 percent. This estimate is based on the general assessment made by American Express (Gilligan 39) and on the fact that we have an opportunity to significantly reduce air travel costs by eliminating business-class travel. However, these measures are likely to be unpopular with employees. To gain acceptance for such changes, management will need to sell employees on the need for moderation in T&E allowances.

Four Ways to Trim Expenses

By researching what other companies are doing to curb T&E expenses, the accounting department has identified four prominent opportunities that should enable Electrovision to save about $6 million annually in travel-related costs.

Institute Tighter Spending Controls

A single individual should be appointed director of travel and entertainment to spearhead the effort to gain control of the T&E budget. More than a third of all U.S. companies now employ travel managers ("Businesses Use Savvy Managers" 4). The director should be familiar with the travel industry and should be well versed in both accounting and information technology. The director should also report to the vice president of operations. The director's first priorities should be to establish a written T&E policy and a cost-control system.

Electrovision currently has no written policy on travel and entertainment, a step that is widely recommended by air travel experts (Smith D4). Creating a policy would clarify management's position and serve as a vehicle for communicating the need for moderation.

Reducing Electrovision's Travel and Entertainment Costs   P a g e **5**

Moreno supports her argument with objective facts and sound reasoning.

The recommendations are realistic, noting both the benefits and the risks of taking action.

Moreno creates a forceful tone by using action verbs in the third-level subheadings of this section. This approach is appropriate to the nature of the study and the attitude of the audience. However, in a status-conscious organization, the imperative verbs might sound a bit too presumptuous coming from a junior member of the staff.

At a minimum, the policy should include the following:

- All travel and entertainment should be strictly related to business and should be approved in advance.

- Except under special circumstances to be approved on a case-by-case basis, employees should travel by coach and stay in mid-range business hotels.

- The T&E policy should apply equally to employees at all levels.

To implement the new policy, Electrovision will need to create a system for controlling T&E expenses. Each department should prepare an annual T&E budget as part of its operating plan. These budgets should be presented in detail so that management can evaluate how T&E dollars will be spent and can recommend appropriate cuts. To help management monitor performance relative to these budgets, the director of travel should prepare monthly financial statements showing actual T&E expenditures by department.

The director of travel should also be responsible for retaining a business-oriented travel service that will schedule all employee business trips and look for the best travel deals, particularly in airfares. In addition to centralizing Electrovision's reservation and ticketing activities, the agency will negotiate reduced group rates with hotels and rental car firms. The agency selected should have offices nationwide so that all Electrovision facilities can channel their reservations through the same company. This is particularly important in light of the dizzying array of often wildly different airfares available between some cities. It's not uncommon to find dozens of fares along commonly traveled routes (Rowe 30). In addition, the director can help coordinate travel across the company to secure group discounts whenever possible (Barker 31; Miller B6).

Reduce Unnecessary Travel and Entertainment

One of the easiest ways to reduce expenses is to reduce the amount of traveling and entertaining that occurs. An analysis of last year's expenditures suggests that as much as 30 percent of Electrovision's travel and entertainment is discretionary. The professional staff spent $2.8 million attending seminars and conferences last year. Although these gatherings are undoubtedly beneficial, the company could save money by sending fewer representatives to each function and perhaps by eliminating some of the less valuable seminars.

Similarly, Electrovision could economize on trips between headquarters and divisions by reducing the frequency of such visits and by sending fewer people on each trip. Although there is often no substitute for face-to-face meetings, management could try to resolve more internal issues through telephone, electronic, and written communication.

Electrovision can also reduce spending by urging employees to economize. Instead of flying business class, employees can fly coach class or take advantage of discount fares. Rather than ordering a $50 bottle of wine, employees can select a less expensive bottle or dispense with

---

In addition to making key points easy to find, bulleted lists help break up the text to relieve the reader's eye.

Moreno lists the steps needed to implement her recommendations.

Moreno takes care not to overstep the boundaries of her analysis. For instance, she doesn't analyze the value of the seminars that employees attend every year, so she avoids any absolute statements about reducing travel to seminars.

alcohol entirely. People can book rooms at moderately priced hotels and drive smaller rental cars.

Obtain Lowest Rates from Travel Providers

Apart from urging employees to economize, Electrovision can also save money by searching for the lowest available airfares, hotel rates, and rental car fees. Currently, few employees have the time or knowledge to seek out travel bargains. When they need to travel, they make the most convenient and comfortable arrangements. A professional travel service will be able to obtain lower rates from travel providers.

Judging by the experience of other companies, Electrovision may be able to trim as much as 30 to 40 percent from the travel budget simply by looking for bargains in airfares and negotiating group rates with hotels and rental car companies. Electrovision should be able to achieve these economies by analyzing its travel patterns, identifying frequently visited locations, and selecting a few hotels that are willing to reduce rates in exchange for guaranteed business. At the same time, the company should be able to save up to 40 percent on rental car charges by negotiating a corporate rate.

The possibilities for economizing are promising; however, making the best travel arrangements often requires trade-offs such as the following:

- The best fares might not always be the lowest. Indirect flights are usually cheaper, but they take longer and may end up costing more in lost work time.

- The cheapest tickets often require booking 14 or even 30 days in advance, which is often impossible for us.

- Discount tickets are usually nonrefundable, which is a serious drawback when a trip needs to be canceled at the last minute.

Replace Travel with Technological Alternatives

Less-expensive travel options promise significant savings, but the biggest cost reductions over the long term might come from replacing travel with virtual meeting technology. Both analysts and corporate users say that the early kinks that hampered online meetings have largely been worked out, and the latest systems are fast, easy to learn, and easy to use (Solheim 26). For example, WebEx (a leading provider of webconferencing services) offers everything from simple, impromptu team meetings to major online events with up to 3,000 participants ("Online Meeting Solutions").

One of the first responsibilities of the new travel director should be an evaluation of these technologies and a recommendation for integrating them throughout Electrovision's operations.

By pointing out possible difficulties and showing that she has considered all angles, Moreno builds reader confidence in her judgment.

Note how Moreno makes the transition from section to section. The first sentence under the second heading on this page refers to the subject of the previous paragraph and signals a shift in thought.

The Impact of Reforms

By implementing tighter controls, reducing unnecessary expenses, negotiating more favorable rates, and exploring alternatives to travel, Electrovision should be able to reduce its T&E budget significantly. As Table 1 illustrates, the combined savings should be in the neighborhood of $6 million, although the precise figures are somewhat difficult to project.

Table 1
Electrovision Can Trim Travel and Entertainment Costs
by an Estimated $6 Million per Year

SOURCE OF SAVINGS	ESTIMATED SAVINGS
Switching from business-class to coach airfare	$2,300,000
Negotiating preferred hotel rates	940,000
Negotiating preferred rental car rates	460,000
Systematically searching for lower airfares	375,000
Reducing interdivisional travel	675,000
Reducing seminar and conference attendance	1,250,000
TOTAL POTENTIAL SAVINGS	**$6,000,000**

To achieve the economies outlined in the table, Electrovision will incur expenses for hiring a director of travel and for implementing a T&E cost-control system. These costs are projected at $115,000: $105,000 per year in salary and benefits for the new employee and a one-time expense of $10,000 for the cost-control system. The cost of retaining a full-service travel agency is negligible, even with the service fees that many are now passing along from airlines and other service providers.

The measures required to achieve these savings are likely to be unpopular with employees. Electrovision personnel are accustomed to generous T&E allowances, and they are likely to resent having these privileges curtailed. To alleviate their disappointment

- Management should make a determined effort to explain why the changes are necessary.

- The director of corporate communication should be asked to develop a multifaceted campaign that will communicate the importance of curtailing T&E costs.

- Management should set a positive example by adhering strictly to the new policies.

- The limitations should apply equally to employees at all levels in the organization.

An informative title in the table is consistent with the way headings are handled throughout this report, and it is appropriate for a report to a receptive audience.

The in-text reference to the table highlights the key point the reader should get from the table.

Including financial estimates helps management envision the impact of the suggestions, even though the estimated savings are difficult to project accurately.

Note how Moreno calls attention in the first paragraph to items in the following table, without repeating the information in the table.

She uses a descriptive heading for the last section of the text. In informational reports, this section is often called "Summary"; in analytical reports, it is called "Conclusions" or "Conclusions and Recommendations."

Moreno summarizes her conclusions in the first two paragraphs—a good approach because she organized her report around conclusions and recommendations, so readers have already been introduced to them.

Presenting the recommendations in a list gives each one emphasis.

CONCLUSIONS AND RECOMMENDATIONS

Electrovision is currently spending $16 million per year on travel and entertainment. Although much of this spending is justified, the company's costs are high relative to competitors' costs, mainly because Electrovision has been generous with its travel benefits.

Electrovision's liberal approach to travel and entertainment was understandable during years of high profitability; however, the company is facing the prospect of declining profits for the next several years. Management is therefore motivated to cut costs in all areas of the business. Reducing T&E spending is particularly important because the bottom-line impact of these costs will increase as airline fares increase.

Electrovision should be able to reduce T&E costs by as much as 40 percent by taking four important steps:

1. *Institute tighter spending controls.* Management should hire a director of travel and entertainment who will assume overall responsibility for T&E activities. Within the next six months, this director should develop a written travel policy, institute a T&E budget and a cost-control system, and retain a professional, business-oriented travel agency that will optimize arrangements with travel providers.

2. *Reduce unnecessary travel and entertainment.* Electrovision should encourage employees to economize on T&E spending. Management can accomplish this by authorizing fewer trips and by urging employees to be more conservative in their spending.

3. *Obtain lowest rates from travel providers.* Electrovision should also focus on obtaining the best rates on airline tickets, hotel rooms, and rental cars. By channeling all arrangements through a professional travel agency, the company can optimize its choices and gain clout in negotiating preferred rates.

4. *Replace travel with technological alternatives.* With the number of computers already installed in our facilities, it seems likely that we could take advantage of desktop videoconferencing and other distance-meeting tools. Technological alternatives won't be quite as feasible with customer sites, since these systems require compatible equipment at both ends of a connection, but such systems are certainly a possibility for communication with Electrovision's own sites.

Because these measures may be unpopular with employees, management should make a concerted effort to explain the importance of reducing travel costs. The director of corporate communication should be given responsibility for developing a plan to communicate the need for employee cooperation.

Moreno doesn't introduce any new facts in this section. In a longer report she might have divided this section into subsections, labeled "Conclusions" and "Recommendations," to distinguish between the two.

MLA style lists references alphabetically by the author's last name, and when the author is unknown, by the title of the reference. (See Appendix B for additional details on preparing reference lists.)

WORKS CITED

Barker, Julie. "How to Rein in Group Travel Costs." *Successful Meetings* Feb. 2011: 31. Print.

"Businesses Use Savvy Managers to Keep Travel Costs Down." *Christian Science Monitor* 17 July 2008: 4. Print.

Dahl, Jonathan. "2000: The Year Travel Costs Took Off." *Wall Street Journal* 29 Dec. 2007: B6. Print.

Gilligan, Edward P. "Trimming Your T&E Is Easier Than You Think." *Managing Office Technology* Nov. 2008: 39–40. Print.

Miller, Lisa. "Attention, Airline Ticket Shoppers." *Wall Street Journal* 7 July 2007: B6. Print.

Phillips, Edward H. "Airlines Post Record Traffic." *Aviation Week & Space Technology* 8 Jan. 2007: 331. Print.

"Product Overview: Cisco WebEx Meeting Center," *Webex.com*. 2011. WebEx, n.d. 2 February 2011. Web.

Rowe, Irene Vlitos. "Global Solution for Cutting Travel Costs." *European Business* 12 Oct. 2008: 30. Print.

Smith, Carol. "Rising, Erratic Airfares Make Company Policy Vital." *Los Angeles Times* 2 Nov. 2007: D4. Print.

Solheim, Shelley. "Web Conferencing Made Easy." *eWeek* 22 Aug. 2008: 26. Web.

"Travel Costs Under Pressure." *Purchasing* 15 Feb. 2007: 30. Print.

Moreno's list of references follows the style recommended in the *MLA Style Manual*. The box below shows how these sources would be cited following APA style.

REFERENCES

Barker, J. (2011, February). How to rein in group travel costs. *Successful Meetings,* p. 31.

Businesses use savvy managers to keep travel costs down. (2008, July 17). *Christian Science Monitor,* p. 4.

Dahl, J. (2007, December 29). 2000: The year travel costs took off. *Wall Street Journal,* B6.

Gilligan, E. (2008, November). Trimming your T&E is easier than you think. *Managing Office Technology,* pp. 39–40.

Miller, L. (2007, July 7). Attention, airline ticket shoppers. *Wall Street Journal,* B6.

Phillips, E. (2007, January 8). Airlines post record traffic. *Aviation Week & Space Technology,* p. 331.

Rowe, I. (2008, October 12). Global solution for cutting travel costs. *European,* p. 30.

Smith, C. (2007, November 2). Rising, erratic airfares make company policy vital. *Los Angeles Times,* D4.

Solheim, S. (2008, August 22). Web conferencing made easy. *eWeek,* p. 26.

Travel costs under pressure. (2007, February 15). *Purchasing,* p. 30.

WebEx.com. (2011). *Product Overview: Cisco WebEx Meeting Center.* Retrieved from http://www.webex.com/product-overview/index.html

In the body of the letter, you may also highlight important points or sections of the report, make comments on side issues, give suggestions for follow-up studies, and offer any details that will help readers understand and use the report. You may also want to acknowledge help given by others. The conclusion of the transmittal letter often includes a note of thanks for having been given the report assignment, an expression of willingness to discuss the report, and an offer to assist with future projects.

Table of Contents

The table of contents (often titled simply "Contents") indicates in outline form the coverage, sequence, and relative importance of the information in the report. The headings used in the text of the report are the basis for the table of contents. Depending on the length and complexity of the report, you may need to decide how many levels of headings to show in the contents; it's a trade-off between simplicity and completeness. Contents that show only first-level heads are easy to scan but could frustrate people looking for specific subsections in the report. Conversely, contents that show every level of heading—down to the fourth or fifth level in detailed reports—identify all the sections but can intimidate readers and blur the focus by detracting from your most important message points. Where the detailed table of contents could have dozens or even hundreds of entries, consider including two tables: a high-level table that shows only major headings, followed by a detailed table that includes everything (as this and many other textbooks do). No matter how many levels you include, make sure readers can easily distinguish between them.

To save time and reduce errors, use the table of contents generator in your word-processing software.

Also, take extra care to verify that your table of contents is accurate, consistent, and complete. Even minor errors could damage your credibility if readers turn to a given page and don't find what they expect to see there, or if they find headings that seem similar to those in the table of contents but aren't worded quite the same. To ensure accuracy, construct the table of contents after your report is complete, thoroughly edited, and proofed. This way, the headings and subheadings aren't likely to change or move from page to page. And if at all possible, use the automatic features in your word-processing software to generate the table of contents. Doing so helps improve accuracy by eliminating typing mistakes, and it keeps your table current in the event that you have to repaginate or revise headings late in the process.

If you will be creating a PDF file of the report for electronic distribution, you can make life easier for your readers by making the entries in the table of contents clickable links.

List of Illustrations

If you have more than a handful of illustrations in your report, or if you want to call attention to them, include a list of illustrations after the table of contents. For simplicity's sake, some reports refer to all visuals as *illustrations* or *exhibits*. In other reports, as in Moreno's Electrovision report, tables are labeled separately from other types of visuals, which are called *figures*. Regardless of the system you use, be sure to include titles and page numbers.

If you have enough space on a single page, include the list of illustrations directly beneath the table of contents. Otherwise, put this list on the page after the contents page. When tables and figures are numbered separately, they should also be listed separately.

Synopsis or Executive Summary

A synopsis is a brief preview of the most important points in your report.

A **synopsis** is a brief overview (one page or less) of a report's most important points, designed to give readers a quick preview of the contents (see Figure 13.2). It's often included in long informational reports dealing with technical, professional, or academic subjects and can also be called an **abstract**. Because it's a concise representation of an entire report, it may be distributed separately to a wide audience; interested readers can then request a copy of the entire report. A synopsis or an abstract is not a lengthy element, but take your time with it. In a sense, it's an advertisement for the entire report, so you want it to represent the report accurately.

The phrasing of a synopsis can be either informative or descriptive. An *informative synopsis* presents the main points of the report in the order in which they appear in the text. A *descriptive synopsis*, on the other hand, simply tells what the report is about, using only moderately greater detail than the table of contents; the actual findings of the report are omitted. Here are examples of statements from each type:

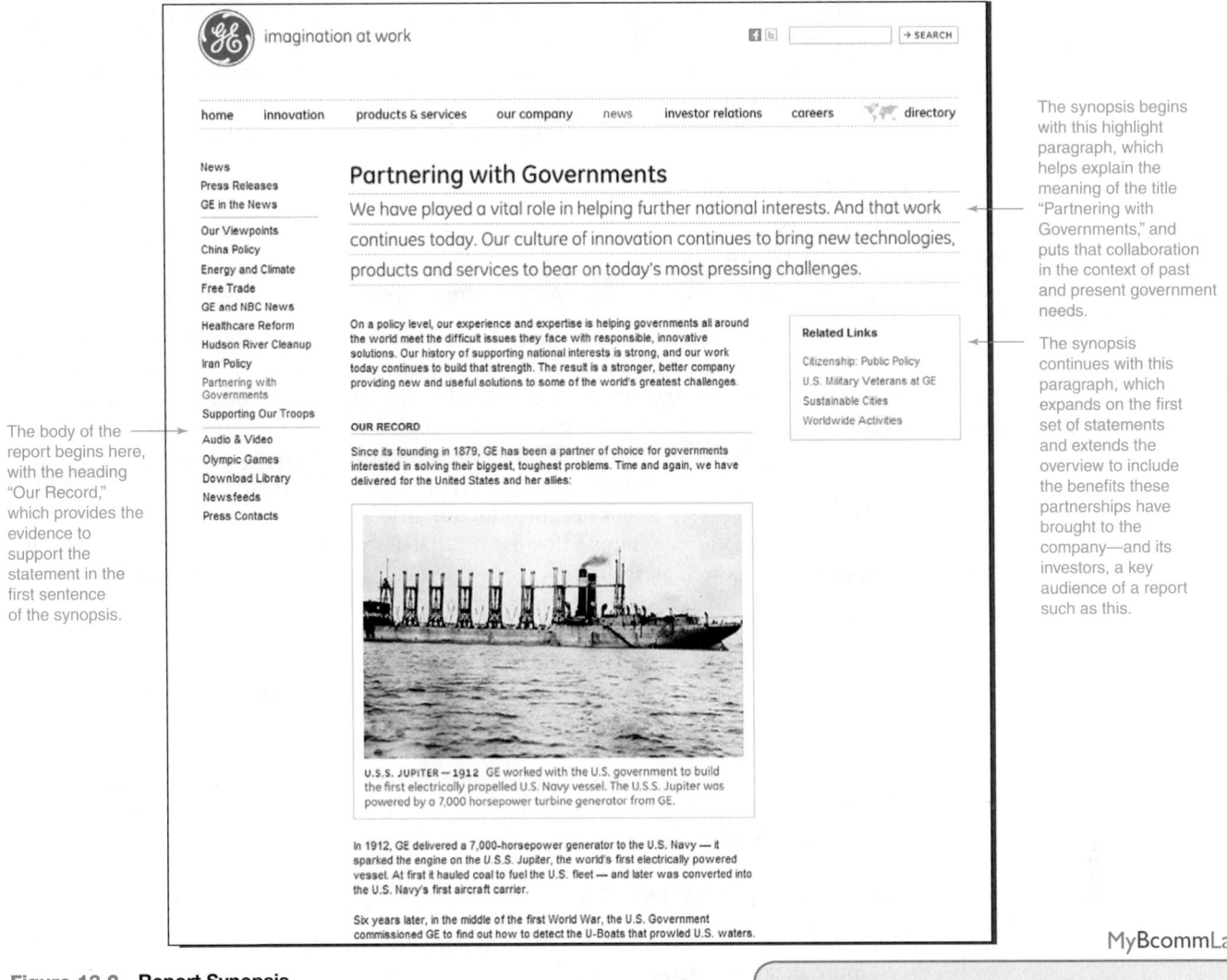

Figure 13.2   Report Synopsis
This position paper by General Electric starts with a brief synopsis that offers an overview of the document's content.
Source: www.ge.com/news/our_viewpoints/partnering_with_gov.html.

Apply Figure 13.2's key concepts by revising a new document. Go to Chapter 13 in www.pearsoninternationaleditions.com/mybcommlab and select Document Makeovers.

Informative Synopsis

Sales of super-premium ice cream make up 11 percent of the total ice cream market.

Descriptive Synopsis

This report contains information about super-premium ice cream and its share of the market.

The way you handle a synopsis reflects the approach you use in the text. If you're using the indirect approach in your report, you're better off with a descriptive synopsis because an informative synopsis "gives away the ending" of your report. No matter which type of synopsis you use, be sure to present an accurate picture of the report's contents.[4]

Many report writers prefer to include an **executive summary** instead of a synopsis or an abstract. Whereas a synopsis is a "prose table of contents" that outlines the main points of the report, an executive summary is a fully developed "mini" version of the report itself. An executive summary is more comprehensive than a synopsis; it can contain headings, well-developed transitions, and even visual elements. It is usually organized in the same way as the report, using a direct or an indirect approach, depending on the audience's receptivity.

An executive summary is a "mini" version of your report.

Executive summaries are intended for readers who lack the time or motivation to study the complete text. As a general rule, the length of an executive summary should be proportionate to the length of the report. A brief business report may have only a one-page or shorter executive summary. Longer business reports may have a two- or three-page summary. Anything longer, however, might cease to be a summary.[5]

Many reports require neither a synopsis nor an executive summary. Length is usually the determining factor. Most reports of fewer than 10 pages either omit such a preview or combine it with the letter of transmittal. However, if your report is over 20 or 30 pages long, you'll probably want to include either a synopsis or an executive summary as a convenience for readers. Which one you provide depends on the traditions of your organization.

TEXT OF THE REPORT

No matter how many separate elements are in a formal report, the heart of the report is still the introduction, body, and close.

The heart of a report is composed of three main parts: the introduction, body, and close. Chapter 14 describes the content of these sections in more detail, but here are a few considerations to bear in mind as you prepare a formal report:

- **Introduction.** A good introduction prepares your readers to follow and comprehend the information that follows. It invites audience members to continue reading by telling them what the report is about, why they should be concerned, and how the report is organized. If your report has a synopsis or an executive summary, minimize redundancy by balancing the introduction with the material in your summary, as Linda Moreno does in her Electrovision report. For example, Moreno's executive summary is fairly detailed, so she keeps her introduction brief.
- **Body.** This section contains information that supports your conclusions and recommendations as well as your analysis, logic, and interpretation of the information. See the body of Linda Moreno's Electrovision report for an example of the types of supporting details commonly included in this section.
- **Close.** The close of your report should summarize your main ideas, highlight your conclusions or recommendations (if any), and list any courses of action that you expect readers to take or that you will be taking yourself. This section may be labeled "Summary" or "Conclusions and Recommendations." In reports that use the direct approach, the close is relatively brief. In contrast, with the indirect approach, you may be using this section to present your conclusions and recommendations for the first time, in which case this section might be fairly extensive.

SUPPLEMENTARY PARTS

Supplementary parts follow the text of the report and provide information for readers who seek more detailed discussion. For online reports, you can put supplements on separate webpages and allow readers to link to them from the main report pages. Supplements are more common in long reports than in short ones, and they typically include appendixes, a bibliography, and an index.

Appendixes

Use an appendix for materials that are too lengthy or detailed for the body or not directly relevant to all audience members.

An **appendix** contains materials related to the report but not included in the text because they are too long or perhaps not relevant to everyone in the audience. If your company has an intranet, shared workspaces, or other means of storing and accessing information online, consider putting your detailed supporting evidence there and referring readers to those sources for more detail.

The content of report appendixes varies widely, including any sample questionnaires and cover letters, sample forms, computer printouts, statistical formulas, financial statements and spreadsheets, copies of important documents, and multipage illustrations that would break up the flow of text. You might also include a glossary as an appendix or as a separate supplementary part.

If you have multiple categories of supporting material, give each type a separate appendix. An appendix is usually identified with a letter and a short, descriptive title. All appendixes should be mentioned at appropriate places in the text and listed in the table of contents.

Bibliography

A bibliography fulfills your ethical obligation to credit your sources, and it allows readers to consult those sources for more information.

To fulfill your ethical and legal obligation to credit other people for their work and to assist readers who want to research your topic further, include a **bibliography**, a list of the secondary sources you consulted when preparing your report. In her Electrovision report, Linda Moreno labeled her bibliography "Works Cited" because she listed only the works that were mentioned in the report. You might call this section "References" if it includes works consulted but not mentioned in your report. Moreno uses the author–date system to format her bibliographic sources. An alternative is to use numbered footnotes (at the bottom of the page) or endnotes (at the end of the report). For more information on citing sources, see Appendix B, "Documentation of Report Sources."

In addition to providing a bibliography, some authors prefer to cite references in the report text. Acknowledging your sources in the body of your report demonstrates that you have thoroughly researched your topic. Furthermore, mentioning the names of well-known or important authorities on the subject helps build credibility for your message. Such source references should be handled as smoothly as possible. One approach, especially for internal reports, is simply to mention a source in the text:

> According to Dr. Lewis Morgan of Northwestern Hospital, hip replacement operations account for 7 percent of all surgeries performed on women age 65 and over.

However, if your report will be distributed to outsiders, include additional information on where you obtained the data. You are probably familiar with citation methods suggested by the Modern Language Association (MLA) or the American Psychological Association (APA). *The Chicago Manual of Style* is a reference often used by typesetters and publishers. All these sources encourage the use of in-text citations (inserting the author's last name and a year of publication or a page number directly in the text).

Index

An **index** is an alphabetical list of names and subjects mentioned in a report, along with the pages on which they occur (see the indexes in this book for examples). If you think your readers will need to access specific points of information in a lengthy report, consider including an index that lists all key topics, product names, markets, or important persons— whatever is relevant to your subject matter. As with your table of contents, accuracy in an index is critical. The good news is that you can also use your word-processing software to compile the index. Just be sure to update the index (and any other automatically generated elements, such as the table of contents) right before you produce and distribute your report.

If your report is lengthy, an index can help readers locate specific topics quickly.

Producing Formal Proposals

Proposals addressed to external audiences, including potential customers and investors, are nearly always formal. For smaller projects and situations in which you already have a working relationship with the audience, a proposal can be less formal and skip some of the components described in this section.

Formal proposals contain many of the same components as other formal reports (see Figure 13.3 on the next page). The difference lies mostly in the text, although a few of the prefatory parts are also different. With the exception of an occasional appendix, most proposals have few supplementary parts. As always, if you're responding to an RFP, follow its specifications to the letter, being sure to include everything it asks for and nothing it doesn't ask for.

3   LEARNING OBJECTIVE

Identify the major components of formal proposals.

Formal proposals must have a high degree of polish and professionalism.

PREFATORY PARTS

The cover, title fly, title page, table of contents, and list of illustrations are handled the same way in a formal proposal as in other formal reports. However, you'll want to handle other prefatory parts a bit differently, such as a copy of the RFP, the synopsis or executive summary, and the letter of transmittal.

Copy of or Reference to the RFP

RFPs usually have specific instructions for referring to the RFP itself in your proposal because the organizations that issue RFPs need a methodical way to track all their active RFPs and the incoming responses. Some organizations require that you include a copy of the entire RFP in your proposal; others simply want you to refer to the RFP by name or number. Just make sure you follow the instructions in every detail. If the RFP offers no specific instructions, use your best judgment, based on the length of the RFP and whether you received a printed copy or accessed it online.

An RFP may require you to include a copy of the RFP in your prefatory section; be sure to follow its instructions carefully.

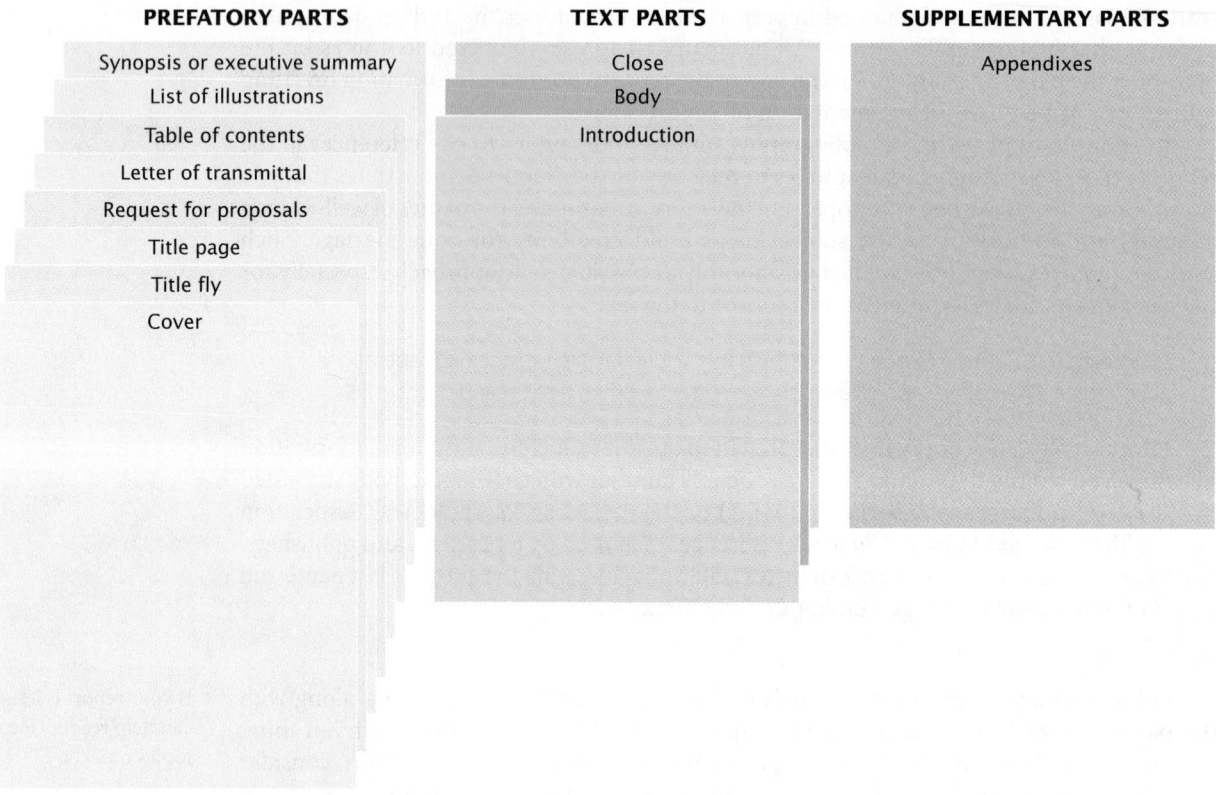

PREFATORY PARTS	TEXT PARTS	SUPPLEMENTARY PARTS
Synopsis or executive summary	Close	Appendixes
List of illustrations	Body	
Table of contents	Introduction	
Letter of transmittal		
Request for proposals		
Title page		
Title fly		
Cover		

Figure 13.3 Parts of a Formal Proposal
As with formal reports, you can select from a variety of components to complete a formal proposal.

Synopsis or Executive Summary

Although you may include a synopsis or an executive summary for your reader's convenience when your proposal is quite long, these components are often less useful in a formal proposal than they are in a formal report. If your proposal is unsolicited, your transmittal letter will already have caught the reader's interest, making a synopsis or an executive summary redundant. It may also be less important if your proposal is solicited because the reader is already committed to studying your proposal to find out how you intend to satisfy the terms of a contract. The introduction of a solicited proposal would provide an adequate preview of the contents.

Letter of Transmittal

The way you handle the letter of transmittal depends on whether the proposal is solicited or unsolicited. If the proposal is solicited, approach the letter of transmittal as a positive message, highlighting those aspects of your proposal that may give you a competitive advantage. If the proposal is unsolicited, approach the letter as a persuasive message that must convince the reader that you have something worthwhile to offer, something that justifies the time required to read the entire proposal.

TEXT OF THE PROPOSAL

Just as with reports, the text of a proposal is composed of three main parts: the introduction, body, and close. As Chapter 12 notes, the content and depth of each part depend on whether the proposal is solicited or unsolicited, formal or informal. Here's a brief review:[6]

- **Introduction.** This section presents and summarizes the problem you intend to solve and your solution to that problem, including any benefits the reader will receive from your solution.
- **Body.** This section explains the complete details of the solution: how the job will be done, how it will be broken into tasks, what method will be used to do it (including the required equipment, material, and personnel), when the work will begin and end, how

much the entire job will cost (including a detailed breakdown, if required or requested), and why you are qualified.

- **Close.** This section emphasizes the benefits that readers will realize from your solution, and it urges readers to act.

Figure 13.4 provides an example of an informal proposal.

Proofreading Reports and Proposals

After you have assembled all the components of your report or proposal, revised the entire document's content for clarity and conciseness, and designed the document to ensure readability and a positive impression on your readers, you have essentially produced your document in its final form. Now you need to review it thoroughly one last time, looking

4 LEARNING OBJECTIVE

Describe an effective plan for proofreading reports and proposals.

O'Donnell & Associates, Inc.

1793 East Westerfield Road, Arlington Heights, Illinois 60005
(847) 398-1148 Fax: (847) 398-1149 Email: dod@ix.netcom.com

July 30, 2012

Ms. Joyce Colton, P.E.
AGI Builders, Inc.
1280 Spring Lake Drive
Belvidere, Illinois, 61008

Subject: Proposal No. F-0087 for AGI Builders, Elgin Manufacturing Campus

Dear Ms. Colton:

O'Donnell & Associates is pleased to submit the following proposal to provide construction testing services for the mass grading operations and utility work at the Elgin Manufacturing Campus, 126th St., Elgin, Illinois. Our company has been providing construction-testing services in the Chicago area since 1972 and has performed numerous large-scale geotechnical investigations across Illinois, including more than 100 at O'Hare International Airport, Midway Airport, Meig's Field, and other airports.

Background

It is our understanding that the work consists of two projects: (1) the mass grading operations will require approximately six months, and (2) the utility work will require approximately three months. The two operations are scheduled as follows:

Mass Grading Operation   September 2012–February 2013
Utility Work   March 2013–May 2013

Proposed Approach and Work Plan

O'Donnell & Associates will perform observation and testing services during both the mass grading operations and the excavation and backfilling of the underground utilities. Specifically, we will perform field density tests on the compacted material as required by the job specifications using a nuclear moisture/density gauge. We will also conduct appropriate laboratory tests such as ASTM D-1557 Modified Proctors. We will prepare detailed reports summarizing the results of our field and laboratory testing. Fill materials to be placed at the site may consist of natural granular materials (sand), processed materials (crushed stone, crushed concrete, slag), or clay soils. O'Donnell & Associates will provide qualified personnel to perform the necessary testing.

The opening paragraph serves as an introduction.

Headings divide the proposal into logical segments for easy reading.

The work plan describes the scope of the project and outlines specific tests the company will perform.

The introduction grabs the reader's attention by highlighting company qualifications.

The project background section acknowledges the two projects and their required timeline.

(continued)

Figure 13.4 Informal Solicited Proposal
This proposal was submitted by Dixon O'Donnell, vice president of O'Donnell & Associates, a geotechnical engineering firm that conducts a variety of environmental testing services. As you review this document, pay close attention to the specific items addressed in the proposal's introduction, body, and close.

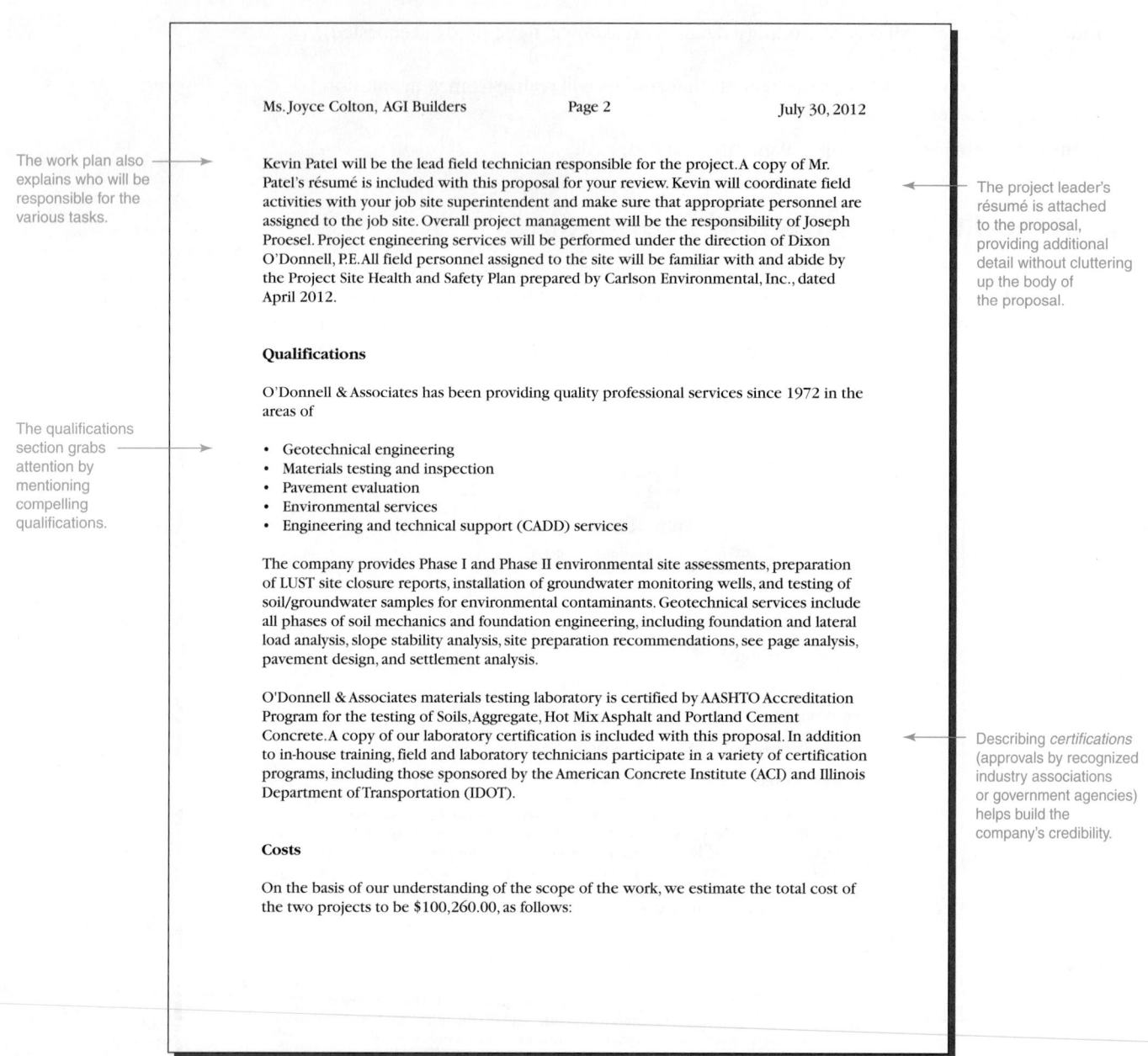

The work plan also explains who will be responsible for the various tasks.

The qualifications section grabs attention by mentioning compelling qualifications.

The project leader's résumé is attached to the proposal, providing additional detail without cluttering up the body of the proposal.

Describing *certifications* (approvals by recognized industry associations or government agencies) helps build the company's credibility.

Ms. Joyce Colton, AGI Builders   Page 2   July 30, 2012

Kevin Patel will be the lead field technician responsible for the project. A copy of Mr. Patel's résumé is included with this proposal for your review. Kevin will coordinate field activities with your job site superintendent and make sure that appropriate personnel are assigned to the job site. Overall project management will be the responsibility of Joseph Proesel. Project engineering services will be performed under the direction of Dixon O'Donnell, P.E. All field personnel assigned to the site will be familiar with and abide by the Project Site Health and Safety Plan prepared by Carlson Environmental, Inc., dated April 2012.

Qualifications

O'Donnell & Associates has been providing quality professional services since 1972 in the areas of

- Geotechnical engineering
- Materials testing and inspection
- Pavement evaluation
- Environmental services
- Engineering and technical support (CADD) services

The company provides Phase I and Phase II environmental site assessments, preparation of LUST site closure reports, installation of groundwater monitoring wells, and testing of soil/groundwater samples for environmental contaminants. Geotechnical services include all phases of soil mechanics and foundation engineering, including foundation and lateral load analysis, slope stability analysis, site preparation recommendations, see page analysis, pavement design, and settlement analysis.

O'Donnell & Associates materials testing laboratory is certified by AASHTO Accreditation Program for the testing of Soils, Aggregate, Hot Mix Asphalt and Portland Cement Concrete. A copy of our laboratory certification is included with this proposal. In addition to in-house training, field and laboratory technicians participate in a variety of certification programs, including those sponsored by the American Concrete Institute (ACI) and Illinois Department of Transportation (IDOT).

Costs

On the basis of our understanding of the scope of the work, we estimate the total cost of the two projects to be $100,260.00, as follows:

(continued)

Figure 13.4 **Informal Solicited Proposal** *(continued)*

for inconsistencies, errors, and missing components. Proofing can catch minor flaws that might diminish your credibility—and major flaws that might damage your career.

Proofreading the text portions of your report is essentially the same as proofreading any other business message—you check for typos, spelling errors, and mistakes in punctuation. However, reports often have elements that may not be included in other messages, so don't forget to proof your visuals thoroughly and make sure they are positioned correctly. If you need specific tips on proofreading documents, look back at Chapter 6 for some reminders on what to look for when proofreading text and how to proofread like a pro.

Ask for proofreading assistance from someone who hasn't been involved in the development of your proposal; he or she might see errors that you've been overlooking.

Whenever possible, arrange for someone with "fresh eyes" to proofread the report, somebody who hasn't been involved with the text so far. At this point in the process, you are so familiar with the content that your mind will fill in missing words, fix misspelled words, and subconsciously compensate for other flaws, without you even being aware of it. Someone else might see mistakes that you've passed over a dozen times without noticing. An ideal approach is to have two people review it, one who is an expert in the subject matter and one who isn't. The first person can ensure its technical accuracy, and the second can ensure that a wide range of readers will understand it.[7]

Ms. Joyce Colton, AGI Builders   Page 3   July 30, 2012

Cost Estimates

Cost Estimate: Mass Grading	Units	Rate ($)	Total Cost ($)
Field Inspection			
Labor	1,320 hours	$38.50	$ 50,820.00
Nuclear Moisture Density Meter	132 days	35.00	4,620.00
Vehicle Expense	132 days	45.00	5,940.00
Laboratory Testing			
Proctor Density Tests	4 tests	130.00	520.00
(ASTM D-1557)			
Engineering/Project Management			
Principal Engineer	16 hours	110.00	1,760.00
Project Manager	20 hours	80.00	1,600.00
Administrative Assistant	12 hours	50.00	600.00
Subtotal			**$ 65,860.00**

Cost Estimate: Utility Work	Units	Rate ($)	Total Cost ($)
Field Inspection			
Labor	660 hours	$ 38.50	$ 25,410.00
Nuclear Moisture Density Meter	66 days	5.00	2,310.00
Vehicle Expense	66 days	45.00	2,970.00
Laboratory Testing			
Proctor Density Tests	2 tests	130.00	260.00
(ASTM D-1557)			
Engineering/Project Management			
Principal Engineer	10 hours	110.00	1,100.00
Project Manager	20 hours	80.00	1,600.00
Administrative Assistant	15 hours	50.00	750.00
Subtotal			**$ 34,400.00**

Total Project Costs			**$100,260.00**

This estimate assumes full-time inspection services. However, our services may also be performed on an as-requested basis, and actual charges will reflect time associated with the project. We have attached our standard fee schedule for your review. Overtime rates are for hours in excess of 8.0 hours per day, before 7:00 a.m., after 5:00 p.m., and on holidays and weekends.

A clear and complete itemization of estimated costs builds confidence in dependability of the project's financial projections.

To give the client some budgetary flexibility, the proposal offers an alternative to the fixed-fee approach—which may lower any resistance to accepting the bid.

(continued)

Figure 13.4   Informal Solicited Proposal *(continued)*

Distributing Reports and Proposals

All the distribution issues explored in Chapter 6 apply to reports and proposals, but pay particular attention to the length and complexity of your documents. For physical distribution, consider spending the few extra dollars for a professional courier or package delivery service, if that will help your document stand apart from the crowd. The online tracking offered by FedEx, UPS, and other services can verify that your document arrived safely. On the other hand, if you've prepared the document for a single person or small group, delivering it in person can be a nice touch. In addition to answering any immediate questions about it, you can promote the results in person—reminding the recipient of the benefits contained in your report or proposal.

For electronic distribution, unless your audience specifically requests a word-processor file, provide documents as PDF files. Many people are reluctant to open word-processor files these days, particularly from outsiders, given the greater vulnerability of such files to macro viruses and other contaminations. Moreover, using PDF files lets you control how your document is displayed on your audience's computer, ensuring that your readers see

5   LEARNING OBJECTIVE

Describe the decision process for distributing reports and proposals.

Using portable document format (PDF) is a common and relatively safe way to distribute reports electronically.

The brief close emphasizes the bidder's qualifications and asks for a decision.

Ms. Joyce Colton, AGI Builders   Page 4   July 30, 2012

Authorization

With a staff of over 30 personnel, including registered professional engineers, resident engineers, geologists, construction inspectors, laboratory technicians, and drillers, we are confident that O'Donnell & Associates is capable of providing the services required for a project of this magnitude.

If you would like our firm to provide the services as outlined in this proposal, please sign this letter and return it to us along with a certified check in the amount of $10,000 (our retainer) by August 14, 2011. Please call me if you have any questions regarding the terms of this proposal or our approach.

The call to action clarifies the steps needed to put the project in motion.

Sincerely,

Dixon O'Donnell

Dixon O'Donnell
Vice President

Enclosures

Accepted for AGI BUILDERS, INC.

By_____   Date _____

The customer's signature will make the proposal a binding contract.

Figure 13.4   Informal Solicited Proposal *(continued)*

your document as you intended. Review and commenting features in Adobe Acrobat and other systems make PDFs a handy way to gather input from a team of reviewers, too. In addition, making documents available as downloadable PDF files is almost universally expected these days, if only for the sake of convenience.

If your company or client expects you to distribute your reports via a web-based content management system, intranet, or extranet, be sure to upload the correct file(s) to the correct online location. Verify the onscreen display of your report after you've posted it, too; make sure graphics, charts, links, and other elements are in place and operational.

When you've completed your formal report or proposal and sent it off to your audience, your next task is to wait for a response. If you don't hear from your readers within a week or two, you might want to ask politely whether the report arrived. (Some RFPs specify a response time frame. In such a case, *don't* pester the recipient ahead of schedule, or you'll hurt your chances.) In hope of stimulating a response, you might ask a question about the report, such as "How do you think accounting will react to the proposed budget increase?" You might also offer to answer any questions or provide additional information. To review the ideas presented in this chapter, see "Checklist: Producing Formal Reports and Proposals."

✓ Checklist   Producing Formal Reports and Proposals

A. Prefatory parts.
- Use your company's standard report covers, if available.
- Include a concise, descriptive title on the cover.
- Include a title fly only if you want an extra-formal touch.
- On the title page, list (1) report title; (2) name, title, and address of the group or person who authorized the report; (3) name, title, and address of the group or person who prepared the report; and (4) date of submission.
- Include a copy of the letter of authorization, if appropriate.
- If responding to an RFP, follow its instructions for including a copy or referring to the RFP by name or tracking number.
- Include a letter of transmittal that introduces the report.
- Provide a table of contents in outline form, with headings worded exactly as they appear in the body of the report.
- Include a list of illustrations if the report contains a large number of them.
- Include a synopsis (brief summary of the report) or an executive summary (a condensed, "mini" version of the report) for longer reports.

B. Text of the report.
- Draft an introduction that prepares the reader for the content that follows.
- Provide information that supports your conclusions, recommendations, or proposals in the body of the report.
- Don't overload the body with unnecessary detail.
- Close with a summary of your main idea.

C. Supplementary parts.
- Use appendixes to provide supplementary information or supporting evidence.
- List in a bibliography any secondary sources you used.
- Provide an index if your report contains a large number of terms or ideas and is likely to be consulted over time.

ON THE JOB: SOLVING COMMUNICATION DILEMMAS AT GARAGE TECHNOLOGY VENTURES

Source: Courtesy of Guy Kawasaki.

You recently joined Guy Kawasaki and the rest of the team at Garage Technology Ventures in Palo Alto. Part of your responsibilities includes screening executive summaries of business plans submitted by start-up companies seeking financing. Review the criteria discussed in the chapter-opening vignette on page 449 to address the following challenges.

1. You've just received an intriguing executive summary from a start-up company whose technology reduces the cost of providing Internet service by nearly 30 percent, an amount that would spark interest from just about every Internet service provider in the world. The financial projections in the executive summary are realistic—and quite positive. Even if this investment panned out only half as well as the numbers suggest, it would bring in a sizable amount of cash when the company eventually goes public. The patented technological solution is sound, too; you used to work as a network engineer, and these people know what they're doing. There is just one problem: the submission is entirely anonymous. The document describes, in vague terms, four experienced technical and business specialists but without

giving their names or their specific work experiences. A note attached to the plan apologizes for the secrecy but says the four principles in the new firm can't reveal themselves until they get financing and can therefore leave their current jobs. What should you do?
   a. Reject the submission without a second thought; you can't invest in them if you don't know who they are.
   b. Pass it on to Kawasaki and the other managing directors for their consideration, like any other promising business plan.
   c. Forward it to another networking company in the Garage portfolio and ask them to explore bringing this technology to market.
   d. Write a message to the email address provided in the plan, stating that Garage might be interested, but only if the people behind the plan are willing to reveal themselves. If they refuse or don't respond, toss out the plan.

2. Review these "grabs" presented in three executive summaries. Discuss their strengths and weaknesses and decide which one of the three you would forward to Kawasaki and the other directors.
   a. **Company A:** Pardon our bullish tone, but this is the best investment opportunity you are likely to see this year. As one of our board members recently said, we are already on track to out-Apple Apple and out-Google Google.
   b. **Company B:** Cooling the huge data centers that power the Internet costs millions of dollars a year and consumes

massive amounts of energy. Our low-temperature server technology pays for itself in less than a year by reducing energy bills and extending the life of data center hardware.

   c. **Company C:** Our travel-search website has already proven so popular that last month we had 140,000 site visitors. By the way, we have interest from three other investment firms, so our advice would be to jump on this opportunity!

3. You are finalizing this year's portfolio update report for the company's partners and investors, an important document that summarizes the performance over the last year of all the companies in which Garage has an investment stake. Accuracy and clarity are essential with this document, because the information it contains can lead to significant changes in investment and oversight strategies for the companies in the portfolio. Which of the following proofreading strategies should you use to make sure your report is free of errors?

   a. Take advantage of technology. Double-check the settings in your word-processing software to make sure every checking tool is activated as you type, including the spell checker, grammar checker, and style checker. When you're finished with the first draft, run each of these tools again, just to make sure the computer didn't miss anything.

   b. Recognize that no report, particularly a complex 60-page document with multiple visuals, is going to be free of errors. Include a statement on the title page apologizing for any errors that may still exist in the report. Provide your email address and invite people to send you a message when they find errors.

   c. As soon as you finish typing the first draft, immediately review it for accuracy while the content is still fresh in your mind. After you've done this, you can be reasonably sure that the document is free from errors. If you wait a day or two, you'll start to forget what you've written, thereby lowering your chances of catching errors.

   d. Put the report aside for at least a day and then proofread it carefully. Also, recruit two colleagues to review it for you—one who can review the technical and financial accuracy of the material and one who has a good eye for language and clarity.

4. Looking over past editions of the annual performance report, you see that it has always had the generic main title of "Annual Performance Review," followed by a subtitle that summarizes the overall performance of the companies in the portfolio. Which of the following subtitles would be most effective and most appropriate for this year's report, a year in which half the companies in the portfolio experienced major technical or legal setbacks, and only two met their revenue projections?

   a. A Year We'd Rather Forget

   b. We Can't Continue at This Rate

   c. A Year of Serious Challenges

   d. A Portfolio in Crisis

LEARNING OBJECTIVES CHECKUP

Assess your understanding of the principles in this chapter by reading each learning objective and studying the accompanying exercises. For fill-in-the-blank items, write the missing text in the blank provided; for multiple-choice items, circle the letter of the correct answer. You can check your responses against the answer key on page AK-2.

Objective 13.1: Describe the process of revising formal reports and proposals.

1. Which of the following is *not* one of the four major tasks involved in completing business reports and proposals?

   a. Revising the report's organization, style, tone, and readability

   b. Formatting the report

   c. Deciding which visuals to create for the report

   d. Proofreading the report

Objective 13.2: Identify the major components of formal reports.

2. In what situation should you consider including a letter or memo of authorization in a formal report?

   a. If you're getting paid to write the report

   b. If you received written authorization to write the report

   c. If the audience outranks you

   d. If you outrank the audience

3. What is the purpose of including a letter of acceptance in a formal report?

   a. It reminds your audience what you previously agreed to address in the report and why you were assigned to write it.

   b. It makes your report feel more formal and official.

   c. It prevents others from taking credit for your work.

   d. It summarizes the key points of your report for people who are too busy to read the report itself.

4. A letter or memo of _____ is a specialized form of a cover letter that introduces your report to the audience.

5. A/an _____ is a brief overview (usually one page or less) of a report's most important points.

6. A/an _____ _____ is a fully developed "mini" version of the report itself.

7. Which of the following may contain headings, visual aids, and enough information to help busy executives make quick decisions?

   a. An executive summary

   b. A synopsis

   c. Both

   d. Neither

8. Which of the following is *not* a typical supplementary part of a formal report?
   a. Appendixes
   b. Bibliography
   c. Letter of authorization
   d. Index

Objective 13.3: Identify the major components of formal proposals.

9. If you've submitted a proposal that is in response to an RFP, and the RFP doesn't include specific instructions for referring to the RFP, what steps can you take to make sure the recipient understands which RFP you're responding to?
   a. Include the formal title of the RFP (and its reference number, if it has one) as a footnote in the first appendix of your report.
   b. If the RFP is short, include it with the other prefatory parts of your proposal; if the RFP is lengthy, include just the introductory page(s) from it.
   c. Include the entire RFP in the body of your proposal, no matter how long it is.
   d. The RFP was written by someone else, so you can ignore it in your report.

10. How should you handle the letter of transmittal for an unsolicited proposal?
    a. Treat the letter as a routine message; businesspeople get proposals all the time, so they don't expect anything more than a simple announcement that identifies you and your proposal.
    b. Treat the letter as a positive message, highlighting the good news that you have to offer in the proposal.
    c. Treat the letter as a persuasive message, persuading the reader that your report offers information of value.
    d. Don't waste the reader's time with a letter of transmittal; get right to the point with the body of your proposal.

Objective 13.4: Describe an effective plan for proofreading reports and proposals.

11. The following sentence appears in your first draft of a report that analyzes perceived shortcomings in your company's employee health benefits: "Among the many criticisms and concerns expressed by the workforce, at least among the 376 who responded to our online survey (out of 655 active employees), the issues of elder care, health insurance during retirement, and the increased amount that employees are being forced to pay every month as the company's contribution to health insurance coverage has declined over the past two years were identified as the most important." You realize that this 69-word sentence could be shorter, more direct, and more powerful. Which of these revisions is the most effective?
    a. The employees who responded to our online survey (376 out of 655 active employees) identified these three issues as the most important: elder care, insurance coverage after they retire, and rising monthly payments.
    b. Elder care, insurance coverage after they retire, and rising monthly payments were the three most important issues identified in our survey of employees regarding their complaints and criticisms of health care benefits. Out of a current active workforce of 655 people, 376 employees completed the online survey. They complained about quite a range of issues, but these three were the most important to them overall.
    c. The top three employee concerns: elder care, insurance coverage after they retire, and increases in the amounts that employees pay every month for health insurance.
    d. Based on responses from 376 employees (out of 655) who responded to an online survey, the top three concerns our employees have regarding their health benefits are elder care, insurance coverage after they retire, and increases in the monthly cost of insurance.

Objective 13.5: Describe the decision process for distributing reports and proposals.

12. Why are PDF files a universally popular format for distributing reports electronically?
    a. Senders appreciate the ability to maintain control over how their documents appear on the receiving end.
    b. Receivers are often reluctant to open word-processor files.
    c. Most businesspeople expect most reports to be distributed as PDF files.
    d. All of the above are true.

13. What is the best strategy when you've sent a formal proposal in response to an RFP but you haven't heard back within a week or two?
    a. Immediately follow up with the recipient, regardless of the response window specified in the RFP; doing so is a sign that you're hungry for the business.
    b. Never pester a proposal recipient under any circumstances, even if you have to wait months for a response.
    c. Remove the project from your workload planner and get on with something else; if you haven't heard back in a week or two, you're not going to get the contract.
    d. If the response time frame specified in the RFP has passed, follow up with a question related to the content of the proposal or an offer to answer any questions.

MyBcommLab

LEARNING OBJECTIVES

1 Describe the process of revising formal reports and proposals. [page 450]

2 Identify the major components of formal reports. [page 450]

3 Identify the major components of formal proposals. [page 471]

4 Describe an effective plan for proofreading reports and proposals. [page 473]

5 Describe the decision process for distributing reports and proposals. [page 475]

CHAPTER OUTLINE

Revising Reports and Proposals

Producing Formal Reports
Prefatory Parts
Text of the Report
Supplementary Parts

Producing Formal Proposals
Prefatory Parts
Text of the Proposal

Proofreading Reports and Proposals

Distributing Reports and Proposals

 **Checklist**

**Producing Formal Reports
and Proposals**

A. Prefatory parts.
- Use your company's standard report covers, if available.
- Include a concise, descriptive title on the cover.
- Include a title fly only if you want an extra-formal touch.
- On the title page, list (1) report title; (2) name, title, and address of the group or person who authorized the report; (3) name, title, and address of the group or person who prepared the report; and (4) date of submission.
- Include a copy of the letter of authorization, if appropriate.
- If responding to an RFP, follow its instructions for including a copy or referring to the RFP by name or tracking number.
- Include a letter of transmittal that introduces the report.

KEY TERMS

abstract Name usually given to a synopsis that accompanies long technical, professional, or academic reports

appendix Supplementary section that contains materials related to the report but not included in the text because they are too long or perhaps not relevant to everyone in the audience

bibliography A list of the secondary sources consulted in the preparation of a report

executive summary A complete but summarized version of the report; may contain headings, well-developed transitions, and even visual elements

index An alphabetical list of names and subjects mentioned in a report, along with the pages on which they occur

letter of acceptance Message written in response to a letter of authorization

letter of authorization Written authorization to prepare a report

letter of transmittal A specialized form of cover letter that introduces a report to the audience

synopsis A brief overview (one page or less) of a report's most important points, designed to give readers a quick preview of the contents

title fly A single sheet of paper with only the title of the report on it

title page Page that includes the report title; the name, title, and address of the person or organization that authorized the report (if anyone); the name, title, and address of the person or organization that prepared the report; and the date on which the report was submitted

- Provide a table of contents in outline form, with headings worded exactly as they appear in the body of the report.
- Include a list of illustrations if the report contains a large number of them.
- Include a synopsis (brief summary of the report) or an executive summary (a condensed, "mini" version of the report) for longer reports.

B. Text of the report.
- Draft an introduction that prepares the reader for the content that follows.
- Provide information that supports your conclusions, recommendations,

or proposals in the body of the report.
- Don't overload the body with unnecessary detail.
- Close with a summary of your main idea.

C. Supplementary parts.
- Use appendixes to provide supplementary information or supporting evidence.
- List in a bibliography any secondary sources you used.
- Provide an index if your report contains a large number of terms or ideas and is likely to be consulted over time.

APPLY YOUR KNOWLEDGE

To review chapter content related to each question, refer to the indicated Learning Objective.

1. Is an executive summary a persuasive message? Explain your answer. [LO-2]
2. Under what circumstances would you include more than one table of contents in a report? [LO-2]
3. If you included a bibliography in your report, would you also need to include in-text citations? Please explain. [LO-2]
4. How would you report on a confidential survey in which employees rated their managers' capabilities? Both employees and managers expect to see the results. Would you give the same report to employees and managers? What components would you include or exclude for each audience? Explain your choices. [LO-2]
5. If you were submitting a solicited proposal to build a small shopping center, would you include as references the names and addresses of other clients for whom you recently built similar facilities? Where in the proposal would you include these references? Why? [LO-3]

PRACTICE YOUR SKILLS

Message for Analysis

Message 13.A: Executive Summaries [LO-2]
To access this document for this exercise, go to http://real-time-updates.com/ebc10, click on Student Assignments, and select Chapter 13, page 481, Message 13.A. Download this PDF file, which is the executive summary of *Dietary Guidelines for Americans*, a publication from the U.S. Center for Nutrition Policy and Promotion. Using the information in this chapter, analyze the executive summary and offer specific suggestions for revising it.

Exercises

Active links for all websites in this chapter can be found on MyBcommLab; see your User Guide for instructions on accessing the content for this chapter. Each activity is labeled according to the primary skill or skills you will need to use. To review relevant chapter content, you can refer to the indicated Learning Objective. In some instances, supporting information will be found in another chapter, as indicated.

1. **Revising for Clarity and Conciseness [LO-1]** Revise the following sentence to make it clearer and more direct. Feel free to break it into two sentences, if you prefer.

   This job requires someone with both tact and perseverance, because you don't have authority over other people, but your success depends on getting them to perform certain tasks, and you need to persuade them to perform these tasks and not be afraid to follow up to make sure the tasks get done.

2. **Producing Formal Reports; Collaboration: Team Projects [LO-2], Chapter 2** You and a classmate are helping Linda Moreno prepare her report on Electrovision's travel and entertainment costs (see "Report Writer's Notebook" on page 453). This time, however, the report is to be informational rather than analytical, so it will not include recommendations. Review the existing report and determine what changes would be needed to make it an informational report. Be as specific as possible. For example, if your team decides the report needs a new title, what title would you use? Now draft a transmittal memo for Moreno to use in conveying this informational report to Dennis McWilliams, Electrovision's vice president of operations.

3. **Producing Formal Reports [LO-2]** You are president of the Friends of the Library, a nonprofit group that raises funds and provides volunteers to support your local library. Every February, you send a report of the previous year's activities and accomplishments to the County Arts Council, which provides an annual grant of $1,000 toward your group's summer reading festival. Now it's February 6, and you've completed your formal report. Here are the highlights:

   - Back-to-school book sale raised $2,000.
   - Holiday craft fair raised $1,100.
   - Promotion and prizes for summer reading festival cost $1,450.
   - Materials for children's program featuring local author cost $125.
   - New reference databases for library's career center cost $850.
   - Bookmarks promoting library's website cost $200.

   Write a letter of transmittal to Erica Maki, the council's director. Because she is expecting this report, you can use the direct approach. Be sure to express gratitude for the council's ongoing financial support.

4. **Producing Formal Reports [LO-2]** Government reports vary in purpose and structure. Read through the Department of Education's report "Helping Your Child Become a Reader," available at www.ed.gov. What is the purpose of this document? Does the title communicate this purpose? What type of report is this, and what is the report's structure? Which prefatory and supplementary parts are included? Now analyze the visuals. What types of visuals are included in this report? Are they all necessary? Are the titles and legends sufficiently informative? How does this report take advantage of the online medium to enhance readability?

5. **Distributing Reports; Communication Ethics: Resolving Ethical Dilemmas [LO-5], Chapter 1** You submitted what you thought was a masterful report to your boss over three weeks ago. The report analyzes current department productivity and recommends several steps that you think will improve employee output without increasing individual workloads. Brilliant, you thought. But you haven't heard a word from your boss. Did you overstep your boundaries by making recommendations that might imply that she has not been doing a good job? Did you overwhelm her with your ideas? You'd like some feedback. In your last email to her, you asked if she had read your report. So far you've received no reply. Then yesterday, you overheard the company vice president talk about some productivity changes in your department. The changes were ones that

you recommended in your report. Now you're worried that your boss submitted your report to senior management and will take full credit for your terrific ideas. What, if anything, should you do? Should you confront your boss about this? Should you ask to meet with the company vice president? Discuss this situation with your teammates and develop a solution to this sticky situation. Present your solution to the class, explaining the rationale behind your decision.

EXPAND YOUR SKILLS

Critique the Professionals

Browse the websites of several companies to find a downloadable PDF file of a report, white paper, company backgrounder, product overview, or other document at least two pages long. Evaluate the design and production quality of this document. Does the layout enhance the message or distract your attention from it? It what ways do design elements convey the company's brand image? Does the document strike you as "under-designed" or "over-designed" for its intended purpose? Using whatever medium your instructor requests, write a brief summary of your analysis. Be sure to include a link to the document.

Sharpening Your Career Skills Online

Bovée and Thill's Business Communication Web Search, at http://businesscommunicationblog.com/websearch, is a unique research tool designed specifically for business communication research. Use the Web Search function to find a website, video, PDF document, or PowerPoint presentation that offers advice on producing formal reports and proposals. Write a brief email message to your instructor, describing the item that you found and summarizing the career skills information you learned from it.

IMPROVE YOUR GRAMMAR, MECHANICS, AND USAGE

The following exercises help you improve your knowledge of and power over English grammar, mechanics, and usage. Turn to the "Handbook of Grammar, Mechanics, and Usage" at the end of this book and review all of Sections 2.10 (Quotation Marks), 2.11 (Parentheses), and 2.12 (Ellipses). Then look at the following 10 items. Circle the letter of the preferred choice in the following groups of sentences. (Answers to these exercises appear on page AK-4.)

1. a. She has written the article (5 Tips for the Business Manager) in this month's *Harvard Business Review*.
   b. She has written the article "5 Tips for the Business Manager" in this month's *Harvard Business Review*.
   c. She has written the article "5 Tips for the Business Manager . . ." in this month's *Harvard Business Review*.

2. a. His meeting notes . . . see Appendix 2 . . . reveal very interesting details.
   b. His meeting notes (see Appendix 2) reveal very interesting details.
   c. His meeting notes "see Appendix 2" reveal very interesting details.

3. a. The office will be open on Saturday as well for the duration of the conference (January 16 through January 24).
   b. The office will be open on Saturday as well for the duration of the conference "January 16 through January 24."
   c. The office will be open on Saturday as well for the duration of the conference (January 16 through January 24.)

4. a. "My first salary . . ." he wrote in his memoirs, ". . . was two dollars a day."
   b. "My first salary," he wrote in his memoirs, "was two dollars a day."
   c. "My first salary" he wrote in his memoirs "was two dollars a day."

5. a. The phrase "let the cat out of the bag" means "to reveal a secret".
   b. The phrase "let the cat out of the bag" means to reveal a secret.
   c. The phrase let the cat out of the bag means "to reveal a secret."

6. a. Her husband (the one who drives the white Mercedes) is the head of a major publishing house.
   b. Her husband (the one who drives the white Mercedes), is the head of a major publishing house.
   c. Her husband . . . the one who drives the white Mercedes . . . is the head of a major publishing house.

7. a. "Gather ye rosebuds while ye may," is the first line of a famous poem.
   b. ". . . Gather ye rosebuds while ye may" is the first line of a famous poem.
   c. "Gather ye rosebuds while ye may . . ." is the first line of a famous poem.

8. a. Can you remember who said, "Let them eat cake?"
   b. Can you remember who said, "Let them eat cake"?

9. a. Envelope detectors can be used to separate the two patterns. (More on envelope detection in Chapter 4).
   b. Envelope detectors can be used to separate the two patterns. (More on envelope detection in Chapter 4.)

10. a. His autobiography starts off, "This may sound like a fairy tale . . . ," and when you finish the book, you feel like it is!
    b. His autobiography starts off, "This may sound like a fairy tale, . . ." and when you finish the book, you feel like it is!
    c. His autobiography starts off, "This may sound like a fairy tale . . ." and when you finish the book, you feel like it is!

For additional exercises focusing on quotation marks, parentheses, and ellipses, visit MyBcommLab. Click on Chapter 13, click on "Additional Exercises to Improve Your Grammar, Mechanics, and Usage," and then click on 19. Punctuation D.

CASES

Short Formal Reports Requiring No Additional Research

PORTFOLIO BUILDER

1. Message Strategies: Informational Reports   As the newest member of the corporate training division of Paper Products, Inc., you have been asked to investigate and analyze the merits of creating online courses for the company's employees. The president of your company thinks e-learning might be a good employee benefit as well as a terrific way for employees to learn new skills that they can use on the job. You've already done your research, and here's a copy of your notes:

- Online courses open up new horizons for working adults, who often find it difficult to juggle conventional classes with jobs and families.
- Adults over 25 now represent nearly half of higher-ed students; most are employed and want more education to advance their careers.
- Some experts believe that online learning will never be as good as face-to-face instruction.
- Online learning requires no commute and is appealing for employees who travel regularly.
- Enrollment in courses offered online by postsecondary institutions is expected to increase from 4 million students in 2009 to 7 million students in 2014.
- E-learning is a cost-effective way to get better-educated employees.
- More than one-third of the $50 billion spent on employee training every year is spent on e-learning.
- At IBM, some 200,000 employees received education or training online last year, and 75 percent of the company's Basic Blue course for new managers is online. E-learning cut IBM's training bill by $350 million last year—mostly because online courses don't require travel.
- There are no national statistics, but a recent report from the *Chronicle of Higher Education* found that institutions are seeing dropout rates that range from 20 to 50 percent for online learners. The research does not adequately explain why the dropout rates for e-learners are higher.
- A recent study of corporate online learners reported that employees want the following things from their online courses: college credit or a certificate; active correspondence with an online facilitator who has frequent virtual office hours; access to 24-hour, seven-day-a-week technical support; and the ability to start a course anytime.
- Corporate e-learners said that their top reason for dropping a course was lack of time. Many had trouble completing courses from their desktops because of frequent distractions caused by coworkers. Some said they could access courses only through the company's intranet, so they couldn't finish their assignments from home.
- Besides lack of time, corporate e-learners cited the following as e-learning disadvantages: lack of management oversight, lack of motivation, problems with technology, lack

of student support, individual learning preferences, poorly designed courses, substandard/inexperienced instructors.

- A recent study by GE Capital found that finishing a corporate online course was dependent on whether managers gave reinforcement on attendance, how important employees were made to feel, and whether employee progress in the course was tracked.
- Sun Microsystems found that interactivity can be a critical success factor for online courses. Company studies showed that only 25 percent of employees finish classes that are strictly self-paced. But 75 percent finish when given similar assignments and access to tutors through email, phone, or online discussion groups.
- Company managers must supervise e-learning just as they would any other important initiative.
- For online learning to work, companies must develop a culture that takes online learning just as seriously as classroom training.
- For many e-learners, studying at home is optimal. Whenever possible, companies should offer courses through the Internet or provide intranet access at home. Having employees studying on their own time will more than cover any added costs.
- Corporate e-learning has flared into a $2.3 billion market, making it one of the fastest-growing segments of the education industry.
- Rather than fly trainers to 7,000 dealerships, General Motors University now uses interactive satellite broadcasts to teach salespeople the best way to highlight features of the new Buick.
- Fast and cheap, e-training can shave companies' training costs while it saves employees' travel time.
- Pharmaceutical companies such as Merck are conducting live, interactive classes over the web, allowing sales reps to learn about the latest product information at home rather than fly to a conference center.
- McDonald's trainers can log into Hamburger University to learn such skills as how to assemble a made-to-order burger or properly place a drink on a tray.
- One obstacle to the spread of online corporate training is the mismatch between what employees really need—customized courses that are tailored to a firm's products and its unique corporate culture—and what employers can afford.
- Eighty percent of companies prefer developing their own online training courses in-house. But creating even one customized e-course can take months, involve armies of experts, and cost anywhere from $25,000 to $50,000. Thus, most companies either stick with classroom training or buy generic courses on such topics as how to give performance appraisals, understanding basic business ethics, and so on. Employers can choose from a wide selection of noncustomized electronic courses.
- For online learning to be effective, content must be broken into short "chunks" with lots of pop quizzes, online discussion groups, and other interactive features that let students

demonstrate what they've learned. For instance, Circuit City's tutorial on digital camcorders consists of three 20-minute segments. Each contains audio demonstrations of how to handle customer product queries, tests on terminology, and "try-its" that propel trainees back onto the floor to practice what they've learned.

- Dell expects 90 percent of its learning solutions to be totally or partially technology enabled.
- The Home Depot has used e-training to cut a full day from the time required to train new cashiers.
- Online training has freed up an average of 17 days every year for Black & Decker's sales representatives.

Your task: Write a short (three to five pages) memo report to the director of human resources, Kerry Simmons, presenting the advantages and disadvantages of e-learning and making a recommendation about whether Paper Products, Inc., should invest time and money in training its employees this way. Be sure to organize your information so that it is clear, concise, and logically presented. Simmons likes to read the "bottom line" first, so be direct: Present your recommendation up front and support your recommendation with your findings.[8]

PORTFOLIO BUILDER

2. Message Strategies: Analytical Reports You've been in your new job as human resources director for only a week, and already you have a major personnel crisis on your hands. Some employees in the marketing department got their hands on a confidential salary report, only to learn that, on average, marketing employees earn less than engineering employees. In addition, several top performers in the engineering group make significantly more money than anybody in marketing. The report was passed around the company instantly by email, and now everyone is discussing the situation. You'll deal with the data

security issue later; for now, you need to address the dissatisfaction in the marketing group.

Case Table 13.1 lists the salary and employment data you were able to pull from the employee database. You also had the opportunity to interview the engineering and marketing directors to get their opinions on the pay situation; their answers are listed in Case Table 13.2.

Your task: The CEO has asked for a short report, summarizing the data and information you have on engineering and marketing salaries. Feel free to offer your own interpretation of the situation as well (make up any information you need), but keep in mind that as a new manager with almost no experience in the company, your opinion might not have a lot of influence.

CASE TABLE 13.1 Selected Employment Data for Engineers and Marketing Staff

Employment Statistic	Engineering Department	Marketing Department
Average number of years of work experience	18.2	16.3
Average number of years of experience in current profession	17.8	8.6
Average number of years with company	12.4	7.9
Average number of years of college education	6.9	4.8
Average number of years between promotions	6.7	4.3
Salary range	$58–165K	$45–85K
Median salary	$77K	$62K

CASE TABLE 13.2 Summary Statements from Department Director Interviews

Question	Engineering Director	Marketing Director
1. Should engineering and marketing professionals receive roughly similar pay?	In general, yes, but we need to make allowances for the special nature of the engineering profession. In some cases, it's entirely appropriate for an engineer to earn more than a marketing person.	Yes.
2. Why or why not?	Several reasons: (1) Top engineers are extremely hard to find, and we need to offer competitive salaries; (2) the structure of the engineering department doesn't provide as many promotional opportunities, so we can't use promotions as a motivator the way marketing can; (3) many of our engineers have advanced degrees, and nearly all pursue continuing education to stay on top of the technology.	Without marketing, the products the engineers create wouldn't reach customers, and the company wouldn't have any revenue. The two teams make equal contributions to the company's success.
3. If we decide to balance pay between the two departments, how should we do it?	If we do anything to cap or reduce engineering salaries, we'll lose key people to the competition.	If we can't increase payroll immediately to raise marketing salaries, the only fair thing to do is freeze raises in engineering and gradually raise marketing salaries over the next few years.

PORTFOLIO **BUILDER**

3. Message Strategies: Analytical Reports Spurred on in part by the success of numerous television shows and even entire cable networks devoted to remodeling, homeowners across the country are redecorating and rebuilding like never before. Many people are content with superficial changes, such as new paint or new accessories, but some are more ambitious. These homeowners want to move walls, add rooms, redesign kitchens, convert garages to home theaters—the big stuff.

With many consumer trends, publishers try to create magazines that appeal to carefully identified groups of potential readers and the advertisers who'd like to reach them. The do-it-yourself (DIY) market is already served by numerous magazines, but you see an opportunity in those homeowners who tackle the heavy-duty projects. Case Tables 13.3 through 13.5 summarize the results of some preliminary research you asked your company's research staff to conduct.

Your task: You think the data show a real opportunity for a "big projects" DIY magazine, although you'll need more extensive research to confirm the size of the market and refine the editorial direction of the magazine. Prepare a brief analytical report that presents the data you have, identifies the opportunity or opportunities you've found (suggest your own ideas based on the tables), and requests funding from the editorial board to pursue further research.

CASE TABLE 13.3	Rooms Most Frequently Remodeled by DIYers

Room	Percentage of Homeowners Surveyed Who Have Tackled or Plan to Tackle at Least a Partial Remodel
Kitchen	60
Bathroom	48
Home office/study	44
Bedroom	38
Media room/home theater	31
Den/recreation room	28
Living room	27
Dining room	12
Sun room/solarium	8

CASE TABLE 13.4	Average Amount Spent on Remodeling Projects

Estimated Amount	Percentage of Surveyed Homeowners
Under $5K	5
$5–10K	21
$10–20K	39
$20–50K	22
More than $50K	13

CASE TABLE 13.5	Tasks Performed by Homeowner on a Typical Remodeling Project

Task	Percentage of Surveyed Homeowners Who Perform or Plan to Perform Most or All of This Task Themselves
Conceptual design	90
Technical design/architecture	34
Demolition	98
Foundation work	62
Framing	88
Plumbing	91
Electrical	55
Heating/cooling	22
Finish carpentry	85
Tile work	90
Painting	100
Interior design	52

Short Formal Reports Requiring Additional Research

PORTFOLIO **BUILDER**

4. Message Strategies: Analytical Reports Like any other endeavor that combines hardnosed factual analysis and creative freethinking, the task of writing business plans generates a range of opinions.

Your task: Find at least six sources of advice on writing successful business plans (focus on start-up businesses that are likely to seek outside investors). Use at least two books, two magazine or journal articles, and two websites or blogs. Analyze the advice you find and identify points where most or all the experts agree and points where they don't agree. Wherever you find points of significant disagreement, identify which opinion you find most convincing and explain why. Summarize your findings in a brief formal report.

TEAM **SKILLS**   PORTFOLIO **BUILDER**

5. Message Strategies: Analytical Reports Anyone looking at the fragmented 21st-century landscape of media and entertainment options might be surprised to learn that poetry was once a dominant medium for not only creative literary expression but philosophical, political, and even scientific discourse. Alas, such is no longer the case.

Your task: With a team of fellow students, your challenge is to identify opportunities to increase sales of poetry—any kind of poetry, in any medium. The following suggestions may help you get started:

- Research recent bestsellers in the poetry field and try to identify why they have been popular.
- Interview literature professors, professional poets, librarians, publishers, and bookstore personnel.
- Conduct surveys and interviews to find out why consumers don't buy more poetry.
- Attend a few poetry slams or readings and talk to the participants about their poetry buying needs and habits.
- Review professional journals that cover the field of poetry, including *Publishers Weekly* and *Poets & Writers*, from both business and creative standpoints.

Summarize your recommendations in a brief formal report; assume that your target readers are executives in the publishing industry.

PORTFOLIO BUILDER

6. Message Strategies: Analytical Reports   After 15 years in the corporate world, you're ready to strike out on your own. Rather than building a business from the ground up, however, you think that buying a franchise is a better idea. Unfortunately, some of the most lucrative franchise opportunities, such as the major fast-food chains, require significant start-up costs—some more than a half-million dollars. Fortunately, you've met several potential investors who seem willing to help you get started in exchange for a share of ownership. Between your own savings and money from these investors, you estimate that you can raise from $350,000 to $600,000, depending on how much ownership share you want to concede to the investors.

You've worked in several functional areas already, including sales and manufacturing, so you have a fairly well-rounded business résumé. You're open to just about any type of business, too, as long as it provides the opportunity to grow; you don't want to be so tied down to the first operation that you can't turn it over to a hired manager and expand into another market.

Your task: To convene a formal meeting with the investor group, you need to first draft a report that outlines the types of franchise opportunities you'd like to pursue. Write a brief report, identifying five franchises that you would like to explore further. (Choose five based on your own personal interests and the criteria already identified.) For each possibility, identify the nature of the business, the financial requirements, the level of support the company provides, and a brief statement of why you could run such a business successfully (make up any details you need). Be sure to carefully review the information you find about each franchise company to make sure you can qualify for it. For instance, McDonald's doesn't allow investment partnerships to buy franchises, so you won't be able to start up a McDonald's outlet until you have enough money to do it on your own.

For a quick introduction to franchising, see How Stuff Works (www.howstuffworks.com/franchising). You can learn more about the business of franchising at Franchising.com (www.franchising.com) and search for specific franchise opportunities at Francorp Connect (www.francorpconnect.com). In addition, many companies that sell franchises, such as Subway, offer additional information on their websites.

PORTFOLIO BUILDER

7. Message Strategies: Informational Reports   Health care costs are a pressing concern at every level in the economy, from individual households up through companies of all sizes on up to state and federal governments. Many companies that want to continue offering or to start offering some level of health insurance to their employees are struggling with a cost spiral that seems out of control.

Your task: Identify five ways that companies are reducing the cost of providing health care insurance for their employees (other than eliminating this benefit entirely). Compile your findings in a brief report that includes at least one real-life example for each of the five ways.

PORTFOLIO BUILDER

8. Message Strategies: Analytical Reports.   After several false starts over the past few years, tablet computers seem to have finally caught on among business users. In addition to Apple's popular iPad, seemingly every computer company on the planet is looking to get a share of this market. Will they be a passing fad? A cool toy or a serious business tool?

Your task: Prepare a short analytical report that compares the advantages and disadvantages of tablet computers for traveling salespeople.

Long Formal Reports Requiring No Additional Research

PORTFOLIO BUILDER

9. Message Strategies: Informational Reports   As a researcher in your state's consumer protection agency, you're frequently called on to investigate consumer topics and write reports for the agency's website. Thousands of consumers have arranged the purchase of cars online, and millions more do at least some of their research online before heading to a dealership. Some want to save time and money, some want to be armed with as much information as possible before talking to a dealer, while others want to completely avoid the often-uncomfortable experience of negotiating prices with car salespeople. In response, a variety of online services have emerged to meet these consumer needs. Some let you compare information on various car models, some connect you to local dealers to complete the transaction, and some complete nearly all of the transaction details for you, including negotiating the price. Some search the inventory of thousands of dealers, whereas others search only a single dealership or a network of affiliated dealers. In other words, a slew of new tools are available for car buyers, but it's not always easy to figure out where to go and what to expect. That's where your report will help.

By visiting a variety of car-related websites and reading magazine and newspaper articles on the car-buying process, you've compiled a variety of notes related to the subject:

- **Process overview.** The process is relatively straightforward and fairly similar to other online shopping experiences, with two key differences. In general, a consumer identifies the make and model of car he or she wants, and then the online car-buying service searches the inventories of car dealers nationwide and presents the available choices. The consumer chooses a particular car from that list, and the service handles the communication and purchase details with the dealer. When the paperwork is finished, the consumer then visits the dealership and picks up the car. The two biggest differences with online auto buying are that (1) you can't actually complete the purchase over the Internet (in most cases, you must visit a local dealer to pick up the car and sign the papers, although in some cities, a dealer or a local car-buying service will deliver it to your home), and (2) in most states, it's illegal to purchase a new car from anyone other than a franchise dealer (i.e., you can't buy directly from the manufacturer, the way you can buy a Dell computer directly from Dell, for instance).

- **Information you can find online (not all information is available at all sites).** The information you can find online includes makes, models, colors, options, option packages (often, specific options are available only as part of a package; you need to know these constraints before you select your options), photos, specifications (everything from engine size to interior space), fuel efficiency estimates, performance data, safety information, predicted resale value, reviews, comparable models, insurance costs, consumer ratings, repair and reliability histories, available buyer incentives and rebates, true ownership costs (including fuel, maintenance, repairs, etc.), warranty information, loan and lease payments, and maintenance requirements.

- **Advantages of shopping online.** Advantages of shopping online include shopping from the comfort and convenience of home, none of the dreaded negotiating at the dealership (in many cases), the ability to search far and wide for a specific car (even nationwide, on many sites), rapid access to considerable amounts of data and information, and reviews from both professional automotive journalists and other consumers. In general, online auto shopping reduces a key advantage that auto dealers used to have: control of most of the information in the purchase transaction. Now consumers can find out how reliable each model is, how quickly it will depreciate, how often it is likely to need repairs, what other drivers think of it, how much the dealer paid the manufacturer for it, and so on.

- **Changing nature of the business.** The relationship between dealers and third-party websites (such as CarsDirect .com and Vehix.com) continues to evolve. At first, the relationship was antagonistic, as some third-party sites and dealers frequently competed for the same customers, and each side made bold proclamations about driving the other out of business. However, the relationship is more collaborative in many cases now, with dealers realizing that some third-party sites already have wide brand awareness and nationwide audiences. As the percentage of new car sales that originate via the Internet continues to increase, dealers are more receptive to working with third-party sites.

- **Comparing information from multiple sources.** Consumers shouldn't rely solely on the information from a single website. Each site has its own way of organizing information, and many have their own ways of evaluating car models and connecting buyers with sellers.

- **Understanding what each site is doing.** For instance, some search thousands of dealers, regardless of ownership connections. Others, such as AutoNation, search only affiliated dealers. A search for a specific model might yield only a half-dozen cars on one site but dozens of cars on another site. Find out who owns the site and what their business objectives are, if you can; this will help you assess the information you receive.

- **Leading websites.** Consumers can check out a wide variety of websites, some of which are full-service operations, offering everything from research to negotiation; others provide more specific and limited services. For instance, CarsDirect (www.carsdirect.com) provides a full range of services, whereas Carfax (www.carfax.com) specializes in uncovering the repair histories of individual used cars. Case Table 13.6 lists some of the leading car-related websites.

Your task: Write an informational report, based on your research notes. The purpose of the report is to introduce consumers to the basic concepts of integrating the Internet into their car-buying activities and to educate them about important issues.[9]

CASE TABLE 13.6 **Leading Automotive Websites**

Site	URL
AutoAdvice	www.autoadvice.com
Autobytel	www.autobytel.com
Autos.com	www.autos.com
AutoVantage	www.autovantage.com
Autoweb	www.autoweb.com
CarBargains	www.carbargains.com
Carfax	www.carfax.com
CarPrices.com	www.carprices.com
Cars.com	www.cars.com
CarsDirect	www.carsdirect.com
CarSmart	www.carsmart.com
Consumer Reports	www.consumerreports.org
eBay Motors	www.motors.ebay.com
Edmunds	www.edmunds.com
iMotors	www.imotors.com
IntelliChoice	www.intellichoice.com
InvoiceDealers	www.invoicedealers.com
JDPower	www.jdpower.com
Kelley Blue Book	www.kbb.com
MSN Autos	http://autos.msn.com
PickupTrucks.com	www.pickuptrucks.com
The Car Connection	www.thecarconnection.com
Vehix.com	www.vehix.com
Yahoo! Autos	http//autos.yahoo.com

PORTFOLIO BUILDER

10. Message Strategies: Informational Reports Your company is the largest private employer in your metropolitan area, and the 43,500 employees in your workforce have a tremendous impact on local traffic. A group of city and county transportation officials recently approached your CEO with a request to explore ways to reduce this impact. The CEO has assigned you the task of analyzing the workforce's transportation habits and attitudes as a first step toward identifying potential solutions. He's willing to consider anything from subsidized bus passes to company-owned shuttle buses to telecommuting, but the decision requires a thorough understanding of employee transportation needs. Case Tables 13.7 through 13.11 summarize data you collected in an employee survey.

Your task: Present the results of your survey in an informational report, using the data provided in Case Tables 13.7 through 13.11.

CASE TABLE 13.7 **Employee Carpool Habits**

Frequency of Use: Carpooling	Portion of Workforce
Every day, every week	10,138 (23%)
Certain days, every week	4,361 (10%)
Randomly	983 (2%)
Never	28,018 (64%)

CASE TABLE 13.8 **Use of Public Transportation**

Frequency of Use: Public Transportation	Portion of Workforce
Every day, every week	23,556 (54%)
Certain days, every week	2,029 (5%)
Randomly	5,862 (13%)
Never	12,053 (28%)

CASE TABLE 13.9 **Effect of Potential Improvements to Public Transportation**

Which of the Following Would Encourage You to Use Public Transportation More Frequently (check all that apply)	Portion of Respondents
Increased perceptions of safety	4,932 (28%)
Improved cleanliness	852 (5%)
Reduced commute times	7,285 (41%)
Greater convenience: fewer transfers	3,278 (18%)
Greater convenience: more stops	1,155 (6%)
Lower (or subsidized) fares	5,634 (31%)
Nothing could encourage me to take public transportation	8,294 (46%)

Note: This question was asked of respondents who use public transportation randomly or never, a subgroup that represents 17,915 employees, or 41 percent of the workforce.

CASE TABLE 13.10 **Distance Traveled to/from Work**

Distance You Travel to Work (one way)	Portion of Workforce
Less than 1 mile	531 (1%)
1–3 miles	6,874 (16%)
4–10 miles	22,951 (53%)
11–20 miles	10,605 (24%)
More than 20 miles	2,539 (6%)

CASE TABLE 13.11 **Is Telecommuting an Option?**

Does the Nature of Your Work Make Telecommuting a Realistic Option?	Portion of Workforce
Yes, every day	3,460 (8%)
Yes, several days a week	8,521 (20%)
Yes, random days	12,918 (30%)
No	18,601 (43%)

Long Formal Reports Requiring Additional Research

PORTFOLIO BUILDER

11. Message Strategies: Informational Reports The partners in your accounting firm have agreed to invest some of the company's profits in the stock market. A previous team effort identified two leading companies in each of five different industries:

- Boeing; Lockheed Martin (aerospace, defense)
- Hewlett-Packard; Dell (computers and software)
- Barnes & Noble; Amazon (retailing)
- UPS; FedEx (delivery and logistics)

The partners have already done an in-depth financial analysis of all 10 firms, and they have asked you to look for more qualitative information, such as

- Fundamental philosophical differences in management styles, launch and handling of products and services, marketing of products and services, and approach to e-commerce that sets one rival company apart from the other
- Future challenges that each competitor faces
- Important decisions made by the two competitors and how those decisions affected their company
- Fundamental differences in each company's vision of its industry's future (for instance, do they both agree on what consumers want, what products to deliver, and so on?)
- Specific competitive advantages of each rival
- Past challenges each competitor has faced and how each met those challenges
- Strategic moves made by one rival that might affect the other

- Company success stories
- Brief company background information
- Brief comparative statistics, such as annual sales, market share, number of employees, number of stores, types of equipment, number of customers, sources of revenue, and so on

Your task: Select two competitors from the preceding list (or another list provided by your instructor) and write a long formal informational report comparing how the two companies are addressing the topics outlined by the partners. Of course, not every topic will apply to each company, and some will be more important than others—depending on the companies you select. The partners will invest in only one of the two companies in your report. (*Note:* Because these topics require considerable research, your instructor may choose to make this a team project.)

PORTFOLIO BUILDER

12. Message Strategies: Analytical Reports As a college student and an active consumer, you may have considered one or more of the following questions at some point in the past few years:

a. What criteria distinguish the top-rated MBA programs in the country? How well do these criteria correspond to the needs and expectations of business? Are the criteria fair for students, employers, and business schools?
b. Which of three companies you might like to work for has the strongest corporate ethics policies?
c. What will the music industry look like in the future? What's next after online stores such as Apple iTunes and digital players such as the iPod?
d. Which industries and job categories are forecast to experience the greatest growth—and therefore the greatest demands for workers—in the next 10 years?
e. What has been the impact of Starbucks's aggressive growth on small, independent coffee shops? On midsized chains or franchises? In the United States or in another country?
f. How large is the "industry" of major college sports? How much do the major football or basketball programs contribute—directly or indirectly—to other parts of a typical university?
g. How much have minor league sports—baseball, hockey, arena football—grown in small- and medium-market cities? What is the local economic impact when these municipalities build stadiums and arenas?

Your task: Answer one of these questions, using secondary research sources for information. Be sure to document your sources in the correct form. Make conclusions and offer recommendations where appropriate.

PORTFOLIO BUILDER

13. Message Strategies: Analytical Reports An observer surveying the current consumer electronics landscape and seeing Apple products everywhere might be surprised to learn that during part of the company's history, it was regarded by some as a fairly minor player in the computer industry—and at times a few pundits even wondered whether the company would survive.

Your task: In a two- to three-page report, identify the reasons Apple has been successful and explain how other companies can apply Apple's strategies and tactics to improve their business results.

Formal Proposals

PORTFOLIO BUILDER

14. Message Strategies: Proposals Presentations can make or break both careers and businesses. A good presentation can bring in millions of dollars in new sales or fresh investment capital. A bad presentation might cause a number of troubles, from turning away potential customers to upsetting fellow employees to derailing key projects. To help business professionals plan, create, and deliver more effective presentations, you offer a three-day workshop that covers the essentials of good presentations:

- Understanding your audience's needs and expectations
- Formulating your presentation objectives
- Choosing an organizational approach
- Writing openings that catch your audience members' attention
- Creating effective graphics and slides
- Practicing and delivering your presentation
- Leaving a positive impression on your audience
- Avoiding common mistakes with Microsoft PowerPoint
- Making presentations online using webcasting tools
- Handling questions and arguments from the audience
- Overcoming the top 10 worries of public speaking (including How can I overcome stage fright? and I'm not the performing type; can I still give an effective presentation?)

Here is some additional information about the workshop:

- **Workshop benefits:** Students will learn how to prepare better presentations in less time and deliver them more effectively.
- **Who should attend:** Top executives, project managers, employment recruiters, sales professionals, and anyone else who gives important presentations to internal or external audiences.
- **Your qualifications:** 18 years of business experience, including 14 years in sales and 12 years in public speaking. Experience speaking to audiences as large as 5,000 people. More than a dozen speech-related articles published in professional journals. Have conducted successful workshops for nearly 100 companies.
- **Workshop details:** Three-day workshop (9 A.M. to 3:30 P.M.) that combines lectures, practice presentations, and both individual and group feedback. Minimum number of students: 6. Maximum number of students per workshop: 12.
- **Pricing:** The cost is $3,500, plus $100 per student. 10 percent discount for additional workshops.
- **Other information:** Each attendee will have the opportunity to give three practice presentations that will last from three to five minutes. Everyone is encouraged to bring PowerPoint files containing slides from actual business presentations. Each attendee will also receive a workbook and a digital video recording of his or her final class presentation. You'll also be available for phone or email coaching for six months after the workshop.

Your task: Identify a company in your local area that might be a good candidate for your services. Learn more about the company by visiting its website so you can personalize your proposal. Using the information listed earlier in this exercise, prepare a sales proposal that explains the benefits of your training and what students can expect during the workshop.

PORTFOLIO BUILDER

15. Message Strategies: Proposals For years, a controversy has been brewing over the amount of junk food and soft drinks being sold through vending machines in local schools. Schools benefit from revenue-sharing arrangements, but many parents and health experts are concerned about the negative effects of these snacks and beverages. You and your brother have almost a decade of experience running espresso and juice stands in malls and on street corners, and you'd love to find some way to expand your business into schools. After a quick brainstorming session, the two of you craft a plan that makes good business sense while meeting the financial concerns of school administrators and the nutritional concerns of parents and dietitians. Here are the notes from your brainstorming session:

- Set up portable juice bars on school campuses, offering healthy fruit and vegetable drinks along with simple healthy snacks.
- Offer schools 30 percent of profits in exchange for free space and long-term contracts.
- Provide job training opportunities for students (during athletic events, etc.).
- Provide detailed dietary analysis of all products sold.
- Establish a nutritional advisory board composed of parents, students, and at least one certified health professional.
- Assure schools and parents that all products are safe (e.g., no stimulant drinks, no dietary supplements, and so on).
- Support local farmers and specialty food preparers by buying locally and giving these vendors the opportunity to test market new products at your stands.

Your task: Based on the ideas listed, draft a formal proposal to the local school board, outlining your plan to offer healthier alternatives to soft drinks and prepackaged snack foods. Invent any details you need to complete your proposal.

PORTFOLIO BUILDER

16. Message Strategies: Proposals Seems like everybody in the firm is frustrated. On the one hand, top executives complain about the number of lower-level employees who want promotions but just don't seem to "get it" when it comes to dealing with customers and the public, recognizing when to speak out and when to be quiet, knowing how to push new ideas through the appropriate channels, and performing other essential but difficult-to-teach tasks. On the other hand, ambitious employees who'd like to learn more feel that they have nowhere to turn for career advice from people who've been there. In between, a variety of managers and midlevel executives are overwhelmed by the growing number of mentoring requests they're getting, sometimes from employees they don't even know.

You've been assigned the challenge of proposing a formal mentoring program—and a considerable challenge it is:

- The number of employees who want mentoring relationships far exceeds the number of managers and executives willing and able to be mentors. How will you select people for the program?
- The people most in demand for mentoring also tend to be some of the busiest people in the organization.
- After several years of belt tightening and staff reductions, the entire company feels overworked; few people can imagine adding another recurring task to their seemingly endless to-do lists.
- What's in it for the mentors? Why would they be motivated to help lower-level employees?
- How will you measure success or failure of the mentoring effort?

Your task: Identify potential solutions to the issues (make up any information you need) and draft a proposal to the executive committee for a formal, companywide mentoring program that would match selected employees with successful managers and executives.

REFERENCES

1. Adapted from "Writing a Compelling Executive Summary," Garage Technology Ventures, accessed 9 March 2011, www.garage.com; "Crafting Your Wow! Statement," Garage Technology Ventures, accessed 9 March 2011, www.garage .com; Guy Kawasaki website, accessed 9 March 2011, www .guykawasaki.com.

2. John Morkes and Jakob Nielsen, "Concise, Scannable, and Objective: How to Write for the Web," UseIt.com, accessed 13 November 2006, www.useit.com.

3. Michael Netzley and Craig Snow, *Guide to Report Writing* (Upper Saddle River, N.J.: Prentice Hall, 2001), 57.

4. Oswald M. T. Ratteray, "Hit the Mark with Better Summaries," *Supervisory Management*, September 1989, 43–45.

5. Netzley and Snow, *Guide to Report Writing*, 43.

6. Alice Reid, "A Practical Guide for Writing Proposals," accessed 31 May 2001, http://members.dca.net/areid/ proposal.htm.

7. Toby B. Gooley, "Ocean Shipping: RFPs That Get Results," *Logistics Management*, July 2003, 47–52.

8. Adapted from "Home Depot Says E-Learning Is Paying for Itself," *Workforce Management*, 25 February 2004, www .workforce.com; Robert Celaschi, "The Insider: Training," *Workforce Management*, August 2004, 67–69; Joe Mullich, "A Second Act for E-Learning," *Workforce Management*, February 2004, 51–55; Gail Johnson, "Brewing the Perfect Blend," *Training*, December 2003, 30+; Tammy Galvin, "2003 Industry Report," *Training*, October 2003, 21+; William C. Symonds, "Giving It the Old Online Try," *BusinessWeek*, 3 December 2001, 76–80; Karen Frankola, "Why Online Learners Drop Out," *Workforce*, October 2001, 52–60; Mary Lord, "They're Online and on the Job; Managers and Hamburger Flippers Are Being E-Trained at Work," *U.S. News & World Report*, 15 October 2001, 72–77.

9. Adapted from Ieva M. Augstums, "Buyers Take the Driver's Seat," *Dallas Morning News*, 20 February 2004, www .highbeam.com; Jill Amadio, "A Click Away: Automotive Web Sites Are Revved Up and Ready to Help You Buy," *Entrepreneur*, 1 August 2003, www.highbeam.com; Dawn C. Chmielewski, "Car Sites Lend Feel-Good Info for Haggling," *San Jose Mercury News*, 1 August 2003, www .highbeam.com; Cromwell Schubarth, "Autoheroes Handle Hassle of Haggling," *Boston Herald*, 24 July 2003, www .highbeam.com; Rick Popely, "Internet Doesn't Change Basic Shopping Rules," *Chicago Tribune*, 28 February 2004, www.highbeam.com; Matt Nauman, "Walnut Creek, Calif., Firm Prospers as Online Car Buying Becomes More Popular," *San Jose Mercury News*, 21 June 2004, www .highbeam.com; Cliff Banks, "e-Dealer 100," *Ward's Dealer Business*, 1 April 2004, www.highbeam.com; Cars.com website, accessed 30 June 2004, www.cars.com; CarsDirect website , accessed 30 June 2004, www.carsdirect.com.

Designing and Delivering Oral and Online Presentations

LEARNING OBJECTIVES   After studying this chapter, you will be able to

1 Highlight the importance of presentations in your business career and explain how to adapt the planning step of the three-step process to presentations

2 Describe the tasks involved in developing a presentation after completing the planning step

3 Describe the six major design and writing tasks required to enhance your presentation with effective visuals

4 Outline four major tasks involved in completing a presentation

5 Describe four important aspects of delivering a presentation in today's social media environment

MyBcommLab   Where you see MyBcommLab in this chapter, go to www.pearsoninternationaleditions.com/mybcommlab for additional activities on the topic being discussed.

ON THE JOB: COMMUNICATING AT PRINCIPATO-YOUNG ENTERTAINMENT

Talent agent Peter Principato coaches his comedian clients to hone their presentations before pitching movie and TV show ideas to studio executives.
Source: Alexander Sibaja/Hulton Archive/Getty Images.

The Serious Side of the Comedy Business

The business of being funny can be profoundly unfunny these days, particularly for comedians who want to break into movies and television shows. Fewer movies are being made, and the audience for television and online shows is so fragmented that trying to build a fan base is an uphill struggle. Making the situation even worse for comedians, many of whom are writers at heart, is the seemingly unstoppable growth of reality shows, which require neither writers nor actors in any conventional sense.

Talent agent Peter Principato knows this landscape as well as anyone, and as he puts it, "There's less and less real estate every year." Studios are increasingly reluctant to "green light" projects, particularly with the young and not-quite-top-of-the-marquee talent that is the specialty of Principato-Young Entertainment, the Beverly Hills company he co-founded with producer Paul Young. But comedy is in Principato's blood, so he works overtime to make his clients successful, even in this challenging environment.

In the entertainment industry, the road to success often starts with "the pitch," a brief presentation to one or more studio executives by an individual writer, actor, director, or producer or by a team of these people. If the executive is intrigued by the concept, it might be discussed further within the studio, and eventually a decision will be made about funding production.

With so much riding on this brief presentation, you can imagine that it's a high-anxiety event for the presenters, requiring vital communication skills. In fact, the ability to pitch effectively is so important that it has its own slang term: being "good in a room."

Pitches can fall flat for a number of reasons, whether the concept is just not a good fit for a particular studio, the idea is so unusual that the executives are unwilling to risk investing in it, or the pitch is just poorly presented. A presenter may fail by being unable to summarize what a new show or movie idea is all about, by smothering the executives in too many details, or by trying too hard to sell the concept.

The pointers Principato gives his clients constitute good advice for presentations in any industry, but they're vital in the entertainment industry. First, come up with a single compelling sentence that describes the show or movie. If presenters can't do this, chances are they haven't thought the idea out well enough, or the idea is so complicated that it would be too risky or too expensive to attempt. This one-line summary is essential for another reason, in that the first studio executive to hear the pitch will usually need to share it with other executives or potential financiers before a decision can be made. A catchy,

succinct idea is a lot easier to repeat than a rambling, confused concept.

Second, expand on that one sentence with a single paragraph that builds interest by substantiating the concept and helping the listener envision what the show or movie would be like. Third, for a proposed series, explain how the concept would play out, week by week, by describing several episodes. Fourth, fill in the "big picture," such as by describing how the show would look on screen or by rounding out the main characters.

You've probably noticed how this advice follows the classic AIDA model of getting attention, building interest, increasing desire, and asking for a decision, which is what makes Principato's advice valuable for just about any profession.

The funny business is tough and getting tougher, but Principato is clearly doing something right. Principato-Young continues to expand and attract more of the young comedians who might be box office stars for the next several decades. And his love of comedy and comedians continues to motivate Principato himself. As he describes it, having his job "is like getting to hang out with your favorite band."[1]

Planning a Presentation

You might not pitch the next Oscar winner to a studio executive as Peter Principato (profiled in the chapter opener) hopes to do, but wherever your career takes you, speeches and presentations will offer important opportunities to put all your communication skills on display, including research, planning, writing, visual design, and interpersonal and nonverbal communication. Presentations also let you demonstrate your ability to think on your feet, grasp complex business issues, and handle challenging situations—all attributes that executives look for when searching for talented employees to promote.

Planning presentations is much like planning other business messages: You analyze the situation, gather information, select the right medium, and organize the information (see Figure 14.1 on the next page). Gathering information for oral presentations is essentially the same as it is for written communication projects. The other three planning tasks have some special applications when it comes to oral presentations; they are covered in the following sections.

On the subject of planning, be aware that preparing a professional-quality business presentation can take a considerable amount of time. Nancy Duarte, whose design firm has years of experience creating presentations for corporations, offers this rule of thumb: For a one-hour presentation that uses 30 slides, allow 36 to 90 hours to research, conceive, create, and practice.[2] Not every one-hour presentation justifies a week or two of preparation, of course, but the important presentations that can make your career or your company certainly can.

ANALYZING THE SITUATION

As with written communications, analyzing the situation involves defining your purpose and developing an audience profile (see Table 14.1 on the next page). The purpose of most of your presentations will be to inform or to persuade, although you may occasionally need to make a collaborative presentation, such as when you're leading a problem-solving or brainstorming session.

In addition to following the audience analysis advice in Chapter 4, try to anticipate the likely emotional state of your audience members. Figure 14.2 on page 495 offers tips for dealing with a variety of audience mindsets.

1   LEARNING OBJECTIVE

Highlight the importance of presentations in your business career, and explain how to adapt the planning step of the three-step process to presentations.

The three-step process adapts easily to speeches and presentations.

Creating a high-quality presentation for an important event can take many days, so be sure to allow enough time.

MyBcommLab

- Access this chapter's simulation entitled Developing Oral & Online Presentations located at www.pearsoninternationaleditions .com/mybcommlab.

1 Plan →	2 Write →	3 Complete

Analyze the Situation

Define your purpose and develop a profile of your audience, including their likely emotional states and language preferences.

Gather Information

Determine audience needs and obtain the information necessary to satisfy those needs.

Select the Right Medium

Choose the best medium or combination of media for delivering your presentation, including handouts and other support materials.

Organize the Information

Define your main idea, limit your scope and verify timing, select the direct or indirect approach, and outline your content.

Adapt to Your Audience

Adapt your content, presentation style, and room setup to the audience and the specific situation. Be sensitive to audience needs and expectations with a "you" attitude, politeness, positive emphasis, and bias-free language. Plan to establish your credibility as required.

Compose Your Presentation

Outline an attention-getting introduction, body, and close. Prepare supporting visuals and speaking notes.

Revise the Message

Evaluate your content and speaking notes.

Master Your Delivery

Choose your delivery mode and practice your presentation.

Prepare to Speak

Verify facilities and equipment, including online connections and software setups. Hire an interpreter if necessary.

Overcome Anxiety

Take steps to feel more confident and appear more confident on stage.

Figure 14.1 **The Three-Step Process for Developing Oral and Online Presentations**
Although you rarely "write" a presentation or speech in the sense of composing every word ahead of time, the tasks in the three-step writing process adapt quite well to the challenge of planning, creating, and delivering oral and online presentations.

TABLE 14.1	Analyzing Audiences for Oral Presentations

Task	Actions
To determine audience size and composition	• Estimate how many people will attend. • Identify what they have in common and how they differ. • Analyze the mix of men and women, age ranges, socioeconomic and ethnic groups, occupations, and geographic regions represented.
To predict the audience's probable reaction	• Analyze why audience members are attending the presentation. • Determine the audience's general attitude toward the topic: interested, moderately interested, unconcerned, open-minded, or hostile. • Analyze the mood that people will be in when you speak to them. • Find out what kind of backup information will most impress the audience: technical data, historical information, financial data, demonstrations, samples, and so on. • Consider whether the audience has any biases that might work against you. • Anticipate possible objections or questions.
To gauge the audience's experience	• Analyze whether everybody has the same background and level of understanding. • Determine what the audience already knows about the subject. • Decide what background information the audience will need to better understand the subject. • Consider whether the audience is familiar with the vocabulary you intend to use. • Analyze what the audience expects from you. • Think about the mix of general concepts and specific details you will need to present.

Supportive: Reward their goodwill with a presentation that is clear, concise, and upbeat; speak in a relaxed, confident manner.

Interested but neutral: Build your credibility as you present compelling reasons to accept your message; address potential objections as you move forward; show confidence in your message but a willingness to answer questions and concerns.

Uninterested: Use the techniques described in this chapter to get their attention and work hard to hold it throughout; find ways to connect your message with their personal or professional interests; be well organized and concise.

Worried: Don't dismiss their fears or tell them they are mistaken for feeling that way; if your message will calm their fears, use the direct approach; if your message will confirm their fears, consider the indirect approach to build acceptance.

Hostile: Recognize that angry audiences care deeply but might not be open to listening; consider the indirect approach to find common ground and to diffuse anger before sharing your message; work to keep your own emotions under control.

Figure 14.2   Planning for Various Audience Mindsets
Try to assess the emotional state of your audience ahead of time so you can plan your presentation approach accordingly.

As you analyze the situation, also consider the circumstances. Is the audience in the room or online? How many people will be present, and how will they be seated? Can you control the environment to minimize distractions? What equipment will you need? Such variables can influence not only the style of your presentation but the content itself.

REAL-TIME UPDATES
Learn More by Watching This Video

Dealing with the Difficult Four

Get advice on dealing with four difficult audience members: the Resister, the Expert, the Dominator, and the Rambler. Go to http://real-timeupdates.com/ebc10 and click on Learn More. If you are using MyBcommLab, you can access Real-Time Updates within each chapter or under Student Study Tools.

SELECTING THE RIGHT MEDIUM

The task of selecting the right medium might seem obvious. After all, you are speaking, so it's an oral medium. However, you have an array of choices these days, from live, in-person presentations to *webcasts* (online presentations that people either view live or download later from your website), *screencasts* (recordings of activity on computer displays with audio voiceover), or *twebinars* (the use of Twitter as a *backchannel*—see page 515—for real-time conversation during a web-based seminar[3]).

ORGANIZING YOUR PRESENTATION

Organizing a presentation involves the same tasks as organizing a written message: Define your main idea, limit your scope, select the direct or indirect approach, and outline your content. Keep in mind that when people read written reports, they can skip back and forth if they're confused or don't need certain information. However, in an oral presentation, audiences are more or less trapped in your time frame and sequence. For some presentations, you should plan to be flexible and respond to audience feedback, such as skipping over sections the audience doesn't need to hear and going into more detail in other sections.

Defining Your Main Idea

If you've ever heard a speaker struggle to get his or her main point across ("What I really mean to say is . . ."), you know how frustrating such an experience can be for an audience.

Knowing your audience's state of mind will help you adjust both your message and your delivery.

Try to learn as much as you can about the setting and circumstances of your presentation, from the size of the audience to seating arrangements.

If you can't express your main idea in a single sentence, you probably haven't defined it clearly enough.

To avoid that struggle, figure out the one key message you want audience members to walk away with. Then compose a one-sentence summary that links your subject and purpose to your audience's frame of reference. Here are some examples:

> Convince management that reorganizing the technical support department will improve customer service and reduce employee turnover.
>
> Convince the board of directors that we should build a new plant in Texas to eliminate manufacturing bottlenecks and improve production quality.
>
> Address employee concerns regarding a new health-care plan by showing how the plan will reduce costs and improve the quality of their care.

Each of these statements puts a particular slant on the subject, one that directly relates to the audience's interests. By focusing on your audience's needs and using the "you" attitude, you help keep their attention and convince them that your points are relevant.

Limiting Your Scope

Limiting you scope helps ensure that your presentation fits the allotted time and that you maintain the audience's attention level.

The only sure way to measure the length of your presentation is to complete a practice run.

Limiting your scope is important with any message, but it's particularly vital with presentations, for two reasons. First, for most presentations, you must work within strict time limits. Second, the longer you speak, the more difficult it is to hold the audience's attention levels, and the more difficult it is for your listeners to retain your key points.[4] Even if you are not given a time limit, keep your presentation as short as possible, taking only as much of the audience's time as you need to accomplish your purpose.

The only sure way to know how much material you can cover in a given time is to practice your presentation after you complete it. As an alternative, if you're using conventional structured slides (see page 503) you can figure on 3 or 4 minutes per slide as a rough guide.[5] Of course, be sure to factor in time for introductions, coffee breaks, demonstrations, question-and-answer sessions, and anything else that takes away from your speaking time.

Viewing time constraints as a creative challenge can actually help you develop more effective presentations. Limitations can force you to focus on the most essential message points that are important to your audience.[6] (See Case 1 on page 524 for the special twist on time-constrained presentations known as *pecha-kucha*.)

Choosing Your Approach

Organize short presentations the same way you would a letter or brief memo; organize long presentations as you would a report or proposal.

With a well-defined main idea to guide you and a clear idea about the scope of your presentation, you can begin to arrange your message. If you have 10 minutes or less, organize your presentation much as you would a letter or other brief message: Use the direct approach if the subject involves routine information or good news and use the indirect approach if the subject involves bad news or persuasion. Plan your introduction to arouse interest and to give a preview of what's to come. For the body of the presentation, be prepared to explain the who, what, when, where, why, and how of your subject. In the final section, review the points you've made and close with a statement that will help your audience remember the subject of your speech (see Figure 14.3).

Longer presentations are organized more like reports. If the purpose is to motivate or inform, you'll typically use the direct approach and a structure imposed naturally by the subject: comparison, importance, sequence, chronology, geography, or category (as discussed in Chapter 11). If your purpose is to analyze, persuade, or collaborate, organize your material around conclusions and recommendations or around a logical argument. Use the direct approach if the audience is receptive and the indirect approach if you expect resistance.

Using a storytelling model can be a great way to capture and hold the audience's attention.

No matter what the length, look for opportunities to integrate storytelling (see page 145) into the structure of your presentation. The dramatic tension (not knowing what will happen to the "hero") at the heart of effective storytelling is a great way to capture and keep the audience's attention.

Progress Update: August 2012

Purpose: To update the Executive Committee on our product development schedule

I.   Review goals and progress.
   A. Mechanical design:
      1. Goal: 100%
      2. Actual: 80%
      3. Reason for delay: Unanticipated problems with case durability
   B. Software development:
      1. Goal: 50%
      2. Actual: 60%
   C. Material sourcing:
      1. Goal: 100%
      2. Actual: 45% (and materials identified are at 140% of anticipated costs)
      3. Reason for delay: Purchasing is understaffed and hasn't been able to research sources adequately.
II. Discuss schedule options.
   A. Option 1: Reschedule product launch date.
   B. Option 2: Launch on schedule with more expensive materials.
III. Suggest goals for next month.
IV. Q&A

MyBcommLab

Apply Figure 14.3's key concepts by revising a new document. Go to Chapter 14 in www.pearsoninternationaleditions.com/mybcommlab and select Document Makeovers.

Figure 14.3   Effective Outline for a 10-Minute Presentation
Here is an outline of a short presentation that updates management on the status of a key project; the presenter has some bad news to deliver, so she opted for an indirect approach to lay out the reasons for the delay before sharing the news of the schedule slip.

Preparing Your Outline

A presentation outline helps you organize your message and serves as the foundation for delivering your speech. Prepare your outline in several stages:[7]

- State your purpose and main idea and then use these elements to guide the rest of your planning.
- Organize your major points and subpoints in logical order, expressing each major point as a single, complete sentence.
- Identify major points in the body first, then outline the introduction and close.
- Identify transitions between major points or sections, then write these transitions in full-sentence form.
- Prepare your bibliography or source notes; highlight those sources you want to identify by name during your talk.
- Choose a compelling title. Make it brief, action oriented, and focused on what you can do for the audience.[8]

Many speakers like to prepare both a detailed *planning outline* (see Figure 14.4 on the next page) and a simpler *speaking outline* that provides all the cues and reminders they need in order to present their material. To prepare an effective speaking outline, follow these steps:[9]

- Start with the planning outline and then strip away anything you don't plan to say directly to your audience.
- Condense points and transitions to key words or phrases.

In addition to planning your speech, a presentation outline helps you plan your speaking notes.

You may find it helpful to create a simpler speaking outline from your planning outline.

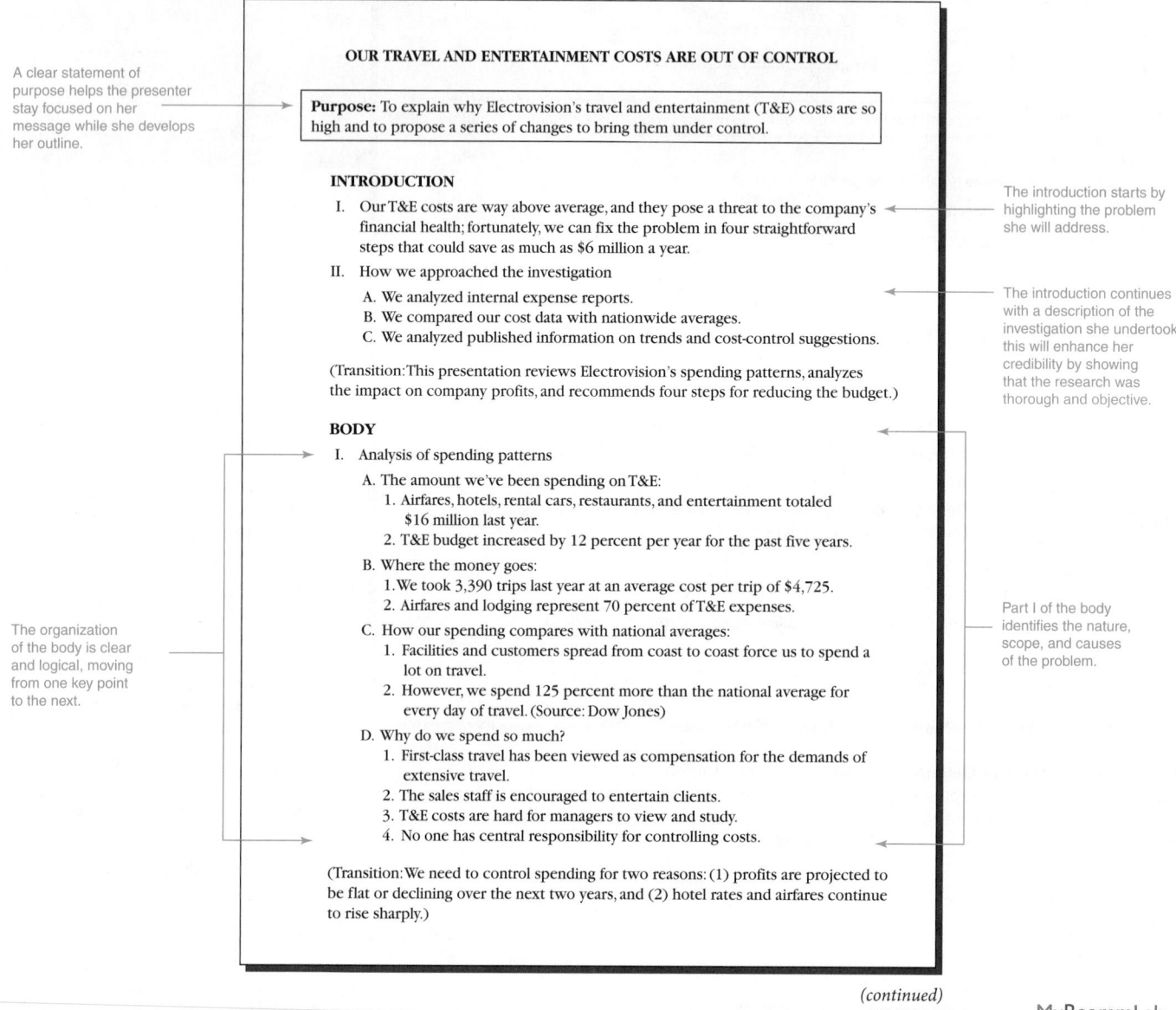

A clear statement of purpose helps the presenter stay focused on her message while she develops her outline.

OUR TRAVEL AND ENTERTAINMENT COSTS ARE OUT OF CONTROL

Purpose: To explain why Electrovision's travel and entertainment (T&E) costs are so high and to propose a series of changes to bring them under control.

INTRODUCTION

I.   Our T&E costs are way above average, and they pose a threat to the company's financial health; fortunately, we can fix the problem in four straightforward steps that could save as much as $6 million a year.

II. How we approached the investigation
   A. We analyzed internal expense reports.
   B. We compared our cost data with nationwide averages.
   C. We analyzed published information on trends and cost-control suggestions.

(Transition: This presentation reviews Electrovision's spending patterns, analyzes the impact on company profits, and recommends four steps for reducing the budget.)

BODY

I.   Analysis of spending patterns
   A. The amount we've been spending on T&E:
      1. Airfares, hotels, rental cars, restaurants, and entertainment totaled $16 million last year.
      2. T&E budget increased by 12 percent per year for the past five years.
   B. Where the money goes:
      1. We took 3,390 trips last year at an average cost per trip of $4,725.
      2. Airfares and lodging represent 70 percent of T&E expenses.
   C. How our spending compares with national averages:
      1. Facilities and customers spread from coast to coast force us to spend a lot on travel.
      2. However, we spend 125 percent more than the national average for every day of travel. (Source: Dow Jones)
   D. Why do we spend so much?
      1. First-class travel has been viewed as compensation for the demands of extensive travel.
      2. The sales staff is encouraged to entertain clients.
      3. T&E costs are hard for managers to view and study.
      4. No one has central responsibility for controlling costs.

(Transition: We need to control spending for two reasons: (1) profits are projected to be flat or declining over the next two years, and (2) hotel rates and airfares continue to rise sharply.)

The introduction starts by highlighting the problem she will address.

The introduction continues with a description of the investigation she undertook; this will enhance her credibility by showing that the research was thorough and objective.

The organization of the body is clear and logical, moving from one key point to the next.

Part I of the body identifies the nature, scope, and causes of the problem.

(continued)

MyBcommLab

Figure 14.4   Effective Outline for a 30-Minute Presentation
This outline clearly identifies the purpose and the distinct points to be made in the introduction, body, and close. Notice also how the speaker has written her major transitions in full-sentence form to be sure she can clearly phrase these critical passages when it's time to speak.

Apply Figure 14.4's key concepts by revising a new document. Go to Chapter 14 in www.pearsoninternationaleditions.com/mybcommlab and select Document Makeovers.

- Add delivery cues, such as places where you plan to pause for emphasis or use visuals.
- Arrange your notes on numbered cards or use the notes capability in your presentation software.

Developing a Presentation

2   **LEARNING OBJECTIVE**

Describe the tasks involved in developing a presentation after completing the planning step.

Although you usually don't write out a presentation word for word, you still engage in the writing process—developing your ideas, structuring support points, phrasing your transitions, and so on. Depending on the situation and your personal style, the eventual presentation might follow your initial words closely, or you might express your thoughts in fresh, spontaneous language.

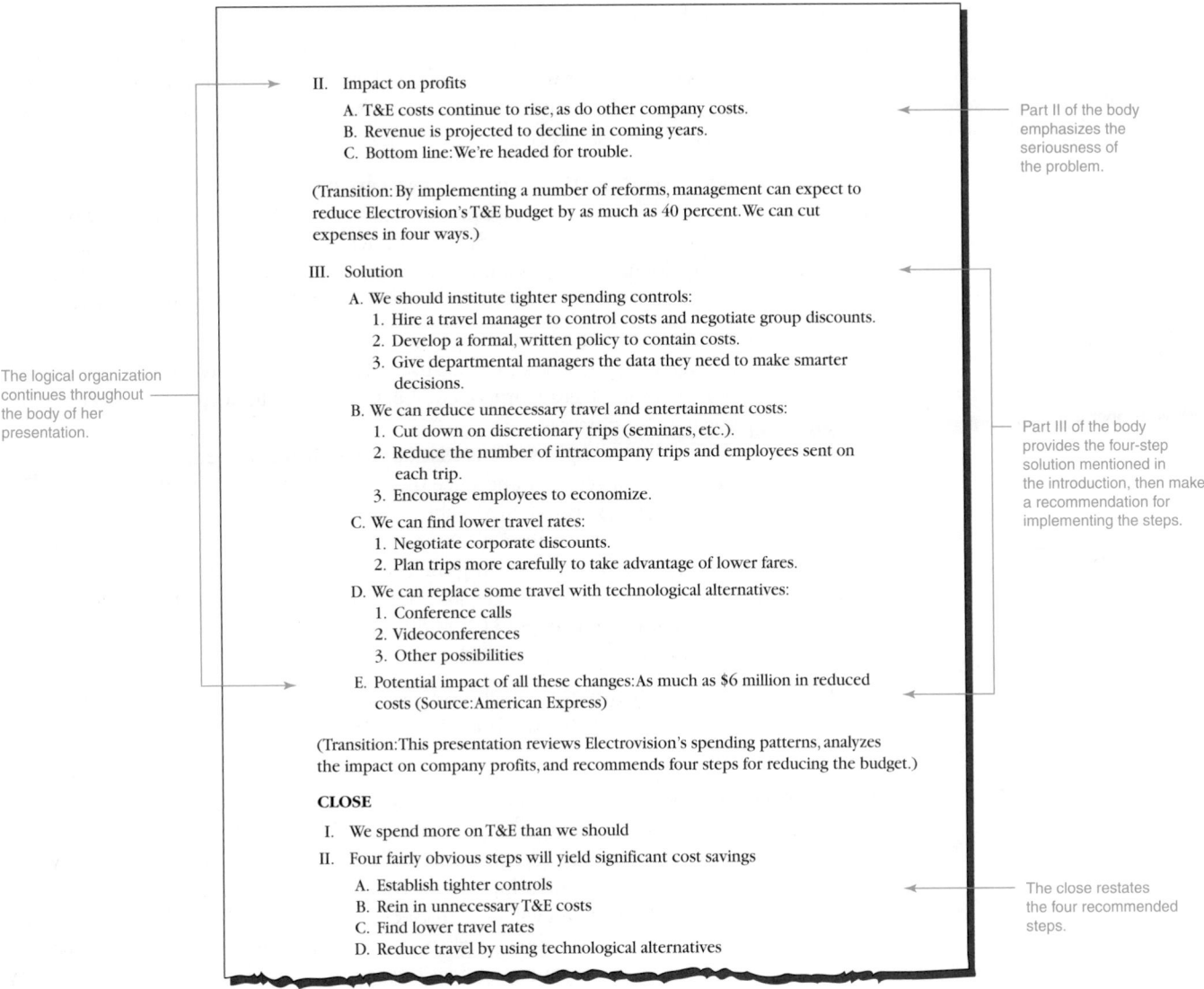

The logical organization continues throughout the body of her presentation.

II. Impact on profits

   A. T&E costs continue to rise, as do other company costs.
   B. Revenue is projected to decline in coming years.
   C. Bottom line: We're headed for trouble.

(Transition: By implementing a number of reforms, management can expect to reduce Electrovision's T&E budget by as much as 40 percent. We can cut expenses in four ways.)

III. Solution

   A. We should institute tighter spending controls:
      1. Hire a travel manager to control costs and negotiate group discounts.
      2. Develop a formal, written policy to contain costs.
      3. Give departmental managers the data they need to make smarter decisions.
   B. We can reduce unnecessary travel and entertainment costs:
      1. Cut down on discretionary trips (seminars, etc.).
      2. Reduce the number of intracompany trips and employees sent on each trip.
      3. Encourage employees to economize.
   C. We can find lower travel rates:
      1. Negotiate corporate discounts.
      2. Plan trips more carefully to take advantage of lower fares.
   D. We can replace some travel with technological alternatives:
      1. Conference calls
      2. Videoconferences
      3. Other possibilities
   E. Potential impact of all these changes: As much as $6 million in reduced costs (Source: American Express)

(Transition: This presentation reviews Electrovision's spending patterns, analyzes the impact on company profits, and recommends four steps for reducing the budget.)

CLOSE

I. We spend more on T&E than we should

II. Four fairly obvious steps will yield significant cost savings

   A. Establish tighter controls
   B. Rein in unnecessary T&E costs
   C. Find lower travel rates
   D. Reduce travel by using technological alternatives

Annotations:
- Part II of the body emphasizes the seriousness of the problem.
- Part III of the body provides the four-step solution mentioned in the introduction, then makes a recommendation for implementing the steps.
- The close restates the four recommended steps.

Figure 14.4   Effective Outline for a 30-Minute Presentation *(continued)*

ADAPTING TO YOUR AUDIENCE

Your audience's size, the venue (in person or online), your subject, your purpose, your budget, and the time available for preparation all influence the style of your presentation. If you're speaking to a small group, particularly people you already know, you can use a casual style that encourages audience participation. Use simple visuals and invite your audience to interject comments. Deliver your remarks in a conversational tone, using notes to jog your memory if necessary.

Adapting to your audience involves a number of issues, from speaking style to technology choices.

If you're addressing a large audience or if the event is important, establish a more formal atmosphere. During formal presentations, speakers are often on a stage or platform, standing behind a lectern and using a microphone so that their remarks can be heard throughout the room or captured for broadcasting or webcasting.

COMPOSING YOUR PRESENTATION

Like written documents, oral presentations are composed of distinct elements: the introduction, the body, and the close.

Presentation Introduction

An effective introduction arouses interest in your topic, establishes your credibility, and prepares the audience for the body of your presentation.

A good introduction arouses the audience's interest in your topic, establishes your credibility, and prepares listeners for what will follow. That's a lot to accomplish in the first few minutes, so give yourself plenty of time to develop the words and visuals you'll use to get your presentation off to a great start.

Getting Your Audience's Attention Some subjects are naturally more interesting to some audiences than others. If you will be discussing a matter of profound significance that will personally affect the members of your audience, chances are they'll listen, regardless of how you begin. All you really have to do is announce your topic, and you'll have their attention. Other subjects call for more imagination. Here are six ways to arouse audience interest:[10]

Spend some time thinking about the best way to capture the audience's attention and interest with your opening remarks.

- Unite the audience around a common goal.
- Tell a compelling story that illustrates an important and relevant point. If your entire presentation is structured as a story, of course, you'll want to keep the interest high by not giving away the ending yet.
- Pass around a product sample or otherwise appeal to listeners' senses.
- Ask a question that will get your audience thinking about your message.
- Share an intriguing, unexpected, or shocking detail.
- Open with an amusing observation about yourself, the subject matter of the presentation, or the circumstances surrounding the presentation—but make sure any humorous remarks are relevant, appropriate, and not offensive to anyone in the audience. In general, avoid humor when you and the audience don't share the same native language or culture; it's too easy for humor to fall flat or backfire.

Regardless of which technique you choose, make sure you can give audience members a reason to care and to believe that the time they're about to spend listening to you will be worth their while.[11]

Building Your Credibility Audiences tend to decide within a few minutes whether you're worth listening to, so establishing your credibility quickly is vital.[12] If you're not a well-known expert or haven't already earned your audience's trust in other situations, you'll need to build credibility in your introduction. If someone else will introduce you, he or she can present your credentials. If you will be introducing yourself, keep your comments brief, but don't be afraid to mention your accomplishments. Your listeners will be curious about your qualifications, so tell them briefly who you are, why you're there, and how they'll benefit from listening to you. You might say something like this:

I'm Karen Whitney, a market research analyst with Information Resources Corporation. For the past five years, I've specialized in studying high-technology markets. Your director of engineering, John LaBarre, asked me to talk about recent trends in computer-aided design so that you'll have a better idea of how to direct your research efforts.

This speaker establishes credibility by tying her credentials to the purpose of her presentation. By mentioning her company's name, her specialization and position, and the name of the audience's boss, she lets her listeners know immediately that she is qualified to tell them something they need to know.

If you will be introduced by a master of ceremonies or another speaker, that person may be able to briefly itemize your qualifications as a way to build your credibility with the audience.
Source: © Exactostock/SuperStock.

Previewing Your Message In addition to arousing audience interest and establishing your credibility, a good introduction gives your audience members a preview of what's ahead, helping them understand the structure and content of your message. A report reader can learn these things by looking at the table of contents and scanning the headings, but in a presentation, you need to provide that framework with a preview.

Your preview should summarize the main idea of your presentation, identify major supporting points, and indicate the order in which you'll develop those points. Tell your listeners in so many words, "This is the subject, and these are the points I will cover." Once you've established the framework, you can be confident that the audience will understand how the individual facts and figures are related to your main idea as you move into the body of your presentation. If you are using an indirect approach, your preview can discuss the nature of your main idea without disclosing it.

Offer a preview to help your audience understand the importance, the structure, and the content of your message.

Presentation Body

The bulk of your presentation is devoted to a discussion of the main points in your outline. No matter what organizational pattern you're using, your goals are to make sure that the organization of your presentation is clear and your that presentation holds the audience's attention.

Connecting Your Ideas   In written documents, you can show how ideas are related with a variety of design clues: headings, paragraph indentions, white space, and lists. However, with oral communication—particularly when you aren't using visuals for support—you have to rely primarily on spoken words to link various parts and ideas.

For the links between sentences and paragraphs, use one or two transitional words: *therefore, because, in addition, in contrast, moreover, for example, consequently, nevertheless,* or *finally*. To link major sections of a presentation, use complete sentences or paragraphs, such as "Now that we've reviewed the problem, let's take a look at some solutions." Every time you shift topics, be sure to stress the connection between ideas by summarizing what's been said and previewing what's to come. The longer your presentation, the more important your transitions. Your listeners need clear transitions to guide them to the most important points. Furthermore, they'll appreciate brief interim summaries to pick up any ideas they may have missed.

Use transitions generously to help the audience follow and process your messages, particularly in longer presentations.

Holding Your Audience's Attention   A successful introduction will have grabbed your audience's attention; now the body of your presentation needs to hold that attention. Here are a few helpful tips for keeping the audience tuned into your message:

- Keep relating your subject to your audience's needs.
- Anticipate—and answer—your audience's questions as you move along so people don't get confused or distracted.
- Use clear, vivid language and throw in some variety; repeating the same words and phrases over and over puts people to sleep.
- Show how your subject is related to ideas that audience members already understand, and give people a way to categorize and remember your points.[13]
- If appropriate, encourage participation by asking for comments or questions.
- Illustrate your ideas with visuals, which enliven your message, help you connect with audience members, and help them remember your message more effectively (see "Enhancing Your Presentation with Effective Slides," pages 502–509).

The most important way to hold an audience's attention is to show how your message relates to their individual needs and concerns.

Presentation Close

The close of a speech or presentation has two critical jobs to accomplish: making sure your listeners leave with the key points from your talk clear in their minds and in the appropriate emotional state. For example, if the purpose of your presentation was to warn company managers that their out-of-control spending threatens the company's survival, you want them to leave with that message ringing in their ears—and with enough concern for the problem to stimulate changes in their behavior.

Plan your close carefully so that your audience leaves with a clear summary of your main idea and in an emotional state that is appropriate to your purpose.

Restating Your Main Points   Use the close to succinctly restate your main points, emphasizing what you want your listeners to do or to think. For example, to close a presentation on your company's executive compensation program, you could repeat your specific recommendations and then conclude with a memorable statement to motivate your audience to take action:

When you repeat your main idea in the close, emphasize what you want your audience to do or to think.

REAL-TIME UPDATES
Learn More by Listening to This Podcast

Keep audiences tuned in with engaging presentations

Explore the value of effective business presentations and what separates ho-hum presentations from those that really engage audiences. Go to http://real-timeupdates.com/ebc10 and click on Learn More. If you are using MyBcommLab, you can access Real-Time Updates within each chapter or under Student Study Tools.

We can all be proud of the way our company has grown. However, if we want to continue that growth, we need to take four steps to ensure that our best people don't start looking for opportunities elsewhere:

- First, increase the overall level of compensation
- Second, establish a cash bonus program
- Third, offer a variety of stock-based incentives
- Fourth, improve our health insurance and pension benefits

By taking these steps, we can ensure that our company retains the management talent it needs to face our industry's largest competitors.

Repetition of key ideas, as long as you don't overdo it, greatly improves the chance that your audience will hear your message in the way you intended.

Ending with Clarity and Confidence   If you've been successful with the introduction and body of your presentation, your listeners now have the information they need, and they're in the right frame of mind to put that information to good use. Now you're ready to end on a strong note that confirms expectations about any actions or decisions that will follow the presentation—and to bolster the audience's confidence in you and your message one final time.

Plan your final statement carefully so you can end on a strong, positive note.

Some presentations require the audience to reach a decision or agree to take specific action, in which case the close provides a clear wrap-up. If the audience agrees on an issue covered in the presentation, briefly review the consensus. If they don't agree, make the lack of consensus clear by saying something like, "We seem to have some fundamental disagreement on this question." Then be ready to suggest a method of resolving the differences.

If you expect any action to occur as a result of your speech, be sure to explain who is responsible for doing what. List the action items and, if possible within the time available, establish due dates and assign responsibility for each task.

Make sure your final remarks are memorable and have the right emotional tone.

Make sure your final remarks are memorable and expressed in a tone that is appropriate to the situation. For example, if your presentation is a persuasive request for project funding, you might emphasize the importance of this project and your team's ability to complete it on schedule and within budget. Expressing confident optimism will send the message that you believe in your ability to perform. Conversely, if your purpose was to alert the audience to a problem or risk, false optimism will undermine your message.

Whatever final message is appropriate, think through your closing remarks carefully before stepping in front of the audience. You don't want to wind up on stage with nothing to say but "Well, I guess that's it."

Enhancing Your Presentation with Effective Slides

3 **LEARNING OBJECTIVE**

Describe the six major design and writing tasks required to enhance your presentation with effective visuals.

Thoughtfully designed visuals create interest, illustrate complex points, and help the audience absorb information.

Slides and other visuals can improve the quality and impact of your presentations by creating interest, explaining points that are difficult to explain in words alone, adding variety, and increasing the audience's ability to absorb and remember information.

You can select from an assortment of visuals to enhance oral presentations. Don't overlook "old-school" technologies such as overhead transparencies, chalkboards, whiteboards, and flipcharts—they can all have value in the right circumstances. However, the medium of choice for most business presentations is an electronic slide presentation using Microsoft PowerPoint, Apple Keynote, Google Docs, or similar software. Electronic presentations are easy to edit and update; you can add sound, photos, video, and animation; they can be incorporated into online meetings, webcasts, and *webinars* (a common term for web-based seminars); and you can record self-running presentations for trade shows, websites, and other uses.

Electronic presentations are practically universal in business today, but their wide-spread use is not always welcome. You may have already heard the expression "death by PowerPoint," which refers to the agonizing experience of sitting through too many poorly conceived and poorly delivered slide shows. In the words of presentation expert and author Garr Reynolds, "most presentations remain mind-numbingly dull, something to be endured by presenter and audience alike."[14]

That's the bad news. The good news is that presentations can be an effective communication medium and an experience that is satisfying, and sometimes even enjoyable, for presenter and audience alike. Follow Reynolds's advice and start with the mindset of *simplicity* (clear ideas presented clearly) and *authenticity* (talking *with* your audience about things they care about, rather that talking at them or trying to be a "performer"), and you'll be well on your way to becoming an effective presenter.

> Focus on making your presentations simple and authentic.

CHOOSING STRUCTURED OR FREE-FORM SLIDES

Perhaps the most important design choice you face when creating slides is whether to use conventional **structured slides** or the looser, **free-form slides** that many presentation specialists now advocate. Compare the two rows of slides in Figure 14.5 on the next page. The structured slides in the top row follow the same basic format throughout the presentation; in fact, they're based directly on the templates built into PowerPoint. The free-form slides in the bottom row don't follow a rigid structure.

REAL-TIME UPDATES
Learn More by Watching This Video

Get a quick video tour of Garr Reynolds's *Presentation Zen*

Fellow designer Matt Helmke offers a succinct overview of Reynolds's groundbreaking book on presentation design. Go to http://real-timeupdates.com/ebc10 and click on Learn More. If you are using MyBcommLab, you can access Real-Time Updates within each chapter or under Student Study Tools.

However, choosing a free-form design strategy does not mean you can just randomly change the design from one slide to the next. Effectively designed slides should still be unified by design elements such as color and typeface selections, as Figures 14.5c and 14.5d show. Also, note how Figure 14.5d combines visual and textual messages to convey the point about listening without criticizing. This complementary approach of pictures and words is a highlight of free-form design.

> Structured slides are usually based on templates that give all the slides in a presentation the same general look (which usually involves a lot of bullet points); free-form slides are much less rigid and emphasize visual appeal.

Structured Slides

Both design strategies have advantages and disadvantages, and one or the other can be a better choice for specific situations. Structured slides have the advantage of being fast and easy to create: You simply choose an overall design theme, select a template, and start typing. Given the speed and ease of creating them, structured slides can be a more practical choice for routine presentations such as project status updates, where your slides are likely to be used only one time.

> Structured slides are often the best choice for project updates and other routine information presentations, particularly if the slides are intended to be used only once.

Of course, making things easier on the presenter won't necessarily make them easy for the audience, but if you're in a schedule crunch, going the structured route might save the day because at least you'll have *something* ready to show.

Also, because more information can usually be packed on each slide, structured slides can be more effective at conveying complex ideas or sets of interrelated data to the right audiences. For example, if you are talking to a group of executives who must decide where to make budget cuts across the company's eight divisions, at some point in the presentation they probably will want to see summary data for all eight divisions on a single slide for easy comparison. Such a slide would be overcrowded by the usual definition, but this might be the only practical way to get a "big picture" view of the situation. (The best solution is probably some high-level, summary slides supported by a detailed handout, as "Creating Effective Handouts" on page 510 explains.)

The primary disadvantage of structured design is that mind-numbing effect Garr Reynolds describes, caused by text-heavy slides that all look alike. Slide after slide of dense, highly structured bullet points with no visual relief can put an audience to sleep.

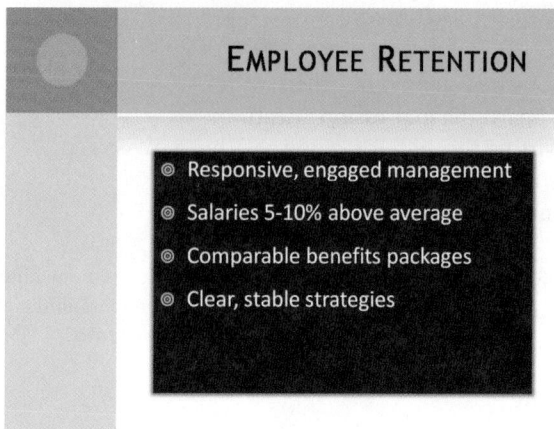

Figure 14.5a

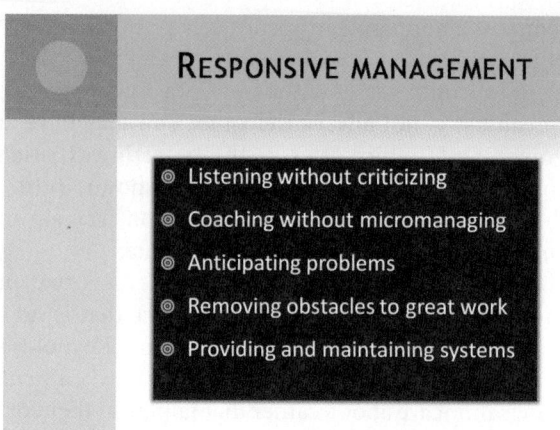

Figure 14.5b

Figure 14.5c

Figure 14.5d

Figure 14.5 **Structured Versus Free-Form Slide Design**
Compare the rigid, predictable design of the two slides in the top row with the more dynamic free-form designs in the bottom row. Although the two free-form slides don't follow the same design structure, they are visually linked by color and font choices. (Note that Figure 14.5d is a humorous way of conveying the first bullet point in Figure 14.5b.)

Free-Form Slides

Free-form slide designs can overcome the drawbacks of text-heavy structured design and fulfill three criteria that researchers have identified as important for successful presentations: (1) providing complementary information through both textual and visual means, (2) limiting the amount of information delivered at any one time to prevent cognitive overload, and (3) helping viewers process information by identifying priorities and connections.[15] (Of course, well-designed structured slides can also meet these criteria, but the constraints of prebuilt templates make doing so more of a challenge.)

With appropriate imagery, free-form designs can also create a more dynamic and engaging experience for the audience. Given their ability to excite and engage, free-form designs are particularly good for motivational, educational, and persuasive presentations—particularly when the slides will be used multiple times and therefore compensate for the extra time and effort often required to create them.

Free-form slides do have several potential disadvantages, however. First, effectively designing slides with both visual and textual elements is more creatively demanding and more time-consuming than simply typing text into preformatted templates. The emphasis on visual content also requires more images, which take time to find.

Second, because far less textual information tends to be displayed on-screen, the speaker is responsible for conveying more of the content. Ideally, of course, this is how

Well-designed free-form slides help viewers understand, process, and remember the speaker's message.

Free-form slides can require more skill and time to create, and they put more demands on the speaker during the presentation.

a presentation *should* work, but presenters sometimes find themselves in less than ideal circumstances, such as being asked to fill in for a colleague on short notice.

Third, if not handled carefully, the division of information into smaller chunks can make it difficult to present complex subjects in a cohesive, integrated manner. For instance, if you're discussing a business problem that has five interrelated causes, it might be helpful to insert a conventional bullet-point slide as a summary and reminder after discussing each problem on its own.

REAL-TIME UPDATES
Learn More by Watching This Video

Way beyond bullet points: A stunning example of free-form slide design

See how a creative mind can transform electronic slides into something far more compelling than conventional bullet points. Go to http://real-timeupdates.com/ebc10 and click on Learn More. If you are using MyBcommLab, you can access Real-Time Updates within each chapter or under Student Study Tools.

DESIGNING EFFECTIVE SLIDES

Despite complaints about "death by PowerPoint," the problem is not with the software itself (or with Apple Keynote or any other presentation program). It is just a tool and, like other tools, can be used well or used poorly. Unfortunately, lack of design awareness, inadequate training, schedule pressures, and the instinctive response of doing things the way they've always been done can lead to ineffective slides and lost opportunities to really connect with audiences.

> Use presentation software wisely to avoid the "death by PowerPoint" stigma that presentations have in the mind of many professionals.

Another reason for ineffective slides, and one that appears to be increasingly common, is the practice of treating slide sets as standalone documents that can be read on their own, without a presenter. (The emergence of websites such as SlideShare, discussed in "Business Communication 2.0: Presentations Get Social" on page 509, might be contributing to the phenomenon, too, by making it so easy to share slide sets.) These "slideument" hybrids that try to function as both presentation visuals and printed documents don't work well as either: They have too much information to be effective visuals and too little to be effective reports (in addition to being clumsy to read).

> "Slideuments" are hybrids that try to function as both presentation slides and readable documents—and usually fail at both tasks.

As "Creating Effective Handouts" on page 510 explains, the ideal solution is to create an effective slide set and a separate handout document that provides additional details and supporting information. This way, you can optimize each piece to do the job it is really meant to do. An alternative is to use the notes field in your presentation software to include your speaking notes for each slide. Anyone who gets a copy of your slides can at least follow along by reading your notes, although you will probably need to edit and embellish them to make them understandable by others.

> Rather than packing your slides with enough information to make them readable as standalone documents, complement well-designed slides with printed handouts.

Designing Slides Around a Key Visual

With both structured and free-form design strategies, it is often helpful to structure specific slides around a key visual that helps organize and explain the points you are trying to make. For example, a pyramid suggests a hierarchical relationship, and a circular flow diagram emphasizes that the final stage in a process loops back to the beginning of the process. Figure 14.6 on the next page shows six of the many types of visual designs you can use to organize information on a slide.

> Organizing a slide around a key visual can help the audience quickly grasp how ideas are related.

Writing Readable Content

One of the most common mistakes beginners make—and one of the chief criticisms leveled at structured slide designs in general—is stuffing slides with too much text. Doing so overloads the audience with too much information too fast, takes attention away from the speaker by forcing people to read more, and requires the presenter to use smaller type.

> Use slide text sparingly and only to emphasize key points, not to convey your entire message.

Effective text slides supplement your words and help the audience follow the flow of ideas (see Figure 14.7 on page 507). Use text to highlight key points, summarize and preview your message, signal major shifts in thought, illustrate concepts, or help create interest in your spoken message.

Creating Charts and Tables for Slides

Charts and tables for presentations need to be simpler than visuals for printed documents. Detailed images that look fine on the printed page can be too dense and too complicated for

> Charts and tables for presentations need to be simpler than visuals for printed documents.

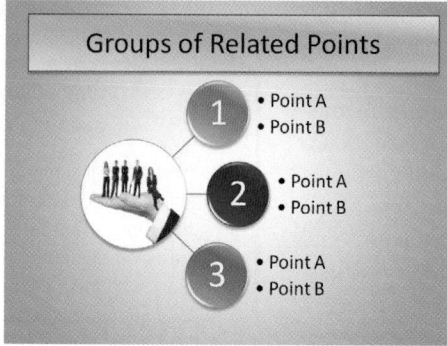

Figure 14.6a

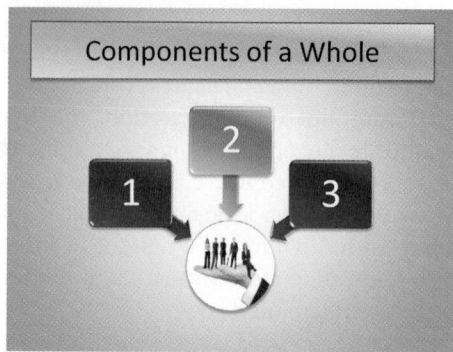

Figure 14.6b

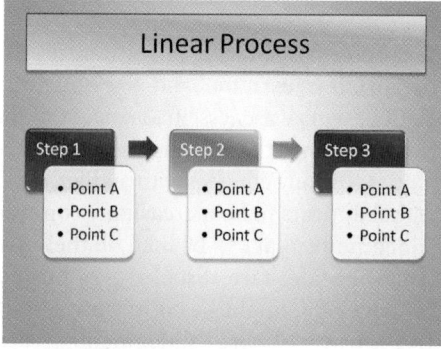

Figure 14.6c

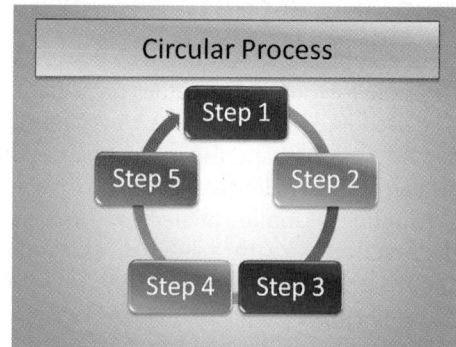

Figure 14.6d

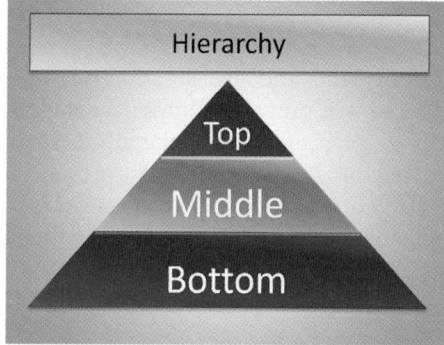

Figure 14.6e

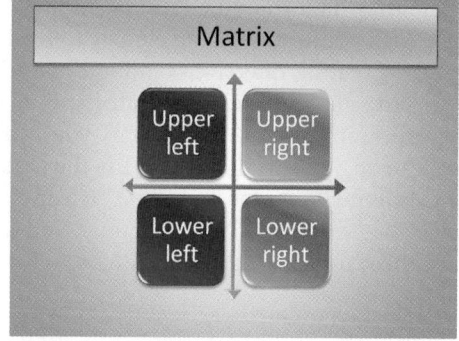

Figure 14.6f

Figure 14.6 **Using a Key Visual to Organize Points on a Slide**
Simple graphical elements such as these "SmartArt" images in Microsoft PowerPoint make it easy to organize slide content using a key visual. Whether you're trying to convey the relationship of ideas in a hierarchy, a linear process, a circular process, or just about any other configuration, a key visual can work in tandem with your written and spoken messages to help audiences get your message.

presentations. Remember that your audience will view your slides from across the room—not from a foot or two away, as you do while you create them. Keep the level of detail to a minimum, eliminating anything that is not absolutely essential. If necessary, break information into more than one chart or table. If necessary, provide detailed versions of charts and tables in a handout.

Selecting Design Elements

Color is more than just decoration; colors have meanings themselves, based on both cultural experience and the relationships that you established between the colors in your designs.

As you create slides, pay close attention to the interaction of color, background and foreground designs, artwork, typefaces, and type styles.

- **Color.** Color is a critical design element that can grab attention, emphasize important ideas, create contrast, influence acceptance of your ideas, improve retention, and stimulate a variety of emotions (see Table 14.2 on page 508).[16] Color is powerful, so use it carefully.

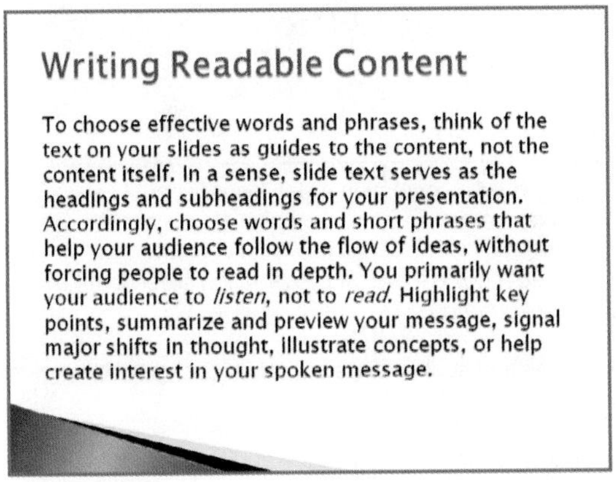

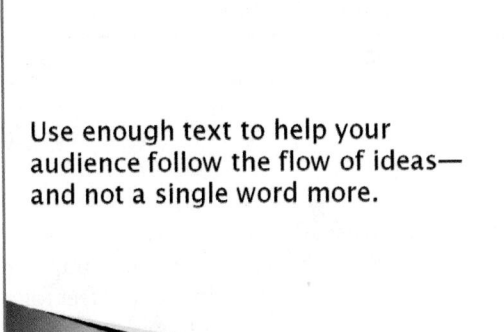

Figure 14.7a

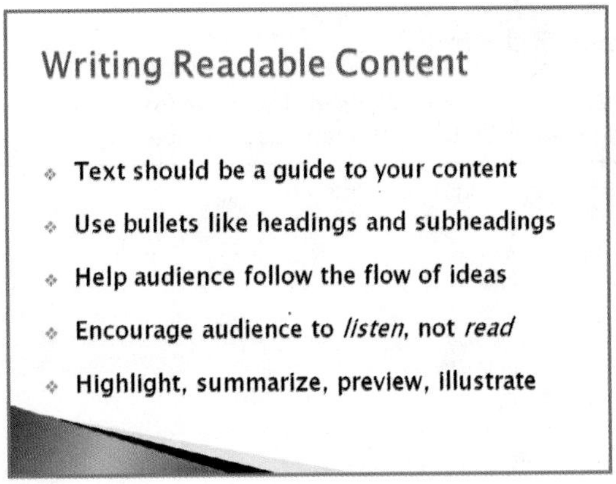

Figure 14.7b

Figure 14.7c

Figure 14.7d

Figure 14.7 Writing Text for Slides

Effective text slides are clear, simple guides that help the audience understand and remember the speaker's message. Notice the progression toward simplicity in these slides: Figure 14.7a is a paragraph that would distract the audience for an extended period of time. Figure 14.7b offers concise, readable bullets, although too many slides in a row in this structured design would become tedious. Figure 14.7c distills the message down to a single thought that is complete on its own but doesn't convey all the information from the original and would need embellishment from the speaker. Figure 14.7d pushes this to the extreme, with only the core piece of the message to serve as an "exclamation point" for the spoken message. Figure 14.7c, and especially Figure 14.7d, could be made even more powerful with a well-chosen visual that illustrates the idea of following the flow.

- **Background designs and artwork.** All visuals have two layers of design: the *background* and the *foreground*. The background is the equivalent of paper in a printed document, and the elements in the foreground are the essential content of your slides. Make sure the background stays in the background and doesn't distract viewers or compete with the foreground. (Note that many of the template designs in presentation software have backgrounds that are too distracting for serious business use.)

  Make sure the background of your slides stays in the background; it should never get in the way of the informational elements in the foreground.

- **Foreground designs and artwork.** The foreground contains the unique text and graphic elements that make up each individual slide. Foreground elements can be either functional or decorative. *Functional artwork* includes photos, technical drawings, charts, and other visual elements containing information that's part of your message. In contrast, *decorative artwork* simply enhances the look of your slides and should be using sparingly, if at all.

- **Typefaces and type styles.** Type is harder to read on-screen than on the printed page, so you need to choose fonts and type styles with care. Sans serif fonts are usually easier to read than serif fonts. Use both uppercase and lowercase letters, with generous space between lines of text, and limit the number of fonts to one or two per slide. Choose font

  Many of the typefaces available on your computer are difficult to read on screen, so they aren't good choices for presentation slides.

TABLE 14.2	Color and Emotion	
Color	Selected Emotional Associations in U.S. Business Culture (Can Vary in Other Cultures, Sometimes Significantly)	Best Uses
Blue	Peaceful, soothing, tranquil, cool, trusting	Background for presentation slides (usually dark blue); safe and conservative
White	Neutral, innocent, pure, wise	Font color of choice for most presentation slides that have a dark background
Yellow	Warm, bright, cheerful, enthusiastic	Text bullets and subheadings on a dark background
Red	Passionate, dangerous, active, painful	To promote action or stimulate the audience; seldom used as a background. ("In the red" specifically refers to financial losses.)
Green	Assertive, prosperous, envious, relaxed	Highlight and accent color. (Green symbolizes money in the United States but not in other countries.)

Source: Adapted from Claudyne Wilder and David Fine, *Point, Click & Wow* (San Francisco: Jossey-Bass Pfeiffer, 1996), 63, 527.

sizes that are easy to read from anywhere in the room, usually between 28 and 36 points, and test them in the room if possible. A clever way to test readability at your computer is to stand back as many feet from the screen as your screen size in inches (17 feet for a 17-inch screen, for example). If the slides are readable at this distance, you're probably in good shape.[17]

Maintaining design consistency is critical because audiences start to assign meaning to visual elements beginning with the first slide. For instance, if yellow is used to call attention to the first major point in your presentation, viewers will expect the next occurrence of yellow to also signal an important point. The *slide master* feature makes consistency easy to achieve because it applies consistent design choices to every slide in a presentation.

Design inconsistencies confuse and annoy audiences; don't change colors and other design elements randomly throughout your presentation.

Adding Animation and Multimedia

Today's presentation software offers many options for livening up your slides, including sound, animation, video clips, transition effects, and hyperlinks. Think about the impact that all these effects will have on your audience, and use only those special effects that support your message.[18]

You can animate just about everything in an electronic presentation, but resist the temptation to do so; make sure an animation has a purpose.

Functional animation involves motion that is directly related to your message, such as a highlight arrow that moves around the screen to emphasize specific points in a technical diagram. Such animation is also a great way to demonstrate sequences and procedures. In contrast, *decorative animation*, such as having a block of text cartwheel in from offscreen, needs to be used with great care. These effects don't add any functional value, and they easily distract audiences.

If you use transitions between slides, make sure they are subtle; they should do nothing more than ease the eye from one slide to the next.

Slide transitions control how one slide replaces another, such as having the current slide gently fade out before the next slide fades in. Subtle transitions like this can ease your viewers' gaze from one slide to the next, but many of the transition effects now available are little more than distractions and are best avoided. **Slide builds** control the release of text, graphics, and other elements on individual slides. With builds, you can make key points appear one at a time rather than having all of them appear on a slide at once, thereby making it easier for you and the audience to focus on each new message point.

Hyperlinks let you build flexibility into your presentations.

A *hyperlink* instructs your computer to jump to another slide in your presentation, to a website, or to another program entirely. Using hyperlinks is also a great way to build flexibility into your presentations so that you can instantly change the flow of your presentation in response to audience feedback.

BUSINESS COMMUNICATION 2.0

Presentations Get Social

When you're looking for creative inspiration, collaboration, or feedback, don't limit yourself to the people in your office. With a presentation sharing website such as SlideShare (www.slideshare.net), you can learn from and collaborate with the entire world. Sometimes described as "YouTube for Power-Point," SlideShare offers free storage and controlled access for presentation slides; it now hosts thousands of presentations, with more added every day.

If you'd like to find presentations on just about any topic imaginable, you can search for slides by keyword, browse by category, select popular topics from a tag cloud, or sort by popularity. For inspiration and design ideas, simply browse until something catches your eye. You can view any publicly available presentation in the viewer window right on the Slide-Share website or download presentations to your computer (if the person who contributed a presentation allows it to be downloaded).

If you want to share your slides, you can upload presentations as a guest or create a profile much as you can on a social networking site. With your profile established, you can continue to add new presentations to your *slidespace* and expand your online community by adding new contacts. As with Flickr and some other content-sharing sites, SlideShare lets you set various levels of access permission, from "your eyes only" to selected contacts to the entire world. This controlled-sharing aspect is a great way to share slides with conference attendees, business partners, and team members. You can also embed your presentations in your blog so all your blog visitors can see them, or embed them on an intranet so that only your coworkers can see them.

In the spirit of community, SlideShare offers tools to alert your followers on Twitter and your contacts on LinkedIn and other social networking sites. With SlideShare, your friends, fans, and customers can see your inspiring content as soon as you publish it.

CAREER APPLICATIONS

1. Visit SlideShare and find two presentations on the same business topic, such as public relations, financial matters, leadership, or even giving presentations. View and compare the two presentations in terms of content. Which presentation is clearer? More credible? More convincing? What specific steps did this presenter take to ensure clarity and confidence?
2. Now compare those two presentations in terms of their visual design. Do their designs help or hinder the communication effort? If you see any weaknesses, what improvements would you suggest?

Source: Adapted from SlideShare, accessed 12 February 2011, www.slideshare.net.

Source: Used with permission of SlideShare Inc.

Multimedia elements offer the ultimate in active presentations. Using audio and video clips can be a great way to complement your textual message. Just be sure to keep these elements brief and relevant, as supporting points for your presentation, not as replacements for it.

Completing a Presentation

The completion step for presentations involves a wider range of tasks than most printed documents require. Make sure you allow enough time to test your presentation slides, verify equipment operation, practice your speech, and create handout materials. With a first draft of your presentation in hand, revise your slides to make sure they are readable, concise, consistent, and fully operational (including transitions, builds, animation, and multimedia). Complete your production efforts by finalizing your slides, creating handouts, choosing your presentation method, and practicing your delivery.

4 LEARNING OBJECTIVE

Outline four major tasks involved in completing a presentation.

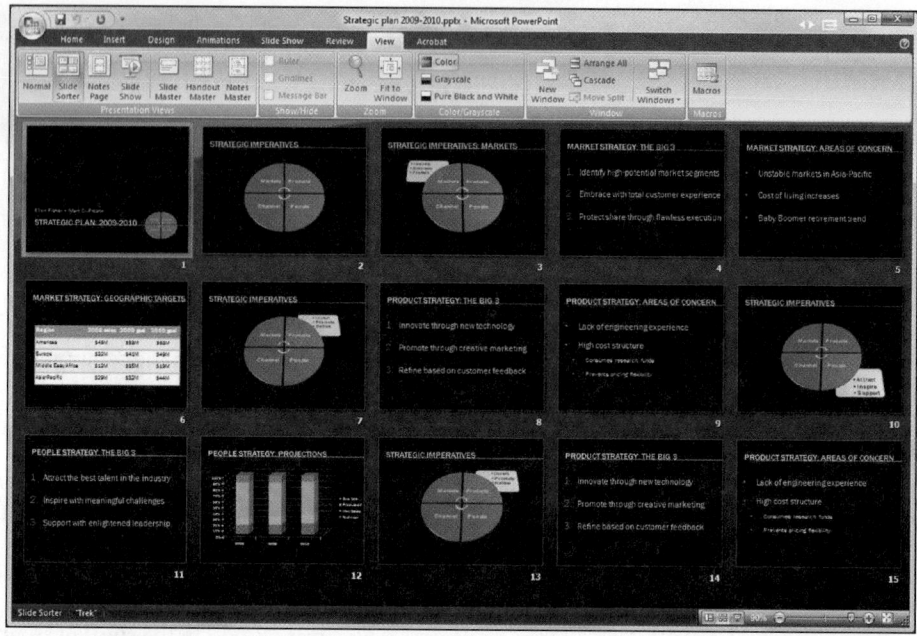

Figure 14.8 Slide Sorter View
Examining *thumbnails* of slides on one screen is the best way to check the overall design of your final product. The slide sorter also makes it easy to ponder the order and organization of your presentation; you can change the position of any slide simply by clicking and dragging it to a new position.

FINALIZING YOUR SLIDES

Electronic presentation software can help you throughout the editing and revision process. As Figure 14.8 shows, the *slide sorter* view (different programs have different names for this feature) lets you see some or all of the slides in your presentation on a single screen. Use this view to add and delete slides, reposition slides, check slides for design consistency, and verify the operation of any effects. Moreover, the slide sorter is a great way to review the flow of your story.[19]

In addition to using content slides, you can help your audience follow the flow of your presentation by creating slides for your title, agenda and program details, and navigation:

- **Title slide(s).** You can make a good first impression with one or two title slides, the equivalent of a report's cover and title page (see Figures 14.9a and 14.9b).
- **Agenda and program details.** These slides communicate the agenda for your presentation and any additional information the audience might need (see Figures 14.9c and 14.9d).
- **Navigation slides.** To tell your audience where you're going and where you've been, you can use a series of **navigation slides** based on your outline or agenda. As you complete each section, repeat the agenda slide but indicate which material has been covered and which section you are about to begin (see Figure 14.10). This sort of slide is sometimes referred to as a *moving blueprint*. As an alternative to the repeating agenda slide, you can insert a simple *bumper* slide at each major section break, announcing the title of the section you're about to begin.[20]

Navigation slides help your audience keep track of what you've covered already and what you plan to cover next.

CREATING EFFECTIVE HANDOUTS

Use handout materials to support the points made in your presentation and to offer the audience additional information on your topic.

Handouts, any printed materials you give the audience to supplement your talk, should be considered an integral part of your presentation strategy. Handouts can include detailed charts and tables, case studies, research results, magazine articles, and anything else that supports the main idea of your presentation.

Figure 14.9a

Figure 14.9b

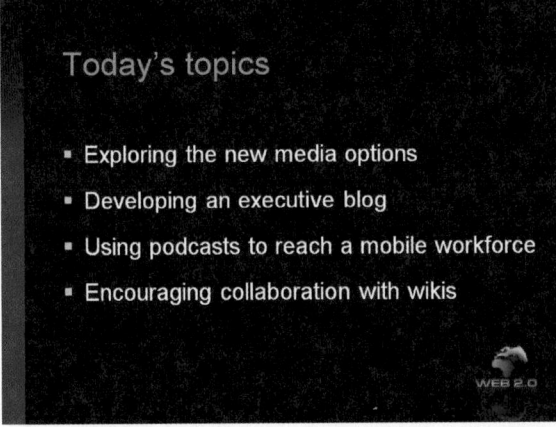

Figure 14.9c

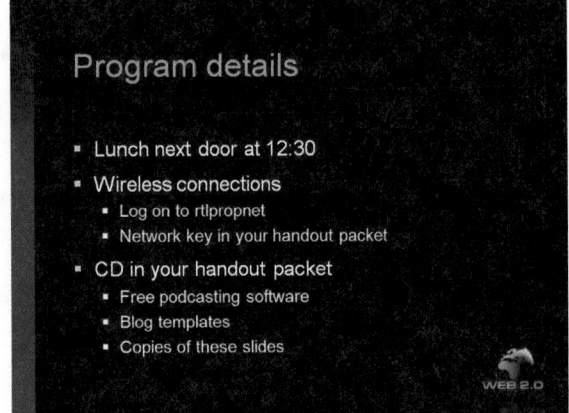

Figure 14.9d

Figure 14.9   Navigation and Support Slides
You can use a variety of navigation and support slides to introduce yourself and your presentation, to let the
audience know what your presentation will cover, and to provide essential details.

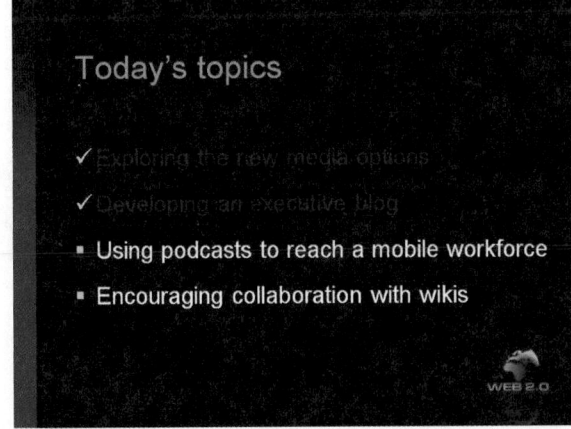

Figure 14.10a

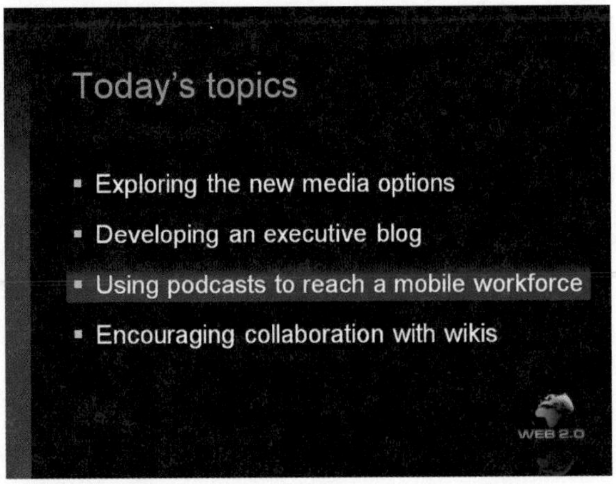

Figure 14.10b

Figure 14.10   Moving Blueprint Slides
Here are two of the ways you can use a *blueprint slide* as a navigational aid to help your audience stay on
track with the presentation. Figure 14.10a visually "mutes" and checks off the sections of the presentation that
have already been covered. In contrast, Figure 14.10b uses a sliding highlight box to indicate the next section
to be covered.

✓ Checklist   Enhancing Presentations with Visuals

A. Plan your presentation visuals.
- Make sure you and your message, not your visuals, remain the focus of your presentation.
- Follow effective design principles, with an emphasis on simplicity and authenticity.

B. Choose structured or free-form slides.
- Structured slides using bullet-point templates are easy to create, require little design time or skill, and can be completed in a hurry. Best uses: routine, internal presentations
- Free-form slides make it easier to combine textual and visual information, to create a more dynamic and engaging experience, and to maintain a conversational connection with the audience. Best uses: motivational, educational, and persuasive presentations

C. Design effective slides.
- Avoid the temptation to create "slideuments," slides that are so packed with information that they can be read as standalone documents.
- Use a key visual to organize related ideas in a clear and meaningful way.
- Write text content that will be readable from everywhere in the room.
- Write short, active, parallel phrases that support, not replace, your spoken message.
- Limit the amount of text so that your audience can focus on listening, not reading.
- Use color to emphasize important ideas, create contrast, isolate visual elements, and convey intended nonverbal signals.
- Limit color to a few compatible choices and use them consistently.

- Make sure your slide background doesn't compete with the foreground.
- Use decorative artwork sparingly and only to support your message.
- Emphasize functional artwork—photos, technical drawings, charts, and other visual elements containing information that is part of your message.
- Choose typefaces that are easy to read on-screen; limit the number of typefaces and use them consistently.
- Use slide masters to maintain consistency throughout your presentation.
- Use functional animation when it can support your message.
- Make sure slide transitions are subtle, if used at all.
- Use builds carefully to control the release of information.
- Use hyperlinks and action buttons to add flexibility to your presentation.
- Incorporate multimedia elements that can help engage your audience and deliver your message.

D. Complete slides and support materials.
- Review every slide carefully to ensure accuracy, consistency, and clarity.
- Make sure that all slides are fully operational.
- Use the slide sorter to verify and adjust the sequence of slides, if needed.
- Have a backup plan in case your electronic presentation plan fails.
- Create navigation and support slides.
- Create handouts to complement and support your presentation message.

REAL-TIME UPDATES
Learn More by Watching This Video

Five easy tips to add a professional finish to your slides

Learn some simple techniques pros use to create and edit high-quality images for PowerPoint presentations. Go to http://real-timeupdates.com/ebc10 and click on Learn More. If you are using MyBcommLab, you can access Real-Time Updates within each chapter or under Student Study Tools.

Plan your handouts as you develop your presentation so that you use each medium as effectively as possible. Your presentation should paint the big picture, convey and connect major ideas, set the emotional tone, and rouse the audience to action (if that is relevant to your talk). Your handouts can then carry the rest of the information load, providing the supporting details that audience members can consume at their own speed, on their own time. You won't need to worry about stuffing every detail into your slides, because you have the more appropriate medium of printed documents to do that. As Garr Reynolds puts it, "Handouts can set you free."[21]

For a quick review of the key steps in creating effective visuals, see "Checklist: Enhancing Presentations with Visuals." For the latest information on presentation design, visit http://real-timeupdates.com/ebc10 and click on Chapter 14.

CHOOSING YOUR PRESENTATION METHOD

Speaking from carefully prepared notes is the easiest and most effective delivery mode and should be used for nearly all speeches and presentations.

With all your materials ready, your next step is to decide which method of speaking you want to use. Speaking from notes, with the help of an outline, note cards, or visuals, is nearly always the most effective and easiest delivery mode. This approach gives you something to refer to and still allows for plenty of eye contact, a natural speaking flow, interaction with the audience, and improvisation in response to audience feedback.

In contrast, reciting your speech from memory is usually a bad idea. Even if you can memorize the entire presentation, you will sound stiff and overly formal because you are "delivering lines," rather than talking to your audience. However, memorizing a quotation, an opening statement, or a few concluding remarks can bolster your confidence and strengthen your delivery.

Reading a speech is necessary in rare instances, such as when delivering legal information, policy statements, or other messages that must be conveyed in an exact manner. However, for all other business presentations, reading is a poor choice because it limits your interaction with the audience and lacks the fresh, dynamic feel of natural talking.

Another important decision at this point is preparing the venue where you will speak. In many instances, you won't have much of a choice, and in some situations, you won't even be able to visit the venue ahead of time. However, if you do have some control over the environment, think carefully about the seating for the audience, your position in the room, and the lighting. For instance, dimming the lights is common practice for many presenters, but dimming the lights too far can hamper the nonverbal communication between you and your audience and therefore limit opportunities for interaction.[22]

PRACTICING YOUR DELIVERY

Practicing your presentation is essential. Practice helps ensure that you appear polished and confident, reduces anxiety, gives you the chance to smooth out any rough spots, and lets you verify the operation of slides and equipment. A test audience can tell you if your slides are understandable and whether your delivery is effective. A day or two before you're ready to step on stage for an important talk, make sure you and your presentation are ready:

- Can you present your material naturally, without reading your slides?
- Could you still make a compelling and complete presentation if you experience an equipment failure and have to proceed without using your slides at all?
- Is the equipment working, and do you know how to work it?
- Is your timing on track?
- Can you easily pronounce all the words you plan to use?
- Have you anticipated likely questions and objections?

If you're addressing an audience that doesn't speak your language, consider using an interpreter. Send your interpreter a copy of your speech and visuals as far in advance of your presentation as possible. If your audience is likely to include persons with hearing impairments, be sure to team up with a sign-language interpreter as well.

> The more you practice, the more confidence you'll have in yourself and your material.

> You'll know you've practiced enough when you can present the material at a comfortable pace, in a natural and conversational tone, and without relying on your slides for every message point.

Delivering a Presentation

It's showtime. This section offers practical advice for four important aspects of delivery: overcoming anxiety, handling questions responsively, embracing the backchannel, and giving presentations online.

5   LEARNING OBJECTIVE

Describe four important aspects of delivering a presentation in today's social media environment.

OVERCOMING ANXIETY

Even seasoned pros get a little nervous before a big presentation—and that is a good thing. Nervousness is an indication that you care about your audience, your topic, and the occasion. These techniques will help you convert anxiety into positive energy:[23]

- **Stop worrying about being perfect.** Successful speakers focus on making an authentic connection with their listeners, rather than on trying to deliver a note-perfect presentation.
- **Know your subject.** The more familiar you are with your material, the less panic you'll feel.
- **Practice, practice, practice.** The more you rehearse, the more confident you will feel.
- **Visualize success.** Visualize mental images of yourself in front of the audience, feeling confident, prepared, and able to handle any situation that might arise.[24] Bear in mind that your audience wants you to succeed, too.

> Practice is the best antidote for anxiety; it gives you confidence that you know your material and that you can recover from any glitches you might encounter.

- **Remember to breathe.** Tension can lead people to breathe in a rapid and shallow fashion, which can create a lightheaded feeling. Breathe slowly and deeply to maintain a sense of calm and confidence.
- **Be ready with your opening line.** Have your first sentence memorized and on the tip of your tongue.
- **Be comfortable.** Dress appropriately but as comfortably as is appropriate. Drink plenty of water ahead of time to hydrate your voice (bring a bottle of water with you, too).
- **Take a three-second break.** If you sense that you're starting to race, pause and arrange your notes or perform some other small task while taking several deep breaths. Then start again at your normal pace.
- **Concentrate on your message and your audience, not on yourself.** When you're busy thinking about your subject and observing your audience's response, you tend to forget your fears.
- **Maintain eye contact with friendly audience members.** Eye contact not only makes you appear sincere, confident, and trustworthy but can give you positive feedback as well.
- **Keep going.** Things usually get better as you move along, with each successful minute giving you more and more confidence.

HANDLING QUESTIONS RESPONSIVELY

Don't leave the question-and-answer period to chance: Anticipate potential questions and think through your answers.

The question-and-answer (Q&A) period is one of the most important parts of an oral presentation. It gives you a chance to obtain important information, to emphasize your main idea and supporting points, and to build enthusiasm for your point of view. When you're speaking to high-ranking executives in your company, the Q&A period will often consume most of the time allotted for your presentation.[25]

Whether or not you can establish ground rules for Q&A depends on the audience and the situation. If you're presenting to upper managers or potential investors, for example, you will probably have no say in the matter: Audience members will likely ask as many questions as they want, whenever they want, to get the information they need. On the other hand, if you are presenting to your peers or a large public audience, try to establish some guidelines, such as the number of questions allowed per person and the overall time limit for questions.

Don't assume that you can handle whatever comes up without some preparation.[26] Learn enough about your audience members to get an idea of their concerns and think through answers to potential questions.

When people ask questions, pay attention to nonverbal signals to help determine what each person really means. Repeat the question to confirm your understanding and to ensure that the entire audience has heard it. If the question is vague or confusing, ask for clarification; then give a simple, direct answer.

If you don't have a satisfactory answer to an important question from the audience, offer to provide it after the presentation.

If you are asked a complex or difficult question, answer carefully. Offer to meet with the questioner afterward if the issue isn't relevant to the rest of the audience or if giving an adequate answer would take too long. If you don't know the answer, don't pretend that you do. Instead, offer to get a complete answer as soon as possible or ask someone in the audience to volunteer information.

Be on guard for audience members who use questions to make impromptu speeches or to take control of your presentation. Without offending the questioner, find a way to stay in control. You might admit that you and the questioner have differing opinions and, before calling on someone else, offer to get back to the questioner after you've done more research.[27]

If you ever face hostile questions, respond honestly and directly while keeping your cool.

If a question ever puts you on the hot seat, respond honestly but keep your cool. Look the person in the eye, answer the question as well as you can, and keep your emotions under control. Defuse hostility by paraphrasing the question and asking the questioner to confirm that you've understood it correctly. Maintain a businesslike tone of voice and a pleasant expression.[28]

When the time allotted for your presentation is almost up, prepare the audience for the end by saying something like, "Our time is almost up. Let's have one more question."

After you reply to that last question, summarize the main idea of the presentation and thank people for their attention. Conclude with the same confident demeanor you've had from the beginning.

EMBRACING THE BACKCHANNEL

Many business presentations these days involve more than just the spoken conversation between the speaker and his or her audience. Using Twitter and other electronic media, audience members often carry on their own parallel communication during a presentation via the **backchannel**, which presentation expert Cliff Atkinson defines as "a line of communication created by people in an audience to connect with others inside or outside the room, with or without the knowledge of the speaker."[29] Chances are you've participated in a backchannel already, such as when texting with your classmates or live-blogging during a lecture.

The backchannel presents both risks and rewards for business presenters. On the negative side, for example, listeners can research your claims the instant you make them and spread the word quickly if they think your information is shaky. The backchannel also gives contrary audience members more leverage, which can lead to presentations spinning out of control. On the plus side, listeners who are excited about your message can build support for it, expand on it, and spread it to a much larger audience in a matter of seconds. You can also get valuable feedback during and after presentations.[30]

By embracing the backchannel, rather than trying to fight or ignore it, presenters can use this powerful force to their advantage. Follow these tips to make the backchannel work for you:[31]

- **Integrate social media into the presentation process.** For example, you can set up a formal backchannel yourself using tools such as BackNoise (http://backnoise.com), create a website for the presentation so that people can access relevant resources during or after the presentation, create a Twitter hashtag that everyone can use when sending tweets, or display the Twitterstream during Q&A so that everyone can see the questions and comments on the backchannel.
- **Monitor and ask for feedback.** Using a free service such as Tweetdeck, you can monitor in real time what the people in the audience are writing about. To avoid trying to monitor the backchannel while speaking, you can schedule "Twitter breaks," during which you review comments and respond as needed.
- **Review comments to improve your presentation.** After a presentation is over, review comments on audience members' Twitter accounts and blogs to see how you can improve your content or your presentation habits.
- **Automatically tweet key points from your presentation while you speak.** Add-ons for presentation software can send out prewritten tweets as you show specific slides during a presentation. By making your key points readily available, you make it easy for listeners to retweet and comment on your presentation.
- **Establish expectations with the audience.** Explain that you welcome audience participation, but to ensure a positive experience for everyone, ask that comments be civil, relevant, and productive.

GIVING PRESENTATIONS ONLINE

The benefits of online presentations are considerable, including the opportunity to communicate with a geographically dispersed audience at a fraction of the cost of travel. However, the challenges for a presenter can be significant, thanks to that layer of technology between you and your audience. Many of those "human moments" that guide and encourage

Twitter and other social media are dramatically changing business presentations by making it easy for all audience members to participate in the *backchannel*.

Resist the urge to ignore or fight the backchannel; instead, learn how to use it to your advantage.

REAL-TIME UPDATES
Learn More by Watching This Video

Maximize the rewards of the backchannel and minimize the risks

This webinar hosted by author Cliff Atkinson outlines the principles of the social media backchannel and analyzes a real-life presentation where the backchannel spurred an audience revolt and what presenters can learn from this. Go to http://real-timeupdates.com/ebc10 and click on Learn More. If you are using MyBcommLab, you can access Real-Time Updates within each chapter or under Student Study Tools.

Online presentations let you reach a wider audience, but the lack of direct contact forces you to take a more active role in engaging your audience.
Source: © Flirt/SuperStock.

you through an in-person presentation won't travel across the digital divide. For instance, it's often difficult to tell whether audience members are bored or confused because your view of them is usually confined to small video images (and sometimes not even that).

To ensure successful online presentations, keep the following advice in mind:

- **Consider sending preview study materials ahead of time.** Some presenters advise against giving out your slides ahead of time, however, because doing so gives away the ending of your presentation.
- **Keep your presentation as simple as possible.** Break complicated slides down into multiple slides if necessary, and keep the direction of your discussion clear so that no one gets lost.
- **Ask for feedback frequently.** Many online viewers will be reluctant to call attention to themselves by interrupting you to ask for clarification. Also, setting up a backchannel via Twitter or as part of your online meeting system gives viewers a chance to ask questions without interrupting.
- **Consider the viewing experience from the audience members' point of view.** Will they be able to see what you think they can see? For instance, webcast video is often displayed in a small window, so viewers may miss important details.
- **Allow plenty of time for everyone to get connected and familiar with the screen they're viewing.** Build extra time into your schedule to ensure that everyone is connected and ready to start.

Finally, don't get lost in the technology. Use these tools whenever they'll help but remember that the most important aspect of any presentation is getting the audience to receive, understand, and embrace your message. For the latest information on online presentations, visit http://real-timeupdates.com/ebc10 and click on Chapter 14.

ON THE JOB: SOLVING COMMUNICATION DILEMMAS AT PRINCIPATO-YOUNG ENTERTAINMENT

Source: Alexander Sibaja/Hulton Archive/Getty Images.

You share Peter Principato's love of comedy, and now you get to learn from his decades of experience in the business. You've joined Principato-Young as an apprentice talent manager, working side by side with Principato to coach comedians through their careers and to pitch TV and movie ideas to studio executives.

Principato was struck by the rapport you established with Lysette Laria, a new client, and he has asked you to team up with Laria to pitch a new weekly situation comedy she created, tentatively called "You Just Missed Me." In it she will play a character on the run from the mob, who hides in plain sight in various professions—impersonating a new character every week and generally making a mess of every job she steps into.

1. You and Laria know how important an attention-getting opening is when it comes to pitching a new show. You have a meeting with a studio executive next week, and you've brainstormed five possibilities. Which of these should you use?
   a. You don't want to miss "You Just Missed Me"!
   b. "You Just Missed Me" gives comic treatment to a fear that many of us have or can imagine having: being uncovered as a fraud.

c. Just imagine what it would be like to go to work in disguise every day with the fear that your real identity might be uncovered.

d. M.A.S.H., Cheers, Seinfeld, Friends, The Office—which sitcom is next to join these classics in the pantheon of money-making shows?

e. Imagine all the trouble you could get into by clumsily faking your way through a new profession every day of your life, all while running from a bunch of bad guys who are as clueless as they are heartless.

2. When Laria first described her show's concept to Principato, he chuckled at the comic possibilities but then went glum when he stopped to consider the cost and complexity of producing a show set in a different location every episode. He knows any studio executive will have the same reservations. How should you and Laria handle this objection in your pitch next week?

a. Emphasize that if the show turns out to be as popular as you honestly believe it will be, it will generate high ratings, which will lead to higher advertising rates, which will then pay for the higher production costs.

b. See if you can identify any other successful shows that have had to use a variety of sets and use them as justification for whatever "You Just Missed Me" is likely to cost.

c. Explain to the studio executive that you will adapt the episode storylines to fit the studio's existing sets, whatever those are.

d. Do some research to find out which shows and movies this studio has produced in the past and which of those sets are still available. Then sketch out two or three episodes that could adapt these specific resources to help keep costs down.

3. You've seen Laria perform in comedy clubs a dozen times, and on stage she is witty, chatty, and relaxed. Unfortunately, off stage she is withdrawn and fidgety, giving the impression that she is either terrified to be in someone's presence or so bored she can't wait to leave. Neither impression will help in a pitch meeting where you're trying to sell her as the capable star of a show that will cost millions of dollars to produce. How should you handle the situation?

a. As awkward as Laria is in one-on-one settings, she will be the star of the show, so she simply has to step up and perform in the pitch meeting. Let her give the presentation and just hope her on-stage persona somehow comes through. Or hope that the studio executive finds her quirky personality appealing somehow.

b. Send her for some emergency training sessions so that she can become "good in a room." Then let her give the presentation.

c. You are comfortable giving presentations and actually enjoy meeting with executives, so you should give the presentation yourself. Laria will come along, but only as a prop and proof that she exists, without saying anything beyond simple introductions.

d. You should give the bulk of the presentation but plan it so that Laria can weave in a few of her comedy routines along the way, as though she were on stage. This will show off her talents without draining the life out of the presentation.

4. Principato warned you that some studio executives can be blunt, but that didn't prepare you for the shock you received after you and Laria gave your pitch. The executive sat silently for a long moment and then without even looking at you, asked in a derisive tone, "Seriously? Is that the best you can do?" How should you respond to this hostile question?

a. Respond with confidence, saying "Yes, it absolutely is the best."

b. Respond with a question, asking the executive if he has specific concerns about the show.

c. Respond with an air of submissive respect, saying "Well, if you don't like it, I suppose we could tweak the format or come up with something else."

d. Respond with confidence, saying "Yes, it absolutely is the best, and we're happy to walk out of here and pitch it to another studio."

LEARNING OBJECTIVES CHECKUP

Assess your understanding of the principles in this chapter by reading each learning objective and studying the accompanying exercises. For fill-in-the-blank items, write the missing text in the blank provided; for multiple-choice items, circle the letter of the correct answer. You can check your responses against the answer key on page AK-2.

Objective 14.1: Highlight the importance of presentations in your business career, and explain how to adapt the planning step of the three-step process to presentations.

1. If you are facing an audience that is apprehensive about what you might have to say in a presentation, which of the following approaches is best?

a. Even if your presentation will confirm their worst fears, use the direct approach to confront the negative emotions head-on.

b. If your message will calm their fears, use the direct approach; if your message will confirm their fears, consider the indirect approach to build acceptance.

    c. Ignore the emotional undercurrents and focus on the practical content of your message.

    d. Diffuse the situation with a humorous story that dismisses the audience members' fears.

2. If you are using a conventional structured slide design, roughly how many slides should you plan to use in a 30-minute presentation?

    a. 100–150

    b. 30–40

    c. 60–65

    d. 8–10

3. A/an _____ outline is similar to an outline for a written memo or report, whereas a/an _____ outline is a simplified version designed to help you during the delivery of your presentation.

Objective 14.2: Describe the tasks involved in developing a presentation after completing the planning step.

4. Which of the following is the best way to arouse interest in a presentation to a group of fellow employees on the importance of taking ownership of the problem whenever a customer calls in with a complaint?

    a. "If customers leave, so do our jobs."

    b. "Everything we want as employees of this company—from stable jobs to pay raises to promotional opportunities—depends on one thing: satisfied customers."

    c. "How are customers supposed to get their problems solved if we keep passing the buck from one person to the next without ever doing anything?"

    d. "The company's profit margins depend on satisfied customers, and it's up to us to make sure those customers are satisfied."

5. If you suspect that your audience doesn't really care about the topic you plan to discuss, how can you generate interest in your presentation?

    a. Look for ways to help them relate to the information on a personal level, such as helping the company ensure better job security.

    b. Speak louder and, if possible, use lots of sound effects and visual special effects in your presentation.

    c. Show your passion for the material by speaking faster than normal and pacing the room in an excited fashion.

    d. Show that you care about their feelings by saying up front that you don't really care about the topic either, but you've been assigned to talk about it.

6. If you're giving a presentation in a subject area that you've researched thoroughly but in which you don't have any hands-on experience (suppose your topic is coordinating a major facility relocation or hiring a tax attorney, for instance), which of these steps should you take to build credibility?

    a. During your introduction, explain that your presentation is the result of research that you've done and briefly explain the extent of the research.

    b. Explain that you don't have any experience in the subject area, but you've done some research.

    c. Emphasize that you know a great deal about the subject matter.

    d. Sidestep the issue of credibility entirely in the introduction and let your knowledge shine through during the body of your presentation.

7. Which of the following would do the best job of holding an audience's attention during a presentation on the growing importance of social networking in corporate communication? In this particular case, the audience members are all managers of the same company, but they represent a half dozen countries and speak four different native languages (although they all have basic English skills).

    a. "Social networks are now an important feature in the corporate communication landscape."

    b. "Successful managers around the world now view social networks as an essential tool in their communication efforts."

    c. "Millions of customers and employees are now hip to the latest wave to blow through corporate communication, the clumsily named but nevertheless vital social network."

    d. "I personally get dozens of interesting social networking updates every day, which is solid evidence of how important social networks have become."

8. Your company recently relocated from another state, and the owners are eager to begin building a positive relationship with the local community. You've been asked to speak to employees about volunteering in various community organizations. Which of the following statements does the best job of communicating the owners' wishes while appealing to employees' personal interests?

    a. "Becoming involved in community organizations is a great way for you and your families to meet new people and feel more at home in your new city."

    b. "Becoming involved in community organizations shows our new neighbors that we're an organization of positive, caring people—and it's a great way for you and your families to meet new people and feel more at home in your new city."

    c. "We really owe it to our new community to give back by volunteering."

    d. "The owners feel it is vital for us to become more involved in the community."

9. Which of these techniques is mentioned in the chapter as a way to hold an audience's attention during a presentation?

    a. Speak louder than average

    b. Tell people that management expects them to pay attention

    c. Use clear and vivid language

    d. None of the above

Objective 14.3: Describe the six major design and writing tasks required to enhance your presentation with effective visuals.

10. Which of the following is an advantage of structured slide designs over free-form designs?

    a. Structured designs are more colorful and therefore keep audience attention better.

    b. People are accustomed to structured designs, so they are more comfortable with them.

    c. Structured slides are generally easier to create than free-form slides.

    d. Structured slides are cheaper.

11. Which of the following is a benefit of organizing a slide around a key visual such as a pyramid or a circular flow diagram?
    a. Slides without key visuals are always boring and repetitive.
    b. The key visual shows how the various ideas are related, making it easier for viewers to grasp your message.
    c. With a key visual to rely on, the speaker doesn't have to know the subject matter quite as thoroughly.
    d. You can use the key visual for every slide, making your presentation more consistent.

12. Which of the following is a problem that results from cramming too much text on a slide?
    a. It forces the audience members to spend more time reading than listening to speaker.
    b. It forces the presenter to use smaller type on the slide.
    c. It overloads the audience with too much information too fast.
    d. All of the above are problems that result from cramming too much text on a slide.

13. Charts and tables used for electronic presentations should be
    a. Simpler than charts and tables used for printed documents.
    b. More complex than charts and tables used for printed documents.
    c. Exactly the same as charts and tables used for printed documents.

14. Slide _____ control how one slide replaces another, whereas slide _____ control how text and graphical elements are revealed on an individual slide.

15. Why is consistent use of colors, typefaces and type treatments, size, and other design elements important in presentations?
    a. Consistency is not important; in fact, it's a sign of a dull presentation.
    b. Consistency shows that you're a smart businessperson who doesn't waste time on trivial details.
    c. Consistency simplifies the viewing and listening process for your audience and enables them to pay closer attention to your message rather than spending time trying to figure out your visuals.
    d. Consistency shows that you're a team player who can follow instructions.

Objective 14.4: Outline four major tasks involved in completing a presentation.

16. How does the completion stage of the three-step writing process differ between reports and presentations?
    a. Completion is exactly the same for reports and presentations.
    b. Presentations are never proofread or tested ahead of time; doing so would destroy the spontaneity of your delivery.
    c. You never revise presentation slides because they're locked in place once you create them.
    d. The completion state for presentations involves a wider range of tasks, including testing your presentation slides, verifying equipment operation, practicing your speech, and creating handout materials.

17. What advice would you give to a novice presenter regarding practicing before a big presentation?
    a. Don't practice—it destroys the spontaneity you need to give an upbeat presentation.
    b. Make multiple practice runs, a half dozen if needed, to make sure you can deliver the material smoothly and confidently.
    c. Write out a script and memorize it word for word; you can't risk forgetting any key points.
    d. One practice session is adequate; use the extra time to polish your presentation slides instead.

18. What is the best approach to developing handout materials?
    a. Create them after you've planned, developed, and tested your presentation so that you can see which points are confusing and could benefit from additional support.
    b. Wait until you give the presentation and then ask your viewers what they would like to see in terms of additional information.
    c. Always follow the lead of whatever the more experienced presenters in your department do; they've already set audience expectations.
    d. Plan your handouts as you plan and create your slides so that you maintain an effective balance between information that you'll cover during the presentation and information that is better suited to a printed handout.

Objective 14.5: Describe four important aspects of delivering a presentation in today's social media environment.

19. Which of the following is an effective way to respond if you feel nervous right before giving a presentation?
    a. Think up a short joke to begin your presentation; the audience's laughter will help you relax.
    b. Begin your presentation by telling people that you're nervous and asking them to be sympathetic if you make any mistakes.
    c. Begin your presentation by telling the audience how much you dislike speaking in public; most of them dislike public speaking, too, so they'll be more sympathetic toward you.
    d. Remind yourself that everybody gets nervous and that being nervous simply means you care about doing well; use the nervousness to be more energetic when you begin speaking.

20. Which of these actions should you take when an audience member asks you a question?
    a. Observe the questioner's body language and facial expression to help determine what the person really means.
    b. Nod your head or show some other sign that you acknowledge the question.
    c. Repeat the question to confirm your understanding and to ensure that the entire audience has heard it.
    d. Do all of the above.

21. If you receive a question that is important and relevant to the topic you're presenting but you lack the information needed to answer it, which of the following would be the best response?
    a. "I'm sorry; I don't know the answer."
    b. "You've asked an important question, but I don't have the information needed to answer it properly. I'll

research the issue after we're finished here today and then send everyone an email message with the answer."

   c. "Let me get back to you on that."

   d. "I'd really like to stay focused on the material that I prepared for this presentation."

22. What is the best strategy for using the Twitter-enabled backchannel in a presentation?

   a. Build automated Twitter feeds into your presentation slides that send out capsule points as you move through the presentation, but ignore whatever audience members might be doing on Twitter and stay focused on your presentation.

   b. Announce up front that the use of Twitter and other messaging tools is forbidden during the presentation; the audience's job is to pay attention to you, the speaker.

   c. Embrace the backchannel fully, including building in automated feeds from your presentation, providing a hashtag for everyone to use making it easy to follow tweets related to the presentation, and take occasional Twitter breaks to check for feedback and questions from the audience.

   d. Ignore it; you can't stop people from tweeting during a presentation, so you might as well just accept that they are going to do so.

23. Which of the following is a disadvantage of conducting presentations online?

   a. The lack of audio communication

   b. The inability of most people to participate, since businesses have different Internet connection speeds

   c. The inability to use PowerPoint slides online

   d. The shortage (or sometimes complete lack) of nonverbal signals such as posture, which can provide vital feedback during a presentation

24. Which of the following is an advantage of online presentations?

   a. Lower costs as a result of less travel

   b. More opportunities for employees to meet customers in person

   c. The ability to multitask during meetings

   d. All of the above

MyBcommLab

CHAPTER OUTLINE

Planning a Presentation
Analyzing the Situation
Selecting the Right Medium
Organizing Your Presentation

Developing a Presentation
Adapting to Your Audience
Composing Your Presentation

Enhancing Your Presentation with Effective Slides
Choosing Structured or Free-Form Slides
Designing Effective Slides

Completing a Presentation
Finalizing Your Slides
Creating Effective Handouts
Choosing Your Presentation Method
Practicing Your Delivery

Delivering a Presentation
Overcoming Anxiety
Handling Questions Responsively
Embracing the Backchannel
Giving Presentations Online

 **Checklist**

Enhancing Presentations with Visuals

A. Plan your presentation visuals.
- Make sure you and your message, not your visuals, remain the focus of your presentation.
- Follow effective design principles, with an emphasis on simplicity and authenticity.

B. Choose structured or free-form slides.
- Structured slides using bullet-point templates are easy to create, require little design time or skill, and can be completed in a hurry. Best uses: routine, internal presentations
- Free-form slides make it easier to combine textual and visual information, to create a more dynamic and engaging experience, and to maintain a conversational connection with the audience. Best uses: motivational, educational, and persuasive presentations

LEARNING OBJECTIVES

1 Highlight the importance of presentations in your business career, and explain how to adapt the planning step of the three-step process to presentations. [page 493]

2 Describe the tasks involved in developing a presentation after completing the planning step. [page 498]

3 Describe the six major design and writing tasks required to enhance your presentation with effective visuals. [page 502]

4 Outline four major tasks involved in completing a presentation. [page 509]

5 Describe four important aspects of delivering a presentation in today's social media environment. [page 513]

KEY TERMS

backchannel A social media conversation that takes place during a presentation, in parallel with the speaker's presentation

free-form slides Presentation slides that are not based on a template, often with each slide having a unique look but unified by typeface, color, and other design choices; tend to be much more visually oriented than structured slides

navigation slides Noncontent slides that tell your audience where you're going and where you've been

slide builds Similar to slide transitions, these effects control the release of text, graphics, and other elements on individual slides

slide transitions Software effects that control how one slide replaces another on-screen

structured slides Presentation slides that follow the same design templates throughout and give all the slides in a presentation the same general look; they emphasize textual information in bullet-point form

C. Design effective slides.
- Avoid the temptation to create "slideuments," slides that are so packed with information that they can be read as standalone documents.
- Use a key visual to organize related ideas in a clear and meaningful way.
- Write text content that will be readable from everywhere in the room.
- Write short, active, parallel phrases that support, not replace, your spoken message.
- Limit the amount of text so that your audience can focus on listening, not reading.
- Use color to emphasize important ideas, create contrast, isolate visual elements, and convey intended nonverbal signals.
- Limit color to a few compatible choices and use them consistently.
- Make sure your slide background doesn't compete with the foreground.
- Use decorative artwork sparingly and only to support your message.
- Emphasize functional artwork—photos, technical drawings, charts, and other visual elements containing information that is part of your message.

- Choose typefaces that are easy to read on-screen; limit the number of typefaces and use them consistently.
- Use slide masters to maintain consistency throughout your presentation.
- Use functional animation when it can support your message.
- Make sure slide transitions are subtle, if used at all.
- Use builds carefully to control the release of information.
- Use hyperlinks and action buttons to add flexibility to your presentation.
- Incorporate multimedia elements that can help engage your audience and deliver your message.

D. Complete slides and support materials.
- Review every slide carefully to ensure accuracy, consistency, and clarity.
- Make sure that all slides are fully operational.
- Use the slide sorter to verify and adjust the sequence of slides, if needed.
- Have a backup plan in case your electronic presentation plan fails.
- Create navigation and support slides.
- Create handouts to complement and support your presentation message.

APPLY YOUR KNOWLEDGE

To review chapter content related to each question, refer to the indicated Learning Objective.

1. Why is it important to limit the scope of presentations? [LO-1]

2. How can visually oriented free-form slides help keep an audience engaged in a presentation? [LO-3]

3. Is it ethical to use design elements and special effects to persuade an audience? Why or why not? [LO-3]

4. Why is speaking from notes almost always the best method of delivery? [LO-4]

5. How does embracing the backchannel reflect the "you" attitude? [LO-5]

PRACTICE YOUR SKILLS

Messages for Analysis

Message 14.A: Improving a Presentation Slide

To access this PowerPoint presentation, visit http://real-timeupdates.com/ebc10, click on Student Assignments, and select Chapter 14, page 522, Message 14.A. Revise the text on these slides to make them more effective for presentation use.

Message 14.B: Analyzing Animation

To access this PowerPoint presentation, visit http://real-timeupdates.com/ebc10, click on Student Assignments, and select Chapter 14, page 522, Message 14.B. Download and watch the presentation in slide show mode (after you select Slide Show from the View menu, simply click your mouse to advance through the slides). After you've watched the presentation, identify at least three ways in which various animations, builds, and transitions either enhanced or impeded your understanding of the subject matter.

Exercises

Active links for all websites in this chapter can be found on MyBcommLab; see your User Guide for instructions on accessing the content for this chapter. Each activity is labeled according to the primary skill or skills you will need to use. To review relevant chapter content, you can refer to the indicated Learning Objective. In some instances, supporting information will be found in another chapter, as indicated.

1. **Presentations: Planning a Presentation [LO-1]** Select one of the following topics. Then research your topic as needed and prepare a brief presentation (5-10 minutes) to be given to your class.

   a. What I expect to learn in this course

   b. Past public speaking experiences: the good, the bad, and the ugly

   c. I would be good at teaching _____.

   d. I am afraid of _____.

   e. It's easy for me to _____.

   f. I get angry when _____.

   g. I am happiest when I _____.

   h. People would be surprised if they knew that I _____.

   i. My favorite older person

   j. My favorite charity

   k. My favorite place

   l. My favorite sport

   m. My favorite store

   n. My favorite television show

   o. The town you live in suffers from a great deal of juvenile vandalism. Explain to a group of community members why juvenile recreational facilities should be built instead of a juvenile detention complex.

   p. You are speaking to the Humane Society. Support or oppose the use of animals for medical research purposes.

   q. You are talking to civic leaders of your community. Try to convince them to build an art gallery.

   r. You are speaking to a first-grade class at an elementary school. Explain why they should brush their teeth after meals.

   s. You are speaking to a group of traveling salespeople. Convince them that they should wear their seatbelts while driving.

   t. You are speaking to a group of elderly people. Convince them to adopt an exercise program.

   u. Energy issues (supply, conservation, alternative sources, national security, global warming, pollution, etc.)

   v. Financial issues (banking, investing, family finances, etc.)

   w. Government (domestic policy, foreign policy, Social Security taxes, welfare, etc.)

   x. Interesting new technologies (virtual reality, geographic information systems, nanotechnology, bioengineering, etc.)

   y. Politics (political parties, elections, legislative bodies and legislation, the presidency, etc.)

   z. Sports (amateur and professional, baseball, football, golf, hang gliding, hockey, rock climbing, tennis, etc.)

2. **Presentations: Planning and Developing; Collaboration: Team Projects [LO-1], [LO-2], Chapter 2** With a team of three other students, prepare a detailed outline (including descriptions of any visuals you would plan to use) for a 10-minute presentation on the advantages of attending your college or university. The presentation would be delivered by someone from the admissions office, and the audience would be visiting high school students and their family members. After completing the outline together, each team member should individually develop a 60-second introduction to the presentation. Meet again, have each team member give his or her introduction, and then discuss which was most effective and why. Be prepared to discuss your conclusion with the class.

3. **Presentations: Planning, Developing, and Delivering [LO-1] [LO-2] [LO-3]** Identify a company whose prospects look bright over the next few years because of highly competitive products, strong leadership, fundamental changes in the market, or any other significant reason. Prepare a

five-minute speech, without visuals, explaining why you think this company is going to do well in the near future.

4. **Presentations: Planning and Developing; Collaboration: Team Projects [LO-1], [LO-2], Chapter 2** You've been asked to give an informative 10-minute talk on vacation opportunities in your home state. Draft your introduction, which should last no more than 2 minutes. Then pair off with a classmate and analyze each other's introductions. How well do these two introductions arouse the audience's interest, build credibility, and preview the presentation? Suggest how these introductions might be improved.

5. **Presentations: Planning and Developing [LO-1], [LO-2]** Locate the transcript of a speech, either online or through your school library. Good sources include Yahoo's directory of commencement speeches (http://dir.yahoo.com/Education/Graduation/Speeches) and the publication *Vital Speeches of the Day*. (Recent years of *Vital Speeches of the Day* are available in the ProQuest database; ask at your library.) Many corporate websites also have archives of executives' speeches; look in the "investor relations" section. Examine both the introduction and the close of the speech you've chosen and then analyze how these two sections work together to emphasize the main idea. What action does the speaker want the audience to take? Next, identify the transitional sentences or phrases that clarify the speech's structure for the listener, especially those that help the speaker shift between supporting points. Using these transitions as clues, list the main message and supporting points; then indicate how each transitional phrase links the current supporting point to the succeeding one. Prepare a two- to three-minute presentation summarizing your analysis for your class.

6. **Presentations: Designing Presentation Visuals [LO-3]** Look through recent issues (print or online) of several business publications to find articles discussing challenges that a specific company or industry is facing. Using the articles and the guidelines discussed in this chapter, create three to five slides on Google Docs, summarizing these issues.

7. **Presentations: Designing Presentation Visuals [LO-3]** Find a business-related slide presentation on SlideShare (www.slideshare.net) and analyze the design. Do you consider it primarily structured or free form? Does the design help the audience understand and remember the message? Why or why not? What improvements would you suggest to the design?

8. **Presentations: Mastering Delivery; Nonverbal Communication: Analyzing Nonverbal Signals [LO-5], Chapter 2** Observe and analyze the delivery of a speaker in a school, work, or other setting. What type of delivery did the speaker use? Was this delivery appropriate for the occasion? What nonverbal signals did the speaker use to emphasize key points? Were these signals effective? Which nonverbal signals would you suggest to further enhance the delivery of this oral presentation? Why?

9. **Presentations: Delivering a Presentation; Communication Ethics: Making Ethical Choices [LO-5], Chapter 1** Think again about the oral presentation you observed and analyzed in the previous activity. How could the speaker have used nonverbal signals to unethically manipulate the audience's attitudes or actions?

10. **Presentations: Delivering a Presentation; Collaboration: Team Projects; Media Skills: Microblogging [LO-5], Chapter 2, Chapter 7** In a team of six students, develop a 10-minute slide presentation on any topic that interests you. Nominate one person to give the presentation; the other five will participate via a Twitter backchannel. Create a webpage that holds at least one downloadable file that will be discussed during the presentation, and set up a backchannel on BackNoise (http://backnoise.com) or a similar service. Practice using the backchannel, including using a hashtag for the meeting and having the presenter ask for audience feedback during a "Twitter break." Be ready to discuss your experience with the entire class. For information on getting started on Twitter, visit http://real-timeupdates.com/ebc10, click on Student Assignments, and then click on Twitter Screencast.

EXPAND YOUR SKILLS

Critique the Professionals

Visit the TED website at www.ted.com/talks and listen to any presentation that interests you. Compare the speaker's delivery and visual support materials with the concepts presented in this chapter. What works? What doesn't work? Using whatever medium your instructor requests, write a brief summary of your analysis.

Sharpen Your Career Skills Online

Bovée and Thill's Business Communication Web Search, at http://businesscommunicationblog.com/websearch, is a unique research tool designed specifically for business communication research. Use the Web Search function to find a website, video, PDF document, podcast, or presentation that offers advice on creating and delivering business presentations. Write a brief email message to your instructor or a post for your class blog, describing the item that you found and summarizing the career skills information you learned from it.

IMPROVE YOUR GRAMMAR, MECHANICS, AND USAGE

The following exercises help you improve your knowledge of and power over English grammar, mechanics, and usage. Turn to the "Handbook of Grammar, Mechanics, and Usage" at the end of this book and review all of Sections 3.1 (Capitalization), 3.2 (Underscores and Italics), and 3.3 (Abbreviations). Then look at the following 10 items. Circle the letter of the preferred choice in the following groups of sentences. (Answers to these exercises appear on page AK-4.)

1. **a.** See that the book is mailed to Doctor J. Thorndyke, NH 1, Scottsdale, AZ 85251.
   b. See that the book is mailed to Doctor J. Thorndyke, National Highway 1, Scottsdale, Arizona 85251.
   c. See that the book is mailed to Dr. J. Thorndyke, NH 1, Scottsdale, AZ 85251.

2. **a.** He graduated with an MS degree from the Massachusetts Institute of Technology.
   b. He graduated with a Master of Science degree from the Massachusetts Institute of Technology.

3. **a.** Willard Wright (a journalist from The Economist) will interview him on Friday.
   b. Willard Wright (a journalist from *The Economist*) will interview him on Friday.
   c. Willard Wright (a journalist from The *Economist*) will interview him on Friday.

4. **a.** The museum is on the corner of Berlie and Hudson streets.
   b. The museum is on the corner of Berlie and Hudson Streets.

5. **a.** I will have the report ready by 8 p.m. this evening, PST, so please give me a call by then.
   b. I will have the report ready by 8 this evening, PST, so please give me a call by then.
   c. I will have the report ready by 8 p.m., PST, so please give me a call by then.

6. **a.** Which band do you think will get the *Rolling Stone* magazine award for Best Debut Album of the Year?
   b. Which band do you think will get the *Rolling Stone magazine* award for *Best Debut Album of the Year*?
   c. Which band do you think will get the *Rolling Stone magazine* award for Best Debut Album of the Year?

7. **a.** The new Innovation Center will be inaugurated on Jul. 3, 2012, less than one yr. from now.
   b. The new Innovation Center will be inaugurated on July 3, 2012, less than one year from now.
   c. The new Innovation Center will be inaugurated on Jul. 3, 2012, less than one year from now.

8. **a.** We are meeting the boss on wednesday at the JFK Center in LA.
   b. We are meeting the boss on Wednesday at the JFK Center in LA.
   c. We are meeting the boss on Wednesday at the jfk center in Los Angeles.

9. **a.** You should learn the difference between *p.a.* (which means "every year") and PA (which means "Personal Assistant").
   b. You should learn the difference between *p.a.* (which means "every year") and *PA* (which means "Personal Assistant").
   c. You should learn the difference between *p.a.* (which means *every year*) and PA (which means *Personal Assistant*).

10. **a.** Our first factory was located on the East coast.
    b. Our first factory was located on the east coast.
    c. Our first factory was located on the East Coast.

For additional exercises focusing on mechanics, visit MyBcommLab. Click on Chapter 14, click on Additional Exercises to Improve Your Grammar, Mechanics, and Usage, and then click on 20. Capitals or 21. Word division.

CASES

PRESENTATION SKILLS   PORTFOLIO BUILDER

1. Presentations: Planning a Presentation [LO-1], [LO-2]
Pecha-kucha is a style of presentation that might be the ultimate in creative constraint: The speaker is limited to 20 slides, each of which is displayed for exactly 20 seconds before automatically advancing. PechaKucha Nights, which are open to the public, are now put on in cities all over the world. Visit www.pecha-kucha .org for more information on these events or to view some archived presentations.

Your task: Select one of the subjects from Exercise 1 on page 522 and develop a *pecha-kucha* style presentation with 20 slides, each designed to be displayed for 20 seconds. Use the slide timing capabilities in your presentation software to control the timing. Make sure you practice before presenting to your class so that you can hit the precise timing requirements.[32]

PRESENTATION SKILLS
SOCIAL NETWORKING SKILLS

2. Presentations: Planning a Presentation [LO-1], [LO-2] You know those times when you're craving Thai food or the perfect fruit smoothie, but you don't know where to go? Or when you're out shopping or clubbing and want to let your friends know where you are? Foursquare's location-based services connect you with friends and companies that offer products and services of interest.

Your task: Create a brief presentation explaining the Foursquare concept and its features and benefits (visit http://foursquare .com/ for more information). List two Foursquare competitors and give a brief assessment of which of the three you would recommend to your classmates.[33]

PRESENTATION SKILLS   TEAM SKILLS

3. Presentations: Planning a Presentation; Collaboration: Team Projects [LO-1], Chapter 2 In your job as a business development researcher for a major corporation, you're asked to gather and process information on a wide variety of subjects. Management has gained confidence in your research and analysis skills and would now like you to begin making regular presentations at management retreats and other functions. Topics are likely to include the following:

- Offshoring of U.S. jobs
- Foreign ownership of U.S. firms
- Employment issues involving workers from other countries
- Tax breaks offered by local and state governments to attract new businesses
- Economic impact of environmental regulations

Your task: With a team assigned by your instructor, choose one of the topics from the list and conduct enough research to familiarize yourself with the topic. Identify at least three important issues that anyone involved with this topic should know about. Prepare a 10-minute presentation that introduces the topic, comments on its importance to the U.S. economy, and discusses the issues you've identified. Assume that your audience is a cross-section of business managers who don't have any particular experience in the topic you've chosen.

PRESENTATION SKILLS

4. Planning, Designing, and Creating Presentation Slides [LO-1], [LO-2], [LO-3], [LO-4]   Read the "On the Job" vignette about Southwest Airlines on page 214 in Chapter 7 and decide whether free-form or structured slides would be the most effective way to present this story to an audience of customer service agents to help them understand the power of social media.

Your task: Using whichever design approach you think is better, create a brief presentation (slides and speaking notes) to tell the story.

PRESENTATION SKILLS   TEAM SKILLS

5. Planning, Designing, and Creating Presentation Slides; Collaboration: Team Projects [LO-1], [LO-2], [LO-3], [LO-4], Chapter 2   Changing a nation's eating habits is a Herculean task, but the physical and financial health of the United States depends on it. You work for the USDA Center for Nutrition Policy and Promotion (www.cnpp.usda.gov), and it's your job to educate people on the dangers of unhealthy eating and the changes they can make to eat more balanced and healthful diets.

Your task: Visit http://real-timeupdates.com/ebc10, click on Student Assignments, select Chapter 14, page 525, Case 5, and download the *Dietary Guidelines for Americans*. With a team assigned by your instructor, develop a presentation no longer than 15 minutes, using free-form slides, that conveys the key points from Chapter 3 of the *Guidelines*, "Food and Food Components to Reduce." The objectives of your presentation are to alert people to the dangers of excessive consumption of the five components discussed in the chapter and to let them know what healthy levels of consumptions are. This chapter has a lot of information, but you don't need to pack it all into your slides; you can assume that the chapter will be available as a handout to anyone who attends your presentation. Create as many slides as you need, along with speaking notes that someone outside your team could use to give the presentation. You can use images from the *Guidelines* PDF, the websites of the U.S. Department of Agriculture and the U.S. Department of Health and Human Services, or a non-government source such as Creative Commons (http://creativecommons.org). Make sure you follow the usage and attribution guidelines for any photos you find on non-government sites.

PRESENTATION SKILLS   PORTFOLIO BUILDER

6. Presentations: Designing Presentation Visuals [LO-3]
Depending on the sequence your instructor chose for this course, you may have covered up to a dozen chapters or so at this point

and learned or improved many valuable skills. Think through your progress and identify five business communication skills that you've either learned for the first time or developed during this course.

Your task: Create a six-slide presentation, with a title slide and five slides that describe each of the five skills you've identified. Be sure to explain how each skill could help you in your career. Use any visual style that you feel is appropriate for the assignment.

REFERENCES

1. John Bowe, "Funny = Money," *New York Times*, 30 December 2010, www.nytimes.com; Stephanie Palmer Taxy, Good in a Room website, accessed 13 March 2011, www.goodinaroom.com; Mike Fleming, "A Banner Day for Two Former Assistants," Deadline Hollywood, 20 January 2011, www.deadline.com.

2. Nancy Duarte, *Slide:ology: The Art and Science of Creating Great Presentations* (Sebastopol, Calif.: O'Reilly Media, 2008), 13.

3. Amber Naslund, "Twebinar: GE's Tweetsquad," 4 August 2009, www.radian6.com/blog.

4. Carmine Gallo, "How to Deliver a Presentation Under Pressure," *BusinessWeek* online, 18 September 2008, www.businessweek.com.

5. Sarah Lary and Karen Pruente, "Powerless Point: Common PowerPoint Mistakes to Avoid," *Public Relations Tactics*, February 2004, 28.

6. Garr Reynolds, *Presentation Zen* (Berkeley, Calif.: New Riders, 2008), 39–42.

7. Sherwyn P. Morreale and Courtland L. Bovée, *Excellence in Public Speaking* (Fort Worth, Tex.: Harcourt Brace College Publishers, 1998), 234–237.

8. John Windsor, "Presenting Smart: Keeping the Goal in Sight," *Presentations*, 6 March 2008, www.presentations.com.

9. Morreale and Bovée, *Excellence in Public Speaking*, 241–243.

10. Adapted from Eric J. Adams, "Management Focus: User-Friendly Presentation Software," *World Trade*, March 1995, 92.

11. Carmine Gallo, "Grab Your Audience Fast," *BusinessWeek*, 13 September 2006, 19.

12. Walter Kiechel III, "How to Give a Speech," *Fortune*, 8 June 1987, 180.

13. *Communication and Leadership Program* (Santa Ana, Calif.: Toastmasters International, 1980), 44, 45.

14. Reynolds, *Presentation Zen: Simple Ideas on Presentation Design and Delivery*, 10.

15. Cliff Atkinson, "The Cognitive Load of PowerPoint: Q&A with Richard E. Mayer," Sociablemedia.com, accessed 22 December 2008, www.sociablemedia.com.

16. "The Power of Color in Presentations," 3M Meeting Network, accessed 25 May 2007, www.3m.com/meetingnetwork/readingroom/meetingguide_power_color.html.

17. Duarte, *Slide:ology: The Art and Science of Creating Great Presentations*, 152.

18. Sarah Lary and Karen Pruente, "Powerless Point: Common PowerPoint Mistakes to Avoid," *Public Relations Tactics*, February 2004, 28.

19. Reynolds, *Presentation Zen: Simple Ideas on Presentation Design and Delivery*, 85.

20. Jerry Weissman, *Presenting to Win: The Art of Telling Your Story* (Upper Saddle River, N.J.: Pearson Prentice Hall, 2006), 162–163.

21. Reynolds, *Presentation Zen: Simple Ideas on Presentation Design and Delivery*, 66.

22. Reynolds, *Presentation Zen: Simple Ideas on Presentation Design and Delivery*, 208.

23. Richard Zeoli, "The Seven Things You Must Know About Public Speaking," *Forbes*, 3 June 2009, www.forbes.com; Morreale and Bovée, *Excellence in Public Speaking*, 24–25.

24. Jennifer Rotondo and Mike Rotondo, Jr., *Presentation Skills for Managers* (New York: McGraw-Hill, 2002), 9.

25. Rick Gilbert, "Presentation Advice for Boardroom Success," *Financial Executive*, September 2005, 12.

26. Rotondo and Rotondo, *Presentation Skills for Managers*, 151.

27. Teresa Brady, "Fielding Abrasive Questions During Presentations," *Supervisory Management*, February 1993, 6.

28. Robert L. Montgomery, "Listening on Your Feet," *The Toastmaster*, July 1987, 14–15.

29. Cliff Atkinson, *The Backchannel* (Berkeley, Calif.: New Riders, 2010), 17.

30. Atkinson, *The Backchannel*, 51, 68–73.

31. Olivia Mitchell, "10 Tools for Presenting with Twitter," Speaking About Presenting blog, 3 November 2009, www.speakingaboutpresenting.com; Atkinson, *The Backchannel*, 51, 68–73, 99.

32. Adapted from PechaKucha20x20 website, accessed 4 August 2010, www.pecha-kucka.org; Reynolds, *Presentation Zen: Simple Ideas on Presentation Design and Delivery*, 41.

33. Adapted from Foursquare website, accessed 4 August 2010, http://foursquare.com; Christina Warren, "Foursquare Reaches 100 Millions Checkins," Mashable, 20 July 2010, http://mashable.com.

PART 5

Writing Employment Messages and Interviewing for Jobs

The same techniques you use to succeed in your career can also help you launch and manage that career. Understand the employer's perspective on the hiring process so that you can adapt your approach and find the best job in the shortest possible time. Learn the best ways to craft a résumé and the other elements in your job search portfolio. Understand the interviewing process to make sure you're prepared for every stage and every type of interview.

Stephan Coburn/Fotolia, LLC-Royalty Free

LEARNING OBJECTIVES After studying this chapter, you will be able to

1 List eight key steps to finding the ideal opportunity in today's job market

2 Explain the process of planning your résumé, including how to choose the best résumé organization

3 Describe the tasks involved in writing your résumé, and list the major sections of a traditional résumé

4 Characterize the completing step for résumés, including the six most common formats in which you can produce a résumé

MyBcommLab Where you see MyBcommLab in this chapter, go to www.pearsoninternationaleditions.com/mybcommlab for additional activities on the topic being discussed.

ON THE JOB: COMMUNICATING AT ATK

ATK's Carl Willis oversees the company's efforts to use advanced statistical analysis to predict workforce needs.
Source: Courtesy of ATK.

Focusing an Obsession with Accuracy on the Challenges of Talent Management

One could say ATK is in the business of accuracy. Whether it's rocket motors for NASA, missiles and munitions for the U.S. Army, or ammunition for law enforcement and sporting uses, customers depend on ATK for accuracy and overall performance. Failure is not an option, because as the company says, "Our customers' lives depend on the products we make."

Over the past few years, the multifaceted Minneapolis aerospace and defense company has been applying that obsession with accuracy and performance to one of the toughest problems any business faces: attracting, hiring, and keeping the quality employees who make business success possible. Along the way, ATK is one of a small but growing cadre of firms revolutionizing the practice of human resources (HR).

In the eyes of some professionals in finance, manufacturing, sales, and other data-driven functional areas, HR suffers from a "reputational deficit," to put it politely. Most other functional areas have long since adopted information technology to improve decision making and demonstrate their contribution to the bottom line. However, HR is still viewed by some as a "soft" function that might do a fine job of processing employee paperwork but can't really prove how well it's doing the critical job of finding the right employees and making sure they stay on board. The information systems being used tend to focus on recordkeeping, compliance verification, and other important but not terribly strategic tasks.

Carl Willis, ATK's vice president of human resources, oversees the company's efforts in the emerging field of *predictive workforce analytics*, the use of statistical modeling to help a company keep its business needs and employee skill sets in alignment. Balancing this complex equation of supply and demand is particularly vital for a company such as ATK, where many jobs are highly specialized and the departure of a single employee can sometimes cause significant problems. ATK's system is so advanced that it can predict the "flight risk" of individual employees, and it was able to predict with remarkable accuracy the number of employees who would take early retirement before a particular retirement benefit was set to expire. Being able to predict such events with accuracy allows a company to ramp up hiring and focus on specific types of skills it will need to bring in.

At a broader level, the aerospace and defense sector is facing a shortage of key talent in the near future, as its aging workforce heads into retirement. ATK is counting on predictive analytics to help it characterize the skills required to perform those jobs and identify new employees who can provide them when the time comes.

With updated tools in hand, a new generation of HR professionals is poised to make a more strategic contribution, armed with the data to prove it.[1]

www.atk.com

Finding the Ideal Opportunity in Today's Job Market

The efforts made by ATK (profiled in the chapter opener) show the importance that top companies place on finding the right employees and the investments they are willing to make in both personnel and technology to attract and keep valuable talent. Whether you'll be looking for your first professional job on graduation or you're already in the middle of a career, you need to put as much thought and care into finding the right job as employers put into finding the right employees.

Identifying and landing the ideal job can be a long and difficult process, particularly in today's tough employment markets. Fortunately, the skills you're developing in this course will give you a competitive advantage. This section offers a general job-search strategy with advice that applies to just about any career path you might want to pursue. As you craft your personal strategy, keep these two guidelines in mind:

- **Get organized.** Your job search could last many months and involve multiple contacts with dozens of companies. You need to keep all the details straight to make sure you don't miss opportunities or make mistakes such as losing someone's email address or forgetting an appointment.
- **Start now and stick to it.** Even if you are a year or more away from graduation, now is not too early to get started with some of the essential research and planning tasks. If you wait until the last minute, you will miss opportunities and you won't be as prepared as the candidates you'll be competing against.

1 LEARNING OBJECTIVE

List eight key steps to finding the ideal opportunity in today's job market.

WRITING THE STORY OF YOU

Take the time now to explore the possibilities, find your passion, and identify appealing career paths. If you haven't yet, read the career-planning Prologue that starts on page 31, and particularly the "What Do You Want to Do?" section on page 33, to help identify the nature of the work you'd like to do, if not a specific profession.

Next, using the advice on creating a personal brand on page 37, begin writing the "story of you": the things you are passionate about, the skills you possess, your ability to help an organization reach its goals, the path you've been on so far, and the path you want to follow in the future. Think in terms of an image or a theme you'd like to project. Are you academically gifted? An effective leader? A well-rounded professional with wide-ranging talents? A creative problem solver? A technical wizard? Writing your story is a valuable planning exercise that helps you think about where you want to go and how to present yourself to target employers.

What's your story? Employers will want to know where you've been and where you want to go.

MyBcommLab

- Access this chapter's simulation entitled Cover Letters & Resumes located at www.pearsoninternationaleditions .com/mybcommlab.

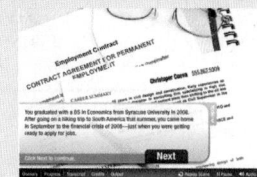

LEARNING TO THINK LIKE AN EMPLOYER

Now that you know your side of the hiring equation a little better, switch sides and look at it from an employer's perspective. To begin with, recognize that companies take risks with

Employers judge their recruiting success by *quality of hire*, and you can take steps to be—and look like—a high-quality hire.

every hiring decision—the risk that the person hired won't meet expectations and the risk that a better candidate has slipped through their fingers. Many companies judge the success of their recruiting efforts by *quality of hire*, a measure of how closely new employees meet the company's needs.[2] What steps can you take to present yourself as the low-risk, high-reward choice, as someone who can make a meaningful contribution to the organization?

Your perceived ability to perform the job is obviously an essential part of your potential quality as a new hire. However, hiring managers consider more than just your ability to handle the responsibilities you'll be given. They want to know if you'll be reliable and motivated, if you're somebody who "gets it" when it comes to being a professional in today's workplace. A great way to get inside the heads of corporate recruiters is to "eavesdrop" on their professional conversations by reading periodicals such as *Workforce Management* (www.workforce.com) and blogs such as Fistful of Talent (www.fistfuloftalent.com) and The HR Capitalist (www.hrcapitalist.com).

Follow the online conversations of professional recruiters to learn what their hot-button issues are.

RESEARCHING INDUSTRIES AND COMPANIES OF INTEREST

Learning more about professions, industries, and individual companies is easy with the library and online resources available to you. Don't limit your research to easily available sources, however. Companies are likely to be impressed by creative research, such as interviewing their customers to learn more about how the firm does business. "Detailed research, including talking to our customers, is so rare it will almost guarantee you get hired," explains the recruiting manager at Alcon Laboratories.[3]

Table 15.1 lists some of the many websites where you can learn more about companies and find job openings. Start with The Riley Guide, www.rileyguide.com, which offers

TABLE 15.1	**Selected Job-Search Websites**	
Website*	**URL**	**Highlights**
Riley Guide	www.rileyguide.com	Vast collection of links to both general and specialized job sites for every career imaginable; don't miss this one—it could save you hours of searching
TweetMyJobs.com	http://tweetmyjobs.com	The largest Twitter job board, with thousands of channels segmented by geography, job type, and industry
CollegeRecruiter.com	www.collegerecruiter.com	Focused on opportunities for graduates with less than three years of work experience
Monster	http://home.monster.com	One of the most popular job sites, with hundreds of thousands of openings, many from hard-to-find small companies; extensive collection of advice on the job search process
MonsterCollege	http://college.monster.com	Focused on job searches for new college grads; your school's career center site probably links here
CareerBuilder	www.careerbuilder.com	One of the largest job boards; affiliated with more than 150 newspapers around the country
Jobster	www.jobster.com	Uses social networking to link employers with job seekers
USAJOBS	www.usajobs.opm.gov	The official job search site for the U.S. government, featuring everything from jobs for economists to astronauts to border patrol agents
IMDiversity	www.imdiversity.com	Good resource on diversity in the workplace, with job postings from companies that have made a special commitment to promoting diversity in their workforces
Dice.com	www.dice.com	One of the best sites for high-technology jobs
Net-Temps	www.net-temps.com	Popular site for contractors and freelancers looking for short-term assignments
Internship Programs.com	http://internshipprograms.com	Posts listings from companies looking for interns in a wide variety of professions
Simply Hired Indeed	www.simplyhired.com www.indeed.com	Specialized search engines that look for job postings on hundreds of websites worldwide; they find many postings that aren't listed on job board sites such as Monster

Note: This list represents only a small fraction of the hundreds of job-posting sites and other resources available online; be sure to check with your college's career center for the latest information.

Sources: TweetMyJob.com, accessed 3 November 2011, http://tweetmyjob.com; The Riley Guide, accessed 3 November 2011, www.rileyguide.com; SimplyHired website, accessed 3 November 2011, www.simplyhired.com; Indeed website, accessed 3 November 2011, www.indeed.com; CollegeRecruiter.com, accessed 3 November 2011, www.collegerecruiter.com; Jobster website, accessed 3 November 2011, www.jobster.com; InternshipPrograms.com, accessed 3 November 2011, http://internshipprograms.com.

advice for online job searches as well as links to hundreds of specialized websites that post openings in specific industries and professions. Your college's career center placement office probably maintains an up-to-date list as well.

To learn more about contemporary business topics, peruse some of these leading business periodicals and newspapers with significant business sections (in some cases, you may need to go through your library's online databases to gain full access):

Wall Street Journal: http://online.wsj.com/public/us
New York Times: www.nyt.com
USA Today: www.usatoday.com
Bloomberg Businessweek: www.businessweek.com
Business 2.0: http://money.cnn.com/magazines/business2
Fast Company: www.fastcompany.com
Fortune: http://money.cnn.com/magazines/fortune
Forbes: www.forbes.com

Employers expect you to be familiar with important developments in their industries, so stay on top of business news.

In addition, thousands of bloggers, microbloggers, and podcasters offer news and commentary on the business world. To identify some that you might find helpful, start with directories such as Technorati (http://technorati.com/business) for blogs or Podcast Alley (www.podcastalley.com; select the "Business" genre) for podcasts. AllTop (http://alltop.com) is another good resource for finding people who write about topics that interest you. In addition to learning more about professions and opportunities, this research will help you get comfortable with the jargon and buzzwords currently in use in a particular field—including essential *keywords* to use in your résumé (see "Composing Your Résumé" on page 540).

TRANSLATING YOUR GENERAL POTENTIAL INTO A SPECIFIC SOLUTION FOR EACH EMPLOYER

An important aspect of the quality-of-hire challenge is trying to determine how well a candidate's attributes and experience will translate to the challenges of a specific position. As Jim Schaper, CEO of the Alpharetta, Georgia, software company Infor Global Solutions, puts it, "We try to determine if newly minted graduates can apply knowledge they've already gained."[4] Customizing your résumé to each job opening is an important step in showing employers that you will be a good fit. From your initial contact all the way through the interviewing process, in fact, you will have opportunities to impress recruiters by explaining how your general potential translates to the specific needs of the position.

An essential task in your job search is presenting your skills and accomplishments in a way that is relevant to the employer's business challenges.

For example, instead of following up with just a simple thank-you note after interviewing with Detroit-based InStar Services, Mary Berman offered a plan showing how she could help the company during her first 60 days on the job.[5] Berman could offer such a plan because she researched the company to find out its needs and she understands her own capabilities well enough to match them to those needs.

TAKING THE INITIATIVE TO FIND OPPORTUNITIES

When it comes to finding the right opportunities, the easiest ways are not always the most productive ones. The major job boards such as Monster and classified services such as Craigslist might have thousands of openings—but many thousands of job seekers are looking at and applying for these same openings. Moreover, posting job openings on these sites is often a company's last resort, after it has exhausted other possibilities.

Instead of searching through the same job openings as everyone else, take the initiative and go find opportunities. Identify the companies you want to work for and focus your efforts on them. Get in touch with their human resources departments (or individual managers if possible), describe what you can offer the company, and ask to be considered if any opportunities come up.[6] Your message might appear right when a company is busy looking for someone but hasn't yet advertised the opening to the outside world.

Don't hesitate to contact interesting companies even if they haven't advertised job openings to the public yet—they might be looking for somebody just like you.

Start thinking like a networker now; your classmates could turn out to be some of your most important business contacts.

Networking is a mutually beneficial activity, so look for opportunities to help others in some way.

BUILDING YOUR NETWORK

Networking is the process of making informal connections with mutually beneficial business contacts. Networking takes place wherever and whenever people communicate: at industry functions, at social gatherings, at alumni reunions—and all over the Internet, from LinkedIn and Twitter to Facebook and Google +. In addition to making connections through social media tools, you can get yourself noticed by company recruiters. Although the overall percentage of new hires identified through social media is still fairly small and varies across industries and job categories, a majority of companies now use social media to look for promising candidates.[7] As more candidates get connected and more companies use these media, the percentage of hires found via LinkedIn and other sites is likely to rise.

Networking is more essential than ever, because the vast majority of job openings are never advertised to the general public. To avoid the time and expense of sifting through thousands of applications and the risk of hiring complete strangers, most companies prefer to ask their employees for recommendations first.[8] The more people who know you, the better chance you have of being recommended for one of these hidden job openings.

Start building your network now, before you need it. Your classmates could end up being some of your most valuable contacts, if not right away then possibly later in your career. Then branch out by identifying people with similar interests in your target professions, industries, and companies. Read news sites, blogs, and other online sources. Follow industry leaders on Twitter. You can also follow individual executives at your target companies to learn about their interests and concerns.[9] Be on the lookout for career-oriented *Tweet-ups*, in which people who've connected on Twitter get together for in-person networking events. Connect with people on LinkedIn and Facebook, particularly in groups dedicated to particular career interests. Depending on the system and the settings on individual users' accounts, you may be able to introduce yourself via private messages. Just make sure you are respectful of people and don't take up much of their time.[10]

Participate in student business organizations, especially those with ties to professional organizations. Visit *trade shows* to learn about various industries and rub shoulders with people who work in those industries.[11] Don't overlook volunteering; you not only meet people but also demonstrate your ability to solve problems, manage projects, and lead others. You can do some good while creating a network for yourself.

Remember that networking is about people helping each other, not just about other people helping you. Pay close attention to networking etiquette: Try to learn something about the people you want to connect with, don't overwhelm others with too many messages or requests, be succinct in all your communication efforts, don't give out other people's names and contact information without their permission to do so, never email your résumé to complete strangers, don't assume you can send your résumé to everyone you meet, and remember to say thank you every time someone helps you.[12]

To become a valued network member, you need to be able to help others in some way. You may not have any influential contacts yet, but because you're actively researching a number of industries and trends in your own job search, you probably have valuable information you can share via your social networks, blog, or Twitter account. Or you might simply be able to connect one person with another who can help. The more you network, the more valuable you become in your network—and the more valuable your network becomes to you.

Finally, be aware that your online network reflects on who you are in the eyes of potential employers, so exercise some judgment in making connections. Also, some employers are beginning to contact people in a candidate's network for background information, even if the candidate doesn't list those people as references.[13]

SEEKING CAREER COUNSELING

Your college's career center probably offers a wide variety of services, including individual counseling, job fairs, on-campus interviews, and job listings. Counselors can give you advice on career planning and provide workshops in job search techniques, résumé preparation, job readiness training, interview techniques, self-marketing, and more.[14] You can also find career planning advice online. Many of the websites listed in Table 15.1 offer articles and online tests to help you choose a career path, identify essential skills, and prepare to enter the job market.

AVOIDING MISTAKES

While you're making all these positive moves to show employers you will be a quality hire, take care to avoid the simple blunders that can torpedo a job search, such as not catching mistakes in your résumé, misspelling the name of a manager you're writing to, showing up late for an interview, tweeting something unprofessional, leaving embarrassing images or messages open to public view on your social media accounts, failing to complete application forms correctly, asking for information that you can easily find yourself on a company's website, or making any other error that could flag you as someone who is careless, clueless, or disrespectful. For example, nearly half of all employers now check out candidates' social networking profiles—and a third have rejected candidates because of what they've found.[15]

To understand why even a minor mistake can hurt your chances, look at the situation from a recruiter's point of view. At KeyBank, for instance, a recruiter typically has 25 to 30 open positions at any given time.[16] If a hundred people are applying for each position—and the number can be much higher in a slow job market—a single recruiter could be considering 2,500 to 3,000 candidates at once. As recruiters work to narrow down the possibilities, even a seemingly inconsequential mistake on your part can give them a reason to bump you out of the candidate pool.

REAL-TIME UPDATES
Learn More by Reading This Article

Follow these people to a new career

Alison Doyle maintains a great list of career experts to follow on Twitter. Go to http://real-timeupdates.com/ebc10 and click on Learn More. If you are using MyBcommLab, you can access Real-Time Updates within each chapter or under Student Study Tools.

Don't overlook the many resources available through your college's career center.

Don't let a silly mistake knock you out of contention for a great job.

REAL-TIME UPDATES
Learn More by Reading This Article

Try these Facebook apps in your job search

These Facebook apps can supply automated job alerts, let you upload your résumé, and perform other helpful functions for your job search. Go to http://real-timeupdates.com/ebc10 and click on Learn More. If you are using MyBcommLab, you can access Real-Time Updates within each chapter or under Student Study Tools.

Planning a Résumé

Although you will create many messages during your career search, your résumé will be the most important document in this process. You will be able to use it directly in many instances, adapt it to a variety of uses such as an e-portfolio, and reuse pieces of it in social networking profiles and online application forms.

Writing a résumé is one of those projects that really benefits from multiple planning, writing, and completing sessions spread out over several days or weeks. You are trying to summarize a complex subject (yourself!) and present a compelling story to complete strangers in a brief document. Follow the three-step writing process (see Figure 15.1 on the next page) and give yourself plenty of time.

2 LEARNING OBJECTIVE

Explain the process of planning your résumé, including how to choose the best résumé organization.

ANALYZING YOUR PURPOSE AND AUDIENCE

A **résumé** is a structured summary of a person's education, employment background, and job qualifications. Before you begin writing a résumé, make sure you understand its true function—as a brief, persuasive business message intended to stimulate an employer's interest in meeting you and learning more about you (see Table 15.2). In other words, the purpose of a résumé is not to get you a job but rather to get you an interview.[17]

As you conduct your research on various professions, industries, companies, and individual managers, you will have a better perspective on your target readers and their

Once you view your résumé as a persuasive business message, it's easier to decide what should and shouldn't be in it.

1 Plan → **2 Write** → **3 Complete**

Analyze the Situation
Recognize that the purpose of your résumé is to get an interview, not to get a job.

Gather Information
Research target industries and companies so that you know what they're looking for in new hires; learn about various jobs and what to expect; learn about the hiring manager, if possible.

Select the Right Medium
Start with a traditional paper résumé and develop scannable, electronic plain-text, PDF, and online versions, as needed. Consider using PowerPoint and video for your e-portfolio.

Organize the Information
Choose an organizational model that highlights your strengths and downplays your shortcomings; use the chronological approach unless you have a strong reason not to.

Adapt to Your Audience
Plan your wording carefully so that you can catch a recruiter's eye within seconds; translate your education and experience into attributes that target employers find valuable.

Compose the Message
Write clearly and succinctly, using active, powerful language that is appropriate to the industries and companies you're targeting; use a professional tone in all communications.

Revise the Message
Evaluate content and review readability and then edit and rewrite for conciseness and clarity.

Produce the Message
Use effective design elements and suitable layout for a clean, professional appearance; seamlessly combine text and graphical elements. When printing, use quality paper and a good printer.

Proofread the Message
Review for errors in layout, spelling, and mechanics; mistakes can cost you interview opportunities.

Distribute the Message
Deliver your résumé, carefully following the specific instructions of each employer or job board website.

Figure 15.1   Three-Step Writing Process for Résumés
Following the three-step writing process will help you create a successful résumé in a short time. Remember to pay particular attention to the "you" attitude and presentation quality; your résumé will probably get tossed aside if it doesn't speak to audience needs or if it contains mistakes.

information needs. Learn as much as you can about the individuals who may be reading your résumé. Many professionals and managers are bloggers, Twitter users, and LinkedIn members, for example, so you can learn more about them online even if you've never met them. Any bit of information can help you craft a more effective message.

By the way, if employers ask to see your "CV," they're referring to your *curriculum vitae*, the term used instead of *résumé* in academic professions and in many countries outside

TABLE 15.2	Fallacies and Facts About Résumés
Fallacy	**Fact**
The purpose of a résumé is to list all your skills and abilities.	The purpose of a résumé is to kindle employer interest and generate an interview.
A good résumé will get you the job you want.	All a résumé can do is get you in the door.
Your résumé will always be read carefully and thoroughly.	In most cases, your résumé needs to make a positive impression within 30 or 45 seconds; only then will someone read it in detail. Moreover, it will likely be screened by a computer looking for keywords first—and if it doesn't contain the right keywords, a human being may never see it.
The more good information you present about yourself in your résumé, the better, so stuff your résumé with every positive detail you can think of.	Recruiters don't need that much information about you at the initial screening stage, and they probably won't read it.
If you want a really good résumé, have it prepared by a résumé service.	You have the skills needed to prepare an effective résumé, so prepare it yourself—unless the position is especially high level or specialized. Even then, you should check carefully before using a service.

the United States. Résumés and CVs are essentially the same, although CVs can be much more detailed. If you need to adapt a U.S.-style résumé to CV format, or vice versa, career expert Alison Doyle offers advice on her website, www.alisondoyle.com.

GATHERING PERTINENT INFORMATION

If you haven't been building an employment portfolio thus far, you may need to do some research on yourself. Gather all the pertinent personal history you can think of, including the dates, duties, and accomplishments from any previous jobs you've held. Compile relevant educational experience that adds to your qualifications—formal degrees, skills certificates, academic awards, or scholarships. Also, gather any relevant information about school or volunteer activities that might be relevant to your job search, including offices you have held in any club or professional organization, presentations given, and online or print publications. You probably won't use every piece of information you come up with, but you'll want to have it at your fingertips before you begin composing your résumé.

SELECTING THE BEST MEDIUM

You should expect to produce your résumé in several media and formats. "Producing Your Résumé" on page 545 explores the various options.

ORGANIZING YOUR RÉSUMÉ AROUND YOUR STRENGTHS

Although there are a number of ways to organize a résumé, most are some variation of chronological, functional, or a combination of the two. The right choice depends on your background and your goals, as the following sections explain.

The Chronological Résumé

In a **chronological résumé**, the work experience section dominates and is placed immediately after your contact information and introductory statement. The chronological approach is the most common way to organize a résumé, and many employers prefer this format because it presents your professional history in a clear, easy-to-follow arrangement.[18] If you're just graduating from college and have limited professional experience, you can vary this chronological approach by putting your educational qualifications before your experience.

> The chronological résumé is the most common approach, but it might not be right for you at this stage in your career.

Develop your work experience section by listing your jobs in reverse chronological order, beginning with the most recent one and giving more space to the most recent positions. For each job, start by listing the employer's name and location, your official job title, and the dates you held the position (write "to present" if you are still in your most recent job). Next, in a short block of text, highlight your accomplishments in a way that is relevant to your readers. Doing so may require "translating" the terminology used in a particular industry or profession into terms that are more meaningful to your target readers. If the general responsibilities of the position are not obvious from the job title, provide a little background to help readers understand what you did. See Figures 15.2 (page 536) and 15.3 (page 537) for examples of ineffective and effective approaches.

The Functional Résumé

A **functional résumé**, sometimes called a *skills résumé*, emphasizes your skills and capabilities, identifying employers and academic experience in subordinate sections. This arrangement stresses individual areas of competence rather than job history. The functional approach also has three advantages: (1) Without having to read through job descriptions, employers can see what you can do for them, (2) you can emphasize earlier job experience, and (3) you can deemphasize any lengthy unemployment or lack of career progress. However, you should be aware that because the functional résumé can obscure your work history, many employment professionals are suspicious of it.[19] If you don't believe the chronological format will work for you, consider the combination résumé instead.

> The functional résumé is often considered by people with limited or spotty employment history, but many employers are suspicious of this format.

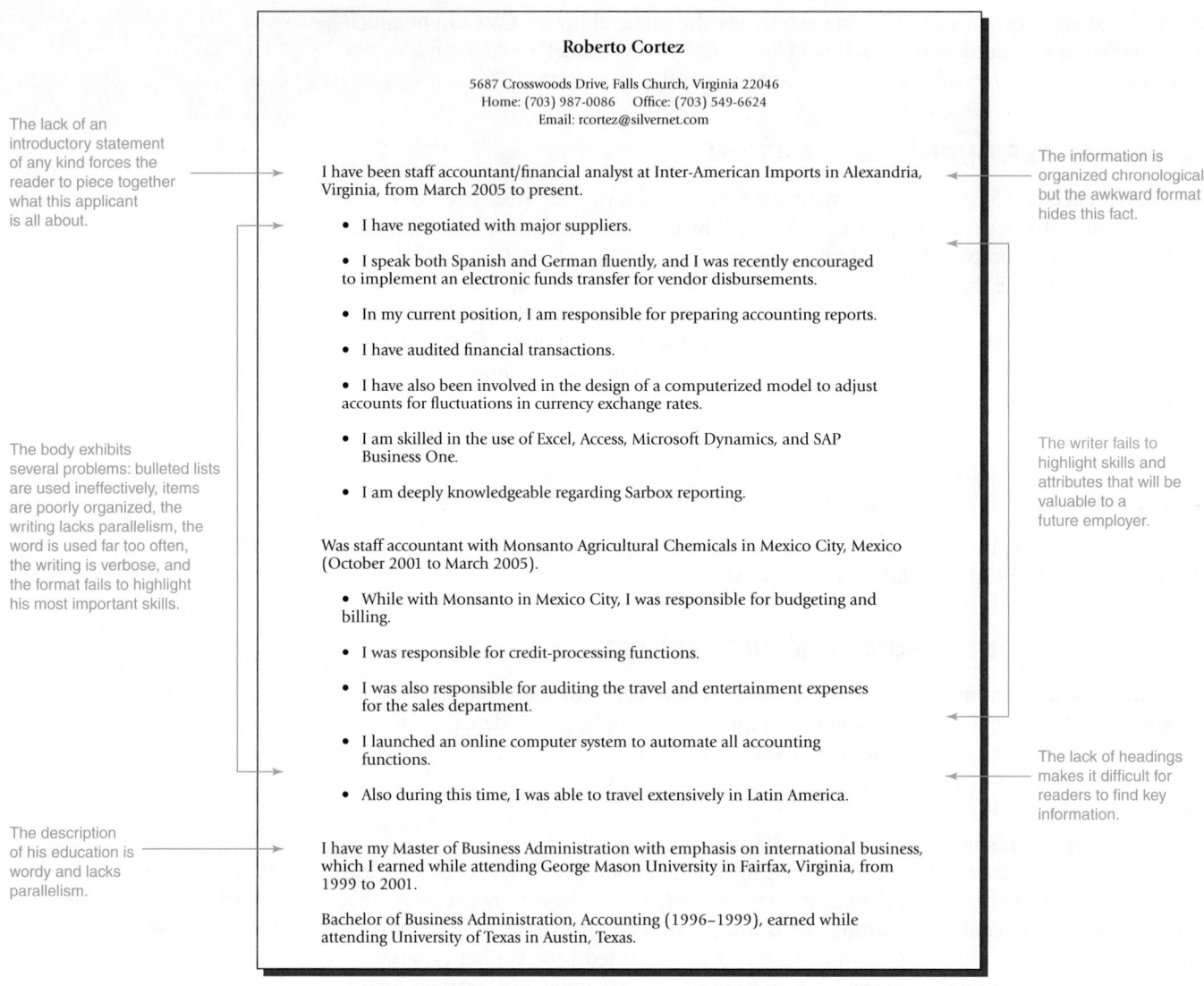

The lack of an introductory statement of any kind forces the reader to piece together what this applicant is all about.

The body exhibits several problems: bulleted lists are used ineffectively, items are poorly organized, the writing lacks parallelism, the word is used far too often, the writing is verbose, and the format fails to highlight his most important skills.

The description of his education is wordy and lacks parallelism.

The information is organized chronologically, but the awkward format hides this fact.

The writer fails to highlight skills and attributes that will be valuable to a future employer.

The lack of headings makes it difficult for readers to find key information.

Roberto Cortez

5687 Crosswoods Drive, Falls Church, Virginia 22046
Home: (703) 987-0086   Office: (703) 549-6624
Email: rcortez@silvernet.com

I have been staff accountant/financial analyst at Inter-American Imports in Alexandria, Virginia, from March 2005 to present.

- I have negotiated with major suppliers.

- I speak both Spanish and German fluently, and I was recently encouraged to implement an electronic funds transfer for vendor disbursements.

- In my current position, I am responsible for preparing accounting reports.

- I have audited financial transactions.

- I have also been involved in the design of a computerized model to adjust accounts for fluctuations in currency exchange rates.

- I am skilled in the use of Excel, Access, Microsoft Dynamics, and SAP Business One.

- I am deeply knowledgeable regarding Sarbox reporting.

Was staff accountant with Monsanto Agricultural Chemicals in Mexico City, Mexico (October 2001 to March 2005).

- While with Monsanto in Mexico City, I was responsible for budgeting and billing.

- I was responsible for credit-processing functions.

- I was also responsible for auditing the travel and entertainment expenses for the sales department.

- I launched an online computer system to automate all accounting functions.

- Also during this time, I was able to travel extensively in Latin America.

I have my Master of Business Administration with emphasis on international business, which I earned while attending George Mason University in Fairfax, Virginia, from 1999 to 2001.

Bachelor of Business Administration, Accounting (1996–1999), earned while attending University of Texas in Austin, Texas.

Figure 15.2   Ineffective Chronological Résumé
This chronological résumé exhibits a wide range of problems. The language is self-centered and unprofessional, and the organization forces the reader to dig out essential details—and today's recruiters don't have the time or the patience for that. Compare this with the improved version in Figure 15.3.

The Combination Résumé

If you don't have a lot of work history to show, consider a combination résumé to highlight your skills while still providing a chronological history of your employment.

A **combination résumé** meshes the skills focus of the functional format with the job history focus of the chronological format (see Figure 15.4 on page 538). The chief advantage of this format is that it allows you to focus attention on your capabilities when you don't have a long or steady employment history, without raising concerns that you might be hiding something about your past.

As you look at a number of sample résumés, you'll probably notice many variations on the three basic formats presented here. Study these other options in light of the effective communication principles you've learned in this course and the unique circumstances of your job search. If you find one that seems like the best fit for your unique situation, by all means use it.

ADDRESSING AREAS OF CONCERN

Frequent job changes and gaps in your work history are two of the more common issues that employers may perceive as weaknesses.

Many people have gaps in their careers or other issues that could be a concern for employers. Here are some common issues and suggestions for handling them in a résumé:[20]

- **Frequent job changes.** If you've had a number of short-term jobs of a similar type, such as independent contracting and temporary assignments, try to group them under

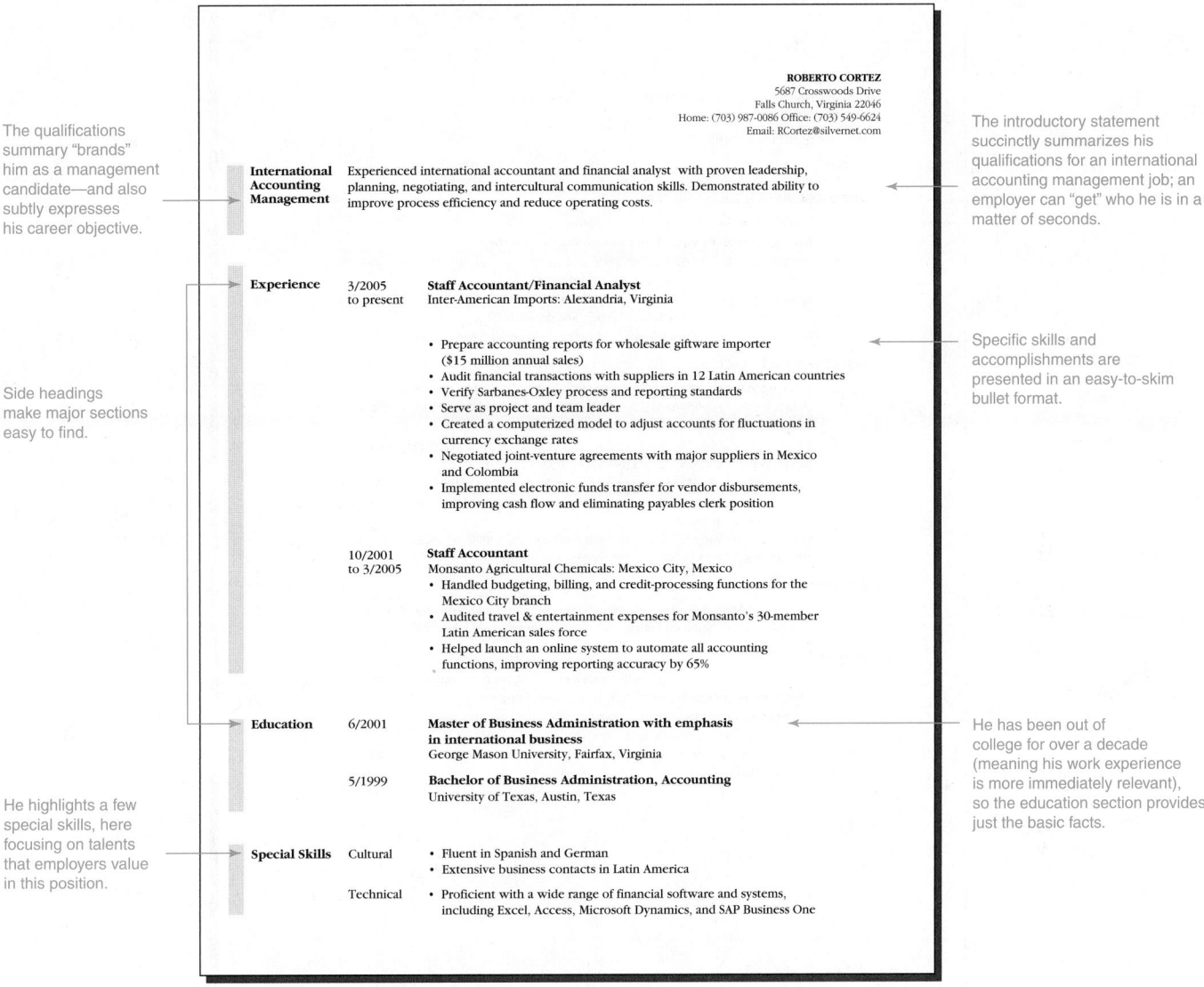

The qualifications summary "brands" him as a management candidate—and also subtly expresses his career objective.

Side headings make major sections easy to find.

He highlights a few special skills, here focusing on talents that employers value in this position.

The introductory statement succinctly summarizes his qualifications for an international accounting management job; an employer can "get" who he is in a matter of seconds.

Specific skills and accomplishments are presented in an easy-to-skim bullet format.

He has been out of college for over a decade (meaning his work experience is more immediately relevant), so the education section provides just the basic facts.

ROBERTO CORTEZ
5687 Crosswoods Drive
Falls Church, Virginia 22046
Home: (703) 987-0086 Office: (703) 549-6624
Email: RCortez@silvernet.com

International Accounting Management
Experienced international accountant and financial analyst with proven leadership, planning, negotiating, and intercultural communication skills. Demonstrated ability to improve process efficiency and reduce operating costs.

Experience
3/2005 to present
Staff Accountant/Financial Analyst
Inter-American Imports: Alexandria, Virginia

- Prepare accounting reports for wholesale giftware importer ($15 million annual sales)
- Audit financial transactions with suppliers in 12 Latin American countries
- Verify Sarbanes-Oxley process and reporting standards
- Serve as project and team leader
- Created a computerized model to adjust accounts for fluctuations in currency exchange rates
- Negotiated joint-venture agreements with major suppliers in Mexico and Colombia
- Implemented electronic funds transfer for vendor disbursements, improving cash flow and eliminating payables clerk position

10/2001 to 3/2005
Staff Accountant
Monsanto Agricultural Chemicals: Mexico City, Mexico
- Handled budgeting, billing, and credit-processing functions for the Mexico City branch
- Audited travel & entertainment expenses for Monsanto's 30-member Latin American sales force
- Helped launch an online system to automate all accounting functions, improving reporting accuracy by 65%

Education
6/2001
Master of Business Administration with emphasis in international business
George Mason University, Fairfax, Virginia

5/1999
Bachelor of Business Administration, Accounting
University of Texas, Austin, Texas

Special Skills
Cultural
- Fluent in Spanish and German
- Extensive business contacts in Latin America

Technical
- Proficient with a wide range of financial software and systems, including Excel, Access, Microsoft Dynamics, and SAP Business One

Figure 15.3 Effective Chronological Résumé
This version does a much better job of presenting the candidate's ability to contribute to a new employer. Notice in particular how easy it is to scan through this résumé to find sections of interest.

a single heading. Also, if past job positions were eliminated as a result of layoffs or mergers, find a subtle way to convey that information (if not in your résumé, then in your cover letter). Reasonable employers understand that many professionals have been forced to job hop by circumstances beyond their control.
- **Gaps in work history.** Mention relevant experience and education you gained during employment gaps, such as volunteer or community work.
- **Inexperience.** Mention related volunteer work and membership in professional groups. List relevant course work and internships.
- **Overqualification.** Tone down your résumé, focusing exclusively on the experience and skills that relate to the position.
- **Long-term employment with one company.** Itemize each position held at the firm to show both professional growth and career growth within the organization and increasing responsibilities along the way.
- **Job termination for cause.** Be honest with interviewers and address their concerns with proof, such as recommendations and examples of completed projects.
- **Criminal record.** You don't necessarily need to disclose a criminal record or time spent incarcerated on your résumé, but you may be asked about it on job application forms. Laws regarding what employers may ask (and whether they can conduct

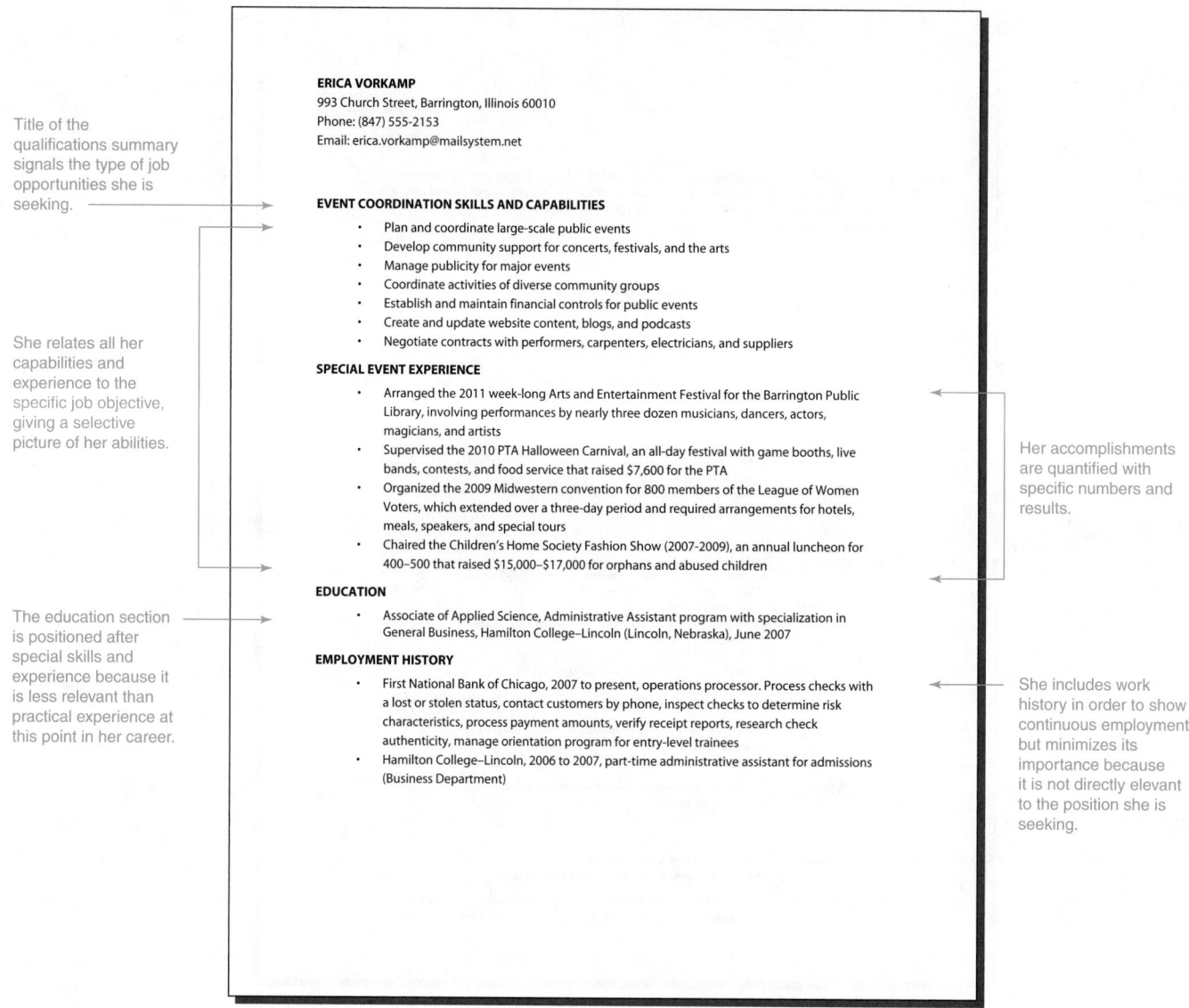

Title of the qualifications summary signals the type of job opportunities she is seeking.

She relates all her capabilities and experience to the specific job objective, giving a selective picture of her abilities.

The education section is positioned after special skills and experience because it is less relevant than practical experience at this point in her career.

ERICA VORKAMP
993 Church Street, Barrington, Illinois 60010
Phone: (847) 555-2153
Email: erica.vorkamp@mailsystem.net

EVENT COORDINATION SKILLS AND CAPABILITIES
- Plan and coordinate large-scale public events
- Develop community support for concerts, festivals, and the arts
- Manage publicity for major events
- Coordinate activities of diverse community groups
- Establish and maintain financial controls for public events
- Create and update website content, blogs, and podcasts
- Negotiate contracts with performers, carpenters, electricians, and suppliers

SPECIAL EVENT EXPERIENCE
- Arranged the 2011 week-long Arts and Entertainment Festival for the Barrington Public Library, involving performances by nearly three dozen musicians, dancers, actors, magicians, and artists
- Supervised the 2010 PTA Halloween Carnival, an all-day festival with game booths, live bands, contests, and food service that raised $7,600 for the PTA
- Organized the 2009 Midwestern convention for 800 members of the League of Women Voters, which extended over a three-day period and required arrangements for hotels, meals, speakers, and special tours
- Chaired the Children's Home Society Fashion Show (2007-2009), an annual luncheon for 400–500 that raised $15,000–$17,000 for orphans and abused children

EDUCATION
- Associate of Applied Science, Administrative Assistant program with specialization in General Business, Hamilton College–Lincoln (Lincoln, Nebraska), June 2007

EMPLOYMENT HISTORY
- First National Bank of Chicago, 2007 to present, operations processor. Process checks with a lost or stolen status, contact customers by phone, inspect checks to determine risk characteristics, process payment amounts, verify receipt reports, research check authenticity, manage orientation program for entry-level trainees
- Hamilton College–Lincoln, 2006 to 2007, part-time administrative assistant for admissions (Business Department)

Her accomplishments are quantified with specific numbers and results.

She includes work history in order to show continuous employment but minimizes its importance because it is not directly elevant to the position she is seeking.

Figure 15.4   Combination Résumé

With her limited work experience in her field of interest (event coordinator), Erica Vorkamp opted for a combination résumé to highlight her skills. Her employment history is complete and easy to find, but it isn't featured to the same degree as the other elements. Notice how she uses the title of the introductory statement to identify the job opportunities she is looking for.

MyBcommLab

Apply Figure 15.4's key concepts by revising a new document. Go to Chapter 15 in www.pearsoninternationaleditions.com/mybcommlab and select Document Makeovers.

a criminal background check) vary by state and profession, but if you are asked and the question applies to you, you are legally bound to answer truthfully. Use the interview process to explain any mitigating circumstances and to emphasize your rehabilitation and commitment to being a law-abiding, trustworthy employee.[21]

Writing a Résumé

3   LEARNING OBJECTIVE

Describe the tasks involved in writing your résumé, and list the major sections of a traditional résumé.

As you follow the three-step process to develop your résumé, keep four points in mind. First, treat your résumé with the respect it deserves. A single mistake or oversight can cost you interview opportunities. Second, give yourself plenty of time. Don't put off preparing your résumé until the last second and then try to write it in one sitting. Third, learn from good models. You can find sample résumés online at college websites and on job boards such as

Monster and CareerBuilder. Fourth, don't get frustrated by the conflicting advice you'll read about résumés. Résumés are as much art as science, and there is more than one way to be successful with them. Consider the alternatives and choose the approach that makes the most sense to you, given everything you know about successful business communication.

If you feel uncomfortable writing about yourself, you're not alone. Many people, even accomplished writers, find it difficult to write their own résumés. If you get stuck, find a classmate or friend who is also writing a résumé and swap projects for a while. By working on each other's résumés, you might be able to speed up the process for both of you.

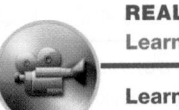

REAL-TIME UPDATES
Learn More by Watching This Video

Learn to use LinkedIn's résumé builder

See how to build and customize a résumé on LinkedIn and then use it on other social networking sites. Go to http://real-timeupdates.com/ebc10 and click on Learn More. If you are using MyBcommLab, you can access Real-Time Updates within each chapter or under Student Study Tools.

If you're uncomfortable writing your own résumé, see if you can trade with a classmate and write each other's résumé.

KEEPING YOUR RÉSUMÉ HONEST

Estimates vary, but one comprehensive study uncovered lies about work history in more than 40 percent of the résumés tested.[22] And dishonest applicants are getting bolder all the time—going so far as to buy fake diplomas online, pay computer hackers to insert their names into prestigious universities' graduation records, and sign up for services that offer phony employment verification.[23]

Applicants with integrity know they don't need to stoop to lying. If you are tempted to stretch the truth, bear in mind that professional recruiters have seen every trick in the book, and frustrated employers are working aggressively to uncover the truth. Nearly all employers do some form of background checking, from contacting references and verifying employment to checking criminal records and sending résumés through verification services.[24] Employers are also beginning to craft certain interview questions specifically to uncover dishonest résumé entries.[25]

More than 90 percent of companies that find lies on résumés refuse to hire the offending applicants, even if that means withdrawing formal job offers.[26] And if you do sneak past these filters and get hired, you'll probably be exposed on the job when you can't live up to your own résumé. Given the networked nature of today's job market, lying on a résumé could haunt you for years—and could force you to keep lying throughout your career to hide the original misrepresentations on your résumé.[27]

Résumé fraud has reached epidemic proportions, but employers are fighting back with more rigorous screening techniques.

ADAPTING YOUR RÉSUMÉ TO YOUR AUDIENCE

The importance of adapting your résumé to your target readers' needs and interests cannot be overstated. In a competitive job market, the more you look like a good fit, the better your chances of securing interviews. Address your readers' business concerns by showing how your capabilities meet the demands and expectations of the position and of the organization as a whole. For example, if you are applying for work in public relations (PR), you would need to know that an internal corporate PR department and an independent PR agency perform many of the same tasks, but the outside agency must also sell its services to multiple clients. Consequently, it needs employees who are skilled at attracting and keeping paying customers, in addition to being skilled at PR.

Adapting to your readers can mean customizing your résumé, sometimes for each job opening. However, the effort can pay off in more interviewing opportunities.

Use what you've learned about your target readers to express your experience using the terminology of the hiring organization. For instance, military experience can help you develop many skills that are valuable in business, but military terminology can sound like a foreign language to people who aren't familiar with it. Isolate the important general concepts and present them in common business language. Similarly, educational achievements in other countries might not align with the standard U.S. definitions of high schools, community colleges, technical and trade schools, and universities. If necessary, include a brief statement explaining how your degree or certificate relates to U.S. expectations—or how your U.S. degree relates to expectations in other countries, if you're applying for work abroad.

Translate your past accomplishments into a compelling picture of what you can do for employers in the future.

Military service and other specialized experiences may need to be "translated" into terms more readily understandable by your target readers.

COMPOSING YOUR RÉSUMÉ

Draft your résumé using short, crisp phrases built around strong verbs and nouns.

Write your résumé using a simple and direct style. Use short, crisp phrases instead of whole sentences and focus on what your reader needs to know. Avoid using the word *I*, which can sound both self-involved and repetitious by the time you outline all your skills and accomplishments. Instead, start your phrases with strong action verbs such as these:[28]

accomplished	assumed	coordinated	explored	initiated
achieved	budgeted	created	forecasted	installed
administered	chaired	demonstrated	generated	introduced
approved	changed	developed	identified	investigated
arranged	compiled	directed	implemented	joined
assisted	completed	established	improved	launched
maintained	participated	recommended	set up	supervised
managed	performed	reduced	simplified	systematized
motivated	planned	reorganized	sparked	targeted
operated	presented	resolved	streamlined	trained
organized	proposed	saved	strengthened	transformed
oversaw	raised	served	succeeded	upgraded

For instance, you might say, "Created a campus organization for students interested in entrepreneurship" or "Managed a fast-food restaurant and four employees." Whenever you can, quantify the results so that your claims don't come across as empty puffery. Don't just say you're a team player or detail oriented—show you are by offering concrete proof.[29] Here are some examples of phrasing accomplishments using active statements that show results:

Avoid Weak Statements	Use Active Statements That Show Results
Responsible for developing a new filing system	Developed a new filing system that reduced paperwork by 50 percent
I was in charge of customer complaints and all ordering problems	Handled all customer complaints and resolved all product order discrepancies
I won a trip to Europe for opening the most new customer accounts in my department	Generated the highest number of new customer accounts in my department
Member of special campus task force to resolve student problems with existing cafeteria assignments	Assisted in implementing new campus dining program that balances student wishes with cafeteria capacity

Providing specific supporting evidence is vital but make sure you don't go overboard with small details.[30]

Include relevant *keywords* in your introductory statement, work history, and education sections.

In addition to clear writing with specific examples, the particular words and phrases you use throughout your résumé are critically important. The majority of résumés are now subjected to *keyword searches* in an applicant tracking system or other database, in which a recruiter searches for résumés most likely to match the requirements of a particular job. Résumés that don't match the requirements closely may never be seen by a human reader, so it is essential to use the words and phrases that a recruiter is most likely to search for. (Although most experts used to advise including a separate *keyword summary* as a standalone list, the trend nowadays is to incorporate your keywords into your introductory statement and other sections of your résumé.)[31]

Identifying these keywords requires some research, but you can uncover many of them while you are researching various industries and companies (see page 530). The trick is to study job descriptions carefully and to understand your target audience's needs. In contrast to the action verbs that catch a human reader's attention, keywords that catch a computer's attention are usually nouns that describe the specific skills, attributes, and experiences an employer is looking for in a candidate. Keywords can include the business and technical terms associated with a specific profession, industry-specific jargon, names or types of products or systems used in a profession, job titles, and college degrees.[32] Follow the Real-Time Updates link on this page to see a helpful list of ideas for compiling keywords for your career search.

Finally, beware of clichés that are used on so many résumés and social media profiles that they've probably lost most of their impact. For example, LinkedIn recently identified these 10 buzzwords and phrases as the most overused: *extensive experience, innovative, motivated, results-oriented, dynamic, proven track record, team player, fast-paced, problem solver,* and *entrepreneurial*.[33] Instead of *saying* you are all these things, *show* how you are, using solid evidence.

REAL-TIME UPDATES
Learn More by Reading This Article

Find the keywords that will light up your résumé

This list of tips and tools will help you find the right keywords to customize your résumé for every opportunity. Go to http://real-timeupdates.com/ebc10 and click on Learn More. If you are using MyBcommLab, you can access Real-Time Updates within each chapter or under Student Study Tools.

Name and Contact Information

Your name and contact information constitute the heading of your résumé; include the following:

- Name
- Physical address (both permanent and temporary, if you're likely to move during the job search process; however, if you're posting a résumé in an unsecured location online, leave off your physical address for security purposes)
- Phone number(s)
- Email address
- The URL of your personal webpage, e-portfolio, or social media résumé (if you have one)

Be sure that everything in your résumé heading is well organized and clearly laid out on the page.

If the only email address you have is through your current employer, get a free personal email address from one of the many services that offer them. It's not fair to your current employer to use company resources for a job search, and it sends a bad signal to potential employers. Also, if your personal email address is anything like precious.princess@ something.com or PsychoDawg@something.com, get a new email address for your business correspondence.

> Be sure to provide complete and accurate contact information; mistakes in this section of the résumé are surprisingly common.

> Get a professional-sounding email address for business correspondence (such as firstname.lastname@something .com), if you don't already have one.

Introductory Statement

Of all the parts of a résumé, the brief introductory statement that follows your name and contact information probably generates the most disagreement. You can put one of three things here:[34]

- **Career objective.** A career objective identifies either a specific job you want to land or a general career track you would like to pursue. Some experts advise against including a career objective because it can categorize you so narrowly that you miss out on interesting opportunities, and it is essentially about fulfilling your desires, not about meeting the employer's needs. In the past, most résumés included a career objective, but in recent years more job seekers are using a qualifications summary or a career summary. However, if you have little or no work experience in your target profession, a career objective might be your best option. If you do opt for an objective, word it in a way that relates your qualifications to employer needs. Avoid such self-absorbed statements as "A fulfilling position that provides ample opportunity for career growth and personal satisfaction."
- **Qualifications summary.** A qualifications summary offers a brief view of your key qualifications. The goal is to let a reader know within a few seconds what you can deliver. You can title this section generically as "Qualifications Summary" or "Summary of Qualifications," or if you have one dominant qualification, you can use that as the title (see the career summary in Figure 15.4 on page 538 for an example). Consider using a qualifications summary if you have one or more important qualifications but don't yet have a long career history. Also, if you haven't been working long but your

> You can choose to open with a career objective, a qualifications summary, or a career summary.

> If you have a reasonably focused skill set but don't yet have a long career history, a qualifications summary is probably the best type of introductory statement for you.

college education has given you a dominant professional "theme," such as multimedia design or statistical analysis, you can craft a qualifications summary that highlights your educational preparedness.

- **Career summary.** A career summary offers a brief recap of your career, with the goal of presenting increasing levels of responsibility and performance. A career summary can be particularly useful for executives who have demonstrated the ability to manage increasingly larger and more complicated business operations—a key consideration when companies look to hire upper-level managers.

Education

If you are early in your career, your education is probably your strongest selling point.

If you're still in college or have recently graduated, education is probably your strongest selling point. Present your educational background in depth, choosing facts that support your "theme." Give this section a heading such as "Education," "Technical Training," or "Academic Preparation," as appropriate. Then, starting with the most recent, list the name and location of each school you have attended, the month and year of your graduation (say "anticipated graduation in _____" if you haven't graduated yet), your major and minor fields of study, significant skills and abilities you've developed in your course work, and the degrees or certificates you've earned. If you're still working toward a degree, include in parentheses the expected date of completion. Showcase your qualifications by listing courses that have directly equipped you for the job you are seeking and indicate any scholarships, awards, or academic honors you've received.

The education section should also include relevant training sponsored by business or government organizations. Mention high school or military training only if the associated achievements are pertinent to your career goals.

Whether you list your grade point average depends on the job you want and the quality of your grades. If you don't show your GPA on your résumé—and there's no rule saying you have to—be prepared to answer questions about it during the interview process because many employers will assume that your GPA is not spectacular if you didn't list it on your résumé. If you choose to show a grade point average, be sure to mention the scale, especially if it isn't a four-point scale. If your grades are better within your major than in other courses, you can also list your GPA as "Major GPA" and include only those courses within your major.

Work Experience, Skills, and Accomplishments

When you describe past job responsibilities, identify the skills and knowledge that you can apply to a future job.

Devote the most space to jobs that are related to your target position.

Like the education section, the work experience section should focus on your overall theme in a way that shows how your past can contribute to an employer's future. Use keywords to call attention to the skills you've developed on the job and to your ability to handle increasing responsibility.

List your jobs in reverse chronological order, starting with the most recent. Include military service and any internships and part-time or temporary jobs related to your career objective. Include the name and location of the employer, and if readers are unlikely to recognize the organization, briefly describe what it does. When you want to keep the name of your current employer confidential, you can identify the firm by industry only ("a large video game developer"). If an organization's name or location has changed since you worked there, state the current name and location and include the old information preceded by "formerly. . . ." Before or after each job listing, state your job title and give the years you worked in the job; use the phrase "to present" to denote current employment. Indicate whether a job was part time.

Devote the most space to the jobs that are related to your target position. If you were personally responsible for something significant, be sure to mention it. Facts about your skills and accomplishments are the most important information you can give a prospective employer, so quantify them whenever possible.

REAL-TIME UPDATES
Learn More by Reading This Article

Watch a résumé pro rework an introductory statement

Whichever style of introductory statement you choose to include, it must be concise, concrete, and reader-focused. Follow the revisions in this real-life example to see how to craft an effective statement. Go to http://real-timeupdates.com/ebc10 and click on Learn More. If you are using MyBcommLab, you can access Real-Time Updates within each chapter or under Student Study Tools.

One helpful exercise is to write a 30-second "commercial" for each major skill you want to highlight. The commercial should offer proof that you really do possess the skill. For your résumé, distill the commercials down to brief phrases; you can use the more detailed proof statements in cover letters and as answers to interview questions.[35]

If you have had a number of part-time, temporary, or entry-level jobs that don't relate to your career objective, you have to use your best judgment when it comes to including or excluding them. Too many minor and irrelevant work details can clutter your résumé, particularly if you've been in the professional workforce for a few years. However, if you don't have a long employment history, including these jobs shows your ability and willingness to keep working.

Activities and Achievements

Include activities and achievements outside of a work context only if they make you a more attractive job candidate. For example, traveling, studying, or working abroad and fluency in multiple languages could weigh heavily in your favor with employers who do business internationally.

Include personal accomplishments if they suggest special skills or qualities that are relevant to the jobs you're seeking.

Because many employers are involved in their local communities, they tend to look positively on applicants who are active and concerned members of their communities as well. Consider including community service activities that suggest leadership, teamwork, communication skills, technical aptitude, or other valuable attributes.

You should generally avoid indicating membership or significant activity in religious or political organizations (unless, of course, you're applying to such an organization) because doing so might raise concerns for people with differing beliefs or affiliations. However, if you want to highlight skills you developed while involved with such a group, you can refer to it generically as a "not-for-profit organization."

Finally, if you have little or no job experience and not much to discuss outside of your education, indicating involvement in athletics or other organized student activities lets employers know that you don't spend all your free time hanging around your apartment playing video games. Also consider mentioning publications, projects, and other accomplishments that required relevant business skills.

Personal Data and References

In nearly all instances, your résumé should not include any personal data beyond the information described in the previous sections. When applying to U.S. companies, never include any of the following: physical characteristics, age, gender, marital status, sexual orientation, religious or political affiliations, race, national origin, salary history, reasons for leaving jobs, names of previous supervisors, names of references, Social Security number, or student ID number.

When applying to U.S. companies, your résumé should not include any personal data such as age, marital status, physical description, or Social Security number.

Note that standards can vary in other countries. For example, you might be expected to include your citizenship, nationality, or marital status.[36] However, verify such requirements before including any personal data.

The availability of references is usually assumed, so you don't need to put "References available upon request" at the end of your résumé. However, be sure to have a list of several references ready when you begin applying for jobs. Prepare your reference sheet with your name and contact information at the top. For a finished look, use the same design and layout you use for your résumé. Then list three or four people who have agreed to serve as references. Include each person's name, job title, organization, address, telephone number, email address (if the reference prefers to be contacted by email), and the nature of your relationship.

Prepare a list of references but don't include them on your résumé.

Completing a Résumé

 LEARNING OBJECTIVE

Characterize the completing step for résumés, including the six most common formats in which you can produce a résumé.

Completing your résumé involves revising it for optimum quality, producing it in the various forms and media you'll need, and proofreading it for any errors before distributing it or publishing it online. Producing and distributing a résumé used to be fairly straightforward;

SHARPENING YOUR CAREER SKILLS

Don't. Just Don't.

Even though employment recruiters might think they've seen it all by now, innovative job applicants still keep finding new ways to get their résumés tossed into the recycling bin. Here are a few examples for your amusement—and warning, if you're inclined to share a little too much information:

- The passing of a beloved pet is never easy, but should grief over a departed cat keep someone out of the workforce for three months? That's how one job applicant explained a three-month gap in his employment history.
- One applicant's résumé arrived in an envelope that had a picture of a car on it, along with an explanation saying it would be a gift for the hiring manager.
- A person's family medical history is obviously important to him or her, but it's not something to put on a résumé, as one job seeker did, for reasons unknown.
- In a valiant effort to cram as many mistakes as possible onto a single page, one creative candidate included a full body photo of herself—in thigh-high boots, no less—and used oversized, fluorescent pink paper. This résumé probably did look pretty as it fluttered off a recruiter's desk into the recycling bin.
- Expressing strong interest in a job is good, but not if that interest is expressed like this: "to keep my parole officer from putting me back in jail."

- One applicant's mother was proud of her, to be sure, but including a letter from her with a résumé made the applicant look like, well, a child.

These cringe-inducing blunders are worth more than a quick chuckle: They're a great reminder of why it is crucial to understand the purpose of a résumé and the effect a résumé has on hiring managers.

CAREER APPLICATIONS

1. Is it a good idea to "show some personality" in your résumé? Explain your answer.
2. How should you handle the employment section of your résumé if you really did take three months off work to grieve the loss of a pet?

Sources: Adapted from Rosemary Haefner, "Biggest Resume Mistakes," CNN.com, 21 May 2007, www.cnn.com; Sue Campbell, "Eight Worst Resume Mistakes," 1st-Writer.com, www.1st-writer.com; "150 Funniest Resume Mistakes, Bloopers, and Blunders Ever," The Best Article Every Day blog, 2 June 2008, www.bspcn.com; "Hiring Managers Share Top 12 Wackiest Resume Blunders in New CareerBuilder.com Survey," CareerBuilder.com, 25 April 2007, www.careerbuilder.com.

---

you printed it on quality paper and mailed or faxed it to employers. However, the advent of **applicant tracking systems** (databases that let managers sort through incoming applications to find the most promising candidates), social media, and other innovations has dramatically changed the nature of résumé production and distribution. Be prepared to produce several versions of your résumé, in multiple formats and multiple media.

Even if most or all of your application efforts take place online, starting with a traditional paper résumé is still useful, for several reasons. First, a traditional printed résumé is a great opportunity to organize your background information and identify your unique strengths. Second, the planning and writing tasks involved in creating a conventional résumé will help you generate blocks of text that you can reuse in multiple ways throughout the job search process. Third, you'll never know when someone might ask for your résumé during a networking event or other in-person encounter, and you don't want to let that interest fade in the time it might take for the person to get to your information online.

Most of your application efforts will take place online, but starting with a traditional paper résumé is still useful.

REVISING YOUR RÉSUMÉ

Avoid the common errors that will get your résumé excluded from consideration.

Ask professional recruiters to list the most common mistakes they see on résumés, and you'll hear the same things over and over again. Keep your résumé out of the recycling bin by avoiding these flaws:

- Too long or too wordy
- Too short or sketchy
- Difficult to read
- Poorly written
- Displaying weak understanding of the business world in general or of a particular industry or company

- Poor-quality printing or cheap paper
- Full of spelling and grammar errors
- Boastful
- Gimmicky design

The ideal length of your résumé depends on the depth of your experience and the level of the positions for which you are applying. As a general guideline, if you have fewer than 10 years of professional experience, try to keep a conventional printed résumé to one page. Recruiters appreciate brevity, and presenting yourself in a single page shows your ability to write concise, focused, audience-oriented messages.[37] For online résumé formats, you can always provide links to additional information. If you have more experience and are applying for a higher-level position, you may need to prepare a somewhat longer résumé.[38] For highly technical positions, longer résumés are often the norm as well because the qualifications for such jobs can require more description.

If your employment history is brief, keep your résumé to one page.

PRODUCING YOUR RÉSUMÉ

No matter how many media and formats you eventually choose for producing your résumé, a clean, professional-looking design is a must. Unless you have some experience in graphic design and you're applying in a field such as advertising or retail merchandising, where visual creativity is viewed as an asset, resist the urge to "get creative" with your résumé layout.[39] Recruiters and hiring managers want to skim your essential information in a matter of seconds, and anything that distracts or delays them will work against you. Moreover, complex layouts can confuse an applicant tracking system, which can result in your information getting garbled.

Effective résumé designs are simple, clean, and professional— not gaudy, "clever," or cute.

Fortunately, good résumé design is not difficult to achieve. As you can see in Figures 15.3 and 15.4, good designs feature simplicity, order, effective use of white space, and clear typefaces. If your résumé will be viewed online in any format, use a typeface such as Georgia, which was designed for on-screen display, rather than the traditional Times New Roman, which was designed for printing and doesn't render as sharply on screen.[40] Make subheadings easy to find and easy to read, placing them either above each section or in the left margin. Use lists to itemize your most important qualifications. Color is not necessary by any means, but if you add color, make it subtle and sophisticated, such as a thin horizontal line under your name and address. The most common way to get into trouble with résumé design is going overboard (see Figure 15.5 on the next page).

Depending on the companies you apply to, you might want to produce your résumé in as many as six formats (all are explained in the following sections):

Be prepared to produce several versions of your résumé in multiple media.

- Printed traditional résumé
- Printed scannable résumé
- Electronic plain-text file
- Microsoft Word file
- Online résumé, also called a multimedia résumé or social media résumé
- PDF file

Unfortunately, there is no single format or medium that works for all the situations you will encounter, and employer expectations continue to change as technology evolves. Find out what each employer or job posting website expects, and provide your résumé in that specific format.

As you produce your résumé in various formats, you will encounter the question of whether to include a photograph of yourself on or with your résumé. For print or electronic documents that you will be submitting to employers or job websites, the safest advice is to avoid photos. The reason is that seeing visual cues of the age, ethnicity, and gender of candidates early in the selection process exposes employers to complaints of discriminatory hiring practices. In fact, some employers won't even look at résumés that include photos, and some applicant tracking systems automatically discard résumés with any kind of extra files.[41] However, photographs are acceptable for social media résumés and other online formats where you are not actually submitting a résumé to an employer.

Do not include or enclose a photo in résumés that you send to employers or post on job websites.

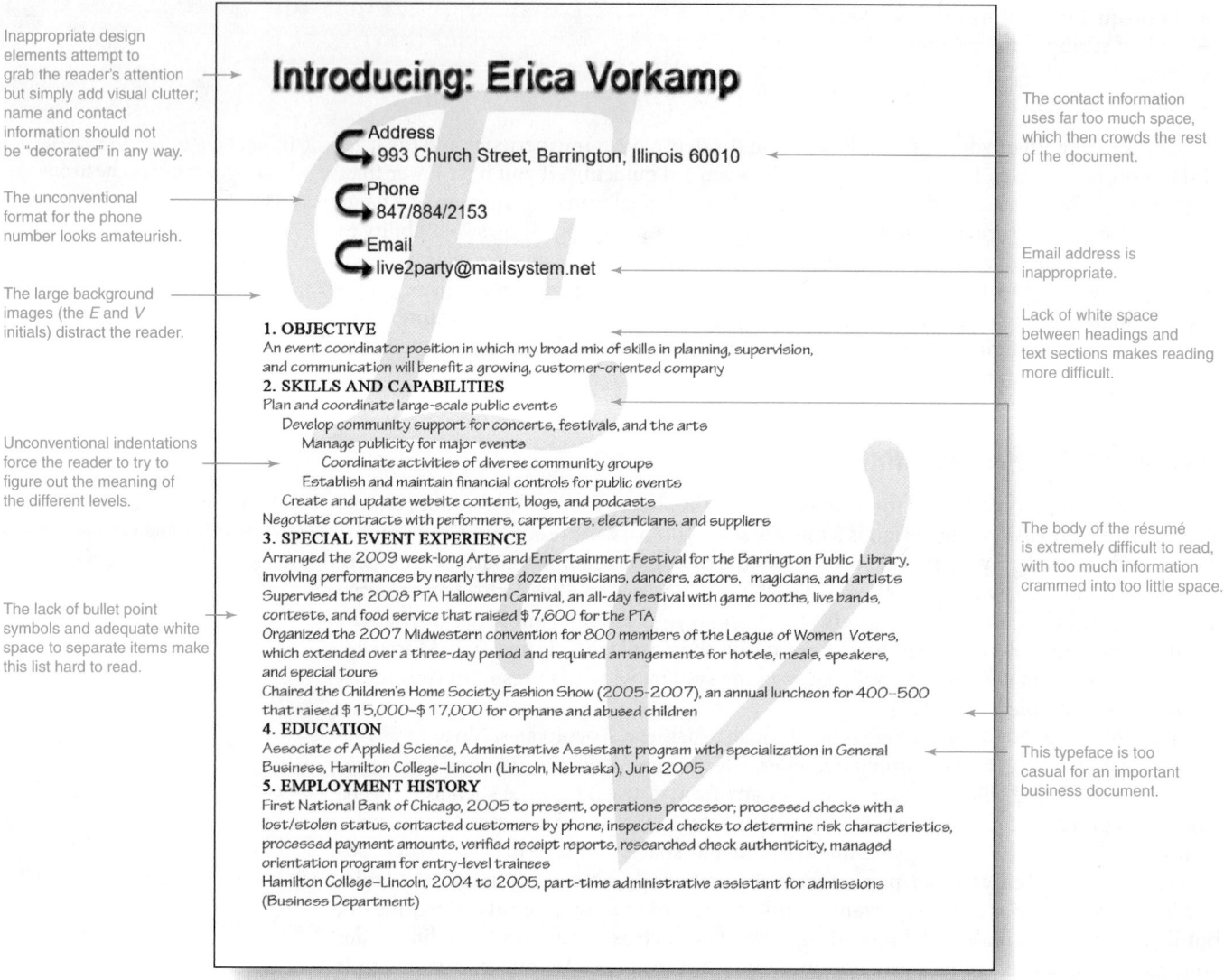

Inappropriate design elements attempt to grab the reader's attention but simply add visual clutter; name and contact information should not be "decorated" in any way.

The unconventional format for the phone number looks amateurish.

The large background images (the *E* and *V* initials) distract the reader.

Unconventional indentations force the reader to try to figure out the meaning of the different levels.

The lack of bullet point symbols and adequate white space to separate items make this list hard to read.

The contact information uses far too much space, which then crowds the rest of the document.

Email address is inappropriate.

Lack of white space between headings and text sections makes reading more difficult.

The body of the résumé is extremely difficult to read, with too much information crammed into too little space.

This typeface is too casual for an important business document.

Introducing: Erica Vorkamp

Address
993 Church Street, Barrington, Illinois 60010

Phone
847/884/2153

Email
live2party@mailsystem.net

1. OBJECTIVE
An event coordinator position in which my broad mix of skills in planning, supervision, and communication will benefit a growing, customer-oriented company

2. SKILLS AND CAPABILITIES
Plan and coordinate large-scale public events
Develop community support for concerts, festivals, and the arts
Manage publicity for major events
Coordinate activities of diverse community groups
Establish and maintain financial controls for public events
Create and update website content, blogs, and podcasts
Negotiate contracts with performers, carpenters, electricians, and suppliers

3. SPECIAL EVENT EXPERIENCE
Arranged the 2009 week-long Arts and Entertainment Festival for the Barrington Public Library, involving performances by nearly three dozen musicians, dancers, actors, magicians, and artists
Supervised the 2008 PTA Halloween Carnival, an all-day festival with game booths, live bands, contests, and food service that raised $7,600 for the PTA
Organized the 2007 Midwestern convention for 800 members of the League of Women Voters, which extended over a three-day period and required arrangements for hotels, meals, speakers, and special tours
Chaired the Children's Home Society Fashion Show (2005-2007), an annual luncheon for 400-500 that raised $15,000-$17,000 for orphans and abused children

4. EDUCATION
Associate of Applied Science, Administrative Assistant program with specialization in General Business, Hamilton College-Lincoln (Lincoln, Nebraska), June 2005

5. EMPLOYMENT HISTORY
First National Bank of Chicago, 2005 to present, operations processor; processed checks with a lost/stolen status, contacted customers by phone, inspected checks to determine risk characteristics, processed payment amounts, verified receipt reports, researched check authenticity, managed orientation program for entry-level trainees
Hamilton College-Lincoln, 2004 to 2005, part-time administrative assistant for admissions (Business Department)

Figure 15.5   Ineffective Résumé Design
This résumé tries too hard to be creative and eye-catching, resulting in a document that is difficult to read—and that probably won't get read. Recruiters have seen every conceivable design gimmick, so don't try to stand out from the crowd with unusual design. Instead, provide compelling, employer-focused information that is easy to find.

MyBcommLab

Apply Figure 15.5's key concepts by revising a new document. Go to Chapter 15 in www.pearsoninternationaleditions.com/mybcommlab and select Document Makeovers.

In addition to these six main formats, some applicants create PowerPoint presentations, videos, or even infographics to supplement a conventional résumé. Two key advantages of a PowerPoint supplement are flexibility and multimedia capabilities. For instance, you can present a menu of choices on the opening screen and allow viewers to click through to sections of interest. (Note that most of the things you can accomplish with PowerPoint can be done with an online résumé, which is probably more convenient for most readers.)

A video résumé can be a compelling supplement as well, but be aware that some employment law experts advise employers not to view videos, at least not until after candidates have been evaluated solely on their credentials. The reason for this caution is the same as with photographs. In addition, videos are more cumbersome to evaluate than paper or electronic résumés, and some recruiters refuse to watch them.[42] However, not all companies share this concern over videos, so you'll have to research their individual preferences. In fact, Zappos (see page 560) actually encourages applicant videos and provides a way to upload videos on its job application webpage.[43]

Rather than following any conventional textual structure, an infographic résumé attempts to convey a person's career development and skill set graphically through a visual metaphor such as a timeline or subway map or as a poster with an array of individual elements (see Figure 15.6 on the next page). A well-designed infographic could be an intriguing element of the job-search package for candidates in certain situations and professions because it can definitely stand out from traditional résumés and can show a high level of skill in visual communication. However, infographics are likely to be incompatible with most applicant tracking systems and with the screening habits of most recruiters, so while you might stand out with an infographic, you might also get tossed out if you try to use an infographic in place of a conventional résumé. In addition, successful infographics require skills in graphical design, and if you lack those skills, you'll need to hire a designer.

If you're applying for work in a graphics or design-related field, definitely consider an infographic as an element in your package because it can demonstrate some of the key talents that will be expected from people in your line of work. If you're applying in other fields, consider whether a visual approach might help you stand out or communicate key strengths in ways that a conventional résumé can't. In virtually every situation, however, an infographic should complement a conventional résumé, not replace it.

Producing a Traditional Printed Résumé

The traditional paper résumé still has a place in this world of electronic job searches, if only to have a few copies ready whenever one of your networking contacts asks for one. Avoid basic, low-cost white bond paper intended for general office use and gimmicky papers with borders and backgrounds. Choose a heavier, higher-quality paper designed specifically for résumés and other important documents. White or slightly off-white is the best color choice. This paper is more expensive than general office paper, but you don't need much, and it's a worthwhile investment.

Use high-quality paper when printing your résumé.

When you're ready to print your résumé, use a well-maintained, quality printer. Don't tolerate any streaks, stray lines, or poor print quality. You wouldn't walk into an interview looking messy, so make sure your résumé doesn't look that way, either.

Printing a Scannable Résumé

You might encounter a company that prefers *scannable résumés*, a type of printed résumé that is specially formatted to be compatible with optical scanning systems that convert printed documents to electronic text. These systems were quite common just a few years ago, but their use appears to be declining rapidly as more employers prefer email delivery or website application forms.[44] A scannable résumé differs from the traditional format in two major ways: it should always include a keyword summary, and it should be formatted in a simpler fashion that avoids underlining, special characters, and other elements that can confuse the scanning system. If you need to produce a scannable résumé, search online for "formatting a scannable résumé" to get detailed instructions.

Some employers still prefer résumés in scannable format, but most now want electronic submissions.

Creating a Plain-Text File of Your Résumé

A *plain-text file* (sometimes known as an ASCII text file) is an electronic version of your résumé that has no font formatting, no bullet symbols, no colors, no lines or boxes, or other special formatting. The plain-text version can be used in two ways. First, you can include it in the body of an email message, for employers who want email delivery but don't want file attachments. Second, you can copy and paste the sections into the application forms on an employer's website.

A plain-text version of your résumé is simply a computer file without any of the formatting that you typically apply using a word processor.

A plain-text version is easy to create with your word processor. Start with the file you used to create your résumé, use the "Save As" choice to save it as "plain text" or whichever similarly labeled option your software has, and verify the result by using a basic text editor (such as Microsoft Notepad). If necessary, reformat the page manually, moving text and inserting space as needed. For simplicity's sake, left-justify all your headings rather than trying to center them manually.

Make sure you verify the plain-text file that you create with your word processor; it might need a few manual adjustments using a text editor such as NotePad.

Creating a Word File of Your Résumé

In some cases, an employer or job-posting website will want you to upload a Microsoft Word file or attach it to an email message. (Although there are certainly other word processors on the market, Microsoft Word is the de facto standard in business these days.) This method of transferring information preserves the design and layout of your résumé and

Some employers and websites want your résumé in Microsoft Word format; make sure your computer is thoroughly scanned for viruses first, however.

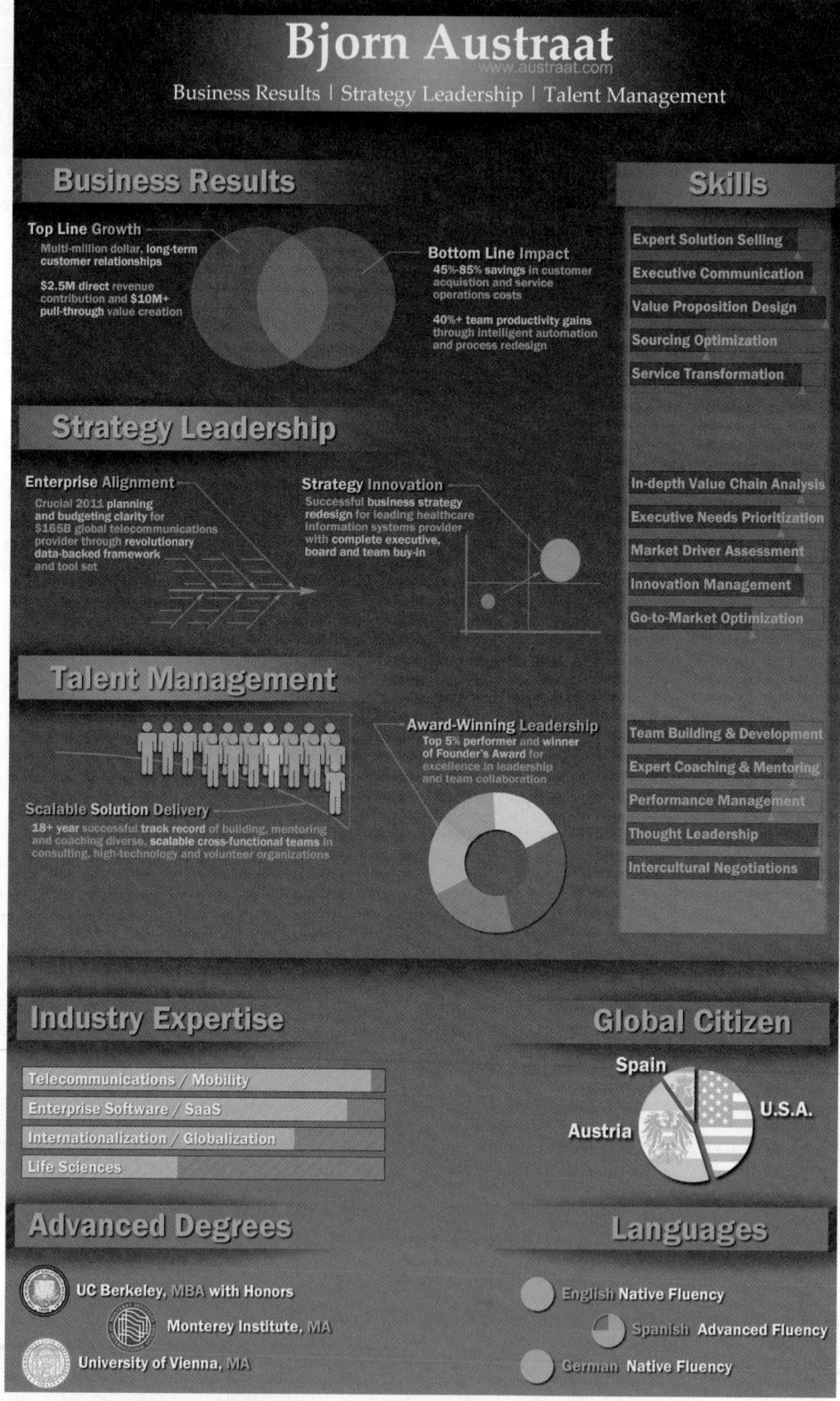

Figure 15.6 Infographic Résumé
A well-designed infographic can be an intriguing part of a job-search package in some professions. However, an infographic should always complement a conventional résumé, not try to replace it.
Source: © Bjorn Austraat 2011.

saves you the trouble of creating a plain-text version. However, before you submit a Word file to anyone, make sure your computer is free of viruses. Infecting a potential employer's computer will not make a good first impression.

Creating a PDF Version of Your Résumé

Creating a PDF file is a simple procedure, but you need the right software. Adobe Acrobat (not the free Adobe Reader) is the best-known program, but many others are available, including some free versions. You can also use Adobe's online service, at http://createpdf .adobe.com, to create PDFs without buying software.

Creating an Online Résumé

A variety of terms are used to describe online résumés, including *personal webpage*, *e-portfolio*, *social media résumé*, and *multimedia résumé*. Whatever the terminology used on a particular site, all these formats provide the opportunity to expand on the information contained in your basic résumé with links to projects, publications, screencasts, online videos, course lists, social networking profiles, and other elements that give employers a more complete picture of who you are and what you can offer (see Figure 15.7).

A good place to start is your college's career center. Ask whether the career center (or perhaps the information technology department) hosts online résumés or e-portfolios for students.

A commercial hosting service is another good possibility for an online résumé. For instance, the free service VisualCV (www.visualcv.com) lets you build an online résumé with video clips and other multimedia elements. This site is a good place to see numerous

> You have many options for creating an online résumé, from college-hosted e-portfolios to multimedia résumés on commercial websites.

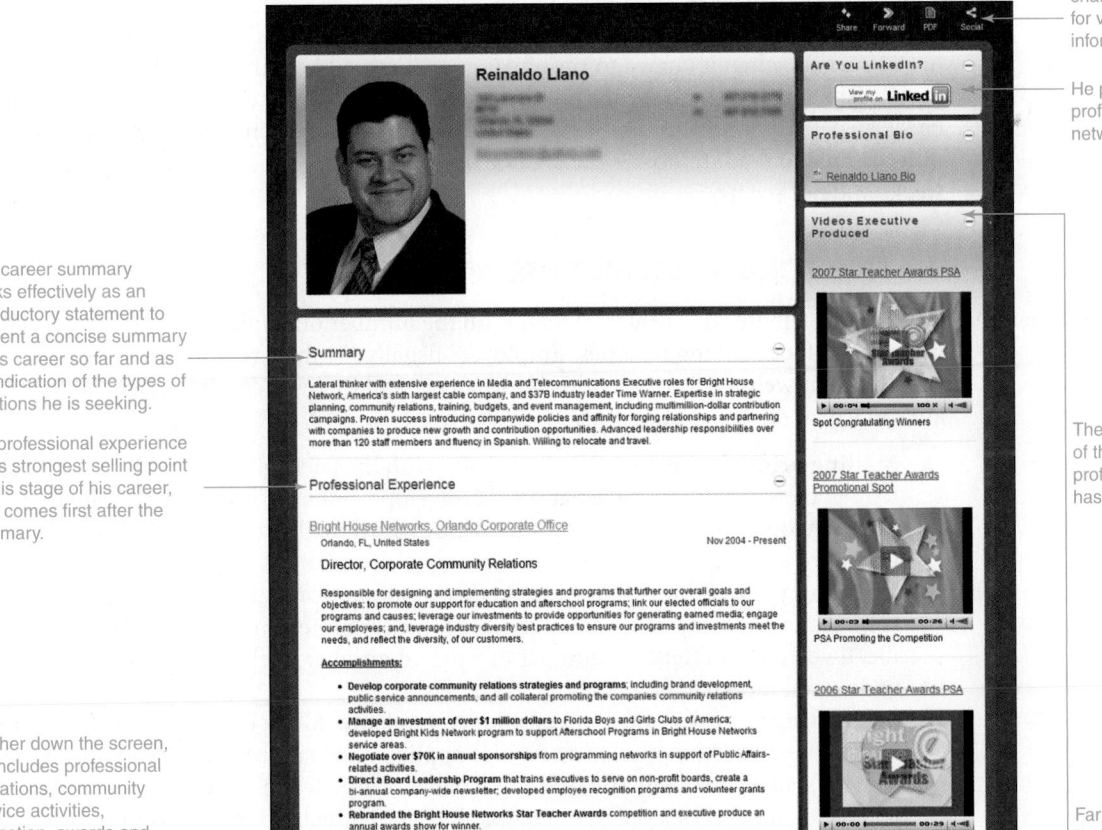

The career summary works effectively as an introductory statement to present a concise summary of his career so far and as an indication of the types of positions he is seeking.

His professional experience is his strongest selling point at this stage of his career, so it comes first after the summary.

Farther down the screen, he includes professional affiliations, community service activities, education, awards and recognition, and links to news media articles in which his work was highlighted.

The site's social media sharing button makes it easy for viewers to copy his information to their networks.

He prominently links to his profile on the social network LinkedIn.

The multimedia capabilities of the site allow him to embed professional videos that he has produced.

Farther down the screen, he links to other work projects, such as brochures and photos of promotional items he has produced.

Figure 15.7 Online Résumé
Reinaldo Llano, a corporate communications executive in the media industry, used the résumé hosting website VisualCV to create and present this multimedia/social media résumé.
Source: Used with permission of VisualCV.

examples, from students just about to enter the workforce full-time all the way up to corporate CEOs.[45]

Regardless of the approach you take to creating an online résumé, keep these helpful tips in mind:

- **Remember that your online presence is a career-management tool.** The way you are portrayed online can work for you or against you, and it's up to you to create a positive impression. Most employers now conduct online searches to learn more about promising candidates, and 70 percent of those who do have rejected applicants because of information they dug up online.[46]
- **Take advantage of social networking.** Use whatever tools are available to direct people to your online résumé, such as including the URL of your online résumé on the "Info" tab on your Facebook page.
- **During the application process, don't expect or ask employers to retrieve a résumé from your website.** Submit your résumé using whatever method and medium each employer prefers. If employers then want to know more about you, they will likely do a web search on you and find your site, or you can refer them to your site in your résumé or application materials.

PROOFREADING YOUR RÉSUMÉ

Your résumé can't be "pretty good" or "almost perfect"—it needs to be *perfect*, so proofread it thoroughly and ask several other people to verify it, too.

Employers view your résumé as a concrete example of your attention to quality and detail. Your résumé doesn't need to be good or pretty good—it needs to be *perfect*. Although it may not seem fair, just one or two errors in a job application package are enough to doom a candidate's chances.[47]

Your résumé is one of the most important documents you'll ever write, so don't rush or cut corners when it comes to proofreading. Check all headings and lists for clarity and parallelism and be sure that your grammar, spelling, and punctuation are correct. Double-check all dates, phone numbers, email addresses, and other essential data. Ask at least three other people to read it, too. As the creator of the material, you could stare at a mistake for weeks and not see it.

DISTRIBUTING YOUR RÉSUMÉ

When distributing your résumé, pay close attention to the specific instructions provided by every employer, job website, or other recipient.

How you distribute your résumé depends on the number of employers you target and their preferences for receiving résumés. Employers usually list their requirements on the career pages of their websites, so verify this information and follow it carefully. Beyond that, here are some general distribution tips:

- **Mailing printed résumés.** Take some care with the packaging. Spend a few extra cents to mail these documents in a flat 9 × 12 envelope, or better yet, use a Priority Mail flat-rate envelope, which gives you a sturdy cardboard mailer and faster delivery for just a few more dollars.
- **Emailing your résumé.** Some employers want applicants to include the text of their résumés in the body of an email message; others prefer an attached Microsoft Word file. If you have a reference number or a job ad number, include it in the subject line of your email message.
- **Submitting your résumé to an employer's website.** Many employers, including most large companies, now prefer or require applicants to submit their résumés online. In some instances, you will be asked to upload a complete file. In others, you will need to copy and paste sections of your résumé into individual boxes in an online application form.
- **Posting your résumé on job websites.** You can post your résumé (or create one online, on some sites) on general-purpose job websites such as Monster (http:// home.monster.com and http://college.monster.com) and CareerBuilder (www .careerbuilder.com), on more specialized websites such as Jobster (www.jobster.com) or Jobfox (www.jobfox.com), or with staffing services such as Volt (http://jobs.volt .com). Roughly 100,000 job boards are now online, so you'll need to spend some time

looking for sites that specialize in your target industries, regions, or professions.[48] Before you upload your résumé to any site, however, learn about its confidentiality protection. Some sites allow you to specify levels of confidentiality, such as letting employers search your qualifications without seeing your personal contact information or preventing your current employer from seeing your résumé. Don't post your résumé to any website that doesn't give you the option of restricting the display of your contact information. Only employers that are registered clients of the service should be able to see your contact information.[49]

Don't post a résumé on any public website unless you understand its privacy and security policies.

For a quick summary of the steps to take when planning, writing, and completing your résumé, refer to "Checklist: Writing an Effective Résumé." For the latest information on résumé writing, visit http://real-timeupdates.com/ebc10 and click on Chapter 15.

✓ Checklist   Writing an Effective Résumé

A. Plan your résumé.
- Analyze your purpose and audience carefully to make sure your message meets employers' needs.
- Gather pertinent information about your target companies.
- Select the best medium by researching the preferences of each employer.
- Organize your résumé around your strengths, choosing the chronological, functional, or combination structure. (Be careful about using the functional structure.)

B. Write your résumé.
- Keep your résumé honest.
- Adapt your résumé to your audience to highlight the qualifications each employer is looking for.
- Choose a career objective, qualifications summary, or career summary as your introductory statement—and make it concise, concrete, and reader-focused.

- Use powerful language to convey your name and contact information, introductory statement, education, work experience, skills, work or school accomplishments, and activities and achievements.

C. Complete your résumé.
- Revise your résumé until it is clear, concise, and compelling.
- Produce your résumé in all the formats you might need: traditional printed résumé, scannable, plain-text file, Microsoft Word file, PDF, or online/multimedia/social media.
- Proofread your résumé to make sure it is absolutely perfect.
- Distribute your résumé using the means that each employer prefers.

ON THE JOB: SOLVING COMMUNICATION DILEMMAS AT **ATK**

Source: Courtesy of ATK.

You work as a recruiter in the human resources department at ATK's Minneapolis headquarters, where part of your responsibility involves using the applicant tracking system to identify promising job candidates. Your current task is finding candidates to fill a staff accountant position in the corporate finance group.

1. You've learned to pay close attention to the introductory statement on résumés to make sure you match applicants' interests with appropriate job openings. You've selected four résumés for the accountant position. Which of the following is the most compelling statement for this position?

a. Career objective: An entry-level financial position in a large company
b. Qualifications summary: Proven track record of using accounting and financial talent and business savvy in shepherding companies toward explosive growth
c. Qualifications summary: Solid academic grounding in business administration with experience in cash management and basic accounting procedures
d. Career objective: To learn all I can about accounting in an exciting environment with a company whose reputation is as outstanding as ATK's

2. Of the education sections included in the résumés, which of the following is the most effective?

a. **Morehouse College, Atlanta, GA, 2007–2010.** Received BA degree with a major in Business Administration and a minor in Finance. Graduated with a 3.65 grade point average. Played varsity football and basketball. Worked 15 hours per week in the library.

Coordinated the local student chapter of the American Management Association. Member of Alpha Phi Alpha social fraternity.

b. **I attended Wayne State University in Detroit, Michigan, for two years and then transferred to the University of Michigan at Ann Arbor, where I completed my studies.** My major was economics, but I also took many business management courses, including employee motivation, small business administration, history of business start-ups, and organizational behavior. I selected courses based on the professors' reputation for excellence, and I received mostly A's and B's. Unlike many college students, I viewed the acquisition of knowledge—rather than career preparation—as my primary goal. I believe I have received a well-rounded education that has prepared me to approach management situations as problem-solving exercises.

c. **University of Connecticut, Storrs, Connecticut. Graduated with a BA degree in 2011.** Majored in Physical Education. Minored in Business Administration. Graduated with a 2.85 average.

d. **North Texas State University and University of Texas at Tyler.** Received BA and MBA degrees. I majored in business as an undergraduate and concentrated in financial management during my MBA program. Received a special $2,500 scholarship offered by Rotary international recognizing academic achievement in business courses. I also won the MEGA award in 2009. Dean's List.

3. Which of the résumés does the best job of portraying each candidate's work experience?

a. **McDonald's, Peoria, IL, 2004–2005. Part-time cook.** Worked 15 hours per week while attending high school. Prepared all menu items. Received employee-of-the-month award for outstanding work habits. **University Grill, Ames, IA, 2007–2011. Part-time cook.** Worked 20 hours per week while attending college. Prepared hot and cold sandwiches. Helped manager purchase ingredients. Trained new kitchen workers. Prepared work schedules for kitchen staff.

b. Although I have never held a full-time job, I have worked part-time and during summer vacations throughout my high school and college years. During my freshman and sophomore years in high school, I bagged groceries at the A&P store three afternoons a week, where I was generally acknowledged as one of the hardest-working employees. During my junior and senior years, I worked at the YMCA as an after-school counselor for elementary school children. I know I made a positive difference in their lives because I still get letters from some of them. During summer vacations while I was in college, I did construction work for a local homebuilder. The job paid well, and I also learned a lot about carpentry. I also worked part-time in college in the student cafeteria.

c. **Macy's Department Store, Sherman Oaks, CA, Summers, 2002–2005. Sales Consultant, Furniture Department.** Interacted with a diverse group of customers while endeavoring to satisfy their individual needs and make their shopping experience efficient and enjoyable. Under the direction of the sales manager, prepared employee schedules and completed departmental reports. Demonstrated computer skills and attention to detail while assisting with inventory management, working the cash register, and handling a variety of special orders and customer requests. Received the CEO Award (for best monthly sales performance) three times.

d. **Athens, GA, Civilian Member of Public Safety Committee, January–December 2009.**

- Organized and promoted a lecture series on vacation safety and home security for the residents of Athens, GA; recruited and trained seven committee members to help plan and produce the lectures; persuaded local businesses to finance the program; designed, printed, and distributed flyers; wrote and distributed press releases; attracted an average of 120 people to each of three lectures

- Developed a questionnaire to determine local residents' home security needs; directed the efforts of 10 volunteers working on the survey; prepared written report for city council and delivered oral summary of findings at town meeting; helped persuade city to fund new home security program

- Initiated the Business Security Forum as an annual meeting at which local business leaders could meet to discuss safety and security issues; created promotional flyers for the first forum; convinced 19 business owners to fund a business security survey; arranged press coverage of the first forum

4. While you are analyzing four résumés suggested by your applicant tracking system, a fellow employee hands you a résumé (see next page) and says this person would be great for the opening in accounting. What action will you take?

a. Definitely recommend that ATK take a look at this outstanding candidate.

b. Reject the application. He doesn't give enough information about when he attended college, what he majored in, or where he has worked.

c. Review the candidate's web-based e-portfolio, in which he has posted many of his school projects. If the assessment contains the missing information and the candidate sounds promising, recommend him for a closer look. If vital information is still missing, send the candidate an email requesting additional information. Make the decision once you receive all necessary information.

d. Consider the candidate's qualifications relative to those of other applicants. Recommend him if you cannot find three or four other applicants with more directly relevant qualifications.

Darius Jaidee
809 N. Perkins Rd, Stillwater, OK 74075
Phone: (405) 369-0098
Email: dariusj@okstate.edu

Career Objective: To build a successful career in financial management

Summary of Qualifications: As a student at the University of Oklahoma, Stillwater, completed a wide variety of assignments that demonstrate skills related to accounting and management. For example:

Planning skills: As president of the university's foreign affairs forum, organized six lectures and workshops featuring 36 speakers from 16 foreign countries within a nine-month period. Identified and recruited the speakers, handled their travel arrangements, and scheduled the facilities.

Communication skills: Wrote more than 25 essays and term papers on various academic topics, including at least 10 dealing with business and finance. As a senior, wrote a 20-page analysis of financial trends in the petroleum industry, interviewing five high-ranking executives in accounting and finance positions at ConocoPhillip's refinery in Ponca City, Oklahoma, and company headquarters in Houston, Texas.

Accounting and computer skills: Competent in all areas of Microsoft Office, including Excel spreadsheets and Access databases. Assisted with bookkeeping activities in parents' small business, including the conversion from paper-based to computer-based accounting (Peachtree software). Have taken courses in accounting, financial planning, database design, web design, and computer networking.

For more information, including employment history, please access my e-portfolio at http://dariusjaidee.com.

LEARNING OBJECTIVES CHECKUP

Assess your understanding of the principles in this chapter by reading each learning objective and studying the accompanying exercises. For fill-in-the-blank items, write the missing text in the blank provided; for multiple-choice items, circle the letter of the correct answer. You can check your responses against the answer key on page AK-3.

Objective 15.1: List eight key steps to finding the ideal opportunity in today's job market.

1. How does writing the "story of you" help you plan your job search and craft your résumé?
   a. It helps you focus your résumé on your needs, rather than on the employer's.
   b. It helps you think about where you want to go and how to present yourself to target employers.
   c. It allows you to avoid writing a traditional structured résumé.
   d. It helps you plan the speech you should make at the beginning of every job interview.

2. _____ _____ _____ is a measure of how closely new employees meet a company's needs.

3. What is the first step that employers usually take when they need to find candidates to interview for a job opening?
   a. They search online for personal websites and e-portfolios that might contain information about potential candidates.
   b. They look inside the company for likely candidates.
   c. They post job openings on job boards such as Monster .com and CareerBuilder.com.
   d. They run ads in the local newspaper.

4. Which of these most accurately characterizes the respective approaches that employers use to find new employees and employees use to find new opportunities?
   a. Employers and employees look in the same places, in the same general sequence.
   b. The respective approaches of employers and employees is essentially opposite, with employers starting inside the firm and gradually moving toward help wanted ads as a last resort and employees starting with help wanted ads and moving in the other direction.
   c. Because websites are the only places that employers now communicate news of job openings, the web is the only place employees should look.
   d. The approaches of employees and employers have nothing in common.

5. Which of the following best describes the process of networking as it applies to your career?
   a. Making sure you are plugged into the online scene so that you don't miss out on any new Internet developments
   b. Making connections with a broad sphere of mutually beneficial business contacts
   c. Asking as many people as possible to alert you to interesting job opportunities
   d. Making sure you get to know everyone in your company shortly after accepting a new position

6. If you don't yet have significant work experience but still want to become a valued network member, which of the following tactics should you consider?
   a. Limit your networking to people whose work experience is similar to yours so that you can share similar information.
   b. Create a convenient, foldable, business-card-size version of your résumé that you can give to everyone you meet so they don't have to carry a full-size copy of your résumé.
   c. Avoid networking until you have enough work experience to be able to offer insider tips on the job market in your industry.
   d. Research recent trends in the business world in order to have interesting and useful information at your fingertips whenever you encounter people in your network.

Objective 15.2: Explain the process of planning your résumé, including how to choose the best résumé organization.

7. A/an _____ résumé highlights employment experience, listing jobs in reverse order from most recent to earliest.

8. A/an _____ résumé focuses on a person's particular skills and competencies, without itemizing his or her job history.

9. A/an _____ résumé uses elements of both the chronological and functional formats.

10. Which of the following is an advantage of the chronological résumé?
    a. It helps employers easily locate necessary information.
    b. It highlights your professional growth and career progress.
    c. It emphasizes continuity and stability in your employment background.
    d. It performs all of these communication functions.

11. Why are many employers suspicious of the functional résumé?
    a. It allows applicants to hide or downplay lengthy periods of unemployment or a lack of career progress.
    b. It doesn't scan into computer databases as effectively as other résumé formats.
    c. It doesn't provide any information about education.
    d. It encourages applicants to include accomplishments that were the result of teamwork rather than individual efforts.

12. Which of the following is a disadvantage of the combination résumé?
    a. It is impossible to convert to scannable format.
    b. It tends to be longer than other formats and can be repetitious.
    c. It doesn't work for people who have extensive job experience.
    d. The combination résumé has no disadvantages.

Objective 15.3: Describe the tasks involved in writing your résumé, and list the major sections of a traditional résumé.

13. Which of the following sections should be included in any résumé, regardless of the format you've chosen?
    a. Contact information, education, and work experience
    b. Contact information, education, and personal references
    c. Personal data, contact information, and education
    d. Education, personal references, and career objectives

14. Why do some experts recommend against using a career objective as the introductory statement on your résumé?
    a. It can limit your possibilities as a candidate, particularly if you want to be considered for a variety of positions.
    b. It shows that you're selfish and thinking only about your own success.
    c. It shows that you're unrealistic, since no one can plan a career that might last for 40 or 50 years.
    d. It helps focus you as a candidate in the minds of potential employers.

15. How does a qualifications summary differ from a career summary?
    a. They are identical.
    b. A qualifications summary offers a brief view of your most important skills and attributes, whereas a career summary is a recap of your career progress.
    c. No one uses a qualifications summary anymore, whereas a career summary is still popular.
    d. The career summary is best for recent graduates, whereas the qualifications summary is best for people with a decade or two of experience.

16. Which should come first on your résumé, your education or your work experience?
    a. Education should come first.
    b. Work experience should come first.
    c. It depends on which is more meaningful to an employer, given where you are in your career at this moment.
    d. The best résumés today use a two-column format in which education and work experience are listed side by side.

17. How much personal data should you put on a résumé aimed at U.S. employers?
    a. You should list your age, marital status, and physical handicaps that might require special accommodation.
    b. You should list your age, marital status, a general assessment of your health (without mentioning any specific problems), and religious affiliation.
    c. You should not list any personal data on your résumé.
    d. You should not list anything related to health or nationality, but you should list age, gender, and salary history (assuming you've had at least one full-time job).

Objective 15.4: Characterize the completing step for résumés, including the six most common formats in which you can produce a résumé.

18. Which of the following best describes the level of quality you should achieve when producing your résumé?
    a. With the advent of email and social networking, most companies are much more relaxed about grammar, spelling, and other old-school concerns, so don't sweat the details.
    b. The typical recruiter in a major corporation sees so many résumés on any given day that most errors pass by unnoticed.
    c. Your résumé needs to be perfect.
    d. Your résumé should reflect your work habits, so if you're more of a strategic thinker and don't worry about insignificant details, make sure your résumé reflects that.

19. Most résumés are now subjected to _____ _____ in an applicant tracking system or other database, in which a recruiter looks for résumés most likely to match the requirements of a particular job

20. A/an _____ _____ version of your résumé has the same content as a traditional résumé but has had all the formatting removed so that it can be easily emailed or copied into online forms.

21. Which of these is a significant advantage of online, multimedia, or social media résumés?
    a. You can expand on the information contained in your basic résumé with links to projects, publications, screencasts, online videos, course lists, social networking profiles, and other elements.
    b. You can build up your résumé over time and don't have to worry about having every little detail in place when you launch your job search.
    c. You can use lots of color.
    d. You can use the flexibility of the web to provide extensive details on your life history.

MyBcommLab

Log on to www.pearsoninternationaleditions.com/mybcommlab to access study and assessment aids associated with this chapter. If you are not using MyBcommLab, you can access the Real-Time Updates http://real-timeupdates.com/ebc10.

LEARNING OBJECTIVES

1. List eight key steps to finding the ideal opportunity in today's job market. [page 529]
2. Explain the process of planning your résumé, including how to choose the best résumé organization. [page 533]
3. Describe the tasks involved in writing your résumé, and list the major sections of a traditional résumé. [page 538]
4. Characterize the completing step for résumés, including the six most common formats in which you can produce a résumé. [page 543]

KEY TERMS

applicant tracking systems Computer systems that capture and store incoming résumés and help recruiters find good prospects for current openings

chronological résumé The most common résumé format; it emphasizes work experience, with past jobs shown in reverse chronological order

combination résumé Format that includes the best features of the chronological and functional approaches

functional résumé Format that emphasizes your skills and capabilities while identifying employers and academic experience in subordinate sections; many recruiters view this format with suspicion

networking The process of making connections with mutually beneficial business contacts

résumé A structured, written summary of a person's education, employment background, and job qualifications

 **Checklist**

Writing an Effective Résumé

A. **Plan your résumé.**
- Analyze your purpose and audience carefully to make sure your message meets employers' needs.
- Gather pertinent information about your target companies.
- Select the best medium by researching the preferences of each employer.
- Organize your résumé around your strengths, choosing the chronological, functional, or combination structure. (Be careful about using the functional structure.)

B. **Write your résumé.**
- Keep your résumé honest.
- Adapt your résumé to your audience to highlight the qualifications each employer is looking for.
- Choose a career objective, qualifications summary, or career summary as your introductory statement—and make it concise, concrete, and reader-focused.
- Use powerful language to convey your name and contact information, introductory statement, education, work experience, skills, work or school accomplishments, and activities and achievements.

C. **Complete your résumé.**
- Revise your résumé until it is clear, concise, and compelling.
- Produce your résumé in all the formats you might need: traditional printed résumé, scannable, plain-text file, Microsoft Word file, PDF, or online/multimedia/social media.
- Proofread your résumé to make sure it is absolutely perfect.
- Distribute your résumé using the means that each employer prefers.

APPLY YOUR KNOWLEDGE

To review chapter content related to each question, refer to the indicated Learning Objective.

1. How can you "think like an employer" if you have no professional business experience? [LO-1]

2. If you were a team leader at a summer camp for children with special needs, should you include this in your employment history if you are applying for work that is unrelated? Explain your answer. [LO-3]

3. Can you use a qualifications summary if you don't yet have extensive professional experience in your desired career? Why or why not? [LO-3]

4. Some people don't have a clear career path when they enter the job market. If you're in this situation, how would your uncertainty affect the way your write your résumé? [LO-3]

5. Between your sophomore and junior years, you quit school for a year to earn the money to finish college. You worked as a loan-processing assistant in a finance company, checking references on loan applications, typing, and filing. Your manager made a lot of the fact that he had never attended college. He seemed to resent you for pursuing your education, but he never criticized your work, so you thought you were doing okay. After you'd been working there for six months, he fired you, saying that you'd failed to be thorough enough in your credit checks. You were actually glad to leave, and you found another job right away at a bank, doing similar duties. Now that you've graduated from college, you're writing your résumé. Will you include the finance company job in your work history? Explain. [LO-3]

PRACTICE YOUR SKILLS

Message for Analysis

Read the following résumé information and then (1) analyze the strengths or weaknesses of the information and (2) revise the résumé so that it follows the guidelines presented in this chapter.

Message 15.A: Writing a Résumé [LO-3]

Sylvia Manchester
765 Belle Fleur Blvd.
New Orleans, LA 70113
(504) 312-9504
smanchester@rcnmail.com

PERSONAL: Single, excellent health, 5'7", 136 lbs.; hobbies include cooking, dancing, and reading.

JOB OBJECTIVE: To obtain a responsible position in marketing or sales with a good company.

EDUCATION: BA degree in biology, University of Louisiana, 1998. Graduated with a 3.0 average. Member of the varsity cheerleading squad. President of Panhellenic League. Homecoming queen.

WORK EXPERIENCE

Fisher Scientific Instruments, 2004 to now, field sales representative. Responsible for calling on customers and explaining the features of Fisher's line of laboratory instruments. Also responsible for writing sales letters, attending trade shows, and preparing weekly sales reports.

Fisher Scientific Instruments, 2001–2003, customer service representative. Was responsible for handling incoming phone calls from customers who had questions about delivery, quality, or operation of Fisher's line of laboratory instruments. Also handled miscellaneous correspondence with customers.

Medical Electronics, Inc., 1998–2001, administrative assistant to the vice president of marketing. In addition to handling typical secretarial chores for the vice president of marketing, I was in charge of compiling the monthly sales reports, using figures provided by members of the field sales force. I also was given responsibility for doing various market research activities.

New Orleans Convention and Visitors Bureau, 1995–1998, summers, tour guide. During the summers of my college years, I led tours of New Orleans for tourists visiting the city. My duties included greeting conventioneers and their spouses at hotels, explaining the history and features of the city during an all-day sightseeing tour, and answering questions about New Orleans and its attractions. During my fourth summer with the bureau, I was asked to help train the new tour guides. I prepared a handbook that provided interesting facts about the various tourist attractions, as well as answers to the most commonly asked tourist questions. The Bureau was so impressed with the handbook they had it printed up so that it could be given as a gift to visitors.

University of Louisiana, 1995–1998, part-time clerk in admissions office. While I was a student in college, I worked 15 hours a week in the admissions office. My duties included filing, processing applications, and handling correspondence with high school students and administrators.

Exercises

Active links for all websites in this chapter can be found on MyBcommLab; see your User Guide for instructions on accessing the content for this chapter. Each activity is labeled according to the primary skill or skills you will need to use. To review relevant chapter content, you can refer to the indicated Learning Objective. In some instances, supporting information will be found in another chapter, as indicated.

1. **Career Management: Researching Career Opportunities [LO-1]** Based on the preferences you identified in your career self-assessment (see page 34 in the Prologue) and the academic, professional, and personal qualities you have to offer, perform an online search for a career that matches your interests (starting with the websites listed in Table 15.1). Draft a brief report for your instructor, indicating how the career you select and the job openings you find match your strengths and preferences.

2. **Message Strategies: Writing a Résumé; Collaboration: Team Projects [LO-3], Chapter 2** Working with another student, change the following statements to make them more effective for a résumé by using action verbs.

   a. Have some experience with database design.

   b. Assigned to a project to analyze the cost accounting methods for a large manufacturer.

c. I was part of a team that developed a new inventory control system.

d. Am responsible for preparing the quarterly department budget.

e. Was a manager of a department with seven employees working for me.

f. Was responsible for developing a spreadsheet to analyze monthly sales by department.

g. Put in place a new program for ordering supplies.

3. **Message Strategies: Writing a Résumé [LO-3]** Using your team's answers to Exercise 2, make the statements stronger by quantifying them. (Make up any numbers you need.)

4. **Message Strategies: Writing a Résumé; Communication Ethics: Resolving Ethical Dilemmas [LO-3], Chapter 1** Assume that you achieved all the tasks shown in Exercise 2 not as an individual employee but as part of a work team. In your résumé, must you mention other team members? Explain your answer.

5. **Completing a Résumé [LO-4]** Using your revised version of the résumé in Message for Analysis 15.A, create a plain-text file that Sylvia Manchester could use to include in email messages.

6. **Completing a Résumé [LO-4]** Imagine that you are applying for work in a field that involves speaking in front of an audience, such as sales, consulting, management, or training. Using material you created for any of the exercises or cases in Chapter 14, record a two- to three-minute video demonstration of your speaking and presentation skills. Record yourself speaking to an audience, if one can be arranged.

EXPAND YOUR SKILLS

Critique the Professionals

Locate an example of an online résumé (a sample or an actual résumé) from VisualCV (www.visualcv.com) or a similar website. Analyze the résumé using the guidelines presented in this chapter. Using whatever medium your instructor requests, write a brief analysis (no more than one page) of the résumé's strengths and weaknesses, citing specific elements from the résumé and support from the chapter. If you are analyzing a real résumé, do not include any personally identifiable data, such as the person's name, email address, or phone number, in your report.

Sharpening Your Career Skills Online

Bovée and Thill's Business Communication Web Search, at http://businesscommunicationblog.com/websearch, is a unique research tool designed specifically for business communication research. Use the Web Search function to find a website, video, PDF document, podcast, or PowerPoint presentation that offers advice on creating an effective résumé. Write a brief email message to your instructor, describing the item that you found and summarizing the career skills information you learned from it.

IMPROVE YOUR GRAMMAR, MECHANICS, AND USAGE

The following exercises help you improve your knowledge of and power over English grammar, mechanics, and usage. Turn to the "Handbook of Grammar, Mechanics, and Usage" at the end of this book and review all of Sections 4.1 (Frequently Confused Words), 4.2 (Frequently Misused Words), and 4.3 (Frequently Misspelled Words). Then look at the following 10 items. Underline the preferred choice within each set of parentheses. (Answers to these exercises appear on page AK-4.)

1. The Board's decision to cut costs will (*affect, effect*) all of us.

2. You should follow your manager's (*advice, advise*).

3. You will (*loose, lose*) your job if you carry on like this.

4. The director will decide the appointment based on (*whoever, whomever*) applies for the position.

5. I have made (*a lot, alot*) of progress on my book today.

6. We have (*recieved, received*) all the reports from your team on time.

7. I read the meeting notes, and found them (*incomprehensible, uncomprehensible*).

8. There is no (*necessity, neccessity*) for separate permissions for this.

9. Thomas Edison (*discovered, invented*) the light bulb.

10. We have all been ordered to go (*for, to*) the director's office.

For additional exercises focusing on frequently confused, misused, or misspelled words, visit MyBcommLab. Click on Chapter 15, click on Additional Exercises to Improve Your Grammar, Mechanics, and Usage, and then click on 21. Frequently confused words, 22. Frequently misused words, or 23. Frequently misspelled words.

CASES

CAREER SKILLS   **EMAIL SKILLS**

1. Career Planning: Researching Career Opportunities [LO-1] Knowing the jargon and "hot button" issues in a particular profession or industry can give you a big advantage when it comes to writing your résumé and participating in job interviews. You can fine-tune your résumé for both human readers and applicant tracking systems, sound more confident and informed in interviews, and present yourself as a professional-class individual with an inquiring mind.

Your task: Imagine a specific job category in a company that has an informative, comprehensive website (to facilitate the research you'll need to do). This doesn't have to be a current job opening, but a position that you know exists or is likely to exist in this company, such as a business systems analyst at Apple or a brand manager at Unilever.

Explore the company's website and other online sources to find the following: (1) A brief description of what this job entails, with enough detail that you could describe it to a fellow student. (2) Some of the terminology used in the profession or the industry, both formal terms that might serve as keywords on your résumé and informal terms and phrases that insiders are likely to use in publications and conversations. (3) An ongoing online conversation among people in this profession. For example, this might be a LinkedIn Group, a popular industry or professional blog that seems to get quite a few comments, or an industry or professional publication that attracts a lot of comments. (4) At least one significant issue that will affect people in this profession or companies in this industry over the next few years. For example, if your chosen profession involves accounting in a publicly traded corporation, upcoming changes in international financial reporting standards would be a significant issue. Similarly, for a company in the consumer electronics industry, the recycling and disposal of *e-waste* is an issue. Write a brief email message summarizing your findings and explaining how you could use this information on your résumé and during job interviews.

CAREER SKILLS   TEAM SKILLS

2. Planning a Résumé [LO-2] If you haven't begun your professional career yet or you are pursuing a career change, the employment history section on your résumé can sometimes be a challenge to write. A brainstorming session with your wise and creative classmates could help.

Your task: In a team assigned by your instructor, you will help each other evaluate your employment histories and figure out the best way to present your work backgrounds on a résumé. First, each member of the team should compile his or her work history, including freelance projects and volunteer work if relevant, and share this information with the team. After allowing some time for everyone to review each other's information, meet as a team (in person if you can, or online otherwise). Discuss each person's history, pointing out strong spots and weak spots, and then brainstorm the best way to present each person's employment history.

Note: If there are aspects of your employment history you would rather not share with your teammates, substitute a reasonably similar experience of the same duration.

CAREER SKILLS   TEAM SKILLS

3. Writing a Résumé [LO-3] The introductory statement of a résumé requires some careful thought, both in deciding which of the three types of introductory statement (see page 541) to use and what information to include in it. Getting another person's perspective on this communication challenge can be helpful. In this activity, in fact, someone else is going to write your introductory statement for you, and you will return the favor.

Your task: Pair off with a classmate. Provide each other with the basic facts about your qualifications, work history, education, and career objectives. Then meet in person or online for an informal interview, in which you ask each other questions to flesh

out the information you have on each other. Assume that each of you has chosen to use a qualifications summary for your résumé. Now write each other's qualifications summary and then trade them for review. As you read what your partner wrote about you, ask yourself if this feels true to what you believe about yourself and your career aspirations. Do you think it introduces you effectively to potential employers? What might you change about it?

PRESENTATION SKILLS   PORTFOLIO BUILDER

4. Message Strategies: Completing a Résumé [LO-4] Creating presentations and other multimedia supplements can be a great way to expand on the brief overview that a résumé provides.

Your task: Starting with any version of a résumé that you've created for yourself, create a PowerPoint presentation that expands on your résumé information to give potential employers a more complete picture of what you can contribute. Include samples of your work, testimonials from current or past employers and colleagues, videos of speeches you've made, and anything else that tells the story of the professional "you." If you have a specific job or type of job in mind, focus your presentation on that. Otherwise, present a more general picture that shows why you would be a great employee for any company to consider. Be sure to review the information from Chapter 14 about creating professional-quality presentations.

REFERENCES

1. Adapted from *ATK Corporate Profile*, accessed 23 March 2011, www.atk.com; Ed Frauenheim, "Weapons-Maker ATK Practices Personnel Precision," *Workforce Management*, March 2011, 22–23, 26; Ed Frauenheim, "Numbers Game: Companies Utilize Data to Predict Workforce Needs," *Workforce Management*, March 2011, 20–21; Orca-Eyes website, accessed 23 March 2011, www.orcaeyes.com.
2. Courtland L. Bovée and John V. Thill, *Business in Action*, 5th ed. (Boston: Pearson Prentice Hall, 2011), 241–242.
3. Anne Fisher, "How to Get Hired by a 'Best' Company," *Fortune*, 4 February 2008, 96.
4. Jim Schaper, "Finding Your Future Talent Stars," *BusinessWeek*, 2 July 2010, www.businessweek.com.
5. Eve Tahmincioglu, "Revamping Your Job-Search Strategy," MSNBC.com, 28 February 2010, www.msnbc.com.
6. Tahmincioglu, "Revamping Your Job-Search Strategy."
7. Rita Pyrillis, "The Bait Debate," *Workforce Management*, February 2011, 18–21.
8. Jessica Dickler, "The Hidden Job Market," CNNMoney.com, 10 June 2009, http://money.cnn.com.
9. Tara Weiss, "Twitter to Find a Job," *Forbes*, 7 April 2009, www.forbes.com.
10. Miriam Saltpeter, "Using Facebook Groups for Job Hunting," Keppie Careers blog, 13 November 2008, www.keppiecareers.com.
11. Anne Fisher, "Greener Pastures in a New Field," *Fortune*, 26 January 2004, 48.
12. Liz Ryan, "Etiquette for Online Outreach," Yahoo! Hotjobs website, accessed 26 March 2008, http://hotjobs.yahoo.com.

13. Eve Tahmincioglu, "Employers Digging Deep on Prospective Workers," MSNBC.com, 26 October 2009, www.msnbc.com.

14. Career and Employment Services, Danville Area Community College website, accessed 23 March 2008, www.dacc.edu/career; Career Counseling, Sarah Lawrence College website, accessed 23 March 2008, www.slc.edu/occ/index.php; Cheryl L. Noll, "Collaborating with the Career Planning and Placement Center in the Job-Search Project," *Business Communication Quarterly* 58, no. 3 (1995): 53–55.

15. Erica Swallow, "How to: Spruce Up a Boring Résumé," Mashable, accessed 21 July 2011, http://mashable.com.

16. Fay Hansen, "Recruiters Bear a Bigger Load as Hiring Takes Off," *Workforce Management*, May 2010, www.workforce.com.

17. Randall S. Hansen and Katharine Hansen, "What Résumé Format Is Best for You?" QuintCareers.com, accessed 7 August 2010, www.quintcareers.com.

18. Hansen and Hansen, "What Résumé Format Is Best for You?"

19. Katharine Hansen, "Should You Consider a Functional Format for Your Resume?" QuintCareers.com, accessed 7 August 2010, www.quintcareers.com.

20. Kim Isaacs, "Resume Dilemma: Criminal Record," Monster.com, accessed 23 May 2006, www.monster.com; Kim Isaacs, "Resume Dilemma: Employment Gaps and Job-Hopping," Monster.com, accessed 23 May 2006, www.monster.com; Susan Vaughn, "Answer the Hard Questions Before Asked," *Los Angeles Times,* 29 July 2001, W1–W2.

21. John Steven Niznik, "Landing a Job with a Criminal Record," About.com, accessed 23 May 2006, http://jobsearchtech.about.com.

22. "How to Ferret Out Instances of Résumé Padding and Fraud," *Compensation & Benefits for Law Offices,* June 2006, 1+.

23. "Resume Fraud Gets Slicker and Easier," CNN.com, accessed 11 March 2004, www.cnn.com.

24. Cari Tuna and Keith J. Winstein, "Economy Promises to Fuel Résumé Fraud," *Wall Street Journal*, 17 November 2008, http://online.wsj.com; Lisa Takeuchi Cullen, "Getting Wise to Lies," *Time*, 1 May 2006, 59; "Resume Fraud Gets Slicker and Easier"; Employment Research Services website, accessed 18 March 2004, www.erscheck.com.

25. "How to Ferret Out Instances of Résumé Padding and Fraud."

26. Jacqueline Durett, "Redoing Your Résumé? Leave Off the Lies," *Training*, December 2006, 9; "Employers Turn Their Fire on Untruthful CVs," *Supply Management*, 23 June 2005, 13.

27. Cynthia E. Conn, "Integrating Writing Skills and Ethics Training in Business Communication Pedagogy: A Résumé Case Study Exemplar," *Business Communication Quarterly*, June 2008, 138–151; Marilyn Moats Kennedy, "Don't Get Burned by Résumé Inflation," *Marketing News*, 15 April 2007, 37–38.

28. Rockport Institute, "How to Write a Masterpiece of a Résumé."

29. Lora Morsch, "25 Words That Hurt Your Resume," CNN.com, 20 January 2006, www.cnn.com.

30. Liz Ryan, "The Reengineered Résumé," *BusinessWeek*, 3 December 2007, SC12.

31. Katharine Hansen, "Tapping the Power of Keywords to Enhance Your Resume's Effectiveness," QuintCareers.com, accessed 7 August 2010, www.quintcareers.com.

32. Hansen, "Tapping the Power of Keywords to Enhance Your Resume's Effectiveness."

33. Jolie O'Dell, "LinkedIn Reveals the 10 Most Overused Job-Hunter Buzzwords," Mashable, 14 December 2010, http://mashable.com.

34. Dave Johnson, "10 Resume Errors That Will Land You in the Trash," BNET, 22 February 2010, www.bnet.com; Anthony Balderrama, "Resume Blunders That Will Keep You from Getting Hired," CNN.com, 19 March 2008, www.cnn.com; Michelle Dumas, "5 Resume Writing Myths," Distinctive Documents blog, 17 July 2007, http://blog.distinctiveweb.com; Kim Isaacs, "Resume Dilemma: Recent Graduate," Monster.com, accessed 26 March 2008, http://career-advice.monster.com.

35. Karl L. Smart, "Articulating Skills in the Job Search," *Business Communication Quarterly* 67, no. 2 (June 2004): 198–205.

36. "When to Include Personal Data," ResumeEdge.com, accessed 25 March 2008, www.resumeedge.com.

37. Eve Tahmincioglu, "Looking for a Job in 2011? Here's How to Stand Out," MSNBC.com, 3 January 2011, http://today.msnbc.com.

38. "Résumé Length: What It Should Be and Why It Matters to Recruiters," *HR Focus*, June 2007, 9.

39. Rachel Zupek, "Seven Exceptions to Job Search Rules," CNN.com, 3 September 2008, www.cnn.com.

40. Swallow, "How to: Spruce Up a Boring Résumé."

41. John Hazard, "Resume Tips: No Pictures, Please and No PDFs," Career-Line.com, 26 May 2009, www.career-line.com; "25 Things You Should Never Include on a Resume," HR World website 18 December 2007, www.hrworld.com.

42. John Sullivan, "Résumés: Paper, Please," *Workforce Management*, 22 October 2007, 50; "Video Résumés Offer Both Pros and Cons During Recruiting," *HR Focus*, July 2007, 8.

43. Jobs page, Zappos website, accessed 24 March 2011, http://about.zappos.com/jobs.

44. Nancy M. Schullery, Linda Ickes, and Stephen E. Schullery, "Employer Preferences for Résumés and Cover Letters," *Business Communication Quarterly*, June 2009, 163–176.

45. VisualCV website, accessed 10 August 2010, www.visualcv.com.

46. Elizabeth Garone, "Five Mistakes Online Job Hunters Make," *Wall Street Journal*, 28 July 2010, http://online.wsj.com.

47. "10 Reasons Why You Are Not Getting Any Interviews," *Miami Times*, 7–13 November 2007, 6D.

48. Deborah Silver, "Niche Sites Gain Monster-Sized Following," *Workforce Management*, March 2011, 10–11.

49. "Protect Yourself From Identity Theft When Hunting for a Job Online," *Office Pro*, May 2007, 6.

LEARNING OBJECTIVES After studying this chapter, you will be able to

1 Explain the purposes of application letters, and describe how to apply the AIDA organizational approach to them

2 Describe the typical sequence of job interviews, the major types of interviews, and what employers look for during an interview

3 List six tasks you need to complete to prepare for a successful job interview

4 Explain how to succeed in all three stages of an interview

5 Identify the most common employment messages that follow an interview, and explain when you would use each one

MyBcommLab Where you see MyBcommLab in this chapter, go to www.pearsoninternationaleditions.com/mybcommlab for additional activities on the topic being discussed.

ON THE JOB: COMMUNICATING AT **ZAPPOS**

Zappos CEO Tony Hsieh makes sure the company's interviewing process finds the candidates who are compatible with an offbeat customer- and colleague-focused culture.
Source: Brad Swonetz/Redux.

Unconventional Approaches to Finding Unconventional Employees

When a company communicates its core values with the help of a cartoon amphibian named Core Values Frog, you can guess the company doesn't quite fit the stuffy corporate stereotype. While it is passionately serious about customer satisfaction and employee engagement, the Las Vegas–based online shoe and clothing retailer Zappos doesn't take itself too seriously. In fact, one of the 10 values the frog promotes is "Create fun and a little weirdness."

Fun and a little weirdness can make a workplace more enjoyable, but CEO Tony Hsieh's commitment to employees runs much deeper than that. The company makes frequent reference to "the Zappos Family," and it embraces the ideals of taking care of one another and enjoying time spent together in numerous ways. These activities can range from parades in the workplace and other goofy events to the Wishez program, in which employees can ask one another to fulfill personal wishes, whether lighthearted desires such as getting backstage access at concerts or serious matters such as getting help during tough financial times.

To find employees who will thrive in and protect the unconventional Zappos culture, the company takes an unorthodox path when it comes to recruiting and interviewing. For example, in stark contrast to the companies that refuse to look at videos as part of job application packages, Zappos encourages applicants to send videos of themselves and even provides an upload facility on its website's application page.

The interviewing process is designed to find passionate, free-thinking candidates who fit the culture, from the offbeat antics to the serious commitment to customers and fellow employees. Some of the questions interviewees can expect to encounter include "What was the best mistake you made on the job?" and "On a scale of 1 to 10, how weird are you?"

Speaking of offbeat interviews, the company recently screened software engineering candidates using 30-minute coding challenges, in which the first programmer to solve the problem was "fast-tracked to Vegas" for the next round of interviews. Coding contests are not all that unusual for recruiting programmers, but it's unlikely that many feature an open bar, as the Zappos competition did.

A strong customer- and employee-focused culture, a strong commitment to maintaining that culture, and a recruiting strategy that finds the right people for that culture—this relentless focus on doing business the Zappos way keeps paying off. The company continues to grow and continues to be ranked as one of the best places in work in the United States.[1]

www.zappos.com

Submitting Your Résumé

Whether you plan to apply to Zappos (profiled in the chapter opener) or any other company, your résumé in some form will usually be the centerpiece of your job-search package. However, it needs support from several other employment messages before, during, and after the interview process. These messages can include application letters, job-inquiry letters, application forms, and follow-up notes.

1 LEARNING OBJECTIVE

Explain the purposes of application letters and describe how to apply the AIDA organizational approach to them.

WRITING APPLICATION LETTERS

Whenever you mail, email, hand-deliver, or upload your résumé, you should include an **application letter**, also known as a *cover letter*, to let readers know what you're sending, why you're sending it, and how they can benefit from reading it. (Although this message is often not a printed letter anymore, many professionals still refer to it as a letter.) Take the same care with your application letter that you took with your résumé. A poorly written application letter can prompt employers to skip over your résumé, even if you are a good fit for a job.[2] Staffing specialist Abby Kohut calls the application letter "a writing-skills evaluation in disguise" and emphasizes that even a single error can get you bounced from contention.[3]

The best approach for an application letter depends on whether you are sending a **solicited application letter** to apply for an identified job opening or are *prospecting* with an **unsolicited application letter**—taking the initiative to write to companies even though they haven't announced a job opening that is right for you.[4] In many ways, the difference between the two is like the difference between solicited and unsolicited proposals (see page 394). Figure 16.1 on the next page shows an application message written in response to a posted job opening. The writer knows exactly what qualifications the organization is seeking and can "echo" those attributes back in his message.

Prospecting is more challenging because you don't have the clear target you have with a solicited message. You will need to do more research to identify the qualities that a company would probably seek for the position you hope to occupy (see Figure 16.2 on page 563). Also, search for news items that involve the company, its customers, the profession, or the individual manager to whom you are writing. Using this information in your application letter helps you establish common ground with your reader—and it shows that you are tuned in to what is going on in the industry.

For either type of letter, follow these tips to be more effective:[5]

- Resist the temptation to stand out with gimmicky application letters; impress with knowledge and professionalism instead.
- If the name of an individual manager is at all findable, address your letter to that person, rather than something generic such as "Dear Hiring Manager." Search LinkedIn, the company's website, industry directories, Twitter, and anything else you can think of to find an appropriate name. Ask the people in your network if they know a name. If another applicant finds a name and you don't, you're at a disadvantage.
- Clearly identify the opportunity you are applying for or expressing interest in.
- Show that you understand the company and its marketplace.

Always accompany your résumé with an application message (letter or email) that motivates the recipient to read the résumé.

An unsolicited application letter is more challenging because you must identify the qualities the company would likely be looking for in the position you would like to get.

MyBcommLab

- Access this chapter's simulation entitled Interviewing located at www.pearsoninternationaleditions.com/mybcommlab.

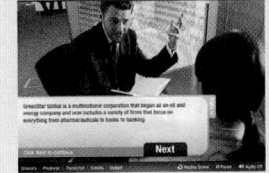

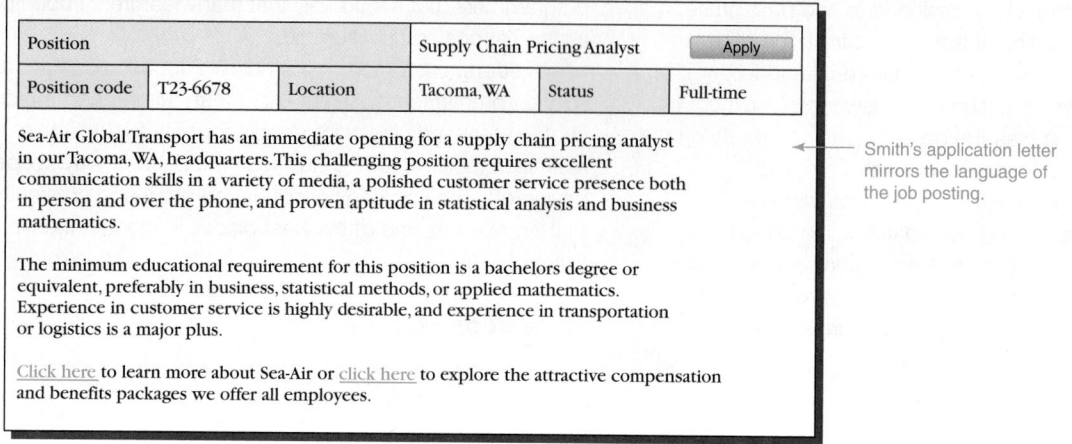

Position			Supply Chain Pricing Analyst		Apply
Position code	T23-6678	Location	Tacoma, WA	Status	Full-time

Sea-Air Global Transport has an immediate opening for a supply chain pricing analyst in our Tacoma, WA, headquarters. This challenging position requires excellent communication skills in a variety of media, a polished customer service presence both in person and over the phone, and proven aptitude in statistical analysis and business mathematics.

The minimum educational requirement for this position is a bachelors degree or equivalent, preferably in business, statistical methods, or applied mathematics. Experience in customer service is highly desirable, and experience in transportation or logistics is a major plus.

Click here to learn more about Sea-Air or click here to explore the attractive compensation and benefits packages we offer all employees.

Smith's application letter mirrors the language of the job posting.

27225 Eucalyptus Avenue
Long Beach, CA 90806
March 13, 2012

Sea-Air Global Transport
5467 Port of Tacoma Rd., Suite 230
Tacoma, WA 98421

Dear Hiring Manager:

Sea-Air Global Transport consistently appeared as a top transportation firm in the research I did for my senior project in global supply chain management, so imagine my delight when I discovered the opening for an export pricing analyst in your Tacoma headquarters (Position Code: T23-6678). With a major in business and a minor in statistical methods, my education has been ideal preparation for the challenges of this position.

In fact, my senior project demonstrates most of the skills listed in your job description, including written communication skills, analytical abilities, and math aptitude. I enjoyed the opportunity to put my math skills to the test as part of the statistical comparison of various freight modes.

As you can see from my résumé, I also have more than three years of part-time experience working with customers in both retail and commercial settings. This experience taught me the importance of customer service, and I want to start my professional career with a company that truly values the customer. In reviewing your website and reading several articles on Lloyd's List and other trade websites, I am impressed by Sea-Air's constant attention to customer service in this highly competitive industry.

My verbal communication skills would be best demonstrated in an interview, of course. I would be happy to meet with a representative of your company at their earliest convenience. I can be reached at dalton.k.smith@gmail.com or by phone at (562) 555-3737.

Sincerely,

Dalton Smith

The first sentence grabs attention by indicating knowledge of the company and its industry.

The reference to his résumé emphasizes his customer service orientation and also shows he has done his homework by researching the company.

The letter doesn't include a handwritten signature because it was uploaded to a website along with his résumé.

The opening paragraph identifies the specific job for which he is applying.

In this discussion of his skills, he echoes the qualifications stated in the job posting.

In the close, he politely asks for an interview in a way that emphasizes yet another job-related skill.

Figure 16.1   Solicited Application Message
In this response to an online job posting, Dalton Smith highlights his qualifications while mirroring the requirements specified in the posting. Following the AIDA model, he grabs attention immediately by letting the reader know that he is familiar with the company and the global transportation business.

- Never volunteer salary history or requirements unless an employer has asked for this information.
- Keep it short—no more than three paragraphs. Keep in mind that all you are trying to do at this point is move the conversation forward one step.
- Show some personality, while maintaining a business-appropriate tone. The letter gives you the opportunity to balance the facts-only tone of your résumé.
- Project confidence without being arrogant.

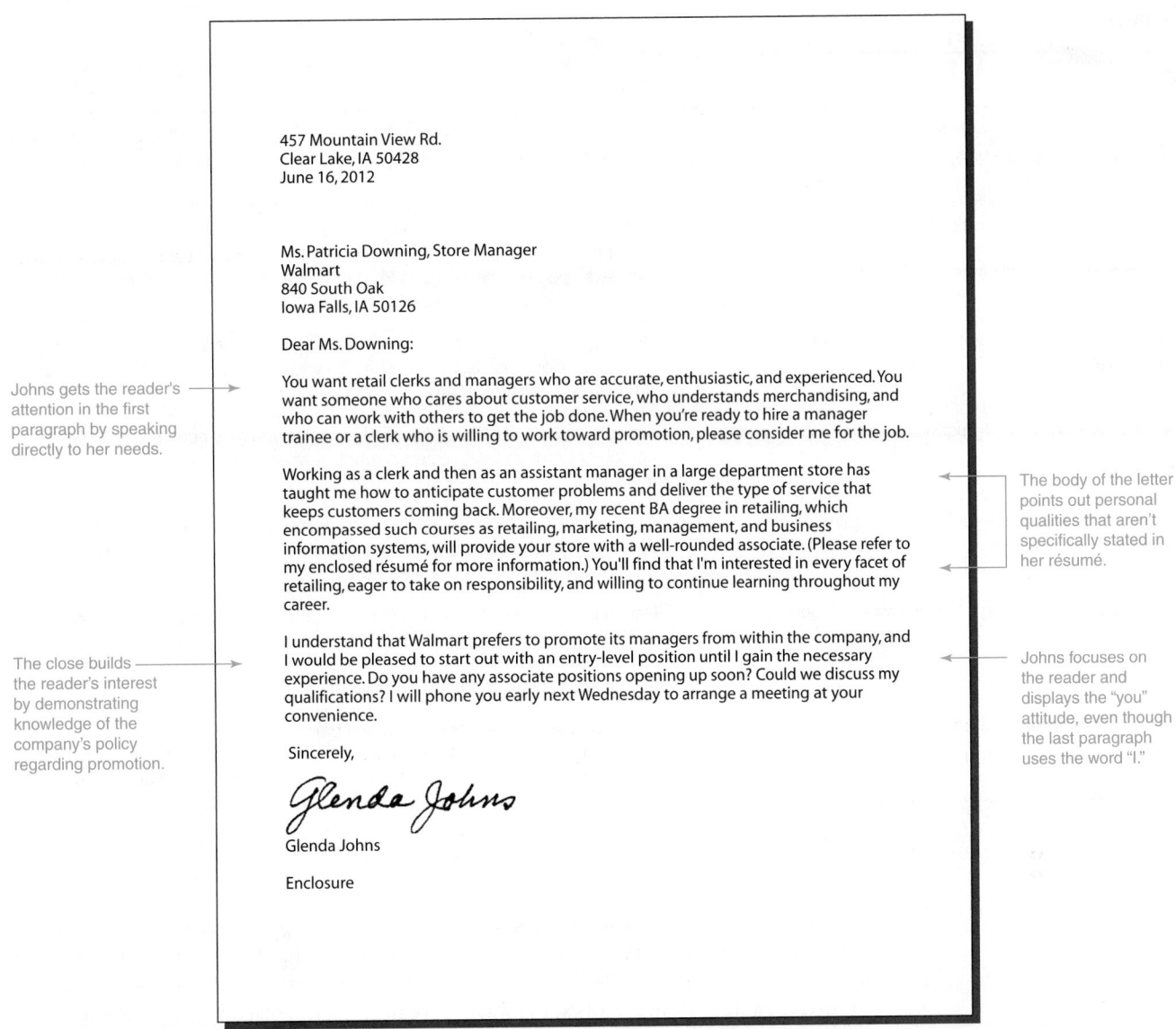

457 Mountain View Rd.
Clear Lake, IA 50428
June 16, 2012

Ms. Patricia Downing, Store Manager
Walmart
840 South Oak
Iowa Falls, IA 50126

Dear Ms. Downing:

You want retail clerks and managers who are accurate, enthusiastic, and experienced. You want someone who cares about customer service, who understands merchandising, and who can work with others to get the job done. When you're ready to hire a manager trainee or a clerk who is willing to work toward promotion, please consider me for the job.

Working as a clerk and then as an assistant manager in a large department store has taught me how to anticipate customer problems and deliver the type of service that keeps customers coming back. Moreover, my recent BA degree in retailing, which encompassed such courses as retailing, marketing, management, and business information systems, will provide your store with a well-rounded associate. (Please refer to my enclosed résumé for more information.) You'll find that I'm interested in every facet of retailing, eager to take on responsibility, and willing to continue learning throughout my career.

I understand that Walmart prefers to promote its managers from within the company, and I would be pleased to start out with an entry-level position until I gain the necessary experience. Do you have any associate positions opening up soon? Could we discuss my qualifications? I will phone you early next Wednesday to arrange a meeting at your convenience.

Sincerely,

Glenda Johns

Glenda Johns

Enclosure

Johns gets the reader's attention in the first paragraph by speaking directly to her needs.

The close builds the reader's interest by demonstrating knowledge of the company's policy regarding promotion.

The body of the letter points out personal qualities that aren't specifically stated in her résumé.

Johns focuses on the reader and displays the "you" attitude, even though the last paragraph uses the word "I."

Figure 16.2 Unsolicited Application Letter
Glenda Johns's experience as a clerk and an assistant manager gives her a good idea of the qualities that Walmart is likely to be looking for in future managers. She uses these insights to craft the opening of her letter.

Because application letters are persuasive messages, the AIDA approach you learned in Chapter 10 is ideal, as the following sections explain.

Getting Attention

The opening paragraph of your application letter has two important tasks to accomplish: (1) clearly stating your reason for writing and (2) giving the recipient a reason to keep reading. Why would a recruiter want to keep reading your letter instead of the hundred others piling up on his or her desk? Because you show some immediate potential for meeting the company's needs. You've researched the company and the position, and you know something about the industry and its current challenges. Consider this opening:

The opening paragraph of your application letter needs to clearly convey the reason you're writing and give the recipient a compelling reason to keep reading.

With the recent slowdown in corporate purchasing, I can certainly appreciate the challenge of new fleet sales in this business environment. With my high energy level and 16 months of new-car sales experience, I believe I can produce the results you listed as vital in the job posting on your website.

TABLE 16.1	Tips for Getting Attention in Application Letters
Tip	**Example**
Unsolicited Application Letters Show how your strongest skills will benefit the organization.	If you need a regional sales specialist who consistently meets sales targets while fostering strong customer relationships, please consider my qualifications.
Describe your understanding of the job's requirements and show how well your qualifications fit them.	Your annual report stated that improving manufacturing efficiency is one of the company's top priorities for next year. Through my postgraduate research in systems engineering and consulting work for several companies in the industry, I've developed reliable methods for quickly identifying ways to cut production time while reducing resource use.
Mention the name of a person known to and highly regarded by the reader.	When Janice McHugh of your franchise sales division spoke to our business communication class last week, she said you often need promising new marketing graduates at this time of year.
Refer to publicized company activities, achievements, changes, or new procedures.	Today's issue of the Detroit News reports that you may need the expertise of computer programmers versed in robotics when your Lansing tire plant automates this spring.
Use a question to demonstrate your understanding of the organization's needs.	Can your fast-growing market research division use an interviewer with two years of field survey experience, a B.A. in public relations, and a real desire to succeed? If so, please consider me for the position.
Use a catchphrase opening if the job requires ingenuity and imagination.	Haut monde—whether referring to French, Italian, or Arab clients, it still means "high society." As an interior designer for your Beverly Hills showroom, not only could I serve and sell to your distinguished clientele, but I could do it in all these languages. I speak, read, and write them fluently.
Solicited Application Letters Identify where you discovered the job opening; describe what you have to offer.	Your job posting on Monster.com for a cruise-line social director caught my eye. My eight years of experience as a social director in the travel industry would allow me to serve your new Caribbean cruise division well.

This applicant does a smooth job of mirroring the company's stated needs while high-lighting his personal qualifications, along with evidence that he understands the broader market. He balances his relative lack of experience with enthusiasm and knowledge of the industry. Table 16.1 highlights some ways you can spark interest and grab attention in your opening paragraph. All these openings demonstrate the "you" attitude, and many indicate how the applicant can benefit the employer.

Building Interest and Increasing Desire

Use the middle section of your application letter to expand on your opening and present a more complete picture of your strengths.

The middle section of your application letter presents your strongest selling points in terms of their potential benefit to the organization, thereby building interest in you and creating a desire to interview you. As with the opening, the more specific you can be in the middle section, the better. And back up your assertions with some convincing evidence of your ability to perform:

Poor

I completed three college courses in business and managerial communication, earning an A in each course, and have worked for the past year at Imperial Construction.

Improved

Using the skills gained from three semesters of college training in business and managerial communication, I developed a collection system for Imperial Construction that reduced annual bad-debt losses by 25 percent. By emphasizing a win–win scenario for the company and its clients with incentives for on-time payment, the system was also credited with improving customer satisfaction.

When writing a solicited letter, be sure to discuss each requirement specified in the advertisement. If you are deficient in any of these requirements, stress other solid selling points to help strengthen your overall presentation.

Don't restrict your message to just core job duties. Also highlight personal characteristics that apply to the targeted position, such as your diligence or your ability to work hard, learn quickly, handle responsibility, or get along with people, using concrete examples:

> While attending college full time, I worked part-time during the school year and up to 60 hours a week each summer in order to be totally self-supporting while in college. I can offer your organization the same level of effort and perseverance.

Mention your salary requirements at this stage only if the organization has asked you to state them. If you don't know the salary that's appropriate for the position and someone with your qualifications, you can find typical salary ranges at the Bureau of Labor Statistics website, **www.bls.gov**, or a number of commercial websites. If you do state a target salary, tie it to the value you offer:

Don't bring up salary in your application letter unless the recipient has asked you to include your salary requirements.

> For the past two years, I have been helping a company similar to yours organize its database marketing efforts. I would therefore like to receive a salary in the same range (the mid-60s) for helping your company set up a more efficient customer database.

Toward the end of this section, refer the reader to your résumé by citing a specific fact or general point covered there:

> As you can see in the attached résumé, I've been working part time with a local publisher since my sophomore year. During that time, I've used client interactions as an opportunity to build strong customer service skills.

Motivating Action

The final paragraph of your application letter has two important functions: to ask the reader for a specific action (usually an interview) and to facilitate a reply. Offer to come to the employer's office at a convenient time or, if the firm is some distance away, to meet with its nearest representative or arrange a telephone interview. Include your email address and phone number, as well as the best time to reach you. Alternatively, you can take the initiative and say that you will follow up with a phone call. Refer again to your strongest selling point and, if desired, your date of availability:

In the final paragraph of your application letter, respectfully ask for specific action and make it easy for the reader to respond.

> After you have reviewed my qualifications, could we discuss the possibility of putting my marketing skills to work for your company? Because I will be on spring break the week of March 8, I would like to arrange a time to talk then. I will call in late February to schedule a convenient time when we could discuss employment opportunities at your company.

After editing and proofreading your application letter, give it a final quality check by referring to "Checklist: Writing Application Letters." Then send it along with your résumé promptly, especially if you are responding to an advertisement or online job posting.

FOLLOWING UP AFTER SUBMITTING A RÉSUMÉ

Deciding if, when, and how to follow up after submitting your résumé and application letter is one of the trickiest

REAL-TIME UPDATES
Learn More by Exploring This Interactive Website

How much are you worth?

Find real-life salary ranges for a wide range of jobs. Go to http://real-timeupdates.com/ebc10 and click on Learn More. If you are using MyBcommLab, you can access Real-Time Updates within each chapter or under Student Study Tools.

✔ Checklist | Writing Application Letters

- Take the same care with your application letter that you took with your résumé.
- If you are *prospecting* using an unsolicited message, do deep research to identify the qualities the company likely wants.
- For solicited messages in response to a posted job opening, word your message in a way that echoes back the qualifications listed in the posting.
- Open the letter by capturing the reader's attention in a businesslike way.
- Use specific language to clearly state your interests and objectives.

- Build interest and desire in your potential contribution by presenting your key qualifications for the job.
- Link your education, experience, and personal qualities to the job requirements.
- Outline salary requirements only if the organization has requested that you provide them.
- Request an interview at a time and place that is convenient for the reader.
- Make it easy to comply with your request by providing your complete contact information and good times to reach you.
- Adapt your style for cultural variations, if required.

Think creatively about a follow-up message; show that you've continued to add to your skills or that you've learned more about the company or the industry.

parts of a job search. First and foremost, keep in mind that employers continue to evaluate your communication efforts and professionalism during this phase, so don't say or do anything to leave a negative impression. Second, adhere to whatever instructions the employer has provided. If a job posting says "no calls," for example, don't call. Third, if the job posting lists a *close date*, don't call or write before then, because the company is still collecting applications and will not have made a decision about inviting people for interviews. Wait a week or so after the close date. If no close date is given and you have no other information to suggest a timeline, you can generally contact the company starting a week or two after submitting your résumé.[6] Keep in mind that a single instance of poor etiquette or clumsy communication can undo all your hard work in a job search, so maintain your professional behavior every step of the way.

When you follow up by email or telephone, you can share an additional piece of information that links your qualifications to the position (keep an eye out for late-breaking news about the company, too) and ask a question about the hiring process as a way to gather some information about your status. Good questions to ask include:[7]

- Has a hiring decision been made yet?
- Can you tell me what to expect next in terms of the hiring process?
- What is the company's timeframe for filling this position?
- Could I follow up in another week if you haven't had the chance to contact me yet?
- Can I provide any additional information regarding my qualifications for the position?

Whatever the circumstances, a follow-up message can demonstrate that you're sincerely interested in working for the organization, persistent in pursuing your goals, and committed to upgrading your skills.

If you don't land a job at your dream company on the first attempt, don't give up. You can apply again if a new opening appears, or you can send an updated résumé with a new unsolicited application letter that describes how you have gained additional experience, taken a relevant course, or otherwise improved your skill set. Many leading employers take note of applicants who came close but didn't quite make it and may extend offers when positions open up in the future.[8]

Understanding the Interviewing Process

2 **LEARNING OBJECTIVE**

Describe the typical sequence of job interviews, the major types of interviews, and what employers look for during an interview.

An **employment interview** is a formal meeting during which both you and the prospective employer ask questions and exchange information. The employer's objective is to find the best talent to fill available job openings, and your objective is to find the right match for your goals and capabilities.

As you get ready to begin interviewing, keep two vital points in mind. First, recognize that the process takes time. Start your preparation and research early; the best job offers usually go to the best-prepared candidates. Second, don't limit your options by looking at only a few companies. By exploring a wide range of firms and positions, you might uncover great opportunities that you would not have found otherwise. You'll increase the odds of getting more job offers, too.

Start preparing early for your interviews—and be sure to consider a wide range of options.

THE TYPICAL SEQUENCE OF INTERVIEWS

Most employers interview an applicant multiple times before deciding to make a job offer. At the most selective companies, you might have a dozen or more individual interviews across several stages.[9] Depending on the company and the position, the process may stretch out over many weeks, or it may be completed in a matter of days.[10]

Employers start with the *screening stage*, in which they filter out applicants who are unqualified or otherwise not a good fit for the position. Screening can take place on your school's campus, at company offices, via telephone (including Skype or another Internet-based phone service), or through a computer-based screening system. Time is limited in screening interviews, so keep your answers short while providing a few key points that differentiate you from other candidates. If your screening interview will take place by phone, try to schedule it for a time when you can be focused and free from interruptions.[11]

During the screening stage of interviews, use the limited time available to differentiate yourself from other candidates.

The next stage of interviews, the *selection stage*, helps the organization identify the top candidates from all those who qualify. During these interviews, show keen interest in the job, relate your skills and experience to the organization's needs, listen attentively, and ask insightful questions that show you've done your research.

During the selection stage, continue to show how your skills and attributes can help the company.

If the interviewer agrees that you're a good candidate, you may receive a job offer, either on the spot or a few days later by phone, mail, or email. In other instances, you may be invited back for a final evaluation, often by a higher-ranking executive. The objective of the *final stage* is often to sell you on the advantages of joining the organization.

During the final stage, the interviewer may try to sell you on working for the firm.

COMMON TYPES OF INTERVIEWS

Employers can use a variety of interviewing methods throughout the interviewing process, and you need to recognize the different types and be prepared for each one. These methods can be distinguished by the way they are structured, the number of people involved, and the purpose of the interview.

Structured versus Unstructured Interviews

In a **structured interview**, the interviewer (or a computer program) asks a series of questions in a predetermined order. Structured interviews help employers identify candidates who don't meet basic job criteria, and they make it easier for the interview team to compare answers from multiple candidates.[12]

A structured interview follows a set sequence of questions, allowing the interview team to compare answers from all candidates

In contrast, in an **open-ended interview**, the interviewer adapts his or her line of questioning based on the answers you give and any questions you ask. Even though it may feel like a conversation, remember that it's still an interview, so keep your answers focused and professional.

In an open-ended interview, the interviewer adapts the line of questioning based on your responses and questions.

Panel and Group Interviews

Although one-on-one interviews are the most common format, some employers use panel or group interviews as well. In a **panel interview**, you meet with several interviewers at once.[13] Try to make a connection with each person on the panel and keep in mind that each person has a different perspective, so tailor your responses accordingly.[14] For example, an upper-level manager is likely to be interested in your overall business sense and strategic perspective, whereas a potential colleague might be more interested in your technical skills and ability to work in a team. In a **group interview**, one or more interviewers meet with several candidates simultaneously. A key purpose of a group interview is to observe how the candidates interact with potential peers.[15]

In a panel interview, you meet with several interviewers at once; in a group interview, you and several other candidates meet with one or more interviewers at once.

Behavioral, Situational, Working, and Stress Interviews

Perhaps the most common type of interview these days is the **behavioral interview**, in which you are asked to relate specific incidents and experiences from your past.[16] Generic

In a behavioral interview, you are asked to describe how you handled situations from your past.

interview questions can often be answered with "canned" responses, but behavioral questions require candidates to use their own experiences and attributes to craft answers. Studies show that behavioral interviewing is a much better predictor of success on the job than traditional interview questions.[17] To prepare for a behavioral interview, review your work or college experiences to recall several instances in which you demonstrated an important job-related attribute or dealt with a challenge such as uncooperative team members or heavy workloads. Get ready with responses that quickly summarize the situation, the actions you took, and the outcome of those actions.[18]

In situational interviews, you're asked to explain how you would handle various hypothetical situations.

A **situational interview** is similar to a behavioral interview except that the questions focus on how you would handle various hypothetical situations on the job. The situations will likely relate to the job you're applying for, so the more you know about the position, the better prepared you'll be.

In a working interview, you actually perform work-related tasks.

A **working interview** is the most realistic type of interview: You actually perform a job-related activity during the interview. You may be asked to lead a brainstorming session, solve a business problem, engage in role playing, or even make a presentation.[19]

The theory behind stress interviews is to let recruiters see how you handle yourself under pressure.

The most unnerving type of interview is the **stress interview**, during which you might be asked questions designed to unsettle you, or you might be subjected to long periods of silence, criticism, interruptions, or even hostile reactions by the interviewer. The theory behind this approach is that you'll reveal how well you handle stressful situations, although some experts find the technique of dubious value.[20] If you find yourself in a stress interview, recognize what is happening and collect your thoughts for a few seconds before you respond.

INTERVIEW MEDIA

Expect to use a variety of media when you interview, from in-person conversations to virtual meetings.

Expect to be interviewed through a variety of media. Employers trying to cut travel costs and the demands on staff time now interview candidates via telephone, email, instant messaging, virtual online systems, and videoconferencing, in addition to traditional face-to-face meetings (see Figure 16.3).

Treat a telephone interview as seriously as you would an in-person interview.

To succeed at a telephone interview, make sure you treat it as seriously as an in-person interview. Be prepared with a copy of all the materials you have sent to the employer, including your résumé and any correspondence. In addition, prepare some note cards with key message points you'd like to make and questions you'd like to ask. If possible, arrange to speak on a landline so you don't have to worry about mobile phone reception problems.

Figure 16.3 Finding Real Jobs in a Virtual World
Virtual job fairs, such as the Working Worlds event hosted by Luxembourg's GAX Technologies, allow candidates and recruiters to interact without the time and expense of travel.
Source: Used with permission of GAX.

And remember that you won't be able to use a pleasant smile, a firm handshake, and other nonverbal signals to create a good impression. A positive, alert tone of voice is therefore vital.[21]

Email and IM are also sometimes used in the screening stage. Although you have almost no opportunity to send and receive nonverbal signals with these formats, you do have the major advantage of being able to review and edit each response before you send it. Maintain a professional style in your responses, and be sure to ask questions that demonstrate your knowledge of the company and the position.[22]

> When interviewing via email or IM, be sure to take a moment to review your responses before sending them.

Many employers use video technology for both live and recorded interviews. For instance, Zappos often uses video interviews on Skype to select the top two or three finalists for each position and then invites those candidates for in-person interviews.[23] With recorded video interviews, an online system asks a set of questions and records the respondent's answers. Recruiters then watch the videos as part of the screening process.[24] Prepare for a video interview as you would for an in-person interview—including dressing and grooming—and take the extra steps needed to become familiar with the equipment and the process. If you're interviewing from home, arrange your space so that the webcam doesn't pick up anything distracting or embarrassing in the background. During a video interview, remember to sit up straight and focus on the camera.

> In a video interview, speak to the camera as though you are addressing the interviewer in person.

Online interviews can range from simple structured questionnaires and tests to sophisticated job simulations that are similar to working interviews (see Figure 16.4). In the banking industry, for example, Atlanta-based SunTrust and Cleveland-based National City use computerized simulations to see how well candidates can perform job-related tasks and decision-making scenarios. These simulations help identify good candidates, give applicants an idea of what the job is like, and reduce the risk of employment discrimination lawsuits because they closely mimic actual job skills.[25]

> Computer-based virtual interviews range from simple structured interviews to realistic job simulations to meetings in virtual worlds.

WHAT EMPLOYERS LOOK FOR IN AN INTERVIEW

Interviews give employers the chance to go beyond the basic data of your résumé to get to know you and to answer two essential questions. The first is whether you can handle the responsibilities of the position. Naturally, the more you know about the demands

> Suitability for a specific job is judged on the basis of such factors as
> - Academic preparation
> - Work experience
> - Job-related personality traits

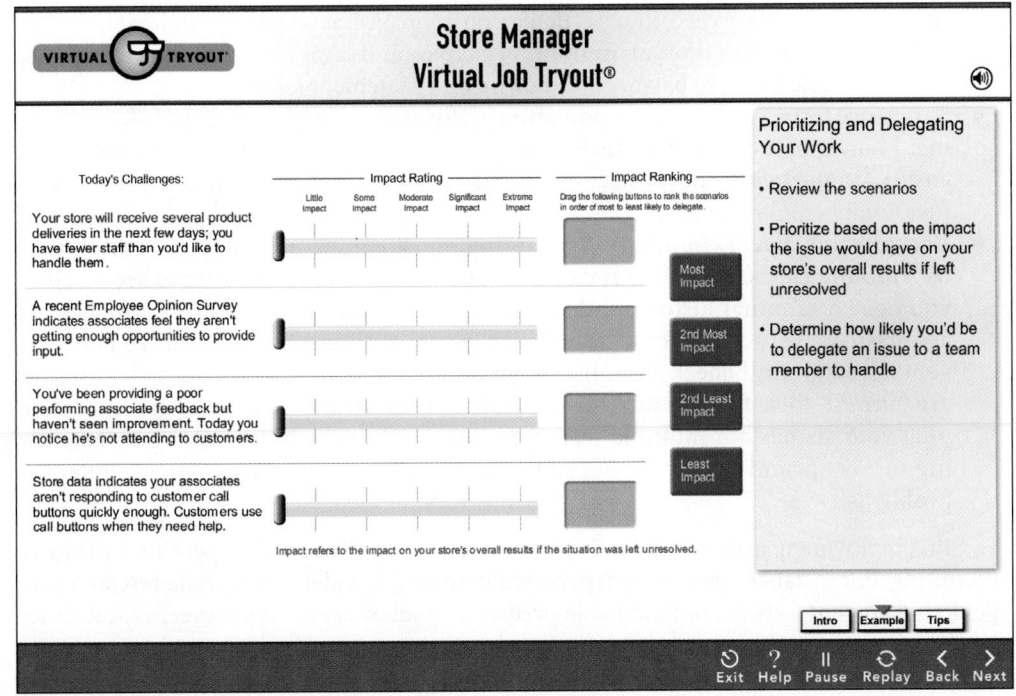

Figure 16.4 Job Task Simulations
Computer-based job simulations are an increasingly popular approach to testing job-related skills.
Source: Used with permission of Shaker Consulting Group.

of the position, and the more you've thought about how your skills match those demands, the better you'll be able to respond.

The second essential question is whether you will be a good fit with the organization and the target position. This line of inquiry includes both a general and a specific aspect. The general aspect concerns your overall personality and approach to work. All good employers want people who are confident, dedicated, positive, curious, courteous, ethical, and willing to commit to something larger than their own individual goals. The specific aspect involves the fit with a particular company and position. Just like people, companies have different "personalities." Some are intense; others are more laid back. Some emphasize teamwork; others expect employees to forge their own way and even compete with one another. Expectations also vary from job to job within a company and from industry to industry. An outgoing personality is essential for sales but less so for research, for instance.

> Compatibility with an organization and a position is judged on the basis of personal background, attitudes, and style.

PREEMPLOYMENT TESTING AND BACKGROUND CHECKS

> Preemployment tests attempt to provide objective, quantitative information about a candidate's skills, attitudes, and habits.

In an effort to improve the predictability of the selection process, many employers now conduct a variety of preemployment evaluations and investigations. Here are types of assessments you are likely to encounter during your job search:[26]

- **Integrity tests.** Integrity tests attempt to measure how truthful and trustworthy a candidate is likely to be.
- **Personality tests.** Personality tests are designed to gauge such aspects as attitudes toward work, interests, managerial potential, dependability, commitment, and motivation.
- **Cognitive tests.** Cognitive tests measure a variety of attributes involved in acquiring, processing, analyzing, using, and remembering information. Typical tests involve reading comprehension, mathematics, problem solving, and decision making.
- **Job knowledge and job skills tests.** These assessments measure the knowledge and skills required to succeed in a particular position. An accounting candidate, for example, might be tested on accounting principles and legal matters (knowledge) and asked to create a simple balance sheet or income statement (skills).
- **Substance tests.** A majority of companies perform some level of drug and alcohol testing. Many employers believe such testing is necessary to maintain workplace safety, ensure productivity, and protect companies from lawsuits, but others view it as an invasion of employee privacy.
- **Background checks.** In addition to testing, most companies conduct some sort of background check, including reviewing your credit record, checking to see whether you have a criminal history, and verifying your education. Moreover, you should assume that every employer will conduct a general online search on you. To help prevent a background check from tripping you up, verify that your college transcripts are current, look for any mistakes or outdated information in your credit record, plug your name into multiple search engines to see whether anything embarrassing shows up, and scour your social network profiles and connections for potential problems.

Preemployment assessments are a complex and controversial aspect of workforce recruiting. For instance, even though personality testing is widely used, some research suggests that current tests are not a reliable predictor of job success.[27] However, expect to see more innovation in this area and greater use of testing in general in the future as companies try to reduce the risks and costs of poor hiring decisions.

If you're concerned about any preemployment test, ask the employer for more information or ask your college career center for advice. You can also get more information from the Equal Employment Opportunity Commission, at www.eeoc.gov.

Preparing for a Job Interview

Now that you're armed with insights into the interviewing and assessment process, you're ready to begin preparing for your interviews. Preparation will help you feel more confident and perform better under pressure, and preparation starts with learning about the organization.

3   **LEARNING OBJECTIVE**

List six tasks you need to complete to prepare for a successful job interview.

LEARNING ABOUT THE ORGANIZATION AND YOUR INTERVIEWERS

Today's employers expect serious candidates to demonstrate an understanding of the company's operations, its markets, and its strategic and tactical challenges.[28] You've already done some initial research to identify companies of interest, but when you're invited to interview, it's time to dig a little deeper (see Table 16.2). Making this effort demonstrates your interest in the company, and it identifies you as a business professional who knows the importance of investigation and analysis.

Interviewers expect you to know some basic information about the company and its industry.

In addition to learning about the company and the job opening, learn as much as you can about the managers who will be interviewing you, if you can get their names. Search LinkedIn in particular; many professionals have profiles on the popular business networking site. Think about ways to use whatever information you find. For example, if you learn that an interviewer lists membership in a particular professional organization, you might ask him or her whether the organization is a good forum for people to learn about vital issues in the profession or industry. This question gives the interviewer an opportunity to talk about his or her own interests and experiences for a moment, which builds rapport and might reveal vital insights into the career path you are considering. Just make sure your questions are sincere and not uncomfortably personal.

TABLE 16.2	Investigating an Organization and a Job Opportunity

Where to Look and What You Can Learn

- *Company website, blogs, and social media accounts:* Overall information about the company, including key executives, products and services, locations and divisions, employee benefits, job descriptions
- *Competitors' websites, blogs, and social media accounts:* Similar information from competitors, including the strengths these companies claim to have
- *Industry-related websites and blogs:* Objective analysis and criticism of the company, its products, its reputation, and its management
- *Marketing materials (print and online):* The company's marketing strategy and customer communication style
- *Company publications (print and online):* Key events, stories about employees, new products
- *Your social network contacts:* Names and job titles of potential contacts within a company
- *Periodicals (newspapers and trade journals, both print and online):* In-depth stories about the company and its strategies, products, successes, and failures; you may find profiles of top executives
- *Career center at your college:* Often provides a wide array of information about companies that hire graduates
- *Current and former employees:* Insights into the work environment

Points to Learn About the Organization

- Full name
- Location (headquarters and divisions, branches, subsidiaries, or other units)
- Ownership (public or private; whether it is owned by another company)
- Brief history
- Products and services
- Industry position (whether the company is a leader or a minor player; whether it is an innovator or more of a follower)
- Key financial points (such as stock price and trends, if a public company)
- Growth prospects (whether the company is investing in its future through research and development; whether it is in a thriving industry)

Points to Learn About the Position

- Title
- Functions and responsibilities
- Qualifications and expectations
- Possible career paths
- Salary range
- Travel expectations and opportunities
- Relocation expectations and opportunities

Asking questions of your own is as important as answering the interviewer's questions. Not only do you get vital information, but you show initiative and curiosity.
Source: © Exactostock/SuperStock.

You can expect to face a number of common questions in your interviews, so be sure to prepare for them.

THINKING AHEAD ABOUT QUESTIONS

Planning ahead for the interviewer's questions will help you handle them more confidently and successfully. In addition, you will want to prepare insightful questions of your own.

Planning for the Employer's Questions

Many general interview questions are "stock" queries that you can expect to hear again and again during your interviews. Get ready to face these five at the very least:

- **What is the hardest decision you've ever had to make?** Be prepared with a good example (that isn't too personal), explaining why the decision was difficult, how you made the choice you made, and what you learned from the experience.
- **What is your greatest weakness?** This question seems to be a favorite of some interviewers, although it probably rarely yields useful information. One good strategy is to mention a skill or attribute you haven't had the opportunity to develop yet but would like to in your next position.[29]
- **Where do you want to be five years from now?** This question tests (1) whether you're merely using this job as a stopover until something better comes along and (2) whether you've given thought to your long-term goals. Your answer should reflect your desire to contribute to the employer's long-term goals, not just your own goals. Whether this question often yields useful information is also a matter of debate, but be prepared to answer it.[30]
- **What didn't you like about previous jobs you've held?** Answer this one carefully: The interviewer is trying to predict whether you'll be an unhappy or difficult employee.[31] Describe something that you didn't like in a way that puts you in a positive light, such as having limited opportunities to apply your skills or education. Avoid making negative comments about former employers or colleagues.
- **Tell me something about yourself.** One good strategy is to *briefly* share the "story of you" (see page 529), quickly summarizing where you have been and where you would like to go—in a way that aligns your interests with the company's. Alternatively, you can focus on a specific skill that you know is valuable to the company, share something business-relevant that you are passionate about, or offer a short summary of what colleagues or customers think about you.[32] Whatever tactic you choose, this is not the time to be shy or indecisive, so be ready with a confident, memorable answer.

Continue your preparation by planning a brief answer to each question in Table 16.3. You can also find typical interview questions at websites such as InterviewUp, **www.interviewup .com**, where candidates share actual questions they have faced in recent interviews.[33]

Look for ways to frame your responses as brief stories rather than as dry facts or statements.

As you prepare answers, look for ways to frame your responses as brief stories (again, 30 to 90 seconds) rather than simple declarative answers.[34] Cohesive stories tend to stick in the listener's mind more effectively than disconnected facts and statements.

Planning Questions of Your Own

Remember that an interview is a two-way conversation: The questions you ask are just as important as the answers you provide. By asking insightful questions, you can demonstrate your understanding of the organization, you can steer the discussion into areas that allow you to present your qualifications to best advantage, and you can verify for yourself whether this is a good opportunity. Plus, interviewers expect you to ask

REAL-TIME UPDATES
Learn More by Watching This Video

Study the classics to ace your next interview

No, not Homer and Ovid—classic interview questions. Prepare answers to these old standbys so you can respond with clarity and confidence. Go to http://real-timeupdates.com/ebc10 and click on Learn More. If you are using MyBcommLab, you can access Real-Time Updates within each chapter or under Student Study Tools.

TABLE 16.3	**Twenty-Five Common Interview Questions**

Questions About College

1. What courses in college did you like most? Least? Why?
2. Do you think your extracurricular activities in college were worth the time you spent on them? Why or why not?
3. When did you choose your college major? Did you ever change your major? If so, why?
4. Do you feel you did the best scholastic work you are capable of?
5. How has your college education prepared you for this position?

Questions About Employers and Jobs

6. What jobs have you held? Why did you leave?
7. What percentage of your college expenses did you earn? How?
8. Why did you choose your particular field of work?
9. What are the disadvantages of your chosen field?
10. Have you served in the military? What rank did you achieve? What jobs did you perform?
11. What do you think about how this industry operates today?
12. Why do you think you would like this particular type of job?

Questions About Work Experiences and Expectations

13. Do you prefer to work in any specific geographic location? If so, why?
14. What motivates you? Why?
15. What do you think determines a person's progress in a good organization?
16. Describe an experience in which you learned from one of your mistakes.
17. Why do you want this job?
18. What have you done that shows initiative and willingness to work?
19. Why should I hire you?

Questions About Work Habits

20. Do you prefer working with others or by yourself?
21. What type of boss do you prefer?
22. Have you ever had any difficulty getting along with colleagues or supervisors? With instructors? With other students?
23. What would you do if you were given an unrealistic deadline for a task or project?
24. How do you feel about overtime work?
25. How do you handle stress or pressure on the job?

Sources: Adapted from InterviewUp website, accessed 6 April 2008, www.interviewup.com; *The Northwestern Endicott Report* (Evanston, Ill.: Northwestern University Placement Center).

questions and tend to look negatively on candidates who don't have any questions to ask. For a list of good questions that you might use as a starting point, see Table 16.4 on the next page.

BOLSTERING YOUR CONFIDENCE

Interviewing is stressful for everyone, so some nervousness is natural. However, you can take steps to feel more confident. Start by reminding yourself that you have value to offer the employer, and the employer already thinks highly enough of you to invite you to an interview.

The best way to build your confidence is to prepare thoroughly and address shortcomings as best you can—in other words, take action.

If some aspect of your appearance or background makes you uneasy, correct it if possible or offset it by emphasizing positive traits such as warmth, wit, intelligence, or charm. Instead of dwelling on your weaknesses, focus on your strengths. Instead of worrying about how you will perform in the interview, focus on how you can help the organization succeed. As with public speaking, the more prepared you are, the more confident you'll be.

POLISHING YOUR INTERVIEW STYLE

Competence and confidence are the foundation of your interviewing style, and you can enhance them by giving the interviewer an impression of poise, good manners, and good judgment. You can develop an adept style by staging mock interviews with a friend or using an interview simulator. Record these mock interviews so you can evaluate yourself. Your college's career center may have computer-based systems for practicing interviews as well (see Figure 16.5 on the next page).

Staging mock interviews with a friend is a good way to hone your style.

After each practice session, look for opportunities to improve. Have your mock interview partner critique your performance or critique yourself if you're able to record your

TABLE 16.4	Ten Questions to Consider Asking an Interviewer
Question	**Reason for Asking**
1. What are the job's major responsibilities?	A vague answer could mean that the responsibilities have not been clearly defined, which is almost guaranteed to cause frustration if you take the job.
2. What qualities do you want in the person who fills this position?	This will help you go beyond the job description to understand what the company really wants.
3. How do you measure success for someone in this position?	A vague or incomplete answer could mean that the expectations you will face are unrealistic or ill defined.
4. What is the first problem that needs the attention of the person you hire?	Not only will this help you prepare, but it can signal whether you're about to jump into a problematic situation.
5. Would relocation be required now or in the future?	If you're not willing to move often or at all, you need to know those expectations now.
6. Why is this job now vacant?	If the previous employee got promoted, that's a good sign. If the person quit, that might not be such a good sign.
7. What makes your organization different from others in the industry?	The answer will help you assess whether the company has a clear strategy to succeed in its industry and whether top managers communicate this to lower-level employees.
8. How would you define your organization's managerial philosophy?	You want to know whether the managerial philosophy is consistent with your own working values.
9. What is a typical workday like for you?	The interviewer's response can give you clues about daily life at the company.
10. What systems and policies are in place to help employees stay up to date in their professions and continue to expand their skills?	If the company doesn't have a strong commitment to employee development, chances are it isn't going to stay competitive very long.

Sources: Adapted from Joe Conklin, "Turning the Tables: Six Questions to Ask Your Interviewer," *Quality Progress*, November 2007, 55; Andrea N. Browne, "Keeping the Momentum at the Interview; Ask Questions, Do Your Research, and Be a Team Player," *Washington Post*, 29 July 2007, K1; Marilyn Sherman, "Questions R Us: What to Ask at a Job Interview," *Career World*, January 2004, 20; H. Lee Rust, *Job Search: The Complete Manual for Jobseekers* (New York: American Management Association, 1979), 56.

Figure 16.5 Interview Simulators
Experts advise you to practice your interview skills as much as possible. You can use a friend or classmate as a practice partner, or you might be able to use one of the interview simulators now available, such as this system from Perfect Interview. Ask at your career center, or search online for "practice interviews" or "interview simulators."
Source: Used with permission of Interview Simulators, from Perfect Interview LLC.

COMMUNICATING ACROSS CULTURES

Successfully Interviewing Across Borders

Interviewing for a job in another country can be one of the most exciting steps in your career. To succeed, you need to pay especially close attention to personal appearance, an awareness of what interviewers are really trying to learn about you, and what you should learn about the organization you're hoping to join.

Some countries and cultures place a much higher importance on dress and personal grooming than many employees in the United States are accustomed to; moreover, expectations of personal appearance can vary dramatically from country to country. Ask people who've been to the country and observe local businesspeople when you arrive. Many people interpret inappropriate dress as more than a simple fashion mistake; they view it as an inability or unwillingness to understand another culture.

Whether or not these things should matter isn't the issue; they do matter, and successful job candidates learn how to respond to different expectations. For instance, business image consultant Ashley Rothschild points out that you could get away with wearing a boldly colored suit in Italy but probably not in Japan. Business professionals do tend to dress formally in Italy, but as a worldwide fashion leader, the country has a broad definition of what is appropriate business attire.

Smart recruiters always analyze both nonverbal signals and verbal messages to judge whether an applicant truly has the qualities necessary for a job. In international employment situations, you'll probably be under even closer scrutiny. Recruiters abroad will want to know if you really have what it takes to succeed in unfamiliar social settings, how your family will handle the transition, and whether you can adapt your personal work style and habits enough to blend in with the hiring organization.

Remember to ask plenty of questions and do your research, both before and after the interview. Some employees view overseas postings as grand adventures, only to collide headfirst with the reality of what it's like to live and work in a completely different culture. For instance, if you've grown accustomed to the independent work style you enjoy in your current job or in school, could you handle a more structured work environment with a hierarchical chain of command? Make sure to get a sense of the culture both within the company and within its social community before you commit to a job in another country.

CAREER APPLICATIONS

1. Explain how you could find out what is appropriate dress for a job interview in South Africa.
2. Would it be appropriate to ask an interviewer to describe the culture in his or her country? Explain your answer.

Sources: Adapted from Jean-Marc Hachey, "Interviewing for an International Job," excerpt from *The Canadian Guide to Working and Living Overseas*, 3rd ed., accessed 23 February 2004, www.workingoverseas.com; Rebecca Falkoff, "Dress to Impress the World: International Business Fashion," Monster .com, accessed 23 February 2004, www.monster.com; Mary Ellen Slater, "Navigating the Details of Landing an Overseas Job," *Washington Post*, 11 November 2002, E4.

---

practice interviews, using the list of warning signs shown in Table 16.5 on the next page. Pay close attention to the length of your planned answers as well. Interviewers want you to give complete answers, but they don't want you to take up valuable time or test their patience by chatting about minor or irrelevant details.[35]

In addition to reviewing your answers, evaluate your nonverbal behavior, including your posture, eye contact, facial expressions, and hand gestures and movements. Do you come across as alert and upbeat or passive and withdrawn? Pay close attention to your speaking voice as well. If you tend to speak in a monotone, for instance, practice speaking in a livelier style, with more inflection and emphasis. And watch out for "filler words" such as *uh* and *um*. Many people start sentences with a filler without being conscious of doing so. Train yourself to pause silently for a moment instead as you gather your thoughts and plan what to say.

> Evaluate the length and clarity of your answers, your nonverbal behavior, and the quality of your voice.

PRESENTING A PROFESSIONAL IMAGE

Clothing and grooming are important elements of preparation because they reveal something about your personality, professionalism, and ability to sense the unspoken "rules" of a situation. Inappropriate dress is a common criticism leveled at interviewees, so stand out by looking professional.[36] Your research into various company, industries, and professions should give you insight into expectations for business attire. If you're not sure what to wear and the company hasn't provided any guidance, refer to Table 2.4 on page 93 for tips on selecting appropriate business attire or ask someone who works in the same industry. And don't be afraid to call the company for advice.

> Dress conservatively and be well groomed for every interview.

TABLE 16.5	Warning Signs: 25 Attributes That Interviewers Don't Like to See

1. Poor personal appearance
2. Overbearing, overaggressive, or conceited demeanor; a "superiority complex"; a know-it-all attitude
3. Inability to express ideas clearly; poor voice, diction, or grammar
4. Lack of knowledge or experience
5. Poor preparation for the interview
6. Lack of interest in the job
7. Lack of planning for career; lack of purpose or goals
8. Lack of enthusiasm; passive and indifferent demeanor
9. Lack of confidence and poise; appearance of being nervous and ill at ease
10. Insufficient evidence of achievement
11. Failure to participate in extracurricular activities
12. Overemphasis on money; interest only in the best dollar offer
13. Poor scholastic record
14. Unwillingness to start at the bottom; expecting too much too soon
15. Tendency to make excuses
16. Evasive answers; hedging on unfavorable factors in record
17. Lack of tact
18. Lack of maturity
19. Lack of courtesy and common sense, including answering mobile phones, texting, or chewing gum during the interview
20. Being critical of past or present employers
21. Lack of social skills
22. Marked dislike for schoolwork
23. Lack of vitality
24. Failure to look interviewer in the eye
25. Limp, weak handshake

Sources: Adapted from "Employers Reveal Outrageous and Common Mistakes Candidates Made in Job Interviews, According to New CareerBuilder Survey," CareerBuilder .com, 12 January 2011, www.careerbuilder.com; *The Northwestern Endicott Report* (Evanston, Ill.: Northwestern University Placement Center).

You don't need to spend a fortune on interview clothes, but your clothes must be clean, pressed, and appropriate. The following conservative look will serve you well in most business interview situations:[37]

- Neat, "adult" hairstyle
- Conservative business suit (for women, that means no exposed midriffs, short skirts, or plunging necklines) in a dark solid color or a subtle pattern such as pinstripes
- Solid color shirt for men (white in more conservative professions); coordinated blouse for women
- Conservative tie (classic stripes or subtle patterns) for men
- Limited jewelry (men, especially, should wear very little jewelry)
- No visible piercings other than one or two earrings (for women only)
- No visible tattoos
- Stylish but professional-looking shoes (no extreme high heels or casual shoes)
- Clean hands and nicely trimmed fingernails
- Little or no perfume or cologne (some people are allergic, and many people are put off by strong smells)
- Subtle makeup (for women)
- Exemplary personal hygiene

If you want to be taken seriously, dress and act seriously.

Remember, an interview is not the place to express your individuality or to let your inner rebel run wild. Send a clear signal that you understand the business world and know how to adapt to it. You won't be taken seriously otherwise.

BEING READY WHEN YOU ARRIVE

When you go to your interview, take a small notebook, a pen, a list of the questions you want to ask, several copies of your résumé (protected in a folder), an outline of what you have learned about the organization, and any past correspondence about the position. You may also want to take a small calendar, a transcript of your college grades, a list of references, and a portfolio containing samples of your work, performance reviews, and certificates of achievement.[38] Think carefully if you plan to use a tablet computer or any other device for note taking or reference during an interview. You don't want to waste any of the interviewer's time fumbling with it. Also, turn

Make a positive first impression with careful grooming and attire. You don't need to spend a fortune on new clothes, but you do need to look clean, prepared, and professional.
Source: © Blend Images/Alamy.

✓ Checklist   Planning for a Successful Job Interview

- Learn about the organization, including its operations, markets, and challenges.
- Learn as much as you can about the people who will be interviewing you, if you can find their names.
- Plan for the employer's questions, including questions about tough decisions you've made, your perceived shortcomings, what you didn't like about previous jobs, and your career plans.
- Plan questions of your own to find out whether this is really the job and the organization for you and to show that you've done your research.
- Bolster your confidence by removing as many sources of apprehension as you can.

- Polish your interview style by staging mock interviews.
- Present a professional appearance with appropriate dress and grooming.
- Be ready when you arrive and bring along a pen, paper, a list of questions, copies of your résumé, an outline of your research on the company, and any correspondence you've had regarding the position.
- Double-check the location and time of the interview and map out the route beforehand.
- Relax and be flexible; the schedule and interview arrangements may change when you arrive.

off your mobile phone; in a recent survey of hiring professionals, answering calls or texting while in an interview were identified as the most common mistakes made by job candidates.[39]

Be sure you know when and where the interview will be held. The worst way to start an interview is to be late, and arriving in a stressed-out state isn't much better. Check the route you will take, but don't rely on time estimates from a bus or subway service or from an online mapping service. If you're not familiar with the route, the safest choice is to travel to the location a few days before the interview, if possible, to verify it for yourself. Leave yourself plenty of time for unforeseen problems.

When you arrive, remind yourself that you are fully prepared and confident and then try to relax. You may have to wait, so bring along something business oriented to read. If company literature is available in the lobby, read it while you wait. At every step, show respect for everyone you encounter. If the opportunity presents itself, ask a few questions about the organization or express enthusiasm for the job. Refrain from smoking before the interview (nonsmokers can smell smoke on the clothing of interviewees) and avoid chewing gum or otherwise eating or drinking in the lobby (or at any point during the interview). Anything you do or say while you wait may well get back to the interviewer, so make sure your best qualities show from the moment you enter the premises. To review the steps for planning a successful interview, see "Checklist: Planning for a Successful Job Interview."

> Be ready to go the minute you arrive at the interviewing site; don't fumble around for your résumé or your list of questions.

Interviewing for Success

At this point, you have a good sense of the overall process and know how to prepare for your interviews. The next step is to get familiar with the three stages that occur in some form in all interviews: the warm-up, the question-and-answer session, and the close.

4   LEARNING OBJECTIVE

Explain how to succeed in all three stages of an interview.

THE WARM-UP

Of the three stages, the warm-up is the most important, even though it may account for only a small fraction of the time you spend in the interview. Studies suggest that many interviewers, particularly those who are poorly trained in interviewing techniques, make up their minds within the first 20 seconds of contact with a candidate.[40] Don't let your guard down if it appears that the interviewer wants to engage in what feels like small talk; these exchanges are every bit as important as structured questions.

Body language is crucial at this point. Stand or sit up straight, maintain regular but natural eye contact, and don't fidget. When the interviewer extends a hand, respond with a firm but not overpowering handshake. Repeat the interviewer's name when you're introduced ("It's a pleasure to meet you, Ms. Litton"). Wait until you're asked to be seated or the

> The first minute of the interview is crucial, so stay alert and be on your best business behavior.

Recognize that you could face substantial questions as soon as your interview starts, so make sure you are prepared and ready to go.

interviewer has taken a seat. Let the interviewer start the discussion, and be ready to answer one or two substantial questions right away. The following are some common openers:[41]

- Why do you want to work here?
- What do you know about us?
- Tell me a little about yourself.

THE QUESTION-AND-ANSWER STAGE

Questions and answers usually consume the greatest part of the interview. Depending on the type of interview, the interviewer will likely ask about your qualifications, discuss some of the points mentioned in your résumé, and ask about how you have handled particular situations in the past or would handle them in the future. You'll also be asking questions of your own.

Dealing with Questions

Listen carefully to questions before you answer.

Let the interviewer lead the conversation and never answer a question before he or she has finished asking it. Not only is this type of interruption rude, but the last few words of the question might alter how you respond. As much as possible, avoid one-word yes-or-no answers. Use the opportunity to expand on a positive response or explain a negative response. If you're asked a difficult question or the offbeat questions that companies such as Zappos and Google are known to use, pause before responding. Think through the implications of the question. For instance, the recruiter may know that you can't answer a question and only wants to know how you'll respond under pressure.

Whenever you're asked if you have any questions, or whenever doing so naturally fits the flow of the conversation, ask a question from the list you've prepared. Probe for what the company is looking for in its new employees so that you can show how you meet the firm's needs. Also try to zero in on any reservations the interviewer might have about you so that you can dispel them.

Listening to the Interviewer

Paying attention to both verbal and nonverbal messages can help you turn the question-and-answer stage to your advantage.

Paying attention when the interviewer speaks can be as important as giving good answers or asking good questions. Review the tips on listening offered in Chapter 2. The interviewer's facial expressions, eye movements, gestures, and posture may tell you the real meaning of what is being said. Be especially aware of how your answers are received. Does the interviewer nod in agreement or smile to show approval? If so, you're making progress. If not, you might want to introduce another topic or modify your approach.

Handling Potentially Discriminatory Questions

Federal, state, and local laws prohibit a wide variety of interview questions.

A variety of federal, state, and local laws prohibit employment discrimination on the basis of race, ethnicity, gender, age (at least if you're between 40 and 70), marital status, religion, national origin, or disability. Interview questions designed to elicit information on these topics are potentially illegal.[42] Table 16.6 on the next page compares some questions that are acceptable for employers to ask with questions that can land an employer in legal trouble if the questions are asked in order to gather information that can be used to discriminate in the hiring decision.[43]

Think about how you might respond if you were asked a potentially unlawful question.

If an interviewer asks a potentially unlawful question, consider your options carefully before you respond. You can answer the question as it was asked, you can ask tactfully whether the question might be prohibited, you can simply refuse to answer it, or you can try to answer "the question behind the question."[44] For example, if an interviewer inappropriately asks whether you are married or have strong family ties in the area, he or she might be trying to figure out if you're willing to travel or relocate—both of which are acceptable questions. Only you can decide which is the right choice based on the situation.

Even if you do answer the question as it was asked, think hard before accepting a job offer from this company if you have alternatives. Was the off-limits question possibly accidental (it happens) and therefore not really a major concern? If you think it was intentional, would you want to work for an organization that condones illegal or discriminatory questions or that doesn't train its employees to avoid them?

SHARPENING YOUR CAREER SKILLS
Make Sure You Don't Talk Yourself out of a Job

Even well-qualified applicants sometimes talk themselves right out of an opportunity by making avoidable blunders during a job interview. Take care to avoid these all-too-common mistakes:

- **Being defensive.** An interview isn't an interrogation, and the interviewer isn't out to get you. Treat interviews as business conversations, an exchange of information in which both sides have something of value to share. You'll give (and get) better information that way.
- **Failing to ask questions.** Interviewers expect you to ask questions, both during the interview and at its conclusion, when they ask if you have any questions. If you have nothing to ask, you come across as someone who isn't really interested in the job or the company. Prepare a list of questions before every interview.
- **Failing to answer questions—or trying to bluff your way through difficult questions.** If you can't answer a question, don't try to talk your way around it or fake your way through it. Remember that sometimes interviewers ask strange questions just to see how you'll respond. What kind of fish would you like to be? How would you go about nailing jelly to the ceiling? Why are manhole covers round? Some of these questions are designed to test your grace under pressure, whereas others are used to get you to think through a logical answer. (Manhole covers are round because a circle is the only shape that can't fall through an open hole of slightly smaller size, by the way.) Don't act like the question is stupid or refuse to answer it. As Lynne Sarikas, director of the MBA Career Center at Northeastern University, explains, these questions offer an opportunity to "demonstrate quick thinking, poise, creativity, and even a sense of humor."

- **Freezing up.** The human brain seems to have the capacity to just freeze up in stressful situations. An interviewer might have asked you a simple question, or perhaps you are halfway through an intelligent answer, and poof!—all your thoughts disappear and you can't organize words in any logical order. Try to quickly replay the last few seconds of the conversation in your mind to see if you can recapture the conversational thread. If that fails, you're probably better off explaining to the interviewer that your mind has gone blank and asking him or her to repeat the question. Doing so is embarrassing but not as embarrassing as chattering on and on with no idea of what you're saying, hoping you'll stumble back onto the topic.
- **Failing to understand your potential to contribute to the organization.** Interviewers care less about your history than about how you can help their organization in the future. Be sure to understand ahead of time how your skills can help the company meet its challenges.

CAREER APPLICATIONS

1. What should you do if you suddenly realize that something you said earlier in the interview is incorrect or incomplete? Explain your answer.
2. How would you answer the following question: "How do you respond to colleagues who make you angry?" Explain your answer.

Sources: Adapted from "Because You Asked: Interviews Get a Little Strange," ManageSmarter, 25 September 2008, www.managesmarter.com; Thomas Pack, "Good Answers to Job Interview Questions," *Information Today*, January 2004, 35+; John Lees, "Make Them Believe You Are the Best," *The Times* (London), 21 January 2004, 3; "Six Interview Mistakes," Monster.com, accessed 23 February 2004, www.monster.com.

If you believe an interviewer's questions to be unreasonable, unrelated to the job, or an attempt to discriminate, you have the option of filing a complaint with the EEOC (www.eeoc.gov) or with the agency in your state that regulates fair employment practices.

THE CLOSE

Like the warm-up, the end of the interview is more important than its brief duration would indicate. These last few minutes are your last opportunity to emphasize your value to the organization and to correct any misconceptions the interviewer might have. Be aware that many interviewers will ask whether you have any more questions at this point, so ask one or two from the list you brought or ask a question related to something that came up during the interview.

Concluding Gracefully

You can usually tell when the interviewer is trying to conclude the session. He or she may ask whether you have any more questions, check the time, summarize the discussion, or simply tell you that the allotted time for the interview is up. When you get the signal, be sure to thank the interviewer for the opportunity and express your interest in the organization.

Conclude an interview with courtesy and enthusiasm.

TABLE 16.6	Acceptable Versus Potentially Discriminatory Interview Questions
Interviewers may ask this . . .	**But not this**
What is your name?	What was your maiden name?
Are you over 18?	When were you born?
Did you graduate from high school?	When did you graduate from high school?
[No questions about race are allowed.]	What is your race?
Can you perform [specific tasks]?	Do you have physical or mental disabilities? Do you have a drug or alcohol problem? Are you taking any prescription drugs?
Would you be able to meet the job's requirement to frequently work weekends?	Would working on weekends conflict with your religion?
Do you have the legal right to work in the United States?	What country are you a citizen of?
Have you ever been convicted of a felony?	Have you ever been arrested?
This job requires that you speak Spanish. Do you?	What language did you speak in your home when you were growing up?

Sources: Adapted from Deanna G. Kucler, "Interview Questions: Legal or Illegal?" *Workforce Management*, www.workforce.com; "Illegal Interview Questions," *USA Today*, 29 January 2001, www.usatoday.com; "Dangerous Questions," *Nation's Business*, May 1999, 22.

If you can do so comfortably, try to pin down what will happen next, but don't press for an immediate decision.

If this is your second or third visit to the organization, the interview may end with an offer of employment. If you have other offers or need time to think about this offer, it's perfectly acceptable to thank the interviewer for the offer and ask for some time to consider it. If no job offer is made, the interview team may not have reached a decision yet, but you may tactfully ask when you can expect to know the decision.

Discussing Salary

Research salary ranges in your job, industry, and geographic region before you try to negotiate salary.

If you receive an offer during the interview, you'll naturally want to discuss salary. However, let the interviewer raise the subject. If asked your salary requirements during the interview or on a job application, you can say that your requirements are open or negotiable or that you would expect a competitive compensation package.[45]

How far you can negotiate depends on several factors, including market demand for your skills, the strength of the job market, the company's compensation policies, the company's financial health, and whether you have other job offers. Remember that you're negotiating a business deal, not asking for personal favors, so focus on the unique value you can bring to the job. The more information you have, the stronger your position will be.

Negotiating benefits may be one way to get more value from an employment package.

If salary isn't negotiable, look at the overall compensation and benefits package. You may find flexibility in a signing bonus, profit sharing, retirement benefits, health coverage, vacation time, and other valuable elements.[46]

Keeping careful records of your job interviews is essential.

To review the important tips for successful interviews, see "Checklist: Making a Positive Impression in Job Interviews."

REAL-TIME UPDATES
Learn More by Watching This PowerPoint Presentation

Should you accept? Evaluating a job offer

Explore the many steps needed to determine whether a job offer is right for you, your family, and your future. Go to http://real-timeupdates.com/ebc10 and click on Learn More. If you are using MyBcommLab, you can access Real-Time Updates within each chapter or under Student Study Tools.

INTERVIEW NOTES

Maintain a notebook or simple database with information about each company, interviewers' answers to your questions, contact information for each interviewer, the status of thank-you notes and other follow-up communication, and upcoming interview appointments. Carefully organized notes will help you decide which company is the right fit for you when it comes time to choose from among the job offers you receive.

✓ **Checklist** **Making a Positive Impression in Job Interviews**

A. Be ready to make a positive impression in the warm-up stage.
- Be alert from the moment you arrive; even initial small talk is part of the interviewing process.
- Greet the interviewer by name, with a smile and direct eye contact.
- Offer a firm (not crushing) handshake if the interviewer extends a hand.
- Take a seat only after the interviewer invites you to sit or has taken his or her own seat.
- Listen for clues about what the interviewer is trying to get you to reveal about yourself and your qualifications.
- Exhibit positive body language, including standing up straight, walking with purpose, and sitting up straight.

B. Convey your value to the organization during the question-and-answer stage.
- Let the interviewer lead the conversation.
- Never answer a question before the interviewer finishes asking it.
- Listen carefully to the interviewer and watch for nonverbal signals.
- Don't limit yourself to simple yes-or-no answers; expand on the answer to show your knowledge of the company (but don't ramble on).
- If you encounter a potentially discriminatory question, decide how you want to respond before you say anything.
- When you have the opportunity, ask questions from the list you've prepared; remember that interviewers expect you to ask questions.

C. Close on a strong note.
- Watch and listen for signs that the interview is about to end.
- Quickly evaluate how well you've done and correct any misperceptions the interviewer might have.
- If you receive an offer and aren't ready to decide, it's entirely appropriate to ask for time to think about it.
- Don't bring up salary but be prepared to discuss it if the interviewer raises the subject.
- End with a warm smile and a handshake and thank the interviewer for meeting with you.

For the latest information on interviewing strategies, visit http://real-timeupdates .com/ebc10 and click on Chapter 16.

Following Up After the Interview

Staying in contact with a prospective employer after an interview shows that you really want the job and are determined to get it. Doing so also gives you another chance to demonstrate your communication skills and sense of business etiquette. Following up brings your name to the interviewer's attention once again and reminds him or her that you're actively looking and waiting for the decision.

5 LEARNING OBJECTIVE

Identify the most common employment messages that follow an interview and explain when you would use each one.

Any time you hear from a company during the application or interview process, be sure to respond quickly. Companies flooded with résumés may move on to another candidate if they don't hear back from you within 24 hours.[47]

THANK-YOU MESSAGE

Write a thank-you message within two days of the interview, even if you feel you have little chance of getting the job. In addition to demonstrating good etiquette, a thank-you message gives you the opportunity to reinforce the reasons you are a good choice for the position and lets you respond to any negatives that might've arisen in the interview.[48] Acknowledge the interviewer's time and courtesy, convey your continued interest, reinforce the reasons that you are a good fit for the position, and ask politely for a decision (see Figure 16.6 on the next page).

A thank-you message is more than a professional courtesy; it's another chance to promote yourself to an employer.

Depending on the company and the relationship you've established with the interviewer, the thank-you message can be handled via letter or email. Be brief and sound positive without sounding overconfident.

MESSAGE OF INQUIRY

If you're not advised of the interviewer's decision by the promised date or within two weeks, you might make an inquiry. A message of inquiry (which can be handled by email

Use the model for a direct request when you write an inquiry about a hiring decision.

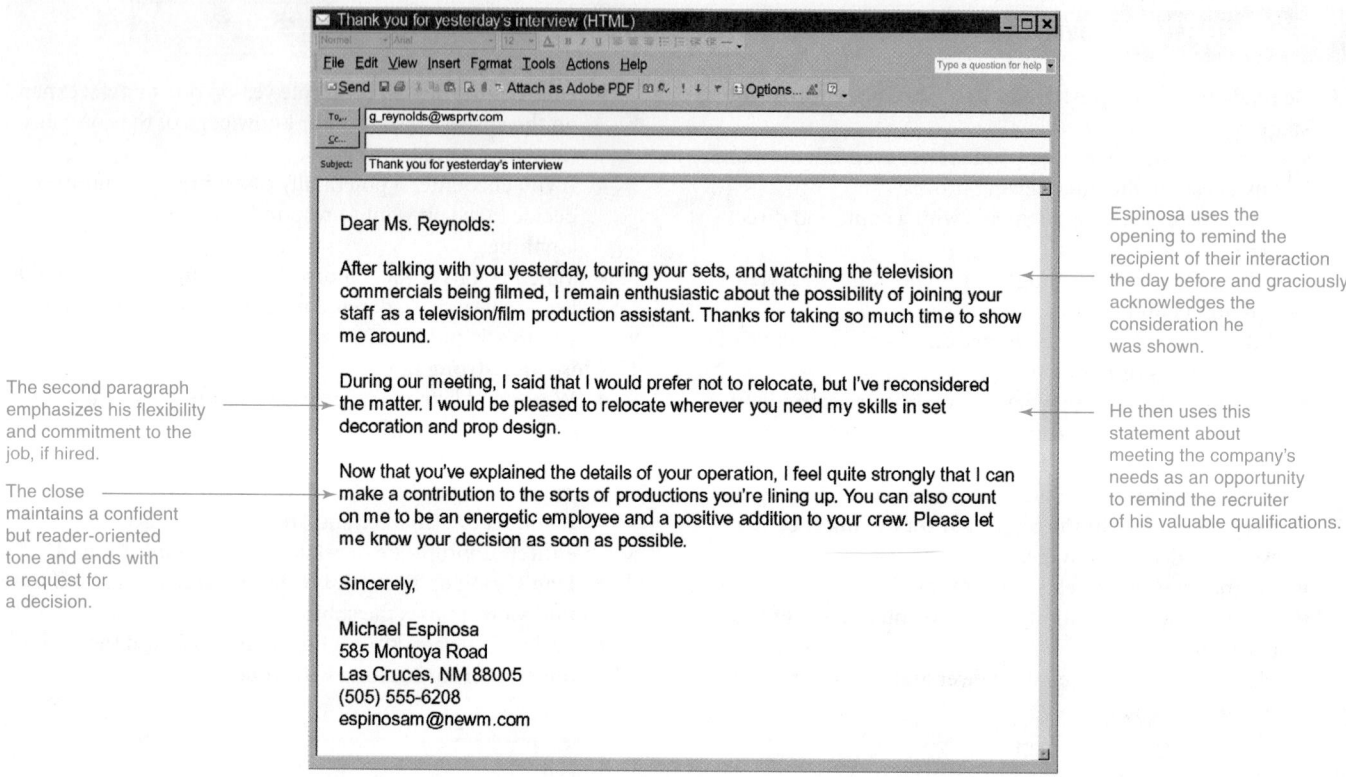

The second paragraph emphasizes his flexibility and commitment to the job, if hired.

The close maintains a confident but reader-oriented tone and ends with a request for a decision.

Espinosa uses the opening to remind the recipient of their interaction the day before and graciously acknowledges the consideration he was shown.

He then uses this statement about meeting the company's needs as an opportunity to remind the recruiter of his valuable qualifications.

MyBcommLab

Figure 16.6   Thank-You Message
In three brief paragraphs, Michael Espinosa acknowledges the interviewer's time and consideration, expresses his continued interest in the position, explains a crucial discussion point that he has reconsidered, and asks for a decision.

Apply Figure 16.6's key concepts by revising a new document. Go to Chapter 16 in www.pearsoninternationaleditions.com/mybcommlab and select Document Makeovers.

if the interviewer has given you his or her email address) is particularly appropriate if you've received a job offer from a second firm and don't want to accept it before you have an answer from the first. The following message illustrates the general model for a direct request:

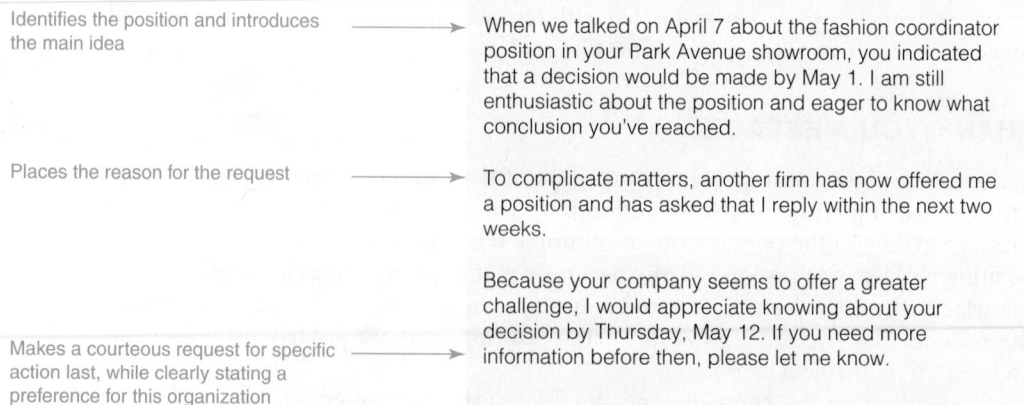

Identifies the position and introduces the main idea

When we talked on April 7 about the fashion coordinator position in your Park Avenue showroom, you indicated that a decision would be made by May 1. I am still enthusiastic about the position and eager to know what conclusion you've reached.

Places the reason for the request

To complicate matters, another firm has now offered me a position and has asked that I reply within the next two weeks.

Makes a courteous request for specific action last, while clearly stating a preference for this organization

Because your company seems to offer a greater challenge, I would appreciate knowing about your decision by Thursday, May 12. If you need more information before then, please let me know.

REQUEST FOR A TIME EXTENSION

If you receive a job offer while other interviews are still pending, you can ask the employer for a time extension. Open with a strong statement of your continued interest in the job, ask for more time to consider the offer, provide specific reasons for the request, and assure the reader that you will respond by a specific date (see Figure 16.7).

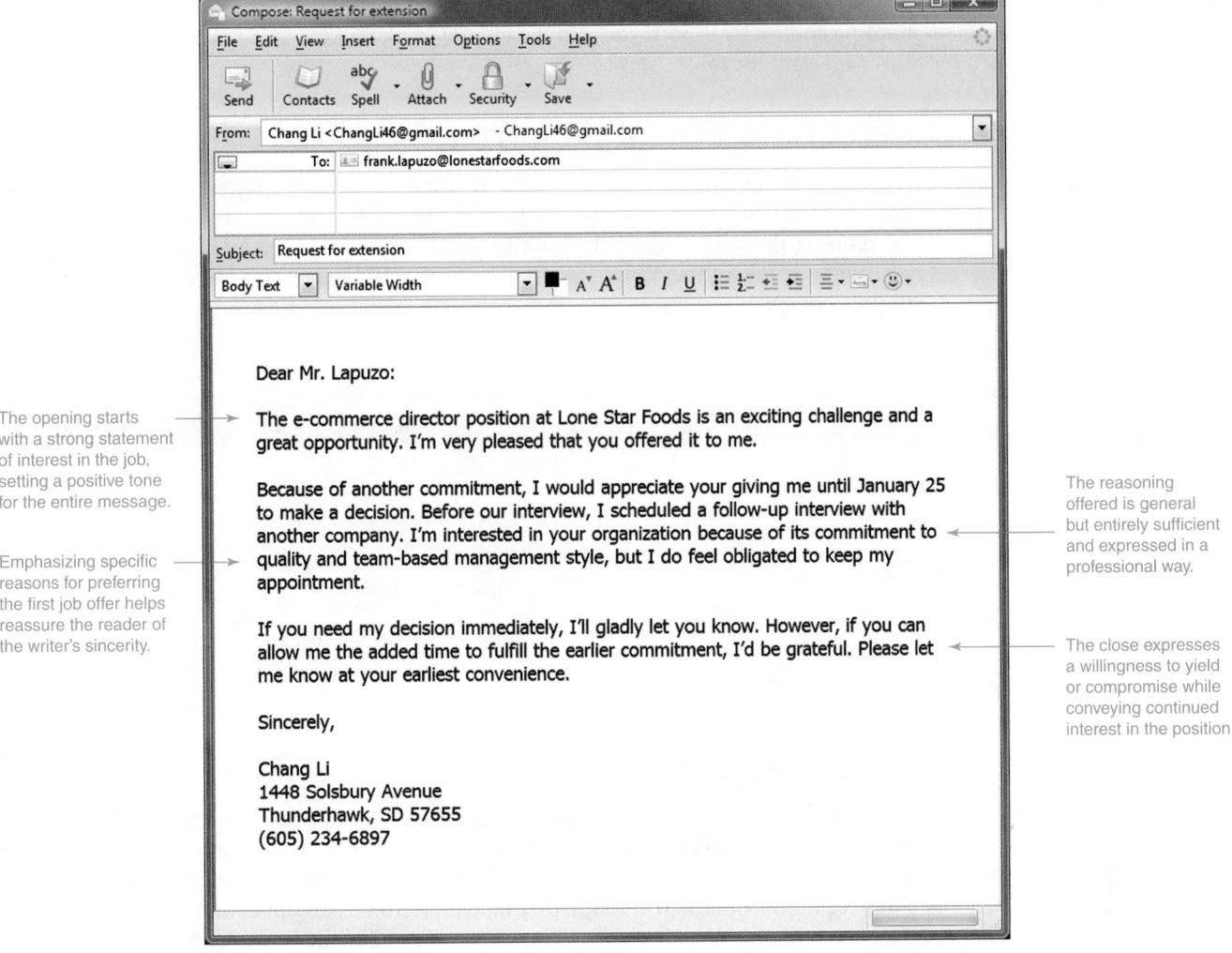

The opening starts with a strong statement of interest in the job, setting a positive tone for the entire message.

Emphasizing specific reasons for preferring the first job offer helps reassure the reader of the writer's sincerity.

The reasoning offered is general but entirely sufficient and expressed in a professional way.

The close expresses a willingness to yield or compromise while conveying continued interest in the position.

Figure 16.7 Request for a Time Extension
If you need to request more time to make a decision about a job offer, make sure to reaffirm that you are still interested in the job.

MyBcommLab

Apply Figure 16.7's key concepts by revising a new document. Go to Chapter 16 in www.pearsoninternationaleditions.com/mybcommlab and select Document Makeovers.

LETTER OF ACCEPTANCE

When you receive a job offer that you want to accept, reply within five days. Begin by accepting the position and expressing thanks. Identify the job that you're accepting. In the next paragraph, cover any necessary details. Conclude by saying that you look forward to reporting for work. As always, a positive letter should convey your enthusiasm and eagerness to cooperate:

Use the model for positive messages when you write a letter of acceptance.

I'm delighted to accept the graphic design position in your advertising department at the salary of $2,875 per month.

Confirms the specific terms of the offer with a good-news statement at the beginning

Enclosed are the health insurance forms you asked me to complete and sign. I've already given notice to my current employer and will be able to start work on Monday, January 18.

Covers miscellaneous details in the middle

The prospect of joining your firm is exciting. Thank you for giving me this opportunity, and I look forward to making a positive contribution.

Closes with another reference to the good news and a look toward the future

Written acceptance of a job offer can be considered a legally binding contract.

Be aware that a job offer and a written acceptance of that offer can constitute a legally binding contract, for both you and the employer. Before you send an acceptance letter, be sure you want the job.

LETTER DECLINING A JOB OFFER

If you decide to decline a job offer, do so tactfully, using the model for negative messages.

After all your interviews, you may find that you need to write a letter declining a job offer. Use the techniques for negative messages (see Chapter 9): Open warmly, state the reasons for refusing the offer, decline the offer explicitly, and close on a pleasant note, expressing gratitude. By taking the time to write a sincere, tactful letter, you leave the door open for future contact:

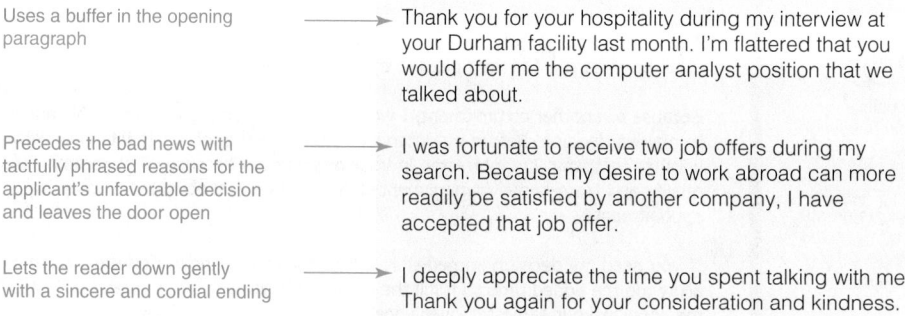

Uses a buffer in the opening paragraph → Thank you for your hospitality during my interview at your Durham facility last month. I'm flattered that you would offer me the computer analyst position that we talked about.

Precedes the bad news with tactfully phrased reasons for the applicant's unfavorable decision and leaves the door open → I was fortunate to receive two job offers during my search. Because my desire to work abroad can more readily be satisfied by another company, I have accepted that job offer.

Lets the reader down gently with a sincere and cordial ending → I deeply appreciate the time you spent talking with me. Thank you again for your consideration and kindness.

LETTER OF RESIGNATION

Letters of resignation should always be written in a gracious and professional style that avoids criticism of your employer or your colleagues.

If you get a job offer and are currently employed, you can maintain good relations with your current employer by writing a letter of resignation to your immediate supervisor. Follow the approach for negative messages and make the letter sound as positive as possible, regardless of how you feel. Don't take this letter as an opportunity to vent any frustrations you may have. Say something favorable about the organization, the people you work with, or what you've learned on the job. Then state your intention to leave and give the date of your last day on the job. Be sure you give your current employer at least two weeks' notice:

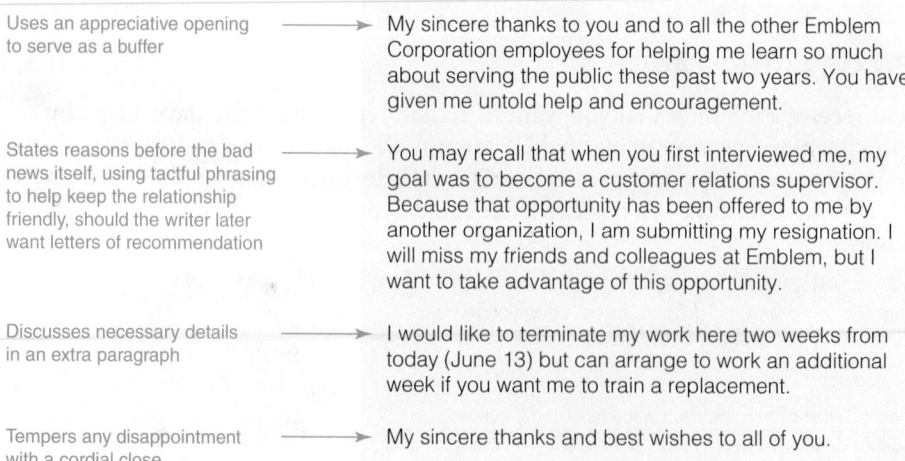

Uses an appreciative opening to serve as a buffer → My sincere thanks to you and to all the other Emblem Corporation employees for helping me learn so much about serving the public these past two years. You have given me untold help and encouragement.

States reasons before the bad news itself, using tactful phrasing to help keep the relationship friendly, should the writer later want letters of recommendation → You may recall that when you first interviewed me, my goal was to become a customer relations supervisor. Because that opportunity has been offered to me by another organization, I am submitting my resignation. I will miss my friends and colleagues at Emblem, but I want to take advantage of this opportunity.

Discusses necessary details in an extra paragraph → I would like to terminate my work here two weeks from today (June 13) but can arrange to work an additional week if you want me to train a replacement.

Tempers any disappointment with a cordial close → My sincere thanks and best wishes to all of you.

To verify the content and style of your follow-up messages, consult the tips in "Checklist: Writing Follow-up Messages."

✔ Checklist | Writing Follow-Up Messages

A. Thank-you messages.
- Write a brief thank-you letter within two days of the interview.
- Acknowledge the interviewer's time and courtesy.
- Restate the specific job you're applying for.
- Express your enthusiasm about the organization and the job.
- Add any new facts that may help your chances.
- Politely ask for a decision.

B. Messages of inquiry.
- If you haven't heard from the interviewer by the promised date, write a brief message of inquiry.
- Use the direct approach: main idea, necessary details, specific request.

C. Requests for a time extension.
- Request an extension if you have pending interviews and need time to decide about an offer.
- Open on a friendly note.
- Explain why you need more time and express continued interest in the company.
- In the close, promise a quick decision if your request is denied and ask for a confirmation if your request is granted.

D. Letters of acceptance.
- Send this message within five days of receiving the offer.
- State clearly that you accept the offer, identify the job you're accepting, and confirm vital details such as salary and start date.
- Make sure you want the job; an acceptance letter can be treated as a legally binding contract.

E. Letters declining a job offer.
- Use the indirect approach for negative messages.
- Open on a warm and appreciative note and then explain why you are refusing the offer.
- End on a sincere, positive note.

F. Letters of resignation.
- Send a letter of resignation to your current employer as soon as possible.
- Begin with an appreciative buffer.
- In the middle section, state your reasons for leaving and actually state that you are resigning.
- Close cordially.

ON THE JOB: SOLVING COMMUNICATION DILEMMAS AT ZAPPOS

Source: Brad Swonetz/Redux.

You recently joined the human resources department at Zappos headquarters in Las Vegas. You're looking to hire experienced customer support specialists who remain calm when things get chaotic and who are comfortable communicating in the Zappos style with a diverse range of customers. Using what you know about job applications and interviewing, address these challenges. (To learn more about working at Zappos, you can visit **http://about.zappos.com/jobs**.)

1. Because written communication skills are such an important part of the job, you pay close attention to application letters, particularly unsolicited letters from candidates who have taken the initiative to contact Zappos even without a job opening being posted. Based on the following opening paragraphs, which of these four candidates has done the best job of capturing your attention and interest?

   a. With 4.5 years of customer service experience, solid performance reviews, and a firm commitment to excellence in customer service, I trust I don't sound overconfident when I say that I posses the qualities a fine organization such as Zappos needs to help achieve its goals and objectives.

   b. You do wacky. I do wacky. Let's make this happen.

   c. Given your reputation for hiring the coolest cats in town, the big question is why the heck don't I work there yet? I'm driven, way smarter than average, and would feel right at home in Vegas, baby!

   d. In addition to being an enthusiastic Zappos customer, I am also a customer service professional myself. A brilliant idea came to me last week while I was having yet another satisfying interaction with your customer support crew: I want to be part of the team that can create such positive experiences for customers.

2. You like to put applicants at ease right away, so you usually start interviews by asking an offbeat question to break the tension while also prompting the candidate to reveal something about his or her personality and knowledge. Which of these questions would you choose to start an interview?

   a. Who is the most ridiculously demanding customer you ever encountered?

   b. If we gave you a jetpack to fly all over town surprising customers with product deliveries, would you take the job?

c. Ever have one of those days when life seems like one endless job interview?

d. So . . . buying that weekly lottery ticket still hasn't worked out, eh?

3. Zappos likes employees who can think on their feet, even when faced with outlandish questions and circumstances. Which of these questions would you use to judge a candidate's ability to grasp a problem and begin developing a solution?

a. You're a scientist with the Environmental Protection Agency, specializing in toxic waste from electronic products. You're testifying before a congressional committee, and a senator wants to know how many mobile phone batteries will be thrown away in the next 10 years. Without access to any additional information, how would you start to construct an estimate of this number?

b. Guess how old I am.

c. Why do telephone numbers in movies and TV shows always start with 555?

d. How would you explain the concept of a human family to a creature from another planet?

4. At the end of each interview, you make a point to ask candidates if they have any questions for you. Which of the following responses impresses you the most?

a. No, thanks. I think I'm all set. You've done a wonderful job of answering whatever questions I might've come in with.

b. Oh, I don't need to take any more of your time. I'm a pretty good independent thinker. If I have any questions, I'll just look you up online when I get back to home.

c. Absolutely. Can you give me the inside scoop? Is this fun Zappos family environment stuff for real or just a show to impress people on the outside?

d. Yes, thanks, I do. Now that Amazon has acquired Zappos, do you think there will be opportunities to spread the Zappos spirit through the entire Amazon operation? Or is there a risk that the Zappos spirit might be lost now that it's part of a much larger company?

LEARNING OBJECTIVES CHECKUP

Assess your understanding of the principles in this chapter by reading each learning objective and studying the accompanying exercises. For fill-in-the-blank items, write the missing text in the blank provided; for multiple-choice items, circle the letter of the correct answer. You can check your responses against the answer key on page AK-3.

Objective 16.1: Explain the purposes of application letters, and describe how to apply the AIDA organizational approach to them.

1. What is the primary reason for sending an application letter?
   a. To encourage the reader to look at your résumé
   b. To ask for a job
   c. To itemize your qualifications
   d. To ask for an application form

2. Why are unsolicited application letters more challenging to write than solicited application letters?
   a. Nobody wants to receive unsolicited application letters.
   b. With an unsolicited letter, you have to do the research to identify the qualities the company would likely be looking for in the position you would like to get.
   c. Solicited application letters are shorter, making it more likely than recruiters will bother to read them.
   d. Unsolicited letters do not lend themselves to the AIDA model.

3. Which of the following is a good technique to gain attention in the opening paragraph of any application letter?
   a. Make sure you "jump off the page" with an eye-catching design.
   b. Explain how you have some immediate potential to meet the company's needs.

   c. Invoke a sense of dramatic mystery by withholding either the job you are applying for or some key facts about yourself.
   d. Go deep—structure your letter more along the lines of a comprehensive informational report.

4. What are the two vital functions of the final paragraph of an application letter?
   a. To ask the reader for an interview (or other appropriate action) and to express how happy you would be to work for the company
   b. To ask the reader for an interview (or other appropriate action) and to make it easy for the reader to reply
   c. To ask the reader for an interview (or other appropriate action) and to state your salary expectations
   d. To encourage the reader to read your résumé and to highlight at least three key points from your résumé

Objective 16.2: Describe the typical sequence of job interviews, the major types of interviews, and what employers look for during an interview.

5. Which of these interview stages happens first?
   a. The selection stage
   b. The screening stage
   c. The filtering stage
   d. The sorting stage

6. A/an _____ interview, often used in the screening stage, features a series of prepared questions in a set order.

7. How does a behavioral interview differ from a situational interview?
   a. A behavioral interview asks you to relate incidents and experiences from your past, whereas a situational interview puts you in actual work situations and asks you

to perform some task, such as leading a brainstorming session.

b. They are essentially the same thing, although behavioral interviews are generally conducted by a computer rather than a live interviewer.

c. A situational interview asks you to relate incidents and experiences from your past, whereas a behavioral interview asks how would you respond to various hypothetical situations in the future.

d. A behavioral interview asks you to relate incidents and experiences from your past, whereas a situational interview asks how would you respond to various hypothetical situations in the future.

8. What are the two most important factors that employers look for during interviews?

a. Fit with the organization and motivation

b. Motivation and ability to perform the job

c. Motivation and years of experience

d. Ability to perform the job and compatibility with the organization

9. Which of the following preemployment tests might you encounter while applying for jobs?

a. Integrity tests

b. Substance tests

c. Personality tests

d. All of the above

Objective 16.3: List six tasks you need to complete to prepare for a successful job interview.

10. If an interviewer asks you to describe your biggest weakness, which of the following is a good strategy for your response?

a. The interviewer is just trying to rattle you, so what you say is less important than staying cool and calm while you say it.

b. Frame your response in terms of skills you plan to develop in the future, specifically a skill that will benefit the company.

c. Respectfully explain to the interviewer that the question is illegal.

d. Explain that you don't have any major weaknesses.

11. What is the best strategy for asking questions of your own during an interview?

a. Try to ask all of them at the beginning of the interview so that you don't run out of time.

b. Wait until after the interview and then email your questions to the interviewer.

c. Try to work your questions in naturally throughout the course of the interview.

d. Wait until the interviewer asks if you have any questions.

12. If you believe that you have a particular disadvantage related to some aspect of your appearance, interviewing skills, job skills, or work experience, how should you handle the situation when preparing for an interview?

a. Plan to make a joke about your weakness early in the interview; this will break the tension and allow you to focus on the interviewer's questions.

b. Compensate by focusing on your strengths, both while you're preparing and during the interview.

c. Correct the perceived shortcoming if possible; if not, focus on your positive attributes.

d. Ignore the situation; there's nothing you can do about a weakness at this point.

13. If you're not sure what style of clothing to wear to a particular interview and you're not able to ask someone at the company for advice, what should you do?

a. Dress in a fairly conservative style; it's better to be a little too dressy than too casual.

b. Dress as you would like to dress on the job.

c. Dress in an eye-catching style that will make a lasting impression on the interviewer.

d. Arrive early with several different changes of clothes; try to see what people there are wearing, then find a place to change into whichever outfit you have that most closely matches.

Objective 16.4: Explain how to succeed in all three stages of an interview.

14. Studies show that many interviewers, particularly those with poor training, make up their minds about candidates

a. In the first 20 seconds of the interview

b. In the final 20 seconds of the interview

c. On the basis of the résumé

d. On the basis of the cover letter

15. Which of the following is an advisable response to an interviewer who asks you about your marital status, how many children you have, and what their ages are?

a. Answer the questions; it is perfectly within the interviewer's right to ask you such personal questions, even if they are not directly related to the job you are applying for.

b. Tell the interviewer that such questions are illegal and threaten to sue for invasion of privacy.

c. Sidestep the questions by asking if the interviewer has some specific concerns about your commitment to the job, your willingness to travel, or some other factor.

d. If you want the job, refuse to answer the questions but promise that you won't report the illegal questioning to the EEOC.

16. What should you do if the interviewer tells you the salary for the job being offered?

a. Always take whatever the company offers.

b. Respond with a figure higher than what is offered.

c. Respond with a figure lower than what is offered.

d. Ask if there is any room to negotiate on salary.

Objective 16.5: Identify the most common employment messages that follow an interview, and explain when you would use each one.

17. Following a job interview, you should send a thank-you message

a. Within two days after the interview

b. Only if you think you got the job

c. That follows the AIDA organizational model

d. That does all of the above

18. A letter declining a job offer should follow

a. The direct approach

b. The AIDA model

c. A negative news approach

d. The polite plan

MyBcommLab

Log on to www.pearsoninternationaleditions
.com/mybcommlab to access study and
assessment aids associated with this chapter.
If you are not using MyBcommLab, you can
access the Real-Time Updates http://real-
timeupdates.com/ebc10.

 **Checklist**

**Making a Positive Impression in Job
Interviews**

**A. Be ready to make a positive impression
in the warm-up stage.**
- Be alert from the moment you arrive;
  even initial small talk is part of the
  interviewing process.
- Greet the interviewer by name, with
  a smile and direct eye contact.
- Offer a firm (not crushing) handshake
  if the interviewer extends a hand.
- Take a seat only after the interviewer
  invites you to sit or has taken his or
  her own seat.

LEARNING OBJECTIVES

1. Explain the purposes of application letters, and describe how to apply the AIDA organizational approach to them. [page 561]
2. Describe the typical sequence of job interviews, the major types of interviews, and what employers look for during an interview. [page 566]
3. List six tasks you need to complete to prepare for a successful job interview. [page 571]
4. Explain how to succeed in all three stages of an interview. [page 577]
5. Identify the most common employment messages that follow an interview, and explain when you would use each one. [page 581]

KEY TERMS

application letter Message that accompanies a résumé to let readers know what you're sending, why you're sending it, and how they can benefit from reading it

behavioral interview Interview in which you are asked to relate specific incidents and experiences from your past

employment interview Formal meeting during which you and an employer ask questions and exchange information

group interviews Interview in which one or more interviewers meet with several candidates simultaneously

open-ended interview Interview in which the interviewer adapts his or her line of questioning based on the answers you give and any questions you ask

panel interview Interview in which you meet with several interviewers at once

situational interview Similar to a behavioral interview, except the questions focus on how you would handle various hypothetical situations on the job

solicited application letter Message sent in response to an announced job opening

stress interview Interview in which you might be asked questions designed to rattle you or you might be subjected to long periods of silence, criticism, interruptions, and or hostile reactions by the interviewer

structured interview Interview in which the interviewer (or a computer) asks a series of prepared questions in a set order

unsolicited application letter Message sent to an organization that has not announced an opening

working interview Interview in which you perform a job-related activity

- Listen for clues about what the interviewer is trying to get you to reveal about you and your qualifications.
- Exhibit positive body language, including standing up straight, walking with purpose, and sitting up straight.

B. Convey your value to the organization during the question-and-answer stage.
- Let the interviewer lead the conversation.
- Never answer a question before the interviewer finishes asking it.
- Listen carefully to the interviewer and watch for nonverbal signals.
- Don't limit yourself to simple yes-or-no answers; expand on the answer to show your knowledge of the company (but don't ramble on).
- If you encounter a potentially discriminatory question, decide how you want to respond before you say anything.

- When you have the opportunity, ask questions from the list you've prepared; remember that interviewers expect you to ask questions.

C. Close on a strong note.
- Watch and listen for signs that the interview is about to end.
- Quickly evaluate how well you've done and correct any misperceptions the interviewer might have.
- If you receive an offer and aren't ready to decide, it's entirely appropriate to ask for time to think about it.
- Don't bring up salary but be prepared to discuss it if the interviewer raises the subject.
- End with a warm smile and a handshake and thank the interviewer for meeting with you.

APPLY YOUR KNOWLEDGE

To review chapter content related to each question, refer to the indicated Learning Objective.

1. How can you distinguish yourself from other candidates in a screening interview and still keep your responses short and to the point? Explain. [LO-2]

2. How can you prepare for a situational or behavioral interview if you have no experience with the job for which you are interviewing? [LO-2]

3. If you lack one important qualification for a job but have made it past the initial screening stage, how should you prepare to handle this issue during the next round of interviews? Explain your answer. [LO-3]

4. What is an interviewer likely to conclude about you if you don't have any questions to ask during the interview? [LO-3]

5. Why is it important to distinguish unethical or illegal interview questions from acceptable questions? Explain. [LO-4]

PRACTICE YOUR SKILLS

Messages for Analysis

Read the following messages and then (1) analyze the strengths or weaknesses of each document and (2) revise each document so that it follows this chapter's guidelines.

Message 16.A: Writing an Application Letter [LO-1]

I'm writing to let you know about my availability for the brand manager job you advertised. As you can see from my enclosed résumé, my background is perfect for the position. Even though I don't have any real job experience, my grades have been outstanding, considering that I went to a top-ranked business school.

I did many things during my undergraduate years to prepare me for this job:

- Earned a 3.4 out of a 4.0, with a 3.8 in my business courses
- Elected representative to the student governing association
- Selected to receive the Lamar Franklin Award
- Worked to earn a portion of my tuition

I am sending my résumé to all the top firms, but I like yours better than any of the rest. Your reputation is tops in the industry, and I want to be associated with a business that can pridefully say it's the best.

If you wish for me to come in for an interview, I can come on a Friday afternoon or anytime on weekends when I don't have classes. Again, thanks for considering me for your brand manager position.

Message 16.B: Writing Application Follow-up Messages [LO-1]

Did you receive my résumé? I sent it to you at least two months ago and haven't heard anything. I know you keep résumés on file, but I just want to be sure that you keep me in mind. I heard you are hiring health-care managers

and certainly would like to be considered for one of those positions.

Since I last wrote you, I've worked in a variety of positions that have helped prepare me for management. To wit, I've become lunch manager at the restaurant where I work, which involved a raise in pay. I now manage a waitstaff of 12 girls and take the lunch receipts to the bank every day.

Of course, I'd much rather be working at a real job, and that's why I'm writing again. Is there anything else you would like to know about me or my background? I would really like to know more about your company. Is there any literature you could send me? If so, I would really appreciate it.

I think one reason I haven't been hired yet is that I don't want to leave Atlanta. So I hope when you think of me, it's for a position that wouldn't require moving. Thanks again for considering my application.

Message 16.C: Thank-You Message [LO-5]

Thank you for the really marvelous opportunity to meet you and your colleagues at Starret Engine Company. I really enjoyed touring your facilities and talking with all the people there. You have quite a crew! Some of the other companies I have visited have been so rigid and uptight that I can't imagine how I would fit in. It's a relief to run into a group of people who seem to enjoy their work as much as all of you do.

I know that you must be looking at many other candidates for this job, and I know that some of them will probably be more experienced than I am. But I do want to emphasize that my two-year hitch in the Navy involved a good deal of engineering work. I don't think I mentioned all my shipboard responsibilities during the interview.

Please give me a call within the next week to let me know your decision. You can usually find me at my dormitory in the evening after dinner (phone: 877-9080).

Message 16.D: Letter of Inquiry [LO-5]

I have recently received a very attractive job offer from the Warrington Company. But before I let them know one way or another, I would like to consider any offer that your firm may extend. I was quite impressed with your company during my recent interview, and I am still very interested in a career there.

I don't mean to pressure you, but Warrington has asked for my decision within 10 days. Could you let me know by Tuesday whether you plan to offer me a position? That would give me enough time to compare the two offers.

Message 16.E: Letter Declining a Job Offer [LO-5]

I'm writing to say that I must decline your job offer. Another company has made me a more generous offer, and I have decided to accept. However, if things don't work out for me there, I will let you know. I sincerely appreciate your interest in me.

Exercises

Active links for all websites in this chapter can be found on MyBcommLab; see your User Guide for instructions on accessing the content for this chapter. Each activity is labeled according to the primary skill or skills you will need to use. To review relevant chapter content, you can refer to the indicated Learning Objective. In some instances, supporting information will be found in another chapter, as indicated.

1. **Career Management: Preparing for Interviews [LO-3]** Google yourself, Bing yourself, scour your social networking profiles, review your Twitter messages, and explore every other possible online source you can think of that might have something about you. If you find anything potentially embarrassing, remove it if possible. Write a summary of your search-and-destroy mission (you can skip any really embarrassing details in your report to your instructor!).

2. **Career Management: Researching Target Employers [LO-3]** Select a medium or large company (one that you can easily find information on) where you might like to work. Use online sources to gather some preliminary research on the company; don't limit your search to the company's own website.

    a. What did you learn about this organization that would help you during an interview there?

    b. What online sources did you use to obtain this information?

    c. Armed with this information, what aspects of your background do you think might appeal to this company's recruiters?

    d. Based on what you've learned about this company's culture, what aspects of your personality should you try to highlight during an interview?

3. **Career Management: Interviewing; Collaboration: Team Projects [LO-4], Chapter 2** Divide the class into two groups. Half the class will be recruiters for a large chain of national department stores, looking to fill manager trainee positions (there are 16 openings). The other half of the class will be candidates for the job. The company is specifically looking for candidates who demonstrate these three qualities: initiative, dependability, and willingness to assume responsibility.

    a. Have each recruiter select and interview an applicant for 10 minutes.

    b. Have all the recruiters discuss how they assessed the applicant in each of the three desired qualities. What questions did they ask or what did they use as an indicator to determine whether the candidate possessed the quality?

    c. Have all the applicants discuss what they said to convince the recruiters that they possessed each of these qualities.

4. **Career Management: Interviewing [LO-3]** Write a short email to your instructor, discussing what you believe are your greatest strengths and weaknesses from an employment perspective. Next, explain how these strengths and weaknesses would be viewed by interviewers evaluating your qualifications.

5. **Career Management: Interviewing [LO-3]** Prepare written answers to 10 of the questions listed in Table 16.3.

6. **Message Strategies: Employment Messages, Communication Ethics: Resolving Ethical Dilemmas [LO-5], Chapter 1** You have decided to accept a new position with a competitor of your company. Write a letter of resignation to your supervisor, announcing your decision.

    a. Will you notify your employer that you are joining a competing firm? Explain.

    b. Will you use the direct or the indirect approach? Explain.

    c. Will you send your letter by email, send it by regular mail, or place it on your supervisor's desk?

EXPAND YOUR SKILLS

Critique the Professionals

Visit LinkedIn Answers at www.linkedin.com/answers (open a free LinkedIn account if required). In the Browse panel, click on Career and Education and then Job Search. Browse both Open Questions and Closed Questions to find three job-search insights that you didn't know before. Using whatever medium your instructor requests, write a brief summary (no more than one page) of what you learned.

Sharpening Your Career Skills Online

Bovée and Thill's Business Communication Web Search, at http://businesscommunicationblog.com/websearch, is a unique research tool designed specifically for business communication research. Use the Web Search function to find a website, video, PDF document, or PowerPoint presentation that offers advice on interviewing. Write a brief email message to your instructor, describing the item that you found and summarizing the career skills information you learned from it.

IMPROVE YOUR GRAMMAR, MECHANICS, AND USAGE

The following exercises help you improve your knowledge of and power over English grammar, mechanics, and usage. Turn to the "Handbook of Grammar, Mechanics, and Usage" at the end of this book and review all of Section 3.4 (Numbers). Then look at the following 10 items. Circle the letter of the preferred choice in the following groups of sentences. (Answers to these exercises appear on page AK-4.)

1. a. We will need one memory card, four hard drives and 15 monitors.

    b. We will need one memory card, four hard drives and fifteen monitors.

    c. We will need 1 memory card, 4 hard drives and 15 monitors.

2. a. Nearly 12 million people use our product in this country alone.

    b. Nearly twelve million people use our product in this country alone.

    c. Nearly 12,000,000 million people use our product in this country alone.

3. a. The report was almost 1,200 pages, and yet she had it on my desk by 5:00 p.m.
   b. The report was almost 1200 pages, and yet she had it on my desk by five o'clock in the evening.
   c. The report was almost 1,200 pages, and yet she had it on my desk by five o'clock p.m.

4. a. The deadline for submission is 6/11, but I don't think we can submit before 6/15.
   b. The deadline for submission is June 11, but I don't think we can submit before June 15.
   c. The deadline for submission is 6/11, but I don't think we can submit before June 15.

5. a. Over 30 percent of our users are working individuals.
   b. Over thirty percent of our users are working individuals.
   c. Of our users, over thirty percent are working individuals.

6. a. Two-thirds of the participants at the conference are male.
   b. 2/3 of the participants at the conference are male.
   c. 2 thirds of the participants at the conference are male.

7. a. At the conference, we handed out 30 2-page brochures, and 55 four-page brochures.
   b. At the conference, we handed out 30 two-page brochures, and 55 four-page brochures.
   c. At the conference, we handed out thirty 2-page brochures, and 55 four-page brochures.

8. a. The doors should be 42 inches wide by 48 and three-fourths inches long by 9/15 inches deep.
   b. The doors should be 42 inches wide by 48-3/4 inches long by 9/15 inches deep.
   c. The doors should be 42 inches wide by 48-12/16 inches long by 9/15 inches deep.

9. a. The preview copy was delivered to 200 Heller Drive, Suite 7, Santa Cruz, CA 95064.
   b. The preview copy was delivered to 200 Heller Drive, Suite seven, Santa Cruz, CA 95064.
   c. The preview copy was delivered to two hundred Heller Drive, Suite seven, Santa Cruz, CA 95064.

10. a. The results of the customer satisfaction survey are out: 64.8% are happy with our service, 18.75% are not happy, 17% are undecided, and the error is 0.55%.
    b. The results of the customer satisfaction survey are out: 64.8% are happy with our service, 18.75% are not happy, 17.0% are undecided, and the error is .55%.
    c. The results of the customer satisfaction survey are out: 64.80% are happy with our service, 18.75% are not happy, 17.00% are undecided, and the error is 0.55%.

For an overall review of your grammar, mechanics, and usage skills, visit MyBcommLab. Click on Chapter 16, click on Additional Exercises to Improve Your Grammar, Mechanics, and Usage, and then click on 25. Grammar and Usage.

CASES

Writing Application Letters

EMAIL SKILLS

1. Message Strategies: Employment Messages (Application Letters) [LO-1] Use one of the websites listed in Table 15.1 on page 530 to find a job opening in your target profession. If you haven't narrowed down to one career field yet, chose a business job for which you will have at least some qualifications at the time of your graduation.

Your task: Write an email message that would serve as your application letter if you were to apply for this job. Base your message on your actual qualifications for the position, and be sure to "echo" the requirements listed in the job description. Include the job description in your email message when you submit it to your instructor.

EMAIL SKILLS

2. Message Strategies: Employment Messages (Application Letters) [LO-1] You've applied yourself with vigor and resolve for four years, and you're just about to graduate with your business degree. While cruising the web to relax one night, you stumble on something called Google Earth. You're hooked instantly by the ability to zoom all around the globe and look at detailed satellite photos of places you've been to or dreamed of visiting. You can even type in the address of your apartment and get an aerial view of your neighborhood. You're amazed at the three-dimensional renderings of major U.S. cities. Plus, the photographs and maps are linked to Google's other search technologies, allowing you to locate everything from ATMs to coffees shops in your neighborhood.

You've loved maps since you were a kid, and discovering Google Earth is making you wish you'd majored in geography. Knowing how important it is to follow your heart, you decide to apply to Google anyway, even though you don't have a strong background in geographic information systems. You do have a ton of passion for maps and a good head for business.

Your task: Visit http://earth.google.com and explore the system's capabilities. (You can download a free copy of the software.) In particular, look at the business and government applications of the technology, such as customized aerial photos and maps for real estate sales, land use and environmental impact analysis, and emergency planning for homeland security agencies. Be sure to visit the Community pages as well, where you can learn more about the many interesting applications of this technology. Draft an application email to Google, asking to be considered for the Google Earth team. Think about how you could help the company develop the commercial potential of this product line and make sure your enthusiasm shines through in the message.

Interviewing

TEAM SKILLS   BLOGGING SKILLS

3. Career Management: Researching Target Employers [LO-3] Research is a critical element of the job-search process. With information in hand, you increase the chance of finding the right opportunity (and avoiding bad choices), and you impress interviewers in multiple ways by demonstrating initiative, curiosity, research and analysis skills, an appreciation for the complex challenges of running a business, and willingness to work to achieve results.

Your task: With a small team of classmates, use online job listings to identify an intriguing job opening that at least one member of the team would seriously consider pursuing as graduation approaches. (You'll find it helpful if the career is related to at least one team member's college major or on-the-job experience so that the team can benefit from some knowledge of the profession in question.) Next, research the company, its competitors, its markets, and this specific position to identify five questions that would (1) help the team member decide if this is a good opportunity and (2) show an interviewer that you've really done your homework. Go beyond the basic and obvious questions to identify current, specific, and complex issues that only deep research can uncover. For example, is the company facing significant technical, financial, legal, or regulatory challenges that threaten its ability to grow or perhaps even survive in the long term? Or is the market evolving in a way that positions this particular company for dramatic growth? In a post for your class blog, list your five questions, identify how you uncovered the issue, and explain why each is significant.

TEAM SKILLS

4. Career Management: Interviewing [LO-4] Interviewing is a skill that can be improved through practice and observation.

Your task: You and all other members of your class are to write letters of application for an entry-level or management-trainee position that requires an engaging personality and intelligence but a minimum of specialized education or experience. Sign your letter with a fictitious name that conceals your identity. Next, polish (or create) a résumé that accurately identifies you and your educational and professional accomplishments.

Now, three members of the class who volunteer as interviewers divide up all the anonymously written application letters. Then each interviewer selects a candidate who seems the most convincing in his or her letter. At this time, the selected candidates identify themselves and give the interviewers their résumés.

Each interviewer then interviews his or her chosen candidate in front of the class, seeking to understand how the items on the résumé qualify the candidate for the job. At the end of the interviews, the class decides who gets the job and discusses why this candidate was successful. Afterward, retrieve your letter, sign it with the right name, and submit it to the instructor for credit.

TEAM SKILLS

5. Career Management: Interviewing [LO-4] Select a company in an industry in which you might like to work and then identify an interesting position within the company. Study the company and prepare for an interview with that company.

Your task: Working with a classmate, take turns interviewing each other for your chosen positions. Interviewers should take notes during the interview. When the interview is complete, critique each other's performance. (Interviewers should critique how well candidates prepared for the interview and answered the

questions; interviewees should critique the quality of the questions asked.) Write a follow-up letter thanking your interviewer and submit the letter to your instructor.

Following Up After an Interview

LETTER WRITING SKILLS

6. Message Strategies: Employment Messages (Request for a Time Extension) [LO-5] Because of a mix-up in your job application scheduling, you accidentally applied for your third-choice job before going after the one you really wanted. What you want to do is work in retail marketing with the upscale department store Neiman Marcus in Dallas; what you have been offered is a job with Longhorn Leather and Lumber, 65 miles away in the small town of Commerce, Texas.

You review your notes. Your Longhorn interview was three weeks ago with the human resources manager, R. P. Bronson, who has just written to offer you the position. The store's address is 27 Sam Rayburn Drive, Commerce, TX 75428. Mr. Bronson notes that he can hold the position open for 10 days. You have an interview scheduled with Neiman Marcus next week, but it is unlikely that you will know the store's decision within this 10-day period.

Your task: Write to Mr. Bronson, requesting a reasonable delay in your consideration of his job offer.

LETTER WRITING SKILLS   EMAIL SKILLS

7. Message Strategies: Employment Messages (Letter Declining a Job Offer) [LO-5] Fortunately for you, your interview with Neiman Marcus (see Case 6) went well, and you've just received a job offer from the company.

Your task: Write a letter to R. P. Pronson at Longhorn Leather and Lumber, declining his job offer, and write an email message to Clarissa Bartle at Neiman Marcus, accepting her job offer. Make up any information you need when accepting the Neiman Marcus offer.

LETTER WRITING SKILLS

8. Message Strategies: Employment Messages (Letters of Resignation) [LO-5] Leaving a job is rarely stress free, but it's particularly difficult when you are parting ways with a mentor who played an important role in advancing your career. A half-dozen years into your career, you have benefited greatly from the advice, encouragement, and professional connections offered by your mentor, who also happens to be your current boss. She seemed to believe in your potential from the very beginning and went out of her way on numerous occasions to help you. You returned the favor by becoming a stellar employee who has made important contributions to the success of the department your boss leads.

Unfortunately, you find yourself at a career impasse. You believe you are ready to move into a management position, but your company is not growing enough to create many opportunities. Worse yet, you joined the firm during a period of rapid expansion, so there are many eager and qualified internal candidates at your career level interested in the few managerial jobs that do become available. You fear it may be years before you get the chance to move up in the company. Through your online networking activities, you found an opportunity with a firm in another industry and have decided to pursue it.

Your task: You have a close relationship with your boss, so you will announce your intention to leave the company in a private, one-on-one conversation. However, you also recognize the need to write a formal letter of resignation, which you will hand to your boss during this meeting. This letter is addressed to your boss, but as formal business correspondence that will become part of your personnel file, it should not be a "personal" letter. Making up whatever details you need, write a brief letter of resignation.

REFERENCES

1. Adapted from "Wishez Is Live," Zappos Family blog, 17 November 2010, http://blogs.zappos.com; Tony Hsieh, "Amazon & Zappos, 1 Year Later," Zappos CEO & COO blog, 22 July 2010, http://blogs.zappos.com; Zaoops Jobs page, accessed 25 March 2011, http://about.zappos.com/jobs; Todd Raphael, "7 Interview Questions from Zappos," Todd Raphael's World of Talent blog, 22 July 2010, http://community.ere.net; Jeffrey M. O'Brien, "Zappos Knows How to Kick It," *Fortune*, 22 January 2009, http://about.zappos.com/press-center; "Zappos Family Seattle Coding Challenge and Tech Tweet Up," Zappos Family blog, 22 March 2011, http://blogs.zappos.com.

2. Matthew Rothenberg, "Manuscript vs. Machine," The Ladders, 15 December 2009, www.theladders.com; Joann Lublin, "Cover Letters Get You in the Door, So Be Sure Not to Dash Them Off," *Wall Street Journal*, 6 April 2004, B1.

3. Lisa Vaas, "How to Write a Great Cover Letter," The Ladders, 20 November 2009, www.theladders.com.

4. Alison Doyle, "Introduction to Cover Letters," About.com, accessed 13 August 2010, http://jobsearch.about.com.

5. Doyle, "Introduction to Cover Letters"; Vaas, "How to Write a Great Cover Letter"; Toni Logan, "The Perfect Cover Story," *Kinko's Impress* 2 (2000): 32, 34.

6. Lisa Vaas, "How to Follow Up a Résumé Submission," The Ladders, 9 August 2010, www.theladders.com.

7. Alison Doyle, "How to Follow Up After Submitting a Resume," About.com, accessed 13 August 2010, http://jobsearch.about.com; Vaas, "How to Follow Up a Résumé Submission."

8. Anne Fisher, "How to Get Hired by a 'Best' Company," *Fortune*, 4 February 2008, 96.

9. Fisher, "How to Get Hired by a 'Best' Company."

10. Sarah E. Needleman, "Speed Interviewing Grows as Skills Shortage Looms; Strategy May Help Lock in Top Picks; Some Drawbacks," *Wall Street Journal*, 6 November 2007, B15.

11. Scott Beagrie, "How to Handle a Telephone Job Interview," *Personnel Today*, 26 June 2007, 29.

12. John Olmstead, "Predict Future Success with Structured Interviews," *Nursing Management*, March 2007, 52–53.

13. Fisher, "How to Get Hired by a 'Best' Company."

14. Erinn R. Johnson, "Pressure Sessions," *Black Enterprise*, October 2007, 72.

15. "What's a Group Interview?" About.com Tech Careers, accessed 5 April 2008, http://jobsearchtech.about.com.

16. Fisher, "How to Get Hired by a 'Best' Company."

17. Katherine Hansen, "Behavioral Job Interviewing Strategies for Job-Seekers," QuintCareers.com, accessed 13 August 2010, www.quintcareers.com.

18. Hansen, "Behavioral Job Interviewing Strategies for Job-Seekers."

19. Chris Pentilla, "Testing the Waters," *Entrepreneur*, January 2004, www.entrepreneur.com; Terry McKenna, "Behavior-Based Interviewing," *National Petroleum News*, January 2004, 16; Nancy K. Austin, "Goodbye Gimmicks," *Incentive*, May 1996, 241.

20. William Poundstone, "Beware the Interview Inquisition," *Harvard Business Review*, May 2003, 18+.

21. Peter Vogt, "Mastering the Phone Interview," Monster.com, accessed 13 December 2006, www.monster.com; Nina Segal, "The Global Interview: Tips for Successful, Unconventional Interview Techniques," Monster.com, accessed 13 December 2006, www.monster.com.

22. Segal, "The Global Interview: Tips for Successful, Unconventional Interview Techniques."

23. Barbara Kiviat, "How Skype Is Changing the Job Interview," *Time*, 20 October 2009, accessed 13 August 2010, www.time.com.

24. HireVue website, accessed 4 April 2008, www.hirevue.com; in2View website, accessed 4 April 2008, www.in2view.biz; Victoria Reitz, "Interview Without Leaving Home," *Machine Design*, 1 April 2004, 66.

25. Gina Ruiz, "Job Candidate Assessment Tests Go Virtual," *Workforce Management*, January 2008, accessed 14 August 2010, www.workforce.com; Connie Winkler, "Job Tryouts Go Virtual," *HR Magazine*, September 2006, 131–134.

26. Jonathan Katz, "Rethinking Drug Testing," *Industry Week*, March 2010, 16–18; Ashley Shadday, "Assessments 101: An Introduction to Candidate Testing," *Workforce Management*, January 2010, accessed 14 August 2010, www.workforce.com; Dino di Mattia, "Testing Methods and Effectiveness of Tests," *Supervision*, August 2005, 4–5; David W. Arnold and John W. Jones, "Who the Devil's Applying Now?" *Security Management*, March 2002, 85–88; Matthew J. Heller, "Digging Deeper," *Workforce Management*, 3 March 2008, 35–39.

27. Frederick P. Morgeson, Michael A. Campion, Robert L. Dipboye, John R. Hollenbeck, Kevin Murphy, and Neil Schmitt, "Are We Getting Fooled Again? Coming to Terms with Limitations in the Use of Personality Tests in Personnel Selection," *Personnel Psychology* 60, no. 4 (Winter 2007): 1029–1049.

28. Austin, "Goodbye Gimmicks."

29. Rachel Zupek, "How to Answer 10 Tough Interview Questions," CNN.com, 4 March 2009, www.cnn.com; Barbara Safani, "How to Answer Tough Interview Questions Authentically," The Ladders, 5 December 2009, www.theladders.com.

30. Nick Corcodilos, "How to Answer a Misguided Interview Question," *Seattle Times*, 30 March 2008, www.seattletimes.com.

31. Katherine Spencer Lee, "Tackling Tough Interview Questions," *Certification Magazine*, May 2005, 35.

32. Scott Ginsberg, "10 Good Ways to 'Tell Me About Yourself,'" The Ladders, 26 June 2010, www.theladders.com.

33. InterviewUp website, accessed 13 August 2010, www.interviewup.com.

34. Joe Turner, "An Interview Strategy: Telling Stories," Yahoo! HotJobs, accessed 5 April 2008, http://hotjobs.yahoo.com.

35. "A Word of Caution for Chatty Job Candidates," *Public Relations Tactics*, January 2008, 4.

36. "Employers Reveal Outrageous and Common Mistakes Candidates Made in Job Interviews, According to New CareerBuilder Survey," CareerBuilder.com, 12 January 2011, www.careerbuilder.com.

37. Randall S. Hansen, "When Job-Hunting: Dress for Success," QuintCareers.com, accessed 5 April 2008, www.quintcareers.com; Alison Doyle, "Dressing for Success," About.com, http://jobsearch.about.com.

38. William S. Frank, "Job Interview: Pre-Flight Checklist," *The Career Advisor*, accessed 28 September 2005, http://careerplanning.about.com.

39. "Employers Reveal Outrageous and Common Mistakes Candidates Made in Job Interviews, According to New CareerBuilder Survey."

40. T. Shawn Taylor, "Most Managers Have No Idea How to Hire the Right Person for the Job," *Chicago Tribune*, 23 July 2002, www.ebsco.com.

41. "10 Minutes to Impress," *Journal of Accountancy*, July 2007, 13.

42. Steven Mitchell Sack, "The Working Woman's Legal Survival Guide: Testing," Findlaw.com, accessed 22 February 2004, www.findlaw.com.

43. Mark Henricks, "3 Interview Questions That Could Cost Your Company $1 Million," BNET, 8 March 2011, www.bnet.com.

44. Todd Anten, "How to Handle Illegal Interview Questions," Yahoo! HotJobs, accessed 7 August 2009, http://hotjobs.yahoo.com.

45. "Negotiating Salary: An Introduction," *Information Week* online, accessed 22 February 2004, www.informationweek.com.

46. "Negotiating Salary: An Introduction."

47. Lisa Vaas, "Resume, Meet Technology: Making Your Resume Format Machine-Friendly," The Ladders, accessed 13 August 2010, www.theladders.com.

48. Joan S. Lublin, "Notes to Interviewers Should Go Beyond a Simple Thank You," *Wall Street Journal*, 5 February 2008, B1.

Format and Layout of Business Documents

The format and layout of business documents vary from country to country. In addition, many organizations develop their own variations of standard styles, adapting documents to the types of messages they send and the kinds of audiences they communicate with. The formats described here are the most common approaches used in U.S. business correspondence, but be sure to follow whatever practices are expected at your company.

First Impressions

Your documents tell readers a lot about you and about your company's professionalism. So all your documents must look neat, present a professional image, and be easy to read. Your audience's first impression of a document comes from the quality of its paper, the way it is customized, and its general appearance.

PAPER

To give a quality impression, businesspeople consider carefully the paper they use. Several aspects of paper contribute to the overall impression:

- **Weight.** Paper quality is judged by the weight of four reams (each a 500-sheet package) of letter-size paper. The weight most commonly used by U.S. business organizations is 20-pound paper, but 16- and 24-pound versions are also used.
- **Cotton content.** Paper quality is also judged by the percentage of cotton in the paper. Cotton doesn't yellow over time the way wood pulp does, plus it's both strong and soft. For letters and outside reports, use paper with a 25 percent cotton content. For memos and other internal documents, you can use a lighter-weight paper with lower cotton content. Airmail-weight paper may save money for international correspondence, but make sure it isn't too flimsy.[1]
- **Size.** In the United States, the standard paper size for business documents is 8½ by 11 inches. Standard legal documents are 8½ by 14 inches. Executives sometimes have heavier 7-by-10-inch paper on hand (with matching envelopes) for personal messages such as congratulations.[2] They may also have a box of note cards imprinted with their initials and a box of plain folded notes for condolences or for acknowledging formal invitations.
- **Color.** White is the standard color for business purposes, although neutral colors such as gray and ivory are sometimes used. Memos can be produced on pastel-colored paper to distinguish them from external correspondence. In addition, memos are sometimes produced on various colors of paper for routing to separate departments. Light-colored papers are appropriate, but bright or dark colors make reading difficult and may appear too frivolous.

CUSTOMIZATION

For letters to outsiders, U.S. businesses commonly use letterhead stationery, which may be either professionally printed or designed in-house using word processing templates and graphics. Letterhead typically contains the company name, logo, address, telephone and fax numbers, general email address, website URL, and possibly one or more social media URLs.

In the United States, businesses always use letterhead for the first page of a letter. Successive pages are usually plain sheets of paper that match the letterhead in color and quality. Some companies use a specially printed second-page letterhead that bears only the company's name.

APPEARANCE

Nearly all business documents are produced using an inkjet or laser printer; make sure to use a clean, high-quality printer. Certain documents, however, should be handwritten (such as a short informal memo or a note of condolence). Be sure to handwrite, print, or type the envelope to match the document. However, even a letter on the best-quality paper with the best-designed letterhead may look unprofessional if it's poorly produced. So pay close attention to all the factors affecting appearance, including the following:

- **Margins.** Business letters typically use 1-inch margins at the top, bottom, and sides of the page, although these parameters are sometimes adjusted to accommodate letterhead elements.
- **Line length.** Lines are rarely justified, because the resulting text looks too formal and can be difficult to read.
- **Character spacing.** Use proper spacing between characters and after punctuation. For example, U.S. conventions include leaving one space after commas, semicolons, colons, and sentence-ending periods. Each letter in a person's initials is followed by a period and a single space. However, abbreviations such as U.S.A. or MBA may or may not have periods, but they never have internal spaces.

- **Special symbols.** Take advantage of the many special symbols available with your computer's selection of fonts. In addition, see if your company has a style guide for documents, which may include particular symbols you are expected to use.
- **Corrections.** Messy corrections are unacceptable in business documents. If you notice an error after printing a document with your word processor, correct the mistake and reprint. (With informal memos to members of your own team or department, the occasional small correction in pen or pencil is acceptable, but never in formal documents.)

Letters

All business letters have certain elements in common. Several of these elements appear in every letter; others appear only when desirable or appropriate. In addition, these letter parts are usually arranged in one of three basic formats.

STANDARD LETTER PARTS

The letter in Figure A.1 shows the placement of standard letter parts. The writer of this business letter had no letterhead available but correctly included a heading. All business letters typically include these seven elements.

Heading

The elements of the letterhead make up the heading of a letter in most cases. If letterhead stationery is not available, the heading includes a return address (but no name) and starts 13 lines from the top of the page, which leaves a 2-inch top margin.

Date

If you're using letterhead, place the date at least one blank line beneath the lowest part of the letterhead. Without letterhead, place the date immediately below the return address. The standard method of writing the date in the United States uses the full name of the month (no abbreviations), followed by the day (in numerals, without *st*, *nd*, *rd*, or *th*), a comma,

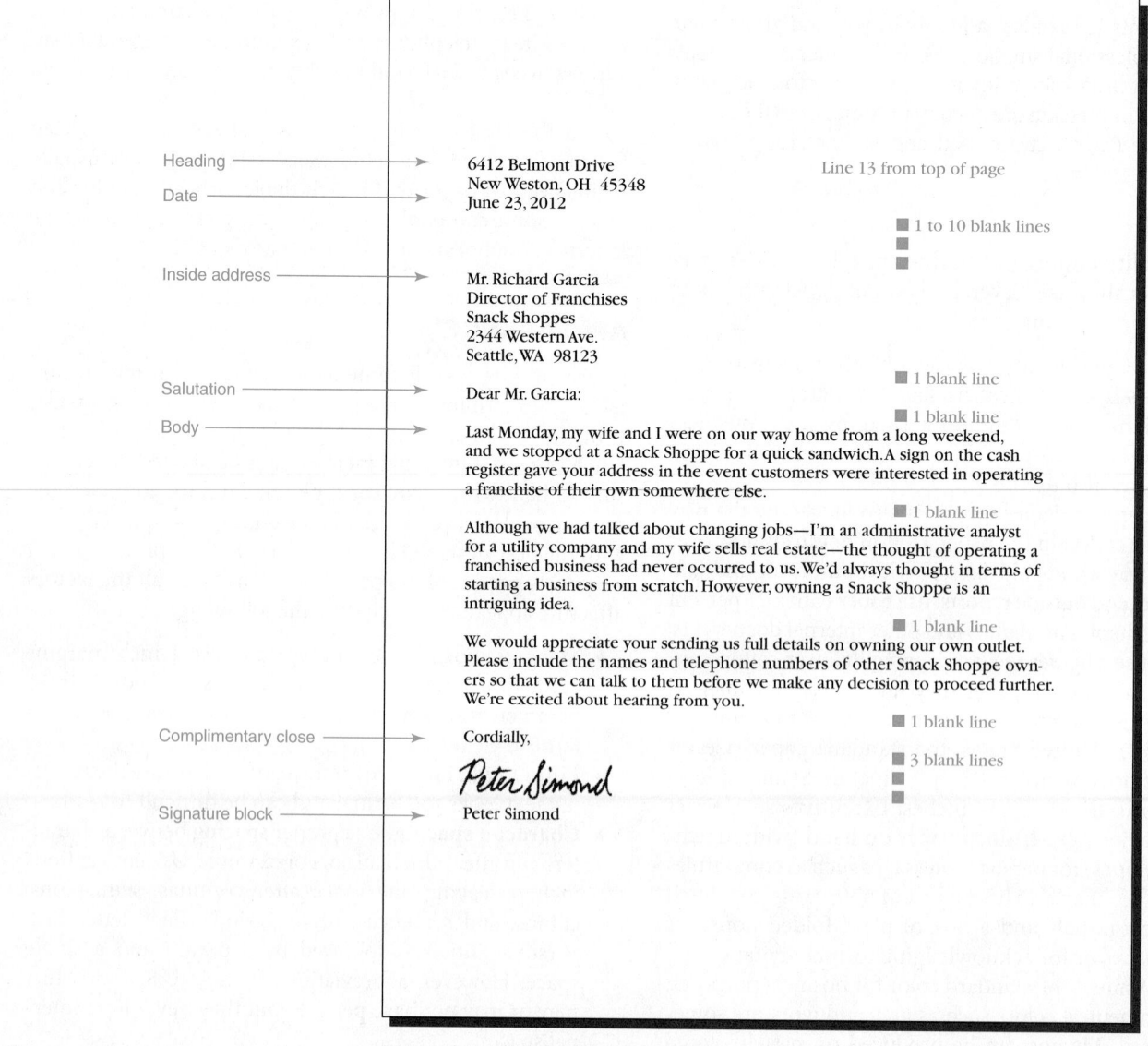

Figure A.1 Standard Letter Parts

TABLE A.1   Common Date Forms

Convention	Description	Date—Mixed	Date—All Numerals
U.S. standard	Month (spelled out) day, year	July 14, 2012	7/14/12
U.S. government and some U.S. industries	Day (in numerals) month (spelled out) year	14 July 2012	14/7/12
European	Replace U.S. solidus (diagonal line) with periods	14 July 2012	14.7.2012
2012 International standard	Year month day	2012 July 14	2012,7,14

and then the year: July 14, 2012 (7/14/2012). Some organizations follow other conventions (see Table A.1). To maintain the utmost clarity in international correspondence, always spell out the name of the month in dates.[3]

Inside Address

The inside address identifies the recipient of the letter. For U.S. correspondence, begin the inside address at least one line below the date. Precede the addressee's name with a courtesy title, such as *Dr., Mr.,* or *Ms.* The accepted courtesy title for women in business is *Ms.,* although a woman known to prefer the title *Miss* or *Mrs.* is always accommodated. If you don't know whether a person is a man or a woman (and you have no way of finding out), omit the courtesy title. For example, *Terry Smith* could be either a man or a woman. The first line of the inside address would be just *Terry Smith*, and the salutation would be *Dear Terry Smith*. The same is true if you know only a person's initials, as in *S. J. Adams.*

Spell out and capitalize titles that precede a person's name, such as *Professor* or *General* (see Table A.2 on the next page for the proper forms of address). The person's organizational title, such as *Director,* may be included on this first line (if it is short) or on the line below; the name of a department may follow. In addresses and signature lines, don't forget to capitalize any professional title that follows a person's name:

Mr. Ray Johnson, Dean

Ms. Patricia T. Higgins

Assistant Vice President

However, professional titles not appearing in an address or signature line are capitalized only when they directly precede the name:

President Kenneth Johanson will deliver the speech.

Maria Morales, president of ABC Enterprises, will deliver the speech.

The Honorable Helen Masters, senator from Arizona, will deliver the speech.

If the name of a specific person is unavailable, you may address the letter to the department or to a specific position within the department. Also, be sure to spell out company names in full, unless the company itself uses abbreviations in its official name.

Other address information includes the treatment of buildings, house numbers, and compass directions (see Table A.3

on page A-5). The following example shows all the information that may be included in the inside address and its proper order for U.S. correspondence:

Ms. Linda Coolidge, Vice President
Corporate Planning Department
Midwest Airlines
Kowalski Building, Suite 21-A
7279 Bristol Ave.
Toledo, OH 43617

Canadian addresses are similar, except that the name of the province is usually spelled out:

Dr. H. C. Armstrong
Research and Development
Commonwealth Mining Consortium
The Chelton Building, Suite 301
585 Second St. SW
Calgary, Alberta T2P 2P5

The order and layout of address information vary from country to country. So when addressing correspondence for other countries, carefully follow the format and information that appear in the company's letterhead. However, when you're sending mail from the United States, be sure that the name of the destination country appears on the last line of the address in capital letters. Use the English version of the country name so that your mail is routed from the United States to the right country. Then, to be sure your mail is routed correctly within the destination country, use the foreign spelling of the city name (using the characters and diacritical marks that would be commonly used in the region). For example, the following address uses *Köln* instead of *Cologne*:

H. R. Veith, Director	Addressee
Eisfieren Glaswerk	Company name
Blaubachstrasse 13	Street address
Postfach 10 80 07	Post office road
D-5000 Köln I	District, city
GERMANY	Country

For additional examples of international addresses, see Table A.4 on page A-6.

Be sure to use organizational titles correctly when addressing international correspondence. Job designations vary around the world. In England, for example, a managing director is often what a U.S. company would call its chief executive officer or president, and a British deputy is the equivalent of a vice president. In France, responsibilities are

TABLE A.2	Forms of Address	
Person	**In Address**	**In Salutation**
Personal Titles		
Man	Mr. [first & last name]	Dear Mr. [last name]:
Woman*	Ms. [first & last name]	Dear Ms. [last name]:
Two men (or more)	Mr. [first & last name] and Mr. [first & last name]	Dear Mr. [last name] and Mr. [last name] *or* Messrs. [last name] and [last name]:
Two women (or more)	Ms. [first & last name] and Ms. [first & last name]	Dear Ms. [last name] and Ms. [last name] *or* Mses. [last name] and [last name]:
One woman and one man	Ms. [first & last name] and Mr. [first & last name]	Dear Ms. [last name] and Mr. [last name]:
Couple (married with same last name)	Mr. [husband's first name] and Mrs. [wife's first name] [couple's last name]	Dear Mr. and Mrs. [last name]:
Couple (married with different last names)	Mr. [first & last name of husband] Ms. [first & last name of wife]	Dear Mr. [husband's last name] and Ms. [wife's last name]:
Couple (married professionals with same title and same last name)	[title in plural form] [husband's first name] and [wife's first name] [couple's last name]	Dear [title in plural form] [last name]:
Couple (married professionals with different titles and same last name)	[title] [first & last name of husband] and [title] [first & last name of wife]	Dear [title] and [title] [last name]:
Professional Titles		
President of a college or university	[title] [first & last name], President	Dear [title] [last name]:
Dean of a school or college	Dean [first & last name] *or* Dr., Mr., *or* Ms. [first & last name], Dean of [title]	Dear Dean [last name]: *or* Dear Dr., Mr., *or* Ms. [last name]:
Professor	Professor *or* Dr. [first & last name]	Dear Professor *or* Dr. [last name]:
Physician	[first & last name], M.D.	Dear Dr. [last name]:
Lawyer	Mr. *or* Ms. [first & last name], Attorney at Law	Dear Mr. *or* Ms. [last name]:
Military personnel	[full rank, first & last name, abbreviation of service designation] (add *Retired* if applicable)	Dear [rank] [last name]:
Company or corporation	[name of organization]	Ladies and Gentlemen: *or* Gentlemen and Ladies:
Governmental Titles		
President of the United States	The President	Dear Mr. *or* Madam President:
Senator of the United States	The Honorable [first & last name]	Dear Senator [last name]:
Cabinet member	The Honorable [first & last name]	Dear Mr. *or* Madam Secretary:
Attorney General	The Honorable [first & last name]	Dear Mr. *or* Madam Attorney General:
Mayor	The Honorable [first & last name], Mayor of [name of city]	Dear Mayor [last name]:
Judge	The Honorable [first & last name]	Dear Judge [last name]:

*Use *Mrs.* or *Miss* only if the recipient has specifically requested that you use one of these titles; otherwise *always* use *Ms.* in business correspondence. Also, never refer to a married woman by her husband's name (e.g., Mrs. Robert Washington) unless she specifically requests that you do so.

TABLE A.3	Inside Address Information	
Description	**Example**
Capitalize building names.	Empire State Building
Capitalize locations within buildings (apartments, suites, rooms).	Suite 1073
Use numerals for all house or building numbers, except the number one.	One Trinity Lane; 637 Adams Ave., Apt. 7
Spell out compass directions that fall within a street address.	1074 West Connover St.
Abbreviate compass directions that follow the street address.	783 Main St., N.E., Apt. 27

assigned to individuals without regard to title or organizational structure, and in China the title *project manager* has meaning, but the title *sales manager* may not.

To make matters worse, businesspeople in some countries sign correspondence without their names typed below. In Germany, for example, the belief is that employees represent the company, so it's inappropriate to emphasize personal names.[4] Use the examples in Table A.4 as guidelines when addressing correspondence to countries outside the United States.

Salutation

In the salutation of your letter, follow the style of the first line of the inside address. If the first line is a person's name, the salutation is *Dear Mr.* or *Ms. Name*. The formality of the salutation depends on your relationship with the addressee. If in conversation you would say "Mary," your letter's salutation should be *Dear Mary*, followed by a colon. Otherwise, include the courtesy title and last name, followed by a colon. Presuming to write *Dear Lewis* instead of *Dear Professor Chang* demonstrates a disrespectful familiarity that the recipient will probably resent.

If the first line of the inside address is a position title such as *Director of Personnel*, then use *Dear Director*. If the addressee is unknown, use a polite description, such as *Dear Alumnus, Dear SPCA Supporter,* or *Dear Voter*. If the first line is plural (a department or company), then use *Ladies and Gentlemen* (look again at Table A.2). When you do not know whether you're writing to an individual or a group (for example, when writing a reference or a letter of recommendation), use *To whom it may concern.*

In the United States some letter writers use a "salutopening" on the salutation line. A salutopening omits *Dear* but includes the first few words of the opening paragraph along with the recipient's name. After this line, the sentence continues a double space below as part of the body of the letter, as in these examples:

Thank you, Mr. Brown,   Salutopening Body
for your prompt payment of your bill.

Congratulations, Ms. Lake!   Salutopening Body
Your promotion is well deserved.

Whether your salutation is informal or formal, be especially careful that names are spelled correctly. A misspelled name is glaring evidence of carelessness, and it belies the personal interest you're trying to express.

Body

The body of the letter is your message. Almost all letters are single-spaced, with one blank line before and after the salutation or salutopening, between paragraphs, and before the complimentary close. The body may include indented lists, entire paragraphs indented for emphasis, and even subheadings. If it does, all similar elements should be treated in the same way. Your department or company may select a format to use for all letters.

Complimentary Close

The complimentary close begins on the second line below the body of the letter. Alternatives for wording are available, but currently the trend seems to be toward using one-word closes, such as *Sincerely* and *Cordially*. In any case, the complimentary close reflects the relationship between you and the person you're writing to. Avoid cute closes, such as *Yours for bigger profits*. If your audience doesn't know you well, your sense of humor may be misunderstood.

Signature Block

Leave three blank lines for a written signature below the complimentary close, and then include the sender's name (unless it appears in the letterhead). The person's title may appear on the same line as the name or on the line below:

Cordially,

Raymond Dunnigan
Director of Personnel

Your letterhead indicates that you're representing your company. However, if your letter is on plain paper or runs to a second page, you may want to emphasize that you're speaking legally for the company. The accepted way of doing that is to place the company's name in capital letters, a double

TABLE A.4	International Addresses and Salutations		
Country	**Postal Address**	**Address Elements**	**Salutations**
Argentina	Sr. Juan Pérez Editorial Internacional S.A. Av. Sarmiento 1337, 8° P.C. C1035AAB BUENOS AIRES–CF ARGENTINA	S.A. = Sociedad Anónima (corporation) Av. Sarmiento (name of street) 1337 (building number) 8° - 8th. P = Piso (floor) C (room or suite) C1035AAB (postcode + city) CF = Capital Federal (federal capital)	Sr. = Señor (Mr.) Sra. = Señora (Mrs.) Srta. = Señorita (Miss) Don't use given names except with people you know well.
Australia	Mr. Roger Lewis International Publishing Pty. Ltd. 166 Kent Street, Level 9 GPO Box 3542 SYDNEY NSW 200 AUSTRALIA	Pty. Ltd. – Proprietory Limited (corp.) 166 (building number) Kent Street (name of street) Level (floor) GPO Box (P.O. box) City + state (abbrev.) + postcode	Mr. and Mrs. used on first contact. Ms. not common (avoid use). Business is informal—use given name freely.
Austria	Herrn Dipl.-Ing.J.Gerdenitsch International Verlag Ges.m.b.H. Glockengasse 159 1010 WIEN AUSTRIA	Herrn – To Mr. (separate line) Dipl.-Ing. (engineering degree) Ges.m.b.H. (a corporation) Glockengasse (street name) 159 (building number) 1010 (postcode + city) WIEN (Vienna)	Herr (Mr.) Frau (Mrs.) Fräulein (Miss) obsolete in business, so do not use. Given names are almost never used in business.
Brazil	Ilmo. Sr. Gilberto Rabello Ribeiro Editores Internacionais S.A. Rua da Ajuda, 228–6° Andar Caixa Postal 2574 20040–000 RIO DE JANEIRO–RJ BRAZIL	Ilmo. = Ilustrissimo (honorific) Ilma. = Ilustrissima (hon. female) S.A. – Sociedade Anônima (corporation) Rua = street, da Ajuda (street name) 228 (building number) 6° = 6th. Andar (floor) Caixa Postal (P.O. box) 20040–000 (postcode + city)–RJ (state abbrev.)	Sr. = Senhor (Mr.) Sra. = Senhora (Mrs.) Srta. = Senhorita (Miss) Family name at end, e.g., Senhor Ribeiro (Rabello is mother's family name) Given names are readily used in business.
China	Xia Zhiyi International Publishing Ltd. 14 Jianguolu Chaoyangqu BEIJING 100025 CHINA	Ltd. (limited liability corporation) 14 (building number) Jianguolu (street name), lu (street) Chaoyangqu (district name) (city + postcode)	Family name (single syllable) first. Given name (2 syllables) second, sometimes reversed. Use Mr. or Ms. at all times (Mr. Xia).
France	Monsieur LEFÈVRE Alain Éditions Internationales S.A. Siège Social Immeuble Le Bonaparte 64–68, av. Galliéni B.P. 154 75942 PARIS CEDEX 19 FRANCE	S.A. = Société Anonyme (corporation) Siège Social (head office) Immeuble (building + name) 64–68 (building occupies 64, 66, 68) av. = avenue (no initial capital) B.P. = Boîte Postale (P.O. box) 75942 (postcode + city) CEDEX (postcode for P.O. box)	Monsieur (Mr.) Madame (Mrs.) Mademoiselle (Miss) Best not to abbreviate. Family name is sometimes in all caps with given name following.
Germany	Herrn Gerhardt Schneider International Verlag GmbH Schillerstraße 159 44147 DORTMUND GERMANY	Herrn = To Mr. (on a separate line) GmbH (inc.—incorporated) –straße (street—'β' often written 'ss') 159 (building number) 44147 (postcode – city)	Herr (Mr.) Frau (Mrs.) Fräulein (Miss) obsolete in business. Business is formal: (1) do not use given names unless invited, and (2) use academic titles precisely.
India	Sr. Shyam Lal Gupta International Publishing (Pvt.) Ltd. 1820 Rehaja Centre 214, Darussalam Road Andheri East MUMBAI–400049 INDIA	(Pvt.) (privately owned) Ltd. (limited liability corporation) 1820 (possibly office #20 on 18th floor) Rehaja Centre (building name) 214 (building number) Andheri East (suburb name) (city + hyphen + postcode)	Shri (Mr.), Shrimati (Mrs.) but English is common business language, so use Mr., Mrs., Miss. Given names are used only by family and close friends.

(continued)

Country	Postal Address	Address Elements	Salutations
Italy	Egr. Sig. Giacomo Mariotti Edizioni Internazionali S.p.A. Via Terenzio, 2120138 MILANO ITALY	Egr. = Egregio (honorific) Sig. = Signor (not nec. a separate line) S.p.A. = Società per Azioni (corp.) Via (street) 21 (building number) 20138 (postcode + city)	Sig. = Signore (Mr.) Sig.ra = Signora (Mrs.) Sig.a (Ms.) Women in business are addressed as Signora. Use given name only when invited.
Japan	Mr. Taro Tanaka Kokusai Shuppan K.K. 10–23, 5-chome, Minamiazabu Minato-ku TOKYO 106 JAPAN	K.K. = Kabushiki Kaisha (corporation) 10 (lot number) 23 (building number) 5-chome (area #5) Minamiazabu (neighborhood name) Minato-ku (city district) (city + postcode)	Given names are not used in business. Use family name + job title. Or use family name + "-san" (Tanaka-san) or more respectfully, add "-sama" or "-dono."
Korea	Mr. Kim Chang-ik International Publishers Ltd. Room 206, Korea Building 33–4 Nonhyon-dong Kangnam-ku SEOUL 135–010 KOREA	English company names common Ltd. (a corporation) 206 (office number inside the building) 33–4 (area 4 of subdivision 33) -dong (city neighborhood name) -ku (subdivision of city) (city + postcode)	Family name is normally first but sometimes placed after given name. A two-part name is the given name. Use Mr. or Mrs. in letters, but use job title in speech.
Mexico	Sr. Francisco Pérez Martínez Editores Internacionales S.A. Independencia No. 322 Col. Juárez 06050 MEXICO D.F.	S.A. – Sociedad Anónima (corporation) Independencia (street name) No. = Número (number) 322 (building number) Col. = Colonia (city district) Juárez (locality name) 06050 (postcode + city) D.F. = Distrito Federal (federal capital)	Sr. = Señor (Mr.) Sra. = Señora (Mrs.) Srta. = Señorita (Miss) Family name in middle: e.g., Sr. Pérez (Martínez is mother's family). Given names are used in business.
South Africa	Mr. Mandla Ntuli International Publishing (Pty.) Ltd. Private Bag X2581 JOHANNESBURG 2000 SOUTH AFRICA	Pty. = Proprietory (privately owned) Ltd. (a corporation) Private Bag (P.O. Box) (city + postcode) or (postcode + city)	Mnr. = Meneer (Mr.) Mev. = Mevrou (Mrs.) Mejuffrou (Miss) is not used in business. Business is becoming less formal, so the use of given names is possible.
United Kingdom	Mr. N. J. Lancaster International Publishing Ltd. Kingsbury House 12 Kingsbury Road EDGEWARE Middlesex HA8 9XG ENGLAND	N. J. (initials of given names) Ltd. (limited liability corporation) Kingsbury House (building name) 12 (building number) Kingsbury Road (name of street/road) EDGEWARE (city—all caps) Middlesex (county—not all caps) HA8 9XG	Mr. and Ms. used mostly. Mrs. and Miss sometimes used in North and by older women. Given names—called Christian names—are used in business after some time. Wait to be invited.

space below the complimentary close, and then include the sender's name and title four lines below that:

Sincerely,
WENTWORTH INDUSTRIES

Helen B. Taylor
President

If your name could be taken for either a man's or a woman's, a courtesy title indicating gender should be included, with or without parentheses. Also, women who prefer a particular courtesy title should include it:

Mrs. Nancy Winters
(Ms.) Juana Flores

Ms. Pat Li
(Mr.) Jamie Saunders

ADDITIONAL LETTER PARTS

Letters vary greatly in subject matter and thus in the identifying information they need and the format they adopt. The letter in Figure A.2 on the next page shows how these additional parts should be arranged. The following elements may be used in any combination, depending on the requirements of the particular letter:

- **Addressee notation.** Letters that have a restricted readership or that must be handled in a special way should include such addressee notations as *PERSONAL, CONFIDENTIAL, or PLEASE FORWARD*. This sort of notation appears a double space above the inside address, in all-capital letters.

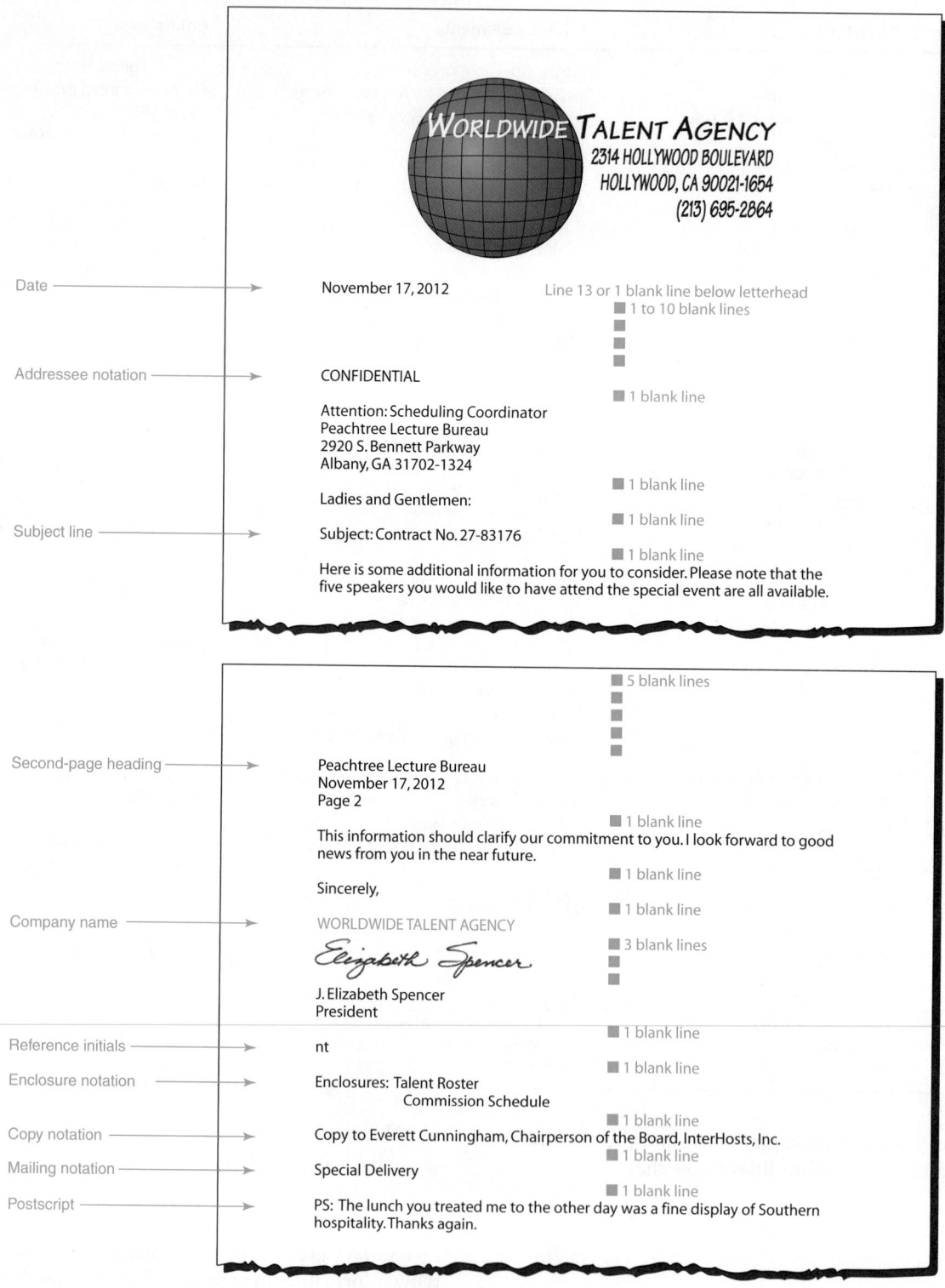

Figure A.2 Additional Letter Parts

- **Attention line.** Although not commonly used today, an attention line can be used if you know only the last name of the person you're writing to. It can also direct a letter to a position title or department. Place the attention line on the first line of the inside address and put the company name on the second.[5] Match the address on the envelope with the style of the inside address. An attention line may take any of the following forms or variants of them:

  Attention Dr. McHenry

  Attention Director of Marketing

  Attention Marketing Department

- **Subject line.** The subject line tells recipients at a glance what the letter is about (and indicates where to file the letter for future reference). It usually appears below the salutation, either against the left margin, indented (as a paragraph in the body), or centered. It can be placed above the salutation or at the very top of the page, and it can be underscored. Some businesses omit the word *Subject*, and some organizations replace it with *Re:* or *In re:* (meaning "concerning" or "in the matter of"). The subject line may take a variety of forms, including the following:

Subject: RainMaster Sprinklers
About your February 2, 2012, order
FALL 2012 SALES MEETING
Reference Order No. 27920

- **Second-page heading.** Use a second-page heading whenever an additional page is required. Some companies have second-page letterhead (with the company name and address on one line and in a smaller typeface). The heading bears the name (person or organization) from the first line of the inside address, the page number, the date, and perhaps a reference number. Leave two blank lines before the body. Make sure that at least two lines of a continued paragraph appear on the first and second pages. Never allow the closing lines to appear alone on a continued page. Precede the complimentary close or signature lines with at least two lines of the body. Also, don't hyphenate the last word on a page. All the following are acceptable forms for second-page headings:

Ms. Melissa Baker
May 10, 2012
Page 2

Ms. Melissa Baker, May 10, 2012, Page 2

Ms. Melissa Baker-2-May 10, 2012

- **Company name.** If you include the company's name in the signature block, put it a double space below the complimentary close. You usually include the company's name in the signature block only when the writer is serving as the company's official spokesperson or when letterhead has not been used.
- **Reference initials.** When businesspeople keyboard their own letters, reference initials are unnecessary, so they are becoming rare. When one person dictates a letter and another person produces it, reference initials show who helped prepare it. Place initials at the left margin, a double space below the signature block. When the signature block includes the writer's name, use only the preparer's initials. If the signature block includes only the department, use both sets of initials, usually in one of the following forms: *RSR/sm*, *RSR:sm*, or *RSR:SM* (writer/preparer). When the writer and the signer are different people, at least the file copy should bear both their initials as well as the typist's: *JFS/RSR/sm* (signer/writer/preparer).

- **Enclosure notation.** Enclosure notations appear at the bottom of a letter, one or two lines below the reference initials. Some common forms include the following:

Enclosure
Enclosures (2)
Enclosures: Résumé
               Photograph
               Brochure

- **Copy notation.** Copy notations may follow reference initials or enclosure notations. They indicate who's receiving a *courtesy copy* (*cc*). Recipients are listed in order of rank or (rank being equal) in alphabetical order. Among the forms used are the following:

cc: David Wentworth, Vice President
Copy to Hans Vogel
748 Chesterton Road
Snohomish, WA 98290

- **Mailing notation.** You may place a mailing notation (such as *Special Delivery* or *Registered Mail*) at the bottom of the letter, after reference initials or enclosure notations (whichever is last) and before copy notations. Or you may place it at the top of the letter, either above the inside address on the left side or just below the date on the right side. For greater visibility, mailing notations may appear in capital letters.
- **Postscript.** A postscript is presented as an afterthought to the letter, a message that requires emphasis, or a personal note. It is usually the last thing on any letter and may be preceded by *P.S.*, *PS.*, *PS:*, or nothing at all. A second afterthought would be designated *P.P.S.* (post postscript).

LETTER FORMATS

A letter format is the way of arranging all the basic letter parts. Sometimes a company adopts a certain format as its policy; sometimes the individual letter writer or preparer is allowed to choose the most appropriate format. In the United States, three major letter formats are commonly used:

- **Block format.** Each letter part begins at the left margin. The main advantage is quick and efficient preparation (see Figure A.3).
- **Modified block format.** Same as block format, except that the date, complimentary close, and signature block start near the center of the page (see Figure A.4 on page A-11). The modified block format does permit indentions as an option. This format mixes preparation speed with traditional placement of some letter parts. It also looks more balanced on the page than the block format does. (Note: The address and contact information in the left margin of this letter is part of this company's particular stationery design; other designs put this information at the top or bottom of the page.)

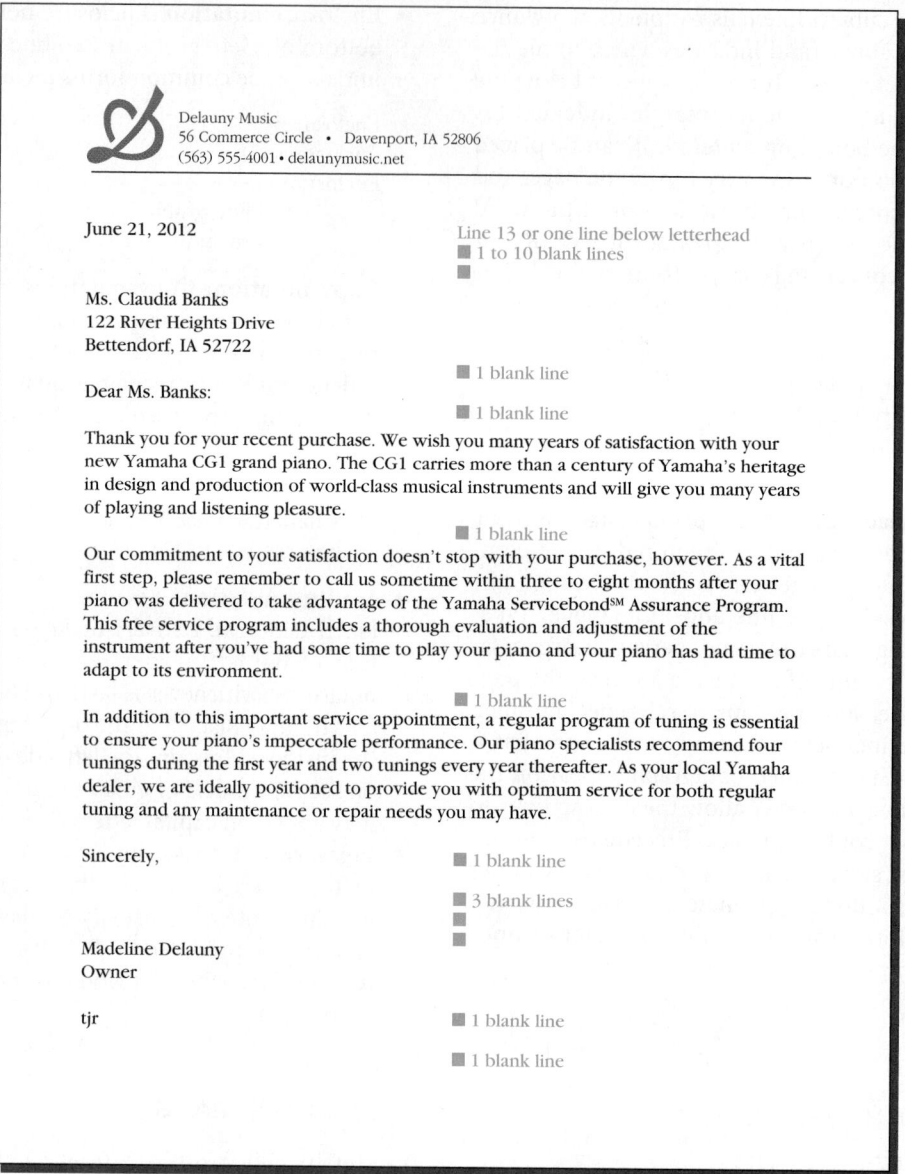

Figure A.3 Block Letter Format

- **Simplified format.** Instead of using a salutation, this format often weaves the reader's name into the first line or two of the body and often includes a subject line in capital letters (see Figure A.5 on page A-12). This format does not include a complimentary close, so your signature appears immediately below the body text. Because certain letter parts are eliminated, some line spacing is changed.

These three formats differ in the way paragraphs are indented, in the way letter parts are placed, and in some punctuation. However, the elements are always separated by at least one blank line, and the printed name is always separated from the line above by at least three blank lines to allow space for a signature. If paragraphs are indented, the indention is normally five spaces. The most common formats for intercultural business letters are the block style and the modified block style.

In addition to these three letter formats, letters may also be classified according to their style of punctuation. *Standard*, or *mixed, punctuation* uses a colon after the salutation (a comma if the letter is social or personal) and a comma after the complimentary close. *Open punctuation* uses no colon or comma after the salutation or the complimentary close. Although the most popular style in business communication is mixed punctuation, either style of punctuation may be used with block or modified block letter formats. Because the simplified letter format has no salutation or complimentary close, the style of punctuation is irrelevant.

Envelopes

For a first impression, the quality of the envelope is just as important as the quality of the stationery. Letterhead and envelopes should be of the same paper stock, have the same color ink,

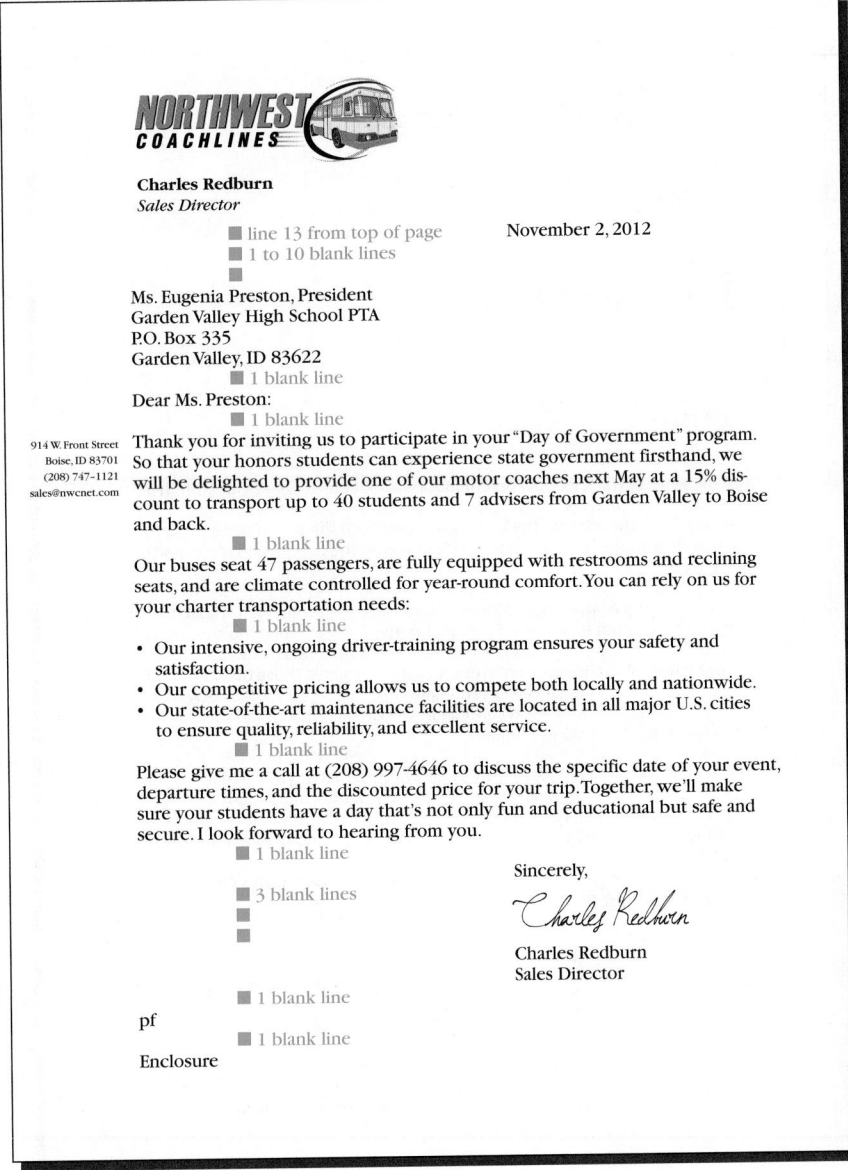

Figure A.4   Modified Block Letter Format

and be imprinted with the same address and logo. Most envelopes used by U.S. businesses are No. 10 envelopes (9½ inches long), which are sized for an 8½-by-11-inch piece of paper folded in thirds. Some occasions call for a smaller, No. 6¾, envelope or for envelopes proportioned to fit special stationery. Figure A.6 on page A-13 shows the two most common sizes.

ADDRESSING THE ENVELOPE

No matter what size the envelope, the address is always single-spaced with all lines aligned on the left. The address on the envelope is in the same style as the inside address and presents the same information. The order to follow is from the smallest division to the largest:

1. Name and title of recipient
2. Name of department or subgroup
3. Name of organization
4. Name of building
5. Street address and suite number, or post office box number
6. City, state, or province, and zip code or postal code
7. Name of country (if the letter is being sent abroad)

Because the U.S. Postal Service uses optical scanners to sort mail, envelopes for quantity mailings, in particular, should be addressed in the prescribed format. Everything is in capital letters, no punctuation is included, and all mailing instructions of interest to the post office are placed above the address area (see Figure A.6). Canada Post requires a similar format, except that only the city is all in capitals, and the postal code is placed on the line below the name of the city. The post office scanners read addresses from the bottom up, so if a letter is to be sent to a post office box rather than to a street address, the street address should appear on the line

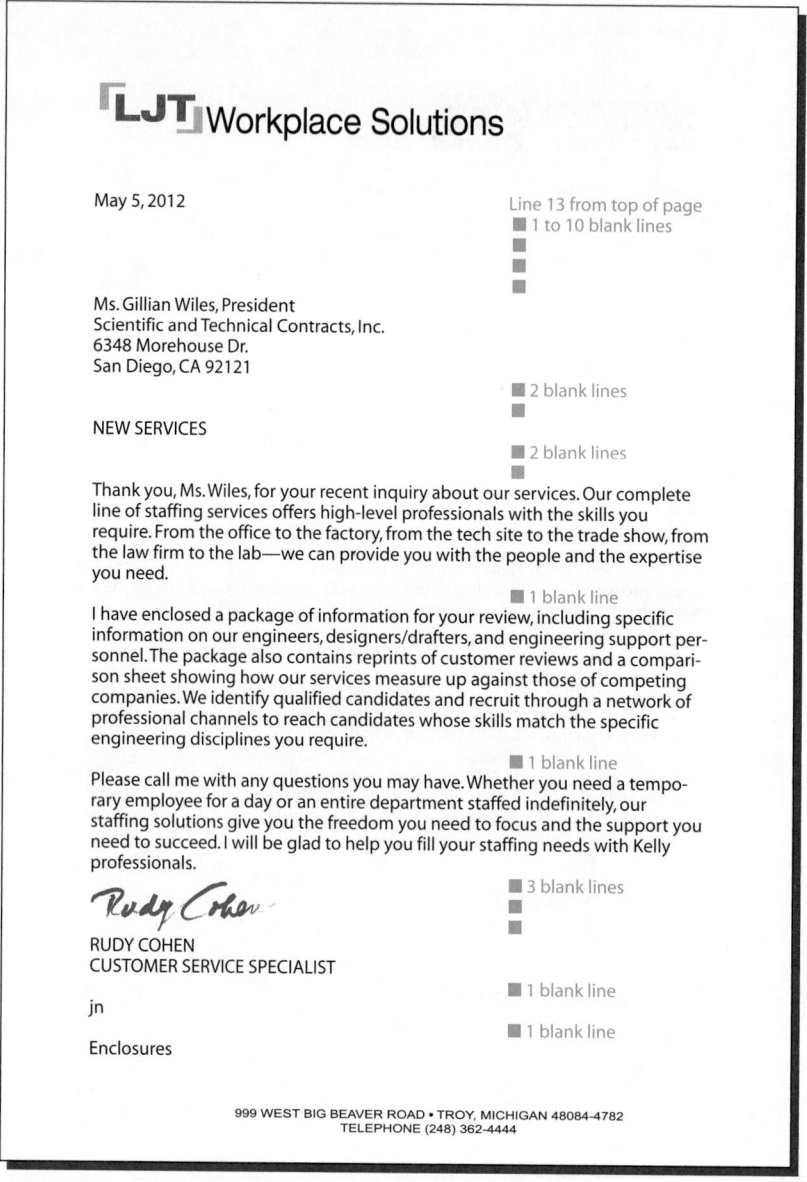

Figure A.5   Simplified Letter Format

above the box number. Figure A.6 also shows the proper spacing for addresses and return addresses.

The U.S. Postal Service and the Canada Post Corporation have published lists of two-letter mailing abbreviations for states, provinces, and territories (see Table A.5 on the next page). Postal authorities prefer no punctuation with these abbreviations. Quantity mailings should always follow post office requirements. For other letters, a reasonable compromise is to use traditional punctuation, uppercase and lowercase letters for names and street addresses, but two-letter state or province abbreviations, as shown here:

Mr. Kevin Kennedy
2107 E. Packer Dr.
Amarillo, TX 79108

Canadian postal codes are alphanumeric, with a three-character "area code" and a three-character "local code" separated by a single space (K2P 5A5). Zip and postal codes should be separated from state and province names by one space. Canadian postal codes may be treated the same or may be put in the bottom line of the address all by itself.

FOLDING TO FIT

The way a letter is folded also contributes to the recipient's overall impression of your organization's professionalism. When sending a standard-size piece of paper in a No. 10 envelope, fold it in thirds, with the bottom folded up first and the top folded down over it (see Figure A.7 on page A-14); the open end should be at the top of the envelope and facing out. Fit smaller stationery neatly into the appropriate envelope simply by folding it in half or in thirds. When sending a standard-size letterhead in a No. 6¾ envelope, fold it in half from top to bottom and then in thirds from side to side.

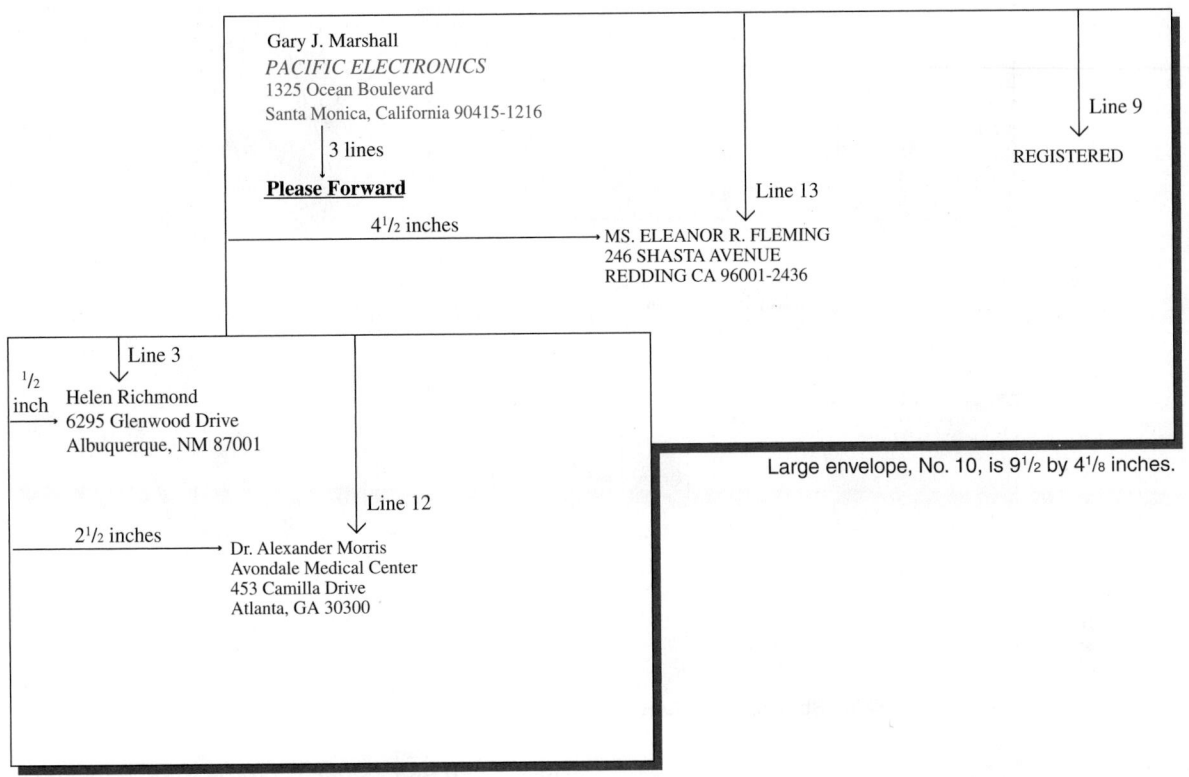

Figure A.6   Prescribed Envelope Format

TABLE A.5	Two-Letter Mailing Abbreviations for the United States and Canada

State/ Territory/ Province	Abbreviation	State/ Territory/ Province	Abbreviation	State/ Territory/ Province	Abbreviation
United States		Massachusetts	MA	Tennessee	TN
Alabama	AL	Michigan	MI	Texas	TX
Alaska	AK	Minnesota	MN	Utah	UT
American Samoa	AS	Mississippi	MS	Vermont	VT
Arizona	AZ	Missouri	MO	Virginia	VA
Arkansas	AR	Montana	MT	Virgin Islands	VI
California	CA	Nebraska	NE	Washington	WA
Canal Zone	CZ	Nevada	NV	West Virginia	WV
Colorado	CO	New Hampshire	NH	Wisconsin	WI
Connecticut	CT	New Jersey	NJ	Wyoming	WY
Delaware	DE	New Mexico	NM	**Canada**	
District of Columbia	DC	Maryland	MD	Alberta	AB
Florida	FL	New York	NY	British Columbia	BC
Georgia	GA	North Carolina	NC	Manitoba	MB
Guam	GU	North Dakota	ND	New Brunswick	NB
Hawaii	HI	Northern Mariana	MP	Newfoundland and Labrador	NL
Idaho	ID	Ohio	OH	Northwest Territories	NT
Illinois	IL	Oklahoma	OK	Nova Scotia	NS
Indiana	IN	Oregon	OR	Nunavut	NU
Iowa	IA	Pennsylvania	PA	Ontario	ON
Kansas	KS	Puerto Rico	PR	Prince Edward Island	PE
Kentucky	KY	Rhode Island	RI	Quebec	QC
Louisiana	LA	South Carolina	SC	Saskatchewan	SK
Maine	ME	South Dakota	SD	Yukon Territory	YT

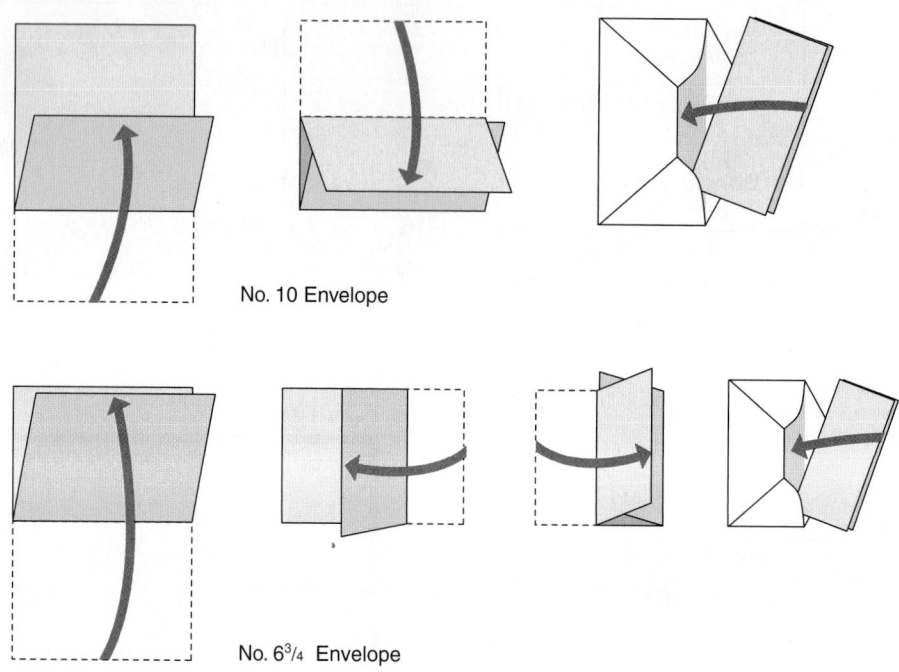

No. 10 Envelope

No. 6³/₄ Envelope

Figure A.7 Folding Standard-Size Letterhead

INTERNATIONAL MAIL

Postal service differs from country to country, so it's always a good idea to investigate the quality and availability of various services before sending messages and packages internationally. Also, compare the services offered by delivery companies such as UPS and FedEx to find the best rates and options for each destination and type of shipment. No matter which service you choose, be aware that international mail requires more planning than domestic mail. For example, for anything beyond simple letters, you generally need to prepare *customs forms* and possibly other documents, depending on the country of destination and the type of shipment. You are responsible for following the laws of the United States and any countries to which you send mail and packages.

The U.S. Postal Service currently offers four classes of international delivery, listed here from the fastest (and most expensive) to the slowest (and least expensive):

- **Global Express Guaranteed** is the fastest option. This service, offered in conjunction with FedEx, provides delivery in one to three business days to more than 190 countries and territories.
- **Express Mail International** guarantees delivery in three to five business days to a limited number of countries, including Australia, China, Hong Kong, Japan, and South Korea.
- **Priority Mail International** offers delivery guarantees of 6 to 10 business days to more than 190 countries and territories.
- **First Class Mail International** is an economical way to send correspondence and packages weighing up to four pounds to virtually any destination worldwide.

To prepare your mail for international delivery, follow the instructions provided at www.usps.com/international.

There you'll find complete information on the international services available through the U.S. Postal Service, along with advice on addressing and packaging mail, completing customs forms, and calculating postage rates and fees. The *International Mail Manual*, also available on this website, offers the latest information and regulations for both outbound and inbound international mail. For instance, you can click on individual country names to see current information about restricted or prohibited items and materials, required customs forms, and rates for various classes of service.[6] Various countries have specific and often extensive lists of items that may not be sent by mail at all or that must be sent using particular postal service options.

Memos

Electronic media have replaced most internal printed memos in many companies, but you may have occasion to send printed memos from time to time. These can be simple announcements or messages, or they can be short reports using the memo format (see Figure A.8).

On your document, include a title such as MEMO or INTEROFFICE CORRESPONDENCE (all in capitals) centered at the top of the page or aligned with the left margin. Also at the top, include the words *To, From, Date,* and *Subject*—followed by the appropriate information—with a blank line between as shown here:

MEMO

TO:
FROM:
DATE:
SUBJECT:

Carnival's standard memo stationary includes the company logo followed by a title indicating that this is a memo. —→

The four standard memo heads are used. —→

Because it is an internal memo, the writer does not begin with a salutation. —→

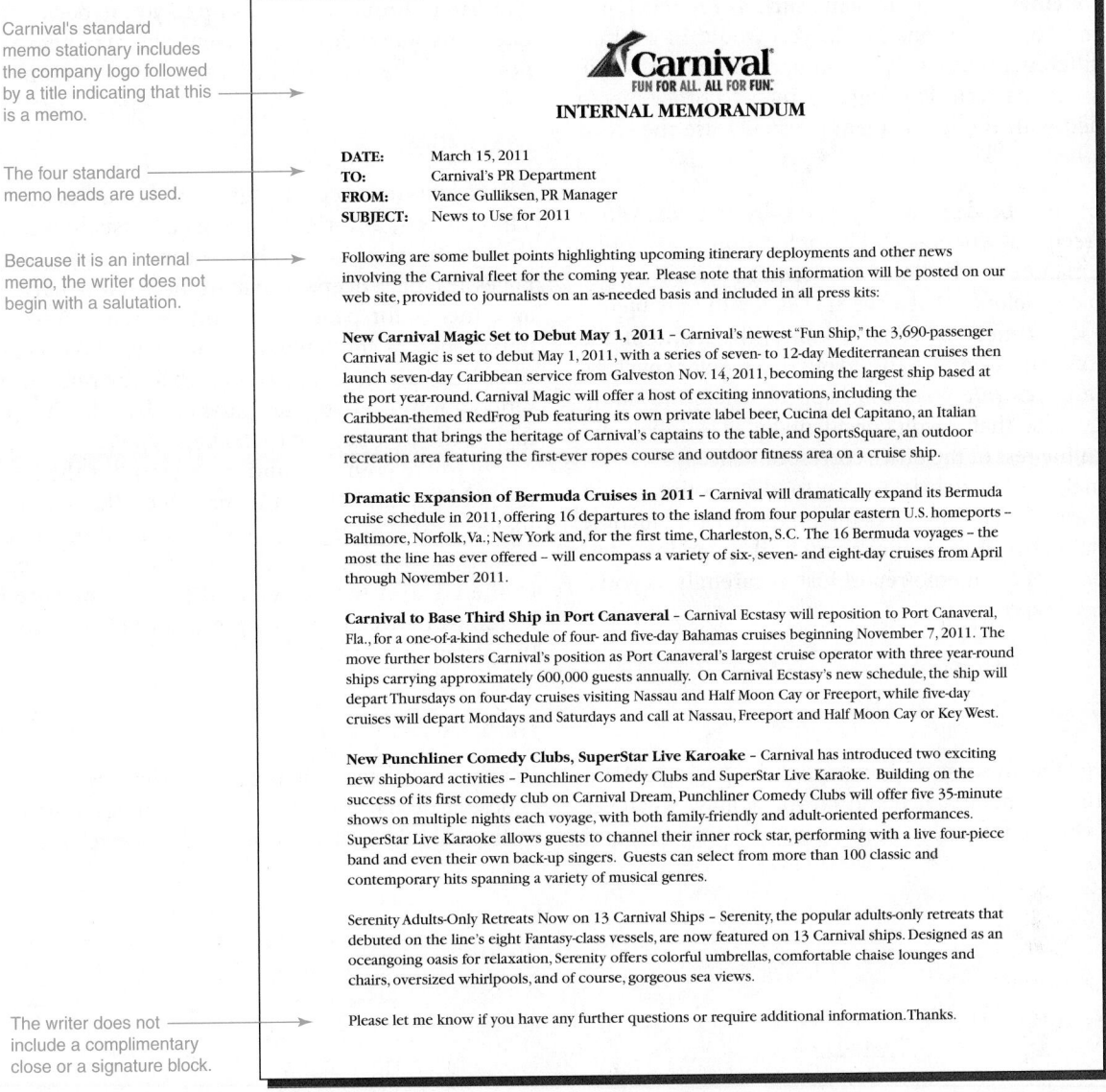

Carnival
FUN FOR ALL. ALL FOR FUN.

INTERNAL MEMORANDUM

DATE: March 15, 2011
TO: Carnival's PR Department
FROM: Vance Gulliksen, PR Manager
SUBJECT: News to Use for 2011

Following are some bullet points highlighting upcoming itinerary deployments and other news involving the Carnival fleet for the coming year. Please note that this information will be posted on our web site, provided to journalists on an as-needed basis and included in all press kits:

New Carnival Magic Set to Debut May 1, 2011 – Carnival's newest "Fun Ship," the 3,690-passenger Carnival Magic is set to debut May 1, 2011, with a series of seven- to 12-day Mediterranean cruises then launch seven-day Caribbean service from Galveston Nov. 14, 2011, becoming the largest ship based at the port year-round. Carnival Magic will offer a host of exciting innovations, including the Caribbean-themed RedFrog Pub featuring its own private label beer, Cucina del Capitano, an Italian restaurant that brings the heritage of Carnival's captains to the table, and SportsSquare, an outdoor recreation area featuring the first-ever ropes course and outdoor fitness area on a cruise ship.

Dramatic Expansion of Bermuda Cruises in 2011 – Carnival will dramatically expand its Bermuda cruise schedule in 2011, offering 16 departures to the island from four popular eastern U.S. homeports – Baltimore, Norfolk, Va.; New York and, for the first time, Charleston, S.C. The 16 Bermuda voyages – the most the line has ever offered – will encompass a variety of six-, seven- and eight-day cruises from April through November 2011.

Carnival to Base Third Ship in Port Canaveral – Carnival Ecstasy will reposition to Port Canaveral, Fla., for a one-of-a-kind schedule of four- and five-day Bahamas cruises beginning November 7, 2011. The move further bolsters Carnival's position as Port Canaveral's largest cruise operator with three year-round ships carrying approximately 600,000 guests annually. On Carnival Ecstasy's new schedule, the ship will depart Thursdays on four-day cruises visiting Nassau and Half Moon Cay or Freeport, while five-day cruises will depart Mondays and Saturdays and call at Nassau, Freeport and Half Moon Cay or Key West.

New Punchliner Comedy Clubs, SuperStar Live Karoake – Carnival has introduced two exciting new shipboard activities – Punchliner Comedy Clubs and SuperStar Live Karaoke. Building on the success of its first comedy club on Carnival Dream, Punchliner Comedy Clubs will offer five 35-minute shows on multiple nights each voyage, with both family-friendly and adult-oriented performances. SuperStar Live Karaoke allows guests to channel their inner rock star, performing with a live four-piece band and even their own back-up singers. Guests can select from more than 100 classic and contemporary hits spanning a variety of musical genres.

Serenity Adults-Only Retreats Now on 13 Carnival Ships – Serenity, the popular adults-only retreats that debuted on the line's eight Fantasy-class vessels, are now featured on 13 Carnival ships. Designed as an oceangoing oasis for relaxation, Serenity offers colorful umbrellas, comfortable chaise lounges and chairs, oversized whirlpools, and of course, gorgeous sea views.

Please let me know if you have any further questions or require additional information. Thanks.

The writer does not include a complimentary close or a signature block. —→

Figure A.8   Short Report Using the Memo Format

Sometimes the heading is organized like this:

MEMO

TO: FROM:
DATE: SUBJECT:

The following guidelines will help you effectively format specific memo elements:

- **Addressees.** When sending a memo to a long list of people, include the notation *See distribution list* or *See below* in the *To* position at the top; then list the names at the end of the memo. Arrange this list alphabetically, except when high-ranking officials deserve more prominent placement. You can also address memos to groups of people—*All Sales Representatives, Production Group, New Product Team.*
- **Courtesy titles.** You need not use courtesy titles anywhere in a memo; first initials and last names, first names, or even initials alone are often sufficient. However, use

a courtesy title if you would use one in a face-to-face encounter with the person.
- **Subject line.** The subject line of a memo helps busy colleagues quickly find out what your memo is about, so take care to make it concise and compelling.
- **Body.** Start the body of the memo on the second or third line below the heading. Like the body of a letter, it's usually single-spaced with blank lines between paragraphs. Indenting paragraphs is optional. Handle lists, important passages, and subheadings as you do in letters.
- **Second page.** If the memo carries over to a second page, head the second page just as you head the second page of a letter.
- **Writer's initials.** Unlike a letter, a memo doesn't require a complimentary close or a signature, because your name is already prominent at the top. However, you may initial the memo—either beside the name appearing at the top of the memo or at the bottom of the memo.

● **Other elements.** Treat elements such as reference initials and copy notations just as you would in a letter. One difference between letters and memos is that while letters use the term *enclosure* to refer to other pieces included with the letter, memos usually use the word *attachment*.

Memos may be delivered by hand, by the post office (when the recipient works at a different location), or through interoffice mail. Interoffice mail may require the use of special reusable envelopes that have spaces for the recipient's name and department or room number; the name of the previous recipient is simply crossed out. If a regular envelope is used, the words *Interoffice Mail* appear where the stamp normally goes, so that it won't accidentally be stamped and mailed with the rest of the office correspondence.

Informal, routine, or brief reports for distribution within a company are often presented in memo form. Don't include report parts such as a table of contents and appendixes, but write the body of the memo report just as carefully as you'd write a formal report.

Reports

Enhance the effectiveness of your reports by paying careful attention to their appearance and layout. Follow whatever guidelines your organization prefers, always being neat and

consistent throughout. If it's up to you to decide formatting questions, the following conventions may help you decide how to handle margins, headings, and page numbers.

MARGINS

All margins on a report page should be at least 1 inch wide. The top, left, and right margins are usually the same, but the bottom margins can be 1½ times deeper. Some special pages also have deeper top margins. Set top margins as deep as 2 inches for pages that contain major titles: prefatory parts (such as the table of contents or the executive summary), supplementary parts (such as the reference notes or bibliography), and textual parts (such as the first page of the text or the first page of each chapter).

If you're going to bind your report at the left or at the top, add half an inch to the margin on the bound edge (see Figure A.9): The space taken by the binding on left-bound reports makes the center point of the text a quarter inch to the right of the center of the paper. Be sure to center headings between the margins, not between the edges of the paper.

HEADINGS

If you don't have a template supplied by your employer, choose a design for headings and subheadings that clearly distinguishes the various levels in the hierarchy. The first-level

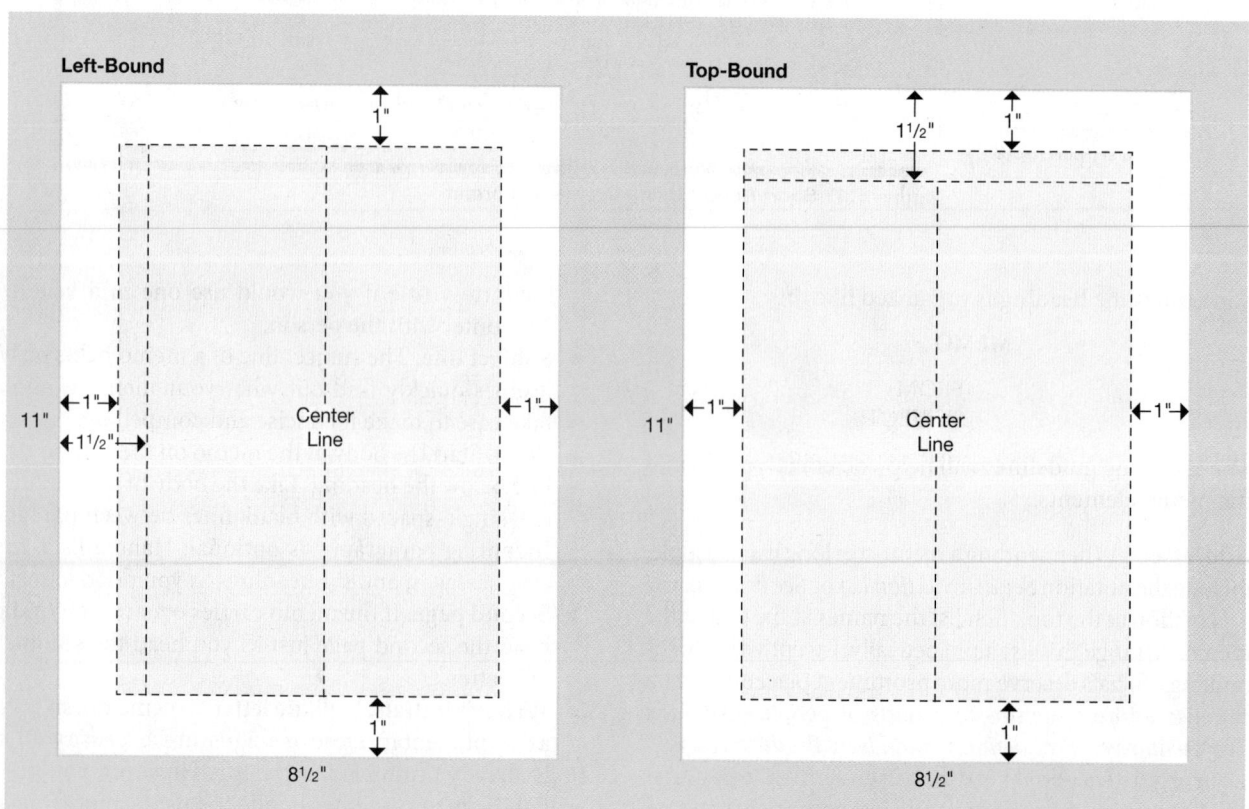

Figure A.9 Margins for Formal Reports

headings should be the most prominent, on down to the lowest-level subheading.

PAGE NUMBERS

Every page in a report is counted; however, not all pages show numbers. The first page of the report, normally the title page, is unnumbered. All other pages in the prefatory section are numbered with a lowercase roman numeral, beginning with *ii* and continuing with *iii, iv, v,* and so on. Start numbering again with arabic numerals (1, 2, and so on) starting at the first page of the body.

You have many options for placing and formatting the page numbers, although these choices are usually made for you in a template. If you're not using a standard company template, position the page number where it is easy to see as the reader flips through the report. If the report will be stapled or otherwise bound along the left side, for instance, the best place for the page number is the upper right or lower right corner.

Documentation of Report Sources

By providing information about your sources, you improve your own credibility as well as the credibility of the facts and opinions you present. Documentation gives readers the means for checking your findings and pursuing the subject further. Also, documenting your report is the accepted way to give credit to the people whose work you have drawn from.

What style should you use to document your report? Experts recommend various forms, depending on your field or discipline. Moreover, your employer or client may use a form different from those the experts suggest. Don't let this discrepancy confuse you. If your employer specifies a form, use it; the standardized form is easier for colleagues to understand. However, if the choice of form is left to you, adopt one of the styles described here. Whatever style you choose, be consistent within any given report, using the same order, punctuation, and format from one reference citation or bibliography entry to the next.

A wide variety of style manuals provide detailed information on documentation. These publications explain the three most commonly used styles:

- American Psychological Association, *Publication Manual of the American Psychological Association*, 6th ed. (Washington, D.C.: American Psychological Association, 2009). Details the author-date system, which is preferred in the social sciences and often in the natural sciences as well.
- *The Chicago Manual of Style*, 16th ed. (Chicago: University of Chicago Press, 2010). Often referred to only as "*Chicago*" and widely used in the publishing industry; provides detailed treatment of source documentation and many other aspects of document preparation.
- Joseph Gibaldi, *MLA Style Manual and Guide to Scholarly Publishing*, 3rd ed. (New York: Modern Language Association, 2008). Serves as the basis for the note and bibliography style used in much academic writing and is recommended in many college textbooks on writing term papers; provides a lot of examples in the humanities.

For more information on these three guides, visit http://real-timeupdates.com/ebc10 and click on Appendix B. Although many schemes have been proposed for organizing the information in source notes, all of them break the information into parts: (1) information about the author (name), (2) information about the work (title, edition, volume number), (3) information about the publication (place, publisher), (4) information about the date, and (5) information on relevant page ranges.

The following sections summarize the major conventions for documenting sources in three styles: *The Chicago Manual of Style* (Chicago), the *Publication Manual of the American Psychological Association* (APA), and the *MLA Style Manual* (MLA).

Chicago Humanities Style

The Chicago Manual of Style recommends two types of documentation systems. The *documentary-note*, or *humanities*, style gives bibliographic citations in notes—either footnotes (when printed at the bottom of a page) or endnotes (when printed at the end of the report). The humanities system is often used in literature, history, and the arts. The other system recommended by *Chicago* is the *author-date* system, which cites the author's last name and the date of publication in the text, usually in parentheses, reserving full documentation for the reference list (or bibliography). For the purpose of comparing styles, this section concentrates on the humanities system, which is described in detail in *Chicago*.

IN-TEXT CITATION— *CHICAGO* HUMANITIES STYLE

To document report sources in text, the humanities system relies on superscripts—arabic numerals placed just above the line of type at the end of the reference:

> Toward the end of his speech, Myers sounded a note of caution, saying that even though the economy is expected to grow, it could easily slow a bit.[10]

The superscript lets the reader know how to look for source information in either a footnote or an endnote (see Figure B.1 on the next page). Some readers prefer footnotes so that they can simply glance at the bottom of the page for information. Others prefer endnotes so that they can read the text without a clutter of notes on the page. Also, endnotes relieve the writer from worrying about how long each note will be and how much space it will take away from the page. Both footnotes and endnotes are handled automatically by today's word processing software.

For the reader's convenience, you can use footnotes for **content notes** (which may supplement your main text with asides about a particular issue or event, provide a cross-reference to another section of your report, or direct the

	NOTES
Journal article with volume and issue numbers	1. Jonathan Clifton, "Beyond Taxonomies of Influence," *Journal of Business Communication* 46, no. 1 (2009): 57–79.
Brochure	2. BestTemp Staffing Services, *An Employer's Guide to Staffing Services,* 2d ed. (Denver: BestTemp Information Center, 2011), 31.
Newspaper article, no author	3. "Might Be Harder Than It Looks," *Los Angeles Times,* 30 January 2009, sec. A, p. 22.
Annual report	4. The Walt Disney Company, *2010 Annual Report* (Burbank, Calif.: The Walt Disney Company, 2011), 48.
Magazine article	5. Kerry A. Dolan, "A Whole New Crop" *Forbes,* 2 June 2008, 72–75.
Television broadcast	6. Daniel Han, "Trade Wars Heating Up Around the Globe," *CNN Headline News* (Atlanta: CNN, 5 March 2002).
Internet, World Wide Web	7. "Intel—Company Capsule," Hoover's Online [cited 19 June 2011], 3 screens; available from www.hoovers.com/intel/-ID_13787-/free-co-factsheet.xhtml.
Book, component parts	8. Sonja Kuntz, "Moving Beyond Benefits," in *Our Changing Workforce,* ed. Randolf Jacobson (New York: Citadel Press, 2001), 213–27.
Unpublished dissertation or thesis	9. George H. Morales, "The Economic Pressures on Industrialized Nations in a Global Economy" (Ph.D. diss., University of San Diego, 2001), 32–47.
Paper presented at a meeting	10. Charles Myers, "HMOs in Today's Environment" (paper presented at the Conference on Medical Insurance Solutions, Chicago, Ill., August 2001), 16–17.
Online magazine article	11. Leo Babauta, "17 Tips to Be Productive with Instant Messaging," in *Web Worker Daily* [online] (San Francisco, 2007 [updated 14 November 2007; cited 14 February 2008]); available from http://webworkerdaily.com.
CD-ROM encyclopedia article, one author	12. Robert Parkings, "George Eastman," *The Concise Columbia Encyclopedia* (New York: Columbia University Press, 1998) [CD-ROM].
Interview	13. Georgia Stainer, general manager, Day Cable and Communications, interview by author, Topeka, Kan., 2 March 2011.
Newspaper article, one author	14. Evelyn Standish, "Global Market Crushes OPEC's Delicate Balance of Interests," *Wall Street Journal,* 19 January 2002, sec. A, p. 1.
Book, two authors	15. Miriam Toller and Jay Fielding, *Global Business for Smaller Companies* (Rocklin, Calif.: Prima Publishing, 2001), 102–3.
Government publication	16. U.S. Department of Defense, *Stretching Research Dollars: Survival Advice for Universities and Government Labs* (Washington, D.C.: GPO, 2002), 126.

Figure B.1   Sample Endnotes—Chicago Humanities Style

reader to a related source). Then you can use endnotes for **source notes** (which document direct quotations, paraphrased passages, and visual aids). Consider which type of note is most common in your report, and then choose whether to present these notes all as endnotes or all as footnotes. Regardless of the method you choose for referencing textual information in your report, notes for visual aids (both content notes and source notes) are placed on the same page as the visual.

BIBLIOGRAPHY— *CHICAGO* HUMANITIES STYLE

The humanities system may or may not be accompanied by a bibliography (because the notes give all the necessary bibliographic information). However, endnotes are arranged in order of appearance in the text, so an alphabetical bibliography can be valuable to your readers. The bibliography may be titled *Bibliography, Reference List, Sources, Works Cited* (if you include only those sources you actually cited in your report), or *Works Consulted* (if you include uncited sources as well). This list of sources may also serve as a reading list for those who want to pursue the subject of your report further, so you may want to annotate each entry—that is, comment on the subject matter and viewpoint of the source, as well as on its usefulness to readers. Annotations may be written in either complete or incomplete sentences. (See the annotated list of style manuals earlier in this appendix.) A bibliography may also be more manageable if you subdivide it into categories (a classified bibliography), either by type of reference (such as books, articles, and unpublished material) or by subject

BIBLIOGRAPHY

Journal article with volume and issue numbers	Clifton, Jonathan. "Beyond Taxonomies of Influence." *Journal of Business Communication* 46, no. 1 (2009): 57–79.
Online magazine article	Babauta, Leo. "17 Tips to Be Productive with Instant Messaging," In *Web Worker Daily* [online], San Francisco, 2007 [updated 14 November 2007, cited 14 February 2008]. Available from http://webworkerdaily.com.
Brochure	BestTemp Staffing Services. *An Employer's Guide to Staffing Services.* 2d ed. Denver: BestTemp Information Center, 2011.
Newspaper article, no author	"Might Be Harder Than It Looks." *Los Angeles Times,* 30 January 2009, sec. A, p. 22.
Magazine article	Dolan, Kerry A. "A Whole New Crop," *Forbes*, 2 June 2008, 72–75.
Television broadcast	Han, Daniel. "Trade Wars Heating Up Around the Globe." *CNN Headline News.* Atlanta: CNN, 5 March 2002.
Internet, World Wide Web	"Intel—Company Capsule." *Hoover's Online* [cited 19 June 2011]. 3 screens; Available from www.hoovers.com/intel/-ID_13787-/free-co-factsheet.xhtml.
Book, component parts	Kuntz, Sonja. "Moving Beyond Benefits." In *Our Changing Workforce*, edited by Randolf Jacobson. New York: Citadel Press, 2001.
Unpublished dissertation or thesis	Morales, George H. "The Economic Pressures on Industrialized Nations in a Global Economy." Ph.D. diss., University of San Diego, 2001.
Paper presented at a meeting	Myers, Charles. "HMOs in Today's Environment." Paper presented at the Conference on Medical Insurance Solutions, Chicago, Ill., August 2001.
CD-ROM encyclopedia article, one author	Parkings, Robert. "George Eastman." *The Concise Columbia Encyclopedia.* New York: Columbia University Press, 1998. [CD-ROM].
Interview	Stainer, Georgia, general manager, Day Cable and Communications. Interview by author. Topeka, Kan., 2 March 2011.
Newspaper article, one author	Standish, Evelyn. "Global Market Crushes OPEC's Delicate Balance of Interests." *Wall Street Journal,* 19 January 2002, sec. A, p. 1.
Book, two authors	Toller, Miriam, and Jay Fielding. *Global Business for Smaller Companies.* Rocklin, Calif.: Prima Publishing, 2001.
Government publication	U.S. Department of Defense. *Stretching Research Dollars: Survival Advice for Universities and Government Labs.* Washington, D.C.: GPO, 2002.
Annual report	The Walt Disney Company, *2010 Annual Report,* Burbank, Calif.: The Walt Disney Company, 2011.

Figure B.2   Sample Bibliography—Chicago Humanities Style

matter (such as government regulation, market forces, and so on). Following are the major conventions for developing a bibliography according to *Chicago* style (see Figure B.2):

- Exclude any page numbers that may be cited in source notes, except for journals, periodicals, and newspapers.
- Alphabetize entries by the last name of the lead author (listing last name first). The names of second and succeeding authors are listed in normal order. Entries without an author name are alphabetized by the first important word in the title.
- Format entries as hanging indents (indent second and succeeding lines three to five spaces).
- Arrange entries in the following general order: (1) author name, (2) title information, (3) publication information, (4) date, (5) periodical page range.

- Use quotation marks around the titles of articles from magazines, newspapers, and journals. Capitalize the first and last words, as well as all other important words (except prepositions, articles, and coordinating conjunctions).
- Use italics to set off the names of books, newspapers, journals, and other complete publications. Capitalize the first and last words, as well as all other important words.
- For journal articles, include the volume number and the issue number (if necessary). Include the year of publication inside parentheses and follow with a colon and the page range of the article: *Journal of Business Communication* 46, no. 1 (2009): 57–79. (In this source, the volume is 46, the number is 1, and the page range is 57–79.)
- Use brackets to identify all electronic references: [Online database] or [CD-ROM].

- Explain how electronic references can be reached: Available from www.spaceless.com/WWWVL.
- Give the citation date for online references: Cited 23 August 2010.

APA Style

The American Psychological Association (APA) recommends the author-date system of documentation, which is popular in the physical, natural, and social sciences. When using this system, you simply insert the author's last name and the year of publication within parentheses following the text discussion of the material cited. Include a page number if you use a direct quotation. This approach briefly identifies the source so that readers can locate complete information in the alphabetical reference list at the end of the report. The author-date system is both brief and clear, saving readers time and effort.

IN-TEXT CITATION—APA STYLE

To document report sources in text using APA style, insert the author's surname and the date of publication at the end of a statement. Enclose this information in parentheses. If the author's name is referred to in the text itself, then the name can be omitted from parenthetical material.

> Some experts recommend both translation and back-translation when dealing with any non-English-speaking culture (Clifton, 2009).
>
> Toller and Fielding (2001) make a strong case for small companies succeeding in global business.

Personal communications and interviews conducted by the author would not be listed in the reference list at all. Such citations would appear in the text only.

> Increasing the role of cable companies is high on the list of Georgia Stainer, general manager at Day Cable and Communications (personal communication, March 2, 2011).

LIST OF REFERENCES—APA STYLE

For APA style, list only those works actually cited in the text (so you would not include works for background or for further reading). Following are the major conventions for developing a reference list according to APA style (see Figure B.3):

- Format entries as hanging indents.
- List all author names in reversed order (last name first), and use only initials for the first and middle names.
- Arrange entries in the following general order: (1) author name, (2) date, (3) title information, (4) publication information, (5) periodical page range.
- Follow the author name with the date of publication in parentheses.
- List titles of articles from magazines, newspapers, and journals without underlines or quotation marks.

- Capitalize only the first word of the title, any proper nouns, and the first word to follow an internal colon.
- Italicize titles of books, capitalizing only the first word, any proper nouns, and the first word to follow a colon.
- Italicize titles of magazines, newspapers, journals, and other complete publications. Capitalize all the important words in the title.
- For journal articles, include the volume number (in italics) and, if necessary, the issue number (in parentheses). Finally, include the page range of the article: *Journal of Business Communication, 46*(1), 57–79. (In this example, the volume is 46, the number is 1, and the page range is 57–79.)
- Include personal communications (such as letters, memos, email, and conversations) only in text, not in reference lists.
- Electronic references include author, date of publication, title of article, name of publication (if one), volume, date of retrieval (month, day, year), and the source.
- For electronic references, indicate the actual year of publication.
- For webpages with extremely long URLs, use your best judgment to determine which URL from the site to use. For example, rather than giving the URL of a specific news release with a long URL, you can provide the URL of the "Media relations" webpage.
- APA citation guidelines for social media are still evolving. For the latest information, visit the APA Style Blog at http://blog.apastyle.org/apastyle.
- For online journals or periodicals that assign a digital object identifier (DOI), include that instead of a conventional URL. If no DOI is available, include the URL of the publication's home page (such as http://online.wsj.com for the *Wall Street Journal*).

MLA Style

The style recommended by the Modern Language Association of America is used widely in the humanities, especially in the study of language and literature. Like APA style, MLA style uses brief parenthetical citations in the text. However, instead of including author name and year, MLA citations include author name and page reference.

IN-TEXT CITATION—MLA STYLE

To document report sources in text using MLA style, insert the author's last name and a page reference inside parentheses following the cited material: (Matthews 63). If the author's name is mentioned in the text reference, the name can be omitted from the parenthetical citation: (63). The citation indicates that the reference came from page 63 of a work by Matthews. With the author's name, readers can find complete publication information in the alphabetically arranged list of works cited that comes at the end of the report.

REFERENCES

Journal article with volume and issue numbers
Clifton, J. (2009). Beyond Taxonomies of Influence. *Journal of Business Communication 46* (1), 57.

Online magazine article
Babauta, L. (2007, November 14), 17 tips to be productive with instant messaging. *Web Worker Daily*. Retrieved from http://webworkerdaily.com

Brochure
BestTemp Staffing Services. (2011). *An employer's guide to staffing services* (2d ed.) [Brochure]. Denver, CO: BestTemp Information Center.

Newspaper article, no author
Might be harder than it looks. (2009, January 30). *Los Angeles Times*, p. A22.

Magazine article
Dolan, K. A. (2008, June 2). A whole new crop. *Forbes*, 72–75.

Television broadcast
Han, D. (2002, March 5). Trade wars heating up around the globe. *CNN Headline News*. [Television broadcast]. Atlanta, GA: CNN.

Internet, World Wide Web
Hoover's Online. (2011). *Intel—Company Capsule*. Retrieved from http://www.hoovers.com/intel/-ID_13787-/free-co-factsheet.xhtml

Book, component parts
Kuntz, S. (2001). Moving beyond benefits. In Randolph Jacobson (Ed.), *Our changing workforce* (pp. 213–227). New York, NY: Citadel Press.

Unpublished dissertation or thesis
Morales, G. H. (2001). *The economic pressures on industrialized nations in a global economy*. Unpublished doctoral dissertation, University of San Diego.

Paper presented at a meeting
Myers, C. (2001, August). *HMOs in today's environment*. Paper presented at the Conference on Medical Insurance Solutions, Chicago, IL.

CD-ROM encyclopedia article, one author
Parkings, R. (1998). George Eastman. On *The concise Columbia encyclopedia*. [CD-ROM]. New York, NY: Columbia University Press.

Interview
Cited in text only, not in the list of references.

Newspaper article, one author
Standish, E. (2002, January 19). Global market crushes OPEC's delicate balance of interests. *Wall Street Journal*, p. A1.

Book, two authors
Toller, M., & Fielding, J. (2001). *Global business for smaller companies*. Rocklin, CA: Prima Publishing.

Government publication
U.S. Department of Defense. (2002). *Stretching research dollars: Survival advice for universities and government labs*. Washington, DC: U.S. Government Printing Office.

Annual report
The Walt Disney Company. (2011). *2010 Annual Report*. Burbank, CA: The Walt Disney Company.

Figure B.3   Sample References—APA Style

Some experts recommend both translation and back-translation when dealing with any non-English-speaking culture (Clifton 57).

Toller and Fielding make a strong case for small companies succeeding in global business (102–03).

LIST OF WORKS CITED—MLA STYLE

The *MLA Style Manual* recommends preparing the list of works cited first so that you will know what information to give in the parenthetical citation (for example, whether to add a short title if you're citing more than one work by the same author, or whether to give an initial or first name if you're citing two authors who have the same last name). The list of works cited appears at the end of your report, contains all the works that you cite in your text, and lists them in alphabetical order. Following are the major conventions for developing a reference list according to MLA style (see Figure B.4 on the next page):

- Format entries as hanging indents.
- Arrange entries in the following general order: (1) author name, (2) title information, (3) publication information, (4) date, (5) periodical page range.
- List the lead author's name in reverse order (last name first), using either full first names or initials. List second and succeeding author names in normal order.
- Use quotation marks around the titles of articles from magazines, newspapers, and journals. Capitalize all important words.

WORKS CITED

Journal article with volume and issue numbers

Clifton, Jonathan. "Beyond Taxonomies of Influence." *Journal of Business Communication* 46, 1 (2009): 57–79.

Online magazine article

Babauta, Leo. "17 Tips to Be Productive with Instant Messaging," *Web Worker Daily* 14 Nov. 2007. 14 Feb. 2008. http://webworkerdaily.com

Brochure

BestTemp Staffing Services. *An Employer's Guide to Staffing Services*. 2d ed. Denver: BestTemp Information Center, 2011.

Newspaper article, no author

"Might Be Harder Than It Looks." *Los Angeles Times,* 30 Jan. 2009: A22.

Magazine article

Dolan, Kerry A. "A Whole New Crop" *Forbes*, 2 June 2008: 72–75.

Television broadcast

Han, Daniel. "Trade Wars Heating Up Around the Globe." *CNN Headline News*. CNN, Atlanta. 5 Mar. 2002.

Internet, World Wide Web

"Intel—Company Capsule." *Hoover's Online*. 2011. Hoover's Company Information. 19 June 2011 http://www.hoovers.com/intel/-ID_13787/free-co-factsheet.xhtml

Book, component parts

Kuntz, Sonja. "Moving Beyond Benefits." *Our Changing Workforce*. Ed. Randolf Jacobson. New York: Citadel Press, 2001. 213–27.

Unpublished dissertation or thesis

Morales, George H. "The Economic Pressures on Industrialized Nations in a Global Economy." Diss. U of San Diego, 2001.

Paper presented at a meeting

Myers, Charles. "HMOs in Today's Environment." Conference on Medical Insurance Solutions. Chicago. 13 Aug. 2001.

CD-ROM encyclopedia article, one author

Parkings, Robert. "George Eastman." *The Concise Columbia Encyclopedia*. CD-ROM. New York: Columbia UP, 1998.

Interview

Stainer, Georgia, general manager, Day Cable and Communications. Telephone interview. 2 Mar. 2011.

Newspaper article, one author

Standish, Evelyn. "Global Market Crushes OPEC's Delicate Balance of Interests." *Wall Street Journal,* 19 Jan. 2002: A1.

Book, two authors

Toller, Miriam, and Jay Fielding. *Global Business for Smaller Companies*. Rocklin, CA: Prima Publishing, 2001.

Government publication

United States. Department of Defense. *Stretching Research Dollars: Survival Advice for Universities and Government Labs*. Washington: GPO, 2002.

Annual report

The Walt Disney Company, *2010 Annual Report*. Calif.: The Walt Disney Company, 2011.

Figure B.4   Sample Works Cited—MLA Style

- Italicize the names of books, newspapers, journals, and other complete publications, capitalizing all main words in the title.
- For journal articles, include the volume number and the issue number (if necessary). Include the year of publication inside parentheses and follow with a colon and the page range of the article: *Journal of Business Communication* 46, 1 (2009): 57. (In this source, the volume is 46, the number is 1, and the page is 57.)
- Electronic sources are less fixed than print sources, and they may not be readily accessible to readers. So citations for electronic sources must provide more information. Always try to be as comprehensive as possible, citing whatever information is available (however, see the note in the right column about extremely long URLs).

- The date for electronic sources should contain both the date assigned in the source (if no date is shown, write "n.d." instead) and the date accessed by the researcher.
- The URL for electronic sources must be as accurate and complete as possible, from access-mode identifier (such as http or ftp) to all relevant directory and file names. If the URL is extremely long, however, use the URL of the website's home page or the URL of the site's search page if you used the site's search function to find the article. Beginning with its 2009 edition, the MLA Style Manual no longer requires writers to include URLs for materials retrieved online. However, follow whatever guidelines your instructor gives you in this regard.
- Also beginning in 2009, MLA style requires you to indicate the medium of publication. For most sources, this will be "Web" or "Print," but you may also cite "CD-ROM" and other media, as appropriate.

APPENDIX C — Correction Symbols

Instructors often use these short, easy-to-remember correction symbols and abbreviations when evaluating students' writing. You can use them too, to understand your instructor's suggestions and to revise and proofread your own letters, memos, and reports. Refer to the Handbook of Grammar, Mechanics, and Usage (pp. H-1–H-25) for further information.

Content and Style

Acc	Accuracy. Check to be sure information is correct.
ACE	Avoid copying examples.
ACP	Avoid copying problems.
Adp	Adapt. Tailor message to reader.
App	Follow proper organization approach. (Refer to Chapter 4.)
Assign	Assignment. Review instructions for assignment.
AV	Active verb. Substitute active for passive.
Awk	Awkward phrasing. Rewrite.
BC	Be consistent.
BMS	Be more sincere.
Chop	Choppy sentences. Use longer sentences and more transitional phrases.
Con	Condense. Use fewer words.
CT	Conversational tone. Avoid using overly formal language.
Depers	Depersonalize. Avoid attributing credit or blame to any individual or group.
Dev	Develop. Provide greater detail.
Dir	Direct. Use direct approach; get to the point.
Emph	Emphasize. Develop this point more fully.
EW	Explanation weak. Check logic; provide more proof.
Fl	Flattery. Avoid compliments that are insincere.
FS	Figure of speech. Find a more accurate expression.
GNF	Good news first. Use direct order.
GRF	Give reasons first. Use indirect order.
GW	Goodwill. Put more emphasis on expressions of goodwill.
H/E	Honesty/ethics. Revise statement to reflect good business practices.
Imp	Imply. Avoid being direct.
Inc	Incomplete. Develop further.
Jar	Jargon. Use less specialized language.
Log	Logic. Check development of argument.

Neg	Negative. Use more positive approach or expression.
Obv	Obvious. Do not state point in such detail.
OC	Overconfident. Adopt humbler language.
OM	Omission.
Org	Organization. Strengthen outline.
OS	Off the subject. Close with point on main subject.
Par	Parallel. Use same structure.
Pom	Pompous. Rephrase in down-to-earth terms.
PV	Point of view. Make statement from reader's perspective rather than your own.
RB	Reader benefit. Explain what reader stands to gain.
Red	Redundant. Reduce number of times this point is made.
Ref	Reference. Cite source of information.
Rep	Repetitive. Provide different expression.
RS	Resale. Reassure reader that he or she has made a good choice.
SA	Service attitude. Put more emphasis on helping reader.
Sin	Sincerity. Avoid sounding glib or uncaring.
SL	Stereotyped language. Focus on individual's characteristics instead of on false generalizations.
Spec	Specific. Provide more specific statement.
SPM	Sales promotion material. Tell reader about related goods or services.
Stet	Let stand in original form.
Sub	Subordinate. Make this point less important.
SX	Sexist. Avoid language that contributes to gender stereotypes.
Tone	Tone needs improvement.
Trans	Transition. Show connection between points.
UAE	Use action ending. Close by stating what reader should do next.
UAS	Use appropriate salutation.
UAV	Use active voice.
Unc	Unclear. Rewrite to clarify meaning.
UPV	Use passive voice.
USS	Use shorter sentences.
V	Variety. Use different expression or sentence pattern.
W	Wordy. Eliminate unnecessary words.
WC	Word choice. Find a more appropriate word.
YA	"You" attitude. Rewrite to emphasize reader's needs.

Grammar, Mechanics, and Usage

Ab	Abbreviation. Avoid abbreviations in most cases; use correct abbreviation.
Adj	Adjective. Use adjective instead.
Adv	Adverb. Use adverb instead.
Agr	Agreement. Make subject and verb or noun and pronoun agree.
Ap	Appearance. Improve appearance.
Apos	Apostrophe. Check use of apostrophe.
Art	Article. Use correct article.
BC	Be consistent.
Cap	Capitalize.
Case	Use cases correctly.
CoAdj	Coordinate adjective. Insert comma between coordinate adjectives; delete comma between adjective and compound noun.
CS	Comma splice. Use period or semicolon to separate clauses.
DM	Dangling modifier. Rewrite so that modifier clearly relates to subject of sentence.
Exp	Expletive. Avoid expletive beginnings, such as it is, there are, there is, this is, and these are.
F	Format. Improve layout of document.
Frag	Fragment. Rewrite as complete sentence.
Gram	Grammar. Correct grammatical error.
HCA	Hyphenate compound adjective.
lc	Lowercase. Do not use capital letter.
M	Margins. Improve frame around document.
MM	Misplaced modifier. Place modifier close to word it modifies.
NRC	Nonrestrictive clause (or phrase). Separate from rest of sentence with commas.
P	Punctuation. Use correct punctuation.
Par	Parallel. Use same structure.
PH	Place higher. Move document up on page.
PL	Place lower. Move document down on page.
Prep	Preposition. Use correct preposition.
RC	Restrictive clause (or phrase). Remove commas that separate clause from rest of sentence.
RO	Run-on sentence. Separate two sentences with comma and coordinating conjunction or with semicolon.
SC	Series comma. Add comma before *and*.
SI	Split infinitive. Do not separate *to* from rest of verb.
Sp	Spelling error. Consult dictionary.
S-V	Subject-verb pair. Do not separate with comma.
Syl	Syllabification. Divide word between syllables.
WD	Word division. Check dictionary for proper end-of-line hyphenation.
WW	Wrong word. Replace with another word.

Proofreading Marks

Symbol	Meaning	Symbol Used in Context	Corrected Copy
═	Align horizontally	meaningful result	meaningful result
‖	Align vertically	1. Power cable 2. Keyboard	1. Power cable 2. Keyboard
bf	Boldface	Recommendations bf	**Recommendations**
≡	Capitalize	Pepsico, Inc.	PepsiCo, Inc.
][	Center	] Awards Banquet [	Awards Banquet
◡	Close up space	self- confidence	self-confidence
ℯ	Delete	harrassment and abuse	harassment
ds	Double-space	text in first line text in second line ds	text in first line text in second line
∧	Insert	turquoise shirts	turquoise and white shirts
∨	Insert apostrophe	our teams goals	our team's goals
∧	Insert comma	a, b and c	a, b, and c
⹀	Insert hyphen	third quarter sales	third-quarter sales
⊙	Insert period	Harrigan et al	Harrigan et al.
∨ ∨	Insert quotation marks	This team isn't cooperating.	This "team" isn't cooperating.
#	Insert space	real estate testcase	real estate test case
ital	Italics	Quarterly Report ital	*Quarterly Report*
/	Lowercase	TULSA, South of here	Tulsa, south of here
⌴	Move down	Sincerely,	Sincerely,
⊏	Move left	Attention: ⊏ Security	Attention: Security
⊐	Move right	February 2, 2010 ⊐	February 2, 2010
⌐	Move up	THIRD-QUARTER SALES	THIRD-QUARTER SALES
STET	Restore	staff talked openly and frankly STET	staff talked openly
∫	Run lines together	Manager, Distribution	Manager, Distribution
ss	Single space	text in first line text in second line	text in first line text in second line
⬭	Spell out	COD	cash on delivery
sp	Spell out	sp Assn. of Biochem. Engrs.	Association of Biochemical Engineers
⌐	Start new line	Marla Fenton, Manager, Distri-bution	Marla Fenton, Manager, Distribution
¶	Start new paragraph	¶ The solution is easy to determine but difficult to implement in a competitive environment like the one we now face.	The solution is easy to determine but difficult to implement in a competitive environment like the one we now face.
∼	Transpose	airy, light, casual tone	light, airy, casual tone

Handbook of Grammar, Mechanics, and Usage

The rules of grammar, mechanics, and usage provide the guidance every professional needs in order to communicate successfully with colleagues, customers, and other audiences. Understanding and following these rules helps you in two important ways. First, the rules determine how meaning is encoded and decoded in the communication process. If you don't encode your messages using the same rules your readers or listeners use to decode them, chances are your audiences will not extract your intended meaning from your messages. Without a firm grasp of the basics of grammar, mechanics, and usage, you risk being misunderstood, damaging your company's image, losing money for your company, and possibly even losing your job. In other words, if you want to get your point across, you need to follow the rules of grammar, mechanics, and usage. Second, apart from transferring meaning successfully, following the rules tells your audience that you respect the conventions and expectations of the business community.

You can think of *grammar* as the agreed-upon structure of a language, the way that individual words are formed and the manner in which those words are then combined to form meaningful sentences. *Mechanics* are style and formatting issues such as capitalization, spelling, and the use of numbers and symbols. *Usage* involves the accepted and expected way in which specific words are used by a particular community of people—in this case, the community of businesspeople who use English. This handbook can help you improve your knowledge and awareness in all three areas. It is divided into the following sections:

- **Diagnostic Test of English Skills.** Testing your current knowledge of grammar, mechanics, and usage helps you find out where your strengths and weaknesses lie. This test offers 50 items taken from the topics included in this handbook.
- **Assessment of English Skills.** After completing the diagnostic test, use the assessment form to highlight the areas you most need to review.
- **Essentials of Grammar, Mechanics, and Usage.** This section helps you quickly review the basics. You can study the things you've probably already learned but may have forgotten about grammar, punctuation, mechanics (including capitalization, abbreviation, number style, and word division), and vocabulary (including frequently confused words, frequently misused words, frequently misspelled words, and transitional words and phrases). Practice sessions throughout this section help you test yourself and reinforce what you learn. Use this

essential review not only to study and improve your English skills but also as a reference for any questions you may have during this course.

Diagnostic Test of English Skills

Use this test to determine whether you need more practice with grammar, punctuation, mechanics, or vocabulary. When you've answered all the questions, ask your instructor for an answer sheet so that you can score the test. On the Assessment of English Skills form (page H-3), record the number of questions you answered incorrectly in each section.

The following choices apply to items 1–5. Write in each blank the letter of the choice that best describes the part of speech that is underlined.

- **A.** noun
- **B.** pronoun
- **C.** verb
- **D.** adjective
- **E.** adverb
- **F.** preposition
- **G.** conjunction
- **H.** article

_____ **1.** The new branch location will be decided <u>by</u> next week.

_____ **2.** We must hire only <u>qualified</u>, ambitious graduates.

_____ **3.** After their <u>presentation,</u> I was still undecided.

_____ **4.** See <u>me</u> after the meeting.

_____ **5.** Margaret, pressed for time, turned in <u>unusually</u> sloppy work.

In the blanks for items 6–15, write the letter of the word or phrase that best completes each sentence.

_____ **6.** (A. Russ's, B. Russ') laptop was stolen last week.

_____ **7.** Speaking only for (A. me, B. myself), I think the new policy is discriminatory.

_____ **8.** Of the five candidates we interviewed yesterday, (A. who, B. whom) do you believe is the best choice?

_____ **9.** India has increased (A. it's, B. its) imports of corn and rice.

_____ **10.** Anyone who wants to be (A. their, B. his or her) own boss should think about owning a franchise.

_____ **11.** If the IT department can't (A. lie, B. lay) the fiber-optic cable by March 1, the plant will not open on schedule.

_____ 12. Starbucks (A. is, B. are) opening five new stores in San Diego in the next year.

_____ 13. The number of women-owned small businesses (A. has, B. have) increased sharply in the past two decades.

_____ 14. Greg and Bernyce worked (A. good, B. well) together.

_____ 15. They distributed the supplies (A. among, B. between) the six staff members.

The following choices apply to items 16–20. Write in each blank the letter of the choice that best describes the sentence structure problem with each item.

A. sentence fragment
B. comma splice
C. misplaced modifier
D. fused sentence
E. lack of parallelism
F. unclear antecedent

_____ 16. The number of employees who took the buyout offer was much higher than expected, now the entire company is understaffed.

_____ 17. The leader in Internet-only banking.

_____ 18. Diamond doesn't actually sell financial products rather it acts as an intermediary.

_____ 19. Helen's proposal is for not only the present but also for the future.

_____ 20. When purchasing luxury products, quality is more important than price for consumers.

For items 21–30, circle the letter of the preferred choice in each of the following groups of sentences.

21. A. What do you think of the ad slogan "Have it your way?"
　　B. What do you think of the ad slogan "Have it your way"?

22. A. Send copies to Jackie Cross, Uniline, Brad Nardi, Peale & Associates, and Tom Griesbaum, MatchMakers.
　　B. Send copies to Jackie Cross, Uniline; Brad Nardi, Peale & Associates; and Tom Griesbaum, MatchMakers.

23. A. They've recorded 22 complaints since yesterday, all of them from long-time employees.
　　B. They've recorded 22 complaints since yesterday; all of them from long-time employees.

24. A. We are looking for two qualities in applicants: experience with computers and an interest in people.
　　B. We are looking for two qualities in applicants; experience with computers and an interest in people.

25. A. At the Center for the Blind the clients we serve have lost vision, due to a wide variety of causes.
　　B. At the Center for the Blind, the clients we serve have lost vision due to a wide variety of causes.

26. A. Replace your standard lightbulbs with new, compact fluorescent bulbs.
　　B. Replace your standard lightbulbs with new, compact, fluorescent bulbs.
　　C. Replace your standard lightbulbs with new compact fluorescent bulbs.

27. A. Blue Cross of California may have changed its name to Anthem Blue Cross but the company still has the same commitment to California.
　　B. Blue Cross of California may have changed its name to Anthem Blue Cross, but the company still has the same commitment to California.

28. A. Only eight banks in this country—maybe nine can handle transactions of this magnitude.
　　B. Only eight banks in this country—maybe nine—can handle transactions of this magnitude.

29. A. Instead of focusing on high-growth companies, we targeted mature businesses with only one or two people handling the decision making
　　B. Instead of focusing on high growth companies, we targeted mature businesses with only one or two people handling the decision-making.

30. A. According to board president Damian Cabaza "having a crisis communication plan is a high priority."
　　B. According to board president Damian Cabaza, "Having a crisis communication plan is a high priority."

For items 31–40, select the best choice from among those provided.

31. A. At her previous employer, Mary-Anne worked in Marketing Communications and Human Resources.
　　B. At her previous employer, Mary-Anne worked in marketing communications and human resources.

32. A. By fall, we'll have a dozen locations between the Mississippi and Missouri rivers.
　　B. By Fall, we'll have a dozen locations between the Mississippi and Missouri Rivers.

33. A. The Board applauded President Donlan upon her reelection for a fifth term.
　　B. The board applauded president Donlan upon her reelection for a fifth term.
　　C. The board applauded President Donlan upon her re-election for a fifth term.

34. A. If you want to travel to France, you need to be au courant with the business practices.
　　B. If you want to travel to France, you need to be "au courant" with the business practices.

35. A. As the company's CEO, Thomas Spurgeon handles all dealings with the FDA.
　　B. As the company's C.E.O., Thomas Spurgeon handles all dealings with the F.D.A.

36. A. The maximum speed limit in most states is 65 mph.
　　B. The maximum speed limit in most states is 65 m.p.h.

37. A. Sales of graphic novels increased nine percent between 2008 and 2009.
　　B. Sales of graphic novels increased 9 percent between 2008 and 2009.

38. A. Our store is open daily from nine a.m. to seven P.M.
　　B. Our store is open daily from 9:00 A.M. to 7:00 P.M.

39. A. The organizing meeting is scheduled for July 27, and the event will be held in January 2012.
　　B. The organizing meeting is scheduled for July 27th, and the event will be held in January, 2012.

40. **A.** We need six desks, eight file cabinets, and 12 trashcans.
    B. We need 6 desks, 8 file cabinets, and 12 trashcans.

For items 41–50, write in each blank the letter of the word that best completes each sentence.

_____ **41.** Will having a degree (A. affect, B. effect) my chances for promotion?

_____ **42.** Try not to (A. loose, B. lose) this key; we will charge you a fee to replace it.

_____ **43.** I don't want to discuss my (A. personal, B. personnel) problems in front of anyone.

_____ **44.** Let us help you choose the right tie to (A. complement, B. compliment) your look.

_____ **45.** The repairman's whistling (A. aggravated, B. irritated) all of us in accounting.

_____ **46.** The bank agreed to (A. loan, B. lend) the Smiths $20,000 for their start-up.

_____ **47.** The credit card company is (A. liable, B. likely) to increase your interest rate if you miss a payment.

_____ **48.** The airline tries to (A. accommodate, B. accomodate) disabled passengers.

_____ **49.** Every company needs a policy regarding sexual (A. harrassment, B. harassment).

_____ **50.** Use your best (A. judgment, B. judgement) in selecting a service provider.

Assessment of English Skills

In the space provided, record the number of questions you answered incorrectly.

Questions	Skills Area	Number of Incorrect Answers
1–5	Parts of speech	_____
6–15	Usage	_____
16–20	Sentence structure	_____
21–30	Punctuation	_____
31–40	Mechanics	_____
41–50	Vocabulary	_____

If you had more than two incorrect answers in any of the skills areas, focus on those areas in the appropriate sections of this handbook.

Essentials of Grammar, Mechanics, and Usage

The following sentence looks innocent, but is it really?

We sell tuxedos as well as rent.

You sell tuxedos, but it's highly unlikely that you sell rent—which is what this sentence says. Whatever you're selling, some people will ignore your message because of a blunder like this. The following sentence has a similar problem:

Vice President Eldon Neale told his chief engineer that he would no longer be with Avix, Inc., as of June 30.

Is Eldon or the engineer leaving? No matter which side the facts are on, the sentence can be read the other way. Now look at this sentence:

The year before we budgeted more for advertising sales were up.

Confused? Perhaps this is what the writer meant:

The year before, we budgeted more for advertising. Sales were up.

Or maybe the writer meant this:

The year before we budgeted more for advertising, sales were up.

These examples show that even short, simple sentences can be misunderstood because of errors on the part of the writer. As you've learned in numerous courses over your schooling, an English sentence consists of the parts of speech being combined with punctuation, mechanics, and vocabulary to convey meaning. Making a point of brushing up on your grammar, punctuation, mechanics, and vocabulary skills will help ensure that you create clear, effective business messages.

1.0 Grammar

Grammar is the study of how words come together to form sentences. Categorized by meaning, form, and function, English words fall into various parts of speech: nouns, pronouns, verbs, adjectives, adverbs, prepositions, conjunctions, articles, and interjections. You will communicate more clearly if you understand how each of these parts of speech operates in a sentence.

1.1 NOUNS

A **noun** names a person, a place, a thing, or an idea. Anything you can see or detect with one of your senses has a noun to name it. Some things you can't see or sense are also nouns—ions, for example, or space. So are things that exist as ideas, such as accuracy and height. (You can see that something is accurate or that a building is tall, but you can't see the idea of accuracy or the idea of height.) These names for ideas are known as **abstract nouns**. The simplest nouns are the names of things you can see or touch: *car*, *building*, *cloud*, *brick*; these are termed **concrete nouns**. A few nouns, such as *algorithm*, *software*, and *code*, are difficult to categorize as either abstract or concrete but can reasonably be considered concrete even though they don't have a physical presence.

1.1.1 Proper Nouns and Common Nouns

So far, all the examples of nouns have been **common nouns**, referring to general classes of things. The word *building* refers to a whole class of structures. Common nouns such as *building* are not capitalized.

If you want to talk about one particular building, however, you might refer to the Glazier Building. The name is capitalized, indicating that *Glazier Building* is a **proper noun**.

Here are three sets of common and proper nouns for comparison:

Common	Proper
city	Kansas City
company	Blaisden Company
store	Books Galore

1.1.2 Nouns as Subject and Object

Nouns may be used in sentences as subjects or objects. That is, the person, place, thing, or idea that is being or doing (subject) is represented by a noun. So is the person, place, idea, or thing that is being acted on (object). In the following sentence, the nouns are underlined:

The <u>web designer</u> created the <u>homepage</u>.

The web designer (subject) is acting in a way that affects the homepage (object). The following sentence is more complicated:

The <u>installer</u> delivered the <u>carpet</u> to the <u>customer</u>.

Installer is the subject. *Carpet* is the object of the main part of the sentence (acted on by the installer), and *customer* is the object of the phrase *to the customer*. Nevertheless, both *carpet* and *customer* are objects.

1.1.3 Plural Nouns

Nouns can be either singular or plural. The usual way to make a plural noun is to add *s* or *es* to the singular form of the word:

Singular	Plural
file	files
tax	taxes
cargo	cargoes

Many nouns have other ways of forming the plural. Some plurals involve a change in a vowel (*mouse/mice, goose/geese, woman/women*), the addition of *en* or *ren* (*ox/oxen, child/children*), the change from *y* to *ies* (*city/cities, specialty/specialties*), or the change from *f* to *v* (*knife/knives, half/halves*; some exceptions: *fifes, roofs*). Some words of Latin origin offer a choice of plurals (*phenomena/phenomenons, indexes/indices, appendixes/appendices*). It's always a good idea to consult a dictionary if you are unsure of the correct or preferred plural spelling of a word.

The plurals of compound nouns are usually formed by adding *s* or *es* to the main word of the compound (*fathers-in-law, editors-in-chief, attorneys-at-law*).

Some nouns are the same whether singular or plural (*sleep, deer, moose*). Some nouns are plural in form but singular in use (*ethics, measles*). Some nouns are used in the plural only (*scissors, trousers*).

Letters, numbers, and words used as words are sometimes made plural by adding an apostrophe and an *s* (*A's, Ph.D.'s, I's*). However, if no confusion would be created by leaving off the apostrophe, it is common practice to just add the *s* (*1990s, RFPs, DVDs*).

1.1.4 Possessive Nouns

A noun becomes possessive when it's used to show the ownership of something. Then you add *'s* to the word:

the man's car · · · · · · the woman's apartment

However, ownership does not need to be legal:

the secretary's desk · · · · · · the company's assets

Also, ownership may be nothing more than an automatic association:

a day's work · · · · · · the job's prestige

An exception to the rule about adding *'s* to make a noun possessive occurs when the word is singular and already has two "s" sounds at the end. In cases like the following, an apostrophe is all that's needed:

crisis' dimensions · · · · · · Mr. Moses' application

When the noun has only one "s" sound at the end, however, retain the *'s*:

Chris's book · · · · · · Carolyn Nuss's office

With compound (hyphenated) nouns, add *'s* to the last word:

Compound Noun	Possessive Noun
mother-in-law	mother-in-law's
mayor-elect	mayor-elect's

To form the possessive of plural nouns, just begin by following the same rule as with singular nouns: add *'s*. However, if the plural noun already ends in an *s* (as most do), drop the one you've added, leaving only the apostrophe:

the clients' complaints · · · · · · employees' benefits

To denote joint possession by two or more proper nouns, add the *'s* to the last name only (*Moody, Nation, and Smith's* ad agency). To denote individual possession by two or more persons, add an *'s* to each proper noun (*Moody's, Nation's, and Smith's* ad agencies).

1.1.5 Collective Nouns

Collective nouns encompass a group of people or objects: *crowd, jury, committee, team, audience, family, couple, herd, class*. They are often treated as singular nouns. (For more on collective nouns, see Section 1.3.4, Subject-Verb Agreement.)

1.2 PRONOUNS

A **pronoun** is a word that stands for a noun; it saves repeating the noun:

> Employees have some choice of weeks for vacation, but *they* must notify the HR office of *their* preference by March 1.

The pronouns *they* and *their* stand in for the noun *employees*. The noun that a pronoun stands for is called the **antecedent** of the pronoun; *employees* is the antecedent of *they* and *their*.

When the antecedent is plural, the pronoun that stands in for it has to be plural; *they* and *their* are plural pronouns because *employees* is plural. Likewise, when the antecedent is singular, the pronoun has to be singular:

> We thought the contract had expired, but we soon learned that *it* had not.

1.2.1 Multiple Antecedents

Sometimes a pronoun has a double (or even a triple) antecedent:

> Kathryn Boettcher and Luis Gutierrez went beyond *their* sales quotas for January.

If taken alone, *Kathryn Boettcher* is a singular antecedent. So is *Luis Gutierrez*. However, when together they are the plural antecedent of a pronoun, so the pronoun has to be plural. Thus the pronoun is *their* instead of *her* or *his*.

1.2.2 Unclear Antecedents

In some sentences the pronoun's antecedent is unclear:

> Sandy Wright sent Jane Brougham *her* production figures for the previous year. *She* thought they were too low.

To which person does the pronoun *her* refer? Someone who knew Sandy and Jane and knew their business relationship might be able to figure out the antecedent for *her*. Even with such an advantage, however, a reader might receive the wrong meaning. Also, it would be nearly impossible for any reader to know which name is the antecedent of *she*.

The best way to clarify an ambiguous pronoun is usually to rewrite the sentence, repeating nouns when needed for clarity:

> Sandy Wright sent her production figures for the previous year to Jane Brougham. Jane thought they were too low.

The noun needs to be repeated only when the antecedent is unclear.

1.2.3 Pronoun Classes

Personal pronouns consist of *I, you, we/us, he/him, she/her, it*, and *they/them*.

Compound personal pronouns are created by adding *self* or *selves* to simple personal pronouns: *myself, ourselves, yourself, yourselves, himself, herself, itself, themselves*. Compound personal pronouns are used either *intensively*, to emphasize the identity of the noun or pronoun (I *myself* have seen the demonstration), or *reflexively*, to indicate that the subject is the receiver of his or her own action (I promised *myself* I'd finish by noon). Compound personal pronouns are used incorrectly if they appear in a sentence without their antecedent:

> Walter, Virginia, and *I* (not *myself*) are the top salespeople.
>
> You need to tell *her* (not *herself*) about the mixup.

Relative pronouns refer to nouns (or groups of words used as nouns) in the main clause and are used to introduce clauses:

> Purina is the brand *that* most dog owners purchase.

The relative pronouns are *which, who, whom, whose*, and *what*. Other words used as relative pronouns include *that, whoever, whomever, whatever*, and *whichever*.

Interrogative pronouns are those used for asking questions: *who, whom, whose, which*, and *what*.

Demonstrative pronouns point out particular persons, places, or things:

> *That* is my desk.   *This* can't be correct.

The demonstrative pronouns are *this, these, that*, and *those*.

Indefinite pronouns refer to persons or things not specifically identified. They include *anyone, someone, everyone, everybody, somebody, either, neither, one, none, all, both, each, another, any, many*, and similar words.

1.2.4 Case of Pronouns

The case of a pronoun tells whether it's acting or acted upon:

> *She* sells an average of five packages each week.

In this sentence, *she* is doing the selling. Because *she* is acting, *she* is said to be in the **nominative case**. Now consider what happens when the pronoun is acted upon:

> After six months, Ms. Browning promoted *her*.

In this sentence, the pronoun *her* is acted upon and is thus said to be in the **objective case**.

Contrast the nominative and objective pronouns in this list:

Nominative	Objective
I	me
we	us
he	him
she	her
they	them
who	whom
whoever	whomever

Objective pronouns may be used as either the object of a verb (such as *promoted*) or the object of a preposition (such as *with*):

> Rob worked with *them* until the order was filled.

In this example, *them* is the object of the preposition *with* because Rob acted upon—worked with—them. Here's a sentence with three pronouns, the first one nominative, the second the object of a verb, and the third the object of a preposition:

> He paid *us* as soon as the check came from *them.*

He is nominative; *us* is objective because it's the object of the verb *paid; them* is objective because it's the object of the preposition *from.*

Every writer sometimes wonders whether to use *who* or *whom:*

> (*Who, Whom*) will you hire?

Because this sentence is a question, it's difficult to see that *whom* is the object of the verb *hire.* You can figure out which pronoun to use if you rearrange the question and temporarily try *she* and *her* in place of *who* and *whom:* "Will you hire *she?*" or "Will you hire *her?*" *Her* and *whom* are both objective, so the correct choice is "Whom will you hire?" Here's a different example:

> (*Who, Whom*) logged so much travel time?

Turning the question into a statement, you get:

> He logged so much travel time.

Therefore, the correct statement is:

> Who logged so much travel time?

1.2.5 Possessive Pronouns

Possessive pronouns work like possessive nouns—they show ownership or automatic association:

> her job   their preferences
>
> his account   its equipment

However, possessive pronouns are different from possessive nouns in the way they are written. Possessive pronouns never have an apostrophe:

Possessive Noun	Possessive Pronoun
the woman's estate	her estate
Roger Franklin's plans	his plans
the shareholders' feelings	their feelings
the vacuum cleaner's attachments	its attachments

The word *its* is the possessive of *it.* Like all other possessive pronouns, *its* has no apostrophe. Some people confuse *its* with *it's,* the contraction of *it is.* (Contractions are discussed in Section 2.9, Apostrophes.)

1.2.6 Pronoun-Antecedent Agreement

Like nouns, pronouns can be singular or plural. Pronouns must agree in number with their antecedents—a singular antecedent requires a singular pronoun:

> The president of the board tendered *his* resignation.

Multiple antecedents require a plural pronoun:

> The members of the board tendered *their* resignations.

A pronoun referring to singular antecedents connected by *or* or *nor* should be singular:

> Neither Sean nor Terry made his quota.

But a pronoun referring to a plural and a singular antecedent connected by *or* or *nor* should be plural:

> Neither Sean nor the twins made *their* quotas.

Formal English prefers the nominative case after the linking verb *to be:*

> It is *I.*   That is *he.*

However, for general usage it's perfectly acceptable to use the more natural "It's me" and "That's him."

1.3 VERBS

A **verb** describes an action or acts as a link between a subject and words that define or describe that subject:

> They all *quit* in disgust.
> Working conditions *were* substandard.

The English language is full of **action verbs.** Here are a few you'll often run across in the business world:

verify	perform	fulfill
hire	succeed	send
leave	improve	receive
accept	develop	pay

You could undoubtedly list many more.

The most common linking verbs are all the forms of *to be:* I *am, was,* or *will be;* you *are, were,* or *will be.* Other words that can serve as linking verbs include *seem, become, appear, prove, look, remain, feel, taste, smell, sound, resemble, turn,* and *grow:*

> It *seemed* a good plan at the time.
>
> She *sounds* impressive at a meeting.
>
> The time *grows* near for us to make a decision.

These verbs link what comes before them in the sentence with what comes after; no action is involved. (See Section 1.7.5 for a fuller discussion of linking verbs.)

An **auxiliary verb** is one that helps another verb and is used for showing tense, voice, and so on. A verb with its helpers is called a **verb phrase.** Verbs used as auxiliaries include *do, did, have, may, can, must, shall, might, could, would,* and *should.*

1.3.1 Verb Tenses

English has three simple verb tenses: present, past, and future.

Present:	Our branches in Hawaii *stock* other items.
Past:	We *stocked* Purquil pens for a short time.
Future:	Rotex Tire Stores *will stock* your line of tires when you begin a program of effective national advertising.

With most verbs (the regular ones), the past tense ends in *ed*, and the future tense always has *will* or *shall* in front of it. But the present tense is more complex, depending on the subject:

	First Person	Second Person	Third Person
Singular	I stock	you stock	he/she/it stocks
Plural	we stock	you stock	they stock

The basic form, *stock*, takes an additional *s* when *he, she,* or *it* precedes it. (See Section 1.3.4 for more on subject-verb agreement.)

In addition to the three simple tenses, the three **perfect tenses** are created by adding forms of the auxiliary verb *have*. The present perfect tense uses the past participle (regularly the past tense) of the main verb, *stocked*, and adds the present-tense *have* or *has* to the front of it:

(I, we, you, they) *have stocked.*

(He, she, it) *has stocked.*

The past perfect tense uses the past participle of the main verb, *stocked*, and adds the past-tense *had* to the front of it:

(I, you, he, she, it, we, they) *had stocked.*

The future perfect tense also uses the past participle of the main verb, *stocked*, but adds the future-tense *will have:*

(I, you, he, she, it, we, they) *will have stocked.*

Verbs should be kept in the same tense when the actions occur at the same time:

When the payroll checks *came in*, everyone *showed up* for work.

We *have found* that everyone *has pitched* in to help.

When the actions occur at different times, you may change tense accordingly:

The shipment *came* last Wednesday, so if another one *comes* in today, please return it.

The new employee *had been* ill at ease, but now she *has become* a full-fledged member of the team.

1.3.2 Irregular Verbs

Many verbs don't follow some of the standard patterns for verb tenses. The most irregular of these verbs is *to be*:

Tense	Singular	Plural
Present:	I *am*	we *are*
	you *are*	you *are*
	he, she, it *is*	they *are*
Past:	I *was*	we *were*
	you *were*	you *were*
	he, she, it *was*	they *were*

The future tense of *to be* is formed in the same way that the future tense of a regular verb is formed.

The perfect tenses of *to be* are also formed as they would be for a regular verb, except that the past participle is a special form, *been*, instead of just the past tense:

Present perfect:	you have been
Past perfect:	you had been
Future perfect:	you will have been

Here's a sampling of other irregular verbs:

Present	Past	Past Participle
begin	began	begun
shrink	shrank	shrunk
know	knew	known
rise	rose	risen
become	became	become
go	went	gone
do	did	done

Dictionaries list the various forms of other irregular verbs.

1.3.3 Transitive and Intransitive Verbs

Many people are confused by three particular sets of verbs:

lie/lay   sit/set   rise/raise

Using these verbs correctly is much easier when you learn the difference between transitive and intransitive verbs.

Transitive verbs require a receiver; they "transfer" their action to an object. Intransitive verbs do not have a receiver for their action. Some intransitive verbs are complete in themselves and need no help from other words (prices *dropped*; we *won*). Other intransitive words must be "completed" by a noun or adjective called a **complement**. Complements occur with linking verbs.

Here are some sample uses of transitive and intransitive verbs:

Intransitive	Transitive
We should include in our new offices a place to *lie* down for a nap.	The workers will be here on Monday to *lay* new carpeting.
Even the way an interviewee *sits* is important.	That crate is full of stemware, so *set* it down carefully.
Salaries at Compu-Link, Inc., *rise* swiftly.	They *raise* their level of production every year.

The workers *lay* carpeting, you *set down* the crate, they *raise* production; each action is transferred to something. In the intransitive sentences, a person *lies down*, an interviewee *sits*, and salaries *rise* without affecting anything else. Intransitive sentences are complete with only a subject and a verb; transitive sentences are not complete unless they also include an object; or something to transfer the action to.

Tenses are a confusing element of the lie/lay problem:

Present	Past	Past Participle
I *lie*	I *lay*	I *have lain*
I *lay* (something down)	I *laid* (something down)	I *have laid* (something down)

The past tense of *lie* and the present tense of *lay* look and sound alike, even though they're different verbs.

1.3.4 Subject-Verb Agreement

Whether regular or irregular, every verb must agree with its subject, both in person (first, second, or third) and in number (single or plural).

	First Person	Second Person	Third Person
Singular	I *am*	you *are*	he/she/it *is*
	I *write*	you *write*	he/she/it *writes*
Plural	we *are*	you *are*	they *are*
	we *write*	you *write*	they *write*

In a simple sentence, making a verb agree with its subject is a straightforward task:

Hector Ruiz *is* a strong competitor. (third-person singular)

We *write* to you every month. (first-person plural)

Confusion sometimes arises when sentences are a bit more complicated. For example, be sure to avoid agreement problems when words come between the subject and verb. In the following examples, the verb appears in italics, and its subject is underlined:

The <u>analysis</u> of existing documents *takes* a full week.

Even though *documents* is a plural, the verb is in the singular form. That's because the subject of the sentence is *analysis*, a singular noun. The phrase *of existing documents* can be disregarded. Here is another example:

The <u>answers</u> for this exercise *are* in the study guide.

Take away the phrase *for this exercise* and you are left with the plural subject *answers*. Therefore, the verb takes the plural form.

Verb agreement is also complicated when the subject is a collective noun or pronoun or when the subject may be considered either singular or plural. In such cases, you often have to analyze the surrounding sentence to determine which verb form to use:

The <u>staff</u> *is* quartered in the warehouse.

The <u>staff</u> *are* at their desks in the warehouse.

The <u>computers</u> and the <u>staff</u> *are* in the warehouse.

Neither the staff nor the <u>computers</u> *are* in the warehouse.

<u>Every</u> computer *is* in the warehouse.

Many a <u>computer</u> *is* in the warehouse.

Did you notice that words such as *every* use the singular verb form? In addition, when an *either/or* or a *neither/nor* phrase combines singular and plural nouns, the verb takes the form that matches the noun closest to it.

In the business world, some subjects require extra attention. Company names, for example, are considered singular and therefore take a singular verb in most cases—even if they contain plural words:

Stater Brothers *offers* convenient grocery shopping.

In addition, quantities are sometimes considered singular and sometimes plural. If a quantity refers to a total amount, it takes a singular verb; if a quantity refers to individual, countable units, it takes a plural verb:

Three hours *is* a long time.

The eight dollars we collected for the fund *are* tacked on the bulletin board.

Fractions may also be singular or plural, depending on the noun that accompanies them:

One-third of the warehouse *is* devoted to this product line.

One-third of the products *are* defective.

To decide whether to use a singular or plural verb with subjects such as *number* and *variety*, follow this simple rule: If the subject is preceded by *a*, use a plural verb:

A number of products *are* being displayed at the trade show.

If the subject is preceded by *the*, use a singular verb:

The variety of products on display *is* mind-boggling.

For a related discussion, see Section 1.7.1, Longer Sentences.

1.3.5 Voice of Verbs

Verbs have two voices, active and passive. When the subject comes first, the verb is in **active voice**; when the object comes first, the verb is in **passive voice**:

Active:	The buyer *paid* a large amount.
Passive:	A large amount *was paid* by the buyer.

The passive voice uses a form of the verb *to be*, which adds words to a sentence. In the example, the passive-voice sentence uses eight words, whereas the active-voice sentence uses only six to say the same thing. The words *was* and *by* are unnecessary to convey the meaning of the sentence. In fact, extra words usually clog meaning. So be sure to opt for the active voice when you have a choice.

At times, however, you have no choice:

Several items *have been taken*, but so far we don't know who took them.

The passive voice becomes necessary when you don't know (or don't want to say) who performed the action; the active voice is bolder and more direct.

1.3.6 Mood of Verbs

Verbs can express one of three moods: indicative, imperative, or subjunctive. The **indicative mood** is used to make a statement or to ask a question:

The secretary mailed a letter to each supplier.

Did the secretary mail a letter to each supplier?

Use the **imperative mood** when you wish to command or request:

Please mail a letter to each supplier.

With the imperative mood, the subject is the understood *you*.

The **subjunctive mood** is used to express doubt or a wish or a condition contrary to fact:

If I *were* you, I wouldn't send that email.

The subjunctive is also used to express a suggestion or a request:

I asked that Rosario *be* [not *is*] present at the meeting.

1.3.7 Verbals

Verbals are verbs that are modified to function as other parts of speech. They include infinitives, gerunds, and participles.

Infinitives are formed by placing a *to* in front of the verb (*to go, to purchase, to work*). They function as nouns. Although many of us were taught that it is "incorrect" to split an infinitive—that is, to place an adverb between the *to* and the verb—that rule is not a hard and fast one. In some cases, the adverb is best placed in the middle of the infinitive to avoid awkward constructions or ambiguous meaning:

Production of steel is expected to *moderately exceed* domestic use.

Gerunds are verbals formed by adding *ing* to a verb (*going, having, working*). Like infinitives, they function as nouns. Gerunds and gerund phrases take a singular verb:

Borrowing from banks *is* preferable to getting venture capital.

Participles are verb forms used as adjectives. The present participle ends in *ing* and generally describes action going on at the same time as other action:

Checking the schedule, the contractor was pleased with progress on the project.

The past participle is usually the same form as the past tense and generally indicates completed action:

When *completed*, the project will occupy six city blocks.

The **perfect participle** is formed by adding *having* to the past participle:

Having completed the project, the contractor submitted his last invoice.

1.4 ADJECTIVES

An **adjective** modifies (tells something about) a noun or pronoun. Each of the following phrases says more about the noun or pronoun than the noun or pronoun would say alone:

an *efficient* staff   a *heavy* price

brisk trade   *light* web traffic

Adjectives modify nouns more often than they modify pronouns. When adjectives do modify pronouns, however, the sentence usually has a linking verb:

They were *attentive*.   It looked *appropriate*.

He seems *interested*.   You are *skillful*.

1.4.1 Types of Adjectives

Adjectives serve a variety of purposes. **Descriptive adjectives** express some quality belonging to the modified item (*tall, successful, green*). **Limiting or definitive adjectives**, on the other hand, point out the modified item or limit its meaning without expressing a quality. Types include:

* Numeral adjectives (one, fifty, second)
* Articles (a, an, the)
* Pronominal adjectives: pronouns used as adjectives (his desk, each employee)
* Demonstrative adjectives: this, these, that, those (these tires, that invoice)

Proper adjectives are derived from proper nouns:

Chinese customs   *Orwellian* overtones

Predicate adjectives complete the meaning of the predicate and are introduced by linking verbs:

The location is *perfect*. Prices are *high*.

1.4.2 Comparative Degree

Most adjectives can take three forms: simple, comparative, and superlative. The simple form modifies a single noun or pronoun. Use the comparative form when comparing two items. When comparing three or more items, use the superlative form:

Simple	Comparative	Superlative
hard	harder	hardest
safe	safer	safest
dry	drier	driest

The comparative form adds *er* to the simple form, and the superlative form adds *est*. (The *y* at the end of a word changes to *i* before the *er* or *est* is added.)

A small number of adjectives are irregular, including these:

Simple	Comparative	Superlative
good	better	best
bad	worse	worst
little	less	least

When the simple form of an adjective has two or more syllables, you usually add *more* to form the comparative and *most* to form the superlative:

Simple	Comparative	Superlative
useful	more useful	most useful
exhausting	more exhausting	most exhausting
expensive	more expensive	most expensive

The most common exceptions are two-syllable adjectives that end in *y*:

Simple	Comparative	Superlative
happy	happier	happiest
costly	costlier	costliest

If you choose this option, change the *y* to *i* and tack *er* or *est* onto the end.

Some adjectives cannot be used to make comparisons because they themselves indicate the extreme. For example, if something is perfect, nothing can be more perfect. If something is unique or ultimate, nothing can be more unique or more ultimate.

1.4.3 Hyphenated Adjectives

Many adjectives used in the business world are actually combinations of words: *up-to-date* report, *last-minute* effort, *fifth-floor* suite, *well-built* engine. As you can see, they are hyphenated when they come before the noun they modify. However, when such word combinations come after the noun they modify, they are not hyphenated. In the following example, the adjectives appear in italics and the nouns they modify are underlined:

> The <u>report</u> is *up to date* because of our team's *last-minute* <u>efforts</u>.

Hyphens are not used when part of the combination is a word ending in *ly* (because that word is usually not an adjective). Hyphens are also omitted from word combinations that are used so frequently that readers are used to seeing the words together:

> We live in a *rapidly shrinking* world.
> Our *highly motivated* employees will be well paid.
> Please consider renewing your *credit card* account.
> Send those figures to our *data processing* department.
> Our new intern is a *high school* student.

1.5 ADVERBS

An **adverb** modifies a verb, an adjective, or another adverb:

Modifying a verb:	Our marketing department works *efficiently*.
Modifying an adjective:	She was not dependable, although she was *highly* intelligent.
Modifying another adverb:	When signing new clients, he moved *extremely* cautiously.

An adverb can be a single word (*clearly*), a phrase (*very clearly*), or a clause (*because it was clear*).

1.5.1 Types of Adverbs

Simple adverbs are simple modifiers:

> The door opened *automatically*.
> The order arrived *yesterday*.
> Top companies were *there*.

Interrogative adverbs ask a question:

> *Where* have you been?

Conjunctive adverbs connect clauses:

> We can't start *until* Maria gets here.
> Jorge tried to explain *how* the new software works.

Words frequently used as conjunctive adverbs include *where, wherever, when, whenever, while, as, how, why, before, after, until,* and *since*.

Negative adverbs include *not, never, seldom, rarely, scarcely, hardly,* and similar words. Negative adverbs are powerful words and therefore do not need any help in conveying a negative thought. Avoid using double negatives like these:

> I don't want no mistakes.
> (Correct: "I don't want any mistakes," or "I want no mistakes.")
> They couldn't hardly read the report.
> (Correct: "They could hardly read the report," or "They couldn't read the report.")
> They scarcely noticed neither one.
> (Correct: "They scarcely noticed either one," or "They noticed neither one.")

1.5.2 Adverb-Adjective Confusion

Many adverbs are adjectives turned into adverbs by adding *ly*: *highly, extremely, officially, closely, really*. In addition, many words can be adjectives or adverbs, depending on their usage in a particular sentence:

The *early* bird gets the worm. [adjective]	We arrived *early*. [adverb]
It was a *hard* decision. [adjective]	He hit the wall *hard*. [adverb]

Because of this situation, some adverbs are difficult to distinguish from adjectives. For example, in the following sentences, is the underlined word an adverb or an adjective?

> They worked <u>well</u>.
> The baby is <u>well</u>.

In the first sentence, *well* is an adverb modifying the verb *worked*. In the second sentence, *well* is an adjective modifying the noun *baby*. To choose correctly between adverbs and adjectives, remember that linking verbs are used to connect an adjective to describe a noun. In contrast, you would use an adverb to describe an action verb:

Adjective	Adverb
He is a *good* worker. (What kind of worker is he?)	He works *well*. (How does he work?)
It is a *real* computer. (What kind of computer is it?)	It *really* is a computer. (To what extent is it a computer?)

Adjective	Adverb
The traffic is *slow*. (What quality does the traffic have?)	The traffic moves *slowly*. (How does the traffic move?)
This food tastes *bad* without salt. (What quality does the food have?)	This food *badly* needs salt. (How much is it needed?)

1.5.3 Comparative Degree

Like adjectives, adverbs can be used to compare items. Generally, the basic adverb is combined with *more* or *most*, just as long adjectives are. However, some adverbs have one-word comparative forms:

One Item	Two Items	Three Items
quickly	more quickly	most quickly
sincerely	less sincerely	least sincerely
fast	faster	fastest
well	better	best

1.6 OTHER PARTS OF SPEECH

Nouns, pronouns, verbs, adjectives, and adverbs carry most of the meaning in a sentence. Four other parts of speech link them together in sentences: prepositions, conjunctions, articles, and interjections.

1.6.1 Prepositions

A preposition is a word or group of words that describes a relationship between other words in a sentence. A simple preposition is made up of one word: *of, in, by, above, below*. A *compound preposition* is made up of two prepositions: *out of, from among, except for, because of*.

A **prepositional phrase** is a group of words introduced by a preposition that functions as an adjective (an adjectival phrase) or as an adverb (adverbial phrase) by telling more about a pronoun, noun, or verb:

> The shipment will be here *by next Friday*.
>
> Put the mail *in the out-bin*.

Prepositional phrases should be placed as close as possible to the element they are modifying:

> Shopping *on the Internet* can be confusing for the uninitiated. (*not* Shopping can be confusing for the uninitiated *on the Internet*.)

Some prepositions are closely linked with a verb. When using phrases such as *look up* and *wipe out*, keep them intact and do not insert anything between the verb and the preposition.

You may have been told that it is unacceptable to put a preposition at the end of a sentence. However, that is not a hard-and-fast rule, and trying to follow it can sometimes be a challenge. You can end a sentence with a preposition as long as the sentence sounds natural and as long as rewording the sentence would create awkward wording:

> I couldn't tell what they were interested in.
>
> What did she attribute it to?
>
> What are you looking for?

Avoid using unnecessary prepositions. In the following examples, the prepositions in parentheses should be omitted:

> All (of) the staff members were present.
>
> I almost fell off (of) my chair with surprise.
>
> Where was Mr. Steuben going (to)?
>
> They couldn't help (from) wondering.

The opposite problem is failing to include a preposition when you should. Consider these two sentences:

> Sales were over $100,000 for Linda and Bill.
>
> Sales were over $100,000 for Linda and for Bill.

The first sentence indicates that Linda and Bill had combined sales over $100,000; the second, that Linda and Bill each had sales over $100,000, for a combined total in excess of $200,000. The preposition *for* is critical here.

When the same preposition can be used for two or more words in a sentence without affecting the meaning, only the last preposition is required:

> We are familiar (with) and satisfied with your company's products.

But when different prepositions are normally used with the words, all the prepositions must be included:

> We are familiar with and interested in your company's products.

Some prepositions have come to be used in a particular way with certain other parts of speech. Here is a partial list of some prepositions that have come to be used with certain words:

according to	independent of
agree to (a proposal)	inferior to
agree with (a person)	plan to
buy from	prefer to
capable of	prior to
comply with	reason with
conform to	responsible for
differ from (things)	similar to
differ with (person)	talk to (without interaction)
different from	talk with (with interaction)
get from (receive)	wait for (person or thing)
get off (dismount)	wait on (like a waiter)

If you are unsure of the correct idiomatic expression, check a dictionary.

Some verb-preposition idioms vary depending on the situation: You agree *to* a proposal but *with* a person, *on* a price, or *in* principle. You argue *about* something, *with* a person, and *for* or *against* a proposition. You compare one item *to* another to show their similarities; you compare one item *with* another to show differences.

Here are some other examples of preposition usage that have given writers trouble:

among/between: *Among* is used to refer to three or more (Circulate the memo *among* the staff); *between* is used to refer to two (Put the copy machine *between* Judy and Dan).

as if/like: *As if* is used before a clause (It seems *as if* we should be doing something); *like* is used before a noun or pronoun (He seems *like* a nice guy).

have/of: *Have* is a verb used in verb phrases (They should *have* checked first); *of* is a preposition and is never used in such cases.

in/into: *In* is used to refer to a static position (The file is *in* the cabinet); *into* is used to refer to movement toward a position (Put the file *into* the cabinet).

1.6.2 Conjunctions

Conjunctions connect the parts of a sentence: words, phrases, and clauses. A coordinating conjunction connects two words, phrases, or clauses of equal rank. The simple coordinating conjunctions include *and, but, or, nor, for, yet,* and *so*. Correlative conjunctions are coordinating conjunctions used in pairs: *both/and, either/or, neither/nor, not only/ but also*. Constructions with correlative conjunctions should be parallel, with the same part of speech following each element of the conjunction:

The purchase was *not only* expensive *but also* unnecessary.

The purchase *not only was* expensive *but also was* unnecessary.

Conjunctive adverbs are adverbs used to connect or show relationships between clauses. They include *however, nevertheless, consequently, moreover,* and *as a result*.

A **subordinate conjunction** connects two clauses of unequal rank; it joins a dependent (subordinate) clause to the independent clause on which it depends (for more on dependent and independent clauses, see Section 1.7.1). Subordinate conjunctions include *as, if, because, although, while, before, since, that, until, unless, when, where,* and *whether*.

1.6.3 Articles and Interjections

Only three articles exist in English: *the, a,* and *an*. These words are used, like adjectives, to specify which item you are talking about. *The* is called the *definite article* because it indicates a specific noun; *a* and *an* are called the *indefinite articles* because they are less specific about what they are referring to.

If a word begins with a vowel (soft) sound, use *an*; otherwise, use *a*. It's *a history*, not *an history, a hypothesis*, not *an hypothesis*. Use *an* with an "h" word only if it is a soft "h," as in *honor* and *hour*. Use *an* with words that are pronounced with a soft vowel sound even if they are spelled beginning with a consonant (usually in the case of abbreviations): *an SEC application, an MP3 file*. Use *a* with words that begin with vowels if they are pronounced with a hard sound: *a university, a Usenet account*.

Repeat an article if adjectives modify different nouns: *The red house and the white house are mine*. Do not repeat an article if all adjectives modify the same noun: *The red and white house is mine*.

Interjections are words that express no solid information, only emotion:

Wow!   Well, well!
Oh, no!   Good!

Such purely emotional language has its place in private life and advertising copy, but it only weakens the effect of most business writing.

1.7 SENTENCES

Sentences are constructed with the major building blocks, the parts of speech. Take, for example, this simple two-word sentence:

Money talks.

It consists of a noun (*money*) and a verb (*talks*). When used in this way, the noun works as the first requirement for a sentence, the **subject**, and the verb works as the second requirement, the **predicate**. Without a subject (who or what does something) and a predicate (the doing of it), you have merely a collection of words, not a sentence.

1.7.1 Longer Sentences

More complicated sentences have more complicated subjects and predicates, but they still have a simple subject and a predicate verb. In the following examples, the subject is underlined once, the predicate verb twice:

Marex and Contron enjoy higher earnings each quarter.

Marex [and] *Contron* do something; *enjoy* is what they do.

My interview, coming minutes after my freeway accident, did not impress or move anyone.

Interview is what did something. What did it do? It *did* [not] *impress* [or] *move*.

In terms of usable space, a steel warehouse, with its extremely long span of roof unsupported by pillars, makes more sense.

Warehouse is what *makes*.

These three sentences demonstrate several things. First, in all three sentences, the simple subject and predicate verb are the "bare bones" of the sentence, the parts that carry the core idea of the sentence. When trying to find the subject and predicate verb, disregard all prepositional phrases, modifiers, conjunctions, and articles.

Second, in the third sentence, the verb is singular (*makes*) because the subject is singular (*warehouse*). Even though the plural noun *pillars* is closer to the verb, *warehouse* is the subject. So *warehouse* determines whether the verb is singular or plural. Subject and predicate must agree.

Third, the subject in the first sentence is compound (*Marex* [and] *Contron*). A compound subject, when connected by *and*, requires a plural verb (*enjoy*). Also, the second sentence shows how compound predicates can occur (*did* [not] *impress* [or] *move*).

Fourth, the second sentence incorporates a group of words—*coming minutes after my freeway accident*—containing a form of a verb (*coming*) and a noun (*accident*). Yet, this group of words is not a complete sentence for two reasons:

- Not all nouns are subjects: *Accident* is not the subject of *coming*.
- Not all verbs are predicates: A verb that ends in *ing* can never be the predicate of a sentence (unless preceded by a form of *to be*, as in *was coming*).

Because they don't contain a subject and a predicate, the words *coming minutes after my freeway accident* (called a **phrase**) can't be written as a sentence. That is, the phrase cannot stand alone; it cannot begin with a capital letter and end with a period. So a phrase must always be just one part of a sentence.

Sometimes a sentence incorporates two or more groups of words that do contain a subject and a predicate; these word groups are called **clauses**:

My <u>interview</u>, because it came minutes after my freeway accident, did not impress or move anyone.

The **independent clause** is the portion of the sentence that could stand alone without revision:

My *interview* did not impress or move anyone.

The other part of the sentence could stand alone only by removing *because.*

(because) It came minutes after my freeway accident.

This part of the sentence is known as a **dependent clause**; although it has a subject and a predicate (just as an independent clause does), it's linked to the main part of the sentence by a word (*because)* showing its dependence.

In summary, the two types of clauses—dependent and independent—both have a subject and a predicate. Dependent clauses, however, do not bear the main meaning of the sentence and are therefore linked to an independent clause. Nor can phrases stand alone, because they lack both a subject and a predicate. Only independent clauses can be written as sentences without revision.

1.7.2 Types of Sentences

Sentences come in four main types, depending on the extent to which they contain clauses. A simple sentence has one subject and one predicate; in short, it has one main independent clause:

Boeing is the world's largest aerospace company.

A **compound sentence** consists of two independent clauses connected by a coordinating conjunction (*and, or, but*, etc.) or a semicolon:

Airbus outsold Boeing for several years, but Boeing has recently regained the lead.

A **complex sentence** consists of an independent clause and one or more dependent clauses:

Boeing is betting [independent clause] that airlines will begin using moderately smaller planes to fly passengers between smaller cities [dependent clause introduced by *that*].

A **compound-complex sentence** has two main clauses, at least one of which contains a subordinate (dependent clause):

Boeing is betting [independent clause] that airlines will begin using moderately smaller planes to fly passengers between smaller cities [dependent clause], and it anticipates that new airports will be developed to meet passenger needs [independent clause].

1.7.3 Sentence Fragments

An incomplete sentence (a phrase or a dependent clause) that is written as though it were a complete sentence is called a **fragment**. Consider the following sentence fragments:

Marilyn Sanders, having had pilferage problems in her store for the past year. Refuses to accept the results of our investigation.

This serious error can easily be corrected by putting the two fragments together:

Marilyn Sanders, having had pilferage problems in her store for the past year, refuses to accept the results of our investigation.

The actual details of a situation will determine the best way for you to remedy a fragment problem.

The ban on fragments has one exception. Some advertising copy contains sentence fragments, written knowingly to convey a certain rhythm. However, advertising is the only area of business in which fragments are acceptable.

1.7.4 Fused Sentences and Comma Splices

Just as there can be too little in a group of words to make it a sentence, there can also be too much:

All our mail is run through a postage meter every afternoon someone picks it up.

This example contains two sentences, not one, but the two have been blended so that it's hard to tell where one ends and the next begins. Is the mail run through a meter every afternoon? If so, the sentences should read:

All our mail is run through a postage meter every afternoon. Someone picks it up.

Perhaps the mail is run through a meter at some other time (morning, for example) and is picked up every afternoon;

All our mail is run through a postage meter. Every afternoon someone picks it up.

The order of words is the same in all three cases; sentence division makes all the difference. Either of the last two cases is grammatically correct. The choice depends on the facts of the situation.

Sometimes these so-called **fused sentences** have a more obvious point of separation:

> Several large orders arrived within a few days of one another, too many came in for us to process by the end of the month.

Here, the comma has been put between two independent clauses in an attempt to link them. When a lowly comma separates two complete sentences, the result is called a **comma splice**. A comma splice can be remedied in one of three ways:

- Replace the comma with a period and capitalize the next word: ". . . one another. Too many . . ."
- Replace the comma with a semicolon and do not capitalize the next word: ". . . one another; too many . . ." This remedy works only when the two sentences have closely related meanings.
- Change one of the sentences so that it becomes a phrase or a dependent clause. This remedy often produces the best writing, but it takes more work.

The third alternative can be carried out in several ways. One is to begin the sentence with a subordinating conjunction:

> Whenever several large orders arrived within a few days of one another, too many came in for us to process by the end of the month.

Another way is to remove part of the subject or the predicate verb from one of the independent clauses, thereby creating a phrase:

> Several large orders arrived within a few days of one another, too many for us to process by the end of the month.

Finally, you can change one of the predicate verbs to its *ing* form:

> Several large orders arrived within a few days of one another, too many coming in for us to process by the end of the month.

In many cases, simply adding a coordinating conjunction can separate fused sentences or remedy a comma splice:

> You can fire them, or you can make better use of their abilities.
>
> Margaret drew up the designs, and Matt carried them out.
>
> We will have three strong months, but after that sales will taper off.

Be careful with coordinating conjunctions: Use them only to join simple sentences that express similar ideas.

Also, because they say relatively little about the relationship between the two clauses they join, avoid using coordinating conjunctions too often: *and* is merely an addition sign; *but* is just a turn signal; *or* only points to an alternative. Subordinating conjunctions such as *because* and *whenever* tell the reader a lot more.

1.7.5 Sentences with Linking Verbs

Linking verbs were discussed briefly in the section on verbs (Section 1.3). Here, you can see more fully the way they function in a sentence. The following is a model of any sentence with a linking verb:

> A *(verb)* B.

Although words such as *seems* and *feels* can also be linking verbs, let's assume that the verb is a form of *to be*:

> A *is* B.

In such a sentence, A and B are always nouns, pronouns, or adjectives. When one is a noun and the other is a pronoun, or when both are nouns, the sentence says that one is the same as the other:

> She is president.
>
> Rachel is president.
>
> She is forceful.

Recall from Section 1.3.3 that the noun or adjective that follows the linking verb is called a *complement*. When it is a noun or noun phrase, the complement is called a *predicate nominative*, when the complement is an adjective, it is referred to as a *predicate adjective*.

1.7.6 Misplaced Modifiers

The position of a modifier in a sentence is important. The movement of *only* changes the meaning in the following sentences:

> Only we are obliged to supply those items specified in your contract.
>
> We are obliged only to supply those items specified in your contract.
>
> We are obliged to supply only those items specified in your contract.
>
> We are obliged to supply those items specified only in your contract.

In any particular set of circumstances, only one of those sentences would be accurate. The others would very likely cause problems. To prevent misunderstanding, place such modifiers as close as possible to the noun or verb they modify.

For similar reasons, whole phrases that are modifiers must be placed near the right noun or verb. Mistakes in placement create ludicrous meanings:

> Antia Information Systems bought new computer chairs for the programmers with more comfortable seats.

The anatomy of programmers is not normally a concern of business writers. Obviously, the comfort of the chairs was the issue:

> Antia Information Systems bought programmers the new computer chairs with more comfortable seats.

Here is another example:

> I asked him to file all the letters in the cabinet that had been answered.

In this ridiculous sentence, the cabinet has been answered, even though no cabinet in history is known to have asked a question. *That had been answered* is too far from *letters* and too close to *cabinet*. Here's an improvement:

> I asked him to file in the cabinet all the letters that had been answered.

The term **dangling modifier** is often used to refer to a clause or phrase that because of its position in the sentence seems to modify a word that it is not meant to modify. For instance:

> Lying motionless, co-workers rushed to Barry's aid.

Readers expect an introductory phrase to modify the subject of the main clause. But in this case it wasn't the *co-workers* who were lying motionless but rather *Barry* who was in this situation. Like this example, most instances of dangling modifiers occur at the beginning of sentences. The source of some danglers is a passive construction:

> To find the needed information, the whole book had to be read.

In such cases, switching to the active voice can usually remedy the problem:

> To find the needed information, you will need to read the whole book.

1.7.7 Parallelism

Two or more sentence elements that have the same relation to another element should be in the same form. Otherwise, the reader is forced to work harder to understand the meaning of the sentence. When a series consists of phrases or clauses, the same part of speech (preposition, gerund, etc.) should introduce them. Do not mix infinitives with participles or adjectives with nouns. Here are some examples of nonparallel elements:

> Andersen is hiring managers, programmers, and people who work in accounting. [nouns not parallel]
>
> Andersen earns income by auditing, consulting, and by bookkeeping. [prepositional phrases not parallel]
>
> Andersen's goals are to win new clients, keeping old clients happy, and finding new enterprises. [infinitive mixed with gerunds]

2.0 Punctuation

On the highway, signs tell you when to slow down or stop, where to turn, and when to merge. In similar fashion, punctuation helps readers negotiate your prose. The proper use of punctuation keeps readers from losing track of your meaning.

2.1 PERIODS

Use a period (1) to end any sentence that is not a question, (2) with certain abbreviations (such as U.S.), and (3) between dollars and cents in an amount of money.

2.2 QUESTION MARKS

Use a question mark after any direct question that requests an answer:

> Are you planning to enclose a check, or shall we bill you?

Don't use a question mark with commands phrased as questions for the sake of politeness:

> Will you send us a check today.

A question mark should precede quotation marks, parentheses, and brackets if it is part of the quoted or parenthetical material; otherwise, it should follow:

> This issue of *Inc.* has an article titled "What's Your Entrepreneurial IQ?"
>
> Have you read the article "Five Principles of Guerrilla Marketing"?

Do not use the question mark with indirect questions or with requests:

> Mr. Antonelli asked whether anyone had seen Nathalia lately.

Do not use a comma or a period with a question mark; the question mark takes the place of these punctuation marks.

2.3 EXCLAMATION POINTS

Use exclamation points after highly emotional language. Because business writing almost never calls for emotional language, you will seldom use exclamation points.

2.4 SEMICOLONS

Semicolons have three main uses. One is to separate two closely related independent clauses:

> The outline for the report is due within a week; the report itself is due at the end of the month.

A semicolon should also be used instead of a comma when the items in a series have commas within them:

> Our previous meetings were on November 11, 2009; February 20, 2010; and April 28, 2011.

Finally, a semicolon should be used to separate independent clauses when the second one begins with a conjunctive adverb such as *however*, *therefore*, or *nevertheless* or a phrase such as *for example* or *in that case*:

> Our supplier has been out of part D712 for 10 weeks; however, we have found another source that can ship the part right away.
>
> His test scores were quite low; on the other hand, he has a lot of relevant experience.

Semicolons should always be placed outside parentheses.

Events Northwest has the contract for this year's convention (August 23–28); we haven't awarded the contract for next year yet.

2.5 COLONS

Use a colon after the salutation in a business letter. You should also use a colon at the end of a sentence or phrase introducing a list or (sometimes) a quotation:

> Our study included the three most critical problems: insufficient capital, incompetent management, and inappropriate location.

A colon should not be used when the list, quotation, or idea is a direct object of the verb or preposition. This rule applies whether the list is set off or run in:

> We are able to supply
>
> staples
>
> wood screws
>
> nails
>
> toggle bolts

> This shipment includes 9 DVDs, 12 CDs, and 4 USB flash drives.

Another way you can use a colon is to separate the main clause and another sentence element when the second explains, illustrates, or amplifies the first:

> Management was unprepared for the union representatives' demands: this fact alone accounts for their arguing well into the night.

However, in contemporary usage, such clauses are frequently separated by a semicolon.

Like semicolons, colons should always be placed outside parentheses.

> He has an expensive list of new demands (none of which is covered in the purchase agreement): new carpeting, network cabling, and a new security system.

2.6 COMMAS

Commas have many uses; the most common is to separate items in a series:

> He took the job, learned it well, worked hard, and succeeded.
>
> Put paper, pencils, and paper clips on the requisition list.

Company style may dictate omitting the final comma in a series. However, if you have a choice, use the final comma; it's often necessary to prevent misunderstanding.

A second place to use a comma is between independent clauses that are joined by a coordinating conjunction (*and*, *but*, or *or*).

> She spoke to the sales staff, and he spoke to the production staff.
>
> I was advised to proceed, and I did.

A third use for the comma is to separate a dependent clause at the beginning of a sentence from an independent clause:

> Because of our lead in the market, we may be able to risk introducing a new product.

However, a dependent clause at the end of a sentence is separated from the independent clause by a comma only when the dependent clause is unnecessary to the main meaning of the sentence:

> We may be able to introduce a new product, although it may involve some risk.

A fourth use for the comma is after an introductory phrase or word:

> Starting with this amount of capital, we can survive in the red for one year.
>
> Through more careful planning, we may be able to serve more people.
>
> Yes, you may proceed as originally planned.

However, with short introductory prepositional phrases and some one-syllable words (such as *hence* and *thus*), the comma is often omitted:

> Before January 1 we must complete the inventory.
>
> Thus we may not need to hire anyone.
>
> In July we will complete the move to Tulsa.

Fifth, paired commas are used to set off nonrestrictive clauses and phrases. A **restrictive clause** is one that cannot be omitted without altering the meaning of the main clause, whereas a **nonrestrictive clause** can be:

> The *Time Magazine* website, which is produced by Steve Conley, has won several design awards. [nonrestrictive: the material set off by commas could be omitted]
>
> The website that is produced by Steve Conley has won several design awards. [restrictive: no commas are used before and after *that is produced by Steve Conley* because this information is necessary to the meaning of the sentence—it specifies which website]

A sixth use for commas is to set off appositive words and phrases. (An **appositive** has the same meaning as the word it is in apposition to.) Like nonrestrictive clauses, appositives can be dropped without changing or obscuring the meaning of the sentence:

> Conley, a freelance designer, also produces the websites for several nonprofit corporations.

Seventh, commas are used between adjectives modifying the same noun (coordinate adjectives):

> She left Monday for a long, difficult recruiting trip.

To test the appropriateness of such a comma, try reversing the order of the adjectives: *a difficult, long recruiting trip*. If the order cannot be reversed, leave out the comma (a *good old friend* isn't the same as an *old good friend*). A comma should not be used when one of the adjectives is part of the noun. Compare these two phrases:

a distinguished, well-known figure

a distinguished public figure

The adjective-noun combination of *public* and *figure* has been used together so often that it has come to be considered a single thing: *public figure*. So no comma is required.

Eighth, commas are used both before and after the year in sentences that include month, day, and year:

It will be sent by December 15, 2012, from our Cincinnati plant.

Some companies write dates in another form: 15 December 2012. No commas should be used in that case. Nor is a comma needed when only the month and year are present (December 2012).

Ninth, commas are used to set off a variety of parenthetical words and phrases within sentences, including state names, dates, abbreviations, transitional expressions, and contrasted elements:

They were, in fact, prepared to submit a bid.

Habermacher, Inc., went public in 1999.

Our goal was increased profits, not increased market share.

Service, then, is our main concern.

The factory was completed in Chattanooga, Tennessee, just three weeks ago.

Joanne Dubiik, M.D., has applied for a loan from First Savings.

I started work here on March 1, 2003, and soon received my first promotion.

Tenth, a comma is used to separate a quotation from the rest of the sentence:

Your warranty reads, "These conditions remain in effect for one year from date of purchase."

However, the comma is left out when the quotation as a whole is built into the structure of the sentence:

He hurried off with an angry "Look where you're going."

Finally, a comma should be used whenever it's needed to avoid confusion or an unintended meaning. Compare the following:

Ever since they have planned new ventures more carefully.

Ever since, they have planned new ventures more carefully.

2.7 DASHES

Use dashes to surround a comment that is a sudden turn in thought:

Membership in the IBSA—it's expensive but worth it—may be obtained by applying to our New York office.

A dash can also be used to emphasize a parenthetical word or phrase:

Third-quarter profits—in excess of $2 million—are up sharply.

Finally, use dashes to set off a phrase that contains commas:

All our offices—Milwaukee, New Orleans, and Phoenix—have sent representatives.

Don't confuse a dash with a hyphen. A dash separates and emphasizes words, phrases, and clauses more strongly than commas or parentheses can; a hyphen ties two words so tightly that they almost become one word.

When using a computer, use the em dash symbol. When typing a dash in email, type two hyphens with no space before, between, or after.

A second type of dash, the en dash, can be produced with computer word processing and page-layout programs. This kind of dash is shorter than the regular dash and longer than a hyphen. It is reserved almost exclusively for indicating "to" or "through" with numbers such as dates and pages: *2011–2012, pages 30–44.*

2.8 HYPHENS

Hyphens are mainly used in three ways. The first is to separate the parts of compound words beginning with such prefixes as *self-, ex-, quasi-,* and *all-*:

self-assured	quasi-official
ex-wife	all-important

However, do not use hyphens in words that have prefixes such as *pro, anti, non, re, pre, un, inter,* and *extra*:

prolabor	nonunion
antifascist	interdepartmental

Exceptions occur when (1) the prefix occurs before a proper noun or (2) the vowel at the end of the prefix is the same as the first letter of the root word:

pro-Republican	anti-American
anti-inflammatory	extra-atmospheric

When in doubt, consult your dictionary.

Hyphens are used in some types of spelled-out numbers. For instance, they are used to separate the parts of a spelled-out number from *twenty-one* to *ninety-nine* and for spelled-out fractions: *two-thirds, one-sixth* (although some style guides say not to hyphenate fractions used as nouns).

Certain compound nouns are formed by using hyphens: *secretary-treasurer, city-state.* Check your dictionary for compounds you're unsure about.

Hyphens are also used in some compound adjectives, which are adjectives made up of two or more words. Specifically, you should use hyphens in compound adjectives that come before the noun:

an interest-bearing account	well-informed executives

However, you need not hyphenate when the adjective follows a linking verb:

> This account is interest bearing.
>
> Their executives are well informed.

You can shorten sentences that list similar hyphenated words by dropping the common part from all but the last word:

> Check the costs of first-, second-, and third-class postage.

Finally, hyphens may be used to divide words at the end of a typed line. Such hyphenation is best avoided, but when you have to divide words at the end of a line, do so correctly (see Section 3.5). Dictionaries show how words are divided into syllables.

2.9 APOSTROPHES

Use an apostrophe in the possessive form of a noun (but not in a pronoun):

> On his desk was a reply to Bette *Ainsley's* application for the *manager's* position.

Apostrophes are also used in place of the missing letter(s) of a contraction:

Whole Words	Contraction
we will	we'll
do not	don't
they are	they're

2.10 QUOTATION MARKS

Use quotation marks to surround words that are repeated exactly as they were said or written:

> The collection letter ended by saying, "This is your third and final notice."

Remember: (1) When the quoted material is a complete sentence, the first word is capitalized. (2) The final comma or period goes inside the closing quotation marks.

Quotation marks are also used to set off the title of a newspaper story, magazine article, or book chapter:

> You should read "Legal Aspects of the Collection Letter" in *Today's Credit*.

Quotation marks may also be used to indicate special treatment for words or phrases, such as terms that you're using in an unusual or ironic way:

> Our management "team" spends more time squabbling than working to solve company problems.

When you are defining a word, put the definition in quotation marks:

> The abbreviation *etc.* means "and so forth."

When using quotation marks, take care to insert the closing marks as well as the opening ones.

Although periods and commas go inside any quotation marks, colons and semicolons generally go outside them. A question mark goes inside the quotation marks only if the quotation is a question:

> All that day we wondered, "Is he with us?"

If the quotation is not a question but the entire sentence is, the question mark goes outside:

> What did she mean by "You will hear from me"?

For quotes within quotes, use single quotation marks within double:

> As David Pottruck, former co-CEO of Charles Schwab, told it, "I assembled about 100 managers at the base of the Golden Gate Bridge and gave them jackets emblazoned with the phrase 'Crossing the Chasm' and then led them across the bridge."

Otherwise, do not use single quotation marks for anything, including titles of works—that's British style.

2.11 PARENTHESES AND BRACKETS

Use parentheses to surround comments that are entirely incidental or to supply additional information:

> Our figures do not match yours, although (if my calculations are correct) they are closer than we thought.
>
> These kinds of supplements do not require FDA (Food and Drug Administration) approval.

Parentheses are used in legal documents to surround figures in arabic numerals that follow the same amount in words:

> Remittance will be One Thousand Two Hundred Dollars ($1,200).

Be careful to put punctuation marks (period, comma, and so on) outside the parentheses unless they are part of the statement in parentheses. And keep in mind that parentheses have both an opening and a closing mark; both should always be used, even when setting off listed items within text: *(1)*, not *1)*.

Brackets are used for notation, comment, explanation, or correction within quoted material:

> In the interview, multimillionaire Bob Buford said, "One of my major influences was Peter [Drucker], who encourages people and helps them believe in themselves."

Brackets are also used for parenthetical material that falls within parentheses:

> Drucker's magnum opus (*Management: Tasks, Responsibilities, Practices* [Harper & Row, 1979]) has influenced generations of entrepreneurs.

2.12 ELLIPSES

Use ellipsis points, or three evenly spaced periods, to indicate that material has been left out of a direct quotation. Use them only in direct quotations and only at the point where material was left out. In the following example, the first sentence is quoted in the second:

The Dow Jones Industrial Average fell 276.39 points, or 2.6%, during the week to 10292.31.

According to the *Wall Street Journal*, "The Dow Jones Industrial Average fell 276.39 points . . . to 10,292.31."

The number of dots in ellipses is not optional; always use three. Occasionally, the points of an ellipsis come at the end of a sentence, where they seem to grow a fourth dot. Don't be fooled: One of the dots is a period. Ellipsis points should always be preceded and followed by a space.

Avoid using ellipses to represent a pause in your writing; use a dash for that purpose:

At first we had planned to leave for the conference on Wednesday—but then we changed our minds. [not *on Wednesday . . . but then*]

3.0 Mechanics

The most obvious and least tolerable mistakes that a business writer makes are probably those related to grammar and punctuation. However, a number of small details, known as writing mechanics, demonstrate the writer's polish and reflect on the company's professionalism.

When it comes to mechanics, also called *style*, many of the "rules" are not hard and fast. Publications and organizations vary in their preferred styles for capitalization, abbreviations, numbers, italics, and so on. Here, we'll try to differentiate between practices that are generally accepted and those that can vary. When you are writing materials for a specific company or organization, find out the preferred style (such as *The Chicago Manual of Style* or Webster's *Style Manual*). Otherwise, choose a respected style guide. The key to style is consistency: If you spell out the word *percent* in one part of a document, don't use the percent sign in a similar context elsewhere in the same document.

3.1 CAPITALIZATION

With capitalization, you can follow either an "up" style (when in doubt, capitalize: *Federal Government, Board of Directors*) or a "down" style (when in doubt, use lowercase: *federal government, board of directors*). The trend over the last few decades has been toward the down style. Your best bet is to get a good style manual and consult it when you have a capitalization question. Following are some rules that most style guides agree on.

Capital letters are used at the beginning of certain word groups:

- **Complete sentence:** Before hanging up, he said, "We'll meet here on Wednesday at noon."
- **Formal statement following a colon:** She has a favorite motto: Where there's a will, there's a way.
- **Phrase used as sentence:** Absolutely not!
- **Quoted sentence embedded in another sentence:** Scott said, "Nobody was here during lunch hour except me."

- **List of items set off from text:** Three preliminary steps are involved:

  Design review
  Budgeting
  Scheduling

Capitalize proper adjectives and proper nouns (the names of particular persons, places, and things):

Darrell Greene lived in a Victorian mansion.

We sent Ms. Larson an application form, informing her that not all applicants are interviewed.

Let's consider opening a branch in the West, perhaps at the west end of Tucson, Arizona.

As office buildings go, the Kinney Building is a pleasant setting for TDG Office Equipment.

We are going to have to cancel our plans for hiring French and German sales reps.

Larson's name is capitalized because she is a particular applicant, whereas the general term *applicant* is left uncapitalized. Likewise, *West* is capitalized when it refers to a particular place but not when it means a direction. In the same way, *office* and *building* are not capitalized when they are general terms (common nouns), but they are capitalized when they are part of the title of a particular office or building (proper nouns). Some proper adjectives are lowercased when they are part of terms that have come into common use, such as *french fries* and *roman numerals*.

Titles within families or companies as well as professional titles may also be capitalized:

I turned down Uncle David when he offered me a job. I wouldn't be comfortable working for one of my relatives.

We've never had a president quite like President Sweeney.

People's titles are capitalized when they are used in addressing a person, especially in a formal context. They are not usually capitalized, however, when they are used merely to identify the person:

Address the letter to Chairperson Anna Palmer.

I wish to thank Chairperson Anna Palmer for her assistance.

Anna Palmer, chairperson of the board, took the podium.

Also capitalize titles if they are used by themselves in addressing a person:

Thank you, Doctor, for your donation.

Always capitalize the first word of the salutation and complimentary close of a letter:

Dear Mr. Andrews: *Yours* very truly,

The names of organizations are capitalized, of course; so are the official names of their departments and divisions. However, do not use capitals when referring in general terms to a department or division, especially one in another organization:

Route this memo to Personnel.

Larry Tien was transferred to the Microchip Division.

Will you be enrolled in the Psychology Department?

Someone from the personnel department at EnerTech stopped by the booth.

Capitalization is unnecessary when using a word like *company, corporation*, or *university* alone:

The corporation plans to issue 50,000 shares of common stock.

Likewise, the names of specific products are capitalized, although the names of general product types are not:

Apple Inc.   Xerox machine

Tide laundry detergent

When it comes to government terminology, here are some guides to capitalization: (1) Lowercase *federal* unless it is part of an agency name; (2) capitalize names of courts, departments, bureaus, offices, and agencies but lowercase such references as *the bureau* and *the department* when the full name is not used; (3) lowercase the titles of government officers unless they precede a specific person's name: *the secretary of state, the senator, the ambassador, the governor, and the mayor* but *Mayor Gonzalez* (Note: style guides vary on whether to capitalize *president* when referring to the president of the United States without including the person's name); capitalize the names of laws and acts: *the Sherman Antitrust Act, the Civil Rights Act*; (4) capitalize the names of political parties but lowercase the word *party: Democratic party, Libertarian party*.

When writing about two or more geographic features of the same type, it is now accepted practice to capitalize the common noun in addition to the proper nouns, regardless of word order:

Lakes Ontario and Huron

Allegheny and Monongahela Rivers

Corson and Ravenna Avenues

The names of languages, races, and ethnic groups are capitalized: Japanese, Caucasian, Hispanic. But racial terms that denote only skin color are not capitalized: black, white.

When referring to the titles of books, articles, magazines, newspapers, reports, movies, and so on, you should capitalize the first and last words and all nouns, pronouns, adjectives, verbs, and adverbs, and capitalize prepositions and conjunctions with five letters or more. Except for the first and last words, do not capitalize articles:

Economics During the Great War

"An Investigation into the Market for Long-Distance Services"

"What Successes Are Made Of"

When *the* is part of the official name of a newspaper or magazine, it should be treated this way too:

The Wall Street Journal

Style guides vary in their recommendations regarding capitalization of hyphenated words in titles. A general guide is to capitalize the second word in a temporary compound (a compound that is hyphenated for grammatical reasons and not spelling reasons), such as *Law-Abiding Citizen*, but to lowercase the word if the term is always hyphenated, such as *Son-in-law*).

References to specific pages, paragraphs, lines, and the like are not capitalized: *page 73, line 3*. However, in most other numbered or lettered references, the identifying term is capitalized:

Chapter 4   *Serial No. 382-2203*   *Item B-11*

Finally, the names of academic degrees are capitalized when they follow a person's name but are not capitalized when used in a general sense:

I received a bachelor of science degree.

Thomas Whitelaw, Doctor of Philosophy, will attend.

Similarly, general courses of study are not capitalized, but the names of specific classes are:

She studied accounting as an undergraduate.

She is enrolled in Accounting 201.

3.2 UNDERSCORES AND ITALICS

Usually a line typed underneath a word or phrase either provides emphasis or indicates the title of a book, magazine, or newspaper. If possible, use italics instead of an underscore. Italics (or underlining) should also be used for defining terms and for discussing words as words:

In this report, *net sales* refers to after-tax sales dollars.

The word *building* is a common noun and should not be capitalized.

Also use italics to set off foreign words, unless the words have become a common part of English:

Top Shelf is considered the *sine qua non* of comic book publishers.

Chris uses a laissez-faire [no italic] management style.

3.3 ABBREVIATIONS

Abbreviations are used heavily in tables, charts, lists, and forms. They're used sparingly in prose. Here are some abbreviation situations to watch for:

- In most cases do not use periods with acronyms (words formed from the initial letter or letters of parts of a term): *CEO, CD-ROM, DOS, YWCA, FDA*; but *Ph.D., M.A., M.D.*
- Use periods with abbreviations such as *Mr., Ms., Sr., Jr., a.m., p.m., B.C.*, and *A.D.*
- The trend is away from using periods with such units of measure as *mph, mm*, and *lb*.
- Use periods with such Latin abbreviations as *e.g., i.e., et al.*, and *etc.* However, style guides recommend that you avoid using these Latin forms and instead use their English equivalents (*for example, that is, and others*, and *and so on*, respectively). If you must use these abbreviations, such as in parenthetical expressions or footnotes, do not put them in italics.

- Some companies have abbreviations as part of their names (*&, Co., Inc., Ltd.*). When you refer to such firms by name, be sure to double-check the preferred spelling, including spacing: *AT&;T; Barnes & Noble; Carson Pirie Scott & Company; PepsiCo; Kate Spade, Inc.; National Data Corporation; Siemens Corp.; Glaxo Wellcome PLC; US Airways; U.S. Business Reporter.*
- Most style guides recommend that you spell out *United States* as a noun and reserve *U.S.* as an adjective preceding the noun modified.

One way to handle an abbreviation that you want to use throughout a document is to spell it out the first time you use it, follow it with the abbreviation in parentheses, and then use the abbreviation in the remainder of the document.

3.4 NUMBERS

Numbers may be correctly handled many ways in business writing, so follow company style. In the absence of a set style, however, generally spell out all numbers from one to nine and use arabic numerals for the rest.

There are some exception*s* to this general rule. For example, never begin a sentence with a numeral:

Twenty of us produced 641 units per week in the first 12 weeks of the year.

Use numerals for the numbers one through nine if they're in the same list as larger numbers:

Our weekly quota rose from 9 to 15 to 27.

Use numerals for percentages, time of day (except with o'clock), dates, and (in general) dollar amounts:

Our division is responsible for 7 percent of total sales.

The meeting is scheduled for 8:30 a.m. on August 2.

Add $3 for postage and handling.

When using numerals for time, be consistent: It should be *between 10:00 a.m. and 4:30 p.m.*, not *between 10 a.m. and 4:30 p.m.* Expressions such as *4:00 o'clock* and *7 a.m. in the morning* are redundant.

Use a comma in numbers expressing thousands (1,257), unless your company specifies another style. When dealing with numbers in the millions and billions, combine words and figures: 7.3 million, 2 billion.

When writing dollar amounts, use a decimal point only if cents are included. In lists of two or more dollar amounts, use the decimal point either for all or for none:

He sent two checks, one for $67.92 and one for $90.00.

When two numbers fall next to each other in a sentence, use figures for the number that is largest, most difficult to spell, or part of a physical measurement; use words for the other:

I have learned to manage a classroom of 30 twelve-year-olds.

She won a bonus for selling 24 thirty-volume sets.

You'll need twenty 3-inch bolts.

In addresses, all street numbers except One are in numerals. So are suite and room numbers and zip codes. For street names that are numbered, practice varies so widely that you should use the form specified on an organization's letterhead or in a reliable directory. All the following examples are correct:

One Fifth Avenue	297 Ninth Street
1839 44th Street	11026 West 78 Place

Telephone numbers are always expressed in numerals. Parentheses may separate the area code from the rest of the number, but a slash or a hyphen may be used instead, especially if the entire phone number is enclosed in parentheses:

382-8329   (602/382-8329)   602-382-8329

Percentages are always expressed in numerals. The word *percent* is used in most cases, but % may be used in tables, forms, and statistical writing.

Ages are usually expressed in words—except when a parenthetical reference to age follows someone's name:

Mrs. Margaret Sanderson is seventy-two.

Mrs. Margaret Sanderson, 72, swims daily.

Also, ages expressed in years and months are treated like physical measurements that combine two units of measure: *5 years 6 months.*

Physical measurements such as distance, weight, and volume are also often expressed in numerals: *9 kilometers, 5 feet 3 inches, 7 pounds 10 ounces.*

Decimal numbers are always written in numerals. In most cases, add a zero to the left of the decimal point if the number is less than one and does not already start with a zero:

1.38   .07   0.2

In a series of related decimal numbers with at least one number greater than one, make sure that all numbers smaller than one have a zero to the left of the decimal point: 1.20, 0.21, 0.09.

Simple fractions are written in words, but more complicated fractions are expressed in figures or, if easier to read, in figures and words:

two-thirds   9/32   2 hundredths

Most style guides recommend that you use a comma with numbers consisting of four digits: *2,345*, not *2345*.

When typing ordinal numbers, such as *3rd edition* or *21st century,* your word processing program may automatically make the letters *rd* (or *st, th,* or *nd*) into a superscript. Do yourself a favor and turn that formatting function off in your "Preferences," as superscripts should not be used in regular prose or even in bibliographies.

3.5 WORD DIVISION

In general, avoid dividing words at the end of lines. When you must do so, follow these rules:

- Don't divide one-syllable words (such as *since, walked,* and *thought*), abbreviations (*mgr.*), contractions (*isn't*), or numbers expressed in numerals (*117,500*).

- Divide words between syllables, as specified in a dictionary or word-division manual.
- Make sure that at least three letters of the divided words are moved to the second line: *sin-cerely* instead of *sincere-ly*.
- Do not end a page or more than three consecutive lines with hyphens.
- Leave syllables consisting of a single vowel at the end of the first line (*impedi-ment* instead of *imped-iment*), except when the single vowel is part of a suffix such as *-able, -ible, -ical,* or *-ity* (*re-spons-ible* instead of *re-sponsi-ble*).
- Divide between double letters (*tomor-row*), except when the root word ends in double letters (*call-ing* instead of *cal-ling*).
- Wherever possible, divide hyphenated words at the hyphen only: instead of *anti-inde-pendence*, use *anti-independence*.
- Whenever possible, do not break URLs or email addresses. If you must break a long URL or email address, do not insert a hyphen at the end of the first line.

4.0 Vocabulary

Using the right word in the right place is a crucial skill in business communication. However, many pitfalls await the unwary.

4.1 FREQUENTLY CONFUSED WORDS

Because the following sets of words sound similar, be careful not to use one when you mean to use the other:

Word	Meaning
accede	to comply with
exceed	to go beyond
accept	to take
except	to exclude
access	admittance
excess	too much
advice	suggestion
advise	to suggest
affect	to influence
effect	the result
allot	to distribute
a lot	much or many
all ready	completely prepared
already	completed earlier
born	given birth to
borne	carried
capital	money; chief city
capitol	a government building
cite	to quote
sight	a view
site	a location

Word	Meaning
complement	complete amount; to go well with
compliment	expression of esteem; to flatter
corespondent	party in a divorce suit
correspondent	letter writer
council	a panel of people
counsel	advice; a lawyer
defer	to put off until later
differ	to be different
device	a mechanism
devise	to plan
die	to stop living; a tool
dye	to color
discreet	careful
discrete	separate
envelop	to surround
envelope	a covering for a letter
forth	forward
fourth	number four
holey	full of holes
holy	sacred
wholly	completely
human	of people
humane	kindly
incidence	frequency
incidents	events
instance	example
instants	moments
interstate	between states
intrastate	within a state
later	afterward
latter	the second of two
lead	a metal; to guide
led	guided
lean	to rest at an angle
lien	a claim
levee	embankment
levy	tax
loath	reluctant
loathe	to hate
loose	free; not tight
lose	to mislay
material	substance
materiel	equipment
miner	mineworker
minor	underage person

Word	Meaning
moral	virtuous; a lesson
morale	sense of well-being
ordinance	law
ordnance	weapons
overdo	to do in excess
overdue	past due
peace	lack of conflict
piece	a fragment
pedal	a foot lever
peddle	to sell
persecute	to torment
prosecute	to sue
personal	private
personnel	employees
precedence	priority
precedents	previous events
principal	sum of money; chief; main
principle	general rule
rap	to knock
wrap	to cover
residence	home
residents	inhabitants
right	correct
rite	ceremony
write	to form words on a surface
role	a part to play
roll	to tumble; a list
root	part of a plant
rout	to defeat
route	a traveler's way
shear	to cut
sheer	thin, steep
stationary	immovable
stationery	paper
than	as compared with
then	at that time
their	belonging to them
there	in that place
they're	they are
to	a preposition
too	excessively; also
two	the number
waive	to set aside
wave	a swell of water; a gesture

Word	Meaning
weather	atmospheric conditions
whether	if
who's	contraction of "who is" or "who has"
whose	possessive form of who

In the preceding list, only enough of each word's meaning is given to help you distinguish between the words in each group. For more complete definitions, consult a dictionary.

4.2 FREQUENTLY MISUSED WORDS

The following words tend to be misused for reasons other than their sound. Reference books (including the *Random House College Dictionary*, revised edition; Follett's *Modern American Usage*; and Fowler's *Modern English Usage*) can help you with similar questions of usage:

a lot: When the writer means "many," *a lot* is always two separate words, never one.

aggravate/irritate: *Aggravate* means "to make things worse." Sitting in the smoke-filled room *aggravated* his sinus condition. *Irritate* means "to annoy." Her constant questions *irritated* [not *aggravated*] me.

anticipate/expect: *Anticipate* means "to prepare for": Macy's *anticipated* increased demand for athletic shoes in spring by ordering in November. In formal usage, it is incorrect to use *anticipate* for *expect*: I *expected* (not *anticipated*) a better response to our presentation than we actually got.

compose/comprise: The whole comprises the parts:

> The company's distribution division *comprises* four departments.

It would be incorrect usage to say

> The company's distribution division *is comprised of* four departments.

In that construction, *is composed of* or *consists of* would be preferable. It might be helpful to think of *comprise* as meaning "encompasses" or "contains."

continual/continuous: *Continual* refers to ongoing actions that have breaks:

> Her *continual* complaining will accomplish little in the long run.

Continuous refers to ongoing actions without interruptions or breaks:

> A *continuous* stream of paper came out of the fax machine.

convince/persuade: One is *convinced* of a fact or that something is true; one is *persuaded* by someone else to do something. The use of *to* with *convince* is unidiomatic—you don't convince someone to do something, you persuade them to do it.

correspond with: Use this phrase when you are talking about exchanging letters. Use *correspond to* when you mean "similar to." Use either *correspond with* or *correspond to* when you mean "relate to."

dilemma/problem: Technically, a *dilemma* is a situation in which one must choose between two undesirable alternatives. It shouldn't be used when no choice is actually involved.

disinterested: This word means "fair, unbiased, having no favorites, impartial." If you mean "bored" or "not interested," use uninterested.

etc.: This abbreviated form of the Latin phrase *et cetera* means "and so on" or "and so forth," so it is never correct to write "and etc." The current tendency among business writers is to use English rather than Latin.

example/sample: An example is a model to be followed or one item that represents a group. A sample is a preview of a product or another entity, intended to demonstrate the product's qualities. In statistics, a sample is selected to represent the characteristics of a larger population.

flaunt/flout: To flaunt is to be ostentatious or boastful; to flout is to mock or scoff at.

impact: Avoid using impact as a verb when influence or affect is meant.

imply/infer: Both refer to hints. Their great difference lies in who is acting. The writer implies, the reader infers, sees between the lines.

lay: This word is a transitive verb. Never use it for the intransitive lie. (See Section 1.3.3.)

lend/loan: Lend is a verb; loan is a noun. Usage such as "Can you loan me $5?" is therefore incorrect.

less/fewer: Use less for uncountable quantities (such as amounts of water, air, sugar, and oil). Use fewer for countable quantities (such as numbers of jars, saws, words, pages, and humans). The same distinction applies to much and little (uncountable) versus many and few (countable).

liable/likely: Liable means "responsible for": I will hold you liable if this deal doesn't go through. It is incorrect to use liable for "possible": Anything is likely (not liable) to happen.

literally: Literally means "actually" or "precisely"; it is often misused to mean "almost" or "virtually." It is usually best left out entirely or replaced with figuratively.

many/much: See less/fewer.

regardless: The less suffix is the negative part. No word needs two negative parts, so don't add ir (a negative prefix) to the beginning. There is no such word as irregardless.

try: Always follow with *to*, never *and*.

verbal: People in the business community who are careful with language frown on those who use *verbal* to mean "spoken" or "oral." Many others do say "verbal agreement." Strictly speaking, *verbal* means "of words" and therefore includes both spoken and written words. Follow company usage in this matter.

4.3 FREQUENTLY MISSPELLED WORDS

All of us, even the world's best spellers, sometimes have to check a dictionary for the spelling of some words. People who have never memorized the spelling of commonly used words must look up so many that they grow exasperated and give up on spelling words correctly.

Don't expect perfection and don't surrender. If you can memorize the spelling of just the words listed here, you'll need the dictionary far less often and you'll write with more confidence:

absence	convertible
absorption	corroborate
accessible	criticism
accommodate	
accumulate	definitely
achieve	description
advantageous	desirable
affiliated	dilemma
aggressive	disappear
alignment	disappoint
aluminum	disbursement
ambience	discrepancy
analyze	dissatisfied
apparent	dissipate
appropriate	
argument	eligible
asphalt	embarrassing
assistant	endorsement
asterisk	exaggerate
auditor	exceed
	exhaust
bankruptcy	existence
believable	extraordinary
brilliant	
bulletin	fallacy
	familiar
calendar	flexible
campaign	fluctuation
category	forty
ceiling	
changeable	gesture
clientele	grievous
collateral	
committee	haphazard
comparative	harassment
competitor	holiday
concede	
congratulations	illegible
connoisseur	immigrant
consensus	incidentally
convenient	indelible

independent
indispensable
insistent
intermediary
irresistible

jewelry
judgment
judicial

labeling
legitimate
leisure
license
litigation

maintenance
mathematics
mediocre
minimum

necessary
negligence
negotiable
newsstand
noticeable

occurrence
omission

parallel
pastime
peaceable
permanent
perseverance
persistent
personnel
persuade
possesses
precede

predictable
preferred
privilege
procedure
proceed
pronunciation
psychology
pursue

questionnaire

receive
recommend
repetition
rescind
rhythmical
ridiculous

salable
secretary
seize
separate
sincerely
succeed
suddenness
superintendent
supersede
surprise

tangible
tariff
technique
tenant
truly

unanimous
until

vacillate
vacuum
vicious

4.4 TRANSITIONAL WORDS AND PHRASES

The following sentences don't communicate as well as they could because they lack a transitional word or phrase:

> Production delays are inevitable. Our current lag time in filling orders is one month.

A semicolon between the two sentences would signal a close relationship between their meanings, but it wouldn't even hint at what that relationship is. Here are the sentences again, now linked by means of a semicolon, with a space for a transitional word or phrase:

> Production delays are inevitable; _____, our current lag time in filling orders is one month.

Now read the sentence with *nevertheless* in the blank space. Then try *therefore, incidentally, in fact,* and *at any rate* in the blank. Each substitution changes the meaning of the sentence.

Here are some transitional words (conjunctive adverbs) that will help you write more clearly:

accordingly	furthermore	moreover
anyway	however	otherwise
besides	incidentally	still
consequently	likewise	therefore
finally	meanwhile	

The following transitional phrases are used in the same way:

as a result	in other words
at any rate	in the second place
for example	on the other hand
in fact	to the contrary

When one of these words or phrases joins two independent clauses, it should be preceded by a semicolon and followed by a comma:

> The consultant recommended a complete reorganization; moreover, she suggested that we drop several products.

Answer Keys

ANSWER KEY FOR "LEARNING OBJECTIVES CHECKUP"

Chapter 1

1. b
2. b
3. c
4. d
5. b
6. a
7. a
8. Interactive and conversational
9. sense, select, perceive
10. d
11. information, people (*or* recipients *or* receivers *or* audiences)
12. a
13. c
14. d
15. dilemma, lapse

Chapter 2

1. d
2. d
3. constructive
4. d
5. a
6. a
7. b
8. parliamentary
9. virtual
10. telepresence
11. decode
12. c
13. d
14. a
15. d
16. d
17. c
18. a
19. a

Chapter 3

1. d
2. d
3. c
4. a
5. c
6. d
7. ethnocentrism
8. stereotyping
9. b
10. a
11. c
12. b
13. nonverbal
14. a
15. d
16. a
17. b
18. b

Chapter 4

1. b
2. c
3. a
4. general purpose
5. b
6. a
7. c
8. c
9. d
10. d
11. richness
12. d
13. a
14. b
15. d
16. direct
17. indirect
18. a
19. a

Chapter 5

1. a
2. d
3. d
4. b
5. c
6. c
7. passive
8. active
9. b
10. b
11. c
12. a
13. a
14. c
15. c
16. examples
17. differences, similarities
18. a
19. b
20. boilerplate

Chapter 6

1. d
2. a
3. c
4. a
5. b
6. d
7. d
8. b
9. b
10. a
11. c
12. b
13. white space
14. c
15. a
16. c
17. d
18. a
19. b

Chapter 7

1. b
2. b
3. c
4. UGC site

5. c
6. community participation
7. a
8. c
9. a
10. a
11. c
12. d
13. b
14. a
15. c
16. d
17. c
18. d
19. c
20. vidcast/vodcast
21. a

Chapter 8

1. b
2. a
3. d
4. c
5. b
6. d
7. c
8. direct
9. a
10. b
11. the good news
12. d
13. d
14. b
15. a
16. d
17. c

Chapter 9

1. h
2. d
3. c
4. a
5. a
6. c
7. c
8. buffer
9. c
10. d
11. b
12. c
13. c
14. c
15. b

16. a
17. d

Chapter 10

1. b
2. d
3. d
4. b
5. c
6. d
7. c
8. emotional
9. logical
10. b
11. b
12. c
13. c
14. b
15. a
16. a
17. a
18. d

Chapter 11

1. a
2. informational
3. analytical
4. proposals
5. d
6. d
7. primary
8. secondary
9. a
10. c
11. d
12. a
13. c
14. d
15. a
16. b
17. information architecture
18. a
19. b
20. a

Chapter 12

1. d
2. b
3. c
4. c
5. a
6. c

7. a
8. b
9. d
10. d
11. localizing
12. b
13. d
14. b
15. d
16. d
17. d
18. data visualization
19. c
20. d
21. c

Chapter 13

1. c
2. b
3. a
4. transmittal
5. synopsis
6. executive summary
7. a
8. c
9. b
10. c
11. d
12. d
13. d

Chapter 14

1. b
2. d
3. planning, speaking
4. b
5. a
6. a
7. b
8. a
9. c
10. c
11. b
12. d
13. a
14. transitions, builds
15. c
16. d
17. b
18. d
19. d
20. d
21. b

22. c
23. d.
24. a

Chapter 15

1. b
2. quality of hire
3. b
4. b
5. b
6. d
7. chronological
8. functional
9. combination
10. d

11. a
12. b
13. a
14. a
15. b
16. c
17. c
18. c
19. keyword searches
20. plain text
21. a

Chapter 16

1. a
2. b

3. b
4. b
5. b
6. structured
7. d
8. d
9. d
10. b
11. c
12. c
13. a
14. a
15. c
16. d
17. a
18. c

ANSWER KEY FOR "IMPROVE YOUR GRAMMAR, MECHANICS, AND USAGE" EXERCISES

Chapter 1

1. superior's (1.1.4)
2. fish (1.1.3)
3. 2000s (1.1.3)
4. Jameses, faxes (1.1.3)
5. companies (1.1.3)
6. duties (1.1.3)
7. members' (1.1.4)
8. brothers-in-law, ventures (1.1.3, 1.1.4)
9. analyses (1.1.3)
10. Les's, month's (1.1.4)

Chapter 2

1. its (1.2.5)
2. their (1.2.5)
3. its (1.2.5)
4. their (1.2.1)
5. his or her (1.2.3)
6. his or her (1.2.3)
7. a, them (1.2.3, 1.2.4)
8. who (1.2.4)
9. whom (1.2.4)
10. its (1.2.5)

Chapter 3

1. a (1.3.1)
2. b (1.3.1)
3. a (1.3.1)
4. a (1.3.5)
5. b (1.3.5)
6. a (1.3.4)
7. a (1.3.4)
8. b (1.3.4)

9. a (1.3.4)
10. b (1.3.4)

Chapter 4

1. better (1.4.1)
2. most appropriate (1.4.1)
3. most effective (1.4.1)
4. biggest (1.4.1)
5. expensively designed, low-budget (1.4.2)
6. cross-references (1.4.2)
7. ten-year-old (1.4.2)
8. high-handed, devil-may-care (1.4)
9. small plastic (1.4)
10. usual warm, friendly (1.4)

Chapter 5

1. well (1.5)
2. surely (1.5)
3. sick (1.5)
4. well (1.5)
5. good (1.5)
6. better (1.5.2)
7. better (1.5.2)
8. any (1.5.1)
9. ever (1.5.1)
10. can, any (1.5.1)

Chapter 6

1. approaching (1.6.1)
2. home (1.6.1)
3. reply to (1.6.1)
4. told (1.6.1)
5. between (1.6.1)

6. to (1.6.1)
7. from (1.6.1)
8. as (1.6.1)
9. not to (1.6.1)
10. on (1.6.1)

Chapter 7

1. b (1.6.2)
2. b (1.6.1)
3. b (1.6.1)
4. b (1.6.1)
5. a (1.6.1)
6. a (1.6.1)
7. a (1.6.3)
8. b (1.6.2)
9. a (1.6.3)
10. b (1.6.3)

Chapter 8

1. b (1.7.3)
2. a (1.7.2)
3. b (1.7.6)
4. a (1.7.4)
5. b (1.7.4)
6. b (1.7.6)
7. b (1.7.6)
8. b (1.7.4)
9. a (1.7.3)
10. b (1.7.2)

Chapter 9

1. c (2.6)
2. a (2.6)
3. a (2.6)

4. a (2.6)
5. b (2.6)
6. c (2.6)
7. b (2.6)
8. b (2.6)
9. a (2.6)
10. b (2.6)

Chapter 10

1. a (2.4)
2. a (2.5)
3. c (2.4)
4. a (2.5)
5. b (2.5)
6. b (2.4)
7. a (2.4)
8. c (2.4)
9. b (2.4)
10. c (2.5)

Chapter 11

1. a (2.1)
2. a (2.2)
3. a (2.1)
4. a (2.1)
5. b (2.2, 2.3)
6. b (2.1)
7. b (2.2, 2.1)
8. a (2.2)
9. b (2.2)
10. a (2.2, 2.3)

Chapter 12

1. b (2.7)
2. a (2.8)
3. c (2.7)
4. a (2.8)
5. a (2.7)
6. b (2.7)
7. c (2.8)
8. a (2.8, 2.7)
9. c (2.8, 2.7)
10. a (2.8)

Chapter 13

1. b (2.10)
2. b (2.11)
3. a (2.11)
4. b (2.10)
5. a (2.10)
6. a (2.11)
7. c (2.10, 2.12)
8. b (2.10)
9. b (2.11)
10. c (2.10, 2.12)

Chapter 14

1. c (3.1, 3.3)
2. a (3.1, 3.3)
3. b (3.2)
4. a (3.1)
5. c (3.3)

6. a (3.1, 3.2)
7. b (3.1, 3.3)
8. b (3.1, 3.3)
9. a (3.2)
10. c (3.1)

Chapter 15

1. affect (4.1)
2. advice (4.1)
3. lose (4.1)
4. whoever (4.1)
5. a lot (4.2)
6. received (4.3)
7. incomprehensible (4.2)
8. necessity (4.3)
9. invented (4.2)
10. to (4.2)

Chapter 16

1. c (3.4)
2. a (3.4)
3. a (3.4)
4. b (3.4)
5. a (3.4)
6. a (3.4)
7. b (3.4)
8. b (3.4)
9. a (3.4)
10. c (3.4)

Brand, Organization, Name, and Website Index

Subject Index